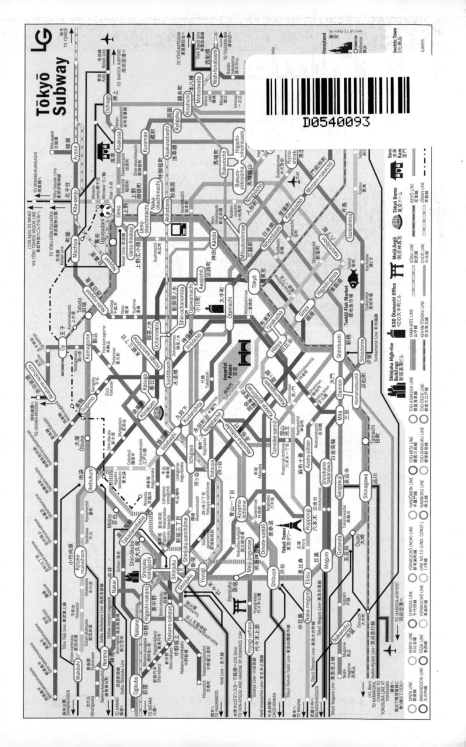

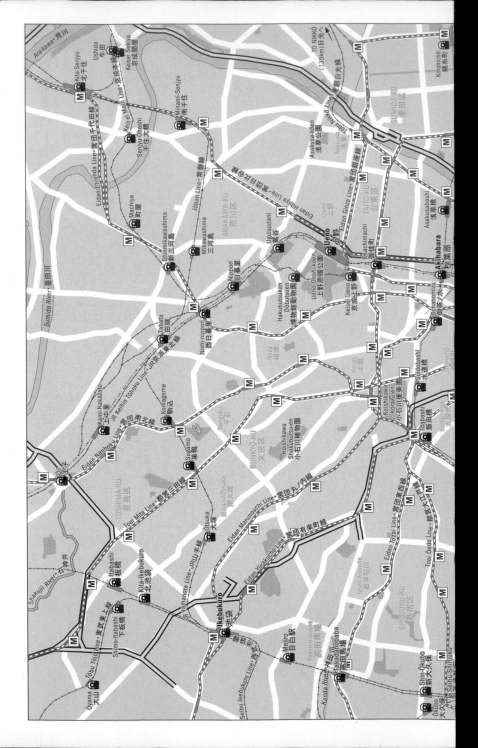

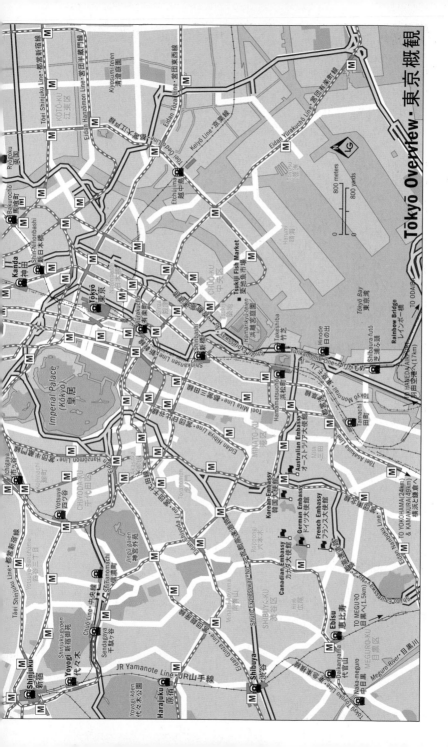

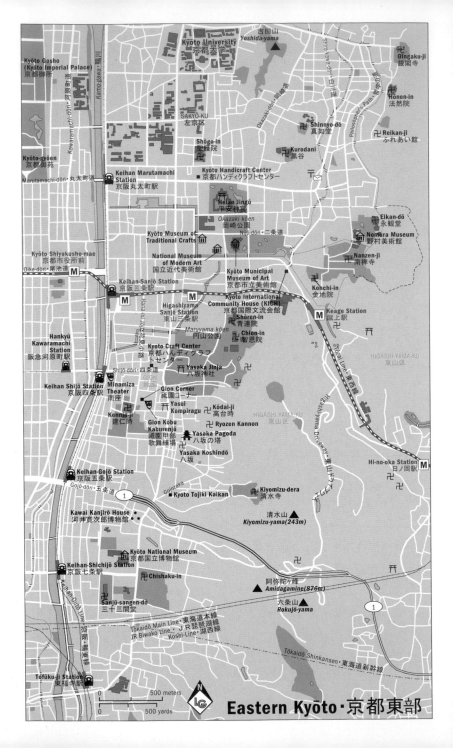

Eastern Kyōto・京都東部

LET'S GO

■ THE RESOURCE FOR THE INDEPENDENT TRAVELER

"The guides are aimed not only at young budget travelers but at the indepedent traveler; a sort of streetwise cookbook for traveling alone."

—*The New York Times*

"Unbeatable; good sight-seeing advice; up-to-date info on restaurants, hotels, and inns; a commitment to money-saving travel; and a wry style that brightens nearly every page."

—*The Washington Post*

"Lighthearted and sophisticated, informative and fun to read. [Let's Go] helps the novice traveler navigate like a knowledgeable old hand."

—*Atlanta Journal-Constitution*

"A world-wise traveling companion—always ready with friendly advice and helpful hints, all sprinkled with a bit of wit."

—*The Philadelphia Inquirer*

■ THE BEST TRAVEL BARGAINS IN YOUR PRICE RANGE

"All the dirt, dirt cheap."

—*People*

"Anything you need to know about budget traveling is detailed in this book."

—*The Chicago Sun-Times*

"Let's Go follows the creed that you don't have to toss your life's savings to the wind to travel—unless you want to."

—*The Salt Lake Tribune*

■ REAL ADVICE FOR REAL EXPERIENCES

"The writers seem to have experienced every rooster-packed bus and lunar-surfaced mattress about which they write."

—*The New York Times*

"A guide should tell you what to expect from a destination. Here Let's Go shines."

—*The Chicago Tribune*

"[Let's Go's] devoted updaters really walk the walk (and thumb the ride, and trek the trail). Learn how to fish, haggle, find work—anywhere."

—*Food & Wine*

LET'S GO PUBLICATIONS

TRAVEL GUIDES

Alaska 1st edition **NEW TITLE**
Australia 2004
Austria & Switzerland 2004
Brazil 1st edition **NEW TITLE**
Britain & Ireland 2004
California 2004
Central America 8th edition
Chile 1st edition
China 4th edition
Costa Rica 1st edition
Eastern Europe 2004
Egypt 2nd edition
Europe 2004
France 2004
Germany 2004
Greece 2004
Hawaii 2004
India & Nepal 8th edition
Ireland 2004
Israel 4th edition
Italy 2004
Japan 1st edition **NEW TITLE**
Mexico 20th edition
Middle East 4th edition
New Zealand 6th edition
Pacific Northwest 1st edition **NEW TITLE**
Peru, Ecuador & Bolivia 3rd edition
Puerto Rico 1st edition **NEW TITLE**
South Africa 5th edition
Southeast Asia 8th edition
Southwest USA 3rd edition
Spain & Portugal 2004
Thailand 1st edition
Turkey 5th edition
USA 2004
Western Europe 2004

CITY GUIDES

Amsterdam 3rd edition
Barcelona 3rd edition
Boston 4th edition
London 2004
New York City 2004
Paris 2004
Rome 12th edition
San Francisco 4th edition
Washington, D.C. 13th edition

MAP GUIDES

Amsterdam
Berlin
Boston
Chicago
Dublin
Florence
Hong Kong
London
Los Angeles
Madrid
New Orleans
New York City
Paris
Prague
Rome
San Francisco
Seattle
Sydney
Venice
Washington, D.C.

COMING SOON:
Road Trip USA

LET'S GO

JAPAN

2004

TERESA ELSEY EDITOR
MEGUMI GORDON ASSOCIATE EDITOR
ANDRES WEI-CHIAO SU ASSOCIATE EDITOR
JULIA ELIZABETH TWAROG ASSOCIATE EDITOR

RESEARCHER-WRITERS
MATTHEW D. FIRESTONE   MAIKO NAKARAI
TOMOHIRO HAMAKAWA   ANNALISE NELSON
MAX GOLDEN LIN   NICK TOPJIAN
DANIEL MORALES   JAKUB WRZESNIEWSKI

SERENA TAN MAP EDITOR
LAUREN E. BONNER MANAGING EDITOR

ST. MARTIN'S PRESS ☒ NEW YORK

HELPING LET'S GO If you want to share your discoveries, suggestions, or corrections, please drop us a line. We read every piece of correspondence, whether a postcard, a 10-page email, or a coconut. **Address mail to:**

Let's Go: Japan
67 Mount Auburn Street
Cambridge, MA 02138
USA

Visit Let's Go at **http://www.letsgo.com,** or send email to:

feedback@letsgo.com
Subject: "Let's Go: Japan"

In addition to the invaluable travel advice our readers share with us, many are kind enough to offer their services as researchers or editors. Unfortunately, our charter enables us to employ only currently enrolled Harvard students.

HOW TO USE THIS BOOK

INTRODUCTORY MATERIAL. The first chapter, **Discover Japan** (p. 1), introduces the country that brought you sushi and *samurai*, complete with **Suggested Itineraries** (p. 5) to guide your trip. The **Essentials** section (p. 9) contains practical advice on renewing your passport, booking your tickets, packing your bags, and everything else under the rising sun. Make up for falling asleep in seventh-grade social studies with a flip through **Life and Times** (p. 75), a quick introduction to the people, places, and faces in the pages to come. And if you're already intrigued by the isles, our section on **Alternatives to Tourism** (p. 57) suggests some opportunities to extend your stay by volunteering, studying, or working.

THE LAY OF THE LAND. We plop you down first in **Tōkyō** (p. 110), capital, population center, and beating heart of modern Japan. From there, it's on to the surrounding **Kantō** (p. 206) region, north to, well, **Northern Honshū** (p. 267), and a quick U-turn back to **Central Honshū** (p. 324). Your next stop is historic and heady **Kansai** (p. 392); if you can bear to leave, **Western Honshū** (p. 479) is there to round out the big island. Small **Shikoku** (p. 525) is up next, with southern island **Kyūshū** (p. 579) on deck. Ferry down to tropical paradise **Okinawa** (p. 636), then discover the meaning of "country of contrasts" in remote, northernmost **Hokkaidō** (p. 667).

PHONE CODES AND TELEPHONE NUMBERS. Area codes for each region appear opposite the name of the region and are denoted by the ☎ icon. Phone numbers in text are also preceded by the ☎ icon.

TRANSPORTATION. Both arrival and departure cities generally list information on transportation connections. Parentheticals usually provide the trip duration, followed by the frequency, then the price; unless otherwise noted, the price is for a one-way trip. For general information on getting there, getting around, and getting it on, consult the **Essentials** (p. 9) section.

PRICE DIVERSITY. Our researchers list establishments in order of value from best to worst, with absolute favorites denoted by the *Let's Go* thumbs-up (📖). Since the best value doesn't always mean the cheapest price, we've incorporated a system of price ranges for accommodations and food; see p. xvi for details.

SCHOLARLY ARTICLES. We brought in the experts to give you the low-down on Japanese history and contemporary life. Ted Bestor tackles Tōkyō through the ages (p. 203), while Tomie Hahn explores Japanese aesthetics (p. 102) and Merry White reports on coffeehouses and caffeine culture (p. 406).

SPECIAL FEATURES. Our own researchers tried their hands at in-depth reporting with twin perspectives on climbing Mt. Fuji (p. 246), a look at the atomic bombing of Hiroshima (p. 486), a primer on Hokkaidō's native Ainu (p. 695), an essential "Japanglish" guide for non-Japanese speakers (p. 737), and much more.

THE AFTERMATH. The **Appendix** (p. 726) contains a Japanese glossary, pronunciation guide, and phrasebook for when the international language of charades just isn't cutting it, as well as a climate table, a measurement conversion chart, and a table of national holidays. Flip to the **Inside Back Cover** for quick reference on phone codes, time zones, and our price diversity scheme.

A NOTE TO OUR READERS The information for this book was gathered by *Let's Go* researchers from May through August of 2003. Each listing is based on one researcher's opinion, formed during his or her visit at a particular time. Those traveling at other times may have different experiences since prices, dates, hours, and conditions are always subject to change. You are urged to check the facts presented in this book beforehand to avoid inconvenience and surprises.

ABOUT LET'S GO

GUIDES FOR THE INDEPENDENT TRAVELER

Budget travel is more than a vacation. At *Let's Go*, we see every trip as the chance of a lifetime. If your dream is to grab a knapsack and a machete and forge through the jungles of Brazil, we can take you there. Or, if you'd rather enjoy the Riviera sun at a beachside cafe, we'll set you a table. If you know what you're doing, you can have any experience you want—whether it's camping among lions or sampling Tuscan desserts—without maxing out your credit card. We'll show you just how far your coins can go, and prove that the greatest limitation on your adventure is not your wallet, but your imagination. That said, we understand that you may want the occasional indulgence after a week of hostels and kebab stands, so we've added "Big Splurges" to let you know which establishments are worth those extra euros, as well as price ranges to help you quickly determine whether an accommodation or restaurant will break the bank. While we may have diversified, our emphasis will always be on finding the best values for your budget, giving you all the info you need to spend six days in London or six months in Tasmania.

BEYOND THE TOURIST EXPERIENCE

We write for travelers who know there's more to a vacation than riding double-deckers with tourists. Our researchers give you the heads-up on both world-renowned and lesser-known attractions, on the best local eats and the hottest nightclub beats. In our travels, we talk to everybody; we provide a snapshot of real life in the places you visit with our sidebars on topics like regional cuisine, local festivals, and hot political issues. We've opened our pages to respected writers and scholars to show you their take on a given destination, and turned to lifelong residents to learn the little things that make their city worth calling home. And we've even given you Alternatives to Tourism—ideas for how to give back to local communities through responsible travel and volunteering.

OVER FORTY YEARS OF WISDOM

When we started, way back in 1960, Let's Go consisted of a small group of well-traveled friends who compiled their budget travel tips into a 20-page packet for students on charter flights to Europe. Since then, we've expanded to suit all kinds of travelers, now publishing guides to six continents, including our newest guides: *Let's Go: Japan* and *Let's Go: Brazil*. Our guides are still annually researched and written entirely by students on shoe-string budgets, adventurous travelers who know that train strikes, stolen luggage, food poisoning, and marriage proposals are all part of a day's work. Even as you read this, work on next year's editions is well underway. Whether you're reading one of our new titles, like *Let's Go: Puerto Rico* or *Let's Go Adventure Guide: Alaska*, or our original best-seller, *Let's Go: Europe*, you'll find the same spirit of adventure that has made *Let's Go* the guide of choice for travelers the world over since 1960.

GETTING IN TOUCH

The best discoveries are often those you make yourself; on the road, when you find something worth sharing, please drop us a line. We're Let's Go Publications, 67 Mt. Auburn St., Cambridge, MA 02138, USA (feedback@letsgo.com).

For more info, visit our website: www.letsgo.com.

CONTENTS

RESEARCHER-WRITERS

Matthew D. Firestone   *Northern Honshū, Kantō, Okinawa*

Matt, whose many travels to exotic locales have landed him in bamboo prison more times than he can count, found Japan a fresh challenge. Nevertheless, he scuba dived, bungee-jumped, and mountain climbed from Okinawa to Tōhoku, making friends at every turn, downing copious amounts of *rāmen*, and learning Japanese on the road. An aspiring biological anthropologist, he researched *Britain and Ireland 2002* and wrote for *Costa Rica* and *Thailand 2003*.

Tomohiro Hamakawa   *Kyūshū*

Having cut his teeth on *Southeast Asia* and *Thailand 2003*, this veteran researcher was only too ready to uncover his home country for *Let's Go*. A student of social anthropology and an ardent traveler with a passion for international development, his next globehop will take him to China to participate in NGO work. First off the blocks, Tomo's dedication, idealism, and consistently heartfelt copy set the standard for the rest of Team Japan to follow.

Max Golden Lin   *Tōkyō*

Max stood on the Roppongi Hills Sky Deck, realized the sheer scale of the sprawling metropolis below, and somehow still managed to research and write the most dazzling new copy this office has ever seen. A composer and mathematician when he's not tearing up the dance floor or squandering his pocket change on arcade games, our favorite wordsmith gave his mind, soul, and sanity to *Let's Go*, asking only for our love in return. We were glad to oblige. Every day.

Daniel Morales   *Shikoku, Kyūshū, Kantō*

This published *haiku* poet and Haruki Murakami fan put his literary aspirations and hyperactive subconscious to work on the roads of Shikoku, braving Japanese motorists and feeding his love of jazz and beer in neighborhood bars. New to *Let's Go* but not to Japan, Dan's research drew from his experience in East Asian Studies and internship in Okayama. After graduation, he hopes to try his hand at driving monster trucks or, failing that, working in publishing.

Maiko Nakarai   *Central Honshū, Kantō*

A Tōkyō native, our savvy, stylish urban girl proved herself just as comfortable with folk culture as frenzied crowds when we plunked her down in Japan's heartland. Her familiarity with the terrain showed in the ease with which she traveled, while her total dedication to the job was apparent in her meticulous research. Always a pleasure to work with, she says she aspires to do something to help bridge Japan and the US. We'd like to suggest she already has.

Annalise Nelson   *Kansai*

Researcher for *France 2002* and editor of *France 2003*, Annalise converted her ample experience into an avalanche of delightful and thorough copy. A scholar of the humanities, her academic interests in history and culture made her the ideal choice for our Kyōto itinerary; her cheerful disposition and willingness to oblige made her the ideal choice for an office sweetheart. We're sorry to bid her *au revoir*, but a consulting job in Paris awaits.

Nick Topjian   *Hokkaidō, Northern Honshū*

If Nick ever loses his shadow, look for it strumming a guitar as it wanders Hokkaidō. This *Let's Go* vet *(Eastern Europe 2001* and *Europe 2003)* drizzled some special sauce on researcher prowess and love for Japan, braving all things scenic, secluded, and sketchy to get the job done. Whether with brown bears or members of a barnyard band, Nick made friends everywhere he traipsed, making us confident our island country has not seen the last of this *gaijin.*

Jakub Wrzesniewski   *Kansai, Western Honshū*

With a *Let's Go* resume the length of a *shinkansen* train, this researcher for *Southeast Asia 2001, Southwest USA 2002,* and *USA 2003* and co-editor for *Southwest USA 2003* went out on the road ready to teach his editors a thing or two. Always an enigma, this travel-hardened vet with a thirst for international relations never failed to amaze us. Kuba scarcely ever lacked fresh insights, so his auspicious swan song hardly occasioned lengthy editing.

CONTRIBUTING WRITERS

Tomie Hahn has garnered degrees in art history, music performance, and ethnomusicology, and now writes about Japanese culture, monster trucks, dance, and technology as culture. A proponent of practicing what she preaches, she also performs traditional *nihon buyō* dance and plays the *shakuhachi* (bamboo flute). Her article on Japanese aesthetics in modern culture is on p. 102.

Ted Bestor is a professor of anthropology and Japanese studies at Harvard University. He first visited Tōkyō in the late 1960s, and has been hooked on the city ever since, writing about urban culture and history, markets and economic organization, food culture, the fishing industry, and popular culture. His two books about the city are *Neighborhood Tōkyō* and *Tsukiji: The Fish Market at the Center of the World.* His article on the historical traces left in Tōkyō is on p. 203; he also lent his expertise to our Tsukiji walking tour on p. 164.

Merry White is a professor of anthropology at Boston University. She studies the social construction of adolescence in Japan and the US, education, family policy and reform, and group membership and marginality in Japan. Her most recent book is *Perfectly Japanese: Making Families in an Era of Upheaval.* Currently researching coffeehouse culture in Japan, her article on p. 406 delves into the history of the caffeinated beverage. She shares some of her top picks for a cuppa in Kyōto on p. 408.

ACKNOWLEDGMENTS

LET'S GO

TEAM JAPAN THANKS: Daniel, Maiko, Matt, Max, and Nick; Annalise, Kuba, and Tomo. Your passion and dedication were an inspiration to us all. Lauren, for loving us best. Serena, map maven. An ME team that went beyond the call. Prod, for fonts and so much more. Julia and Kathy, roadtrippy podmates. やったー！

TERESA THANKS: Megumi, Andres, and Julia, more than just salarymen. RWs all, some kind of superheroes. Lauren, cheerleader and confidante. Sonja, Luis, Amber, Chris, and Jeff, incongruously grouped, but without whom I couldn't have. Mom, Dad, and Matt, always.

MEGUMI THANKS: Teresa, our battery-powered moonshine; Andres and Julia for always laughing; Thomas and Jeff for customer service; Julia and Kathy for roadtrippiness. A sexy summer crew and Julz, partner in crime. ママ、パパ、Jenny, for consultations and love.

ANDRES THANKS: Teresa, who held it all together. Megumi, Kathy, Julia, and Julia—the best coworkers/podmates. Meredith, for sharing this summer with me. Ruby and Burnett, for good times. Mr. and Mrs. Schweig, for taking care of us. Mom, Dad, and Eric, my family.

JULIA THANKS: Teresa, editrix extraordinaire, amazing Andres and marvelous Megumi. Julia and Kathy (yay floods!), and prod. My whole family: love you more than anything. Amelia for late-night chats and laughs, Edgar for all the fun, insightful Emma, and the Goi family.

SERENA THANKS: Teresa & co., delights to work with. Nathaniel, beacon in the Japanese sea. Jarek, for the buoyant helium.

Editor
Teresa Elsey
Associate Editors
Megumi Gordon, Andres Wei-Chiao Su, Julia Elizabeth Twarog
Managing Editor
Lauren E. Bonner
Map Editor
Serena Tan
Typesetter
Jeffrey Hoffman Yip

Publishing Director
Julie A. Stephens
Editor-in-Chief
Jeffrey Dubner
Production Manager
Dusty Lewis
Cartography Manager
Nathaniel Brooks
Design Manager
Caleb Beyers
Editorial Managers
Lauren Bonner, Ariel Fox, Matthew K. Hudson, Emma Nothmann, Joanna Shawn Brigid O'Leary, Sarah Robinson
Financial Manager
Suzanne Siu
Marketing & Publicity Managers
Megan Brumagim, Nitin Shah
Personnel Manager
Jesse Reid Andrews
Researcher Manager
Jennifer O'Brien
Web Manager
Jesse Tov
Web Content Director
Abigail Burger
Production Associates
Thomas Bechtold, Jeffrey Hoffman Yip
IT Directors
Travis Good, E. Peyton Sherwood
Financial Assistant
R. Kirkie Maswoswe
Associate Web Manager
Robert Dubbin
Office Coordinators
Abigail Burger, Angelina L. Fryer, Liz Glynn

Director of Advertising Sales
Daniel Ramsey
Senior Advertising Associates
Sara Barnett, Daniella Boston
Advertising Artwork Editors
Julia Davidson, Sandy Liu

President
Abhishek Gupta
General Manager
Robert B. Rombauer
Assistant General Manager
Anne E. Chisholm

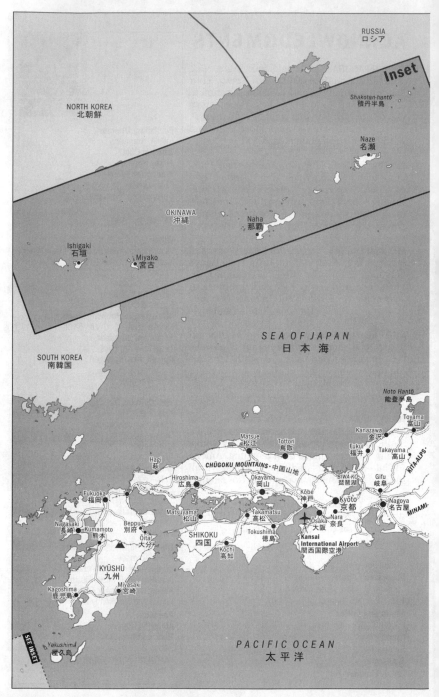

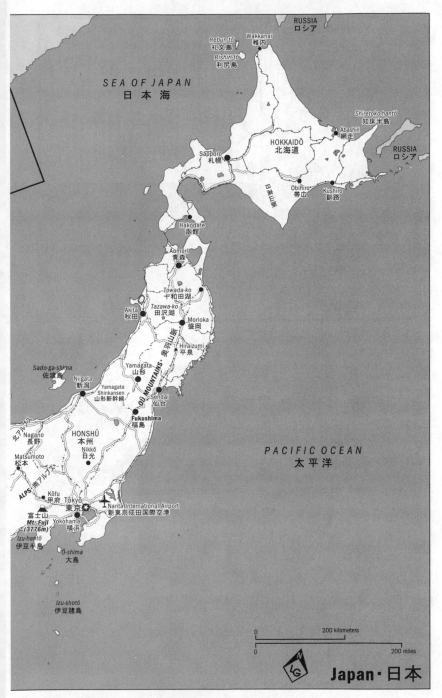

SEA OF JAPAN
日 本 海

RUSSIA
ロシア

Rebun-tō
礼文島
Rishiri-tō
利尻島

Wakkanai
稚内

Shiretoko-hantō
知床半島

HOKKAIDŌ
北海道

Abashiri
網走

RUSSIA
ロシア

Sapporo
札幌

日高山脈

Obihiro
帯広

Kushiro
釧路

Hakodate
函館

Aomori
青森

Towada-ko
十和田湖

Tazawa-ko
田沢湖

Akita
秋田

Morioka
盛岡

奥羽山脈・OU MOUNTAINS・

Hiraizumi
平泉

Sado-ga-shima
佐渡島

Yamagata
山形

Niigata
新潟

Yamagata
Shinkansen
山形新幹線

Sendai
仙台

Fukushima
福島

北アルプス

Nagano
長野

HONSHŪ
本州

Nikkō
日光

PACIFIC OCEAN
太平洋

Matsumoto
松本

ALPS 南アルプス

Kōfu
甲府

Tōkyō
東京

Narita International Airport
新東京成田国際空港

富士山
Mt. Fuji
(3776m)

Yokohama
横浜

Izu-hantō
伊豆半島

Ō-shima
大島

Izu-shotō
伊豆諸島

| | 0 | 200 kilometers |
| | 0 | 200 miles |

Japan・日本

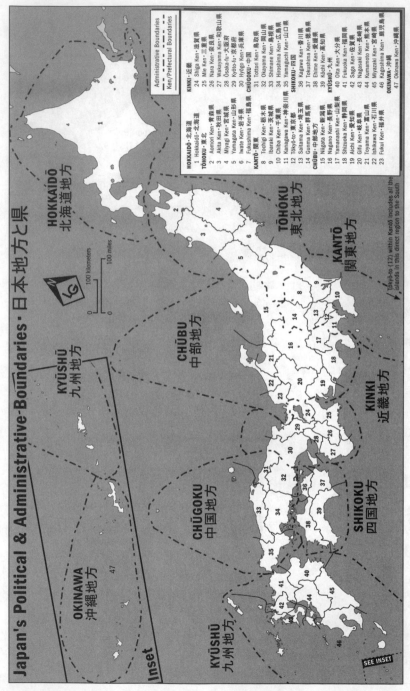

Japan's Political & Administrative-Boundaries・日本地方と県

Inset

HOKKAIDŌ
北海道地方

1

TŌHOKU
東北地方

2

3

5

4

6

7

KANTŌ
関東地方

8

9

10

CHŪBU
中部地方

15

13
14
16

11
12

17
18

21

KYŪSHŪ
九州地方

22

23

20

19

24

29

25

26

27
28

30

32

KINKI
近畿地方

31

33
34

36
35

37

39
38

CHŪGOKU
中国地方

SHIKOKU
四国地方

OKINAWA
沖縄地方

47

41
40

45

42 43
44
46

KYŪSHŪ
九州地方

SEE INSET

N

0   100 miles
0   100 kilometers

HOKKAIDŌ・北海道
1 Hokkaidō・北海道
TŌHOKU・東北
2 Aomori Ken・青森県
3 Akita Ken・秋田県
4 Miyagi Ken・宮城県
5 Yamagata Ken・山形県
6 Iwate Ken・岩手県
7 Fukushima Ken・福島県
KANTŌ・関東
8 Tochigi Ken・栃木県
9 Ibaraki Ken・茨城県
10 Chiba Ken・千葉県
11 Kanagawa Ken・神奈川県
12 Tōkyō-to・東京都
13 Saitama Ken・埼玉県
14 Gunma Ken・群馬県
CHŪBU・中部地方
15 Niigata Ken・新潟県
16 Nagano Ken・長野県
17 Yamanashi Ken・山梨県
18 Shizuoka Ken・静岡県
19 Aichi Ken・愛知県
20 Gifu Ken・岐阜県
21 Toyama Ken・富山県
22 Ishikawa Ken・石川県
23 Fukui Ken・福井県

KINKI・近畿
24 Shiga Ken・滋賀県
25 Mie Ken・三重県
26 Nara Ken・奈良県
27 Wakayama Ken・和歌山県
28 Osaka-fu・大阪府
29 Kyōto-fu・京都府
30 Hyōgo Ken・兵庫県
CHŪGOKU・中国
31 Tottori Ken・鳥取県
32 Okayama Ken・岡山県
33 Shimane Ken・島根県
34 Hiroshima Ken・広島県
35 Yamaguchi Ken・山口県
SHIKOKU・四国
36 Kagawa Ken・香川県
37 Tokushima Ken・徳島県
38 Ehime Ken・愛媛県
39 Kōchi Ken・高知県
KYŪSHŪ・九州
40 Oita Ken・大分県
41 Fukuoka Ken・福岡県
42 Saga Ken・佐賀県
43 Nagasaki Ken・長崎県
44 Kumamoto Ken・熊本県
45 Miyazaki Ken・宮崎県
46 Kagoshima Ken・鹿児島県
OKINAWA・沖縄
47 Okinawa Ken・沖縄県

Tōkyō-to (12) within Kantō includes all the
islands in this direct region to the South

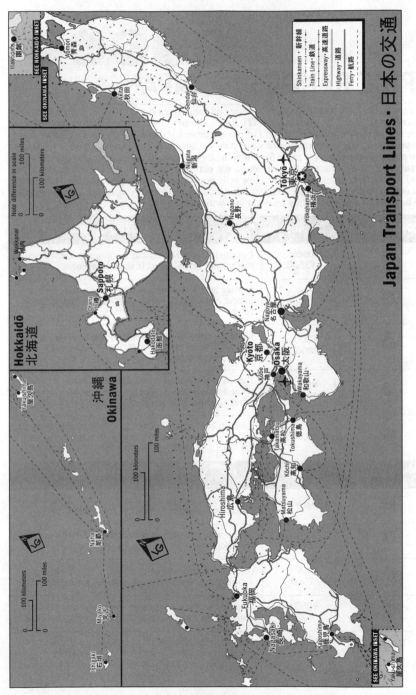

Japan Transport Lines・日本の交通

Shinkansen・新幹線
Train Line・鉄道
Expressway・高速道路
Highway・道路
Ferry・航路

Hokkaidō
北海道

Okinawa
沖縄

SEE HOKKAIDŌ INSET

SEE OKINAWA INSET

Note difference in scale

0　　　100 miles
0　　　100 kilometers

Hakodate 函館

Aomori 青森

Akita 秋田

Sendai 仙台

Niigata 新潟

Nagano 長野

Tokyo 東京

Yokohama 横浜

Nagoya 名古屋

Kyōto 京都

Ōsaka 大阪

Kōbe 神戸

Wakayama 和歌山

Takamatsu 高松

Tokushima 徳島

Kōchi 高知

Matsuyama 松山

Hiroshima 広島

Fukuoka 福岡

Nagasaki 長崎

Kagoshima 鹿児島

Yaku-Shima 屋久島

Wakkanai 稚内

Sapporo 札幌

Otaru 小樽

Hakodate 函館

Yakushima 屋久島

Naha 那覇

Miyako 宮古

Ishigaki 石垣

100 kilometers
100 miles

XV

1 2 3 4 5

PRICE RANGES >> JAPAN

Our researchers list establishments in order of value from best to worst; our favorites are denoted by the Let's Go thumbs-up (🖤). Since the best value is not always the cheapest price, we have incorporated a system of price ranges for quick reference. Our price ranges are based on a rough expectation of what you will spend. For **accommodations,** we base our price range off the cheapest price for which a single traveler can stay for one night. For **restaurants** and other dining establishments, we estimate the average amount that you will spend in that restaurant. The table below tells you what you will *typically* find in Japan at the corresponding price range; keep in mind that a particularly expensive ice cream stand may be marked a ❷, depending on what you will spend.

ACCOMMODATIONS	RANGE	WHAT YOU'RE *LIKELY* TO FIND
❶	under ¥3500	Campsites; youth hostels and dorm rooms. Least expensive capsule hotels. Expect to share a bathroom.
❷	¥3500-5000	Capsule hotels. Less pricy minshuku and ryokan, probably without any meals included. Very basic or older business hotels, usually with limited amenities.
❸	¥5001-8000	Standard, clean business hotels, probably right by the station. Mid-range minshuku and ryokan, possibly with added perks like meals or a bath.
❹	¥8001-15,000	The very nicest ryokan, generally with two meals included. Nicer hotels, including well-known chains, with some extras and additional service.
❺	¥15,000+	Seriously swanky hotels, often in highly desirable areas. If it's a 5 and doesn't have the perks you want, you've paid too much.
FOOD	RANGE	WHAT YOU'RE *LIKELY* TO FIND
❶	under ¥600	Tea, pastries, snacks, and noodle joints. A super casual atmosphere, whether it's carryout or seats at a bar.
❷	¥601-1000	Simple set meals with noodles or rice or a single course. Most likely an informal setting.
❸	¥1001-2500	Local specialty foods, meat dishes, sushi, or set meals with several courses. Sit-down service in a nice place.
❹	¥2501-4000	A somewhat fancy restaurant, probably with multiple-course meals. Much like 3, but with an extra splash of class.
❺	¥4001+	Specialty or gourmet food in a traditional or otherwise luxurious setting. Better be worth writing home about.

DISCOVER JAPAN

Extending from snowy peaks to tropical paradises, encompassing urban cacophony and rural retreats, expressing itself through *kabuki* theater and Kurosawa cinema, Japan packs more inside its borders than you'd think such a tiny slice of real estate could handle. With a strife-filled history and a tendency toward natural disasters, it's a country continually on the make, always ready to rebuild and renew. At the cutting edge of technology and business, this archipelago is also at the forward edge of the globe, greeting the dawn while the rest of the world sleeps.

Unhindered by its late entry onto the world stage, Japan has made up for lost time by spreading an unmistakable culture that seamlessly blends old with new, east with west. Whether the image that flits to mind is of *kimono*-clad hostesses performing tea ceremonies or harried salarymen commuting on high-speed *shinkansen*, people across the globe have vivid impressions of what's distinctly and authentically Japanese. The country has done a brisk trade in exports, spreading sushi, anime, martial arts, and high technology all over the planet, making "Made in Japan" a stamp recognized by consumers of culture the world over.

But as familiar as Japan may seem, it's still an enigma to the outside. Closed to the West until 1853 and separated from continental Asia by both oceans and ideologies, this island nation stands uniquely apart from the rest of the world. From the *samurai* ethos to industrial efficiency, demure *geisha* to collective responsibility, Japan's mystique has fascinated the world for centuries. And as much as Japan stands at the forefront of globalization, it can also be an insular culture that responds better to subtle indirection than pointed inquiries. For every traditional temple or urban imprint you recognize, the country will surprise you by throwing a secluded islet or undiscovered subculture into the mix. As well versed as you may be in *kendō* or *kanji*, your first thought as you step off the plane could still be that you're sure not in Kansas anymore. Neither entirely familiar nor completely foreign, Japan offers an experience you'll find nowhere else, one you owe it to yourself to discover.

FACTS AND FIGURES

CAPITAL: Tōkyō.	**PRICE OF LAND IN GINZA'S MOST EXPENSIVE DISTRICT:** ¥12 million (US$100,000) per square meter.
POPULATION: 127,435,000.	
EARTHQUAKES PER YEAR: 1000.	**ARMS ON A THOUSAND-ARMED KANNON STATUE:** Usually 42.
ACTIVE VOLCANOES: 86.	
CELLULAR PHONES: 81,780,000 (1 for every 1½ people).	**KEYS ON A JAPANESE TYPEWRITER:** About 2400.
VENDING MACHINES: 5,500,400 (1 for every 23 people).	**LICENSED HELLO KITTY PRODUCTS:** 12,000-15,000.
TONS OF FISH TRADED DAILY AT TŌKYŌ'S TSUKIJI MARKET: 2300.	**AVERAGE BUSINESSMAN'S BOWS PER DAY:** 200-300.

TOP TEN LIST

TOP 10 ISLANDS

So you've knocked off the big four. Insatiable island-hoppers still have thousands to choose from. Some *Let's Go* favorites, from Awaji-shima to Zamami-jima:

1. Awaji-shima (p. 525). Wedged between Honshū and Shikoku, this oblong isle boasts Earth's longest suspension bridge.

2. Fukue-jima (p. 595). Gaze toward Asia from these cliffs off Kyūshū, one of Japan's western-most points.

3. Ikuchi-jima (p. 493). Citrus trees dot this Mediterranean-styled isle in the Inland Sea.

4. Iriomote-jima (p. 663). Find truly untrampled territory on this wildest member of the Yaeyamas.

5. Miyajima (p. 494). The Shintō *torii* gate is a don't-miss at Hiroshima's photogenic cousin.

6. Nii-jima (p. 241). Once home to criminal exiles, this speck in the Izu-Shotō chain now attracts Tōkyōites fleeing urban prisons.

7. Odaiba (p. 127). A man-made mass in Tōkyō Bay, this is where business-as-usual turns to unbridled creativity and pure pleasure.

8. Rishiri-tō (p. 721). This dot off Hokkaidō's northernmost tip is marked by a majestic volcano.

9. Sado-ga-shima (p. 276). Exiled literati have long found inspiration on this isle in the Sea of Japan.

10. Zamami-jima (p. 653). Claim your slice of paradise at this laid-back locale in the Keramas.

WHEN TO GO

Japan's geography spans from the sub-arctic to the sub-tropical, so there are no hard and fast rules about the **weather**. Hokkaidō and the north have cool summers and harsh winters, while Kyūshū and Okinawa are warm year-round with limited variation (though they can be plenty hot and humid in summer). The central mountains stay cool in all seasons, with some retaining snow-capped peaks through the hottest months. Honshū's east coast is temperate, and hot in summer, while the Sea of Japan coast gets heavy precipitation blown over from continental Asia. For more on regional variation, consult our climate chart (p. 736).

The Japanese pride themselves on their country's four distinct **seasons** and are connoisseurs of seasonal change. Spring may be the most welcomed season, heralded by the arrival of plum blossoms and the northward creep of cherry blossoms, starting around Tōkyō late in March. The **rainy season** comes in June and lasts three or four weeks. July and August are often miserably hot and humid, and urbanites flee the city for the cooler mountains, seaside, or north. **Typhoon** season spans from May and November, peaking between August and October (p. 17). Fall weather is usually pleasant and clear, so October and November are pleasant, low-season times to visit. Winters are generally mild and sunny, although they're harsh up north and snowy in Central Honshū. Snow sports are prevalent in those areas, so skiers and snowshoers should visit then.

Major **holiday** seasons are **Golden Week** (at the end of April and beginning of May), **Obon** (in July or August), and the week around the **New Year.** While the festivities could be fun, trains and buses will be jammed, accommodations booked solid, and many tourist facilities shut down. If traveling during major holidays, book your bed far in advance and prepare to pay extra for it. Government facilities and offices will be closed on national holidays, while sights and other attractions are more likely to remain open; refer to our table for a full list of important dates (p. 107). Local festivals take place in all seasons and for all reasons, though they're concentrated in the summer. See our **Holidays & Festivals** section (p. 106) for more details on all things celebratory.

WHAT TO DO

With *samurai* strongholds just kilometers from city sprawl and natural wonders, and with a devastatingly smooth and sexy train system connecting it all, Japan has thousands of ways to delight the footloose traveler.

THE GREAT OUTDOORS

Although Japan may be inextricably wedded to images of chaotic concrete and languishing landfills, beyond apocalyptic Tōkyō lies a wonderland for the outdoors lover. On **Ishigaki-jima** (p. 658), enter an alternate dimension of untamed flora and fauna, and take a day to play hide and seek with the tropical fish in the coral reefs. To see the truly untouched reaches of Japan, hack your way through the subtropical wilderness of **Iriomote-jima** (p. 663) and tumble down Urauchigawa's Amazon-esque waters. Shikoku's **Kaifu** (p. 536) will keep the adrenaline flowing as you glide across the break where the Kaifu River and coastline kiss. In the spring, **Furano** (p. 701) croons lavender fields forever, but when winter snow blankets the purple meadows, its mountains beckon skiers. Close to Matsumoto, **Hakuba** (p. 339) lets visitors show off their skills at hiking, biking, mountaineering, skiing, and snowboarding, and right around the corner, a stone's throw from Nagano, **Shiga Kōgen** (p. 331) invites lovers to lie down in the greenery surrounding its lustrous lake. Descend on the mountains of Shiga Kōgen in the winter to swoosh down some of the most acclaimed slopes in Japan, and arguably, the world. At **Towada-ko** (p. 321), see the dual crater lake, formed by a volcanic eruption and now resting on 400m of mountainous rubble, proof that self-destruction sometimes produces ethereal results. **Aso-san** (p. 619), the world's biggest volcanic caldera, comprises five mountains and an outer mountain ring, embracing tourists with a grassy cushion in spring.

DIGESTIBLES & COMESTIBLES

The range of regional variations in Japanese cuisine is matched only by the keen interest the Japanese take in their own local, prefectural, and national foods. Whether sampling delicate dishes of dried tofu or slurping up savory bowls of noodles, you'll find that eating in Japan is as much about the experience—visual, environmental, and auditory—as it is about the food itself. The act of preparing, packaging, and eating *rāmen* is enshrined at the **Yokohama Rāmen Museum** (p. 206). In **Okinawa** (p. 636), be sure to sample local *soba*, made with pure wheat noodles and a rich pork broth. In **Morioka** (p. 304), small bowls of *wanko soba* are at the center of an annual noodle-eating competition. The **Rāmen Stadium** in **Fukuoka** (p. 584) is a noodle aficionado's world tour, transporting you to the far reaches of Honshū, Hokkaidō, and Kyūshū via eight regional varieties.

For Japan's most sought-after beef, head to **Kōbe** (p. 476) where the cows drink beer and get massages to yield surpassingly tender marbled steaks and slices. Browse the vast **Tsukiji** fish market in **Tōkyō** (p. 164), the center of the *sushi* world. In **Kōchi**, try *amego*, featuring large pieces of lightly seared *sashimi* (p. 553). But if all this talk of meat offends your palate or principles, retreat to the Buddhist enclaves of **Kamakura** (p. 219) and **Kyōto** (p. 473) where restaurants specialize in *shōjin ryōri*, a refined (if pricey) vegetarian cuisine. For a less fancy, more filling meal, pop into any *okonomiyaki* joint (p. 292) to

DISCOVER

fry yourself a savory pancake loaded with cabbage and meat or fish. Stock up on traditional sweets and snacks on the **Nakamise** shopping street in **Tōkyō** (p. 178) or at **Kashiya Yokochō** in **Kawagoe** (p. 252). Check out a Japanese bakery for a taste (or worshipful glimpse) of the nation's pillowy, perfectly shaped, perfectly glazed bread. If you're low on cash, enjoy a cheap feast anytime in the basements of department stores, which give an altogether new meaning to the phrase "food court."

TRADITIONAL ARTS

These islands may have embraced modernity without looking back, but traces of an older Japan are thick on the ground. Learn to arrange flowers from the pros at **Tōkyō's** *ikebana* school (p. 190) or take in a show (or an act; let's be realistic here) at Kabuki-za theater (p. 186). **Kyōto** (p. 473) is Japan's playground for the traditional arts—what you can see is limited only by your time and stamina—but *nō* theater, classical dance, and *geisha*-spotting should top your to-do list. The multiple museums in **Kanazawa** (p. 377) preserve crafts, history, and culture in equal measure. Get your freak on in **Tokushima** (p. 528)—dancing crowds gather for August's Awa Odori, but there's participatory footwork every day. When you're ready to get out of the city, you'll find that smaller towns offer equivalent artistic obsessions. **Mashiko** (p. 258) is a potter's paradise, boasting hundreds of kilns and scores of artists, while little **Seto** (p. 345) claims to be the birthplace of the clay arts. Lacquerware is the name of the game in **Kiso-Hirasawa** (p. 344), tucked deep in the Kiso Valley. Some towns specialize, and some towns *specialize:* **Tendo** (p. 286) is one of the latter, churning out chess pieces for all of Japan. **Hirara** (p. 655), in the Okinawan chain, boasts fine clothmakers at work, while nearby **Ishigaki** (p. 658) and other islands pulsate with the sounds of a unique musical tradition.

FESTIVALS

If you're in Japan on a day when there's *not* a festival going on somewhere, frankly, there must be something wrong with you. Every village big enough to have a shrine has at least one annual festival, lasting anywhere from one day to several months. Celebrations range from parades to fireworks to bizarre athletic contests. On January 6 in Kanazawa, the **Kagatobi Dezomeshiki** (p. 377) features scantily-clad firemen who venture into the cold, drinking *sake*, to show the crowds traditional firefighting skills. Each year since 1950, February has heralded the world-famous **Sapporo Snow Festival** (p. 684), an extravaganza of fantastical snow and ice sculptures carved by teams from Japan and dozens of other nations. Hundreds of thousands of spectators gather along the banks of Tōkyō's Sumida River in late July to be blown away by the 20,000 fireworks at the **Sumidagawa Hanabi Taikai** (p. 201). In the **Aomori Nebuta** (p. 317), held from August 2 to 7, gigantic *samurai*-shaped lanterns parade through the streets of Aomori, surrounded by costumed dancers; visitors are free to join in (though you'll need to visit a costume shop if you're planning to dance). At the thunderous **Morioka Sansa Odori** (p. 304) August 1-3, thousands of dancers, drummers, and flautists come together to create an astounding display of performance and sound. August 12-15, in the middle of the Obon festivities, the hugely popular **Awa Odori** draws crowds to Tokushima to watch a parade of fast-paced, frantic dancers—it's also known as the "fool's dance" (p. 528). Dragons come alive, Chinese-style, October 7-9 in Nagasaki for the **Nagasaki Kunichi festival** (p. 619). November 3 is the annual **Matsumoto Oshiro Matsuri** (p. 334), which celebrates the castle with flower shows and festive floats.

DISCOVER

▨LET'S GO PICKS

BEST CAPITALS: Nara (p. 443), **Kyōto** (p. 473), and **Kamakura** (p. 219) all once had a claim to being Japan's *it*-city and have the sites and sights to prove it. **Tōkyō** (p. 110) takes the honors at present, but what the future holds is still open to debate (p. 158).

BEST EXPLOSIVES: The **Sumidagawa Hanabi Taikai** (p. 201), Tōkyō's biggest pyrotechnic show, lights up the city like nothing else. **Aso-san** (p. 619) is the world's biggest volcanic caldera, belching poisonous gas over Kyūshū.

BEST BATHROOMS: The gold- and platinum-tiled beauties at **Kanazawa's Sakuda Gold and Silver Leaf Company** (p. 179) are worth a cool ¥30,000,000.

JUICIEST ATTRACTIONS: Learn about the wonders of Vitamin C at Okinawa's **Nago Pineapple Park** (p. 650). Try the *konatsu* in **Katsurahama** (p. 560)—round like an orange, yellow like a lemon.

SECOND-BEST PLACE TO SEE TRADITIONAL JAPAN: For those who accept some imitations, **Nakamura** (p. 562) self-identifies as "Little Kyōto." **Kawagoe** (p. 252) claims the title "Little Edo"; travelers without time machines will have to take their word for it.

BEST SUNRISE (DISPUTED): Dawn at **Mt. Fuji's** summit is either incredible or pitiful, depending on who you ask (p. 246).

BEST PLACE TO PLAY WITH YOUR FOOD: The mealtime gimmicks at Tōkyō's **Kagaya** (p. 146) include crayon-scrawled menus, choose-your-own international ambiance, and frog costumes. A couple neighborhoods away is **Kappa-bashi-dōri** (p. 178), plastic food central.

MUSEUMS MOST LIKELY TO GIVE YOU A COMPLEX: The **Nawa Insect Museum** (p. 387) in Gifu encases scads of creepy-crawlies, while Freud would have a field day at Uwajima's **Sex Museum** (p. 575).

SUGGESTED ITINERARIES

BEST OF JAPAN (2 MONTHS): A full tour of Japan takes you island-hopping from sprawling metropolises to cultural capitals to rural retreats and back again. Start in the thick of things, with a dip into the mind-boggling urban hotpot that is **Tōkyō** (4 days; p. 110). Once you've caught your breath, daytrip to historic **Kawagoe** (1 day; p. 252). Next stop **Kamakura** (1 day; p. 219) for serious temple-sighting, then try your luck (and hiking boots) against iconic **Mt. Fuji** (2 days; p. 244). Recover from the climb, then start your northward travel with the brilliant shrines at **Nikkō** (1 day; p. 259). Pass through Sendai (p. 286) to reach seaside **Matsushima** (p. 293), then trek inland to the majestic sights of little **Hiraizumi** (1 day; p. 301). Dip into folk-tale culture in **Tōno** (1 day; p. 302) and the surrounding valley for a refresher. Keep moving north, sampling the noodles in **Morioka** (1 day; p. 304), the volcanic crater lake **Towada-ko** (1 day; p. 321), and the *samurai* sights of **Hirosaki** (1 day; p. 314). From Aomori (p. 317), head to **Hakodate** (1 day; p. 670), your introduction to Hokkaidō. Ride the

rails up the coast, visiting **Shikotsu-Toya National Park** (1 day; p. 679) along the way, and ending up in cosmopolitan **Sapporo** (2 days; p. 684). Ship eastward to fishing port **Abashiri** (1 day; p. 709), then take your time poking around vivid, volcanic **Shiretoko National Park** (2 days; p. 715). Change trains at **Asahikawa** (1 day; p. 698) for northerly **Wakkanai** (1 day; p. 719), which puts you in spitting distance of Russia. Ferry out to idyllic **Rishiri-tō** and **Rebun-tō** (2 days; p. 721), then catch the ferry from Otaru or take the train back to Honshū. Either way, end up in **Niigata** (1 day; p. 274), convenient base for culture-rich **Sado-ga-shima** (2 days; p. 276). Castle town **Matsumoto** (1 day; p. 334) is a good first plunge into the Japan Alps. Reemerge at urban **Nagoya** (1 day; p. 324), then wash off the grime at quaint **Takayama** (2 days; p. 345) and tradition-speckled **Kanazawa** (1 day; p. 377). **Nara** (2 days; p. 443), with its horde of historic sights and giant bronze Buddha, is worth a long, awed look. The contrast of über-modern **Ōsaka** (2 days; p. 430) and its serious nightlife may be a shocker, but interna-

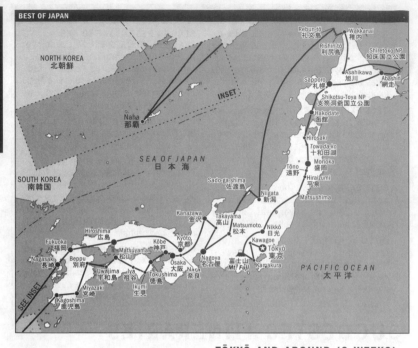

BEST OF JAPAN

tional **Kōbe** (1 day; p. 476) has a cuisine to soothe every taste. Cross the bridge to Shikoku, where **Tokushima** (1 day; p. 528) awaits; then slide down the southeast coast (p. 536) for sand and surf—**Ikumi** (1 day; p. 537) gets our pick. Slip through the vine-bridged **Iya Valley** (1 day; p. 549) on your way to literary **Matsuyama** (2 days; p. 565), and end up in compact, coastal **Uwajima** (1 day; p. 575). Catch the ferry to *onsen*-mad **Beppu** (1 day; p. 635), and continue your tour with a run down to nearly-tropical **Miyazaki** (1 day; p. 635) and a stopover in sunny **Kagoshima** (1 day; p. 619). If you can't get enough paradise, catch a flight or ferry to **Okinawa-hontō** (3 days; p. 636), starting in **Naha** (p. 639). Resume with a stop in **Nagasaki** (2 days; p. 619), and don't leave Kyūshū without slurping noodles in **Fukuoka** (1 day; p. 584). The train runs to **Hiroshima** (2 days; p. 494), where thought-provoking memorials stand witness. End your whirlwind tour in **Kyōto** (4 days; p. 473), prime territory for *geisha*-spotting and steeping in Japanese tradition.

TŌKYŌ AND AROUND (3 WEEKS):
Begin your jaunt through the greater Tōkyō area with a swan-dive into **Shinjuku** (1 day; p. 119), the neon-festooned, concrete cynosure of Tōkyō. Sink or swim as you wade through the crashing tide of people at one of the busiest train stations in the world, and later, mingle with city revelers at one of Shinjuku's many *izakaya* (pubs), or, if you're feeling adventurous, at a joint in Kabukichō. Take a day to appreciate the aging Sensō-ji in **Asakusa** (1 day; p. 117) and buy the folks back home Japanese trinkets and candy galore. Conduct a sociological study of Japan's youth on the shoplined streets of **Harajuku** (p. 117) and, on a Sunday afternoon, the greens of **Yoyogi Park** (1 day; p. 159). Discover the vanguard of Japanese nationalism within the walls of the **Imperial Palace** (1 day; p. 161), and just 24hr. later, feel the throb of fashion and culture that pulsates through **Shibuya** (1 day; p. 118), the virtual epicenter of Japan. Set your inner electronics guru free at the playground of appliances in **Akihabara** (½ day; p. 119), and when you're ready for a taste of the West, **Roppongi** (½ day; p. 118) serves it up in *gaijin*-oriented

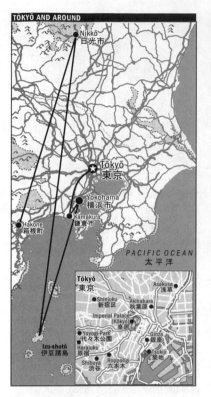

CLASSICAL JAPAN (17 DAYS):

Though disasters, natural and otherwise, have forced the Japanese to rebuild many ancient sites from rubble, history is very much alive in the religious and secular edifices remaining from the feudal past. From Kansai Airport, take the train and cable-car up through the clouds to **Kōya-san** (1 day; p. 467), the mountain home of Shingon Buddhism. After spending the night in temple lodgings (*shukubō*), attend morning services and explore ancient monasteries. Make your pilgrimage east to the cedar-shrouded Shintō heartland of **Ise** (1 day; p. 470), then backtrack to ancient capital **Nara** (1 day; p. 443) where some of Japan's oldest temples await. Begin your **Kyōto** caper (3 days; p. 473) with a Spartan stay at Myōren-ji (p. 404), then sweep through centuries of history at Tō-ji, the Kyōto Imperial Palace, and the Tokugawa castle Nijō-jo. Head west to play *samurai* in feudal fortress **Himeji-jō** (1 day, p. 476), and hop across the Inland Sea to pilgrimage town **Kotohira** (1 day; p. 546). Cross Shikoku to see venerable Kōchi Castle and Chikurin-ji in **Kōchi** (1 day; p. 546). Mosey over to **Matsuyama** for a look at the beautiful castle and a taste of the city's literary heritage (2 days; p. 565), and soak in the oldest hot spring in Japan at **Dogo** (2 days; p. 573). A ferry will take you to Kyūshū; use **Beppu** as a jumping-off point for the ancient rock-carved Buddhist images at Usuki and Kunisaki-hantō (2 days; p. 635). To the west are port cities that reflect Japan's multicultural past: take in the Chinese temples and Dutch colonial heritage at **Nagasaki** (1 day; p. 619), and learn about Japanese Christians at **Shimabara Castle** (1 day; p. 604).

WINTER WONDERLAND (3 WEEKS):

Snowbunnies know that the north of Japan is perfect for cold-weather fun. Warm your toes in **Matsumoto** (2 days; p. 334) before hitting the slopes at **Hakuba** (1 day; p. 339). **Nagano** (1 day; p. 324)

bars, clubs, and restaurants. Rise for an early morning promenade through the fish- and fruit-scented warehouses of **Tsukiji** (1 day; p. 164), and observe the most subtle daily exchange of ¥2.2 billion in the world. Experience a microcosm of Japan's contradictions in **Ginza** (1-2 days; p. 117), through traditional *kabuki* and gold-tinted materialism. Head out of Tōkyō to pay respect to the Buddha of Buddhas at **Kamakura** (2 days; p. 219) and wander around the temples and shops. Catch a train to **Yokohama** and fuel your body at a savory Chinese restaurant and crane your neck at Japan's tallest skyscraper, the 296-foot Landmark Tower (2 days; p. 206). Ease out of your city skin and into the serene slip of **Izu-Shotō,** where you can splash on the beaches (3 days; p. 239). Ogle the opulence that laces the temples of **Nikkō** (2-3 days; p. 259) to prepare for the trip's end: relaxation in the *onsen* and on the slopes of **Hakone** (2 days; p. 229).

hosted the 1998 Winter Olympics and knows a thing or two about snow sports. Jump from there to **Shiga Kōgen** (2 days; p. 331), where 21 ski resorts await; then soak it off in the baths at **Nozawa Onsen** (1 day; p. 332), also home to a skiing museum. **Ura-Bandai** (2 days; p. 272) is all about snowy slopes and serious hikes. If you time it right, you can catch "snow monsters" at **Zaō Onsen** (p. 284), near **Yamagata** (2 days; p. 286), but either way, the weather's fine. **Tazawa-ko** (1 day; p. 310) is in inland Akita Prefecture, Japan's official snowiest spot. Cross over to Hokkaidō for **Niseko** (2 days; p. 677), a winter sports paradise. Land in **Sapporo** (2 days; p. 684) in early February to catch the huge Snow Festival, then ship out to **Daisetsuzan National Park** (2 days; p. 702) for more skiing and snowshoeing. A sightseeing cruise that cuts through the glaciers at **Abashiri** (2 days; p. 709) makes for an unusual ending, though you hardly need an ice breaker when you've seen so much.

THE QUASI-TROPICS (17 DAYS): Don't associate Japan with relaxation? Start your attitude adjustment by surrounding yourself with the lush forests of **Fukue-jima** in the Gotō Islands (2 days; p. 595). You won't want to leave, unless it's to escape the heat in the hot spring town of **Unzen**, where legend has it that a path leads down to hell (1 day; p. 603). Regain Paradise at the base of a live volcano in summery **Kagoshima,** the "Naples of Japan" (2 days; p. 619), and then begin an Okinawan island-hop, starting in the energetic capital of **Naha**, where you can chill to a Ryūkyū pop beat and it's only a bus ride to a beach (3 days; p. 639). Forget your worries on the sun-drenched shores of **Zamami-jima** (2 days; p. 653), then adjust your mask and hold your breath as a menagerie of tropical fish swim by **Ishigaki-jima's** stunning off-shore coral reef (2 days; p. 658). For a change of pace, ride a buffalo cart between the orange-tiled roofs of **Taketomi-jima** (1 day; p. 663). Finally, if you're ready, strap on your hiking boots, grab a kayak, and head for the uncharted interior of Japan's last true wilderness: **Irio-mote-jima** (4 days; p. 663).

ESSENTIALS

FACTS FOR THE TRAVELER

ENTRANCE REQUIREMENTS
Passport (p. 10). Required for citizens of Australia, Canada, Ireland, New Zealand, South Africa, the UK, and the US.
Visa (p. 11). Required only for citizens of South Africa; citizens of Australia, Canada, Ireland, New Zealand, the UK, and the US do not need visas for short stays.
Work Permit (p. 11). Required for all foreigners planning to work in Japan.
International Driving Permit (p. 48). Required for all those planning to drive.

EMBASSIES AND CONSULATES

JAPANESE CONSULAR SERVICES ABROAD

For the addresses of other embassies, contact the Japanese **Ministry of Foreign Affairs** (☎+81-3-3580-3311) or consult www.infojapan.org/about/emb_cons/over.

Australia: Embassy of Japan. 112 Empire Circuit, Yarralumla, Canberra ACT 2600 (☎+61-2-6273-3244; www.japan.org.au). Consulates-General in Brisbane (☎+61-7-3221-5188), Melbourne (☎+61-3-9639-3244), Perth (☎+61-8-9480-1800), and Sydney (☎+61-2-9231-3455).

Canada: Embassy of Japan. 255 Sussex Dr., Ottawa, Ontario K1N 9E6 (☎+1-613-241-8541; www.ca.emb-japan.go.jp). Consulates-General in Edmonton (☎+1-780-422-3752), Montreal (☎+1-514-866-3429), Toronto (☎+1-416-363-7038), and Vancouver (☎+1-604-684-5868).

Ireland: Embassy of Japan. Nutley Bldg., Merrion Centre, Nutley Ln., Dublin 4 (☎+353-1-202-8300; fax 283-8726; www.ie.emb-japan.go.jp).

New Zealand: Embassy of Japan. Majestic Centre, 100 Willis St., P.O. Box 6340, Wellington (☎+64-4-473-1540; www.nz.emb-japan.go.jp). Consulate-General in Auckland (☎+64-9-303-4106). Consulate in Christchurch (☎+64-3-366-5680).

South Africa: Embassy of Japan. 259 Baines St., c/o Frans Oerder St., Groenkloof, 0181, Pretoria (☎+27-12-452-1500; www.japan.org.za). Office of Consul in Cape Town (☎+27-21-425-1695).

UK: Embassy of Japan. 101-104, Piccadilly, London, W1J 7JT (☎+44-20-7465-6500; www.embjapan.org.uk). Consulates-General in London (☎+44-20-465-6500) and Edinburgh (☎+44-131-225-4777).

US: Embassy of Japan. 2520 Massachusetts Ave., N.W. Washington D.C., 20008 (☎+1-202-238-6700; www.embjapan.org). Consulates-General in Anchorage, Atlanta, Boston, Chicago, Denver, Detroit, Honolulu, Houston, Kansas City, Los Angeles, Miami, New Orleans, New York, Portland, San Francisco, and Seattle.

CONSULAR SERVICES IN JAPAN

The Japanese **Ministry of Foreign Affairs** (☎+81-3-3580-3311) can assist travelers in finding embassies in Japan and maintains an online list (www.infojapan.org/about/emb_cons/protocol/index.html). **Embassy Avenue** (www.embassy-avenue.jp) hosts a number of Japanese embassy websites and provides links to others.

Australia: Australian Embassy. 2-1-14, Mita, Minato-ku, Tōkyō 108-8361 (☎+81-3-5232-4111; www.australia.or.jp). Consulates-General in Ōsaka (☎+81-6-6941-9448) and Fukuoka (☎+81-92-734-5055). Consulates in Nagoya (☎+81-52-211-0630), Sapporo (☎+81-11-242-4381), and Sendai (☎+81-22-265-6810).

Canada: Canadian Embassy. 7-3-38, Akasaka, Minato-ku, Tōkyō 107-8503 (☎+81-3-5412-6200; www.canadanet.or.jp). Consulates in Ōsaka (☎+81-6-6212-4910), Fukuoka (☎+81-92-752-6055), and Nagoya (☎+81-52-972-0450).

Ireland: Irish Embassy. Ireland House, 2-10-7, Kōjimachi, Chiyoda-ku, Tōkyō 102-0083 (☎+81-3-3263-0695; www.embassy-avenue.jp/ireland).

New Zealand: New Zealand Embassy. 20-40, Kamiyama-chō, Shibuya-ku, Tōkyō 150-0047 (☎+81-3-3467-2271; www.nzembassy.com/japan).

South Africa: South African Embassy. 414 Zenkyoren Bldg., 4th fl., 2-7-9, Hirakawa-cho, Chiyoda-ku, Tōkyō 102-0093 (☎+81-3-3265-3366; www.rsatk.com).

UK: British Embassy. 1 Ichiban-chō, Chiyoda-ku, Tōkyō 102-8381 (☎+81-3-5211-1100; www.uknow.or.jp). Consulate-General in Ōsaka (☎+81-6-6120-5600). Consulate in Nagoya (☎+81-52-223-5031).

US: United States Embassy. 1-10-5, Akasaka, Minato-ku, Tōkyō 107-8420 (☎+81-3-3224-5000; http://usembassy.state.gov/tokyo). Consulates-General in Osaka (☎+81-6-6315-5900), Sapporo (☎+81-11-641-1115), and Naha (☎+81-98-876-4211). Consulates in Fukuoka (☎+81-92-751-9331) and Nagoya (☎+81-52-203-4011).

TOURIST OFFICES

JAPAN NATIONAL TOURIST ORGANIZATION (JNTO). Charged with promoting tourism in Japan, JNTO operates tourist offices and distributes information.

Japan office: Tōkyō Kōtsū Kaikan Bldg., 2-10-1, Yūraku-chō, Chiyoda-ku, Tōkyō 100-0006 (☎+81-3-3216-1901; www.jnto.go.jp).

Offices abroad: Australia: Level 33, The Chifley Tower, 2 Chifley Sq., Sydney, N.S.W. 2000 (☎+61-2-9232-4522; fax 9232-1494). **Canada:** 165 University Ave., Toronto, Ontario M5H 3B8 (☎+1-416-366-7140; www.japantravelinfo.com). **UK:** Heathcoat House, 20 Savile Row, London, W1S 3PR (☎+44-20-7734-9638; www.seejapan.co.uk). **US:** One Rockefeller Plaza, Ste. 1250, New York, NY 10020 (☎+1-212-757-5640; www.japantravelinfo.com). Additional offices in Chicago (☎+1-312-222-0874), San Francisco (☎+1-415-292-5686), and Los Angeles (☎+1-213-623-1952).

 GUIDED TOURS JNTO produces comprehensive online directories of tour operators who run trips to Japan. For tours from the US and Canada, visit www.jnto.go.jp/eng/TL/index.html. For tours from the UK, Ireland, South Africa, and assorted European destinations, visit www.seejapan.co.uk/ftour.html.

DOCUMENTS AND FORMALITIES

PASSPORTS

Citizens of Australia, Canada, Ireland, New Zealand, South Africa, the UK, and the US need valid passports to enter Japan and to re-enter their home countries. You may be unable to enter Japan if you have less than 6 months before your passport expires. Returning home with an expired passport is illegal, and you may be fined.

Citizens of Australia, Canada, Ireland, New Zealand, the UK, and the US can apply for a passport at any post office, passport office, or court of law. Citizens of South Africa can apply for a passport at any Home Affairs office. Any new passport or renewal applications must be filed well in advance of the departure date, although most passport offices offer rush services for a very steep fee.

Photocopy the page of your passport with your photo, as well as your visas, traveler's check serial numbers and any other important documents. Carry one set of copies in a safe place, apart from the originals, and leave another set at home. Consulates also recommend that you carry an expired passport or an official copy of your birth certificate in a part of your baggage separate from other documents. If you lose your passport, notify the local police and your home government's embassy or consulate. To expedite its replacement, you will need to know all information previously recorded and show ID and proof of citizenship. In some cases, a replacement may take weeks to process and may be valid only for a limited time. Visas stamped in your old passport will be irretrievably lost. In an emergency, ask for temporary traveling papers that will let you return home.

VISAS AND WORK PERMITS

As of August 2003, South Africans need a visa in addition to a valid passport for entrance to Japan; citizens of Australia, Canada, Ireland, New Zealand, the UK, and the US do not. Citizens of Australia, New Zealand, and the US can stay for 90 days without a visa, citizens of Canada up to 3 months, and citizens of Ireland and the UK up to 6 months. The Japanese Ministry of Foreign Affairs provides an online "Guide to Japanese Visas" (www.mofa.go.jp/j_info/visit/visa/index.html).

Single-entry visas cost ¥3000 (US$25), double or multiple-entry visas cost ¥6000 (US$50), and transit visas cost ¥700 (US$6). A temporary visitor's visa allows you to spend 15, 30, or 90 days in Japan. Visas can be purchased from your Japanese consulate or embassy (listed under **Japanese Consular Services Abroad,** on p. 9). US citizens can take advantage of the **Center for International Business and Travel** (CIBT; US ☎800-925-2428), which secures visas for travel to almost all countries for a service charge. Double-check entrance requirements at the nearest embassy or consulate of Japan for up-to-date info before departure. US citizens can also consult the website www.pueblo.gsa.gov/cic_text/travel/foreign/foreignentryreqs.html.

Admission as a visitor does not include the right to work, which is authorized only by a work permit. Entering Japan to study requires a special visa. For more information, see the **Alternatives to Tourism** chapter (p. 57).

IDENTIFICATION

When you travel, always carry at least two forms of identification on your person, including at least one photo ID; a passport combined with a driver's license or birth certificate is usually adequate. Never carry all of your IDs together; split them up in case of theft or loss, and keep photocopies of them in your luggage and at home.

TEACHER, STUDENT, AND YOUTH IDENTIFICATION. The **International Student Identity Card (ISIC),** the most widely accepted form of student ID, provides discounts on some sights, accommodations, and transport; access to a 24hr. emergency line (☎ +44-20-8762-8110); and insurance for US cardholders (see **Insurance,** p. 23). Applicants must be degree-seeking students of a secondary or post-secondary school and be at least 12 years of age. Due to the proliferation of fake ISICs, some services (particularly airlines) require additional proof of identity.

The **International Teacher Identity Card (ITIC)** offers teachers the same insurance coverage as well as similar, but limited, discounts. For travelers who are 25 or under but are not students, the **International Youth Travel Card (IYTC)** offers benefits similar to the ISIC. The **International Student Exchange ID Card (ISE)** provides discounts, medical benefits, and the ability to purchase student airfares.

Each of these cards costs US$22 or equivalent. ISIC and ITIC cards are valid for roughly one and a half academic years; IYTC cards are valid for one year from the date of issue. Many student travel agencies (see p. 37) issue the cards; for a list, contact the **International Student Travel Confederation (ISTC),** Herengracht 479, 1017 BS Amsterdam, the Netherlands (☎ +31-20-421-2800; www.istc.org).

CUSTOMS

Upon entering Japan, you must declare certain items from abroad and pay a duty on the value of those articles if they exceed the allowance established by the **Japanese Customs Service**. Note that goods and gifts purchased at **duty-free** shops are not exempt from duty or sales tax; "duty free" merely means that you need not pay a tax in the country of purchase. Upon returning home, you must declare all articles acquired abroad and pay a duty on the value in excess of your home country's allowance. To expedite your return, register a list of valuables brought from home with customs before traveling, and keep receipts for all goods acquired abroad.

Japan has very strict regulations on importing and possessing **firearms** and other weapons. Persons attempting to bring firearms or swords into Japan may be arrested and the items may be confiscated. As some **medications** cannot be brought into the country, travelers should contact a Japanese embassy or consulate to verify what is legal. US citizens can look at the Confiscation of Prescription Drugs and Other Medications section of the Consular Information Sheet (http://travel.state.gov/japan.html). For specifics on customs regulations, consult the Narita Airport Customs website (www.narita-airport-customs.go.jp.)

MONEY

CURRENCY AND EXCHANGE

The currency chart below is based on August 2003 exchange rates between local currency and Australian dollars (AUS$), Canadian dollars (CDN$), New Zealand dollars (NZ$), South African Rand (ZAR), British pounds (UK£), US dollars (US$), and European Union euros (EUR€). Check the currency converters on financial websites such as www.bloomberg.com and www.xe.com, or look in a large newspaper, for the latest exchange rates.

JAPANESE YEN (¥)	
AUS$1 = ¥77.9	¥1 = AUS$0.0128
CDN$1 = ¥84.3	¥1 = CDN$0.0119
NZ$1 = ¥69.5	¥1 = NZ$0.0144
ZAR1 = ¥16.0	¥1 = ZAR0.0624
UK£1 = ¥188.4	¥1 = UK£0.0053
US$1 = ¥118.2	¥1 = US$0.0085
EUR€1 = ¥131.5	¥1 = EUR€0.0076

As a general rule, it's cheaper to convert money in Japan than at home, but it's wise to bring enough yen to last the first 24-72hr. of your trip. Once you've arrived, **Tōkyō Mitsubishi Bank** (東京三菱銀行), with branches in major cities through the country, provides the widest range of exchange services. You will often find exchange desks in major hotels, although their services may be restricted to guests.

When changing money abroad, try to go to banks that have at most a 5% margin between their buy and sell prices. Since you lose money with every transaction, **convert large sums** (unless the currency is depreciating rapidly), **but no more than you'll need**. Store your money in a variety of forms; ideally, at any given time you will be carrying some cash, some traveler's checks, and an ATM or credit card.

Japan is very much a cash-based society, and the banks are notoriously difficult for short-term visitors to navigate. Although there is always a danger in carrying cash, the risk of theft in Japan is very low, and your stay will be easier and more pleasant if you limit your hours spent at the bank. To prevent disaster, keep small stashes in separate but accessible places; you may want to bring two wallets.

TRAVELER'S CHECKS

Traveler's checks, sold for a small commission at many banks and agencies in the US, are one of the safest means of carrying funds, but can cause inconvenience in Japan. Do not rely on traveler's checks for daily needs, as virtually no stores or restaurants and few banks outside urban centers will accept them; use them only to carry large amounts of cash, and change them in bulk when you get the chance. If you plan to use traveler's checks, buy them in Japanese yen from **Visa,** the most widely recognized brand. A major advantage of traveler's checks is that issuers provide refunds if they are lost or stolen, and many provide toll-free refund hotlines, emergency message services, and stolen credit card assistance. Keep in mind that you will have to present your passport for every traveler's check transaction.

American Express: Checks available with commission at select banks, all AmEx offices, and online (www.americanexpress.com; US residents only). AmEx cardholders can buy checks by phone (US ☎888-269-6669). AAA (see p. 48) offers commission-free checks to members. Available in US, Australian, British, Canadian, Japanese, and Euro currencies. *Cheques for Two* can be signed by either of 2 people traveling together. In the US and Canada ☎800-221-7282; in the UK ☎0800-587-6023; in Australia ☎800-688-022; in New Zealand ☎0508-555-358; elsewhere US collect ☎+1-801-964-6665.

Travelex/Thomas Cook: In the US and Canada call ☎800-287-7362; in the UK call ☎0800-622-101; elsewhere call UK collect ☎+44-1733-318-950.

Visa: Checks available (generally with commission) at banks worldwide. For the nearest office, call Visa's service centers: In the US ☎800-227-6811; in the UK ☎0800-515-884; elsewhere UK collect ☎+44-20-7937-8091. Available in US, British, Canadian, Japanese, and Euro currencies.

CREDIT, DEBIT, AND ATM CARDS

Where they are accepted, **credit cards** often offer superior exchange rates—up to 5% better than the retail rate used by banks and other currency exchange establishments. Credit cards may also offer services such as insurance or emergency help, and are usually required to reserve hotel rooms and rental cars. **MasterCard** and **Visa** are the most welcomed in Japan; **American Express** cards work at some ATMs and at AmEx offices and major airports. Be warned, though, that while department stores and hotels will accept them, most restaurants only take cash.

ATM cards are common in Japan, but even in Tōkyō, ATMs that accept foreign cards are few and far between. With the exception of **Citibank's** few 24hr. machines in major cities, they operate only during business hours. Your best bet is to head for a **post office ATM,** which will probably be equipped for international transactions. ATMs get the same wholesale exchange rate as credit cards, but often limit on the amount of money you can withdraw per day (around US$500), and computer networks sometimes fail. There is typically a surcharge of US$1-5 per withdrawal; most also ATMs charge a transaction fee, paid to the bank that owns the ATM.

Debit cards are as convenient as credit cards but have a more immediate impact on your funds. A debit card can be used wherever its associated credit card company is accepted, yet the money is withdrawn directly from your checking account. Debit cards often function as ATM cards and can be used to withdraw cash from certain ATMs. Ask your bank about restrictions on international use.

The two major international money networks are **Cirrus** (to locate ATMs, US ☎800-424-7787 or www.mastercard.com) and **Visa/PLUS** (to locate ATMs US ☎800-843-7587 or www.visa.com).

GETTING MONEY FROM HOME

If you run out of money while traveling, the easiest and cheapest solution is to have someone back home make a deposit to your credit card or cash (ATM) card. Failing that, consider one of the following options. Note that language barriers and time differences make it surprisingly difficult for friends at home to send money to Japan—plan ahead and consider these methods only as a last resort.

WIRING MONEY. It is possible to arrange a **bank money transfer,** which means asking a bank back home to wire money to a bank in Japan. This is the cheapest way to transfer cash, but it's also the slowest, usually taking several days. You will have to arrange with a Japanese bank to receive money from your bank, a process that may tax limited language skills. Some banks only release funds in local currency, potentially sticking you with a poor exchange rate; ask about this in advance.

Money transfer services are faster than bank transfers, but also much pricier. **Western Union** locations in Japan are limited—besides a lone Nagoya outpost, outlets can only be found in Tōkyō and the neighboring prefectures of Kanagawa and Shizuoka; all are in the offices of Suruga Bank. To find one, visit www.westernunion.com, or call in the US ☎800-325-6000, in Canada ☎800-235-0000, in the UK ☎0800-833-833, in Australia ☎800-501-500, in New Zealand ☎800-27-0000, in South Africa ☎0860-100031, or in Japan ☎+81-12-088-2515. **Travel Express/MoneyGram** offices are scattered through Central Honshū; Tōkyō and Ōsaka have outlets, as do a handful of locations in Aichi, Gifu, Mie, and Shiga prefectures. Search for one at www.moneygram.com, or, in the US, call ☎800-328-5678. Neither **American Express, Travelex,** nor **Thomas Cook** offer money transfers to Japan.

US STATE DEPARTMENT (US CITIZENS ONLY). In dire emergencies only, the US State Department will forward money within hours to the nearest consular office, which will then disburse it according to instructions for a US$15 fee. If you wish to use this service, you must contact the Overseas Citizens Service division of the US State Department (☎+1-202-647-5225; nights, Sundays, and holidays ☎+1-202-647-4000). Other consulates may offer their citizens similar services.

COSTS

The cost of your trip will vary considerably, depending on where you go, how you travel, and where you stay. The most significant expenses will probably be your round-trip **airfare** to Japan (p. 37) and a **railpass** (p. 43). Before you go, spend some time calculating a reasonable per-day **budget** that will meet your needs.

STAYING ON A BUDGET. Generally speaking, a bare-bones day in Japan (camping or sleeping in hostels/guesthouses, buying food at supermarkets) costs about ¥5000 (US$40); a slightly more comfortable day (sleeping in hostels/guesthouses and the occasional budget hotel, eating one meal a day at a restaurant, going out at night) runs ¥9000 (US$75); and for a luxurious day, the sky's the limit. Don't forget to factor in emergency reserve funds (at least US$200) when planning how much you'll need.

SAVING MONEY. Some simpler ways to save money include searching out free entertainment, splitting accommodation and food costs with other trustworthy fellow travelers, and buying food in supermarkets rather than eating out. Make breakfast and lunch your main meals, and skimp on dinner. Stay in big cities on weekends (when many business hotels offer discounts) and at resorts on weekdays (when prices drop). Unless you're prohibited from doing so, do your laundry in the sink. That said, don't go overboard—though staying within your budget is important, don't do so at the expense of your health or a great travel experience.

ESSENTIALS

TIPPING, BARGAINING, AND TAXES

Tipping is not widely practiced in Japan; in fact, handing money to waiters, porters, taxi drivers or bartenders may cause more embarrassment than anything else. The one exception is at high-class Japanese inns, where it is customary to place a gratuity of ¥2000-3000 in an envelope and hand it discreetly to the room attendant. If you want to show your appreciation in another context, you can pull the same money-in-discreet-envelope trick or, preferably, present the person with a small, nicely wrapped gift. Bargaining is not generally accepted, except at certain discount electronics stores and markets. Japan has a 5% consumption tax on all goods; at expensive hotels and restaurants, a service charge of 10-15% may also be added.

SAFETY AND SECURITY

PERSONAL SAFETY

EXPLORING. To avoid unwanted attention, try to blend in as much as possible. Respecting local customs may prevent uncomfortable situations. Familiarize yourself with your surroundings before setting out, and carry yourself with confidence. Check maps in shops and restaurants rather than on the street. If you are traveling alone, be sure someone at home knows your itinerary, and never admit that you're by yourself. When walking at night, stick to busy, well-lit streets and avoid dark alleyways. If you feel uncomfortable, leave as quickly and directly as you can.

SELF DEFENSE. There is no sure-fire way to avoid the threatening situations you might encounter while traveling, but a good self-defense course will give you concrete ways to react to unwanted advances. **Impact, Prepare, and Model Mugging** can refer you to local courses in the US (☎800-345-5425; www.impactsafety.org). Workshops (2-3hr.) start at US$50; full courses (20hr.) run US$350-500.

DRIVING. If you are using a **car,** learn local driving signals and wear a seatbelt. The Japanese drive on the left, so drivers accustomed to right-oriented driving should practice before hitting the highway. Because many roads in Japan do not have names, it can be difficult to navigate some areas; as many Japanese roads are extremely narrow, drivers must use extra caution. Children under 40 lbs. should ride only in carseats, available from most car rental agencies. If your car breaks down, call the police and wait for assistance. For long drives in desolate areas, invest in a cellular phone and a roadside assistance program (see p. 47). Park your vehicle in a garage or well-traveled area, and use a steering wheel locking device in larger cities. **Sleeping in your car** is one of the most dangerous (and often illegal) ways to get your rest. For information on the perils of hitchhiking, see p. 50.

TERRORISM. Terrorism is a serious international concern and Japan is an active participant in international efforts to combat it. At the 2003 G-8 Conference, Japan collaborated with the US in leading talks on a program of initiatives against terrorism, through enhanced aircraft security and assistance to developing countries.

Japan has experienced no major terrorist attacks since 1995, when the religious cult Aum Shinrikyo released sarin gas in the Tōkyō subway, killing 12 people and injuring 5000. This incident marked the most serious terrorist attack in Japan's modern history. Although Aum Shinrikyo has renounced its violent history, it remains on the US State Department's list of foreign terrorist groups.

The Tōkyō Embassy disseminates information through the Embassy Warden System and posts information on threats at the embassy website (www.tokyoacs.com). If you notice suspicious activity while in Japan, contact the local police station (*kōban*) or the emergency dispatchers (☎110).

EARTHQUAKES. Japan experiences frequent earthquakes, most too small to be felt. If a strong earthquake does occur, it will last only one or two minutes. Open a door to provide an escape route and protect yourself by moving underneath a

TRAVEL ADVISORIES. The following government offices provide travel information and advisories by telephone, by fax, or via the web:

Australian Department of Foreign Affairs and Trade: ☎+61-13-00-555135; faxback service 02-6261-1299; www.dfat.gov.au.

Canadian Department of Foreign Affairs and International Trade (DFAIT): In Canada and the US call ☎800-267-8376, elsewhere call ☎+1-613-944-4000; www.dfait-maeci.gc.ca. Call for their free booklet, *Bon Voyage...But.*

New Zealand Ministry of Foreign Affairs: ☎+64-4-439-8000; fax 494-8506; www.mft.govt.nz/travel/index.html.

United Kingdom Foreign and Commonwealth Office: ☎+44-20-7008-0232; fax 7008-0155; www.fco.gov.uk.

US State Department: ☎+1-202-647-5225, faxback +1-202-647-3000; http://travel.state.gov. For *A Safe Trip Abroad*, call ☎+1-202-512-1800.

sturdy doorway, table, or desk. In a coastal or mountainous areas tidal waves and landslides may follow quakes. InterFM (76.1FM), NHK (693AM), and AFN (810AM) are Tōkyō area radio stations that will broadcast emergency information in English; for television, try NHK1, BS1, or BS2, which have bilingual broadcasts.

TYPHOONS. Typhoons are severe tropical storms (equivalent to "hurricanes" in the Atlantic) with very high winds. Typhoons occur from May to November, with the season peaking between August and October. If there is a typhoon, move inside, away from windows, and keep informed on the movement of the storm.

FINANCIAL SECURITY

PROTECTING YOUR VALUABLES. Although Japan has one of the world's lowest crime rates, it's better to be safe than a statistic with no wallet. There are a few steps you can take to minimize the financial risks of traveling. First, **bring as little with you as possible.** Second, buy combination **padlocks** to secure your belongings, either in your pack or in a hostel or train station locker. Keep your traveler's checks and ATM/credit cards in a **money belt**—not a "fanny pack"—along with your passport and ID cards. Due to the cash-based Japanese system, you will probably find it most convenient to travel with a significant amount of cash. This is a widespread practice in Japan, but you should always **keep a small reserve separate from your primary stash.** This should be about US$50 sewn into or stored in the depths of your pack, along with your traveler's check numbers and important photocopies.

CON ARTISTS AND PICKPOCKETS. Never let your passport and your bags out of your sight. Beware of **pickpockets** in city crowds, especially on Japan's notoriously crowded public transportation (but know that even the most honest people to push for space on trains). Never carry your wallet in your back pocket. Be alert in public telephone booths: if you must say your calling card number, do so very quietly; if you punch it in, make sure no one can look over your shoulder.

ACCOMMODATIONS AND TRANSPORTATION. Never leave your belongings unattended; crime occurs in even the most demure-looking hostel or hotel. Bring your own **padlock** for hostel lockers, and never store valuables in a locker.

Be particularly careful on **buses** and **trains.** Carry your backpack in front of you where you can see it. When traveling with others, sleep in alternate shifts. When alone, never stay in an empty train compartment, and use a lock to secure your pack to the luggage rack. Try to sleep on top bunks with your luggage above you (if not in bed with you), and keep important documents and valuables on your person. If traveling by **car,** don't leave valuables in it while you are away.

DRUGS AND ALCOHOL

They barred a certain pot-carrying Beatle from the country for 11 years, so they will have no problem banning you for life. Foreigners found with any amount of marijuana can expect to serve up to seven years in prison, followed by deportation. Penalties for possession of harder drugs are just as unattractive. Remember that you are subject to the laws of the country in which you travel, and it is your responsibility to familiarize yourself with those laws before leaving. A meek "I didn't know it was illegal" will not suffice. If you carry **prescription drugs** while you travel, it is vital to have a copy of the prescriptions and a note from a doctor.

With beer easily available in vending machines, the Japanese **drinking age** of 20 is rarely enforced. While public drunkenness raises few eyebrows, drunk driving laws are among the world's strictest. Having just one drink before getting behind the wheel can get you arrested, fined, and jailed.

HEALTH

Common sense is the simplest prescription for good health. Drink lots of fluids to prevent dehydration and constipation, and wear sturdy shoes and clean socks.

BEFORE YOU GO

In your **passport,** write the names of people you wish to be contacted in an emergency, and list any allergies or medical conditions. Matching a prescription to a foreign equivalent is not always easy or possible, so carry up-to-date, legible prescriptions or a statement from your doctor stating the medication's trade name, manufacturer, chemical name, and dosage. While traveling, keep all medication in your carry-on luggage. For tips on packing a basic **first-aid kit,** see p. 24.

IMMUNIZATIONS AND PRECAUTIONS

Travelers over two years old should make sure that the following vaccines are up to date: MMR (for measles, mumps, and rubella); DTaP or Td (for diptheria, tetanus, and pertussis); OPV (for polio); HbCV (for haemophilus influenza B); and HBV (for hepatitis B). For recommendations on immunizations, consult the CDC (see below) in the US or your country's equivalent, and check with a doctor.

 INOCULATION REQUIREMENTS AND RECOMMENDATIONS. Immunization against Japanese encephalitis (p. 19) is recommended for travelers over one year of age who will spend 30 days or more in locations where the disease occurs, especially rural areas. Japan has no compulsory inoculation requirements for visitors.

USEFUL ORGANIZATIONS AND PUBLICATIONS

The US **Centers for Disease Control and Prevention (CDC;** US ☎877-FYI-TRIP; www.cdc.gov/travel) maintains an international travelers' hotline and an informative website. The CDC's comprehensive booklet *Health Information for International Travel,* an annual rundown of disease, immunization, and general health advice, is free online or US$30 via the Public Health Foundation (US ☎877-252-1200). For quick information on health and other travel warnings, call the **Overseas Citizens Services** (☎+1-317-472-2328, M-F 8:15am-5pm EST; after-hours ☎+1-202-647-4000; toll-free hotline US ☎888-407-4747), or contact a passport agency, embassy, or consulate abroad. For information on medical evacuation services and travel insurance, see the US government's website at http://travel.state.gov/medical.html or the **British Foreign and Commonwealth Office** (www.fco.gov.uk).

For detailed information on travel health, including a country-by-country overview of diseases and a list of travel clinics in the USA, try the **International Travel Health Guide,** by Stuart Rose, MD (US$24.95; www.travmed.com). For general health info, contact the **American Red Cross** (US ☎800-564-1234; www.redcross.org).

MEDICAL ASSISTANCE ON THE ROAD

Hygiene standards are high in Japan, and health care is widely available. Given the cost of drugs, however, try to bring any medications you need with you, and keep a copy of your prescription with you at all times. Both small clinics and large health centers are called "hospitals" in Japan; most of your needs can be served at clinics. You do not usually need an appointment, but the first-come, first-served system may result in long lines. A Japanese-speaking friend, or at least a Japanese note with your name and address, a description of symptoms, and a list of allergies, can be useful if you are not certain that the clinic has English-speaking staff.

American consulates keep lists of English-speaking doctors, dentists, and hospitals in their city. **Jhelp.com,** a nonprofit emergency assistance service, is also a good resource. In an emergency, call their 24hr. toll-free hotline (☎0120-46-1997).

If you are concerned about obtaining medical assistance while traveling, you may wish to employ special support services. The *MedPass* from **GlobalCare, Inc.** (US ☎800-860-1111; www.globalems.com), provides 24hr. international medical assistance, support, and evacuation resources. The **International Association for Medical Assistance to Travelers (IAMAT;** US ☎+1-716-754-4883, Canada ☎+1-519-836-0102; www.cybermall.co.nz/NZ/IAMAT) has free membership, lists English-speaking doctors worldwide, and offers detailed info on immunization requirements and sanitation. If your regular **insurance** policy does not cover travel abroad, you may wish to purchase additional coverage (see p. 23). Those with medical conditions may want to obtain a **Medic Alert** membership (first year US$35, annually thereafter US$20), which includes a stainless steel ID tag engraved with health information, among other benefits, like a 24hr. collect-call number. Contact the Medic Alert Foundation, 2323 Colorado Ave., Turlock, CA 95382, USA (US ☎888-633-4298, outside US ☎+1-209-668-3333; www.medicalert.org).

ONCE IN JAPAN

ENVIRONMENTAL HAZARDS

Visitors to Japan encounter more urban jungle than tropical jungle, but dehydration and sunburn can happen anywhere. Those who travel to rural areas and to the country's northern and southern extremes should be prepared for severe weather.

Heat exhaustion and dehydration: Heat exhaustion leads to nausea, thirst, headaches, and dizziness. Avoid it by drinking fluids, eating salty foods, and avoiding dehydrating beverages. Heat stress can lead to heatstroke, marked by a rising temperature, headache, delirium, and ceased sweating. Cool victims with wet towels and consult a doctor.

Sunburn: If you spend time near water, in the desert, or in the snow, you are at risk of getting burned, even through clouds. If you get burned, drink more fluids than usual and apply an aloe-based lotion. Severe sunburns can lead to sun poisoning, which causes fever, chills, nausea, and vomiting, and should always be treated by a doctor.

Hypothermia and frostbite: A rapid drop in body temperature is the clearest sign of overexposure to cold. Victims may shiver, feel exhausted, have poor coordination or slurred speech, hallucinate, or suffer amnesia. *Do not let hypothermia victims fall asleep.* To avoid hypothermia, keep dry, wear layers, and stay out of the wind. When the temperature is below freezing, watch out for frostbite. If skin turns white or blue, waxy, and cold, do not rub the area. Drink warm beverages, stay dry, and slowly warm the area with dry fabric or steady body contact until a doctor can be found.

High altitude: Allow your body a couple of days to adjust to less oxygen before exerting yourself. Note that alcohol is more potent and UV rays are stronger at high elevations.

INSECT-BORNE DISEASES

Many diseases are transmitted by insects—mainly mosquitoes, fleas, and ticks. Be aware of insects in wet or forested areas; wear pants and long sleeves, tuck your pants into your socks, and use a mosquito net. Use insect repellents like DEET and spray your gear with permethrin (licensed in the US for use on clothing).

Japanese encephalitis: A mosquito-borne disease, most prevalent during rainy season in rural areas near rice fields and livestock pens, Japanese encephalitis causes delirium and flu-like symptoms: chills, headache, fever, and muscle fatigue. Go to a hospital as soon as symptoms appear. Japanese encephalitis is rare in Japan, but has been reported on all islands except Hokkaidō. The transmission season is June-Sept., except in Okinawa, where it extends Apr.-Dec. The risk to most travelers is low—the CDC recommends vaccination only for people intending to spend more than 30 days in rural areas during transmission season. The JE-VAX vaccine, given in 3 shots over a 30-day period, is effective for a year, but has been associated with serious side effects. According to the CDC, infection is unlikely if proper precautions, including using mosquito repellents containing DEET and sleeping under mosquito nets, are taken.

FOOD- AND WATER-BORNE DISEASES

Prevention is the best cure. Don't swear off raw-fish sushi—most establishments serve only the freshest ingredients—but make sure your *sashimi* does not smell putrid. The risk of food poisoning and parasites is never entirely eliminated, as some fish carry toxins which cooking cannot eradicate, although the odds of suffering from sushi are extremely low. Be cautious around raw shellfish, unpasteurized milk, and sauces containing raw eggs. Take care that all the water you drink is clean—tap water is safe throughout Japan, although many Japanese prefer the taste of bottled water. Never drink from a pool of standing water, and it's advisable not to drink from streams. If you are hiking and can't carry enough bottled water with you to last the entire trip, purify your own water by bringing it to a rolling boil or treating it with iodine tablets or solution. Note that some parasites have exteriors that resist iodine treatment, so boiling is more reliable. Always wash your hands before eating or bring a quick-drying purifying liquid hand cleaner.

Traveler's diarrhea: Eating food with unfamiliar ingredients and new kinds of bacteria can upset your stomach for up to 7 days. If you feel nauseous or bloated, try quick-energy, non-sugary foods with protein and carbohydrates. Over-the-counter anti-diarrheals (e.g., Imodium) may counteract the problem. The most dangerous side effect is dehydration: drink water with ½ tsp. of sugar or honey and a pinch of salt, try uncaffeinated soft drinks, or eat salted crackers. If you develop a fever or your symptoms don't go away after 4-5 days, consult a doctor. Consult a doctor immediately for children.

Dysentery: A serious intestinal infection caused by bacteria. Symptoms include bloody diarrhea (sometimes mixed with mucus), fever, and abdominal pain and tenderness. Seek medical help immediately. Dysentery is uncommon in Japan, and can be treated with norfloxacin or ciprofloxacin (commonly known as Cipro).

Cholera: An intestinal disease caused by a bacteria in contaminated food. Most cases in Japan are imported by tourists returning from Southeast Asia, though a few domestic cases have been reported. Symptoms include severe diarrhea, dehydration, vomiting, and muscle cramps. See a doctor immediately; if left untreated, it may be deadly, even within a few hours. Antibiotics are available, but the most important treatment is rehydration. Consider a vaccine (50% effective) if you have stomach problems (e.g., ulcers).

Hepatitis A: A viral infection of the liver acquired primarily through contaminated water. Symptoms include fatigue, fever, loss of appetite, nausea, dark urine, jaundice, vomiting, aches and pains, and light stools. Concerned travelers or those planning to spend over 4 weeks in the country may want to ask about the vaccine (Havrix or Vaqta) or an injection of immune globulin (IG; formerly called gamma globulin).

Giardiasis: Transmitted through parasites in contaminated water and food, and acquired by drinking untreated water from streams or lakes. Symptoms include swollen glands or lymph nodes, fever, rashes or itchiness, and digestive problems.

Typhoid fever: Caused by the salmonella bacteria. The vast majority of cases in Japan are imported from Southeast Asia, but there are occasional domestic cases, usually in spring. While mostly transmitted through contaminated food and water, it can also be acquired by direct contact. Early symptoms include fever, headaches, fatigue, loss of appetite, constipation, and sometimes a rash on the abdomen or chest.

OTHER INFECTIOUS DISEASES

Hepatitis B: A viral infection of the liver transmitted via bodily fluids. Symptoms may not surface for years and include jaundice, lost appetite, fever, and joint pain. A vaccination sequence is recommended for health-care workers, sexually active travelers, and anyone who might need medical treatment abroad; it must begin 6 months before travel.

Hepatitis C: Like Hepatitis B, but the mode of transmission differs. IV drug users, those with occupational exposure to blood, hemodialysis patients, and recipients of blood transfusions are at the highest risk, but it can be spread through sexual contact or sharing items like razors and toothbrushes that may have traces of blood on them.

Severe Acute Respiratory Syndrome (SARS): A viral respiratory illness transmitted through droplets. Early symptoms include fever, chills, headache, and muscle ache. Steroids and antiviral agents have been used as therapy; in some cases, however, SARS is fatal. Japan has been extremely rigorous in screening for SARS infection, and as of August 2003 there had been no confirmed cases in Japan.

AIDS, HIV, AND STDS

Japan has an extremely low rate of AIDS infection, but just as anywhere else, risky behaviors should be avoided. For detailed information on **Acquired Immune Deficiency Syndrome (AIDS)** in Japan, call the **US Centers for Disease Control's** 24hr. hotline at US ☎ 800-342-2437, or contact the **Joint United Nations Programme on HIV/AIDS (UNAIDS)**, 20 ave. Appia, CH-1211 Geneva 27, Switzerland (☎ +41-22-791-3666; fax 22-791-4187). Once in Japan, you can get information from **Japan Helpline AIDS Information** (☎ 0120-46-1995; toll-free; 24hr.) or the **Tōkyō Metropolitan Government AIDS Telephone Service** (☎ 0120-85-812; toll-free; 24hr. recorded English info).

Sexually transmitted diseases (STDs) such as gonorrhea, chlamydia, genital warts, syphilis, and herpes are easier to catch than HIV and can be just as deadly. **Hepatitis B** and **C** can also be transmitted sexually (p. 21). Though condoms may protect you from some STDs, oral or even tactile contact can lead to transmission. If you think you may have contracted an STD, see a doctor immediately.

WOMEN'S HEALTH

The stress of travel can cause women to become vulnerable to **urinary tract** and **bladder infections,** common and uncomfortable bacterial conditions that cause a burning sensation and painful (sometimes frequent) urination. Over-the-counter medicines can sometimes alleviate symptoms, but if they persist, see a doctor. **Vaginal yeast infections** may flare up in hot and humid climates. Wearing loosely fitting trousers or a skirt and cotton underwear will help, as will over-the-counter remedies like Monostat or Gynelotrimin. **Tampons, pads,** and reliable **contraceptive devices** should not be difficult to find in Japan, though your favorite brand may not be stocked—bring extras of anything you can't live without. **Abortions** are safe and legal in Japan. Counseling, advice, and referrals are available through the **Family Planning Federation of Japan,** Hoken Kaikan Shinkan, 1-10, Ichigaya Tamachi, Shinjuku-ku, Tōkyō 162 (☎ +81-3-3269-4041; fax 3269-4750).

TOILETS

The rumors are true—Japan has some pretty "different," sometimes "scary," toilets, from electronic, multi-button "Western" models to traditional super-sanitary ceramic holes-in-the-floor. **Western-style toilets,** found in most modern homes, are raised, with a tank and bowl. Some have flush handles, but others have two basic buttons on top, one marked 大 and the other 小 ("big" and "small" respectively—you get the picture). It's not a disaster if you push the wrong one, but it might not be pretty either. Some high-tech toilets have a bidet, warm-air dryer, heated seat, self-cleaning function, and any number of other innovations. To avoid surprises, don't fool around with buttons you can't read. **Traditional toilets** consist of an

ESSENTIALS

oblong ceramic bowl with a slight hood, set at floor level in a slightly raised platform. Men should stand on the lower portion of the floor and aim for the bowl; women should squat over it, with one foot on either side, facing the hood. This is more sanitary than the Western toilet, since it eliminates contact with the bowl, but keeping your balance can be tricky, and often the toilets are unpleasantly dirty. Many public restrooms, usually marked **W.C.** or ト イ レ (*toire*; toilet), have both types of toilet; a little searching may spare you a potentially traumatizing cultural experience. Be sure to carry **tissues**, as toilet paper is not provided in public restrooms. It's also be a good idea to carry a **handkerchief**—Japan has become environmentally conscious, and most bathrooms don't stock paper towels.

INSURANCE

Travel insurance generally covers medical/health problems, property loss, trip cancellation/interruption, and emergency evacuation. Although your regular policies may well extend to travel-related accidents, you may consider purchasing travel insurance if the cost of potential trip cancellation/interruption is greater than you can absorb. Prices for travel insurance purchased separately generally run about US$50 per week for full coverage, while trip cancellation/interruption may be purchased separately at a rate of about US$5.50 per US$100 of coverage.

Medical insurance (especially university policies) often covers costs incurred abroad; check with your provider. **US Medicare** does not cover foreign travel. **Canadians** are protected by their province's health insurance plan for 90 days after leaving the country; check with the Ministry of Health or Health Plan Headquarters for details. **Homeowners insurance** (or your family's coverage) often covers theft and loss of travel documents (passport, plane ticket, railpass, etc.) up to US$500.

ISIC and **ITIC** (p. 11) provide basic insurance benefits, including US$100 per day of in-hospital sickness for 60 days, US$3000 of accident-related medical reimbursement, and US$25,000 for emergency medical transport. Cardholders can use a toll-free 24hr. helpline (run by insurance provider **TravelGuard**) for medical, legal, and financial emergencies (US and Canada ☎877-370-4742, elsewhere call US collect ☎+1-715-345-0505). **American Express** (US ☎800-528-4800) grants most cardholders car rental insurance (collision and theft, but not liability) and ground travel accident coverage of US$100,000 on flight purchases made with the card.

INSURANCE PROVIDERS. Council and **STA** (see p. 37) offer a range of plans that can supplement your basic coverage. Other private insurance providers in the US and Canada include: **Access America** (US ☎800-284-8300); **Berkely Group/Carefree Travel Insurance** (US ☎800-323-3149; www.berkely.com); **Globalcare Travel Insurance** (US ☎800-821-2488; www.globalcare-cocco.com); and **Travel Assistance International** (US ☎800-821-2828; www.europ-assistance.com). **UK** providers include **Columbus Direct** (☎+44-20-7375-0011). In **Australia**, try **AFTA** (☎+61-2-9264-3299).

PACKING

Pack lightly: Lay out only what you absolutely need, then take half the clothes and twice the money. If you plan to hike, see **Camping and the Outdoors,** p. 28.

LUGGAGE. If you plan to cover most of your itinerary by foot, a sturdy **frame backpack** is unbeatable. (For the basics on buying a pack, see p. 31.) Toting a **suitcase** or **trunk** is fine if you plan to live in one or two cities and explore from there, but not a great idea if you plan to move around frequently. In addition to your main piece of luggage, a **daypack** (a small backpack or courier bag) is useful.

CLOTHING. No matter when you're traveling, it's a good idea to bring a **warm jacket** or wool sweater, a **rain jacket** (Gore-Tex® is both waterproof and breathable), sturdy shoes or **hiking boots,** and **thick socks. Flip-flops** or waterproof sandals are must-haves for grubby hostel showers. You may also want one outfit for going out, and maybe a nicer pair of shoes. If you plan to visit religious or cultural sites, remember something besides tank tops and shorts to be respectful.

CONVERTERS AND ADAPTERS. In Japan, electricity is 100V AC, which should work with 110V North American appliances, though 220/240V electrical appliances may not like it. Japanese plugs are the flat-blade types found in North America, though they may not have the third, round grounding pin. Americans and Canadians should buy an adapter (which changes the shape of the plug) to be able to use three-pronged appliances. New Zealanders and South Africans (who use 220V at home), British and Irish travelers (who use 230V) and Australians (who use 240/250V) need a converter to step down the voltage, as well as a set of adapters.

More puzzling may be Japan's regional differences in electricity frequency (50Hz in eastern Japan; 60Hz in western Japan). Finicky appliances like computers and video cameras may require a transformer to operate properly in the part of Japan that follows a standard different from your own. (Australia, Ireland, New Zealand, South Africa, and the UK follow the 50Hz standard; Canada and the United States use 60Hz.) For more on all things adaptable, visit http://kropla.com/electric.htm.

TOILETRIES. Toothbrushes, towels, soap, deodorant, razors, tampons, and condoms should be available and easy to find, though the brands may be unfamiliar. **Contact lenses**, on the other hand, may be difficult to find, so bring enough extra pairs and solution for your entire trip. Also bring your glasses and a copy of your prescription in case you need emergency replacements.

CELLULAR PHONES. A cell phone can be a lifesaver (literally) on the road; though you may already own a cell phone, it most likely will not work when you arrive at your destination. See p. 36 for information on acquiring a phone in Japan.

FIRST-AID KIT. For a basic first-aid kit, pack: bandages, pain reliever, antibiotic cream, a thermometer, a Swiss Army knife, tweezers, moleskin, decongestant, motion-sickness remedy, diarrhea or upset-stomach medication (Pepto Bismol or Imodium), an antihistamine, sunscreen, insect repellent, burn ointment, and a syringe for emergencies (get an explanatory letter from your doctor).

FILM. Film and developing in Japan are reasonably priced, though many choose to bring film from home and develop it upon returning. Less serious photographers may want to bring a **disposable camera** or two rather than an expensive permanent one. Despite disclaimers, airport security X-rays *can* fog film, so buy a lead-lined pouch at a camera store or ask security to hand-inspect it. Always pack film in your carry-on luggage, since higher-intensity X-rays are used on checked luggage.

OTHER USEFUL ITEMS. For safety purposes, you should bring a **money belt** and small **padlock**. Basic **outdoors equipment** (plastic water bottle, compass, waterproof matches, pocketknife, sunglasses, sunscreen, hat) may also prove useful. **Quick repairs** can be done on the road with a needle and thread; also consider bringing electrical tape for patching tears. If you want to do laundry by hand, bring detergent, a small rubber ball to stop up the sink, and string for a makeshift clothes line. Other things you're liable to forget are: an umbrella; sealable plastic bags (for damp clothes, soap, food, shampoo, and other spillables); an **alarm clock;** safety pins; rubber bands; a **flashlight;** earplugs; garbage bags; a spoon; and a calculator.

IMPORTANT DOCUMENTS. Don't forget your passport, traveler's checks, ATM and/or credit cards, adequate ID, and photocopies of all of the aforementioned in case these documents are lost or stolen (see p. 11). Also check that you have any of the following that might apply to you: a hosteling membership card (see p. 25); driver's license (see p. 11); travel insurance forms; and railpass (see p. 43).

ACCOMMODATIONS

HOSTELS

Travelers will encounter two styles of hostels in Japan. Some resemble Western-style dormitories, with large single-sex rooms accommodating 4 to 8 people, and bunk beds. Others offer traditional Japanese-style rooms, with *tatami* mats and rice paper screens. Hostels sometimes have kitchens for your use, bike rentals, storage areas, transportation to airports, breakfast, and laundry facilities. There can be drawbacks: some close during daytime "lockout" hours, have a curfew, don't accept reservations, impose a maximum stay, or, less frequently, require that you do chores. In Japan, a dorm bed in a hostel will average around ¥3000 a night.

A HOSTELER'S BILL OF RIGHTS. There are certain standard features that we do not include in our hostel listings. Unless we state otherwise, you can expect that every hostel has no lockout, no curfew, free hot showers, some system of secure luggage storage, and no key deposit.

HOSTELLING INTERNATIONAL

Joining the youth hostel association in your own country (listed below) automatically grants you membership privileges in **Hostelling International (HI)**, a federation of national hostelling associations. HI hostels are scattered throughout Japan and are typically less expensive than private hostels. It is a good idea to get a membership card before leaving for Japan, although you can contact the **Japan Youth Hostel Association (JYHA)**, Suidobashi Nishi-guchi Kaikan, 2-20-7, Misaki-chō, Chiyoda-ku, Tōkyō 101-0061 (☎+81-3-3288-1417; www.jyh.or.jp), once in Japan. Some hostels accept reservations via the **International Booking Network**, which takes worldwide reservations online and over the phone (☎+1-202-783-6161; www.hostelbooking.com). The HI umbrella organization's web page (www.iyhf.org) lists the web addresses and phone numbers of all national associations.

Most HI hostels also honor **guest memberships**—you will receive a blank card with space for six validation stamps. Each night you'll pay a nonmember supplement (¥600) and earn one guest stamp; get six stamps, and you earn a one-year membership which gives you access to HI hostels around the world. All prices listed below are valid for **one-year memberships** unless otherwise noted.

Australian Youth Hostels Association (AYHA), Level 3, 10 Mallett St., Camperdown NSW 2050 (☎+61-2-9565-1699; www.yha.org.au). AUS$52, under 18 AUS$16.

Hostelling International-Canada (HI-C), 205 Catherine St. #400, Ottawa, ON K2P 1C3 (☎+1-613-237-7884; www.hihostels.ca). CDN$35, under 18 free.

An Óige (Irish Youth Hostel Association), 61 Mountjoy St., Dublin 7 (☎+353-830-4555; www.irelandyha.org). €25, under 18 €10.50.

Youth Hostels Association of New Zealand, P.O. Box 436, 193 Cashel St., 3rd. Fl. Union House, Christchurch (☎+64-3-379-9970; www.stayyha.org). NZ$40, under 18 free.

Hostels Association of South Africa, 73 St. George's House, 3rd Fl., Cape Town 8001 (☎+27-21-424-2511; www.hisa.org.za). ZAR70, under 18 ZAR40.

Scottish Youth Hostels Association (SYHA), 7 Glebe Crescent, Stirling FK8 2JA (☎+44-1786-891-400; www.syha.org.uk). UK£6.

Youth Hostels Association (YHA; England and Wales), Trevelyon House, Dimple Rd., Matlock, Derbyshire DE4 3YH, UK (☎+44-870-870-8808; www.yha.org.uk). UK£13, under 18 UK£6.50.

Hostelling International Northern Ireland (HINI), 22 Donegall Rd., Belfast BT12 5JN (☎+44-2890-315-435; www.hini.org.uk). UK£10, under 18 UK£6.

Hostelling International-American Youth Hostels (HI-AYH), 733 15th St. NW, #840, Washington, D.C. 20005 (☎+1-202-783-6161; www.hiayh.org). US$25, under 18 free.

> **BOOKING HOSTELS ONLINE** One of the cheapest and easiest ways to ensure a bed for a night is by reserving online. Our website features the **Hostelworld** booking engine; access it at **www.letsgo.com/resources/accommodations.** Hostelworld offers bargain accommodations everywhere from Argentina to Zimbabwe with no added commission.

OTHER TYPES OF ACCOMMODATIONS

MINSHUKU

Minshuku are the Japanese version of a Western bed-and-breakfast. Characterized by their welcoming atmosphere, these family-run guesthouses offer travelers an introduction to Japanese culture with their *tatami* rooms and communal bathrooms and dining areas. Rates are per person; the cheapest minshuku prices begin around ¥4000. The standard price is ¥6000-10,000 (prices include two meals).

Another form of the minshuku is the **kokuminshuku.** *Kokuminshuku* are government-owned lodgings, often located in national parks and resort areas. Created with the aim of promoting tourism in specific areas of Japan, these government-funded facilities win prime realty with beautiful views. Unfortunately, as a result, *kokuminshiku* tend to be set back from the road and require a car to reach. Rooms are large and designed for families and groups; two meals are included in the price. Make advance reservations, especially during Japanese holidays.

RYOKAN

Like minshuku, ryokan are an integral part of the traditional Japanese experience. *Tatami* rooms include minimal furniture and quintessential Japanese art. Many ryokan now include individual bathroom units within the rooms, a TV, and a phone. However, despite these added amenities, ryokan embody Japanese hospitality and charm, with the communal bath serving as the focal point of a stay. Ryokan usually include breakfast and dinner. Note that some only offer a Japanese breakfast, and travelers may discover that *miso* soup and fish are not the way to start the day—that said, everyone should try the authentic breakfast once. Both breakfast and dinner are served within specific time frames, and as it is often unacceptable to request a meal outside of the set hours, plan your day accordingly. Because prices vary considerably between low and high season, and also depend on the grade of the room and meal you choose, be aware of the price selections before making a reservation. On average, ryokan cost ¥8000-10,000 per person, although a very inexpensive ryokan, where meals are not included, might cost ¥4000. Top-of-the-line ryokan can charge exorbitant rates, as much as ¥50,000.

HOTELS

BUSINESS HOTELS. As the name implies, business hotels fulfill the utilitarian role of accommodating business travelers. With clean, Western-style rooms conveniently located by train stations, business hotels are a space for travelers passing through. Rooms are small and include a small bathroom unit, a bed, and a TV. Ask about check-in/out times, which are usually on the early side.

DRAIN YOU OF YOUR LIFE SAVINGS HOTELS. Throughout Japan, particularly in large cities, you will find plush, high-class hotels comparable to those of the elite class around the world. For those who crave reliable service, in English, and the soft touch of Japanese perfection, it might be worth the splurge. Prices start at ¥10,000 and skyrocket past ¥30,000. Hotels include restaurants, bars, pools, fitness centers, shopping arcades, opulent decorations, and plenty of other accessories.

CAPSULE HOTEL. This uniquely Japanese phenomenon emerged in the 1970s as a solution for the drunken businessman who, having missed the last train home, was stranded without a place to sleep. While capsule hotels still function as a place to crash after a festive night, on occasion, sober businessmen and travelers also choose to spend the night in a capsule. Each capsule is approximately 2m by 1m, fitting a bed, phone, TV, and alarm. *Yukatas* (sleeping robes) are provided. Many capsule hotels do not accept women, so female travelers should check ahead.

LOVE HOTEL. A uniquely Japanese derivation of the standard hotel, love hotels offer rooms to those who seek a "rest" for a couple of hours during the day, or a "stay" for the night. You can recognize a love hotel by the embellished architecture with colorful turrets and statues. As most Japanese live in claustrophobia-inducing apartments, and as many young adults continue to live with their parents (and even their parents' parents), it's no wonder that many desire an escape from thin walls and hovering eyes. Liberating visitors not only from the physical confines of space-deprived Japan, love hotels also emancipate the mind from the standard paradigm of hotel interiors. Love hotels range in their offerings, enticing customers with themes from "underwater" to *The Rock* (starring Sean Connery), and with gadgets to satisfy all your unspoken fantasies (moving beds, psychedelic lights, and toys up the wazoo). Discretion is the mantra: customers enter an empty lobby, select a room from pictures on the wall, receive a key from a receptionist behind darkened glass, spend anywhere from 1hr. to a full night, and then leave through a back door. Rental for a few hours runs from ¥3000-5000; overnight stays cost ¥6000-7000. Even if you're not interested in all the perks, the story could be worth the visit, and staying in one is often cheaper than a business hotel.

ACCOMMODATIONS ONLINE Smooth your arrival by searching for your bed ahead of time. **Japanese City Hotel Association** (www.jcha.or.jp) provides a directory of moderately priced hotels throughout Japan, while the **Japanese Inn Group** (www.jpinn.com) lists small, traditional ryokan. **Japan Youth Hostels** (www.jyh.or.jp) has a full listing of their locations on the web. The **Welcome Inn Reservation Center** (www.itcj.or.jp) is devoted to inexpensive accommodations and aimed specifically at foreigners and those who do not speak Japanese.

SHUKUBŌ

Some temples in Japan open their doors to travelers who seek a quiet respite and retreat from the bustle of urban centers and box hotels. Accommodations will be simple and minimal. Although you may be left to your own devices, some *shukubō* will ask that you participate in early morning prayer or meditation. The monks cook a tasty meal of tofu and vegetables (*shojin ryōri*), and, if you're lucky, you might get to join the feast. Many JYHA hostels are actually temples or shrines.

YMCAS AND YWCAS

Young Men's Christian Association (YMCA) lodgings are usually cheaper than a hotel but more expensive than a hostel. Not all YMCA locations offer lodging; those that do are often located in urban downtowns. Many YMCAs accept women and families; some will not lodge those under 18 without parental permission. You can book online at Travel Y's International (www.travel-ys.com) for free. For a listing of YMCAs in Japan, try the **National Council of YMCAs of Japan** (☎+81-3-3293-1921; www.ymcajapan.org/english). The **World Alliance of YMCAs** (☎+41-22-849-5100; www.ymca.int) has listings of YMCAs worldwide.

HOME EXCHANGES

Home exchange offers the traveler various types of homes (houses, apartments, condominiums, villas), plus the opportunity to live like a native and to cut down on housing costs. Contact **HomeExchange.Com** (US ☎800-877-8723; www.homeexchange.com), or **Intervac International Home Exchange**, 12-27-401 Yochomachi Shinjuku, Tōkyō 106-0055 (☎/fax +81-3-3358-7546; www.intervac.com).

LONG-TERM ACCOMMODATIONS

Getting an **apartment** in Japan is an arduous and expensive process best avoided by those not planning on staying for at least two years. In Tōkyō especially, apartments are likely to be difficult to find, inconveniently located, outrageously expensive, or some combination of the three. Besides the rent itself, prospective tenants must be able to front a hefty **security deposit** (*shikikin;* usually one or two months rent, occasionally not refundable) and **key money** (*reikin;* usually two months rent, a gift to the owner of the building, never refundable). You also must be able to supply the name of a **guarantor**, a Japanese citizen willing to accept financial responsibility if you should default. Standard leases run two years.

A common alternative for visitors planning to stay for a few months or a year is to stay in a **gaijin house** or **guesthouse**, an establishment that lets out rooms to foreigners and collects rent by the month. Generally, *gaijin* houses are communal in feel, with shared common areas, kitchens, and bathrooms. Another option is to use an agency that specializes in **monthly apartments** for foreigners, providing a way around many of the restrictions on apartment rental. **J&F Plaza**, 3-12-11, Shinjuku, Shinjuku-ku, Tōkyō 160-0022 (☎+81-3-5366-6356; www.jafplaza.com); **Tōkyō Apartments,** 4-16-12, Kita-Shinjuku, Shinjuku-ku, Tōkyō (☎+81-3-3367-7117; www.tokyoapt.com); and **Tōkyō Room Information**, 1F Nakaya Bldg., 1-42-11, Shin-Koiwa, Katsushika-ku, Tōkyō, 124-0024 (☎+81-3-5607-5508; www.tokyo-room-information.com) are three such agencies. **Openspace** (www.openspace.jp) is an online search service that helps match *gaijin* with rooms in the Tōkyō area.

CAMPING AND THE OUTDOORS

Camping is a popular summer activity in Japan. Typically campers pitch their tents in official **campsites** (kyampu-jo; キャンプ場), often found in national parks. Some are free and some charge a small fee. In addition to restrooms, most sites also provide cooking areas, public phones and vending machines, and occasionally laundry facilities. The season is quite short: most campsites only operate from June to August, and popular locations fill up fast. Increasingly, Japanese campers are using RVs, but traditional camping is also permitted at nearly all sites, even those that bill themselves as **auto-campsites** (auto-kyampu-jo; オートキャンプ場).

An excellent general resource for travelers planning on camping or spending time outdoors is the **Outdoor Japan Page** (www.outdoorjapan.com). It provides a listing of campsite information, organized by prefecture, and suggested nearby hikes. Excellent English campsite listings are available on the **Japan National Tourist Organization** website. See in particular the pamphlet on **"Camping in Japan"** (www.jnto.go.jp/eng/RTG/PTG/804.pdf). The **Kyampu-jo Gaido** (キャンプ場ガイド; www.camping.gr.jp) is a Japanese language listing of campsites with tips and packing lists. **Auto-Kyampu Jōhō** (オートキャンプ情報 ; www.wni.co.jp/cww/docs/autocamp.html) offers listings by region for RV camping.

ENVIRONMENTALLY RESPONSIBLE TOURISM. The idea behind responsible tourism is to leave no trace of human presence. A campstove is safer (and more efficient) than using vegetation to cook, but if you must make a fire, keep it small and use only dead branches or brush. Make sure your campsite is at least 50m from water supplies or bodies of water. If there are no toilet facilities, bury human waste (but not paper) at least 10cm deep and above the high-water line, and 50m or more from water supplies and campsites. Pack your trash in a plastic bag and carry it with you until you reach the next trash receptacle. For more information on these issues, contact one of the organizations listed below.

Earthwatch, 3 Clock Tower Pl. #100, Box 75, Maynard, MA 01754, USA (US ☎800-776-0188 or +1-978-461-0081; www.earthwatch.org).

International Ecotourism Society, 28 Pine St., Burlington, VT 05402, USA (☎+1-802-651-9818; www.ecotourism.org).

National Audubon Society, Nature Odysseys, 700 Broadway, New York, NY 10003 (☎+1-212-979-3000; www.audubon.org).

Tourism Concern, Stapleton House, 277-281 Holloway Rd., London N7 8HN, UK (☎+44-20-7753-3330; www.tourismconcern.org.uk).

USEFUL PUBLICATIONS AND RESOURCES

A variety of publishing companies offer camping, hiking, and biking guidebooks to meet the needs of novice or expert. **Sierra Club Books,** 85 Second St., 2nd Fl., San Francisco, CA 94105, USA (☎+1-415-977-5500; www.sierraclub.org/books) publishes general resource books. **The Mountaineers Books,** 1001 SW Klickitat Way, #201, Seattle, WA 98134, USA (US ☎800-553-4453; www.mountaineersbooks.org) has over 600 titles on hiking, biking, mountaineering, natural history, and conservation. Write or call either company to receive a catalog.

NATIONAL PARKS

Japan's national park system, established during the 1930s, boasts 28 national parks, which cover 5.4% of the country's land area, and 55 quasi-national parks, which account for an additional 3.6%. Although many parks include towns and resorts, regulations on activities within the areas are designed to protect the scenic beauty of remarkable ecosystems such as the jungles of Iriomote-jima and the snowy volcanic ranges of Daisetsuzan. The national parks are administered by the **Ministry of the Environment** (www.env.go.jp/en/index.html), which promotes beautification projects and maintains skiing and hiking trails, shuttle buses and ferries, and campsites and picnic grounds. Similar facilities in the quasi-national parks are maintained by the prefecture, with financial assistance from the Ministry.

POPULAR NATIONAL PARKS

Akan-ko National Park (阿寒国立公園; p. 711). Noted for its spectacular scenery, this mountainous park in eastern Hokkaidō contains an Ainu village. A number of watersports are popular on the three lakes, **Akan-ko, Mashu-ko,** and **Kussharo-ko.** Accommodation is available at a number of *onsen* in the park area. Akan Kohan Onsen, which features in Ainu love stories, has an information line at ☎+81-154-67-2831.

Daisetsuzan National Park (大雪山国立公園; p. 721). The largest of Japan's national parks, Daisetsuzan includes a city and nine towns in central Hokkaidō, and is home to the prefecture's highest mountain. Camping is possible at designated sites throughout the park, including **Shikaribetsu Lake** (☎+81-1566-6-2311) and **Asahidake** (☎+81-166-97-2544). Ranger stations are located in Kamikawa (☎+81-1658-2-2574), Higashikawa (☎+81-166-82-2527) and Kamishihoro (☎+81-1564-2-3337).

Towada-ko Hachimantai National Park (十和田湖八幡平国立公園 ; p. 321). Towada-ko is widely considered one of Japan's most beautiful lakes, and the nearby Oirase Valley is noted for its forests. Information is most readily available from the **Lake Towada Information Center** in Towadako-machi (☎+81-176-75-2425). The Hachimantai plateau, with numerous volcanoes, is an alpine area popular for skiers in the winter.

Unzen-Amakusa National Park (雲仙天草国立公園 ; p. 603). Made up of over 120 islands and a number of active volcanoes, Unzen-Amakusa is a favorite summer destination. The rugged interior is mountainous, while the coastal lowlands are a lush, green forest, filled with breathtaking azaleas during May. A center of Christian activity during a brief window in the 16th century, Unzen-Amakusa also has a number of historical sites.

Iriomote National Park (西表国立公園 ; p. 663). Japan's southernmost national park covers nearly 80% of Okinawa's second-largest island. Japan's largest coral reef is here, as is a dense tropical forest. Iriomote is more wilderness than you can find in the rest of Japan. Snorkeling tours are offered by **Shigetamaru** (☎+81-9808-5-6300). Diving can be arranged through **TA-KE Diving School** (☎+81-9808-5-6871).

WILDERNESS SAFETY

THE GREAT OUTDOORS

Stay warm, stay dry, and stay hydrated. The vast majority of life-threatening wilderness situations can be avoided by following this simple advice. Prepare yourself for an emergency by packing raingear, a hat and mittens, a first-aid kit, a reflector, a whistle, high energy food, and extra water. Dress in wool or warm layers of synthetic materials designed for the outdoors; never rely on cotton for warmth, as it is useless when wet. Check **weather forecasts** and pay attention to the skies when hiking, since weather patterns can change suddenly. Whenever possible, let someone know when and where you are hiking—either a friend, your hostel, a park ranger, or a local hiking organization. Do not attempt a hike beyond your ability. See **Health** (p. 18) for information about outdoor ailments and basic medical concerns.

WILDLIFE

SNAKE ATTACK. Japan's most deadly animal is the yellow-green **habu**, a poisonous snake that lives on all of the Okinawa Islands, except for Miyako. Habu are identifiable by their triangular heads and the large nostril-like aperture below their eyes. They are active at night, and spend most of the day sleeping under rocks or among tree roots. Like most wild animals, a habu will typically not attack unless it feels threatened. Hikers in Okinawa should wear shoes at all times and move slowly away from any snakes they come across; quick, violent gestures will make the snake much more likely to strike. In the event of a bite, remain calm. Immediately press a towel or other cloth against the bite and then immobilize the limb with a splint before heading to the nearest hospital for an anti-venom shot. While the goal is to prevent the spread of venom, **do not apply a tourniquet**—this will cause the venom to pool in one area and, in serious cases, do irreparable harm. In many cases, the habu will bite without injecting poison, but if venom has been released, it is crucial to reach a hospital within 2-3hr.

BEARS. If you are hiking in an area that might be frequented by bears (mountains in Hokkaidō and Northern Honshū), ask rangers for information on bear behavior and obey posted warnings. No matter how cute a bear appears, don't be fooled—they're unpredictable animals not intimidated by humans. If you're close enough for a bear to be observing you, you're too close. If you surprise a bear, speak in soothing tones and back away. Do not run—the bear may identify you as prey and give chase. If you will be traveling extensively in bear-inhabited areas, consider taking **pepper spray**. If a bear attacks, spray its face and eyes. Without pepper spray, different strategies should be used with different species. **Black bears** (black coloration, tall ears, no shoulder hump) are carrion eaters—if you play dead, you are giving them a free meal. The best action is to fight back. **Brown bears** are very protective of their cubs, so don't make any moves toward Baby Bear.

Don't leave food or scented items (trash, toiletries, the clothes you cooked in) near your tent. **Bear-bagging,** hanging edibles and other scented objects from a tree out of paws' reach, is the best way to keep your toothpaste from becoming a condiment. Bears are also attracted to **perfume,** so cologne, scented soap, deodorant, and hairspray should stay at home. For more information, consult *How to Stay Alive in the Woods,* by Bradford Angier (Black Dog & Leventhal Books, $20).

CAMPING AND HIKING EQUIPMENT

WHAT TO BUY...

Good camping equipment is both sturdy and light. Camping equipment is generally more expensive in Australia, New Zealand, and the UK than in North America. Many campsites rent equipment on a nightly basis, but if you are planning to camp frequently, it will probably be more practical to bring your own gear.

Sleeping Bag: Most sleeping bags are rated by season ("summer" means 30-40°F; "four-season" or "winter" often means below 0°F). They are made either of **down** (warmer and lighter, but more expensive, and miserable when wet) or of **synthetic** material (heavier, more durable, and warmer when wet). Prices range US$70-210 for a summer synthetic to US$250-300 for a good down winter bag. **Sleeping bag pads** include foam pads (US$10-30), air mattresses (US$15-50), and Therm-A-Rest self-inflating pads (US$45-120). Bring a **stuff sack** to store your bag and keep it dry.

Tent: The best tents are free-standing (with their own frames and suspension systems), set up quickly, and only require staking in high winds. Low-profile dome tents are the best all-around. Good 2-person tents start at US$90, 4-person at US$300. Seal the seams of your tent with waterproofer, and make sure it has a rain fly. Other tent accessories include a **battery-operated lantern,** a **plastic groundcloth,** and a **nylon tarp.**

Backpack: Internal-frame packs mold better to your back, keep a lower center of gravity, and flex to allow you to hike difficult trails. **External-frame packs** are more comfortable for long hikes over even terrain, as they keep weight higher and distribute it more evenly. Your pack should have a strong padded hip-belt to transfer weight to your legs. Serious backpacking requires a pack of at least 4000 cubic in. (16,000cc), plus 500 cubic in. for sleeping bags in internal-frame packs. Sturdy backpacks cost US$125-420—this is one area where it doesn't pay to economize. Fill up any pack with something heavy and walk around the store with it to get a sense of how it distributes weight. Buy a **waterproof backpack cover** or store your things in plastic bags inside your pack.

Boots: Wear hiking boots with good **ankle support.** They should fit snugly and comfortably over 1-2 pairs of wool socks and thin liner socks. Break in boots over several weeks before you go to save yourself painful and debilitating blisters. It's a good idea to bring a pair of regular shoes for non-hiking segments of your trip, as Japanese shoe-removal etiquette will lose its charm quickly if you're constantly untying and relacing your boots.

Other Items: Synthetic layers, like those made of polypropylene, and a pile jacket will keep you warm even when wet. A **"space blanket"** helps retain body heat and doubles as a groundcloth (US$5-15). Plastic **water bottles** are virtually shatter- and leak-proof. Bring **water-purification tablets** for when you can't boil water. Many campgrounds provide campfire sites, but you may want a small metal grate or grill. For places that forbid fires or the gathering of firewood, you'll need a **camp stove** (the classic Coleman starts at US$45) and a propane-filled **fuel bottle.** Also don't forget a **first-aid kit, pocket-knife, insect repellent, calamine lotion,** and **waterproof matches** or a **lighter.**

...AND WHERE TO BUY IT

The mail-order/online companies listed below offer lower prices than many retail stores, but a visit to a local camping or outdoors store will give you a good sense of the look and weight of certain items. It will be much less costly to purchase these before you leave for Japan, although they will add bulk to your luggage.

Campmor, 28 Parkway, P.O. Box 700, Upper Saddle River, NJ 07458, USA (US ☎888-226-7667; www.campmor.com).

Discount Camping, 880 Main North Rd., Pooraka, South Australia 5095, Australia (☎+61-8-8262-3399; www.discountcamping.com.au).

Eastern Mountain Sports (EMS), 1 Vose Farm Rd., Peterborough, NH 03458, USA (US ☎888-463-6367; www.ems.com).

L.L. Bean, Freeport, ME 04033 (US and Canada ☎800-441-5713, UK ☎0800-891-297; www.llbean.com).

Mountain Designs, 51 Bishop St., Kelvin Grove, Queensland 4059, Australia (☎+61-7-3856-2344; www.mountaindesigns.com).

Recreational Equipment, Inc. (REI), Sumner, WA 98352, USA (US and Canada ☎800-426-4840, elsewhere +1-253-891-2500; www.rei.com).

YHA Adventure Shop, 19 High St., Staines, Middlesex, TW18 4QY, UK (☎+44-1784-458-625; www.yhaadventure.com). One of Britain's largest equipment suppliers.

CAMPERS AND RVS

Renting an RV will always be more expensive than tenting or hosteling, but it's cheaper than staying in hotels and renting a car (see **Rental Cars,** p. 46), and the convenience of bringing along your own bedroom, bathroom, and kitchen makes it an attractive option, especially for older travelers and families with children. Rates vary widely by region, season, and type of RV.

ORGANIZED ADVENTURE TRIPS

Organized adventure tours offer another way of exploring the wild. Activities include hiking, camping, biking, skiing, canoeing, kayaking, rafting, and climbing. Tourism bureaus can suggest parks, trails, and outfitters; other good sources for info are stores and organizations that specialize in outdoor equipment (see above). Visit the Outdoor Japan website (www.outdoorjapan.com) for information and links.

Specialty Travel Index, 305 San Anselmo Ave., #313, San Anselmo, CA 94960 (US ☎800-442-4922 or +1-415-459-4900; info@specialtytravel.com; www.specialtytravel.com). Tours worldwide.

GORPtravel, 6707 Winchester Circle, Ste. 101, Boulder, CO 80301 (US ☎877-440-GORP; http://gorptravel.com/index.html). Tours worldwide; offers cultural immersion, mountain biking and hiking/trekking packages in Japan.

MontBell Outdoor Challenge (M.O.C.), (Japan ☎+81-6-6538-0208; www.montbell.com/english/moc/index.html). Organizes group outdoor activities (with equipment and insurance included); locations in Saitama Prefecture and Shikoku.

KEEPING IN TOUCH

BY MAIL

SENDING MAIL HOME FROM JAPAN

Airmail is the best way to send mail home from Japan. Write "par avion" or 航空 (pronounced *kōkū*) on the front. **Aerogrammes,** printed sheets that fold into envelopes and travel via airmail, are available at post offices. Most post offices will charge exorbitant fees or refuse to send aerogrammes with enclosures. **Surface mail** is by far the cheapest and slowest way to send mail. It takes one to three months to cross the Atlantic and two to four to cross the Pacific—good for items you won't need to see for a while, like souvenirs and other heavy items.

Regular airmail to Europe, North America, and Australasia takes 5-7 days to arrive. Postcards and aerogrammes cost ¥70, letters up to 20g ¥110, packages up to 0.5kg ¥1080, and packages up to 2kg ¥2760.

SENDING MAIL TO JAPAN

Mark envelopes "air mail" or "par avion" or your letter or postcard will never arrive. In addition to the standard postage system, whose rates are listed below, **Federal Express** (Australia ☎ 132-610, US and Canada ☎ 800-247-4747, New Zealand ☎ 0800-73-33-39, UK ☎ 0800-123-800; www.fedex.com) handles express mail services from most home countries to Japan; they can get a letter from New York to Tōkyō in 3 days for US$30, and from London to Tōkyō in 2 days for UK£35.

Australia: Allow 3-4 days for regular airmail to Japan. Postcards and letters up to 20g cost AUS$1; packages up to 0.5kg AUS$6.60, up to 2kg AUS$34. EMS can get a letter to Japan in 2-3 days for AUS$30. www.auspost.com.au/pac.

Canada: Allow 4-7 days for regular airmail to Japan. Postcards and letters up to 30g cost CDN$1.25; packages up to 0.5kg CDN$10, up to 2kg CDN$36. PuroLetter can get a letter to Japan in 3-4 days for CDN$44. www.canadapost.ca.

Ireland: Allow 6-10 days for regular airmail to Japan. Postcards and letters up to 25g cost €0.57; packages up to 0.5kg €5, up to 2kg €20. www.anpost.ie.

New Zealand: Allow 4-10 days for regular airmail to Japan. Postcards/aerogrammes cost NZ$1.50. Letters up to 200g cost NZ$1.50-3.50; small parcels up to 0.5kg NZ$16, up to 2kg NZ$50. www.nzpost.co.nz.

UK: Allow 3-7 days for airmail to Japan. Letters up to 20g cost UK£0.68; packages up to 0.5kg UK£5.21, up to 2kg UK£20.21. UK Swiftair delivers letters one day faster for UK£3.30 more. www.royalmail.com.

US: Allow 4-7 days for regular airmail to Japan. Postcards/aerogrammes cost US$0.70; letters under 1 oz. US$0.80. Packages under 12 oz. cost US$8.40; a 2 lb. package is $14.90. Global Express Mail takes 3-5 days and costs US$20-30 for small packages. US Global Priority Mail delivers flat-rate envelopes in 4-6 days for US$5-9. http://ircalc.usps.gov.

RECEIVING MAIL IN JAPAN

There are several ways to arrange pick-up of letters sent to you by friends and relatives while you are abroad. Mail can be sent via **Poste Restante** (General Delivery) to almost any city or town in Japan with a post office, and is fairly reliable. Address *Poste Restante* letters like so: Hideyoshi TOKUGAWA, Poste Restante, Yonezawa-shi, Yamagata-ken, JAPAN.

The mail will go to a special desk in the central post office, unless you specify a post office by street address or postal code. It's best to use the largest post office, since mail may be sent there regardless. Bring your passport (or other photo ID) for pick-up. It may be safer and quicker, though more expensive, to send mail express or registered. If the clerks insist that there is nothing for you, have them check under your first name as well. *Let's Go* lists post offices in the **Practical Information** section for each city and most towns.

American Express's travel offices throughout the world offer a free **Client Letter Service** (mail held up to 30 days and forwarded upon request) for cardholders who contact them in advance. Address the letter in the same way shown above. Some offices will offer these services to non-cardholders (especially AmEx Traveler's Cheque holders), but call ahead to make sure.

BY TELEPHONE

CALLING HOME FROM JAPAN

A **calling card** is probably the cheapest bet, although a few of Japan's payphones accept only coins. You can frequently call collect without a company's calling card by calling their access number and following the instructions. **To obtain a calling card** from your telecommunications service, contact the company directly. **To call home with a calling card,** contact the operator for your service provider in Japan.

Let's Go has recently partnered with ekit.com to provide a calling card that offers a number of services, including email and voice messaging. Before purchasing any calling card, always be sure to compare rates with other cards, and to make sure it serves your needs (a local phonecard is generally better for local calls, for instance). For more information, visit www.letsgo.ekit.com.

Because of problems surrounding fake telephone cards and international phone calls, Japan has a limited number of phones from which you can make international calls. Only specific public phones, identifiable by their silver or bronze coloring, and occasionally, by a sign in English, are usable for international calls. If you aren't using a calling card, you may need to drop your coins as quickly as your words; a helpful chime will inform you that your time is running short. At KDD "credit phones," usually located in hotels, prepaid phone cards and major credit cards can be used for direct international calls, but they are still less cost-efficient. Placing a **collect call** through an international operator (☎0051; most operators speak English) is even more expensive, but may be necessary in an emergency.

PLACING INTERNATIONAL CALLS.

1. The **international dialing prefix.** To dial out of Japan, 0051; **Australia,** 0011; **Canada** or the **US,** 011; the **Republic of Ireland, New Zealand,** or the **UK,** 00; **South Africa,** 09.
2. The **country code** of the country you want to call. To call **Australia,** dial 61; **Canada** or the **US,** 1; the **Republic of Ireland,** 353; **New Zealand,** 64; **South Africa,** 27; the **UK,** 44; **Japan,** 81.
3. The **city/area code.** Let's Go lists the city/area codes for cities and towns in Japan opposite the city or town name, next to a ☎. If the first digit is a zero (e.g., 082 for Hiroshima), omit the zero when calling from abroad (e.g., dial 82 from Canada to reach Hiroshima).
4. The **local number.**

CALLING WITHIN JAPAN

The simplest way to call within the country is to use a coin-operated phone. Phones are located at every train station and many major street corners. **Prepaid phone cards** (available at train station kiosks, vending machines, and convenience stores; ¥500 or ¥1000) usually save time and money in the long run. The computerized phone will tell you how much time, in units, you have left when you insert your card and will punch holes along the side of the card to show you how much value is left on your card. Although you will receive change if you insert an extra ¥10 when using coins in a pay phone, you will not receive change for ¥100 coins.

Another kind of prepaid card comes with a Personal Identification Number (PIN) and a toll-free access number. Instead of inserting the card into the phone, call the access number and follow the directions on the card. These cards can be used for international and domestic calls. To use your credit card or pre-paid phone card, dial ☎0055 and enter your card or PIN number before dialing the number you want to reach. For collect calls within Japan dial ☎106. Phone rates tend to be highest in the morning, lower in the evening, and lowest on Sunday and late at night.

To place your call, dial "0" and the city code, followed by the number you are trying to reach. Toll-free numbers begin with ☎ 0120 or ☎ 0088. For directory assistance, dial ☎ 104; for English service M-F 9am-5pm, call ☎ 0120-364-463.

CELLULAR PHONES

Cellular phones (*keitai denwa*; 携帯電話) are central to modern Japanese communication. They are also far more advanced than those in other countries: full-color LCD screens and camera capabilities have been standard for several years already. Most phones are capable of sending and receiving brief e-mails (though entering your message through the keypad can be a pain). Rates are surprisingly low, and even on the popular pre-paid plans, all incoming calls are free.

Standard Japanese cell phones must be registered with proof of residence provided, which makes it difficult for foreign visitors to obtain them. A better choice for the short-term visitor is a **pre-paid phone**, which requires you to buy an inexpensive phone (US$50-60) and phone cards (available at any convenience store) to make calls. **J-Phone** (www.j-phone.com) and **DoCoMo** (www.nttdocomo.com) are two companies that offer this service. **Cellular Abroad** (US ☎ 1-800-287-3020; http://cellularabroad.com/japancellService.html) can provide you with a cell phone prior to your arrival. The phones cost US$249 for a phone valid for 60 days and ¥5000 of talk time. Extensions of service and talk time can be purchased at convenience stores. It is also possible to rent a cell phone on a weekly or daily basis while you are in Japan, for about ¥1500 per day. **Japan Cell Phone Rentals** (☎ +81-120-88-7937; www.jcrcorp.com) offers a bilingual service for English-speaking travelers.

TIME DIFFERENCES

Japan is 9 hours ahead of **Greenwich Mean Time (GMT).** Japan does not observe **daylight savings time,** so countries that do observe it may be an hour off in summer; fall and spring switchover dates vary between countries and may contribute to the confusion. Generally speaking, Japan is 3 hours behind Auckland, 1 hour behind Sydney; 7 hours ahead of Johannesburg; 14 hours ahead of New York; and 17 hours ahead of Vancouver and San Francisco. The World Time Server (www.worldtimeserver.com) can help sort out any lingering uncertainty.

BY EMAIL AND INTERNET

Japan is a wired country, and Internet access is easy to find in the cities, though more of a challenge in rural areas. **Internet cafes,** which charge about ¥400 per hour and frequently supply free drinks or other amenities, and the occasional free Internet terminal at a library or tourist office are listed in the **Practical Information** sections of major cities. For lists of additional cybercafes, check out **Japan Cyber Cafe** (www.kohphangan.com/batik/internet/cafe/japan.html). New on the scene are subscription-based Internet **"hot spots"**—bring your wireless-enabled laptop to a participating cafe or fast food joint and surf to your heart's content. Though in some places it's possible to forge a remote link with your home server, in most cases this is slower (and thus more expensive) than taking advantage of free **web-based email accounts** (e.g., www.hotmail.com and www.yahoo.com). If you are on a longer visit and have purchased a cell phone, you will be able to send and receive short e-mails from your phone for a few yen each.

GETTING TO JAPAN

BY PLANE

When it comes to airfare, a little effort can save you a bundle. Tickets bought from consolidators and standby seating are good deals, but last-minute specials, airfare wars, and charter flights often beat these fares. Hunt around, be flexible, and ask about discounts. Students, seniors, and those under 26 should never pay full price.

AIRFARES

Airfares to Japan peak between June and August; holidays are also expensive. The cheapest times to travel are November and January, but watch out for the December travel season when prices jump up. Midweek (M-Th morning) round-trip flights run US$40-50 cheaper than weekend flights, but they are generally more crowded and less likely to permit frequent-flier upgrades. Not fixing a return date ("open return") or arriving in and departing from different cities ("open-jaw") can be pricier than round-trip flights. Patching one-way flights together is the most expensive way to travel. Flights between Japan's capitals or regional hubs—Tōkyō (Narita Airport), Ōsaka (Kansai International Airport), Nagoya, Fukuoka, and Sapporo (New Chitose Airport)—will tend to be cheaper.

Fares for round-trip flights to Tōkyō Narita or Kansai from the US or Canadian east coast cost, on average, US$900-1200 in the off-season (Jan.-Apr. and Sept.-Nov.); from the US or Canadian west coast, US$700-1000. In the UK the high season is April and May; outside of that period, round-trip tickets from London to Narita run UK£750-900. Australia's off season is September to March, when round-trip tickets on Qantas cost AUS$1600-1800. JAL, however, offers special deals on their online booking service (www.japanair.com/e/travelplan/reservations.php), where you may be able to find rates of AUS$1500 even during high season. Flying from New Zealand to Narita costs NZ$1900-2300 on Air New Zealand or Singapore Air.

If Japan is only one stop on a more extensive globe-hop, consider a round-the-world (RTW) ticket. Tickets usually include at least 5 stops and are valid for about a year; prices range US$1200-5000. Try **Northwest Airlines/KLM** (US ☎800-447-4747; www.nwa.com) or **Star Alliance**, a consortium of 22 airlines including United Airlines (US ☎800-241-6522; www.staralliance.com).

BUDGET AND STUDENT TRAVEL AGENCIES

While knowledgeable agents specializing in flights to Japan can make your life easy and help you save, they may not spend the time to find you the lowest possible fare—they get paid on commission. Travelers holding **ISIC and IYTC cards** (see p. 11) qualify for big discounts from student travel agencies. Most flights from budget agencies are on major airlines, but in peak season some may sell seats on less-reliable chartered aircraft.

USIT, 19-21 Aston Quay, Dublin 2 (☎+353-1-602-1600; www.usitworld.com) Ireland's leading student/budget travel agency has 22 offices throughout Northern Ireland and the Republic of Ireland. Offers programs to work in North America.

CTS Travel, 30 Rathbone Pl., London W1T 1GQ, UK (☎+44-20-7290-0630; www.ctstravel.co.uk). A British student travel agent with offices in 39 countries including the US, Empire State Building, 350 Fifth Ave., Ste. 7813, New York, NY 10118 (US ☎877-287-6665; www.ctstravelusa.com).

STA Travel, 7890 S. Hardy Dr., Ste. 110, Tempe AZ 85284, USA (24hr. reservations and info ☎800-781-4040; www.sta-travel.com). A student and youth travel organization with over 150 offices worldwide (check their website for a listing of all their offices), including US offices in Boston, Chicago, Los Angeles, New York, San Francisco, Seattle, and Washington, D.C. Ticket booking, travel insurance, railpasses, and more. In the UK, walk-in office 11 Goodge St., London W1T 2PF (☎+44-207-436-7779). In New Zealand, Shop 2B, 182 Queen St., Auckland (☎+64-9-309-0458). In Australia, 366 Lygon St., Carlton Vic 3053 (☎+61-3-9349-4344).

Travel CUTS (Canadian Universities Travel Services Limited), 187 College St., Toronto, ON M5T 1P7 Canada (☎+1-416-979-2406; www.travelcuts.com). Offices across Canada and the US in Seattle, San Francisco, Los Angeles, New York, and elsewhere. Also in the UK, 295-A Regent St., London W1B 2H9 (☎+44-20-7255-2191).

✈ FLIGHT PLANNING ON THE INTERNET. Many airlines offer special last-minute deals on the Web—check out the websites for the commercial airlines below for a start (p. 40). Other sites do the legwork and compile the deals for you—try www.bestfares.com, www.flights.com, www.lowestfare.com, www.onetravel.com, and www.travelzoo.com.

■ StudentUniverse (www.studentuniverse.com), **STA** (www.sta-travel.com), and **Orbitz** (www.orbitz.com) provide quotes on student tickets, while **Expedia** (www.expedia.com) and **Travelocity** (www.travelocity.com) offer full travel services. **Priceline** (www.priceline.com) allows you to specify a price, and obligates you to buy any ticket that meets or beats it; be prepared for antisocial hours and odd routes. **Skyauction** (www.skyauction.com) allows you to bid on both last-minute and advance-purchase tickets.

An indispensable resource on the Internet is the *Air Traveler's Handbook* (www.faqs.org/faqs/travel/air/handbook), a comprehensive listing of everything you need to know before you board a plane.

JAPANESE TRAVEL AGENCIES

Travel agencies that specialize in travel to Japan may be the best informed on deals and specials specific to the area, and can help with railpasses, accommodations, and package deals, as well as airfares and general travel. **Japan Travel Bureau, Nippon Travel Agency,** and **Kintetsu International** are the big dogs; smaller specialty travel agencies like **IACE Travel** (US ☎800-872-4223 or +1-212-972-3200; www.iace-usa.com) are worth checking out as well.

JAPAN TRAVEL BUREAU (JTB)

Japan head office: 2-3-11, Higashi Shinagawa, Shinagawa-ku, Tōkyō 140-8602 (☎+81-3-5796-5446; www.jtb.co.jp).

Offices abroad: Australia: JTB Australia Pty. Ltd., Level 12, 500 Collins St., Melbourne 3000 (☎+61-3-8623-0000; www.japantravel.com.au). **Canada:** Branch offices in Toronto (☎+1-800-268-5942) and Vancouver (☎+1-800-663-0229). Online at www.jtbi.ca. **UK:** JTB UK Ltd. 95 Cromwell Rd., London SW7 4JT (☎+44-20-7663-6148; www.accessjapan.co.uk). **US:** Branch offices in Atlanta (☎+1-404-262-3014), Chicago (US ☎800-669-5824), Hasbrouck Heights, NJ (☎+1-201-288-5007), Manhattan (US ☎800-235-3523), San Francisco (☎+1-415-986-4764), San Jose (☎+1-408-727-6800), and Torrance, CA (☎+1-310-618-0961). Online at www.jtbusa.com.

NIPPON TRAVEL AGENCY (NTA)

Japan head office: Shimbashi Ekimae Bldg., 2-20-15, Shimbashi, Minato-ku, Tōkyō 105-8606 (www.nta.co.jp).

Offices abroad: Australia: Head Office, Level 9, 135 Kings St., Sydney, NSW 2000 (☎+61-2-9338-2300). Branches in Melbourne (☎+61-3-9629-7722) and Queensland (Gold Coast ☎+61-7-5592-1093; Cairns ☎+61-7-4031-5844). **Canada:** Head Office, Ste. 950, 1140 West Pender St., Vancouver, BC, V6E 4G1 (☎+1-604-685-4663; fax 687-4664). Branches in Alberta (☎+1-403-762-0777) and Ontario (☎+1-416-594-9209). **New Zealand:** Auckland Branch Office, Level 25, Fay Richwhite Bldg., 151 Queen St., P.O. Box 105-260 Auckland Central (☎+64-9-309-5750; fax 302-0061). **UK:** Head Office, 3rd Fl., Skyline House, 200 Union St., London SE1 OLW (☎+44-20-7902-2700; fax 7902-2727). **US:** Head Office, 1025 West 190th St., Ste. 300, Gardena, CA 90248 (☎+1-310-768-0017; fax 323-4032). Branches in Honolulu (☎+1-808-596-4200), Las Vegas (☎+1-702-791-7665), Los Angeles (☎+1-310-630-0898), New Jersey (☎+1-201-325-8484), New York (☎+1-212-445-0840), Orlando (☎+1-407-281-0775), and San Francisco (☎+1-415-543-3233).

KINTETSU INTERNATIONAL

Headquarters: 1325 Ave. of the Americas, Ste. 2002, New York, NY 10019, USA (☎+1-212-259-9600; www.kintetsu.com). Also in Chicago (☎+1-630-250-8840), Los Angeles (☎+1-562-924-4600), New Jersey (☎+1-201-288-4567), San Francisco (☎+1-415-922-7171), San Jose (☎+1-408-544-2440).

COMMERCIAL AIRLINES

The commercial airlines' lowest regular offer is the **APEX** (Advance Purchase Excursion) fare, which provides confirmed reservations and allows "open-jaw" tickets. Generally, reservations must be made seven to 21 days ahead of departure, with seven- to 14-day minimum-stay and up to 90-day maximum-stay restrictions. These fares carry hefty cancellation and change penalties (fees rise in summer). Book peak-season APEX fares early; by May you will have a hard time getting your desired departure date. Use **Microsoft Expedia** (http://msn.expedia.com) or **Travelocity** (www.travelocity.com) to get an idea of the lowest published fares, then use the resources outlined here to try and beat them. Low-season fares should be appreciably cheaper than the **high-season** (mid-June to Aug.) ones listed here.

TRAVELING FROM NORTH AMERICA

Basic round-trip fares to Japan range roughly US$450-1000. Standard commercial carriers offer the most convenient flights, but they may not be the cheapest, unless you manage to grab a special promotion or airfare war ticket. Foreign carriers may be a better deal, if any of their limited departure points are convenient.

Air Nippon: ☎+81-3-5462-1941; www.ananet.or.jp/ank.

All Nippon Airways (ANA): ☎+81-3-5756-5679; www.ana.co.jp.

Japan Airlines Co. Ltd. (JAL): ☎+81-3-5460-7286; www.jal.co.jp.

TRAVELING FROM THE UK AND IRELAND

British Airways: ☎+44-860-011-747; www.british-airways.co.jp.

Virgin Atlantic: ☎+44-1293-747-747; www.virgin-atlantic.com.

Royal Dutch Airlines (KLM): ☎+44-8705-074-074; www.klm.com/uk_en/.

TRAVELING FROM AUSTRALIA AND NEW ZEALAND

Air New Zealand: New Zealand ☎0800-737-000; www.airnz.co.nz.

Qantas Air: Australia ☎131-313, New Zealand ☎0800-808-767; www.qantas.com.au. Flights from Australia and New Zealand to Tōkyō.

Singapore Air: Australia ☎131-011, New Zealand ☎0800-808-909; www.singaporeair.com. Connections through Singapore.

TRAVELING FROM SOUTH AFRICA

Lufthansa: ☎+27-861-842-538; www.lufthansa.co.za.

British Airways: ☎+27-860-011-747; www.british-airways.com/regional/sa. Cape Town and Johannesburg to Tōkyō with connections through London.

Virgin Atlantic: ☎+27-1293-747-747; www.virgin-atlantic.com. Johannesburg to Tōkyō with connections through London.

Air France: ☎+27-11-770-1601; www.airfrance.com/za. Johannesburg to Paris; connections to Tōkyō.

AIR COURIER FLIGHTS

Those who travel light should consider courier flights. Couriers help transport cargo on international flights by using their checked luggage space for freight. Generally, couriers must travel with carry-ons only and deal with complex flight restrictions. Most flights are round-trip, with short fixed-length stays (usually one week) and a limit of a one ticket per issue. These flights usually operate only out of major gateway cities, mostly in North America. Round-trip courier fares from the US to Japan run about US$500-700. Most flights leave from New York, Los Angeles, San Francisco, or Miami in the US; and from Montreal, Toronto, or Vancouver in Canada. Generally, you must be over 21 (in some cases 18). In summer, popular destinations usually require an advance reservation of about two weeks (you can usually book up to two months ahead). Super-discounted fares are common for "last-minute" flights (three to 14 days ahead). The organizations below provide members with lists of opportunities and courier brokers for an annual fee.

Air Courier Travel Club: www.globalcourierguide.com. Flights from New York to Tōkyō. Lifetime membership $35.

Air Courier Association, 350 Indiana St. #300, Golden, CO 80401, USA (US ☎800-282-1202; www.aircourier.org). To Tōkyō US$204-388. 1-year membership US$49.

International Association of Air Travel Couriers (IAATC), P.O. Box 980, Keystone Heights, FL 32656, USA (☎+1-352-475-1584; www.courier.org). 1-year membership US$45.

STANDBY FLIGHTS

Traveling standby requires considerable flexibility in arrival and departure dates and cities. Companies dealing in standby flights sell vouchers rather than tickets, along with the promise to get to your destination (or near it) within a certain window of time (typically 1-5 days). You call in before your specific window of time to hear your flight options and the probability that you will be able to board each flight. You then decide which flights you want to try to make, show up, present your voucher, and board if space is available. You may receive a monetary refund only if every available flight within your date range is full; if you opt not to take an available (but perhaps less convenient) flight, you can only get credit toward future travel. Carefully read agreements with any company offering standby flights as tricky fine print can leave you in a lurch. To check on a company's service record in the US, call the Better Business Bureau (☎+1-212-533-6200).

TICKET CONSOLIDATORS

Ticket consolidators, or "bucket shops," buy unsold tickets in bulk from airlines and sell them at discounted rates. The best place to look is in the travel section of any major newspaper, where many bucket shops place tiny ads. Call quickly, as availability is extremely limited. Not all bucket shops are reliable, so insist on a receipt that gives full details of restrictions, refunds, and tickets, and pay by credit card (in spite of the 2-5% fee) so you can stop payment if you never receive your tickets. For more info, see www.travel-library.com/air-travel/consolidators.html.

ESSENTIALS

TRAVELING FROM THE US AND CANADA

Travel Avenue (US ☎ 800-333-3335; www.travelavenue.com) searches for best available published fares and then uses several consolidators to attempt to beat that fare. Other consolidators worth trying are **Rebel** (US ☎ 800-227-3235; www.rebeltours.com) and **Cheap Tickets** (US ☎ 800-377-1000; www.cheaptickets.com). Yet more consolidators on the web include **Flights.com** (www.flights.com); **TravelHUB** (www.travelhub.com); and **Club Tripmakers** (US ☎ 888-398-4733; www.clubtripmakers.com). Keep in mind that these are only suggestions to get you started in your research; *Let's Go* does not endorse any of these agencies. As always, be cautious, and research companies before you hand over your credit card number.

CHARTER FLIGHTS

Charters are flights a tour operator contracts with an airline to fly extra loads of passengers during peak season. Charter flights fly less frequently than major airlines, make refunds difficult, and are almost always fully booked. Schedules and itineraries may also change or be cancelled at the last moment (as late as 48 hours before the trip, and without a full refund), and check-in, boarding, and baggage claim are often much slower. They can, however, be cheaper. **Discount clubs** and **fare brokers** offer members savings on last-minute charter and tour deals.

BY BOAT

Japan is accessible by boat from Asia, and overnight ferries can save you money without much lost time. The fares below are one-way for adult foot passengers unless otherwise noted. Ferries run year-round from all destinations.

TRAVELING TO SOUTH KOREA

Kampu Ferry Service: (☎+81-832-24-3000), **Shimonoseki** to **Pusan** (14½hr., daily in both directions; departs 6pm, arrives 8:30am; ¥8500).

Beetle: (☎+81-92-281-2315), **Fukuoka** to **Pusan** (3hr., 4 per day in both directions; ¥13,000, round-trip ¥24,000).

Camelia Line: (☎+81-92-262-2323), **Fukuoka** to **Pusan** (3hr., M-W overnight from Fukuoka, Tu-Th-Su overnight from Pusan; ¥13,000, round-trip ¥24,000).

TRAVELING TO CHINA

China Express Line: (☎+81-6-6536-6541), **Ōsaka/Kōbe** to **Tientsin** (2 days, weekly in both directions; departs Kōbe midnight F, departs Tientsin midnight W; from ¥20,000); **Ōsaka/Kōbe** to **Shanghai** (2 days, weekly from Shanghai, every other week from Ōsaka/Kōbe; departs Kōbe midnight Tu, departs Shanghai midnight Sa; ¥20,000).

Shanghai Ferry Service: (☎+81-78-321-5791), **Ōsaka** to **Shanghai** (2 days, weekly F from Ōsaka, Tu from Shanghai; departs midnight, arrives 10:30am; from ¥20,000).

TRAVELING TO TAIWAN

Arimura Sangyo: (Naha ☎+81-98-869-1320). Boats depart weekly; schedules change seasonally, so call the Naha office. **Ōsaka** to **Keelung** (¥72,000); **Naha** to **Keelung** (¥26,900); **Nagoya** to **Kaohsiung** (¥77,900); **Naha** to **Kaohsiung** (¥29,300).

TRAVELING TO RUSSIA

FESCO: (☎+81-3-5541-7511), **Fushiki** to **Vladivostok** (2½ days, departs Sa from Vladivostok, W from Fushiki; departs 6pm, arrives 9:30am in both directions; ¥28,000).

Higashi Nihonkai Ferry: (☎+81-3-3249-4412), **Wakkanai** to **Korsakof** (5½hr., several times per week, ¥20,000).

GETTING AROUND JAPAN
BY PLANE

Japan has a well-developed domestic air system, with five major airports and dozens of smaller, regional ones. Although more expensive than the train, traveling by plane saves time and can prove very convenient. Routes are available between most major cities. For anyone planning to make multiple intra-Japan flights during their stay, ANA and JAL both offer a bargain **"Visit Japan" fare** (see p. 48).

ANA Domestic Flight Information: Japan toll-free ☎0120-029-222; US toll-free ☎800-235-9262; UK ☎+44-20-7478-1900; South Africa ☎+27-11-884-5167.

JAL Domestic Reservations: Japan toll-free ☎0120-25-5971; US toll-free ☎800-525-3663; UK ☎+44-8457-747-700; Australia ☎+61-2-9272-1111; South Africa ☎+27-11-884-9719)

Japan Air System (part of the JAL Group): domestic reservations ☎+81-3-5457-5566.

BY TRAIN

JR EAST INFOLINE ☎03-3423-0111 (daily 10am-6pm)

Formerly a centralized national system, since 1987 Japan's railways have been operated by a number of smaller local operators under the collective name of **JR** (Japan Railways). Cooperation between them is smooth, and together they provide extensive, efficient and on-time service year-round, making rail the most popular means of getting around the country. Though it is highly convenient, travel by train can get very expensive. Discounted tickets are sometimes available from special counters in the station (not the official ones—look around for a vendor).

TRAIN TYPES. Futsū (regular; 普通) trains operate on local lines, stopping at each station. **Kaisoku** (rapid service; 快速) trains stop only at selected stations; they travel at the same speed as **kyūkō** (ordinary express; 急行), which go longer distances. Local trains are best avoided during rush hour (7:30am-9:30am and 5pm-7pm), when they become insanely crowded. **Tokkyū** (special express; 特急) trains stop only at major stations, making long-distance trips more efficient, though the **shinkansen** (bullet train; 新幹線) provides by far the quickest service along its separate, continuously welded tracks, which allow it to travel at speeds up to 186mph.

TICKET TYPES. Several types of tickets are available on most trains. The most important difference is between the **regular** and **Green Car** (first-class; gurin-sha; グリーン車) fares. Most travelers will want a regular **unreserved fare** (jiyū-seki; 自由席), which is the least expensive and most flexible in terms of departure time. You are not, however, guaranteed a seat in a non-reserved car the way you are when you purchase the regular **reserved fare** (shitei-seki; 指定席). Although all *shinkansen*, with the exception of the Nozomi Line, have a few unreserved cars, during holidays it's best to reserve your seat. If you can't stand cigarette smoke, reserve a non-smoking car (kin'en-sha; 禁煙車). When you enter the platform, you'll either put your ticket through a machine or hand it to the conductor. Make sure you get it back—you'll need it to get off without being fined.

RAILPASSES. JR offers a number of railpass options, which grant almost unlimited use of the JR system. Non-Japanese citizens traveling under "temporary visitor" status and Japanese nationals living abroad permanently are eligible to purchase a pass. Temporary visitors are those who declare "sightseeing" on their immigration forms and who stay in Japan for under 90 days. You will be required to show proof of your status at several points during the purchase process and you may be asked at any point during your journey to display your passport. There are several kinds of **Japan Rail Passes,** which differ in duration and area covered.

JAPAN RAIL PASS OPTIONS				
Region	Duration	Regular Fare*	Green Car Fare*	Restrictions
		Adult/Child/Youth (12-25)	Adult/Child	
All-Japan	7-day	¥28,300/¥14,150	¥37,800/¥18,900	All JR trains except Nozomi shinkansen; all domestic JR ferries
	14-day	¥45,100/¥22,550	¥61,200/¥30,600	
	21-day	¥57,700/¥28,850	¥79,600/¥39,800	
JR East	5-day	¥20,000/¥10,000/¥16,000	¥28,000/¥14,000	Not valid for the Tōkaidō Shinkansen and the Sanyō shinkansen lines
	10-day	¥32,000/¥16,000/¥25,000	¥44,800/¥22,400	
	4 days in 1 month	¥20,000/¥10,000/¥16,000	¥28,000/¥14,000	
JR Kyūshū	5-day	¥15,000		Excludes JR Kyūshū bus lines and international ferries
	7-day	¥20,000		
JR West Kansai (Kyōto-Ōsaka-Kōbe-Nara-Himeji)	1-day	¥2000/¥1000		
	2-day	¥4000/¥2000		
	3-day	¥5000/¥2500		
	4-day	¥6000/¥3000		
JR West Sanjo (Ōsaka-Okayama-Hiroshima-Hakata)	4-day	¥20,000/¥10,000		
	8-day	¥30,000/¥15,000		
JR Hokkaidō	3-day	¥14,000/¥7000	¥20,000/¥10,000	
*prices are subject to change				

You must obtain an **exchange order** for your railpass before you arrive in Japan. Passes are available from JTB Corp., Nippon Travel Agency, Kinki Nippon Tourist, Tōkyū Tourist Corporation, Japan Airlines, All Nippon Airways, and Jalpak. For a **listing of dealers,** see JR's Rail Pass website (www.japanrailpass.net/eng/en05.html). When you arrive in Japan, turn in your exchange order and an application at an exchange office. The order must be exchanged within three months of purchase. When you turn in your exchange order, you must specify a date within the next month when you will begin using your pass.

Cheaper, though less convenient than a railpass, are **Seishun 18** tickets. The 5-packs of tickets cost ¥11,500 and each ticket allows 24hr. of travel on local and limited express trains. Sold at major train stations around school holidays, the tickets are valid when university students are out of school—from March to early April, mid-July to early September, and mid-December to mid-January.

PURCHASING TICKETS. Reserved-seat tickets can be purchased from the **Midori-no-madoguchi** (Green Ticket Window; 緑の窓口) in your departure station, or from the **"View Plazas"** (Travel Information Centers). Tickets can only be refunded before the departure of the train specified on the ticket. Regular fare tickets can be purchased from automatic **ticket vending machines.** Once you have determined the appropriate fare from the posted map, insert coins or bills and press the button that corresponds to your fare. All important information, including departure station, destination, and fare, will be printed on your ticket. If you accidentally purchase a ticket for the wrong fare, ask a JR employee to change it before you board

> **JAPAN RAIL PASS EXCHANGE OFFICE LOCATIONS**
> **In Honshū:** Misawa, Sendai, Yamagata, Fukushima, Niigata, Kanazawa, Narita Airport, Tōkyō Station, Ueno Station, Shinjuku Station, Shibuya Station, Ikebukuro Station, Yokohama, Shin-Yokohama, Odawara, Mishima, Shizuoka, Hamamatsu, Nagoya, Kyōto, Shin-Ōsaka, Ōsaka, Kansai Airport, Sannomiya, Okayama, Hiroshima, Shimonoseki.
> **In Kyūshū:** Kokura, Hakata, Nagasaki, Kumamoto, Oita, Miyazaki, Nishikagoshima.
> **In Shikoku:** Takamatsu, Matsuyama.
> **In Hokkaidō:** Sapporo, New Chitose Airport, Hakodate, Kushiro, Obihiro, Asahikawa.

the train. If you can't find anyone to help you read the station listings, you can buy the cheapest fare and pay the difference at your destination. Before the exit gate of most train stations you'll find a Compensation Machine (乗り越し器), where you can make things right. If there is no machine, tell the worker at the exit window.

Most *shinkansen* have unreserved cars, but reserved seating is recommended during holidays and tourist season. Tickets can be purchased at the departure station or reserved online through **JR's World Eki-net** (www.world.eki-net.com), which requires registration and credit card information, but will allow you to reserve tickets for any itinerary starting at Narita Airport.

BOARDING A TRAIN. When you enter the platform, proceed to the appropriate area, which depends on what type of ticket you have purchased. If you will be traveling Green Car or reserved, line up with the other people who will be in your car. Show someone your ticket if you are confused by the signage, and they can probably direct you to the right place.

BY BUS

Because Japan is known for its efficient rail transportation, travelers often overlook buses as a means of long-distance travel. To some extent, this is justified— the bus system tends to be more difficult for foreigners to navigate, not the least because of the limited amount of information available in English. **JR passes** are valid on local JR buses and some highway routes, as well as on trains. The local JR operators are **JR Hokkaidō Bus, JR Bus Tōhoku** (www.jrbustohoku.co.jp), **JR Bus Kantō** (www.jrbuskanto.co.jp), **JR Tokai Bus** (www.jrtbinm.co.jp), **West Japan JR Bus** (www.nishinihonjrbus.co.jp), **Chūgoku JR Bus** (www.chugoku-jrbus.co.jp), and **JR Kyūshū Bus** (www.jrkbus.co.jp). Numerous private companies run buses as well— consult with the tourist office for the best option where you're traveling.

Local transportation is also often by train or subway, but local buses fill in the gaps and may be the only means of transport in some places. *Let's Go* describes local buses in the listings for individual cities. Two systems exist for payment on buses. On some, you enter at the front of the bus and pay your fare at that time. On others, you enter at the back and take a ticket; the fare is collected when you exit.

BY BOAT

Though slower than air and train travel, ferry services are a popular means of intercity and island-to-island transportation. Trips vary from brief hydrofoil excursions to longer journeys in small ocean liners. On overnight trips, those paying the cheapest fares unroll their futons on a massive communal sleeping area. Paying more will get you a dorm-style bed or a private room. You will probably be charged for bringing a car or motorcycle; bicycles can be brought on board for free.

The **Shin Nihon Kai Ferry Company** has reservation centers in Ōsaka (☎+81-6-6345-2921), Tōkyō (☎+81-3-3543-5500), Sapporo (☎+81-11-241-7100), and Nagoya (☎+81-52-566-1661); the **Blue Highway Ferry Company** has reservation centers in Tōkyō (☎+81-3-3578-1127), Hokkaidō (☎+81-144-34-3121), Kōchi (☎+81-88-831-0520), and south Kyūshū (☎+81-994-73-0661). The **Kansai Kisen Ferry Company** offers services between Ōsaka and cities in Shikoku and Kyūshū; it has offices in Ōsaka (☎+81-6-6572-5181), Matsuyama (☎+81-89-967-7180), and Beppu (☎+81-977-22-2181). The *JR Jikokuhyo* timetable has a comprehensive listing of routes, schedules and fares; for something in English, try the **Japan Long Distance Ferry Association**'s brochure.

BY CAR

Driving in Japan makes sense in some situations. It does not make sense in major cities, where roads are narrow and frequently congested, and parking is scarce and expensive. It makes little sense to drive from city to city, as expressways can charge tolls of about US$1 per mile, making it more expensive to travel by car than by bus or train. Driving can be, however, a good option for exploring rural areas like the interior and southern coast of Shikoku, the San-in coast of Western Honshū, or rural areas of Hokkaidō. Rural roads are often unpaved, and mountainous areas close roads in winter. If you anticipate driving in wintery climes, the bilingual *Japan Road Atlas* (¥2890) provides the dates on which some roads close.

GETTING A JAPANESE DRIVER'S LICENSE If you are planning a longer stay in Japan, you should be aware the IDP becomes invalid after one year. You will then have to take the following steps in order to have your foreign driver's license converted into a **Japanese license:**

1. Obtain a translation of your foreign driver's license (¥3000) from an office of the Japan Automobile Federation. You may also mail a photocopy of your license to a JAF office and have the translation processed by post for an extra ¥700. Some embassies (not including the US embassy) offer translation services. Be very careful with your copy of the translation, as JAF will be very reluctant to reissue one.

2. Go to a local Driver's License Office and present the following documents: your foreign driver's license (if it does not state the date of issue, bring another document citing the date of issue); passport; resident card or alien registration card; one photo, 2.4 cm x 3 cm (smaller than a normal passport photo, but a photo booth may be available at the office); and the Japanese translation of your driving license.

RENTAL CARS

Car rentals are widespread and easy to find at airports and train stations. Several websites, such as Discover Japan (www.discover-japan.info/book_car/japan_car_hire.html) and Outdoor Japan (www.outdoorjapan.com/travel/travelcarrental.html), offer online search and booking services. Cheaper cars tend to be less reliable and harder to handle on difficult terrain. Less expensive 4WD vehicles tend to be top-heavy, and are more dangerous on particularly bumpy roads.

RENTAL AGENCIES. You can generally make reservations before you leave by calling major international offices in your home country. However, occasionally the price and availability information they give doesn't jive with what the local offices in your country will tell you. Try checking with both numbers to make sure you get the best price and accurate information. Local desk numbers are included in town listings; for home-country numbers, call your toll-free directory.

To rent a car from most establishments in Japan, you need to be at least 18 years old. Small local operations occasionally rent to people under 21, but be sure to ask about the insurance coverage and deductible, and always check the fine print. Two large agencies are **Hertz Japan** (Japan ☎0120-489-882, US reservations ☎800-654-3001; www.hertz.com) and **Nippon Rent-a-Car** (Tōkyō ☎+81-3-3485-7196 for English, Ōsaka ☎+81-6-6232-0919; www.nipponrentacar.co.jp, only in Japanese).

COSTS AND INSURANCE. Rental car prices start at around ¥6500 a day from national companies; expect to pay more for larger cars and for 4WD. Automatics and stick shifts are usually both available, but it is virtually impossible, no matter where you are, to find an automatic 4WD. Some rental packages offer unlimited kilometers; nearly all require that you return the car with a full tank of gas. Many packages include **insurance** against theft and collision. Be aware that cars rented on an **American Express** or **Visa/Mastercard Gold or Platinum** credit cards in Japan might *not* carry the automatic insurance that they would in some other countries; check with your credit card company. Insurance plans almost always come with an **excess** (or deductible) of around ¥50,000, meaning you pay for all damages up to that sum. The excess can often be reduced or waived entirely if you pay an additional charge, around ¥1000 per day. National chains often allow one-way rentals, picking up in one city and dropping off in another, usually with a minimum hire period and a hefty repositioning charge.

ON THE ROAD

In Japan, people drive on the left side of the road, and steering wheels are on the right side of the car. For an enlightening look at the relationship between left-side driving and ancient *samurai* practices, visit www.2pass.co.uk/japan.htm. Seat belts are required. You may not turn at a red light. The pedestrian always has the right of way. If you have consumed even one alcoholic drink, *do not drive*. Penalties are severe and a very small amount of alcohol detected in your breath can get you jailed and fined. **Petrol (gasoline)** prices vary, but average about ¥110-150 per liter in cities and from ¥95 per liter in outlying areas.

> **DRIVING PRECAUTIONS.** When traveling in the summer, bring substantial amounts of **water** (a suggested 5L per person per day) for drinking and for the radiator. For long drives to unpopulated areas, register with police before beginning the trek, and again upon arrival at the destination. When traveling for long distances, make sure tires are in good repair and have enough air, and get good maps. A **compass** and a **car manual** can also be very useful. You should always carry a **spare tire** and **jack, jumper cables, extra oil, flares, a flashlight,** and **heavy blankets** (in case your car breaks down at night or in the winter). If you don't know how to **change a tire,** learn before heading out, especially if you are planning on traveling in deserted areas. If you do have a breakdown, **stay with your car;** if you wander off, there's less likelihood trackers will find you.

Road conditions are generally good, so there should be no need for worry except in mountainous areas during the winter, when you should consider putting chains on your tires. Also, be aware that while expressways have speed limits of 80 km/h, drivers routinely exceed this limit with impunity. While you, of course, as a law-abiding visitor, should *not* do the same, be warned that your Japanese companions on the highway will be zipping along quite briskly.

CAR ASSISTANCE. The Japan Automobile Federation (Kikaishinko Kaikan Biru, 3-5-8 Shiba-kōen, Minato-ku, Tōkyō 105; http://www.jaf.or.jp/e/index_e.htm) has headquarters throughout Japan and publishes a useful book called *Rules of the Road* in six languages—you can pick up a copy for ¥1000.

ESSENTIALS

THE HIDDEN DEAL

TRAVEL TRICKS

First of all, don't dismiss internal flights as too pricey for your budget-traveling pockets. Domestic airports serve most places a traveler would want to go, and frequent flights criss-cross the islands. Prices often compare favorably with ferry or train fares, and the speed of air travel is hard to beat. Both ANA and JAL offer a **"Visit Japan"** fare, which allows the purchase of up to five tickets to any domestic destination the airline flies for only ¥12600 (about US$105) each. "Visit Japan" tickets must be purchased before you arrive in Japan—contact your local ANA or JAL agent.

Railpasses (p. 43) are universally touted as a deal, but get out your calculator before investing. It's nice to be able to hop on any train, but in many cases point-to-point tickets actually cost less. The 7-day All-Japan pass, for example, is a deal only if you spend more than ¥4050 per day on transport. Most passes are good for consecutive days only, so you lose out if you spend more than a few days in one place.

To really save on rail trips, travel like the natives (who are ineligible for railpasses). **Seishun 18** tickets (p. 43) were designed for schoolkids on vacation, but carry no age restriction and are a good deal for cross-country journeys. *Shinkansen* travel isn't included, but the tickets make it possible to cross the whole country (albeit slowly) for just ¥2300.

DRIVING PERMITS AND CAR INSURANCE

INTERNATIONAL DRIVING PERMIT (IDP). If you plan to drive a car while in Japan, you must be over 18 and have an **International Driving Permit (IDP)** in addition to a **valid foreign license** obtained at least three months before arriving in Japan (you may not drive in Japan with only a foreign license). Your IDP, valid for one year, must be issued in your own country before you depart. Buying the permit from the American Automobile Association (AAA) should cost only US$10-20; beware of online scams that charge more. An IDP application requires one or two photos, a current local license, an additional form of identification, and a fee. To apply, contact your home country's Automobile Association.

The US embassy website warns that some American travelers have been told by Japanese police that it is illegal to use an IDP after exiting and returning to Japan, or after 90 days (rather than 1 year) in Japan, or to use a license obtained by mail while in Japan. The conflicting accounts suggest that it may be best to obtain a Japanese license if you plan to drive extensively or regularly during your stay.

CAR INSURANCE. Most credit cards cover standard insurance. If you rent, lease, or borrow a car, you will need a **green card,** or **International Insurance Certificate,** to certify that you have liability insurance that applies abroad. Green cards can be obtained at rental agencies, car dealers, and some travel agents. Rental agencies may let you to purchase insurance when you rent, at a daily rate of around US$8.

BY BICYCLE

Japan is a very bicycle-friendly country. Many urban areas can be efficiently traveled by bicycle, and youth hostels and other shops often rent bikes. *Let's Go* lists bicycle rental outlets in the **Transportation** sections of cities. Travelers planning on spending a long time in one city might find it economical to purchase an inexpensive bicycle and sell it upon their departure.

Serious cyclists, however, will want to get out of the city and hit some real trails. Nearly every rural area of Japan provides good cycling—consult some of the resources below for route suggestions. The **Touring Mapple** guide (Japanese only; www.mapple.co.jp; ¥1600) by Shobunsha is highly recommended. Their bilingual **Road Atlas** (www.mapple.co.jp/Bmap.htm; ¥2857) may also help. One thing to note is that bicycles cannot be taken "as is" on trains—the wheels must be removed and a bike bag used. **Folding bicycles** are increasing in quality and growing in popularity. Cycling may be an economical way to visit an otherwise expensive country. Many cyclists choose to **camp** (p. 28). **Cycling terminals,** found mainly in Hokkaidō, offer basic lodging near bicycle routes for about ¥5000, including meals; there's an online list at www.outdoorjapan.com/activities/cycling/activities-cycling-terminals.html. **Rider houses** cater mostly to motorcyclists, providing basic, informal crash space (often of the floor-sleeping variety) for very low prices (around ¥1000), but it may take persistence and Japanese-language skills to find them.

BICYCLING RESOURCES

Books: Cycling Japan, by Bryan Harrell, Taro Hirowatari, and Hilary Sagar (Kodansha) and **Bicycling in Japan: A Touring Handbook,** by Suzanne Lee (Zievid Press) are recommended by many cyclists. Unfortunately, both are out of print.

Japan Bicycle Promotion Institute, 1-9-3, Akasaka, Minato-ku, Tōkyō 107-0052 (☎03-5572-6410; www.jbpi.or.jp). Provides data and reports. Site has an English section.

Japan Cycling Federation, www.jcf.or.jp, has an event calendar for competitive cyclists.

▨ **Japan Cycling Navigator,** www.t3.rim.or.jp/~sayori. Offers advice, info, recommended routes, housing help, bulletin boards, and lots of links. Oozing with friendly biker spirit.

KANCycling, www.kancycling.com, is a repository of information on biking in Kansai throughout Japan, including detailed route plans.

Ministry of Land, Infrastructure and Transport Bicycling Site, www.mlit.go.jp/road/road/bicycle, is a Japanese-only site providing data and route maps.

Outdoor Japan, www.outdoorjapan.com, devotes a section of its website to cycling, including bicycling tips, suggested courses, and area guides.

BICYCLE TOURS

Those interested in extended cycling trips, but not quite ready to strike out on their own, might consider joining a package tour or an outdoors organization.

Backroads, 801 Cedar St., Berkeley, CA 94710, USA (☎US 800-462-2848 or +1-510-527-1555; www.backroads.com). Operates a 6-day luxury tour around Kyōto and Noto-hantō. US$4000.

Cyclevents, P.O. Box 725, Hilo, HI 96721, USA. (☎US 888-733-9615; www.cyclevents.com). Travels through Central Honshū and the Japan Alps. 11-day trip US$3250.

Free Ride Adventures, 1-4-7, Nagaresimizu, Chelto-no-Mori, Toyohira, Chino, Nagano-ken 391-0213, Japan (☎/fax +81-266-71-6688; www.freerideadventuresjpn.com). Guided mountain bike trips around Nagano. Half- and full-day trips. One-day package ¥7800 per person; discounts for groups.

VeloAsia, 1283 12th Ave., San Francisco, CA 94122, USA (☎+1-415-731-3360; fax 978-428-6440; www.veloasia.com). Company focuses on trips in Vietnam, but offers a 14-day tour in the Kyōto area. US$275-380 per day.

BY FOOT

Though it might not be apparent in the land of ubiquitous public transportation, walking is a viable means of transport throughout Japan. **JNTO** publishes walking guides with recommended courses for Tōkyō, Kyōto, and Nara, available at tourist offices or on the JNTO website (www.jnto.go.jp/eng/RTG/PTG/index.html); a better alternative is to get a decent city map and blaze your own trail.

Even a short trip out of Tōkyō provides opportunities for hoofing it—**Outdoor Japan** (www.outdoorjapan.com) outlines a series of half-day hikes not far from the city in the "Hiking and Camping" section of its website. Japan is rife with opportunities for mountain hikes—besides old standard **Mt. Fuji** (p. 244), the Japan Alps in the Chūbu area of Central Honshū feature numerous worthy peaks. For pious peripatetics, **pilgrimages** are another worthy way to earn some Japanese blisters. Most famous is Shikoku's two-month, 88-temple **Shikoku Henro** route (p. 530), but there's also the 33-temple **Saigoku Kannon** pilgrimage in Kansai and numerous shorter trips, such as the pilgrimage to **Kōya-san** (p. 467) in Wakayama.

Those in search of hiking guidance or companionship on the trail might join a trip with an outdoors group. The **Tsukuba Walking & Mountaineering Club** (http://eve.bk.tsukuba.ac.jp/twmc/), based just outside Tōkyō, runs fairly regular hiking excursions. The **Late Risers Hiking Club Shimane** (www.geocities.com/shimane-hiker) operates in the Chūgoku area. Visitors can sign up to participate through their websites. The **International Adventure Club** (www.iac-tokyo.org) in Tōkyō and the **International Outdoor Club** (www.geocities.com/ioc-kansai) in Kansai operate more formally, and plan kayaking, rafting, and biking outings as well as hikes.

Package tours with walking or hiking components tend to be excessively pricey, but save the idle rich the trouble of planning their trip and the risk of getting lost.

Esprit Travel & Tours, 200 S. San Pedro St., Ste. 506, Los Angeles, CA 90012-5302, USA (US ☎800-377-7481, ☎+1-213-346-9100; www.esprittravel.com). Offers gentle themed walking tours (average 3-6 mi. per day). 12-14 day tours US$3200-6000.

Himalayan Kingdoms, Old Crown House, 18 Market St., Wotton-under-Edge, Gloucestershire, GL12 7AE (☎+44-845-330-8579; www.himalayankingdoms.co.uk). Offers 15-day walking tours in Japan, among numerous other destinations.

Geographic Expeditions, 2627 Lombard St., San Francisco, CA 94123, USA (US ☎800-777-8183, ☎+1-415-922-0448; www.geoex.com). Runs adventure tours all over the world, including 6-14 day walking trips in Japan (US$1800-5800).

Trek Holidays, 8412-109th Street, Edmonton, Alberta T6G 1E2, Canada (US ☎888-456-3522, ☎+1-780-439-0024; www.trekholidays.com). Adventure tours all over the world. 12-day tours about CDN$4000.

Walk Japan Ltd. (+852-2817-6781; www.walkjapan.com). Guides a 12-day tour along the old Nakasendō highway, beginning in Kyōto. About US$1800.

BY THUMB

> **!** Let's Go never recommends hitchhiking as a safe means of transportation, and none of the information presented here is intended to do so.

Let's Go strongly urges you to consider the risks before you choose to hitchhike. Hitching means entrusting your life to a random person who happens to stop, and risking theft, assault, harassment, and unsafe driving. The urban public transportation infrastructure in Japan is so comprehensive and efficient that few visitors should consider any other means of getting around. Nonetheless, some travelers report that Japanese drivers in rural areas are occasionally willing to pick up transients. Depending on circumstances, groups of men and women, and men traveling alone, might consider hitchhiking. Women traveling alone should not hitch.

Hitchhiking is not common in Japan. Hitchers should look neat and wholesome and smile and bow at drivers who stop. Smart hitchers never get into a car that they can't get out of again in a hurry and never let go of their backpacks. If they feel threatened, they insist on being let off, regardless of where they are. Some travelers report that acting as if you are about to open the car door or vomit on the upholstery usually gets a driver to stop. Hitching at night is particularly dangerous and difficult; experienced hitchers stand in well-lit places and expect drivers to be leery. Determined hitchhikers may find Will Ferguson's *The Hitchhiker's Guide to Japan* and *Hokkaido Highway Blues: Hitchhiking Japan* useful resources.

SPECIFIC CONCERNS

WOMEN TRAVELERS

Japan is often referred to as one of the safest countries in the world. Women travelers will usually not feel threatened or uncomfortable. If you are concerned, stay in hostels that offer single rooms that lock from the inside or in religious organizations with rooms for women only. Stick to centrally located accommodations and avoid solitary late-night treks or metro rides. Some women report being groped in crowded Japanese subways and trains—be especially alert during rush hours.

Always carry extra money for a phone call, bus, or taxi. **Hitchhiking** is never safe for lone women, or even for two women together. Look as if you know where you're going and approach older women or couples for directions if you're lost. Dress conservatively, especially in rural areas. Trying to fit in can be effective, but dressing to the style of an obviously different culture may make you ill at ease and conspicuous. Wearing a **wedding band** may help prevent unwanted overtures.

Women will likely find that the greatest threat is the drunk, belligerent businessman, who might taunt nonsensically, but who will probably not cause any physical harm. Your best answer to verbal harassment is no answer at all; feigning deafness, sitting motionless, and staring straight ahead at nothing in particular will do a world of good. The extremely persistent can sometimes be dissuaded by a firm, loud, and very public "Go away!" Don't hesitate to seek out a police officer or a passerby if you are being harassed. A self-defense course will both prepare you for a potential attack and raise your level of awareness of your surroundings (p. 16).

Being A Broad in Japan (Alexandra Press, ¥3000) is a thorough guide to daily life in Japan, intended for those planning longer stays. The website (www.being-a-broad.com) includes some of the book's content and a discussion board.

FROM THE ROAD

SINGLE WOMAN SEEKS FUN, SAFE SOLO TRAVEL

Having lived in Tōkyō for more than ten years, I set out on my travels through Japan confidently. What I discovered along the way neither contradicted my expectations nor completely fulfilled them. Instead, I found that traveling alone as a young woman was an unusual but memorable way to explore my native country.

Lugging around a mountaineering backpack invited strange glances, rude remarks, and even the occasional shove, but an outward appearance of confidence went a long way in inviting help and advice. As I wandered around train stations looking for my connection or sat on the steps of a temple studying my map, I piqued the curiosity of passersby, many looking for a friendly ear.

No matter where you are, traveling as a solo woman has its dangers. Never give your full name to a stranger, choose rooms with locking doors, and be alert at night. But rather than getting paranoid, remember these warnings while keeping an open mind.

Traveling alone for leisure in Japan, especially as a woman, is uncommon and attracts attention, but my advice is simple: Practice common sense, but allow yourself to let your guard down at times and you'll discover some of the best experiences that no travel guide can ever cover.

- Maiko Nakarai

ESSENTIALS

TRAVELING ALONE

There are many benefits to traveling alone, including independence and greater interaction with locals. On the other hand, solo travelers are vulnerable target for harassment and theft. Try not to stand out as a tourist, look confident, and be especially careful in deserted or very crowded areas. Never admit that you are alone and maintain regular contact with someone at home. For more tips, pick up *Traveling Solo* by Eleanor Berman (Globe Pequot Press; US$17) or subscribe to **Connecting: Solo Travel Network,** 689 Park Rd., Unit 6, Gibsons, BC V0N 1V7, Canada (☎604-886-9099; www.cstn.org; membership US$35). **Travel Companion Exchange,** P.O. Box 833, Amityville, NY 11701, USA (US ☎800-392-1256, ☎+1-631-454-0880; www.whytravelalone.com; US$48), links solo travelers with companions.

OLDER TRAVELERS

Older travelers may find that Japan, whose historical and cultural background are backed up with an established travel infrastructure, is an ideal destination. Numerous websites provide info for adventurous and cyber-savvy seniors. The US State Department offers online travel tips (http://travel.state.gov/olderamericans.html).

Senior citizens are often eligible for discounts on transportation, museums, theaters, and accommodations. If you don't see a senior citizen price listed, ask, and you may be delightfully surprised. The books *No Problem! Worldwise Tips for Mature Adventurers*, by Janice Kenyon (Orca Book Publishers; US$16) and *Unbelievably Good Deals and Great Adventures That You Absolutely Can't Get Unless You're Over 50*, by Joan Rattner Heilman (NTC/Contemporary Publishing; US$13) are excellent resources, as are the following organizations:

Elderhostel, 11 Ave. de Lafayette, Boston, MA 02111, USA (US ☎877-426-8056; www.elderhostel.org). Organizes 2- to 3-week "educational adventures" in Japan on varied subjects for those 55+. Prices about US$5500-6000.

The Mature Traveler, P.O. Box 15791, Sacramento, CA 95852, USA (US ☎800-460-6676; www.thematuretraveler.com). Deals, discounts, and travel packages for the 50+ traveler. Subscription US$30.

Seniors Abroad International Homestays, 12533 Pacato Cir. N., San Diego, CA 92128, USA (fax +1-858-487-1492; haev@pacbell.net). Arranges a series of three or four 6-day homestays in different parts of Japan for active Americans over 50.

Travel 50 & Beyond, 1502 Augusta Dr., Ste. 415, Houston, TX 77057, USA (☎+1-713-974-6903; www.travel50andbeyond.com). Magazine devoted to world travel for the older set. Subscription US$12.

BISEXUAL, GAY, AND LESBIAN TRAVELERS

Gay establishments in Japan tend to be extremely underground in nature. While visitors will observe little overt discrimination against homosexuals and bisexuals in Japan, open homosexuality and bisexuality are also rare. Much has been written about fluid gender and sexual roles in Japan's ancient history and contemporary popular culture, but the idea of being openly gay is undesirable to many Japanese, as it challenges social and family norms many still wish to endorse. That said, a lively gay underground does exist, particularly in large cities. Utopia-Asia (http://www.utopia-asia.com/tipsjapn.htm) offers a general overview of the gay scene in Japan; it includes an extensive list of establishments in major Japanese cities.

Listed below are organizations and bookstores that address some specific concerns. **Out and About** (www.planetout.com) offers a bi-weekly newsletter addressing travel concerns and a comprehensive site addressing gay travel concerns.

Gay's the Word, 66 Marchmont St., London WC1N 1AB, UK (☎+44-20-7278-7654; www.gaystheword.co.uk). The largest gay and lesbian bookshop in the UK, with both fiction and non-fiction titles. Mail-order service available.

Giovanni's Room, 1145 Pine St., Philadelphia, PA 19107, USA (☎+1-215-923-2960; www.queerbooks.com). Lesbian/feminist and gay bookstore with mail-order service.

International Lesbian and Gay Association (ILGA), 81 rue Marché-au-Charbon, B-1000 Brussels, Belgium (☎+32-2-502-2471; www.ilga.org). Provides political information, such as homosexuality laws of individual countries.

▼ **FURTHER READING: BISEXUAL, GAY, AND LESBIAN.**
Spartacus International Gay Guide 2001-2002. Bruno Gmunder Verlag (US$33).
Damron Men's Guide, Damron's Accommodations, and *The Women's Traveller.* Damron Travel Guides (US$14-19). For more info, visit www.damron.com.
Ferrari Guides' Gay Travel A to Z, Ferrari Guides' Men's Travel in Your Pocket, and *Ferrari Guides' Inn Places.* Ferrari Publications (US$16-20). Purchase the guides online at www.ferrariguides.com.
The Gay Vacation Guide: The Best Trips and How to Plan Them, Mark Chesnut. Citadel Press (US$15).
Male Homosexuality in Modern Japan: Cultural Myths and Social Realities. Mark McLelland (US$30).

TRAVELERS WITH DISABILITIES

Japan has not always been the most welcoming of countries for people with disabilities. Though things are changing, you may still encounter Japanese unfamiliar with the idea of people with disabilities living and traveling independently.

Japan is gradually becoming more accessible, but travelers may not find the level of accommodations they are accustomed to at home. Those with disabilities should inform airlines and hotels of their needs when making reservations. Train and subway stations often feature numerous stairs, and buses are only gradually being equipped with lifts. Call restaurants, museums, and other facilities to find out if they are accessible. **Guide dog owners** should know that Japan requires a quarantine period and proof of rabies vaccination for dogs entering the country. The Japanese Animal Quarantine Service (☎+81-45-751-5921; www.maff-aqs.go.jp/english/ryoko) can provide more information about these regulations.

USEFUL ORGANIZATIONS

Access Abroad, www.umabroad.umn.edu/access. A website devoted to making study abroad available to students with disabilities. Specific access information for 3 Japanese programs is included. The site is maintained by Disability Services Research and Training, University of Minnesota, University Gateway, Ste. 180, 200 Oak St. SE, Minneapolis, MN 55455, USA (☎+1-612-624-6884; fax 625-5572).

Accessible Activities, http://accessible.jp.org. A publication of the Japanese Red Cross Language Service Volunteers. The online guides to Tōkyō, Kyōto (including Nara), and Kamakura provide extensive accessibility information for hotels, sights, and transportation. The Tōkyō guide includes general info that may be of use to many travelers.

Disabled Peoples' International, 748 Broadway, Winnipeg, Manitoba, Canada R3G 0X3 (+1-204-287-8010; www.dpi.org). Worldwide network of organizations advocating for the disabled. **Japan National Assembly,** Sohyo-kaikan, 3-2-11, Kanda-Surugadai Chiyoda-ku, Tōkyō 101-0062, Japan (☎+81-3-5256-5365; dpi-japan@nifty.ne.jp).

Japan Council on Disability (JD), 117, Komoe Itabashi-ku, Tōkyō 173-0037, Japan (☎+81-3-5287-2346; www.jdnet.gr.jp). Campaigns for the rights of the disabled and publishes a journal. Online information in Japanese only.

(sidebar) **ESSENTIALS**

ESSENTIALS

Society for Accessible Travel & Hospitality (SATH), 347 Fifth Ave., #610, New York, NY 10016, USA (☎+1-212-447-7284; www.sath.org). An advocacy group that publishes free online travel information and the travel magazine *OPEN WORLD* (US$18, free for members). Annual membership US$45, students and seniors US$30.

TOUR AGENCIES

Accessible Journeys, 35 West Sellers Ave. Ridley Park, PA 19078, USA (☎US 800-846-4537, +1-610-521-0339; www.disabilitytravel.com). Designs tours for wheelchair users and slow walkers. No Japan tours currently, but site has tips and forums for all travelers.

Directions Unlimited, 720 N. Bedford Rd., Bedford Hills, NY 10507, USA (☎800-533-5343). Books individual and group vacations for the physically disabled.

Flying Wheels, 143 W. Bridge St., P.O. Box 382, Owatonna, MN 55060, USA (☎+1-507-451-5005; fax 451-1685; www.flyingwheelstravel.com). Specializes in escorted trips to Europe for people with physical disabilities; plans custom accessible trips worldwide.

MINORITY TRAVELERS

Because Japan initially appears to be a homogenous society, it is easy to assume that this non-confrontational country lacks minorities and discrimination. Although Japan's minority citizens constitute only 1% of the nation's population, the number reflects a recent influx of foreigners. In urban areas, the minority population reaches up to 10%. Since the small minority population faces a largely homogenous society, minorities often struggle to receive equal recognition.

There are four prominent minority groups in Japan: the Burakumin (descendents of stigmatized social groups), the Okinawans (whose island was autonomous until 1879), the Ainu (indigenous people of northern Japan), and Korean-Japanese immigrants. More recently, Japan has seen immigrants from China, Southeast Asia, the Middle East, and South America. Although most travelers will stand out as minorities, they can expect greater anonymity in urban areas. Despite this minority status, travelers will find that they are often received exceptionally warmly; onlookers are usually motivated by curiosity rather than ill will.

TRAVELERS WITH CHILDREN

Family vacations often require that you slow your pace and always require that you plan ahead. **Be sure that your child carries some sort of ID** in case of an emergency or in case he or she gets lost. If you rent a car, make sure the rental company provides a car seat for younger children. The CDC provides a webpage with health recommendations for travelers with children (www.cdc.gov/travel/child_travel.htm); *Safe and Sound: Healthy Travel with Children,* by Marlene Coleman (Globe Pequot, US$17), may also be a useful resource.

Museums, tourist attractions, accommodations, restaurants, and transportation services often offer discounts for children; *Let's Go* lists child and student prices where available. Children under two generally fly for 10% of the adult airfare on international flights (this does not necessarily include a seat), while international fares are usually discounted 25% for children from two to 11. JR passes (p. 43) are half-price for children under 12, and discounted for youths.

Kids Web Japan (www.jinjapan.org/kidsweb) is a good website for children to begin learning about the country's geography and culture. **Japan With Kids** (www.tokyowithkids.com) is a useful resource for families spending longer periods in Japan. For more info on family travel, consult one of the following books:

Japan for Kids: The Ultimate Guide for Parents and Their Children, Diane Wiltshire and Jeanne Huey Erickson. Kodansha (US$17).

Kids' Trips in Tokyo: A Family Guide to One-Day Outings, Ivy Maeda, Kitty Kobe, Cynthia Ozeki, and Lyn Sato. Kodansha (US$17).

Adventuring with Children: An Inspirational Guide to World Travel and the Outdoors, Nan Jeffrey. Avalon House Publishing (US$15).

Gutsy Mamas: Travel Tips and Wisdom for Mothers on the Road, Marybeth Bond. Travelers' Tales, Inc. (US$8).

DIETARY CONCERNS

Vegetarians may be concerned about the prevalence of fish in Japanese cuisine, but a wide range of options exist in Japan. There are vegetarian restaurants in nearly every city, and vegetarian entrees are available in most restaurants. "Vegetarian" in Japanese is *"bejitarian"*—see the **Food** section of the **Appendix** (p. 734) for detailed ordering instructions. Vegans will want to avoid most soups, which tend to be made with fish broth: beware dishes that include "bonito," the ubiquitous dried fish flakes (花鰹). The travel section of the **The Vegetarian Resource Group's** website (www.vrg.org/travel) has a lengthy list of organizations and websites for vegetarians traveling abroad. Find vegetarian restaurants at the **Japan Vegetarian Society** website (www.jpvs.org/ep/ep1), while the **Tōkyō Vegetarian Guide** (www.vegietokyo.com) lists vegetarian restaurants in Tōkyō and prints articles on adapting Japanese cuisine. For more information, visit your local bookstore and consult *Vegetarian Asia*, by Teresa Bergen (Noble Poodle Press; US$12).

Travelers who keep kosher should contact local synagogues to find kosher restaurants. In Tōkyō, the **Jewish Community Center**, 3-8-8 Hirō, Shibuya-ku, Tōkyō (☎+81-3-3400-2559; www.jccjapan.or.jp) can put you in contact with Jewish organizations in other cities. Your own synagogue or college Hillel should have access to lists of Jewish institutions across the world. A good general resource is the *Jewish Travel Guide*, edited by Michael Zaidner (Vallentine Mitchell; US$17).

OTHER RESOURCES

Let's Go tries to cover all aspects of budget travel, but we can't put *everything* in our guides. The publishers and websites below can serve as jumping off points for your own research; then try our **Additional Resources** section (p. 107) for a list of some of our favorite books and films about Japan.

TRAVEL PUBLISHERS AND BOOKSTORES

Alexandra Press (☎+81-3-5410-3744; www.alexandrapress.com) publishes and distributes a small selection of books written by internationals living in Japan.

Cheng & Tsui, 25 West St., Boston, MA 02111, USA (☎+1-617-988-2401; www.chengtsui.com). Asian language resources, as well as literature, history, and culture.

Hippocrene Books, Inc., 171 Madison Ave., New York, NY 10016, USA (☎718-454-2366; www.hippocrenebooks.com). Foreign language dictionaries and learning guides.

▓ **Kodansha International,** Otowa YK Building, 1-17-14 Otowa, Bunkyo-ku, Tōkyō, Japan 112-8652 (☎03-3944-6492; www.thejapanpage.com). Major publisher of English-language books on Japanese subjects. Extensive collection includes titles on travel, language, literature, cooking, art, and other subjects.

Shen's Books, 40951 Fremont Blvd., Fremont, CA 94538, USA (US ☎800-456-6660, ☎+1-510-668-1898; www.shens.com). Specializes in international children's books.

Stone Bridge Press, P.O. Box 8208, Berkeley, CA 94707, USA (☎+1-510-524-8732; www.stonebridge.com). Books about Japan, with a focus on contemporary culture.

Travel Books & Language Center, Inc., 4437 Wisconsin Ave. NW, Washington, D.C. 20016, USA (☎800-220-2665; www.bookweb.org/bookstore/travelbks). Over 60,000 titles from around the world.

WORLD WIDE WEB

Almost every aspect of budget travel is accessible via the web. Within 10min. at the keyboard, you can make a hostel reservation, get advice on travel hotspots, or find out how much a train from Kōbe to Kanazawa costs. Listed here are some sites to start off your surfing; other relevant sites are listed throughout the book. Because website turnover is high, use search engines to strike out on your own.

 WWW.LETSGO.COM Our new website now features the online content of our guides. In addition, trial versions of *Let's Go City Guides* are available for download on Palm OS™ PDAs. As always, our website has photos and streaming video, online ordering of our titles, a travel forum buzzing with stories and tips, a newsletter, and links to help you find everything you ever wanted to know about Japan.

THE ART OF BUDGET TRAVEL

How to See the World (www.artoftravel.com). A compendium of great travel tips, from cheap flights to self defense to interacting with local culture.

Travel-Library.com (www.travel-library.com). A fantastic set of links for general information and personal travelogues.

INFORMATION ON JAPAN

Japan.co.jp (www.japan.co.jp). Links to 90,000 sites on all aspects of Japan.

Japan Information Network (www.jinjapan.org). Comprehensive and authoritative information source, with an atlas, statistics, directories, and a databank.

Japan Reference Page (www.japanreference.com). Links to thousands of Japan-related resources, in categories from cinematography to Christianity.

Jim Breen's Japanese Page (www.csse.monash.edu.au/~jwb/japanese.html). A well-researched site with links on art, culture, and language by Japanophile Jim Breen.

The Quirky Japan Homepage (www3.tky.3web.ne.jp/~edjacob). Just what it professes to be, with pages on cool places almost no one visits, crime and conspiracies, love hotels, vending machines, and "seldom asked questions" about Japan.

 PREFECTURES AND CITIES ONLINE

Most prefectures, cities, and towns in Japan have an **official website** (usually with an English section). *Let's Go* frequently lists these website addresses, but since most follow the same format, you can find many more sites on your own. **Prefecture** websites follow the format **www.pref.prefecturename.jp;** the website for Shizuoka Prefecture, for example, is www.pref.shizuoka.jp. **City** websites follow the format **www.city.cityname.prefecturename.jp;** the website for Takamatsu, for example, is www.city.takamatsu.kagawa.jp. **Town** websites follow the format **www.town.townname.prefecturename.jp;** the website for Mashiko, for example, is www.town.mashiko.tochigi.jp.

ALTERNATIVES TO TOURISM

When *Let's Go* started out in 1961, about 1.7 million people in the world were traveling internationally each year; in 2002, nearly 700 million trips were made, projected to be up to a billion by 2010. The Japanese, prolific travelers, have been an active part of this trend, making more than 16 million overseas trips and receiving more than 5 million international visitors in 2002. This dramatic rise in tourism has created an interdependence between the economy, environment, and culture of many destinations and the tourists they host; never before has the traveler's impact on his environment been so significant.

Two rising trends in sustainable travel are ecotourism and community-based tourism. **Ecotourism** focuses on the conservation of natural habitats and using them to build up the economy without exploitation or overdevelopment. The Japanese government, through the Ministry of Agriculture, Forestry, and Fisheries, instituted a "green tourism" initiative in 1994, supporting informed travel to rural areas and city-country interaction. **Community-based tourism** aims to channel tourist yen into the local economy, by emphasizing tours and cultural programs run by members of the host community. The development of local tourist infrastructure in rural Japan is just beginning to blossom—planning a trip that takes advantage of it may take additional research, but can be extremely rewarding. When visiting areas traditionally inhabited by Japan's minority groups—parts of Hokkaidō and Okinawa, for example—be sensitive to the difference between activities that benefit the native populations and activities that exploit or marginalize them.

There are many ways to **volunteer** in the efforts to help with local social and environmental issues in Japan. Opportunities range from cleaning up lakes near Tōkyō to helping run an international peace conference, and can be participated in either on an infrequent basis or as the main component of your trip. Later in this section, we recommend organizations that can help you find projects that best suit your interests, whether you're looking to pitch in for a day or a year.

In addition to volunteering, **studying** at a college or language program is a way to integrate yourself with the communities you visit. Language schools are available throughout Japan; many also offer culture, art, or cooking classes. Some language students have the opportunity for a homestay with a Japanese family, an unparalleled way to learn about Japanese customs and communities. Other travelers structure their trips by the **work** that they can do along the way—either odd jobs as they go, or full-time stints in cities where they plan to stay for some time. You'll find opportunities to teach English all over the country; internships and tourism jobs, on the other hand, may be limited to major cities and tourist areas. Short-term work is legal and not difficult to find, though a work permit is required for employment of any duration.

For more information about sustainable tourism, www.worldsurface.com features photos and personal stories of volunteer experiences. More general information is available at www.sustainabletravel.org. For those who seek more active involvement, Earthwatch International, Operation Crossroads Africa, and Habitat for Humanity offer fulfilling volunteer opportunities all over the world.

A NEW PHILOSOPHY OF TRAVEL

We at *Let's Go* have watched the growth of the 'ignorant tourist' stereotype with dismay, knowing that the majority of travelers care passionately about the state of the communities and environments they explore—but also knowing that even conscientious tourists can inadvertently damage natural wonders, rich cultures, and impoverished communities. We believe the philosophy of **sustainable travel** is among the most important travel tips we could impart to our readers, to help guide fellow backpackers and on-the-road philanthropists. By staying aware of the needs and troubles of local communities, today's travelers can be a powerful force in preserving and restoring this fragile world.

Working against the negative consequences of irresponsible tourism is much simpler than it might seem; it is often self-awareness, rather than self-sacrifice, that makes the biggest difference. Simply by trying to spend responsibly and conserve local resources, all travelers can positively impact the places they visit. Let's Go has partnered with **BEST** (**Business Enterprises for Sustainable Travel,** an affiliate of the Conference Board; see www.sustainabletravel.org), which recognizes businesses that operate based on the principles of sustainable travel. Below, they provide advice on how ordinary visitors can practice this philosophy in their daily travels, no matter where they are.

TIPS FOR CIVIC TRAVEL: HOW TO MAKE A DIFFERENCE

Travel by train when feasible. Rail travel requires only half the energy per passenger mile that planes do. On average, each of the 40,000 daily domestic air flights releases more than 1700 pounds of greenhouse gas emissions.

Use public mass transportation whenever possible; outside of cities, take advantage of group taxis or vans. Bicycles are an attractive way of seeing a community first-hand. And enjoy walking—purchase good maps of your destination and ask about on-foot touring opportunities.

When renting a car, ask whether fuel-efficient vehicles are available. Honda and Toyota produce cars that use hybrid engines powered by electricity and gasoline, thus reducing emissions of carbon dioxide. Ford Motor Company plans to introduce a hybrid fuel model by the end of 2004.

Reduce, reuse, recycle—use electronic tickets, recycle papers and bottles wherever possible, and avoid using containers made of styrofoam. Refillable water bottles and rechargable batteries both efficiently conserve expendable resources.

Be thoughtful in your purchases. Take care not to buy souvenir objects made from trees in old-growth or endangered forests, such as teak, or items made from endangered species, like ivory or tortoise jewelry. Ask whether products are made from renewable resources.

Buy from local enterprises, such as casual street vendors. In developing countries and low-income neighborhoods, many people depend on the "informal economy" to make a living.

Be on-the-road-philanthropists. If you are inspired by the natural environment of a destination or enriched by its culture, join in preserving their integrity by making a charitable contribution to a local organization.

Spread the word. Upon your return home, tell friends and colleagues about places to visit that will benefit greatly from their tourist dollars, and reward sustainable enterprises by recommending their services. Travelers can not only introduce friends to particular vendors but also to local causes and charities that they might choose to support when they travel.

> Before handing your money over to any volunteer or study abroad program, make sure you know exactly what you're getting into. It's a good idea to get the name of **previous participants** and ask them about their experience, as some programs sound much better on paper than in reality. The **questions** below are a good place to start:
> -Will you be the only person in the program? If not, what are the other participants like? How old are they? How much will you interact with them?
> -Are room and board included? If so, what is the arrangement? Will you be expected to share a room? A bathroom? What are the meals like? Do they accommodate any dietary restrictions?
> -Is transportation included? Are there any additional expenses?
> -How much free time will you have? Will you be able to travel around the island?
> -What kind of safety network is set up? Will you still be covered by your home insurance? Does the program have an emergency plan?

ALTERNATIVES TO TOURISM

VOLUNTEERING

Community and volunteerism have always been important in Japan, but it took the massive earthquake that devastated Kōbe in 1995 to really mobilize the nation. Dozens of volunteer aid organizations formed in the wake of the disaster, and volunteerism rates, especially among young people, rose to a new high. Since Japan is a very wealthy nation in worldwide terms, a significant amount of Japanese volunteering takes place abroad, especially in Southeast Asia. There is no shortage, however, of aid organizations focused on domestic issues of concern.

Most volunteers in Japan do so on a short-term basis, at organizations that make use of drop-in or once-a-week volunteers. Environmental work may be the easiest for foreigners to get involved with—clean-up projects do not require advanced language skills, and pollution is such a prevalent issue that projects regularly take place in nearly every part of the country. Bilingual visitors will find their language skills are best used in translating, interpreting, or teaching.

More intensive or long-term volunteer groups may charge a participation fee, especially if the programs are handled through a parent organization that takes care of logistical details. The costs can be surprisingly hefty, although they frequently cover most living expenses and provide a group environment and support system. Organizations usually come in two flavors—religious and non-sectarian—although there are rarely restrictions on participation in either.

Volunteer organizations often operate on tiny staffs and budgets; they may not have the resources to offer English-language information to foreigners who want to participate. Though most of the organizations listed here provide at least some English material, Japanese language skills will open doors. That said, willing hands and hearts are always welcomed, and the persistent will always be able to find some meaningful way to put their skills to work.

ENVIRONMENT

Although Japan is known for its natural beauty, ongoing industrialization coupled with an extremely dense urban population have left some areas with serious pollution problems. Major lawsuits in the 1990s brought an end to many harmful industrial practices, but the effects on the air, water, and forests still impact daily life in many areas, especially on the Pacific coast. Thanks in part to the traditional Shintō respect for nature, environmental consciousness runs high, and grassroots organizations lobby for improved environmental legislation or spend weekends cleaning up their surroundings. Many projects double as nature excursions. English-speaking volunteers are often in demand for translation and publicity work.

AEON Environment Foundation, 5-1-1, Nakase, Mihama-ku, Chiba 261-8515 (☎043-212-6022; www.aeongroup.net/ef). Supports activities to preserve traditional rural communities in Japan, using local volunteers. Also runs reforestation projects abroad.

Animal Refuge Kansai (ARK), 595 Noma Ohara, Nose-chō, Toyono-gun, Ōsaka-fu 563-0131 (☎0727-37-0712; http://members.tripod.com/ARKBARK/index.html). An animal shelter in Nose, near Ōsaka and Kyōto, ARK offers foreign volunteers airfare and basic, shared lodging in exchange for a 3-month commitment.

A SEED Japan, 5-4-23, Shinjuku, Shinjuku-ku, Tōkyō 160-0022 (☎03-5366-7484; www.jca.apc.org/~aseed). Works on environmental issues and social justice, with a focus on recruiting young people. Welcomes participants in its ecology projects; seeks English-speaking volunteers for its international section.

Concordia International Youth Exchange, Heversham House, 2nd fl., 20-22 Boundary Road, Hove, BN3 4ET UK (☎+44 01273 422 218; www.concordia-iye.org.uk). Operates 2- to 4-week volunteer projects all over the world, usually June-Sept. Numerous programs in Japan, most concerned with conservation or agriculture. Participants must be residents of the UK; 18-30 years of age. Fee about UK£100, not including travel.

EcoSIG (www.geocities.com/green_in_japan/index.html). Promotes education and environmental awareness with the publication of an English-language website, newsletter, directory, and guide. Associated with the JET program, though it has many non-JET members. Volunteers sought to serve as officers, help with newsletter distribution, and assist in special projects.

Friends of the Earth Japan, 3-17-24-2F Majiro, Toshima-ku, Tōkyō 171-0031 (☎03-3951-1081; www.foejapan.org). Sponsors events, eco-tours, and hiking trips. Local group activities and projects seek volunteers.

Greenpeace Japan, 8-13-11, NF Bldg. 2F, Nishi-Shinjuku, Shinjuku, Tōkyō 160-0023 (☎03-5338-9800; www.greenpeace.or.jp). Website provides info on environmental and peace issues, with opportunities to participate in local events and cyberactivism.

Japan Environmental Exchange, c/o Venetia International 100, Oi-chō, Tanaka, Sakyo-ku, Kyōto 606-8202 (☎/fax 075-707-6705; www.jca.apc.org/jee). Provides information on environmental issues at meetings and through publications. Monthly hikes in the Kyōto mountains and twice-monthly English study using environmental texts. Membership ¥2000. Volunteers welcome.

Kuril Island Network (KIN), 4-44-13, Izumi, Suginami-ku, Tōkyō 168-0063 (fax 03-3315-6820; www.kurilnature.org). Devoted to conservation in the Kuril Islands, a disputed territory between Japan and Russia. Assistance with web maintenance, design, event planning, translation, and public speaking desired.

NICE Japan, 2-4-2-701, Shinjuku, Shinjuku-ku, Tōkyō 160-0022 (☎03-3358-7140; www.nice1.gr.jp/indexe.html). The "Never-ending International workCamps Exchange" (NICE) places short-term volunteers at weekend or week-long workcamps for environmental clean-up or work with children. Non-residents must apply through the corresponding organization in their country; visit www.unesco.org/ccivs/ for a list.

Yamaguchi Coastal Clean-up Coalition, (http://homepage3.nifty.com/yccc). Organizes 2-4 yearly beach clean-ups in the Yamaguchi area. All are welcome.

PEACE AND DEVELOPMENT

Japan's experience with the atomic bombs at Hiroshima and Nagasaki has made it one of the most peace-conscious nations in the world. The Japanese army was permanently dissolved in 1945; today Japanese peacekeepers and volunteers work for peace all over the world. Many peace-focused organizations also stress sustainable development (usually third-world economic projects creating short-term effects and long-term awareness). Hands-on agricultural and building positions take place in other nations, but volunteers in Japan can support the movement from the administrative side.

▩ **Asian Rural Institute (ARI)**, 442-1, Tsukinokizawa, Nishinasuno-chō, Tochigi 329-2703 (☎0287-36-3111; www.ari.edu). Trains participants from Africa and Asia in 9-month leadership and sustainable agriculture programs. Working visitors may stay for a small fee, except in Apr. Long-term volunteers do farm or office work. ¥30,000 per month. Holds occasional seminars for those interested in NGOs and international cooperation.

Habitat For Humanity Japan, MBE607, 3-28 Kiol-chō, Chiyoda-ku, Tōkyō 102-8557 (☎03-3373-1259; hfhijso@yahoo.co.jp). The Japanese branch of the international organization devoted to building affordable houses for low-income families. Contact the Tōkyō office for information on local projects.

ICA Japan, 2-38-4-102, Seijo, Setagaya-ku, Tōkyō 157 (☎03-3416-3947; http://icajapan.org). Institute of Cultural Affairs Japan. Works with multi-national NGOs to foster international economic development and understanding. Applications for office positions accepted on a rolling basis; intern applications require a longer process, including two essays. Duties include project development, newsletter writing, fundraising, and computer work. Japanese speakers preferred; skilled non-speakers may apply.

Live with Friends on the Earth (LIFE), 2-2-2, Fujimi, Tōkyō-Sanwa Building 201, Chiyoda-ku, Tōkyō 102-0071 (☎03-3261-7855; www.ne.jp/asahi/life/home). Supports sustainablility in India and Indonesia; domestic activities, seminars, and workshops support the mission. Volunteers and interns needed for the Tōkyō office.

Peaceboat, 3-14-3, Takadanobaba, 2F Hattatsu Bldg., Shinjuku-ku, Tōkyō 169-0075 (☎03-3360-0630; www.peaceboat.org). Conducts "peace voyages" of 2-12 weeks, visiting numerous countries to encourage peace education and international cooperation. Awards a peace studies certificate. Volunteer interpreters, English and Spanish teachers, and office staff sought.

Volunteers for Peace, 1034 Tiffany Rd., Belmont, VT 05730, USA (☎+1-802-259-2759; www.vfp.org). Arranges 2- to 3-week placements in work camps all over the world, including numerous programs in Japan. Membership required for registration. Programs average US$200-500.

World Friendship Center, (☎082-503-3191; http://ha7.seikyou.ne.jp/home/wfc/indexE.html). In Hiroshima, near Peace Park. Participates in numerous projects in pursuit of peace and international friendship. Volunteers sort used phone cards, visit nursing homes, and lobby for Amnesty International.

MINORITY ISSUES

Japan appears homogenous, so it's easy to assume that it lacks minorities and the related problems of discrimination. Racial minorities include the indigenous Ainu people, who, much like the American Indians, were pushed farther and farther toward the frontier by the majority; the Korean-Japanese, many of whose families were forcibly relocated to Japan during the pre-WWII colonial era; and the recent immigrants from China, Southeast Asia, and the Middle East. Recently, the plight of children of Filipino mothers and Japanese fathers has garnered attention.

Discrimination can be cultural as well as racial. Two prominent cultural groups are the *Burakumin*, the descendants of stigmatized social groups dating back to feudal times, and the Brazilians, many of whom are racially Japanese but culturally South American. Both groups are often excluded from "Japanese" life.

The majority of travelers will be minorities themselves, which may pose some obstacles to volunteering in this field. Advocacy work is often available with organizations that support low-income laborers. Additionally, Western visitors with knowledge of Spanish and Portuguese can be helpful to organizations dealing with the Latin American and Brazilian populations.

Casa de Amigos, Mishima Catholic Church 12-4 Midori-chō, Mishima (☎0559-75-0221). Run out of a Catholic Church, Casa de Amigos provides assistance to Latin American and Portuguese-speaking foreigners in the Mishima area.

Hand-in-Hand Chiba, 3-5-7 Chuo, Chuo-ku, Chiba, 260-0013 (☎043-224-2154). Provides information and assistance to foreign workers, primarily from mainland Asia, the Middle East and Africa. Multi-lingual volunteers may find a placement in the office.

International Movement Against All Forms of Discrimination and Racism (IMADR), 3-5-11 Roppongi, Minato-ku, Tōkyō 106-0032 (☎03-3586-7447; www.imadr.org). Largely a political group which works toward the passage of anti-discrimination laws and increased understanding of minority issues. The Japan chapter works on issues pertaining to *Burakumin*, Koreans and Ainu. Volunteers with sufficient Japanese language skill may be accepted; inquire with the office for details.

Solidarity Network with Migrants Japan, #203, House 2, Tomisaka Christian Center, 2-17-41, Koishikawa, Bunkyo-ku, Tōkyō (☎03-5802-6033; www.jca.apc.org/migrant-net). Works for immigrants through lobbying and networking. Volunteers help with mailings, web updates, translation, paperwork, event planning, and illustration.

WOMEN'S ISSUES

While women in Japan enjoy political rights identical to men, they have yet to achieve equal social status. Society tends to attribute personal responsibility to women for problems in their families. Women face hiring discrimination and sexual harassment in the workplace, and in many cases earn less than their male counterparts. The situation has only worsened since the collapse of the bubble economy, and pressure for mothers to stay at home remains high.

The view of domestic abuse as a purely private affair has been fought in recent years, particularly after the 2001 passage of the nation's first domestic violence laws, but there is still a level of denial about the issue, and it remains a problem. In a recent government study, 5% of Japanese women reported having been abused. Prefectures and cities have their own counseling centers, which may need volunteers; contact the local agency for information.

Asia-Japan Women's Resource Center, 14-10-311, Sakuragaoka, Shibuya-ku, Tōkyō 150-0031 (☎03-3780-5245; www.jca.ax.apc.org/ajwrc). A general women's issues/activism organization focusing on empowering women throughout Asia. Domestic activities include drop-in centers for Filipino and Thai women. Contact organization for information on specific opportunities.

Asian Women's Center, 3-3-8, Kaiun-chō, Nagata-ku, Kōbe 653-0052 (☎078-735-6131; www.tcc117.org/awep). Supports Asian women, particularly migrant workers from southern Asia, with workshops, study tours, training, and traditional craft sales. Local activities include English classes, counseling, and clothing recycling. Volunteer counselors, office workers, translators, and sales staff sought.

Asia Women's Empowerment Project, 3-3-8 Kaiun-chō, Nagata-ku, Kōbe 653-0052 (☎078-735-6131; www.tcc117.org/awep). Supports Asian women, particularly migrant workers from southern Asia, with workshops, study tours, training, and traditional craft sales. Local activities include English classes, counseling, and clothing recycling. Volunteer counselors, office workers, translators, and sales staff sought.

DigitalEve Japan (info@digitalevejapan.org; www.digitalevejapan.org). The Japanese chapter of DigitalEve International supports women's use of technology through meetings, workshops, events, and an online events. Business- or technology-savvy volunteers should contact by e-mail.

H.E.L.P. Asian Women's Center, 2-23-5, Hyakunin-chō, Shinjuku-ku, Tōkyō (☎03-3368-8855). Offering refuge, help, and legal services to Japanese and Southeast Asian women in crises, H.E.L.P. works to end gender discrimination in Japanese society.

Violence Against Women in War—Network Japan (VAWW-NET Japan), 2-10-10, Shiomi, Koto-ku, Tōkyō 135-8585, (☎/fax 03-5337-4088; www.jca.apc.org/vaww-net-japan). Works on behalf of women forced into military sexual slavery and against sexual violence at US military bases. Seeks volunteers for translation and computer work.

LANGUAGE

Foreigners who do not speak Japanese often encounter language difficulties when they try to conduct their day-to-day business in Japan. Arriving *gaijin* have not always anticipated the linguistic problems they will encounter, and, in an emergency, they may need immediate language assistance. For long-term travelers with high proficiency in Japanese, volunteering at a foreign language help service can be a valuable service to the international community. In addition to the services listed below, many towns and cities have their own multilingual help lines, which may be in need of staff; contact local tourist offices for more information.

Christian Academy Japan, 1-2-14, Shinkawa-chō, Higashi Kurume-shi, Tōkyō 203-0013 (☎0424-75-2200; www.caj.or.jp). Provides an English K-12 education for the children of foreign missionaries. Seeks volunteer teacher's assistants, maintenance workers, and lunchtime supervisors. Inquire through the form on their website.

HELP Line (☎03-3486-7567; http://home.att.ne.jp/sky/helpline). A social services helpline run by the Catholic Society of the Sacred Heart. Volunteers, who must speak Japanese, either answer phones or go to provide services, such as food for the needy or sick or translations for foreigners (especially Spanish and Portuguese speakers).

Japanese Red Cross Language Service Volunteers, 1-1-3 Shibadaimon, Minato-ku, Tōkyō 105-8521 (www.lanserv.gr.jp). Translation and interpretation services and assistance of the disabled. Welcomes English and French speakers and bilingual volunteers.

Sapporo International Communication Plaza Foundation (☎011-211-2105; www.plaza-sapporo.or.jp). Residents of Sapporo can register as Foreign Language Volunteers (¥1000 fee) and assist with interpretation for tourists and at conventions.

Tōkyō English Life Line (TELL), 5-4-22, Minami Aoyama, Minato-ku, Tōkyō 107-0062. (lifeline ☎03-5774-0992, volunteer inquiries 03-3498-0246; www.telljp.com). Provides free English telephone counseling, community outreach, and in-person counseling. 12-week training sessions (60hr.) for telephone counselors begin in Jan. and Sept; a small fee. Counselors must be fluent English speakers. Pre-training interview required.

ELDERLY

If demographic projections prove correct, the elderly will account for 26% of Japan's population by 2015 and 30% by 2030. Japan is the world's fastest-aging industrialized nation, and will have to make significant changes in order to accommodate the elderly population. Volunteering in this sector is an important but underdeveloped area; volunteers may find it especially rewarding to work in an area of service that is just now taking off. There are no national organizations providing placements or listings for this type of volunteer work; long-term visitors interested in working with the elderly should contact their local **elderly care home** (rōjin hōmu; 老人ホーム) for information on how to volunteer. Japanese language skills are likely to be especially important when working with elderly people and the organizations that care for them.

STUDYING ABROAD

Study abroad programs range from basic language and culture courses to college-level classes, often for credit, to training programs in culinary or martial arts. In order to choose a program that best fits your needs, you will want to research all you can before making your decision—determine costs and duration, as well as what kind of students participate in the program and what sort of accommodations are provided. You may also wish to look into the many scholarships available to students traveling in Japan. Some programs may offer partial scholarships or stipends; in other cases you may wish to apply to independent institutions, such as the **Association of International Education, Japan (AIEJ)**, or the **Association of Teachers of Japanese Bridging Project** for funding.

In programs that have large groups of students who speak the same language, there is a trade-off. You may feel more comfortable in the community, but you will not have the same opportunity to practice a foreign language or to befriend other international students. For accommodations, dorm life provides a better opportunity to mingle with fellow students, but there is less of a chance to experience the local scene. If you live with a family, there is a potential to build lifelong friendships with your hosts and to experience day-to-day life in more depth, but conditions can vary greatly from family to family.

UNIVERSITIES

Some American schools still require students to pay them for credits obtained elsewhere. Most university-level study-abroad programs are meant as language and culture enrichment opportunities, and therefore are conducted in Japanese. Still, many programs do offer classes in English and lower-level language courses.

Those relatively fluent in Japanese may find it cheaper to enroll directly in a university abroad, although getting college credit may be more difficult. To enter the Japanese university system, foreigners must first apply to take the **Examination for Japanese University Admission for International Students (EJU)**. There are examination sites throughout Japan, as well as in various East and Southeast Asian countries, including Taiwan, China, Korea, and Singapore. Applications for the First Session are taken in February and March every year, and the test is administered in June; applications for the Second Session are taken in July and August, and the test is administered in November. Check the AIEJ website (www.aiej.or.jp/examination/ efjuafis_e.html) for dates, applications, and fees.

A good resource for finding programs that cater to your particular interests is www.studyabroad.com, which has links to various semester abroad programs based on a variety of criteria, including desired location and focus of study. **Worldwide Classrooms: Library of International Programs** also runs a Japan website (www.worldwide.edu/ci/japan), which offers an extensive if slightly disorganized listing of various educational institutions, from English-language primary/secondary schools to language programs for undergraduate, graduate and postgraduate students. The **AIEJ** website (www.aiej.or.jp/index_e.html) contains search engines for Japanese universities and colleges as well as for international student scholarships. The following is a list of organizations that can help place students in university programs abroad, or that have their own branch in Japan.

AMERICAN PROGRAMS

Antioch Education Abroad, Antioch College, 795 Livermore Street, Yellow Springs, OH 45387-1697, USA (☎+1-937-769-1015, toll-free US ☎ 800-874-7986; www.antiochcollege.edu/aea/index.html). Offers two programs in Kyōto: a summer Field Studies course that explores history, art, literature, legends, and contemporary changes in Kyōto; and a Buddhist Studies course during the fall semester in which students live in monasteries and temples, experience firsthand the practice of Buddhist precepts and meditation, and attend classes in philosophy, history, anthropology, and Japanese.

Associated Kyōto Program (AKP), Smith College, Northampton, MA, 01063, USA (contact Ashley Davis; ☎+1-413-585-3566; www.associatedkyotoprogram.org) runs a full-year study-abroad homestay program at Doshisha University, Kamigyo-Ku, Kyōto, 602-8580, and accepts 40-50 students each year, mostly from sponsoring institutions (see website list). Separate application for scholarships, research grants, and internships.

Brethren Colleges Abroad (BCA), P.O. Box 407, 50 Alpha Drive, Elizabethtown, PA, 17022-0407, USA (☎+1-717-361-6600, toll-free US 866-222-6188; www.bca-net.org). Offers a variety of educational exchanges worldwide, including a homestay language-study program based in Hokusei Gakuen University, Sapporo. Students may choose semester (4-month) or year-long (10-month) programs, attend university courses, and apply for internships.

Earlham College Japan Study (☎+1-765-983-1224; www.earlham.edu/~jpns). A 10-month study abroad program based in Waseda University, Tōkyō. Participants stay with a host family in Tōkyō and spend a month with a family in Shimane Prefecture between terms. Qualified applicants from schools included in the Great Lakes College Association (GLCA) or the Associated Colleges of the Midwest (ACM) are given preference.

Inter-University Center for Japan Language Studies (IUC), Encina Hall Room E009, Stanford University, Stanford, CA 94305, USA (contact Stacey Campbell, Program Manager; ☎+1-650-725-1490; www.stanford.edu/dept/IUC). Offers training in advanced spoken and written Japanese. Students may enroll in a 10-month program (Aug.-July the following year) or a 6-week summer program, both based in Yokohama. Also offers a part-time **Language Tutorial Program for Professionals** (offered summer, June-Aug.; winter, Jan.-Mar.; spring, Apr.-May). Contact the Center in Yokohama: Inter-University Center, Pacifico Yokohama, 5F, 1-1-1, Minato Mirai, Nishi-ku, Yokohama, Japan 220-0012 (☎+81-045-223-2002; www.twics.com/~iucjapan).

Japan Center for Michigan Universities (JCMU), 110 MSU International Center, E. Lansing, MI 48824-1035, USA (☎+1-517-355-4654; www2.isp.msu.edu/jcmu/index.html) runs a 1- or 2-semester academic program on Japanese language and culture, an intensive summer program for language study, and a 2-week May Short Program that gives students a taste of study abroad. Tuition fees and housing fees together are roughly US$7000, US$5200, and US$1000 respectively. The JCMU campus is located in Hikone, Shiga Prefecture, on the shore of Lake Biwa. JCMU also offers an Environment Sciences in Japan Program (ESJ) that surveys environmental issues.

Kentucky Institute for International Studies (KIIS), Murray State University, P.O. Box 9, Murray, KY, 42071, USA (☎+1-270-762-3091; www.kiis.org; or contact Ms. Yoko Hatakeyama, KIIS Japan Program Director, ☎270-762-3419, yoko.hatakeyama@murraystate.edu). Runs study-abroad programs in Tenri, Nara, and Kyōto. Except for Intermediate Conversational Japanese, none of the courses require prior language study. The 2003 program cost was approximately US$3000 including round-trip airfare, tuition, housing, and most transportation and food.

Kyōto Center for Japanese Studies (KCJS), c/o Stanford Overseas Studies, P.O. Box 20346, Stanford, CA 94309, USA (☎+1-650-725-0233; http://kcjs.stanford.edu). Offers a 2-semester academic program at the Stanford Japan Center, 52-2 Hoshoji-chō, Okazaki, Sakyo-ku, Kyōto 606-8333, Japan (☎+81-75-752-7074; office@stanford-jc.or.jp), mainly for undergraduates who have completed 2 or more years of college-level Japanese language study. Tuition roughly US$27,000 for the academic year; housing fees and food total about US$5000 per semester.

Princeton in Ishikawa, c/o Keiko Ono, Department of East Asian Studies, 211 Jones Hall, Princeton University, Princeton, NJ 08544, USA (☎+1-609-258-4279; www.cs.princeton.edu/~mtwebb/pii_website/new/pii.html). Offers an 8-week intensive summer language program in 2nd- and 3rd-year Japanese at Kanazawa City in Ishikawa Prefecture. Accepts about 45 students a year. Basic program cost of US$4000 includes tuition, textbooks, and homestay fees with breakfast and lunch.

Temple University International Programs, 200 Tuttleman Learning Center, 1809 North 13th Street, Philadelphia, PA 19122, USA (☎+1-215-204-0720; www.temple.edu/intl-prog). Offers semester, full-year and 10-week summer programs at Temple University

ALTERNATIVES TO TOURISM

Japan (TUJ) in Tōkyō. Foreign students attend classes with bilingual Japanese students, facilitating cultural exchange and interaction. Special 6-week summer programs in: Japanese Art, Media and Design; Urban Culture; Political Science; and Visual Anthropology.

University of Kansas Summer Institute: Exploring Contemporary Japan, Office of Study Abroad, Lippincott Hall, 1410 Jayhawk Blvd., Rm 108, The University of Kansas, Lawrence, KS 66045-7515, USA (☎+1-785-864-3742; www.ku.edu/~osa). Offers a 5-week summer program in Hiratsuka for language and cultural study. Undergraduate and graduate students welcome. The program fee, approximately US$3600, covers tuition, lodging and breakfast, a stipend for local transportation, and field trip costs.

University of Kentucky Summer Field Seminar in Japan, contact Dr. P.P. Karan, Department of Geography, 1439 Patterson Office Tower, University of Kentucky, Lexington, KY 40506, USA (☎+1-859-257-6953; PPKaran@pop.uky.edu); or Dr. H. Todd Stradford, Department of Geography, 1 University Plaza, UW Platteville, Platteville, WI, 53818, USA (☎+1-608-342-1674; stradfot@uwplatt.edu). The UK Japanese Studies Department and UW Platteville Department of Geography jointly organize a 6-week summer travel abroad program, spent mostly on the campus of IEC Technical College.

Waseda Oregon Programs, Waseda Oregon Office, Portland State University, P.O. Box 751 - WASA, Portland, OR 97207-0751, USA (☎+1-503-725-5726; www.wasedaoregon.org). Offers 8-week summer language immersion programs at Waseda University for students and professionals. Program fee of approximately US$5000 includes tuition, housing, field trips, books, and health insurance. Also offers the Transnational Program at Waseda, a 6-month academic program of 3 months of intensive language study, followed by 3 months of continued language study and comparative culture studies.

JAPAN-BASED PROGRAMS

At a typical Japanese university, the first semester runs April-September and the second October-March. Because this calendar differs from those of many other countries, including the US, foreign students seeking entrance into a Japanese university must plan their schedules accordingly. Some of the institutions listed below, however, offer programs that comply with the American academic calendar. The Japanese Ministry of Foreign Affairs manages a website (www.studyjapan.go.jp/en/index.html) that provides information and advice on looking for and choosing a program in Japan.

Aichi Shukutoku University, 9 Katahira, Nagakute-chō, Aichi-gun, Aichi, 480-1197 (www2.aasa.ac.jp/english). Runs a 9-month, 2-semester academic program combining language study with courses in Japanese art and culture (calligraphy, flower arrangement, literature, etc.). Accepts no more than 30 students each year; offers both dormitory housing and homestays. Tuition and admission fees total about ¥780,000.

Japan Culture and Language Program, Keiwa College, 1270, Tomizuka, Shibata-shi, 957-8585 (contact James Brown; ☎0254-26-3636; www.keiwa-c.ac.jp/Foreign/index.html). Runs a 1-month homestay program in Japanese language and culture. Keiwa College is near Niigata City. The program cost in 2003 was ¥250,000.

Office of International Studies and Exchange, Nagoya University of Foreign Studies, 57, Takenoyama, Iwasaki, Nisshin, Aichi 470-0197 (☎05617-5-1756; www-e.nufs.ac.jp/hl/jljsp/e_31.htm). Offers intensive summer language and culture program with homestays and internship possibilities. Foreign students may enroll in the Japanese Language and Japanese Studies Program (JLJSP) for 1 or 2 semesters.

Ritsumeikan University, Kinugasa Campus: 56-1 Toji-in Kitamachi, Kita-ku, Kyōto, 603-8577 (☎075-465-1111); **Biwako-Kusatsu Campus:** Noji Higashi 1-1-1 Kusatsu, 525-8577 Shiga-ken (☎077-566-1111; www.ritsumei.ac.jp). Runs programs for international students and professionals. The **Study In Kyōto (SKP)** program offers term-time undergraduate courses in Japanese language (upper-elementary to advanced) and culture (address inquiries to the "Office of International Affairs" at the Kinugasa campus; ☎075-465-8230; kokusai@st.ristumai.ac.jp). The 1-month **Summer Japanese Program** is an intensive introduction to Japanese language and culture for college and university students (address inquiries to the "Office of Language Education" at the Kinugasa campus; ☎075-465-7878; gengo@st.ritsumei.ac.jp). Recent additions include the English-language Master's Program in International Technology and Management (since 2001), and a Global Cooperation Program.

Summer Courses in Japanese, International Christian University, 3-10-2, Osawa, Mitaka-shi, Tōkyō 181-8585 (contact Miyuki Yamazaki; ☎0422-33-3501; scj@icu.ac.jp). Runs a 6-week intensive language course for all levels. Students attend class in the morning and may participate in afternoon culture programs.

Summer Session of Asian Studies, Sophia University, 4, Yonban-chō, Chiyoda-ku, Tōkyō 102-008 1 (contact Director Richard A. Gardener, ☎03-3238-4090, c-takeda@hoffman.cc.sophia.ac.jp; or the Asian Studies Program, ☎0305-348-1914, asian@fiu.edu) offers a 4-week summer workshop on Japanese culture and society, making extensive use of sites in cosmopolitan Tōkyō. Foreign students and secondary or college instructors are all welcome (educators may attend weekly workshops).

LANGUAGE SCHOOLS

Unlike American universities, language schools are frequently independently run international or local organizations or divisions of foreign universities that rarely offer college credit. Language schools are a good alternative to university study if you desire a deeper focus on the language or a slightly less rigorous courseload. These programs are also good for younger high school students who might not feel comfortable with older students in a university program.

Experiment in International Living, Kipling Rd., P.O. Box 676, Brattleboro, VT 05302, USA (US ☎800-345-2929; www.usexperiment.org). Runs 3- to 5-week summer programs that offer high-school students cross-cultural homestays and language training in Japan and cost US$1900-5000.

Hokkaidō International Foundation (HIF), Office of the Japanese Program, 14-1, Moto-machi, Hakodate, Hokkaidō, 040-0054 (☎0138-22-0770; www.hif.or.jp/en). Offers an 8-week homestay summer program for Japanese language study (intermediate to advanced) complemented by classes in traditional Japanese arts. Professionals, college students, and graduated high school seniors may apply. Runs the annual 2-week Hokkaidō Cultural Program (tudoi@hif.or.jp) in which exchange students across Japan participate in speech contests, discuss international issues, and visit local schools.

Institute for the International Education of Students (IES), 33 North LaSalle Street, 15th fl., Chicago, IL 60602 USA (☎+1-312-944-1750, US ☎800-995-2300; www.iesabroad.org). A global non-profit organization that sponsors semester and full-year programs in Tōkyō, Nagoya, and Kasugai. Japanese language instruction is available, as well as English-language classes on various topics including business, international studies, and engineering (options vary campus to campus). The Tōkyō campus offers a summer program. IES offers financial aid and scholarships.

OTHER SCHOOLS AND PROGRAMS

Whether your weapon of choice is a *samurai* sword, a sushi knife, or a *nō* fan, Japan has something, possibly in English, for you. Pursuing non-academic studies in Japanese theater, martial arts, or cuisine can not only help you explore special interests but also provide you with a different window into Japanese culture.

ALTERNATIVES TO TOURISM

Aikikai Hombu Dojo (www.aikikai.or.jp/Eng) is home to the Aikikai Foundation and the Aikido World Headquarters. Prospective students must register as a Hombu Member at the reception office. The registration fee is ¥8400; class prices vary. The Aikido Academy 6-month intensive course is held twice a year, beginning in Apr. and Oct.

Akasaka Cooking School, 3-21-14, Akasaka, Minato-ku, Tōkyō (☎03-3582-9074; www.akasaka-cooking.com). Offers 3-4hr. private lessons for non-Japanese on the basics of Japanese home cooking, for ¥10,000 per class, not including cost of ingredients. Call ahead to arrange a date and a menu of 2-3 dishes.

Budo Tours, (contact Sensei Kenshi Uno; www.budotours.com), is based in Imabari and offers personalized, one-on-one instruction for serious martial artists. *Aikidō, iaidō, jūdō, jodo, kappo* healing, karate, *kendō, kyudō, shorinji kempo,* and Zen meditation are all taught. Three packages are offered: the Standard Budo Tour (about US$2600 per week), for a standard hotel room; the Executive Budo Tour (US$3400), for a 5-star hotel room; and the Homestay or Zen Temple Budo Tour (US$2400), in which the client stays with a host family or in a Zen monastery.

Gourmet On Tour, Berkeley Square House, 2F, Berkeley Square, Mayfair, London W1J 6BD, UK (☎+44-20-7396-5550, US ☎800-504-9842; www.gourmetontour.com). Offers over 70 culinary and wine-appreciation tours worldwide, including a 10-day tour package in Japan for US$8000-10,000 (airfare not included). Led by author and culinary instructor Hiroko Shimbo, participants experience food markets and traditional food production, enjoy cooking classes, and sample a variety of regional cuisines. See www.gourmetontour.com/main/AS/schools/AS3_07a.shtml for details.

Noh Training Project (NTP) Programs in Tōkyō, Nomura (Toto-kai) Rehearsal Nō Stage, Horinuchi 3-33-12, Suginami-ku, Tōkyō (☎03-3312-0984). Offers instruction in the techniques of classical *nō* drama for English speakers. There are two 12-14 week sessions, one in the spring and the other in the fall; shorter winter sessions of 3-8 weeks sometimes offered. The full fee is ¥75,000, and for partial participation $60,000; individually, the sessions are ¥2500 each. There is an initial fee of ¥10,000 for all new students that includes the fan cost. For details, contact Instructor Richard Emmert, 2-27-10 Hon-chō, Nakano-ku, Tōkyō 164 (☎03-3373-0553; emmert@gol.com).

Kodokan International Jūdō Center, 1-16-30 Kasuga, Bunkyo-ku, Tōkyō (for English, contact International Department; ☎03-3818-4172; www.kodokan.org). Founded in 1882 by Jigoro Kano, the founder of *jūdō.* The Kodokan Center offers *jūdō* classes in all levels and hosts tournaments. Access to the *dojo* requires an initial charge of ¥8500, plus a monthly fee of ¥5000. Short summer courses in *jūdō* and *kata* are also offered for ¥5500/¥7000. There is also a branch in Ōsaka, the **Kodokan Ōsaka International Jūdō Center,** 4-15-11, Nagata, Jyoto-ku, Ōsaka (☎06-6961-0640).

Le Cordon Bleu Paris Daikan-yama, 28-13 Sarugaku-chō, Shibuya-ku, Tōkyō (☎03-5489-0141; www.cordonbleu.co.jp) offers introductory courses in French cuisine, pastry, catering, and bread baking, as well as diploma programs for Pastry and Cuisine. The school of pastry arts is located at **Le Cordon Bleu Yokohama,** 2-18-1 Takashima, Nishi-ku, Yokohama City, Kanagawa (☎045-440-4720; fax 045-440-4722). Tuition around ¥546,000-700,000.

Sugawara Martial Arts Institute, 3-20-13, Tadao, Machida-shi, Tōkyō (contact Tetsutaka Sugawara; ☎427-94-0972; www.sugawarabudo.com). Offers *aikidō* classes for adults and children, as well as classes for adults in *Tai Chi* and in the classic Japanese sword school *Tenshin Shōden Katori Shintō Ryu.*

A Taste of Culture (contact Elizabeth Andoh, Director & Instructor; ☎/fax 03-5716-5751; www.tasteofculture.com). A culinary facility in Setagaya-ku, Tōkyō. Offers market tours, tasting sessions, cooking classes, and customized programs for food service and hospitality professionals. Classes led by author and culinary instructor Elizabeth Andoh.

Traditional Theatre Training (TTT) Kyōto Performance Institute, Ryukoku University, 520-21, Seta Ōtsu, Shiga-ken (contact Jonah Saltz; ☎0775-43-7875; jonah@rnoc.fks.ryukoku.ac.jp). Runs 2 summer programs: a bilingual 1-week seminar on Kyōto's performance traditions and a 6-week program of performance workshops in *nō, kyogen,* or *nihonbuya.*

WORKING

VISA INFORMATION

Admission to Japan as a visitor does not include the right to work, which is authorized only by a **work permit.** The Japanese Ministry of Foreign Affairs provides an online "Guide to Japanese Visas" (www.mofa.go.jp/j_info/visit/visa/index.html), your best source for information on visa policies and procedures. For a list of regional immigration authorities, go to www.mofa.go.jp/j_info/visit/visa/appendix3.html. Check with your regional Japanese consulate or embassy for further information on work and study visas (see page 9).

Foreigners can receive working visas for employment in a Japanese company, for work in Japan for a foreign company, for entertainment activities (concerts, theater, sports), and for educational activities (foreign language teaching). Although work permits are not required for students at a college or university, **foreign students need special permits to study.**

The visa application process is much smoother and faster if you first obtain a **Certificate of Eligibility,** which is issued before a visa application by a regional immigration authority, in part to verify that the applicant has a legitimate reason for staying in Japan. Travelers can have a Japanese contact secure a certificate from the nearest regional immigration authority. If you apply for a working visa without this certificate, your documents will likely be forwarded to a regional immigration authority in Japan and could take a long time to be processed.

As with volunteering, work opportunities tend to fall into two categories. Some travelers want long-term jobs that allow them to get to know another part of the world as a member of the community, while other travelers seek out short-term jobs to finance the next leg of their travels. In Japan, people who would like long-term employment will find the greatest number of opportunities in the English-teaching sector. There is a plethora of placement agencies and English teaching schools, and job-seekers can always find a bulletin board to advertise themselves as English tutors. A market for professional workers pays for a number of foreigners to live and work in Japan each year; however, with the struggling economy, even professionals will discover that the opportunities have drastically reduced.

Look for English job listings in the *Japan Times, The Daily Yomiuri,* or the *Asahi Shinbun.* You will find the most comprehensive listing in the Monday edition of the *Japan Times.* In the Kansai area (Kyōto, Kōbe, and Ōsaka), try *Kansai Time Out* for regional job listings. The *Tōkyō Journal* is good for job listings and other information on living in Japan pertinent to English-speaking foreigners.

LONG-TERM WORK

If you're planning on spending a substantial amount of time (more than three months) working in Japan, search for a job well in advance. International placement agencies are often the easiest way to find employment abroad, especially for teaching English. **Internships,** usually for college students, are a good way to segue into working abroad, although they are often unpaid or poorly paid (many veterans say the experience, however, is well worth it). Be wary of advertisements or companies that claim the ability to get you a job abroad for a fee—often the same listings are available online or in newspapers, or the listings provided are out of date. Search for a reputable organization; good choices include:

Co-op Japan, c/o University of Victoria, P.O. Box 3025 Stn. CSC, Victoria, BC, Canada V8W 3P2 (☎+1-250-721-8808; http://cjp.coop.uvic.ca). The Co-op's Science and Engineering Placement program coordinates 7- to 11-month research, manufacturing, and industry internships for Canadian science and engineering undergraduates from participating universities. A 1-month language and culture immersion program is included. Internships begin yearly in May.

ICPA (International Computer Professional Association), 1388 Sutter St., Suite 1210, San Francisco, CA 94109, USA (☎800-358-4272; www.icpa.com). Parkwest Bldg., 11th fl., 6-12-1, Nishi-Shinjuku, Shinjuku-ku, Tōkyō 160-0023 (☎+81-3-5325-3218, fax 5325-3219). Helps professionals in technology, marketing, and finance find jobs with large companies. Submit a resume online or send it to one of the addresses above.

International Co-operative Education, 15 Spiros Way, Menlo Park, CA, 94025, USA (☎+1-650-323-4944; www.icemenlo.com). Finds summer jobs in Japan for students. Costs include a $200 application fee and a $600 fee for placement.

JETRO (Japan External Trade Organization), 42nd fl., McGraw-Hill Building, 1221 Ave of the Americas, New York, NY 10020, USA (☎+1-212-997-0400; www.jetro.go.jp). 2-5, Toranomon 2-chōme, Minato-ku, Tōkyō 105-8466 (☎+81-3-3582-5511; fax 3587-0219). 2-12 month commitment. Jobs available in numerous fields, featuring software development and applications, and chemistry and chemical engineering. To apply, contact the program manager nearest you (for a list of programs, look at http://app.jetro.go.jp/database/In3-Japan/In3top.nsf/SCInfo?OpenView). The umbrella organization for this program in the US is the **University of Michigan's Japan Technology Management Program,** 1205 Beal Ave., 2715 IOE Bldg., Ann Arbor, MI 48109, USA (☎+1-734-763-3258; fax 763-0686). Most internships pay upwards of ¥150,000 per month. Depending on the company, participants receive free housing and compensation for work-related travel. Applicants do not need to be US citizens, but must be enrolled in a US college or graduate school for the duration of the internship. Proficiency in Japanese not always required, but most companies seek at least conversational Japanese speakers. Applications available in October.

MOGPA, P.O. Box 131751, Saint Paul, MN 55113, USA (☎+1-651-481-0583; www.interinasia.com). US non-profit assists US undergraduates and recent graduates in getting 6-12 month internships at companies in Japan. Internships are paid or basic living costs are compensated. No fees. Connects participants with apartments or homestays. Intermediate Japanese required (2 years of college or the equivalent). US citizens or permanent residents only. $75 application fee; $900 program fee.

Princeton-in-Asia (PiA), Room 241, Princeton University, 33 Frist Campus Center, Princeton, NJ 08544, USA (☎+1-609-258-3657; www.princeton.edu/%7Epia). A non-profit organization that aims to place college seniors and recent graduates in Japan. Positions range from English teachers to specialized jobs in business, international development, and journalism. Full-year contract begins in late Aug. Participants receive generous salary and subsidized housing. Must be available for interview at Princeton in Jan. $30 application fee ($20 for Princeton students) and $300 internship contribution.

TEACHING ENGLISH

While teaching jobs abroad are rarely well-paid, Japan is one of the few cases in which this is not true. Teaching English in Japan can be lucrative, especially at elite private schools or established institutions. Unfortunately, because living

ONLINE CLASSIFIEDS Get a peek into the Japanese job market by browsing listings on the Internet. More general than the organizations listed below, the following sites may help jump-start your job search. The **Japan Times** (http://job.japantimes.com) offers extensive online classified listings. The **Metropolis** magazine of **Japan Today** profiles one job opening each week and provides listings for others (http://metropolis.japantoday.com/tokyo/recent/jobs.asp). Websites with listings for positions in Japan include **Jobs in Japan** (www.jobsinjapan.com), **Gaijinpot** (www.gaijinpot.com), **CareerCross** (www.careercross.com), **Flipdog** (www.flipdog.com), **Job Dragon** (www.jobdragon.com), and **WorkinJapan.com** (www.daijob.com/wij), though they focus mostly on professional jobs.

costs are so high, much of your income will be siphoned into the cost of supporting yourself. Try to find a program that provides free housing; if you have other contacts in Japan, work them to secure cheap or free housing. By maintaining a prudent lifestyle, a teacher in Japan can save enough to make this a worthwhile venture. Volunteering as a teacher is also a popular option; even unsalaried teachers often get some sort of a daily stipend to help with living expenses.

In almost all cases, you must have at least a bachelor's degree to be a full-fledged teacher, although college undergraduates can often get summer positions tutoring. Schools and companies seeking teachers will usually specify their requirements, but it pays to inquire about jobs even if you do not meet the qualifications. At times, the demand for teachers exceeds the supply, so if an employer needs teachers urgently, you might find yourself hired regardless of technicalities. Most schools hire teachers from within Japan, although well-established places find staff from abroad. Unfortunately, because the Japanese economy has suffered since its peak bubble years of the 80s and early 90s, teaching opportunities are not as ubiquitous as in bygone days. Despite the tighter job market, however, Japanese people will always thirst to learn English, so teaching will remain one of the more reliable, secure posts available to the English-speaking foreigner.

Many schools require a **Teaching English as a Foreign Language (TEFL)** certificate, and in general certified teachers find higher paying jobs. Native English speakers working in private schools are most often hired for English-immersion classrooms where no Japanese is spoken. Placement agencies or university fellowship programs are the best resources for teaching jobs in Japan. The alternative is to make contacts directly with schools or just to try your luck once you arrive in the country. If you are going to try the latter, the best time to show up is several weeks before the start of the school year, which begins in April. **O-Hayo Sensei** (www.ohayosensei.com), a bi-monthly electronic newsletter for English teachers in Japan, lists numerous teaching jobs. The following organizations are extremely helpful in placing teachers in Japan.

JET Program (www.mofa.go.jp/j_info/visit/jet). Established in 1987 as a joint effort by governments of participating countries and the Japanese government, the JET Program is one of the most well-known cultural exchange programs in Japan. College grads work in local government organizations and teach in junior or high schools. 6000+ yearly participants. Offers three types of jobs: Assistant Language Teacher (90% of participants), Coordinator for International Relations, and Sports Exchange Advisor. US citizens, go to www.us.emb-japan.go.jp to apply; Canadian citizens can apply at www.ca.emb-japan.go.jp/jetweb2002/jetindex.html. If you are not a US or Canadian citizen, consult your local Japanese embassy or consulate for an application.

AEON Corporation of Japan, AEON Inter-Cultural USA, 230 Park Ave. #1000, New York, NY 10169, USA (☎+1-212-808-3080; www.aeonet.com). AEON Corporation, Level 66 Mic Centre, 19-29 Martin Place, Sydney, NSW 2000, Australia (☎+61-2-9238-2348,

ALTERNATIVES TO TOURISM

fax 9238-2355). **AEON Japan,** Shinjuku I-Land Tower Bldg. 12F, 6-5-1, Nishi-Shinjuku, Shinjuku-ku, Tōkyō 163-1377 (☎+81-3-5381-1500, fax 5381-1501). There are two divisions of AEON: AEON, for high school, university, and adult education, and AEON Amity, for children's education.

Berlitz Japan, Inc. (http://berlitzjapan.homestead.com). Minimum one year contract. Must be native English speaker. Send references and resume to hr@lc.berlitz.co.jp. Hiring takes place in Japan. May-July are peak demand seasons; Dec-April present fewer opportunities. In cooperation with Sesame Street, the company launched **Berlitz Kids** in 2000, and now offers fun, interactive, cultural lessons to students age 3-16.

ECC Foreign Language Institute, ECC USA Representative Office, c/o Kiyomura & Associates Inc., World Trade Center Bldg., 350 S. Figueroa St., Suite 501, Los Angeles, CA 90071 USA (☎+1-213-626-8170 ext.103; www.ecc.co.jp). Tōkyō Recruitment Office, Sanyamate Bldg., 7-11-10, Nishi-Shinjuku, Shinjuku-ku, Tōkyō 160-0023 (☎+81-3-5330-1585; fax 5330-7084). The academic year follows the Japanese Apr.-Apr. schedule, but teachers and students can join at any point during the year. Applications accepted from within Japan and overseas. One year contract; native English speakers only. Hiring offices in Tōkyō, Nagoya, Ōsaka, Australia, the UK, the US, and Canada. Send resume and cover letter to the office nearest you.

Fulbright English Teaching Assistantship, US Student Programs Division, Institute of International Education, 809 United Nations Plaza, New York, NY 10017, USA (☎212-984-5330; www.iie.org). Competitive program sends college graduates to teach and research in Japan.

GEOS Language System, GEOS Language Corp., Toronto Office, Simpson Tower, Suite 2424, 401 Bay St., Toronto, ON M5H 2Y4, Canada (☎+1-416-777-0109; www.geoscareer.com). GEOS Language Ltd., St. Martin's House, 16 St. Martin's Le Grand, London EC1A 4EN, UK (☎+44-207-397-8401; fax 397-8402). International applications only; apply online or fax a cover letter, resume, and proof of B.A. to your regional office. GEOS has offices in North America, Europe, and Australia and Oceania. Offers positions at 450 schools in Japan, with the potential for advancement. Renewable contract.

Interac Co., Ltd., Foreign Recruiting, Fujibo Bldg. 2F, 2-10-28 Fuijimi, Chiyoda-ku, Tōkyō 102-0071 (www.interac.co.jp). Founded in 1972, Interac provides teachers for hundreds of schools in Japan. Domestic and overseas applicants accepted. Apply online or send an application via email or fax to the Tōkyō Head Office. Interviews in either Tōkyō or a location in Canada, the US, Australia, or the UK. Most jobs are for native English speakers, but some other language positions are available as well.

International Schools Services (ISS), 15 Roszel Rd., Box 5910, Princeton, NJ 08543-5910, USA (☎+1-609-452-0990; www.iss.edu). Hires teachers for more than 200 overseas schools including Japan; candidates should have experience teaching or with international affairs, 2-year commitment expected.

Nova Group, Nova Group Tōkyō Head Office, Box 6036 Shinjuku NS Bldg., 2-4-1, Nishi-Shinjuku, Shinjuku-ku, Tōkyō 163-0823 (☎+81-3-6688-444; www.teachinjapan.com). There are 530 schools English language schools throughout Japan, and nine Nova offices worldwide, in Tōkyō, Ōsaka, London, Paris, Brisbane, Toronto, San Francisco, Chicago, and Boston. Each determines its own recruiting schedule, so contact the office closest to you for further information. Minimum 1 year commitment.

International Schools:

Aoba-Japan International School, Suginami Campus, 2-10-7, Miyamae, Suginami-ku, Tōkyō 168-0081 (☎+81-3-3335-6620; fax 3332-6928). Meguro Campus, 2-10-34, Aobadai, Meguro-ku, Tōkyō 153-0042 (☎+81-3-3461-1442; www.a-jis.com/Eng/EV.asp). A co-educational school of 600 students, pre-K through 9th grade. Caters to students of all nationalities, with a program for kids who know little English. Jobs available between Feb. and Apr. every year; apply online and the office will hold your information for future reference.

Nagoya International School, 2686 Minamihara, Nakashidami, Moriyama-ku, Nagoya, 463-0002 (☎+81-52-736-2025; www.nisjapan.net/nis/index.html).

SHORT-TERM WORK

Traveling for long periods can get expensive, so many travelers try their hand at odd jobs for a few weeks at a time to make some extra cash to carry them through another month or two of touring. No matter how short the duration of work, however, anyone trying to work in Japan needs a working visa. The lone exception to this rule is chores performed in exchange for free or discounted room or board.

Most often, short-term jobs can be found by word of mouth or by talking to the owner of a hostel or restaurant. Some establishments, especially due to the high turnover in the tourism industry, are always eager for help, even if it's only temporary. *Let's Go* tries to list temporary jobs like these whenever possible; look in the Practical Information sections of larger cities, or check out the list below. If you want to work through an established temp agency, **Adecco** (www.adeccocareer.co.jp), **Japan Convention Services** (www.convention.co.jp), and **Manpower** (www.manpower.co.jp), are three large companies worth trying.

Many foreigners work in Japan's nightlife industry. In cities, especially in Tōkyō, foreign men may find work as bouncers, and foreign women as hostesses. Hostesses usually work in a small bar whose owners have cultivated a loyal clientele. There is no physical component to the hostess's job, but she must be conscious of her appearance, laugh at customers' jokes, light their cigarettes, pour drinks, and always be eager for more karaoke. Such subservience can feel degrading, but many women are drawn to the job by the good pay and relative ease of the work.

A number of programs allow foreigners to spend a few months working in Japan; these are most often directed at undergraduate students. These programs are a great way to earn some money while getting acquainted with the country, and can prepare foreigners for the wild experience of traveling in Japan.

WORKING HOLIDAYS Japan has partnered with Australia, New Zealand, Canada, Korea, France, Germany, and the UK to create the **Working Holiday Visa.** This special visa is awarded to young citizens of those countries (ages 18-30) whose purpose for traveling to Japan is mainly tourism, but who would like to be able to work while there. The **Japanese Association for Working Holiday Makers** (☎03-3389-0181; www.jawhm.or.jp) provides job referrals to working holiday visa holders, as well as supplying them with cultural and accommodations information and organizing social events.

Forval Foundation, #411 Tōkyō Central Omotesandō 3-15, Jingumae 4-chōme, Shibuya-ku, Tōkyō 150-0001 (☎+81-3-5474-3699; www.forvalfoundation.org). Places college undergraduates in 8-week summer internships. Application deadline Jan. Japanese proficiency (at least 2 years college credit or equivalent) required. Include airfare from New York to Narita, company housing or homestay, and ¥100,000 per month stipend.

Nambu Foundation, Internship Application Review Committee, 51 East 42nd St., 18th fl., New York, NY 10017, USA (☎+1-212-551-9570; www.nambufound.com). Internships run from June to mid-Aug. Applications due in Jan. Conversational Japanese required. Compensation up to US$1000 on flights, free housing for 2 months, work-related travel expenses, and a stipend of ¥160,000 per month.

Summer Day Camp at ASIJ, The American School in Japan, 1-1-1 Nomizu, Chōfu-shi, Tōkyō 182-0031, Japan (☎+81–42-234-5300 ext. 323; www.asij.ac.jp/sdc/sdc-staff.html). Summer day camp office open M-F 9am-12 and 1-4pm. Summer camp for Tōkyō children. International, English-speaking staff. Every summer, mid-July to mid-Aug. Staff must work at both 2 week sessions; M-F 9am-4pm. Positions include English teacher, swimming instructor, and senior/junior counselors. Housing not provided. ASIJ is a 10min. walk from the Tama Station, 45min. outside of Shinjuku. Hiring starts in Feb. Applicants must have a personal or telephone interview with the director.

Willing Workers On Organic Farms Japan (WWOOF), Kita 16-jō Higashi 16-3-22, Higashi-ku Sapporo 065-0016 (www.wwoofjapan.com). Matches members with host establishments, usually farms, that provide room and board in exchange for 4-6hr. of work per day. Work ranges from raising chickens to chopping wood to making noodles. Membership (US$40) required to browse listings.

FOR FURTHER READING ON ALTERNATIVES TO TOURISM

How to Live Your Dream of Volunteering Overseas, by Collins, DeZerega, and Heckscher. Penguin Books, 2002 (US$17).

International Directory of Voluntary Work, by Whetter and Pybus. Peterson's Guides and Vacation Work, 2000 (US$16).

International Jobs, by Kocher and Segal. Perseus Books, 1999 (US$18).

Invest Yourself: The Catalogue of Volunteer Opportunities, published by the Commission on Voluntary Service and Action (☎ 718-638-8487).

Work Abroad: The Complete Guide to Finding a Job Overseas, by Hubbs, Griffith, and Nolting. Transitions Abroad Publishing, 2000 ($16).

Work Your Way Around the World, by Susan Griffith. Worldview Publishing Services, 2001 (US$18).

ALTERNATIVES TO TOURISM

LIFE AND TIMES

The pregnant silence of the Buddha coexists with 24-hour urban noise; the miniaturization of cell phones and pocket cameras stands in contrast to the space-age scale of the new Kyōto train station. The description "a country of contrasts," while applied so frequently to Asian countries as to be a cliché, remains perhaps the most accurate description of Japan for visitors. On the one hand, there's the famous thread of conformism running through Japanese culture—the uniformly dressed salaryman performing morning calisthenics, the concept of *wa* (which stresses team spirit over personal achievement), and so on. On the other hand, there are the contradictions of youth culture and fashion, with hordes of *kogaru* girls in miniskirt uniforms and loose socks, heavily tanned *ganguro* on platform shoes, *yamumba* with white lipstick and white eyeshadow—individual looks, certainly, but adopted en masse. Voracious borrowers of foreign trends as varied as salsa dancing and gospel singing, the Japanese are yet extremely proud of what they consider uniquely theirs: *sumō*, the *kimono*, the *geisha* tradition, and the tea ceremony, to name a few prominent cultural markers.

At the center of this hybridized culture, however, is a society more nearly homogeneous in race and language than any other, a society whose sense of national identity, though forever altered by World War II, remains strong and vibrant. Recent economic downturns and accelerating modernization have brought out some national self-questioning, and public figures from talk-show host Kitano "Beat" Takeshi (p. 103) to author Murakami Haruki (p. 99) have turned a probing eye on how the Japanese live and function. This country of contrasts, so striking and puzzling to foreigners, confronts its own citizens with a number of difficult questions about what it is to be Japanese in the world today.

LAND

Packing 127 million people into 146,000 sq. mi.—an area the size of California—this island nation boasts a population density 12 times that of the United States. With the **Sea of Japan** to the west, the **East China Sea** to the southwest, and the vast **Pacific Ocean** to the east, Japan truly stands apart from the rest of the world. The four major islands, Hokkaidō, Honshū, Shikoku, and Kyūshū, extend in a long arc just off Asia's eastern coast. **Honshū** is the main island, home to major cities **Ōsaka** and **Nagoya**, historic **Kyōto**, and that sprawling megalopolis, **Tōkyō**. Sparsely-populated **Hokkaidō,** the second-largest and northernmost island, attracts hikers and skiers, while little temple-speckled **Shikoku,** just below Honshū, is a pilgrim's paradise. Southern **Kyūshū**, with its proximity to China and Korea, has long been Japan's point of contact with Asia and boasts archeological sites, tourist resorts, and a pleasant climate. Thousands of smaller islands dot the surrounding waters—the most famous being the subtropical chain known as **Okinawa,** or the Ryūkyū Islands, that trails 650 mi. from the southern edge of Kyūshū almost to Taiwan.

Mount Fuji is a fitting national icon—four-fifths of the land area is mountainous. Where there aren't mountains, there's water: Japan boasts 18,500 mi. of coastline and its chief natural resource is fish. **Lake Biwa,** in the Kansai area, is Japan's largest body of fresh water; other lakes are sprinkled through the northern half of the country. The government and the social structure may be stable, but the ground certainly isn't. Situated at the intersection of a number of tectonic plates, Japan is subject to as many as 1500 **earthquakes** annually, as well as frequent **volcanic eruptions** and **tsunami.**

NAME GAMES. Japan's four main islands are further divided into **regions**. Hokkaidō, Shikoku, and Kyūshū are each a region unto themselves. Honshū is split into five parts: **Tōhoku**, the northern part of the island; **Kantō**, the district surrounding Tōkyō; **Chubu**, the central area; **Kansai**, or Kinki, home to Kyōto, Ōsaka, Nara, and Kōbe; and **Chugoku**, the island's western spur. These regions are once again subdivided into **prefectures**, of which Japan has forty-odd, depending on how you deal with the exceptions.

FLORA AND FAUNA

PLANTS

Dramatic variations in climate from the southern tip to the northern extremity of Japan have resulted in tremendous diversity of plant life. The Ryūkyū and Bonin archipelagoes contain semitropical rainforests of camphor, oaks, ferns, and mulberries, and mangrove swamps can be found on the southern coast of Kyūshū. In Kyūshū, Shikoku, and most of southern Honshū, a laurel forest zone of broad-leafed evergreens is dominated by camphor, pasania, camellia, holly, and native Japanese oaks such as *shī* and *kashi*. In the cool-temperature areas of central and northern Honshū and southern Hokkaidō, deciduous broad-leafed forests of beech, maple, oak, and birch thrive above an undergrowth of various bamboo grasses. In the subalpine regions of central and northern Hokkaidō, characteristic trees are Sakhalin fir, Yezo spruce, and other conifers. Almost 70% of Japan is still covered in forest, although deforestation and pollution continue to take their toll.

COMMON PLANTS. Japanese pine (*matsu*) and cedar (*sugi*) are common throughout the country. Large Japanese pines serve as windbreakers in coastal areas, while small ones are used as *bonsai* and garden trees. The plants most likely to feature in your sightseeing, however, are flowering trees. The cherry tree, a national symbol, blooms in mid-spring in gardens and forests throughout Japan, and following the northward progress of the cherry blossoms (*sakura*) is a popular pastime. Plum blossoms arrive in early spring, hydrangeas in early summer, and chrysanthemums in the fall. Camellias, maples, magnolias, daphnes, and gingkos are also common along streets and in Japanese gardens.

ANIMALS

Once connected to the Asian continent, Japan shares many of the animal species of China and Korea. The subsequent isolation of the islands, and in particular of smaller isles in the Inland Sea and in Okinawa, preserved a number of unique species such as the Japanese giant salamander and the Japanese macaque.

COMMON ANIMALS. Dogs considered native to Japan include the large Akita; the medium-sized Hokkaidō, Kai, Kyūshū and Shikoku dogs; and the small Shiba inu. Tortoiseshell cats are popular pets. Carp are often used for decorative purposes in garden pools. In rural areas cicada (*semi*), large harmless winged insects, produce a loud, screeching clamor during the summer months. Raccoon dogs (*tanuki*) are nocturnal animals resembling badgers that pop up in numerous Japanese folk tales as trickster characters with supernatural powers.

ENDANGERED ANIMALS. Destruction of habitats and the decrease in wild prey have both diminished the numbers of certain Japanese species. There are about 70 species of endangered mammals and 130 endangered birds on the islands. The **Iriomote wildcat** lives only on Iriomote Island in southernmost Okinawa and has become the rarest cat in the world—less than 100 remain today. The **Japanese crested ibis** (*toki*), killed in the past for its beautiful wings, approached extinction in 1981 when only a single bird remained at the conservation center on the island of Sado. More were discovered in China, however, and Japan acquired two in 1999 in hopes of repopulating the species. **Blakiston's fish owl,** Japan's largest owl, lives exclusively in central and eastern Hokkaidō, where deforestation has rendered it a critically endangered species. **Golden eagles** live in mountainous regions throughout the country and currently number less than 300. Other endangered species are the **Japanese otter,** the **albatross,** and the **stork.**

DANGEROUS ANIMALS. Hokkaidō is home to the **brown bear** (*higuma*)—the **Asiatic brown bear** (*tsukinowaguma*) inhabits the other main islands. Although bear attacks are rare, mother bears are known to be protective of their cubs, so keep your distance (p. 30). The **haku snake** of Okinawa is poisonous, but hospitals can provide antivenoms (p. 30). The poisonous **mamushi snake** on the mainland presents less of a threat. At certain times during the summer, be wary of **stinging jellyfish** in off-shore waters. In rural areas, use insect repellent to guard against mosquitoes, which may carry Japanese encephalitis (p. 18).

HISTORY

ORIGINS OF CIVILIZATION. Although the fossil record clearly shows that hominids had arrived in Japan via glacial landbrige as early as 35,000 BC, archaeological evidence of civilization emerges around 10,000 BC, the year commonly recognized as the beginning of the **Jōmon Period,** so named for the distinctive twisted-rope pattern of the era's pots, which are believed to be the world's earliest. Despite their precocity at ceramics, the early Jōmon people made few technological advances, living in the Stone Age until immigrants from Northern China and Korea, displaced by conflict, began arriving in northern Kyūshū around 400 BC.

RAPID DEVELOPMENT. The newcomers brought with them the revolutionizing knowledge of wet rice farming. Later, around 300 BC, they also imported bronze bells, mirrors and weapons, and finally iron, rocketing Japan from Stone Age to Iron Age almost overnight. The new technologies transformed Jōmon society so radically that historians start calling it the **Yayoi Period.** At this point, the predecessor of the modern Japanese language, related to Korean, and a shamanistic, clan-centered religion that would eventually develop into **Shintō** (p. 88) emerged. As time went on, inter-clan conflict led to the formation of over 100 small states throughout the **Yamato** region in Western Honshū.

GREAT BURIAL GROUNDS. By around the year AD 300, a new culture began to form around Nara and Ōsaka. This era is known as the **Yamato,** or **Kofun Period;** *kofun* is the term for the huge keyhole-shaped burial mounds erected for kings. One of the most famous is the tree-covered, triple-moated **Tomb of Nintoku,** measuring 396m long and nearly 30m high. which took 20 years to complete. The tomb and others like it symbolize the power of the Yamato kings over their subjects. Changes in the tombs' contents, notably the inclusion of **weapons** and images of **horses,** which begin to appear around 500, mark the social transformation that accompanied a second influx of foreigners.

THE KOREAN CONNECTION. Japan had close ties with the kingdom of **Mimana,** also known as Paekche, on the Korean peninsula. Paekche was at war with the other two kingdoms of Korea, Koguryo and Silla, and although it had reinforcements from Japan, Paekche ultimately lost the war in the 6th century. In the wake of the defeat, waves of refugees fled to Yamato. The Koreans had

THE LOCAL LEGEND

THE MYTHICAL ORIGINS OF JAPAN

In the beginning, everything was chaos. Suddenly, the Plain of Heaven appeared from the shapeless mass. Within the plain, gods began to materialize spontaneously and the earth began to condense. Ages passed, and the gods realized there was nothing to do. To liven things up, they chose **Izanagi** and **Izanami** to go to earth and make something of it.

At the Bridge of Heaven, Izanagi stuck his jewelled spear into the ubiquitous fog, stirring to see how solid it was, when he hit something on the bottom. When he pulled the spear out, a drop of brine fell from the tip and formed land, Onokoro. Thrilled, Izanagi and Izanami settled there, experimented until they discovered the marriage ceremony, and began having children—or more accurately, islands. One by one, **Awaji, Shikoku, Oki, Kyūshū, Tsushima,** and **Honshū** were born.

The next eight children were gods; the eighth was the fire god, and Izanami died giving birth. Izanagi followed her to the underworld to entreat her return, but when he disobeyed her command not to look into the forbidden castle, she chased him out. Outside, he purified his eyes with water. From the water was born Shintō's supreme Sun Goddess, **Amaterasu Omi-kami,** whose great, great grandson **Jimmu** became the first emperor in 660 BC.

already imported classical Chinese writing in the early 5th century, and in the years surrounding the war, **Confucianism** and **Buddhism** (p. 89) also made their way across the waters. Both would become important to the formation of Japanese state and society. **Prince Shōtoku's 17 Article Constitution,** written in 604, formed the overall basis of the centralized Japanese government for centuries to come and was mainly grounded in Confucian principles of harmony, regularity, and moral development, with Buddhist influences.

THE RISE OF BUDDHISM. There was quite a bit of conflict among various Japanese clans about whether to adopt the outsiders' new ways. The powerful **Soga clan,** a branch of the Imperial line, decided to back Buddhism and used their faith as a tool in the struggle for power over the kingdom. When Soga-no-Umako defeated his anti-Buddhist enemy Mononobe in 587, he built the temple **Hoko-ji,** now known as **Asuka-dera,** near Nara (p. 458). Eventually the Soga became the most powerful leaders in Japan, acting as regents for emperors and essentially ruling the country until a rival group, the Nakatomi, assassinated a Soga leader in 645, removing that family from power. Bearing the new name **Fujiwara,** the coup leader initiated the **Taika Reforms,** which strengthed the role of the emperor and laid the framework for the Chinese-inspired **ritsuryo** system of civil law.

CLASSICAL CULTURE. In 710, **Emperor Shomu** established the first "permanent" capital at Nara, where it remained for a record-breaking 84 years, known now as the **Nara Period.** Buddhism really took off as several new sects made their way from China to the islands of Japan. The arts also flourished. The period's crowning achievement was Emperor Shomu's construction of **Tōdai-ji** and an enormous statue of the Buddha, the **Daibutsu,** whose dedication ceremony drew visitors from India and gifts from as far away as Greece (p. 451). Japan's literary tradition emerged under Chinese influences (p. 99).

THE GOLDEN YEARS (HEIAN PERIOD, 794-1192). In 794, the capital moved to Heian, now known as **Kyōto,** where it was to remain for almost the next 800 years. The role of *tennō*, or emperor, was at last firmly established; he ruled along Confucian lines by virtue of his descent from the Shintō goddess **Amaterasu Ōmi-kami.** The government was essentially based upon the highly centralized model of Tang China, but although the emperor appointed regional governors in place of clan leaders, the clan structure of the Yayoi Period continued to exert great influence. The Fujiwara clan, like the earlier Soga, dominated the government for 200 years through a combination of regencies for child emperors and marriage into the Imperial family. Eventually, the Fujiwara were so powerful that they could force an emperor to give up his throne upon reaching adulthood to another manipulable child. In part because of the Fujiwara influence, the Heian Era was a time of remarkable stability and a golden era in Buddhism's development. The arts and literature flourished, notably with the composition of the **The Tale of Genji** (p. 99).

THE DECLINE OF FUJIWARA POWER. Although Emperor Go-Sanjo, the first emperor in decades not to be born of a Fujiwara mother, made important strides against Fujiwara domination and the *shōen* system, his son **Shirakawa** struck the greatest blow by retiring at an early age and, instituting the role of *insei*, or cloistered emperor, ruling from behind the scenes. The Fujiwara suffered another setback in 1155, when the appointment of **Go-Shirakawa** as Emperor precipitated the **Hōgen Disturbance.** The Fujiwara proved unable to put down this conflict without the help of two warrior clans, the **Taira** and **Minamoto**; power was suddenly in the hands of the warrior families. The Taira, under **Kiyomori,** held the advantage.

RISE OF THE SAMURAI. In 1180, conflict between the Taira and Minamoto families erupted into the **Genpei War,** which ended in 1185 with Minamoto domination. Power now lay in the hands of **Minamoto Yoritomo,** whose life had been spared years ago by his enemy Taira Kiyomori, and his brother **Yoshitsune,** whose military brilliance had led the family to victory. Yoritomo soon did away with his brother, and in Kamakura he created a **bakufu** (literally, tent-government) separate from the Imperial government in Kyōto. From the *bakufu*, he ruled the military houses as shōgun and oversaw the development of a semi-feudal system.

THE EMPEROR STRIKES BACK. Although Japan had been successful in staving off Mongolian attacks in the late 13th century (p. 81), the *bakufu* did not survive long after the invasions. In 1331, **Emperor Go-Daigo** attempted to overthrow the Hōjō, only to be defeated and exiled. He returned, however, and mustered support from among the warrior class. In 1333, he defeated the Hōjō once and for all and began the **Kemmu Restoration,** his attempt to bring back the former glory of the Heian Period. Within a few months, however, his proposed reforms had so angered General **Ashikaga Takauji** that the general imprisoned Go-Daigo. The emperor escaped to the mountains of Yoshino, where he set up the **Southern Court.**

SHŌGUN AND SHUGO AND SHŌEN. Takauji proclaimed his recognition of a separate **Northern Court,** and set up a new *bakufu* in an area of Tōkyō known as **Muromachi.** The courts would remain separate until 1392, in what is known as the **Nambokucho Period.** The dream of ruling the country from one centralized location had proven impossible, so the Muromachi *bakufu* employed a system of delegation, entrusting administration of a given region to an official known as **shugo.** Especially after the assassination of shōgun **Ashikaga Yoshinori** in 1441, the *shugo* gained more and more power and came to be called **shugo-daimyō,** or *shugo/* regional lord. From this point on, although their patronage of the arts produced a number of great developments (p. 99), the Ashikaga shōgun grew weaker and weaker, until all central control was lost and the ten-year **Ōnin War** broke out in 1467. The *shugo-daimyō* abandoned Kyōto to protect their own lands in the provinces, beginningr the **Sengoku Period** of constant war between the 260 *daimyō*. During this time, the entire social order was overturned, as peasants and religious leaders rose up against the *daimyō* in bands called **ikki.**

ARRIVAL OF WESTERNERS. The first Westerners arrived in Japan in 1542; they were Portuguese, and they brought with them guns and Christianity. The warring *daimyō* were eager to adopt the weaponry, but efforts at evangelicization proved

LIFE & TIMES

THE WAY OF THE SAMURAI Samurai, probably the most widely recognized cultural icon of Japan, were prevalent in Japanese society from the **Kamakura Period** until the end of the **Tokugawa.** The word "samurai" comes from the verb "to serve"; samurai began as warriors pledged to serve their regional lord. In the early 1100s, lords began actively recruiting warriors in Kyōto for their private retinues. When the **Minamoto** defeated the rival **Taira** samurai family in the **Genpei War** in 1185, samurai leader **Minamoto Yoritomo** established a samurai government and became the first shōgun. Through the Kamakura and **Muromachi Periods,** samurai eclipsed the court in power, but maintained a separate elite culture. **Nō** and **kabuki** theater developed during this period, as did **tea ceremony, sumi-e ink painting** and **Zen gardens** (p. 101). From the beginning of the Muromachi, the samurai were largely influenced by **Zen Buddhism,** whose worldview and emphasis on self-control the samurai admired. Often monks doubled as warriors and inter-temple battles were not uncommon before the Tokugawa peace. For centuries, however, samurai culture was limited to the elite leadership circles; most samurai were essentially mercenaries, whose loyalty lasted as long as the lord's funds held out. Many samurai-farmers worked their own land when they weren't fighting to supplement their income. It was only in the Edo Period that the samurai class became completely differentiated from peasants. Also around this time, the myth of the samurai began to take shape. Since the Tokugawa-imposed peace kept warriors from actually fighting, they moved to the cities and, living as a privileged class, idealized and embellished the stories of their ancestors. Among the greatest cultural achievements of the Edo Period was romanticization-in-retrospect of the concept **bushidō.** Commonly known as the "way of the warrior," bushidō values justice, loyalty, bravery, benevolence and honesty, as well as the all-important self-control. Even though the samurai class was abolished with the **restoration of Emperor Meiji,** the notion remains popular today among martial arts enthusiasts all over the world. In the 1980s, American businessmen studied Tokugawa samurai **Miyamoto Musashi's** classic **A Book of Five Rings** in hopes of learning the "samurai secrets" behind Japan's incredible economic success.

ineffective due to the lack of priests. All this changed with the arrival of **St. Francis Xavier** in 1549, and the Christian community grew rapidly. So rapidly, in fact, that Tokugawa Ieyasu, feeling threatened, outlawed the religion in 1615 and put many practitioners to death. From this point until the arrival of the Americans in 1853, Japan remained closed to all Westerners except **Dutch traders.**

REUNIFICATION. The chaos of the Sengoku Period was brought to an end by the rise of the **Tokugawa.** Two strong warlords, **Oda Nobunaga** and **Toyotomi Hideyoshi,** gained control over their fellow daimyō, setting Japan on the road to national unification. Nobunaga destroyed the monastery on **Mount Hiei** (p. 427), ending the political independence of the influential monks who had threatened his authority. As part of his anti-Buddhist policy, he embraced the newly arrived Westerners, supporting their religion and adopting their technology, particularly firearms, which helped him achieve his military goals. In 1582, Nobunaga was betrayed and attacked by one of his generals, Akechi Mitsuhide. He committed **seppuku,** suicide by disembowelment, and left the mission to Hideyoshi, his strongest ally.

TOKUGAWA. Hideyoshi made great strides toward unification, but at the time of his death in 1598 he left no adult son to assume his role. He had called upon the five most powerful daimyō to act as regents for his young son **Hideyori,** but con-

flict between them eliminated any hope of cooperation, and in the end **Tokugawa Ieyasu,** the strongest of
the five, gained dominance. In 1600, he defeated his
greatest rival, Ishida Mitsunari, and in 1615 finally
destroyed Hideyori's stronghold. Claiming descent
from the Minamoto clan, Ieyasu soon established his
own *bakufu* in the city of **Edo,** modern-day Tōkyō, in
the Kantō region. Thus began the longest period of
peace in all Japanese history; it is known as either
the **Edo** or **Tokugawa Period** and was a time of great
artistic production. The Tokugawa implemented a
highly effective law for the military houses; *daimyō*
were forced to leave hostages at the shōgunal court
to ensure obedience. Social stratifications were formalized into the legally defined categories of *samurai*, peasant, merchant, and artisan, with the
samurai at the top of the ladder.

WESTERN INCURSION. The Tokugawa regime was
remarkably successful at domestic administration,
but proved unable to withstand a substantial foreign
threat. In 1853, US Commodore **Matthew C. Perry** and
his **"black ships"** arrived in Japan with a letter from
President Fillmore requesting that Japan establish diplomatic relations with the United States. Although it
was supposedly a friendly negotiation, Perry
announced that the Japanese would have one year to
think it over before he returned with an even larger
force. Faced with greatly superior American military
power, the *bakufu* was forced to capitulate, and in
1854 signed the **Kanagawa Treaty,** which gave unfair
trade advantages to the United States. The treaty was
humiliating to the *bakufu*, and created feelings of
inferiority and resentment among the Japanese,
many of whom took up the catch phrase **"sonnō jōi"**
(revere the emperor; expel the barbarians).

THE MEIJI RESTORATION AND MODERNIZATION.
For years already there had been a contingent who
opposed the *bakufu* and were loyal to the emperor.
The failure of the Tokugawa to oppose the Westerners provided impetus for action. In 1867, the last
Tokugawa shogun, **Yoshinobu,** resigned from his position, citing his inability to serve the nation, and in
1868 the loyalists "restored" **Emperor Meiji** to actual
power in what is known as the **Meiji Restoration.** This
period was marked by a striving toward modernization in an effort to establish equality with the West.
The samurai class was abolished, society was
restructured, and the new government, headed by
the Emperor and the **Meiji Oligarchs,** began encourag-
ing industrialization and the adoption of Western-
style capitalism and military practices. In 1899, Japan
ratified the **Meiji Constitution,** which remained in
effect until 1945.

THE LOCAL LEGEND

KHAN GOES DOWN

In 1268, **Kublai Khan** issued
an order to the "king" of Japan,
demanding that he acknowledge
vassalage to the Mongol Empire or
face war with the world's greatest
army. Interestingly, he sent it not
to the emperor in Kyōto, but to the
shōgun at Kamakura, who forwarded it to Kyōto. Neither government responded: Japan's wars to
that point had been exclusively
civil, and no one knew how to deal
with a foreign threat.

Six years later, the Mongols
arrived in **Hakata Bay,** dealing the
Japanese severe damage on the
first day of fighting. That night,
however, the Mongols slept on
their ships, and a freak storm decimated their fleet, forcing the survivors to slink back to the
mainland. Realizing the danger
they'd faced, the Japanese reorga-
nized their forces and began building up defenses. When the
Mongols returned in 1281, they
were held off for months before a
storm wiped out their ships. The
Japanese, believing the wind to
have been sent by the gods to protect the country, called it **kamikaze,** or "divine wind," an image
revived in the World War II era.

Scrolls from the 1290s depicting scenes from the invasion are
on view at the **Fukuoka City
Museum** (p. 590). At **Kushida
Jinja** (p. 591) visitors can see
stone anchors recovered from the
wrecks of the Mongol ships.

NOTIONS OF EMPIRE. The **Sino-Japanese War** of 1895 ended in victory for Japan, as did the **Russo-Japanese War** in 1904. Both were fought over control of Korean ports. With both China and Russia defeated, Japan expanded the Empire and began to occupy **Korea** in 1905, formally annexing the peninsula in 1910. During this period of colonization, the Japanese reaped many economic benefits at the expense of native Korean prosperity and human rights.

RISING (ULTRA-)NATIONALISM. During WWI, Japanese industry provided the Allies with equipment, and the economy grew substantially. Enormous corporate conglomerates, known as **zaibatsu**, dominated the economy; prominent players in this era include the still extant Mitsubishi, Mitsui, and Nissan corporations. Beginning in the late 1920s, with the ascent of **Emperor Hirohito** to the throne, a group of ultra-conservatives came to power, and encouraged a highly nationalistic and militaristic view of the Empire. This was the beginning of an extremely dark period in Japanese history, which the government has yet to fully acknowledge. In what is known as the **Manchurian Incident**, the Japanese army invaded Northeast China in 1931, and in 1932 founded the puppet state of **Manchukuo;** only Italy and Germany extended diplomatic recognition to the "independent" state, and the disapproval of the **League of Nations** led to Japan's withdrawal from the organization in 1933.

APPROACHING THE WAR. Over the next few years, as militarism and nationalism intensified, Japan forged closer and closer ties with Facist Italy and Nazi Germany. In 1937, Japan invaded China proper, leading to the horrific massacre of civilians known as the **Rape of Nanking.** The outbreak of war in Europe lessened international resistance to Japan's aggressive actions, although the Americans, who had not yet entered the war, protested strongly against the incursion into Indo-China in 1940. The Japanese rationale for this invasion was the establishment of the Japanese-led **Great East Asia Co-Prosperity Sphere,** under which the Japanese claimed they would liberate the Asian nations from Western imperialism. Just before the bombing of the American military base at **Pearl Harbor** on December 7, 1941, civilian Prime Minister **Konoe Fumimaro,** the last bastion of moderation, resigned. His post passed to the military-minded **Tōjō Hideki.**

THE "PACIFIC" WAR. The day after the surprise attack, the enraged United States declared war on Japan; Britain followed suit. Four years of bloody naval, land, and air battle in the Pacific ensued; meanwhile, Japan continued fighting in China and Southeast Asia. At the outset, it seemed Japan might be successful: within weeks of the Pearl Harbor attack, Guam, Wake Island, Hong Kong, and Manila had fallen to the Japanese forces, and within months, the Malay peninsula, Singapore, the Dutch East Indies and the Philippines were under Japanese control. All Japanese territories suffered harsh treatment at the hands of the Imperial Army. The **Bataan Death March,** during which tens of thousands of war prisoners and civilians died, is only one of the most notorious incidences of Japanese brutality. The United States struck back with force at the **Battle of Midway** in June 1942, and from this point until the final defeat in 1945, Japan was on the defensive, pushed farther and farther back toward the homeland. Although the United States conducted highly concentrated **fire-bombing** campaigns against Japanese cities, killing and maiming millions of civilians, no combat took place on Japanese soil until 1945, when the two forces faced each other on the **Okinawan Islands.** Desperate to protect the main islands from invasion, the Japanese leadership used Okinawa as a last defense, resulting in enormous military and civilian casualties, as thousands of Okinawan civilians killed themselves rather than fall into the hands of the Americans. Despite the devastating defeat, after which Prime Minister Tōjō resigned, Japan refused to surrender, and on August 6, 1945, President Truman, fearing that the Russians would reach Japan first, ordered the dropping of the atomic bomb **"Little Boy"** on the city of **Hiroshima** (p. 486). Three days later, bombers dropped **"Fat Man"** on **Nagasaki**. Hundreds of thousands died instantly in the horrific conflagrations. On August 15, 1945, Emperor Hirohito made his historic radio broadcast declaring Japan's surrender.

OCCUPATION. Until the final stages of the war, Japanese civilians had been told that they were winning. The terrifying, total devastation of the two A-bombs and Hirohito's announcement shattered their illusions. There was remarkably little resistance when the Americans, commanded by **General Douglas MacArthur**, demobilized and dissolved the Japanese army and began to rebuild the country along democratic lines, purging the conservative leaders who had led the country into war. Tōjō, along with six other military leaders, was executed for war crimes. Psychologically and materially difficult, the occupation years provided nevertheless a comparatively smooth transition from military state to liberal democracy. In 1947, the new, US-approved **Constitution** was adopted, and in 1951, Japan signed the **San Francisco Peace Treaty**, which returned it to the community of nations.

FROM RAGS... The next year, 1952, the occupation ended, as the result of Liberal Party Prime Minister **Yoshida Shigeru's** military pact with the US, allowing for a continued American presence on the islands even after independence. With the exception of Okinawa, which remained under US control until 1972, Japan escaped the messy Cold War process of division; as an anti-Communist stronghold with US backing, it soon began its climb toward economic greatness. Industrial demand created by the **Korean War** provided the kickstart for a program of intensive, government-supervised economic development that would last decades. In 1956, Japan joined the **United Nations**. The **1964 Tōkyō Olympics**, coming just less than twenty years since the total defeat of the nation, were testament to the recovering level of national confidence.

...TO MIRACULOUS RICHES. Whereas material survival had been the priority in the immediate post-war years, in the comfortable years of the mid-1960s, ideology became more important. In line with worldwide trends, Japanese students voiced their dissatisfaction with quality of life and governmental policy, particularly with regard to the environment. By the 1970s, Japan was taking a far more active role in international affairs, starting with re-establishment of relations. Japan's international prominence only increased with the economic growth of the 1980s, and, in 1992, a modification to the Constitution allowed for the deployment of peacekeeping troops to foreign nations. Japan's new economic power inspired emulation around the globe, and catapulted Japan to the top of the finance world. The unprecedented wealth that developed with the rise of the yen in the 1980s drove property values sky high; when the economy hit a major recession in the early 1990s, people said that the **bubble economy** had burst.

BUBBLE AND POST-BUBBLE POLITICS. Politically, the period since 1955 has been dominated by the **Liberal Democratic Party** (LDP), which led the country without interruption from 1955 to 1993, at which point growing anxiety about the economic future prompted voters to back a broad coalition of socialist and left-leaning groups led by Hosokawa Morihiro. The new government's inadequate action in the aftermath of the **1995 Kōbe earthquake**, in which 5000 were killed and many more injured, proved part of its downfall. Where the government failed, however, the Japanese people came through, pouring into the ruined city to help rebuild it. The LDP regained control of the government in 1996 with the election of **Hashimoto Ryūtaro**, who initiated several bold steps to cut the nation's ever-increasing budget, dealt with crises over the presence of US forces in Okinawa (p. 648), and strengthened security ties with the US. His attempt to raise the consumption tax backfired badly when consumer activity suddenly dropped off. He resigned in 1998 with the yen at an eight-year low and the economy in utter disarray.

TODAY

Obuchi Keizo, the high-ranking LDP member who replaced Hashimoto, became Japan's 41st prime minister since the end of the war. At the beginning of 1999, Obuchi formed a coalition with the Liberal Party, and in October, added the political party **New Kōmeitō** (Clean Government) to his coalition, enacting several measures designed to reboot the economy, including a zero-interest policy and a five-year fiscal budget. Public optimism was high, but Obuchi's stroke in early 2000 proved a serious setback. With their leader seriously ill, his cabinet resigned *en masse* in April, and **Mori Yoshiro** was appointed prime minister in his place. Mori declared his intention to follow the path set by Obuchi, and presided over a coalition government, composed of the New Kōmeitō and the new **Conservative Party.** Voters supported Mori in the June 2000 election, but to many commentators, the new government's policies seemed vague and insufficient to effect the rebirth of the country. Statements refering to the divinity of the Japanese people caused great controversy, and Mori resigned from office in 2001 with one of the lowest approval ratings in modern Japanese history.

The **2000 G8 Summit** held in **Nago,** Okinawa, was a major event for Japan. Presided over by Prime Minister Mori, it gave the country an opportunity to voice some of its concerns about the future to the entire globe; Japanese newspapers stressed the need to establish a peaceful world for the 21st century. Meanwhile, the future of the **Imperial Family** changed with the birth of **Princess Aiko** in 2002; although conservatives dislike the idea of a female monarch, unless **Crown Prince Naruhito** and **Princess Masako** have a male child soon, it seems likely that Aiko will take her place as second-in-line to the throne, which has been occupied since 1989 by Hirohito's son, **Emperor Akihito.**

Editorialists greeted the April 2001 election of Mori's replacement, high-energy LDP maverick and pledged reformer **Koizumi Junichiro,** with similar enthusiasm. His initial approval rating was over 80%, and the public looked forward to structural reform and economic and political reinvigoration from the LDP, New Kōmeitō and Conservative Party coalition. Foreign relations, however, were in a difficult place; the visit of former Taiwanese president **Lee Teng-hui (Li Denghui)** had seriously strained relations with China, while controversy over the **Northern Territories** was bringing discussion with Russia to a halt and recent attempts to establish normal relations with North Korea had fallen through. Since Koizumi's 2002 visit to **North Korea,** the prime minister has taken an active role in trying to negotiate down the escalating **nuclear crisis** on the Korean peninsula. However, the admission by North Korean leader **Kim Jong Il** that North Korea had kidnapped 12 Japanese citizens made normalization highly unpopular. Several of the kidnap victims have died, and others now have families and lives in North Korea.

Japan's **2002 Soccer World Cup,** jointly hosted with South Korea, brought the two nations into the limelight and produced a remarkable sense of mutual goodwill. Japan has also taken part in a number of **UN peacekeeping missions,** including operations in Israel, East Timor, and Afghanistan. Koizumi has undeniably shaken things up in many ways: during his tenure the **Diet** has had more female members than ever, and the first female foreign minister, **Tanaka Makiko,** was appointed in 2001. Most of Koizumi's promises for slash-and-burn reform, made during the election, however, have yet to materialize; the economy is still in trouble, and corrupt and factional politics remain to be rooted out. Nevertheless, today his approval is a respectable 50%; personal popularity and the perception held by some voters that he cares more than any of the other politicians have kept him afloat.

A number of issues have been the subject of controversy in Japanese society in recent years, not least of which is the problem of the environment. Japanese **commerical whaling** practices hit the international spotlight during the 2002 Convention on International Trade in Endangered Species. In May 2003, **Tōkyō Electric Power Company (TEPCO)** admitted to covering up maintenance problems and obstructing government inspections. Several TEPCO plants were closed for inspection amid public outcry, causing power shortages in Tōkyō.

Education will always be a major concern in a country that prides itself on the discipline and performance of its students. School violence and bullying, which rose sharply during the 1990s, are still a problem, and lately, despite the nation's consistently high test results, the education system is widely criticized for emphasizing memorization over real learning. A separate movement has been pushing for more accurate history textbooks, especially those that deal with WWII.

In the past few years, the government's refusal to fully acknowledge, among other wartime atrocities, the use of Korean, Chinese, and Filipino women as military sex slaves or **"comfort women"** during WWII has intensified debate on culpability. Nationalism is a lurking concern for the Japanese, who are wary of anything that resembles WWII rhetoric. Early in 2003, Koizumi created a stir when he visited the **Yasukuni Jinja,** a Shintō memorial to the war dead with strong historical links to nationalism and emperor worship. **Emperor Akihito,** however, himself a scientist and the first Japanese Emperor not to claim divine origins, has spoken against this nationalism. New Japanese heros are conquering the world in a different way; to the joy of Japanese fans, star players **Matsui Hideki, Suzuki Ichiro,** and **Nomo Hideo** have taken the American baseball scene by storm, while Japanese **anime** characters are gaining worldwide recognition.

PEOPLE

DEMOGRAPHICS

Long isolated from the outside world, the population of Japan is highly homogenous—as much as 99% of the population is ethnically **Japanese.** The homogen-

IN RECENT NEWS

THE JAPAN-BRAZIL CONNECTION

Brazil hosts the largest community of Japanese outside of Japan (about 7% of the Brazilian population is Japanese). Japan counts Brazilians as its third largest minority group. What connects the homes of samba and sushi, of Carnival and calligraphy?

Japanese immigrants began sailing for Brazil at the turn of the 20th century. The flow of Japanese to the United States had been halted by strained race relations and Teddy Roosevelt's "Gentleman's Agreement," but Brazilian coffee plantations offered ample work for Japanese laborers. About 1.3 million Japanese live in Brazil today.

In the 1980s, the flow reversed. Descendants and families of those immigrants—ethnically Japanese, but culturally Brazilian—returned to Japan to find relief from Brazil's severe recession by taking Japanese factory jobs. Japan, which had been supplying its booming job market with illegal immigrants from Southeast Asia, welcomed the chance to hire authentic "Japanese" instead, and, in 1990, recast its immigration laws to allow Brazilians of Japanese descent to work at unskilled jobs.

Currently, around 200,000 Japanese-Brazilians live in Japan. Perceived as foreigners by the Japanese despite their Asian ethnicity, they walk an intricate identity tightrope.

ity may make for a tight-knit, collectively responsible culture, but it also means that minorities experience more in the way of exclusion or discrimination than they might in a more diverse population.

Small numbers of **Koreans, Chinese, Ainu,** and, recently, **Brazilians** make up most of the minority population. Many of the Koreans came to Japan as laborers around WWII (not necessarily willingly) and couldn't return when the Korean War broke out. The Chinese (both mainlanders and Taiwanese) have trickled into the country since the 1500s; major Chinatowns can be found in Yokohama and Kōbe. The Ainu, native people from Hokkaidō, have largely become assimilated into mainstream Japanese culture, though a few traditional enclaves remain; the Japanese did not officially recognize them as a minority until 1990. The people of the Ryūkyū Islands (Okinawa) also often identify as a separate group.

LANGUAGE

Japan cultivated an oral tradition while isolated from the rest of the world. Consequently, linguists struggle to place the language within one linguistic family. Japan has been associated with the Altaic languages (including Turkish, Mongolian, and Korean; in this category, Japanese is most closely linked with Korean), and also with the languages of the South Pacific. Ainu, the indigenous language of northern Japan puzzles linguists even more, as it does not seem to relate to any other languages.

Because the island layout and mountain ranges segregated the Japanese from each other for so long, there have always been many dialects (hōgen; 方言) within the country. Starting with the transition from ancient to modern Japanese in the 12th century, a standard dialect was imposed on the nation in order to facilitate better communication. From this point, the country adopted the Tōkyō dialect, known as *hyōjungo* (標準語), as the norm, although many regions have maintained their distinct dialect while also learning the Tōkyō dialect. The standardized Japanese incorporates different social styles of speech; the highest form of social stratification through language is *keigo* (honorific speech; 警護).

Although the Japanese language may initially intimidate learners with its three-tier writing system and subtle pitch differences, it is actually an easy language for people to begin studying. Certain aspects of Japanese grammar distinguish it from European languages and make Japanese a simpler language to tackle as a beginner. In Japanese, verbs do not change according to singular or plural subjects. Pronouns are often left out of a sentence. There are no definite articles, and nouns will not change whether referring to singular or plural objects. However, a few conventions of Japanese are quite different from English. While English word order follows a Subject-Verb-Object pattern, Japanese sentences are typically Subject-Object-Verb: "Bashō wrote *haiku*" would be literally translated into Japanese as "Bashō *haiku* wrote." Also in contrast to English, the Japanese version of prepositions, known as particles, come after, not before, their objects. Thus "I am going to Tōkyō" becomes in Japanese "Watashi wa Tōkyō ni iki masu," which literally means "I Tōkyō to am going"; "ni" is the particle corresponding to "to."

Pronunciation of Japanese is not the most challenging feature of the language. Every character is always pronouced and given equal stress. The one exception to this rule is that when saying "desu" or "masu," the u drops off, so that the word sounds more like "des" or "mas." Although command of pitch requires a deeper grasp of the language, a new speaker can ignore the subtlety of pitch differentiation and still be understood by Japanese people. For a few words, pitch intonations can change the meaning of a word and result in funny, or awkward, conversation (*byōin* means both "hospital" and "hairdresser," separated only by the speaker's inflection). However, Japanese people tend to give foreigners the benefit of the doubt, and will usually overlook this type of error.

Travelers will discover that many Japanese people speak some English because the government mandates that all students study English for up to ten years. Tragically for English-speaking travelers, however, the focus of these lessons leans towards reading and writing, and not conversational skills. This emphasis, combined with many non-native speaking teachers, translates into a nation of people who possess literacy in English but struggle to carry on a simple conversation. However, with a little persistence and slow and careful pronunciation of words, English-speaking travelers should be able to find English-speaking Japanese to answer their questions.

Because so few foreigners and travelers take the time to learn any Japanese, if you prepare yourself with a few key phrases, or make any effort to learn the language, your investment will be deeply appreciated and rewarded by the Japanese with whom you interact. A simple "arigatō gozaimasu" (thank you very much) earns foreigners many smiles. If you do not have time to absorb any Japanese before traveling, it is possible to navigate parts of the country (especially more urban areas) by relying on **rōmaji** (the English transliteration of Japanese), which appears on many signs and menus.

THE WRITTEN SYSTEM

Japanese is written vertically, from right to left. Recently, the language also appears horizontally, from left to right. Japanese comprises three systems: hiragana, katakana, and kanji. Anyone seeking to master literacy must learn all of these systems and understand how to properly interweave them to communicate fluently. The first two writing systems, hiragana and katakana, enable students to express words phonetically, and both of these systems are constructed from five vowel sounds. All other sounds in the system are a combination of an English consonant and one of these vowel sounds (for example: with "m," ma, mi, mu, me, mo).

HIRAGANA (ひらがな). Loopy and curvy on the page, this system of 46 characters was initially developed by women in the Heian court, but today serves as the most basic tool to write Japanese. Hiragana builds on five basic vowel sounds:

あ	**a** as in f**a**ther
い	**i** as in mach**i**ne
う	**u** as in tr**u**th
え	**e** as in p**e**nalty
お	**o** as in n**o**

The rest of the characters can be described as an English consonant proceeded by one of these five vowel sounds. The one exception to this summary is the very last hiragana character, ん , pronounced "nn." As this is the first writing system that elementary kids learn in school, beginner level books are usually written in only hiragana. Many times, even higher level books filled with complex ideograms will have **furigana** (振り仮名), the pronunciation of difficult or rare ideograms, printed in hiragana above, or to the right of, the character. Although hiragana can express any sound in Japanese, its primary purpose is to write simple words, conjugations at the end of verbs, and particles of speech.

KATAKANA (カタカナ). The angular lines of this writing system, formerly used by males to the exclusion of hiragana, render katakana sometimes easier than hiragana for foreigners to learn. As with hiragana, 46 characters compose katakana, and these are all based on the same original vowel sounds. Every hiragana character has a katakana counterpart, but katakana characters are employed to write different kinds of words. Katakana is used when writing foreigners' names, borrowed foreign words, company names, and new Japanese words.

KANJI (漢字). The most complicated of the three systems, kanji (ideograms) were introduced to Japan by Buddhist monks. There are tens of thousands of Chinese ideograms incorporated in the Japanese language, although command of only two thousand will equip you with the knowledge to read a newspaper. While many of the ideograms resemble their Chinese counterparts, some have been altered and simplified over the centuries. Each ideogram represents an idea, and not necessarily just one sound, as do the hiragana and katakana characters. Ideograms usually have more than one reading, one taken from the original Chinese pronunciation and others created by the Japanese. The correct reading of an ideogram is determined by the context of the word in which the character is used or the sentence in which it is placed.

RELIGION

Religion in Japan takes a very different form from Western religion, primarily because none of the major religions has been exclusive of any of the others. For centuries a great pluralism existed, resulting in a great deal of interchange between Shintō, Buddhism, and Confucianism, each influencing a different aspect of society. Buddhism is the only religion whose modern adherents often claim it as their only faith: 84% of Japanese identify themselves as Shintō-Buddhist, while many others consider themselves to be areligious participants in Shintō customs. Although there is a small group of devout Christians in Japan, Christian influence has been largely superficial in wider society.

SHINTŌ. Shintō, literally "the way of the gods," is a belief system native to Japan. It did not become an organized practice until the mid-19th century; until that time Shintō had been a highly localized religion of **kami** and **ancestor worship**. According to Shintō, the human spirit never disappears, although it loses its substantiated form after death. Shintō is not nature worship; although there is no clear distinction between material and spiritual existence, *kami* worship does not entail a divinization of nature itself, but rather an awe for forces and objects of nature with a particularly impressive influence over life. The *kami*, closely linked with these natural features and forces, are spirits, not gods in the omniscient, omnipotent Judeo-Christian/Islamic sense; *kami* are highly compatible with other religions. During the classical period the *kami* were seen as guardians of the Buddha, although later the Buddha was considered the manifestation of *kami*.

Shintō has no doctrine or religious texts, although myths are retold in the classical works *Kojiki, Nihonshoki,* and *Manyoshu* (p. 99). During the pre-war era, Shintō was used by the state to garner popular support and justify expansion. The most famous Shintō term in the West is **kamikaze**: the name for the suicidal WWII pilots literally means "divine wind." Until the Japanese defeat in 1945, worshipping the emperor, believed to be descended from the sun goddess Amaterasu Ōmikami, was central to Shintō.

Today, believers value "uprightness, righteousness," "purity of the heart," and the worship of *kami*. Shintō is practiced at shrines, the most important of which is the **Grand Shrine at Ise** (p. 470) where Amaterasu is enshrined. **Purification** of the hands and mouth (*temizu;* 手水) was required of all shrine visitors before the war, but today participation is optional. Using a scoop, visitors pour water from the covered stone basin at the entrance of the shrine into the right hand, then the left. Worshippers next put some water in their mouths and spit it out into the gutter below the basin. The next step is the **offering**, usually a ¥5 coin placed in the collection box, and the **prayer**. Ringing the bell once summons the *kami*, followed by two deep bows, two claps at chest level, and a final bow. In performing the ritual, it is believed that one approaches the way of the *kami*. Priests, male and female since the war, care for shrines and perform rites.

Also important to the practice of Shintō are the many festivals held throughout the year. The two most important are the **New Year**, when people visit a shrine, and **Obon**, a holiday of ancestor worship with strong Buddhist elements (p. 106).

BUDDHISM. Buddhism was founded in India during the 6th century BC by Siddhartha Gautama, a member of a wealthy family who became disillusioned with his privileged life and troubled by world's suffering. Renouncing his home and upbringing, he took up the life of a wandering ascetic. While meditating beneath the bodhi tree, he arrived at a complete understanding of the **Four Noble Truths** regarding the nature of suffering, its cause, its cessation, and the way leading to its cessation. With the cessation of suffering, **nirvana** or enlightenment is achieved.

Buddhism first entered Japan through China and Korea during the 7th and 8th centuries AD. The dominant strain of Buddhism practiced throughout East Asia is called **Mahayana** or **"Greater Vehicle"** Buddhism. With the exception of Shingon, all Japanese sects fall under the Mahayana rubric. Of the earliest Japanese sects, three—**Ritsu, Hossō,** and **Kegon**—survive to the present day and still have their headquarters in Nara. These have been superseded, however, by the more influential schools of Tendai, Pure Land, Nichiren, Zen, and Shingon Buddhism. **Tendai** Buddhism is the Japanese counterpart to Chinese Tient'ai Buddhism, brought to Japan during the 8th century by the monk Saichō, later known as Dengyō Daishi. Tendai Buddhists take the **Lotus Sutra** as their central text, and their rituals combine influences from different Chinese sects. Today the Tendai headquarters are at **Mount Hiei** (p. 427), near Kyōto, where Saichō built his first temple.

Modern Japanese Buddhist practices vary widely, from austere *zazen* meditation to elaborate Shingon rituals to the different devotional chants of Nichirenites and Pure Land Buddhists. **Meditation,** a central aspect of any Buddhist practice, is most heavily emphasized in **Zen** Buddhism. Chinese Ch'an Buddhism reached Japan in the 12th and 13th centuries and developed into the current Rinzai and Soto schools of Zen. The military class in *samurai* Japan favored Zen for its emphasis on discipline. *Zazen* meditation requires long periods of sitting with correct posture, breathing naturally, and stilling the mind. Sometimes the practitioner meditates on **koan,** short riddles or puzzles; one of the most famous is: "What is the sound of one hand clapping?"

Although some have dubbed Buddhism an "atheist" religion, many Buddhists worship Buddhas as deity-like figures. One example of devotional Buddhism is the **Pure Land** or **Jōdo-shu** school, whose adherents venerate the Amida Buddha by reciting the *nembutsu*, or the phrase *namu amida butsu* ("Hail to Amida Buddha"). By putting their faith in the power of Amida to save mankind, they hope to be reborn in the Pure Land where none of the hindrances of this world will prevent them from achieving *nirvana*. **Nichiren** Buddhists have their own chant: *namu myōhō renge kyō* ("Hail to the Lotus Sutra"). Born in the 13th century as a movement seeking to restore the purity of original Tendai teachings, Nichiren Buddhists often denounce other Buddhist sects as heretical.

Founded in the 8th century by Kūkai, now known as Kobo Daishi, **Shingon** is a form of esoteric Buddhism that makes use of elaborate rituals. By meditating on images and performing hand gestures (mudras) and chants (mantras) in rigid

LIFE & TIMES

sequences, Shingon followers hope to bring themselves closer to oneness with Vairocana, the cosmic Buddha, of whom Siddhartha Gautama was one incarnation. Because the truth of Vairocana cannot be expressed in language, Shingon relies heavily on artistic representations of truth, called *mandalas*, for use in meditation. This sect enjoys wide popularity in Japan, and thousands of adherents make the pilgrimage to Mount Kōya in Wakayama Prefecture every year (p. 467).

CHRISTIANITY. Portugese missionaries, including **St. Francis Xavier,** first introduced **Catholicism** to Japan in the 16th century. In its monotheistic exclusivism, Christianity is fundamentally different from Shintō and the native versions of Buddhism, and although there were quite a number of converts, culture clash won out; Christianity was outlawed in 1615, and thousands of Christians were gruesomely executed. For hundreds of years, **crypto-Christians** lived in the Nagasaki area until they were "discovered" in 1865 by a French Catholic missionary.

Around the same time, **Protestant** and **Russian Orthodox** missionaries also came knocking. The Westerners founded many churches and schools, including **Sophia Univeristy,** but couldn't maintain large congregations; many new Japanese sects split off from the Western church. Today, practicing Christians make up less than 1% of Japan's population, but Christmas is a popular secular holiday, and Christian-style weddings are in high fashion.

CULTURE

FOOD AND DRINK

For the Japanese, eating has never been about self-sustenance. Its second priority is the continuation of life; its first is to serve as an art form. Nowhere else will you find so much attention given to detail, presentation, and flavor. A visitor need only glance at the oodles of dishes, in infinite shapes and sizes, to understand the art of Japanese food, and to understand why the dishwasher never infiltrated Japanese kitchens. Unfortunately, because of the popularization of certain Japanese foods (namely sushi and tempura) as elements of Western cuisine, many foreigners believe that this in fact is all Japanese people eat. Experimenting with the full spectrum of Japanese foods will forever alter your conception of eating.

FREQUENTLY SEEN RESTAURANTS. Most restaurants in Japan are specialty restaurants, serving only one genre of food. However, for a general assortment of food, the Japanese eat in **shokudō** (食堂) or **family restaurants** (famirī resutoran; ファミリーレストラン). Located around train stations and touristed areas, *shokudō*, the English equivalent of cafeterias, serve standard Japanese and Western dishes at cheap prices. *Shokudō* find their Westernized and commercialized sister-type in **family restaurants** (Denny's, Jonathon's), which serve a similar combination of Japanese and Western dishes at low prices. Another option in Japan for variety food restaurants is an **izakaya** (居酒屋). Frequented by salarymen seeking a release from perpetual overtime work, *izakaya* provide a menu of small, single-serving dishes and infinite amounts of alcohol. Prices vary considerably depending on the grade of *izakaya*; some are extremely cheap and casual, while others will quickly drain large sums of your money for comparatively small dishes. At night, an *izakaya* will swell with the shouts of happy, rowdy crowds, marked by the synchronized toasts of company gatherings. Although **yakitori-ya** advertise a more specialized menu, they serve as a space for social gatherings in the same way as *izakaya*. You can expect myriad options of what to grill on a skewer, ranging from the traditional chicken (**yakitori,** 焼き鳥) to chicken livers and giblets (**tori kimo yaki,** 鳥肝焼き) to Japanese mushrooms (**shītake,** しいたけ).

SUSHI. A trip to Japan would not be complete without a night at a **sushi-ya** (すし 屋). *Sushi-ya* also fluctuate in price, but it is possible to spend hundreds of dollars on a sushi eating excursion. However, don't let extravagant prices deter you. It is worth some investigating and investing to treat yourself to a transcendental sensory experience at a *sushi-ya*. For an equally character-building (but cheaper) experience, try a **kaiten-zushi-ya,** where sushi dishes parade by you on a conveyor belt from which you can pluck your food of choice.

NOODLES. According to many Japanese, **soba-ya** (そば屋) and **rāmen-ya** (ラーメ ン屋) capture the essence of Japanese eating. Littered throughout Japan, at every train station and in every alley, *soba-ya* and *rāmen-ya* are this nation's favorites for breakfast, lunch, snack, dinner, and even late-night eating. In the morning, time-strapped salarymen will cram into tiny *soba-ya* and *rāmen-ya*, and while standing, slurp a bowl of noodles before hustling off to work.

SPECIALTY RESTAURANTS. Although it is possible to eat *karē* (Japanese curry) at many places besides a **karē-ya,** this specialty restaurant offers a wider variety of this Japanese staple food. Similarly, even though a menu might include a *tonkatsu* dish, it is also common to encounter a **tonkatsu-ya** which serves just *tonkatsu*. While some people like to compare **okonomiyaki** with a Western pancake, it is difficult to draw such parallels while reconciling the difference in flavor and ingredients between the concoction of the West and the islands of Japan. At an **okonomiyaki-ya,** the chef will either cook your *okonomiyaki* in front of you, or you will have the thrill of cooking your own *okonomiyaki* on a grill at your table. With its thick batter and vegetable or meat toppings, an *okonomiyaki* will fill your stomach and stave off hunger for a long time.

Other specialty restaurants include, but are not limited to, **tempura-ya** (extensive menu of *tempura* meals, usually served with white rice or noodles), **unagi-ya** (often serve only *unagi*, or eel, prepared in a sweet soy sauce and placed on a box-shaped container of rice), **sukiyaki-ya** (features *sukiyaki* or *shabu-shabu*, both dishes which you cook at the table, using a pot, meat, and vegetables), and a plethora of **foreign food restaurants.** Despite a long history of isolation, Japan imbibes and incorporates elements of other cultures with remarkable fluidity. Often, the Japanized version of another country's culture seems an improvement from the original, but so expect a different flavor at the numerous **Italian, French, Chinese, ethnic** (Southeast Asian), **yōshoku** (Western food), and **yakiniku** (Korean style barbeque; meat is cooked on a grill at the table) restaurants.

A QUICK BITE. Kissaten (coffee shops), a prevalent Japanese establishment, surround every train station and dot the country's landscape. A cup of coffee or a soft drink can be expensive at a *kissaten*, sometimes costing as much as US$7 for a drink. You will usually find single-serving cakes or other light foods at a *kissaten*. Japanese cakes are constructed with great delicacy and embellished with intricate designs. Despite the elaborate appearance of these cakes, people who are not accustomed to the subtle flavor might find the Japanese interpretation of Western dessert not sweet enough and unfulfilling. **Yatai** and **rotensho,** food stalls that pop up at every festival in Japan, sometimes camp out by train stations for hungry passersby. These stalls will sell anything from chocolate-covered bananas to battered and grilled octopus (**tako-yaki;** たこ焼き).

THE ULTIMATE EATING EXPERIENCE. The zenith of Japanese food is **kaiseki ryōri,** a multi-course meal of traditional Japanese food. Each course is small, allowing the diner to reflect on minutia, from the placeware in which the dish is served to the symbolism of each food. The unifying theme of all the dishes that comprise the *kaiseki* meal often corresponds to the season. *Kaiseki ryōri* is expensive, starting around ¥10,000.

LIFE & TIMES

FOOD

Essentials

ご飯	gohan	A bowl of sticky white rice will accompany most Japanese meals. Although occasionally served with the main dish, it is more traditional to eat the rice at the very end of the meal, with *tsukemono* and *miso* soup.
漬け物	tsukemono	Pickled vegetables; either very salty or sweet; usually eaten at the end of a meal with rice.
味噌汁	miso shiru	*Miso* soup—made with *miso* paste; usually contains tofu, seaweed (wakame), and sometimes onions, *daikon*, potatoes, or carrots.

Rice Dishes (gohan ryōri; ご飯料理)

どんぶり	domburi	A bowl of rice topped with a variety of foods.
かつ丼	katsu-don	A bowl of rice with tonkatsu on top.
牛丼	gyū-don	A bowl of rice with beef on top.
親子丼	oyako-don	A bowl of rice with egg and chicken on top.
おにぎり	onigiri	A triangular rice ball, usually salted and wrapped in seaweed, containing anything from *umeboshi* (pickled plum) to tuna.
カレーラ イス	karê raisu	A Japanese version of curry rice; gravy sauce, thicker than Indian curry, with beef, chicken, or vegetables, poured over rice.

Fish Dishes (sakana ryōri; 魚料理)

刺身	sashimi	Raw fish. Although travelers should always be cautious when consuming anything uncooked, it is fairly safe to eat sashimi in Japan.
焼き	yakizakana	Grilled fish.
うな重	unajū	Marinated in a sweet soy sauce, charcoal-broiled and served on rice, this eel is considered a delicacy in Japan. For those travelers repulsed by the tanks of swimming eel displayed in front of most eel restaurants, it might still be worth accompanying friends there just for the rice, flavored with eel and sauce.
塩焼き	shio-yaki	Salted and broiled fish.
煮魚	ni-zakana	Fish prepared in soy sauce.

Noodle Dishes (menrui; 麺類)

うどん	udon	Thick flour noodles, in a hot or cold broth; can be topped with meats or vegetables.
そば	soba	Thin buckwheat noodles; also served in a hot or cold broth and topped with meats or vegetables.
ラーメン	râmen	Chinese noodles, hot or cold (*hiyashi chūka;* 冷やし中華).
そうめん	sômen	Thin wheat noodles with a sauce (*tsuyu*). Served cold as a summer dish.
焼きそば	yakisoba	Fried noodles mixed with meat, cabbage, and other vegetables.

Nabe Dishes (nabe ryōri; dishes prepared in a thick pot; 鍋料理)

おでん	oden	Fish cakes, *daikon* (and other vegetables), and *konyaku* boiled in a soy sauce and fish-based broth.
すき焼き	sukiyaki	Thinly sliced meat, vegetables, konyaku noodles (*shirataki*), and tofu are prepared in a pot (you can choose to dip these in a beaten egg).
しゃぶ しゃぶ	shabu-shabu	Japanese hot-pot; thinly sliced meat, vegetables, and tofu are briefly immersed in boiling water, then dipped in vinegar or sesame sauce.
ちゃんこ なべ	chanko nabe	The traditional meal of sumo wrestlers, containing tofu, cabbage, and other vegetables.

Meat Dishes (肉料理 ; niku ryōri)

焼き鳥	yakitori	Grilled chicken skewers, marinated in a sweet soy sauce (yakitori sauce). It is possible to have yakitori of numerous types—a range of meats and vegetables—all grilled on skewers.
とんかつ	tonkatsu	Breaded pork cutlets, deep fried and served with rice and cabbage.
肉じゃが	nikujaga	Meat and potatoes, Japanese style, boiled in a sweet soy sauce.

FOOD

Condiments

しょうゆ	shōyu	Soy sauce.
わさび	wasabi	Horseradish.
とんかつ ソース	tonkatsu sosu	Worcestershire sauce.

Fruits (kudamono; 果物)			**Vegetable Dishes** (yasai ryōri; 野菜料理)		
バナナ	banana	Banana.	かぼちゃ	kabocha	Pumpkin.
りんご	ringo	Apple.	ほうれん草	hōrenso	Spinach.
ぶどう	budō	Grapes.	たまねぎ	tamanegi	Onions.
いちご	ichigo	Strawberries.	たけのこ	takenoko	Bamboo shoots.
もも	momo	Peach.	大根	daikon	*Daikon* radish.
メロン	meron	Melon.	きのこ	kinoko	Mushrooms.
栗	kuri	Chestnuts.	いも	imo	Potato.
オレンジ	orenji	Orange.	きゅうり	kyūri	Cucumber.
レモン	remon	Lemon.	野菜いため	yasai itame	Stir-fried vegetables.
すいか	sulka	Watermelon.	サラダ	sarada	Salad.

DRINKS

Travelers will find that the Japanese have cooked up an array of drinks, and are constantly experimenting to create new ones to add to the market. More popular drinks include *oolong* tea (**ūron-cha;** ウーロン茶) and barley tea (**mugi-cha;** 麦茶), sports drinks like **Pocari Sweat,** milk-based drinks like **Calpis Water** (say it aloud, it's fun), coffee drinks, and a variety of sodas. Recent concern with weight and health, especially among women, has provoked the production of drinks geared towards a more health-conscious consumer. Teas have been revived as a drink with slimming effects. There is always a new drink on the market, riding a wave of weight-loss propaganda until disenchantment wins out. The Japanese also imbibe their share of alcoholic drinks, some of which are unique to the country. The standard drink is a *nama biiru* (**draft beer,** 生ビール). Japan is also a country of **sake** drinkers; most drink menus include warm and cold sake, **ume-shu** (梅酒 ; a *sake*-based drink flavored with *ume*, or pickled plum), or **remon-shu** (レモン酒 ; a *sake*-based drink flavored with lemon). Although the drinking age is 20, travelers will discover that this is not a strict drinking age.

> **YOU CAN BUY IT IN A VENDING MACHINE.** Visitors to Japan may be surprised by the bazillions of vending machines and the multitude of goodies sold in them. Without further introduction, *Let's Go* provides this helpful list of things you can buy with that last handful of yen: soda, juice, coffee, tea, vitamin drinks, beer, sake, cigarettes, rice, disposable cameras, film, CDs, candy, gum, ice cream, snacks, bread, cup noodles, hot dogs, stamps, postcards, batteries, newspapers, herbal remedies, pornography, sex toys, fortunes, hot meals, pearl jewelry, paperbacks, fresh flowers, fast food, condoms, eggs, boxer shorts, vegetables, video games, and pajamas.

LIFE & TIMES

CUSTOMS AND ETIQUETTE

A complex web of rules guide the Japanese in their interactions with others. Fortunately for the traveler, the Japanese understand that foreigners cannot possibly know the axioms by which natives govern their lives, and sincerely appreciate foreigners' efforts to practice the customs of Japan. As long as you demonstrate respect, do not be afraid of trying things and making a mistake; remember that it is important to be able to laugh at yourself. The downside to this forgiving attitude is that a foreigner will find it difficult to absolve himself of his status as an outsider.

NEVER STOP BOWING. The Japanese greet everyone—from extended family members to friends to colleagues to superiors—with a bow. As a foreigner, it might feel awkward, but after enough tries, a bow can morph into an intrinsic gesture. The depth and duration of the bow correspond with the participants' relative status (a deeper bow means an inferioir position). For an interesting sociological study, check out a bowing marathon between two elderly women who have run into each other in the street. When you are introduced to someone for the first time, say, **"Hajimemashite. Yoroshiku onegai shimasu"** or **"Korekara osewa ni narimasu."** (Loose translation: "Pleased to meet you.") When you part, if you have been treated kindly or helped, say **"Domo, osewa ni narimashita"** and bow.

Bowing does not take place only when two people initially meet. Bowing is an ingrained movement of the body, and one that you will observe eveywhere you turn while in Japan. The Japanese bow to express innumerable feelings, and this action can serve as an important tool throughout your gallant exploration of Japan. Bow when you say hello; bow when you part; bow when you want to apologize; bow when you are accepting a compliment; bow when you want to say thank you; bow when you enter or exit a room; bow when you know not what else to do; just bow.

NAME CALLING. Japanese people refer to others by using their last name and the suffix "-san" (the equivalent of the English Ms./Mrs./Mr.). Do not use "-san" when talking about yourself or people very close to you (family members or close friends). Continue addressing Japanese people by their last name, plus *san*, unless someone insists that you call them otherwise. Children, very good friends, and pets can be called by their last or first name and the diminutive suffix "-chan."

PUNCTUALITY IS THE SOUL OF WIT. When making arrangements to rendez-vous with other Japanese, remember that Japan is an extremely time-sensitive country. **Do not be late.** In fact, it is a good idea to be early, as many Japanese people consider it normal to show up five or ten minutes early to any engagement. Because the Japanese transportation system provides reliable, punctual services, it is possible for people to plan their travel down to the minute to ensure prompt arrival at the desired destination. If a train is running behind schedule, meaning more than a minute late, an announcer will apologize profusely for the inconvenience; for delays in the morning, train stations will print and distribute "late passes" for company workers to hand into the boss-man to legitimize tardiness.

LET YOUR FEET BREATHE. In Japan, people will always remove their shoes whenever moving from outdoors to indoors. Whenever you enter someone's house, or any building where you see that people have taken off their shoes, **take your shoes off as well.** There will either be a **genkan** (front entrance) where you can remove and leave your shoes, or cubbies or lockers in which you can place your shoes. Normally, slippers will be provided for you to wear once you have taken off your shoes. Note that if you use a bathroom, there will be a separate pair of slippers waiting just inside the door, so remove your general indoor slippers before entering the bathroom and switch into the new pair for your time in the bathroom.

If you enter a *tatami* room, remove your shoes (or slippers) and do not put anything else on. When traveling in Japan, you will be required to remove your shoes numerous times a day. For this reason, it is a good idea to **buy a pair of shoes that you can slip on and off very easily** before your trip. Laces, high boots, or anything complicated will hobble your mobility and graceful style.

IN THE BATHTUB. A far cry from Western-style baths, Japanese bathtubs will make you swoon. Once you immerse yourself in this bathing experience, you will never be able to return to the days of steeping in your own filth. In order to fully appreciate the Japanese bath experience (and not violate some of the most entrenched Japanese traditions), heed our advice. First, **never ever, ever get in the bath without washing your body first.** Whether you are bathing in someone's house, a public bath house, or a classy *onsen* resort, there will always be a station for you to clean yourself before entering the actual bath. If you are at a public bath house or *onsen*, there will be rows of individual stations, all with a small stool, a bucket, some cleansing products, and a faucet and detachable shower head. Fill the bucket with hot water, douse the stool, and then plop yourself down and scrub-a-dub-dub. Do not feel self-conscious about being naked. If you look around, you will notice that *everyone else in the room is naked as well*. After you have washed yourself, give the stool a final douse to clean it off for the next person, and then make your way over to the bath. Be careful, because **floors are slippery when wet,** and these floors are inherently wet. Many people like to rinse off with water at one of the washing stations before leaving.

If you are in the bathtub of someone's house, the setup will be exactly the same, *sans* all of the strangers. It is still important that you wash yourself before getting into the bathtub because a Japanese family will draw the bath once for the day, and everyone will use that water for his or her bath. There will be a folding cover for the bathtub, so when you leave the bath, make sure you place the cover back over the tub in order to keep the water warm for those coming in after you.

MORE ON ONSEN. *Onsen* are often the feature attraction at ryokan or *onsen* resorts. When staying at one of these places, you will be provided with a *yukata* (light Japanese robe) and small hand towel. You can either change into the *yukata* in your room and make your way to the bath in this robe, or you can undress in the dressing room by the baths. The dressing room will often have larger towels, and you can use the small hand towel for washing, or, for the more demure, covering parts of your body. Today, many, but not all, baths are segregated by gender—look for the 女 symbol for the women's entrance, and 男 for the men's.

EATING. When eating at a restaurant or in someone's home, the Japanese maintain the same level of politeness and cleanliness that they exercise in every other sphere of life. Before eating, people say **"Itadakimasu"** (I will eat), and when they are done with the meal, **"Gochisō sama deshita"** (That was a feast). Although many restaurants and homes use forks and knives, at times you will be confronted with only chopsticks (hashi), and it will be up to you to deliver the food from your plate to your mouth with these tools. The good news is that when eating out of bowls (rice, soup, noodles), it is customary, to lift the bowl to your mouth in order to drink the soup or gracefully shovel the food directly into your mouth. If you are using your chopsticks to pick food off a plate and transport it to your mouth, you might consider using your other hand cupped as a safety net under the chopsticks, so that any falling food will be caught in your hand, and not by your lap. It is important that you **do not stick chopsticks upright in your rice bowl,** and also that you **do not pass food from your chopsticks to another person's chopsticks,** as both of these actions are taboos of Buddhist tradition. **When taking food from a communal plate, you should use the other end of your chopsticks,** so as not to spread germs.

DINING OUT. When entering a restaurant, a chorus of **"Irasshaimase"** (Welcome!) will often greet you, followed by **"Nanmei sama desuka"** (how many people are in your party?). You can respond using your fingers, or you could brave **"[Number] mei desu."** Once you are seated, a waitstaff will bring you water or tea and **oshibori** (hot or cold hand towels). The *oshibori* is intended for your hands, and not for you to give yourself a scrubbing in the middle of the restaurant. Men and small children might be able to get away with a forehead wipe, especially during the summer, but most Japanese keep the towels to their hands.

Japanese do not keep napkins at the table, and unless you are in an upper-end Western restaurant, you will probably not find any cloth napkins adorning the tables. The reason for this is threefold: first, the Japanese are incredibly resource-conscious, and do not see the point in wasting limited supplies, and second, the Japanese value cleanliness. They are neat eaters who make sure that everything makes it into their mouths and few crumbs are left on the table. Third, it is customary for the Japanese to carry around handkerchiefs, and so if spillage does occur, people are equipped to clean up themselves.

When ordering, if you cannot read or speak Japanese, there are alternatives to the pointing and praying approach. First, you can ask for an English menu: **"Eigo no menu ga arimasuka."** If the response is negative, hope that there's a display case in the front of the restaurant filled with plastic models of the dishes. This display case just might become your best friend. If the first two options fall through, you might ask for the set meal (teishoku) and hope that you like the dishes included.

Although select restaurants will include a service charge on the bill, most restaurants do not, and **you do not need to tip.** As you exit, you can bow and say, **"Gochiso sama deshita,"** to be polite.

DRINKING. When you go out drinking with Japanese people, always fill other people's drinks and never fill your own glass. Someone will notice your empty glass and fill it for you. Before a round of drinks, it is customary to lift glasses and exclaim, *"Kanpai!"*

IF YOU ARE NOT STANDING, YOU MUST BE... Sitting. While in Japan, prepare yourself for sitting in small chairs or sitting on the floor. Although this should not pose a problem for most people, if you are very tall or have exceptionally long legs, then you might find yourself uncomfortable at some restaurants. *Sēza*, the traditional Japanese way of sitting, requires people to kneel with their legs tucked underneath them. As this will grow increasingly uncomfortable, and as you might sense impending paralysis if you stay in this position for too long, it is acceptable, especially for foreigners, to shift as needed.

TRADING CARDS. Japanese people love their **meishi** (business cards) and will love to collect yours. Be sure to have a stack with you on your travels, and always carry some around with you when you are out. When giving a *meishi*, use both hands, bow, and hand the *meishi* so that the receiver can read it. When receiving a *meishi*, bow, and accept it with both hands. If you put the *meishi* away in front of the giver, make sure that you store it someplace safe and protected. Do not just jam it into your back pocket. If you exchange *meishi* simultaneously, then take the *meishi* with one hand, while offering your *meishi* with the other (make sure it's facing away from you), and bow.

GIVE A LITTLE, LOVE A LITTLE. Gift-giving is supremely important, and when in doubt, it is always safer to buy a gift than to not. **When invited to a person's house, always arrive with a gift.** This can be something simple—fruit, flowers, cookies, or a cake—but it is important that you remember not to show up empty-handed. There are usually department stores (check out the basement level), supermarkets, or fruit or flower shops close to a train station, so you should always be able to find someplace convenient that sells an appropriate gift. If you go on a trip while staying at a Japanese person's house or while working in a Japanese office, remember to bring back a gift. Expect the recipients of the gift to enthusiastically refuse it, sometimes repeatedly, before finally accepting the offering. When you present someone with a gift, you should downplay its value. If you are the recipient of a gift, you should likewise refuse to accept it, and then finally acquiesce, while expressing exuberant gratitude for the present. It is not customary to open gifts in front of the giver, so if it is food or something else that should be opened immediately, you should inform the receiver.

People generally give money (cash) in an envelope for weddings and funerals. As there is an established money-giving hierarchy, ask someone how much money a person of your relationship is expected to give.

THE ARTS

The Japanese aesthetic sense is often explained in terms difficult to translate into Western equivalents, for example—*wabi* (unassuming, simple); *sabi* (rustic, imperfect, serene); *shibui* (refined, tasteful, quiet); *yungen* (mysterious, subtle); and *fura* (beauty in nature). On the other hand, recent years have seen *manga* (comic books), anime, film, and contemporary music flooding onto the international scene in a Japan-pop explosion that requires no translation.

HISTORY

The earliest examples of Japanese art are pottery and clay figures (of animals and humans) from the Jōmon Period, followed by the geometric-design-etched red-clay figures of the Yayoi. But things really got moving with the arrival of Buddhism (p. 89), when architecture and sculpture accelerated in response to the need for temples and images. The Nara Period is known as the "Golden Age of Buddhist Art"; it was also the age of Chinese influence, as everyone marveled at (and copied) the accomplishments of the mighty Tang Dynasty. The Heian Era brought Shingon Buddhism (p. 89), which was less about aesthetics than iconography—the artists prioritized "correct representation" over objective beauty.

Art of the Kamakura Period grew more realistic, imbued with a *samurai* ethos. Muromachi art is said to mark the first appearance of the artistic values traditionally thought of as Japanese—simplicity, subtlety, restraint, and miniaturization among them. The Edo Period featured development in painting and crafts, while modern art has been marked by Western influence and a desire to create a hybrid Japanese art. One constant through the ages has been a sensitivity to the aesthetic possiblities of nature and to the harmony of human interaction with it.

FINE ARTS. The arrival of Buddhism created a need for iconography, and **sculpture** flourished in the 6th and 7th centuries. The "Golden Era" of the late Nara Period, however, produced the most realistic and graceful sculptures, and marked a branching out from wood and bronze to lacquer and clay as materials. In the early Heian, Shingon Buddhist sculptures returned to bulky, less realistic forms, while the Kamakura Period featured bold and lifelike *samurai*-inspired works.

Painting became important during the Heian as Buddhists created expressive **mandalas** (diagrams of the spiritual world), and the **yamoto-e** ("Japanese-style") form of painting appeared. Landscape painting and narrative scroll paintings also

LIFE & TIMES

ARCHITECTURE'S GREATEST HITS

Your first temple will be thrilling; your second shrine fascinating. But after a week or two of sightseeing, many travelers complain of architectural overload. *Let's Go's* primer aspires to enhance your appreciation of that umpteenth pagoda...or to assuage your guilt about skipping it.

• **Shintō shrines** are erected in areas where **kami** (deities) are thought to dwell, and are meant to be unobtrusive and integrated with their natural surroundings. The first shrines were no shrines at all—just nature and a rope marker. Now there are numerous styles of shrine, but no standard form. A **torii** gate stands before a shrine, indicating the lantern-lined path leading to the shrine itself. A pair of **guardian lions** (*komainu*) stand guard either at the gate or in front of the **main hall** (*honden*); at the entrance, you'll find a basin (*chozuya*), at which you can rinse your hands and mouth. Some of Japan's most famous shrines are **Shinmei** (at Ise Shrine; p. 470), **Izumo-Taisha** (near Matsue, p. 516), **Meiji-jingu** (p. 159), and **Yasukuni-jinja** (p. 162).

• If it's flamboyant, ornate or monumental, however, it's most likely a **Buddhist temple**. When Buddhism hopped the pond, it brought a characteristic architecture with it. The typical temple complex includes an earthen wall with **gate,** a **main hall** (kondō), a **lecture hall** (kōdō), a **bell tower** (shōrō), a **sutra depository** (kyōzō), a **pagoda** (tō), and auxiliary buildings to serve the monks and nuns who lived there (dormitories, dining halls). The **pagoda**, originally at the center of the complex, is adapted from the Indian *stupa*, and stores relics of the Buddha. Over time, however, the focus of these temples changed, and, by the Nara Period, it was the **main hall** and the objects for worship it contained that stood at the center. Still later, the arrival of Zen Buddhism emphasized a temple style that was elaborate, symmetrical, and strictly laid-out. Japan's oldest temple is **Horyu-ji,** near Nara (p. 454); other worthy examples are the complexes in **Kamakura** (p. 219), **Nikkō** (p. 259), **Kyōto** (p. 392), and at **Eihei-ji** (p. 376).

• Mostly remnants from the 16th and 17th centuries' squabbles, Japan's **castles** come in three styles—the **mountaintop castle** (*yamajiro*), the **flatland-mountain castle** (*hirayamajiro*), and the **flatland castle** (*hirajiro*). The earliest castles, like **Gifu-jō** (p. 386), are of the mountaintop variety, depending on their location more than their architecture for defense against would-be attackers. At some point, however, daimyo traded natural defenses for fewer stairs, erecting mid-level castles on low mountains or hills; **Himeji-jō** (p. 476) is a typical example. The flatland castle represents the greatest development of defensive walls and moats and was all the rage in the early Edo Period. **Ōsaka-jō** (p. 436) was the first; **Nagoya-jō** (p. 383) and **Matsumoto-jō** (p. 337) are other good specimens. The main structure of every castle is the **donjon**, or main keep; the mess of walls, gates, moats, fortifications, and storehouses that surround it are meant to protect it. Should you manage to breach all those defenses and find yourself inside, don't expect European-style sumptuousness—Japan's castles were strategic military sites, not living spaces, and the Spartanly-appointed interiors show it. For a more comprehensive guide to Japan's castle culture, point your browser to www.obershawonline.com/castle/index.html.

• Though Japan has a rich architectural history, the sights a traveler encounters are too often **replicas** and **reconstructions**. A penchant for natural disasters, coupled with a war-torn past and a predilection for tearing down and rebuilding shrines every 20 years or so (p. 470), have been hard on the furniture.

came into vogue. **Sumi-e,** or Chinese ink painting, arrived during the Muromachi Period. **Ukiyo-e** paintings, perhaps Japan's most recognizable form, were an Edo innovation—originally paintings of the "floating world" (the pleasures of the common people), the school soon turned to woodcuts to satisfy popular demand.

LITERATURE. Japanese literary history begins in the 8th century AD, with the adoption of the Chinese writing system (p. 88). The oldest surviving prose work, the **Record of Ancient Matters** *(Kōjiki)* dates to 712; the historically important **Chronicle of Japan** *(Nihonshoki)* was composed around 720. With the Chinese language came Chinese influence, and early literary works owe a considerable debt to the **Chinese classics.** Japan's first **novel** is said to be **The Tale of the Bamboo Cutter** *(Taketori Monogatari)*, written around 811. Women penned the most important works of the Heian court—Murasaki Shikibu's **Tale of Genji** *(Genji Monogatari)* is a hefty (54-volume) classic work, documenting a nostalgia for things past, while critical Sei Shonagon listed "Annoying Things," "Hateful Things," and hundreds of other things in her disarmingly modern **Pillow Book** *(Makura no Soshi)*.

In the 13th century, history and literature took a more warlike turn, with dashing, romantic samurai tales like the epic **Tale of the Heike** *(Heike Monogatari)* shoving dainty court literature aside. Others retreated from the rapidly changing world; **Essays in Idleness** *(Tsurezuregusa;* 1335) is the work of Buddhist hermit Yoshida Kenko. The **Treasury of the True Dharma Eye** *(Shobogenzo)*, an important Zen text, was one of the first Buddhist writings in Japanese. The 14th century also brought the **Chronicle of the Great Peace** *(Taiheiki)* and a steady stream of *nō* plays. "Make swords, not words," was the motto for the 16th century, but the beginning of the Edo Period brought a literary resurgence. Two famous authors of the period are novelist **Ihara Saikaku,** who described Ōsaka merchant life, and playwright **Chikamatsu Monzaemon,** whose works were meant for the puppet theater but can now be seen on the *kabuki* stage (p. 100).

The 19th century brought the influence of the West, both in forms (the modern Western novel, the political novel) and in ideas (naturalism and romanticism among others). Futabatei Shimei's **Drifting Clouds** *(Ukigumo)*, written in colloquial language, is often called Japan's first modern novel. Two of the great writers of Western-style novels were **Mori Ogai** (who also wrote poetry and plays) and **Natsume Soseki** (a master of the psychological novel), who studied in Germany. The **"I-novel,"** a typically Japanese style of personal fiction, appeared in the 20th century. The militarist 1930s overshadowed a brief **aestheticism** vogue; post-war, an outpouring of **atomic bomb literature** attempted to make sense out of tragedy.

In the decades since, Japanese authors have begun to appear on the international scene. **Kawabata Yasunari** was awarded the Nobel Prize for Literature in 1968; in 1984, **Ōe Kenzaburo** took the same honor. Other popular contemporary authors include **Osaragi Jiro, Mishima Yukio, Tanizaki Jun'ichiro, Abe Kobo,** and **Inoue Yasushi;** very recently, **Murakami Haruki, Yoshimoto Banana,** and **Murakami Ryū** have proven themselves both prolific and popular.

The oldest surviving remnant of the Japanese **poetic tradition** is the **Collection of Ten Thousand Leaves** *(Man'yoshu)*, an anthology of 4516 poems composed by a wide swathe of Japanese, from peasants to emperors, and compiled around AD 770. The Heian Period absorbed the influence of Chinese Tang poetry, but also brought the development of the **tanka**—everyone who was anyone (nobles and priests included) was writing the 31-syllable poems (the lines follow a 5-7-5-7-7 pattern). **A New Collection of Poems Ancient and Modern** *(Shin Kokinshu)* is the medieval poem tome, collected by imperial decree.

LIFE & TIMES

Renga, linked, collective poems, and **haiku,** a popular 17-syllable form, popped up in the Edo Period, with **Bashō** as its most famous practitioner. The traditional forms persist in the present, but Western forms have also been adopted.

TRADITIONAL ARTS

The arts the typical traveler associates with Japan may be those without apparent Western equivalents. Japan has cultivated a long tradition of distinctly Asian (if not purely Japanese) arts. Since 1955, the Japanese Agency of Cultural Affairs has encouraged the preservation of traditional arts by designating "Bearers of Important Intangible National Assets," commonly known as "Living National Treasures" (*ningen kokuho*), in numerous skill areas, from *kabuki* acting to sword-forging to porcelain making. Common to many traditional arts is an emphasis on precision and attention to detail—from the carefully stylized movements of a *nō* actor to the minute folds of an origami crane—an emphasis that reflects, in many ways, the interests of the culture as a whole.

THEATER ARTS

NŌ. The official performance art of the Edo court, *nō* combines elements of drama, music, and dance. An aesthetic experience *par excellence*, it is considered the quintessential Japanese art. A *nō* performance features a single main actor (traditionally, a man), accompanied by secondary actors, a chorus, a flute, and drums. The actors' movements are choreographed from a highly regimented and stylized repertoire of forms. Very few props are used, but the elaborate costumes and masks are Japanese icons. Because performances generally last several hours and are conducted in an archaic Japanese that even natives have difficulty understanding, partaking of a full performance can be a gruelling undertaking.

KYOGEN. Generally performed during the interludes of a *nō* performance, *kyogen* is a form of comic acting that began in the 15th century and was formalized in the 17th. The plays are usually no more than 20-30min. and follow simple comic plots. They require few actors, but feature intricately designed movements and bold costumes, occasionally including masks.

BUNRAKU. *Bunraku* is the traditional puppet theater of Japan, featuring puppets sometimes nearly life-size, controlled by black-robed puppeteers. A narrator recites the story the puppets enact, providing the dialogue, accompanied by a *shamisen*. *Bunraku* was developed in its current form in Ōsaka in the late 19th century, although the tradition of puppetry extends back at least to the early 17th.

KABUKI. Borrowing its plays and amalgamating its techniques from *nō*, *kyogen*, and *bunraku*, *kabuki* may be the most vivid of the traditional performing arts. A theater based on acting (the all-male performers train from childhood) and visual presentation, *kabuki* incorporates song and dance into a formal art. *Kabuki* actors wear extravagant, colorful costumes and elaborate makeup—*kabuki* has been called the world's most beautiful theater art.

RAKUGO. The traditional art of comic storytelling features a single, kneeling storyteller, who uses expressive motions and gestures to communicate his tale. With only a fan and towel as props, the traditionally-dressed performer weaves a short tale with an emphasis on the punchline. *Rakugo* has its roots in a long storytelling tradition; contemporary artists tell both traditional and contemporary stories.

MUSICAL ARTS

TRADITIONAL INSTRUMENTS. Borrowed from China, the **biwa** is a large four- or five-stringed lute used in court music and as a complement to oral recitation. The **shamisen,** a three-stringed, fretless version, often accompanies singers. The **koto** is a type of zither; its thirteen strings are plucked by the musician, who kneels behind it. Flautists will recognize the **shakuhachi,** a form of notched flute.

GAGAKU. *Gagaku* has been the traditional music of the Imperial Court for over a thousand years. The music calls for wind, string, and percussion instruments, including the *shō* (a bamboo pipe instrument), the *wagon* (an early form of *koto*), and *taiko* drums, accompanied by dance (*bugaku*) and vocal performance. The simple, refined melodies are also often heard at Shintō shrines.

BUYŌ. Japanese classical dance comes from two sources: dances extracted from 18th- and 19th-century *kabuki* theater and traditional dances from the Ōsaka and Kyōto pleasure quarters.

OTHER ARTS AND CRAFTS

IKEBANA. *Ikebana* is the art of precise, formal flower arrangement, divided into numerous schools. Key to the art is simplicity and harmony—unlike cluttered Western floral arrangements, the best examples of *ikebana* use as few leaves and stems as possible. Many Japanese homes and businesses feature a fresh *ikebana* arrangement on continual display.

TEA CEREMONY. Developed by Kamakura-period Zen monks trying to keep from nodding off while meditating, tea ceremony (*chadō*) is now an art practiced mainly by young women, who often take classes as preparation for marriage. Tea ceremony works on the principles of simplicity and steps in proper order. Conducted in a teahouse or special room, a tea ceremony begins with the presentation of the tea instruments. The guests are given sweets, and the tea is prepared and served ritually by the host.

BONSAI. Another example of the Japanese affection for the minature, *bonsai* is a common pastime. More than just the torture of trees by pruning, clipping, and binding, the art aspires to the creation of entire miniature landscapes.

PAPER AND HANDICRAFTS. **Origami,** the art of paper folding, originally encompassed both a religious and a gift-giving significance. Now more a triumph of manual gymnastics, the idea of folding 1000 cranes in times of sickness or hardship persists. **Washi** is the term for handmade Japanese paper. **Calligraphy** (*shōdō*) is a prized and popularly practiced art. The term **mingei** is applied to all handmade useful craft objects—baskets, lacquerware, textiles, and pottery, for example.

CURRENT SCENE

FROM J-POP TO JAZZ. Japan today bursts with a cacophony of sounds. A booming domestic music industry, one of the world's largest, turns out hosts of new singers and bands every year. One J-pop factory is run by **Tetsuya Komura,** a major producer, songwriter, and composer since the 1990s who has overseen acts such as dance-pop unit **trf,** pop idol **Namie Amuro,** and three-person band **globe** (of which Komura was a member). Japanese-American singer **Utada Hikaru** had a string of hit singles in 1998 and 1999. With a constantly shifting membership of (at most) thirteen hyperactive girls, **Morning Musume** has turned out such feverishly danceable hits such as "LOVE Machine" (1999) and "Happy Summer Wedding" (2000), and even spawned its own TV show "Hello Morning." Other popular groups include

An ethnologist and performer examines Japanese aesthetics

ne of the most magical phenomena that visitors encounter in Japan is the juxtaposition of ancient and contemporary arts in everyday life. Side by side, these experiences may appear mesmerizing and disorienting. Consider a Zen garden inside a busy shopping center, or perhaps the sounds of a *shamisen* (three-stringed lute) floating from an apartment window near a noisy *pachinko* parlor. There is a playful quality to this experience—the challenge of absorbing several hundred years of aesthetic cultural values, all conflated in the present moment. Looking closer, we can see that the experience of time itself can be crafted creatively on both a small and a large scale.

Over time, Japanese traditional art forms have been passed down orally from teacher to student, in a hierarchical master-disciple relationship found throughout Asia in a variety of forms. This mode of transmission demands a significant amount of time, and relies on patience, disciplined practice, and lived experience. Artists often make comments such as, "You must learn through the body," or, "If we learn quickly, the *kokoro* (heart or spirit) will be missing." In the age of instant coffee and e-mail messages, sentiments such as these connote a vastly different flow of time.

This unique concept of time infuses Japanese art not only in practice but also in philosophy. Consider the concept of *ma*, an artistic approach to space and time deeply influenced by Buddhist thought and essential to Japanese visual and performing arts. *Ma*, "negative" or "open" space, pertains to compositional proportions and reflects a spiritual/philosophical approach to art. "Negative" space and time are believed to be not empty, but expansive and full of energy. Artists employ *ma* as a means of inducing a contemplative state, an awareness of expansive space and time. In the *sumie* (brush painting) tradition, we see *ma* in the negative space, the "blank" area enveloping the brush strokes on rice paper. For example, a scroll painting of a bird perched on an angular tree limb might consist of a dozen brush strokes. Here *ma* exists between the strokes and extends to the empty space of the scroll. A quality of irregularity brings *ma* to the foreground—the brushstrokes, often asymmetrical and deliberately jagged, create a particularly

interesting negative space. Contextualized in the world, the bird's existence draws our attention to the abstract and ephemeral qualities of our own existence.

The concept of *ma* also appears in the traditional performing arts (such as *nō*, *kabuki*, *bunraku*, or *nihon buyo*). For example, *ma* is embodied in the series of still poses choreographed into a piece. The body is rarely "balanced" symmetrically in a pose. Instead, the naturally symmetrical human body is poised so that one leg is forward or bent, each arm held in varied positions, and the torso often turned in opposition to the direction of the feet. Not only is the body's stance irregular, but the "negative space" (*ma*) around the body forms interesting asymmetrical contours, such as the open area bounded by the outstretched arm and torso. During these poses, time freezes momentarily—a temporal *ma* that highlights a moment outside the regular flow of time. The music may employ rests or free tempo to mirror this expanded temporal quality, implying a suspension of time through abstract punctuations of silence.

The Japanese reverence for time is evident in the art of *bonsai*, miniature potted trees. One-hundred-year-old trees, precisely crafted with a long-term vision of growth, bear the marks of their age. Limbs poised asymmetrically like a dancer's, the trees exhibit their constructed "natural" beauty in stance and composed *ma*. Most often a tree is planted off-center, leaving an empty space to create the illusion of expansive landscape. Some *bonsai* even cascade over the edge of the pot—dramatically asymmetrical.

Delightfully, we can appreciate both the new and the old as they coexist in the present. While some Japanese contemporary artists deliberately challenge tradition, others build upon traditional concepts such as *ma*. Observing these contrasts of time and aesthetics in everyday life provides marvelous, even whimsical insights into culture and time. Those aspects of Japan that are modern and technologically advanced reveal the extent of the country's historical and developmental journey into the present. Suddenly, the sight of an 80-year-old woman in an indigo *kimono* riding the bullet train while engrossed in a flashy robot-fantasy *manga* (comic book) seems only a surface incongruity. Playful experiences such as these offer us a space in which to ponder time.

Tomie Hahn is an ethnologist and performer who writes about Japanese culture, monster trucks, dance, and technology as culture.

pop-rock band **GLAY**, the Beatles-flavored **Southern All Stars**, R&B duo **Chemistry**, **Judy and Mary** (a band of four, none of whom are named Judy or Mary), trendy boy-band **SMAP** (Sports Music Assemble People), and jazz-funk trio **Dreams Come True**. Somewhat older Japanese may listen to **Chage and Aska**, a songwriting duo popular since the late '70s, or '80s J-pop queens like Nakamori Akina and Seiko Matsuda. Much older Japanese may listen to **enka**, a genre of sentimental popular song performed by women in formal *kimono*. Singers in this genre include Fuyumi Sakamoto and Sayuri Ishikawa. Although *enka* songs blend Western and Japanese instruments and styles, they are often called *nihon no uta*, "the song of Japan," and are said to express *nihonjin no kokoro* or "the heart/soul of the Japanese people." **Jazz** is also highly popular among Japanese both young and old, and Japan has turned out a number of prominent jazz musicians including saxophonist and clarinettist Keizo Inoue, pianist Toshiko Akiyoshi, jazz crooner Kei Kobayashi, and Brazilian-born bossa nova singer-guitarist Lisa Ono. Film-score composer **Joe Hisaishi** has provided the soundtracks to films by Kitano "Beat" Takeshi and Hayao Miyazaki; the late composer **Toru Takemitsu** was acclaimed worldwide for combining Western orchestral and traditional Japanese instruments in his pieces.

KINEMA. Three directors of the post-WWI era represent a golden age of Japanese cinema. The most well-known of these outside Japan is undoubtedly **Akira Kurosawa**, whose evocations of a feudal past in *Rashomon* (1950) and *The Seven Samurai* (1954) won awards at the time of their release and continue to be cited as influences by filmmakers today. His synthesis of Eastern and Western sensibilities, however, has often appealed more to Western audiences than to Japanese viewers. Many regard **Yasujiro Ozu**'s *shomin-geki* ("common-people's drama"), the most famous of which is *Tokyo Story* (1953), as more typically "Japanese" films for their depictions of middle-class family life. Rounding out the trio of Japanese cinema masters is **Kanji Mizoguchi** whose work, from *Sisters of Gion* (1936) to *Ugetsu* (1954), examines the place of women in Japanese society.

Japan has spawned a number of movie cults in the West, from *roman porno* (romantic pornographic) flicks like *Gate of Flesh* (1964) to serious erotica like *In the Realm of the Senses* (1977), from monster kitsch in *Godzilla* movies to futuristic anime violence in *Akira* (see **Anime**, below). The Hollywood remake of Hideo Nakata's *Ringu* (1998) reflects a growing interest in Japan's thriving **horror** genre. Disturbing spectacles of violence like Kinji Fukasaku's *Battle Royale* (2001) manage to out-gore any mainstream American thriller playing today. On the lighter side, popular **comedies** include Juzo Itami's *Tampopo* (1986), the story of a young man's search for the perfect noodle restaurant, and Yaguchi Shinobu's *Waterboys* (2001) about the adventures of a male high school synchronized swimming team.

SUPER FUN HAPPY FAMILY WISH SHOW! Humiliating game shows and robot cartoons form only a tiny part of the *geinokai* (entertainment world). With its romantic dramas serialized all over Asia, Japan's TV industry is something of a pan-Asian star-machine, sustaining pop groups like SMAP and Morning Musume through their own spin-off shows. One of the most recognizable TV personalities of all is **Kitano "Beat" Takeshi**. This fascinating media character leads a double existence. In the West, he is critically acclaimed as a director of superviolent gangster films such as *Sonatine* (1993) or the Hollywood-made *Brother* (2001). In Japan, however, he has also been a staple of TV comedy for over 15 years, famous for hosting feisty talk shows such as the hit series *Strange Japanese Habits (Koko ga hen Dayo Nihonjin)*. This show sets 50 or so Japanese-speaking foreigners loose to speak openly on a variety of Japanese cultural peculiarities, from fashion to the education system. Other popular TV shows include the comedy/vari-

LIFE & TIMES

ety show *Downtown* starring *manzai* (slapstick comedy) duo Hamada Masatoshi and Matsutomo Hitoshi, and of course the televised cooking competition *Iron Chef*, recently imported to great success in the US and Canada.

A MANGA FOR ALL SEASONS. Just about everyone in Japan, from small children to teenagers to businessmen to housewives, reads comics. Comics *(manga)* and animation (anime) are popular accepted as viable forms of media, entertainment and even education for all age groups. There are educational *manga* about economics, historical *manga* about national or foreign heroes, romances geared toward teenage girls, basketball dramas, many creative genres of erotica, cyberpunk thrillers, martial arts adventures—indeed, something for every person and situation. In the early 20th century, Japanese comics were strongly influenced by Western comics and caricatures, but a uniquely Japanese form began to develop after World War II when Tezuka Osamu, the "god of *manga*," integrated cinematic effects such as close-ups and scene panning into the novel-length *New Treasure Island (Shin-Takara-jima)* of 1947. Nowadays, *manga* account for nearly one-quarter of sales in Japan's publishing industry. Some common terminology: *shōnen manga* are boys' comics, *shōjō manga* girls' comics, and *seinen manga* youth comics (young adult). *Jump*, a magazine and leading publisher of *shōnen manga*, has put out such bestsellers as Akira Toriyama's **Dragonball Z** and Takehiko Inoue's **Slam Dunk.** Tezuka's romance *Knight of the Ribbon (Ribon no kishi)* ushered in the *shōjō manga* genre in the 1950s; popular titles today include Fuyumi Soryō's *Mars #1* and Kaira Yura's *Angelique*. The most popular *manga* often become animated films or TV series; one such adaptation is the classic **Doraemon** series, starring a blue earless robot cat with a taste for red-bean buns and a pouch on his belly full of gadgets from the future.

ANIME. Although the more conservative among the older generation refer disparagingly to rabid anime fans as *otaku* (best translated as "housebroken no-life geek"), animated films and TV series are a staple for young Japanese. The history of anime began in the early 20th century with animated shorts such as Kitayama Seitaro's *Peach Boy* (1918), inspired by contemporary American and European techniques, but based on Japanese folk-tales and traditional images. Animation took on a militaristic shade around World War II when the Imperial army commissioned Mitsuyo Seo to produce the 74-min. *Momotaro's Gods-Blessed Sea Warriors*, in which cute animal sailors representing the Imperial Navy liberated Indonesia and Mylasia from foreign devils with horns. In the post-war period, a number of private animation companies emerged, including Toei Animation Co., which released its first full-length film, *The Tale of the White Serpent (Hakujaden*, marketed in the US as *Panda and the Magic Serpent)* in 1958. At about this time, "god of manga" Osamu Tezuka started Japan's first TV animation studio, Mushi Productions, and turned his comic series *Astro Boy (Tetsuwan Atom)* into an internationally circulated TV series.

In the 1960s and 1970s, anime began to develop the thematic sophistication and variety for which it is known today. The "giant robot" genre blossomed with Toei's adaptation of Go Nagai's manga *Mazinger Z*, a precursor to later series such as *Mobile Suit Gundam* and *Macross (Robotech* in the US). A genre of "magic girl anime" *(mahō shōjō* anime) emerged with the TV debut of *Mahōtsukai Sally* in 1966, inspired by the American sitcom *Bewitched*. **Sailor Moon** is a recent combination of the *mahō shōjō* genre with the *sentai* or "team of heroes" genre. Another major 1970s creation was the comedy series *Lupin Sansei* featuring international thief and scoundrel **Lupin**, whose wild antics and wilder sideburns hit the big screen in the 1978 feature film *Castle of Cagliostro (Cagliostro No Shiro)*. This was the first significant directing job for Hayao Miyazaki, now renowned at home and abroad for such films as **Princess Mononoke** (1997) and **Spir-**

ited Away (2001). Together with Isao Takahata (who directed the poignant WWII drama *Grave of the Fireflies* in 1988), Miyazaki heads **Studio Ghibli,** the leading anime production company in Japan today with Disney as its overseas distributor. The other large production studio is **Gainax,** a leader in episodic science fiction anime as exemplified by **Neon Genesis Evangelion** *(Shin Seiki Evangelion).* The 1982 release of Ridley Scott's *Bladerunner* informed a whole generation of dark futuristic anime films, including Katsuhiro Otamo's **Akira** (1988) and Mamoru Oshī's **Ghost in the Shell** (1995). For more information on the latest anime releases, check out www.manga.com (not a manga site).

MODERN ARCHITECTURE. The Meiji Restoration of 1868 brought the first wave of Western architecture into Japan in the form of Victorian-style banks and schools. When Frank Lloyd Wright completed his rebuilding of Tōkyō's Imperial Hotel in 1922, the **modernist** movement gained its first foothold. The period after World War I saw a number of competing styles, including the nationalistic **Imperial Crown style** and the **International style** influenced by Le Corbusier and Mies van der Rohe. After World War II, Japanese architects began to combine traditional and modern styles in an attempt to reconcile the two. **Tange Kenzo** is famous for his success during this period in fusing traditional Japanese architecture with modernism and Western technical innovations. His most famous works include the Yoyogi National Stadium (which hosted the 1964 Olympic Games in Tōkyō), the Hiroshima Peace Center, and the Tōkyō Cathedral of Saint Mary. Among his students were such future luminaries as Kisho Kurokawa, Arata Isozaki, and Fumihiko Maki. The **Metabolism** movement was launched in 1960 at the World Design Conference in Tōkyō. Critical of Modernism's classicism, Metabolism emphasized the changeability of modern cities. It aimed to create designs that were not static but dynamic, with different parts growing and decaying like parts of an organism—hence the name. Founding members Takashi Asada, Kiyonori Kikutake, and Kisho Kurokawa were soon joined by Fumihiko Maki and Masato Otako. In the 1970s some different responses to urban conditions emerged, one of which was **Ando Tadao**'s minimalism. He rejected the pollution, congestion, and chaos of the urban environment and created a defensive architecture that presented blank walls to the street, concealing sophisticated, poetic spaces inside.

During the real-estate boom of the '80s, many Japanese developers invited foreign architects to design their buildings. One famous product of this period is Philippe Stark's Asahi Super Dry Hall (1989) in Asakusa, Tōkyō, topped by a striking gold-leaf sculpture (which many lovingly refer to as the Golden Turd). The collapse of Japan's economy in the early 1990s slowed architectural development. Even so, there remain many prominent Japanese architects who have produced works both inside and outside Japan: Kenzo's Metropolitan Government Offices in Tōkyō (1991), Kurokawa's Pacific Tower (1992) in Paris, and Tadao's Meditation Space (1995) at the UNESCO complex in Paris.

SPORTS AND RECREATION

SUMŌ. The emblematic Japanese sport, *sumō* is backed by a 2000-year tradition. Professional matches are steeped in ceremony, with long introductions and extended purification rituals prefacing what are often extremely short actual bouts. The extremely large wrestlers (for that, uh, low center of gravity) attempt to either force their opponents out of the ring or force them to touch the ground within the ring with any part of their body other than the soles of their feet. Sumō wrestlers live and train in **stables** *(heya)*, where the gruelling regimen includes early rising, lots of chores, and high-calorie meals. Six **basho,** or wrestling tournaments, each lasting 15 days, are held each year, and these are the best opportunities to see *sumō*. The January, May and September *basho* are in Tōkyō; in March, July, and November, they move to Ōsaka, Nagoya, and Fukuoka, respectively.

MARTIAL ARTS. Budō, or "the martial way," encompasses several separate arts. **Jūdō** is based on jujitsu techniques of the *samurai* and involves grappling and throwing moves. **Kendō** is a form of fencing with two-handed bamboo swords; those who practice it wear elaborate, quilted protective gear. **Kyūdō** is Japanese archery, emphasizing form over accuracy. **Ninjitsu,** the art of spies and assassins, has been wildly exaggerated in recent popular accounts of ninjas, but also has serious practitioners. Though perhaps the most internationally famed Japanese sport, **karate** is not counted among the traditional martial arts: inspired by Chinese kung fu, its current form was developed in 17th-century Okinawa. **Aikidō** is a relative newcomer to the family—more interested in personal and spiritual development than use in combat, the graceful form has no matches or competitions.

BASEBALL. Japan's most popular team sport, baseball has been played in Japan since the 1870s. High school tournaments are followed countrywide and nationally televised. The Japanese professional league has twelve teams, which play in two divisions; the season runs from April to October. Watching the crowd may be half the fun at a professional game—look for organized cheering and the spectacular 7th-inning balloon release.

WESTERN SPORTS. Golf is Japan's ultimate status-conscious sport, with green fees starting in the astronomical range and going up from there. Golfing excursions are often business-related, and the experience is less for physical exercise than an exercise in etiquette and fashion. **Soccer** *(sakkā)* has a short history in Japan; the professional **J. League** was formed only in 1993, but was a surprise sensation, attracting a trendier, more alternative crowd than baseball.

GAMES. Deceptively simple and wildly popular, **go** is the classic Japanese game. Intellectually demanding, the game involves placing black and white stones on the intersections of a gridded board to capture your opponent's pieces. **Mah-jongg,** in contrast, is a fast-paced tile game, often associated with gambling. **Shōgi** is the Japanese version of chess, descended from the same Indian game as Western chess, and employing flat, wooden pieces. **Hanafuda** is a gambling game, featuring cards with pictures of flowers and trees; **sugoroku** resembles backgammon.

PACHINKO. Developed in 1950s Nagoya as a peacetime use for steel sheets and ball bearings, *pachinko* has become a uniquely Japanese pastime. Noisy, gaudy pachinko parlors, where people crowd to play the pinball-like arcade game, can be found all over the country. Unlike pinball, however, *pachinko* is an utterly unskilled game—players release steel balls into the machines and then watch the balls drop through a series of pins, winning more balls if they land in the right holes. *Pachinko* gambling is not strictly legal in Japan, but regulars know where to exchange their token prizes for real cash.

HOLIDAYS AND FESTIVALS

New Year *(Shōgatsu)* is the most important holiday in Japan, and most Japanese do not work from January 1 to January 3. The New Year is seen as a fresh start, and people try to complete all duties in December and then forget the troubles of the old year at *bōnenkai* or "year-forgetting parties." On January 1 it is customary to visit a shrine or temple, and when night comes temples throughout the country ring their bells 108 times to drive away the 108 evil thoughts. Foods eaten during these three days include *toshikoshi soba,* buckwheat noodles representing long life; *ozōni,* soup with *mochi* cakes; *otoso,* sweetened rice wine; and other special foods collectively called *osechi ryōri.* Many Japanese take vacations within or even outside Japan during this time, and so airports are often crowded. Travelers should be aware that the entire country will shut down for the week surrounding New Year—it may be very difficult to find open establishments.

Another important national holiday around this time is **Coming-of-Age Day** (also known as Adult Day) on January 15, when every town and city in Japan holds a *seijin shiki* (adulthood ceremony) for all residents who turned 20 in the previous year. Young women buy or rent *kimono* for the ceremony, and young men wear business suits or dark-colored *kimono*. Government officials give speeches and present gifts to the new adults, who depart together to drink and celebrate.

Children's Day *(Tango no Sekku)* is actually a boy's festival when families wish their sons a good future and decorate their houses with carp streamers and samurai figurines representing strength, power and success. Girls have their own celebration during the **Doll Festival** *(Hina Matsuri)*, also known as the Peach Blossom Festival *(Momo no Sekku)*, when families decorate beautiful *hina* dolls in Heianera *kimono* and display them in the best room of the house. Parents wish their daughters a successful and happy life, and a meal of *chirashizushi* (sashima and vegetables on a bed of sushi rice), rice cakes and sweet sake is eaten. Children's Day falls within a collection of four holidays at the end of April and beginning of May that together form **Golden Week,** one of Japan's busiest holiday seasons.

The other major vacation period falls around the **Obon Festival** during July or August (based on the lunar calendar). During this Buddhist festival, families honor deceased ancestors by holding memorial services, making offerings at temples and hanging lanterns in front of their houses. At the end of the festival, lanterns are set afloat on rivers and seas to guide the ancestors home. It is also a tradition to visit ancestors' graves during the weeks of the **Vernal and Autumnal Equinox Days.**

The festival **Setsubun** ("seasonal division"), marking the day before spring begins, is not a national holiday but is celebrated in many forms throughout the country on February 3. To ward away evil spirits, families may hang fish heads or holly tree leaves outside their door, or scatter roasted beans around the house. Each family member will then pick up the number of beans corresponding to his or her age. It is also customary to shout *oni wa soto, fuku wa uchi* ("Get out Ogre! Come in Happiness!") while performing the bean-throwing rite.

Japanese people also celebrate many Western holidays. Because **Valentine's Day** (Feb. 14) in Japan is a day when women give men gifts (mostly of chocolate), men are expected to reciprocate on **White Day** (Mar. 14). A marshmallow company is said to have started this custom in the '60s—the day is named after the color of the candy—but typical White Day gifts now range from cookies to accessories. While **Christmas** is not a national holiday, a rising number of Japanese have adopted the practices of decorating the house with Christmas lights and giving gifts to friends. Christmas cakes in Japan are usually either sponge cakes covered with strawberries and whipped cream, or Christmas logs with seasonal decorations.

For a table of Japan's national holidays, refer to the **Appendix** (p. 727).

ADDITIONAL RESOURCES

GENERAL HISTORY

Embracing Defeat: Japan in the Wake of World War II, by John W. Dower. A sober, detailed exploration of the US occupation and aftermath. Dower's highly-regarded **War Without Mercy** investigates both American and Japanese racism during the war.

Hirohito and the Making of Modern Japan, by Herbert P. Bix. An award-winning biography, praised for its shocking and extensively researched portrait of the emperor.

History of Japan, by R.H.P. Mason and J.G. Caiger. A comprehensive historical overview.

The Heritage of Japanese Civilization, by Albert M. Craig. A brief history, emphasizing tradition in the arts and in society.

A Modern History of Japan: From Tokugawa Times to the Present, by Andrew Gordon. An appealing, readable modern history.

NONFICTION

The Japan We Never Knew: A Journey of Discovery, by David Suzuki and Keibo Oiwa. The result of interviews with minorities and activists in Japan, Suzuki and Oiwa's book is a thought-provoking look at an often-forgotten side of Japan.

The Material Child: Coming of Age in Japan and America, by Merry White. A cross-cultural study look at adolescents on both sides of the Pacific.

Nightwork: Sexuality, Pleasure, and Corporate Masculinity in a Tokyo Hostess Club, by Anne Allison. A non-sensationalized look at Japanese nightlife, by a Western athropologist who spent time working as a hostess.

Tales of Times Now Past, edited by Marian Ury. A compilation of Japanese and Buddhist stories and fables.

Tokyo: A Spatial Anthropology, by Jinnai Hidenobu. A unique look at the remnants of historical Tokyo through the city's architecture and landscape.

Tsukiji: The Fish Market at the Center of the World, by Theodore C. Bestor. An ethnography of the world's largest seafood market, focusing on its day-to-day workings, its role as Tōkyō's supplier of sushi, changing patterns of Japanese food culture, and its 400-year history. **Neighborhood Tokyo** is Bestor's prize-winning account of daily life in a "traditional" Tokyo district; the book focuses on how residents carve out and sustain a very local, face-to-face sense of community in the midst of the sprawling metropolis.

You Gotta Have Wa, by Robert Whiting. A look into the world of Japanese baseball, with comparisons to the US and reflections on the culture as a whole. Also by Whiting, **Tokyo Underworld** explores organized crime in Japan, emphasizing the role of the US in its development.

FICTION

Audrey Hepburn's Neck, by Alan Brown. A sexy Tōkyō comedy about Japanese men, the women who love them, and the complications that ensue.

Japan Pop!: Inside the World of Japanese Popular Culture, edited by Timothy J. Craig. A collection of scholarly essays on music, comics, anime, television, film, and more.

Kokoro, by Soseki Natsume. A poignant look at loneliness and relationships, by one of the most significant Meiji novelists. **I Am a Cat** and **And Then** are other good choices.

Memoirs of a Geisha, by Arthur Golden. The product of 10 years of research, Golden's novel has been praised as an accurate and intriguing account of Gion life. A film version, buzzed about since 1999, has been stalled by trouble keeping a director.

Narrow Road, by Bashō Matsuo. The *haiku* poet's most famous work, a recounting of a trip to northern Japan, is available in numerous translations.

The Pillow Book, by Sei Shonagon. A very readable collection of lists and sketches by an observant and critical woman of the Heian court.

Snow Country, by Yasunari Kawabata. A masterful story of doomed love by the Nobel Prize-winning author.

The Tale of Genji, by Murasaki Shikibu. The 11th-century court epic is a masterpiece of world literature. The Arthur Waley translation (published in the 1930s) is considered the "classic"; later attempts by Edward Seidensticker (1976) and Royall Tyler (2001) also have their supporters.

Tokyo Stories: A Literary Stroll, translated and edited by Lawrence Rogers. An anthology of short stories featuring the metropolis in the 20th century, in a variety of styles.

The Wind-Up Bird Chronicle, by Haruki Murakami. An epic of alienation, responsibility, and losing your cat by the master of the surreal and the everyday. Also recommended are his **Norwegian Wood** and **Hard-Boiled Wonderland and the End of the World.**

FILM

Battle Royale, directed by Kinji Fukasaku (2001). A highly disturbing, but incredibly thought-provoking film about a class of schoolchildren forced to fight to the death. Frequent, graphic scenes of violence.

Ringu, directed by Hideo Nakata (1998). A supernatural horror film featuring a videotape that kills everyone who watches it. Remade in the US as **The Ring** (2002).

The Seven Samurai, written by Akira Kurosawa (1954). The classic pick for heroic samurai and such, it was also the basis for much of the cinematography and swordplay of Star Wars. **Throne of Blood** (1957), **Kagemusha** (1980), and **Ran** (1985), are other good Kurosawa choices.

Shall We Dance? directed by Masayuki Suo (1996). The sweet, poignant story of a salaryman who takes ballroom dance lessons and changes his life.

Spirited Away, directed by Hayao Miyazaki (2001). The top-grossing anime classic tells the tale of a young girl's fantastic adventures in a magical, breathtakingly animated world. **Princess Mononoke** (1997) is a similarly gripping tale of man, nature, love, and spirits in medieval Japan.

Tampopo, directed by Juzo Itami (1986). A food-fascinated comedy about a truck driver's quest for the perfect noodle.

TRAVEL BOOKS

36 Views of Mount Fuji: On Finding Myself in Japan, by Cathy N. Davidson. A selection of essays by an American professor, lauded for their realism and sensitivity.

Dave Barry Does Japan, by Dave Barry. The American humorist takes on Japanese language, culture, industry, and tourism with his trademark irreverent style.

Hokkaido Highway Blues: Hitchhiking Japan, by Will Ferguson. The more colorful and anecdotal companion to Ferguson's practical, fact-filled **Hitchhiker's Guide to Japan** takes a humorous look at an unusual journey.

The Lady and the Monk: Four Seasons in Kyōto, by Pico Iyer. The penetrating travelogue of a visitor to a Kyōto monastery who falls in love with a married Japanese woman.

Learning to Bow: Inside the Heart of Japan, by Bruce Feiler. A teacher's report on his experiences during a year spent in small-town Japan.

The Roads to Sata: A 2000-Mile Walk Through Japan, by Alan Booth. A hiker's tale of hoofing it from Kyūshū to Hokkaidō.

Sake & Satori: Asian Journals—Japan, by Joseph Campbell. The famous myth critic's notes on his 1950s journey through Asia, including five months in Japan.

Untangling My Chopsticks: A Culinary Sojourn in Kyoto, by Victoria Abbott Riccardi. The memoir of an American woman who spent a year at a traditional cooking school, speckled with recipes and mouthwatering prose.

TŌKYŌ (東京)

> Tōkyō's phone code is **03**.

With 34 million souls calling the metropolitan area home, Tōkyō is the biggest city in the world almost any way the cookie is cut. Japan's capital, a behemoth dynamo, can keep pace with any imagination. Palace strolls and helicopter rides, anime character actors and torture chamber dinners—if Tōkyō's neon voodoo knows a limit, it's better hidden than a *samurai*'s knickers. Yet behind every giggling hostess lies a casualty to the commercial lurch forward, a defeated human signpost here or a club kid in the gutter there.

But given the history, Tōkyō's careless developmental wanderlust makes perfect sense. The city has been burned down and shaken to her knees so many times that the structures remaining hardly fit in with each other. In the mismatched concrete overdrive, only department stores and ownership changes are constant. The scene is no different from a hundred paces than at ten, each district bound by formulaic chains. Zoom out 250m, though, and the chaos trickles into focus, for Tōkyō leaves no important tasks to its sibling cities. Centralization fever has gone to town on these Kantō Plains, where politics, economy, technology, art, and most anything with a cutting edge find their hub and harbor. From the sky, the sea ushers in a new meaning of majesty, surging against the city's off-shore developments with the kind of fear-instilling momentum reserved for movies and the subconscious. Tōkyō is that terrifying law of averages that eradicates color, a modern-day Tower of Babel, a testament to the awesome power of the human spirit when allowed to dream and forced to survive. Welcome to the dizzying megalopolis, unconquerable in a single lifetime. Welcome to Tōkyō.

HIGHLIGHTS OF TŌKYŌ

ASCEND THE HEIGHTS. The Skydeck of **Roppongi Hills Mori Tower** (p. 166) is our pick for getting above it all. The **Tōkyō Tower** (p. 166) and **Sunshine 60** (p. 161) observatories also have their proponents, though a helicopter ride (p. 169) is hard to beat.

PLUMB THE DEPTHS. At the **Lockup** (p. 155), dining has a handcuffed twist. Creatures of the night hit up the clubs in **Roppongi** (p. 195) and **Kabuki-chō** (p. 200).

CROSS THE WATER. The newest bit of Tōkyō real estate, **Odaiba** (p. 118), is the jewel in the city's crown, just across the Rainbow Bridge.

✈ INTERCITY TRANSPORTATION

BY PLANE

For information on international flights to Tōkyō, see p. 37.

NARITA AIRPORT

Narita Airport (☎0476-32-2802, flights 0476-34-5000; www.narita-airport.or.jp), 65km northeast of Tōkyō, serves over 60 domestic and international airlines.

Keisei Line: ☎3831-0131. The quickest and most economical option for travel between the airport and Tōkyō, the **Keisei Skyliner** connects Narita Airport and Ueno Station (56min.; every 30min.; ¥1920, under 12 ¥960). The **Limited Express** takes longer but is significantly cheaper (71min.; every 20 min.; ¥1000, under 12 ¥500).

JR Line: Terminal One ☎0476-33-1630, Terminal Two ☎35-6008. The **Narita Express** runs between Narita Airport and Tōkyō, Shinjuku, Shinagawa, and Ikebukuro Stations (every 30min.; Tōkyō: 1hr., ¥2940; Shinjuku, Shinagawa, Ikebukuro: 80min., ¥3110).

Airport Limousine: ☎3665-7220; www.limousinebus.co.jp. The bus service's extensive network stops at more than 80 hotels and various train stations in Tōkyō (80-120min.; every 15-30min.; ¥3000, under 12 ¥1500).

Taxi: Airport Taxi Management Committee, ☎0476-32-8282. From Narita, there are 2 options. Fixed-fare taxis are ¥17,000 to Tōkyō and Ueno Stations. If you don't mind traveling with 6-7 other passengers, shared taxis to Tōkyō Station cost ¥4000 per person. Both serve other locations for varying prices. From Tōkyō to Narita, a cab takes 70-100min. and costs around ¥25,000. Some companies to try are **Tōkyō MK** (☎5547-5667), **Nisshin Kōtsū** (☎3820-3255), and **Tōkyō Jumbo Hire** (☎5269-3815).

HANEDA AIRPORT

Japan's grand central for domestic flights hangs 60km south of central Tōkyō (☎5757-8111; www.tokyo-airport-bldg.co.jp).

Tōkyō Monorail: www.tokyo-monorail.co.jp/english. Connects you to Hamamatsu-chō on the Tōkyō mainframe (22min.; every 4min. at peak times; adults ¥470, children ¥240).

Keihin Express: www.keikyu.co.jp/english. Just as good as the monorail and slightly faster for Shinjuku and surroundings. Connects to Shinagawa Station (19min., ¥400).

Airport Limousine: See **Narita Airport,** above. Times and prices vary, but the quickest way to get to the JR Yamanote Line is through Tōkyō Station (40min., ¥900).

Taxi: A trip to Shinagawa, the closest JR Yamanote Station, costs about ¥3000.

BY TRAIN

The **JR shinkansen** (bullet train) travels between Tōkyō and major Japanese cities; visit Tōkyō or Ueno Station for details. As for more immediate attractions, the **Odakyū Electric Railway** (www.odakyu-group.co.jp) can haul you to Hakone (¥1150, express ¥2020). See the main office (☎5321-7887) in the west side of Odakyū Shinjuku Station. The **Tōbu Railway** (www.tobu.co.jp) serves Nikkō.

▛ LOCAL TRANSPORTATION

JAPAN RAIL EAST

Tōkyō is a public transportation miracle, and the JR is its heart, arteries, lungs, and spleen. You will rarely be more than 10min. from a station, and trains leave every 4min. or so at peak hours. JR East operates some thirty regular lines, about eight of which matter to Central Tōkyō. The most prominent is the circular **Yamanote Line,** which defines Tōkyō and services every major neighborhood save Odaiba. A round-trip joyride takes 63min. Each line is open roughly 5am-midnight.

JR stations are massive labyrinths with food courts and up to twenty exits. Use the maps to find your destination and the line required to get there. The big number in the station's white bubble is the cost of getting there (the smaller price is for children). Pop your money in the ticket machine and watch the blank buttons light up; hit the one with the desired price, and don't give the frivolous buttons a second thought. Feed the ticket to the entrance turnstiles. The machine will spit it out at the opposite end for you to retrieve. Now find

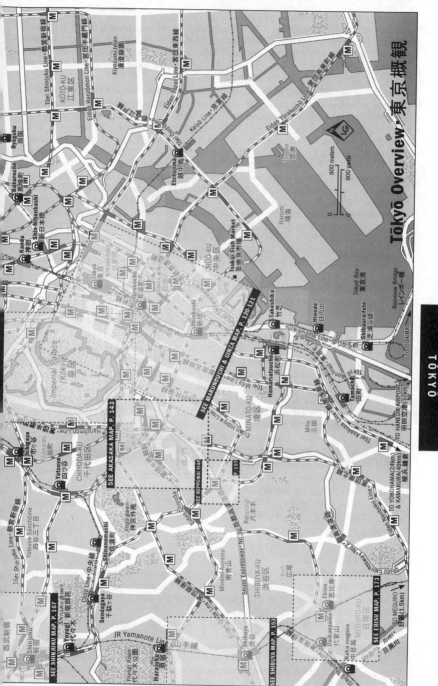

Tōkyō Overview・東京概観

TŌKYŌ

KŌTŌ-KU
江東区

Toei Shinjuku Line・都営新宿線
Eidan Hanzōmon Line・営団半蔵門線
Eidan Tōzai Line・営団東西線
Keiyō Line・京葉線
Eidan Yūrakuchō Line・営団有楽町線

Kyosumi-teien
清澄庭園

Toyosu
豊洲

800 meters
800 yards
0

Ryōgoku
両国

Bakurochō
馬喰町

Shin-Nihonbashi
新日本橋

Kanda
神田

Etchūjima
越中島

Tsukiji Fish Market
築地魚市場

CHŪŌ-KU
中央区

Harumi
晴海

Tōkyō Bay
東京湾

Tōkyō
東京

Yūrakuchō
有楽町

Shinbashi
新橋

SEE MARUNOUCHI & GINZA MAP, P. 120, 121

Takeshiba
竹芝

Hinode
日の出

Shibaura-futō
芝浦ふ頭

Rainbow Bridge
レインボー橋

TO ODAIBA

Shibakōen
芝公園

Yurikamome Line・ゆりかもめ

Imperial Palace
(Kōkyo)
皇居

SEE AKASAKA MAP, P. 143

Hamamatsuchō
浜松町

Tōei Mita Line・都営三田線

MINATO-KU
港区

Eidan Hibiya Line・営団日比谷線

Tamachi
田町

Kōnan
港南

Tōkyō
東京

Ichigaya
市ヶ谷

Eidan Hanzōmon Line

Yotsuya
四ツ谷

Eidan Namboku Line・営団南北線

CHIYODA-KU
千代田区

Mita
三田

TO HANEDA AIRPORT
羽田空港(7km)

P.197

SEE ROPPONGI MAP

Roppongi
六本木

TO YOKOHAMA(24km)
& KAMAKURA(49km)
横浜、鎌倉

Toei Shinjuku Line・都営新宿線

Yotsuya-Sanchōme
四谷三丁目

Shinanomachi
信濃町

Chūō Line・中央線

Jingūgaien
神宮外苑

Minami-Aoyama
南青山

Shūto Expressway・No.2
首都高速2号

SHIBUYA-KU
渋谷区

Hiro-o
広尾

Shūto Expressway・No.2
首都高速2号

Shibuya
渋谷

SEE SHINJUKU MAP, P. 167

Shinjuku-gyoen
新宿御苑

Sendagaya
千駄ヶ谷

Tōyogi
代々木

Ebisu
恵比寿

MEGURO-KU
目黒区

Daikanyama
代官山

TO MEGURO
(1.5km)

SEE EBISU MAP, P. 173

Naka-meguro
中目黒

Meguro River・目黒川

Tōkyū Tōyoko Line・東急東横線

西武新宿
Shinjuku
新宿

JR Yamanote Line
山手線

Yoyogi Kōen
代々木公園

Harajuku
原宿

SEE SHIBUYA MAP, P. 153

the correct platform: every platform sign contains a platform number, a colored stripe, and the name of a line. **Don't pick an express train if it will skip your destination.** At some stations, express trains have their own platforms. At others, an electric sign on the platform announces whether the next train is express (kyūkō; 急行 or kaisoku; 快速) or regular (kakutei; 各亭). A sign above the driver identifies the train as well.

There is a simpler way. Buy the cheapest ticket available (¥130), then ditch your pride and ask the man in the booth which platform is correct. When you pop your charlatan of a ticket into the exit stiles, the machine will reject it with brazen indignance. Take it to the fare adjustment machine and even the balance. Another solution lies in the cartoon penguin you'll see advertising **Suica. Suica iO** is a prepaid card (¥2000) that deducts the correct fare as you travel. It neither costs extra (the ¥500 deposit is refunded when the card is returned) nor saves money, but it'll get you away from price charts. The machines can detect the card through other materials; stash it in your wallet for slick stile style. The regular **iO** card (in denominations of ¥1000, ¥3000, and ¥5000) has to go through the machines like a regular ticket, but prints the names of the stations you've been to on the back of the card and doesn't require a deposit. A **commuter pass** permits unlimited travel between two specified destinations and the stations between them; check with the station master for details. Another alternative is the **Tokunai Free Kippu,** which provides unlimited access to JR non-express trains within the 23 wards for one day (¥730).

Questions? **JR East InfoLine** (☎3423-0111; open daily 10am-6pm) speaks fluent English and is amazing with schedules, routes, fares, purchasing, station facilities, and lost and found. Major stations have JR info centers downstairs from the platforms. The official website (www.jreast.co.jp) is also helpful.

> **JR VS. SUBWAY** A final word of advice: *never confuse the JR with the subway.* Their maps look similar and they occasionally occupy the same building, but that teal Sagami JR Line has nothing to do with the teal Namboku Subway Line you meant to take. A quick run-down of the differences:
> - **Japan Rail East** runs the JR. The subway lines are run by two different companies, with the **Eidan,** or **TRTA** (Tōkyō Rapid Transit Authority), lines comprising the majority and the **Tōei** lines making up the rest. A route mixing the two requires a fresh ticket purchase at the transfer station or a transfer ticket.
> - JR lines are marked by colored bands; subway lines by colored circles.
> - JR exits are named; subway exits are numbered.
> - JR has the Suica Card; the subway has the SF MetroCard.
> - Even though the two systems are not the same, a **Tōkyō Free Kippu** gets you on JR trains within the 23 wards, Tōei subways, Tōei buses, and Eidan subways for a full day (¥1580).

SUBWAY

JR and subway, the bread and butter of intercity transportation. One or the other is almost always a 5min. walk away, and their omnipresence means any given sight is likely walkable from four stations we didn't list. The two are very similar: if you can navigate one you can navigate the other. Train frequency is comparable, and kids (age 6-12) get discounts on both. Even the hours of operation are the same. Subway fares start at ¥130; find information and a seriously useful map at www.tokyometro.go.jp. Subway stations, being underground, are hidden. Entrances are often built into department stores or annexed to JR stations. Fear not: they are clearly marked, despite the various incarnations of the subway emblem (the main one is a circle with a line through it).

TRTA offers coupon tickets valid for three months from purchase: **11-ride tickets** (11 rides for the price of 10), **off-peak tickets** (12 rides for the price of 10, only good M-F 10am-4pm), and **Sa/holiday tickets** (15 tickets for the price of 10, only valid Sa-Su and national holidays). The **Eidan Subway One-day Open Free Ticket** is good on all Eidan subways (¥710). The **One-day Economy Pass** earns the buyer free rides on all Tōei subways, Tōei buses, and Tōei Arakawa Line trams (¥700). The **Common Subway Ticket** is a one-day pass for Eidan and Tōei subways (¥1000).

OTHER TRAINS

Don't bother looking for Odaiba train stations on the JR or subway. They're served by the **Yurikamome**, an entirely different entity, famous for crossing the Rainbow Bridge. The primary mainland terminus is in Shinbashi. It's a little more expensive (at least ¥320 to get to Odaiba), but much less crowded than other trains.

Tōei's **Arakawa Line**, starting from Waseda and wending up through West Ikebukuro and beyond, is actually a trolley. A mere ¥160 will get you as far as you want; hit the stop button before the driver reaches your station. Inexact coinage isn't a problem, but if you want change, put your money in the side slots, not on the conveyor belt. Enter at the front and leave from the back to avoid a scolding.

FERRY

If you prefer to travel with the wind in your hair and the sea at your back, **Suijōbus** (水上バス ; ☎3841-9178; www.suijobus.co.jp/english) cuts through the harbor at a decent clip, rivaling the train in speed. Most ride for pleasure; everyone should try it once to get a true view of Tōkyō. A recorded message calls out the sights in English and Japanese. Launches are about every 45min. The trips to Odaiba and Hamarikyū-teien Gardens (25min., every 45min., ¥920 with garden admission; last ship 3pm) come highly recommended. You'll likely depart from Asakusa, though Hinode Pier (Hamamatsu-chō Station) is feasible too. Other ports include Shinagawa, Harumi, and Wakasu, all next to aquatic-themed sights. Availability between 10am-5pm is a sure bet, but many lines operate 9-10am and 5-7pm as well.

BUSES

The vast majority of tourists never ride a Tōkyō bus. In general, wherever the bus can get you, the trains can do it better. If you do choose the bus, exit only through the back door (except in Tama). Adults pay ¥200, children ¥100. The **Common Bus Card** works on most buses in the Tōkyō metropolitan area (the bus will have a sign). **Tōei Regular Passes** provide unlimited rides on Tōei buses (daypass ¥500).

GIVING BACK

VOLUNTEERING TŌKYŌ

Language barriers and an underdeveloped volunteerism infrastructure can make giving back to Tōkyō a tough nut to crack. An invaluable resource for would-be do-gooders is the **Foreign Executive Women (FEW) Volunteering Directory**, which lists more than 80 Tōkyō-based organizations in want of helping hands. Extensive listings give contact information, mission statements and project lists, and skills and time commitments desired. *(To get a copy, send ¥390 in stamps or ¥1000 in cash—prefered, as the cost of printing and distributing the book is about ¥600—to FEW Volunteering Directory, c/o 1-3-9-202, Shōtō, Shibuya-ku. For updates and more information on FEW, visit www.fewjapan.com.)*

Another place to peruse the guide, as well as to pick up some more volunteering tips, is the **Tōkyō Volunteer Center** (Tonai Borantia Shimin Katsudō Sentā; 都内ボランティア市民活動 センター) in Iidabashi. It's geared towards natives, but fluent English aides can help iron things out; Japanese speakers will find many more doors open.

(Central Plaza 10F, 1-1, Kagurakashi, Shinjuku-ku (☎3235-1171; www.tvac.or.jp). Iidabashi Station West Exit. Turn right and immediately cross a bridge into the big brown building. Open Tu-Sa 9am-9pm, Su 9am-5pm.)

TAXIS

Taxis prowl the streets and line up at JR stations; lit signs in front of the driver indicate availability. Prices vary; usually a base fare of ¥500-650 is charged on top of a hybrid formula of distance and time; ¥80 per 1.5km is one example. Feel free to ask the driver for a price estimate before you get in. Rides get pricier at night. Recent deregulation has set taxi competition ablaze, and the result is unprecedented comfort. Companies are upgrading their fleets with GPS tracking, tinted glass, leather seats, and a bag of chips. These luxury cars tend to be black or blue and often cost no more than regular taxis. It's worth mentioning that taxi drivers are among the nicest people in Tōkyō. They are an excellent hire if you are unsure where exactly your destination is, especially when looking for a hotel late at night. Expect them to know their way, but don't expect them to know road names.

▣ ORIENTATION

Diverse in color, character, and charm, Tōkyō is a sprawling mass of incongruous neighborhoods scrunched side-by-side. Finding a proper "downtown" or "city center" is a challenge; finding the Tōkyō scene you dream about, be it shop-slick Ginza, tradition-steeped Asakusa, or late-night Roppongi, is not.

It's not for nothing that this town has a reputation for being difficult to navigate. In a place where guidebooks throw up their hands at directions and addresses and street names are an endangered species, even long-time residents don't venture out without a map. One tip: public "you-are-here"-style maps don't always have north at the top—they're oriented so that up is the way you face to read them.

TŌKYŌ BY WEB. Unsurprisingly, the big city has an imposing presence online. While your finds are limited only by your search engine and your wanderlust, below are some of our top picks for clicks:

The Tōkyō Convention and Visitors Bureau (www.tcvb.or.jp) and **Tōkyō Tourism Info** (www.tourism.metro.tokyo.jp) may be the standard choices, but they're both content-rich and surf-worthy. The latter, with its **Tōkyō Tourism Webstation** is a good bit glitzier than the former.

Metropolis (http://metropolis.japantoday.com) is Tōkyō's standard English weekly, with feature articles, travel columns, entertainment options, and restaurant reviews. The linked **Visitor's Guide** has listings enough to keep a traveler busy for months. Edgier **TokyoQ** (http://club.nokia.co.jp/tokyoq) has extensive listings of events, nightlife, and restaurants.

Mid-Tōkyō Maps (www.mid-tokyo.com) takes an interactive, cartographic look at the city's history, present, and future. More about concept than content, **superfuturecity** (www.superfuture.com) posts detailed shopping maps and capsule reviews of establishments in Tōkyō neighborhoods.

MAJOR NEIGHBORHOODS

AKASAKA (赤坂)

High on life and short on sights, Japan's modern seat of power plays the salaryman game, but with briefcases akimbo. Akasaka presents itself like a street market, but the merchants are nowhere and the only good for sale is that precious city buzz. **Hie Shrine** is a good central landmark from its vantage up on the hill, and curvy **Sotobori-dōri** is the most obvious eyeline to keep the map intact, though the action is on the west bank. Akasaka's biggest sight, the sprawling **Akasaka Imperial Palace,** lies west, for the eyes of the politically privileged only. The legislative **National Diet**

Building to the east is for everyone, as are the area's hodgepodge of artistic venues. Farther out is **Toranomon,** Akasaka's right-hand man and home to a sight or two. Saunter south for **Ark Hills,** the Roppongi Hills of yesteryear, where breezy terraces and live music can all be found in an impeccable plaza. The Akasaka, Akasaka-mitsuke, Kokkai-gijidōmae, and Tameike-sannō subway stations deliver the crowds.

ASAKUSA (浅草)

The heyday of Asakusa is a hundred years gone, but people who can appreciate the past will still find plenty to do in Tōkyō's old entertainment capital. On any given day, odds are decent that some kind of festival is going on, and performers in traditional *kimono* can still be seen traipsing about. At Tōkyō's northeastern limit, Asakusa's eastern border is the **Sumida River** and the fun stretches west about as far as **Kappa-bashi-dōri.** You'll likely be arriving by subway, either by the Ginza Line or Asakusa Line. The subway lines land at two adjacent but distinct stations in the southeast corner of all the action: the Flamme D'Or sculpture is impossible to miss and the butt of countless jokes. Asakusa is famous for Senso-ji, one of Eastern Japan's oldest temples, still ticking today. Craftsmanship is alive and well here, and the wares being hawked are handmade and charming. There's no doubt that some attractions in this dying carnival are here to stay, and the mood is one of fun.

EBISU (恵比寿)

Ebisu is not Tōkyō's big draw; the neighborhood lacks that special personality that makes a place worth visiting. There are, however, two excellent reasons to come. The first is **Yebisu Garden Place,** a square rivaling Roppongi Hills in scope. The second is nightlife: Ebisu has alternative options good for resubscribing to your belief in Tōkyō's novelty. Nearby **Daikanyama** (a shopping neighborhood for the idle rich) and fine dining are other good reasons to head for this area south of Shibuya.

GINZA (銀座)

Commercial indulgence. Exotic dining. Galleries. Theaters. Visiting Tōkyō's shopping quarters is like walking into a living advertisement. Every bit as flashy as a metropolitan shopping quarter ought to be, **Ginza** is the main district in town and especially famous for its *kabuki* theater. The heart of the action lies at the intersection of **Chūō-dōri** and **Harumi-dōri;** the A3, A5, A8, and A9 exits of the Ginza subway station all lead there. **Yūraku-chō,** literally the "pleasure-having area," lies up north between Ginza and Tōkyō Station. **Hibiya,** to the west and just below the Imperial Palace, is much quieter; to the south lies unremarkable **Shinbashi.** Like all of downtown, the varying districts run right into each other with no transition. Space is limited, after all. The showrooms glow, the designer clothes wow, and the pastries ooze. It's expensive, but you owe it to yourself to see it at least once.

HARAJUKU (原宿) AND AOYAMA (青山)

"R&R" stands for restoration and rebellion out here. The **Meiji-Jingū Gardens** and **Yoyogi Park** are a temple to the body, with fields and stadia galore. Between these two lies a quiet shopping town, the unlikely brooding grounds of teeny-bopper youth and the unholy flock of "beauty" salons that spike their hair. Cell phones at the ready and dressed to shock, the youngsters pour out for a veritable human circus on Sundays. The area in question lies between Shibuya and Shinjuku. The JR Yamanote Line delivers you to Harajuku, Yoyogi Park, or the Meiji-jingū Inner Gardens. A jog east along **Omotesandō-dōri** delivers pedestrians to Omotesandō; the other leg of the "V," **Aoyama-dōri,** beelines for Aoyama and the Meiji-jingū Outer Gardens, adjacent to Akasaka.

IKEBUKURO (池袋)

Nestled in the twilight fade between the modern roar of the west and the tranquil murmur of the northeast Edo-period downtown, Ikebukuro manages to catch a bit of both worlds with a ryokan here and a mega-*depāto* there. **Sunshine City** presides over this fair Tōkyō neighborhood from the east, offering to quench the wanderlust of the casual pedestrians of Sunshine 60-dōri. Ikebukuro is on the JR Yamanote Line, halfway between Shinjuku and Ueno. Subways are just as good. Most of the action lies between the JR station and Sunshine City.

MARUNOUCHI (丸の内)

Urban sprawl doesn't even begin to describe it. No skyscrapers and none of that focused downtown energy can be found here. Tōkyō's business center is a massive blanket of 15-story buildings made of concrete, iron and glass. But there are no absolutes: a little farther east lies the financial district, **Nihonbashi**, a handsome piece of urban charm with a history. On the other side of Tōkyō Station is Tōkyō's largest expanse of man-made beauty, the Imperial Palace. Up north lie **Kanda** and **Jinbōchō**, famous for bookstores and not much else. Moats, swans, and salaryman floods. Come walk the fine line between gritty reality and the heavens.

ODAIBA (お台場)

Amid the urban chaos that is Tōkyō, Odaiba is the eye of the hurricane. The buildings are so far apart, you can actually see the bits of nature the megalopolis failed to smother. Everything on these man-made islands is sterile, modern, bigger, and better. A cinch to navigate but hard to find, Odaiba is accessible only by Yurikamome rail (terminus in Shinbashi Station) and Suijō Waterbus (stations in Asakusa and Hinode Pier). Hardcore hikers can trek 30min. across Rainbow Bridge. (Head south from Hinode Subway Station.) Odaiba is split into halves by the Ariake-Nishi Canal; the Fuji TV building, the giant ferris wheel, and the water's edge mean you won't get lost unless you try. Fresh harbor air and wide open spaces. Bring a date, bring a picnic basket, just bring it.

ROPPONGI (六本木)

With more flavors than an ice cream parlor, Roppongi is small on miles but big on mileage. These days visitors are heading for **Roppongi Hills**, future square extraordinaire with more functions than can be considered decent. But it's with the disappearance of the sun that Roppongi's true claim to fame comes: the infamous nightscene. Roppongi is landlocked to the west of Akasaka, accessible only by the Hibiya and Ōedo subway lines, and not at all by JR. Footsoldiers can make the trek from Azabu-jūban, Nogizaka, and Roppongi-itchōme as well. For better or for shame: here's to decadence, here's to revelry, here's to Roppongi.

SHIBUYA (渋谷)

The true cosmopolitan center is so colossal, it apologizes for the Japanese sense of moderation. Big-name *depāto* and amusement centers rally shamelessly in hearty one-upmanship, growing so universally large that the streets are endowed with a sense of order. A deluge of funseekers and commuters put all other human floods in Tōkyō to shame. A day here might begin with late afternoon shopping, peppered by the odd museum, then on to dinner and some live music. Outdoor cafes are popular holdovers until the clubs get kicking, and lucky rollers finish the night on Love Hotel hill. The most common launching point is the **Hachikō statue**, a tribute to the loyalest canine companion that ever was, though the giant big-screen

TVs are infinitely more noticeable. From here the attractions spread out along an array of broad avenues. Shibuya is on the JR Yamanote Line; the Ginza and Hanzō-mon subway lines and the JR Saikyō Line can get you there as well.

SHINJUKU (新宿)

Jack of all trades and master of none, Shinjuku summarizes the rest of Tōkyō in concise yet towering terms. Populated as it is, it lacks a distinct flavor during the day and is terribly low on sights, partially thanks to offices and government buildings that choose function over glitter. The night is an entirely different matter; though most prefer to blow their bucks on Shibuya or Omotesandō, Kabuki-chō is a life lesson for the timid and a thriller for the daredevils that no one should miss and no one should ever show their grandmother. Shinjuku is in western Tōkyō, north of Harajuku and south of Ikebukuro. Though easily accessed by JR and subway, the stations (all named "Shinjuku") are cut up and strewn about in independent pieces; be careful when meeting friends. Tochōmae, Hatsudai, and anything-with-"Shinjuku"-in-it stations are all in the area.

UENO (上野)

Welcome to Tōkyō's junction, where masses converge quickly and disperse just as quickly. This "upper plains" is one of Japan's major transportation hubs, as a quick glance at this neighborhood will make apparent. Ueno is a hill: up top you'll find a spacious park, a bastion for Tōkyō's museums and a reserve of the old *shita-machi* downtown. At the foot you'll find a mass of disorganized buildings screaming for travelers' attention. Street markets get the job done fast, while karaoke clubs and hostess bars beckon to passing wallets. The dichotomy of the place may be disconcerting, but at least it's easy to find. Ueno Station serves the Keisei Line, the Keihin Tōhoku and Yamanote JR Lines, and the Ginza and Hibiya Subway Lines. The Iriya, Nezu, Inarichō, Minowa, and Okachi-machi Stations are next door, providing shortcuts to institutions on the fringe. JR riders should know that the Kōen Exit deposits you at the park while the Shinobazu and Hirokōji exits take you south, to bright lights and good times.

SMALLER NEIGHBORHOODS

AKIHABARA (秋葉原). Between Ueno and Marunouchi lies the electric heart of Tōkyō. Anything that falls under the category of "appliance," "video game," or "anime" can be found here.

KŌRAKUEN (後楽園). It's home to Tōkyō's big bad baseball stadium; so big that "Tōkyō Dome City" may not be a misnomer after all. A little north of the Imperial Palace, this neighborhood's just outta the park.

MEGURO (目黒). If the words "Parasite Museum" don't pique your interest, skip this residential area, but be forewarned that worms can detect bottled-up morbid curiosity from miles away. It's near the southern tip of the JR Yamanote Line.

RYŌGOKU (両国). The center ring of *sumō* activity in Tōkyō is so hot, the whole neighborhood has melted into one big *sumō* souvenir shop. Try not to laugh at their oversized diapers; *sumō* have more raw horsepower than a tractor on caffeine. It's at the map's easternmost limits.

TŌKYŌ

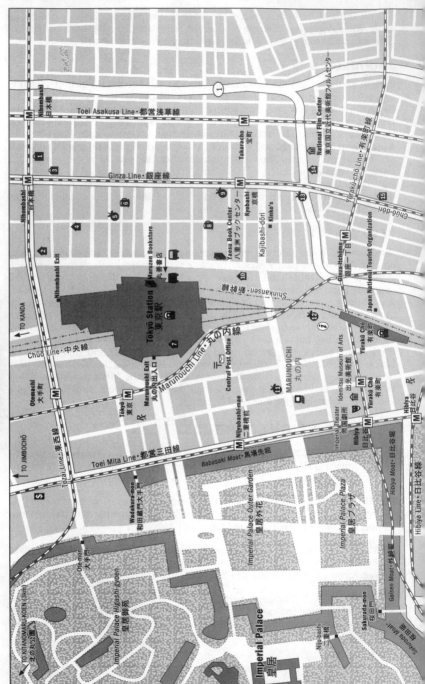

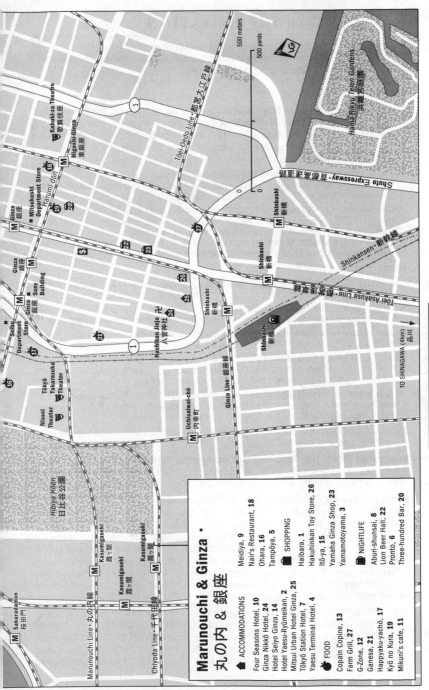

TŌKYŌ

Marunouchi & Ginza
丸の内 & 銀座

ACCOMMODATIONS
Four Seasons Hotel, 10
Ginza Nikkō Hotel, 24
Hotel Seiyo Ginza, 14
Hotel Yaesu-Ryūmeikan, 2
Mitsui Urban Hotel Ginza, 25
Tōkyō Station Hotel, 7
Yaesu Terminal Hotel, 4

FOOD
Copain Copine, 13
Farm Grill, 27
G-Zone, 21
Ganesa, 21
Happyaku-yachō, 17
Kyō no Kura, 19
Mikuni's cafe, 11

Meidiya, 9
Nair's Restaurant, 18
Ohara, 16
Tampōya, 5

SHOPPING
Haibara, 1
Hakuhinkan Toy Store, 26
Itō-ya, 15
Yamaha Ginza Shop, 23
Yamamotoyama, 3

NIGHTLIFE
Aburi-shunsai, 8
Lion Beer Hall, 22
Pronto, 6
Three-hundred Bar, 20

Kabuki-za Theatre
Higashi-Ginza 東銀座
Harumi-dōri
Mitsukoshi Department Store
Ginza 銀座
Ginza 銀座
Sony Building
Seibu Department Store
Tōkyō Takarazuka Theater
Nissei Theater
Hachikan Jinja 八官神社
Shinbashi
Shinbashi 新橋
Shinbashi 新橋
Shinbashi 新橋
Shinbashi 新橋
Uchisaiwai-chō 内幸町
Hibiya Kōen 日比谷公園
Sakuradamon 桜田門
Kasumigaseki 霞ヶ関
Kasumigaseki 霞ヶ関
Kasumigaseki 霞ヶ関
Kasumigaseki 霞ヶ関
Marunouchi Line・丸の内線
Chiyoda Line・千代田線
Ginza Line・銀座線
Tōei Asakusa Line・都営浅草線
Shinkansen・新幹線
Shuto Expressway・首都高速道路
Tōei Oedo Line・都営大江戸線
Hama-Rikyū Teien Gardens 浜離宮庭園
TO SHINAGAWA (4km) 品川
500 meters
500 yards

🛈 PRACTICAL INFORMATION

More a collection of small cities composing the mother of all cities than a monolithic metropolis with a single center, Tōkyō tends to have tourist facilities and services in each area, as well as a centralized set.

ALL OF TŌKYŌ

Tourist Office: Tōkyō's tourist organizations are the **Japan National Tourist Organization** (www.jnto.go.jp), **Tōkyō Metropolitan Government** (www.tourism.metro.tokyo.jp), and **Tōkyō Convention and Visitors Bureau** (www.tcvb.or.jp). The **Tōkyō Visitor's Guide** by *Metropolis* (http://metropolis.japantoday.com), is a must-have: it's an amazing and comprehensive compendium of upcoming events and places to dine, shop, and dance.

Japan National Tourist Organization (JNTO), Tōkyō Kōtsū Kaikan Bldg. 10F, 2-10-1, Yūrakuchō, Chiyoda-ku (☎3201-3331). Yūrakuchō Station. The JR's Kyōbashi Exit puts you right in front. Open M-F 9am-5pm, Sa 9am-noon. Closed Dec. 29-Jan. 3.

Tōkyō Convention & Visitors Bureau (TCVB), Tōkyō Metropolitan Government No. 1 Bldg. 1F (☎5321-3077). Open daily 9:30am-6:30pm. Closed for New Year's holidays. The "Yes! Tōkyō" materials provide transport tips and neighborhood-by-neighborhood coverage. Their regional maps are not as detailed as their big city map (a nearly flawless must-have), but are easier to use, since they filter out Tōkyō's little alleys. TCVB materials are available at all tourist offices.

Tours:

Sunrise Tours (☎5796-5454; www.jtb.co.jp/sunrisetour) makes runs to Nikkō (¥13,500, children ¥11,500) and Mt. Fuji and Hakone (¥15,000/¥13,000). Closed Dec. 28-Jan. 5.

Hato Bus Tours (☎3435-6081; www.hatobus.co.jp). Popular for their Dynamic Tōkyō Tour, which takes visitors to a tea ceremony and some of Tōkyō's gardens. Call for info about other tours.

Japan Gray Line (☎3436-6881; www.jgl.co.jp/inbound/traveler/traveler.htm). Have made a name for themselves with half- and full-day bus tours of Tōkyō.

Jun's Tōkyō Discovery Tours (☎3749-0445; me2@gb3.so-net.ne.jp). For opponents of herd behavior. Totally personalized; it's just you and Tōkyō connoisseur Junko, toodling around as you see fit. For about US$100 a day (8-9hr.), she'll plan your route and take care of meals and transport.

Kimi Information Center, 2-42-3, Ikebukuro, Toshima-ku (☎3986-1604). Also good for one-on-one. They can put you in touch with an English-speaking college student who'll show you around your favorite neighborhood for free. Open M-F 10am-7pm, Sa 10am-4pm.

Embassies and Consulates: If a foreign government has an embassy in Japan, the office is in Tōkyō. See p. 9 for a partial list.

Immigration Office: The **Tōkyō Regional Immigration Bureau** (☎5796-7111) handles visa renewals. Recently moved to the boonies: go to Shinagawa Station and take the Kōnan Exit. Then take the #99 bus to the 6th stop. Open M-F 9am-noon and 1pm-4pm.

Banks and Currency Exchange: Banks in Tōkyō are more abundant than traffic lights; just head to any major street and scan the signs for the characters " 銀行 ." Foreign cash and traveler's checks can be exchanged throughout the city if you have your passport and can provide an address in Japan; Resona Bank also requires a (non-cell) phone number before they'll take your traveler's checks. Banks are the easiest choice for currency exchange—and often the only places that will change traveler's checks. Most banks open for exchange M-F 9am-3pm. Big post offices (see below) will also change money. Most open for exchange weekdays 9am-4pm (Tōkyō Central until 6pm). Major hotels and large department stores will also sometimes cash traveler's checks.

ATM: ATMs that will accept foreign plastic may be a little more difficult to find—your best bets are the international ATMs in post offices. **Citibank** (☎3215-0051; no English) has 24hr. international ATMs. Look at Roppongi Minami Bldg. 2F, 5-1-1, Roppongi, Minato-ku (nearest station: Roppongi, Exit 3); M2F, Kurosawa Bldg. 3F, 6-9-2, Ginza, Chūō-ku (Ginza, Exit A2); Dōgenzaka Kabuto Bldg. 1F, 2-25-12, Dōgenzaka, Shibuya-ku

(Shibuya, Hachikō Exit); Shinjuku Sky Bldg. 1F, 1-18-8, Nishi-shinjuku (Shinjuku, South Exit, East Side). **VISA** Global ATMs can get you cash advances; they're in Narita First Terminal Central Bldg. 1F and Second Terminal Main Bldg. 3F and throughout Tōkyō.

Credit Cards: Toll-free English-speaking numbers, to cancel cards and check balances: **Citibank** ☎0120-110-330; **Mastercard** ☎00531-11-3886; **Visa** ☎00531-44-0022.

American Express: American Express International ☎3220-6100. Available 24hr.

Luggage Storage: Virtually every JR station has a full set of lockers. If you need to put away an elephant and a half, **Tōkyō Station** is probably the best bet. Lockers (☎3212-2441) cost ¥300-600 depending on size; your stash gets fed to woodland creatures at 2am the 3rd day. ¥700 lockers are down a hallway on the right side (as you exit) of the Marunouchi Underground North Exit stiles, and can fit two or three nerds (or a huge backpack); max. 2 days. The station's **cloak room** (☎3201-3386) is open daily 10am-6pm and will hold anything under 30kg for 1 day only; it's on the left, just before the Yaesu Underground Central Exit stiles.

Lost Property: Local police boxes and some stations have lost and found offices. Failing that, try the **Central Lost and Found Office** of the Metropolitan Police (☎3814-4151; 24hr.). The **JR East Infoline** (☎3423-0111; daily 10am-6pm) has English speakers and can help locate anything lost on a JR train. The line's frequently busy; don't give up. For lost items on the subway, call the **TRTA Lost & Found** at ☎3834-5577 (Japanese only). For things lost in **taxis**, call ☎3648-0300 (24hr.; Japanese only).

English-Language Bookstores:

Tower Books, 1-22-14, Jinnan, Shibuya-ku (☎3496-3661), on the 7th fl. of Tower Records Shibuya. Shibuya Station. Hachikō Exit. Walk up the main road, parallel to and just left of the train tracks. On the right, after the Seibu and Marui *depāto*. Has every genre of literature you'd expect to find in a store back home. Open daily 10am-11pm.

Maruzen, 2-3-10, Nihonbashi, Chūō-ku. Nihonbashi Station (☎3272-7211; www.maruzen.co.jp/home/temp). Take Exit A1 and look right, across the street. English titles on the 4th fl. include children's literature, academic texts, magazines, dictionaries, books about Japanese society, and a smattering of bestsellers. Open M-Sa 10am-8pm, Su 10am-7pm. Credit cards accepted.

Yaesu Center, 2-5-1, Yaesu, Chūō-ku (☎3281-1811). Tōkyō Station. Take Yaesu South exit; it's farther south on the opposite side of the main avenue before you. Books in English, German, and French on the 7th fl., mostly textbooks. Open M-Sa 10am-9pm, occasional Su 10am-7pm.

Good Day Books, 1-11-2-3F Ebisu, Shibuya-ku (☎5421-0957; www.gooddaybooks.com), has shelves upon shelves of intriguing used English titles, overflowing into boxes on the floor. Ebisu Station. East Exit (3rd fl.). Descend and U-turn, then pass between Sunkus and Pronto. Turn right on Ebisu-dōri. On the right, on the 3rd fl. Open M-Tu and Th-Sa 11am-8pm; Su 11am-6pm.

Library: National Diet Library (☎3581-2331). Nagata-chō Station. Visible from Exit 2. Japan's biggest, with 12 million volumes. Foreigners may visit, but can't take books out. Open M-Sa 9:30am-5pm. Closed 2nd and 4th Sa and 1st and 3rd M of the month.

Cultural and Religious Centers:

Foreign Residents' Advisory Center Hotline (☎5320-7744) answers general questions about Japan and Japanese culture in pretty good English. Open M-F 9:30am-noon and 1-4pm. Change the phone suffix to 7755 for French (Th only), 7766 for Mandarin (Tu, F), 7730 for Spanish (Th), or 7700 for Korean (W).

Welcome Furoshiki (☎5472-7074; furoshiki@oakassociates.co.jp) is a good way to start a stay; a volunteer will visit you with brochures, recent news, and practical info. Fire away with questions—you have 1hr. before your new friend skedaddles. Call and leave a message to arrange a visit.

Islamic Center Japan, 1-6-11, Ohara, Setagaya-ku (☎3460-6169; http://islamcenter.or.jp/eng). Sasazuka Station (Keiō Line) or Shimokitazawa Station (Odakyū Line). From the first, exit north and head west down the main road toward Chiyoda Bridge. Turn left at the intersection onto Kannana Road, then left after the bus stop onto Inokashira. On the right. Website helps keep Halal.

IN RECENT NEWS

HOUSE RULES

While in Tōkyō, you may see a funny-looking silver trailer that looks like it should be selling hot dogs. Before you try to place an order, take heed: it's actually a smoking lounge.

In October 2002, a law was passed banning outdoor smoking in certain districts of Chiyoda-ku (home of the Imperial Palace and Tōkyō Station). Don't bother guessing whether you're in a safe district or not—the law has fangs, ¥2000 worth, to be precise. Following the law's passage a great deal of controversy ensued, of course; the ever-pressing issue of "freedom to" vs. "freedom from" was brought into question.

Enter the funny-looking silver trailer. Japan Tobacco rallied against the fledgling law with the introduction of "smoking-space" vehicles. According to *Mainichi* newspaper, these trailers come equipped with counters for eating, vending machines, and A/C. Needless to say, some nonsmokers aren't too happy about this creative loophole. As for smokers, this measure just might keep them off the endangered species list.

Other big ticket penalties include public urination (¥10,000), littering (¥50,000), and not picking up after your dog (¥50,000). Big Brother has been talking about installing video cameras to enforce the house rules, but it hasn't happened yet.

Jewish Community of Japan, 3-8-8, Hirō, Shibuya-ku (☎3400-2559; www.jccjapan.or.jp). Shibuya Station. Take Bus #3 to Tōkyō Jo-Gakkan Mae. Website helpful with keeping kosher.

Ticket Agencies: While many venues ticket themselves, most events are also available through **Ticket Pia** (☎5237-9999; www.pia.co.jp/pia/english/ticket.html), which has 600 box offices and 13,000 machines in convenience stores. **CN Playguide** (☎3561-8821; www.a-box.ne.jp) and **Lawson Ticket** (☎3573-1012) are the 2 other big players.

Laundromat: The Tōkyō standard for reclaiming social presentability is ¥200 a load. Drying clothes in the sun is common practice, but individuals who demand fluffiness can have it for ¥100 a load. Many laundromats sell cheap detergent packets for ¥100.

Emergency: Police ☎110. **Fire** or **ambulance** ☎119. **Japan Helpline** (☎0570-000-911; www.jhelp.com) operates 24-7 in fluent English; they can help in emergencies.

Police: Foreign hotline ☎3501-0110. Office at 1-1-2, Kasumigaseki, Chiyoda-ku 100-8929. English-, Chinese-, and Korean-speakers 24hr. Less frequent coverage of Spanish, Thai, Tagalog, Persian, and French. **Metro police department** counseling services ☎3503-8484. Speaks English and Mandarin. Can make appointments for Spanish, Cantonese, Thai, Korean, French, and other languages. Open M-F 8:30am-5pm.

Crisis Lines: Tōkyō English Life Line (☎5774-0992; www.telljp.com) offers English counseling by phone or face-to-face. Open daily 9am-4pm and 7pm-11pm.

Red Cross: Medical center, 4-1-22, Hirō, Shibuya-ku (☎3400-1311). Shibuya Station. **Red Cross HQ** ☎3438-1311. Open M-F 9-5pm. **Blood donation** ☎5485-6011.

Pharmacy: American Pharmacy speaks fluent English and can fill any prescriptions you have, even foreign-issued ones, and can recommend local doctors. **Marunouchi branch:** ☎5220-7716. Tōkyō Station. In the Marunouchi Bldg. basement, across from the Marunouchi South Exit. Open M-F 9am-9pm, Sa 10am-9pm, Su and holidays 10am-8pm. **Ueno branch:** Ueno Station. On the right just before Shinobazu Exit dumps you outside. Open M-F 9am-11pm, Sa-Su and holidays 9am-10:30pm.

Hospital/Medical Services: Hospitals are everywhere. The following information lines can direct you to the nearest one, but if it's not an emergency you may be best off with the Tōkyō Clinic or the International Clinic, where they speak fluent English.

Info Lines: Tōkyō Medical Information Service introduces visitors to medical facilities and practitioners, and explains the Japanese medical system. Their **Emergency Interpretation Service** (☎5285-8185) is open M-F 5pm-8pm; Sa-

Su and holidays 9am-8pm. **Tōkyō English Life Line** (☎5774-0992) staffers speak fluent English and will relay your emergency to the authorities. Available M-F 9am-5pm. **AMDA International Medical Information Center** (☎5285-8088) can offer general help in fluent English. Available M-F 9am-5pm.

St. Luke's International Hospital (Seiroka Byōin), 9-1, Akashichō, Chūō-ku (☎3541-5151). Tsukiji Station. Follow the signs from Exit 3 or 4. Foreigner-friendly. They have emergency services, but the regular hours are limited to M-F 8:30-11:30am.

Tōkyō Clinic, Mori Bldg. 2F, 3-4-30, Shiba-kōen, Minato-ku (☎3436-3028). Kamiyachō Station. From Exit 1, head toward Tōkyō Tower. Brownish/red-brick bldg. across from tower. Perfect English spoken. Dental also. Reception M-F 8:30am-5:30pm (consultations 9am-4:45pm), Sa 9am-noon. Appointment required.

International Clinic, 1-5-9, Azabudai, Minato-ku (☎3583-7831). Roppongi Station. Turn right out of Subway Exit 3. Walk 10sec. and turn right again at the intersection with a sushi restaurant and a 2nd floor Citibank on the corner. Go straight for 10min., stopping at Iigura Katamachi crossing (it has an elevated highway—it's *not* Iigura crossing). Look for a 2-story house with a garden and trees. Excellent English. Open M-F 9am-noon and 2pm-5pm, Sa 9am-noon.

Ishikawa Clinic, 3-2-7, Nishi-Azabu, Minato-ku (☎3401-6340). Roppongi Station. Appointment required. Open M 9am-5pm, Tu and Th 9am-1pm and 3pm-7pm, W and F 9am-1pm.

Yamauchi Dental Clinic, 3-16-10, Shirokanedai, Minato-ku (☎3441-6377). Shirokanedai Station. English-speaking dentists.

Fax and Copy Shops: Tōkyō, world capital of office technology, does not skimp on digital needs. **Kinko's** shops, open 24/7, are absolutely everywhere. To make a quick copy, stop by any convenience store; all have coin-op machines that print on a variety of paper sizes for ¥10 a sheet (more for color). Japanese paper sizes range from B5-A3; this is hassle for cross-cultural folder and hole punch compatibility.

Internet Access: Most **Kinko's** shops (see above) have Internet access, charging ¥200 for 10min. For additional options, see individual neighborhood listings below.

Post Office: Max. weight of packages to be sent abroad is 20kg. Floating your goods home takes up to 2 months and costs up to ¥10,250 for the US. **SAL** airmail ships when there's extra space and costs up to ¥19,550 for the US. **Airmail** costs up to ¥27,150 for the US. **EMS** airmail provides computerized tracking, insurance, and a greater maximum package size and for the US is actually cheaper than regular airmail. Most post offices are open M-F 9am-5pm; several are open 24hr.

Tōkyō Central Post Office, just outside the Marunouchi South Exit of JR Tōkyō Station. General mail open M-F 9am-9pm, Sa-Su and holidays 9am-7pm, Jan. 1-3 9am-12:30pm, Dec. 20 and Dec. 27 9am-5pm. Cash service (ATM) M-F 7am-11:55pm, Sa 12:05am-11:55pm, Su and holidays 12:05am-8pm; closed Jan. 1-3. After Hours Service Box open daily midnight-9am for general mail; M-F 9pm-midnight, Sa-Su and holidays 7pm-midnight for cash service.

Tōkyō International Post Office (☎3241-4877). Tōkyō Station. From the JR's Nihonbashi Exit, walk to the elevated tracks and follow the left edge. It's on your left near the end. Open M-F 9am-7pm, Sa 9am-5pm, Su 9am-12:30pm. After hours window open at all other times.

Postal Code: Postal codes are 7 digits long, and the first 3 are usually unique to a specific ward. There's an online postal code look-up at http://yuujirou.inac.co.jp.

MAJOR NEIGHBORHOODS

AKASAKA

Internet Access: Barbocco, 2-14-3 2F, Nagata-chō, Chiyoda-ku (☎3580-1036). Akasaka-mitsuke Station. Highly visible from the subway station's Sotobori-dōri Exit. An Italian fast food cafe. Free Internet so long as you buy food or a drink. Open M-Sa 11am-9pm. **Net Square,** Copacabana Bldg. 1F, 3-6-4, Akasaka, Minato-ku (☎5545-9020; www.netsquare.jp) is a little farther from the same station. Turn left out of the right mouth of the Sotobori-dōri Exit and head a few blocks down. It's on the left after 3 little side streets. ¥250 for 30min. Open M-Sa 8am-7pm, Su and holidays 10am-7pm.

TŌKYŌ

Post Office: 8-4-17, Akasaka, Minato-ku (☎3478-3423). Aoyama-itchōme Station. Across the street from Exit 4. Open 24hr. After-hours counter in the back.

ASAKUSA

Tourist Office: Asakusa Culture and Sightseeing Center, 2-18-9, Kaminari-mon, Taitō-ku (☎3842-5566). Take Exit 2 from the Ginza Line Station and head to the end of the next block, away from the river. One of Tōkyō's larger TIC's. English maps of the Asakusa area. Pick up a "Welcome Guide to Taitō City": a card on the back gets you local discounts. Terrific English-fluent booth with friendly volunteers. Open daily 10am-5pm.

Tours: Asakusa Rickshaw (Asakusa Jinrikishya), 1-13-10, Kaminari-mon, Taitō-ku (☎3851-9361; www.ebisuya.com). Strapping young men will haul you around Asakusa, explaining local sights as they go. Look for the red rickshaws in front of the tourist office. Tours range from ¥2000 for a 10min. ride (¥3000 for 2 people) to a special ¥15,000 ride for newlyweds. Available in English. The **Asakusa Culture and Sightseeing Center** (see above) gives tours at 1:30 and 3pm on Su; get tickets through their branch at Yūrakuchō Station, but those who simply show up are often welcomed.

Currency Exchange and Bank: Tōkyō-Mitsubishi Bank (☎3851-9361). Traveler's checks changed. No US credit cards accepted.

Internet Access: Internet Cafe Papyrus, 1-35-8, Asakusa, Taitō-ku (☎3842-4687). Asakusa Station. U-turn out of Exit 3 and take a left at the end of the block. Cross 3 little streets and turn left at the end. Building immediately on left; 2nd floor. Tiny, but Internet cafes are a rare species here. ¥100 per 10min. Open M-Sa 10:30am-8pm.

Post Office: 1-1-1 Taitō-ku, Asakusa. From Exit #1 or 2 of the Ginza Line Station, head down the main road, away from the huge golden sculpture. Turn left at the T-intersection; it's on your right after a few mini-blocks. Open 24hr. (late-night window after 7pm).

GINZA

Tourist Office: JNTO headquarters, the best tourist information center in Tōkyō, is in front of Yūrakuchō Station (see **All of Tōkyō,** p. 122).

Internet Access: Woman Excite Café (☎3286-5532; http://woman.excite.co.jp). Ginza Station. From the intersection of Chūō-dōri and Harumi-dōri, head west down Harumi-dōri, away from Mitsukoshi. Enter Seibu behind Ginza Station and go to the 8th fl. Turn left off the escalator; the sign-up desk is in the near-right corner. 1hr. max., drink purchase required. Free. **Kinko's,** 1-5-12, Nishi-Shinbashi, Minato-ku (☎3506-2611). Uchisaiwachō Station. Head straight out of Exit 4. On the right, after the footbridge.

Post Office: Post office outlets pepper the area, but the Tōkyō Central Post Office is only slightly farther than the major branches around here (see **All of Tōkyō,** p. 122).

HARAJUKU AND AOYAMA

Internet Access: Yahoo Internet Cafe, Starbucks Garden Square, 5-11-2, Jingūmae, Shibuya-ku. Harajuku or Omotesandō Station. From either station, go toward the other via Omotesandō-dōri. ESQUISSE Omotesandō is halfway; turn south at its east edge. A block on the right, above Starbucks. Free. Open M-F 7am-10pm, Sa-Su 8am-10pm.

IKEBUKURO

Tourist Office: Less for brochure blitzing and more for service-providing, the **Kimi Information Center,** Oscar Bldg. 8F, 2-42-3, Ikebukuro, Toshima-ku (☎3986-1604; www.kimiwillbe.com) caters to English speakers. Ikebukuro Station. From the West Exit, turn right and cross to KFC, past the police box. Turn left, then make a right at Sumitomo-Mitsui Bank. The 4th right is a narrow alley with an unlabeled elevator lobby on the left; ride to the 8th fl. Free monthly magazine offers job and housing leads, and housing agents help can put up more permanent visitors for a fee. They'll keep mail and take telephone messages (¥3150 for 2 months). Translation services, computer rental, Internet access (¥100 per 10min.), headhunters, bulletin boards, and fax service (¥315 plus phone charge) also available. Open M-F 10am-7pm, Sa 10am-4pm.

Tours: The **Kimi Information Center** (see above) hooks tourists up with local English-starved students who will show them around; individuals need only pay for themselves.

Internet Access: ManBOO! (マンボー), 1-13-11 2F, Higashi-Ikebukuro, Toshima-ku (☎5911-4344). Ikebukuro Station. From the giant Seibu, head down Green Main-dōri. The next main left forks; take the right. Take the 1st right after Cinema Sunshine on the left; it's on the right, above Bar Mysterious. The total Internet/*manga* cafe. ¥380 for 1st hr.; ¥100 for additional 15min.; 3hr. package ¥960 (start 8am-10pm); 5hr. package ¥1160 (start 11pm-3am). For free access, try the 6 computers on the 2nd fl. of the Ikebukuro **Virgin Megastore** (☎5952-5600). Open daily 11am-8pm.

MARUNOUCHI

Tourist Office: Tōkyō Station is a major railway hub and has information booths. However, these are mostly geared toward transportation questions; for a real tourist office, JNTO Headquarters is close by (see **All of Tōkyō**, p. 122).

Tours: Imperial Palace (☎3213-1111, ext. 485 or 486). Tōkyō Station. Head straight out of Marunouchi Central Exit and go down the broad avenue. The gates are on the opposite side of the bridge. Sakashita-mon is slightly uphill on the left, guarded by a police box. Kikyō-mon is more to the right and will be surrounded by guards at the time of the tour. An Imperial Palace tour can be arranged through the Kunaichō (the Imperial Household's administrative branch). Call ahead; it takes a day to print your official visitation permit, and you must come to the Kunaichō at least a day before the tour to pick it up. The Kunaichō is accessible by talking to the guards at Sakashita-mon gate. Tours usually 10am and 1:30pm weekdays and begin at Kikyō-mon gate. See **Marunouchi Sights** (p. 161) for details. Kunaichō open M-F 8:45am-4:30pm. Closed holidays.

Internet Access: Marunouchi Cafe, Fuji Bldg. 1F, 3-2-3, Marunouchi, Chiyoda-ku (☎3212-5025). Tōkyō Station. Take the left mouth of Marunouchi South Exit, cross to the Central Post Office, and keep the post office on your left. At the end, cross the street and turn left. Make your 1st right, then turn left at the brick-floor intersection. It's at the opposite corner of the next intersection. Free lounge with artsy decor and vending machines. Internet free; there's sometimes a lengthy wait. Foreign users must flash a passport and re-register every hr. Open M-Sa 8am-8pm, Sa-Su and holidays 10am-6pm. **Sakura Hotel** (p. 135) has a single computer available for public use. ¥262 for 15min., ¥420 for 30min., ¥630 for 1hr. Black-and-white printing ¥30, color ¥100.

Post Office: The left mouth of the Marunouchi South Exit of the JR Tōkyō Station will put you right across from Tōkyō Central Post Office (see **All of Tōkyō**, p. 122).

ODAIBA

Tours: Seaside Cycle, Seaside Hall, 1-6-1, Daiba, Minato-ku (☎3599-3196). Odaiba Kaihin-Kōen Station. Turn right from the turnstiles, cross to the shoreside street, and turn left. They'll pedal you all over Daiba's parks. 1hr. tour ¥3000, for 2 people ¥5000. If you want the workout, rent your own bike: ¥500 for 1hr., ¥800 for 3hr., ¥1000 per day. Weekends higher. Open M-F 11am-8:30pm, Sa 10:30am-9pm, Su 10am-10pm.

Currency Exchange, Banks, and ATMs: Tōkyō Big Sight has ATMs and changes cash (no traveler's checks). Banks are rare; a branch of **Mizuho Bank** is stashed in the northwest corner of Tōkyō Fashion Town. The post office (see below) has an international ATM.

Internet Access: Broadband Cafe, 2-5-18, Ariake, Kōtō-ku. Kokusai-Tenjijō Seimon Station. Turn left out of the turnstiles and walk straight, all the way down Tōkyō Fashion Town's 2nd fl. plaza. It's on the ground floor of the Panasonic Center. Free Internet with drink purchase. Open Tu-Su 10am-6pm.

TŌKYŌ

Post Office: 1-5-4-301, Daiba, Minato-ku. Odaiba Kaihin-Kōen Station. Turn right, stay on the 2nd fl., and walk toward the arches. It's on the right. General delivery open M-F 9am-5pm; cash service M-F 9am-4pm; international ATM M-F 9am-7pm.

ROPPONGI

Tours: Roppongi Hills launches tours (of just the Hills) from an office in the main plaza; English tours only happen several times a month.

Banks and ATMs: Banks are scarcer than elsewhere, but a **Citibank** at Roppongi Crossing saves the day. VISA Global ATMs in Takehara Bldg. 1F and Kōsaten Arts Shop Bldg.

Internet Access: Manga Hiroba. From Roppongi Crossing, it's 3min. down the left side of Gaien-higashi-dōri. Very well hidden. Comfy stalls for private Googling. Enough *manga* (comics) for several life sentences. 1st hr. ¥380, additional 30min. ¥150. Free drinks. **Shiday** is on the other side of the street, with 3 nice but open computers in the lobby of a karaoke parlor. Internet available daily noon-5am. ¥250 for 15min.

SHIBUYA

Banks and ATMs: No problems finding cash here, especially when plastic is so humbly accepted. Citibank is a consistent option; facing the giant TV from its foot, head left up the tree-lined avenue and fork right a few hundred yards.

Internet Access: Internet cafes in Shibuya are sinfully nice. **Cafe J Net NEWNEW,** 34-5, Udagawachō, Shibuya-ku (☎5458-5935) has so many computers that guests are given coordinates. Shibuya Station. Hachikō Exit. Cross the street to the smaller big TV and head left up the tree-lined avenue. Turn right at the fork, right at the 2nd fork, and right opposite the center of Tōkyū department store. It's on the left, on the 7th fl. Internet gaming, private stalls, office software, free drinks, *manga*, and more. ¥200 sign-up fee. ¥300 per hr. Private stalls ¥460 per hr. 5-12hr. night packages ¥950-2300. Open 24hr. Cash only. **Bagus Internet Manga,** Bldg. 6F, 28-6, Udagawa-chō, Shibuya-ku (☎5428-3217; www.bagus-99.com/manga) has a DVD library, comic books, and Playstation2. Shibuya Station. JR Hachikō Exit. Facing the big TVs, head left down the main road, perpendicular to the tracks. Turn right at the fork. It's a few blocks down, in the Club Sega bldg. Free drinks. 1st hr. ¥450, then ¥70 per 10min. Weekend rates higher. Open 24hr.

Post Office: 1-12-13, Shibuya, Shibuya-ku (☎5469-9907). Shibuya Station. Hachikō Exit. Turn right and cross under the tracks. Go past the main intersection. Look for a towering building on the left. Open 24hr. International ATMs closed 11:55pm-12:05am.

SHINJUKU

Tourist Office: Tōkyō's best-presented tourist information branch (☎5321-3077; www.tourism.metro.tokyo.jp/english/public/tokyo_tocho.html) is under the Tōkyō Metropolitan Government Office buildings. Tochōmae Station. Turn right out of the exit; make a right into the recessed entrance. Inside, it's on the right. Unseemly quantity of maps and brochures. Open daily 9:30am-6pm. Closed for year-end holidays.

Tours: The tourist office above runs 40min. tours of the Tōkyō Metropolitan Government Office, 10am-2:30pm daily. English, Chinese, and Korean tours available.

Bank: Citibank is a good 24hr. option; take the Shinjuku Station's South Exit and turn right, then look below to the 2nd chunk of building on the right next to the bridge.

Internet Access: All Shinjuku's main players offer private closets. Doubles at **Rakuda** (らくだ ; ☎3353-7400; www.raku-da.com) are partially advertised as rest stops. Shinjuku Station. From the East Exit, go straight, bearing right between the driveway islands. Cross the street and go on. Turn right opposite Mitsukoshi, and it's on the left. Women ¥200 for 1st hr., men ¥300. Additional 15min. ¥100. ¥880 for 3hr. (begin

8am-5pm). ¥1080 for 5hr. (begin 10pm-3am). Free drinks. Open 24hr. **ManBOO!** (マ ンボー), 3-15-15 6F, Shinjuku, Shinjuku-ku (☎3209-4957; http://manboo.co.jp) is closer to Kabuki-chō. From the East Exit, turn left and head to the road in front of Prince Hotel. Turn right; it's the middle of the 6th block, after Wendy's. Women ¥100 for 1st hr., men ¥200. Additional 15min. ¥100. ¥780 for 3hr. (begin 8am-11pm). ¥980 for 5hr. (begin 11pm-8am). Free drinks. Open 24hr. In Kabuki-chō, try **Bagus**, 1-21-1 4F, Kabuki-chō, Shinjuku-ku (☎5155-5443; www.bagus-99.com/manga) in the same building as Buttu-Trick Bar (see **Food**). ¥450 for 1st hr., additional 10min. ¥70. Booths ¥500 for 1st hr., additional 10min. ¥80. ¥30 weekend fee. Free drinks. Open 24hr.

Post Office: The main post office is west of the tracks and equipped with an international ATM. Take a right out of the Shinjuku Station South Exit, the next main right down the divided road, and the 3rd right after that a bit before Hotel Kadoya. Open 24hr.

UENO

Tourist Office: 1-60, Ueno Kōen, Taitō-ku (☎3836-3471; www.tourism.metro.tokyo.jp). Underground, in front of the Keisei Ueno Station ticket gate. Pick up a "Welcome Guide to Taitō City": a card on the back earns discounts at local establishments. Maps of Ueno Park are available at the kiosk across from the JR's Kōen Exit.

Internet Access: Break (ブレイク ; www.jr-break.com/ueno), at the station's Hirokōji Exit, next to the Hard Rock Cafe, gives visitors 30min. of free Internet; needless to say, it's very popular. Internet M-F 11am-7:30pm, Sa-Su and holidays 10am-6:30pm.

Post Office: 6-15-1, Ueno, Taitō-ku. From the JR's Hirokōji Exit, head down the alley on the left side of the OICITY building (ma-roo-ee city). It's on the right, halfway down the block. Open M-F 9am-6pm.

SMALLER NEIGHBORHOODS

AKIHABARA

Internet Access: Manga Kissa, 3-7-12, Isamiya, Bldg. 8, 4F, Soto-Kanda, Chiyoda-ku (☎3252-2733). Cosplay-themed Internet cafe 2 flights above Cos Cha (p. 157) on the 4th fl. ("Cosplay" = dressing up like anime characters.) New, totally easy to settle into, and sells *manga*. ¥450 for 1st hr., ¥100 every additional 15min. Includes free drink.

⚑ ACCOMMODATIONS

The city is rich in places to lay sleepy heads, though the prices may make you wince. Look outside established areas and be prepared to commute if you want bargains; if you're splurging to stay in the thick of it, shop around until you find the amenities you desire. Accommodations tax is usually included in the quoted price of cheaper stays, but more upscale places will tack it on to their listed rates.

The **Welcome Inn Reservation Center** (☎3252-1717; www.itcj.or.jp), helps non-Japanese speakers reserve rooms. Find the directory online, venture into a hotel and hope it's a member, or visit the office in the Kōtsū Kaikan Building, easily identifiable from the Kyōbashi Exit of Yūrakuchō Station.

Just off the map is the **Tōkyō International Youth Hostel (HI) ❷** (Tōkyō Kokusai Yūsu Hosuteru; 東京国際ユースホステル), Central Plaza, 1-1, Kagurakashi, Shinjuku-ku (☎3235-1107; www.tokyo-yh.jp). From Iidabashi Station's West Exit, turn right, cross a bridge to the brown building and ride to the 18th floor. One of Tōkyō's two hostels (the other is **Yoyogi**, p. 134) it masquerades as an ordinary hotel. (Breakfast ¥400. Laundry ¥100. Check-in 3pm. Check-out 10am. Lockout 10am-3pm. Curfew 10:30pm. Dorms ¥3500, under 14 ¥2000.)

UNDER ¥3500 (●)	
⚟ Capsule Hotel Asakusa Riverside (131)	AS
Hotel Kinuya Honkan (140)	UN
Hotel New Koyo (131)	AS
Taitō Ryokan (132)	AS
⚟ Yoyogi Youth Hostel (HI) (134)	HA

¥3500-5000 (●)	
Capsule Hotel & Sauna Roby (134)	IK
Capsule Hotel Fontaine Akasaka (130)	AK
Capsule Land Shibuya (137)	SB
Green Plaza Shinjuku (138)	SJ
⚟ Kimi Ryokan (134)	IK
Oriental Capsule Sauna (139)	UN
Ryokan Katsutarō (139)	UN
⚟ Sakura Hotel (135)	MR
⚟ Sawanoya Ryokan (139)	UN

¥5001-8000 (●)	
⚟ Andon Ryokan (131)	AS
Asakusa Central Hotel (133)	AS
Asakusa Plaza Hotel (133)	AS
City Hotel Lornstar (138)	SJ
Hotel Asia Center of Japan (130)	AK
⚟ Hotel Park Inn (137)	SJ
Hotel Pastoral (136)	RP
Hotel Pine Hill (140)	UN
Hotel Suncity (134)	IK
Hotel Tateshina (138)	SJ
Hotel Yaesu-Ryūmeikan (135)	MR
Kadoya Hotel (138)	SJ
Kinuya Hotel (139)	UN
Kyōwa Kaikan (133)	EB
Mayo Viento (137)	SB
Ryokan Shigetsu (132)	AS
Tōkyō Business Hotel (137)	SJ

¥8001-15,000 (●)	
Asakusa View Hotel (133)	AS
Ginza Nikkō Hotel (133)	GZ
Hotel Arca Torre (136)	RP
Hotel Floracion Aoyama (134)	HA
Hotel Ibis (136)	RP
Hotel Listel (138)	SJ
Hotel Rose Garden (138)	SJ
Hotel Theatre (134)	IK
⚟ Hotel Villa Fontaine Roppongi (136)	RP
Mitsui Urban Hotel Ginza (133)	GZ
Nishi Shinjuku Hotel (139)	SJ
Rainbow Hotel (140)	UN
Shibuya City Hotel (136)	SB
Shibuya Tōbu Hotel (137)	SB
Shibuya Tōkyū Inn (137)	SB
Tōkyō Bay Ariake Washington Hotel (135)	OD
Tōkyō Station Hotel (135)	MR
Yaesu Terminal Hotel (135)	MR

¥15,001+ (●)	
Akasaka Excel Hotel Tōkyū (131)	AK
ANA Hotel Tōkyō (131)	AK
⚟ Cerulean Tower Tōkyū Hotel (136)	SB
Four Seasons Hotel (135)	MR
Grand Hyatt Tōkyō (136)	RP
Hotel Century Southern Tower (137)	SJ
Hotel Metropolitan (134)	IK
Hotel New Ōtani Tōkyō (131)	AK
Hotel Nikkō Tōkyō (135)	OD
Hotel Seiyō Ginza (133)	GZ
Keiō Plaza Hotel (138)	SJ
Le Meridien Grand Pacific Tōkyō (136)	OD
Suigetsu Hotel (139)	UN
The Westin (133)	EB

AK Akasaka **AS** Asakusa **EB** Ebisu **GZ** Ginza **HA** Harajuku and Aoyama **IK** Ikebukuro **MR** Marunouchi **OD** Odaiba **RP** Roppongi **SB** Shibuya **SJ** Shinjuku **UN** Ueno

MAJOR NEIGHBORHOODS

AKASAKA

The National Diet makes for an expensive bedfellow, but the local hotels know how to pamper a guest silly.

Hotel Asia Center of Japan (ホテルアジア会館), 8-10-32, Akasaka, Minato-ku (☎3402-6111; www.asiacenter.or.jp). Aoyama-itchōme Station. Take Exit 4. Cross the street and immediately turn right. Proceed a few blocks and turn left at Shinsaka 40 House. Cheaper, snugger, and a little farther than your average Hilton. A new tower goes up Apr. 15, 2004. Laundry ¥200. Reception 24hr. Check-in 2pm. Check-out 11am. Singles ¥7800; doubles from ¥11,800; triples from ¥19,800. Credit cards accepted. ●

Capsule Hotel Fontaine Akasaka (カプセルホテルフォンテーヌ赤坂), 4-3-5, Akasaka, Sumida-ku (☎3583-6554; www.fontaine-akasaka.co.jp). Akasaka-mitsuke Station. Turn right from the left mouth of the subway's Sotobori-dōri Exit and head down

Sotobori-dōri a few blocks. Turn right opposite Hie Shrine's gate. It's at the top of the road and slightly to the right. The standard cubby-hole and sauna are a little more expensive here, but they're rolling with the times and letting in women. Some English spoken. Reception 24hr. Check-in 5pm (but show up whenever). Check-out 10am. Capsules ¥4800 (includes sauna and bath access). Credit cards accepted. ❷

ANA Hotel Tōkyō, 1-12-33, Akasaka, Minato-ku (☎3505-1111; www.anahotels.com/tokyo). Tameike-sannō Station. Right in front of Exit 13, in Ark Hills. Surpasses the local luxury competition in presentation; the lobby feels like an atrium, and the walls seem to glow. All the amenities are there, including a giant swimming pool and fitness room. Familiar, comforting, and far too expensive. Parking ¥1000 per night. Check-in 1pm. Check-out noon. Singles from ¥24,000; doubles from ¥32,000. ❺

Hotel New Ōtani Tōkyō, 4-1, Kioi-chō, Chiyoda-ku (☎3265-1111; www.newotani.co.jpen). Akasaka-mitsuke Station. Take the left mouth of the Sotobori-dōri Exit. Turn left and cross all the way over the intersection under the highway, then over a bridge. It's on the left. One of those executive hotels with every amenity you can name. Conference rooms? Check. Art museum? Check. Bellboys in monkey hats? Check. The circular tower has glass windows and makes for a fun peek 'n' flee. Reception 24hr. Check-in 2pm. Check-out noon. Singles from ¥29,000; doubles from ¥34,000. ❺

Akasaka Excel Hotel Tōkyū, 2-14-3, Nagata-chō, Chiyoda-ku (☎3580-2311; www.ath-jp.com). Akasaka-mitsuke Station. The left mouth of the subway's Sotobori-dōri Exit puts it in view. Horde of restaurants on the 1st and 2nd fl. terrace. Living within spanking distance of the subway isn't too shabby either. Parking ¥500 for 30min. or ¥1500 for 24hr. with 1 night stay. Check-in 2pm. Check-out 11am. Singles from ¥18,000; twins from ¥22,000; doubles from ¥26,000. Credit cards accepted. ❺

ASAKUSA

Quiet, foreigner-friendly Asakusa is an excellent budget choice and, together with Ueno, forms the hotbed for Tōkyō's ryokan. Two of Tōkyō's best options lie up north in nearby Minowa, which is just barely walkable.

🖾 Andon Ryokan, 2-34-11, Nihonzutsumi, Taitō-ku (☎3873-8611; www.andon.co.jp). Minowa Station. Turn left out of Exit #3 and walk a block. At the large confusing intersection, cross to the 9-story building with the white sign. Proceed down the left road (you're on the right side). Take the 2nd right and turn left; it's the glowing teal building. If you don't mind being far out, this brand-new ryokan is ideal. Glows like a lamp. Unbelievably sexy interior: common room like a posh modern jazz club. Cable Internet and DVD player in every room, DVD library, private jacuzzi, tea, and full kitchen. Drawbacks include location, smallish rooms, and an unremarkable guest:bathroom ratio. Home-cooked breakfast ¥300. Laundry ¥200; dryer ¥100. Key deposit ¥1000. Free parking. Reception open 7am-10pm. Check-in 3pm. Check-out 10am. Fluent English spoken. Reservations required. Doubles ¥7800. Extra bed ¥3000. Credit cards accepted. ❸

🖾 Capsule Hotel Asakusa Riverside (カプセルホテル浅草リバサイ度), 2-20-4, Kaminari-mon, Asakusa (☎3844-1155; gyomin@tctu.ne.jp). From the subway stations, walk toward the golden statue until the foot of a bridge. Turn right and look for a green sign. An ideal capsule hotel. Free Japanese bath with a view of the Sumida River (until 1 or 2am). One of the few with capsules for women. TV in capsule for ¥300. Breakfast ¥600. Free lockers. Reception open M-F 3pm-10am, Sa-Su 2pm-10am. Check-in M-F 3pm, Sa-Su 2pm. Check-out 10am. Capsule ¥2900. Credit cards accepted. ❶

Hotel New Koyo (Nyūkōyō; ニュー紅陽), 2-26-13, Nihonzutsumi, Taitō-ku (☎3873-0343; www.newkoyo.com). Minowa Station. Turn left out of Exit 3 and walk a bit. At the confusing intersection, cross to the 9-story building with the white sign. Go down the left road (you're on the right side). Take the 9th right. As cheap and *gaijin*-oriented as Tōkyō gets; perfect for backpackers. Designated hours for showers; walls are thin. Tiny Western- and Japanese-style rooms. Internet ¥15 per min. Free kitchen use (¥2 per min. for stove). Bike rental ¥500 per day. Movie library. Fluent English

TŌKYŌ

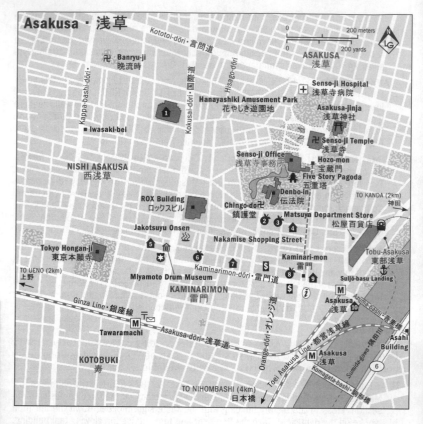

Asakusa・浅草

Kototoi-dōri・言問道

ASAKUSA
浅草

卍 **Banryu-ji**
晩流時

Senso-ji Hospital
浅草寺病院

Hanayashiki Amusement Park
花やしき遊園地

Asakusa-jinja
浅草神社

■ **Iwasaki-bei**

卍 **Senso-ji Temple**
浅草寺

NISHI ASAKUSA
西浅草

Senso-ji Office
浅草寺事務所

Hozo-mon
宝蔵門

Five Story Pagoda
五重塔

Denbo-in
伝法院

TO KANDA (2km)
神田

ROX Building
ロックスビル

Chingo-dōri卍
鎮護堂

Matsuya Department Store
松屋百貨店

Jakotsuyu Onsen

Nakamise Shopping Street

Tobu-Asakusa
東部浅草

Tokyo Hongan-ji
東京本願寺

TO UENO (2km)
上野

Miyamoto Drum Museum

Kaminarimon-dōri・雷門道

Kaminari-mon
雷門

Suijō-basu Landing

Asakusa
浅草

KAMINARIMON
雷門

Ginza Line・銀座線

Tawaramachi

Asakusa-dōri・浅草道

Asahi
Building

KOTOBUKI
寿

TO NIHOMBASHI (4km)
日本橋

Asakusa
浅草

Asakusa・浅草

⌂ ACCOMMODATIONS
Asakusa Central Hotel, **7**
Asakusa Plaza Hotel, **9**
Asakusa View Hotel, **1**
Capsule Hotel Asakusa
    Riverside, **10**
Ryokan Shigetsu, **4**
Taitō Ryokan, **5**

🍴 FOOD
Chinya, **8**
Daikokuya, **2**
Sushiya Street, **6**
Umezono, **3**

spoken. Towels ¥200. Laundry ¥200 (dryer ¥100). Free parking. Reception open 7am-10pm. Check-in noon. Check-out 10am. Reserve 2-3 days in advance. Singles from ¥2500. AmEx/MC/V. ❶

Ryokan Shigetsu (旅館指月), 1-31-11, Asakusa, Taitᵒ-ku (☎3843-2345; www.shigetsu.com). From Exit 1 of the Ginza Line Subway Station, turn right into the shopping arcade. Look left for a road hung with white lanterns; it's on the left. Unlike many ryokan, Shigetsu looks relatively new; it's smart and inviting. Restaurant available. Internet via a lobby computer. Western- and Japanese-style rooms. Breakfast ¥1200. Check-in 3pm. Check-out 10am. Singles from ¥7300; doubles from ¥14,000. ❸

Taitō Ryokan (台東旅館), 2-1-4, Nishi-Asakusa, Taitᵒ-ku (☎3843-2822; jptaito@liberty-house.gr.jp; www.libertyhouse.gr.jp). Tawara-machi Station. Turn left from Exit 3. Head up a bit and turn left at the percussion store. Look for a wooden building on the right. A little dark, but there's a subtle charm. Spacious *tatami* rooms; the owner is down-to-earth. English and Mandarin spoken. Reception 8-10am and 3-10pm. Check-in 3pm. Check-out 10am. No smoking. Reserve by e-mail. ¥3000 per person. Cash only. ❶

Asakusa View Hotel (浅草ビューホテル), 3-17-1, Nishi-Asakusa, Taitō-ku. (☎3847-1111; www.viewhotels.co.jp/asakusa). Tawara-machi Station. Take Exit 3 and turn left. It's on the left many blocks down; the ROX building is halfway. The *crème de la crème* of Asakusa isn't cheap and the lower-end rooms are not very large, but the bath, pool, sushi bar, and restaurants are perks. Short-term parking included. Check-in 1pm, Japanese-style rooms 4pm. Check-out 11am/10am. Singles from ¥13,000; doubles ¥23,000, Japanese-style ¥40,000; triples ¥34,000. Credit cards accepted. ❹

Asakusa Central Hotel (浅草セントラルホテル), 1-5-3, Asakusa, Taitō-ku (☎3847-2222; www.pelican.co.jp). Head straight out of Exit 1 of the Ginza Line Subway Station and go several blocks down the main street. Look right for a blue-lettered sign. Management just changed hands. Spacious Japanese and Western rooms. Comfortable and unremarkable. Breakfast available in restaurant. Check-in 3pm. Check-out 11am. Singles from ¥7800; doubles from ¥11,000. Credit cards accepted. ❸

Asakusa Plaza Hotel (浅草プラザホテル), 1-2-1, Asakusa, Taitō-ku. (☎3845-2621; www.asakusaplaza.jp). Take Exit 1 from the Ginza Line Subway Station and you're looking at it. Park yourself for the night up high. Laundry ¥200; dryer ¥100. Reception until 1am. Check-in 4pm. Check-out 10am. Singles from ¥6000; doubles from ¥10,500; twins from ¥11,000. 10% discount for long stays (more than a week). AmEx/MC/V. ❸

EBISU

A rich neighborhood largely devoid of tourism, Ebisu is not the best place to stay.

Kyowa Kaikan (協和会館), 1-10-5, Ebisu-nishi, Shibuya-ku (☎3464-2262; fax 3464-2202). Ebisu Station. From the West Exit, cross the main street and head down it away from the tracks. Turn right turn at the shrine. It's on the left. A little peace and quiet for the traveler who insists on living in a business hotel near a major station. Rooms surprisingly sufficient. Check-in 4pm. Check-out 10am. Reception open 7am-1am. Curfew 1am. Singles from ¥5500; doubles from ¥11,000. Credit cards accepted. ❸

The Westin, 1-4-1, Mita, Meguro-ku (☎5423-7000; www.westin.co.jp). Ebisu Station. Head for Yebisu Garden Place. The hotel's behind the chateau. Dark chessboard marble and gleam. Checking out the artsy lobby is free; checking in is another matter entirely. Check-in 1pm. Check-out noon. Singles from ¥34,000; doubles from ¥39,000. ❺

GINZA

As the nickname "Silver Seat" suggests, even the cheapest housing around here is lavish and prohibitively expensive for most. If you can afford to burn some yen, however, there are some dreamy places to stay.

Hotel Seiyo Ginza, 1-11-2, Ginza, Chūō-ku (☎3535-1111; www.seiyo-ginza.com). Ginza Station. From Chūō-dōri and Harumi-dōri, head up Chūō-dōri away from San-ai. Turn right just before going under the expressway. Entrance is on the left, behind the driveway. The lap of luxury needs little comment...the price says it all. Reception is difficult to find—it's 2 tables on the 2nd fl., on the right. 24hr. butler service. 2 gourmet restaurants. Check-in 2pm. Check-out noon. Rooms from ¥42,000. AmEx/DC/JCB/MC/V. ❺

Ginza Nikkō Hotel, 8-4-21, Ginza, Chūō-ku (☎3571-8379; www.ginza-nikko-hotel.com). Shinbashi Station. From the Ginza Line, take Exit 5. Head to the right and go straight under the cream-colored bridge. It's several blocks down. Spacious, luxurious, and Western-style: the Ginza standard. Breakfast ¥1600. Reception 24hr. Check-in 1pm. Check-out noon. Singles from ¥12,000; doubles ¥24,000. AmEx/DC/JCB/MC/V. ❹

Mitsui Urban Hotel Ginza, 8-6-15, Ginza, Chūō-ku (☎3297-8611; www.mitsuikanko.co.jp). Shinbashi Station. From the Ginza Line, take Exit 5. Head out to the right and go straight under the cream-colored bridge. Turn right immediately after crossing under and look for a black metal tree. It's a luxury hotel, but the chandeliers and *foie gras* have been replaced with a smarter street-feel. Parking lot. Check-in 1pm. Check-out 11am. Singles from ¥14,000; doubles from ¥21,000. AmEx/DC/JCB/MC/V. ❹

TŌKYŌ

HARAJUKU AND AOYAMA

Hotels are in short supply, but Yoyogi to the northwest provides budget digs.

■ **Yoyogi Youth Hostel (HI)**, Olympic Ctr., 3-1, Kamizono-chō, Yoyogi, Shibuya-ku (☎3467-9163; www.nyc.go.jp/e/users/d2-5.html). Yoyogi Hachiman or Yoyogi-kōen Station. You can't cut through from the Meiji-Jingū Inner Gardens. Trace Yoyogi Park, keeping it on the right. Enter the main gate. Pastels and plazas designed to please; the result combines Easter and Mexican villa. Strict schedule offset by resort-like appearance. Lockers ¥100. Laundry available. Max. stay 3 days. Reception 5-10pm. Check-in 5-10pm. Check-out 7-9am. Lockout 9am-5pm. Curfew 10pm. Reservations required; call or visit www.jyh.or.jp. Closed several days a month. Singles ¥3000; nonmembers ¥4000. ❶

Hotel Floracion Aoyama, 4-17-58, Minami-aoyama, Minato-ku (☎3403-1541; www.floracion-aoyama.com). Omotesandō Station. Take Exit A4, turn right, right again, and left after Yamagiwa Aoyama. Niceish, but the Western singles are a bit small for the price. Parking ¥1000. Singles from ¥9000; doubles from ¥16,000; triples from ¥20,000. ❹

IKEBUKURO

On the JR, Ikebukuro is an excellent place to stay, with a strong but never overpowering urban hustle. Prices are on the money and ryokan offer first-rate value.

■ **Kimi Ryokan** (貴美旅館), 2-36-8, Ikebukuro, Toshima-ku (☎3971-3766; www.kimi-ryokan.jp). Ikebukuro Station. From the West Exit, head toward the police box and cross to KFC. Turn left, continue 3 blocks, and go right at Sumitomo-Mitsui Bank. Take the 4th left, at the major intersection, 3rd right, before the pharmacy, and 1st left. It's on the left in illegible *kanji*. A steal bordering on robbery, the singles are spacious for the price. A stone garden and fuzzy puppy make it homey. Fluent English spoken. In-room Internet for a fee. No breakfast. Shared showers available 24hr. Cypress bath available 4-11pm. Reception 7am-1am. Check-in 3pm. Check-out 11am. Curfew 1am. Reservations helpful. Singles ¥4500; doubles from ¥6500. Cash and traveler's checks only. ❷

Capsule Hotel & Sauna Roby (カプセルホテル＆サウナロビー), 2-7-3, Ikebukuro, Toshima-ku (☎5391-3531). Ikebukuro Station. Follow Kimi Ryokan directions to Sumitomo-Mitsui Bank. It's at the end of the 3rd block, on the left; look for an owl mascot. Roby is on the sunny, pleasant side of capsule Tōkyō. No women or tattoos. See the 2nd fl. for the lobby, 8th fl. for the sauna. Check-in 4pm. Check-out 10am. Capsules ¥4200. Credit cards accepted (sauna cash only). ❷

Hotel Metropolitan (ホテルメトロポリタン), 1-6-1, Nishi-Ikebukuro, Toshima-ku (☎3980-1111; www.itbc.co.jp/hotel). Ikebukuro Station. From the West Exit, stay on the west side of the block, walk to the end of the Metropolitan Plaza, turn right, take the next left, then the *next* left, and the lobby's on the left. Ikebukuro's luxury option fetches decent value: just the regular, shiny stuff. Breakfast ¥1300. Check-in 1pm. Check-out 11am. Singles from ¥16,500; doubles from ¥22,000; Japanese-style ¥60,000. ❺

Hotel Theatre (ホテルテアトル), 1-21-4, Higashi-Ikebukuro, Toshima-ku (☎3988-2251; www.theatres.co.jp/hotel). Ikebukuro Station. From the East Exit, cross slightly to the right to Green Main-dōri. The next main intersection offers 2 lefts; take the 1 on the right. It's on the left opposite HMV. Sunshine-dōri is the heart of Ikebukuro; a night here puts eats and shops right at your feet. The hotel is fine and unremarkable. In-room Internet. Check-in 2pm. Check-out 11am. Singles from ¥8700; doubles from ¥12,000. ❹

Hotel Suncity (ホテルサンシティ), 1-29-1, Nishi-Ikebukuro, Toshima-ku (☎3986-1101; www.h-suncity.com). Ikebukuro Station. From the North Exit, follow the tracks north; it's across the road. Cheapest singles are 11 sq. m of formulaic comfort. Check-in 3pm. Check-out 10am. Singles from ¥7800; doubles ¥12,600; triples ¥15,600. ❸

MARUNOUCHI

Downtown is where famous rich people stay. It is not for budget travelers, and, given the quality of public transportation, there's little need to live there. There are finds just outside urban central, however; read on.

■ **Sakura Hotel,** 2-21-4, Kanda-Jinbōchō, Chiyoda-ku (☎3261-3939; www.sakura-hotel.co.jp). Jinbōchō Station. Turn left out of Exit A1, then left again at the intersection. Head straight and make your 3rd left, then look for the pink canopy. Budget housing that extends a special welcome to foreigners and backpackers. College dorm feel: white linens, a desk, and a TV supply the basic needs. Communal bathroom. Breakfast included with singles, otherwise ¥300. Washer ¥100; dryer ¥100. Reception 24hr. Check-in 1pm. Check-out 11am. English and some French spoken. Dorms ¥3600 per person; singles from ¥5800; doubles ¥7500. AmEx/DC/JCB/MC/V. ❷

Four Seasons Hotel, 1-11-1, Marunouchi, Chiyoda-ku (☎5222-7222; www.fourseasons.com). Tōkyō Station. Turn right from Yaesu Central Exit and go down the main road. A bit past the end of the station, on the right; an unassuming walkway leads to the front. How they managed to hide a luxury hotel in downtown Tōkyō is a mystery, but it's no secret that Four Seasons are jawdroppers. Let's just say you won't be lacking the 42" flat-screen plasma TV with surround sound you demand from any decent hotel. Reception 24hr. Check-in 3pm. Check-out noon. Singles from ¥55,000; doubles ¥60,000. ❺

Tōkyō Station Hotel, 1-9-1, Marunouchi, Chiyoda-ku (☎3231-2511; www.tshl.co.jp). Tōkyō Station. Turn left out of the JR's Yaesu Central Exit; it adjoins the station. High ceilings, immense windows, and thick, dignified carpet are giveaways that this hotel wasn't built yesterday. Variety of restaurants and bars. Some rooms have a view of the Imperial Palace; others showcase the station's interior. Parking included. Reception 24hr. Check-in 2pm. Check-out 11am. Reservations required. Singles from ¥10,000; twins from ¥17,000; doubles ¥23,000; triples ¥30,000. Credit cards accepted. ❹

Yaesu Terminal Hotel, 1-5-14, Yaesu, Chūō-ku (☎3281-2089). Nihonbashi Station. Turn left out of Exit B3. Make the next 2 lefts. The hotel is on the left; the entrance is recessed and invisible from over 10m. Convenient business hotel just far enough from Tōkyō Station to hide among the trees, albeit city trees. Breakfast ¥1500. Reception 24hr. Check-in 2pm. Check-out 10am. Singles from ¥10,800; doubles from ¥15,800; triples ¥19,800. AmEx/DC/JCB/MC/V. ❹

Hotel Yaesu-Ryūmeikan (ホテル八重洲龍名館), 1-3-22, Yaesu, Chiyoda-ku (☎3271-0971). Nihonbashi Station. Take Exit A3 and turn left at the intersection. It's the 2nd building on the left. An excellent choice for living fancy with a restaurant that's cuter than those you typically find in hotels of this caliber. Japanese-style and Western-style rooms available. Breakfast ¥1000. Wheelchair accessible. Check-in 2pm. Check-out 10am. Singles from ¥7000; doubles ¥13,000, with bath from ¥16,000; triples ¥18,500/from ¥21,500. Prices exclude tax. Credit cards accepted. ❸

ODAIBA

Staying by the bay is a bad idea unless you can get a rich uncle or a lovestruck local to foot the bill. What exists is super-nice but also super expensive. Besides, it'll cost you ¥320 and time just to get to the Yamanote Line.

Tōkyō Bay Ariake Washington Hotel, 3-1, Ariake, Kōtō-ku (☎5564-0111; www.ariake-wh.com). Kokusai-Tenjijo Seimon Station. Turn left from the turnstiles and walk straight down Tōkyō Fashion Town's 2nd fl. plaza. Turn right after the down escalator. The most affordable stay in Odaiba is still pretty expensive, but you'll be next door to restaurants run by the Iron Chefs. Parking available for a fee. Reception 24hr. Check-in 2pm. Check-out 10am. Singles from ¥9950; doubles from ¥16,000. Credit cards accepted. ❹

Hotel Nikkō Tōkyō, 1-9-1, Daiba, Minato-ku (☎5500-5500; www.hnt.co.jp). Daiba Station. Turn left out of the turnstiles. Planning to waste buckets of money on a day of luxury? Hotel Nikkō Tōkyō is one of the prettiest places to do it. The architects have taken full advantage of the harborside location; the hotel radiates openness like no other. Creative modern art makes for a shiny finish. Check-in 2pm. Check-out noon. Singles from ¥28,000; doubles from ¥33,000; extra bed ¥5000. ❺

Le Meridien Grand Pacific Tōkyō, 2-6-1, Daiba (☎5500-6711; www.htl-pacific.co.jp). Daiba Station. Turn right out of the turnstiles. Hotel Nikkō stole the direct waterfront location, so Le Meridien carves its niche on a glowing interior. Check-in 3pm. Check-out noon. Singles from ¥26,000; doubles from ¥31,000. ❺

ROPPONGI

Not served by JR, Roppongi is not the most convenient stay. A few mid- to upper-price options are at the main crossing, but value seekers are better off elsewhere.

▨ **Hotel Villa Fontaine Roppongi** (ホテルヴィラフォンテーヌ六本木), 1-6-2, Roppongi, Minato-ku (reservations ☎5339-1200, info ☎3560-1110; www.villa-fontaine.co.jp). Roppongi-itchōme Station. Exit up the right escalator and follow signs. Add a mile to the commute, and suddenly the same prices net extras left and right, from queen-sized beds to LAN connections. Chalk it up to the barren surroundings. Proximity to a subway station? It's *part* of the subway station. Discount fitness club access. Free breakfast 7-9:30am. Coin-op laundry. Check-in 3pm. Check-out 11am. Phone reservations 9am-10pm. Singles from ¥11,900; doubles from ¥14,000; triples ¥21,000. ❹

Hotel Arca Torre (ホテルアルカトーレ), 6-1-23, Roppongi, Minato-ku (☎3404-5111; www.arktower.co.jp). Roppongi Station. From Roppongi Crossing, follow the highway toward Almond Confectionery and beyond. On the left, with frills and fanfare. As centrally located as you can be. Size of the cheapest rooms standard for mid-range hotels, but flatscreen TV and in-room Internet access are a boon. Check-in 3pm. Check-out 10:30am. Singles from ¥11,000; doubles from ¥14,000. Credit cards accepted. ❹

Hotel Ibis, 7-14-4, Roppongi, Minato-ku (☎3403-4411; www.ibis-hotel.com). Roppongi Station. From Roppongi Crossing, head perpendicular to the highway away from Almond Confectionery. It's on the left. This Roppongi standby is comparable to Arca Torre. Breakfast from ¥1300. Parking ¥2100. Check-in 1pm. Check-out 11am. Singles from ¥11,500; doubles ¥14,100; triples ¥24,000. ❹

Hotel Pastoral, 4-1-1, Toranomon, Minato-ku (☎3432-7261; www.pastoral.or.jp). Kamiyachō Station. Head towards Exits 4A and 4B, but duck out through Toranomon 45 Mt. Bldg. and follow signs to the exit. Head straight out of the stairs; the sign peeks through on the left. Over 300 rooms. Distance from Roppongi breeds value. Check-in 2pm. Check-out 10am. Singles from ¥6800; doubles ¥10,600; triples ¥15,500. ❸

Grand Hyatt Tōkyō, 6-10-3, Roppongi, Minato-ku (☎4333-8123; http://tokyo.grand.hyatt.com). Roppongi Station. From the Roppongi Hills Exit, climb the escalators and peek around Mori Tower. In the dead center of Roppongi Hills, the most costly urban development project in Tōkyō's private sector, the Hyatt scoffs at a mere ❺. Prices start in the ¥40,000s; check the website. ❺

SHIBUYA

"Shibuya accommodation" is practically synonymous with "love hotel," at least in the budget range. The nice options aren't even all that nice; price-jacking thrives on the nearby commercial buzz. The cheapest way to stay may be to fall asleep at a private booth in an Internet cafe (p. 128); a soft leathery seat can be yours for 12hr. for as little as ¥2300 if you get there late enough.

▨ **Cerulean Tower Tōkyū Hotel**, Sakuragaoka-chō, Shibuya-ku (☎3476-3000; www.ceruleantower-hotel.com). Shibuya Station. From the West Exit, take the footbridge to the left all the way to the opposite end. Follow the elevated highway to the big tower. Relatively new and the very definition of business sexy. Enormous conference rooms, a massive lounge, and a *nō* theater. See **Nightlife**, p. 188, for the jazz club, **JZ Brat**. Parking included. Check-in 2pm. Check-out noon. Singles from ¥24,000; doubles from ¥34,000. Extra bed ¥4000. Cots free. ❺

Shibuya City Hotel, 1-1, Maruyama-chō, Shibuya-ku (☎5489-1010; www.shibuya-city-hotel.com). Shibuya Station. From the Hachikō Exit, cross the street to the smaller big TVs and head left up the tree-lined avenue. Turn right at the fork and left at the 2nd major fork. It's a block or 2 down on the left. Western rooms, relatively cheap for Shibuya. Cushy and boring; know the price, and you know the hotel. Check-in 3pm. Check-out 11am. Singles from ¥9000; doubles from ¥18,000; triples from ¥22,000. ❹

Shibuya Tōbu Hotel (渋谷東武ホテル), 3-1, Udagawa-chō, Shibuya-ku (☎3476-0111; www.tobuhotel.co.jp/shibuya). Shibuya Station. Take the Hachikō Exit, cross the street, and pass the right side of Starbucks. Bear left between Seibu and OI. It's on the left, past the Parco buildings. Non-luxury, but non-budget. Better-than-sufficient space and 6 restaurants. Proximity to Shibuya Station a slight value boost. Breakfast from ¥1200. Check-in 2pm. Check-out 11am. Singles from ¥11,500; doubles from ¥15,000. ❹

Capsule Land Shibuya (カプセルランド渋谷), 1-19-14, Dōgenzaka, Shibuya-ku (☎3464-1777; www.ps-w.com/landconcept). Shibuya Station. Hachikō Exit or Subway Exit 1. From the JR, cross the street to the smaller big TV and head left up the tree-lined avenue. It's far down on the left. Blue and orange sign. A 140-capsule whopper at the top of Love Hotel hill. Low sketch factor and a full list of amenities, including bath, movies, massage chairs, and coin laundry. Women get dissed on the capsule front, but can stay in single rooms. Capsules ¥3700; singles ¥9500. Credit cards accepted. ❷

Shibuya Tōkyū Inn (渋谷東急イン), 1-24-10, Shibuya, Shibuya-ku (☎3498-0109; www.tokyuhotels.co.jp). Shibuya Station. Near Tōbu Hotel, but after the left between Seibu and OI, it's a few minutes on the right. "Mid-range" means banquet halls and a restaurant. Unsurprising Western rooms. Breakfast ¥950. Parking available. Check-in 3pm. Check-out 10am. Singles from ¥12,000; twins from ¥19,000; doubles ¥20,000. ❹

Mayo Viento (マヨビエント), 1-10-1, Dōgenzaka, Shibuya-ku (☎5458-8342). Shibuya Station. From the West Exit, go under the metal archway with the electric-bulb sign. Take the 2nd left, where the brick ends. It's the 1st building on the right. Automatic gold door looks like a wall. Rooms like someone's pad; the kind of place you enter and crash. Some English spoken. Laundry machines free. Reception 24hr. Reservations not required. Singles from ¥7000 (from ¥9600 F-Sa). Credit cards accepted. ❸

SHINJUKU

Urban as Shinjuku is, housing is surprisingly cheap and abundant as fish spawn. Tours and conferences make their nests here because only Shinjuku has the size, urban proximity, and value they crave. The skyscraping west side offers a little more bellhop for a little more cash, while the east side cuts better deals.

▨ **Hotel Park Inn** (ホテルパークイン新宿), 1-36-5, Shinjuku, Shinjuku-ku (☎3354-9000; http://hotel-parkinn.com). Shinjuku Station. From the East Exit, turn right on Shinjuku-dōri (by Mizuho Bank). Walk 5-10min., then take the 5th left after the 2nd intersection, with Resona Bank. It's the 4th block on the right. Hotel or nightclub? The jet-set, blacklight astro theme is the antithesis to standard Tōkyō floofy. Rooms have big beds and leathery, executive chairs. Parking ¥2400. Check-in 3pm. Check-out 11am. Singles from ¥7980; doubles from ¥8925. Website discounts. V. ❸

Tōkyō Business Hotel (東京ビジネスホテル), 6-3-2, Shinjuku, Shinjuku-ku (☎3356-4605; fax 3356-4606). Shinjuku Station. From the East Exit, turn left and follow the tracks to the main road, just before the Pepe Shinjuku Prince Hotel. Turn right and take a hike; then left just after OIMEN. Take the 1st right, after Park City Isetan; it's the 9th left. Cheapest rooms are smallish, but the price is right. Inviting lobby and public baths. Parking ¥2000. Reception 6am-12:30am. Check-in 4-10pm. Check-out 10am. Lockout 10am-3:30pm. Curfew 12:30am. Singles from ¥5000, with bath ¥7600; twins from ¥12,800; extra beds ¥3000. Discounts for web reservations. ❸

Hotel Century Southern Tower (ホテルセンチュリーサザンタワー), 2-2-1, Yoyogi, Shibuya-ku (☎5354-0111; www.southerntower.co.jp). Shinjuku Station. From the New South Exit, follow the tracks away and cross the bridge. It's in front of the bridge, slightly left. Those not deterred by the price will find big desks, Internet, restaurants, and a bar. Everyone else can sneak into the elevators for a commanding view of Shinjuku. Lobby on 20F. Check-in 2pm. Check-out 11am. Singles from ¥16,000; doubles from ¥22,000; extra bed ¥2000. Credit cards accepted. ❺

Keiō Plaza Hotel (京王プラザホテル), 2-2-1, Nishi-shinjuku, Shinjuku-ku (☎3344-0111; www.keioplaza.com). Shinjuku Station. From the West Exit, follow the underground tunnels to Shinjuku Center Bldg. Exit to the street and get to the left side of a bridge with a divided road. Go straight; it's the 1st big building on the right. Massive and decked with shiny chandeliers; green top-hatted bellboys are the frosting. 25 sq. m for a single is twice the usual Tōkyō offering, but big conventions can tie up the elevators for up to 20min. Breakfast ¥2200. Check-out 11am. In-room Internet. Singles from ¥18,500; doubles from ¥22,000; extra bed ¥4000. Credit cards accepted. ❺

Hotel Listel (ホテルリステル新宿), 5-3-20, Shinjuku, Shinjuku-ku (☎3350-0123; www.listel.co.jp). Shinjuku Station. From the East Exit, turn left and follow the tracks to the main road, just before Pepe Shinjuku Prince Hotel. Turn right, take a hike, and go left just after OIMEN. Take the 1st right, after Park City Isetan. It's on the right, after 6 potential rights. Higher price fetches extra space and fairly large beds in this orangest of hotels. Aromatherapy room. In-room Internet. Parking ¥3000. Check-in 2pm. Check-out 10am. Singles from ¥8500; doubles from ¥14,000. AmEx/DC/JCB/MC/V. ❹

City Hotel Lornstar (シティホテルロンスター), 2-12-12, Shinjuku, Shinjuku-ku (☎3356-6511; www.thehotel.co.jp). Shinjuku Station. From the East Exit, turn right on Shinjuku-dōri, by Mizuho Bank. Walk 5-10min. Take the 1st left after the 2nd main intersection. It's the 4th block on the right. Despite an unfortunate spelling error, this is a tidy, modest, sufficient option. Complimentary breakfast. Reception 24hr. Check-in 2pm. Check-out 10am. Singles ¥7000; doubles ¥8000. ❸

Kadoya Hotel (かどやホテル), 1-23-1, Nishi-shinjuku, Shinjuku-ku (☎3346-2561; www.kadoya-hotel.co.jp). Shinjuku Station. From the West Exit. Follow the underground tunnels to Shinjuku Center Bldg. Exit to the street and get to the left side of a bridge with a divided road. Proceed straight; it's on the left a bit after the 2nd crossing. One of few budget options in Shinjuku outside infamous 2-chōme, with friendly service to boot. The 11 sq. m singles are the rooms you know by heart. Reception 24hr. Check-in 2pm. Check-out 10am. Singles from ¥7200; doubles from ¥11,000; triples from ¥17,000. ❸

Hotel Rose Garden (ホテルローズガーデン新宿), 8-1-3, Nishi-shinjuku, Shinjuku-ku (☎3360-1533; www.hotel-rosegarden.jp). Shinjuku Station. From the West Exit, turn right; follow the tracks to the main road, which goes under the tracks. Turn left; it's on the right, 4 blocks after the temple. Comfy and sequestered; lobby like a conservatory. Breakfast ¥1500. Singles from ¥10,000; twins from ¥23,000; extra bed ¥3000. ❹

Green Plaza Shinjuku (グリーンプラザ新宿), 1-29-2, Kabuki-chō, Shinjuku-ku (☎3207-4923; www.hgpshinjuku.jp). Shinjuku Station. From the East Exit, turn left and follow the tracks to the road that crosses under the tracks. Cross the side and shave the right side of the Pepe Shinjuku Prince Hotel; it's on the right, a few minutes down. Lobby elevators start from B1, not 1F. This clubside property gets heavy traffic in the wee hours. 630 capsules. Impressive rooftop bath and sauna, if that's your cup of hot water. No capsules for women, but there *is* a lady's sauna. No tattoos. Baggage checked, not stored in lockers. Check-in 3pm. Check-out 10am. Capsules ¥4000. ❷

Hotel Tateshina (ホテルたてしな), 5-8-6, Shinjuku, Shinjuku-ku (☎3350-5271; www.tateshina.co.jp). Shinjuku Station. From the East Exit, turn left and follow the tracks up to the main road, just before the Pepe Shinjuku Prince Hotel. Turn right, take a hike; it's the 5th left after OIMEN, on the right. Japanese-style rooms are a rarity this far west. Breakfast ¥800. Parking ¥1500. Free in-room Internet. Reception 5am-1am. Check-in 3:30pm. Check-out 10am. Curfew 1am (doors open 5am). Singles from ¥7500; doubles from ¥11,000; Japanese-style rooms for 4 people from ¥12,800. Discounts with web reservation. Credit cards accepted. ❸

Nishi Shinjuku Hotel (西新宿ホテル), 7-14-14, Nishi-shinjuku, Shinjuku-ku (☎5389-1010; www.nshotel.com). Shinjuku Station. From the West Exit, turn right and follow the tracks to the main road which crosses under the tracks. Turn left, then right after the temple behind the wall. It's the 3rd right, on the right. Ho-hum cheaper choice. The 1960s concrete exterior certainly sticks out. Parking ¥1500. Check-in 2pm. Check-out 11am. Singles from ¥8500; doubles from ¥15,000; triples ¥20,000. ❹

UENO

As a transport hub, Ueno is rich in housing. You can choose from a wealth of ryokan, capsule hotels, motels, and palaces; many, however, may find the quieter, more foreigner-friendly housing in Asakusa more desirable. Prices here range from Tōkyō's cheapest to the sky-scraping. Many foreigners opt for the excellent values next to Ueno's sister stations. Ueno's starboard also has its share of lodging, but the old soldier district feels a little less welcoming.

▨ **Sawanoya Ryokan** (澤の屋旅館), 2-3-11, Yanaka, Taitō-ku (☎3822-2251; www.sawanoya.com). Nezu Station. Turn left out of Exit 1. Not counting the immediate light at your back, turn right at the 3rd traffic light. Hidden on the right at the end of the 4th block. Nothing flashy, but has the delicate touches that betray a business well-loved by its owner. Ultra-quiet and slightly-more-spacious-than-average *tatami* rooms. Impressive dining area/common room. Lion Dance and tea ceremony performed. Western-style breakfast ¥300, Japanese-style ¥900. Laundry ¥200. Reception open 7am-11pm. Check-in 3pm. Check-out 10am. Singles from ¥4700; doubles from ¥8800, with bath ¥9400; triples ¥12,000/¥13,500. Closed Dec. 29-Jan. 3. AmEx/JCB/MC/V. ❷

Suigetsu Hotel (水月ホテル), 3-3-21, Ikenohata, Taitō-ku (☎3822-4611; www.ohgai.co.jp). Nezu Station. Cross the street out of Exit 2, turn right at the T-intersection, and walk past the traffic light. It's on the right, with a *kanji* sign. If money is no object, pamper yourself silly at one of Ueno's finest. Gorgeous courtyard, underground hot springs, tea ceremonies, banquet halls, a sushi bar, and traditional *kaiseki ryōri* dining (i.e., crouching on *tatami* and sampling little Japanese dishlets). Suigetsu rocks it Western-style, Japanese-style, and karaoke-bar-style. Free Internet. Shuttle service. Breakfast included. Laundry service included. Free parking. Check-in 3pm. Check-out 10am. Singles from ¥8900; doubles from ¥13,600; triples from ¥33,000; larger rooms available. Hefty room charges start at ¥7200. Credit cards accepted. ❺

Oriental Capsule Sauna (カプセルオリエンタル), 6-9-9, Ueno, Taitō-ku (☎3833-1501). From the JR's Hirokōji Exit, take the alley right of the one with the silver archway; it's on the left. Capsule hotels can be downers, but the Oriental keeps things fresh: bright lights and fun extras attract many a weary businessman. Dip in the communal baths or sweat your day off in the sauna. Massage ¥3300 for 40min. Men only. Check-in noon. Check-out 10am. Capsule ¥3600, includes bath. Credit cards accepted. ❷

Kinuya Hotel (きぬやホテル), 2-14-28, Ueno, Taitō-ku (☎3833-1911; info@kinuyahotel.jp). Turn right out of the JR's Shinobazu Exit and follow the main road left. Make a hard right onto the major street that merges with this one; it's on the left, nestled in the trees. Alternatively, exit west from Ueno's Keisei Station. Restaurant with a view, 30min. of free Internet access, and a friendly, English-capable staff. Breakfast ¥850. Check-in 1pm. Check-out 10am. Singles ¥7400; doubles ¥10,300. Credit cards accepted. ❸

Ryokan Katsutarō (旅館勝太郎), 4-16-8, Ikenohata, Taitō-ku (☎3821-9808). Nezu Station. Take Exit 2, cross the street, turn right at the T-intersection, and it'll be on your left. Quiet Japanese-style inn resting silently against the posterior of Ueno Park. Rooms are huge and the beds are extra fluffy; it's the kind of space that invites somersaults. In-room Internet access for laptop owners. English spoken. Breakfast ¥500. Check-in 3pm. Check-out 10am. Curfew 11pm. Singles ¥4500; doubles ¥8400, with bath ¥9000; triples ¥12,300/¥13,200; quads ¥16,000/¥17,200. AmEx/MC/V. ❷

TŌKYŌ

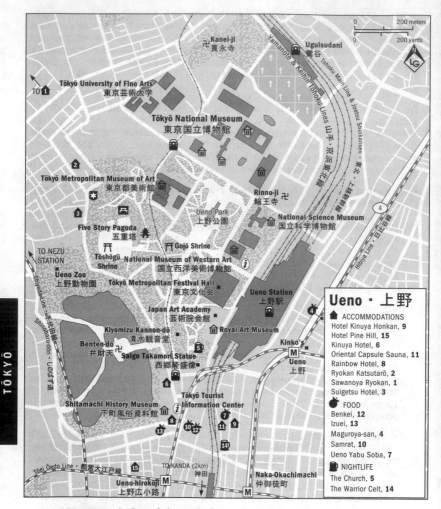

Ueno · 上野

♦ ACCOMMODATIONS
Hotel Kinuya Honkan, 9
Hotel Pine Hill, 15
Kinuya Hotel, 6
Oriental Capsule Sauna, 11
Rainbow Hotel, 8
Ryokan Katsutarō, 2
Sawanoya Ryokan, 1
Suigetsu Hotel, 3

♦ FOOD
Benkei, 12
Izuei, 13
Maguroya-san, 4
Samrat, 10
Ueno Yabu Soba, 7

♦ NIGHTLIFE
The Church, 5
The Warrior Celt, 14

Hotel Pine Hill (ホテルパインヒル上野), 2-3-4, Ueno, Taitō-ku (☎3836-5111; fax 3837-0080). Turn right out of the JR's Shinobazu Exit and follow the main road a bit. Turn right at Matsuzakaya department store and look for the hotel on the right. Business hotel with a spacious lobby. Breakfast ¥630. Private bath. Laundry facilities. Check-in 3:00pm. Check-out 11am. Singles ¥7100; doubles ¥15,500. Credit cards accepted. ❸

Rainbow Hotel (ホテルレインボー), 2-13-1, Ueno, Taitō-ku (☎3833-7716). Turn right out of JR's Shinobazu Exit and follow the main road left; look for a silver building on the other side of the street, past Keisei Station. 3rd fl. lobby. Features include lofty upper-floor rooms for those who like to perch, central location for those who like park ambles as well as city scramble, and wide beds for those who sleep like starfish. Check-in 4pm. Check-out 10am. Singles ¥8930; twins ¥16,800; doubles from ¥10,500. ❹

Hotel Kinuya Honkan (きぬや本館), 6-8-11, Ueno, Taitō-ku (☎3833-1921). Take the JR's Hirokōji Exit and go down the arcade with the silver arch; look for yellow and green writing on the left. The simplicity, friendly reception, and central location accommodate weary travelers who just want to pay and pass out on a piece of *tatami*. No breakfast. Reception open 4:30am-3:30am. Doors locked 3:30-4:30am. Check-in 1pm (capsules 4pm). Check-out 10am. Singles from ¥5700, with bath from ¥10,000; doubles from ¥9300; capsules ¥3100. Credit cards accepted. Capsules ❶; rooms ❸.

LONG-TERM ACCOMMODATIONS

For the long haul, most people choose to live in a guesthouse or *gaijin* house, a blend between a hostel and an apartment, designed with foreigners in mind. The best ones lie outside congested neighborhoods; many long-term visitors choose to steer clear of central Tōkyō entirely and make regular 40min. commutes. Guesthouses typically charge ¥60,000-80,000 per month for a good single. One of the coolest options is **Apple House** (☎0422-51-2277; www.applehouse.ne.jp/english/applehouse.html), run by an awesome group of paint-obsessed youngsters. Extras include a massive group kitchen, in-room Internet, and an exercise machine. **Cozy House** (☎047-379-1539; www.cozyhouse.net) is a much quieter, apartment-like option. Guests are left well enough alone in an unexpected but appreciated surplus of sunshine. **Sakura House** (☎5330-5250; www.sakura-house.com) runs a zillion guesthouses; the good ones (especially the new one in Yoyogi) get filled quickly in the high season, leaving acceptable but cramped crumbs for the rest. **J&F Plaza** (☎5366-6356; http://jafnet.co.jp/plaza/e_top.html) is another big player.

◘ FOOD

When you ask how many restaurants Tōkyō has, numbers like "80,000" and "100,000" start flying around. With that many to choose from, if you can't find something to suit your tastes, well, you're just not trying hard enough. From experimental fusion fare to in-and-out quickie stops, from conveyor-belt sushi bars to five-star dining that pulls out all the stops, Tōkyō's got it. Every area has its own unique flavor, be it authentic Japanese homestyle or international gimmickry of the highest degree. Wherever you are, department stores and station areas are safe bets for reliable eats. Note that some restaurants will charge a "sitting fee" just for the privilege of coming in.

TŌKYŌ

AMERICAN

Frisco Pasta Kitchen (149)	IK ❷
New York Grill (155)	SJ ❺

ASIAN AND PAN-ASIAN

Buttu Trick-Bar (156)	SJ ❸
Chinoise Turandot (144)	AK ❸
Copain Copine (149)	MR ❸
Erawan (145)	EB ❸
▨ Ganesa (146)	GZ ❹
Mugyodon (144)	AK ❸
Oriental Spoon (152)	SB ❹
South China (147)	HA ❸
Tampōya (149)	MR ❸
Tōkyō Daihanten (155)	SJ ❹

BAKERIES AND DESSERT

▨ Naniwaya (151)	RP ❶
▨ Umezono (145)	AS ❷

BEER HALLS AND BREWERIES

Beer Station Ryōgoku (157)	RY ❸
Sunset Beach Brewing Company (150)	OD ❸
World Sports Cafe (154)	SB ❸

CAFES AND SANDWICH SHOPS

+ac (148)	HA ❸
Bagel & Bagel (154)	SB ❶
Ex-café (148)	HA ❷
Mikuni's Cafe (149)	MR ❸
▨ News Deli (147)	HA ❷
Odaiba Cafe (150)	OD ❸
▨ Pita the Great (143)	AK ❶

INDIAN

Moti (152)	RP ❹
Nair's Restaurant (147)	GZ ❷
Samrat (157)	UN ❷

INTERNATIONAL

Amapola (145)	EB ❸
Bistoro Cafe La Rochelle (150)	OD ❸
Christon Cafe (155)	SJ ❸
DEN Rokuen-Tei (153)	SB ❹

ITALIAN

Eno Gusto (150)	OD ❸
Il Forno (150)	OD ❸
Trattoria Al Porto (150)	OD ❹

TŌKYO

IZAKAYA

Maruhachi (154)	SB ❸
Nihonkai Shōya (149)	IK ❹
▨ Tsuki no Shizuku (152)	SB ❹

JAPANESE

Asadaya Ihei (144)	AK ❺
Benkei (157)	UN ❹
Chinya (145)	AS ❺
▨ Daikokuya (144)	AS ❸
▨ Inakaya (151)	RP ❺
▨ Izuei (156)	UN ❸
▨ Kyō no Kura (146)	GZ ❹
Meshiyadon (156)	SJ ❷
Nakamura Ariake (150)	OD ❺
Ohara (147)	GZ ❷
Ótoya (157)	MG ❷
Shunbora (150)	OD ❷
Tenya (144)	AK ❶
▨ Tomoegata (157)	RY ❸
Tonkatsu Wakō (154)	SB ❸
Tsunahachi (155)	SJ ❸
▨ Ueno Yabu Soba (156)	UN ❸
▨ Yakitori Kameya (148)	IK ❸

MEXICAN AND TEXMEX

▨ Cantina La Fiesta (151)	RP ❸
▨ Fonda de la Madrugada (147)	HA ❹

NOODLES

Ichiran (151)	RP ❷
Jangara Rāmen (144)	AK ❸
Kōmen (147)	HA ❷
Kyūjūkyū Tonkō Rāmen (145)	EB ❸
Manrikiya (151)RP	❷
Nagazaka Sarashina (151)RP	❸

SEAFOOD

Bodaiju (154)	SB ❹
Kani Dōraku (155)	SJ ❺
Maguroya-san (156)	UN ❸
Tōkyō Joe's (144)	AK ❺
Uokatsu (151)	RP ❸

SHOPPING STREETS AND FOOD COURTS

▨ G-Zone (146)	GZ ❸
Happyaku-yachō (147)	GZ ❷
Hisago-dōri (145)	AS ❶
▨ Omoide Yokochō (154)	SJ ❸
Sushiya Street (145)	AS ❷

STEAKHOUSES

▨ Farm Grill (146)	GZ ❸
Goodtimes (156)	SJ ❸
Gyūbei (149)	IK ❸
▨ Kushinbō (147)	HA ❸

SUSHI

▨ Bikkuri-zushi (145)	EB ❹
Bikkuri-zushi (152)	RP ❸
Dai Sushi Parco (154)	SB ❸
Ganso Zushi (153)	SB ❷
Hina Sushi (151)	RP ❺
Sakae-zushi (156)	SJ ❸

THEME

▨ Arabian Rock (154)	SJ ❸
Cos Cha (157)	AB ❷
▨ Kagaya (146)	GZ ❸
▨ The Lockup (155)	SJ ❸
Oak World (155)	SJ ❸

AB Akihabara **AK** Akasaka **AS** Asakusa **EB** Ebisu **GZ** Ginza **HA** Harajuku & Aoyama **IK** Ikebukuro **MG** Meguro **MR** Marunouchi **OD** Odaiba **RP** Roppongi **RY** Ryôgoku **SB** Shibuya **SJ** Shinjuku **UN** Ueno

MAJOR NEIGHBORHOODS

AKASAKA

Hungry? Akasaka could feed a small country; a few minutes of random walking is all you need to find a restaurant. The culinary aorta runs west and parallel to Sotobori-dōri, several lanes thick. Start from **Akasaka-mitsuke Station** for budget to mid-range Japanese fare. Finish at Akasaka's toes for international cuisine, including **Korea Town**. Other options include the **Akasaka Excel Hotel Tōkyū**, which is built atop a two-story terrace of all kinds of food, from croissants to oysters. **Ark Hills** has a few fancy aces up its sleeve. A word on local specialties: Akasaka is known for *ryōtei* dining, which involves *kimono*-clad *geisha* and considerable financial loss. And don't be surprised to see poisonous *fugu* (blowfish) swimming freely about in display tanks; dig in, or just marvel at a distance.

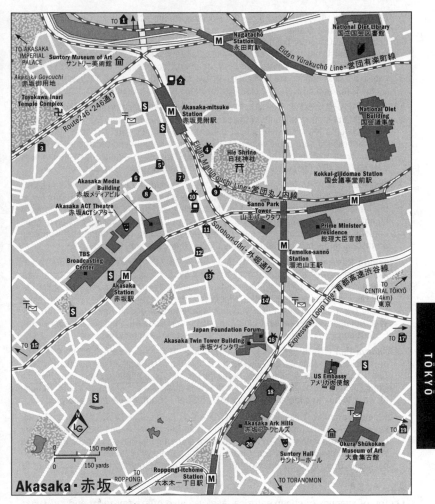

TO **1**

Nagatachō Station
永田町駅

National Diet Library
国立国会図書館

Eidan Yūrakuchō Line・営団有楽町線

TO AKASAKA
IMPERIAL
PALACE

Suntory Museum of Art
サントリー美術館 🏛

Akasaka Goyouchi
赤坂御用地

Toyokawa Inari
Temple Complex 卍

Route 246・246通り

🏛 **2**

Akasaka-mitsuke
Station
赤坂見附駅

3

National Diet
Building
国会議事堂

4

Hie Shrine
日枝神社

5

Kokkai-gijidomae Station
国会議事堂前駅

6

Akasaka Media
Building
赤坂メディアビル

8

7

Eidan Marunouchi Line・営団丸ノ内線

9

Akasaka ACT Theatre
赤坂ACTシアター

10

Sannō Park
Tower
山王パークタワー

Prime Minister's
residence
総理大臣官邸

11

Sotobori-dōri・外堀通り

TBS
Broadcasting
Center

12

Tameike-sannō
Station
溜池山王駅

13

Akasaka Station
赤坂駅

14

Expressway Loop Line・首都高速渋谷線

TO
CENTRAL TŌKYŌ
(4km)
東京

TO **15**

Japan Foundation Forum

Akasaka Twin Tower Building
赤坂ツインタワー

16

TO **17**

US Embassy
アメリカ大使館

18

Akasaka Ark Hills
赤坂アークヒルズ

Ōkura Shūkokan
Museum of Art
大倉集古館 🏛

TO **19**

N

20

Suntory Hall
サントリーホール

0   150 meters
0   150 yards

Akasaka・赤坂

TO
ROPPONGI

Roppongi-itchōme
Station
六本木一丁目駅

TO TORANOMON

TŌKYŌ

🍽 **Pita the Great** (ピタザグレイ
ト), ATT Shinkan 2F, 2-1-1,
Akasaka, Minato-ku (☎5563-
0851). Tameike-sannō Station.
Take Exit 12. Keep bearing right
and don't cross any streets.
English sign. Vegetarians rejoice: a
fellow *gaijin* has heard your cries in
meat-ridden Japan. Pita is made
fresh before your eyes in the tiny
shop; ¥500 gets stuffings from
falafel to blueberries. Open daily
11:30am-6pm. Cash only. ❶

Akasaka・赤坂

🏠 ACCOMMODATIONS
Akasaka Excel Hotel Tōkyū, **2**
ANA Hotel Tōkyō, **18**
Capsule Hotel Fontaine Akasaka, **6**
Hotel Asia Center of Japan, **15**
Hotel New Otani Tōkyō, **1**

🍸 NIGHTLIFE
Bill's Café and Bar, **5**
Bob's Lounge, **14**
Dubliners', **17**
Hobgoblin, **12**
Jambo, **7**

🍴 FOOD
Asadaya Ihei, **10**
Chinoise Turandot, **20**
Jangara Rāmen, **9**
Mugyodon, **13**
Pita the Great, **16**
Tenya, **8**
Tōkyō Joe's, **4**

🛍 SHOPPING
Japan Sword, **19**
Kofutsuya, **11**
Toraya, **3**

Tōkyō Joe's (東京ジョーズ), 2-13-5, Nagatachō, Chiyoda-ku (☎3508-0325). Akasaka-mitsuke Station. Take the left mouth of the Sotobori-dōri Exit. Turn right and head 100-200m down the main street. Look for crab signs on the opposite side. Stone crab specialists have set up saloon in Akasaka. Western atmosphere an excellent backdrop for guests to get intimate with tasty, dead crustaceans. Dinner feast ¥8000; adherents to the "less is more" credo might try 3 claws for ¥3600. Open M-F 11:30am-3pm and 5pm-11pm, Sa-Su 11:30am-11pm. Reservations required. Credit cards accepted. ❺

Tenya (てんや), 5-1-4, Akasaka, Minato-ku (☎5570-9831). Akasaka-mitsuke Station. Turn right out of the left mouth of the subway station's Sotobori-dōri Exit and head down Sotobori-dōri a few blocks. Turn right opposite Hie Shrine's gate. It's at the top of the road. Knocks *tempura* to the *rāmen* level in the price department, and the locals love it. Quick, clean, and cheap. The *jyōtendon* gets you 2 pieces of shrimp and some bonuses over rice (¥540). *Tempura*-eel bowl ¥690. Open daily 11am-10pm. Cash only. ❶

Mugyodon (ムギョドン), 2-17-74, Akasaka, Sumida-ku (☎3586-6478). Akasaka Station. Take Exit 2 and head downhill. Make the 1st right at Pasteria Piena. Turn left at the T-intersection; it's on the 2nd fl. of the building with the red awning and lanterns. A humble, tasty representation of local Korea Town fare. Spicy hot-pot concoction of beef, burdock, carrots, sprouts, and noodles ¥1600. If it's 8pm on F, there's belly-dancing downstairs in the other restaurant. Open M-Sa 5pm-12:30am. Cash only. ❸

Jangara Rāmen (じゃんがらラメン ; ☎3595-2130; www.kyusyujangara.co.jp). Akasaka-mitsuke Station. Take the left mouth of the Sotobori-dōri Exit. Turn right and walk down the main street, halfway to Tameike-sannō Station; it's on the other side of the street, just past Hie Jinja's 2nd and main gates. Widely considered to offer the best *rāmen* in Tōkyō, Jangara is a popular chain with superior noodle texture and flavor. Pick a broth, pick your toppings, and pick a seat amid the pop-clutter. Open M-Th and Sa 10:45am-2am, F 10:45am-3:30am, Su and holidays 10:45am-1am. Cash only. ❸

Asadaya Ihei (浅田屋伊兵), 3-6-4, Akasaka, Minato-ku (☎3585-6606; www.asadayaihei.co.jp). Akasaka-mitsuke Station. Take the right mouth of the Sotobori-dōri Exit. Turn left and walk past 3 cross-alleys. It's on the left, with blue *noren* (curtains) and illegible *kanji*. One of several polished *ryōtei* restaurants in Akasaka. Set course ¥5500, though it's easy to run up a larger tab. Open M-Sa 5:30pm-10pm. Credit cards accepted. ❺

Chinoise Turandot (Yusenkyō; 遊仙境), Ark Mori Bldg. 2F, 1-12-32, Akasaka, Minato-ku (☎3568-7190). Tameike-sannō Station. Take Exit 13 and head up the stairs into Ark Hills. It's on the farther end of the main plaza ground floor. Classic Chinese food meets Western professional snaziness. Classics like *mabo* tofu (¥1800) and Peking duck (¥500 per piece). Open M-Sa 11:30am-2:30pm and 5:30pm-10pm. Credit cards accepted. ❸

ASAKUSA

On top of avenues of cheap eateries, Asakusa also offers *tempura* and *sukiyaki* specialist restaurants. Gourmet restaurants flock to the top of mostly-offices **Asahi Building.** If you'd prefer to skip the appetizer and main course and head straight to triple dessert, you're in luck: **Nakamise** shopping street is full of authentic and mouth-watering Japanese sweets and snacks. For do-it-yourself types, a full supermarket **(Akafudadō)** lies right in front of Tawara-machi Station.

■ **Daikokuya** (大黒家), 1-38-10, Asakusa, Taitō-ku (☎3844-1111). Head straight out of Exit 1 of the Ginza Line Subway Station and turn right into the shopping arcade. As you proceed, look left for a road with white lanterns. Head down it; the restaurant is on the left. Despite having moved to a larger location, Daikokuya still can't fit all the locals lining up for *tempura*, but the wait is brief, and the food is worth it. Go with the basics and get 4 pieces of *ebi* (shrimp) *tempura* (¥1800), or mix it up with *sashimi* and fried veggies. English menu available. Open Su-F 11:30am-8:30pm, Sa and holidays 11:30am-9pm. Reservations may help, but aren't necessary. No credit cards. ❸

▨ **Umezono** (梅園 ; ☎3841-7580). Asakusa Station. Head straight out of Exit 1 from the Ginza Line Subway Station and turn right into the shopping arcade. Look left for a road hung with white lanterns. The lanterns are hung on Umezono. An excellent place for dessert. *Mochi* (Japanese flour snack, often filled with sweet red bean paste) ¥150 a piece. Shaved ice with ice cream and syrup ¥470. Open 10am-8pm daily. Cash only. ❷

Chinya (ちんや), 1-3-4, Asakusa, Taitō-ku (☎3841-0010; www.chinya.co.jp). Take Exit 1 from the Ginza Line Subway station. Head straight out and past the shopping alley; it's on the right, labeled in *hiragana*. 4 floors of *sukiyaki* and *shabu shabu* served by *kimono*-clad hostesses await those who prefer the finer things in life to the thickness of their wallets. Has been around for over 100 years and has a history as a *sukiyaki* specialist. ¥2500 and way, way up for *sukiyaki* or *shabu shabu*. Open M-Sa 11:45am-9:15pm, Su and holidays 11:30am-9:00pm. Reservations required for private room. ❺

Sushiya Street. Tawara-machi Station. Take Exit 3 and turn left. Turn right at the percussion store. Sushiya is on the left, a very short ways down. If you're looking for cheap eats, this small shopping avenue has a variety of quick and filling meals to offer. Indian food, *okonomiyaki*, sushi, curry rice, and *tempura* dishes ¥500-1000. ❷

Hisago-dōri. Tawara-machi Station. Take Exit 3 and turn left. Head down the main street to the ROX building. Go behind it and to the end of the broadway. Like Sushiya Street, this place has small eateries offering quick bites; it feels less welcoming, but the excellent Chinese restaurant on the right cooks up heaping bowls of *rāmen* (¥500). Open M-Sa 11am-3am, Su 11am-midnight. Closed 1st and 3rd M of every month. Cash only. ❶

EBISU

The station is surrounded by cheap eats, but your best bet is to head to Yebisu Garden Place. An actual chateau lies at the head of the plaza, with innards so royal you might lose track of your ¥4200 meal. Fancy fish and other tasties can be had 39 stories up in the towers. Decent restaurants line the way northeast towards Ebisu Prime Square. **Matsuzakaya** (松坂屋) is a basic supermarket, providing all your basic needs. (Ebisu Station. West Exit, West Side. Take the main road away from the tracks. Turn left after Starbucks. Open 10am-10pm.)

▨ **Bikkuri-zushi** (びっくり寿司 ; ☎5795-2333). Ebisu Station. East Exit (3rd fl.). Descend and U-turn, then pass between Sunkus and Pronto. Cross the main street, Ebisu-dōri, to the fun looking building on the tip of the triangle. The name means "surprise sushi." Someone's doing something savvy at Tsukiji every morning. Friendly chefs go the extra mile, leaving long coattails on the salmon and serving tuna icy (but not frozen). Encapsulated chefs work under bright lights and a roof that appears stolen from a *nō* theater. The standard twin *nigiri* cavort around ¥300-500. Open daily 11:00am-6am. ❹

Kyūjyūkyū Tonkō Rāmen (九十九とんこうラメン), 1-1-36, Hirō, Shibuya-ku (☎5466-9566). Ebisu Station. West Exit, East Side. Turn left, take the next right, cross a bridge, then take the footbridge to the right side of the road you would be on if you went to the opposite corner. Head uphill. On the right, in red. Regular *rāmen* too healthy for you? ¥900 cheese ramen: slurp that. Wild hot with the locals; if only they had more seats. Open daily 11:00am-5am. ❸

Amapola (アマポーラ), City Square Ebisu 1F, 3-1-24, Ebisu-minami, Shibuya-ku (☎3793-7721). Ebisu Station. West Exit, East Side. Go down the main road, away from the tracks. A few minutes on the left, with international flags and Christmas lights. Mediterranean cuisine has fled east to a warm local reception. *Paella* from ¥1600, fish from ¥1800. Open daily 11:30am-midnight. Credit cards accepted. ❸

Erawan (エラワン), 1-1-39, Hirō, Shibuya-ku (☎3409-8001). Ebisu Station. West Exit, East Side. Follow the directions for Kyūjyūkyū, then head uphill. On the right, in Ebisu Prime Square. Fancy Thai food amid color-changing columns. Meats, curry, noodles, vegetables, and seafood dishes ¥1000-1600. Open daily 11:30am-4:30pm and 5:30-11pm. Reservations recommended. Credit cards accepted. ❸

GINZA

Oh mercy. The victuals here are not only good, they're also served in uncompromisingly creative atmospheres. Questing for international cuisine? Look no further. Much of it is on the expensive side but it's *so* worth it. The east side of the train tracks is dedicated to food and gets particularly intriguing in the two-block stretch around Ganesa. For cheaper eats, most department stores offer food in either the basement or the top floors. At night, stalls peddling *yakitori* spring from the ground at **Yakitori Alley,** the triangle of land containing Happyaku-yachō.

■ **Kagaya** (カガヤ), 2-15-12, Shinbashi, Minato-ku (☎3591-2347; www1.ocn.ne.jp/ ~kagayayy). Shinbashi Station. Take the JR's Karasumori Exit and turn right out of the turnstiles (careful, some misleading signs go to the Shiodome Exit). Leave the station and cross a narrow street, then head away from the tracks down the only street that goes under them. After passing another cross street and a small alley on the right, look on the right for the hidden, bright white sign on the ground with a bunny, frog, and teddy bear. Anyone with a shred of appreciation for Japanese humor must come here. Without spoiling too much, let's say that the night will involve live entertainment including acting, costumes, surprises, and games so addictive you may lose track of your meal. Food is of the home-cooked, delicious variety and comes in 4 packages, ranging from light (¥1000) to make-me-a-feast (¥2500) to all-you-can-drink-wasted. Honestly, more worthwhile than the Imperial Palace. Bring friends if you can. Call ahead, but drop in if you can't. Open M-Sa from 6pm till the cows come home. Su negotiable. ❸

■ **Farm Grill,** Ginza Nine Sangōkan Bldg. 2F, 8-5, Ginza, Chūō-ku (☎5568-6156). Shinbashi Station. From the intersection of Chūō-dōri and Harumi-dōri, head south all the way down Chūō-dōri, away from Miko and Mitsukoshi department store. The entrance is under the expressway, a little to the left. If you only see one shrine in Japan, see the Farm Grill shrine to all-you-can-eat crab and steak. This "California Buffet" has diversity (ever seen spicy *gyōza* at a buffet?), and more importantly, quality. Dinner ¥2500, all-you-can-eat-and-drink (alcohol included) ¥3800. Lunch (also all-you-can-drink, but no alcohol) ¥1000. Open M-Sa 11:30am-2pm and 5-11pm; Su 11:30am-1pm and 5-11pm. Reservations not required. AmEx/DC/JCB/MC/V. ❸

■ **G-Zone,** 1-2-3, Ginza, Chūō-ku. Kyōbashi Station. From the intersection of Chūō-dōri and Harumi-dōri, head away from San-ai up Chūō-dōri, all the way to the expressway. Look for "La Boheme" under the expressway. A hip new dining complex (opened April 2003), hot on decor and an unqualified eye-catcher. 4 themed restaurants joined by what can only be described as one long, theme-park-esque artificial cave. **La Boheme** serves Italian fare (☎5224-3616), **Zest Cantina** dishes out Tex-Mex (☎5524-3621), **Monsoon Cafe** covers the non-Japanese Asian base (☎5524-3631), while **Gonpachi** delivers the local goods (☎5524-3641). Meal prices center around ¥1000. No sweatpants, running shorts, or sandals. 20+ after 6pm. Open daily 11:30am-5am. Credit cards accepted. ❸

■ **Kyō no Kura,** Ginza Kotei Bldg. B1, 5-9-1, Ginza, Chūō-ku (☎3571-6556). Ginza Station. From the intersection of Chūō-dōri and Harumi-dōri, head east down Harumi-dōri. In the basement of the building at the near corner of the 2nd block. Classy and upscale, it fits right into Ginza. Japanese food is the name of the game and they play the classic favorites. *Soba* upwards of ¥780. *Sashimi* platter ¥1280. Call ahead; it's usually packed. Open M-Sa 11:30am-2pm and 4:30-11pm, Su noon-11pm. AmEx/DC/JCB/MC/V. ❹

■ **Ganesa,** Pacific Ginza Bldg. 6F, 7-2-20, Ginza, Chūō-ku (☎5568-4312). Ginza Station. From the intersection of Chūō-dōri and Harumi-dōri, head down Chūō-dōri away from Wok and Mitsukoshi department store. Make the 2nd right and proceed to the elevated expressway. Turn left and look left for the Pacific Ginza Bldg. One of those ideas so novel it makes you utter your favorite expletive in delight. Incredibly sexy ambience: candlelight illuminates circular, translucent tents in which guests are seated side-by-side on low platforms. Pan-Asian cuisine served with grace (in small portions). Spicy

Korean noodles and *harumaki* (spring rolls) ¥800. A classy *izakaya* and not a standard restaurant: 1-drink min. Open M-Tu 6-11:30pm, W-Th 6pm-4am, F and days before holidays 6pm-5am, Sa 5-11:30pm. Reservations recommended. Credit cards accepted. ❹

Nair's Restaurant (ナイルレストラン), 4-10-7, Ginza, Chūō-ku (☎3541-8246). Higashi-Ginza Station. U-turn out of Exit A2. Turn left at the corner. It's on the left. The Indian fare here is best served spicy. Reputation built on the popular Murgi Lunch combo: curry, chicken, rice, and peas for ¥1400. The staff speaks English; try giving them a "what's up?" Open M and W-Sa 11:30am-9:30pm, Su 11:30am-8:30pm. ❸

Happyaku-yachō, 2-1-18, Yūraku-chō, Chiyoda-ku (☎3580-8845). Ginza or Hibiya Station. From either subway station, take Exit A1 and make 2 lefts. It's on the right, under the train tracks, with huge lanterns. No-frills beer and Japanese-style fried chicken, served in a casual atmosphere. In historic Yakitori Alley. Chicken/rice combo ¥800. Beer from ¥400. Japanese menu. Open daily 11am-10pm. AmEx/DC/JCB/MC/V. ❷

Ohara (おはら), 1-6-3, Yūraku-chō, Chiyoda-ku. (☎5501-3590). Hibiya Station. Take Exit A4. A popular eatery serving such Japanese favorites as *tonkatsu* (pork; ¥690), *yakiniku* (barbecue; ¥750), and cold *udon* noodles (¥640). Open M-Sa 11am-1am, Su and holidays 11am-11pm. Cash only. ❷

HARAJUKU AND AOYAMA

Restaurants here are sparser than in the rest of Tōkyō. Decent-sized clusters are located around **Gaien-mae Station** and the Harajuku end of **Omotesandō-dōri**. Offshoots to the main roads sometimes plop food right in front of you. Department stores are, as always, a reliable source of sustenance. **Kinokuniya** is a fine piece of supermarket with a twist: male elevator operators. My, how the tables turn.

🈂 **Kuishinbō** (くいしんぼう), 2-7-21, Kita-Aoyama, Minato-ku (☎3402-2984). Gaien-mae Station. Take Exit 3, bend right out of the exit, and scramble uphill. It's on the right, opposite Aoyama KY Bldg. Juicy hunks of cow in a quickie budget setting. The wait is slight, but the slavering is great. Steak strips from ¥680; combo that bovine for ¥320 more. Open daily 11am-10:30pm. Reservations not required, but it gets busy. ❸

🈂 **News Deli**, SJ Bldg. 1F, 3-6-26, Kita-Aoyama, Minato-ku (☎3407-1715). Omotesandō Station. From Exit B4, walk away from the main intersection and make the next right. It's on the right. A restaurant this high on energy is rare; chalk it up to the staff or the bumpin' music. Creative desserts ¥550. Pasta, sandwiches, rice combos ¥880. Curry ¥980. Open M-F 10am-2am, Sa 11am-2am, Su 11am-11pm. Cash only. ❷

🈂 **Fonda de la Madrugada**, Vila Bianca B1, 2-33-11, Jingūmae, Shibuya-ku (☎5410-6288; www.fonda-m.com). Harajuku Station. Take either exit and turn left, following the road 500m. Turn right at the intersection with Itokin. On the left, after the sidestreet after the parking lot. Perfect Mexican restaurant, replete with genuine *hacienda* feelin'. Staff recs include *jalapeños rellenos* with cream cheese (¥900), and tacos that forego cheese and lettuce for extra meat (¥1000). *Margaritas congelados* (¥1200) and tortilla soup (¥1000) are even better. Reservations helpful. Open daily 5:30pm-5am. Credit cards accepted. ❹

South China (Nangokushuka; 南国酒家), 6-35-3, Jingūmae, Shibuya-ku (☎3400-0031). Harajuku Station. Turn right from the Omotesandō Exit. Take the footbridge to the opposite corner and head straight out the stairs; it's at the end of the block in big white *kanji*. Genuine Chinese food with a smattering of the gourmet poppycock that gets your wallet shanghai-ed. Fried noodles from ¥1200. Multiple course meals from ¥5000. Open 11:30am-10:30pm. AmEx/DC/JCB/MC/V. ❸

Kōmen (光麺), 6-2-8, Jingūmae, Shibuya-ku (☎5468-6344). Harajuku Station. Turn right out of the Omotesandō Exit. Take the footbridge and go perpendicular to the station. Head down the main street; take the 2nd right after the Gap; it's on the left in yellow electric *kanji*. The winner of "Best Rāmen in Tōkyō 2003" engages diners in

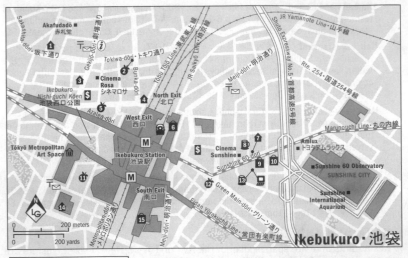

Ikebukuro · 池袋

Ikebukuro · 池袋

🏠 ACCOMMODATIONS
Capsule Hotel & Sauna Roby, **3**
Hotel Metropolitan, **14**
Hotel Suncity, **4**
Hotel Theatre, **7**
Kimi Ryokan, **1**
🍴 FOOD
Frisco Pasta Kitchen, **12**
Gyūbei, **11**
Nihonkai Shōya, **2**
Yakitori Kameya, **5**
🍸 NIGHTLIFE
Drum Kan, **8**
Mysterious, **13**
🛍 SHOPPING
HMV, **9**
Tōbu Department Store, **6**
Seibu Department Store, **15**
Tōkyū Hands, **10**

kettle culture with giant vats and a hint of ambience. Noodles are delightfully eggy. The *jyukusei* broth (¥730) is recommended. Toppings ¥120-230. Open daily 11am-5am. ❷

+ac (Tōkyō Apartment Café), Green Fantasia 1F, 1-11-11, Jingūmae, Shibuya-ku (☎3401-4101). Harajuku Station. Turn right from the Omotesandō Exit. Take the footbridge and go perpendicular to the station. Head down the main street 1min. or so; on the left. This clever cafe is hip enough to draw Harajuku's pre-gamers. The newspaper in front is actually the menu, with a very satisfactory drink list. ¥550 for beer, ¥650-750 for finer things. The food is so original that the menu's incomprehensible; try Chā-shū Tacos (¥650), or Goya Chanpuru (¥750). Open Su-Th 11am-1am, F-Sa 11am-2am. ❸

Ex-café, 1-12-6, Jingūmae, Shibuya-ku. (☎5770-2775). Harajuku Station. Turn right out of the Omotesandō Exit. Take the footbridge and go perpendicular to the station. Head down the stairs to the main street. Go left before Laforet, then left again. On the left. A shiny space for afternoon cake and tea. Open Su-Tu and Th-Sa 11:30am-11pm. ❷

IKEBUKURO

Ikebukuro diners should stick to the clusters. Sunshine City is full of options, as is the enormous Seibu next to the station. Sunshine 60-dōri has colorful choices on top of suitable ambulatory foodstuffs. For grocery needs, **Akafudadō** (赤札堂), near Kimi Ryokan, packs fresh meat and produce. (Open daily 10am-5am.)

🍱 **Yakitori Kameya** (焼とりかめや), 1-20-3, Nishi-Ikebukuro, Toshima-ku (☎3982-9458). Ikebukuro Station. From the West Exit, turn right and walk past the police box to the KFC. Turn left, it's at the end of the 1st block on the left after crossing. Beer food so tasty you can call it dinner. Acclaimed barbecue sauce draws businessmen; friendly baseball-themed setting attracts families. Asparagus rolls (¥470) and chicken *yakitori* (¥320) to die for. ¥200 sit-down fee. Open M-Sa noon-midnight, Su noon-10pm. ❸

Gyūbei (牛兵衛), 1-10-2 1F, Nishi-Ikebukuro, Toshima-ku (☎3983-7676). Ikebukuro Station. From the West Exit, find a street flush and center opposite the Metropolitan Plaza. Beef fans should try Gyūbei's choice strips, engineered to high deliciousness. For lunch, the E set (¥980) is among the most popular, including 3 pieces of steak, *kimchi*, veggies, and rice. Solid dinner combos from ¥3500, typically cooked over grills in the tables. Open daily 11:30am-2:30pm and 5pm-midnight. Credit cards accepted. ❸

Frisco Pasta Kitchen (フリスコパスタキッチン), 1-26-2, Minami-Ikebukuro, Toshima-ku (☎3980-9337). Ikebukuro Station. From the giant Seibu, head down Green Main-dōri; it's the end of the 2nd block on the right. Screaming "USA!" at the top of its lungs, FPK offers the cheapest eats in town. With tortilla crisps for pizza dough and low alcohol content in the drinks, it all makes sense. Pasta is substantial, and the pastaria's young-ish diners report satisfaction. Appetizers ¥280-450. Pizza or pasta ¥480-680. Cocktails up to ¥360. Sit-down fee. Open daily noon-midnight. ❷

Nihonkai Shōya (二本海庄や), 1-42-7, Nishi-Ikebukuro, Toshima-ku (☎3987-9861). Ikebukuro Station. From the West Exit, turn right and cross past the police box to KFC. Turn right, then take the 2nd left at Hotel Suncity. It's at the end of the 4th block on the left, just before Tokiwa-dōri. This bamboo-forest seafood *izakaya* sticks out for ambience and a fishy menu diverse enough to make Neptune cry. Sushi feasts ¥3000; crab feast ¥5000; little dishes much cheaper. Open daily 11:30am-1:30am, 5pm-late. ❹

MARUNOUCHI

Noon draws hungry Marunouchi businessfolk out into the daylight to feast on business noodles at business lunchstands. Some places are designed for speed and only have counters, no seats; truly a case of eat-and-run. You can join the salarymen throughout the city, though the restaurants are particularly concentrated along the west side of the tracks, from Yaesu South Exit down through Ginza. The station-side banks of the Imperial Palace moat host swankier spots and international cuisine; fine dining also finds a home atop the new Marunouchi Building. **Meidiya** is a strange little market with alternative foodstuffs: wine, canned consomme, whiskey, and cheese are among their offerings, as well as standard fruit, cereal, and snacks. (Kyōbashi Subway Station. Take Exit 7 and turn left twice.)

Copain Copine, 3-6-1, Marunouchi, Chiyoda-ku (☎3217-3777). Tōkyō Station. Turn left out of the JR's Yaesu South Exit and walk straight ahead, following the closer edge of the train tracks south. It's on the left, a short walk ahead. The Marunouchi masses have spoken, and Copain Copine is a winner. The spacious dining hall and Korean menu are both unique for the area and draw ample visitors. Try *chijimi* for ¥700 and up, or the egg/meat ramen for ¥880. If you're feeling saucy, a hot-pot-esque combo of meat and vegetables awaits you for ¥2000 (serves 2-3). Open daily 11am-2pm and 5-10:30pm. Dec. 24-31 open until 3am. AmEx/DC/JCB/MC/V. ❸

Mikuni's Cafe, Furukawa Sogo Bldg. 1F, 2-6-1, Marunouchi, Chiyoda-ku. (☎5220-3921). Tōkyō Station. Take the left mouth of Marunouchi South Exit and cross to the Central Post Office. Proceed, keeping the post office on your left. At the end, cross the street and turn left. Make the 1st right, then go left at the brick-floor intersection. It's at the end of the block on the left. Has that casual flair that distinguishes good cafes from the rest. Smartly dressed waiters bring pasta to resting shoppers, while busier customers hit up the bakery. Spaghetti ¥1000. Croissant or glazed raisin bread ¥160-180. Open M-F 7am-10:30pm, Sa-Su 11:30am-8:30pm. Credit cards accepted. ❸

Tampōya, Masaya Bldg. 5F, 3-2-16, Nihonbashi, Chiyoda-ku (☎6202-0101). Tōkyō Station. Take Yaesu Central Exit look for a silver building to the right of a building with a yellow and black neon sign. Head between the buildings and look left after crossing one street. Sweet ambient lighting and a black iron/bamboo curtain theme. Pan-Asian cuisine and a deluge of cocktails populate the menu (English available). House recom-

TŌKYŌ

mendations designated in green; try the spring rolls (¥560) or the Peking Duck (¥580). Servings are à la carte and small, so order a few dishes for a full meal. Open M-Sa 5-11:30pm. Reservations not required. Sit-down fee ¥500. Credit cards accepted. ❸

ODAIBA

Odaiba is different from the rest of Tōkyō: only a handful of restaurants stand alone; food courts are the way to go. The fifth floor of **Decks, Aqua City,** and the second and third floors of **Venus Fort** each have forkloads of international mid-range restaurants. **Tōkyō Fashion Town** has all that and a bag of fast food. The three major hotels each have a full menu of *le fancy stuff*. And there are a lot of Italian cafes.

Bistoro Cafe La Rochelle, Ariake Park Bldg. 2F, 3-1-28, Ariake, Kōtō-ku (☎5564-0007). Kokusai-Tenjijo Seimon Station. Turn left out of the turnstiles and walk straight all the way down Tōkyō Fashion Town's 2nd fl. plaza. Turn right after the escalator down. It's in the near entrance of the Ariake Washington Hotel. Iron Chef France knows how to party: with a full set of silk cushions, his restaurant looks like James Bond's love nest. Who would have thought a master chef would offer his work à la buffet? Lunch M-F ¥1300, Sa-Su ¥1800. Dinner ¥3000. Open daily 11am-3pm (last order 2pm) and 5-10pm (last order 9pm). Closed 1st and 3rd M of every month. AmEx/MC/V. ❸

Trattoria Al Porto, Ariake Park Bldg. 2F, 3-1-28, Ariake, Kōtō-ku (☎5564-0002). Follow directions for Bistoro Cafe La Rochelle. Where Iron Chef Italy struts his pasta. The profusion of 2-seaters suggests the, how do you say, *amore*. Noodles ¥1500; main courses ¥1600-2800. Dinner ¥3800 or ¥5000. Open daily 11am-3pm (last order 2pm) and 5-10pm (last order 9pm). Closed 2nd and 4th M of the month. Credit cards accepted. ❹

Nakamura Ariake (中村有明), Ariake Park Bldg. 2F, 3-1-28, Ariake, Kōtō-ku (☎3599-3636). Follow directions for Bistoro Cafe La Rochelle. It's hard not to splurge on Iron Chef Japan's place after flying all the way here. Interior has an impressive wooden glow. Lunch items ¥1200-4800. Dinner courses ¥3500-8000. Open daily 11am-3:30pm (last order 3pm) and 5-10pm (last order 9pm). AmEx/DC/JCB/MC/V. ❺

Sunset Beach Brewing Company, 1-6-1, Daiba, Minato-ku (☎3599-6655). Odaiba Kaihin-Kōen Station. On the 5th fl. of Decks (p. 182). Part beer and all buffet. Too delicate for outright gorging, but a very tasty choice. Lunch ¥1200. All-you-can-soft-drink ¥380. Open daily 11am-11pm (no entry after 10pm). Credit cards accepted. ❸

Odaiba Cafe, 1-3-5-105, Daiba, Minato-ku (☎5531-2771). Odaiba Kaihin-Kōen Station. Turn right out of the turnstiles and trot downstairs. Turn left at the intersection, it's on the right at the T-junction. Spic-and-span "American" restaurant. Menu looks more like an Italian chef was trapped in a seafood truck. Pasta and soup ¥1500. Scallops ¥2000. Sexy bar and frequent live jazz suggest the bayside cafe moonlights as a casual nightclub. Open daily 11:30am-11pm. Credit cards accepted. ❸

Il Forno, Palette Town Venus Fort 2A, Aomi, Kōtō-ku (☎3599-2211). Aomi Station. On the 2nd fl. of Venus Fort, identifiable from the station. One of the bigger trattorias in the area and one with ambience, thanks to the lack of daylight in Venus Fort. Pasta and drink ¥1280, with seafood ¥1580. Open daily 11am-11pm. Credit cards accepted. ❸

Shunbora (旬坊), 1-6-1, Daiba, Minato-ku (☎3599-6586). Odaiba Kaihin-Kōen Station. Turn right from the turnstiles and go down. U-turn and make the next right; look left for *kanji*. A Japanese eatery nestled against the bosom of shameless commercialism. *Soba* and *tempura* under ¥1000. Open daily 10am-10pm. AmEx/DC/JCB/MC/V. ❷

Eno Gusto, 1-3-3-102, Daiba, Minato-ku (☎5531-0747). Odaiba Kaihin-Kōen Station. Turn right out of the turnstiles and go downstairs. Turn left at the intersection; it's on the right, past the T-junction. Further proof that Italian cafes and harbors were made for each other. Pasta ¥800-1100. Open daily 11:30am-10pm. Credit cards accepted. ❸

ROPPONGI

Roppongi is the place to go for international food, prepared by Roppongi's multi-national crowd. No top-echelon finery, but home-made budgety goodness is all over **Azabu-jūban** shopping street. Roppongi Hills is loaded with options, and many of the "bars" on **Gaien Higashi-dōri** are primarily restaurants, moonlighting incognito. For supermarkets, try **Marché** at Roppongi Crossing, or **FOO:D Magazine** next to Roppongi Hills. **Seifu**, on Azabu-jūban Shōtengai, is smaller but open 24hr.

- ■ **Inakaya** (田舎家), 5-3-4 1F, Roppongi, Minato-ku (☎3408-5040). Roppongi Station. From Roppongi Crossing, head perpendicular to the highway toward Marché. Make the 2nd right, just before the ROI Bldg. Take the 1st right, then the 1st left. Immediately on the right; look for *kanji*. Unabashed energy. Specializes in *robatayaki* dining, in which guests sit around a chef like junior woodchucks at a campfire. Buckets of fresh meats and vegetables are prepared and served from a distance with a huge spatula. Half-restaurant, half-show, all *sake*, and all very uniquely Japanese. Open daily 5pm-5am. ❺

- ■ **Cantina La Fiesta**, 3-15-23 2F, Roppongi, Minato-ku (☎3475-4412; www.lafiesta-tokyo.com). Roppongi Station. From Roppongi Crossing, head toward Marché. Take the 4th left; it's on the right. This cantina is the real thing. Chicken *chimichangas* unearthly good. Genuinely friendly service; full *colleción* of tequila and sangria. Webpage coupon. Open M-Th 11:30am-2pm and 5pm-1am, F 11:30am-2pm, and 5pm-5am, Sa 11:30am-5am, Su 11:30am-1am. No reservations or hesitations required. ❸

- ■ **Naniwaya** (浪花家 ; ☎3583-4975). Azabu-jūban Station. Turn left from Exit 5A, follow the main road up and turn left at Jomo gas station. A block down, on the left. Legend has it they invented *taiyaki*, the biggest pastry fad this side of the Pacific. This one-hit specialist shack, on Azabu-jūban, has cranked out red-bean-filled fish-shaped pancakes since 1909. Locals drool up to 30min. for a fresh batch, then snap up 20 and scurry home. *Taiyaki* are dessert: just a few will ruin dinner and make the day worthwhile. 2 *taiyaki* min. to eat inside. Open M and W-Su 11am-7pm. Closed 3rd W of the month. ❶

- **Nagazaka Sarashina** (水坂更科 ; ☎3585-1676). Azabu-jūban Station. Turn left out of Exit 5A, then follow the main road up and turn left at the Jomo gas station. Take the 2nd left at the nut store. A hit for those who believe that the best noodle is a homemade noodle. The authenticity and the service make for quality slurping. *Tempura soba* goes for ¥2350 (about double generic *tempura soba* prices). Special thick eely noodles ¥770. Other prices run the gamut. Open daily 11am-9pm. ❸

- **Hina Sushi** (雛鮨), Denki Bldg. B1, 6-1-20, Roppongi, Minato-ku (☎3403-9112). Roppongi Station. From Roppongi Crossing, follow the highway toward Almond Confectionery. It's on the left, after Hotel Arca Torre. Contrary to popular belief, sushi doesn't have to be served over a bar. A favorite place to get authentically sushified. A course ¥3980; B course ¥4480. Open M-F 11:30am-2:30pm and 5-11pm; Sa-Su noon-10pm. ❺

- **Manrikiya** (萬力屋), 2-3-2, Azabu-jūban, Minato-ku (☎3452-5510). Azabu-jūban Station. Follow directions for Nagazaka. The *kanji* sign's on the right. Precious is the dumpling that brings tidings of joy. Tasty is the soup that warms the heart. Rare is the Tōkyō eatery with a staff that cares. Open daily 11:30am-2pm and 5-10pm. Cash only. ❷

- **Uokatsu** (魚可津 ; ☎3401-7959). Azabu-jūban Station. Turn left out of Exit 5A, then follow the main road up and turn left at the Jomo gas station. Take the 1st right, across from the nut store, and it's the 2nd block, on the right. Half restaurant, half fish market. ¥600-900 for the basics, combo ¥380 extra. Staff favorite combo ¥1800. Open Tu-Su 11:30am-2pm and 5-11pm (last order 10pm). ❸

- **Ichiran** (一蘭), 4-11-11 2F, Roppongi, Minato-ku (☎3796-7281). Roppongi Station. From Roppongi Crossing, head perpendicular to the highway, away from Almond Confectionery. It's the 3rd block on the right, across from Hotel Ibis. A gimmicky, quickie *rāmen* chain perfect for individuals who abhor social interaction. Ordinary counter, only with partitions and *noren* (curtains) hiding customer from cook. Guests take a lunch ticket from a machine and check a chart for blue, unoccupied stalls. Deposit the ticket through the *noren*, and the *rāmen* returns equally anonymously. Open 24hr. ❷

Moti, Roppongi Hama Bldg. 3F, 6-2-35, Roppongi, Minato-ku (☎3479-1939). Roppongi Station. From Roppongi Crossing, follow the highway towards Almond Confectionery. It's on the left, near Roppongi Hills. The samosas aren't the spiciest and the curry can be overly buttery, but spacious circumstances and a solid menu make amends. Immodest hunks of *naan*. Most curries ¥1300. Open daily 11:30am-10pm. ❹

Bikkuri-zushi (びっくり寿司), 3-14-9 1F, Roppongi, Minato-ku (☎3402-8541). Roppongi Station. From Roppongi Crossing, run away from the highway, toward Marché. A few blocks down on the left, at the end of the

Shibuya・渋谷

♠ ACCOMMODATIONS

Capsule Land Shibuya, **43**	Shibuya City Hotel, **35**
Cerulean Tower Tōkyū Hotel, **46**	Shibuya Tōbu Hotel, **10**
Hotel Floracion Aoyama, **33**	Shibuya Tōkyū Inn, **29**
Mayo Viento, **44**	Yoyogi Youth Hostel (HI), **8**

🍴 FOOD

+ac, **1**	Kushinbō, **34**
Bagel & Bagel, **24**	Maruhachi, **39**
Bodaiju, **45**	News Deli, **31**
Dai Sushi Parco, **16**	Oriental Spoon, **16**
DEN Rokuen-Tei, **16**	South China, **2**
Ex-café, **1**	Tonkatsu Wakō, **22**
Ganso Zushi, **26**	Tsuki no Shizuku, **36**
Kōmen, **6**	World Sports Cafe, **23**

🍸 NIGHTLIFE

300 Coins Bar, **14**	Club Xanadu, **25**
Club Asia, **37**	D-Zone, **32**
Club Atom, **41**	Gaspanic, **28**
Club Eggsite, **9**	J-Pop Cafe, **19**
Club Quattro, **21**	JZ Brat, **47**
Club Vras, **41**	Loop, **30**
Club Womb, **40**	Paradise Macau, **13**
	The Pink Cow, **18**

🛍 SHOPPING

100 Yen Plaza, **27**	Parco, **12**
Kiddy Land, **7**	Shibuya Mark City, **42**
Laforet, **4**	Shiseidō Garden C, **5**
Mandarake, **20**	Three Minutes of Happiness, **11**
Obutsudan, **38**	Tōkyū Hands, **15**
	Tower Records, **17**

block opposite ROI. A *kaiten-zushi* among clubs, the pinnacle of strategic placement. "Bikkuri" means "surprise," appropriate because picking sushi is like picking lottery numbers; some pieces aren't worth the ¥130 charged, while the ¥350 salmon is entirely up to par. Open daily 11am-5am. ❸

SHIBUYA

Getting fed is as simple as a frolic through the food courts, where upscale and downscale dwell together in harmony; **Parco** department store is especially strong in the mid-range. The basement of **Tōkyū Plaza,** 1-2-2, Dōgenzaka, is a supermarket-gone-wild. (☎3463-3851. Shibuya Station. From the West Exit, it's left of the metal ark with the electric sign. Open daily 10am-8:30pm.) Enthusiasts might call the 8th floor **Tsuji Cooking Academy** (☎3463-3565) to book a class.

🔲 **Tsuki no Shizuku,** Skyline Bldg. B1F, 2-29-20, Dōgenzaka (☎5459-6140). Shibuya Station. From the Hachikō Exit, cross the street to the smaller big TV and head left up the tree-lined avenue. Turn right at the fork. It's a few blocks down on left; look for mossy green panels. Before the term "tofu-specialist *izakaya*" sends you packing, consider its immense popularity. The interior's a gorgeous labyrinth of private tables with designer waterfalls, glass floors, and a sushi bar. Set courses ¥3000-4500. Open M-Sa 4:30pm-4am, Su and holidays 4:30pm-2am. Reservations helpful. Credit cards accepted. ❹

Oriental Spoon (オリエンタルスプーン) Parco Part 1-8F, Udagawa-chō, Shibuya-ku (☎3464-6644). Shibuya Station. From the Hachikō Exit, cross the street and head up past the right side of Starbucks. Bear left between Seibu and OI, and it's a few minutes down on the left. Also the name of a techno album, "Nouvelle Asia Fusion Cuisine" means the boys upstairs are playing with their food. There's no saying what will happen to a menu at a food laboratory, but staff recommendations save the day. Expect to pay about ¥4000 for a full dinner. Open daily 11am-midnight. Credit cards accepted. ❹

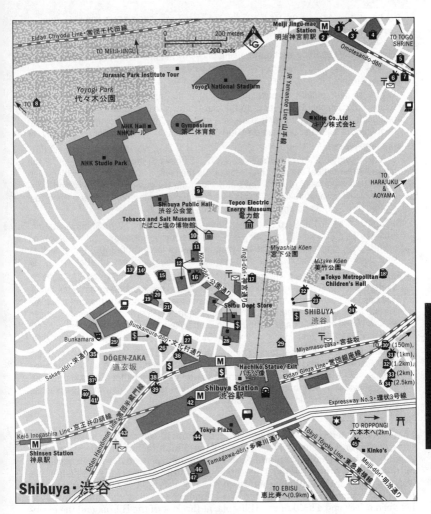

Shibuya · 渋谷

■ **Ganso Zushi** (元祖寿司), 2-29-14, Dōgenzaka, Shibuya-ku (☎ 3462-0400). Shibuya Station. From the Hachikō Exit, cross to the smaller big TV and head left up the tree-lined avenue. Turn right at the fork and left opposite the ONE OH NINE building, before the 2nd main fork. It's a few steps down on the left, with a rotating sign. *Kaiten-zushi* at a price so low, it's eerie. Most platters ¥99. The sushi is satisfactory enough, but experts will be able to taste the lowered quality. Corn *maki* and mayonnaise-splattered salmon are, shall we say, unorthodox. Open daily 11:30am-10pm. Cash only. ❷

DEN Rokuen-Tei, Parco Part 1-8F, Udagawa-chō, Shibuya-ku (☎ 6415-5489). Shibuya Station. Next to Oriental Spoon. Experimental restaurants must come in pairs: this neighbor to Oriental Spoon plays with grilled meat, seafood, and tofu. Rooftop garden suggests the good life. Open daily 11am-midnight. Credit cards accepted. ❹

Dai Sushi Parco, Part 1-8F, Udagawa-chō, Shibuya-ku (☎5784-1717). Shibuya Station. Next to Oriental Spoon and DEN Rokuen-Tei. *Kaiten-zushi* à la sexy, Dai Sushi proves that a fish-hauling conveyor belt doesn't have to look like a stop-'n'-go station for salarymen. Platters run ¥150-550; for those gauging prices by the international salmon standard, it's ¥250. Open daily 11am-midnight. Credit cards accepted. ❸

Tonkatsu Wakō (とんかつ和幸 ; ☎5766-3578). Shibuya Station. From the Hachikō Exit, cross right under the tracks and turn left at the main intersection. Next to World Sports Cafe. Friendly Wakō sticks to the classic items in Japanese fryers, but the end product is deeper than the gold and crispy standard. Cushy and comfy, a good retreat from Shibuya's streets. Set meals ¥1000-1400. Open daily 10am-10pm. Cash only. ❸

World Sports Cafe (ワールドスポーツカフェ東京), World Sports Plaza East B1F, 1-16-9, Shibuya, Shibuya-ku (☎3407-7337). Shibuya Station. Cross right under the tracks and turn left at the main intersection. On the right, a little ways down with big lettering. Throw one back with the boys and watch the big game. The giant TV and (relatively) ample seating make this a veritable community center, only for beer. Open Tu-F 5:30pm-4:30am; Sa-Su and holidays 11:30am-4:30am. ❸

Bodaiju (菩提樹), 3-9-10, Shibuya, Shibuya-ku (☎5485-1123). Shibuya Station. From the East Exit, go right on Meiji-dōri and cross the expressway. 1 block down, on the left. Daily supplement of fried and breaded marine life ¥1500-3500. Turf as well as surf: steaks ¥1900-3900. *Tatami* cells and wicker walls. Open daily 11:30am-10pm. ❹

Bagel & Bagel, Star Plaza Aoyama 1F, 1-10-3, Shinjuku, Shinjuku-ku (☎5766-0910). Shibuya Station. From the Hachikō Exit, turn right and cross under tracks. Truck uphill, way past the main intersection. Turn left opposite the police box; it's the 2nd block, on the left. Nothing cures afternoon tummy jibblies quite like a syndicated cafe. Advertised as New York-style, but mango and pumpkin-seed bagels hint at Tōkyō's influence. Sandwiches ¥280-540. Open M-F 8am-9pm; Sa-Su and holidays 10am-8pm. Cash only. ❶

Maruhachi, 2-10-12, Dōgenzaka, Shibuya-ku (☎3476-5739). Shibuya Station. From the Hachikō Exit, cross the street to the smaller big TV and head left up the tree-lined avenue. Turn left at the fork and it's uphill several blocks; look for a door with a star. Pop *izakaya* with a Caribbean shack o' fun feel. Unique dishes: mayonnaise-drenched shrimp ¥850. Open daily 5pm-7am. Credit cards accepted. ❸

SHINJUKU

Shinjuku is something of a culinary wasteland; notwithstanding, no other region is quite so fervently themed. The Oriental Wave Building and the Musashino-kan Building (where The Lockup and Kani Dōraku are, respectively) offer veritable carnivals for a pretty penny. The department stores, especially Takashiyama Times Square, are loaded but shut down as early as 8pm. For budget options, try the block around Suehirotei theater. West Shinjuku trekkers will find themselves between a fork and a hard place; Hilltopia, at the foot of the Hilton, and the circular part of Shinjuku Hand Tower aren't overly lovable, but salvation is salvation.

◙ Omoide Yokochō (思い出横丁). Shinjuku Station. From the East Exit, turn left and hug the tracks. Go under them and immediately turn left down the side alley; there's a *kanji* sign above the alley. Why do things taste better skewered and roasted over coals? The tiny *yakitori* shacks on this back alley awaken the stomach; one whiff of "Memory Sidestreet" is likely to elicit drool. Japanese menus can be confusing, but ordering *yakitori setto* is likely to work. A few sushi and noodle restaurants have found their way to the side alley as well. Open daily. Varying hours, but 4pm-midnight is hot. A few open at 6am for breakfast. Beware sit-down fees. Surprisingly expensive. ❸

◙ Arabian Rock, 1-16-3 2F, Kabuki-chō, Shinjuku-ku (☎5292-5512). Shinjuku Station. From the East Exit, turn left and follow the tracks to the main road that crosses under the tracks. Cross the street and turn right. It's on the left 4 blocks down, blaring Arabian music. Taking themed *izakaya* above and beyond, Arabian Rock has a magic lamp to open the door and hires belly dancers as waitresses. Satin curtains and pillows drape the interior. The line extends out the door and down the stairs; this could very well be Shinjuku's hottest food ticket. Open M-Sa 5pm-5am, Su and holidays 5pm-midnight. ❸

🈺 **The Lockup,** Oriental Wave Bldg. 5F, 5-17-13, Shinjuku, Shinjuku-ku (☎5272-7055; http://r.gnavi.co.jp/g528902). Shinjuku Station. From the East Exit, turn left and follow the tracks to the main road, just before Pepe Shinjuku Prince Hotel. Turn right; it's in the Oriental Wave Bldg., many blocks down on the left. Naughty diners wind through the freaky, creaky foyer to be led, handcuffed, to prison cells. Not quite an *izakaya*, it's the kind of place where you call appetizers and drinks a meal. Good luck leaving; you may have to beg the temptress-guards to lead you out. Open M-Th 5pm-1am, F-Sa 5pm-5am, Su and holidays 5pm-midnight. Reservations helpful. Credit cards accepted. ❸

Tōkyō Daihanten (東京大飯店), Oriental Wave Bldg. 3-4F, 5-17-13, Shinjuku, Shinjuku-ku (☎3202-0123; www.tokyoudaihanten.com). Same building as The Lockup. The ultimate South Chinese restaurant is a social center for Tōkyō's Chinese. For ¥600 it can be your *shūmai* center, or at least your house of shrimp dumplin's. Tea costs money. 10% service fee. Dim sum available M-F 5pm-9:30pm, Sa-Su and holidays 11:30am-9:30pm. 4th fl. is for group functions, but there's also a ¥1500 lunch buffet M-F 11:30am-2:30pm. 3rd fl. open daily 11:30am-10:30pm. AmEx/DC/JCB/MC/V. ❹

Christon Cafe, Oriental Wave Bldg. 8-9F, 5-17-13, Shinjuku, Shinjuku-ku (☎5287-2426;www.ug-gu.co.jp). Same building as The Lockup. Unless you count pigging out on wafers at Communion, the Oriental Cafe is a one-in-a-lifetime chance to snarf food in a convincing cathedral environment. Euro-hybrid cuisine with Japanese twists; think *paella* and pasta. Open M-Sa 5pm-5am, Su 5pm-11pm. Reservations helpful. ❸

Tsunahachi (つな八), 3-31-8, Shinjuku, Shinjuku-ku (☎3352-1012; www.tunahachi.co.jp). Shinjuku Station. From the East Exit, head straight, bearing slightly right between the driveway islands. Cross the street and go on. Turn right at the end of Mitsukoshi; it's the traditional-looking shack on the left. 100% grandparent approved and full to the brim for lunch, Tsunahachi does all kinds of *tempura*. Eggplants, peppers, yams, whole fish: the fryer stops for no thing. Mix masters should try the combo plates from ¥1300, a good way to taste deep-fried rainbow. Open daily 11:15am-10pm. ❸

Kani Dōraku (かに道楽), 3-27-10, Shinjuku, Shinjuku-ku (☎3350-0393; www.jri-jp.com). Shinjuku Station. From the East Exit, head straight, bearing slightly right between the driveway islands. Cross the street and look for a giant crab. Entrance is to the right of the crab building. Crustaceans in the soup, crustaceans in the *tempura*, crustaceans in the tofu; the kitchen has a seriously tasty infestation on its hands. The *nō*-theater-esque setting is a hoot. The only thing lacking is quantity; you leave with a half-empty stomach. Grab a crab *kaiseki* for ¥4300 to sample crabulent creativity. 10% add-on fee. Open daily 11:30am-midnight (last order 11pm). Credit cards accepted. ❺

New York Grill, Park Hyatt Hotel. 52F, 3-7-1-2, Nishi-shinjuku, Shinjuku-ku (☎5323-3458). Shinjuku Station. From the South Exit, turn right and follow the main road 10min.; look for 3 towers. Dizzying heights and big chunks of beef; is this what the Japanese think of America? The ever-changing menu whispers sweet nothings like "pumpkin puree," "ham couscous," and "sea urchin butter." Brunch ¥5800. Lunch ¥4600. Dinner ¥10,000-15,000. For dessert, try the 235m-high view through floor-to-ceiling glass. Open daily 11:30am-2:30pm and 5:30-10:30pm. Reservations helpful. Credit cards accepted. ❺

Oak World (オークワールド), 1-21-1 2F, Kabuki-chō, Shinjuku-ku (☎5272-2670; www.bld-group.com/oakworld). Shinjuku Station. From the East Exit, turn left and follow the tracks to the main road that crosses under the tracks. Turn right, skip the 2 roads at the base of Pepe Shinjuku Prince Hotel, and make the next left. Turn left into the wide plaza; it's on the left. "Theme-park Restaurant" is an apt title for table magic, ride simulators, and heavily atmospheric dining in the Italian, Japanese, and Chinese Zones. Sprawling, huge, and eerily empty at times. Open daily 5pm-5am. ❸

TŌKYŌ

Buttu Trick-Bar (ブッツトリックバー), 1-21-1 3F, Kabuki-chō, Shinjuku-ku (☎5292-2206; www.ug-gu.co.jp). Shinjuku Station. Follow Oak World directions up to the left after Pepe Shinjuku. It's on the left, opposite Koma Theater. What's the trick? The gig is primarily a restaurant, and a massive one at that. A giant buddha presides over pan-Asian cuisine, offering such interesting dishes as octopus-*don* (¥780). More restaurant than *izakaya*, more Indiana Jones than bar. Open daily 5pm-5am. ❸

Goodtimes, 5-24-59, Sendagaya, Shibuya-ku (☎3226-1701; www.nre.co.jp). Shibuya Station. Right outside the New South Exit. Has the spirit and looks of an American grill down cold; the only thing different is the distinctly Japanese steak sauce. The ¥1500 steak combo is a solid choice; though the salad bar is a little weak, its existence at all is surprising. Open M-Sa 11am-11pm, Su 11am-10pm. AmEx/DC/JCB/MC/V. ❸

Sakae-zushi (栄寿司), 1-13-4, West Shinjuku, Shinjuku-ku (☎3343-1616). Shinjuku Station. From the main Shinjuku post office, exit out the wider south side. Head straight past the "Slot" building; it's at the end of the block on the right. This branch misses the pretty award by a long shot, but it may be the only player in the area's mess of fry-boy hats and *pachinko* parlors. Standard slices of tuna and salmon ¥250. Open M-Sa 11:30am-midnight; Su and holidays noon-9pm. Cash only. ❸

Meshiyadon (めしや丼 ; ☎5367-8737). Shinjuku Station. From the East Exit, turn right on Shinjuku-dōri, by Mizuho Bank. Walk 5-10min. Take the 5th left after the 2nd main intersection. It's the 5th block on the right. A good budget alternative for late night munchery. Specialties include *unagi* (eel) and beef bowls. They may not be Tōkyō's choicest, but the job gets done. *Unagi* bowls ¥770. Open 24hr. ❷

UENO

Most restaurants in Ueno lie to the south, out of the Shinobazu Exit, hidden in the pedestrian maze among the skyscrapers. Culinary treasures speckle the area, some of which have century-long histories and look completely out of place among the *pachinko* parlors. Eel is a particularly hot local item. **Akafudadō,** up away from the action, is all over your grocery needs like a salaryman at a hostess bar. (Nezu Station. Across the intersection from Exit 1. Open daily 10am-11pm.)

▨ **Ueno Yabu Soba,** 6-9-16, Taitō-ku, Ueno (☎3831-4728). Take the JR's Hirokōji exit and go down the arcade with the silver arch to the 4-way pedestrian intersection. It's the store with the traditional Japanese look. A 110-year-old class act smack in the midst of urban chaos. The delicate Japanese setting and peaceful traditional music perfectly complement the slurping of noodles. *Soba* noodles start at ¥650; the *tempura-soba* is especially good (¥1700). Open Su-Tu and Th-Sa 11:30am-8:30pm. Cash only. ❸

▨ **Izuei,** 2-12-22, Taitō-ku, Ueno (☎3831-0954). Turn right out of the JR's Shinobazu Exit and follow the main road left. Where the main roads merge, look across the street. One of the area's oldest restaurants, Izuei specializes in eel slices. Fancier than your typical *unagi-ya*: each of the 7 floors features a different style; a good tuck-in will cost upwards of ¥1500. The Japanese menu is a bit daunting—most everything's eel and most dishes within a category vary only in size. Open 11am-9:30pm. Credit cards accepted. ❸

Maguroya-san, 4-12-1, Taitō-ku, Higashi-Ueno (☎3844-2732). Head straight out of the Iriya exit of JR Ueno Station and cross the street. Shift right a bit to keep going straight. Cross the next street, truck under the bridge, and pass 3 side streets; it's on your left. If you thought tuna existed only in canned or sushi form, think again. The fish flourishes unencumbered by Western stereotypes on an unremarkable street. Interior beautiful and relatively spacious. Tuna dumplings ¥500. 5 slices of *sashimi* ¥500. Tuna feasts ¥2990 a head. Open daily 11:30am-10:30pm. Credit cards accepted. ❸

Samrat (Samurāto), Oak Building 2F, 8-9-4, Ueno, Taitō-ku (☎5688-3226). Take the JR's Shinobazu Exit and walk down the Ameyoko arcade (it has an archway with red letters). Bear right at the fork and take the 1st right. Look left for the sign. Japan's subtle flavors may have left you in dire need of spice, and Samrat provides the much-needed party in your mouth. Standard Indian fare with huge chunks of *naan* in a cafe setting. Individual dishes available, but the 2-curry set dinner (¥890) is overwhelmingly popular; the 3-curry set is for fickle types. Open daily 11am-10pm. Cash only. ❷

Benkei, 4-5-10, Ueno, Taitō-ku (☎3831-2283). Take the JR's Shinobazu Exit and cross the street. Walk such that you're on the left side of the main road. Turn left after passing the ABAB building, and look for blue characters on white. Benkei offers eel at the same prices as Izuei (¥1500 for a simple eel/rice combo), but also features *sukiyaki* and *shabu shabu* on the second floor (¥2500 for an enormous plate of cook-it-yourself meat). Open daily 11:30am-9:50pm. Closed the 3rd M of every month. ❹

SMALLER NEIGHBORHOODS

AKIHABARA

Cos Cha, Bldg. 8 2F, 3-7-12, Isamiya, Soto-Kanda, Chiyoda-ku (☎3253-4560). Akihabara Station. Going down Chūō-dōri away from the station, turn left at the shop labeled "Kirara". Then take your 2nd right, pass one alley, and scan the 2nd fl. on the left for the image of a winged waitress in the window. "Cos" is short for "cosplay," the act of dressing up like anime characters. The waitresses at this novelty cafe don full anime waitress garb and even act the part, behaving more feminine than usual. The cafe is new and the environs are a little stark, but the food is tasty. The menu covers burgers, coffee, pastries, and rotating specials for lunch (see if you've arrived on a beef curry day). Good stuff runs ¥800-1000. Open daily 11am-10pm. AmEx/DC/JCB/MC/V. ❷

MEGURO

Ōtoya (大戸や), Sezāru Meguro 2F, 1-2-22, Shimomeguro, Meguro-ku (☎5719-1581). Meguro Station. From the West Exit, follow the main road away from the station. 2min. down on the left, on the 2nd fl. with a *kanji* sign. Running into this massive chain is inevitable, but getting acquainted is an excellent idea for the budget traveler. *Jako-gohan*, a traditional dish of hundreds of miniscule fish over rice, is an affordable way to load up on protein (¥210); just brush out that baleen before breaching the exit. ¥630 for *soba*, ¥430 for *udon*. Open daily 10am-11pm. Cash only. ❷

RYŌGOKU

🏯 **Tomoegata**, 2-18-15, Ryōgoku, Sumida-ku (☎3632-5600). Ryōgoku Station. Head straight out of the JR's West Exit and bear left under the tracks, straight along the main road. Make the 3rd left, opposite the blue building. Look for *kanji* signs. Ever wonder how *sumō* wrestlers grow to be as large as tanks without becoming sofa-ridden? In addition to their rigorous workout, they eat *chanko-nabe*, a hot-pot concoction of beef and mixed veggies as tasty as it is low on fat. Tomoegata's smallest "service" size *chanko-nabe* run ¥800; it may be worth a trip to Ryōgoku just to experience the flavor of raw nutrition. Open daily 11:30am-10pm. AmEx/MC/V/JCB. ❸

Beer Station Ryōgoku (ビヤステーション両国), 1-3-20, Yokoami, Sumida-ku (☎3623-5252; www.newtokyo.co.jp). Ryōgoku Station. Take the JR's West Exit and turn right. Built into the station. Beer Station Ryōgoku is aptly named; it's as large as you think a beer station would be and has full party rooms on the upper levels. Visitors can take their choice of differently-themed dining areas, or just drop by for souvenirs and *sumō*-themed snacks. Less expensive are sushi platters from ¥880, pork *katsu* (deep-fried) over noodles

IN RECENT NEWS

DIET NO MORE

Tōkyō is the wellspring of Japan's prosperity, and a quarter of the population has come for a sip. The little prefecture that could has grown overloaded, and the National Diet (Japan's legislative body) has proposed a solution: relocation. Tōkyō may not be the capital for long.

The idea is drastic, but far from crazy. Several problems would be solved, the first being overpopulation. At 33 million people, Tōkyō is fatter than a *sumō* wrestler on a binge. Water and electric supplies are overtaxed. Housing costs make New York and Paris look like bargains. Theoretically, an intrepid entourage would follow the government out, alleviating all these nasty symptoms. The best diet for Tōkyō may be no Diet at all.

The second problem is more dire: the city sits inconveniently atop a major fault line, and a serious quake would leave Tōkyō upcreek *sans* paddle. "Big ones" come regularly (the last was in 1923), and the Kōbe quake of '95 was a terrible reminder that Tōkyō is overdue. Reports estimate that a Kōbe-sized quake in the capital would be 10 to 16 times more devastating, with property losses of ¥100,000 to ¥160,000 billion.

Though relocation was first proposed in 1964, political gears began whirring in earnest around 1990. In 2003, the tractor wheels are turning too, paving the way for potential Parliament Cities in several areas around Tōkyō.

for ¥800, and, of course, beer from ¥550. Open M-F 4:30-11pm, Sa 11:30am-11pm, Su and holidays 11:30am-10pm. AmEx/DC/JCB/MC/V. ❸

◙ SIGHTS

MAJOR NEIGHBORHOODS

AKASAKA

NATIONAL DIET BUILDING (NIHON NO KOKKAI; 日本の国会 **).** The National Diet is Japan's legislative body, consisting of a House of Councillors and a House of Representatives. Center stage for all the hot, sweaty political action is draped in the finest of frilly decor, and visitors are invited to ogle and sigh, musing wistfully and basking in the glory. English tours pass by statues, intricate marble floors and royal red carpet, imperial chambers, and the Chamber of the House of Councillors itself. No reservations necessary. *(1-7-1, Nagatachō, Chiyoda-ku. Nagatachō Station. Turn right out of Exit 1 and cross the crosswalk to the other side of the main street. The visitors' gate is the 1st opening on the near side of the building. Open for tours M-F 9:30am-4pm. Free.)*

TOYOKAWA INARI TEMPLE COMPLEX (豊川稲荷 **).** Temples are a dime a dozen in Japan; the Inari Temple isn't the biggest, but with lots of nifty figurines and colorful banners, the flavor is unique. You can almost groove to the daily chanting (3pm). The English brochure is unusually fluent. *(1-4-7, Moto-Akasaka, Minato-ku. Akasaka-mitsuke Station. Take the left mouth of the Sotobori-dōri Exit and turn left. Cross under the 1st segment of elevated highway and turn left immediately. Look for the gate farther uphill, at the corner. ☎3408-3414. Open daily 6am-5pm. Free.)*

HIE SHRINE (日枝神社 **).** Religious franchises? Believe it. There are more than 3400 Hie shrines throughout Japan. The specialties of this particular branch are its grandiose hilltop real-estate, a chicken coop, and two gates bigger than a whale on stilts. One leads to a run of bright orange gates that literally requires running: thar be mosquitoes here. *(2-10-5, Nagatachō, Chiyoda-ku. Akasaka-mitsuke Station. Take the left mouth of the Sotobori-dōri Exit. Turn right and walk a few minutes down the main street; there's a massive gate on the other side. ☎3581-2471; www.hiejinja.net. Open daily 5am-6pm. Free.)*

ASAKUSA

SENSO-JI (浅草寺 **).** If you only see one temple in Tōkyō, this is the one to see. Asakusa's main attraction draws tourists from Japan's farthest reaches. You may notice the modern-day pilgrims engaging in certain rituals; feel free to join in. The washing of hands is thought to cleanse the spirit to make the self presentable to Kannon (the god of compassion, to whom Senso-ji is devoted). The smoke in front of the temple is thought to have healing powers and is pulled towards the body for good health. Shed your shoes and head inside to pay your respects or simply goggle at the altar. You could also try feeding the pigeon hordes (¥100), reading the excellent English brochure about the temple's history and the surrounding buildings, or visiting the **Denbo-in,** the locked building with the famous garden opposite the temple and to the side. Ideally you should call days ahead to see if you can get in, and even then, odds are good that you'll be rejected. *(2-3-1, Asakusa, Taitō-ku. From Exit 1 of the Ginza Line Subway Station, go straight and turn right onto the shopping arcade. Follow it straight through to get to the temple. ☎ 3842-0181. Open daily 6am-5pm.)*

JAKOTSUYU ONSEN. Hot springs are popular throughout Japan, but this one is particularly special; the locals drilled deep, just so they could have one smack in the center of town. If the main pool is too hot for you, the bunny pool to the side is a nice 42°C. The *onsen* is very hidden, so much so that the street it's on hasn't yet been discovered by Tōkyō's mapmakers. *(1-11-11, Asakusa, Taitō-ku. Head straight out of Exit 1 of the Ginza Line Subway Station and go straight several blocks. Turn right onto Sushiya walking arcade, then take your 1st left, 1st right, and 1st left. ☎ 3841-8645. Open Su-M and W-Sa 1pm-midnight. ¥400. Towels ¥30.)*

GINZA

HAMA-RIKYŪ TEIEN GARDENS (浜離宮庭園). Ducks have a universal appeal: some like to feed them, some like to skewer them, and the Tokugawa Shōgunate loved pumping them full of lead, so much so that they dedicated 250,000 sq. m of seafront property to it. Gun-toting has since been replaced by peonies, and the ducks are much happier. Floating down to the gardens by waterbus is a popular tourist activity. *(1-1, Hama-rikyū Teien, Chūō-ku. Shinbashi Station. March 15min. southwest to Tōkyō Bay; we recommend the waterbus from Asakusa instead. Open daily 9am-5pm. ¥300, 65+ ¥150, elementary students or younger free.)*

SONY BUILDING. The flashy promotional site at the heart of Ginza is used by many a local as a rendezvous. Eight stories dedicated to publicizing a corporate giant have to be at least noticeable, right? Phones, TVs, cars, and other gadgets of the future are paraded shamelessly throughout the building's helical layout. *(5-3-1, Ginza, Chūō-ku. Ginza Station. From the Ginza, Hibiya, or Marunouchi Line, take Exit B9. ☎ 3573-2371; www.sonybuilding.jp. Open daily from 11am.)*

HIBIYA PARK (HIBIYA KŌEN; 日比谷公園). About a century ago, some clever engineer decided to turn the ruins of a castle into something the public could appreciate. Moats were shaped into a pond and ramparts become exotic flowerbeds; the resulting park is a welcome breather from the monotony of central Tōkyō's architectural grind. The park is open walking grounds; try the recommended route to hit all the checkpoints. *(Hibiya Station. Turn left out of Exit A10 from the Chiyoda or Hibiya Line. Make a quick left; the entrance to the park is on the left. Open 24hr. Free.)*

HARAJUKU AND AOYAMA

YOYOGI PARK (YOYOGI KŌEN; 代々木公園). Too big to talk about as a whole, Yoyogi Park rivals the Imperial Palace complex in size. In the northeast, next to Harajuku Station, lies **Meiji Jingū Shrine** (明治神宮), dedicated to Emperor Meiji of Restoration fame. Instead of the usual *omikuji* printed at fortune cookie factories, the shrine distributes *waka* composed by the Meiji and his missus. *(1-1, Yoyogi Kamizono-chō, Shibuya-ku. ☎ 3379-5511; www.meijijingu.or.jp. Open daily 7am-10pm. Free.)* In the neighborhood lie the **Treasure Museum** (Takara-mono-dono; 宝物殿) and the **Treasure Museum Annex** (Meiji Jingū Bunkakan; 明

治神宮文化館), a warehouse for the imperial couple's stuff. *(1-1, Yoyogi Kami-zono-chō, Shibuya-ku. ☎3379-5875; www.meijijingu.or.jp/jingu/guide/09.htm. Open daily 9am-5pm. Closed 3rd F of the month. ¥500, college and high school students ¥200, junior high and younger free.)* Winding around counterclockwise, you'll come to the **National Olympics Memorial Youth Center**, an ex-Olympic site and a location for massive youth events. At the south end of the park lies **Yoyogi National Stadium.** The rest of the park is a broad expanse of cheerful public space; unlike other parks, it's empty, ideal for escaping not just Tōkyō but society. Call park administration (☎3469-6081) to reserve fields or the cycling center (☎3465-6855; closed M) for routes and biking buddies.

MEIJI-JINGŪ OUTER GARDENS. It looks shriny, it sounds shriny, but it smells like sports in what ought to be called the Meiji-Jingū Outfield. On the Gaienmae side of things, you'll find **Jingū Baseball Stadium #1** (Jingū Kyūjō; 神宮球場), home to the Yakult Swallows. *(☎3404-8999. Purchase tickets at the stadium or through the usual agencies. Seats generally from ¥1500, kids ¥500.)* The stadium is not to be confused with **Jingū Baseball Stadium #2** to the north, a college ballpark best caught in the morning. **Prince Chichibu Rugby Stadium** *(☎3408-4495)* is best caught for a different sport entirely. Switching up to Kokuritsu-Kyōgijō Station, the **Tōkyō Metropolitan Gymnasium** (Tōkyō Taiikukan; 東京体育館) is prime grounds for vaulting here and somersaulting there, flipping all the ding-dong-day. Some facilities are even open to the public. *(1-17-1, Sendagaya, Shibuya-ku. ☎5474-2111; www.tef.or.jp. Open daily 9am-9pm. Closed around New Year and 3rd M of the month. Swimming pool ¥450, middle school students and younger ¥200; track ¥150/¥80 for 2hr.; weight room ¥350 for 2hr.)* The **National Stadium** is right next door. Shoot for the center to see the **Meiji Memorial Picture Gallery** (p. 172). The old **Jingū Pool** complex has been frosted over for hotter trends, the **Jingū Skate Rink** (神宮スケートリンク) being the exemplar. *(5, Kasumigaoka, Shinjuku-ku. ☎3403-3456. Open M-F noon-6pm, Sa-Su and holidays 10am-6pm. Last entry 5pm. ¥1300, ¥1000 after 3pm; middle-school students and younger ¥900/¥700; skate rental ¥500.)* Round up eleven other players and a reservation, and you could be playing soccer at the **Jingū-Gaien Foot-sul Club** (神宮外苑フットサルクラブ) instead. Showing up and hoping for an empty court is also viable. *(12, Kasumigaoka, Shinjuku-ku. ☎3403-0923. Open daily 7am-11pm. ¥4000-12,000 per hr. per field.)*

JURASSIC PARK INSTITUTE TOUR. Bigger *is* better. Animatronic mayhem has come to Japan in the form of dinosaurs with sharp, nasty claws. Costumed park guides direct guests through the studio's six main chambers (modeled after the institute in the movie), where an actor interacts with dinosaurs. To say more would be a spoiler. The robots are impressive in size, and the technology is good, though far from magical; small children will be tricked. Be prepared to commit about an hour, as the only exits mid-tour are amusement park wuss escapes. Non-Japanese speakers will be completely in the dark regarding plot. *(Harajuku Station. Turn right from the Omotesandō Exit and go right across the footbridge. Pass the Yoyogi Park gates and the Yoyogi National Stadium on the left. ☎3460-1049; www.jurassicparktour.com. Open daily 8am-9pm. ¥2800, 3-year-olds to elementary school students ¥1500.)*

TOGO SHRINE. A naval genius from the last century, Admiral Togo had the *cojones* to study seven years in Britain and then sink one of their ships—legally, as it turned out. His deeds have scored him a nice niche in the trees with a pond to boot. There's a flea market two Sundays a month and, on August 16th, the locals throw the Mitama-matsuri festival down by the water. *(1-5-3, Jingūmae, Shibuya-ku. Turn right from the Omotesandō Exit. Take the footbridge and go perpendicular to the sta-tion. Head down the stairs and the main street. Make a left at the intersection at the bot-tom of the hill. Cross under the main gate 2 blocks on the left, then take the right path over the lake. ☎3403-3591. Open daily 6am-5pm. Free.)*

IKEBUKURO

▨SUNSHINE INTERNATIONAL AQUARIUM (SUNSHINE KOKUSAI SUIZOKUKAN; サンシャイン国際水族館).

Japan being an island country, the tanks here display specimens that may even be new to hardened sea biscuits. The giant spider crabs are jawdroppers, and the regularly scheduled ray feedings are downright adorable. Presentation is original too; otters poke their heads through holes in mock ice and scuba divers play with eels that look downright dangerous. Other high points include hyperactive jellyfish, sea lion shows, gross insects, and a tarantula. *(Sunshine City World Import Mart Bldg. 10F, 3-1-3, Higashi-Ikebukuro, Toshima-ku. Ikebukuro Station. Take the East Exit and head to Sunshine 60, the tallest building in Ikebukuro. On the roof of the 3rd of Sunshine City's 4 buildings. ☎3989-3466; www.sunshinecity.co.jp. Open M-F 10am-6pm, Sa-Su and holidays 10am-6:30pm; Jul. 19-Aug. 31 10am-8:30pm; Aug. 13-Aug. 17 10am-9:30pm. Behind-the-scenes tours at 1, 3pm. ¥1600, elementary students and children ¥800. Combo ticket with Sunshine 60 Observatory ¥1900, age 4-12 ¥1000.)*

SUNSHINE 60 OBSERVATORY (SUNSHINE 60 TENBŌDAI; サンシャイン 60 展望台).

Right on par with Tōkyō's other towers, Sunshine scrapes 240m. While the view isn't nearly as mind-boggling as Roppongi's, being farther from the center of Tōkyō makes it more colorful and healthy-looking. All visitors should get a bird's-eye view of Tōkyō at least once, and Sunshine 60 falls just a shade behind Mori Tower. The elevator has an interesting ace up its sleeve. *(3-1-1, Higashi-Ikebukuro, Toshima-ku. Ikebukuro Station. Take the East Exit. It's the tallest building in Ikebukuro. Elevator departs from B1. ☎3989-3457; www.sunshinecity.co.jp. Open daily 10am-8:30pm, until 9:30pm July 21-Aug. 31. ¥620, ages 4-12 ¥310. Lounge admission ¥700.)*

MARUNOUCHI

IMPERIAL PALACE (KŌKYO; 皇居).

Arguably the most prominent site in the entire country, Japan's old HQ is so large that the grounds are walkable from at least nine different subway stations. It's breathtaking even from the outside, where an unending stretch of thick outer wall and an imposing moat are complemented by greenery and the occasional swan. The palace's contradictory presence right in the middle of modern Tōkyō hints at how quickly the country has evolved.

The area around the palace is accessible only by a special tour (see **Marunouchi Tours,** p. 127). Be warned that it can be a dull 1¼hr. if you don't speak Japanese; native visitors experience an empathy with the palace's historical importance that the average foreigner may not, and the ferro-concrete palace is not exactly the acme of architectural endeavor. The tour stops in front of highlights including the **Fujimi-yagura** watch-tower, the **Kunaichō Chōsha,** the Imperial Household's administrative headquarters, and the **Seimon-tetsu Bridge.**

The **East Gardens,** on the other hand, are open for all to enjoy. Kids and zealots will enjoy scampering up the **Honmaru** ramparts to behold Tōkyō's treetops. Also native to the East Gardens are gardens for random meandering and the **Sannomaru Shozōkan,** a museum where items from the imperial collections are kept on display. Every autumn the officials here hold a traditional *gagaku* musical performance; call ahead for details. Though **Kitanomaru Kōen** lies within the moat of the Imperial Palace grounds, it is actually a separate entity. While that momentous, royal air can't be found there, bright, shiny museums (p. 172) make up for the lack. *(Info for the East Garden only: ☎3213-2050. Tōkyō Station. Take the Marunouchi Central exit and head down the broadest avenue. Turn right at the bridge, then left at the next main avenue. Follow it to the palace grounds. Gagaku info ☎3213-1111; limited English spoken. Open Tu-Th and Sa-Su Mar.-Oct. 9am-4pm; Nov.-Feb. 9am-1:30pm. Closed Dec. 23 and Dec. 28-Jan. 3. Free.)*

TŌKYŌ

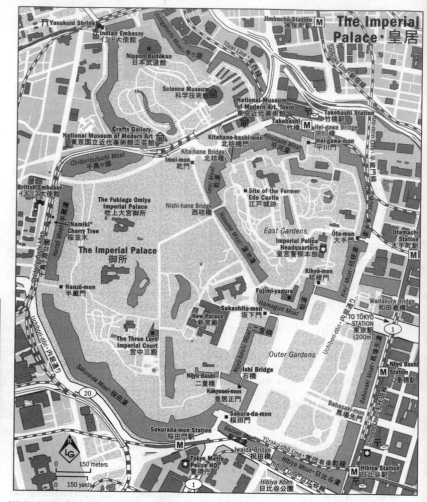

The Imperial Palace·皇居

Jimbochō Station 神保町駅 M

Yasukuni Shrine

Indian Embassy インド大使館

Nippon Budokan 日本武道館

Science Museum 科学技術館

National Museum of Modern Art, Tokyo 東京近代美術館

Takebashi Station 竹橋駅

Takebashi 竹橋

Crafts Gallery, National Museum of Modern Art 東京国立近代美術館工芸館

Kitahane-bashi-mon 北桔橋門

Kita-hane Bridge 北桔橋

Imel-mon 乾門

Hei-gawa Bridge 平川橋

Hei-gawa-mon 平川門

Chidoribufuchi Moat 千鳥ヶ淵

British Embassy イギリス大使館

Site of the Former Edo Castle 江戸城跡

The Fukiage Omiya Imperial Palace 吹上大宮御所

Nishi-hane Bridge 西桔橋

East Gardens

Ōte-mon 大手門

Otemachi Station 大手町駅

"Namiki" Cherry Tree 桜並木

Imperial Police Headquarters 皇宮警察本部

The Imperial Palace 御所

Kikyō-mon 桔梗門

Hanzō-mon 半蔵門

Fujimi-yagura 富士見櫓

Wadakura Bridge 和田倉橋

Sakashita-mon 坂下門

New Palace 新宮殿

TO TŌKYŌ STATION 東京駅 (200m)

The Three Lord Imperial Court 宮中三殿

Outer Gardens

Niyū Bashi Station 二重橋駅

Ishi Bridge 石橋

Nijū Bashi 二重橋

Kōkyosei-mon 皇居正門

Babasaki-mon 馬場先門

Sakura-da-mon 桜田門

Sakurada-mon Station 桜田門駅

Iwaida-Bridge 祝田橋

Yūraku-chō Line·営団有楽町線

Tokyo Metro Police HQ 警視庁

Hibiya Moat 日比谷濠

Hibiya Station 日比谷駅 M

Hibiya Kōen 日比谷公園

0   150 meters

0   150 yards

YASUKUNI SHRINE (YASUKUNI JINJA; 靖国神社). Two enormous archways and a gargantuan statue define the equally leviathan path leading to this tribute to Japanese warriors of times past. The shrine is unusual in that it is a religious war memorial; instead of a single deity, the spirits of thousands of unnamed soldiers who perished from the beginning of the Meiji Restoration and to the end of WWII are honored. Come April 21-23 or October 17-20 to witness special imperial rites. *(www.yasukini.or.jp. Kudanshita Station. Head straight out of Exit 2 and proceed several blocks. Look right for the giant rusty archway that leads to the shrine. Always open. Free.)*

TŌKYŌ STOCK EXCHANGE (TŌKYŌ SHŌKEN TORIHIKISHO; 東京証券取引 所). Open outcry trading has given way to computers, so don't come here expecting anything other than dead silence. The stock exchange is open to visitors, however, and the financially inclined may find something of interest. The ground floor museum gives a brief history, and the upper levels are full of computers with basic economic tutorials. The information terrace is a circular catwalk around the floor—perfect for financial voyeurs since the walls are made of glass. *(2-1, Nihonbashi Kabutochō, Chūō-ku. ☎ 3665-1881; www.tse.or.jp. Nihonbashi Station. Head straight out of Exit D2 for several minutes and then turn right at the post office. Cross under the highway and take not the immediate right but the one after. Look for the colorful signs advertising the Exchange's "Arrows" program. 1-day advance reservations required for group or English-language tours. Open M-F 9am-4:30pm. Closed holidays and Dec. 31-Jan. 3. Free.)*

ODAIBA

◙ŌEDO-ONSEN MONOGATARI (大江戸温泉物語). This hatchling hot springs is already the talk of the town. With restaurants, foot massages, shopping, food courts, and a museum in the house, it's more like a hot-spring theme park. The locals are piling in so fast, they have a sectioned parking lot. Very hot stuff. *(2-57, Aomi, Kōtō-ku. Telecom Center Station. Turn left from the turnstiles and left down the escalator. U-turn; it's all the way down the broad sidewalk. Entrance on the left. ☎ 5500-1126; www.ooedoonsen.jp. Open daily 11am-9am. ¥2700, age 4 through elementary school ¥1500. ¥1500 surcharge past 2am. Morning admission (5-7am) ¥1500. Night admission (6pm-2am) ¥1900.)*

FERRIS WHEEL (DAIKANRANSHA; 大観覧車). Up, up, and away. This 115m circle of joy is Odaiba's defining landmark and one of the world's largest wheels. A round-trip takes 16min., which partially explains why all the locals bring their dates here. The nearby hyperdrop and hypershoot cost ¥500. *(Aomi Station. Cross through the top floor of Mega Web in Palette Town plaza or go down the street with the water to your right, turn left at the intersection, and make a left down an alley. ☎ 5500-2655; www.daikanransha.com. Open Su-Th 10am-10pm, F-Sa 10am-2pm. ¥900, 6-person gondola ¥3000.)*

MEGA WEB. It looks like a car dealership from the outside, but what Toyota has created is really a car fiesta. Take a spin in auto-drive around the track (¥200), or test-drive a new model (¥300, Japanese or international license required). Drive simulators, a 3-D theater, and a history garage round it out. The nifty car elevator is worth a gander; select a car from an electronic menu and stay put while complicated machinery brings the car to you. *(Palette Town, 1, Aomi, Kōtō-ku. Aomi Station. Mega Web is the east half of Palette Town Plaza, right in front of the station. You may end up crossing through Venus Fort. ☎ 3599-0808; www.megaweb.gr.jp. Open daily 11am-9pm. Free.)*

ODAIBA PARKS. Odaiba is one of the few places in Tōkyō where people can fling themselves in haphazard directions without colliding with anyone else. **Daiba Park** is a grassy diamond-shaped peninsula sticking out of the harbor where no grassy diamond-shaped peninsula ought to be. *(1-10, Daiba, Minato-ku. ☎ 5500-2455.)* **Odaiba Kaihin Park** is a strip along the harbor, perfect for meandering and observing leaping fish. **Shiokaze Park** is more or less an enormous poppy field, perfect for running toward your long-lost lover in slow motion. All are open for the public to enjoy.

FUJI TV BUILDING. Glossing over the gift shops and studio promenade on the 5th and 7th floors, the big draw for this architectural dream is its titanium observation deck 123.45m off the ground. *(Daiba Station. Look for the Lego-like building from anywhere in Odaiba. Open Tu-Su 10am-8pm. Closed Tu when M is a holiday. Tickets sold until 7pm. ¥500.)*

RAINBOW BRIDGE. Named for the colored lights that illuminate it at night, this funky multitasker carries roads, rails, and walkers from Tōkyō proper to Odaiba. A walk across takes 30min. *(Open to walkers Apr.-Oct. 9am-9pm; Nov.-Mar. 10am-6pm. Last entry 30min. before close. Closed 3rd M of the month. Pedestrians ¥100.)*

PANASONIC CENTER. Tech-nuts can bathe in the light of high-def TV and the latest in Panasonic gadgetry, though the dinosaur museum (p. 175) is the real sight here. *(2-5-18, Ariake, Kōtō-ku. Kokusai-Tenjijō Seimon Station. Turn left out of the turnstiles and walk straight down Tōkyō Fashion Town's 2nd fl. plaza. It's toward the end. ☎ 3599-2500; www.panasonic-center.com. Open Tu-Su 10am-6pm.)*

BREAKFAST OF CHAMPIONS

If it's true that understanding what people eat helps you understand their culture, it's clear that the key to the Japanese psyche is linked to the catch of the day. The average Japanese citizen consumes about 70kg (150 lb.) of seafood each year; stomach digits like that, and a person begins to fathom what it means to be an island nation. Fish are every bit as essential to the Japanese diet as rice, only they've got fins and a survival instinct. Sushi happens; **Tsukiji Fish Market** makes it happen. Not even the Imperial Palace captures the spirit of Japan with such acuity.

START: Tsukiji Shijō subway station.

FINISH: Tsukiji subway station.

DURATION: 2hr.

WHEN TO GO: The market is open Monday-Saturday, starting bright and early—a 5am start is best.

Imagine the clockwork of a nation focused into one little dock. Every year thousands of foreign visitors come to watch the gears turn. The hitch? The action goes down at 5am. Tsukiji is a dish best served early in an itinerary, when wakeful jet lag victims can turn their affliction to their advantage. Tsukiji is equally viable as an afterparty to a hard night out; just don't end up sleeping amid the fishes.

A subway ride to Tsukiji Shijō and two rights out of Exit A1 deliver lickety-split. A taxi to "Tsukiji ichiba no seimon" is quicker. Other alternatives are Tsukiji, Higashi Ginza, and Shintomi-chō subway stations; just follow your inner lemming to the river. The "Ichi Ichi" bus from Shinbashi Station is first with the locals. A satisfying visit will require at least a couple of hours; plan to be at the marketplace by 6:30am at the latest. The market is closed on Sundays, the second and fourth Wednesdays of the month, Japanese national holidays, the period around New Year's, Obon, and a few random gaps in between. Call ahead (☎3541-1111; Japanese only) or check the online calendar (www.shijou.metro.tokyo.jp; also Japanese only).

Finally, a few basic principles. Tsukiji is an exercise in dodgeball; carts, porters, and anyone in galoshes has the right-of-way. Traffic is so tricky that leaping and hiding in niches will likely be required. Groups will almost certainly get separated. Large backpacks, sandals, and aggressive bargaining are bad ideas. Bringing children is an even worse idea. Flash photography in the vicinity of the auctions is absolutely forbidden.

SEIMON (MAIN GATE). Hit up the guard boxes at the gate on the western side of the marketplace, just across from the Asahi Shinbun (Asahi Newspaper) building, for an English brochure and a map. There are similar boxes by the gates of the **Kaikōbashi entrance** and the **Kachidoki entrance,** both on the market's northern edge.

1 WHARFSIDE. Weave eastward along the only open street, all the way to the **Sumida River's** edge, to get a fresh start with the recently arrived tuna chilling out wharfside. Tsukiji is laid out in a series of crescent-shaped layers; the wharf is the surface of the onion.

2 TUNA AUCTIONS. Head slightly inland into the next two layers, open tents where fish auctions take place amid an eerie fog of death (read "ice being vaporized"). Most visitors will find only a group of wholesale inspectors planning out their strategy; this is done by picking at the dead fish with miniature sickles to determine their quality. Reign in the horses for just a couple minutes and bells will sound the start of an auction; some involve wooden podiums and loudspeakers, some do not. The auctions are highly ritualized and thoroughly entertaining, involving rhythmic finger gesturing. Seafood auctions generally happen between 5:30 and 6:30am.

3 MIDDLEMAN'S MARKETING PLACE. The tuna are dragged off to their fates. Follow them into the next layer, a curving series of stalls under a shed roof. Different aisles feature different forms of sealife requiring different styles of preparation; throat slitting is a particularly gruesome and yet incredibly engaging affair.

4 UOGASHI YOKOCHŌ. Follow the crescents west (away from the river) and turn right down another main road before entering the lettered packaging areas. Proceed with a somewhat lengthy walk to arrive at **Uogashi Yokochō,** a series of small streets for refueling human beings.

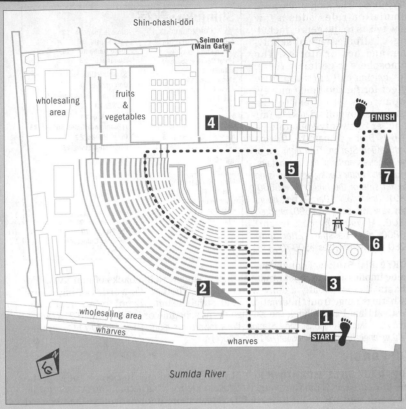

Shin-ohashi-dōri

Seimon (Main Gate)

wholesaling area

fruits & vegetables

4

FINISH

5

7

6

3

2

1

wholesaling area

wharves

wharves

START

Sumida River

The tiny restaurants here get crowded, but the sushi joints among them get creative, serving *tamago* (egg) piping hot and *ebi* (shrimp) topped with a hundred unhatched *ebi* babies. Some may want to save their appetites for the **Outer Marketplace.**

5 KAIKŌBASHI EXIT. Blow this fishstick stand via the **Kaikōbashi Exit,** a bridge one-third of the way back to the river.

6 NAMIYOKE SHRINE. Exit the market, and immediately on the right you'll see the **Namiyoke Shrine,** where memorials to various species of fish and large stone eggs are protected by twin lions.

7 OUTER MARKETPLACE. Head away from the shrine perpendicular to its gate. Duck right two blocks down to enter the **Outer Marketplace.** Most will want to shelve the retail shops and beeline for the sushi bars, renowned for the freshness of their fish. Ultra-fresh sushi has a slightly different taste—you'll know when you try it. How to tell if a place is good? The size of the proprietor's welcome may well be proportional to the quality of the food.

TSUKIJI HONGAN-JI. End your tour with a stop at this just-off-the-map Indian-inspired Buddhist temple, constructed in 1617, before ducking into Tsukiji Subway Station and heading back to bed.

Based on Theodore C. Bestor's Tsukiji: the Fish Market at the Center of the World *(University of California Press, 2004).*

WALKING TOUR

JOYPOLIS. The king of carnival simulation rides adds a few new twists to the genre, including a halfpipe, virtual skydiving, and horror stories. The atmosphere is certainly there, but critics call sims too little effect for far too much money. Japanese youth seem to disagree, as Joypolis draws a fair number of twenty-somethings. *(1-6-1, Daiba, Minato-ku. Odaiba Kaihin-Kōen Station. Turn right out of the turnstiles and shimmy downstairs. U-turn and enter Decks; Joypolis is on the far side of the building. ☎5500-1801. Open daily 10am-11pm, hours may vary with season. ¥500, children ¥300. All-you-can-ride passport ¥3800, night passport (after 5pm) ¥2800. Individual rides ¥500-700.)*

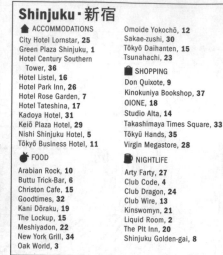

Shinjuku・新宿

♠ ACCOMMODATIONS
City Hotel Lornstar, 25
Green Plaza Shinjuku, 1
Hotel Century Southern Tower, 36
Hotel Listel, 16
Hotel Park Inn, 26
Hotel Rose Garden, 7
Hotel Tateshina, 17
Kadoya Hotel, 31
Keiō Plaza Hotel, 29
Nishi Shinjuku Hotel, 5
Tōkyō Business Hotel, 11

🍴 FOOD
Arabian Rock, 10
Buttu Trick-Bar, 6
Christon Cafe, 15
Goodtimes, 32
Kani Dōraku, 19
The Lockup, 15
Meshiyadon, 22
New York Grill, 34
Oak World, 3

Omoide Yokochō, 12
Sakae-zushi, 30
Tōkyō Daihanten, 15
Tsunahachi, 23

🛍 SHOPPING
Don Quixote, 9
Kinokuniya Bookshop, 37
OIONE, 18
Studio Alta, 14
Takashimaya Times Square, 33
Tōkyū Hands, 35
Virgin Megastore, 28

🌃 NIGHTLIFE
Arty Farty, 27
Club Code, 4
Club Dragon, 24
Club Wire, 13
Kinswomyn, 21
Liquid Room, 2
The Pit Inn, 20
Shinjuku Golden-gai, 8

TŌKYŌ BIG SIGHT. Though the name implies Japan's most ornate shrine, balanced on the backs of four living elephants, this is actually a convention center. Whether it's worth visiting varies; gatherings range from "International Industrial Cleaning Expo" to "Amateur Radio Festival Ham Fair." Check the English event schedule or info booth. *(3-21-1, Ariake, Kōtō-ku. Kokusai-Tenjijō Seimon Station. Walk toward the giant saw. ☎5530-1111; www.bigsight.jp/english. Admission usually ¥1000-2000.)*

ROPPONGI

ROPPONGI HILLS MORI TOWER. Tōkyō's latest attempt to breach the sky, the one that screams "I am Roppongi Hills! Hear me roar!" is actually an artistic softie. Most will start with a lift to **Tōkyō City View**, a more informative but limited 52nd story alternative to the literal high point of Roppongi Hills, the **Sky Deck.** It's shorter than Tōkyō Tower, but an open air heliport is a dizzying experience and there are no glass middlemen to stop viewers from making eye contact with Tōkyō. For once, the city's slummy shell hardly matters; visitors will be overwhelmed by the sheer accomplishment of man. A quick retreat downstairs leads to the **Mori Art Museum,** newly open as of October 2003. The inaugural exhibition, featuring Monet, Matisse, Yoko Ono, Andy Warhol, and Mr. 5th-century-sculptor-dude, lasts until January 2004. *(☎6406-6100. Open Su-W 10am-10pm, Th-Sa 10am-midnight.)* The **Roppongi Hills Club** and **Academy Hills Roppongi** downstairs are exclusive business doodads best left for the exclusively lame. *(6-10-1, Roppongi, Minato-ku. Roppongi Station. Take the Roppongi Hills Exit and ride the escalators up to the main plaza. Entrance to the left, connected to Mori Tower. www.moriartscenter.org. Open daily 9am-1am. Tokyo City View ☎6406-6652. ¥1500, students ¥1000, age 4 to junior high ¥500. More for Sky Deck.)*

TŌKYŌ TOWER. Mine is bigger. An insulting 13m taller than the Eiffel Tower, it seems *le student* has barely outstripped *le teacher*. Last April, fate finally delivered the tower a much needed kick in the pants, planting the Roppongi Hills Sky Deck, a contender better in every respect, directly beside it. The **Special Observatory** is only 12m higher than the newcomer's; even with fixed binoculars, it isn't worth the extra ¥420 and the sacrifice of open air. *(Observatories open daily 9am-10pm. 150m main observatory ¥820, junior high and elementary school students ¥460, younger children ¥310. 250m special observatory additional ¥600/¥400/¥350.)* The tower extras are mostly rip-offs; the oversized holograms in the **Mysterious Walking Zone** are

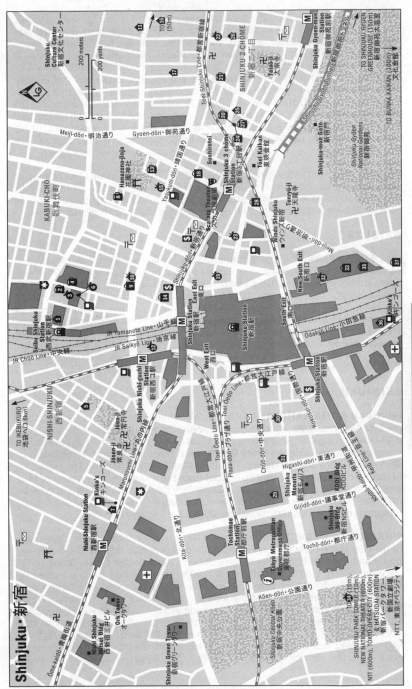

TŌKYŌ

impressive but far too few. The **Trick Art Gallery** starts off with a fantastic illusion, but the rest are so textbook that only children will be impressed. Only the **Wax Museum** carries any weight, with exhibits ranging from the Last Supper to medieval torture. **The Forest of Information** and **Statistics Plaza** are free sideshows. *(All open daily 10am-9pm. Mysterious Walking Zone ¥410, children ¥300. Trick Art Gallery ¥400/¥300. Wax Museum ¥870/¥460.)* Connoisseurs will appreciate the rarity of the fish in the **aquarium;** the rest will bemoan the depressing Chinese-restaurant presentation. *(Open Aug. 1-15 10am-8pm; Mar. 16-July 31 and Aug. 16-Nov. 15 10am-7pm; Nov. 16-Mar. 15 10am-6pm. ¥1000, seniors and age 4 through middle school ¥500.)* The bottom line is an uncreative money maker: the Tōkyō Tower is likely to disappoint. *(4-2-8, Shibakōen, Minato-ku. Kamiya-chō Station. From Exit 3, follow the main road 5min. ☎3433-5111; www.tokyotower.co.jp. Main observatory + extras + special exhibit combo ¥2150.)*

ZŌJŌ-JI (増上寺). Though it's a major temple, Zōjō-ji is likely to only interest the architecturally inclined. It's a hotspot on New Year's Eve and Setsubun. *(4-7-35, Shibakōen, Minato-ku. ☎3432-1431. Akabanebashi Station. From the road just north of Tōkyō Tower, head to the bottom of the hill, shift right and continue straight; it's the 2nd right.)*

SHIBUYA

NHK STUDIO PARK. Not just for filming, NHK Studio Park allows visitors to sample all things TV. Try your hand as a news anchor, or generate sound effects with household objects. Costumes and wigs allow vicarious thrills, and no-glasses 3D movies intrigue the future-oriented (the technology is innovative but not perfect). The main draw, of course, is watching live studios in action. Tromping through takes about an hour. *(2-2-1, Jinnan, Shibuya-ku. Shibuya or Harajuku Station. From Shibuya, take the Hachikō Exit, cross the street, and head up past the right side of Starbucks. Bear left between Seibu and OI. Go all the way down; the studio is vast. ☎3485-8034; www.nhk.or.jp/studiopark. Open daily 10am-6pm. Closed 3rd M of each month except Aug. and Dec. 25-Dec. 31. ¥200, junior high and high school students ¥150, elementary and younger free.)*

SHINJUKU

SHINJUKU GYŌEN NATIONAL GARDENS. Most major neighborhoods have their pockets of green; some would argue that Shinjuku's is the belle of the ball. With 20,000 trees, it's got ample strolling grounds at the very least and is a tribute to Japanese pond design. **Shinjuku Gyōen Greenhouse** (Shinjuku Gyoen Daionshitsu; 新宿御苑大温室) lies aloof at the top, full of exotic plants, not flowers. The collection of Santa Cruz lily pads are especially cool, each big enough to ferry a bevy of froggies. *(11 Naito-chō, Shinjuku-ku. Shinjuku Station. From the South Exit, turn left and follow the main road/bridge for 5min. ☎3350-0151; www.shinjukugyoen.go.jp. Open Tu-Su 9am-4:30pm. Greenhouse open 11am-3:30pm. Closed Dec. 29-Jan. 3. ¥200; ages 6-14 ¥50).*

SHINJUKU PARK TOWER (新宿パークタワー). Shinjuku's three challenges to the clouds are certainly eye-catching. Visitors generally stick to the first seven floors and the bitter top. The biggest draw is **Living Design Center Ozone** (3-7F; www.ozone.co.jp), an information center on the art of interior decoration. Restaurants and cafes fill out the basement, while the first floor showcases professional photography in **Gallery One** and the **Atrium.** (Open almost daily 10:30am-6:30pm. Free.) The first place to get struck by lightning will be the **Park Hyatt Tōkyō** (☎5322-1234; www.parkhyatttokyo.com), on floors 39-52 and recommended to those with ¥49,000 to burn. To go the whole 235m, see **New York Grill** under **Food.** *(3-7-1, Nishi-shinjuku, Shinjuku-ku. ☎5322-6640; www.shinjukuparktower.com. Shinjuku Station. From the South Exit, turn right and follow the main road 10min.; the 3 pointy-tipped towers are unmistakable.)*

SHINJUKU CENTRAL PARK (SHINJUKU CHŪŌ KŌEN; 新宿中央公園).

There isn't much to see here. Aside from a little shrine and a mini-museum, other high points include jungle-like foliage and interesting waterfall effects. The playground in the south end of the park has a jungle gym and a splash pool; kids may have a blast. *(Tōchōmae Station. Across from the Tōkyō Metropolitan Government Office. Free.)*

UENO

UENO PARK (UENO KŌEN; 上野公園).

Strap your boots on and get an early start: Ueno Kōen is Ueno's trademark sight, and it'll take a full day to appreciate everything it has to offer. Several major museums call the park home (see p. 176 for individual listings). If you're just meandering, you might walk to the center of the park's three lakes and ring the gong at 400-year-old temple **Benten-dō.** Also of interest is **Kiyomizu Kannon-dō,** which was transferred from the top of the hill to its current location in 1694. *(Closes 4pm. English explanation of temple history ¥100.)* Farther uphill lies the **Tōshōgū Shrine,** dedicated to Tokugawa Ieyasu, of grand unification fame. Majestic gates and a 100-stone-lantern-salute lead up to the gorgeous building. Ask the info booth for a free English leaflet. *(Entry ¥200.)* A little farther down, a striking series of orange gateways takes you to **Gojō Shrine.** The dioramas are drab, but the courtyard is nice; for a surprise, check out the little stone building that looks like a bathroom hut. Toward the base of the park lies a larger-than-life statue of **Saigō Takamori,** a legendary Japanese military man. Check out the nearby **Royal Art Museum** if you have time; though the building is small and no English labels are provided, its rotating and very focused exhibits just might be your cup of tea. A **fountain** in the center of the park turns on intermittently. *(Take the JR Kōen Exit. Info center ☎3827-9420. Pick up an English map and check for special events at the information center, just across the street and to the right. Most attractions closed M and after 5pm.)*

UENO ZOO (UENO DŌBUTSUEN; 上野動物園).

Tōkyō's biggest zoo features over 60 different exhibits: the pandas, lesser pandas, Japanese birds, and giant anteaters may be particularly novel to Westerners. Don't miss half the zoo: the park comprises an East Garden and a West Garden connected by monorail. *(9-83, Ueno Park, Taitō-ku. Enter the park from the JR's Kōen Exit and plow straight ahead. ☎3828-5171. Open Tu-Su 9:30am-5pm. Closed Dec. 29-Jan. 1. ¥600, over 65 ¥300, ages 12-14 ¥200, under 11 free. Disabled individuals and attendant free. Free for all on Mar. 20, Apr. 29, and Oct. 1.)*

THE BIG SPLURGE

FLOAT LIKE A BUTTERFLY

As one of the world's largest metropolises and a city rife with history, Tōkyō can offer new sights and thrills to visitors for months on end. But can you handle it? Think about those tired feet, those trees destined to become JR tickets. Forget ambulatory sightseeing. How'd you like to see the whole of Tōkyō in the span of minutes?

Excel Air operates a heliport right next to the Tōkyō Disney Resort and offers helicopter cruises of the city. Except for the shorter daytime "Dream Course," the route passes Tōkyō Disney, the Ginza shopping district, Tōkyō Tower, the Imperial Palace, the Tōkyō Dome, and Akihabara. Both day and night trips are offered; the Sunset Course flies at twilight, while the Pearl and Diamond Courses depart at night. The day flight is cheaper, but frankly, the curtain of nightfall does wonders for Tōkyō's blemishes. *(Toyo Central Bldg. 9F, 4-1-13, Toyo, Kōtō-ku. ☎047-380-5555; www.excel-air.com. Maihama Station; JR Keiō Line). Reservations required, up to 2 months ahead. Call ☎047-380-3353 1-3hr. ahead to confirm weather allows flights. Dream Course ¥3900, ¥2900 for children. 2pm-sunset. Sunset Course ¥8000/¥5000. Every 15min. during twilight. Pearl Course M-Th ¥9800/¥8800, F-Su ¥12,500/¥8800. Every 15min. sunset-9pm. Diamond Course M-Th ¥14,800/¥12,600, F-Su ¥18,000/¥12,600. Tax included.)*

THE LOCAL LEGEND

ICHABOD INVERTED

The *samurai* spirit: unswerving, selfless, and, in the case of Taira no Masakado, powerful enough to rocket a decapitated head across Japan. Before defying the laws of physics, Masakado defied the 10th-century court. Luckily, the neighborhood deity granted him a holy light blessing, which left him only one weakness: a small spot on his temple that the light had missed. It was like a sloppy sunscreen job, SPF invincible.

With the gods behind him, Masakado began a winning streak to make the Yomiuri Giants jealous. He killed off his uncles and conquered the Eastern provinces, declaring himself emperor. But that kind of power gets to a *samurai*'s head, and Masakado blabbed his weakness to lover-girl Kikyō-no-mae. She betrayed him, and he was captured and decapitated.

Then his legacy truly began. Masakado's decapitated head refused to rot, glowering with ferocity. In AD 940 it got tired of sitting on a pike and flew home in an unholy streak. A monk shot him short and he landed in present day Tōkyō, where locals buried his head in a mound of dirt.

Tōkyōites made him their guardian and built the Kanda Myōjin shrine for his remains. When neglected his wrath knows no bounds: he's blamed for the 1923 earthquake and a string of corporate suicides. Tōkyōites today still pay their respects at Kanda Myōjin.

SMALLER NEIGHBORHOODS

AKIHABARA

KANDA MYŌJIN SHRINE. This festive-looking shrine has a unique flavor. Radiant vermilion columns and a pair of guardian archers welcome visitors, who come to pay respects to three gods enshrined within. Pick up an English brochure from the shop for full details. The locals make a pilgrimage here on New Year's Day—it could be fun to tag along. *(2-16-2, Soto-Kanda, Chiyoda-ku. ☎3254-0753. Akihabara Station. Take the JR's Electric Town Exit and head up the main street, Chūō-dōri. Take a left at the 1st major intersection, with the big black building. The street bends right and uphill; the 1st right after the Yushima Seidō walls leads through a pale green archway towards the shrine. Free.)*

YUSHIMA SEIDŌ (湯島聖堂). The Yushima Seidō is a walled compound constructed for the study of Confucianism. The main building, or *taisei-den*, consists of an empty plaza that may strike visitors as an apt arena for some martial arts action. A larger-than-life statue of Confucius, outside in the compound's garden, is a reminder that the plaza is actually intended for pacifistic ends. *(Akihabara Station. Take the JR's Electric Town Exit and head up Chūō-dōri. Take a left at the 1st major intersection, with the big black building. The street bends right and uphill. You'll see the garden's walls shortly; entrances are on the opposite side. Open summer 9:30am-5pm; winter 9:30am-4pm. Free.)*

OFF THE MAP

TŌKYŌ DISNEY. Japanese tourists no longer need to go abroad for their taste of mousy magic: they now happily sink their cameras into Tōkyō DisneySea Park and Tokyo Disneyland Park, where tots pose with Mickey, sulky goths melt in their shoes, and everyone hops on rides loaded with animatronic fuzzies. **Tōkyō Disneyland** is the same as its Western counterparts, with wider avenues, a slightly altered layout, and prettier decorations. Smaller **DisneySea Park** features six internationally-themed waterfronts and centerpiece "Mysterious Island," a (fake) volcano. The basic idea is the same but a touch more adult-oriented; while many prefer Disneyland, the ability to drink *sake* and beer at DisneySea tips the scales for others. *(www.tokyodisneyresort.com. Maihama Station, on the JR Keiō Line. Transfer from Tōkyō Station. Just follow the signs. 1-Day Passport for 1 park: 18+ ¥5500, 12-17 ¥4800, ages 4-11 ¥3700. After 6pm on non-holiday weeknights ¥2900. After 3pm most weekends ¥4500/¥3900/¥3000. 2-Day Passport allowing 1 day at each park: ¥9800/*

¥8600/¥6700. 3-Day Passport allowing 1 day at each park, 3rd day dual-park access: ¥13,700/ ¥12,000/¥9300. 4-Day Passport allowing 1 day at each park, 3rd and 4th day dual-park access: ¥17,200/¥15,100/¥11,600.)

🏛 MUSEUMS AND GALLERIES

As a general rule, Tōkyō's museums have last admission 30min. before the museum closes. Many offer group discounts, and those that do define a group as more than 20 people. Those closed on Mondays close on Tuesdays when Monday is a national holiday. Until sales cease on February 29, 2004, visitors will almost certainly want to purchase a **Grutt** (☎ 3443-0051; www.rekibun.or.jp), short for "Good for Round Tour Ticket of Museum" (say *"gurutto"* very precisely, or the docents will rue the day Commodore Perry forced open their pristine harbors). This ¥1800 passport to culture will get you into every major museum in Tōkyō for one month (but not the special exhibits). The Grutt can be purchased at most participating museums, all of which bear big Grutt posters; it's also sold at major convenience stores, major stations, ticketing agencies, and major tourist offices. Hope that the sponsoring organization starts a similar deal when this one expires.

MAJOR NEIGHBORHOODS

AKASAKA

SUNTORY MUSEUM OF ART (SUNTORII BIJUTSUKAN; サントリー美術館).
The museum holds paintings, ceramics, and other sundry goods primarily associated with Japanese everyday life. The whole exhibit rotates: what's here today may be gone tomorrow. *(Tōkyō Suntory Bldg. 11F, 1-2-3, Moto-Akasaka, Minato-ku. Akasaka-mitsuke Station. Exit B is right next to the museum. Use the first elevator on the left. ☎ 3470-1073; www.suntory.co.jp/sma. Open Tu-Th and Sa-Su 10am-5pm, F 10am-7pm. ¥800, college and high school students ¥600, middle and elementary school students ¥400.)*

ŌKURA SHŪKOKAN MUSEUM OF ART (大倉集古館). Glued to the side of the Ōkura Hotel, the museum houses some 2000 works of art. The courtyard, with its giant shrine guard statues and lots of littler statues, is worth a passing glance. *(2-10-3, Toranomon, Minato-ku. Roppongi-itchōme Station. Take Exit 3 and head towards the uphill portion of Ark Hills. It's the closest building on the street between the 2 segments of the Ōkura Hotel. ☎ 3583-0781; www.hotelokura.co.jp/tokyo. Open Apr.-Oct. Tu-Th and Sa 10am-4:30pm, F 10am-5:30pm; Nov.-Mar. Tu-Sa 10am-4:30pm. Closed during exhibit rotations. ¥800, college and high-school students and 65+ ¥500, middle-school students and younger free.)*

ASAKUSA

MIYAMOTO DRUM MUSEUM (MIYAMOTO TAIKO-KAN; 宮本太鼓館). A ticket and an elevator ride to the fourth floor of the Miyamoto Japanese Percussion and Festival Store will land you in *taiko* (drum) heaven. The room is full of drums, ranging from historic *wadaiko* (Japanese drums) to steel drums to powwow drums to the curious Jingling Johnny. The museum is as interested in spreading the love as it is in preserving culture; vistitors are allowed to play a good three-quarters of the drums. (Red dots mark off-limit skins.) Full English subtitles mean you might learn something too. *(Saisensōten Bldg. 4F, 2-1-1, Nishi-Asakusa, Taitō-ku. Tawara-machi Station. Turn left out of Exit 3. Walk a bit and look for the building with a portable shrine on display. ☎ 3842-5622. Open W-Su 10am-5pm. ¥300.)*

EBISU

▨ TŌKYŌ METROPOLITAN MUSEUM OF PHOTOGRAPHY (TŌKYŌ-TO SHASHIN BIJUTSUKAN; 東京都写真美術館). The quality of a visit here is entirely dependent on the current exhibit; fortunately, the Metropolitan Government has unparalleled taste, and on any given day the dice are loaded toward thought-stirring, provocative material. *(Yebisu Garden Place, 1-13-3, Mita, Meguro-ku. Ebisu Station. Take the Skywalk to Yebisu Garden Place. In the back, on the right. ☎ 3280-0099; www.tokyo-photo-museum.or.jp. Open Tu-W and Sa-Su 10am-6pm, Th-F 10am-8pm. Closed Dec. 28-Jan. 4. ¥500, under 18 and 65+ ¥250. Half that for regular gallery.)*

BEER MUSEUM YEBISU (TŌKYŌ BAKUSHU KINENKAN; 恵比寿麦酒記念館). Hardly the Willy Wonka Factory of beers, the Beer Museum is an honest pedagogical effort that will be completely lost on those unable to read Japanese. The Magic Vision "Theater," a series of three holographic screens, portrays a battle between "Gambrinus, King of Beer, and The Evil One of the Forest" for the "heart of the beautiful Beer Fairy." Completely uninformative monitors portray overflowing beer, as if to painfully remind guests that the Tasting Lounge isn't free. Still, ¥200-250 for a decent glass isn't bad. *(4-20-1, Shibuya-ku. Ebisu Station. Take the Skywalk to Yebisu Garden Place. To the far left, behind Mitsukoshi. ☎ 5423-7255; www.sapporobeer.co.jp/Brewery/ebisu. Open Tu-Su 10am-6pm. Last entry 5pm. Closed for New Year. Free.)*

HARAJUKU AND AOYAMA

MEIJI MEMORIAL PICTURE GALLERY (MEIJI-JINGŪ SEITOKU KINEN KAIGAKAN; 明治神宮聖徳記念絵画館). The strokes will be familiar to connoisseurs of traditional Asian art, but the ironclads and moustaches of Emperor Meiji's day paint a whole different picture. His holiness' horse, stuffed and preserved, is a scream and a half. Two sizeable wings give visitors good mileage, though the museum may have hurt earphone sales by providing such full bilingual captions. *(Meiji-Jingu Outer Garden 9, Kasumigaoka, Shinjuku-ku. ☎ 3401-5179; www.meijijingu.or.jp. ¥500, students ¥300, children ¥200. Headsets ¥300 and ¥1700 deposit.)*

ŌTA MEMORIAL MUSEUM (ŌTA KINEN BIJUTSUKAN; 大田記念美術館). Hiding behind the front-line shops of Harajuku is a dedicated collection of *ukiyo-e* art. The fee is high, but the artwork is unique, depicting commoners doing common things. Imagine if Renaissance painters captured family fights at dinner instead of religious icons—now give it a Japanese spin. Limited paintings on display, but (nearly) full English subtitles betray an honest desire to spread the love. *(1-10-10, Jingūmae, Shibuya-ku. Harajuku Station. Turn right from the Omotesandō Exit. Take the bridge and go perpendicular to the station. Go down the stairs and the main street. Turn left before Laforet, then left again. It's on the right. ☎ 3403-0880. Open 10:30am-5:30pm. ¥700, ¥1000 during special exhibits; college and high school students ¥500.)*

SPIRAL HALL (スパイラルホール). Spiral Hall is like a *depāto* with the stores clipped out: they've been replaced with a spiral stairwell, halls hosting events, and a splash of artwork. One of Aoyama's few landmarks, it's worth a peek if you're in the area. *(Omotesandō Station. U-turn out of Exit B1 and it's immediately on the right.)*

MARUNOUCHI

NATIONAL MUSEUM OF MODERN ART, TŌKYŌ (TŌKYŌ KOKURITSU KINDAI BIJUTSUKAN; 東京近代美術館). One moment you think you're looking at a traditional painting of women from the Imperial Court, but then you realize that they're looking through a telescope and the painting was done 50 years

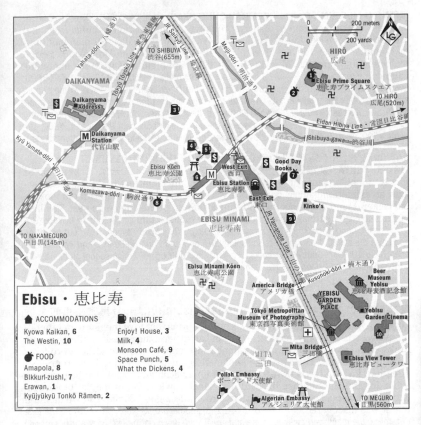

Ebisu・恵比寿

ACCOMMODATIONS
Kyowa Kaikan, **6**
The Westin, **10**

FOOD
Amapola, **8**
Bikkuri-zushi, **7**
Erawan, **1**
Kyūjyūkyū Tonkō Rāmen, **2**

NIGHTLIFE
Enjoy! House, **3**
Milk, **4**
Monsoon Café, **9**
Space Punch, **5**
What the Dickens, **4**

ago. The "Momat," as the acronym would have it, has a few surprises for those unfamiliar with modern art of the Asian variety; displays range from black and white photography to depictions of World War II. Their **crafts gallery** is actually in a different but nearby building; just follow the main road away from the station. (*3-1, Kitanomaru Kōen, Chiyoda-ku. Takebashi Station. Take Exit A1 and cross the bridge, then look right.* ☎ *5777-8600; www.momat.go/jp. Open Tu-Th and Sa-Su 10am-5pm, F 10am-8pm. ¥420, students ¥130, under 15 and over 65 free. Extra fee for special exhibits.*)

SCIENCE MUSEUM (KAGAKU GIJUTSUKAN; 科学技術管). Unlike the natural science museum in Ueno, this museum is geared entirely around interactivity. Optics, motor vehicles, electricity, and everything else you learned about in science class are literally just a touch away. The exhibits are shy on English explanations, but the museum's vast range of buttons and levers communicate to patrons in the universal language of science. The exhibit halls are numerous, so grab an English map from information. (*2-1, Kitanomaru Kōen, Chiyoda-ku. Takebashi Station. Take exit A1 and cross the bridge. Pass the modern art museum on your right and turn right onto street leading you uphill into Kitanomaru Park. Look for a tall white building on your right.* ☎ *3 8544; www.jsf.or.jp. Open daily 9:30am-4:50pm. Closed Dec. 29-Jan. 3. ¥600, high sch junior high school students ¥400, elementary school students and children ¥250.*)

IDEMITSU MUSEUM OF ARTS (IDEMITSU BIJUTSUKAN; 出光美術館). The Idemitsu Museum has no permanent displays; rotating exhibitions keep things fresh and thematically focused. Pottery and paint seem to carry the day. Utopian paintings by Tomioka Tessai, the last literati (Jan. 10-Mar. 7, 2004) and Momoyama Period tea-ceremony ceramics (Mar. 13-May 30, 2004) are highlights from the upcoming calendar. *(Teigeki Bldg. 9F, 3-1-1, Marunouchi, Chiyoda-ku. ☎ 3213-9402 or 5777-8600; www.idemitsu.co.jp/museum. Hibiya Station. The Mita Line's B2 Exit takes you to the correct street; from other lines, take Exit A9. Head for the corner nearest the moat and look for the Imperial Theater; it's black with a kanji sign, a few blocks down. Turn right down that street; the elevator for the Idemitsu Museum has its own foyer on the left, a few doors past the theater. ¥800, students ¥500. Open Tu-Su 10am-5pm. Closed year-end, New Year's, and during exhibit rotations.)*

NATIONAL FILM CENTER (TŌKYŌ KOKURITSU KINDAI BIJUTSUKAN FIRUMUSENTĀ; 東京国立近代美術館、フィルムセンター). A branch of The National Museum of Modern Art, the film museum features regular screenings, an exhibition gallery, and a library. The gallery is peppered with old movies, old cameras, and old projectors, offering a glimpse of the cinematic past. The lack of English explanations leave all but the most diehard film buffs a little bored. *(3-7-6, Kyōbashi, Chūō-ku. ☎ 3561-0830; www.momat.go.jp. Takarachō Station. Head out of exit A4 and cross the street; it's on the left. Screenings Tu-F at 3 and 7pm, Sa-Su at 1 and 4pm. Gallery open Tu-Su 10:30am-6pm. ¥200, college students and over 65 ¥70, high school students ¥40, under 15 free. Library open Tu-F 10:30am-6pm.)*

MEGURO

■ **PARASITOLOGICAL MUSEUM (MEGURO KISEICHŪKAN; 目黒寄生虫館).** Love kittens and bunnies? Have a look at the worms that love them too, but for different reasons. The only museum of its kind anywhere, the parasite collection here ranks in the world's top five. Pustulent worm explosions and afflicted rodents float in pickle jars. The Japanese explanations instruct viewers how to prevent infection; knowledge is power, and the ¥400 English guidebook can help you get some. It's not the Smithsonian, but the sheer gawk value of a 8.8m tapeworm extends the appeal of the museum's two rooms to a good 30min. Did we mention that it was discovered in a person? *(4-1-1, Shimomeguro. Meguro Station. From the East Exit, follow the main road away from the station. 10min. down on the left, after a river crossing and a bridge. ☎ 3716-1264. Open Tu-Su 10am-5pm. Closed Dec. 29-Jan. 4. Free.)*

THE INSTITUTE FOR NATURE STUDY, NATIONAL SCIENCE MUSEUM TŌKYŌ (KYŌIKUKAN; 教育館). A compulsive need to rough it might lead you to Kyōiku-kan, where bugs and ravens will either make you feel at peace with nature or scare the living daylights out of you. Gardens are everywhere in Tōkyō, but the Kyōiku-kan is an unengineered preserve, meaning it smells like raw salad. Deep enough to shed the city and a favorite spot for long walks through overflowing plant life. *(5-~1-5, Shirokanedai, Minato-ku. Meguro Station. Head straight out of the East Exit and follow the ~~~ht. Turn left at the main road. Go straight 5min. and under the highway. Trace the edge of ~~~ keeping it on your left. Another few minutes down, around the corner. Not clearly ~~~176. Open Tu-Su 9am-4pm; up to 1hr. extra during the summer. Closed the day ~~~ nd New Year season. ¥210, high school students and younger ¥60.)*

~N TEIEN ART MUSEUM (TŌKYŌ-TO TEIEN BIJUTSUKAN;
Drool at the Art Deco exhibits, but remember to drool at
~~~piece of Art Deco where a prince used to live. Completed
~~~largely the work of Frenchman Henri Rapin, though the
~~~dded some Asian touches. *(5-21-9, Shirokanedai, Minato-ku.
~~~aight out of the East Exit and follow the bend to the right. Turn left at the
~~~ 5min. and under the highway. At the far tip of the sidewalk triangle, look*

left for the museum gates. ☎ *3443-0201; www.teien-art-museum.ne.jp. Open daily 10am-6pm. Closed 2nd and 4th W of the month, New Year, and during exhibit rotations. ¥200, college students ¥160, high school and junior high and 65+ ¥100. Disabled individuals and attendant free.)*

ODAIBA

◪NATIONAL MUSEUM OF EMERGING SCIENCE AND INNOVATION (NIHON KAGAKU MIRAIKAN; 日本科学未来間). The stuffy connotations of the word "museum" do an injustice to this "warehouse of supreme awesomeness." Instead of exalting igneous rocks, the displays treat modern breakthroughs. Expect full English explanations and exhibits involving walk-through models, interactivity, and live elements like interviews and robot demos. Unversed in optoelectronics? The museum is overstaffed with free-roaming brains. Presentation is as intelligent as the content. Try the virtual rides or the seventh floor dome theater. *(2-41, Aomi, Kōtō-ku. Funeno-Kagakukan Station. Head down the road so the bay is on your right. Turn left at the 1st stoplight.* ☎ *3570-9151; www.miraikan.jst.go.jp. Open Su-M and W-Sa 10am-5pm. ¥500, under 19 ¥200. 2 kids under 6 free with adult. Disabled individuals and caretaker free.)*

◪DINOSAUR FACTORY (HAYASHIBARA SHIZEN KAGAKU HAKUBUTSUKAN; 林原自然科学博物館). The Dinosaur Factory is less about worshiping the beasts and more about serious saurian research. Detailed explanations explore the process from fossils to facts; even dinosaur connoisseurs will learn much. Clever digital guides explain everything in fluent English; costumed guides are also extremely knowledgeable. It's not quite brontosaurus-sized, but still truly exemplary. *(Panasonic Center 3F, 2-5-18, Ariake, Kōtō-ku. Kokusai-Tenjijō Seimon Station. Turn left out of the turnstiles and walk straight down Tōkyō Fashion Town's 2nd fl. plaza. It's inside the Panasonic Center toward the end of the plaza.* ☎ *3599-2500; www.dinosaurfactory.jp. Open Tu-Su 11am-6pm. ¥800, senior and junior high students ¥400, elementary school students ¥200, under 6 and disabled individuals with caretaker free.)*

MUSEUM OF MARITIME SCIENCE (FUNE NO KAGAKUKAN; 船の科学館). Most nautical museums are afterthoughts lumped on a ship; Tokyo's, on the other hand, is the real deal. Learn about hydrodynamics and engine technology through interactive exhibits. Intricate models cover caravels to carriers, and some have consoles for guests to play with. Written labels are in Japanese, but earphones can be rented (¥500). The Yotei-maru and the Soya, moored across the way, are part of the museum and contain a 3-D theater and 1950s models of Tōkyō. *(3-1, Higashi-Yashio, Shinagawa-ku. Funeno-Kagakukan Station.* ☎ *5500-1336; www.funenokagakukan.or.jp. It's a giant ship, visible from the station; the entrance's on the far side. Open M-F 10am-5pm, Sa-Su 10am-6pm. Main bldg., Yotei-maru, and Soya ¥1000, age 5 through junior high ¥600.)*

SHIBUYA

TEPCO ELECTRIC ENERGY MUSEUM (DENRYOKUKAN; 電力館). The folks at Tepco seem convinced that everybody hates electricity and present the topic almost argumentatively. No need to convince them otherwise: their eight-story fun shack is a flashy and original best foot forward. Quiz shows, TV mazes, and buttons abound at a museum that seems more geared toward entertainment than education; labels are in Japanese, in any case. The electricity lab holds demos and the theater shows recent releases on Mondays. *(1-12-10, Jinnan, Shibuya-ku. Shibuya Station. From the Hachikō Exit, cross the street and walk 5min., past the right side of Starbucks. On the left at the bend.* ☎ *3477-1191; www.denryokukan.com. Open Th-Tu 10am-6pm. Free.)*

TOBACCO AND SALT MUSEUM (TABAKO TO SHIO NO HAKUBUTSUKAN; た こと塩の博物館). Right on par with the Weasel and Butter Museum, Tobacco and salt do have an obscure relationship, but only in Japan—visit out why. The museum is primarily historical; tobacco factoid videos and collection on the second floor give patrons something to chew on, while the third floor portrays all things sodium chloride with dioramas of its production and microscopic views of its chemical structure. The museum's appeal could use some spicing up, but then a visit isn't exactly expensive. *(1-16-8, Jinnan, Shibuya-ku. Shibuya Station. From the Hachikō Exit, cross the street and head past the right side of Starbucks. Bear left between Seibu and OI; it's a few minutes down on the right, past the Parco buildings. ☎ 3476-2041; www.jtnet.ad.jp/WWW/JT/Culture/museum/WelcomeJ.html. Open Tu-Su 10am-6pm. Closed M, the 1st Tu in June, and Dec. 29-Jan3. ¥100, high school and younger ¥50.)*

SHINJUKU

NTT INTERCOMMUNICATION CENTER. Feel like a game of creative hardball? The ICC is fresher than a plucked lemon. NTT's contribution to the arts revolves around "dialogue between art and science." In the past this has meant bodies on TV monitors that writhe when stepped on, and computer-improvised music that incorporates live sampling from the audience. Some features struggle to encompass both art and science, while others walk the thin line between genius and inanity. Exhibits rotate every three months. *(Tōkyō Opera City Tower 4F, Nishi-shinjuku, Shinjuku-ku. Hatsudai Station. In front of the station, inside Tokyo Opera City. Only some elevators go to 4F. Alternatively, take Shinjuku Station South Exit, turn right, and walk 15min. ☎ 0120-144-199 or ☎ 5353-0800; www.ntticc.or.jp. Open Tu-Su 10am-6pm. ¥800; college and high school students ¥600; junior high and elementary ¥400. Free for disabled, their attendants, and 65+.)*

UENO

TŌKYŌ NATIONAL MUSEUM (TŌKYŌ KOKURITSU HAKUBUTSUKAN; 東京国立博物館 **).** The big daddy of Tōkyō's museums has 2500-odd pieces of Asian cultural history on regular display—less than 3% of what the curators have in storage. There's something here for everyone: traditional Japanese garb, intricate writing boxes, swords, and pottery are among the items you'll see, and while the collection of official stamps may be beyond your attention span, *samurai* armor has a certain universal appeal. You'll be faced with three of the museum's six buildings when you enter the complex: the **Honkan,** or Japanese art museum, is in front of you, the **Toyokan** to your right contains antiquities on top of that, and the **Hyokeikan** to your left is mostly important for the building itself. National treasures abound behind it all in the **Horyuji Homotsukan,** and the **Heiseikan** in the back and to the left is home to the museum's special exhibits. *(13-9, Ueno Kōen, Taitō-ku. Enter the park from the JR's Kōen Exit and head straight to the middle of a giant, tree-lined causeway. The museum is the momentous looking building on your right. ☎ 3822-1111; www.tnm.jp. Open Tu-Su 9:30am-5:00pm, last entry 4:30pm. Closed Dec. 29-Jan. 1. ¥420; students ¥70; over 65, middle school students and younger and disabled individuals and attendant free. Extra fee for special exhibits.)*

SHITAMACHI HISTORY MUSEUM (下町風俗資料館 **).** Mosey down pondside and see what central Tōkyō was like before it was quashed in the quake of 1923. A small sum gets you access to model buildings, kitchenware, and bug zappers of ~~yore~~. The museum is highly interactive: if you have kids, if you are a kid, or if ~~you're~~ just a highly immature individual, this museum is bound to be loads of fun. ~~You can cr~~awl around most of the exhibits if you take off your shoes, and the sec~~ond floor is fill~~ed with nifty toys. To understand the meaning of addiction, try your ~~hand at a floor~~ of *pachinko*. *(2-1, Ueno Kōen, Taitō-ku. Trace the southern edge of ~~the pond tow~~ard the city and look for a white building. ☎ 3823-7451; www.taitoc~~ity... Op~~en 9:30AM-4:30PM. Closed Dec. 29-Jan. 3. ¥300, children ¥100.)*

~~NATIONAL MU~~SEUM (KOKURITSU KAGAKU HAKABUTSUKAN; 国立科~~学~~ **)** ~~The curat~~ors know how visitors want their exhibits, and they know ~~how to... di~~nosaurs, giant crabs, a narwhal, and an enormous seal wow ~~the kids too~~ impatient to read the signs and the tourists who are too illit~~erate to... The~~ explanations are in English, but they're far shorter than their

Japanese counterparts). The new building (under construction as of publication) looks to be incredible, especially for children. Upcoming special exhibits include one about the making of Star Wars, tentatively set for March-June of 2004. *(7-20, Ueno Park, Taitō-ku. Enter Ueno Kōen from the JR's Kōen Exit. Turn right after the 1st set of buildings and look for a whale statue. ☎ 3822-0111, weekends 3822-0114; www.kahaku.go.jp/ english/index.html. Open Tu-Su 9am-4:30pm, extended until about 2hr. after sunset on 1st and 3rd Sa of the month if the night is clear. Closed Dec. 28-Jan. 1. ¥420, grade school students ¥70. Roughly half-price for nighttime admission; grade school students get nighttime admission free.)*

NATIONAL MUSEUM OF WESTERN ART (国立西洋美術館). Do you live and breathe Western art? Make up for getting on the wrong plane by seeing the Matsukata Collection. The works are predominantly French and rotate in the New Wing every three months. Highlights include Rodin sculptures and special exhibits. Ask reception for an English brochure explaining the museum's past or a Japanese calendar of upcoming exhibitions. *(7-7, Ueno Kōen, Taitō-ku. Enter the park from the JR's Kōen Exit. Bear slightly right and pass the park's info center. ☎ 3828-5131; www.nmwa.go.jp. Open Tu-Th and Sa-Su 9:30am-5pm, F 9:30am-8pm. Closed Dec. 28-Jan. 4. ¥420, university students ¥130, high school students ¥70, junior high school students and younger free. Free for all on the 2nd and 4th Sa of each month and Nov. 3. Extra fee for special exhibitions.)*

SMALLER NEIGHBORHOODS

RYŌGOKU

■ **EDO-TŌKYŌ MUSEUM** (江戸東京博物館). Set a few hours aside for this monster: the new, seven-story Edo-Tōkyō Museum is a must-see and about as big as they come. Start by picking up tickets and a set of headphones (ask about the special exhibit!), then let the escalators ferry you up to the sixth floor, where a huge, old-style bridge invites you to begin your exploration. The name pretty much says it all; the museum is about the old city, and inside you'll find intricate models of Tōkyō's streets and buildings as they were 100-200 years ago. Rather than a series of halls with items frozen behind glass, the museum is like a giant vault with plenty of interactive elements. Come get your learn on about fires, waterworks, transportation, and toothbrushes from your great-great-grandfather's day. Most displays have a healthy dose of English explanation, but if you want the full story, the volunteer booth on the sixth floor offers tours in several languages. Be warned that the full story is long; tours last at least 1hr. *(1-4-1, Yokoami, Sumida-ku. ☎ 3626-9974; www.edo-tokyo-museum.or.jp. Ryōgoku Station. Turn right out of the JR's West Exit and right down the walkway with black and white triangles. Open Tu-Su 9:30am-5:30pm. Closed Dec. 28-Jan. 4. ¥600, college students ¥480, high school and junior high students and over 65 ¥300, elementary school students and younger and the disabled free. Extra fee for special exhibitions.)*

⌐ SHOPPING

If it exists, you can buy it somewhere in the city. While the big players in Tōkyō retail are the omnipresent department stores *(depāto)* and the towering new malls and shopping complexes, enough quirky boutiques and small enterprises exist to satisfy any shopper's appetites and to make a convert of most reluctant tag-alongs.

MAJOR NEIGHBORHOODS

AKASAKA

Shopping in Akasaka is easy, as long as the desired goods can be classified "lunch" or "dinner" and can be found on a menu. Fans of more permaner̄ should drag their unwilling husbands to Ginza.

TŌKYŌ

Toraya (とらや), 4-9-22, Akasaka, Minato-ku (☎3408-4121). Aoyama-itchōme Station. Take Exit 4 and head straight a few blocks. It's on the right, past the black Sōgetsu Foundation building. The museum-like atmosphere and technicians in lab coats will have you thinking you wandered into an antique pharmacy. While they don't deal in medicine, they do prescribe *wagashi*, artistic blobs of confectionery joy. Not to be devoured by the dozen, *wagashi* possess a *haiku*-like delicacy that artists celebrate and Japanese bring home to mom. *Yokan*, a red-bean specialty, runs about ¥1500. Open M-F 8:30am-8pm, Sa-Su and holidays 8:30am-6pm. AmEx/DC/JCB/MC/V.

Japan Sword (Nihon Tōken; 日本刀剣) 3-8-1, Toranomon, Minato-ku (☎3434-4321; www.japansword.co.jp). Toranomon Station. Take Exit 2. 5min. down the main street, on the left. Screw them firearms; swords are sharper, shinier, and *samurai*-approved. What's not to like? Anyone looking for something to hang on the mantle will be happy to know that a few Japanese smiths are still hammering out these classic beauties. It does get expensive: the priciest sword in the shop, a *katana* used by a Tokugawa clansman, will set you back ¥2,800,000. For most, this is a museum with price tags. The 3rd fl. features old Japanese armor. Open M-F 9:30am-6pm, Sa 9:30am-5pm. Credit cards accepted. Of course.

Kofutsuya (小払屋), 2-6-24, Akasaka, Minato-ku (☎3583-0058). Akasaka-mitsuke Station. Take the left mouth of Sotobori-dōri and turn right. Head down a ways and turn right opposite Hie Shrine's giant white gate. Pass one little street and look left. The *kimono*-clad women schlepping about Akasaka can't do it barefoot; Kofutsuya supplies the sandals they need. Prices in the tens of thousands of yen; can run up to ¥73,000. Worth a visit just to see the cobblers in the back turn chunks of wood into elite footwear.

ASAKUSA

No brand names here. Asakusa's tradesmen are famous for their handiwork. Welcome to souvenir central.

■ **Nakamise Shopping Street.** Walk straight out of Exit 1 from the Ginza Line Subway Station; it's on your right. The true market for Japanese snacks and candy—never mind that "Candyman Sidestreet" poser in Ueno. Everything's delicious and souvenir-worthy, as what you'll see is likely indigenous to Asia. Sweet-tooths will appreciate the Japanese version of peanut brittle for about ¥200 per bag. Other foodstuffs include sweet paste griddled into animal shapes (¥250 per bag), sugar-sprinkled soybean skewers (*kibidango*; ¥300), and a substance known as *oboru* that merchants stretch out using their feet (¥1100). In many of the shops and in the surrounding area, you'll find fine craft products, including parasols, fans, and cloths. Most shops open daily 10am-6pm.

Fujiya, 2-2-15, Asakusa, Taitō-ku (☎3841-2283). Asakusa Station. From the Ginza Line part of the station, take Exit 1. Proceed a little and take a right into the shopping arcade. Continue to a cross street where the signs have blue and orange trim. Turn right, then left. It's on the left. Offers craftsman Keiji Kawakami's *tenugui*, towel-shaped cloths decorated with original art. The *tenugui* betray immense originality and skill; most run ₀00-3000 and make ideal souvenirs. Open M-W and F-Su 10am-6:30pm.

hi-dōri. Tawaramachi Station. Take Exit 1 and head away from the nearest ion. The next main street is Kappa-bashi-dōri. You know those plastic rep- e in Japanese restaurants? Welcome to plastic food central. Named ating green imps of Japanese legend, this street is home to restau- al: you can also get chopsticks, lanterns, or a waitress uniform. kusa, Taitō-ku, is a nice example of a plastic food workshop. It's e right, parallel to Senso-ji. Delightful sushi key chains ¥600.

akusa, Taitō-ku (☎3844-7511). Take Exit 1 from Asakusa Station. treet in front of you and look right for a shopping avenue. Look to *its* with a bamboo awning and fans in the display case. A paper special- d in 1856, Kurodaya folds everything from handmade postcards (from

¥60) to gorgeous gold-dusted fans (up to ¥3000).
Figurines, origami paper, and wall hangings also on
sale. Open Tu-Su 11am-7pm. MC/V accepted for purchases over ¥3000.

EBISU

If you're loaded, so is Yebisu Garden Place. **Glass
Square** is a particularly nice place to gallivant. Those
who can afford it should visit **Daikanyama Address,** a
miniature square about a 10min. walk to the west.

Yebisu Garden Place (恵比寿ガーデンプレイス),
4-20, Ebisu, Shibuya-ku (☎5423-7111; www.garden-
place.co.jp). Ebisu Station. Take the skywalk to this
brand new square with flair – the main reason to visit
Ebisu in the daytime. YGP has a baseball stadium's
worth of promenades and fancy shops; the true specialties, however, are the photography and beer museums (p. 172). If the 39th fl. dining doesn't mooch your
moolah fast enough, you can dine French-like in the
garden's sizeable chateau. Grab a map from information for store details; the size of the square makes it
prime grounds for meandering tourists. Hours vary, but
11am-7:30pm will find most places open. Restaurants
are generally done by 11pm.

GINZA

Ginza is renowned for its orchidaceous shop-filled
roads. On any given day you're likely to find hordes
of women in their late 20s and 30s hopping happily
from store to store. Standard department stores
abound, but Ginza is irresistible advertising grounds
for big corporations, and a few of their unique gems
beckon seductively.

Yamaha Ginza Shop (ヤマハ銀座店), 7-9-14, Ginza,
Chūō-ku (☎3572-3188). From the intersection of
Chūō-dōri and Harumi-dōri, head south down Chūō-
dōri, away from Wok and Mitsukoshi department store.
It's on the left a few blocks down. Along with the usual
equipment, albums, and sheet music you'd find in any
music megastore, Yamaha also has live classical performances: don't be surprised to stumble in on a concert in progress. If you'll be in Tōkyō for a while, the
Yamaha Popular Music School, affectionately dubbed
PMS, offers lessons. Open daily 10:45am-7pm.

Hakuhinkan Toy Store (博品館), 8-8-11, Ginza,
Chūō-ku (☎3571-8008). From the intersection of
Chūō-dōri and Harumi-dōri, head south down Chūō-
dōri, away from Wok and Mitsukoshi department
store. It's all the way down on the right, just before
you hit the expressway. Multiple floors of rugrat
heaven. Stock up on giant Pocky and tabs that will
make your tongue glow blue at clubs. Magicians,
dolls, and candy may elicit happy childhood memories. Open daily 11am-8pm.

THE HIDDEN DEAL

IF I HAD ¥100...

A common perception about
Japan—one that generally holds
true—is that it's an incredibly
expensive country. Food is expensive, land is expensive, clothes
are expensive—even small daily
items are overpriced.

Despair not! Happily running
against this trend are the ever-
diversifying ¥100 stores. With
over 150 stores nationwide, the
100 Yen Shop Daisō chain has
outlets in most cities and even
some smaller towns. As the name
suggests, every item in these
stores costs ¥100. But what is
stunning, especially considering
Japan's sagging economy, is the
sheer variety and relative quality
of the items available. Daisō
shops sell everything: food, candles, hangers, plates, socks,
underwear, umbrellas, stationery,
accessories, toys, computer
games, postcards, stickers, bags,
party goods, batteries, CDs, cosmetics...any necessity or novelty
the budget traveler might desire.

In the late 1990s, privately
owned ¥100 stores began crop-
ping up in cities and neighborhoods, but the selection of goods
was severely limited, largely unattractive, and obviously cheap. The
Daisō chain has revamped this
image, expanding the range of
items enormously and improving
quality and fashionability. The Japanese now rely on these stores for
daily items that are much more
expensive elsewhere—and wise
travelers should follow suit.

Itō-ya (伊東屋), 2-7-15, Ginza, Chūo-ku (☎3561-8311; www.ito-ya.co.jp). Ginza Station. From the Chūō-dōri and Harumi-dōri, head up Chūō-dōri away from San-ai. Look for a huge paper clip on the right, past Matsuya department store. Japan is famous for wacky pens and origami, but the grand-daddy stationery-fest on Chūō-dōri is short on surprises. It is, however, beyond practical: anything you could possibly need is here, from art supplies to locks and clocks. Open M-Sa 10am-7pm, Su 10:30am-7pm.

Sake Plaza (日本酒造会館), 1-1-21, Nishi-Nihonbashi, Minato-ku (☎3519-2091; www.japansake.or.jp). Toranomon Station. Take Exit 8 and head straight. Turn left at Resona Bank, and then right at the gas station (not the hard right down the tiny alley). It's on the left. A store and a sight in one, most of Sake Plaza is a circle of shelves with hundreds of unique *sake* bottles. What you can actually buy is restricted to two or three refrigerators and costs ¥380-3000. Japanese readers will delight in a thorough explanation of *sake* and a 4th-floor library dedicated to the stuff. Open M-F 10am-6pm. Cash only.

HARAJUKU AND AOYAMA

Creative local spending habits lead to creative options for foreigners. The stroll from Harajuku to Omotesandō Station is full of expensive boutiques for the discriminating dresser. A right turn down Aoyama-dōri and the second, main left after Spiral Hall gets you started on **Kotto Street,** the best place in town for antiques.

▓ **Oriental Bazaar,** 5-9-13, Jingūmae, Shibuya-ku (☎3400-3933). Harajuku or Omotesandō Station. From the former, turn right out of Omotesandō Exit. Take the footbridge and go perpendicular to the station. Head several minutes down the main street. It's on the 6th block on the right after the main intersection; look for an unmistakable Oriental gate. The "biggest art and antique store in Tōkyō" has carp streamers (¥980), short swords (¥7800), and 24cm *daruma* dolls (¥1300). Stuff to put on your nightstand sold as well. Very foreigner-friendly. Open Su-W and F-Sa 10am-7pm. Credit cards accepted for purchases over ¥2000. Traveler's checks okay.

Elvis & Rockabilly Collector's Shop (Erubisu & Rokabirii Senmonten; エルビス＆ロ カビリー専門店) 1-8-21, Jingūmae, Shibuya-ku (☎3479-6229). Harajuku Station. Turn right out of the Omotesandō Exit. Take the footbridge and go perpendicular to the station. Head down the stairs and the main street and turn left at the major intersection at the base of the hill. It's on the left 1 street after Laforet. People who think vinyl is the real deal may love this store tender. Practically a museum; Kiss paraphernalia and other remnants of the past populate the basement. Open 11am-7pm.

Shiseidō Garden C, 4-26-18, Jingūmae, Shibuya-ku (☎5474-1534). Harajuku Station. Turn right out of Omotesandō Exit. Take the footbridge and go perpendicular to the station. Head down the stairs and the main street. At the bottom on the left, the 3rd block after the intersection with the Gap. Everyone loves to smear goo on his or her face, it's just that girls prefer make-up while boys choose mud. Shiseidō Garden C is fresh out of mud. It does, however, have 2 lengthy aisles lined with mirrors and racks of cosmetics. Fully interactive—smear away to your heart's content. Skin care make-up sessions from ¥3000. Open Tu-Su 11am-7:30pm. Closed 2nd Tu of every month.

Kiddy Land, 6-1-9, Jingūmae, Shibuya-ku (☎3409-3431). Harajuku Station. Turn right out of Omotesandō Exit. Take the footbridge and go perpendicular to the station. Head several minutes down the main street. On the 4th block on the right after the intersection with the Gap. Toys for kids and cute fluffery for closet kids with a soft spot for Japanese quirkiness. Open daily 10am-9pm.

Snoopy Town Shop, 1-14-27, Jingūmae, Shibuya-ku (☎5770-4501). Harajuku Station. Opposite Omotesandō Exit. The peppy beagle has a massive following in Japan. A good meeting point and the definitive place to pick up a giant Snoopy. Open daily 11am-8pm; 10am-9pm during the summer.

Bell Commons Aoyama, 2-14-6, Kita-Aoyama, Minato-ku (☎3475-8121). Gaien-mae Station. From Exit B1, it's a few steps down the base of the fork, on the right. Open space and dangling beauty down the center of the building may have you thinking for a brief second that you aren't in a *depāto*. Trite shops for the rich remind you how wrong you are. The 5th fl. food court is unusually fancy. Open daily from 11am.

Laforet, 1-11-6, Jingūmae, Shibuya-ku (☎3475-0411). Harajuku Station. Turn right out of Omotesandō Exit. Take the footbridge and go perpendicular to the station. Head down the stairs and the main street. Turn left at the major intersection at the base of the hill. Popular *depāto* for girlie young things. Open 11am-8pm.

IKEBUKURO

The area has giant **Seibu** and **Parco** department stores, but the true shopping mecca is the maze-like retail carnival that is **Sunshine City.**

Sunshine City (サンシャインシティ ; ☎3989-3331; www.sunshinecity.co.jp). Ike-bukuro Station East Exit. Cross slightly to the right to Green Main-dōri. The next main intersec-tion offers 2 lefts; take the right fork. At the end of the hubbub before the expressway, take the underpass. Sunshine City, Ikebukuro's main attraction, is a collection of 4 buildings with united basements, including the famous **Sunshine 60 Building** (p. 161). Visitors can easily get happily lost for a full day. By and large, the place is stuffed silly with shopping; most visitors spend most of their time navigating **Shopping Center Alpa** underneath Sunshine 60 and Sunshine City Prince Hotel. The mall is rife with *depāto* fashion and home to the food court of the titans. Kids goggle at the multi-colored **water fountain** show for hours. On the 2nd fl. of the **World Import Building,** a minor shopping spree in its own right is **Namjatown,** a theme park with a pan-Japan "*gyōza* stadium." The **rooftop aquarium** (p. 161) is the most worthwhile sight here; ignore ads for the dead-and-gone Planetarium. The far building, the **Bunka Kaikan Building,** houses a convention center, a theater, and the **Ancient Orient Museum.** This last quadruplet can be ominously vacant; feel free to skip it. Most of the complex open daily 10am-8pm; restaurants stay open up to 2hr. later; sights keep their own hours.

Tōkyū Hands (東急ハンズ), 1-28-10, Higashi-Ikebukuro, Toshima-ku (☎3980-6111). Ikebukuro Station. From the East Exit, cross to the right to Green Main-dōri. The next main inter-section offers 2 lefts; take the right fork. It's at the end of the hubbub on the right, before the expressway. This chain is so crafty that each branch stocks a unique inventory. Here it's games: toys, dartboards, and magic tricks, with a pet shop up top. Other goods, like stationery and hardware, abound. Open daily 10am-8pm. Credit cards accepted.

HMV, Humax Pavilion Ikebukuro Sunshine 60-dōri 2F (☎5953-6711). Ikebukuro Station. From the East Exit, cross slightly to the right to Green Main-dōri. The next main intersection offers 2 lefts; take the one to the right. The music behemoth is on the right, easily spotted in the city throb. Open daily 10:30am-10:30pm. Credit cards accepted.

MARUNOUCHI

There isn't much shopping around Tōkyō Station, but a quick jaunt east will get you to Nihonbashi, where traditional sophistication can be bought on Chūō-dōri.

▨ **Yamamotoyama** (山本山), 2-5-2, Nihonbashi, Chūō-ku (☎3281-0010; www.yamamo-toyama.co.jp). Nihonbashi Station. U-turn out of exit B1. Cross one street and look on the right for display cases of tea. Warning: one sip of Yamamotoyama's quality green tea may leave the average Westerner painfully aware that he's been drinking Brand X all along. This stuff's good. Stop by for a refresher; the store is actually a cafe hybrid and has more than just free samples. ¥250 will net you a 2-tea platter with a blobula of tasty green dessert. Impeccable sleek, tea-garden-esque atmosphere. English literature for guests to peruse. Canisters of tea from ¥2500. Open daily 9:30am-5:30pm. Credit cards accepted.

TŌKYŌ

Haibara (榛原), 7-6-2, Nihonbashi, Chūō-ku (☎3272-3801). Nihonbashi Station. U-turn out of exit B8. Look for the store's English sign at 2nd/3rd-story height. If you thought the Egyptians were good with papyrus, check out what these guys can do. Haibara is a 200-year-old paper specialist. Their shelves are stocked with fans (¥600-12,000), ornate money envelopes (¥300-3500), paper dancers, and straight-up rolls of paper. Open daily 9:30am-5:30pm. Credit cards accepted.

ODAIBA

Half the buildings in Odaiba are malls. Everything is modern and credit cards are as good as cash, but originality is in short supply as Japan's personality takes a backseat to 21st-century standards.

Decks, 1-6-1, Daiba, Minato-ku (☎3599-6500). Odaiba Kaihin-Kōen Station. Turn right out of the turnstiles and go downstairs. U-turn; it's the big *depāto* on the right. Candy and toys in "little Hong Kong" on the 4th fl., where lanterns and carnival games emulate the ex-colony's streets. See the ground level avenue between Decks and Joypolis for **Condomania,** a smurf-sized shack selling novelty rubbers and all things phallic. 5th-fl. food court. Hours vary by store; most open daily 11am-9pm. Credit cards accepted.

Aqua City. Odaiba Kaihin-Kōen Station. Turn right out of the turnstiles and ooze downstairs. U-turn and walk halfway to Daiba Station. It's on the right. A colorful shell with trite department filling; a little classier and more American than most places in Tōkyō. Check out **Ocean Globe Street,** a flashback to the '60s and home of Longboard Cafe and the Capt. Santa Museum shop. Otherwise it's clothes, music, and *manga* as usual.

Venus Fort, 1, Palette Town, Aomi, Kōtō-ku (☎3599-0700). Aomi Station. Visible from the station and labeled in English. This "theme park for women" uses the intimidating feminist title to disguise a shopping mall. Anyone who's been to Caesars Palace, Las Vegas, will recognize the morphing sky projected on the ceiling; the atmosphere may make shoppers forget the time. Offers women's accessories, fine clothing, and a cheese shop. Open daily 11am-9pm; food courts open 11am-11pm. Credit cards accepted.

Sun Walk, 1, Palette Town, Aomi, Kōtō-ku (☎3599-1749; www.sunwalk.net). Aomi Station. On the 1st fl. under Venus Fort, easily identifiable from the station. A world apart from Venus Fort upstairs, Sun Walk offers sporting gear for sporting youth. Fast food and other random shops dot the way. Most shops open daily 11am-8pm or 10pm.

ROPPONGI

Roppongi Hills has the usual whoop-dee-doo required by Japanese shopping laws, but the choice cut is Azabu-jūban, a pleasant breather ripe with Japanese snacks and goods, perfect for non-cheesy souvenirs. Follow the thinnest tentacle at Roppongi Crossing south and make a right at the tip of Azabu-jūban Station.

Roppongi Hills (六本木ヒルズ). Roppongi Station. Roppongi Hills Exit. When asked where tourists to Japan ought to go, the current top three answers among natives are: 1. Disneyland; 2. Roppongi Hills; 3. Blank stares. Ranked somewhere between Mickey Mouse and a total loss for words, Roppongi Hills is easily Tōkyō's hottest trend. The Mori family's vision for the future is too broad to easily define, but includes more than 200 retailers and restaurants, adorned with art ranging from an oversize spider to designer gardens. Visitors can pick up a guide from any shop, outdoor assistant, or info boxlet.

■ **Azabu-jūban Shōtengai** (麻布十版商店街). Azabu-jūban Station. Turn left out of Exit 5A, then follow the main road up and turn left at the Jomo gas station. The main street is a few steps down. *Shōtengai* is Japanese for "shopping street"; Tōkyō has millions, only they're vertical and called *depāto*. The last horizontal rebel is a blessing to franchise-sick foreigners. A partial list of who's on tenth: a peanut candy specialist, a cracker specialist, small eats such as lunchbox *bentō* and *onigiri* (rice balls), tea canisters, assorted Eastern-medicine mojo, *yukata*, fancy *geta*, and so many laundromats, you have to wonder what exactly they're laundering. Shops generally open at 10am and close at 7 or 8pm. Most are closed Tu, a few on Su. Bring cash, not plastic.

SHIBUYA

The economic slump-dom of Japan still knows how to serve a consumerist feast, and while Ginza is the wine and cheese, Shibuya is the main course. 80% *depāto*, 20% entertainment media, 0% practical value: Shibuya's part of a balanced splurge.

Department Store Madness. None of the *depāto* are terribly special; all feature oodles of clothing, shoes, and accessories. Most are open daily 10am-9pm and have international food courts at the top and bottom, which stay open 1hr. later. Multiple branches are common: witness 109, 109-2, and ONE OH NINE, as well as Parco I, II, and III.

Tōkyū Plaza (☎3463-3851) features quick Japanese eateries on B2 while the 9th fl. has finer international restaurants.

Shibuya 109 (☎3477-5111) has rather orthodox women's clothing.

Junior Station 109-2 (☎3477-8111), across the street, is for younger women (if floor maps with colored stars sound appealing, you qualify).

Shibuya Mark City (☎3780-6503) is flatter, longer, and polished silly.

Parco (☎3464-5111) has three buildings, which have children's clothes and some artistic venues on top of the normal fare, including **Cine Quinto** (☎3477-5905).

Shibuya Seibu (☎3462-0111) is probably the biggest, with household goods and a pet shop.

Three Minutes of Happiness, Rika Bldg., 3-5, Udagawa-chō, Shibuya-ku (☎5459-1851). Shibuya Station. From the Hachikō Exit, cross the street and head past the right side of Starbucks. Bear left between Seibu and OI, and it's a few minutes down on the right, past the Parco buildings. While this unique thrift store is cheery in itself, the happiness advertised comes from the unusual inventory, including alterna-snacks and cheap clothes. The spirit is best captured by the rack of plastic bananas. Not just a gag store: shopping here can satisfy daily needs. Open daily 11am-9pm. Credit cards accepted.

Obutsudan (お仏壇), Seimon Bldg., 2-28-4, Dōgenzaka, Shibuya-ku (☎6415-7676). Shibuya Station. Take the Hachikō Exit or Subway Exit 1. From the JR, cross the street to the smaller big TV and head left up the tree-lined avenue. Go left at the fork and it's several blocks uphill on the right; *kanji* sign. Step inside and soft classical music steals you away. Buddhist incense, Buddhist home shrines, iridescent Buddhist lanterns, and figurines of the little baldy himself.

Mandarake, Shibuya Beam B2, 31-2, Udagawa-chō, Shibuya-ku (☎3477-0777). Shibuya Station. From the Hachikō Exit, cross the street and head 5min. past the right side of Starbucks. Bear left between the 2 Seibus. Bear right at the police box; it's on the left, down a striking cave. Incredible *manga* store disguised as a nightclub, Mandarake's location down stairwell after stairwell makes it the world's least handicap-friendly institution. Non-stop aisles make you wonder how many cartoonists an island nation can hold. Costumes, dolls, and ¥350,000 Godzilla models. Open daily noon-8pm.

Tōkyū Hands, 12-18, Udagawa-chō, Shibuya-ku (☎5489-5111). Shibuya Station. Same directions as Mandarake; after the right at the police box, it's 1-2 blocks down on the right. Tōkyō engineers have discovered how to stock a store with every usable product in the dictionary. Pick up the English index in the lobby. Never suffer again for want of urethane or anchor plugs. Or tweezers. Open daily 11am-9pm. Credit cards accepted.

100 Yen Plaza (☎5459-3601). Shibuya Station. From the Hachikō Exit, cross the street to the smaller big TV and head left up the tree-lined avenue. Bear right at the fork, and it's ahead on the right. The mega-version of the chain where everything costs ¥100.

Tower Records, 1-22-14, Jinnan, Shibuya-ku (☎3496-3661). Shibuya Station. From the Hachikō Exit, cross the street and head up past the right side of Starbucks. A short walk ahead, after both OIs. It's on the right. The mega-branch of Tower Records in Shibuya stands 7-stories tall and is commonly used as a landmark. Open daily 10am-11pm.

SHINJUKU

Too poor for Ginza? Too normal for Harajuku? Shinjuku, declared the favorite locale for actual purchases by many a sensible yet trendy shopper, offers a fresh selection that even beer-chugging, sports-loving males can stomach.

▓ **Don Quixote** (ドンキホーテ), 1-12-6, Okubo, Shinjuku-ku (☎5292-7411; www.donki.com). Shinjuku Station. From the East Exit, turn left and follow the tracks to the main road that crosses under the tracks. Turn right and look for an electric billboard with a penguin in a Santa hat. Store name in Japanese. As the name and penguin suggest, the wares show little consistency. Currently the shelves hold such fun items as sexy bunny ears, a burping flytrap, snorkel masks, boxing gloves, and very creative underwear specimens. Extremely crowded, but entirely worth it. Open daily 10am-8pm.

OIONE, 3-5-6, Shinjuku, Shinjuku-ku (☎3354-0101; www.0101.co.jp/onejuku). Shinjuku Station. From the South Exit, turn left and follow the main road/bridge. Go left at Virgin Megastore, it's on the right, 4th block. Say "ma-roo-ee one." The ugly duckling in the Marui family is, incidentally, the most interesting. The punk *depāto* offers such goodies as designer *kimono* with attitude and undies with angel wings. The kind of fashion that flips the bird at the rest. Open almost daily 11am-8pm. Credit cards accepted.

Studio Alta (スタジオアルタ), 3-33-10, Shinjuku, Shinjuku-ku (☎3350-1209). Shinjuku Station. Take the East Exit; it's left of Mizuho Bank. Trendy department store gets 20-somethings to the party in style. Especially fun is the hat store by the foyer, offering uniquely Japanese caps. Open daily 11am-8pm (restaurants open 8am-11pm).

Takashimaya Times Square, 5-24-2, Sendagaya, Shibuya-ku (☎5361-1122; www.takashimaya.co.jp/shinjuku/index_times.html). Shinjuku Station. In front of the New South Exit. The attention-begging behemoth, visible from anywhere in southern Shinjuku, offers something to cater to everyone's needs, and the "restaurant park" floors have most competitors beat for volume. **Tōkyū Hands,** engulfed like amoeba feed, is especially good for outdoorsy needs and anything craft-related. The **Kinokuniya** annex has a decent share of English literature. Open daily 10am-8pm.

Virgin Megastore, 3-1-13 B1F-3F, Shinjuku, Shinjuku-ku (☎3353-0056). Shibuya Station. From the South Exit, turn left and follow the main road/bridge. It's at the next major intersection. 29 megastores are smeared across the country; it's old hat, but with Japanese pop stars on the billboards. Open daily 10am-11pm. Credit cards accepted.

UENO

Ueno has a history of merchants aiming to make it rich on the area's high-volume traffic. While it lacks in standard merchandising, you'll find a host of street vendors eager to make a buck.

Ameya-yokochō. From the JR's Shinobazu Exit, look for the red archway above this street. "Candyman Sidestreet" is named for the times after World War II, when black market merchants provided Ueno Station refugees with sweets and the other sundry odds that make life more colorful. Come today and you'll find candy, shoes, American clothing, fruit, nuts, dried seafood, and even an arcade of stuffed animal cranes. This isn't a night market though—get there by 8pm, or you'll find the carnival has trickled to a halt.

Motorbike Shop Street. Turn left out of the JR's Iriya Exit. Head up a block and say *vroom*. A focal point of Tōkyō's motorcycling community, this avenue means business and is recommended for biking enthusiasts only. Hardcore fans may fall in love with the streets lined with shop after shop of gloves, helmets, and pretty silver engines.

SMALLER NEIGHBORHOODS

AKIHABARA

Akihabara Electric Town. Akihabara Station. Take the Electric Town Exit and turn right to exit the station. Head to the left to get to Chūō-dōri, where the festivities are. Don't let the name fool you; "Electric Town" is a bunch o' stores, not a happy community of animatronic elves. That said, if you can plug it in, you can find it here. Akihabara is *the* definitive place to get appliances and electronics. The complexes on the 1st half of the main street are loaded with fans, TVs, digicams, rice cookers, washing machines, toilet lids, stereos, DVD players, telephones, laptops, and those three-prong to two-prong converters you've been looking for since you stepped off the plane. **Laox** is a major player here and owns several of the appliance orgies you'll walk by. Farther down the street lie anime megastores and video game heaven. Hardcore gamers and moths will be drawn to **Azobit** for their gleaming displays of the latest and greatest titles.

MEGURO

Dear Bear, 2-13-29 1F, Kamiōsaki, Shinagawa-ku (☎5789-7766). Meguro Station. Head straight out of the East Exit and follow the bend to the right. Turn left at the main road; it's on the left, a bit before the elevated expressway. Teddies of the world unite. ¥1000 bears sit next to their ¥20,000 aristocrat counterparts. Visit during a sale to witness firsthand the power of fuzzy lovables over the Japanese heart. Open daily 11am-7pm.

■ ENTERTAINMENT

THEATER

Aoyama Theatre, 5-53-1, Jingūmae Shibuya-ku (☎3797-5678; www.aoyama.org). Shibuya Station. 10min. walk; it's across from Aoyama University. Shibuya's sexy 1200-seater is a technical marvel, and its intimate **Round Theatre** gives spectators the 360-degree view. Eclectic offerings from dance and drama to film and concerts.

■ **Bunkamura,** 2-24-1, Dōgenzaka, Shibuya-ku (☎3477-9111). Shibuya Station. From the Hachikō Exit, cross the street to the smaller big TV and head left up the tree-lined avenue. Turn right at the fork and left at the 2nd fork. Entrance on the right, immediately after Tōkyū department store. Bunkamura, or "Culture Village," is the only appropriate name for this catch-all of artistic showcasing. The basement features a **museum of international art,** with rotations every 2-3 months. The 1st fl. **Theatre Cocoon** fields plays. Famous Japanese classical musicians bang they keys and toot they horns in the 3rd-fl. **Orchard Hall,** and 2 6th-fl. **cinemas** play acclaimed international movies (subtitles in Japanese; ¥1800, students ¥1500, seniors ¥1000.) Prices vary with content for Bunkamura's venues. Bunkamura Ticket Center ☎3477-9999 (10am-5:30pm), or visit them on the 1st fl. (10am-7pm). Unlike Information, they may not speak English.

Haiyuza Gekijō (俳優座劇場), 4-9-2, Roppongi, Minato-ku (☎3470-2880; www.haiyuzagekijou.co.jp). Roppongi Station. From Roppongi Crossing, follow the highway away from Almond Confectionery. Take the 1st left; it's immediately on the left. The 300-seater is a leader in contemporary Japanese drama. Tickets ¥5200, students ¥2600. Call or hit the usual suspects (Ticket PIA or Lawson) for tickets.

Imperial Theater (Teikoku Gekijyō; 帝国劇場), 3-1-1, Marunouchi, Chiyoda-ku (☎3213-7221). Hibiya Station. The Mita Line's B2 exit takes you straight there; from other lines, take Exit A9. Head for the corner nearest the moat and look for the theater's vertical *kanji* sign. Tired of drunken caterwauling at karaoke bars? The Imperial Theater is the place for big-name, professional musicals. B-seat tickets run ¥3000-

THE LOCAL STORY

THE BEST MEDICINE

Patrick Harlan was born in Montana and raised by wolves in Colorado Springs. After a few years of working for the Japanese, he decided he'd rather tickle them silly; at 32, Patrick is now a successful Japanese comedian.

On coming to Japan: After graduating from Harvard with a degree in Comparative Religion, I was naturally flooded with lucrative and enticing job offers in the always-in-demand field of religion comparing. Nevertheless, I turned my back on the easy money and chose to come to Japan to teach English. It worked out marvelously. "Teaching English" is actually a misnomer. It should be called "Getting Japanese People to Pay You to Learn Japanese."

On becoming a comic: After a couple of years I joined a Japanese amateur theater group and started DJ'ing on FM radio. By this point my mastery of the language was so complete that once during a live broadcast on an international gymnastics tournament I tried to say "He did well on the parallel bars" and ended up saying "He did well with the uncircumcised penis." This may have been my first unintentional foray into Japanese comedy. Shortly thereafter I decided to pursue my long-suppressed dream of being an actor, only here in Japan. I was young, talented, out of debt, and obviously insane....Then a miracle happened! An image of the Virgin

6000; try NTT's *terezābu* service for tickets (☎3201-7777; 9am-5:30pm). Groups larger than 15 should call the theater's group reservation center (☎3216-2008; 9am-6pm).

Kabuki-za Theater (歌舞伎座 ; ☎5565-6000; www.kabuki-za.co.jp). Higashi-Ginza Station. Take exit 3 and voilà. *The* place to see *kabuki* in Tōkyō; Ginza is famous for this theater. Tickets ¥2400-16,000; make phone reservations at least a day in advance, or else you'll have to do it in person. Daytime shows everyday except when between programs. *Makumi-seki* "one act" tickets also available and run in the upper hundreds, depending on the act. English earphone guides for full show ¥650.

National Nō Theatre (Kokuritsu Nogakudo; 国立能楽堂), 4-18-1, Sendagaya Shibuya-ku (☎3423-1331). Sendagaya Station. Cross the street, turn right, and follow the tracks. Take the 3rd, unassuming left. It's the 1st right. Main entrance at the end of block on left. As the name suggests, this is the *nō* theater to visit. The on-stage speed limit of about 2cm a year may have you nodding, but the theater does put you close to the cast's awe-inspiring masks. Reserve tickets 1 day in advance at ☎3230-3000 (10am-5pm); on-site tickets possible but not guaranteed. Tickets from ¥1700.

New National Theater (Shin-kokuritsu Gekijyō; 新国立劇場), 1-1-1, Honchō, Shibuya-ku (☎5351-3011; www.nntt.jac.go.jp). Hatsudai Station. It's in front of the exit. The theatrical glue-on to Tōkyō Opera City is ultra-impressive in its own right, featuring grade A acoustics and fully reconfigurable everything. Opera, ballet, dance, and drama take over the 3 stages, designated the Opera House, the Playhouse, and The Pit. "Z Seats" always seem to go for ¥1500; the cost of seeing and being seen varies as much as ¥20,000. Try the box office (☎5352-9999) for tickets.

Nissei Theater (Nissei Gekijyō; 日生劇場), 1-1-1, Yūrakuchō, Chiyoda-ku (☎3503-3111; www.nissaytheatre.or.jp). Hibiya Station. Turn left from Exit A13. "Yūrakuchō" literally means "district of pleasure-having"—it's bound to have shows going on, and, thanks to the Nissei, one of them is sure to be opera. Cheapest seats ¥4000-5000. Try Ticket Pia (☎0570-02-9999) or CN Playguide (☎5802-9990 or 5802-9999).

Shinjuku Culture Center (Shinjuku Bunka Sentā, 新宿文化センター), 6-14-1, Shinjuku, Shinjuku-ku (☎3350-1141; www.shinjukubunka.or.jp). Shinjuku Station. From the East Exit, turn left and follow the tracks to the main road, just before Pepe Shinjuku Prince Hotel. Turn right, take a hike, and turn left at the OIMEN intersection. Take the 1st major right; it's the

4th block on the right. Ballet, opera, musicals, and occasional flamenco happen in backdoor Shinjuku. Tickets usually at the door.

Suehirotei (末廣亭), 3-6-12, Shinjuku, Shinjuku-ku. (☎3351-2974; http://suehirotei.com). Shinjuku Station. From the East Exit, head to Mizuho Bank. Turn right, then take the 1st left after the intersection with Isetan and OICITY. It's the 2nd block on the left, with a *kanji* sign. Your venue for *rakugo:* Japanese funny-men weave tongue-in-cheek comedy in a medium-sized lecture hall. Amusing anecdotal stories are in the lesson plan; the objective is a good chuckle, not a pants-wetting. Non-Japanese speakers might give it a skip. ¥2700, elementary school ¥1800, students ¥2200, 65+ ¥2500. Tickets at the door. Open daily noon-4:30pm and 5-9pm.

The Square, 1-23-1, Azuma-bashi, Sumida-ku (☎5608-5391). Asakusa Station. Take Exit 4 and cross the bridge. On the 4th fl. of the building with the golden sculpture. Right under the Flamme D'Or lies The Square, a venue for...well, it's a venue. The flexible space is rented out for plays, music performances, lectures, fashion shows, and more. The sound and light capabilities of the space are truly immersive; call to see what's up and come see for yourself. **P3 cafe night** is currently hot, with full audiences coming to hear the live music for ¥1000-3000 a head, depending on the band.

Tōkyō Metropolitan Art Space (Tōkyō Geijutsu Gekijyō; 東京芸術劇場), 1-8-1, Nishi-Ikebukuro, Toshima-ku (☎5391-2111). Ikebukuro Station. From the West Exit, shave past the right of Mizuho Bank, then steer slightly left through the Art Space's small outdoor plaza. Theater, concert hall, dance studio, and exhibition gallery in one concrete sushi roll. The concert hall, with 2000 seats and a pipe organ, and the 841-seat theater are the biggest selling features. The foyer is a sight in itself, featuring a big green waterfall and gold cubes suspended from the ceiling. Call for tickets; showing up works, too.

Tōkyō Takarazuka Theater (東京宝塚歌劇 ; ☎5251-2001; http://kageki.hankyu.co.jp). Hibiya Station. U-turn out of exit A4. Make the next left and head straight (roughly; there's a kink where you cross an upcoming road); it's on the right. Cross-dressing worked for Shakespeare, and now it's working for women. Takarazuka is a form of musical with an all-female cast. Try the usual suspects for tickets: Ticket Pia (☎0570-02-9999), CN Playguide (☎03-5802-9955), or Lawson Ticket (☎0570-00-0023). Box office open Su-Tu and Th-Sa 10am-6pm.

Mary appeared on a tortilla in Ecuador! Meanwhile, here in Japan, I met a struggling Japanese comedian looking for a partner. On a whim we joined forces and the rest is history.

On the Japanese sense of humor: I think the human "sense" of humor is fairly similar worldwide. Everybody likes puns, put-downs, and scenes with drunks stumbling into open manholes. The Japanese "style" of humor, however, may be unique. Westerners tell jokes. Japanese do not. America has stand-up comics. Japan has seated storytellers, and two-person comedy acts called *manzai*. In *manzai*, a straight man sets up a joke, the funny guy completes it, and the straight man adds a *tsukkomi*, or rebuke, often accompanied by a slap to the funny guy's face, shoulder, or head. Gives a new meaning to the term "punch line."

On being a foreign comic: My partner and I perform *manzai*, with me as the (allegedly) funny man. Our act often plays on cultural differences and silly prejudices and misconceptions. As an American I'm given a lot of leeway in what I can do and say on screen and stage, and merely using antiquated Japanese or flubbing my lines is often good enough for a laugh. Plus, there are lots of shows looking for a "token foreigner." It's like being the coach's son on a Little League team. You can't hit, run, or throw, but you're always in the lineup.

Want to see Patrick perform? Check local magazines, watch TBS or NHK TV on a weekend, or tune in to J-Wave, 81.3 FM on Friday.

CINEMA

You'll find standard theaters all over Tōkyō, though Shibuya and Shinjuku are especially good bets. Check *Metropolis* magazine (http://metropolis.japantoday.com/tokyo/recent/movies.asp) for the latest on schedules and locations. Whether it's evidence of a massive price-fixing scheme or mere coincidence, nearly all Tōkyō movie theaters boast the same super-sized prices: ¥1800 for a show, with college and high school students getting off for ¥1500 and younger kids and seniors paying ¥1000.

Cinema Mediage (☎5531-7878; www.mediage.jp). Odaiba Kaihin-Kōen Station. On the east side of Aqua City. One of Tōkyō's best. Ultra-modern and far vaster than anything on the mainland. 3034 different chairs in which to ogle 13 different screens. Premier seats from ¥2200 (Sa-Su ¥2500). Open daily 11am-11pm.

Virgin Cinema, Keyakizaka Complex, 6-10-2, Roppongi, Minato-ku (☎5775-6090). Roppongi Station. Take the Roppongi Hills Exit; go up the escalators and left around the central tower. Tōkyō's newborn movie theater screams in THX surround. Definitive box office hits (often in English with subtitles) and stadium seating. Open til the wee hours. Superb caramel popcorn (¥400). Late night shows ¥1800. Ladies ¥1000 on W. 1st day of the month ¥1000. Premiers ¥3000. Open Su-W 10am-midnight, Th-Sa 10am-5pm.

MUSIC

CONCERT HALLS

Suntory Hall, 1-13-1, Akasaka, Minato-ku (☎3584-9999; www.suntory.co.jp/suntoryhall). Tameike-sannō Station. Take Exit 13, cross a small street and head straight up the stairs towards ANA Hotel. Follow the signs to Suntory Hall into Ark Hills. Look here for some of Tōkyō's major musical events, ranging from *taiko*-pounding fun to Western orchestras. Box office open M-Sa 10am-7pm, Su and holidays 10am-6pm (7pm on concert days). Tickets can usually be purchased in person 1hr. before the event.

Tōkyō Metropolitan Festival Hall (Tōkyō Bunka Kaikan), Ueno (☎5815-5452; www.t-bunka.jp). Across the street from the JR's Kōen exit. Host to various ballet performances and classical concerts and the home venue of the **Tōkyō Metropolitan Symphony Orchestra.** Schedule of events available 2 months in advance. Call ahead for tickets; the cheapest usually run around ¥2000.

Tōkyō Opera City (東京オペシティ), 3-20-2, Nishi-shinjuku, Shinjuku-ku (☎5353-0788; www.tokyooperacity.co.jp). Hatsudai Station. In front of the station; alternatively, walk 15min. west from Shinjuku Station's South Exit. Tōkyō's musical pup has been internationally hailed as a miracle of acoustic design, attracting an all-star list of performers from A to Yo-Yo. More than a premier venue for classical music, it's attracted extras to the tune of shops, restaurants, and an art gallery (☎5353-0756). For information about TOC's most creative partner, see the **NTT Intercommunication Center** (p. 176). For tickets call ☎5353-9999, Tu-Su 10am-6pm, and pick them up within a week.

JAZZ

JZ Brat, 26-1, Sakuragaoka-chō, Shibuya-ku (☎5728-0168; www.jzbrat.com). Shibuya Station. From the West Exit, take the footbridge to the left to the end. Follow the elevated highway and turn left after Cerulean Tower Hotel. A classy jazz club with serious talent. Rather expensive—it's glued to a luxury hotel. 1st set 7:30pm; 2nd 9:30pm. Special events F at midnight. Live music and DJs Sa. Heineken ¥800. Cover from ¥3000. Open M-Th 6pm-midnight, F 6pm-4am, Sa 8pm-4am (standing room only).

The Pit Inn, 2-12-4 B1, Shinjuku, Shinjuku-ku (☎3354-2024; www.pit-inn.com). Shinjuku Station. From the South Exit, turn right and follow the main road/bridge. Take the 3rd left after Virgin Megastore; it's the 5th block on the right. Head down to the basement. No-nonsense, eyes-forward, ears-alert jazz house with room for about 100. Instrumentation varies; check the website. Reputedly a definitive place for young artists to make a name for themselves. Cover ¥3000; daytime cover ¥1300 (Sa-Su ¥2500); includes 1 drink. Tickets at the door. Open almost daily 2:30pm-5pm, 7pm-show end.

CONTEMPORARY

Crocodile (クロコダイル), 6-18-8 B1, Jinnan, Shibuya-ku (☎3499-5205; www.music.co.jp/~croco). Shibuya or Harajuku Station. Between the 2 stations, on Meiji-dōri's east side. Alternative music in a spacious, very stage-focused bar. Daily schedule includes blues, salsa, pop, and cowboy music. Beer from ¥550. Hard stuff ¥650. Live music at 8pm. Open daily 6pm to just after the show (usually 10:30-11pm).

Club Quattro (Kurabu Kuatoro; ☎3477-8750). Shibuya Station. From the Hachikō Exit, cross the street and head 5min. past the right side of Starbucks. Bear left between the 2 Seibu's and left at the fork with the police box. It's on the left, 2 flights up. Hot ticket to Japanese groups whose names we love: "Jazztronik," "Gorilla Attack," and "Mamalade Rag" among them. Too snazzy to be an appetizer, Club Quattro is a main course. Live performances daily, starting 5:30-10pm (usually 7 or 7:30pm). Doors open 1hr. early. Ticket prices vary (about ¥2500-5500); call or go through a ticket office to be safe.

Club Eggsite, 2-1-821, Udagawa-chō, Shibuya-ku (☎3496-1785). Shibuya Station. From Hachikō Exit, cross the street and head past the right side of Starbucks. Bear left between Seibu and Oi. Go the whole way down and look right for a spiral stairwell. The Parco buildings are a halfway mark. Less of a showroom than Quattro, Eggsite is just large enough to stretch the limits of "intimate." Soul, funk, rock, and anything else the rising stars of the rising sun can manage. Live performances daily, usually starting between 6:30 and 7:30pm, running until about 10pm. Doors open 30min. early. Ticket prices usually in the ¥2000s; get them at the door, or call ☎3496-1561. Ticket Pia and Lawson (p. 124) are viable too.

Zepp, 1, Palette Town, Aomi, Koto-ku (☎3599-0710; www.zepp.co.jp). Aomi Station. Follow directions to the ferris wheel (p. 163). Between the wheel and the station. Standing room only. 2709-person capacity. Shows daily.

OTHER

EST (エスト), 1-14-14, Shibuya, Shibuya-ku (www.shibuyaeast.co.jp). Shibuya Station. From the East Exit, turn left and head up the main road; it's almost immediately on the right after the crossing. A game parlor. Each floor of bowling has a different theme; the glow-in-the-dark experience on 3 is quality. **Bowling** (☎3409-4721) ¥500-600 per game or ¥4000 per lane per hr. **Billiards** (☎3409-2451) ¥300-340 per 30min. per person, ¥150-170 additional 15min. **Ping pong** (☎3409-9810) ¥600-750 per 30min. per table, ¥300-375 per additional 15min. **Karaoke** (☎3409-4723) ¥50-450 per 30min. Open Su-Th 10am-4:30am, F-Sa 10am-5:30am.

Leisure Land (東京レジャーランド), 1, Palette Town, Aomi, Kōtō-ku (☎3570-5657). Aomi Station. Next to the ferris wheel (p. 163). Bowling lanes, batting cages, video games, karaoke, billiards tables, and table tennis are all stuffed together in this large den of innocent hedonism. Bowling ¥300-600. Karaoke ¥200-500. Billiards ¥600 per hr. per person or ¥600 per 30min. per table. Open 24hr.

Tōkyō Metropolitan Children's Hall (Tōkyō Jidō Kaikan; 東京児童会館), 1-18-24, Shibuya, Shibuya-ku (☎3409-6361). Shibuya Station. From the Hachikō Exit, cross under the tracks and turn left at the next main intersection. Head up Meiji-dōri and turn right at the intersection after World Sports Plaza. Not to be confused with a daycare, the 5-story Children's Hall is a place for parents to bring their kids and actually spend time

TŌKYŌ

with the little buggers. Crafts, events, music corners, playgrounds, and a mini-theater. Resources for high-schoolers include scientific crafts and a lounge. Open daily June-July 9am-6pm; Aug.-May 9am-5pm. Closed holidays and 2nd and 4th M of the month. Free.

ARTS

FLOWER ARRANGING

Sōgetsu Foundation, 7-2-21, Akasaka, Minato-ku (☎3408-1209; www.sogetsu.or.jp). Aoyama-itchōme Station. Take Exit 4 and head straight a few blocks. Look for a big building with glass panels on the right. Arranging flowers is just an *adorable* little hobby for grannies, right? Tell that to the bad-mamma-jamma *iemoto* masters and their mammoth *ikebana* headquarters. With 4 bilingual textbooks for different grades and 169 branches, the Foundation presents *ikebana* like the fully-developed art form it is. Don't just smell the roses; take a class and use them to express yourself. International classes ¥3150, held every M 10am-noon. Call ahead. Advanced classes also available.

TEA CEREMONY

Seisei-an (清静庵 ; ☎3265-1111). Akasaka-mitsuke Station. Turn left out of the left mouth of Sotobori-dōri Exit and keep going. Cross all the way over the large intersection and over the bridge. It's on the 7th fl. of the Hotel New Otani Tōkyō, which is on your left. Traditional tea ceremony ¥1000. Just show up; call ahead if you're bringing a posse. Ceremony takes about 1hr. Open Th-Sa 11am-4pm.

AVANT-GARDE POTPOURRI

■ **The Japan Foundation Forum** (Kokusai Kōryū Kikin; 国際交流基金), Akasaka Twin Tower 1F, 2-17-22, Akasaka, Minato-ku (☎5562-3892). Tameike-sannō Station. Take Exit 12. Keep turning right; it's across the street on the 1st fl. of the Akasaka Twin Tower. More or less a huge chamber with a first-rate lighting system, the ideal catwalk for artists with big dreams. Creativity is in short supply in Tōkyō, but this clean slate is one place where painters, sculptors, photographers, and *butō* dancers make good things happen. Prices vary. Open Tu-Sa 11am-7:30pm. Reception open daily.

SPORTS

BASEBALL

■ **Tōkyō Dome City** (Tōkyō Dōmu Shiti; 東京ドームシティ) 1-3-61, Kōraku, Bunkyō-ku (☎5800-9999; www.tokyo-dome.co.jp). Suidobashi Station. The dome is gargantuan; you can't miss it. They don't call it a city for nothing. The big arena for Japan's national pastime (that would be baseball, though *sumō* is right up there) is such a smashing hit that it even has its own **theme park** and a fully decked-out hotel. The Yomiuri Giants have a dynasty going, so root for the home team. As a pre-game warm-up, ¥400 will get you into the Dome's **baseball museum,** where fans can gaze upon the Hall of Fame and engage in virtual batting practice. Allergic to baseball? Try Dome City's roller coasters and rides, which run in the ¥600 neighborhood. Food, gift shops, and a spa are just a step away. Parking is available at ¥300 for 30min., but spots fill up quickly.

MARTIAL ARTS

Nippon Budōkan (日本武道館), 2-3, Kitanomaru Kōen (☎3216-5100; www.nippon-budokan.or.jp). Kudanshita Station. Head straight out of exit 2 and turn left to get through the gate. Turn right through another gate and you'll walk into it. The *budōkan* was constructed for the judo events of the 1964 Olympics and is every bit as impressive as an Olympic venue ought to be. Still an arena for frequent martial arts contests, especially weekends. Tickets sometimes available from the office.

SUMŌ

■ **Kokugikan** (国技館), 1-3-28, Yokoami, Sumida-ku (☎3623-5111; www.sumo.or.jp). Ryōgoku Station. Take the JR's West Exit and turn right. The Kokugikan is the monster with the teal roof; enter from the left side, towards the main road. If you're lucky enough to be in Tōkyō at the right time, a *sumō* tournament at the Kokugikan is one of the most uniquely Japanese experiences a tourist can have. The stadium's museum allows visitors to feast their eyes on champions of yore. (Free. Open M-F 10am-4:30pm.) 15-day *sumō* tournaments go up Jan., May, and Sept. Events start at 8:30am with the amateurs and run to 6pm. Ticket reservation center ☎5237-9310, but unless you speak Japanese you're better off with Ticket PIA or CN Ticket Outlet. Masu "box" seats from ¥9200; chair seats from ¥3600; same-day tickets ¥2100, ages 3-15 ¥200.

⬛ NIGHTLIFE

Expect from Tōkyō the nightscene you'd expect from any major world city. Foreigners tend to head straight to Roppongi and never look back, but those who branch out come face to face with the true diversity of Tōkyō after lights out. All nightspots are either 18+, 20+, or general admission; but carding is extremely rare. All *izakaya* (pubs) have an unpublished one drink minimum.

AKASAKA

Too old to go clubbing in Roppongi? Too young to start *pachinko*-popping in Kanda? Akasaka's night scene, much like its geography, is sandwiched somewhere between the two. Young professionals come for the bars, and the scene is very international and very much alive. You can come here to chill, but the West Tōkyō thrills are just a hop-skip away.

■ **Hobgoblin,** Tamondo Bldg. B1, 2-13-19, Akasaka, Minato-ku (☎6229-2636; www.hobgoblin-tokyo.com). Akasaka Station. Take Exit 2 and head downhill. Make the 1st right at Pasteria Plena. It's farther down on the left. Offering "authentic British comfort food" by day, the Hobgoblin becomes an international party pub at night. Young businessmen and a hopping bar make for an atmosphere that's full but not packed, busy but not rowdy. No cover. Open M-F 11am-2pm, Sa and holidays 5pm-1am.

Bill's Café and Bar, 3-6-11, Akasaka, Minato-ku (☎3586-8018). Akasaka-mitsuke Station. Take the right mouth of Sotobori-dōri Exit. Turn left and head down several blocks. Turn right at the subway and Derriere, then take the next left. It's on the right, with very open windows. Dark, jazzy, and English-speaking. Beer taps, shelves of liquor, and a long counter give it a Western-world feel. No cover. Open M-F 6pm-1am, Sa 7pm-1am.

Bob's Lounge, Akasaka Flora Bldg. 8F, 2-12-12, Akasaka, Minato-ku (☎3586-2688; http://plaza11.mbn.or.jp/~bobson). Tameike-sannō Station. Take Exit 11 and turn right at the top of the stairs. Take the rightmost street at the intersection. It's on the left; look for a sign on the ground. Dressed like a cowboy, and genteel like one too, Bob runs his "home-sweet-home" with a little Okinawa Sunshine (code for the *shamisen*) and more character than the Japanese language has *kanji*. Pub designed for international communication; group conversations in English (more or less a casual class) with fluent individuals at center stage. Bourbon whiskey and scotch ¥500 for a single, ¥800 for a double. No cover, except on "International Party Night" (W), featuring all you can eat, drink, and sing: men ¥3000, women ¥2500. Open M-F 11am-2pm and 7pm-midnight.

Jambo, Social Akasaka Bldg. B1F, 3-11-7, Akasaka, Minato-ku (☎3224-0365). Akasaka-mitsuke Station. Take the right mouth of the Sotobori-dōri Exit. Turn left; it's on the right after crossing 2 streets. Bright colors and African chow make for a unique *izakaya*. Open M-Sa 6pm-2am.

TŌKYŌ

Dubliners', New Toranomon Bldg. 1F, 1-1-18, Toranomon, Minato-ku (☎5501-1536). Toranomon Station. Head straight out of Exit 8 and look left. Homesick? Dubliners' looks like a pub fell out of a plane and landed in Japan. Don't expect an international scene. Specialties include Irish alcohol, of course. Open M-F 8am-11:30pm.

ASAKUSA

Rickshaws and nightlife don't usually go hand-in-hand, and the Asakusa night air can get a little chilly. Packets of 30- to 50-somethings arrive on weekend nights to patronize their favorite *izakaya*. **Rokku-dōri** has loads of *pachinko* parlors, video arcades, and even a famous strip club, **Rokku-za.**

Kamiya Bar (神谷バー), 1-1-1, Asakusa, Taitō-ku. (☎3841-5400; www.kamiya-bar.com). Asakusa Station. Take the JR's Exit 3 and make a U-turn. The sign is on the left, in *kanji*. One of Tōkyō's oldest (since 1880) and a popular after-work gathering spot. Oddly enough, there's no actual bar; the lights are bright and people come with friends to share beer and stories over a table. Most of the action is on the 1st floor; Asahi action will cost you ¥410, Bass ¥510. Open Su-Tu and Th-Sa 11:30am-10pm.

Brewery Pub Sumidagawa, Asahi Beer Annex Bldg. 3F, 1-23-26, Azuma-bashi, Sumida-ku (☎5608-3831). Asakusa Station. Take Exit 4 and cross the bridge. Look for a 4-story cylinder to the right of the golden statue. A brightly lit, sit-down microbrewery outside the Asahi building. Small groups come to finish off the day with anything from sausage to sushi. Open M-F 11:30am-1:30pm and 5pm-10pm; Sa-Su 11:30am-10pm.

EBISU

Break free from the herd with a flourish. Ebisu has clubs, bars, live music, and even some retro entertainment. What it lacks in luster, it makes up for with a juicy twist of color.

What the Dickens, Roob 6-4F, 1-13-3, Ebisu-nishi, Shibuya-ku (☎3780-2099). Ebisu Station. West Exit, West Side. Cross the main street to the street between Wendy's and KFC. It's at the end of the 1st block after the road bends right. A mixed mess of around 100 crowd this poppa bear cabin to listen to live rock, blues, and jazz. Perch on the 2nd fl. and laugh at the mortals below. Logs and good acoustics—who would have thought? Casual dress. No cover. Open Tu-W 5-11pm, Th-Sa 5pm-2am, Su 3pm-midnight.

Milk, Roob 6-B1, 1-13-3, Ebisu-nishi, Shibuya-ku. (☎5458-2826; www.milk-tokyo.co). Ebisu Station. West Exit, West Side. Same place as What the Dickens. Unlabeled; on the left before the elevator. Sometimes DJ, sometimes live; always original. Bite-sized club, good for focused churning. Sizeable bar area lets cool cats rock from a distance. Casual dress. 18+. Cover usually ¥2500 (1 free drink). Open almost daily 9pm-5am.

Enjoy! House, Daikanyama Techno Bldg. 2F, 2-9-9, Ebisu-nishi, Shibuya-ku (☎5489-1591; fax 5489-1591). Ebisu Station. West Exit, West Side. Head to the right of the escalator and cross straight to the road by the J-phone building, right of the Nova sign. At the 5-armed intersection, take the 2nd road from the left. On the left. Is it a pub? Is it a club? Interior like a mini-brothel with bar and dance floor. The cushy half, in red satin, is incredibly intimate. The dance half blasts music with serious kickback, usually techno, house, or world. "Odd" dress recommended. 1 drink min.; owner recommends 2. 18+. No cover. Happy Hour 1-7pm. Open Su and Tu-Th 1pm-2am, F-Sa 1pm-4am.

Space Punch, SATO Bldg. 1F., 1-13-5, Ebisu-nishi, Shibuya-ku (☎3496-2484). Ebisu Station. From the West Exit, cross the main street and head down it away from the tracks. Turn right at the shrine and circle around it. More creative than a drunk monkey with a typewriter, Space Punch is a chrome escape pod loaded with toys. So removed it missed the last decade, the alcoholic tunnel of astrojoy features a disco ball and '80s tunes. Rock, pop, R&B, and techno also. Better for a night off than a night of getting it on. Beer ¥500; harder stuff up to ¥1000. Casual dress. No cover. Open M-Sa 8pm-3am.

Monsoon Café, Marix Ebisu Bldg. 1F-2F, 4-4-6, Ebisu, Shibuya-ku (☎5789-3811; www.global-dining.com). Ebisu Station. East Exit (3rd fl.). Descend and U-turn, then pass between Sunkus and Pronto. Turn right down the main street, Ebisu-dōri. At the main intersection, go up past the right side of Kinko's; it's farther down on the right. An Asian fusion staple in Tōkyō; the Ebisu branch gets packed with hungry, thirsty guests in the evening before the nightlife heats up. Open daily 11:30am-5am.

GINZA

The lands to the left have stolen the show, but fun-oriented Ginza has managed to secure a modest slice of nightlife for itself. Ginza is famous for upper-class hostess bars, where the college-educated lasses are excellent conversationalists.

Three-hundred Bar, Fazenda Bldg. B1, 5-9-11, Ginza, Chūō-ku (☎3572-6300). Ginza Station. From Chūō-dōri and Harumi-dōri, head east down Harumi-dōri, away from the green frogs. Take the 2nd right and look for an electric "¥300" sign on the ground. A colorful bastion of cheap drinks and youth in an expensive and older area. The ¥300 gets you a golden ticket, which you can redeem for mixed drinks and food. Plentiful lighting and reggae music say "chill," not "rave." No cover. Open daily until 5am.

Lion Beer Hall (ライオンビヤホール), 7-9-20, Ginza, Chūō-ku (☎3571-2590). Ginza Station. From the intersection of Chūō-dōri and Harumi-dōri, head south on Chūō-dōri, away from Wok and Mitsukoshi department store. It's the 1st entrance in the 3rd building on the left. One big *izakaya*. Raging in late evening. Half-pint of Guiness ¥500. Medium-sized Sapporo ¥730. *Shūmai* (dumplings) ¥680. Crab/shrimp pilaf ¥1000.

HARAJUKU AND AOYAMA

Many long-term foreign residents eventually eschew the glamor of major nightlife districts for the nuggets around Omotesandō Station. Shibuya, Roppongi, and Shinjuku shout too loudly; Omotesandō is a place to be, not to be seen. Institutions here tend to be more creative, smaller, and chiller, with a 20-something crowd and a low sketch factor. The night is silent, but that's because treasure is buried deep.

▧ **Dancing-Monkey,** Minami-Aoyama Homes B1F, 6-2-2, Minami-Aoyama, Minato-ku (☎6418-4242; www.global-dining.com). Omotesandō Station. From Exit B1, go forward and turn left at the T-intersection. Very far down on the left, past 5 left turns. One of Tōkyō's best ideas. Fundamentally a late-night deli/bar/diner; at heart, it's very much a dancing monkey. Eating area full of nacho-fiesta-colored seats and silver astro tables on a zebra-stripe floor, finished with a color-morphing bar. Upbeat looping rhythms; staff redefines cool. Wide selection of cake is the cherry on top of a hard night out. Visit the bathroom to reach out and shock someone. Open daily 11:30am-5am.

▧ **The Orbient,** Crystal Bldg. B1F-B2F, 3-5-12, Kita-Aoyama, Minato-ku (☎5775-2555; www.orbient.jp). Ditches typical club flavor for uncompromised classiness; guests explore rooms from "Goldfinger" to "vampire lust," while dancing, chatting, or flirting. Different nights bring different DJs; check the website. Also a restaurant. Dress snappy. Cover usually ¥3000 for men, ¥2000 for women (2 free drinks). Women get no cover Sa and free drinks before 8:30pm Tu and F-Su. Open some Tu and W-Su 7pm-1am.

▧ **The Pink Cow,** 1-3-18, Shibuya, Shibuya-ku (www.thepinkcow.com). Shibuya Station or Omotesandō Station. From the former, take the East Exit. Take the leftmost of the 3 avenues extending past the police box on the opposite side. Take the 1st left after Yachiyo Bank, then the 2nd right; it's on the right. The Cow typically hosts a refreshingly up-front crew of college-aged, street-smart foreigners. No backalley pub to drown your sorrows, the Cow is bright and catchy. Occasional concerts, wine-tasting, and art shows. Genuine Californian cuisine from a genuinely Californian owner during the day; the menu is part vegetarian, of course. Just moved from Harajuku, the new Cow is 4 times bigger than the old one, holding 150-300 people; hopefully the flavor will remain the same.

TŌKYŌ

Oh! God, 6-7-18 B1, Jingūmae, Shibuya-ku (☎3406-3206; www.oh-god-jp.com). Hara-juku Station. Turn right out of the Omotesandō Exit. Take the footbridge perpendicular to the station and head several minutes down the main street. Take the 3rd right after the intersection with the Gap; it's at the T-intersection. For decades, man has struggled with the choice between curling up at home with dinner and a movie and maintaining a social front. Half American diner and half French cafe, Oh! God offers all of the above. The Tex-Mex starved can mosey next door to **Zest Cantina** before the film. No cover. Movies at 9pm, midnight, 3am. Extra 6pm screening F-Su. Open daily 6am-6pm.

Loop, 2-1-13 B1, Shibuya, Shibuya-ku. (☎3797-9933; www.baseplanning.co.jp/loop). Shibuya Station or Omotesandō Station. From the former, take East Exit. Take the left-most of the 3 avenues past the police box on the opposite side. It's on the right, next to 7-Eleven, just before Aoyama University. Totally average in every conceivable aspect. Mid-size. Mid-price. Mid-popularity (almost full). Mixed clientele. A healthy schedule of DJs and a slightly younger crowd. 20+. Cover generally ¥2000-3000 with 1 free drink; pay in full once or check other clubs for ¥500 coupons. Open almost daily 10pm-5am.

Club Mix, 3-6-19 B1F, Kita-Aoyama, Minato-ku (☎3797-1313; www.at-mix.com). Omotesandō Station. From Exit B2, U-turn, cross a little street, and take the next left down an alley. It's on the left. Perfect for a good drink and pumpin' trance. Though they aren't particularly strong, bartender's-choice drinks (¥800) are recommended. Camara-derie is high and becoming a regular pays off; the dancing, on the other hand, is goofy at best. Worst layout ever conceived, with guests squeezing past each other and being hit by opening doors. 1.8L pitchers ¥3000. Casual dress; hats are in. Su-Th cover gen-erally ¥2000, F-Sa ¥2500. 2 free drinks. Open (almost) daily 10pm-late.

D-Zone, 5-47-6, Jingūmae, Shibuya-ku. (☎3407-6845). Omotesandō Station. From Exit B4, walk away from the main intersection and make the 6th right (the 3rd after Kinokuniya). Tromp all the way to the bitter bend; it's on the left. A mid-size dance bar booming with house and techno. Popular but standard shtick. Few locals. Beer ¥600. Casual dress. No cover. "Open til late."

IKEBUKURO

Warm but not hot, Ikebukuro late night pulses steadily without flatlining. Proxim-ity to the true hotspots pays off, and the evening game is all abuzz.

■ **Mysterious** (ミステリアス), 1-13-11 B2F, Higashi-Ikebukuro, Toshima-ku (☎5954-7381). Ikebukuro Station. From the giant Seibu, head down Green Main-dōri. The next main left forks; bear right. It's the 1st right after Cinema Sunshine on the left; it's on the right. Travel through time and space (a.k.a. 2 flights of stairs) to reach Tōkyō's newest gimmick, an *izakaya* from outer space. Daylight is out and blacklight is in; the silver-wrapped waitresses wave guests in like airplanes. Combo platters, named for planets, start at ¥2500. Cocktail menu explained with gibberish alien symbols; all drinks original (¥800). Pineapple stars and glowing mock-ice-cubes complement the soothing astro-drift music. ¥500 sit-down fee, then a 10% extra charge. Casual dress. No cover. Open M-Th 5pm-1am, F-Sa 5pm-5am, Su and holidays 5pm-midnight. Credit cards accepted.

Drum Kan, Suzuki Bldg. 2F, 1-14-15, Higashi-Ikebukuro, Toshima-ku (☎3982-6188). Ikebukuro Station. From the East Exit, cross slightly to the right to Green Main-dōri. The next main intersection offers 2 lefts; take the right one. Turn left opposite HMV, just before Hotel Theater. It's on the left. No tables here; just pull a seat up to a drum can. The sexy red bar works too. Tries to be American, posting flags and playing heavy metal and rock; through some stroke of subtlety it succeeds. Blue neon and fake trees with X-mas lights do justice to the canned theme. Drafts from ¥380; cocktails ¥500. R&B, rare groove, soul, disco classics, rock, and more. 10% discount with flyer. Open daily 7pm-4am.

MARUNOUCHI

The metropolitan hustle of central Tōkyō sets with the sun; there's little reason to come at night, especially if you're under thirty. Even the activities that the lingering salarymen engage in are hotter elsewhere; go to Ueno or Ginza for hostess clubs. The one possible exception is the West Exit of Kanda Station, a major player in *pachinko* and *izakaya*.

Aburi-shunsai, 3-3-4, Nihonbashi, Chūō-ku (☎5202-4129). Tōkyō Station. Take Yaesu Central Exit and check the skyline for a big silver building to the right of a building with a yellow and black neon sign. Head between the buildings and look on the right after crossing one street. The local workforce fills the *izakaya* to get their post-work fish-on. Open M-Th and Sa-Su 5pm-1am, F and holidays 5pm-4am. AmEx/DC/JCB/MC/V.

Pronto, 2-4-10, Yaesu, Chūō-ku. (☎6202-0571; www.pronto.co.jp). Tōkyō Station. Take Yaesu Central Exit and cross the main road before you. Head down the road directly perpendicular to the southern tip of the roof over the tracks (the tip on your left, facing the station). It's at the end of the block on the right. Franchise cafe and bar. Casual-jazzy. Open M-F 7am-11:30pm, Sa-Su 7am-5pm. Credit cards accepted.

ODAIBA

Zepp (p. 189), Leisureland (p. 189), and the ferris wheel (p. 163) could make for a fun nighttime excursion, but let's face it. Go to Roppongi. Do not pass Go. Don't even think about collecting $200.

ROPPONGI

Only in Roppongi (and perhaps neighboring Akasaka) do the internationals come close to forming a majority. Populated by small to mid-size bars with dance floors, the east end of **Gaien-higashi-dōri** is the name of the game. The true clubs are a quick fade off the main. Hostess clubs are in residence, though not in Ueno-esque proportions; some are even packaged for tourist consumption. Regardless of what the night brings, Roppongi is very talkative; individuals fluent in the international language of flirtation should have no trouble getting around or getting it on.

Roppongi wins the intensity award, but is it as sketchy as they say? Loaded with foreigners who believe it, legend becomes reality. Scattered huntresses and human billboards form the kernel of truth; obnoxious drunkards provide snow for the snowball. The institutions themselves are mostly fine; some are even proactively against the grain. The best night to come is Thursday, when bars and clubs cut the most special deals. Half the places will be empty; come weekends to see Roppongi in full, overcrowded decadence. Smart shoppers hit the Happy Hours around 9pm, but the real Roppongi doesn't fire up until 11pm and shifts into top gear around 3am. Quieter places pop their tops early, wrapping up shop by 2am.

Velfarre, 7-14-22, Roppongi, Minato-ku (☎3402-8000; http://velfarre.avex.co.jp). Roppongi Station. From Roppongi Crossing, head perpendicular to the highway away from Almond Confectionery. It's the 1st left, after 7th Heaven. Look for a big staircase on the left. Pronounced *vell-fa-rei*, Velfarre is definitive. Roppongi's big name club purportedly outsizes anything else Tōkyō has to offer while maintaining an entirely professional attitude. The huge main chamber boasts a total light job. Guest DJs pump techno, trance, and hard house to freely flowing glow sticks. Oddly, the titan club has an early bedtime. Dress smart casual. 18+. Cover generally ¥3000 with 2 free drinks. After Hours cover ¥3500 with 1 free drink. Repeat lady visitors (gotta prove it) get in for ¥1000 with 1 free drink. Usually open Th-Su 7pm-1am, sometimes W. After Hours open Su 5am-1pm.

Lexington Queen, Third Goto Bldg. B1F, 3-13-14, Roppongi, Minato-ku (☎3401-1661; www.lexingtonqueen.com). Roppongi Station. From Roppongi Crossing, head down the main street, toward Marché's. Take the 2nd left, after Friday's; it's on the right. Rop-

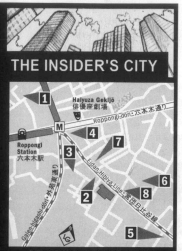

THE INSIDER'S CITY

Haiyuza Gekijō
俳優座劇場

Roppongi-dōri 六本木本通り

Roppongi
Station
六本木駅

Eidan-Hibiya Line 営団日比谷線

Gaien-higashi-dōri 外苑東通り

CRAWL AROUND THE WORLD

The guests aren't from these parts, and neither are half the hosts. Designed for an early Thursday night, at 30min. per bar, you'll finish this global toast to com-buddery in time for the last train.

1 **Salsa Sudada.** Dance before coordination checks out. A 6:30-7pm arrival should land you a salsa lesson.

2 **Hub Roppongi 2nd.** A flight to the British ales for refueling.

3 **Quest.** Discover the Aussie bar under Gaien-higashi-dōri for 7pm-9:30pm Happy Hour.

4 **Powerhouse.** Regulars from Cameroon to Turkey. Happy Hour 8-10pm; ladies free.

5 **Bernd's Bar.** German import. Your Kostritzer is showing.

6 **El Café Latino.** Back to square *uno*. Remember how to salsa?

7 **Alcatraz BC.** A jaunt to San Fran for *izakaya* behind bars.

8 **Club Gitanos.** American-style club. Dance til night's done.

pongi's starlet demands diamonds but reciprocates in spades. The clubbers that make it happen are young and feet-on-fire. A must-hit for visiting stars, with photos to prove it. A few quirks: a penchant for *every* genre of music, a request list, and an in-house sushi bar. The only thing missing is size. 7 drinks ¥4000; ¥3000 for 5; ¥2500 for 3; ¥2000 for 2. Shots ¥100 on Th. Snappy dress. 18+. Men's cover ¥4000, women ¥3000. Ladies free entry and drinks M, free entry and 2 drinks Th. Open daily 8pm-5am.

Gaspanic Club, 3-10-5 3-5F, Roppongi, Minato-ku (☎3402-7054). Roppongi Station. From Roppongi Crossing, head down the main street away from the highway, toward Marché's. Turn left after the first block; it's on the left. One of Roppongi's best choices for boppin', franchise-loving youth and arguably the best of the Gaspanic lot. Perhaps it's the young staff's penchant for attacking guests with a big welcome; perhaps it's the ¥400 Happy Hour drinks, the cheapest around. It may even be the ceiling handrails, which have saved many a bartop dancer a nasty bruise. Whatever it is, it's not the music, Western radio's "100 Most Regurgitated." The staff is pushy with alcohol, which gets old quickly. Happy Hour daily 6pm-9:30pm and all-day Th. Casual dress. Strictly 18+. No cover. 1 drink min. well-enforced. Open daily 6pm-5am.

Alcatraz BC, 3-13-12 2F, Roppongi, Minato-ku. (☎5410-0012; www.alcatraz.ne.jp). Roppongi Station. From Roppongi Crossing, head down the main street away from the highway, toward Marché's. Take the 2nd left, after Friday's. Look for torches on the right. Patrons of this kink-fest *izakaya* are seated in atmospheric prison cells and served by policewomen in pleather skirts. Let the drool and alcohol flow. A sister shop in Shibuya has a similar mental ward/nurse outfit theme. Open Su-Tu 6pm-11pm, W-Sa 6pm-5am.

Motown House (☎5474-4605; www.motown-house.com). Roppongi Station. From Roppongi Crossing, head down the main street away from the highway, toward Marché's. At the end of the 1st block on the left. Places like this are everywhere, but excellent acoustics and sexy clientele set it apart. The locals know it. Savvy foreigners know it. If only the mixed mingling were complemented by something other than English pop hits. Drafts ¥800. Casual dress. No cover. Open daily 6pm-5am.

Queen B, 3-15-23 3F, Roppongi, Minato-ku. (☎3478-4488; www.queenb-tokyo.com). Roppongi Station. From Roppongi Crossing, head down the main street away from the highway, toward Marché's. Turn left at Bikkuri Sushi, opposite the ROI Bldg.; it's on the right.

Roppongi・六本木

▲ ACCOMMODATIONS
Hotel Arca Torre, **13**
Hotel Ibis, **3**
Hotel Villa Fontaine
 Roppongi, **5**

● FOOD
Bikkuri-zushi, **16**
Cantina La Fiesta, **17**
Hina Sushi, **14**
Ichiran, **20**
Inakaya, **1**
Marché, **10**
Moti, **19**

■ NIGHTLIFE
Bar Drop, **7**
Bar, Isn't It?, **4**
Club Garden, **12**
Fiesta, **6**
Gaspanic Club, **8**
Lexington Queen, **9**
Motown House, **11**
Propaganda, **15**
Queen B, **18**
Soul Sonic Boogie, **22**
Velfarre, **2**
Wall Street House, **21**

Roppongi・六本木

One of few transsexual institutions outside Kabukichō, and one of the friendliest hostess bars in town. Some hostesses speak nearly perfect English, and the all-you-can-drink (for 90min.) house bottle system means payment is fire and forget. 9-10:30pm cover ¥9000, 10:30pm-midnight ¥10,500, midnight-4am ¥12,000.

Club Garden, 3-13-12 B1, Roppongi, Minato-ku (☎3475-6969; www.club-garden.com). Roppongi Station. From Roppongi Crossing, head down the main street away from the highway, toward Marché's. Take the 2nd left; it's on the right. Roppongi could use more serious clubs. This new contender boasts a sushi bar and no-genre-barred music. Whether it takes off, only time will tell, but fortune cookies predict good things. 18+. No sandals, no shorts. Men's cover Su-Th ¥3000, F-Sa ¥3500; women Su-W and F-Sa ¥2000, Th free. Includes 2 drinks. Discount with flyer. Open daily 7pm-til late.

Propaganda, 3-14-9 2F, Roppongi, Minato-ku (☎3423-0988). Roppongi Station. From Roppongi Crossing, head down the main street away from the highway, toward Marché's. A few blocks down on the left, above the sushi joint, opposite the ROI Bldg. Popular *early* in the night and a chilling joint for 30-somethings, with an unusual concentration of loners and pairs of women. Great cocktails, most ¥1000. The citrusy Shanghai Sling is especially good. Happy Hour daily 6pm-9pm. Ladies' Night every W (drinks half-price). Open daily 6pm-5am, but has begun clean-up as early as 3am.

Wall Street House, Imperial Roppongi Bldg. B2F, 5-16-52, Roppongi, Minato-ku (☎3586-0874; www.wsjapan.com). Roppongi Station. From Roppongi Crossing, head down the main street away from the highway, towards Marché's. Turn right at the end of the ROI Bldg. Turn left into the white-tiled plaza and follow your ears. A bar with a dance floor. Foreigners and locals mingle. Ladies drink free Th. Print the webpage for a free drink F-Sa 6pm-9pm; bring it Su for ¥500 drinks for women and ¥300 off drinks for men. Casual dress. No cover. Open daily "6pm 'til you pass out."

Bar, Isn't It? MT Bldg. 3F, 3-8-18, Roppongi, Minato-ku (☎3746-1598). Roppongi Station. From Roppongi Crossing, head down the main street away from the highway, towards Marché's. Turn left after the 1st block. Go straight; it's on the right after a slight bend. Whatever it is, this bar/nightclub/comedy club is a massive Michelangelo meets Alice-in-Wonderland mindjob of a venue; certainly the most creative place for a cocktail, if not the hottest late on a Th. Comedy shows, generally 7pm Th, are the real draw. Not always in English; call ahead. Casual dress. Show cover ¥2000 (1 free drink). Cover F-Sa from 9pm ¥1000 (1 drink). Otherwise no cover. Open Th-Sa 6pm-late.

TŌKYŌ

Bar Drop, Com Roppongi 4F, 3-11-5, Roppongi, Minato-ku (☎5772-9188). Roppongi Station. From Roppongi Crossing, follow the highway away from Almond Confectionery. Take the 1st right; it's on the right. This new kid on the block lays claim to "smooth house, tough disco, and twisted beats." Whatever you call it, the DJ is pretty good. Candlelight alongside discolight, Bar Drop has unrealized potential. Happy Hour Th 8pm-11pm, drinks ¥500. Casual dress. No cover. Open daily until about 6am.

Hub Roppongi 2nd, Torikatsu Bldg. B1F, 5-2-5, Roppongi (☎3478-0803). Roppongi Station. From Roppongi Crossing, head down the main street away from the highway, towards Marché's. It's several blocks down on the right, next to McD's. The most visible chain of British pubs in Tōkyō is one of the most popular, duking it out with Hobgoblin. 30-year-old Brits and friends chat it up over pints of Guinness (¥850). Happy Hour daily 5pm-8pm. Casual dress. No cover. Open M-Th 5pm-2am, F-Sa 5pm-5am, Su 5pm-1am.

Soul Sonic Boogie, 5-18-2 B1F, Roppongi, Minato-ku (☎3584-7890; www.soulsonicboogie.com). Roppongi Station. From Roppongi Crossing, head down the main street away from the highway, towards Marché's. Way past the hubbub, in unmistakable glowing blue. Venue is nothing special, but it may be the only place for soul, funk, and hits from decades past. You risk an empty club unless you come in the AM on F or Sa night. Casual dress. F-Sa cover 9pm-11pm ¥1500 (1 drink included), 11pm-5am ¥2500 (2 drinks); Tu-Th 8pm-4am ¥1000 (1 drink). Open Tu-Th 8pm-4am, F-Sa 9pm-5am.

Fiesta, Taimei Bldg. 5F, 3-11-6, Roppongi, Minato-ku. (☎5410-3008; www.nightfever.com/fiesta). Roppongi Station. From Roppongi Crossing, head down the main street away from the highway, towards Marché's. First block on the left. Unlike most private-room karaoke joints, Fiesta is a karaoke bar; one person's lungs fill the entire place with joy or despair. There are English titles, but you may be performing for a local audience. ¥3000 cover includes 3 drinks and karaoke. Open M-W 7pm-4am, Th-Sa 7pm-5am.

SHIBUYA

The music is live, the clubs are hot, and the love hotels heat up even quicker. Not quite as sleazy as Roppongi, Shibuya draws a crowd that's a little younger and a little more local. Most of the action is focused in Dōgenzaka, with the rest of the area buzzing but not quite dead. High tide is 1am; 11pm may feel a little dry, and swimming upstream against the homebound current requires the agility of a salmon. Club covers run ¥2500-3000 and usually include a drink. Otherwise, a beer will set you back ¥500-6000, the hard stuff up to ¥1000. A word about the "legal" drugs sold on the street: "No." Be plenty suspicious that they advertise in English.

▧ **Club Womb,** 2-16, Murayama-chō, Shibuya-ku (☎5459-0039; www.womb.co.jp). Shibuya Station. Hachikō Exit. Cross the street to the smaller big TV and head left up the tree-lined avenue. Turn right at the fork, left at the 2nd fork, and left before Shibuya City Hotel. Turn right after Club Asia, then make an immediate left. Totally unmarked, it's 20-30m down on the left; look for the bouncer. Our single favorite club in Tōkyō. 2 tiers of soundproof dance lounge overlook the main floor. Unmatched sound: famous DJs on weekends, aided by a carefully engineered sound system. Controlled, incredibly attractive crowd, leagues beyond the human droolfest in the rest of Shibuya. Lower foreigner quotient than most venues. Drafts ¥500, cocktails ¥600. 20+. Cover varies, around ¥3500 *sans* free drink. Flyers earn discounts. Open daily about 11pm-5am.

Club Xanadu, Fhontis Bldg. B1, 2-23-12, Dōgenzaka, Shibuya-ku (☎5489-3750; www.xanadu.ne.jp). Shibuya Station. Follow the directions for Club Asia up to Shibuya City Hotel. It's on the left down a narrow stairwell, before the hotel. Budget clubbing: undercutting the competition as much as 3-fold, Xanadu nets half the foreign scene.

The DJs rock and the drinks are strong enough to topple your tipsy; the only thing missing is the total light engineering package. Come 7-9pm for Happy Hour prices or darts. Casual dress. 20+. Cover varies; ¥3000 and a free drink is common. Women often pay less and score an extra drink. Open W-Su 7pm-5am.

Club Vras, Dr. Jeekahn's 1F, 2-4, Maruyama-chō, Shibuya-ku (☎3770-5457; www.vras.net). Shibuya Station. Follow the directions for Club Asia to Shibuya City Hotel. Turn left before the hotel. It's uphill on the right, in club central. With barely enough light to check out the crowd, this thumper of a blackbox is for serious dancers. Perfect for shedding the world and melting into the techno sermon of the DJ. No dress code. 18+. Su-Th ¥2000; F-Sa ¥2500 (1 free drink). Open daily 10pm-5am.

Club Atom, Dr. Jeekahn's 4-6F, 2-4, Maruyama-chō, Shibuya-ku (☎3476-7811; jeekahns@gate01.com). Shibuya Station. Follow the directions for Club Asia to Shibuya City Hotel. Turn left before the hotel; it's uphill on the right. Each floor has a unique flavor, but Dr. Jeekahn's prescription is swank through and through. Dress code prohibits sandals but not shorts. 20+. Cover ¥3000 (2 free drinks). Open F-Sa 10pm-5am.

Plug, 1-23-13, Jinnan, Shibuya-ku (☎5428-9188; www.plug.tv). Shibuya Station. Hachikō Exit. Trace the left edge of the tracks away from the station, to Drunkard's Alley. Halfway down on the left of a sketchy alley. The little club of ruby-red light and mirrors calls itself an "expression basement." Home to a chill crowd dressed like music video extras, and they have the moves, to boot. Totally unlike the crowd on Dōgenzaka. Good place to chat. 20+. Cover varies, usually ¥2500 with 1 free drink. Open daily 7pm-5am.

Club Asia, 1-8, Maruyama-chō, Shibuya-ku (☎5458-1996; www.clubasia.co.jp). Shibuya Station. From the Hachikō Exit, cross the street to the smaller big TV and head left up the tree-lined avenue. Go right at the 1st fork, left at the 2nd. Turn left before Shibuya City Hotel; it's uphill on the right. Huge—no other club in the neighborhood comes close. The different moods of the three chambers let dancers time out without bailing out. Sound and lights on par with the neighbors; not the orgy some clubs this size are. Younger, Japanese crowd. Cover varies; ¥3000 and a free drink is the weekend norm. Open daily 11pm-5am. **Club Vuenos** (☎5458-5963), across the street, is owned by the same folks, but long lines there are prohibitive. Open daily 10pm-dawn.

300 Coins Bar, Noa Shibuya Bldg. B1, 36-2, Udagawa-chō, Shibuya-ku (☎3463-3039). Shibuya Station. From the Hachikō Exit, cross the street and head 5min. past the right side of Starbucks. Bear left between the 2 Seibus, and right at the fork with the police box. On the left, past Tōkyū Hands. Far enough from the neon heat, where children of the night prowl freely, a ¥300 oasis bumps to white plaster and soft-pumping DJ beats. A good place to shoot the funk and limbo below average Shibuya alcohol prices. The food is ¥300 too. Casual dress. No cover. Open daily 4pm-11:30pm (last order 11pm).

J-Pop Cafe, 31-2, Udagawa-chō (☎5456-5767). Shibuya Station. Follow directions for 300 Coins up to the police box, then bear left; it's on the right, the 7th floor of Shibuya BEAM. 1 part cafe, 2 parts upscale youth pre-game and afterparty, the ruby red and funky antenna lamps belong on a music video set. Open M-Th 5pm-midnight, F 5pm-4am, Sa 11:30am-4am, Su 11:30am-midnight.

Gaspanic, 21-7 B1, Udagawa-chō, Shibuya-ku (☎3462-9099). Shibuya Station. From the Hachikō Exit, head down the left of Starbucks, a few doors down. The main branch is in Roppongi, but this one has such an obvious location that it drips with international youth. Happy Hour Th 6-9pm, drinks ¥400. Casual dress. Open daily 6pm-5am.

Paradise Macau, 39-5 1F, Udagawa-chō, Shibuya-ku (☎3780-5231; www.kiwagroup.co.jp). Shibuya Station. Follow directions to the 300 Bar and turn left. Thatch and glowing lamps convert the restaurant/bar into a classy, open-air hangout. Mixed Asian cuisine with a Caribbean feel. Open M-Th 11:30am-11pm; F-Su 11:30am-5am.

TŌKYŌ

SHINJUKU

Lights out over Shinjuku: the stuff of legends, the stuff of infamy. Even schoolchildren know of **Kabuki-chō**, the famous red-light underbelly of Tōkyō, where sightseeing innocents wander alongside a supersized bucket of sketch. Tucked within is the club district, littered with teenage bums. Equally well known is gay/lesbian **Shinjuku 2-chōme**, so concentrated it's nearly an institution. The alternative action centers outside tiny bar **Advocates**, permeating a handful of nearby nightspots.

Liquid Room, Humax Pavilion, 1-20-1 7F, Kabuki-chō, Shinjuku-ku (☎3200-6831; www.liquidroom.net). Shinjuku Station. From the East Exit, turn left and follow the tracks to the main road that crosses under the tracks. Turn right, skip the roads forking at the base of Pepe Shinjuku Prince Hotel, and make the next left. It's on the opposite side of the wide plaza; follow the road past Club Code and look left for the elevator. No consistent theme; check the website to avoid unplanned collisions with men-only night or ¥7000 cover night. Some guest DJs and performers, broad in genre. 20+. Cover varies, generally ¥3000+, sometimes twice that. Frequent discounts on advance tickets; check website for providers. Open daily; doors open anywhere from 5:30pm-midnight.

Club Code, 1-19-2 4F, Kabuki-chō, Shinjuku-ku (☎3209-0702; www.clubcomplex-code.com). Shinjuku Station. Follow directions for Liquid Room. The 1800-person capacity outdoes Club Asia threefold, but the scene isn't particularly savory. Officially all-mix, but hard-house and trance frequently carry the night. Casual dress. Cover varies greatly; ¥3500 including 1 drink is standard weekends. Flyer discounts frequent. Occasional discounts for women Sa. Open daily 8pm-5am.

Club Dragon, 2-12-4 B1, Shinjuku, Shinjuku-ku. (☎3341-0606). Shinjuku Station. From the South Exit, turn right and follow the main road/bridge. Take the 3rd left after Virgin Megastore. It's the 5th block on the right; head to the basement. In a sea of bars, Club Dragon is lonely for fellow clubs but not patrons. Perhaps Tōkyō's premier gay club, it's small but happening. Women welcome F-Su. DJ spins disco/house. M-Th drinks ¥500. Casual or flamboyant dress. 18+. Cover includes 1 drink (2 drinks 8-11pm), men ¥1000, women ¥2000. Open M-Th 6pm-5am, F-Sa 9pm-6am, Su 5pm-5am.

Arty Farty, 2-11-7 2F, Shinjuku, Shinjuku-ku (☎5362-9720; www.arty-farty.net). Shinjuku Station. Follow Club Dragon directions to Virgin Megastore. Take the 2nd right after passing Resona Bank; it's on the right with advertising out front. The general store/American West facade disguises one of Tōkyō's longest bars, very possibly gay Tōkyō's finest on Sa. Come weekends for DJ club and a line. ¥500 drinks. Casual or creative dress. Sa gay men only. No cover. Happy Hour F-Su 5pm-9pm. Open daily 5pm-5am.

Kinswomyn, 2-15-10 3F, Shinjuku, Shinjuku-ku (☎3354-8720). Shinjuku Station. From the South Exit, turn right and follow the main road/bridge. Take the 4th left after Virgin Megastore, opposite Shinjuku-mon gate to Shinjuku National Gardens. It's the 7th right (after the cluster around Advocates), on the left, 3rd fl. The renowned lesbian bar is cozy, and chatty, just full enough to meet plenty of others in a comfortable atmosphere. Women only. Drinks from ¥700. Casual dress. No cover. Open M and W-Su 8pm-4am.

Shinjuku Golden-gai (新宿ゴールデン街). Shinjuku Station. East Exit. Turn left and follow the tracks up to the main road that crosses under the tracks. Cross the road and turn right. Turn left before the left to Hanazono Shrine. It's the 4th left; the arch is labeled. Objectively it's a dinky alley lined with 10-seater flashback bars from the WWII era, but for perceptive dreamers Golden-gai's history as a birthplace of ideas might make all the difference. Frequented by artists and philosophers.

Club Wire, 5-17-6 B1, Shinjuku, Shinjuku-ku. (☎3207-6953; www8.ocn.ne.jp/~club-wire). Shinjuku Station. From the East Exit, turn left and follow the tracks to the main road, just before Pepe Shinjuku Prince Hotel. Turn right. The Oriental Wave Bldg. is many blocks down; turn left immediately after it, towards Hanazono Shrine. Make an unofficial-looking right midway down the path and look for the bouncer. All-mix–new mix, DJ mix, jazz mix. This bite-sized club dares to party where no club has partied before: shrine grounds. Casual dress. 18+. Cover ¥2000 with 1 drink M-Th, usually ¥2500 with 2 drinks F-Sa. Open 9pm-5am; open as early as 6:30pm Su for events.

UENO

It isn't Shibuya or Shinjuku, but Ueno has its share of nocturnal attractions. Sunset sees the emergence of Japan's salarymen, who head south down Chūō-dōri to Okachi-machi, where the *mama-sans* and their bevy of hostesses await. Walk this way if you want to sing karaoke or be pounced on by beautiful 20-somethings, but be forewarned: while they aren't prostitutes, these women *are* after your money. Advertise your poverty and you can safely cruise the local bar scene.

■ **The Church,** 1-57 B1, Ueno Kōen, Taitō-ku (☎ 5807-1957; www.tokyo-church.com). Take the JR's Shinobazu Exit and turn right. At the intersection, look across the street; it's left of the movie theater. Locals and foreigners converge on this spacious venue to chat over imported beers and listen to live music, also a mix of East and West. The crowd is younger than Ueno's regulars and the atmosphere perfect for unwinding after a hard day. Prices reasonable: bottle of Old Speckled Hen ¥700. Live music F and Sa. Casual dress. No cover. Open M-F 11:30am-2am, Sa-Su 11:30am-5am.

The Warrior Celt, 6-9-22, Ueno, Taitō-ku (☎ 3836-8588; www.warriorcelt.com). From the JR's Hirokōji Exit head down the pedestrian arcade with the silver archway; it's a little ways down on your right. Petite in size, but big on love. A core of regulars are enshrined in paint on the walls. Top off your Belhaven Scottish Ale with live music (Tu, F, Sa) and you'll feel like a million yen in no time. Casual dress. No cover. 1-drink min. Happy Hour 5-7pm. Open Su-M 5pm-1am, Tu-Sa 5pm-5am, though the party often lasts longer.

■ FESTIVALS AND EVENTS

The city known for workaholic salarymen has a lighter side, and it's the rare day there isn't something festive going on. Up to 5000 firemen appear in the January 6 **Dezome-shiki Festival,** which showcases rescue techniques and ladder-top acrobatics. The **Tōkyō International Anime Fair** (www.taf.metro.tokyo.jp), slated for March 25-28 in 2004, is always the cause of cartoon mayhem. Ueno claims Japan's famous *sakura,* or cherry blossoms, which explode into brilliant pink-dom in late March and early April. The **Ueno Cherry Blossom Festival** is near the Ueno Park ponds.

Tōkyō's big three festivals go up in late spring, each featuring a parade of *mikoshi* (portable shrines) and traditionally dressed celebrants. Every even year on the last weekend before May 15, Kanda Myōjin shrine hosts the **Kanda Festival.** Call ☎ 3213-4499 (Japanese only) for times. Asakusa's most famous festival is the **Sanja Festival,** the third weekend of May; get yourself to Asakusa Shrine, next to Sensō-ji, for primetime viewing. Every odd year from June 10-16, the Hie Shrine hosts the **Sanno Festival.** Just go to Akasaka-mitsuke Station and follow the hubbub.

If you're around on the last Saturday of July, park yourself on the banks of the Sumida River for the **Sumidagawa Hanabi Taikai** (Sumida Fireworks Big Show)—the impact of 20,000 fireworks cannot be exaggerated enough. Numerous lesser **pyrotechnic displays** light up the summer skies; for a list, explore the Tōkyō Convention and Visitor's Bureau website (www.tcvb.or.jp). The annual **Samba Carnival,** on the last Saturday of August, gathers dancers and spectators on Kaminari-mon-dōri for

TŌKYŌ

Brazilian abandon in its multi-colored glory. Late August also brings Shikoku's **Awa Odori** dancers, inviting a crowd of up to 10,000 to get it on around Koenji Station, and the smooth sounds of the **Tōkyō Jazz Festival** (www.tokyo-jazz.com).

Mid-November brings **Rooster Fair** (Tori-no-ichi; www.torinoichi.jp), for which celebrants purchase bamboo rakes. The most prominent festivities are at the Ōtori Shrine in Asakusa. The annual **Tōkyō International Film Festival** (www.tiff-jp.net), Asia's largest, is typically in late October or early November. Asakusa celebrates **Hagoita-Ichi** at Asakusa Kannon Temple in mid-December, with merchants selling handmade symbolic wooden paddles. The **Tōkyō Millenario** (www.nifty.com/millenario), a young pup in the city's festival scene, is an illuminating end-of-year event in Marunouchi, featuring light sculptures and glitz to spare.

The **Metropolis Visitors' Guide** (http://metropolis.japantoday.com/vg/events.asp) can tell you what time the festivities go down, as well as clue you in to many more events than are listed here. **Tōkyō Tourism Info** has an extensive online events search (www.tourism.metro.tokyo.jp/english/eventsearch) for Tōkyō and surrounding areas; the **Tōkyō Visitor and Convention Bureau** has a listing of the biggies (www.tcvb.or.jp/en/infomation/6event/event_top.html).

An anthropologist uncovers the city behind the skyscrapers

"**G**et out of the city!" I've been told many times. Tōkyō is not the "real" Japan, say guidebooks and casual acquaintances. To experience Japanese culture in its undiluted forms one must get out into the countryside, they tell me. Simply untrue—Tōkyō *is* Japan: the main line, the pure source. Samuel Johnson said "When one is tired of London, one is tired of life, for there is in London all that life can afford." Ditto for Tōkyō.

But it's a hard city to find. It's easy to be overwhelmed by the densely packed grays and browns stretching from horizon to horizon. The newcomer's typical first views of the city—from the windows of an airport bus or a *shinkansen* (bullet train)—are disappointing. Many visitors quickly infer that the city is a huge, sprawling, indistinct jumble.

You have to learn to read the city in a different way to appreciate it, to learn to see it the way a resident sees it. Tōkyō is a city of places, regions, neighborhoods, not of linear order, nor great vistas, nor easily accessible monuments. Tōkyō is experienced by its residents at a micro-scale that is hard for visitors to grasp at first, and this scale is organized around a particular experience of urban space, social life, culture, and history.

The first point to bear in mind—both for getting around and for understanding the background of the city—is the long-standing distinction between *shitamachi* (the low-lying regions near the Sumida River, east of the central city) and *yamanote* (the hilly districts west of the central city). *Shitamachi* was historically the merchant district while *yamanote* was the *samurai* district of the city; today *yamanote* is the quintessential middle-class region of the city, and it gives its name to one of the major transportation arteries around which Tōkyō is oriented.

The central core of Tōkyō is surrounded by a loop rail line (the Yamanote Line) and a recently completed loop subway line (the O-Edo Line); a dozen subway lines crisscross inside these loops and another dozen private railroads extend outward from these loop lines. Major districts of Tōkyō (such as Shinjuku, Shibuya, Shinagawa, Ueno, or Ikebukuro) are stops on the Yamanote Line where the circles and spokes connect. These and other districts are the major way-stations and landmarks for Tōkyōites navigating their city. The Yamanote loop defines one important side of the city: middle-class Tōkyō and the suburbs that developed in the 20th century, west of the old city.

The Yamanote loop stands in contrast to the Sumida River, which runs north-south just to the east of modern central Tōkyō (e.g., the Ginza, Nihonbashi, Marunouchi). The Sumida River defines the other historically significant half of the city, the older mercantile *shitamachi* districts of Edo (as Tōkyō was known before 1868). Until the early 20th century, the river was the city's lifeline, lined by markets, merchant districts, and pleasure quarters. In the 20th century, as Tōkyō converted to a city of rail and moved toward the west, the river fell into disuse, but the Sumida (particularly the far bank, "East of the River") retained an air of old-fashioned mercantile life. The river has recently been revitalized, and in popular imagination it still evokes the older cultural traditions of the city.

Around these two arteries of Tōkyō past and present—the Yamanote loop and the linear Sumida—the city is laid out as a patchwork of distinct regions: Tōkyōites navigate the city by thinking of key districts, sub-districts, and sub-sub-districts. Instead of looking for linear connections (for example, streets with sequential numbering), Tōkyōites see the city as made up of regions, each with a general character. Tōkyō addresses identify regions, districts, and places within places. To know that a shop or restaurant is located in Shinjuku's Kabuki-chō (a raucous entertainment district) or in Minato-ku's Akasaka 5-chōme (where politicians and elite businesspeople entertain each other in discrete elegance), is more important (from a distance, at least) than knowing precisely where each shop is on a single grid. And the entire address system is set up accordingly, to identify districts and then places within districts. Famously, street names and street addresses are rarely used. Reaching the district, then finding the specific place, is a perfectly sensible way to navigate an immense metropolis. And often the key district, the place that begins the associations of place and character, is centered on a rail or subway station.

Underneath the high-rise complexes, above the high-speed subway lines, in between the elevated highways, Tōkyō is built on a pre-industrial city, evident both in the landscape as a whole and in the organization of urban life around districts and neighborhoods.

The twists, turns, and contours of the modern city reflect its origins as a castle town called Edo, established in the late 14th century. Tokugawa Ieyasu, who unified Japan during the late 16th-century civil wars, occupied Edo in 1590, and immediately made the town his headquarters, recognizing its strategic advantages commanding both the Kantō Plain, Japan's largest agricultural region, and a great bay; better yet, it was far-removed from the intrigues of the imperial capital in Kyōto, several hundred miles southwest. Ieyasu was named shōgun (supreme military ruler) in 1603, and during the following century and a half, Edo grew from 10,000 or 15,000 residents to almost a million.

The social and cultural structure of the city was created by the dynamic interaction of a warrior elite with an increasingly wealthy and sophisticated merchant class, which divided the city between the somewhat hilly districts of *yamanote* (literally, "the foothills") west of the castle where *samurai* lived, and the lively merchants' districts in *shitamachi* ("beneath the castle") east of the castle along the Sumida River. Many cultural landmarks of Japanese life—woodblock prints, *kabuki* drama, *sumō* wrestling, *geisha*, and sushi—originated in the *shitamachi* districts of Edo, products of the area's spendthrift culture. In pre-modern times, the *samurai* districts were characterized by careful attention to duty, obligation, status, and austere formality, while the *shitamachi* districts were colorful, carefree, and devil-may-care. These stereotypes were no doubt as overdrawn in the Tokugawa Period as they are today, but nonetheless, the differentiation of the groups—now cast in terms of the lifestyles, relationships, and entertainments of white-collar salaried employees in *yamanote*, and those of self-employed merchants, artisans, and industrialists in *shitamachi*—remain a key distinction in today's Tōkyō.

During the first century of Tokugawa rule, the structure of Edo was transformed not only by massive population growth, but also by the defensive needs of the castle. Moats were dug and rivers were rechanneled to create a spiral of defensive waterways around the castle. The excavated dirt filled in the bay along the mouth of the Sumida River, creating islands and canals which served as markets and merchant districts. Bridges and gates—guarding entryways to the city as well as setting off one neighborhood from the next—were part of the city's defensive structure, as was a street plan of narrow, twisting streets, which prevented large mobs from gathering and which, if the castle ever came under attack, would confuse would-be invaders. Much of this street-plan remains: canals filled, bridges dismantled, streets widened, but confusing twists and turns left intact.

When the Emperor Meiji moved his court from Kyōto to Edo (renamed Tōkyō, meaning "Eastern Capital") in 1872, all political power was consolidated into a single national capital for the first time in roughly eight centuries. The Emperor occupied the highest symbolic ground in Japanese civilization, and the Imperial Palace was considered the central point in the city. Ever since the 1870s, to visit Tōkyō is "going up" (a naïve newcomer to the city is called an "*onobori-san*," or "up-comer") and to leave for the provinces is "going down." Railway schedules still orient themselves in this fashion, rather than specifying trains as north- or south-bound, and Tōkyō Station, just in front of the Imperial Palace, is the zero-point for all calculations of rail distance.

Since the 1870s, Tōkyō has undergone dizzying social, cultural, economic, and physical changes, which is one reason that so little of the city's history is immediately visible. The city has been destroyed and rebuilt repeatedly—even a short list gives a sense of the impermanence of Edo and Tōkyō: the Ansei earthquake of 1856 destroyed much of the old Tokugawa city; a new western-style city was built around the Ginza, Hibiya, and Tsukiji in the late 1860s as Japan opened to foreigners; a great fire in the Ginza district wiped out the foreign finery in 1872; new districts of offices, shops, and government ministries were built in ornate Victorian redbrick or elegant beaux arts styles (a few examples of which survive around Nihonbashi, Marunouchi, and Kasumigaseki); the Victorian city almost entirely disappeared in the massive earthquake that struck Tōkyō and Yokohama in 1923, killing perhaps 100,000 and destroying roughly 700,000 buildings. A new, modern city—incorporating contemporary styles of functionalist and art deco design—was built during the 1920s as the capital of a growing Japanese empire in a building boom that was to culminate in the 1940 Tōkyō Olympics, timed to coincide with the purported 2600th anniversary of the founding of the Japanese imperial dynasty.

The Olympics never came, because of World War II, and in 1945, American air raids destroyed the city once again, leaving much of it little more than rubble. In the 1940s and 1950s, Tōkyō rebuilt haphazardly, and by the early 1960s Japan was eager to celebrate its return to peace and prosperity with the 1964 Tōkyō Olympics. In preparation, new subways, parks, stadia, and highways were built, many of the latter atop the last surviving canals and moats of the old castle town. Since 1964, reconstruction has continued almost continuously, mostly through redevelopments of particular districts, such as the skyrise complex west of Shinjuku Station, the Ark Hills complex in Akasaka, the new island of Odaiba in Tōkyō Bay, or the Roppongi Hills complex that opened in 2003. And, in the background of all new construction lurks the certainty that sooner or later the city will be struck by another major earthquake; seismologists estimate that an earthquake the magnitude of the one that occurred in 1923 will re-occur every 65 to 70 years.

So, on the macro-scale, Tōkyō is perpetually impermanent. But some things survive, among them a focus on places. The pre-industrial city was organized around neighborhoods centered on particular occupations, often established as a feudal guild. Although circumstances have obviously changed (and, in many cases, the locations as well), there are still areas in Tōkyō known for a particular trade: Tsukiji, the fish market (which moved from Nihonbashi in 1923); Jinbo-chō, the book district; Ningyo-chō, the doll district; Kiba, the lumber district; Kappabashi, the restaurant supply (and plastic food model) district; Tawara-machi, a district for Buddhist and Shintō paraphernalia; and the most famous (and least traditional) of them all: Akihabara, the electronics district.

And though such specialized neighborhoods are fewer and fewer, many older sections of the city mix residences with shops and workshops, sustaining neighborhoods where home, work, and community ties intermingle. This is where ordinary life can be seen, along a shopping street, by the gates of an elementary school, in the activities of volunteer firefighters supervising summer festivals. Tōkyō neighborhoods, at least in the older parts of town, are dense networks of institutions, economic ties, local politics, friendships, feuds, and gossip. A relatively large percentage of Tōkyō's residents are employed in family-owned firms—retail shops, restaurants, small workshops—and these are the backbone of old-fashioned community life.

Even in the suburbs, something of this pattern of neighborhood life has been re-created. As the city expanded outward throughout the 20th century (from a population of about 7 million at the start of World War II to about 12 million today, and more than twice that if you count the entire metropolitan region), it recreated a city organized around circles-and-spokes, districts, and sub-districts. Trains, not cars, are the means of daily transportation for millions of Tōkyōites, and suburban train stations are the kernels from which long tendrils of shopping streets stretch out into surrounding residential areas, creating the mix of shopping and street life that gives neighborhoods their character.

The modern city of Tōkyō—especially the ultra-modern city—will present itself to you without any effort on your part: Roppongi Hills, the enormous high-rise complex, almost a self-contained city, that opened in 2003; the clusters of department stores and arcades around Shinjuku Station; the bright lights of the Ginza; the Ferris wheels, shopping arcades, and hotels of Odaiba. But to understand the micro-scale of the contemporary city—strike out for an afternoon of neighborhood watching. Take an old subway line, the Ginza Line, for example, to Tawara-machi or Inari-chō between Ueno and Asakusa, and walk around the wholesale districts for Buddhist altars and visit Kappabashi (the district for restaurant supplies), then walk toward Ueno Station along some of the back streets. You won't see anything spectacular, but you will see the combination of homes, workshops, and community life typical of older Tōkyō. On the O-Edo Line, get off at Ryōgoku to visit the Edo-Tōkyō Museum, and then walk around the commercial district around the station, and perhaps spot a few *sumō* wrestlers who frequent the area; or get off at Monzennaka-chō, visit its famous temples and then wander through the surrounding neighborhoods, which include the old lumber district. Take a suburban railroad from one of the major hubs a few stops out to find yourself in a typical white-collar residential district of no particular fame (for example, the Inokashira Line out of Shibuya to Higashi Matsubara, or the Den'entoshi Line from Oimachi to Togoshi Kōen).

In these or a thousand other places you will sooner or later find yourself on a local shopping street. The *tatami* maker has almost certainly disappeared, the public bath house may no longer be open, and the liquor store may now be part of the 7-Eleven chain of *konbini* (convenience stores), but an hour or two spent watching people shop, watching women walking their children home, watching the comings-and-goings of people engaged in ordinary activities of daily life will demonstrate why Tōkyōites find their city so livable. It's not just the bright lights and the main streets. It's the back streets as well.

As an old Japanese proverb puts it, "sumeba, Miyako," which roughly translates as "no matter where you live, there is the capital."

Ted Bestor is Professor of Anthropology and Japanese Studies at Harvard University. He first visited Tōkyō in the late 1960s, and has been hooked on the city ever since. He is the author of many articles and two books about the city: Neighborhood Tōkyō *and* Tsukiji: The Fish Market at the Center of the World.

KANTŌ (関東)

In Japan's rush toward modernization, the impressive urban center of Tōkyō has grown to symbolize the country's success. But while technology has gradually erased hints of culture, tradition, and nature in Japan's capital, its neighboring towns have clung to their unique flavors, making the region around Tōkyō culturally rich. But Kantō, literally "east of the barrier," is also framed in opposition to historically important Kansai, "west of the barrier," and sometimes struggles to assert itself as a worthy tourist destination. To the metropolis's south lie Yokohama, a sprawling city in its own right, and temple-speckled Kamakura. Scenic Izu Hantō, Hakone's hot springs, and towering Mt. Fuji lie to its west; farther south are the seven islands of Izu-shotō. Up north find the merchant houses of Kawagoe and the sprawling natural scenery of Chichibu-Tama National Park; and farther north, pottery mecca Mashiko and the temples at Nikkō. Whichever way you turn, you'll find towns and cities that outdo Tōkyō with their cultural vivacity, historic atmosphere, and natural beauty.

HIGHLIGHTS OF KANTŌ

SOCIAL CLIMBING. Yokohama's Landmark Tower, centerpiece of the city's new Minato Mirai 21 development (p. 214), tops Tōkyō's highest skyscrapers.

HIGHER AND HIGHER. Iconic **Mt. Fuji** (p. 244) towers over the Kantō plain, inspiring locals and visitors alike to scale the volcanic slopes.

ARCHITECTURAL EXTRAVAGANCE. Learn the meaning of "opulence" among the historic and fantastic temples of **Nikkō** (p. 259).

YOKOHAMA   ☎045

The most famous American in Yokohama is Matthew Perry. Not the Matthew Perry from the television show *Friends* or such hit movies as *Fools Rush In* and *Three to Tango*, but Commodore Matthew C. Perry, who commanded the fleet of American ships that sailed into Yokohama Bay in 1859. This foreign incursion forced Japan to repeal its policy of exclusion, opening the country to trade, modern technology, and foreign cultures, and quickly making Yokohama a hub of international exchange. After the 1923 earthquake and WWII bombing, however, the city was forced to rebuild from rubble. In the last few decades, Yokohama has worked to strengthen its economy, preserve its history, and make itself independent from Tōkyō, the other city on the bay. The area around the port has been the center of redevelopment, and Japan's second largest city now sports Japan's tallest skyscraper, the 296 ft. Landmark Tower.

ON THE WEB   Yokohama: www.welcome.city.yokohama.jp

█ TRANSPORTATION

INTERCITY TRANSPORTATION

Trains: Shin-Yokohama Station is on the Tōkaido **Shinkansen** Line, which runs from Tōkyō to Fukuoka. Trains depart about every 10min, 6am-11pm. To: **Tōkyō** (15min., ¥1320); **Nagoya** (1½hr., ¥9950); **Kyōto** (2hr., ¥12,590); **Shin-Ōsaka** (2¼hr.,

¥13,430); **Hiroshima** (3¾hr., ¥17,740). The main JR line through the city is the **Negishi Line**, part of the Keihin Tōhoku Line. The cheapest way to get to Tōkyō is the **Tōkyū-Tōyoko Line** from Sakuragichō through Takashima-chō and Yokohama Station to Tōkyō Shibuya (45min., every 5-10min., ¥270). The Yokosuka Line runs to **Kamakura** (30min., ¥330) and Tōkyō Shinagawa Station.

Buses: YCAT, 2-19-12, Takashima, Nishi-ku (☎459-4800). The terminal is just off the East Exit of Yokohama Station. Go down the escalator and through Porta. Take a right before Sogō department store and take the escalators. Buses go to both Tōkyō airports. To **Narita** (90min.; every 15min.; ¥3500, round-trip ¥6500; children ¥1750/¥3150), **Haneda** (30min.; every 8-10min.; ¥560/¥1000, children ¥280/¥500. The **Narita Express (NEX)** to Narita departs from Yokohama Station (regular 2½hr., ¥1890; limited express 1½hr., ¥4180). Buy tickets at the green window on the east side of the station.

LOCAL TRANSPORTATION

Trains: The Minato Mirai 21 Line is scheduled to open in February 2004 and will run from Tōkyō Shibuya to Shin-Yokohama, Yokohama, the Minato Mirai 21 (MM21) Central District, and the Kannai area before terminating at a new Motomachi-Chinatown stop.

Subway: The Yokohama Municipal subway is more expensive and slower than the city JR lines. To **Shin-Yokohama** (20min. from Yokohama Station, every 10min., ¥230).

Buses: Local buses charge ¥210 within the city, but most sights are within walking distance of JR stations. Useful lines run to **Yamate** (#11 or 20 run from Sakuragichō Station to Minato-no-Mieru Oka Kōen-mae), to **Yamashita Park** (#8, 11, 20, 58, 89, 109, 125, 131 from Sakuragichō Station to Chūka-gai Iriguchi; weekdays the #26 from Sakuragichō Station to Marine Tower-mae), and along Hon-chō-dōri which becomes Nihon Ōdōri Ave. (parallel to the JR line and the bay). Many will become less useful when the MM21 line opens. Bus terminals are outside Yokohama (East Exit) and Sakuragichō stations. **100 Yen Buses** (www.hamarin-unet.ocn.ne.jp) run weekends and during tourist seasons (Apr. 26-May 5, July 19-Aug.31, Dec. 20-Jan. 7). ¥100 (elementary school students ¥50) per trip. The 4 lines connect MM21 with the rest of the city.

Ferries: The **Sea Bass** has 3 stops: near **Yokohama Station East Exit,** 1-10, Kinko-chō, Kanagawa-ku (☎453-7047), on the edge of **MM21,** 1-3, Minato Mirai, Nishi-ku, (☎223-2120), and at **Yamashita Park,** in front of the Yamashita Park Area (☎661-0347). Ferries run from 10am to around 7pm (¥350-600). Buy tickets at the dock.

Taxis: Heiwa Transportation Company, 3-33, Ōda-chō, Naka-ku (☎633-8181).

Car Rental: Toyota Rent-a-Car, 3-6-7, Shin-Yokohama, Kōhoku-ku (☎470-0100). From the north side of the *shinkansen* terminal of Shin-Yokohama Station, walk up to the end of the block and take a right. Toyota Rent-a-Car will be to your right on the 1st fl.

Bike Rental: Marine Tower Rent-a-Cycle, 15, Yamashita-chō, Naka-ku (☎641-7838). Take the #26 or #47 bus to the Marine Tower-mae stop and the it's across the street. Make rental arrangements on the ground floor. ¥300 for up to 2hr., ¥500 for 4hr., ¥900 for 8hr. or full day. Leave ID or a ¥10,000 bill as collateral. Open 10am-6pm.

◩◪ ORIENTATION AND PRACTICAL INFORMATION

Minato Mirai 21 (MM21) is becoming the center of the city, situated between the newer part of town, around Yokohama Station, and older parts to the south, around Kannai, Chinatown, and into the hills around Yamate and Motomachi.

Tourist Office: There are 4 tourist information centers. The **Kanagawa Prefectural Tourist Association,** 1, Sanbo Bldg., Yamashita-chō, Naka-ku (☎681-0007), has its office below the Silk Museum. It's bigger than the other offices and helpful for information on the whole prefecture. At Yokohama Station, look on the east side of the station for an **information center** (☎441-7300). For info on MM21, visit the **Minato Mirai 21 Infor-**

KANTŌ

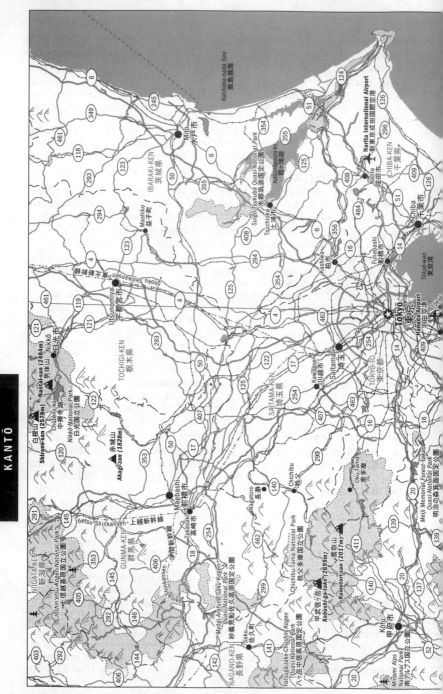

KANTŌ

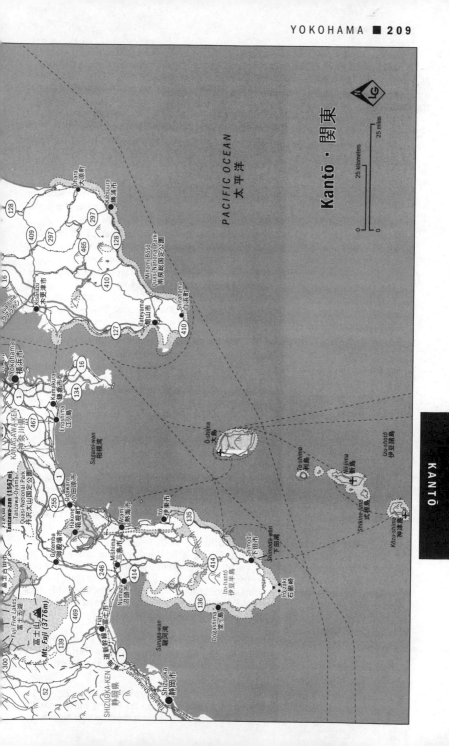

Kantō · 関東

PACIFIC OCEAN
太平洋

KANTŌ

mation Center outside Sakuragichō Station, 1-1-62, Sakuragichō, Naka-ku (☎211-0111). At Shin-Yokohama Station, look for the **Shin-Yokohama Tourist Information** (☎473-2895; open 10am-1pm) next to the railway police office.

Currency Exchange: World Currency Shop, 1-chōme, Minamiyuki, Nishi-ku (☎317-6271), on the west side of Yokohama Station. Open M-Sa 11:00am-7pm. As you come into the station's main west entrance, look for the escalator on the right. It's in the corner of the 2nd floor of the CIAL shopping center. One of few places open on Sa.

ATM: 24hr. International Citibank ATM on the 2nd fl. of the building housing the Yokohama Bay Sheraton. From Yokohama Station, exit the west side and take the stairs to the Sheraton; the ATM is on your left. Citibank offices are on the 8th fl. of the building.

Luggage Storage: There are coin lockers in nearly all of the stations. At Yokohama Station, they are toward the east side and right from the Information Desk. From ¥300. In some stations, such as Sakuragichō, the only larger-size lockers are inside the ticket-taking machines. Ask the station attendant to pass through to use the lockers.

English-language Bookstore: Takahashi Shoten Books and Stationery, 2-85 2F, Motomachi, Naka-ku (☎664-7371). Offers a good selection of English-language periodicals and books, especially travel guides and Japanese language learning books.

Library: Yokohama City Central Library, 1, Oimatsu-chō, Nishi-ku (☎262-7341). From Sakuragichō Station, head toward Noge down Hirato-Sakuragi Rd. and take a right on Noge Hon-dōri. It's on your left shortly before Nogeyama Park. Quiet study room in the basement and carrels on the 4th floor. Open Tu-F 9:30am-8:30pm, Sa-M 9:30am-5pm.

Emergency: Police ☎110. Fire or ambulance ☎119.

Police: Kanagawa Prefectural Police Department, 2-4, Kaigan-dōri, Naka-ku (☎211-1212; www.police.pref.kanagawa.jp).

Fax Office: There are two **Kinko's** stores. One is 5min. from the West Exit of Yokohama Station, 1-11-111, Kitasaiwai-chō, Nishi-ku (☎322-3377). Walk straight 2 blocks, and then take a left; it's at the end of the block on your right. The other is in the Kannai area, 4-36, Hon-chō, Naka-ku (☎640-5381). Exit Kannai Station and walk toward the bay. Take a left on Hon-chō-dōri and it's at the intersection with Bashamichi. Open 24hr.

Internet Access: There are plenty of locations in the main areas around Yokohama Station, Isezaki-chō and Noge-chō; Internet is harder to come by in other areas, but look for the Kinko's stores (see above). ▩**Animi,** 4-2-7, Minato Mirai, Nishi-ku (☎222-3316; www.animi.jp) isn't close to any stations, but you can walk or bus from Sakuragichō (15min.). Use the moving walkways and drop down to Minato Mirai Ōdori. ¥100 per hr. Hot dogs ¥250; soft drinks ¥250. **pl@net II Manga Kiss,** 1-2-1 5F, Minamisaiwai, Nishi-ku (☎311-0088). From Yokohama Station, exit on the west side and walk right, bearing right at the fork at Play City Carrot. It's on the 5th fl. of the building at the end of the block on the left. First 30min. ¥230, ¥100 every 15min. after that. Open 24hr.

Post Office: Yokohama Central Post Office, 2-14-2, Takashima, Nishi-ku (☎461-1381). From Yokohama Station's East Exit, head up the stairs, and take a right. The post office is across the street. Open 24hr. **Sakuragichō Post Office,** 1-1, Sakuragichō, Naka-ku (☎201-3716). From Sakuragichō, exit toward MM21 and head right. The post office is on the 3rd fl. in the building across from the Washington Hotel. Open M-F, 9am-6pm. **ATM** on the 1st floor, open M-F 9am-9pm; Sa-Su 9am-7pm. **Postal Code:** 220.

🏠 ACCOMMODATIONS

All the snazzy new hotels are around the Minato Mirai 21 area, but they also require loads of yen. Echigoya and the Kanagawa Youth Hostel are the cheapest options and aren't too far from train stations.

Yokohama Royal Park Hotel Nikkō, 2-2-1-3, Minato Mirai, Nishi-ku (☎221-1111; www.yrph.com). Sakuragichō Station. From the station take the moving walkways to the Landmark Building. With guest rooms on floors 52-67, your stay will be your highest-alti-

Yokohama · 横浜

♠ ACCOMMODATIONS

Business Inn Kannai, 10
Hotel New Grand, 11
Navios Yokohama, 4
Pan Pacific Hotel, 2
Star Hotel, 12
Yokohama Royal Park Hotel Nikkō, 3
Yokohama Sakuragichō
Washington Hotel, 6

🍴 FOOD

Beer Next, 5
Heichinro, 14
Maxim, 16
Shei Shei, 17
Spice Market, 18
Takasagoya, 9
Yamate Ju-Ban Kan, 19

🍸 NIGHTLIFE

Airegin, 7
Gaspanic, 1
Kushiba, 8
Windjammer, 15
Zorba, 13

Tōkyō Bay
東京湾

400 meters
400 yards

TO TŌKYŌ (30km)
東京

TO YOKOSUKA (34km)

TO YOKOSUKA

Rinkō Kōen
臨港パーク

Sea Bass

Nippon Maru
日本丸

Yokohama-Cosmo World
横浜コスモワールド

Yokohama Shinkō
横浜新港

Yokohama World Porters
横浜ワールド

Nippon Maru Memorial Park
日本丸メモリアルパーク

Yokohama Art Museum
横浜美術館

Mitsubishi Minato Mirai
Industrial Museum
三菱みなとみらい技術館

Yokohama Maritime Museum
横浜マリタイムミュージアム

Landmark Tower

Cosmo Clock
コスモクロック

Tokyu Toyoko Line
東京急行線

Animi

Kinko's

Yokohama Archives of Cultural History
横浜開港資料館

Silk Museum
シルク博物館

Hikawa Maru
氷川丸

Sea Bass

Marine Tower
マリンタワー

Yamashita Kōen
山下公園

Yokohama Doll Museum
横浜人形の家

Harbour View Park
ハーバービュー公園

Kanagawa Prefectural
Tourist Association

Zenrin-mon
善隣門

Tenchi-mon
天長門

Foreigner's Cemetary
外国人墓地

Kantei-byo
関帝廟

Kita Mon
北門

Japan Newspaper Museum

Yokohama Kōen
横浜公園

City Hall
市庁舎

Yokohama Stadium
横浜スタジアム

Museum of Cultural History

Yokohama City Central Library
横浜市中央図書館

Iseyama-Jinja
伊勢山皇大神社

Kamonyama Kōen
掃部山公園

Nogeyama Zoo
野毛山動物園

Nogeyama Kōen
野毛山公園

Keihin Kyuko Line · 京浜急行線

Ōdori Kōen
大通公園

Takashimachō
高島町

Tobe
戸部

Sakuragichō
桜木町

Hinodechō
日ノ出町

Koganechō
黄金町

Kannai
関内

Yokohama
横浜

KANTŌ

tude night in Japan. But the Royal Park doesn't rely on height to impress the ladies—the lobby's museum-like appearance is mirrored in the high-quality rooms. Fitness club and pool, restaurants and lounges, and specialty shops. Parking ¥1500. Check-in 2pm. Check-out noon. Singles from ¥29,000; doubles ¥33,000; twins ¥39,000. Executive suites add ¥5000, bling bling. Bay views have a ¥1000 min. additional charge. ➎

Navios Yokohama, 2-1-1, Shinkō-chō, Naka-ku (☎633-6001). Sakuragichō Station. From the station, cross Kisha-michi Promenade, pass Unga Park Navios, and look left. A 10min. walk. Location is a bit inconvenient, but you'll be minutes from shopping centers, food courts, Cosmo World theme park, and MM21. The 3rd fl. Seamen's Club offers billiards and booze, and looks out over the Bay bridge and shopping centers. Breakfast ¥900. Check-in 2pm. Check-out 10am. Singles ¥8000; doubles ¥16,000; twins ¥15,000; Japanese-style rooms ¥18,000. Credit cards accepted. ➌

Pan Pacific Hotel, 2-3-7, Minato Mirai, Nishi-ku (☎682-2222; www.panpacific.com). Sakuragichō Station. From the station, take the moving walkway to Landmark Plaza Shopping Center. Walk through the plaza connecting with Queen's Square shopping center; it's at the end. Contemporary hotel in MM21; impressive lobby sports palms and a ceiling mural. Houses expensive French, Chinese, and Japanese restaurants and an Italian cafe. Check-in 2pm. Check-out 11am. Rooms from ¥35,000. ➎

Hotel New Grand, 10, Yamashita-chō, Naka-ku (☎681-1841; www.hotel-newgrand.co.jp). Sakuragichō Station. From the station take the #26 bus to Marine Tower-mae; the hotel is on the same block. Alongside Yamashita Park, it's an affordable luxury hotel, offering great views of the bay and MM21. Parking ¥1000. Check-in 2pm. Check-out noon. Singles from ¥10,000 with shower, ¥16,000 with bath; doubles from ¥29,000 in the main building and ¥31,000 in the New Grand Tower. ➍

Echigoya Ryokan, 1-14, Ishikawa-chō, Naka-ku (☎641-4700). Ishikawa-chō Station. From the station South Entrance, walk to the right down Motomachi-dōri. After 2 blocks, Echigoya will appear on the 2nd floor of a building on the right side. Although the lobby is cluttered with small toys, the rooms are all spacious *tatami* rooms. Not close to the city center, but it's still pretty hip. Curfew midnight. Reserve up to 3 months ahead. ➌

Kanagawa Youth Hostel (HI), 1, Momijigaoka, Nishi-ku (☎241-6503). Sakuragichō Station. From the station, exit toward Noge and take a right immediately, following the JR line about 2 blocks. Take a left at the 1st stoplight, go over the small bridge and up the hill, and it's on the right. Single-sex dorms. Public bath. Managers are very particular—fold your sheets and pay on time, or risk being barked at. Breakfast ¥530, at 7:30am. Towels ¥150-¥200. Laundry ¥200. Check-in 5pm. Check-out 10am. Lockout 10am-5pm. Curfew 11pm. Members ¥3050; nonmembers ¥4000. ➊

Business Inn Kannai, 2-3-9, Suehiro-chō, Naka-ku (☎261-5255). Kannai Station. From the North Exit, cross the street heading away from the bay and take a right. Take a left 1 street before Isezaki Mall Shopping Street, and it's on the 2nd block. Male-only capsule hotel in the slightly-shady-at-night Isezaki-chō district. Rooms with locker, 2 towels, and a gown. Reception holds bags. Nice 6th-fl. bath area and game room. Reception until 4am. Check-in 4pm. Check-out 11am. Lockout 11am-4pm. ¥3600. ➋

Star Hotel, 11, Yamashita-chō, Naka-ku (☎651-3111; www.starhotel.co.jp). It's easiest to take a cab, but you can also take the #26 bus from Sakuragichō Station to Marine Tower-mae. If you're looking for something along Yamashita Park a bit more reasonable than the Hotel New Grand, try the Star. Rooms fairly standard. Summer rooftop beer garden; set meals from ¥4000 include 2hr. all-you-can-drink. Parking ¥1000. Breakfast ¥1300, lunch ¥1000, dinner ¥2500. Check-in 2pm. Check-out 11am. Weekdays singles from ¥9000; twins ¥14,000; doubles ¥15,000. Weekend rates higher. ➍

Yokohama Sakuragichō Washington Hotel, 1-1-67, Sakuragichō, Naka-ku (☎683-3111; reservations ☎221-0489; www.yokohama-s-wh.com). Sakuragichō Station. From the station East Exit, walk straight ahead. It's across the street to the right.

Lobby on the 5th fl. Outside Sakuragichō Station and within walking distance of Minato Mirai 21 and the Kannai area. The convenience continues inside, with a Family Mart, restaurants, and stores in the building. Check-in 2pm. Check-out 10am. Singles from ¥9500; doubles ¥16,000; twins ¥20,000. Add ¥2000 for a bayside view. ❹

FOOD

The restaurants in Yokohama are like the temples in Kamakura—there are lots, and the best are hard to find. Make sure you try a bowl of Yokohama-style *rāmen*, a soy-based broth with spinach, *nori* (seaweed), and pork tenderloin. Most shopping centers have food courts.

Beer Next, Akarenga 2 3F, 1-1-2, Shinkō, Naka-ku (☎226-1961). Sakuragichō. From the station cross the Kisha-michi Promenade. The Red Brick Warehouses are at the far end of the island, and Beer Next is in the larger one. Combines refurnished warehouse atmosphere, great beer, and solid food. Half a rotisserie chicken ¥1300. Pizzas and pastas for the same price. Wash it down with Guinness (¥550) or other beers. For dessert, accept nothing less than their creme brulee (¥700). Open daily 11am-11pm. ❸

Takasagoya (たかさご家), 2-13, Jōbanchō, Naka-ku. (☎228-0308). Kannai Station. From the station, exit the bay side of the South Exit and head left, but make a quick right down a bush-lined walkway. It's on the left of the next block. Yokohama-style noodles. Simple menu—*rāmen*, cabbage *rāmen*, pork *rāmen*, and spring onion *rāmen*. 3 sizes of the regular (¥600, ¥700, ¥800) and pork tenderloin (¥800, ¥900, ¥1000). ❷

Shei Shei, 138, Yamashita-chō, Naka-ku (☎681-5554). From the Kanteibyō, walk 1 block down and take a left onto the smaller alley-like Hong Kong Rd. It's on your left. Visit this 3-table restaurant at lunch for their ¥500 specials—usually chicken, beef, fish or spicy tofu with rice and soup. Dinner won't cost much more. ❷

Maxim, 143, Yamashita-chō, Naka-ku (☎212-2322). From Zenrin Gate at the head of the main Chinatown road, Maxim is a short walk to the right. A perfect dessert after gorging on Chinese food. Bubble tea ¥250. Sweet dumpling ¥80. Open 10am-9pm. ❶

Yamate Jūban-kan, 247, Yamate-chō (☎621-4466). Next to the Yamate Museum on Yamate Hon-dōri; plan on stopping by during your tour of Yamate. A good 30min. walk from the Ishikawa-chō JR Station, or take a bus from Sakuragichō Station or Yokohama Station to Motomachi Kōen-mae and it's a block down the street on your right. Cafe on the 1st fl. and French gour-

THE HIDDEN DEAL

THE O-BENTO BAR

At the far end of the Motomachi shopping street, past all of the Lacoste and Luis Vuitton stores, past the foreigner bars and gourmet French restaurants, a small restaurant serves up the most famous of all Japanese lunchtime foods: the *bento* box lunch.

Referred to casually as "O-bento" in Japan, these are a treasure chest of Japanese snacks, with rice and radish thrown in on the side. All made portable in a rectangular plastic container, rubber-banded to keep it together.

Marin offers a variety of different Japanese and Chinese foods in its boxes, making a perfect snack for a long day of shopping. Choose four items for ¥550, five items for ¥650, or six items for ¥780. Among the choices are vegetables cooked *tempura* style, chicken meatballs, lotus hearts, fried tofu, cooked seaweed, radish chunks, pieces of fried chicken, spinach, bean sprouts, and more.

You can take your o-bento to go or go one flight of stairs down, to the spiral staircase that shoots up behind the counter to the second floor tables. Better yet, at night this bastion of the *bento* becomes a bar, serving up *sho-chu, sake,* whiskeys and beer. *(1-87, Motomachi. From Ishikawa-chō Station, walk down Motomachi-dōri. When you see the Maedabashi Bridge on your left, take a right and your 1st left; it's on the 2nd block on the right. ☎651-0057. Open M-Sa 11am-4pm for bento, bar open 7pm-3am.)*

met restaurant on the 2nd. Cafe specialty coffees from ¥440. Soup and salad lunches around ¥1300. Make reservations to eat upstairs—the Kaika Steak set meals (from ¥4800) are famous. Open daily 11am-9pm. ❹

Spice Market, 4-179, Motomachi-chō, Naka-ku (☎641-0043). Ishikawa-chō Station. From the station, walk up Motomachi-dōri and it's on the left, 2 blocks after Nishin-no-hashi St. A brand-new basement Thai/Chinese restaurant with cushiony chairs and dim-colored lighting. Menu organized by cooking style; the fried dishes, like fried tofu (¥450) and Nampla chicken, are small but tasty. You have to order drinks with your food—juice or soda ¥500, teas ¥350, cocktails ¥650. Some regional beers on tap; Hemp Seed Beer from Niigata and some Thai beers available bottled (¥600). ❸

Heichinrō, 149, Yamashita-chō, Naka-ku (☎681-3001; www.heichin.com). Kannai Station. Exit the station on the south side and walk past Yokohama Stadium, turning left through the gate. After 3 blocks, bear right through the main Chinatown gate; it's on the 2nd block. One of Chinatown's nicest restaurants, with backlit flower arrangements and hordes of microphone-wearing waiters. The Yum Cha menu includes spring rolls, dumplings, and tapioca (¥380-900). Set courses ¥4000-15,000; individual dishes ¥1800-3200. Open daily 11am-11pm. Reservations recommended. Credit cards accepted. ❹

⦿ SIGHTS

Nearly all of the museums in Yokohama mention their relevance to the opening of the port. They are scattered all over, but even Minato Mirai 21 has a good selection of cultural activities. Most of the non-museum sights are the green spaces that border port areas, or architecturally interesting buildings both new and old.

MINATO MIRAI 21

■ **LANDMARK TOWER.** The Landmark Tower is Yokohama's attempt to one-up Tōkyō's massive skyscrapers—it looms over the rest of the bay skyline. At 296 ft. tall and 70 floors, it's Japan's tallest skyscraper. It is the centerpiece of Yokohama's MM21 district and contains everything a human needs, short of a school system. Most floors contain office space, but the tower also houses the Yokohama Royal Park Hotel and the Landmark Shopping Center. There are two ways to get to the top. You'll pay to take the under-10-second ride to the second highest floor—the elevator is the fastest in the world—but there are plenty of ways to entertain yourself once there: caricaturists, performing monkeys, and cafes are only part of the fun, and the view alone is well worth it. On a clear day you can see Mt. Fuji in the distance and North Korea building up stocks of nuclear warheads. A night view is just as thrilling—the earth looks like a vast web of lights stretching to Tōkyō. The other way to get sky-high involves at least as much money as the first. From the lobby of the Royal Park Hotel, take the elevator to the 68th or the 70th floor. The 68th floor has three restaurants: **Le Ciel** ❺, a French restaurant; **Shikitei** ❺, a Japanese restaurant; and **Kō-en** ❺, a Chinese restaurant. Each will set you back ¥2000-3000 for lunch or ¥6000-¥8000 for dinner. Reservations are a must. The 70th floor holds banquet rooms and the **Sirius Sky Lounge** ❹. Sirius offers an expensive lunch buffet (¥3500, seniors ¥3000, elementary school students ¥2000). On the 69th floor is the **Sky Garden**. *(From Sakuragichō Station take the covered moving walkways to the entrance for the Sky Garden. http://www.landmark.ne.jp. Sky garden open M-F 10am-9pm, Sa 10am-10pm; July 20-Aug. 31 daily 10am-10pm. ☎ 222-5030. ¥1000, high school students and seniors ¥800, elementary and junior high students ¥500, children 4 and above ¥200.)*

■ **MITSUBISHI MINATO MIRAI INDUSTRIAL MUSEUM.** The technology exhibited in this museum is incredibly diverse. You'll be blown away by Mitsubishi's technological know-how as soon as you enter, as there's a huge Wind Power Generator swirling in the entrance. Nearly all of the exhibits, save video presentations, are translated into English, so it's easy to follow along. There are plenty of interactive games and displays and an impressive collection of scale model trains, boats, and airplanes. The highlight, however, is the helicopter simulators, which take you over the Grand Canyon and Mt. Fuji. *(Mitsubishi Jūko Yokohama Bldg., 3-3-1, Minato Mirai, Nishi-ku. From Sakuragichō Station, take the moving walkway and go down the stairs to Minato Mirai Ōdori. It's on the corner of the next block. ☎ 224-9031; www.mhi.co.jp/museum. Open Tu-Su 10am-5:30pm. ¥500; junior high and high school students ¥300; elementary school ¥200.)*

YOKOHAMA MODERN MUSEUM OF ART. The building that houses the Yokohama Modern Museum of Art is incredible in its own right, with an impressive columned entrance gallery. The museum has six galleries, three drawn from its own permanent collection. Displays generally feature a link to Yokohama, focusing on photography. The other three galleries house rotating exhibits, which emphasize Yokohama's role in Japan's cultural history. *(3-4-1, Minato Mirai, Nishi-ku. From Sakuragichō Station, take the moving walkways and go down the stairs on the left to Minato Mirai Ōdori. Take a right at the corner and a left on the Grand Mall Park; the museum is on your left. ☎ 221-0306; www.art-museum.city.yokohama.jp. Open Su-W and F-Sa 10am-6pm. ¥500; high school or college students ¥300; elementary or middle school students ¥100.)*

⬛ NIPPON MARU AND MARITIME MUSEUM. Parked in the famous No. 1 stone dock of Yokohama, which dates back to 1898, the **Nippon Maru Training Ship** is an example of pre-war nautical engineering. It carries the world's longest working diesel engines and has racked up 54 years of training Japanese sailors, transporting war supplies, and taking repatriation voyages. The Japanese audio that plays overhead while you tour the boat has an English equivalent. If you're lucky, you'll see volunteer sailors furling or unfurling the sails. Across from the dock is the **Yokohama Maritime Museum,** which has five exhibits tracing the history of the Nippon Maru, the port of Yokohama. *(Open July-Aug. 10am-6:15pm; Nov.-June 10am-4:45pm.)* A display of scale-model ships follows the evolution from wooden Edo-era seacraft to ocean-liners and modern oil tankers. *(2-1-1, Minato Mirai, Nishi-ku. From Sakuragichō Station, take the moving walkways toward the Landmark Tower, but take the stairs on the right after the escalators. Entrance to the Nippon Maru is straight ahead. ☎ 221-0280. Open Tu-Su 10am-5pm; July-Aug. 10am-6:30pm; Nov.-Feb. 10am-4:30pm. ¥600, elementary and junior high students ¥300. Admission to Nippon Maru includes museum entrance.)*

IN RECENT NEWS

PORT OF THE FUTURE

Five decades after WWII, Yokohama is rebuilding, with the Minato Mirai 21 development project. Started in 1981, shortly after Mitsubishi Heavy Industries, Ltd. decided to relocate its Yokohama shipyard, Minato Mirai 21 is connecting the public and private sectors to develop the waterfront.

The goal is a complete revitalization of Yokohama's port that still maintaining Yokohama's history. New developments are designed around remains from previous eras—namely stone docks and brick warehouses.

The development is the perfect way to consolidate Yokohama—slated to open in February 2004, it will run from T⁻ky⁻ Shibuya through Yokohama to the new Motomachi CHinatown Station, between Yamata and Motomachi, Chinatown, and the harbor.

The district is meant to beautify the area. Height regulations for buildings are based on distance from the port—the closer you get, the lower the buildings, allowing a view of the port from the top of every building, and allowing viewers from the port to see the whole city. All of the areas bordering the port are grassy, and over 40% of the total land area have been designated as green areas.

WIth earthquake-proof berths for trade, massive emergency water tanks, and the Yokohama Marine Disaster Prevention Complex, it's clear that this development was built to last.

COSMO WORLD. You'll probably notice part of Cosmo World as soon as you get to Yokohama: the Cosmo Clock 21, the world's largest timepiece and third largest ferris wheel. A variety of other rides include log flumes, roller coasters, and merry-go-rounds. There are also some food options and a Beer Terrace during the summer. Cosmo World is open all night on New Year's Eve and has lengthened hours during holidays. *(2-8-1, Shinkō, Naka-ku. From Sakuragichō Station, walk along the moving walkway, then take the stairs down to the right. Walk along Sakura-dōri past the Nippon Maru, and Cosmo World will be on your right. There is also another section in the Shinkō District. To get there, just cross the bridge farther up Sakura-dōri and it'll be on your right. ☎ 641-6591; www.senyo.co.jp. Open Mar. 21-Nov. 30 M-F 11am-9pm, Sa-Su 11am-10pm; Dec. 1-Mar. 19 M-F 11am-8pm, Sa-Su 11am-9pm. Admission free. Rides vary in price up to ¥700.)*

KANNAI AREA

■ **YOKOHAMA ARCHIVES OF HISTORY.** This museum chronicles events using materials from the archives. Everything except the special exhibit is translated, making this the best of Yokohama's historical museums. The old British Consulate building was established as the Archives in 1981; the Tamasuka Tree in the courtyard is supposedly grown from the roots of the tree depicted in the painting of Perry's landing—the last living witness of the signing of the Kanagawa Treaty between the US and Japan in 1854. Displays trace the opening of Yokohama port and its repercussions on the country. The Great Kantō Earthquake is also covered. *(3, Nihon Ōdori, Naka-ku. From Kannai Station's South Exit, walk toward Yokohama stadium and turn left onto Minato Ōdori, then right after the stadium and your 1st left. At the 2nd light take a right; the Archives will be on your right. ☎ 201-2100; www.kaikou.city.yokohama.jp. Open Tu-Su 9:30am-5pm. ¥200, elementary and junior high school students ¥100; reading room only ¥100.)*

NEWSPARK: THE JAPAN NEWSPAPER MUSEUM. Newspark commemorates Yokohama as the home of the first Japanese newspaper. A series of exhibits show the role of newspapers in Japan's history. Many second floor displays are untranslated, but the comic books, newspapers, maps, and other printed materials are still fun to look at. The third-floor exhibits about the historical importance of newspapers have much more English. Fourth floor exhibits explain how contemporary news is gathered, including a rather silly dramatization of a modern newsroom. The museum's old printing blocks and presses are especially impressive. *(11, Nihon Ondōri, Naka-ku. From Kannai Station, exit the south side and take a left before the stadium. At the edge of the stadium take a right and the 1st left onto Nihon Ōdori. The museum is on the 3rd block on the right. ☎ 661-2040; www.pressnet.or.jp/newspark/English_0.html. Open Tu-Su 10am-5pm. ¥500, high school students ¥300, elementary and junior high students ¥100.)*

YOKOHAMA PREFECTURAL MUSEUM OF CULTURAL HISTORY. This museum follows the history of Kanagawa Prefecture from its earliest periods to the modern day. While the English translation is usually limited to a summary at the beginning of displays, some impressive scale models and dioramas don't require much explanation. If you haven't visited Kamakura, this can be a great way to experience its central attraction—through a scale model of the Butsuden from Engaku-ji and a full-sized model of the Shariden. *(5-60, Minaminakadōri, Naka-ku. From Kannai Station, exit on the north side and follow the tracks, taking the 2nd right onto Bashamichi Ave. The museum is 6 blocks on the left. ☎ 201-0926. Open Tu-Su 9:30am-4:30pm. ¥300, students under 20 ¥200.)*

YAMASHITA PARK AREA AND CHINATOWN

YAMASHITA PARK. Opened in 1930, this park allows picturesque strolls along the port. More recently, the park has become the center of the July 20 fireworks festival. Fountains and statues are sprinkled through the park; the statue of the water goddess was donated by San Diego, Yokohama's sister city. The **Hikawa Maru**, a 1930s ocean liner, is docked near the park and open to visitors. The ship isn't as great as the Nippon Maru, but its lobby evokes old ocean liner movies. The Beer Garden is open during the summer; entrance is ¥200. *(Yamashita Kōenchisaki, Yamash-ita-chō, Naka-ku. ☎641-4362; www.hmk.co.jp. Open 9:30am-6pm, later during the summer. ¥800, with Marine Tower ¥1300, with Marine Tower and Doll Museum ¥1550; elementary and junior high students ¥400/¥650/¥750; ages 3-5 ¥300/¥450/¥450.)*

MARINE TOWER. If you've been to the top of the Landmark Tower, the view from the Marine Tower isn't as exciting, but it's one that you can't get from the Landmark: you can see all of the MM21 skyline and Yamashita Park. Your ticket also gets you into a small exhibit of mechanical toys and discounts admission to **Birdpia**, an aviary of international birds you can feed. *(15, Yamashita-chō, Naka-ku. Take the #26 bus from Sakuragichō Station to Marine Tower-mae. ☎641-7838; www.hmk.co.jp. Open daily Jan.-Feb. 10am-7pm; Mar.-July and Sept.-Dec. 10am-9pm; Aug. 10am-10pm. ¥1300, elementary school students ¥650, ages 3-5 ¥450.)*

SILK MUSEUM. The two floors of this exhibit are both very impressive—the first shows the process of silk-making, and the second delineates silk's role in Japanese history. The first floor displays live silkworms and *kimono* woven from silk produced by the museum's worms. The second floor has a great display of Japanese fashion. *(No. 1 Silk Center Bldg., Yamashita-chō, Naka-ku. Kannai Station. Exit south, pass the stadium and take a left. It's on the right after the 4th light. Alternately, take a Yamashita Park-bound bus to Osanbashi. ☎641-0841; www.silkmuseum.or.jp. Open Tu-Su 9am-4:30pm. ¥500, seniors ¥300, high school and college students ¥200, elementary and junior high ¥100.)*

YAMATE/MOTOMACHI AREA

YAMATE, MOTOMACHI, AND THE HARBOR VIEW PARK. While most of the Western-style buildings in this area were destroyed by the 1923 earthquake, buildings from elsewhere have been moved here in an effort to historicize the city. The **Yamate Museum** has the best display of actual artifacts from when the bluff around Motomachi was inhabited by foreigners. *(247, Yamate-chō, Naka-ku. ☎622-1188. Open 11am-4pm. ¥200, students ¥150.)* The Foreigner's Cemetery is not open to the public, but a walk along the fence will strike travelers with the weight of the city's history. You can take a bus to Minato-no-mieru Oka-mae, and walk from there back to Motomachi, or walk from Ishikawa-chō Station up to the Italian Hill houses and then around to the Harbor View Park. None of the houses are individually striking, but it's a nice walk and each house has its high points—plus they're all free. The **Ehrismann Residence** exemplifies the beginnings of modern architecture. *(1-77-4, Motomachi-chō, Naka-ku. ☎211-1101. Open 9:30am-5pm. Free.)* **Berrick Hall** is an interesting Spanish-style building with stucco walls and a tiled roof. *(72, Yamate-chō, Naka-ku. ☎663-5685. Open 9:30am-5pm. Free.)* Pick up a map of the Western-style houses at any one of them. The **Harbor View Park** offers the closest view of the Yokohama Bay Bridge, a nice sight on a misty day, and a rose garden to walk through.

◨ SHOPPING

Yokohama is blanketed in shopping centers, to the extent that even hard-core consumers find it unnecessary to go to Tōkyō. **Yokohama Station** has an expansive array, both above and below ground, including Lumine, Porta, the Diamond, and Joinus. **Minato Mirai 21** has huge retail complexes. The **Landmark Plaza,** connected to the Landmark Tower, offers plenty of stores, but as if five floors weren't enough, all three of Queen's Tower buildings have a **Queen's Square** shopping area in the basement. Cross to the Shinkō District and you'll find the **World Porter's** with a grocery store and food court on the first level, and more shops above. The **Red Brick Warehouses** look like museums, but they too are shopping centers. Closer to

Chinatown, **Motomachi-dōri** has shops from Louis Vuitton to exclusive *o-bento* restaurants. South of Kannai Station you can find **Isezaki-chō**, a smallish shopping street lined with restaurants, bars, *pachinko* parlors, and Manga Kiss stores.

 NIGHTLIFE

Nightlife centers on Kannai and the areas near Chinatown, but it's safe to assume that Minato Mirai 21 will develop its own nighttime flavor in the near future.

Windjammer, 215, Yamashita-chō, Naka-ku (☎662-3966). Kannai Station. From the South Exit, take a right and pass the stadium, taking another right on the 2nd block through the green and white Chinatown gate. It's on the left of the 2nd block. All aboard for a jazz cruise, mateys! Hardwood planks and pictures of ships deck the walls. Jazz performances every night. Main dishes from ¥1300, beer on tap ¥600, Heineken ¥700, Guinness ¥750. Cover Su-Th ¥300, F-Sa ¥500. Open M-Sa 6pm-2am, Su 6pm-1am.

Kushiba (くしば), Benzo Bldg. 2F, 3-48, Benten-dōri, Naka-ku (☎663-4774; www.kushiba.net). Kannai Station. From the North Exit, follow Kannai Ōdori 7 blocks, and turn right. It's on the 2nd fl. on the right. A cozy dimly-lit bar offering varied music and drink specials. Tu all drinks ¥300. W is "Ladies Day"—drinks are ¥100 for women. Good selection of international beers and liqueurs. Open daily 5pm-midnight.

Airegin, 5-60, Sumiyoshi-chō, Naka-ku (☎641-9191; www.angel.ne.jp/~air-gin). Kannai Station. From the North Exit, walk up Kannai Ōdori Avenue to the 1st stoplight and take a left. Airegin is on the right of the 2nd block, on the 4th fl. Small, cozy jazz bar filled with so much jazz paraphernalia that it's a mystery how they got the piano up to the 4th fl. Free M night workshops—the same night as the everything-for-¥500 drink special. Cover usually ¥2000-2300; depends on band. Open 3:30-6:30pm (no live band, no cover), 7:45-10:30pm (live band, cover). Credit cards accepted.

Zorba), 201, Yamashita-chō, Naka-ku (☎681-7766). Kannai Station. From the South Exit, pass the stadium and take a left through the green and white Chinatown gate. Take your 3rd left, and it's on the corner, on the right of the 2nd block. A tiny shot bar and a great last stop. Try the feta cheese or Greek salad (¥800) to replace some lipids after a long night out. Yebisu on tap, Greek selection (Mycos) in the bottle, and a nice array of liquors. Open 11am-6pm (cafe), 6pm-4am (bar). Credit cards accepted.

Gaspanic, 4-8-1, Minato Mirai, Nishi-ku (☎680-0291; www.gaspanic.co.jp). Quite a walk from Sakuragichō Station, but the Minato Mirai Line will improve things. On the east side of Jack Mall, at the end of Grand Mall Park. One of Yokohama's most famous bars. Huge neon sign draws crowds nearly nightly. Happy Hour daily 6-9:30pm, all drinks ¥300. Th drinks ¥300 all night. No open-toed shoes or sandals allowed. Game at Gamepanic (open 10am-midnight) or snack at the cafe (open Su-W 11am-midnight, Th-Sa 10am-midnight), below the bar. Open Su-W 6pm-12am, Th-Sa 6pm-5am.

FESTIVALS AND EVENTS

Yokohama has a tremendous **fireworks display** on July 20 in the harbor, close to Yamashita Park, but the 6000 rounds of fireworks are visible from almost anywhere along the bay. Hotels with good views fill up in advance, so make reservations or forage for space in Yamashita Park. The **Port Opening Commemorative Festival** on June 1 and 2 celebrates Yokohama as an international port. There are fireworks, though not on July's scale, and some museums allow free entrance.

DAYTRIPS FROM YOKOHAMA

SHIN-YOKOHAMA RĀMEN MUSEUM. Entering the Rāmen Museum feels like entering a movie theater—but what you don't know is that you'll be playing a part in a historical documentary. On the first floor, you'll be swept through the history of Japan's most famous noodle. Imported from China, freeze-dried or pan-fried and sold as instant *rāmen* in bags from 1958, cupped in a portable bowl beginning in 1971—these noodles have many forms and flavors. There's little English on the displays, but they're still visually interesting. You can see *rāmen*-creating utensils, the evolution of *rāmen* packaging, *rāmen* ingredients, and unique regional versions. There's a souvenir store for instant *rāmen*, bowls, and utensils. The basement, however, is the museum's real feature. The bottom two floors are a pseudo-amusement park and museum, built in the style of 1958 Tōkyō. It's like a Disney ride, as the vendors of the Dime Store or the Shot Bar play along with the illusion. *Kami-shibai* or "paper play" performances—an old Japanese method of storytelling—occur weekdays around 1:30, 3:30, and 7:30pm. Seven *rāmen* restaurants represent regional variations. One is a limited-term restaurant selected by staff members. A Japanese pamphlet lists each *rāmen* by thickness of the soup and noodles. All stores serve regular bowls (around ¥900) and "mini" bowls (¥550); the latter are designed to allow visitors to slurp several samples. *(2-14-21, Shin-Yokohama, Kōhoku-ku. Shin-Yokohama Station. From the north side of the station walk up the right side and go 2 blocks; take a left and your 1st right. It's on the left. ☎471-0503; www.raumen.co.jp. Open M-F 11am-11pm, Sa 10:30am-11pm. ¥300, elementary students ¥100.)*

KAMAKURA (鎌倉)　　　　☎0467

For many Japanese, Kamakura is a tourist destination or vacation stop an hour south of the capital. During the warm months, crowds of uniformed middle and high schoolers swarm the city to visit the dozens of temples and shrines between the coast to the south and forested hills to the north. The beaches are a hot windsurfing spot and are open for swimming during the summer—Natsume Soseki's most famous novel, *Kokoro*, opens with swimmers on the Kamakura beaches—but the religious sites are year-round attractions. For every temple that gets thousands of visitors in one day, however, there are three or four quieter shrines for the lone visitor to stumble upon. The giant brass Daibutsu, Kamakura's most famous attraction, was constructed in 1252 to replace a wooden Buddha destroyed by storms. Much like this artifact, the city itself is built to withstand tsunamis and typhoons during the summer. Other past disasters have included fires, occurring in nearly every temple over the last 700 years, and most recently the Great Kantō Earthquake. Given the city's hardiness through all these trials, it's a good bet that Kamakura and its temples will be around for another 1000 years.

ON THE WEB	Kamakura: www.city.kamakura.kanagawa.jp

📠 TRANSPORTATION

Trains: Kamakura Station, 1-1-1, Ko-machi (☎24-1725), located at the center of town between Hachimangu Shrine and the coast. The **JR Yokosuka Line** runs through Kamakura. To **Tōkyō** (1hr., every 5-10min., ¥890) and **Yokohama** (30min., every 5-10min., ¥330). The private **Enoden Line** starts from Kamakura and heads west to **Enoshima** (25min., every 12min., ¥250) and **Hase** (10min., every 12min., ¥190).

Local Buses: Bus fare is ¥170 for most destinations and ¥190 for more remote areas. Six bus stops are gathered at the concourse. Buses from the #2 post run north toward Kenchōji and Engakuji; the #3 runs southeast through Anyoin, Myohoji, and Ankokuronji; the #4 and #5 run towards Hachimangu and continue on to Sugimotodera and Jomyoji; the #6 runs southwest to Hase and the Daibutsu.

Taxis: Taxis line up on either side of Kamakura Station and are available at some of the main sights. Alternatively, you can call **Kamakura Taxi** (☎22-0496).

Car Rental: Nippon Rental Car Urban Net, 2-22-15, Yuigahama (☎23-2761).

KANTO

Bike Rental: Rent-a-Cycle (鎌倉の名所めぐりは、レンタサイクルで !), 1-1, Komachi (☎24-2319), on the east side of Kamakura Station to the right around the corner and up an incline from the locker room. Weekdays 1st hr. ¥500, additional hr. ¥250; full-day ¥1500. Weekends ¥550/¥250/¥1600. Open daily 8:30am-5pm.

⚡ ORIENTATION

Kamakura Station is in the city's center, a short walk from **Hachiman-gū** and the main shopping areas. **Komachi-dōri,** the main strip, starts at the station and runs toward the shrine. Before arriving at Kamakura Station, the JR Yokosuka Line (blue) stops at **Kita-Kamakura,** just above a small cluster of temples. Some of the oldest temples lie to the east, accessible by foot or bus. More buses and the Enoden train line run west along the coast, connecting Kamakura Station with Hase, Eno-shima, and other beaches perfect for windsurfing.

❓ PRACTICAL INFORMATION

Tourist Office: Tourist Information Center, on the east side of Kamakura Station, directly to the right after exiting. They have a list of lodgings. For English maps you're better off at **City Hall** (鎌倉市役所), 18-10, Onari-machi (☎23-3000). Go through the underpass west of Kamakura Station, take your 1st right and go 1 block. Cross the street, staying left, and pass the police box. Go up the incline and it's ahead on the left.

Tours: The **Odakyu** counter (☎24-2714; www.enoden.co.jp) is left of the east side of Kamakura Station. They run 4 bus tours around Kamakura. Half-day tour in morning ¥2470, afternoon ¥2250; 4hr. tour ¥4400; 6hr. tour ¥6900. In Japanese only.

Banks and Currency Exchange: There are several banks on the east side of Kamakura Station. Change money on the 2nd fl. of the **Bank of Yokohama,** 1-6-21, Komachi (☎23-3131), right of the station. If you don't have your passport, try the **Bank of Tōkyō Mitsubishi,** 1-5-4, Komachi (☎22-2390), straight ahead from the East Exit.

ATM: Post office ATMs (see below) handle international transactions and accept AmEx.

Luggage Storage: Next to Kamakura Station's East Exit. Small ¥300, medium ¥400.

Library: Kamakura Public Library, 20-35, Onarimachi (☎25-2611). From Kamakura Station west side, go toward Kinokuniya, take a left at the light, walk 5min. past the school, and take your 1st right; it's at the end of the street on the left. English-language periodicals. Open M-W and Sa 9am-5pm, Th-F 9am-7pm.

Emergency: Police ☎110. Fire or ambulance ☎119.

Police: 1-8-4, Komachi (☎23-0110). From Kamakura Station east side, cross the bus concourse and take a left on Wakamiya-oji; the office is at the 1st corner on the right.

24hr. Pharmacy: Family Mart, 1-2-16, Komachi (☎22-4123). From Kamakura Station east side, walk down the street to the right; Family Mart is on the right after Starbucks.

Internet Access: There are no Internet cafes or Kinko's stores in Kamakura. The access point closest to Kamakura and Kita-Kamakura is in Ōfuna, 10min. and ¥150 away on the Yokosuka Line. To get to **Manga Kiss,** 1-11-20, Ishihara Bldg., 4th fl. (☎42-2883), exit Ōfuna Station on the east side and head to the right for a few minutes; it's in the building opposite the monorail. First 30min. ¥250, every 15min. after that ¥100.

Post Office: Kamakura Post Office, 1-10-3, Komachi (☎22-0418). Cross the bus concourse on Kamakura Station's east side; it's on Wakamiya-oji, 1 block right. Open M-F 9am-7pm; Sa 9am-3pm. The **After Hours Counter** has stamps and postcards, and postal **ATMs.** Open M-F 8am-9pm, Sa 9am-7pm, Su 9am-7pm. **Postal Code:** 248.

Kamakura · 鎌倉

🔺 ACCOMMODATIONS
Classical Hotel Ajisai, **3**
Hotel New Kamakura, **6**
Kamakura Kagetsuen
   (HI), **13**
Shangri La Tsuruoka
   City Pension, **5**

🍴 FOOD
Amish Cooking, **2**
Ashinaya, **10**
De Niimes Taru Taru, **7**
Furusato Kamakura, **9**
Kamatama Udon, **12**
Marion Crepes, **11**
Milk Hall, **4**
Motomachi Union, **8**
Yamasato, **1**

🏠 ACCOMMODATIONS

There are plenty of choices along Wakamiya-oji and Dankazura, but most accommodations in the center of town have hefty price tags. Hotel New Kamakura, however, is a steal right next to the station. The Kamakura Kagetsuen on the beach is another good option, a 7min. walk from Hase Station.

Hotel New Kamakura, 13-2, Onari (☎ 22-2230). From Kamakura Station west side, walk to the right along the Yokosuka Line; it's on your left—look for the parking lot. The hotel motto, "Zero Minutes from the Station!" is almost true: you can see (and sometimes hear) the station from the hotel. Run by a family with friendliness in their genes. Talk to the parking attendant to book a room. 2 shared baths. Laundry ¥200. Check-out 10am. If you're a lone ranger, ask for room #26 (¥3500), separate from the main buildings. Singles ¥4000 weekdays, ¥5000 weekends; Western- and Japanese-style twins ¥10,000/¥12,000; Japanese-style rooms in new building ¥18,000. ❷

Kamakura Kagetsuen (HI), 27-9, Sakanoshita (☎25-1236; www.kamakuranet.ne.jp/ ~hase.yh). From Hase Station, cross the tracks and follow them right 1 block. Take a left, then a right at the road along the beach; the hostel is a few minutes farther. Dormitory-style. Breakfast 7:30-8am, dinner 6-7pm. Check-in 3:30-8pm, no later than 6pm for dinner. Check-out 10am. Lockout 11pm-7am. Rates skyrocket during festivals or high season, so book up to 3 months in advance. ¥3150, nonmembers ¥4150. This is the cheaper section of Kagetsuen Hotel, which offers bunkbeds or a Japanese-style setup (¥6500, weekends ¥7500, 2 meals included). ❶

Shangri La Tsuruoka City Pension (シャングリラ鶴岡), 1-9-29, Yukinoshita (☎25-6363). From Kamakura Station east side, cross the bus concourse, turn left on Wakamiya-oji, and walk 5min.; it's on the left, 3rd fl. On Dankazura, famous for azaleas and cherry trees. Close to sights (2min. to Hachiman-gū). Singles and doubles are identical rooms (2 beds). Check-in 3-9pm. Check-out 10am. Reserve 1 month ahead for weekends. High-season singles ¥8500; doubles ¥15,000; deluxe twins ¥17,000; quads ¥30,000. Low-season ¥8000/¥13,000/¥16,000/¥26,000. Credit cards accepted. ❸

Classical Hotel Ajisai, 1-12-4, Yukinoshita (☎22-3492). From Kamakura Station east side, cross the bus concourse and turn left on Wakamiya-oji; it's on the right near Hachiman-gū Shrine. All doubles with fridge, TV, and hot water dispenser. 4th fl. rooms have views of cherry trees and the shrine. From ¥6500 per person; with breakfast ¥7500. ❸

🍴 FOOD

The neighborhood around Kamakura Station has plenty of restaurants and bars—try **Komachi-dōri,** more like a shopping mall than a street, for varied options. There are restaurants around and even inside some temples, so keep your eyes open.

📖 Kamatama Udon (釜卵うどん屋), 3-7-21, Hase (☎22-2264). From Hase Station, take a right, pass the light, and it's on your left. Why visit the Daibutsu when you can eat it? The featured dish is Buddha *udon* (¥800), a bowl of noodles resembling the Buddha's face, with an egg for the 3rd eye. Perfect place for lunch between the Hase Kannon and the Daibutsu. Standard bowl from ¥500. Summer special: Bukkake *udon* with corn, cucumber, spring onions, egg, and red ginger. English menu. Open 11am-5pm. ❶

Motomachi Union, 1-7-13, Komachi (☎24-8211). From Kamakura Station east side, cross the bus concourse and turn left on Watamiya-oji; it's on the left before Dankazura and the 2nd *torii*. Standard grocery store on 1st fl., but 2nd fl. has a cafe, household goods and international beers, wines, and liquor. Coffee, tea, and juices from ¥300. Cake and coffee ¥500. Open daily 10am-11pm. Credit cards accepted. ❷

De Niimes Taru Taru (デ・ニームタルタル), Matsuhide Bldg. 2F, 1-5-6, Komachi-dōri (☎24-9352). Exit Kamakura Station's east side and head toward Komachi-dōri; look for the Heineken sign. Italian-Asian *izakaya*. Cozy place for a drink, snack, or light meal. Cocktails and Heineken ¥600. Wide assortment of whiskeys and liquors from ¥500. Pizza and pastas from ¥800. English menus. Open daily 5pm-2am. ❸

Amish Cooking, 2-4-23, Yukinoshita (☎25-2533). From Kamakura Station, follow Komachi-dōri past the shopping area. It's on the left, across from Yabusame Rd. Quaint cafe decorated with quilts and New England crafts. Thick ham sandwich ¥700. Huge bowl of clam chowder ¥750. Cake from ¥400. Open daily 11am-4pm. Credit cards accepted. ❷

Furusato Kamakura (ふる里), 2-12, Onarimachi (☎23-3328). From Kamakura Station west side, head left on Onarimachi-dōri; it's on the first left corner. Basic *okonomiyaki* (pork, cabbage, eggs) from ¥600; with rice cakes from ¥800; with fried *soba* from ¥750. If you're not that hungry, try the "healthies"—the *okonomiyaki* "skin" with toppings like *kimchi* with shrimp or cuttlefish. Open Tu-Su. ❷

Milk Hall (ミルク・ホール), 2-3-8, Komachi. (☎22-1179; www.milkhall.co.jp). From Kamakura Station east side, walk 2 blocks down Komachi-dōri, take a left and then the next left. It's on the right in a small alley. Groovy jazz cafe connected to an antique store, **Full House.** French salon meets *tapas* bar. Coffee and cocktails ¥550-1000. *The Milk Hall Times* has info on antique meetings and live jazz. Open daily 11am-11pm. ❷

Yamasato (山里), 321, Yamanouchi (☎22-2156). From Kita-Kamakura Station, walk along the north of the tracks and take a left on Meigetsuin-dōri; it's on the 1st corner on the left. Japanese sweets and noodles. *Kaki-gōri* (shaved ice) from ¥500 in summer. Warm rice cakes from ¥500 in winter. Open daily from 10:30am. Last order 5pm. ❷

Ashinaya (あしなや), 1-4-18, Komachi (☎22-1011). Exit Kamakura Station east side and walk to the right; it's across from Starbucks. Kick back with a huge bowl of *rāmen* and catch the latest Hanshin Tigers game. Basic bowl ¥500; *samamen, miso rāmen,* butter *rāmen* ¥730. Open M 11am-9pm; Tu-Su 11am-10pm. Closed some Tu. ❶

Marion Crepes, 1-16-20, Hase (☎23-8819). From Hase Station, take a right, go past the stoplight, and look for the blue awning; it's on the main street towards the Daibutsu. Everything is ¥200-450. Open Su-F 10am-5:50pm, Sa 10am-6:30pm. ❶

⊙ SIGHTS

The temples around Kamakura are its main attractions. In the city proper, the biggest draw is **Hachiman-gū Tsurugaoka,** the shrine built by Minamoto Yoritomo when he established the first shōgunate in Kamakura. Farther north and closer to Kita-Kamakura Station are **Engaku-ji** and **Kenchō-ji,** the top two of the five great Zen temples of Kamakura. To the southwest and closer to the shore is the famous **Daibutsu.** Near that is the eleven-headed **Hase Kannon.** The sights may look dauntingly spread out, but trains, buses, and your feet will propel you quickly from one to the next.

TSURUGAOKA HACHIMAN-GŪ SHRINE (鶴岡八幡宮)

2-1-31, Yukinoshita. From Kamakura Station east side, cross the bus concourse, and take a left on Wakamiya-oji; it leads directly to the shrine. ☎22-0315; http://hachimangu.or.jp.

The original Hachiman-gū Shrine is closer to shore, but when Minamoto Yoritomo established the first Kamakura shōgunate in 1185, he had this new shrine dedicated in thanks for the Minamoto victory over the Taira family. **Dankazura,** the avenue approaching Hachiman-gū from the south, extends between two of the shrine's three red *torii* gates (the third is farther south, near the beach). The bridge to the grounds spans a narrow channel connecting the two parts of **Genpei Pond,** designed by Yoritomo's wife. Coming up to the shrine, you'll cross **Yabusame,** the avenue on which the annual Horse Archery Contest is held. The first red shrine building is the **Mai-den,** where Yoritomo forced Shizuka, the wife of his brother and rival Yoshitsune, to dance for him and his *samurai.* To the left of the steps leading to the main shrine is a **gingko tree,** the site of the third shōgun Sanetomo's assassination. **Hongu,** the main shrine building, was dedicated to the 15th emperor of Japan to elevate Kamakura's importance in relation to Kyōto. Left of the Hongu, the **Homotsu-den** houses portable shrines, screen paintings, a set of armor, and several masks. (Open 9am-4pm. Adults ¥100, elementary school students ¥50.) Heading back down the steps, don't miss the black-lacquered **Shirahata Shrine** to the right of the main shrine; it's the Minamoto family shrine. Follow the path back toward Yabusame and the **Kamakura National Treasure Museum,** 1-1, Yukinoshita (☎22-0753) will be on your left. It has a permanent collection of Kamakura-era statues and a rotating exhibit. (¥300, elementary and middle school students ¥100.) Hachiman-gū hosts dozens of festivals through the year. The New Year's Day festival brings in nearly 2 million people. On the second Sunday in April, dancing

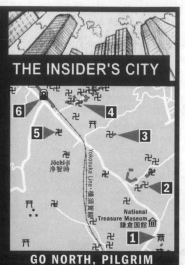

THE INSIDER'S CITY

Jōchi-ji 浄智時

Yokosuka Line - 横須賀線

National Treasure Museum 鎌倉国館

GO NORTH, PILGRIM

Head to north Kamakura for a concentrated look at some of the town's most beautiful temples.

1 Approach **Hachiman-gū** from Dankazura, passing the two red gates and a row of cherry trees. Spend some time exploring the large complex (p. 223).

2 Meander among lovely juniper bushes at **Kenchō-ji,** Kamakura's top-rated Zen temple, and its oldest (p. 224).

3 Admire the bamboo groves and hydrangea at **Meigetsu-in,** and ponder the rock garden (p. 224).

4 Heavily-wooded **Engaku-ji,** the second of Kamakura's top five Zen temples, holds regular *zazen* sessions (p. 225).

5 **Tōkei-ji** was famous as a refuge for women running from their husbands. Today, the mossy gravestones of these women stand behind the temple under tall cypress trees (p. 225).

6 Hop on a JR train at Kita-Kamakura back to Tōkyō or Kamakura (p. 229).

on the Mai-den commemorates Lady Shizuka. The third Sunday in April is the Horseback Archery festival, once meant to keep the skills of *samurai* sharp. The Grand Festival is on September 15, with more horseback archery on the 16th.

OTHER SIGHTS

■**DAIBUTSU (KOTOKU-IN; 大仏).** As a visitor approaches Kotoku-in, the Daibutsu's green head looms through the main gate, obscured by pine trees. Over 13m tall and weighing more than 121 tons, the statue is one of Kamakura's most impressive artifacts. Minamoto Yoritomo first dreamed of building a Buddha in Kamakura to rival the famous one in Nara, but he never lived to see his dream come to fruition. Idanono Tsub-one, a lady of his court, worked with a priest to fulfill his wish. They raised enough money for a wooden sculpture in 1243, but this was later destroyed by a storm. The current bronze Buddha dates from 1252 and has also seen its share of storms: a tsunami in 1498 destroyed the wooden covering. Now the Buddha sits, aged by time and weather, gazing out to the coast. *(4-2-28, Hase. From Hase Station, take a right and follow the right side of the street 10min. ☎22-0703. Open daily Apr.-Sept. 7am-6pm; Oct.-Mar. 7am-5:30pm. ¥200, students ¥150. You can enter the hollow Daibutsu daily 8:00am-4:30pm; ¥20.)*

KENCHŌ-JI (建長寺). The oldest of Kamakura's five famous Zen temples, Kenchō-ji was founded in 1253 by **Rankei Doryu,** a Chinese monk. The seven **juniper trees** in front of the Butsuden date back at least to the 14th century; according to legend, they grew from seeds Rankei brought from China. These gnarled, towering trees and the Bonsho bell are the only objects remaining from the original temple. Passing the trees, let your eyes adjust to the darkness of the **Butsuden** building, and the face of the wooden Buddha will appear. The grounds are usually overrun with schoolchildren and tourists, but if you follow the path to the left of the Hojo, it leads through quiet forests and up stairs to the Han-sobo. The **Ten-en Hiking Trail** starts to the right of the Hansobo. It takes about 2hr. to finish, but if you just walk up the first two sets of stairs, you'll get a nice view of Kencho-ji through the trees. The temple holds *zazen* meditation sessions on Fridays and Saturdays from 5pm at the Hojo. The first time, you'll pay ¥300 for a copy of the text, but after that just show the text and it's free. *(8, Yamanouchi. From Kita-Kamakura Station, walk along the north side of the tracks; 10min. past Meigetsuin-dōri, Kenchō-ji will be on your left. ☎ 22-0981; www.kenchoji.com. Open daily 8:30am-4:30pm. ¥300, children ¥100.)*

MEIGETSU-IN (明月院). Meigetsu-in is what remains of the older temple Zenko-ji; the rest was destroyed during the Meiji purges in 1868. In front of the main hall lies a rock garden whose largest rock is perfectly aligned with a circular window on the main hall. Covered with foliage and flowers, Meigetsu-in is usually quieter than other temples, but in June the number of visitors skyrockets with the blooming of the **hydrangea** which lines the stairs up to the main gate. At other times of the year, the temple's maze-like setup and array of plants—from Dr. Seuss-like bushes to bamboo trees and irises—create a charming atmosphere. *(189, Yamanouchi. From Kita-Kamakura Station, follow the north side of the Yokosuka Line, take a left on Meigetsuin-dōri, and walk to the end. 15min. from Kenchō-ji. ☎24-3437. Open daily July-May 9am-4pm; June 8:30am-4:30pm. ¥300.)*

HASE-DERA (長谷寺). Although the grounds at Hase-dera are slightly more artificial than those of Kamakura's other temples, the main attraction, the Hase Kannon, is worth the trip. Legend has it that in 721 a monk named Tokudo carved two 11-headed statues of the Kannon from one camphor tree. One statue was thrown into the sea and washed up 15 years later in Nagai; from there it was moved to Kamakura. In 1342, Ashikaga Takauji, founder of the Muromachi shōgunate, paid for the gold leaf which covers the statue today. A much smaller replica of the Kannon stands in front of the Real McCoy—for a long time, the original was hidden from the public. The **Jizō-dō**, up the stairs on the way to the Kannon, is lined with rows of Jizō statues, blessing babies who were aborted, died young, or were stillborn. Left of the Kannon-dō, the **Homotsukan treasure house** houses artifacts such as calligraphy by Toyotomi Hideyoshi. Before taking a break at the picnic tables overlooking Yuigahama beach, check out the **Kyozo,** a rotating sutra storage facility. *(3-11-2, Hase. From Hase Station, take a right and then a left at the stoplight. ☎22-6300; www.hasedera.jp. Open daily Mar.-Sept. 8am-5:30pm; Oct.-Feb. 8am-4:30pm. ¥300, age 12 or younger ¥100. Treasure house open Tu-Su 9am-4pm.)*

ENGAKU-JI (円覚寺). Set in the wooded, hilly area around Kita-Kamakura Station, this temple is the most picturesque of the five great Zen temples. The enclosing trees give the enormous grounds an intimate feel. **Tokimune Hojo,** shōgun during the 13th-century Mongol invasions, founded Engaku-ji to commemorate the struggle. After seeing the double-tiered **Sanmon gate,** continue to the **Butsuden,** completely restructured after the 1923 earthquake. The Buddha, however, is the 14th-century original. To the right and up a steep staircase is the **Ōgane,** the original bell, donated in 1301. The **Hojo** features a garden with statues of the Kannon, many rescued from the earthquake. One of the more interesting buildings, the **Shari-den,** is off limits to the public except during the first four days of November and January. **Tokumine's mausoleum,** on the left as you approach the back of the temple, is open to visitors. *(409, Yamanouchi. From Kita-Kamakura Station, follow the Yokosuka line less than 1min.; the temple is on your left. ☎22-0478. Open daily Apr.-Oct. 8am-5pm; Nov.-Mar. 8am-4pm. ¥200, children ¥100. Mausoleum entrance ¥100; ¥500 with tea and sweets. Morning zazen at the Butsuden: Apr.-Oct. 5:30am-6:30am; Nov.-Mar. 6am-7am. Sermons at the Hojo: 2nd and 4th Su of the month 9am-10am.)*

TŌKEI-JI (東慶寺). Founded by Tokumine Hojo's widow, Kakusan-ni, as a nunnery, Tōkei-ji is often called "the divorce temple" or "running-away temple." The Kamakura shōgunate recognized it as a refuge women could go to escape an unwanted marriage, by either becoming a nun or waiting for her husband to agree to a divorce. The **Homotsu-den** has manuscripts written by women who fled to Tōkei-ji. The path through the temple leads to a cemetery next to a beautiful moss-covered cliff. The cemetery itself is shaded by a canopy of incredibly tall cypress trees. *(1367, Yamanouchi. From Kita-Kamakura Station, follow the road on the side of the station opposite Engaku-ji for 5min., and take a right at the light. Tokei-ji is past the driveway and up the stairs. ☎22-1663; www.tokeiji.com. Open daily 8:30am-5pm. ¥100, Homotsu-den ¥300.)*

SUGIMOTO-DERA (杉本寺). Founded in 734, Sugimoto-dera is believed to be Kamakura's oldest temple. Its name derives from the **three Kannon statues** it houses: during a fire in the 12th century, these statues are said to have hidden underneath a giant Japanese cedar tree. While the buildings are not as impressive as others in Kamakura, the unkempt, unraked grounds have their own charm. The staircase bypasses the original moss-covered set of stairs, blocked off with bamboo. See if you can find a hidden pathway or two (hint: one begins to the right of the red guardian statues). The Kannon themselves are not in very good condition and can't rival the Hase Kannon. Sugimoto-dera provides easy access to Jomyo-ji and Hokoku-ji, a few minutes farther down the same road on the left and right respectively. *(703, Nikaido. From Kamakura Station, take the #23, 24, or 26 bus from bus stop #5, and get off at Sugimotodera. Follow the road to your left, and the entrance is up a set of stairs. ☎22-3463. Open daily 8am-4:30pm. ¥200, elementary school students ¥100.)*

JŌCHI-JI (浄智寺). The fourth of the five great Zen temples, Jōchi-ji shares some of Tokei-ji's cypress forests and adds some bamboo, but ultimately isn't as impressive. Like many local temples, it was rebuilt after the 1923 earthquake. Continue up the road from Jochi-ji to access the **Daibutsu Hiking Trail.** *(1402, Yamano-uchi. From Kita-Kamakura, follow the road on the side of the station opposite Engaku-ji for 5min. Jochi-ji is shortly after the stoplight on your right. ☎ 22-3943. Open daily 9am-4pm. ¥150, children ¥80.)*

■ HIKING

Seven different hiking trails criss-cross the Kamakura area; the two most famous are the **Ten-en Hiking Course** (天園) and the **Daibutsu Hiking Course** (大仏). The first runs over the mountain between Zuisen-ji and Kenchō-ji, through one of the most scenic spots in Kanagawa Prefecture, and takes about 2hr. to complete. The Daibutsu Hiking Course starts down the street from the Daibutsu, to the right of the tunnel, and runs to Jochi-ji via Zeniarai Benzaiten and Genjiyama Park.

■ DAYTRIP FROM KAMAKURA

ENO-SHIMA

Half an hour from Kamakura Station on the Enoden Line is the island of Eno-shima, a perfect half-day trip if you've exhausted the hidden secrets of Kamakura and want to relax on the beach. From Enoshima Station, take a left onto the street that runs through the center of town, past the carnival-style game centers, and follow it for 25min. through the underpass and across the bridge.

Enoshima's main attractions center on the three buildings of **Eno-shima Shrine**— Hetsunomiya, Nakatsunomiya, and Okutsunomiya (you'll see them in this order)—which form a triangle on the island. Visitors usually circle Eno-shima clockwise with the option of taking a set of **escalators** up the first portion of the hilly island. *(Open 9am-4:30pm. ¥350, children ¥170.)* Eno-shima's most famous attraction is the nude statue of **Benten,** the Buddhist goddess of music and literature. Considered one of the three great depictions of Benten, the pasty nude is in a building separate from the Hetsunomiya. *(Open 9am-4:30pm. ¥150, junior high and high school students ¥100, elementary school students ¥50.)* Continuing around the island, the two other shrine buildings are less striking. The **Samuel Cocking Garden** is a botanical garden with displays of flowers from around the globe; an **Observation Tower/ Lighthouse** is accessible through the garden. *(☎23-0623. Garden and tower ¥500, children ¥250; garden only ¥200, children ¥100.)* There are plenty of places to enjoy noodles or ice cream on the way to the rugged cliff coast, Eno-shima's other attraction. The Iwaya Caves are at the farthest point, but the stairs on the return trip are brutal—you may be satisfied with admiring the waves, cliffs, and fishermen from above. *(Caves open 9am-5pm. ¥500, children ¥200.)*

NARITA (成田)   ☎ 0476

Sixty kilometers northeast of Tōkyō, Narita is home to an amiable older community that chats on the streets and in the stores. Its proximity to Narita Airport attracts visitors and crew members who join Japanese tourists in strolling the main street, Omotesandō. The city is centered geographically and spiritually around its main attraction, Narita-san Shinsho-ji. Narita is a perfect stop for those with early flights or long layovers, and for those only visiting Tōkyō, it may be worth the daytrip to experience a glimpse of traditional Japan.

TRANSPORTATION AND PRACTICAL INFORMATION. The fastest and cheapest way of traveling between downtown Tōkyō and Narita is to take the Keisei Limited Express (☎03-3831-0131; Ueno: 65min., ¥810; Tōkyō: 75min., ¥900; Shinjuku: 95min., ¥940; every 10-15min.). Depending on where you stay, the JR may be more convenient (Ueno: 90min., ¥890; Tōkyō: 100min., ¥1110; Shinjuku: 120min., ¥1280; every 15-30 min.). Both companies also service Narita Airport (Keisei: 10min., every 10-20min., ¥250; JR: 10min., every hr., ¥230). For transportation between Tōkyō and Narita Airport, see p. 110.

Just outside JR Narita Station's East Exit, the **Narita City Tourist Association,** 839, Hanazaki-chō, provides free maps and brochures. (☎24-3198. Open daily 8:30am-5:15pm.) The **Narita Tourist Pavilion,** on Omotesandō, has three floors of exhibitions and displays on Narita's history. (☎24-3232. Open Tu-Su Oct.-May 9am-5pm; June-Sept. 10am-6pm.) At both locations, you can apply for a free **Narita Welcome Card** to receive local discounts. In an emergency, call ☎110 for **police,** ☎119 for **fire** or **ambulance.** Other services include: **police,** 839-1, Hanazaki-chō; **Drug Store Avin,** 538, Hanazaki-chō (☎22-0041; open daily 9am-7pm); **Media Gate Internet Saloon,** 550, Kami-chō (☎22-1922; www.mediagate.ne.jp; ¥100 per 10min.; open daily 8am-midnight); and the **post office,** 3-15, Mabashi (☎24-0024; fax 24-0025; open M-F 9am-5pm, cash service M-F 9am-5:30pm, Sa 9am-12:30pm). **Postal code:** 286.

ACCOMMODATIONS. Numerous hotels and ryokan can be found near Narita Station, along Omotesandō, and closer to Narita Airport. **Center Hotel Narita ❸,** 922, Hanasaki-chō, is a spotless new hotel where the comfortable rooms have TVs, hairdryers, and bathrooms. Pass through the underground path of Keisei Narita station and take a right. (☎23-1133; www.narita.com/center. Continental breakfast included. Coin laundry. Fax service. Check-in 3pm. Check-out 10am. Singles ¥6000.) Simple Japanese rooms await at **Ohmiya Ryokan ❷,** 384, Naka-chō, home to an amazing beautiful wooden bath. Look diagonally left across from the Tourist Pavillion. (☎22-0119. Reservations required. ¥5000 per person; student group discount ¥3800-4000 per person. Room sizes and rates flexible.) At **Ryokan Ohgiya ❸,** 474, Saiwai-chō, spacious *tatami* rooms are decorated with scrolls, pottery, and flower arrangements and overlook a picturesque garden and pond. The owners are friendly and helpful. From the main fork on Omotesandō, continue left for 200m. (☎22-1161; www.root.or.jp/ohgiya. Coin laundry. Shuttle service to Narita Station. Check-in 2pm. Check-out 10am. Curfew 11pm. Singles ¥6000, with bath ¥7000.) Across from Naritaya International Food Store, near the East Exit of Keisei Narita Station, **Narita Kenkō Center ❶,** 802-1, Hanasaki-chō, is an option for the more adventurous, equipped with 5 baths, 2 saunas, massage chairs, relaxation corners, TV, games, a restaurant (food ¥700-1500), and myriad places to nap. It's not quite the traditional place to stay, but nevertheless a bed (or mattress) to sleep on. (☎23-1126; fax 23-0885. Open 24hr. ¥2000 entrance fee, ¥700 service charge, ¥1000 additional overnight fee. 4-person private room ¥7000, 7-person ¥13,000. Towels, robes, and soap provided.) **Business Hotel Tsukuba ❸,** 847, Hanasaki-chō, is a very basic option close to JR Narita Station. Take a left with the station's East Exit behind you. (☎22-1234; fax 24-4858. Reception 6am-midnight. Singles ¥5500).

FOOD. Restaurants, generally serving traditional Japanese food, line Narita's main road, **Omotesandō.** For snacks while strolling, try **Amataro,** 525, Hanasaki-chō, across from **The Barge Inn,** where they flip *imagawa yaki* (sweet beanpaste-filled treats; ¥80) on a special grill (open daily 9am-6pm). Heading back into Omotesandō from Narita-san Park, tasty souvenirs can be found at **Mitsubashi Shoten,**

100m past Narita-san Shinsho-ji's main entrance (sweets and *tsukemono*; open daily 9am-5pm) or **Abe Shoten,** 503-4, Kami-chō (open daily 9am-6pm), which boasts over 40 types of homemade rice crackers.

Amidst Narita's countless eel shops, **Kawatoyo ❸,** 386, Naka-chō, remains the only true specialist, preparing raw eel in the open. Their *unaju* (¥1300-1800) is unbeatable. (Open Tu-Su 10am-11pm, also open M in Jan., May, and Sept.) In business for 70 years, **Sushi Man ❸** has expanded from serving locals to welcoming crew members from around the globe. (☎22-0465. Sushi sets ¥1000-2500; rolls ¥600-1200; lunch sets ¥800. Open M and W-Su 11am-10pm. AmEx/MC/V.) Those who discover **Miyoshima ❶,** 368-2, Naka-chō, behind the main road, are pleasantly surprised at the opportunity to enjoy tea and sweets (¥500-600) atop a wooden deck with water beneath their feet and bamboo trees swaying overhead. (Green tea, coffee, ice cream ¥500. Open M-Tu and Th-Su 10am-5pm.) Flight crews crowd **Rāmen Bayashi ❷,** 533-13, Hanasaki-chō, back for another helping of the more than 20 types of *rāmen* noodles (¥550-850). The Red Chilli Pepper Soup Noodle is the specialty; beer (¥300-400) is a great complement. (☎24-3631. Open daily 10:30am-8:30pm.) Using milk from their nearby farm, **Milky House ❶,** 601-2, Azuma-chō, scoops up homemade soft-serve and ice cream (¥280-380). Turn left from Narita-san Shinsho-ji and look across from the first parking lot. (☎23-6584; www.yume-bokujo.com. Open M-F 10am-5pm, Sa-Su 9am-5pm. Closed Th Dec.-Feb.)

◪ SIGHTS. Narita's traditional sights, with Shinsho-ji as their centerpiece, could cause you to forget how close you are to über-modern Tōkyō. With the East Exit of JR Narita Station behind you, turn left after the rotary to enter Narita's main road, **Omotesandō.** From Keisei Narita Station, turn right after the rotary and keep going straight. Omotesandō is lined with endless souvenir shops and restaurants, many of which seem identical, but don't miss out on hidden gems like **Amataro** (see **Food**). Upon reaching a fork with a tall monument, keep right and head down the winding hill towards Narita's primary attraction, **Narita-san Shinsho-ji** (☎22-2111; www.naritasan.or.jp). Attracting tourists and faithfuls, this is the main temple of the Shingon Sect of esoteric Buddhism. Founded in 940 and dedicated to Fudo Myō, the god of fire, Narita-san's elaborate gates open to historic buildings such as the **Three Storied Pagoda.** Enter and view the majestic interiors of the **Daihondō** (Great Main Hall) and **Daitō** (Great Pagoda of Peace) with their extravagant decorations. Then stroll through peaceful **Narita-san Park,** gazing into ponds, walking by waterfalls, and enjoying the beautiful greenery. To learn about Narita-san's past, venture into the **Narita-san Reikokan Museum** to see its displays of history, folklore and archaeology. (☎22-0234. Open Tu-Su 9am-4pm. ¥300, ages 12-18 ¥150, under 12 free.) The **Narita-san Museum of Calligraphy** offers traditional scrolls. (☎24-0774. Open Tu-Su 9am-4pm. ¥500, age 16-22 ¥300, under 16 free.) Both are in the park.

◪◪ ENTERTAINMENT AND FESTIVALS. Both local Japanese and crew members on layover flock to British pub ◪**The Barge Inn,** 538, Hamasaki-chō, on Omotesandō, on weekend nights. Upstairs are dark wooden tables and chairs, walls lined with old books, comfortable couches, a fireplace, pool tables, darts, and foosball. Live music starts at 9pm and quickly transforms the place into a noisy dance floor. (☎23-2546. Beers ¥400-800. Spirits and cocktails ¥500. Meals ¥1000-1500. Happy Hour 5-8pm, all drinks ¥400. Open M-Th 4pm-2am, F-Su 10am-2am.) Turn left after Keisei Narita's rotary to find **The Cage** (☎24-1414), a small karaoke bar.

Narita-san Shinsho-ji hosts several major festivals. **Goma,** the sacred fire rite, and **Yakuyoke Oharai,** prayers for protection from evil, are held during Hatsumode on January 1. Famous *sumō* wrestlers and film stars arrive to throw beans wishing good fortune on **Setsubun,** around February 3. The famous **Gion Festival** is in early July (July 2-4 in 2004), and **chrysanthemum exhibitions** begin in early November.

HAKONE (箱根)   ☎ 0460

A mountainous area southwest of Tōkyō, Hakone is a favorite tourist resort best known for its numerous hot springs and breathtaking views. The gateway towns of **Odawara** and **Hakone-Yumoto** serve as convenient starting points for the commonly taken counter-clockwise tour of the area, which ends by famous **Lake Ashi**.

ON THE WEB	Hakone: www.kankou.hakone.kanagawa.jp

⊏ TRANSPORTATION

Trains: The **Odakyu Express** (☎ 5-6255) runs from Tōkyō Shinjuku to Hakone-Yumoto (110min., every 10-20 min., ¥1150). The expensive **JR Shinkansen Kodama** connects Tōkyō and Odawara (40min., every 20-30 min., ¥3640). The **Tōkaidō Line** also runs between these 2 stations (90min., every 10-30min., ¥1450). Because the JR only runs to Odawara, transfer to Odakyu lines for Hakone-Yumoto.

Local Transportation: The typical path around Hakone uses the Tozan Railway (☎ 5-5033), cable car (☎ 2-2049), ropeway (☎ 2-3052), buses (☎ 0465-22-4145 and ☎ 0465-22-3166) and boats (☎ 3-6022 and 3-6351). Costs add up, so the best option is to purchase package excursion passes. The **Hakone Free Pass** offers unlimited use of the Tozan Railway, Tozan Bus, ropeway, cruise boat, cable car and Odakyu Hakone Express Bus for 3 days. Purchased at Shinjuku, the price includes a return ticket. The pass also provides discounts at 30 tourist attractions. (☎ 03-3481-0103; www.odakyu-group.co.jp; at Shinjuku ¥5500, at Odawara or Hakone-Yumoto ¥4130, children half-price.) Weekdays, the **Hakone Weekday Pass** provides the same benefits for 2 days (at Shinjuku ¥4700, at Odawara or Hakone-Yumoto ¥3410). The **Hakone Free Coupon**, provides unlimited use of several transportation lines for 4 days, but is less convenient than the other passes. (☎ 0465-22-3166; www.izuhakone.co.jp; ¥3100, under 12 ¥1560.)

◩ THE ROUTE

ODAWARA (小田原) TO HAKONE-YUMOTO (箱根湯本). From Odawara, take the **Hakone Tozan Railway** (13min., every 20-30min., ¥300) to Hakone Yumoto, the starting point for the loop around Hakone's sights. Hakone Station, a major transportation hub, is surrounded by *onsen*, hotels, and souvenir shops. Turn left outside the station, cross the first bridge, and head up the steep slope to find the small **Hakone Local Museum**, 266, Yumoto, where paintings, pictures, and cultural artifacts illustrate Hakone's history. (☎ 5-7601. Japanese info only. Open Su-Tu and Th-Sa 9am-4:30pm. Closed last M of the month and Dec. 28-Jan. 4. ¥200, under 16 ¥100.) **Onsen spas,** good for relaxation after long train rides, are numerous here.

The **tourist information center** (☎ 5-6202), near the buses outside the train station, distributes free maps. For more assistance, walk 5min. toward the souvenir stores to the **Hakone Tourist Information Service**, 698, Yumoto, which has English speakers and houses the **Hakone Folk Crafts Hall**. (☎ 5-8911; www.hakone.or.jp/town. Open daily 9:30am-6pm. Free.) **Yajikita no Yu ❸**, 694, Yumoto, offers cheap sleeps and several indoor and open-air *onsen*. Turn left after the Tourist Information Service and take the first right. (☎ 5-6666; fax 5-5750. Check-in 3pm. Check-out 10am. Curfew midnight. Bath only ¥900, under 12 ¥500. Closed Th. 4-person room ¥16,000; 1- or 2-person room ¥12,000, available weekdays only.) Farther from the station, **Minshuku Takasugi ❷** has comfortable Japanese-style rooms. (☎ 5-6565. Check-in 3pm. Check-out 10am. Curfew 11pm. ¥5000, students ¥4500.) At **Manju Ya Nano Hana ❹**, 705, Yumoto, you can watch workers making *manju* (sweet beanpaste-filled cakes), sold on the first floor for ¥80. The second floor is a cute cafe, where plants, lanterns, pottery, and traditional sweets (¥700-850) create a soothing atmosphere. (☎5-7737. 1st fl. open daily 8am-6pm. 2nd fl. 9:30am-5:30pm. Closed 3rd Th of the month.)

HAKONE-YUMOTO (箱根湯本) TO CHŌKOKU NO MORI (彫刻の森). The **Hakone Tozan Railway** continues from Hakone-Yumoto to Chōkoku no Mori, where the main attraction is the ▧**Hakone Open-Air Museum**, 1121, Ninotaira. Turn left out of Chōkaku no Mori Station and walk ahead 100m. You emerge from a tunnel to discover a sweeping, scenic, monument-spotted forest view. Over 100 permanent outdoor exhibits by international sculptors speckle the 70,000 sq. m park. The **Picasso Pavillion** gathers 230 sculptures, paintings, and ceramics by the modernist master while works by humanist sculptor **Henry Moore** are displayed in an enclave. The museum also includes art galleries, teahouses, souvenir shops, and playgrounds. (☎2-1161; www.hakone-oam.or.jp. Open daily Mar.-Nov. 9am-5pm; Dec.-Feb. 9am-4pm. ¥1600, college and high school students and 65+ ¥1100, elementary and junior high students ¥800.) Cheap lodgings and a relaxing *onsen* meet at **Choraku ❷**, 525, Kowakidani, 5min. past the museum (☎2-2192; fax 2-4533. Bath ¥500. Check-in 3pm. Check-out 10 am. Curfew 11pm. ¥5000.)

CHŌKOKU NO MORI (彫刻の森) TO GŌRA (強羅). The **Hakone Tozan Railway** ends its winding ascent at Gora. **Gōra Park** is most easily reached by riding the cable car one stop to **Kōen Shimo**, but is also a 200m walk from Gōra Station. Apart from the usual greenery, flowers, fountains, and benches, the park boasts a French rock garden, an English rose garden, a greenhouse, and special flower exhibitions. (☎2-2825. Open daily July 20-Aug. 31 9am-9pm; Sept. 1-July 19 9am-5pm. ¥500, under 12 free.) At Kōen Kami Station, or just outside the eastern exit of the park, is the **Hakone Museum of Art**, 1300, Gōra, which features Japanese ceramics from the Jōmon to the Edo Period. Pathways lead through bamboo gardens, bush clover paths, and moss gardens with bridges and teahouses. (☎2-2623. Open Su-W and F-Sa Apr.-Nov. 9:30am-4:30pm; Dec.-Mar. 9:30am-4pm. Closed Jan. 6-12, and Dec. 25-31. ¥900, high school students ¥400, 65+ ¥700, middle school and under free.)

Services near the station include: a **tourist office**, a **post office**, 1300, Gōra (☎2-2182; open M-F 9am-5pm), and a **police box**, through the underground tunnel to your left. Dining options in Gōra are fairly limited. **Tamura Ginkatsutei ❸**, 1300-5732, Gora, serves standard Japanese fare: *tonkatsu, unajyu, soba* and vegetarian tofu cutlet for around ¥2000. Head down the stairs through the underground tunnel, take the first right turn, then take the first left after the taxi service station. (☎2-1440. Open Su-Tu and Th-Sa 11am-2:30pm and 5pm-9pm.)

GŌRA (強羅) TO SŌUN-ZAN (早雲山) AND ŌWAKUDANI (大涌谷). At Gōra, the cable car takes over, for the steep journey to Sōun-zan (10min., every 15-30min., ¥410). No special attractions there, save the view of sprawling neighboring mountains and towns from 767m up. Then change to the ropeway and hop onto a 12-person, newly renovated gondola to Ōwakudani (7min., every 1min.). Just before Ōwakudani Station the gondolas pass directly over an enormous, steaming, black-and-red cratered valley, remnant of a past volcanic eruption.

Straight out of the station and to the left is the **Ōwakudani Nature Trail**, a 630m trek through the valley. Contrary to what the name suggests, an established cement road runs through greenery, smoldering rocks, and murky *onsen* springs. Eggs blackened by *onsen* brewings are sold at a stand on the trail (¥500 per pack of 6). Though the sights are unique, the volcano emits poisonous gas, and signs warn travelers against staying too long. A section of the trail is closed due to a recent landslide. **Gokuraku Cha-ya ❷**, near the trailhead, serves noodles, *tempura*, and *katsudon* (¥700-1100) in a simple hall. (☎4-7015. Open daily 9:30am-3:30pm.)

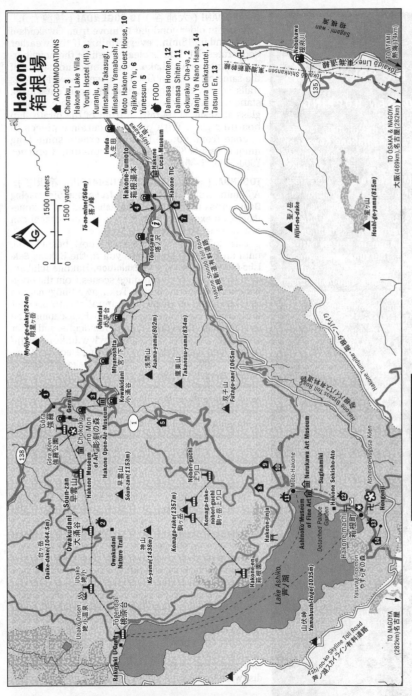

THE BIG SPLURGE

ONSEN HOPPING

Nestled in Hakone's forests, luxury resort **Hakone Kowaki-en Yunessun** is like an amusement park with spas instead of rides. The **Mori No Yu** zone offers traditional *onsen* overlooking gardens and mountains. Try soaking in an authentic wooden *taru buro*, a stone bath, a cypress bath, or the largest open-air garden bath in Hakone. The **Yunessun** swimsuit zone boasts over 20 types of co-ed open-air bath. Hop from a rose-scented bath to a *sake* bath; then try ancient Roman baths complete with Turkish foot baths. Float in the Dead Sea bath, which uses salt from the Mediterranean, or sit under the spray of waterfalls.

Complete your experience by exploring the cool forest pathways and Japanese shrines—or continue it by spending the night. Comfortable singles at the attached **B&B Pension Hakone** are a reasonable way to extend your stay. *(1297, Ninotaira. Hop on the bus to Hakone-machi and Moto-Hakone or get off the cable car at Kowaki-en Station, climb the stairs, and keep heading up the mountain. ☎0460-2-4123; www.yunessun.com. Mori No Yu open daily Mar.-Oct. 9am-7pm; Nov.-Feb. 9am-6pm. Yunessun open daily 9am-8pm. Mori No Yu ¥1800, under 12 ¥900. Yunessun ¥3500/¥1700. Both zones ¥4000/¥2000. B&B Pension Hakone: ☎0460-7-7800; www.pensionhakone.com. Singles ¥4000, Sa and some high-season dates ¥5000.)*

ŌWAKUDANI (大涌谷) TO TŌGENDAI (桃源台). Transfer to older gondolas to move from Ōwakudani to Tōgendai (18min., every 1min.). If the weather cooperates, Mt. Fuji is clearly visible; the neighboring mountains and Lake Ashi, though not sights of the same caliber, can also be viewed. Several hiking trails, equally good for short walks, begin outside the station. Paint your own teacup, bowl, plate, or *sake* glass at **Rakuyaki U-Craft**, in front of the pirate ship boarding gate. With over 100 ceramic pieces to choose from, you're bound to create something unique. (☎4-8887. Open daily 9am-4pm. Ceramics ¥900-1500. 20-30min. to fire.)

TŌGENDAI (桃源台) TO HAKONE-MACHI (箱根町). A 30min. cruise by **Hakone** or **Izuhakone Sightseeing Boat** across the famous **Lake Ashi** lands at Hakone-machi, an expensive resort area. Hakone-machi can also be reached by **bus.**

Turn left, with Hakone-machi Port behind you, until an English sign guides you to the **Hakone Sekisho-Ato (Checkpoint) and Exhibition,** Hakone Ichiban-chō. Displays there reproduce scenes from the original checkpoint, run by the Tokugawa Shōgunate to regulate guns entering the capital and to prevent lords' wives taken hostage in Edo from escaping. The exhibition displays armor, guns, handcuffs, and other *samurai* artifacts. (☎3-6635; www.hakone.or.jp/town. Open daily Feb.-Nov. 9am-5pm; Dec.-Jan. 9am-4:30pm. ¥300, under 12 ¥150.) The **Hakone Detached Palace Garden** is upstairs from the exhibition, and offers magnificent views of Lake Ashi. To find **Ashinoko Nogusa Park,** 223, Hakone, turn right with the port behind you and left at the first light, take the first right turn, and follow the road 100m. In addition to thirteen gardens of flowers collected from around the world, you'll see the temple **Hongen-ji.** (☎3-7686. Open daily 9am-4pm. ¥1000, college students ¥700, high school and junior high students ¥500, elementary students ¥300.)

Services include a **police station** across from the port and a **post office,** 79, Hakone-machi, diagonally across from the port. (☎3-6181. Open M-F 9am-5pm.) **Minshuku Yamabushi ❷,** 433, Hakone, has clean *tatami* rooms overlooking Lake Ashi. Their stone *onsen* is particularly soothing. Turn right out of Hakone-machi Port and left at the light with a sign reading "Green House Pension," or take the bus to Ashikawa Iriguchi. (☎3-6890. Check-in 3pm. Check-out 10am. ¥4000.) For affordable fresh seafood, a rarity in pricey Hakone, head to welcoming 🏮**Daimasa Honten ❸,** 63, Hakone, across from the Hakone Hotel. *Donburi* (rice bowls) with fish, including tuna, eel, *aji*, and *chirashi* are filling choices (¥1000). *Sashimi* and broiled fish sets are served on beautiful dishware for ¥2000-2500. (☎3-6723. Open daily 11am-

4pm, dinner available by reservation.) Most restaurants in the Hakone-machi and Moto-Hakone region close by 5pm. Fortunately, **Tatsumi En ❷**, 187, Hakone, serves Korean-style barbecue (¥700-900) along with basic rice and noodle dishes (¥600-800) until late. Walk past the first traffic light after turning right with Hakone-machi Port behind you. (☎3-6292. Open daily 5pm-1am).

HAKONE-MACHI (箱根町) TO MOTO-HAKONE (元箱根).

The **Suginamiki**, a narrow stone road lined by cedars, begins across from the Hakone Detached Palace Garden's parking lot and leads 2km to Moto-Hakone, where the main attraction is **Hakone Jinja**, 80-1, Moto-Hakone. From the bus station or pier, head 500m left, with Lake Ashi behind you, to the enormous red *torī* gate. A walk through a lantern-illuminated wooden tunnel leads to steep stairs and the main hall. (☎3-7123; fax 3-6669. Treasure hall open daily 9:30am-4pm. Free; treasure hall ¥300.) Across from Moto-Hakone Port, which serves the Hakone Kanko pirate ship, is **Narukawa Art Museum**, 570, Moto-Hakone, which features modern Japanese paintings. Displays change four times a year, and an observatory looks out over Lake Ashi and Hakone Jinja. (☎3-6828; www.narukawamuseum.co.jp. Open daily 9am-5pm. ¥1200, under 15 ¥600.) Although the **Ashinoko Museum of Fine Art**, 1, Hakone, isn't a uniquely Japanese experience, the Picassos, van Goghs, Renoirs, and Monets make it worthwhile. The museum is across from Narukawa Art Museum, to your left. (☎3-1600. Open daily 9am-5pm. ¥1100, high school students ¥900.)

The area's best accommodation option is **Hakone Lake Villa Youth Hostel (HI) ❶**, 103-354, Moto-Hakone, which has an *onsen*, neat Western and Japanese rooms, a balcony, and a lounge. From Futako Jaya bus stop, two stops before Moto-Hakone (coming from Hakone-Yumoto), head downhill 50m, and continue down a dirt road. The hostel is to your right before you reach the main road again. (☎3-1610. Check-in 4pm-10pm. Check-out 7am-10am. Members ¥2900.) Tucked into the serene mountains is ▨**Kuranju ❸**, 133-19, Moto-Hakone, whose spectacular open-air bath overlooks Hakone. Western-style rooms are spacious and clean, with private bathrooms. From Moto-Hakone or Ashinokōen-mae bus stops, call the hotel for pickup. (☎3-7881; fax 3-7292. Check-in 3-6pm. Check-out 10am. Weekdays ¥5500, weekends ¥7000.) **Moto Hakone Guest House ❷**, 103, Moto-Hakone, caters solely to foreign visitors, offering simple Japanese-style rooms. From Ashinokōen-mae bus stop, one stop before Moto-Hakone (coming from Hakone-Yumoto), head downhill 20m and turn left. (☎3-7880; fax 3-6578. Check-in 3pm. Check-out 10am. Coin laundry. Reservations required. ¥5000, higher weekends, holidays, and high season.) Amidst the jungle of overpriced food, Daimasa fortunately has a smaller second store in Moto-Hakone. Like most other area restaurants, **Daimasa Shiten ❷**, 65-2, Moto Hakone, is only open for lunch. The friendly owner welcomes foreigners, and is willing to cater to individual needs. Behind fish store Uwoshin, Daimasa has a patio seating about 15. (☎3-6224. *Donburi* with fish ¥1000. Open daily 11am-4pm.) To get from Moto-Hakone back to Hakone Yumoto, take the Ōdawara Iki bus (30min., every 30min., ¥930). To return to Atami, take the Atami Iki bus.

IZU HANTŌ (伊豆半島)

Sandwiched between Sagami Bay on the east and Suruga Bay on the west, Izu Hantō is 80km southwest of Tōkyō. Beaches on both coasts, mountains in the interior, and over 2000 hot springs make the peninsula a popular tourist destination.

AT A GLANCE	
CLIMATE: Pleasantly warm during the summer, mild during the winter.	**GATEWAYS:** Atami (p. 234), Mishima (p. 236), Numazu.
HIGHLIGHTS: Natural hot springs, extensive scenic beaches, interior mountains.	**WHEN TO GO:** Due to its proximity to Tōkyō, Izu Hantō gets crowded on weekends and holidays.

KANTŌ

TRANSPORTATION

From Tōkyō, the **JR Tōkaidō Line** runs to Atami and Mishima (Atami: 120min., ¥1890; Mishima: 140min., ¥2210). The *shinkansen* (Atami: 40min., ¥4080; Mishima 50min., ¥4400) and limited express (Atami: 80min., ¥3770) are significantly faster but also expensive. Atami begins with the string of towns lining Izu Hantō's east coast, ending with Shimoda and Irozaki at the tip of the peninsula. The **Itō Line** starts in Atami and runs along the east coast, connecting the many small towns through Shimoda (90-110min., every hr., ¥1890). From Itō, the **Izu Kyuko Railways** (☎0557-53-1115) also runs to Shimoda (60-80min., every 30-60min., ¥1570). Rental cars (¥5000 for 12hr.) can be found near the Atami, Mishima, and Itō train stations.

ACCOMMODATIONS

Seven youth hostels dot the Izu Hantō area (www.jyh.or.jp/english/toukai). Unless otherwise noted, they offer breakfast for ¥600 and dinner for ¥1000.

Amagi Harris Court (HI), 28-1, Nashimoto, Kawazu-chō, Kamo-gun (☎0558-35-7253). From Kawazu Station, take the Suzenji Iki bus to Gigein. Members ¥3200, nonmembers ¥4200. ❶

Izukogen Aoikaze (HI), 1250-34, Yawatano, Itō (☎0557-51-3785). From JR Izu-kōgen Station, take the Shaboten Kōen Iki bus to Omuro Kōgen. ¥3200/¥4200. ❶

Gensu (HI), 289, Shimogamo, Izu-chō, Minami, Kamo-gun (☎0558-62-0035). From Shimoda Station, take bus 3 to Shimogamo Yakuba-mae. No meals. ¥2900/¥3900. ❶

Kiya Ryokan (HI), 388, Waraho, Naka, Izu-chō, Tagata-gun (☎0558-83-0146). From Shuzenji Station, take the Juzo-do Iki bus to Waraho. ¥2900/¥3900. ❶

Sanyoso (HI), 73-1, Naka, Matsuzaki-chō, Kamo-gun (☎/fax 0558-42-0408). From Shimoda Station, take the Dogashima Iki bus to Youth Hostel-mae. ¥2900/¥3900. ❶

Shuzenji (HI), 4279-152, Shuzenji, Shuzenji-chō, Tagata-gun (☎0588-72-1222; fax 72-1771). From Shuzenji Station, take the #6 New Town Iki bus to New Town Guchi. Closed Jan. 18-22 and May 30-June 3. ¥2900/¥3900. ❶

Takasagoya Ryokan (HI), 790-1, Toi, Toi-chō, Tagata-gun (☎/fax 0558-98-0200). From Shuzenji Station, take the Toi Iki bus to Toi-baba. ¥2850/¥3850. ❶

ATAMI (熱海)　　　☎0557

To get to the rest of Izu Hantō, you'll have to pass through the fancy resort town of Atami. While beds are expensive, Atami is blessed with beautiful sights, *onsen*, and beaches. Its preeminent attraction is the **◨MOA Museum,** 26-2, Momoyama-chō, a 5min. bus ride from Atami Station (MOA Museum Iki; every 15-20min., ¥160), whose over ten rooms boast paintings, lacquered plates, pottery, and statuary. The view across Atami's woods and the ocean is breathtaking, and the golden tearoom and *nō* theater magnificent. (☎84-2511; www.moaart.or.jp. Open M-W and F-Su 9:30am-4:30pm. ¥1600, 65+ ¥1200, college and high school students ¥800, under 15 free. Discounted tickets at the tourist office.) Within walking distance of Atami Station is **Ōyu Geyser,** one of the world's three largest geysers. Until 1924, water spouted regularly at prolonged intervals; today, unfortunately, the hot water is artificially powered. If that's not steamy enough, the **seven hot springs walk** leads you past the rest of Atami's spouts. **Atami Sunbeach** is open in the summer.

From Tōkyō, reach Atami by local **JR Tōkaidō Line** (120min., every 10-30 min., ¥1890) or *shinkansen* (85min., 6 per day, ¥3190). The **tourist office,** 11-1, Tawara

Hon-chō, in the station building, has maps and pamphlets; staffers speak basic English. (☎81-2033. Open daily Apr.-Sept. 9:30am-6pm; Oct.-Mar. 9:30am-5:30pm.) In an emergency, call ☎110 for **police,** ☎119 for **fire** or **ambulance. Police** are to the right of Atami Station, and the **post office,** 4-10, Tawara Hon-chō, is farther down, on Heiwa St. (☎81-2033. Open M-F 9am-5pm.) **Postal code:** 413.

Ritzy ryokan and upscale hotels fill Atami. A cheap, bland option is the (not particularly) **Fancy Business Hotel ❷,** 10-10 Sakimi-chō, a right turn after passing through Heiwa St. on your left. (☎82-6211. Check-in 3pm. Check-out 10am. ¥4800.) Farther down the street is casual **Izu no Tyaya ❶,** 7-48, Sakimi-chō, which serves standard *teishoku* (set meals), including *udon* noodles (¥450), curry (¥500), and spaghetti (¥500-550) for amazingly low prices. (☎81-2612. Open M-Tu and Th-Su 9:30am-7pm.)

MISHIMA (三島)　　　　☎055

A gateway to central Izu Hantō, Mishima offers gorgeous rivers and ponds. Its main sight, **Mishima Taisha**, 2-1-5, Omiya-chō, sprawls over 50,000 sq. m, with a historic main shrine, a worship hall, an inner shrine, and a *koi* pond. Elegant engravings, statues, and other treasures surround the buildings. (☎975-0172; fax 975-4476.) The city park, **Rakujuen**, is just meters from Mishima Station. Bridges and stepping stones cross the park's pond and streams, pathways lead through the vegetation, and the **Rakujukan** hall hosts an exhibition. (☎975-2570. Open Apr.-Oct. Tu-Su 9am-5pm; Nov.-Mar. 9am-4:30pm. Closed Dec. 27-Jan. 2. ¥300, under 15 ¥50.)

Both the local JR **train** (150min., ¥2210) and *shinkansen* "Kodama" (60min., ¥3890) connect Tōkyō and Mishima. From Atami, take the **Itō Line** two stops (15min., every 20-30min., ¥320). The **tourist office**, 2-29, Ichiban-chō, is by the station's south exit. (☎971-5000; www.mishima-kanko.com. Open daily 9am-5pm.) There are two **post offices** near Mishima Station: Eki-mae Post Office, 8-12, Ichiban-chō (☎975-4695; open M-F 9am-5pm) and Chuo Post Office, 5-5, Chuo-chō (☎975-2101; open M-F 9am-5pm). **Mishima Green Hotel ❶**, 9-35, Kotobuki-chō, awkwardly places Western beds atop *tatami* mats, but low rates justify the oddity. Take a right with Mishima Station's South Exit behind you, go straight, and take a left at the intersection with the 7-Eleven. (☎975-6211; fax 975-3242. Check-in 3pm. Check-out 10am. Curfew midnight. Singles ¥3980; semi-doubles ¥6700.)

ITŌ (伊東)　　　　☎0557

Midway between Atami and Shimoda, Itō is a transport center for many of Izu Hantō's sights. Itō itself has little to offer besides cheap lodgings. The only sight is the unspectacular **Kinoshita Mokutaro Kinenkan**, 2-11-5, Yukawa, which displays paintings and artifacts in the converted house of a doctor/artist. (☎36-7454. Open Tu-Su Apr.-Sept. 9am-4:30pm; Oct.-Mar. 9am-4pm. Closed Dec. 28-Jan. 4. ¥100, under 15 ¥50.) More worthwhile is the **Jogasaki Coast,** accessible by #3 Kaiyō Kōen Iki bus (30min., every hr., ¥700). Jagged cliffs, formed by lava and eroded by waves, overlook the ocean and Izu-Shotō. Travelers nervously shuffle across a 48m-long suspension bridge 23m above the water; a 9km hiking trail is nearby.

Itō has several festivals of note, including the comical **Tarai-nori Kyōsō** (Washtub Boat Race). It's held the first Sunday of July at Itō Spa; participants sit in wooden washtubs and race down Matsukawa River using enlarged rice scoop-shaped oars. Celebrations of **Anjin Matsuri** (William Adams Festival), from August 8-10, include parades and fireworks in commemoration of the British shipwright.

The **Izu Line** runs between Atami and Itō (25min., every 30-60min., ¥320). From Tōkyō, the **Limited Express** "Odoriko" or "Super View Odoriko" connects through to Itō (105min., 5 per day, ¥4090-4390). The **Itō City Tourist Association**, 1-8-3, Yukawa, is inside Itō Station and offers numerous pamphlets and maps. (☎37-6105. Open daily 9am-5pm.) Other services include: **police** box, to your right outside Itō Station; **coin lockers** (¥300-400); Seifu **supermarket** and **drug store** (☎37-7185; supermarket open daily 9am-11pm, drug store daily 9am-9pm), reached by heading down the road to the right of the station; and the **post office**, 1-11-18, Yukawa (☎36-8119; www.japanpost.jp/itoekimae; open M-F 9am-5pm). **Postal Code:** 414.

By far the best option for inexpensive stays is **⬛Yamaki Ryokan ❷**, 4-7, Higashi Matsubara-chō, a gorgeous old building with pleasant gardens, a wooden interior, and an *onsen* spa. (☎37-4123; www.ito-yamaki.co.jp. Check-in 3pm. Check-out 10am. ¥5000.) The **Itō Station Business Hotel ❷**, 1-9-18, Yukawa, is in front of the train station (☎37-2233; coin laundry; check-in 4pm; check-out 10am; curfew 11:30pm; singles ¥5000, twins ¥8000, semi-doubles ¥8800) while **Business Hotel Itō ❷**, 2-2-16, Yukawa, is a left turn from the station to the waterfront, then right and down 5min. (☎36-1515; check-in 4pm; check-out 10am; ¥5000). **Iribune ❸**, 1-9-18, Yukawa, serves sushi (¥680-2000) and impressive *sashimi* boats (¥5000) from next to the Itō Station Business Hotel. (☎38-5383. Open daily 10am-10pm.)

SHIMODA （下田） ☎0558

With gorgeous views of the ocean, the mountains, and the Izu-Shotō islands, Shimoda is an attractive resort loaded with historical significance. The Kanagawa Treaty, negotiated by American Matthew Perry, opened the ports of Shimoda and Hakodate to American trade and was signed at Ryosen-ji in 1856. Townsend Harris, the first Western diplomat allowed to live in Japan, also kept house in Shimoda. Less tourist-oriented than the towns to the north, Shimoda is dotted with museums, temples, parks, and restaurants.

☞ TRANSPORTATION

From Tōkyō, both local JR **trains** (4hr., every 30min., ¥3780) and the *shinkansen* "Odoriko" (170min., 5 per day, ¥6160) serve Shimoda. **Izu Kyūkō Railways** runs along the east coast of Izu Hantō, connecting Itō and Shimoda (80min., every 30min., ¥1570). Some trains run directly from Atami to Shimoda (100min., every 30-60min., ¥1890). For local transportation, try the **rental cycle** store down the road from the post office. (☎22-1099. ¥500 per hr., ¥2000 per day.)

◪ PRACTICAL INFORMATION

The **Izukyu Travel Shimoda tourist desk**, 1-1-3, Nishihongo, is inside Shimoda Station. (☎22-3200. Open daily 9am-5:30pm.) Turn left outside the station to find a more comprehensive **tourist office**, 1-1, Sotogaoka, with English speakers. (☎22-1531. Open daily 10am-5pm.) For a guided tour in English, contact Mr. Takashi Fuki at the **Volunteer English Guide Association**. (☎23-5151; maimai-h@i-younet.ne.jp.) In an emergency, call ☎110 for **police**, ☎119 for **fire** or **ambulance**. The **post office** is at 2-4-20, Nichōme. (☎22-0601. Open M-F 9am-7pm.) **Postal code:** 415.

◪ ACCOMMODATIONS

Although beds near Shimoda Station tend to be in pricey resort hotels, two youth hostels (**Gensu** and **Sanyoso**, p. 234) are just bus rides away.

Kokumin Shukusha New Shimoda, 1-4-13, Nishi Hongo (☎23-0222; fax 22-0025). Turn right outside Shimoda Station, take another right at the 1st light, and go straight 150m. Nothing about New Shimoda actually seems new. Nevertheless, it's cheap lodging with a large *onsen*, near the station. *Tatami* rooms are fairly spacious. Friendly owner. Check-in 3pm. Check-out 10am. Curfew 10pm. ¥4500, ¥7000 with 2 meals. ❷

Shimoda Station Hotel, 1-1-3, Nishi Hongo (☎22-8885). Next to Shimoda Station, this business hotel's sole selling point is convenience. Simple rooms with unit baths, TV, and telephone. Check-in 4pm. Check-out 9:30am. Singles ¥5800; doubles ¥9800. ❸

Minshuku Chosanmaru, 713, Kichisami (☎23-3430; www.mjnet.ne.jp/chosan.) Take the Irozaki-bound bus to Kisami stop. (10min.) If you don't mind the distance from the station, Chosanmaru offers inexpensive Japanese-style lodging, complete with stone *onsen* bath, just 5min. from the beach. ¥4000. ❷

Shimoda Tokyu Hotel, 5-12-1, Shimoda (☎22-2411). An upscale resort with pleasant views overlooking the ocean, rooms here are clean and spacious. The hotel's restaurant serves a full-course seafood dinner, and a bar's attached. ¥13,500 with two meals. ❹

◖ FOOD

Shimoda's numerous sushi bars and restaurants serve fish fresh from the nearby ocean, and are clustered along Mai-mai St., to the south of Shimoda Station.

KANTŌ

Uminchu, 1-4-3, Higashihongo (☎22-5500; fax 22-3555). Behind Shimoda Station. Spacious wooden interior and hanging straw curtains. Frequented by both locals and tourists. Appetizers like *yakitori* (¥240), *tempura* (¥460-620), and salad (¥620-780) as well as seafood *donburi* (¥850-1360). Wide selection of cocktails, beer, and *sake* (¥380). Open M-Tu and Th-Su 10am-10:30pm. ❷

Ryutaro, 1-13-9, Shimoda (☎22-4124). Across the street from the tourist office. Specializes in curry, offering over 15 types in various portions over rice or noodles (¥600-900). Try their specialty *kurofune* curry (¥900) or their homemade soft-serve ice cream. Open daily 10:30am-8pm. Closed every 2nd and 4th W of the month. ❷

Tontei, 1-4-3 2F, Higashihongo (☎22-5655). Above Uminchu, behind the station. Mainly serves *tonkatsu* (breaded pork cutlets) using a recipe unchanged since the store opened in 1965. Food ¥1100-1300. Open M-Tu and Th-Su 5pm-8pm. ❸

Kinuma, 1-13, Shimoda. On Mai-mai St. down from the tourist office. Serves fresh seafood and *tonkatsu*. Tuna, squid, and *aji donburi* ¥1000; *sashimi* sets slightly more expensive (¥1500). Open M-Tu and Th-Su 11am-9pm. ❸

🄖 SIGHTS

Most of Shimoda's sights are centered around the history of Commodore Matthew Perry, the opening of Japan to foreign trade and Sino-Japanese relations.

RYŌSEN-JI. This is where American Commodore Matthew Perry and Japanese ambassador Daigaku Hayashi concluded the 13 articles of the Shimoda Treaty, which opened the ports of Japan. Today, the temple and its gardens are full of white and purple American jasmines. The treasure hall holds paintings depicting Commodore Perry's arrival, including some showing Japanese perceptions of the foreigner. Downstairs is an impressive collection of relics and paintings. *(3-12-12, Shimoda. ☎22-0657; fax 22-6355. Open daily 8:30am-5pm. ¥500, under 17 ¥150.)*

CHŌRAKU-JI. Another historical landmark, Chōraku-ji saw the signing of the Russo-Japan Treaty of Peace and Amity in 1854. The old museum's two exhibition rooms hold dynamic pictures, 19th century carts and chairs, and a poignant multi-panel painting depicting the bombing of Hiroshima and Nagasaki, though the Ryōsen-ji treasure hall has better exhibitions. *(3-13-19, Shimoda. Behind Ryōsen-ji. ☎22-0731. Open daily 9am-5pm. ¥200, middle school students ¥100, under 12 ¥50.)*

SHIMODA PARK. Famous for its 3 million *ajisai* (hydrangeas), Shimoda Park's vast grounds cover a hill. From the top you can look over the nearby sea and, weather permitting, see several of the Izu islands. Monuments commemorating the opening of Japan are scattered throughout the park. Just outside, by the waterfront, is the monument to Perry's landing, also of symbolic importance.

HOFUKU-JI. The museum adjacent to the temple displays historical materials pertaining to Shimoda's tragic heroine, the *geisha* Okichi, including her *kimono*, dishware, paintings, and calligraphy; it's also her gravesite. *(1-18-26, Shimoda. ☎22-0960. Open daily 8am-5pm. ¥300, middle and high school students ¥150, under 12 free.)*

ZUSHU SHIMODA KYODO SHIRYOKAN. This overpriced museum has intriguing paintings, scrolls, and artifacts, but many are similar to those in Ryōsenji's treasure hall. *(4-8-13, Shimoda. Turn left with Ryōsen-ji behind you. ☎23-2500. Open daily 8:30am-5pm. ¥1000, college and high school students ¥800, elementary and middle school ¥500.)*

NESUGATA-SAN. Known as "sleeping sight mountain" because it resembles a sleeping woman when viewed from downtown Shimoda, Nesugata-san promises scenic views of Izu's seven islands, neighboring mountains, and Shimoda harbor and beach. *(1-3-2, Higashihon-chō. Take the ropeway, which departs from behind the train station, for the 3min. trip up. ☎22-1211. ¥1000, under 12 ¥500.)*

SHIRAHAMA BEACH. A 15min. bus ride from Shimoda Station, Shirahama is one of Izu's prettiest white sand beaches. *(Take the #7 Tokai bus, ☎0557-36-1112, or Izu Shimoda bus, ☎0558-22-2567, to Shirahama Kaigan (15min., every 25-30min, ¥320).)*

🎵 🎭 ENTERTAINMENT AND FESTIVALS

Bay cruises are a popular way to see the Shimoda area. The **Black Ship** circles the coast of southern Izu. (19, Sotogaoka. ☎22-1511; fax 22-9291. 20min.; every 30min.; ¥920, under 12 ¥460.) Another cruise services Shimoda and Irozaki (40min.; 3 per day; ¥1530, under 12 ¥770). For fun after hours, check out **Jajah,** 3-13-8, Shichiken-chō. Hidden behind famous Perry Rd., Jajah plays mainly soul and R&B, attracting friendly locals for weekend drinks. (☎27-1611. Open daily 7pm-2am. Drinks ¥500-700.) **Cheshire Cat,** 1-13-11, Shimoda, a trendy bar on Mai-mai St., offers good company and live jazz (Th-Su). In addition to drinks (¥500-700), they serve a good selection of appetizers and meals for ¥550-800. (☎23-3239. Open daily 11am-1am.) Shimoda's famous **Blackship Festival** (3rd F-Su in May), in Shimoda Park, commemorates the man, the ship, the legend. Parades feature the US Navy band and fireworks. The **Okichi Festival** (Mar. 27) honors Okichi, with *geisha* from all over Japan congregating to celebrate her tragic life.

IROZAKI (石廊崎)

At the southernmost tip of the Izu peninsula lies the charming cape town of Irozaki. From atop the town's famous 60m cliffs, you can gaze down across the Pacific Ocean and to Izu's seven islands in the distance. Take the #4 Tokai bus, headed to Irozaki, until the end. (☎0557-36-1112. 40-50min., every 30min., ¥930.) Near the bus stop, across from the lighthouse, is the **Irozaki Jungle Park,** whose five greenhouses boast over 3000 types of tropical plants, flowers, and animals. (☎65-0050. Open daily 8:30am-4:50pm. ¥900.)

IZU-SHOTŌ (伊豆諸島)

The chain of islands speckling the Pacific between the Izu and Chiba peninsulas, south of Tōkyō, are collectively known as Izu-Shotō or the Izu Seven Islands. Their warm climate, beautiful beaches, good fishing, and diverse watersports make them a popular retreat for mainlanders. On weekends, the islands get packed with families, friends, and young couples looking to take advantage of the sunshine. The largest and closest island to Tōkyō is **Ō-shima,** known best for its diving. Then follows the tiny island of **To-shima;** farther south are surf-happy **Nii-jima** and newly formed **Shikine-jima.** Down the line are **Kozu-shima** and **Miyake-jima,** whose residents had to be evacuated after a volcanic eruption. **Mikura-jima** is still farther south, and the last island of the chain is **Hachijō-jima.** (That's eight islands, if you're counting, but Shikine-jima showed up too late to get its own number.)

KANTŌ

AT A GLANCE	
HIGHLIGHTS: Beaches, diving, surfing, and fishing, all within reach of Tōkyō.	**GATEWAYS:** Ferries depart from Tōkyō (p. 110), Atami (p. 234), Itō (p. 236), and Shimoda (p. 237).
CAMPING: Free campsites on the islands often provide bathrooms, showers, cooking facilities, and tents.	**WHEN TO GO:** Try weekdays and non-holidays. The islands closer to Tōkyō, namely Ō-shima, are crowded from July to August and on weekends.
TOURIST INFO: Izu Seven Islands Tourist Federation, ☎03-3436-6955.	

⎕ TRANSPORTATION

Flights: For not much more than the cost of a ferry, a short flight can whisk you away from the workaday world. **ANA** serves **Ō-shima** (35min., 3 per day, ¥8700); **Miyake-jima** (45min., 2 per day, ¥10,800); and **Hachijō-jima** (45min., 4 per day, ¥12,550) from Tōkyō Haneda airport. **Shin-Chuo Koku** (☎0422-31-4191; www.central-air.co.jp) offers service to **Ō-shima** (35min., 2-4 per day); **Kozu-shima** (55min., 3-7 per day); and **Nii-jima** (45min., 4-8 per day), from Tōkyō Chofu airport.

Ferries: Tokai Kisen, (☎03-5472-9999 (information) and ☎5472-9009 (reservations); www.tokaikisen.co.jp). **Shinshin Kisen,** (☎0558-22-2626). Open M-Tu and Th-Su 7:30am-5pm. See details on specific routes and schedules in individual listings below.

Ports: Trips to Izu-shotō start at the docks of Tōkyō, Atami, Itō, or Shimoda.

Tōkyō Takeshiba Port: (☎03-3433-1251). 1min. from Yurikamome Takeshiba Station; 7min. from JR Hamamatsu-chō Station; 10min. from Toei Oedo Line Daimon Station. Open daily 7am-11pm.

Atami Port: (☎0557-82-2131). Take the #8 bus from Atami-ko Station (15min., every 20min., ¥220) or 10min. by taxi. Open daily 8am-5pm.

Itō Port: (☎0557-37-1125). 5min. by taxi (around ¥620) from Itō Station. Open daily 8am-5pm.

Shimoda Port: (☎0558-22-2626). 7 min. by taxi (around ¥870) from Shimoda Station, 20min. by foot. Open M-Tu and Th-Su 7:30am-5pm.

Ō-shima: Moto-machi Port and Okada Port. ☎04992-2-2311. **To-shima:** ☎04992-9-0193. **Nii-jima:** ☎04992-5-0187. **Shikine-jima:** ☎04992-7-0357. **Kozu-shima:** ☎04992-8-1111. **Miy-ake-jima:** ☎04994-6-1131. **Hachijō-jima:** ☎04996-2-1211.

Ō-SHIMA (大島) ☎04992

After a few years, months, or weeks of Tōkyō's harried pace and towering sky-scrapers, many residents and visitors are ready for a break. Although Ō-shima is only 120km south of one of the world's busiest cities, the two bear little resemblance. In the island's center stands **Mt. Mihara** (Mihara Yama; 三原山), an active volcano. It's striped with hiking routes, and a 1hr. climb from the bus stop lands you at its summit, where you can pace the circumference (45min.) or just enjoy the views. Buses run from Moto-machi Port (30min., 6 per day, ¥860) and Ō-shima Park (20min., 2 per day, ¥840). From Mt. Mihara, you can drive through the **Ajisai Rainbow Road,** lined with flowers in summer, to reach **Ō-shima Park** (Ō-shima Kōen; 大島公園). The park's zoo is home to geese, sheep, turtles, deer, and camels, many of which roam freely. (☎2-9111. Open daily 8:30am-5pm. Free.) Next door is the **Camellia Garden and Museum** (Tsubaki-en and Shiryokan; 椿園と資料館), with over 480 types of camellia. (☎2-9111. Open daily 9am-4:30pm. Free.) If the zoo isn't enough wildlife, the **Squirrel Village** (Risu Mura; リス村) raises squirrels, rabbits, chipmunks, and ducks. Hand-feeding and petting are encouraged. (Bus from Moto-machi Port: 20min, ¥240. ☎2-2543. Open daily 9am-4:30pm. ¥630, under 12 ¥420.)

Moto-machi Port is not just a transportation hub; the area is home to museums and *onsen*. The **Izu Ō-shima Museum of Volcanoes** (Kazan Hakubutsukan; 火山博物館), 617, Aza Kanda Yashiki, illustrates volcanic history through pictures and text, accompanied by volcanic rock and seismometers. A 30min. movie (11am, 2pm, 4pm) goes into depth, while a simulator capsule lets you experience an eruption. (☎2-4103. Open daily 9am-5pm. ¥500, under 15 ¥250.) Also nearby is **Palais La Mer** (パレラメール), 2-20-1, Moto-machi, which displays over 4200 types of shells. (☎2-3111. Open daily 9am-5pm. ¥400, under 15 ¥200.) A 3min. walk left of the port lands you at **Moto-machi Hama no Yu** (元町浜の湯), Aza Tonchi Batake, an open-air spa overlooking the Pacific, with Mt. Miyake looming in the background. (☎2-2870. Bathing suit required. Open daily 1-7pm. ¥400, under 12 ¥240.) Farther down the road is **Island Center Gojinka Onsen** (アイランドセンター御神火温泉), 1-8, Aza Nakano Hara. Its higher price gets you a jacuzzi, sauna, sun deck, rest area, and herb spa, although the ocean views are through glass. (☎2-0909; fax 2-7222. Open daily 9am-9pm. Closed 2nd Th and F of the month. ¥1000, under 12 ¥600.)

Ō-shima's beaches are famous for spectacular diving and swimming. Closest to Moto-machi Port is **Kobo Hama Beach** (弘法浜遊泳場). Because of its location, this beach crowds quickly on weekends. Quieter, equally pretty options are **Ou no Hama Beach** (王の浜遊泳場) and **Hi no De Beach** (日の出遊泳場). **Wakō Marine** (和光マリン), 86, Okata Kawa no Michi, offers aspiring divers one-on-one lessons. Friendly professionals help you take the plunge, providing guidance as you enjoy Ō-shima's diverse marine life. (☎2-9528; www.wakohmarine.com. Open daily 8am-6pm. Free shuttle from your accommodations. Lessons ¥13,000.)

Ō-shima is accessible by **ferry** from Tōkyō (105min., ¥6200-7100; weekend overnight ferry 8hr., ¥3810-4760), Atami (100min., ¥2750-4500), and Itō (90min., ¥2390-3500). Depending on the weather, boats dock at either Moto-machi Port (☎2-2311) or Okata Port (☎2-8132); call **Tokai Kisen** beforehand to confirm. **Flights** are also available (see **Transportation**, above). Once on the island, five bus lines shuttle the tourist crowds (daypass ¥1800); unfortunately, the routes are few and largely inconvenient. For those hoping to hit many sights, renting a car is a better option. **Toyota Rental Car,** 1-17-2, Moto-machi, is across from Moto-machi Port (☎2-1611; fax 2-2844. Open daily 5:30am-6pm. 12hr. from ¥5000.) Rental bikes and motorcycles are available at both ports from **Maruhisa** (Moto-machi: ☎2-3317; Okata: 2-8353). If you're really stuck, several **taxi** companies serve the island (Ō-shima Kankō Jidōsha: ☎2-1051; Kumeya Taxi: 2-8932). The **Ō-shima Tourist Office,** 1-3-3, Moto-machi, is right of Moto-machi Port (☎2-2177; www.izu-oshima.or.jp. Open daily 8:30am-5:15pm.) A smaller office is inside Okata Port, but it's only open when ferries dock there. In an emergency, call ☎110 for **police,** ☎119 for **fire** or **ambulance. Police** and **post offices** are near both ports. (Ō-shima Post Office: 4-1-6, Moto-machi. ☎2-1901. Open M-F 9am-5pm and Sa 9am-noon. Okata Post Office: 17-18, Okata Aza Enokido. ☎2-8041. Open M-F 9am-5pm.)

Ō-shima has 62 **minshuku,** which charge a standard rate (1 person ¥4200, with 2 meals ¥7350; 2 or more people with 2 meals ¥6300 per person), and which can be reserved by the tourist office. Of the bunch, 🅂**Chinzan ❷,** 4-19-52, Moto-machi, is a cozy gem with unforgettable meals, newly renovated *tatami* rooms, and kind owners. (Ō-shima Shiten Mae bus stop. ☎2-1488. Check-in 3pm. Check-out 10am. ¥3500, with 2 meals ¥6300.) The **Umi no Furusato Mura ❶** campsite is a good place to rough it. (6-person tents ¥4000 and ¥300 per person; 5-person tents ¥2000/¥200.)

Across from Squirrel Village, **Sankichi ❸,** 56-16, Aza Tsubai Zuki, draws locals with mouthwatering sushi. Their specialty *omakase jizakana* set (¥1600) includes fish indigenous to Ō-shima. (☎2-1944. Most meals ¥1260-2200. Open M-Tu and Th-Su 11am-2pm and 4:30-9pm.) For tasty *rāmen,* try **Izushichi ❶,** with branches in Moto-machi and Okata Ports. The unique salt-based soup (¥600-700) is worth a taste. (Moto-machi: ☎2-0701; Okata: ☎2-8132. Open 9am-5pm when there's a ferry in port.). Another favorite is diner-like **Hyotan ❸,** 1-17, Moto-machi, left of Moto-machi Port. For ¥1200, you can stuff yourself silly on a bowl topped with fresh seafood. (☎2-2383. Open daily 7am-3pm.)

NII-JIMA (新島)   ☎04992

Once a site of exile for mainland criminals, small Nii-jima is 150km south of Tōkyō and 36km southeast of Shimoda. Although remnants of Nii-jima's history remain in the execution ground and exiles' cemetery, it now attracts tourists with its beaches and turquoise waves. A 5min. walk from Nii-jima port leads you to popular **Maehama Beach's** 4km of white sand. Behind the tourist office is **Yunohama Hot Springs.** Despite its bad imitation of Greek architecture, it boasts an amazing view of the Pacific—which you can enjoy from one of the six outdoor spas. (Showers

KANTŌ

and lockers ¥100 each. Bathing suit required. Open 24hr. Free.) On the other side of the island is **Habushiura Beach**, a stellar surfing spot. Surrounded by wave-eroded cliffs and looking out on an endless horizon, the sight is worth the trek.

If the weather isn't cooperating, the recently renovated **Nii-jima Village Museum**, 2-36-3, Honson, has exhibits on Nii-jima's environment, history, and culture. A special exhibit displays handmade surfboards. (☎5-7070; www.niijima.com/museum. Open Tu-Su 9am-5pm. ¥300, under 18 ¥150, 70+ free.) At the **Glass Art Center**, a 10min. walk from Nii-jima port, craftsmen blow glass into sculptures. (☎5-1540; www.niijimaglass.com. Open M and W-Su 9am-4:30pm. Workshops available.) A great way to leave your mark in Japan is through the **"My Memory In 10,000 People"** campaign. For ¥1000, the tourist office will hand you a block of coga rock (indigenous to Nii-jima) and let you etch whatever you please. The personalized pebbles are then planted in walls and sights throughout the island. (☎5-0048. Open M-F 8:30-5pm and Sa-Su 8:30-noon. Mention "My Memory" at the tourist office.)

Getting to Nii-jima requires one of two ferries, depending on which port you're coming from. From Tōkyō (140min., 3 per day, ¥8000-9200; weekend overnight ferry 8¾hr., ¥5120-6400) or Ō-shima (45-90min., 2 per day, ¥2100), take the **Tokai Kisen** ferries (☎03-5472-9999); from Shimoda (2¾-4hr., 1 per day, ¥3600), use the **Shinshin Kisen** service (☎0558-22-2626). Flights between Nii-jima and Chofu Airport in Tōkyō are another possibility (p. 240). When you arrive at Nii-jima port, the **tourist office** is in sight, just across the road. (☎5-0048. Open M-F 8:30am-5pm, Sa-Su 8:30am-noon.) As there is no public transportation, renting a bicycle is a good way to get around. **Nakata Rental** has both bikes and cars. (☎5-0215. Bikes ¥500 for 1hr., ¥1500 per day. Cars ¥5000 for 2hr., ¥12,000 per day.) In an emergency, call ☎110 for **police**, ☎119 for **fire** or ambulance. The **post office**, 1-7-2, Honson (☎5-0088. Open M-F 8:30am-4:30pm) and **police** are near the town center.

All accommodations on the island are arranged through the tourist office. The set rate for minshuku is ¥5250, with two meals ¥7350. For groups over two, a discounted rate of ¥5250/¥6300 per person applies. Hotels start at ¥8000 per person for a group of four, and pensions at ¥7500. Another option is to camp at one of Nii-jima's two free campgrounds. The **Wadahama Camp Site ❶** is on the west side of Nii-jima, past Maehama Beach, and the **Habushiura Camp Site ❶** (☎5-1340) is on the east coast near Habushiura Beach. Both provide bathrooms, showers, and cooking facilities. Because Nii-jima is so small, dining options are fairly limited. You may want to eat where you're staying; however, several restaurants are clustered on the central street, including fried-chicken-and-barbecue **Yuhama-Tei ❷** (☎5-1308; meals ¥600-1000) and sushi bar **Eisushi ❸** (☎5-0913; meals ¥1000-¥1500).

OTHER ISLANDS

If hanging out with the Tōkyō tourist crowds isn't your idea of a vacation, strike out for one of the less popular Izu islands. You'll find less in the way of activities and sightseeing, but if doing nothing sounds like the kind of break you need, one of these specks in the sea might be your best choice.

TO-SHIMA (利島). Tiny To-shima has an area of 4.2 sq. km. Unlike most of the other islands, To-shima has no beaches; it's occupied by a dormant volcano and many smaller mountains. During the winter, 200,000 camellia flowers bloom, blanketing the entire island with a lush, red mat. *(Ferries depart from Tōkyō (2½hr., ¥5300-8200) and Shimoda (1½-5½hr., ¥3600). No ferry W.)*

SHIKINE-JIMA (式根島). Itsy-bitsy Shikine-jima (3.9 sq. km) was connected to nearby Nii-jima until an earthquake and tsunami in 1703 separated the two. This small island has gorgeous white sand beaches around its 12km circumference, sweeping views of its surrounding ocean and islands, and a host of natural *onsen*. *(Daily ferries run from Tōkyō (2¾hr., ¥6400-9200) and Shimoda (3½hr., ¥3600). No ferry W. The tourist association (☎04992-7-0170) can help arrange accommodations.)*

KOZU-SHIMA (神津島). Farther south than Nii-jima and Shikine-jima lies Kozu-shima, an island boasting 19 sq. km and plenty to do. There are beaches for swimming, routes for hiking, extinct volcano Mt. Tenjo for climbing, and relaxing *onsen* for soaking. *(Ferries run once a day from Tōkyō (3¼hr., ¥6790-9800) and Shimoda (2½-4½hr., ¥3600; no W ferry). While the tourist association (☎04992-8-0321, www.fsinet.or.jp/~kouzu) is useful for finding a place to stay, 2 free campsites are also available.)*

MIYAKE-JIMA (三宅島). Although Miyake-jima is home to beaches, *onsen*, and scenic vistas, the volcano Osu-Yama erupted in 2002, forcing residents to evacuate the island. Currently, **no visitors are allowed onto the island.** Inquire with the tourist association (☎04994-6-1144; www.miyake-jima.gr.jp) for up-to-date info.

MIKURA-JIMA (御蔵島). Mikura-jima is famous for dolphin-watching and other types of exotic flora and fauna, but this small, mountainous island has little else to offer. The ecologically fragile isle has recently begun laying out guidelines intended to limit tourism's impact on the wildlife. *(A ferry runs from Tōkyō, departing at night and arriving at Mikura-jima in the morning (7½hr., 1 per day Tu-Su, ¥8040). M and W-Su, the return ferry departs for Tōkyō at 1:25pm, arriving in the evening.)*

HACHIJŌ-JIMA (八丈島). The most southerly of the Izu Islands, Hachijō-jima is 297km south of Tōkyō. Beaches line the island's coasts, and two dormant volcanoes, Mihara-Yama and Hachijo-Fuji, occupy the center. *Onsen* and scenic spots are scattered

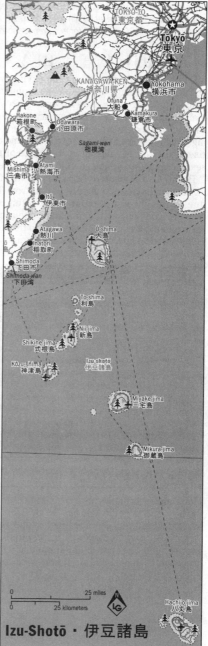

Izu-Shotō・伊豆諸島

KANTŌ

throughout Hachijō-jima, and there's a botanical garden. *(A ferry runs from Tōkyō every night and departs from Hachijō-jima the following morning (11hr., ¥8980). Contact the tourist association (☎04996-2-1377) for accommodations or use the free campsite.)*

MT. FUJI (富士山)   ☎0555

Mt. Fuji (3776m), dominating the skyline with its perfect conical summit, is the quintessential image of Japan. The mountain has always been regarded as a sacred place, and over 1000 years of written records detail pilgrimages to the summit. Matsuo Bashō, Japan's 17th-century traveling poet laureate, visited the mountain several times during his journeys, writing, "My souvenir from Edo is the refreshingly cold wind of Fuji-san I brought home on my fan." Today, witnessing the sunrise at the top of Fuji-san is still a rite of passage; during the summer climbing season, Japanese young and old flock to the mountain in droves.

Bashō also remarked, "In a way it was fun not to see Fuji-san in foggy rain." Though the mountain is only 100km from Tōkyō, it's rarely visible from the city, due to the shroud of clouds that often blankets the peak. But regardless of whether you can see the mountain, the ascent is well-marked and fairly manageable, and most climbers reach the top by sunrise. Although the volcanic slopes are bleak and desolate, views from the summit are breathtaking, and if you have cooperative weather, watching the sun break the horizon from the crater is magical.

AT A GLANCE

TIPS: Most climbers try to reach the summit for sunrise, the best time to see the mountain, since morning sun tends to burn off low-lying cloud cover.

GATEWAYS: Though **Kawaguchi, Fuji-Yoshida, Subashiri,** and **Gotemba** are at the base of the mountain, the most popular gateway is **Kawaguchi 5th Station.**

CLIMATE: Even in summer, temperatures at the peak can be below freezing. As a rule, it's about 20° cooler than Tōkyō. Winds and rain make the mountain feel a lot colder than it is—dress warmly.

CAMPING: Camping is not allowed on the mountain, though there are plenty of campsites at the base of the mountain.

WHEN TO GO: From July 1 to August 31, the mountain is heavily trafficked with tourists, which slows the ascent considerably. It's best to climb on Sunday night or during the week. Climbs just outside this season avoid the masses, but the summit is capped in ice much of the year. Only attempt an off-season climb if you have significant climbing experience and equipment for sub-zero conditions.

▛ TRANSPORTATION

There are multiple ways of reaching the mountain's various stations. From **Tōkyō,** the best option is the **Keiō bus** (☎03-5376-2222), which runs to Kawaguchi 5th station from Shinjuku Bus Terminal, a 2min. walk from the West Exit of JR Shinjuku Station (2½hr., 15 per day during climbing season, ¥2600). If you arrive late enough, you can start hiking immediately to catch the sunrise. The bus can also drop you at the 1st station if you want to start from the base. Coming from the Fuji-go-ko region, take the **Fuji Kyūkō bus** (☎72-2911) which connects Kawaguchi-ko Station to Kawaguchi-ko 5th station (55min., 5 per day, ¥1700). Buses also connect Subashiri to Subashiri 5th station (55min., about 5 per day, ¥1200) and Gotemba to Gotemba 5th station (45min., 5 per day, ¥1080). **Ōsaka** and **Kyōto** are connected by *shinkansen* to Mishima and Shin-Fuji stations, where you can catch the bus to Fuji-no-miya (Mishima) 5th station (2hr., about 5 per day, ¥2400).

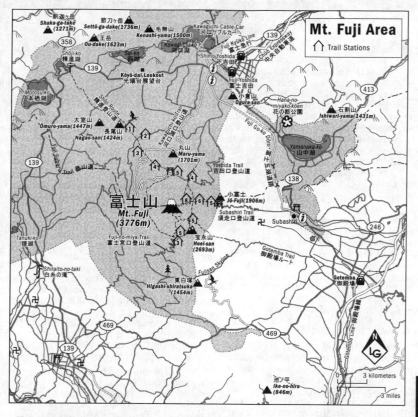

🛈 PRACTICAL INFORMATION

Information: The **tourist information center** in Tōkyō, in the Yuraku Station near the Kyobashi Exit (☎03-3201-3311), is the best place to pick up English pamphlets, as well as recommended timetables for reaching the summit by sunrise. 24hr. taped English info (climbing season only) ☎23-3000. You can also call the **Fuji Safety Guidance Center** at Kawaguchi 6th station (☎24-6223).

Emergency: Police ☎110. Fire or ambulance ☎119.

Stations: There are four main routes to the top of the mountain. Each is serviced by 10 stations, though the 5th stations are the usual starting points. The **Kawaguchi-ko route** is easily reached from Tōkyō and coincides with the **Yoshida route,** which starts from Fuji-Yoshida, for the majority of the climb. The **Subashiri route** starts from Subashiri, later joining the Yoshida route. The **Gotemba route,** which starts in Gotemba, is significantly longer than the others. The **Fuji-no-miya (Mishima) route,** which connects to the Gotemba route near the summit, is easiest to reach from western Japan.

Maps: All the paths are well-marked, and you shouldn't have any problem finding the way. You can pick up an English map at any of the stations, as well as from all of the tourist offices in Fuji-go-ko (see p. 249).

The Climb of a Lifetime

The day was young. Hopping a 1pm local bus from Shinjuku (a Tōkyō district), my buddy Aaron and I left on a mission to conquer Japan's most iconic sight, its tallest, most majestic volcano—Mount Fuji (*Fuji-san* to the natives). Having spent the last few days comfortably ensconced in the metropolis, we knew we were in for a serious physical challenge. The plan: to climb Fuji all through the night in order to witness its 4:30am sunrise at the peak. The supplies: bottled water, multiple layers of clothing, canned oxygen, cameras, and a supply of Snickers.

We reached the mountain by 4pm and began our psychological preparation. This consisted of shouting things like "Who's the man?" and responding with things like "I'm the man!" Ignoring the howling wind and sky of swirling clouds, we started chatting with some hikers we met at the base camp. To our surprise, these tired souls reported that they'd encountered vicious storms and biting cold the night before, and as a result, they'd only made it two-thirds of the way up Fuji. What a bummer! We pushed on.

6pm: We watched the sun set from about 800 feet up, and the view was unbelievable. Imagine looking down from the mountain to see a bed of fluffy clouds below you rather than land. The sun sank slowly into that puffy whiteness, scattering its rays in every direction. It was unreal. Eventually darkness set in, and we began our ascent in earnest.

For the next few hours, Aaron and I hiked and climbed with relative ease. There were almost no other hikers on the trail, mainly because we had gotten a big jump start on the morning tour groups. As the night progressed, our position on the mountain grew more and more stunning. Looking up, we could see the mountain's peak silhouetted against a backdrop of clear sky; looking down, we saw a glowing bed of clouds, lit only by the stars above.

11pm: By late in the evening, the two of us were freezing cold and incredibly tired. With the altitude affecting our breathing, and the weight of our packs growing, we were climbing in spurts and stopping at some of the mountain huts. Occasional encounters with other climbers let us laugh at our shared situation, but in the end it was the view that comforted us most.

By midnight, we could barely move and breathe at the same time. To make matters worse, we suddenly noticed literally hundreds and hundreds of lights massing below us on the trail. I turned to Aaron: "The tour groups! They're catching up!" Resembling crowds of marching ants, the flocks of Japanese tourists were about an hour behind our schedule. We were determined not to let them catch up.

1:30am: Having reached the final rest stop before the last stretch to the peak, Aaron and I slipped in the front door and sat on the floor, only to find were in a private inn. Without hesitation, the innkeeper kicked us out, stranding us out in the bitter cold. What did we do with an hour to kill in the below zero weather? We snuck back into the inn and bundled up like quiet mice, trying to sneak in a few minutes of sleep. In a complete daze caused by physical strain, sleep deprivation, and unbearable cold, we sat there, patiently waiting to time our arrival at the peak for sunrise.

Little did we know, the ants were on their way, and by 3:30am, it was too late. We were awoken from our stolen naps by a herd of flashlight-toting oldies. Knowing that the time to continue upward had arrived, we entered the herd and patiently ascended with them to the Fuji summit.

Witnessing the Fuji sunrise at 4:30am was one of the most beautiful, yet painful, moments of my life. None of the pictures I took could ever do the view justice. Overcome with pure satisfaction, I thought to myself: "This is my Everest, my story of a lifetime." As Aaron and I descended, an old Japanese man shared a Japanese proverb with us: "Everyone climbs Fuji once, but only a fool does climbs twice." I won't be a fool.

- Nick Topjian

The Let's Not Go Guide

I woke up late in the afternoon on the floor of my friend's sweltering Tōkyō apartment, wondering if the pounding in my head was the trapped echo of last night's Roppongi techno or a subconscious premonition that there was some reason to roll out of bed on this otherwise unremarkable Sunday morning. After feeding my growing vending machine addiction with my usual canned breakfast of three iced coffees, I came to the realization that my editors had scheduled me to spend the upcoming night solo climbing the venerable Fuji-san. Shaking off the final remnants of last night, I realized that my current stock of mountaineering equipment consisted of two T-shirts, a ragged fleece, my old running shoes, and half a bottle of warm Pocari Sweat. Let me be the first to tell you that this is not the method of preparation recommended by experts. They say you should get plenty of rest, drink lots of non-dehydrating fluids, and exercise mildly before the climb. My pre-hike regimen consisted of sprinting wildly through the streets of Shinjuku, flailing my arms and screaming obscenities to flag down the last bus for Fuji-san.

Arriving at Kawaguchi-ko 5th Station on a cold, wet, and misty Sunday evening is about as atmospheric as a candle-lit dinner for two at a sewage treatment plant. Since the only ambient light emanated from the wall of vending machines that marked the trailhead, I spent the first part of the hike stumbling through a low-lying cloud bank like a drunken bovine. I had been aware that Mt. Fuji wasn't particularly blessed with dashing good-looks, but after the first few hours of traipsing across a volcanic charcoal landscape, I realized the true desolation of Fuji-san's slopes. Although much of the ascent was about as enjoyable as that time when my friend thought it would be funny to switch my minty-fresh toothpaste with a squeeze-tube of *wasabi*, a few moments are worth mentioning:

2:17am: In a single act of pure, concentrated, scientific genius, I discover that Pocari Sweat glows fluorescent purple when exposed to the beam of my flashlight.

2:18am: In a moment of unchecked, blinding rage, I realize that Pocari Sweat phosphorescence is significantly brighter then the flashlight I bought at the ¥100 shop.

3:11am: After reading a sign advertising oxygen canisters for only ¥1200, I am amused by the thought of meeting someone gullible enough to spend that much for air in a can.

3:12am: Upon spotting a devastatingly attractive Japanese girl sucking down said air in a can, I decide to shell out the ¥1200 in hopes of sharpening my linguistic prowess.

3:13am: In another moment of unchecked, blinding rage, I realize that the attractive Japanese girl is in fact Taiwanese, and that the only word we both understand is the universal sound one makes when acknowledging that air in a can sure is good.

Although most of the trek up to the summit was relatively peaceful, sometime around 4:00 am the air began to grow thick with slumbering *gaijin*, about to emerge from their hibernation to catch sunrise from the top of Fuji-san. This was when I pondered the repercussions of hurling myself over the side of the mountain. Instead, I found myself trapped between Andy and Dick, two good ole' boys from the USA who claimed to have learned everything they needed to know about Japanese culture from anime porn and reruns of the Teenage Mutant Ninja Turtles.

Somewhere in the distance, a lone hawk sheds a single tear, and then pens a *haiku* about the sound of one hand clapping.

After an eternity, our motley crew reaches the top of Mt. Fuji, only to find the summit enveloped in a thick layer of impenetrable cloud cover. My thoughts drift to the disturbing fact that the sub-zero temperature has begun to transform my sweat into frozen balls of pure stench. Just then, I realize that someone has had the good business sense to open a *rāmen* shop directly on the mountain's summit. After moderating a heated debate between my wallet and my stomach, I fork over ¥800 and dive into a Cup o' Noodles that costs less than a dollar at my local supermarket. Capitalism has never tasted so good.

After watching the pitiful sunrise, I overhear another *gaijin* commenting on the condition of the human race. And I quote, "No animal alive would subject itself to freezing elements and a total lack of sleep for the privilege of dining on an ¥800 cup of *rāmen*." About halfway down the mountain, just as the torrential downpour began to turn the trail into a veritable landslide of oozing, brown mud, I began to agree with him.

- Matthew D. Firestone

Gear: It's important to have proper clothing for the wind and rain. Bring a warm fleece and an extra waterproof layer or jacket—this in addition to layering a few T-shirts. A pair of gloves and a hat are essential, and if you're doing an overnight climb, you'll need a flashlight (don't forget extra batteries). You can buy food and drinks along the way, but they are exorbitantly expensive, so stock up before your climb. If you need last-minute supplies, there are shops in each of the 5th stations.

ACCOMMODATIONS AND FOOD

Along each of the summit routes are **mountain lodges** where you can crash. Unfortunately, they are quite expensive (¥4000-7000 per night). It's best to trek straight through the night, but if you get tired, the huts are a good fallback option. During the day, you can rest in the huts for up to 1hr. (¥500-1000). Most lodges prepare **food** for their guests, so there are plenty of places to grab a bowl of noodles. Although a cup of instant *rāmen* can cost up to ¥800, your meal comes with a free rest. Lodges also sell bottles of Pocari Sweat (¥500) and instant hot cocoa (¥400).

THE BIG CLIMB

No matter what your expectations, Fuji-san is never quite the way you imagine. At times you'll find beauty in the desolation of the volcanic slopes; other times you'll feel you're being herded like a goat among the countless other climbers. Japanese of all ages climb the mountain, but it's important to respect the difficulty of the climb—at points, you'll have to traverse extremely rocky paths where it is easy to lose your footing and twist your ankle. There's also the chance of altitude sickness; if you're not adequately prepared for the cold, you risk hypothermia. For two accounts of climbing the venerable Fuji-san, see p. 246.

Almost everyone starts from a 5th station, though you can also start from the base stations. Much of the area leading up to the 5th stations is covered in scenic forests. From Kawaguchi, Subashiri, and Fujinomiya 5th stations, it takes about 4½-5hr. of non-stop climbing to reach the summit. From Gotemba 5th station, it's about 8hr. During the summer months, sunrise is usually around 4-5am. It's best to start climbing at 8-10pm so you have plenty of time to rest along the way. If you reach the summit too early, you'll feel the full force of the low temperatures, so keep track of your pace along the way. If you're planning to stay in a lodge, start in the afternoon so you can get plenty of rest before being woken early in the morning. At the top, you can circumnavigate the crater in about 1hr.; the official summit is marked by **Fuji Weather Station** on the southwest side. The descending trails lead directly to the Kawaguchi-ko, Subashiri and Gotemba routes, and it only takes about 2hr. to reach the 5th stations, even at a leisurely pace.

FUJI FIVE LAKES (富士五湖) ☎0555

Although **Fuji Five Lakes** (Fuji-go-ko) is only 100km from Tōkyō's urban jungle, the region brims with dense, coniferous forests and rolling green hills. The area's showcase attraction is undeniably **Mt. Fuji,** but scattered on the north side of the mountain are a series of five lakes connected by hiking trails where you can soak up the full beauty of the towering summit. The region is popular with older Japanese couples looking to escape the modern grind, and the area has a pleasant holiday feel. On a clear day, Fuji-san casts its reflection on the tranquil lakes below.

TRANSPORTATION. Fuji-go-ko is well serviced by public transportation, and it's very easy to get to the region from Tōkyō, as well as to move between the lakes. Driving from Tōkyō, follow the **Chuo National Expressway** via Ōtsuki, which

AT A GLANCE

HIGHLIGHTS: The principal attraction is **Fuji-san** (p. 244), though there are outdoor activities around the lakes.

GATEWAYS: Fuji-Yoshida is the main transportation hub, though Kawaguchi-ko offers the best range of tourist services and accommodations.

CAMPING: There are numerous campsites, but be prepared for nightly temperature drops and frequent precipitation.

CLIMATE: The climate is temperate, though slightly colder than Tōkyō.

WHEN TO GO: Cherry blossoms and stunning foliage make spring and fall the most popular times to visit the lakes. Summer draws hordes to Fuji-san, while winter leaves the area quiet. The annual **Yoshida-no-hi-matsuri** (Aug. 26-27), marking the end of climbing season, features a *mikoshi* procession and a bonfire.

takes you to Kawaguchi. From Tōkyō Shinjuku Bus Terminal in the Yasuda Seimei Second Building West Side (a 2min. walk from Shinjuku JR Station's West Exit), **Keiō Busline** (☎03-5376-2222) runs buses to **Fuji-Yoshida** and **Kawaguchi** (about 2hr., 15 per day, ¥1700); some continue to **Yamanaka-ko** and **Motosu-ko**. Fuji-yoshida and Kawaguchi are connected to the smaller lakes by the Fujinomiya-bound bus (1½hr., several per hr., ¥2200). Though the region is connected to Tōkyō via rail, buses are faster. From **Tōkyō Shinjuku**, JR Chūō Line trains run to **Ōtsuki** (2hr., every hr., ¥1280). In Ōtsuki, change to the Fuji Kyūkō Line for **Kawaguchi** (1hr., every 30min., ¥1110). **Fuji-Yoshida** is one stop before Kawaguchi-ko. A direct train from Shinjuku runs Sundays and holidays (about 2hr., ¥2400). For local travel, consider buying a **Yutari Fuji Usshu Free Pass** (3 days, ¥3500) at the bus terminal in Shinjuku. It covers local trains, buses, the cable car, and Kawaguchi-ko cruises.

⬛🔢 ORIENTATION AND PRACTICAL INFORMATION. Heading west from Tōkyō, the first lake, **Kawaguchi-ko**, is the largest and the main gateway to the region. The JR Fujikyu Line stops at **Fuji-Yoshida** and **Kawaguchi-ko** stations, good bases for exploring. Lakes **Sai**, **Shōji**, and **Motosu** lie west of Kawaguchi-ko, and **Yamanaka-ko** is directly east of Fuji-yoshida. From Kawaguchi-ko, a road leading south takes you to the 1st station on Fuji-san. There are three helpful tourist information centers in the area. The **Fuji-Yoshida Tourist Information Service** is left of Fuji-Yoshida Train Station. (☎22-7000. Open daily 9am-5:30pm.) The **Kawaguchi-ko Tourist Information Center** is across from the Kawaguchi-ko train station. (☎72-6700. Open daily 9am-4:30pm.) The **Fuji Information Centre** is a 5min. walk west of the station on the same road as the youth hostel. (☎72-2121. Open daily 8am-6pm.) In an emergency, call ☎110 for **police**, ☎119 for **fire** or **ambulance**. There are **post offices** with **international ATM** access in Fuji-Yoshida and Kawaguchi-ko.

🔢🔢 ACCOMMODATIONS AND FOOD. The cheapest stays in the area are the youth hostels in Fuji-Yoshida and Kawaguchi-ko. The **Kawaguchi-ko Youth Hostel (HI) ❶** (河口湖ユースホステル), 21-28, Funatsu, is about 500km southwest of the train station. Pass the tourist information center, turn left at the 7-Eleven, and then turn right past the post office. Continue walking to the power station, where you make a final left. (☎72-1431. Closed Nov. 1-Mar. 1. Dorms ¥3160.) The **Fuji-Yoshida Youth Hostel (HI) ❶** (富士吉田ユースホステル), 2-339, Shimo Yoshida, Hon-chō, is about half a kilometer south of the train station. From the station, follow the main street, passing three lights, and turn down the alley before Lawson. (☎22-0533. Closed Nov.-Feb. Dorms ¥2960.) If you're looking for privacy, try **Kawaguchi-ko Station Inn ❷** (河口湖ステーツョンイン), across the street from Kawaguchi-ko Station. Private *tatami* rooms have shared Japanese bathing facilities. (☎72-0015. Singles ¥4500, with 2 meals ¥7000.) In Fuji-Yoshida, try **Taikokuya**

KANTŌ

❸ (たいこくや), a traditional inn with a private garden, on the main road in the center of town. (☎22-3378. 2 meals included. Singles ¥6500.) If you plan to **camp**, pick up a camping map and extensive list of sites from the information centers.

Fuji-Yoshida is famous for handmade *teuchi udon*—if you're a fan of good noodles, you absolutely cannot leave without trying them. The *udon* is made and served in the kitchens of villagers every day; the best place to arrange a lunchtime visit is the tourist office in Fuji-Yoshida, where you can find out which households are serving noodles that day. In Kawaguchi-ko, the majority of the restaurants are simple cafes, but the town is also home to ▨**Sanrokuen ❷** (山麓園), a country restaurant that oozes rustic charm and serves up skewers of chicken, steak, quail, boar, trout, shrimp, and scallops that you roast over a charcoal pit. It's beyond delicious. Walk left past the tourist information center and hang a right at the 7-Eleven. Continue on this road for 5-10min., and look for the old barnhouse on your right side with rows of hanging corn outside. (☎73-1000. Open daily 11am-10pm.)

◪◪ **SIGHTS AND OUTDOORS.** Although the main draws for visitors are the mountains and lakes, enjoyable sights nearby are a nice way to unwind between dayhikes. The majestic shrine **Fuji Sengen-jinja,** built to calm locals' fears that an eruption of Fuji would destroy their village, is the major sight in Fuji-Yoshida. Follow the town's main street, Honcho-dōri, to an intersection, turn left, and continue to the stone lantern path and old *torii* (entrance gate). The shrine traditionally served as the starting point for the climb to Fuji-san's summit. In Kawaguchi-ko, it's definitely worth heading to the top of **Tenjō-zan** to take in views of Fuji-san and the lakes. The base of the mountain is on the southeastern shore of Kawaguchi-ko, about 15min. by foot north of the tourist information center. You can hike to the top of the mountain in about 45min., or you can take a quick **cable car** to the summit (runs daily 9am-5:20pm, round-trip ¥700). The other main attraction is the **Ichiku Kubota Art Museum,** about 25min. away by bus. (Open daily Apr.-Nov. 9:30am-5:30pm; Dec.-Mar. 10am-7pm. ¥1300.)

Fuji-go-ko is home to pleasant **hiking,** and it's quite feasible to trek around a few of the smaller lakes in a single day or to walk between lakes along the well-laid paths. Pick up a hiking map from the one of the tourist offices for guidance on the extensive network of well-marked trails. Since **Kawaguchi-ko** lies at the center of the area, it's one of the most popular destinations for dayhikers and cyclers. A number of water sports are available on the lake, including boating, windsurfing, and fishing. Outdoors operators along the shore can provide you with any rental equipment your heart desires. **Yamanaka-ko** offers the best windsurfing in the region and a 35min. hovercraft tour (¥900). **Sai-ko** is surrounded by dense forest, and is a popular campsite. Impressive caves near the main entrance road were formed by prehistoric lava flows. **Motosu-ko** is the least touristed and least spoiled of the five lakes. You'll recognize the view of Fuji-san from its shores from the back of the ¥5000 note. Small **Shōji-ko** is the most beautiful of the lakes, and is an extremely popular fishing spot for *herabuna* (carp).

SAITAMA (埼玉) ☎048

Born May 1, 2001, Saitama City merged three formerly independent cities: Urawa, Omiya, and Yono. Although Saitama is most often associated with its sprawling residential neighborhoods, in recent years it has expanded as an important business city, busy transportation hub, and blossoming art and cultural mecca.

◪◪ **TRANSPORTATION AND PRACTICAL INFORMATION.** Thirty kilometers northwest of Tōkyō, Saitama houses workers who commute to the capital. **Omiya Station,** Saitama's transport hub, is serviced by the JR Keihin Tōhoku, Saikyō,

Tobu Noda, and Kawagoe lines, as well as three *shinkansen* lines. From Tōkyō Station, take the Keihin Tōhoku Line (44min., every 5-10min., ¥540). The **Saitama City International Division** tourist office is in Saitama City Hall. (☎829-1236. Open M-F 8:30am-5pm.) In an emergency, call ☎110 for **police,** ☎119 for **fire** or **ambulance.**

Other services include: **luggage storage** in train station lockers (¥300-400); **Saitama Municipal Hospital,** 2460, Mimuro (☎873-4111); **Internet access** at @ **Comic Internet Cafe,** MM Building, 2-1, Miyamachi (☎647-8855; open 24hr.; ¥200 for 30min., ¥100 additional 15min.); and the **Omiya Post Office,** 7-1-12, Bessho and **Urawa Central Post Office,** 2-19-5, Takasgo (both open M-F 9am-5pm). **Postal code:** 330.

☎❖ ACCOMMODATIONS AND FOOD. Places to stay are numerous in Saitama. **Sanko-en ❸,** 3-50, Takahana-chō, is an attractive *ryokan* with clean, spacious *tatami* rooms. (☎641-1887; www.ryokan-sankouen.co.jp. Check-in 3pm. Check-out 10am. Parking free. Singles ¥5000, with breakfast ¥5500, with 2 meals ¥6500.) **Sanrakusou ❸,** 3-84, Dote-chō, also has simple Japanese rooms in an older building. Turn right with Kita Omiya Station behind you, then left at the first light. (☎644-4411; www.businessryokan-sanrakusou.co.jp. Breakfast ¥500. Laundry free. Parking free. Check-in 3pm. Check-out 10am. Singles ¥5000, with breakfast ¥5500, with 2 meals ¥6500.) Renovated in 2000, **Satsuki Ryokan ❸,** 1-376, Takahana-chō, has well-lit rooms and a spacious bath. Turn left out of Kita Omiya Station, take the first right, then third left. (☎647-5577; www5d.biglobe.ne.jp/~satsuki. Laundry available. Check-in 3pm. Check-out 10am. Singles ¥5000, with breakfast ¥5500, with 2 meals ¥6500.) Next to Naka Urawa Station, **Plaza Hotel Urawa ❸,** 1-1-1, Shika Tebukuro, is an upscale business hotel. Rooms have a bathroom, shower, TV, A/C, and fridge. (☎647-3300. Breakfast ¥500. Check-in 3pm. Check-out 10am. Parking free. Singles ¥6900; doubles ¥10,200; twins ¥11,400; triples ¥17,100. AmEx/MC/V.) Outside JR Omiya Station's East Exit, **Park Plaza Omiya ❶,** 1-119-1, Omiya Naka-chō, is a capsule hotel, though you wouldn't know from the name. (☎643-5811; fax 643-3137. ¥3500.)

Restaurants line the back streets around Omiya and Urawa Stations. At **◪Kaito ❷,** you can cook *takoyaki* (octopus balls) at your table and add more than 20 ingredients, from cheese and sausage, to shrimp and *mochi* (¥550-690). From JR Omiya Station's East Exit, walk through the smaller alley (Suzuran-dōri) until you hit a larger road, then turn left. (☎649-1155. Beer ¥480, cocktails ¥400. Open daily 11:30am-11pm.) Although *kamameshi* (a rice dish) is often found at train stations, it's rare to find a restaurant that specializes in it. **Torizen ❷,** however, serves it up with shrimp, eggs, or vegetables (¥850). Look on Suzuran-dōri, across from Ōmiya Station's East Exit. (☎641-2049. Open M and W-Su 11am-10pm.) Inside Saitama Super Arena, follow the smell of freshly baked bread to **Weston ❶,** a cute bakery selling handmade pastries. (☎601-3133. Open daily 8am-11pm.)

◙◪ SIGHTS AND ENTERTAINMENT. With the help and approval of Yoko Ono, the fascinating **◪John Lennon Museum** in Saitama Super Arena has collected over 130 of the Beatle's belongings in the only museum of its kind. Nine chronological zones depict the details of Lennon's personal and professional life with displays of his guitars, handwritten lyrics, sketches, clothes, and pictures. Created to commemorate what would have been his 60th birthday, the inspiring museum ends with the Final Room, a peaceful space dedicated to Lennon's words, lyrics, and music. (2-27, Kamiochiai. ☎601-0009; www.taisei.co.jp/museum. Open M and W-Su 11am-6pm. ¥1500, high school and college students ¥1000, under 15 ¥500.) A 20min. walk from JR Ōmiya Station, **Ōmiya Park** (Ōmiya Kōen; 大宮公園) consists of ponds and gardens, and contains a pool, museum, track, baseball field, and soccer field. The only sight of particular interest, however, is **Hikawa Jinja** (氷川神社). Although there are now about 250 "Hikawa Jinja" shrines sprinkled around the Kantō area, this one has the longest history—2400 years—and is considered the main shrine. The grounds include red stone *torī* gates, wooden buildings, and an elaborate entrance. (4-407, Takahana-chō. Open daily 9am-5pm. Free.)

Tucked in the residential neighborhood behind Ōmiya Kōen Station, **Bonsai Village** (Bonsai Mura; 盆栽村) is a 3- or 4-block area home to eight major *bonsai* gardens. After the 1923 earthquake, many bonsai artists moved their works to Omiya, where Bonsai Village was officially established in 1925. Currently, over 100,000 *bonsai* trees are cultivated within the compact space. As all the gardens are within blocks of each other, a stroll through the area lets you enjoy a multitude of the unique Japanese plants. (Call individual gardens for info: Fuyou-en, ☎666-2400; Syōto-en, ☎652-1033; Kyūka-en, ☎663-0423; Mansei-en, ☎663-2636; Tojū-en, ☎663-3899. Free.) On the main road of Bonsai Village, the small **Cartoon Art Museum** (Manga Kaikan; 漫画会館) honors Kitazawa Rakuten, an influential figure in modern Japanese cartoon art. Displays include his paintings, brushes and paints, and exhibits on the development of cartoons since the Nara Era. (150, Bonsai-chō. ☎663-1541; manga-kaikan@city.saitama.jp. Open Tu-Su 9am-4:30pm. Free.)

At the **Saitama Museum of Modern Art,** in Kita Urawa Park, displays include works by contemporary artists, as well as submissions from locals. The community-friendly museum hosts lectures and interactive workshops. (9-30-1, Tokiwa, Urawa-ku. 3min. from Kita Urawa Station's West Exit. Open Tu-Su 10am-5:30pm. Free.) The **Saitama Arts Foundation** hosts dance, theater, music, and art in four halls. (3-15-1, Kamimine. ☎858-5502; www.saf.or.jp.)

KAWAGOE (川越)   ☎049

With its sprawling flatlands and rural residential neighborhoods, Saitama Prefecture may initially seem to have little to offer to the traveler. But hidden behind its bad reputation is Kawagoe, a charming town reminiscent of an older Japan. Affectionately called "Little Edo," Kawagoe is a don't-miss daytrip from Tōkyō. The town derives its fame from its main attraction, **kurazukuri,** black merchant houses designed to protect residents against fire, a common threat back in the day. A lighted candle left inside the sealed clay buildings deprived potential fires of the oxygen needed to burn. Although there were once over 200 *kurazukuri,* they proved to be less fire-resistant than merchants had hoped, as a sweeping 1893 fire destroyed most of them. Today, 30-odd buildings line **Chūō-dōri,** 1km north of Kawagoe Station. Sixteen of these are protected as Important Cultural Properties.

It's a 500m walk from the *kurazukuri* to Kawagoe's other major attraction, **Kita-In,** 1-20-1, Kosenba-chō, built in AD 830. The temple is best known for its **Gohyaku Rakan,** 540 statues of Buddha's disciples, whose individual features are said to express every possible human emotion. With delicate gardens, elaborate carvings, and a magnificent golden chandelier, Kita-In's sights and significance make it an impressive visit. (☎222-0859. Open daily 9am-4pm. ¥400, under 15 ¥200.) Other sights are concentrated around Chūō-dōri and the *kurazukuri.* Just after the first traffic light is a warehouse displaying the grandiose **dashi float** used during Kawagoe's annual **festival** (3rd weekend of Oct.). Down the road to your left is **Renkei-ji,** a serene temple with a Buddha to rub for good luck. Another 5min. down Chūō-dōri lands you in front of Kawagoe's symbol, **Toki no Kane,** a 16m bell tower used to tell time and warn villagers of fires. The original wooden structure burnt down in 1893, but it was rebuilt, and currently rings four times a day, at 6am, noon, 3pm, and 6pm. Across the road is the **Kurazukuri Shiryōkan,** 7-9, Saiwai-chō, housed in one of the first *kurazukuri* rebuilt after the devastating fire. In addition to its intriguing historic artifacts, its narrow, winding staircase will pump adrenaline to your smallest nerve-endings. (☎225-4287. Open Tu-Su 9am-5pm. Closed 4th F of the month. ¥100, college and high school students ¥50.) Also nearby is the **Hattori Minzoku Shiryōkan**, 6-8, Saiwai-chō, whose limited exhibitions (clocks, sandals, candles) are worth a quick peek. (☎222-0337. Open Tu-Su 10am-4pm. Free.)

At the end of the road featuring the *kurazukuri*, a small alley bustles with vendors selling handmade sweets and rice cakes. This ◪**Kashiya Yokochō** consists of over 70 candy stores, and the narrow street overflows with hundreds of varieties of hard candies, nostalgic snacks, and traditional confectionery stores. A stroll through the area is a sweet trip back to Edo times, enjoyable for all the senses.

There are several ways to get to Candy Land from Tōkyō. From Ikebukuro Station, the fastest option is to take the **Tōbu Tōjō Line** to JR Kawagoe Station (32min., every 5min., ¥450). The **Seibu Shinjuku Line** takes longer, but stops at Hon-Kawagoe Station, closer to the *kurazukuri* (45min., every 8-10min., ¥450). From Shinjuku Station, the **JR Saikyō Line** services Kawagoe Station, though it's a slower, more expensive route (50-60min., every 10min., ¥740). If you're in the Saitama area, the **Kawagoe Line** will take you from Ōmiya to Kawagoe (18min., ¥320). By the entrance to the Tobu Tojo Line is the **tourist office**, 39-19, Wakita Honchō. (☎246-2027. Open daily 9am-4:30pm.) Farther from the station, on Chūō-dōri (the middle road of the three that split north of Hon-Kawagoe Station) is another **tourist office**, 7-9, Saiwai-chō, next to the Kurazukuri museum. (☎223-4115. Open Tu-Su 9:30am-4pm.) In an emergency, call ☎110 for **police**, ☎119 for **fire** or **ambulance**. Other services include: a **police box** outside Hon-Kawagoe Station; **Internet access** at **Airs Cafe**, 8-3, Wakita-chō (☎227-7101; open 24hr.; ¥100 for 15min., ¥880 for 3hr.; free drinks); and three **post offices** (open M-F 9am-5pm). **Postal code: 350.**

Although Kawagoe is an easy daytrip, the **Kawagoe New City Hotel ❸**, 17-4, Wakita-chō, provides affordable lodging near Kawagoe Station. (☎225-7711; fax 222-8988. Check-in 3pm. Check-out 10am. Singles ¥6500; twins ¥11,000.) Good dining options surround Chūō-dōri. **Kinchō ❷**, 6-13, Saiwai-chō, across from Toki no Kane, premiered sweet potato *udon* and now specializes in the starchy noodles. Try sweet potato *tempura udon* (¥1260) or sweet potato *seiro* (¥950), made and served by the friendly owner. (☎23-0345. Open Tu-Su 11:30am-7pm.) For *soba*, try the handmade noodles at **Hyakujō ❷**, across from City Hall. (☎226-2616. *Soba* ¥700-1000. Open M-W and F-Su 11am-7:30pm.) **Ichinoya ❸**, 1-18-10, Matsue-chō, decorated with bamboo, stones, flowers, and pillars, is more upscale, but has perfected Kawagoe's specialty, *unagi* (eel; ¥2300). On weekdays, the lunch deal is ¥950. (☎222-0354. Open from 11:30am.) For aesthetically pleasing set lunches with noodles, *sashimi*, *nimono* vegetables, and rice, head to **Hiromu ❸**, by Kashiya Yokochō (lunches ¥1200). **Karama Tei Bar and Restaurant** promises good company and drinks. (☎222-0929. Open Tu-Su 11:30am-2:30pm and 6pm-1am. Drinks from ¥600.)

CHICHIBU-TAMA NATIONAL PARK

(秩父多摩国立公園) ☎0494

Chichibu-Tama National Park covers more than 121,600 hectares and sprawls over Tōkyō, Saitama, Yamanashi, and Nagano prefectures. Stretching 70km east to west, and 35km north to south, with **Mt. Kumotori** (2017m) near its center, the park has stunning greenery and treks for hikers at all levels of experience.

▐▌ ACCOMMODATIONS AND CAMPING

On the two-day hike between Chichibu and Oku-Tama, you can sleep in one of the numerous mountain huts, locate the free emergency hut, or rough it by camping outside. The largest lodge is **Kumotori Sansō ❷** on the Kumotori San Hike. (☎23-3338. Open year-round. ¥3500, with 2 meals ¥6000.)

AT A GLANCE

HIGHLIGHTS: Hiking, camping, scenic views, and shrines.

CAMPING: Camping is possible at several campsites in the park; however, since mountain huts are scattered around the hiking route, it is not a necessity.

GATEWAYS: Chichibu (p. 254) on one end and Oku-Tama (p. 256) on the other.

WHEN TO GO: As conditions get harsh and potentially dangerous in the cold winter, the best time to go is between early spring and late autumn (Apr.-Nov.).

HIKING AND OUTDOORS

KUMOTORI-SAN HIKE. This two-day hike crosses the park, taking you from the **Chichibu** region, through **Chichibu-Tama National Park**, over **Mt. Kumotori**, to the **Oku-Tama** region. As winters can be harsh, it's advisable to hike between April and December. You can leave Tōkyō for Chichibu in the morning, hike through the national park, spend the night at one of the huts or campgrounds on Mt. Kumotori, and return the next night. Start where the **Mitsumine Ropeway** drops you off, and spend day one hiking to Mt. Kumotori. **Kumotori Sansō** (see above) is the main lodge; other mountain huts and campsites are nearby. On day two, hike to the peak of Mt. Kumotori, the highest point in Tōkyō-ken, then descend to Oku-Tama.

NAGATORO RIVER PASSAGE. For an unforgettably exhilarating experience, try shooting the **Arakawa** and **Chichibu rapids** in Nagatoro. **Outdoor Center Nagatoro Funtech,** 960-4 Nagatoro 960-4, offers rentals, lessons, and trial tours for a whole range of watersports. Their staff is experienced at putting beginners at ease, and includes some native English speakers. *(A 5min. walk from Kami Nagatoro Station. ☎66-4165; www.outdoornagatoro.com. Open daily 9am-5pm. Kayaking ¥9500; rafting ¥6500; "river boogie" ¥7000; canyoning ¥19,000; mountain bike ¥6500, rental only ¥1000. AmEx/MC/V.)*

CHICHIBU (秩父)　　　　　☎0494

A gateway to the park, this enclave offers interesting sights and cheap stays. In central Chichibu, the main attraction is 2000-year-old **Chichibu Shrine** (Chichibu Jinja; 秩父神社), 1-1, Banba-chō, known for its iron-clad dragon, which earlier worshippers created to tie down the creature terrorizing them. The buildings are adorned with colorful carvings. *(☎22-0262 or 22-4625. Open daily 9am-5pm. Free.)* Across the street is the **Chichibu Festival Museum** (Chichibu Matsuri Kaikan; 秩父祭会館), 2-8, Banba-chō. The small museum displays two impressive festival floats, decorated with gold and ornaments. *(☎23-1110; fax 23-7345. Open daily 9am-5:15pm. Closed 4th and 5th Tu of the month. ¥400, under 15 ¥200.)* Chichibu is also famous for the **Chichibu Pilgrimage** (Chichibu Fudadokoro 34 Kasho Meguri; 秩父札所34ヵ所巡り), in which devout Buddhists visit the 34 Kannon temples in the area. The full 100km-course (6-10 days) is a true test of one's devotion, though a quick stop at a few of the temples can be quite enjoyable. *(Open daily 8am-5pm.)*

　Chichibu provides easy access to **Mt. Mitsumine** (Mitsumine-san; 三峰山), the starting point for the two-day hike to Oku-Tama (p. 254). Take the Chichibu Railway to Mitsumine Guchi Station (25min., every 30min., ¥460), then transfer to a bus headed towards Chichibu Ko and get off at Owa (15min., every 30min., ¥300). From there, a 2hr. hike up Omotesando Rd. leads to **Mitsumine Shrine** (Mitsumine Jinja; 三峰神社), 298-1, Mitsumine. The Mitsumine Ropeway can give you a jump-start on your ascent (8min.; every 30min.; ¥950, round-trip ¥1650). The shrine itself is hidden high up in the woods. Unfortunately, it's slated to be under construction until July 2004; while visitors can still see the inside, an ugly white cover shrouds it from prying eyes. *(☎55-0241; fax 55-0328. Open daily 9am-5pm.)*

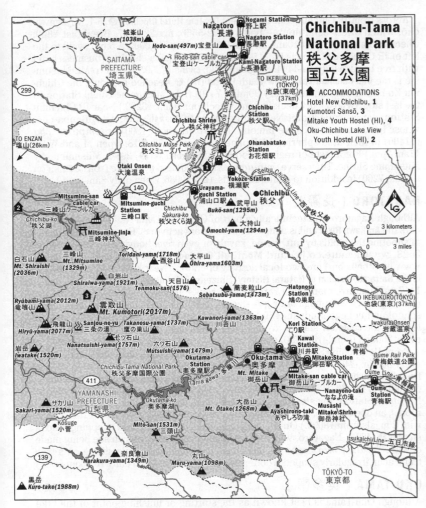

Chichibu-Tama
National Park
秩父多摩
国立公園

⌂ ACCOMMODATIONS
Hotel New Chichibu, 1
Kumotori Sansō, 3
Mitake Youth Hostel (HI), 4
Oku-Chichibu Lake View
Youth Hostel (HI), 2

From Tōkyō, the **Seibu Ikebukuro Line** connects Seibu Ikebukuro and Seibu Chichibu stations. (Local: 110min., every 30-45min., ¥750; Rapid Red Arrow: 90min., every hr., ¥1370.) The **JR Takasaki Line** runs from Ueno Station to Kumagaya Station (75min., every 20-30min., ¥1090), where you transfer to the **Chichibu Railway** to reach Chichibu Station (45min., every 30min., ¥720). The Seibu Chichibu and JR Chichibu stations are 15-20min. apart by foot, and sandwich Chichibu Shrine between them. If you want to access other stations from the Chichibu Railway, note that Ohanabatake Station is significantly closer to Seibu Chichibu Station than the JR Chichibu Station. **Police boxes** and **tourist offices** are near both stations. The Seibu Chichibu tourist office is at 1-16-5, Saka-chō. (☎25-3192; fax 25-2310. Open Tu-Su July-Aug. 9am-6pm; Feb.-June and Sept.-Nov. 9:30am-6pm; Dec.-Jan. 9:30am-5:30pm.) The JR Chichibu tourist office is at 1-7, Miyagawa-chō. (☎24-7538. Open daily Apr.-Nov. 9:30am-6pm; Dec.-Mar. 9:30am-5:30pm.) In an emergency, call ☎110 for **police**, ☎119 for **fire** or **ambulance. Postal code:** 369.

Across from JR Chichibu Station is neat **Dai-Ichi Hotel Chichibu ❸**, 5-1, Miyagawa-chō, which offers semi-double beds. (☎22-5566; fax 22-5567. Breakfast ¥800. Check-in 3pm. Check-out 10am. Singles ¥6000; twins ¥10,000.) A 5min. walk to the left of JR Chichibu Station is **Hotel New Chichibu ❷**, Banba-chō 3-4, a business hotel with free breakfast. (☎24-4444. Singles ¥4830; twins ¥7350.) Closer to Mt. Mitsumine is the **Oku-Chichibu Lake View Youth Hostel (HI) ❶**, reached by riding the Chichibu-Ko-bound bus (30min., every 30min., ¥470) from Mitsumine Guchi Station to the last stop. (☎55-0056. Check-in 3pm. Check-out 10am. ¥3200.) Near JR Chichibu Station, across from Hotel New Chichibu, is **▨Musashiya ❷**, 4-11, Banba-chō, whose handmade noodles are famous. Try *oroshi soba* (¥800) or *tempura soba* (¥1400) in their atmospheric old Japanese house. (☎23-1818. Open M and W-Su 11am-7pm.) For a taste of regional foods, try **Sanroku Tei ❶**, 298-1, Mitsumine, by Mitsumine Shrine. They serve *imo-dengaku* (¥300) and *yamame* (roasted fish on a stick; ¥200) in addition to standard foods. (☎55-0036. Open daily 8am-5pm.)

NAGATORO (長瀞) ☎0494

Although Nagatoro isn't technically a part of Chichibu-Tama National Park, it borders the **Arakawa River** and is a mecca for outdoors activities. Experience the thrills of shooting the rapids by raft, canoe, kayak, or even river bodyboard. **Kanute** (☎66-0528; www.kanute.co.jp) and **MontBell Outdoor Challenge** (☎06-6538-0208; www.montbell.com) are two local activity operators. Near Kami Nagatoro Station is the **Saitama Museum of Natural History** (Shizenshi Hakubutsukan; 自然史博物館), 1417-1, Nagatoro, displaying rare fossils, rocks, minerals, plants, and animals. (☎66-0404; www.kumagaya.or.jp/~sizensi. Open Tu-Su 9am-4:30pm. ¥100, high school and college students ¥50.) A 15min. walk uphill from Nagatoro Station leads to the **cable car** station, from where a short ropeway trip (☎66-0258; 5min.; every 30min.; round-trip ¥720, under 12 ¥360) lands you atop 497m **Mt. Hodo.**

From JR Chichibu Station, take the **Chichibu Railway** to Nagatoro Station (20min., every 30min., ¥460). The **tourist office** (☎66-0307) is in front of the station. Clean, friendly minshuku **Nagatoro-So ❸**, 1504, Nagatoro, is near Kami Nagatoro Station. (☎66-0336; fax 66-2133. 2 meals included. ¥6000.) If you prefer to be closer to Nagatoro Station, **Nagatoro Green Hotel ❸**, 872, Nagatoro, has spacious *tatami* rooms, an open-air spa, and an indoor *onsen*. (☎66-3333; fax 66-0133. From ¥5000, with 2 meals from ¥8000.) On the corner before Nagatoro's main shopping road is **Murata ❶**, 489-1, Nagatoro, which serves handmade *soba* you can see being made on-site. Try their *mori soba* (¥600) or *zaru soba* (¥650) while sitting on a tree trunk at an irregularly shaped wooden table. (☎66-0043. Open daily 10:30am-5pm.)

OKU-TAMA (奥多摩) ☎0428

Although Oku-Tama is best known as the starting or finishing point of the hike through Chichibu-Tama National Park, the region boasts good sights. The main attraction is **Mt. Mitake** (Mitake-san; 御岳山), home to several feasible and popular hikes and the famous **Musashi Mitake Shrine** (Musashi Mitake Jinja; 武蔵御岳神社), 176, Mitake-san. Begin your ascent from Mitake Station on the JR Ome line; the bus stop is on the left, and buses run from there to the Mitake-san cable car station (10min., every 30min., ¥270). The **Mitake-san cable car** (☎78-8121) makes the steep ascent, bringing you to the center of the mountain's sights (6min.; every 30min.; ¥570, round-trip ¥1090). From there, Mitake Shrine is a 25-30min. hike up a paved road to your left. Once you've reached the *torī* gates of the shrine, more than 330 steps still await—only after those will you reach the main building, standing at 929m. Take a peek in the Treasure Hall (open daily 9:30am-4:30pm; ¥300, under 12 ¥150) or just enjoy the view. Construction projects will be ongoing at the shrine until April 2004. (☎78-8500; fax 78-9741). If time permits, a 90min. one-way

hike leads you from Mitake Shrine to the top of neighboring **Mt. Otake** (Otake-san; 大岳山), at 1266m. The sights are amazing, and the hike not too arduous.
You're bound to pass through Ōme Station on the way to Oku-Tama. If you have time, stop by **Ōme Railway Park** (Ōme Tetsudō Kōen; 青梅鉄道公園), 2-155, Katsunuma, whose grounds display ten important locomotives including Japan's first train and the *shinkansen* "Hikari," the first to surpass the speed of 200km/hour. Although the park is packed with children on weekends, train enthusiasts of all ages will appreciate the opportunity to see such significant choo-choos up close. To reach the park, turn left out of Ōme Station, go straight for 5min., take a left and cross over the tracks, then head up the hill along the main road for 10min. (☎22-4678; www.kouhaku.or.jp/ome. Open Tu-Su 9:15am-5pm. ¥100, under 6 free.)
　The only way to get to Oku-Tama is to take the **JR Chuo Line** from Tōkyō or Shinjuku to Tachikawa, and transfer to the **JR Ome Line** to Oku-Tama Station (120min., every 30min., ¥1050). The **Oku-Tama Free Pass** (¥1470) gets you unlimited rides on the Ōme Line and includes a return to Tōkyō. The **tourist information centers** are by Oku-Tama Station (☎83-2152; open daily 8:30am-5pm) and Mitake Station, 332, Mitake Hon-chō (☎78-8836; fax 78-9972; open Tu-Su 8am-4pm). Up on Mt. Mitake, between the cable car stop and Mitake Shrine, the **Mitake Visitors Center**, 38-5, Mitake-san, provides info and maps. (☎78-9363; fax 78-9445. Open Tu-Su 9am-4:30pm.) In an emergency, call ☎110 for **police**, ☎119 for **fire** or **ambulance**. The **post office** is 5min. from Oku-Tama Station. (Open M-F 9am-5pm.) **Postal code:** 198.
　The **Mitake Youth Hostel (HI) ❶**, 57, Mitake-San, whose beautiful wooden building holds 300 years of history, is atop Mt. Mitake, halfway between the cable car dropoff and Mitake Shrine. It offers *tatami* rooms, relaxing baths, and an inviting lobby. (☎78-8501; fax 78-8774. ¥2750.) You can rent small **cottages ❶**, 17, Mitake-San, next to the cable car station. The four cottages have bathrooms, showers, TVs, fridges, microwaves, and cooking facilities. (☎78-9588. Check-in 4pm. Checkout 9:30am. ¥3000 per person; ¥2000 per person for groups larger than 3.) Additionally, more than 25 minshuku and ryokan are scattered along the path to Mitake Shrine. Although dining options are limited around Mt. Mitake and the Oku-Tama region, **Momiji-Ya**, 151, Mitake-San, serves *soba* kneaded right in the cozy restaurant. Enjoy *tororo soba* (¥900) or simple *zaru soba* (¥700) atop wooden tables while watching the master craft the noodles. (☎78-8475. Open daily 10am-5pm.)

TAKASAKI (高崎)　　　　☎027

Takasaki is best known for its *daruma*—fortune trinkets. *Daruma* have two white circles for eyes when you first buy them. You fill in one eye while thinking of a wish; when the wish comes true, you can draw in the other. Takasaki's *daruma* legacy stems from **Shorinzan Daruma Temple** (少林山達磨寺), 296, Hanataka-chō. (☎322-8800; www.daruma.or.jp.) Three-hundred years ago, a shed celebrating Kannon Sama sat on the site of the current temple. When it was swept away in a 17th-century flood, a tree was planted in its place. A man later came upon the tree, following a dream in which a sacred *daruma* instructed him to carve his figure on the tree. Thus began Shorinzan's temple and Takasaki's association with *daruma*.
　The other major sights of Takasaki are clustered on Mt. Kannon and include the statue of **Kannon Sama** (Hakui Dai Kannon; 白衣大観音), which stands 41.8m high. You can go inside the magnificent monument, which has been split into nine floors, and see 20 smaller statues within. (☎322-2269. Open daily 9am-5pm. ¥300, under 12 ¥100.) Nearby is the **Dye Plant Botanical Garden** (Senryo Shokubutsu-en; 染料植物園), 2302-11, Terao-machi, with over 160 types of plants from which colorful dyes are extracted. (☎328-6808. Open Tu-Su 9am-4:30pm.) From Ishidan-Shita bus stop, a 518-step staircase looms ahead, leading to **Shimizu Temple** (清水寺). The temple is said to model more famous Shimizu Temple in Kyōto. (☎323-3214.)

From Tōkyō Ueno, take the **JR Takasaki Line** (105min., every 20-30min., ¥1890) or the *shinkansen* (50min., ¥4290) to Takasaki Station. The **tourist office**, 222, Yashima-chō, is at the east exit. (Open daily 10am-6pm.) In an emergency, call ☎110 for **police, ☎**119 for **fire** or **ambulance.** The **post office**, 118-6, Aramachi, is on Symphony Rd., across from the station. (☎323-4936. Open M-F 9am-5pm.) **Postal code:** 370.

Because Takasaki is a business city, its accommodations are business hotels. The cheapest is **Business Hotel Takizawa** ❷, 1-15, Kaji-chō, 5min. from Takasaki Station on Symphony Rd. (☎323-6177; fax 323-6179. Japanese-style rooms ¥4500; Western-style ¥4800.) New **Central Hotel Takasaki** ❸, closer to the station and also on Symphony Rd., has cleaner, more comfortable rooms. (☎321-7000. Check-in 3pm. Check-out 10am. Singles ¥6300.) **Takasaki Business Hotel** ❷, 3-10-14, Kataoka-chō, has friendly owners, but is 20min. from Takasaki Station. The spacious bath and sauna are perks. (☎326-2828; fax 326-1872. ¥4000, with 2 meals ¥6000.) As you walk toward Mt. Kannon, **Cafe Tesla** ❶, 2-3-6, Yachio, is a great place to grab a bite. Using pure *onsen* water to make their pastries, the bakery has over thirty kinds of soft, savory goods. Take a tray and tongs and choose whatever catches your eye— the custard- or bean paste-filled bread (¥120) is particularly tasty. (☎330-3211. Open daily 7am-8pm or until sold out.) Inside the station, enjoy Indian curry at **Curry Shop Parappa** ❷, 222, Yashima-chō Takasaki Building Montray, with its classy interior and scenic view—painted on the walls. (☎321-5702. Curries ¥750-900. Open daily 11am-9pm.) Across the hall is **Ko-En** ❷, a Chinese restaurant specializing in dumplings and noodles. (☎326-8851. Open daily 11am-9pm.)

MASHIKO (益子)   ☎028

With about 50 potters, over 300 kilns, and countless pottery stores, Mashiko is a mecca for earthen pottery. The village gained its current fame when craftsman Hamada Shōji began working there around 1930, stimulating nationwide attention. Although the kilns are spread widely through the area, the center of the pottery town is the **Ceramic Art Messe** (Tōgei Messe; 陶芸メッセ), 3021, Mashiko, which features pottery by Hamada Shōji and English potter Bernard Leach, as well as current potters of Mashiko. The Messe consists of two museums, the restored former residence and traditional layered kiln of Hamada, and a classroom where you can try some potting (2 hr., takes 4-6 weeks to finish; ¥1100-1600). The Messe complex is a 20min. walk from Mashiko Station along the main street, Jonaizaka, which is lined with pottery stores. From Mashiko and Utsunomiya Stations, the Tōno Bus stops at Tōgei Messe Iriguchi, as an English announcement will kindly tell you, and from there it's a 10min. walk. (☎572-7555; fax 572-7600. Open Su-Tu and Th-Sa Apr.-Oct. 9:30am-5pm; Nov.-Mar. 9:30am-4pm. ¥600, under 12 ¥300.)

Next to the Messe complex is the **Mashiko Yaki Kamamoto Kyōhan Center** (益子焼窯元共販センター), 706-2, O-Aza Mashiko, which gathers different styles of pottery and sells an incredible collection of ceramics. (☎572-4444; www.mashikoyaki.com. Open daily 9am-5:30pm.) Alternatively, browse the endless pottery shops on **Jonaizaka Street.** All sell Mashiko-style pottery, but each has its own unique type. Toward the station is the former home of Higeta Hiroshi, **Kusaki-Zome** (草木染), 2943, Mashiko-machi. In the workshop, you can see 72 vats of indigo dye, set in the ground. (☎572-3162. Open daily 9am-5pm. Free.) **Tsukamoto** (つかもと), 4262, Mashiko, is the largest working kiln in Mashiko, and is on Jonaizaka, past the first light after the small road to the Messe complex. (☎572-3223; www.tsukamoto.net. Reservations sometimes necessary; call ahead.)

The easiest way to get to Mashiko is to take the **shinkansen** from Tōkyō to Utsunomiya (55min., every 20min., ¥4290) and transfer to the Mashiko-bound **Tono Bus** (1hr., every hr., ¥1100). The bus station is outside the East Exit, underneath Miyano-hashi bridge. Alternatively, take the **JR Tōhoku Line** from Ueno to Ōyama

(1¼hr., every 15min., ¥1280), transfer to the **Mito Line**, get off at Shimodate, and transfer to the **Moka Line** to Mashiko (1hr., every hr., ¥1060). For those passing through Utsunomiya, there is a **tourist office**, 1-23, Kawamukai-chō, inside the station, which can provide English brochures about Mashiko, and point you to the bus stop. (☎636-2177. Open daily 8:30am-8pm.) For those arriving at Mashiko Station, the **Mashiko tourist office**, 1539-2, O-Aza Mashiko, to the right of the station, has maps and brochures. (☎570-1120; fax 572-1135. Open daily 9am-5pm.) In an emergency, call ☎110 for **police**, ☎119 for **fire** or **ambulance**. **Postal code:** 321.

Although Mashiko can be seen in a day, there are accommodation options both around Mashiko and near Utsunomiya Station. In Mashiko, **Ōka Rental House ❶**, 3527-3, Mashiko, provides well-equipped cottages. Call to make reservations, and they'll pick you up at Mashiko Station. (☎72-2437. ¥3000.) Another inexpensive option is **Okadaya Ryokan ❷**, on Jonaizaka. (☎572-2016; fax 572-2016. ¥4000, with 2 meals ¥6500.) Staying in Utsunomiya is marginally more expensive, but more convenient for moving around. ▓**Tōyoko Inn Utsunomiya ❸**, 1-4-29, Ima Izumi, is easily the area's best choice. Bright rooms come with TV, fridge, dryer, toiletries, and iron, making this seem more like a real hotel than the chain business hotel it is. (☎624-1045; www.toyoko-inn.com/e_hotel/00056/index.html. Free breakfast. Free Internet. Coin laundry. Check-in 4pm. Check-out 10am. Singles ¥5800; doubles ¥7300; twins ¥8300. AmEx/V.) Restaurants are scarce and unremarkable around the Tōgei Messe. For tea, try **Cake Factory "m," ❶** 1651, Mashiko, on Jonaizaka near Mashiko Station. The smell of freshly baked cake (¥300) and cookies (¥400) is irresistable. (☎572-3146; fax 570-1017. Open Su-Tu and Th-Sa 9:30am-7pm.)

NIKKŌ (日光)   ☎0288

Nikkō is one of Japan's most visited attractions, and for good reason—the unchecked opulence of the temples at Nikkō is an architectural extravaganza. Even if you feel the temples are gaudy and flamboyant, it's impossible to bid Nikkō farewell and remain unaffected. The site's history as a sacred place began with the Buddhist priest Shōdō's establishment of the temple Rinno-ji in the 8th century. The importance of the complex waned with time, but warlord Tokugawa Ieyasau, founder of the Tokugawa shōgunate, requested to be buried at Nikkō before his death in 1616. This kicked back into high gear, causing Rinno-ji and Futarasan-jinja to be revived, and the centerpiece shrine, Tōshō-gū, to be built. Unsatisfied by the first attempt, Ieyasau's grandson put 15,000 craftsmen to work on the bigger, better Tōshō-gū you see today, completed in 1634. Though Nikkō can be seen in a daytrip, it's worth spending a few days is the area, especially since the temple complex is adjacent to **Nikkō National Park**. In addition to offering splendid hiking through old-growth cedar forests, the park is home to pristine lake **Chūzenji-ko** and beautiful waterfalls and hot springs.

ON THE WEB   Nikkō: www.city.nikko.tochigi.jp

▐ TRANSPORTATION

Trains: From Tōkyō, there are two rail approaches to Nikkō. The **Tōhoku** *shinkansen* runs from Ueno to Utsunomiya (50min., every 30min., ¥4600), where you change to the Nikkō-bound rapid train (45min., every 30min., ¥740). If you don't have a railpass, it's cheaper to take the **Tōbu-Nikkō** train from the basement of Matsuya department store, connected to Asakusa Subway Station (rapid train: 2½hr., about 10 per day, ¥1320; limited express 2hr., about 20 per day, ¥2740.) If you're going to explore the national park, buy a 4-day **Nikkō-Kinugawa Free Pass** (¥5740) at the Tōbu ticket window in

KANTŌ

Asakusa. It includes a round-trip ticket on the rapid line, bus travel between Nikkō, Chūzenji, Yumoto, Kinugawa, Kirifuri-kōgen, and Ikari-ko, and discounts at attractions. A 2-day **Nikkō Mini Free Pass** (¥4940) includes a round-trip rail ticket on the rapid line as well as buses between Nikkō, Chūzenji, and Yumoto.

Buses: An efficient and frequent bus line connects JR Tōbu and Nikkō stations to downtown Nikkō and Tōshō-gū, continuing to Yumoto via Chūzenji-ko. The 2hr. trip to Yumoto costs ¥1600 each way, so buy a **free pass** if you'll be traveling in the area.

Taxis: ☎54-1130.

Car Rental: Nippon Rent-a-Car (☎54-0821) in Tōbu Station rents from ¥4500 per day.

■ ◪ ORIENTATION AND PRACTICAL INFORMATION

JR Nikkō Station and adjacent Tōbu Nikkō Station are about 15min. downhill from Tōshō-gū. The approach to the temples is lined with restaurants, hotels, and tourist services. You can walk from one end to the other in about 25min. Heading west from Nikkō via public bus brings you to Chūzenji-ko, the center of Nikkō National Park. The bus line ends west of the lake, at Yumoto Onsen.

Tourist Office: The **Nikkō Tourist Information Center** (☎54-2496) is on the main approach to Tōshō-gū, halfway between the railway stations and the temple complex. The friendly English-speaking staff can book you a room. There's also **Internet access.** (Internet ¥100 per 30min. Open daily 9am-5pm.) Tōbu Nikkō Station has a small **information desk** (☎53-4511) where you can pick up a map. Open daily 8:30am-5pm.

Luggage Storage: There is a storage room in Tōbu Nikkō Station. ¥300-500 per bag.

Emergency: Police ☎110. Fire or ambulance ☎119.

Police: The **Nikkō Police Station,** 2-2-2, Inari-machi (☎53-0110), is 1 block northwest of Tōbu Nikkō Station.

Hospital: There's a small hospital across the street from the public library along the main approach to the temple complex.

Post Office: The **Nikkō Post Office,** a few blocks north of the tourist information center, has **international ATMs** and **currency exchange.** Open M-F 8:45am-5pm. ATM available M-Th 8:45am-6pm, F 8:45am-7pm, Sa-Su 9am-5pm. **Postal Code:** 321.

⌂ ACCOMMODATIONS

Tourism is big business in Nikkō, so you'll find accommodations ranging from budget hostels to cozy inns to upmarket luxury hotels. Most are either along the main approach to Tōshō-gū or slightly west of the temple complex.

Turtle Inn Nikkō (タートルイン日光), 2-16, Takumi-chō (☎53-3168; www.turtle-nikko.com). Follow the main approach to the temple complex, bearing left across the the sacred bridge. At the junction in front of the meeting hall, bear left, walk to the next junction, and bear left. It's 100m down on the left. Though less convenient than some places, you'll sleep in an enormous private *tatami* room with TV and A/C at this delightfully homey inn. English-speaking staff and wonderful home-cooked meals. 2 Japanese baths. Dinner ¥2000. Singles ¥4200. AmEx/MC/V. ❷

Annex Turtle Hotori-An (アネックスタートルほとり庵), 8-28, Takumi-chō (☎53-3663; www.turtle-nikko.com). From Turtle Inn, go down the road until you reach a bridge; cross it. Continue to the right and you'll see the Annex just ahead on your right. Rooms and amenities identical to the Turtle Inn's. The on-site Japanese bath house has scenic views of the Daiya River banks. ❷

Ryokan Aizuya (☎54-0039). Across from the post office on the main approach. A rustic old country building in the heart of Nikkō. Cheapest *tatami* rooms in town. Home-cooked meals and Japanese baths. Singles ¥4000. ❷

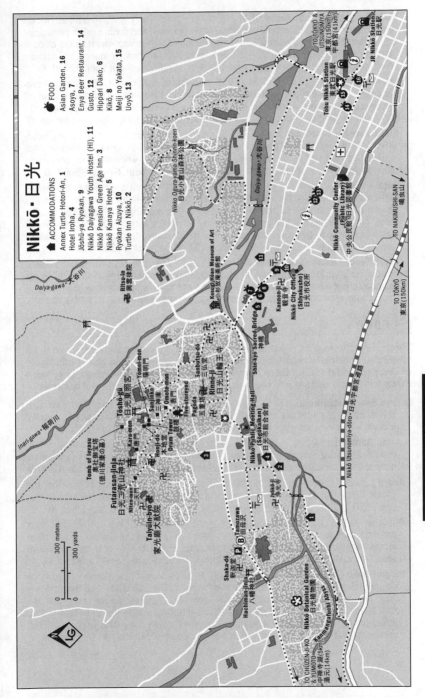

Nikkō · 日光

▲ ACCOMMODATIONS
Annex Turtle Hotori-An, 1
Hotel Iroha, 4
Jōshū-ya Ryokan, 9
Nikkō Daiyagawa Youth Hostel (HI), 11
Nikkō Pension Green Age Inn, 3
Nikkō Kanaya Hotel, 5
Ryokan Aizuya, 10
Turtle Inn Nikkō, 2

🍴 FOOD
Asian Garden, 16
Asoya, 7
Enya Beer Restaurant, 14
Gusto, 12
Hippari Dako, 6
Kikō, 8
Meiji no Yakata, 15
Uoyō, 13

KANTŌ

Nikkō Daiyagawa Youth Hostel (HI) (日光大谷川ユースホステル; ☎54-1974). On a side road behind the Central Post Office. From the main approach, English signs point to the turnoff. Nikkō's cheapest accommodation, but the woman who runs the place is extremely strict. There are better options. Shared bath, kitchen, TV lounge, and laundry machines. Daily lockouts. You must be in bed by 10pm. Check-out 9am. ¥2730. ❶

Jōshū-ya Ryokan (上州屋旅館), 911 Nakahatsuishi (☎54-0155; www.johsyu-ya.co.jp). Next to the post office. A brand-new budget inn with affordable Western- or Japanese-style rooms. A real steal if you have 2 or 3 people in your party. Shared bath, A/C, and TV. Singles ¥4500; doubles ¥3500 per person; triples ¥2980 per person. ❷

Nikkō Pension Green Age Inn (日光ペンショングリーンエイジイン; ☎53-3636). On the west side of the temple complex, near the ticket booth. Pricier than other ryokan, it's right next to the temples. Bavarian facade and wood-trimmed rooms ooze sophistication. Western-style rooms with shared Japanese bath. Singles ¥5800. ❸

Hotel Iroha (ホテルいろは; ☎54-1563). Follow the main approach to the temple complex until you reach the sacred bridge; then bear left and cross the river. Follow this road until you reach the junction in front of the public meeting hall, and bear right. The hotel is 10m ahead on the left. This slightly upmarket hotel offers Western-style or *tatami* rooms with balconies overlooking the nearby Daiya River. A/C, TV, on-premise *onsen*, dining hall, and lounge area. ¥6000-10,000 depending on view. ❸

Nikkō Kanaya Hotel (Nikkō Kanaya Hoteru; 日光金谷ホテル), 1300, Kami-Hatsuishi-machi (☎54-0010; www.kanayahotel.co.jp). On a small turnoff from the main approach, just before the bridge. This 130-year-old hotel is in a class by itself. Elegant rooms with wood decor. An attentive staff caters to your every wish. ¥11,000. ❹

🍴 FOOD

There is no shortage of restaurants in Nikkō, but the city is a virtual ghost town after 8pm. Be sure to try *yuba*, a local type of tofu formed by skimming thin layers of bean curd and rolling them into dense spirals. *Yuba* is excellent as either a candy with sugar and sesame seeds or a flavorful addition to a dish of hot *soba*.

🍴 Enya Beer Restaurant (えんや; ☎30-7785). A few blocks uphill from Tōbu Nikkō Station along the main temple approach. Feast on *teppan-yaki* and *shabu-shabu*, washing it down with a wide selection of imported brews. Open daily 11:30am-10pm. ❸

Asian Garden (☎54-2801). Across the street from Tōbu Nikkō Station. A solid, no-frills Indian restaurant serving up spicy curries and a good variety of vegetarian-friendly dishes. Come for the affordable dinner sets (under ¥1000). Open daily 11am-10pm. ❷

Asoya (あさや; ☎54-0605). On the right side of the road, about 10m before the sacred bridge. Specialty Nikkō *yuba* features in exquisitely presented box sets. Dinner sets ¥1200-2200. *Yuba rāmen* or *soba* under ¥1000. Open daily 11am-10pm. ❷

Gusto (☎50-1232). Centrally located on the main temple approach. It's set back from the road; look for the Skylark sign on the right side. Part of the Skylark chain. Offers Western-style dishes including steak, fried shrimp, and pizza. The only area restaurant open past midnight, it's also dirt cheap. Open M-F 10am-2am, Sa-Su 7am-2am. ❶

Hippari Dako (ひっぱり風凧; ☎53-2933). Heading towards the temple complex, it's on your left a few blocks past the tourist info center. The *mama-san* who runs it has a long, proud history of serving hungry *gaijin*, and she's wallpapered the restaurant with their business cards, photos, t-shirts, and handwritten messages. On entering, you'll be asked (in English) if you're a vegetarian; then she'll churn out *gyōza*, *yakitori*, chicken meatballs, and other homemade goodies as you watch. Open daily 11am-10pm. ❷

Kikō (☎53-3320). Next to Hippari Dako on the right side. No sign, but an English posting in the window advertises homemade Korean cuisine. Run by a Korean woman who will sit you down in her living room and fill you to the brim with homemade dishes like *kimchi rāmen* and Korean hotpot. The setting is about as homey as it gets, and you can watch her preparing your food on her kitchen stove. Open daily 11am-10pm. ❷

Meiji no Yakata (明治の館 ; ☎54-2149). On the west side of Tōbu Nikkō Station. A wonderful bakery and perfect place for coffee or to grab takeaway before the train. Fresh pies, tarts, cheesecakes, and strudels under ¥500. Open daily 9am-8pm. ❶

Uoyō (魚要 ; ☎54-0333). Across from the tourist information center. If you're looking for a change of pace, check out this quaint little restaurant. You can get steaming bowls of *soba* and *udon* with *yuba* and *tempura* for under ¥1000. Open daily 11am-10pm. ❷

⊙ SIGHTS

Although Tōshō-gū is the center of the temple complex, there are several other impressive buildings nearby. Each charges its own entrance fee, but you can save a bit by purchasing a **combination ticket** (¥1250). This does not include admission to the Sleeping Cat, the Tomb of Ieyasu, or any of the area museums. The complex is open April-October daily 8am-4:30pm; November-March daily 8am-3:30pm.

SACRED BRIDGE (SHIN-KYŌ; 神橋). The sacred bridge spanning Daiyagawa is the image plastered on every brochure in the area. The vermilion-lacquered bridge is a 1907 reconstruction of the original 17th-century structure and marks the place where two intertwined snakes are said to have given Shōdō supernatural assistance in crossing the river. The bridge will be under restoration at least through 2004, and is currently surrounded by a "picturesque" metal crate.

RINNŌ-JI (輪王寺). The temple that began Nikkō's reputation as a sacred place is a fitting place to start a tour. Shōdō's original Tendai temple was founded in 766 and erected around 848, though the current structures are 1648 reconstructions. The complex is centered on **Sanbutsu-dō** (Three Buddha Hall), Nikkō's largest temple, which houses golden statues of Amida Nyorai, the Senju-Kannon, and the Batō-Kannon. Other buildings include the **Dai-goma-dō** (Holy Fire Temple), which enshrines over 30 images, including the Five Guardian Buddhist deities, the Twelve Edo Gods, and the Seven Fortune Gods, and the **Gohoten-dō,** which contains the Fudo God and the 1000-armed Senju-Kannon. Rinnō-ji is also home to the **Sorinto Pillar,** a 15m-high memorial inscribed with over 1000 volumes of holy sutra. **Shōdō-en,** a manicured garden of winding paths, ponds, rocks, and plants, is in the compound's southwest. Near the garden, the **Hōmotsu-den** (Treasure Hall) displays sacred artwork. *(Garden and treasure hall ¥300. Open daily 8am-5pm.)*

FIVE-STORIED PAGODA. Through the west gate of Rinnō-ji, you'll enter the Omotesan-dō, which leads to Tōshō-gū. Before the monumental stone *torii*, you'll pass the Five-Storied Pagoda, donated by feudal lord Tadakatsu Sakai in 1650, which enshrines the statue of Five Wisdom Buddha and is marked by the symbols of the zodiac. The original burned down in 1815, but was rebuilt by Sakai's descendants four years later. In an early example of earthquake-proof architecture, the foundationless structure is counterweighted by a free-swinging central pillar.

TŌSHŌ-GŪ (東照宮). Pass through the stone *torii* to approach **Omote-mon** (or **Nio-mon,** Gate of the Deva Kings) and enter Tōshō-gū. Inside, you'll see the **Sanjinko** (Three Sacred Storehouses) on your right and the **Shinkyūsha** (Sacred Stables) on your left. The stables currently house a gift from the government of New

KANTŌ

Zealand—a white horse used in ceremonies. Above the stables, a famous relief of three monkeys depicts the "hear no evil, see no evil, speak no evil" principle of Tendai Buddhism. A few steps farther to the right is the Chinese-gabled **sacred fountain.** Beyond it is the **kyōzō** (sutra library), closed to tourists. After a second *torii* and some stairs, you'll enter the inner precincts of Tōshō-gū. A **drum tower** and a **revolving lantern** await on your left side. Past the drum tower, the **Yakushi-dō** or **Honji-dō,** the largest temple in Tōshō-gū, holds the Yakushi Buddha, flanked by the Sunlight and Moonlight Buddha and the Twelve Sacred Warriors. The temple ceiling is adorned with a painting of a coiled dragon. Although the original was destroyed by fire in 1961, the dragon was repainted by Nampu Katayama. The highlight is watching a monk standing beneath the painting rapping two sticks together: the jangling echo is said to be reminiscent of a roaring dragon.

At the top of a second flight of steps is the **Yomei-mon** (Gate of Sunlight), also known as **Higurashi-mon** (Twilight Gate). Over 10m high, the Chinese-style gate is painted with white lacquer and gold leaf, and features roof brackets carved with creatures from dragons to demigods. On either side are carved panels of natural images. The gate was considered so grandiose by its artists that they installed one of the twelve supporting columns upside down in an act of intentional imperfection. Beyond lies **Kara-mon** (Chinese Gate), the entrance to the inner sanctum. Although it's not as impressive as the Yomei-mon, the Chinese inlay surpasses the Yomei-mon in refinement and elaboration. The **Hon-den** (Main Hall) is reached via the **Hai-den** (Oratory), decorated with carvings and paintings of Heian poets. Farther in is the **Nai-jin** (inner chamber), which houses the Sacred Mirror. This is as far as you're permitted to venture, but just beyond you can see the **Nai-Nai-jin** (innermost chamber), where Ieyasu's spirit rests. On the way out is the **Gama-dō** (Holy Fire Temple), where prayers for peace were made in the Edo Period.

SLEEPING CAT (NEMURI NEKKO) AND THE TOMB OF IEYASU. Through Yomeimon and to the right is a booth selling a combination ticket (¥500) for these two sights. The small **sleeping cat** is renowned for its realism, it's not as impressive as the huge crowds might lead you to believe. Beyond the lintel is a flight of 200 stone steps leading to the beautiful **Tomb of Ieyasu.** The grove around the tomb is peaceful and secluded. Passing underneath the sleeping cat on your way out, look to the left for the **Jin-yōsha,** a storage depot for moveable festival shrines.

FUTARASAN JINJA (二荒山神社 **).** Exiting Tōshō-gū, walk toward the pagoda and follow the path to the right to Futarasan Jinja, a modest red-lacquered shrine that's a breath of fresh air after its ostentatious neighbors. Built by Shōdō in 782, it's dedicated to the three *gongen* (avatars) of Nikkō: Nantai-san, the volcano that created Lake Chūzen-ji; his wife Nyotai; and their son, Taro. Today's structure was rebuilt by Shōgun Hidetada in 1619, and is Nikkō's oldest building.

TAIYŪIN-BYŌ (大院廟 **).** Taiyūin-byō was constructed in memory of Iemitsu Tokugawa, the grandson of Ieyasu who originally commissioned Tōshō-gū. A smaller and less extravagant version of Tōshō-gū, Taiyūin-byō is often hailed as the most appealing of all of Nikkō's temples, featuring in miniature the characteristics of its larger neighbor. The total effect is much more subdued and elegant, and its forested location gives the complex an almost fairy-tale atmosphere.

MUSEUMS. From the sacred bridge, turn right to walk to the **Kosugi Hōan Museum of Art,** which features the local artist's landscapes. *(Open Tu-Su 9:30am-5pm. ¥700.)* Near Omote-mon at the back of the shrine complex is **Nikkō Tōshō-gū Museum of Art.** The wooden facade is striking, but the main attractions are the incredible painted screens inside. *(Open daily Apr.-Oct. 9am-5pm; Nov.-Mar. 9am-4pm. ¥800.)*

▨ HIKING

Before hitting the trails of the national park, there are two quick and easy hikes in Nikkō. Although it only takes about 20min. each way, the hike out to the ▨Gamman-Ga-Fuchi Abyss is a serene wooded path where you'll see colorful swarms of dragonflies in the summer. The abyss is a series of small waterfalls and rapids, while the trail is lined with decaying, moss-covered statues of Jizō, the guardian of deceased and unborn children, pregnant women, and travelers. The Bake-Jizō ridicules hikers who try to count the statues. Continuing past the statues, it's another 20min. to Yashio-no-yu Onsen, a modern bath complex with an outdoor bath. You can also reach the *onsen* by taking a Chūzen-ji-bound bus to Kiyomizu Ichōme.

The other hike in the area is awash in views of the cedar forest around the temple complex. Starting behind Taiyūin-byō, a 3.2km course winds through the hills in the back of the Tōshō-gū, ending at the pristine Takinō Shrine in the middle of the forest. The 2hr. hike can be strenuous, as you have to navigate a series of old stone steps, but the views are rewarding, and it's a great way to escape the crowds.

◗ FESTIVALS

The spectacular Grand Festival, May 17, a re-enactment of the Ieyasu's burial at Tōshō-gū, features over 1000 costumed characters on parade and a display of equestrian archery. A smaller half-day festival takes place October 17. The Yayoi Matsuri on April 16 and 17 features a procession of shrines around Futarasan-jinja.

▨ DAYTRIPS FROM NIKKŌ

Once you've seen Nikkō, the two main areas of interest are Chūzenji-ko and Yumoto, both connected to Nikkō via the Tōbu bus line. There are trails between Chūzenji-ko and Yumoto, and it's feasible to take the bus to one area and hike to the other. The hotels in the park are pricey, so it's best to use Nikkō as a base.

CHŪZENJI-KO (中禅寺湖). About 1hr. west of Nikkō on the bus line is Chūzenji-ko. The lake is fairly uninteresting, and aside from scenic cruises, there isn't much to occupy visitors. At nearby Kegon-no-taki waterfall, an elevator descends to a viewing platform perfectly placed to view the cascade. The falls are a few minutes east of Chūzenji Bus Station. (Open daily May-Sept. 7:30am-6pm; Oct. 7:30am-5pm; Mar.-Apr. and Nov. 8am-5pm; Dec.-Feb. 9am-4:30pm. Roundtrip ¥530.) About 1km to the west, another Futarasan-Jinja, still a center of Buddhist worship, enshrines a statue carved by Shōdō. (Open daily Apr.-Oct. 8am-4:30pm; Nov.-Mar. 8am-3:30pm.) A third Futarasan-Jinja sits on nearby Nantai-san (2484m). Only attempt the 4hr. hike in good weather. (Mountain entrance ¥500.)

Although hiking trails ring the entire perimeter of the lake, the 4.6km northern route takes you to Ryuzyu-no-taki falls, next to the Akanuma Bus Stop. The motion of the water over the rocks is said to resemble a dragon's head. From there, take the bus back to Chūzenji-ko, or continue north through Senjogahara Marsh, a pleasant 6.3km trail of dense forests that leads to Yuno-ko and the Yudaki-no-taki falls, a 110m hot spring cataract. At that point, it's another 2.9km around the lake to the town of Yumoto. This hike is especially recommended in May and June when wildflowers are in bloom, as well as during autumn, when the foliage is spectacular.

KANTŌ

YUMOTO (湯元). Yumoto is about 30min. past Chūzenji-ko by bus, and is the final stop on the Tōbu Line. The main attraction is **Onsen-ji**, a small temple near the hot springs, founded by Shōdō for Yakushinyorai, the Buddha of Healing. Toward the back of the village is **Yu-no-daira**, a sulfur-scented marsh field where hot springs bubble into the ground. If you buy a few eggs from the market, you can sit on the bench there and have a hard-boiled breakfast in about 40min. A 9.6km loop hike starting from the road behind the temple takes you through pastures and up to the surrounding mountains. Three-fourths of the way through the hike, you reach **Kotoku Onsen,** where you can soak in still more baths. If you're planning on camping or hiking extensively in the park, visit the **Nikkō Yumoto Visitor Center** (☎62-2461; www.bes.or.jp/nikko/vc), in town near the waterfront, where you can pick up extensive trail maps as well as a listing of campsites. (Open daily 9am-5pm.)

NORTHERN HONSHŪ

A thicket of summer grasses
Is all that remains
Of the dreams and ambitions
Of ancient warriors.
—Matsuo Bashō in *The Narrow Road to the Deep North*

Walking though the hills near Hiraizumi, recalling the historical dramas that had played out on that very spot, Matsuo Bashō was overcome with the evanescence of human life and civilization. Modern visitors may not be reduced to tears, but despite the factories, train tracks, and occasional cities that now dot the map of Northern Honshū, Old Japan is very much alive there today. The mystical temple Yamadera, already ancient when Bashō visited in the 17th century, crowns one snowy peak, while the villages of the Tōno Valley harbor old thatched-roof houses and rice paddies as far as the eye can see. The big cities, like Aomori, Morioka, Fukushima, aren't too much to write home about—lovely places to live, they lack the luster needed to keep most tourists entertained. Most of the region is mountain, farmland, or forest, while the coast is lined with rocky beaches and fishing villages, and it's in these natural areas that you'll enjoy yourself most.

If you're planning a visit, try to make it in early August so you can catch some of Japan's most colorful festivals and take advantage of the temperate weather— heavy winter snowfalls are great for skiers, but make it hard to hike the gorgeous trails through the national parks and around the lakes Towada-ko and Tazawa-ko. There's no well-trodden *gaijin* trail through the region; the appeal of Tōhoku is the opportunity to stray from the beaten path. Although very few people speak English, if you've got even basic Japanese skills you'll be surprised at how many people are eager to talk with you and hear about your travels. You may suddenly find yourself chatting with the after-work crowd at a small-town *izakaya* and sampling the special local sake, or relaxing in an *onsen* with newfound friends.

HIGHLIGHTS OF NORTHERN HONSHŪ

RĀMENMANIA Slurp up a storm in **Morioka**, city of noodles (p. 304).

YOUR MOVE. Join the game in **Tendō**, chess piece capital of Japan (p. 286).

TIME MACHINE. Marvel at 11th-century splendor in the gardens of Motsu-ji in **Hiraizumi** (p. 301).

AIZU-WAKAMATSU (合津若松)　☎0242

Aizu-Wakamatsu, the oldest city in Fukushima Prefecture, traces its history to Japan's feudal era, when the Matsudaira clan established themselves at the castle Tsuruga-jō. When the clan sided against the Tokugawa shōgunate during the Boshin Civil War, however, a month-long siege left them defeated and Tsuruga-jō burned to the ground. It was rebuilt in the 1960s. Though little other evidence remains of the city's feudal past, the modern downtown is chock-full of cultural sights, and the city is a good base for exploring Ura-Bandai and nearby Kitakata.

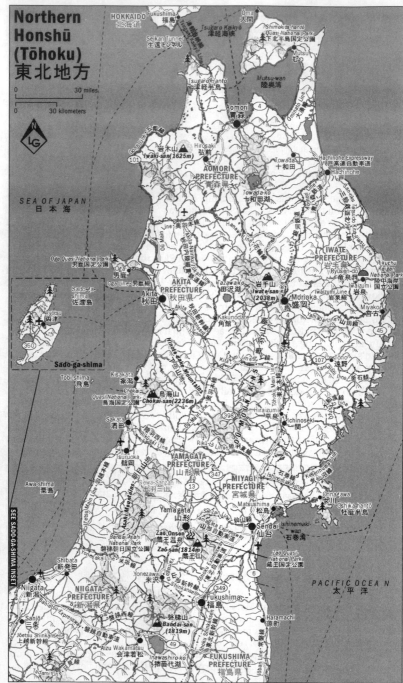

Northern Honshū (Tōhoku)

東北地方

SEE SADO-GA-SHIMA INSET

⌨ TRANSPORTATION. The **Tōhoku shinkansen** runs from Tōkyō or Ueno Station to Koriyama (1½hr., 44 per day, ¥7970), where you'll have to switch to the JR Banetsu Saisen Line (1¼hr., about 6 per day, ¥1110) to reach Aizu-Wakamatsu. From Niigata, take the Ban-etsu Line directly to Aizu-Wakamatsu (2½hr., 2 per day, ¥2210) or the express bus from the Niigata Bus Terminal (1¾hr., 4 per day, ¥2000). From Fukushima, take the shinkansen one stop west to Koriyama and pick up the Ban-etsu Line. From Nikkō, but you have to change trains at Aizu-Tajima (3½hr., ¥3380). If you have a **car**, you can reach Aizu-Wakamatsu from Tōkyō on the Tōhoku Expressway. At the Koriyama Interchange, get on the Ban-etsu Expressway and follow it to the Aizu-Wakamatsu Exit (280km, 4hr.). Niigata connects to Aizu-Wakamatsu via the Ban-etsu Expressway, and Fukushima is just north of the Koriyama Interchange off the Tōhoku Expressway. From Nikkō, take Rte. 119 from the Utsonomiya Interchange.

A network of **public buses** serves Aizu-Wakamatsu, and if you're planning extensive sightseeing, it's worth getting a one-day **free pass** (¥920) at the bus terminal across from the train station. Buses #14 and 15 loop around the city center. Bus #3 runs to Oyaku-en and Aizu-Bukeyashiki. There's **bike rental** a few minutes east of the station, at **Takahashi Rent-a-cycle.** (Open Mar.-Nov. daily 8am-5pm. ¥1000 per day.) For a **taxi**, call **Aizu Taxi** (☎38-1234).

◪⌨ ORIENTATION AND PRACTICAL INFORMATION. Aizu-Wakamatsu lies on an easily navigable grid that runs from the train station in the north to Tsurugajō in the south. The main north-south avenue is **Chūō-dōri,** which intersects **Nanokomachi-dōri** at the city center. **Tourist information** is available at a small booth inside the train station (☎32-0688; open M-Sa 10am-6pm) and at the north gate of the castle (☎27-4005; open daily 8:30am-5:30pm). The **police station** is a 5min. walk west of the train station. There is a nighttime **emergency clinic,** 2-8, Shiro-mae (☎28-1199), at the Hoken Center. **Internet access** is available a few blocks south of the post office at **ePallete,** in the basement of Tsutaya. You can change money at any of the **banks** on Chūō-dōri. The **Central Post Office,** at the intersection of Chūō-dōri and Nanokomachi-dōri, has an **international ATM. Postal code:** 965.

⌨⌨ ACCOMMODATIONS AND FOOD. The best deals on beds are the two youth hostels, but both are inconveniently far from the city center. **Aizu-no-Sato Youth Hostel (HI) ❶** (合津の里ユースホステル), 36, Aizu-Shiokawa-chō (☎0241-27-2054) has simple dorms for ¥2200. Take the JR Ban-etsu Line to Shiokawa Station and walk 10min. For the pleasantly rural **Aizuno Youth Hostel (HI) ❶** (合津野ユースホステル), 88, Aizu-Takada-chō (☎55-1020) take the infrequent JR Tadami Line to Aizu-Takada Station and walk 20min. northwest. (Dorms ¥3200.) A few minutes east of Aizu-Bukeyashiki is **Minshuku Takaku ❸** (民宿多賀来 ; ☎26-6299; singles with 2 meals ¥6000). Close to the train station, there are three business hotels. **Eki-mae Fuji Grand Hotel ❷** (駅前フジグランドホテル), 5-25, Ekimaemachi (☎24-1111; fax 24-3122), is the first hotel when you turn right out of the station, and offers spacious rooms with TV, A/C, and private bath. (Singles ¥4800.) Directly behind the Fuji Grand is **Hotel Alpha One ❷,** 5-8, Ekimae-machi (☎32-6868; fax 32-6822), with identical rooms. (¥4850.) A few minutes east of the station is the **Washington Hotel ❸** (合津若松ワシントンホテル), where singles run ¥5600.

If you're cooking for yourself, there's a **convenience store** next to the train station. There are few restaurants are along the main drag, though some hidden gems lie on Nanokomachi-dōri. One of the most famous places to eat in Aizu-Wakamatsu is **Takino ❷**(田季789 ; ☎25-0808), which specializes in *wappameshi*, a delectable dish of rice, wild herbs, salmon, and salmon eggs lightly steamed in cypress wood. From the post office, head one block east, then two blocks south, then turn left; the restaurant is to the left. (Open daily 11am-9pm.) Equally renowned is **Mitsutaya ❷** (満田屋 ; ☎27-1345), where you can try 8 varieties of *dengaku*, bamboo

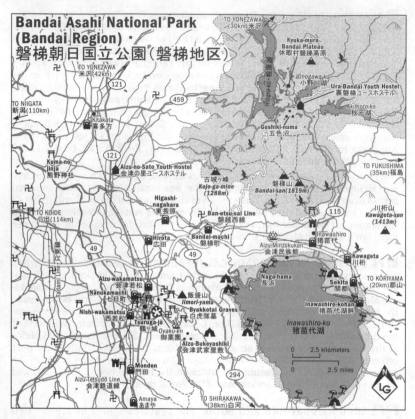

Bandai Asahi National Park (Bandai Region) ·
磐梯朝日国立公園（磐梯地区）

skewers of meats and vegetables grilled in sweet *miso* paste over an open fire. From the post office, head one block south and two blocks west, turning right at the traffic light. It's on the right. (Open daily 10am-5pm.) **Fukuman** ❸ （ふくまん； ☎24-6377) strives to recreate *samurai* meals with an emphasis on fresh fish and local produce. The *kaiseki* chefs serve up exquisite meals, as much a feast for the eyes as for the palate. From the post office, head south and turn left at the fifth traffic light; it's on the left. (Open M and W-Su 11am-2pm and 5-9pm.) For reasonably priced sushi platters, check out **Sushiman** ❷ （寿し万；☎24-1281), one block east of Fuji Grand Hotel in a rustic old building. (Open daily 10am-10pm.)

🔲 **SIGHTS.** Aizu-Wakamatsu's main attraction, **Tsuruga-jō** （鶴ヶ城）, known as Crane Castle, is one of Tōhoku's most famous castles. Although the current castle is a 1965 replica, the original walls are still visible, and the moat them is authentic. Inside are artifacts from the Meiji Restoration. The surrounding park is famous for cherry-blossom viewing and the *rinkaku* tearoom designed by the son of Sen no Rikyu, creator of the Japanese tea ceremony. (☎27-4005. Open daily 8:30am-4:30pm. Tower admission ¥400, tearoom ¥150, combo ¥500.) The **Fukushima Museum,** east of the castle, has local history exhibits. (☎28-6000. Open Tu-Su 9:30am-5pm. ¥260.) The **Aizu Sake History Museum,** 5min. north of Tsuruga-jō, is in a brewery that's been running for 350 years. (☎26-0031. Open daily mid-Mar. to mid-Dec. 8:30am-5pm; mid-Dec. to mid-Mar. 9am-4:30pm. ¥300.)

The **Oyaku-en Botanical Garden** (御薬園) was started by the lords of Aizu in 1670 to grow medicinal herbs for the town. Today, they grow about 400 different kinds of herbs, available for purchase in the gift shop. (Take the bus from platform #4 (15min., every 30min., ¥210.) ☎27-2472. Open daily 8:30am-5pm. ¥310.) Stroll through a tearoom, a rice-cleaning mill, and the housing quarters of **Aizu Bukeyashiki** (会津武家屋敷), a large scale re-creation of a traditional *samurai* residence, modeled after the mansion of Saigo Tanomo, chief retainer of the Aizu clan. (Take the bus from platform #5 (every 30min., 15min., ¥210). ☎28-2525. Open daily Apr.-Nov. 8:30am-5pm; Dec.-Mar. 9am-4:30pm. ¥850.)

The mountain **Iimori-yama** (飯盛山) hosts a memorial to the Byakkotai, or White Tigers, a group of *samurai* youth who committed *seppuku* (disembowelment) here during the Boshin Civil War, mistakenly believing that Tsuruga-jō had been captured. (Always open. Free.) Farther down the hill is the **Sazae-dō**, a six-sided building containing statues of the Goddess of Mercy and a spiral staircase that lets you to ascend and descend without retracing your steps. (☎22-3163. Open daily summer 8:15am-sunset; winter 9:30am-4:30pm. ¥400, students ¥300.) At the base of the hill, **Byakkotai Memorial Hall** displays portraits of the White Tigers and video documentaries. (Open daily Apr.-Nov. 8am-5pm; Dec.-Mar. 8:30am-4:30pm. ¥400.)

■ **FESTIVALS.** For a small regional capital, Aizu-Wakamatsu hosts a number of festivals, with the four main celebrations coordinating with the seasons. The three-day **Autumn Festival** (Sept. 22-24), features a costumed procession around Tsuruga-jō to the tune of a drum-and-fife band, as well as a children's parade and an evening lantern display. Similar festivities occur at the winter **Sainokami**, the **Summer Festival**, and the spring **Higan-jishi**. On July 12, one of three **Rice Planting Festivals** is held at the Isasumi Shrine in Aizu-Takada, featuring Saotome dancers wearing traditional Japanese sedge hats. In the **Higashiyama Spa Summer Festival**, huge colorful tower-floats are placed in the nearby Yugawa River.

KITAKATA (喜多方)　　　　　　☎0241

Kitakata is a pleasant daytrip from Aizu-Wakamatsu, especially if you appreciate the subtle flavors and aromas of nature's perfect food: *rāmen*. Though many towns claim to be the *rāmen* capital, few can take the heat of Kitakata's kitchens. Home to only 37,000 people, Kitakata boasts over 130 *rāmen* restaurants, giving the town one of the world's highest person to *rāmen* shop densities. After slurping down a few bowls, walk them off by exploring the picturesque old storehouses of Kitakata's *kura* districts.

As far as food goes, just follow your nose. Each *rāmen* shop offers a different variation, and half the fun of visiting is seeing what you end up with. Before heading back to Aizu-Wakamatsu, take an hour or so to see some of the 2600 *kura* (storehouses), which feature traditional mud-colored or black-and-white facades or more modern Western-style brick fronts. Since Kitakata merchants were eager to ensure the safety of their *miso*, rice, and *sake*, the popularity of the durable and fireproof *kura* exploded. When you've seen your fill, wind down with a quick visit to the **Yamatogawa Sake Brewing Museum**, 15min. north of the station, where you can sample local *sake* and stroll around the 18th-century brewery. (Open daily 9am-4:30pm. Free.)

Kitakata is connected to Aizu-Wakamatsu by the JR Ban-etsu Line (20min., 1 per hr., ¥320), and the frequent train means that it's possible to head to Kitakata for lunch and be back in Aizu-Wakamatsu by early afternoon. In Kitakata, two main streets run north from the train station—both are lined with countless *rāmen* shops and *kura*. There's a small **tourist information center** outside the train station, where you can pick up an English map. (☎24-2633. Open daily 8:30am-5:15pm.)

NORTHERN HONSHŪ

Bike rental is available on the northeast side of the station. (Open daily 8am-6pm. ¥500 for 2hr. ¥1500 per day.) In case you need to stay, **Kitakata Hotel ❷** across from the station has Western rooms with A/C and TV. (☎22-0139; fax 22-0969. ¥5000.)

URA-BANDAI (裏磐梯)   ☎0241

The 1888 eruption of Bandai-san gave birth to stunning Ura-Bandai, also known as the Bandai-kōgen Plateau. Loved for its ski slopes, the region is quite quiet in summer, when visitors are treated to attractive hikes and lakeside amusements, as well as a chance to climb the volcano itself. A part of Bandai-Asahi National Park, Ura-Bandai can be explored using either Aizu-Wakamatsu or Fukushima as a base.

AT A GLANCE

CLIMATE: The entire area sees extremely long winters—at some resorts you can ski as late as May. In summer, expect mild, temperate weather and frequent rain.

CAMPING: There are campsites throughout the park, but be prepared for frequent summer rains.

HIGHLIGHT: Outside ski season, the main draw for tourists is the **Goshiki-numa** (Five-Colored Lakes) walking trail.

GATEWAY: The nearest transportation hub is the town of **Inawashiro,** though most accommodations are on the plateau near the Goshiki-numa Iriguchi Bus Stop.

⌨ TRANSPORTATION. The two starting points for trips into the park are Aizu-Wakamatsu and Fukushima. From Aizu-Wakamatsu, an infrequent **bus** runs to **Bandai-kōgen-eki** via Goshiki-numa (1½hr., 1 per day, ¥1670). Alternatively, take a bus to Inawashiro (50min., 1 per hr., about ¥1000) and change to a bus for Goshiki-numa Iriguchi and Bandai-kōgen-eki (30min., 1 per hr., around ¥800). From Fukushima, buses run to Bandai-kōgen-eki (3hr., Apr.-Nov. 2-3 per day, ¥2870). The nearest **train** station is **JR Inawashiro Station,** just behind the Inawarisho bus terminal. From Aizu-Wakamatsu, the JR Ban-etsu Line runs to Inawashiro. From Fukushima, first take the local train to Koriyama, where you can pick up the JR Ban-etsu Line. There are also **taxis** (☎0242-32-2950) operating in the area.

▣◪ ORIENTATION AND PRACTICAL INFORMATION. North of Inawashiro, **Goshiki-numa Iriguchi Bus Stop** is the main entrance to the park and the focal point for the area's accommodations. From there, the Goshiki-numa (五色沼) trail is a 5min. walk. At the trail's western end is **Bandai-kōgen Bus Stop,** the jumping-off point for the hike around Lake Hibara and the trek to the top of the volcano.

In winter, expect below-freezing temperatures in the mountains. Even in summer, bring a hat and gloves if you're planning on climbing Bandai-san. The park **visitor's center** is at the Goshiki-numa Iriguchi Bus Stop. (Open daily 8:30am-4pm.) It's the best place for hiking maps and detailed English information.

▥⊡ ACCOMMODATIONS AND FOOD. Though the old building has seen better days, the **Ura-Bandai Youth Hostel (HI) ❶** (裏磐梯ユースホステル) is a cheap choice near the Goshiki-numa trail. (☎32-2811. Bike rental ¥2000 per day. Closed late Nov. to early Apr. Dorms ¥2850.) One of the homiest accommodations in the area is **◪Pension Emu ❷** (ペンション絵夢), across the road from the Goshiki-numa Bus Stop and on the left. The English-speaking owner plays in a rock band and is an avid Beatles fan; his brother paints the dream-like pictures on the walls. (☎32-2228. On-site *onsen*. Singles with bath ¥5000, with 2 meals ¥8500.) Farther up the street on the right is the **Resort Inn ❸**, a good bargain for standard Western rooms. (☎32-2155. 2 meals included. ¥6000.) Classy, villa-style **Fraser Hotel ❹** is

100m down the road from Goshiki-numa Bus Stop. (☎32-3470. 2 meals included. ¥12,000.) The visitor's center has an extensive listing of **campsites**. Pitches cost around ¥500; some campgrounds rent equipment.

Most accommodations serve meals; otherwise options are pretty bleak. Restaurants cluster around both bus stops, but most are expensive, unmemorable cafes. Worth mentioning, however, is sophisticated **Il Regalo** ❸ (イルレガーロ ; ☎32-3607), which serves top-notch Italian cuisine in a Continental dining room. For meals on the go, there's a **convenience store** next door.

🏔 HIKING. The area's most popular hike, **Goshiki-numa**, is a pleasant 1hr. stroll along five swamps that range from light green to chemical blue, colored by minerals melted in the catastrophic eruption. Although the trail is very busy in summer, the hike is the highlight of a visit. The trail begins just behind Goshiki-numa Iriguchi Bus Stop, and finishes near Bandai-kōgen Bus Stop. A 3km loop from Bandai-kōgen Bus Stop runs around the jagged shoreline and forested inlets **Hibara-ko** (檜原湖), the largest of Ura-Bandai's lakes. Campsites and pensions dot the trail.

The hike to the top of **Bandai-san** (1819m) takes about 4hr., so you can get up and down in one day. Views from the summit take in the entire plateau, and the crater is filled with an eerily red-hued lake. The entrance to the ascending trail is just south of Bandai-kōgen Bus Stop. Before tackling the mountain, check with the visitor center about trail conditions and local forecasts.

⛷ SKIING. Ura-Bandai is one of Tōhoku's most popular skiing districts, boasting over 30 separate ski areas. In winter, an extensive network of shuttle buses connects the resorts. **Inawashiro Ski Area** has 16 different trails that appeal to all skill levels; one (extremely difficult) has a 42° slope. **Bandai International Ski Area,** on the eastern side of Bandai-san, has beginner and intermediate trails and a snowboarding school. Popular family destination **Inawashiro Resort Ski Area** offers nine different trails and night skiing, while **Numajiri Ski Area** is Tōhoku's oldest, offering 14 trails and snowboarding and skiing schools. The **Alts Bandai Ski Area** is one of the region's largest. Japan's longest cross-country course (10km) calls **Ura-Bandai Cross Country Ski Area** home, while family-friendly **Urabandai Ski Area** offers a cross-country trail around the crater.

FUKUSHIMA (福島)   ☎0245

Fukushima is a pleasant place to stay the night if you're passing though the Ura-Bandai area. There aren't really any sights, but the downtown area is sparkling and new, and there are a surprising number of cosmopolitan restaurants and cafes. Direct **buses** run from Bandai-kōgen-eki (3hr., Apr.-Nov. 2-3 per day, ¥2870). Fukushima is also on the JR Tōhoku *shinkansen* line between Koriyama and Yonezawa. Buses and trains arrive at JR Fukushima Station, on the west edge of downtown. A small **tourist information** desk in the station has English city maps. (☎25-3722. Open daily 9am-5pm.) **Postal code:** 960.

Although there is no shortage of places to stay, your choices are essentially limited to cookie-cutter business hotels. Across from the West Exit of the station is **Fukushima View Hotel** ❸ (福島ビューホテル), 13-73, Ōta-machi, one of the newest area hotels. Fairly standard Western-style rooms have TV, A/C, and attached bath. Bars and restaurants share the building. (☎31-1111; fax 34-1303. ¥6800.) Just up the road is the **Tōyoko Inn** ❸ (東横イン), which offers smaller rooms in an older building. (☎34-1045; fax 34-1046. ¥5800.) On the other side of the station is the slightly ritzier **Hotel Tatsumiya** ❸, which has equivalent rooms to the View Hotel, but a wider selection of dining and drinking options. (☎22-5111. ¥7000.)

Lots of businessmen pass through Fukushima, so it's not surprising that restaurants have opened up around the station. For fun-to-eat *kaiten-zushi*, head to **Wasabi** ❷ (わさび), in JR Fukushima Station. At ¥100-300 per plate, the high-quality sushi is an incredible bargain, and there's free green tea and *miso* soup. (☎26-3401. Open daily 11am-10pm.) For late-night eats and cheap drinks, **Chuck Wagon Honkey Tonk Saloon ❷** (チャックワゴン), two blocks east of the station, has tasty taco and enchilada platters for ¥680. (☎28-1328. Kirin ¥400. Open daily 5pm-3am.)

NIIGATA (新潟)   ☎025

The prefectural capital of Niigata, one of the largest cities in Northern Honshū, has been an important industrial center and commercial port for centuries. The area receives some of the heaviest winter snowfalls in Asia, but the summer transforms Niigata into an exciting urban playground as city-dwellers shake off the winter chill and descend upon the shopping streets and outdoor arcades in a frenzy. Although most travelers use the city as a gateway to Sado-ga-shima, it's worth spending a night in the city, even if only to stroll the bustling streets and immerse yourself in the fast-paced lifestyle of modern Japan.

ON THE WEB	Niigata City: www.city.niigata.niigata.jp

▛ TRANSPORTATION. The JR Jōetsu **shinkansen** runs via Echigo-Yuzawa (40min., every 15-30min., ¥4730) to Tōkyō, Ueno Station (2hr., ¥10,270). Niigata is also on the **JR Uetsu Line,** which runs hourly via Tsuruoka (2 ¼hr., 1 per hr., ¥3890) to Akita (3¾hr., ¥6510). From Nagano, take the *shinkansen* to Takisaki and transfer to the JR Jōetsu Line. From Ōsaka or Kyōto, take the limited express train as far as Kanazawa and transfer to the JR Hokuriku Line, which runs directly to Niigata (3½hr., 5 per day, ¥14,480). All trains arrive at **JR Niigata Station,** at the southeast corner of the city. A few daily **inter-city buses** connect Niigata to Aizu-Wakamatsu (1¾hr., ¥2000), Kanazawa (4¾hr., ¥4580), Nagano (3½hr., ¥3060), Sendai (4hr., ¥4500), and Yamagata (3¾hr. ¥3500). There are night buses to Tōkyō, Ikebukuro (5¼hr., ¥5250) and Ōsaka/Kyōto (9¼hr., ¥9450). All lines originate at the Bandai Bus Center in the northern part of the city, though most stop at JR Niigata Station before leaving. Buses leave every 15min. from bus stand #6 in front of the train station for **Sado Kisen Ferry Terminal** (15min., ¥180). From the terminal **ferries** (2½hr., 6 per day, ¥2060) and **jetfoils** (1hr., 10 per day, ¥5960, round-trip ¥10,730) go to Sado's main port, Ryōtsu. An **airport** northeast of the city serves Korea, China, Hiroshima, Nagoya, Ōsaka, Sapporo, and Tōkyō. Small planes fly to **Sado Airport.** A bus runs from Niigata Station to the airport (25min., every 30min. 7am-7pm, ¥350).

In the city, an extensive network of **city buses** radiates outwards from the bus station to the residential districts, which are of little interest to the traveler. If you want a rental car, **Eki Rent-a-Car** (☎33-9308), **Nippon Rent-a-Car** (☎32-5789), and **Toyota Rent-a-Car** (☎33-0100) have offices in the station.

▛ ▜ ORIENTATION AND PRACTICAL INFORMATION. The city center is north of the train station, and is divided by the Shinano River into northern and southern sections. North of the river are the majority of the banks and big businesses, while the south is the shopping and entertainment district. The friendly, English-speaking staff of the **tourist information office** outside the Bandai Exit of Niigata Station have a ton of information on Niigata and nearby Sado-ga-shima. If you plan to make the ferry crossing, have the staff phone ahead to make reservations. (☎241-7914. Open daily 8:30am-5:45pm.) There's no shortage of **banks** in the downtown area and along the main street. There is a small **police** booth inside the station. **Internet access** is available on the second floor of the Garesso building, next to the train station, at the **CD Garden.** (☎290-6611. Open daily 10am-9pm. ¥100 for 30min.) The **Central Post Office** is 10min. north of the train station by foot, and has an **international ATM. Postal code:** 950.

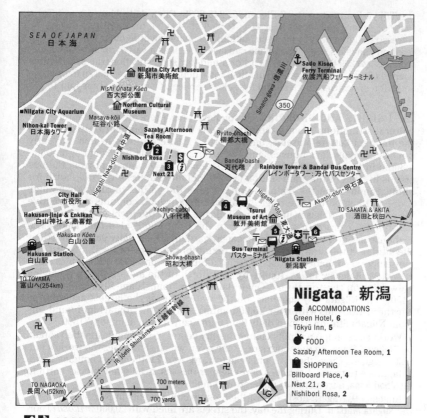

Niigata · 新潟

🏠 ACCOMMODATIONS
Green Hotel, **6**
Tōkyū Inn, **5**

🍴 FOOD
Sazaby Afternoon Tea Room, **1**

🛍 SHOPPING
Billboard Place, **4**
Next 21, **3**
Nishibori Rosa, **2**

🏠🍴 ACCOMMODATIONS AND FOOD. Niigata has an extremely competitive hospitality market, which means it's relatively easy to find a cheap night's lodging. Before settling on a hotel, spend a few minutes wandering around the side streets near the Bandai Exit; since hotels are constantly switching hands, there's a chance you'll stumble on a ridiculously low rate. A few blocks east of the train station, **Green Hotel** ❷ (グリンホテル), 1-4-9, Hanazono, has clean and comfortable Western-style rooms with A/C. (☎246-0431; fax 246-0345. From ¥4500.) Just down the street is the **Single Inn Daiichi** ❷ (シングルイン第 一), 1-6-1, Hanazono, which offers nearly identical rooms. (☎241-3003; fax 241-3003. ¥4500.) A **Hotel Alpha One** ❸, 1-7-18, Hanazono, just down the road, sets the standard with friendly service and bright, spacious rooms. (☎246-5555; fax 245-7550. From ¥5350 per person.) The more upscale **Tōkyū Inn** ❸ (東急イン), 1-2-4, Benten, is also close to the station, and offers more luxurious rooms, with bars and restaurants in the lobby. (☎243-0109; fax 243-0401. From ¥7700.)

Niigata has no shortage of restaurants, and during the warm summer months it feels like the entire city is dining out. The best option for cheap eats is **Mujinzō** ❶ (無尽蔵), an extremely popular neighborhood noodle shop which churns out steaming hot bowls of *rāmen* in record time. There are a number of different noodle shapes and flavors of broth to choose from. It's across the street from the Green Hotel. (☎290-6366. Open daily 11am-10pm.) Another gem is **Rikyūan** ❷ (利休庵), which serves huge wooden tubs of homemade *soba* that will feed two (¥1200), and delicious *una-don* dinner sets for ¥1000. It's around the corner from the Tōkyū Inn next to the 7-Eleven. (☎243-6698. Open daily 11am-10pm.) For a taste of Americana, **Royal Host ❶** (ロヤルホスト), on the first floor of the Garesso Building next to the train station, is a sparkling little diner where you can feast on pancakes, eggs, bacon and sausage as well as a variety of subs and sandwhiches. (☎290-6591. Open 24hr.) For a mid-day sophistication, the **Sazaby Afternoon Tea Room,** on the first floor of Mitsukoshi department store, has an impressive selection of pastries and teas and first-class service. (Open daily 11am-4pm.)

◙ ⌂ **SIGHTS AND SHOPPING.** If you have time, there are several interesting cultural attractions around the city center. The most popular tourist sight is the **Northern Culture Museum,** on the former castle grounds, which currently houses gardens, farmhouses, and tea arbors. (Open daily 8:30am-5pm, 9am-4:30pm in the winter. ¥700.) Tour buses depart for the museum from the bus stands in front of the train station (¥1670 includes admission). Walk north for about 25min. from the train station, or take the #8 bus to Shiyakusho-mae Stop, and just across the river is **Hakusan Park,** which contains an attractive lotus pond and **Hakusan-jinja,** a small shrine where the local god of marriage has lived for more than 400 years. In the park you'll also find **Enkikan,** a teahouse set in a beautifully landscaped garden. (Open daily 9am-5pm.) Near the station, the **Tsurui Museum of Art,** exhibits the work of local modern and contemporary Japanese artists. (Open Tu-Su 10am-5pm. ¥500.) For a bird's-eye city view, **Rainbow Tower,** 10min. by foot north of the station, has a revolving viewpoint on the top floor. (Open daily 10am-5pm, 10am-10pm in summer. ¥450.) The **Niigata City Aquarium,** on the waterfront, is the largest aquarium in Northern Honshū, with over 20,000 animals. Take the Aquarium-bound bus from Niigata Station. (Open daily 9am-5pm, 9am-7pm in summer. ¥1500.)

World-class shopping spots clutter the city center. Your first destination should be **Billboard Place,** on the south side of the river, which showcases the world's hottest designers. Cross the river and head towards **Next 21,** the tallest building in Niigata, home to trendy boutiques. For cheaper threads, head a few blocks north to **Nishibori Rosa,** a tremendous underground mall.

August 7-9, Niigata hosts one of the most exciting events in Northern Honshū, the **Niigata Matsuri.** During the day, the streets are filled with 20,000 *mikoshi* (portable shrines), the most of any festival in Japan. At night, the parades converge on the Bandai bridge, where decorated boats carry illuminated shrines to the sea gods while the sky is lit up by a breathtaking fireworks display.

SADO-GA-SHIMA (佐渡島) ☎0259

In the pre-modern era, the island commonly known as Sado was far enough from Tōkyō that undesirable and out-of-favor intellectuals could be safely banished to its shores. Among the better known exiles were ex-emperor Juntoku, Buddhist priest Nichiren, and Zeami, the actor/playwright who developed *nō* theater. In 1601, a gold rush led to the importation of more criminals and Edo's homeless population to work in the mines. Historically, no one wanted to go to Sado; no wonder that in literature and music, the island is associated with sorrow and loneliness.

In a dramatic reversal, Sado today draws much of its income from tourists who very much do want to come to the island. No wonder, since this popular summer getaway offers a peek into Japan's less-developed past and rural present. Luckily, due to the extensive network of hostels and campsites, Sado is one of the most affordable destinations for the budget traveler in all of Japan. Although you could squeeze in the sights in two or three days, it's best to spend enough time on the island to fully absorb the quiet setting and unharried pace.

AT A GLANCE

HIGHLIGHTS: Splendid isolation, speckled with beaches and cultural attractions.

GATEWAYS: Niigata (p. 274) connects to Sado's east coast port of Ryōtsu (p. 278).

CLIMATE: Most of the year, Sado is cold, though it gets less snowfall than Niigata. Summers are warm.

WHEN TO GO: Summer, with its festivals, is the best time to visit.

TRANSPORTATION

Flights: Kagoshima Air (Niigata ☎025-273-0312, Ryōtsu ☎23-5005) connects Niigata Airport to **Ryōtsu** (15min.; 2-5 per day; ¥7250, 7-day return ¥11,020).

Ferries: From **Sado Kisen Ferry Terminal** there are **ferries** (2½hr., 6 per day, one-way ¥2060) and **jet foils** (1hr., 10 per day, ¥5960, round-trip ¥10,730) to Sado's main ferry port on Ryōtsu. In winter, service is greatly reduced. In summer, make reservations since tickets go quickly. From Naoetsu Port and Teradomari, 7 daily ferries and 2 jet foils run to **Ogi** and **Akadomari** respectively.

Buses: An extensive bus network means you can get almost anywhere via public transportation. Most lines only operate a few times per day. A 1- or 2-day **Free Pass** (¥1500/¥2000) grants unlimited use of public buses. Available at the ferry terminal or the information center in Sawata. From JR Sado Train Station, there are buses every 15min. to **Sado Kisen Ferry Terminal** (15min., ¥180) from bus stand #6. Buses connect Sado Airport to Ryōtsu Ferry Terminal (15min., ¥240).

Rentals: The best way to explore Sado is by car. **Kisen Rent-a-Car** (☎27-5195) has branches in all 3 ferry terminals. From ¥6000 per day. Kisen also rents **motorcycles,** but rent only if you're experienced— many of the coastal routes have blind curves and some are one-lane roads with passing strips. Most hostels rent **bikes** for around ¥1000 per day.

Hitchhiking: Many travelers report that thumbing rides is extremely easy, and the cheapest way to move around the island; however, Let's Go does not recommend hitchhiking.

Tours: Organized bus tours (teiki kankō) are extremely popular among Japanese tourists, and there are number of different tours departing from both Ryōtsu and Ogi.

Sado-ga-shima
佐渡島

ORIENTATION AND PRACTICAL INFORMATION

Most trips to Sado start at Ryōtsu, on the eastern shore. From there, you can head west across the plains to **Sawata** and **Mano,** stopping along the way at temples and cultural attractions. Or, head south to **Ogi,** a convenient base for exploring the southern mountains. Head north to **Aikawa,** the old gold mine capital, to explore the spectacular scenery of the northern mountain chain. There are a few places on the island where you can get information, but it's best to stock up on English pamphlets and maps in Niigata. The **Sado Kisen Ferry Company,** in both ferry terminals, has a great English pamphlet with maps, bus information, and attraction listings. There are also offices in Ryōtsu (p. 278) and Sawata (p. 279). Book lodgings in Niigata or at the ferry terminal in Ryōtsu—hotels fill up fast.

◘ FESTIVALS

On Sado, keep an eye out for *okesa* folk dances, *ondeko* demon drum dances, and the phallic *tsuburosashi* dance. April 28-29, Mano's **Sado Geinō Matsuri** performing arts festival features Sado's traditional dances. Held at Kusukari-jinja in Hamochi town on June 15, the **Hamochi Matsuri** focuses on *okesa* and *tsuburosashi* dances. One of Sado's most popular events, the three-day **Earth Celebration** usually occurs in mid-August, and features the Kodo Drummers of Heaven and performing arts groups from around the world. Sado becomes a veritable Woodstock with workshops, craft exhibits, and other attractions popping up in every corner. The **Kōzan Matsuri** in Aikawa is one of Sado's biggest, and features traditional dance performances, fireworks, and huge parades of floats. It's held July 25-27. **Ogi Mano Matsuri,** a port festival held August 28-30, features folk singing, lion dances, fireworks, and the slightly humorous tub-boat racing.The **Mano Matsuri,** October 15-16, is marked by the *jizō-odori* dancers, who carry huge *jizō* statues on their backs.

RYŌTSU (両津)　　　　　　　　　　　　　　　☎0259

Ryōtsu is the main gateway to Sado and is a pleasant little place to spend a night, though accommodation is cheaper in Mano and Sawata. Ryōtsu is one of the best places to see traditional dances. **Ryōtsu Kaikan** (両津会館) hosts nightly *okesa* and *ondeko* performances from April to September. If you're interested in the history of *nō* theater on the island, just south of Ryōtsu is the **Sado Nō-gaku-no-sato,** a modern museum housing masks, costumes, and robots that perform *nō* every few minutes. (Open daily 8:30am-5pm. ¥800.) Take the Sawata-bound Minami-sen Bus Line #2 to Nō-gaku-no-sato-mae Stop. There are few other sights, as Ryōtsu is mainly a staging point for trips around the island, though the town is near **Mt. Donden** (934m), one of the island's most popular hikes.

In the ferry terminal you'll find all the car rental agents. All buses depart from the adjacent bus stand. Across from the terminal is the **tourist information center.** (☎23-3300. Open Apr.-Sept. daily 8:30am-7pm.) On the same street, a number of **banks** exchange foreign currency and the **post office** has an **international ATM.** In an emergency, call ☎110 for **police;** ☎119 for **fire** or **ambulance.**

The majority of the resort hotels are near Ryōtsu, though the prices are inflated. One exception, 2km north of town, is **Sado Seaside Hotel ❸** (佐渡シーサイドホテル), run by a friendly, English-speaking staff, and offering comfortable *tatami* rooms and *onsen* access. (☎27-7211; fax 27-7213. Free shuttle to the port. ¥5500 per night; ¥10,000 with 2 meals.) Another commendable establishment is the lakeside **Kagetsu Hotel ❸** (花月ホテル), 10min. north of the pier on foot. (☎27-3131; fax 23-4446. From ¥5000 per person.) Ryōtsu has a number of modest restaurants that serve wonderful seafood from the Sea of Japan. At night, visit the **Ebisu** quarter, where you'll find many *izakaya*. Before skipping town, try the delicious meat and noodle dishes at one of the island's best restaurants, **Ajisai ❸** (味彩), near Kagetsu Hotel. (Open M-Tu and Th-Su 11am-2pm and 4pm-10pm.)

CENTRAL SADO   ☎0259

Central Sado, the farm-strewn heart of the island, includes the towns of **Sawata, Niibo, Hatano,** and **Mano,** as well as many historical sights. Temples in the area date back as early as the 8th century. The best-known is **Konpon-ji,** one of 44 headquarters of Nichiren Buddhism, which occupies the grounds where Nichiren Shōnin, the founder of the radical sect, was first brought when he was exiled in 1261. The temple is a few kilometers south of Niibo on the Minami-sen Bus Line. (Open daily 8am-4pm. ¥300.) About 2km east of Konpon-ji near Onogawa Dam is ancient **Seisui-ji,** founded in 808 and modeled after Kiyomizu-dera in Kyōto. In **Mano, Myosen-ji** was erected by Abutsubo Nittoku, Nichiren's first disciple in Sado. It includes a 24m, five-storied pagoda modeled after Tōshō-gū at Nikkō. Just down the road is **Kokubon-ji,** the oldest temple in Sado, founded by Emperor Shōmu in 741. It burned down twice—the last reconstruction was in 1679. The current foundation stones are from the original structure, as is the wooden image of Yakushi Nyorai. Southeast of central Mano, near the Mano Goryō-iriguchi Bus Stop on the Sawata-Ogi Bus Line (#10), is the **Sado Rekishi-Densetsukan** or **Toki-no-Sato,** which houses automated exhibits of Sado's illustrious history. (Open daily 8am-5:30pm. ¥700.) **Sawata** primarily serves as the island's administration center, but it's worth stopping at the **Silver Village** resort on the northeastern edge of town for lunch where you can see a puppet performance .

Two bus lines that connect Ryōtsu to the west coast towns also serve Central Sado. The Minami-sen Line (#2) runs from Ryōtsu along the southern highway via Niibo and Hatano to Mano. The Hon-sen Line (#10) serves the main northern highway, which connects Ryōtsu to Sawata via Sado Airport. Buses run infrequently, so it's useful to rent a bike at one of the hostels. Tourist information is available in Sawata at **Sado Travel Bureau.** (☎57-2126. Open M-Sa 9am-5:30pm, Su 9am-noon.) There are a number of **banks,** but it's the **post office** that has an **international ATM.**

One of the best accommodations on the island is the ◪**Green Village Youth Hostel (HI)** ❶ (グリンヴィレヂユースホステル), just a few minutes from Uryūya Bus Stop on the Minami-sen Line. This family-run hostel is charming and delightfully laid-back, and the *tatami* dorm rooms are as clean and comfy as they come. There's free Internet access, and the seafood dinners (¥1000) are outstanding. (☎22-2719. Hearty breakfast ¥600. Bike rental ¥1000 per day. Dorms ¥2900.) An incredibly welcoming staff make **Kunimisō ❸,** a 15min. walk from Uryūya Bus Stop, one of the most popular minshuku for repeat visitors to the island. If you phone ahead, the owner will pick you up from the bus stop, and if you stay for a few days, you might get to see his puppet collection. (☎22-2316. Meals included. ¥7000 per person.) If you're looking for solitude, the **Sado Hakusan Youth Hostel (HI)** ❶ is in a quiet village near Sawata. Guests can lounge at the nearby *onsen* free of charge. Take the Aikawa-bound bus from Ryōtsu, and get off at the Kubota Stop (40min.). From there, phone the hostel for a ride or walk 25min. (☎52-4422. Breakfast ¥600. Dinner ¥1000. Dorms ¥2400.)

OGI (小木)   ☎0259

Tourists flock en masse to Sado's second port town, Ogi, known for its *tarai-bune* (tub boats), used for harvesting seafood from the rocky coastline. To see what all the fuss is about, head west from the ferry terminal until you find a small jetty where you can take a 10min. jaunt around the harbor in a tub boat. (Open daily 8am-5pm. ¥450.) Farther down the jetty is the departure point for **sightseeing cruises,** which sail along the coastline to the **Sawazaki lighthouse** and the bamboo-fringed islands of **Ya-jima** and **Kyō-jima.** (Open daily Apr. to mid-Nov. 40min. cruise ¥1400.)

If you have a car or bike, there are interesting spots just outside town. Following the road to Shukunegi, you'll come to a solitary Jizō statue presiding over the road. Turn right here, and continue on the side road for another 300m, and you'll come to the steps to **Iwaseya Cave,** which contains the remains of a shrine. Also on the Shukunegi road is the **Sadokoku Ogi Folk Museum,** which has exhibits on the traditional Sado lifestyle. (Open Mar.-Oct. daily 8:30am-5pm, Nov.-Feb. M-F 8:30am-5pm. ¥500.)

To reach Ogi, go first to Sawata or Mano, where you can pick up the hourly bus. Buses arrive at the terminal behind the **post office**, which has an **International ATM**. One block west of the post office is a small **tourist office**, where you can see dance performances. (☎86-3200. Open daily 9:30am-5pm. Performances Mar.-Nov. ¥800 at the door, ¥700 in advance.) If you're looking for **bike rental**, head inland from the ferry terminal toward Hotel New Kihachiya; in front is the **Seaside Villa Shop**. (Open daily 7am-7pm. Bikes from ¥1500 per day.)

The **Ogi Sakuma-sō Youth Hostel ❶** (小木佐久間荘ユースホステル), in a quiet old farmhouse outside town, serves excellent food, and you can use the hot springs for free. From Ogi Port, walk uphill just over 1km until you see the building. (☎86-2565. Dorms from ¥2700.) In town, try **Gonzaya Ryokan ❸**, a traditional inn with beautiful *tatami* rooms. (☎86-3161; fax 86-3162. From ¥5000, with 2 meals ¥7000.) On the other side of the Ogi Peninsula is **Moto-hama Camp ❶**, as cheap as it gets. It's difficult to find; get directions from the tourist office. (Open July 1-Aug. 31. Rental equipment available. ¥1000 per pitch. ¥300 per person.) To sample the region's exquisite seafood, stop at **Sakae-zushi ❷**, behind the Marine Plaza, which has tasty *chirashi* sets for ¥1000. (Open daily 11:30am-10pm.)

AIKAWA (相川)   ☎0259

Although Aikawa was the largest settlement on the island during the gold boom days of Edo, today it's a sleepy little town. Two of the island's most popular destinations, the **Sado gold mines** and **Sekaku-wan,** are just outside of town, which a good base for exploring the northern cape. About 10min. by car or shuttle bus up the mountain is the **Sado Kinzan Gold Mine**, one of the island's most prolific mines during the Edo Period. It has largely been preserved in its original form. Unfortunately, the proprietors have installed kitschy animatronic robots to simulate the harsh working conditions. (Open daily 8am-5pm. ¥700.) About 500m up the same road is **Dōyū no Wareto**, an open-cast strip-mine that literally split the top of the mountain. Today, you can look down into the narrow trenches where the gold ore was extracted. If you have a car, continue up **Osado Skyline Drive**, a spectacular scenic road which ends just outside Ryōtsu. At the foot of the mountain is the **Aikawa Kyōdo Hakubutsukan**, with exhibits on mining culture and a craft studio. (Open daily 8:30am-5pm; closed Sa-Su from Dec-Feb. ¥300.) Nearby the **Sado Hanga-mura Art Museum** exhibits wood-block prints by Sado artists. (Open Mar.-Oct. daily 9am-5pm.) Aikawa is also the base for **Senkaku-wan,** a stunning strip of coastline about 10km north of town, famous for bizarre rock formations. Heading down to the docks in **Tassha** village or **Ageshima-yūen,** you can take a 30min. ride in a glass-bottom boat (open Apr.-Oct., every 30min., ¥850) or a normal boat (open Apr.-Oct., every 30min., ¥700).

Aikawa can be reached from Ryōtsu on the Honsen Line or from Sawata on the Nanaura-Kaigan Line. (1 per hr.) **Shuttle buses** chug up the mountain from the terminal in Aikawa to the mines, though it's also possible to take one of five direct buses from Ryōtsu (1¼hr., ¥860). If you're interested in the boat tours, both Tassha and Ageshima-yūen are located on the Kaifu-sen Bus Line, which connects Aikawa to Iwayaguchi. There is a small **tourist information center** next to the bus terminal. The main street has a **post office** with **International ATM access.**

In Aikawa, pass up the cookie-cutter minshuku for **Dōyū Ryokan ❸** (道遊旅館), an attractive inn with private *tatami* rooms. The ryokan is on a quiet side street near the bus terminal. (¥7000 per night. 2 meals included.) Cheap sleeps and home-cooked meals are yours at **Sado Bell Mer Youth Hostel ❶** (佐渡ベルメール ユースホステル), on a hilltop near Ageshima-yūen on Senkaku-wan. From Aikawa, take the Kaifu-sen bus line north to Minami-Himezu stop and walk 5min. towards the shore. (☎75-2011. ¥3200 per night.) **Familio Sado Aikawa ❷** is a modern resort near Kami-Ogawa on the Kaifu-sen Bus Line. (☎75-1020; fax 86-3162. Twins ¥11,000; quads ¥18,000.) Aikawa isn't well off for restaurants, so try to include meals with your lodgings. Small shops and bakeries sprinkle the main street.

NORTHERN CAPE

North of Senkaku-wan, settlements taper off as the rugged scenery becomes still wilder. The northern cape, also known as Sotokaifu, is home to the tallest mountains on the island, as well as a jagged coastline of rocks, cliffs, gorges, and tiny islets. Since public transportation is pretty infrequent this far north, it's best to rent a car and enjoy driving on the narrow coastal roads, though the Kaifu-sen line and Sotokaifu-sen Line will take you as far as Iwayaguchi from Aikawa and Ryōtsu respectively. The two main attractions are **Futatsu-game,** comprised of two small islands reminiscent of a pair of turtles, and **Ono-game,** a 167m-tall rock, covered in yellow day-lilies in the early summer. At Futatsu-game, a narrow strip of sand serves as a good swimming beach in warm weather and is a popular campsite popular among Japanese families. There is also a hostel near the northwest tip of the island at the Iwayaguchi Bus Stop. The **Soto-kaifu Youth Hostel ❶** (外海府ユースホ ステル) is run by a friendly family, and is perfect for getting away from it all. (☎78-2911. Full board available. Dorms ¥2300.)

YAMAGATA (山形) ☎0236

The capital of Yamagata Prefecture is nestled among mountains. Aside from castle ruins and museums, Yamagata is short on cultural sights, though the city center has shops and a cineplex. Few tourists spend much time in the city itself, but it's a convenient base for daytripping and a good overnight stop if you're heading north.

ON THE WEB	Yamagata City: www.city.yamagata.yamagata.jp

 TRANSPORTATION. JR Yamagata Station is on the southwestern edge of the city. From Sendai, Yamagata can be reached via the JR Senzan Line (1hr., 1 per hr., ¥1110). Yamagata is connected to Yonezawa by the JR Ōu Line (45min., 1 per hr., ¥820) and to Ōmagari (4hr., 1 per hr., ¥2940) via Tazawa-ko and Akita. From Tōkyō, take the JR Yamagata and Tōhoku *shinkansen* (2¾hr., every 10-15min., ¥11,060), which also connects Yamagata to Fukushima.

Next to the railway station is the **bus terminal,** where you can catch **city buses** and **direct shuttles** to Zaō Quasi-National Park and Yamadera. You can also catch **highway buses** to Sendai (about 1hr., every 30min., ¥1000) and Niigata (3¾hr., 8am and 4pm, ¥3500). From nearby Yama-ko Terminal, a **night bus** runs to Asakusa and Ueno in Tōkyō (8hr., 9:30pm, ¥6420). If you're looking to rent a car, try **Eki Rent-a-Car** (☎31-6746), near the station, or **Toyota** (☎25-0100), downtown.

 PRACTICAL INFORMATION. Yamagata lies on a slightly skewed grid, with Yamagata Station at the southwest corner. **Ekimae-dōri** is the major east-west street, starting right at the station. Major north-south axis **Nanoka-machi-dōri** intersects Ekimae-dōri several blocks to the east. The castle grounds are in the northwest, while **Hirashimizu,** a pottery village, is a 20min. bus ride southeast. **Tourist information** is available at an office on the second floor of the station (☎31-7856; open M-F 11am-6pm, Sa-Su 11am-5pm) and at the nearby Coco 21 building (☎24-0043; open M-Sa 9am-5:30pm). You can change money at any of the **banks** downtown, and there's **international ATM** access at the **Central Post Office** on Nanokamachi-dōri and at the small branch north of the station. In an emergency, call ☎110 for **police,** ☎119 for **fire** or **ambulance. Internet access** is available at a small stand on the 5th floor of the station. (¥100 per 15min.) **Postal code:** 990.

🛏🍴 ACCOMMODATIONS AND FOOD. The cheapest sleep in town is **Yamashiroya Ryokan ❷** (山城屋旅館), a few blocks north of the station on the western side of the tracks. The friendly staff provides homestyle meals for a reasonable price. (☎22-3007. Japanese-style rooms ¥4400 per person.) Business hotels cluster within walking distance of the station. One of the cheapest is the **Green Tōhoku ❷** (グリン東北), about 15min. northeast of the station. (☎32-6666. Japanese stylerooms ¥4000 per person; Western-style ¥4500 per person.) **Hotel Sakaeya ❷** (ホテルさかえや), just around the corner from the eastern exit, has standard Westernstyle rooms with private bath. (☎32-2311; fax 32-2310. ¥5000.) The classy **Hotel Castle ❹** (ホテルキャッスル), at the intersection of Eki-mae and Nanoka-machi, has spacious, modern rooms and numerous bars and restaurants. (☎31-3311. From ¥8500 per person.) You can't go ritzier than **Hotel Metropolitan Yamagata ❹** (ホテルメトロポリタン山形) in the train station. (☎28-1111. ¥10,000 per person.)

Many restaurants serve tasty Yonezawa marbled beef as well as the regional delicacy *imoni*, a winter stew of taro, beef, spring onions, and *konnyaku* (vegetable gelatin) simmered in a sweet soy sauce. In the souvenir shops, look for *fukimame*, a surprisingly crispy and sweet confection of boiled peas. The majority of Yamagata's restaurants are on Nanokamachi-dōri, though there are chains in the station. The city is also renowned for its *soba*. At **Shōji-ya ❸** (庄司屋 ; ☎22-1380), you can have it served *ita* style, cooled in ice water and served with *bonito* flake sauce. Box of *ita soba* ¥1600. (Just southwest of city hall. Open Tu-Su 11am-4pm and 5:30-8pm.) Across from the AZ store, off Nanokamachi-dōri, is **Sakaeya Honten ❷** (栄屋本店 ; ☎23-0766), a noodle house famed for chilled *rāmen* salads. (Salad ¥700. Open daily 11:30am-7pm.) Also on Nanokamachi-dōri is **Eleven ❷** (☎41-5626), a small Italian bistro with a selection of pasta dishes (¥800) and wonderful homemade pizzas (¥1000) to choose from. (Open daily 11am-9pm.)

🎡🎭 SIGHTS AND ENTERTAINMENT. Kajo-kōen, former castle grounds, is at the northwestern edge of the city. There's not much to see beyond moats and a gate, as the castle is ruined, ruined, ruined, but locals come for cherry-blossom viewing and sports facilities. (Free.) West of the park is the **City Museum,** once a hospital, and now home to medical artifacts and artworks. (Open Tu-Su 9am-4pm. ¥200.) At the northeast corner of the park, the **Yamagata Art Museum** has a minor collection of European paintings. (Open Tu-Su 10am-5pm. ¥500.) Far north on Nanokamachi-dōri, don't miss the former **Prefectural Office,** an elegant 1916 baroque building. (Open Tu-Su 9am-4:30pm. Free.)

Southeast of the city is the village of **Hirashimizu** (平清水), the center of the region's pottery industry. The district makes a pleasant daytrip, since there are a number of family-run showrooms as well as the renowned **Shichieumon-gama** (七右門窯 ; ☎42-7777), which gives pottery lessons. From Yamagata Station, take a Nishi-Zaō- or Geikō-dai-bound bus to Hirashimizu (20min., 1 per hr., ¥200).

At **Kajo Central,** a 24-story building connected to the train station via a skyway, you'll find restaurants and a 10-screen cineplex. For a nightcap, look no further than 🌙**Night Dew,** a popular *gaijin* hangout. Cover is ¥500, but the best deal is the ¥2500 package that includes 2 karaoke songs and the unlimited drinks you'll need to get through them. (A few blocks east of McDonald's on Nanokamachi-dōri. Free Internet access. Open daily until 5am.)

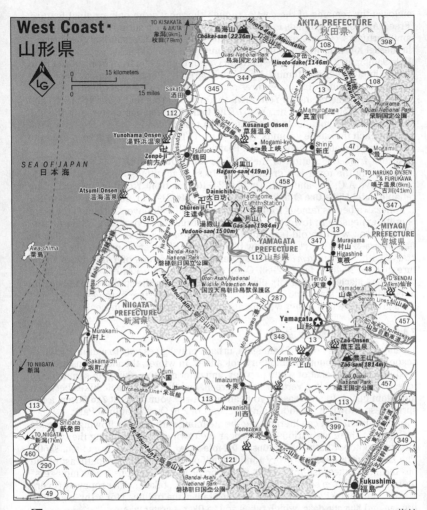

West Coast·
山形県

SEA OF JAPAN
日本海

FESTIVALS. The swirling and folk-singing dancers at **Hanagasa Matsuri** (花笠
祭り ; Aug. 6-8) attract up to 90,000 spectators. In 2005, the city will also host the
third biennial **Yamagata International Documentary Film Festival.** If you're interested
in finding out more or would like to volunteer, contact the organizing committee
at ☎24-8368 or visit www.city.yamagata.yamagata.jp/yidff.

YONEZAWA (米沢)   ☎0238

Yonezawa's history as a castle town began when the Uesugi clan moved house
from Niigata in the 17th century. Weaving its early fame on the silk trade, its main
attractions today are the quiet ruins of the castle and the opportunity to sample
Yonezawa beef. **Matsugaski-kōen** (松ヶ崎公園), about 2km west of the station,

encloses the remains of the castle, though the moat's the only original feature. (Free.) Also on the grounds is **Uesugi-jinja** (上杉神社), a shrine displaying Uesugi family artifacts. (Open Apr.-Nov. daily 9am-4pm. ¥400.) Just south of the shrine is the **Uesugi Kinekan,** which houses more ancestral knick-knacks. (Open Su-M and W-Sa 9am-5pm. ¥300.) Take the Shirabu Onsen-bound bus from Yonezawa-eki to Uesugi-jinja-mae Stop (10min., 1 per hr., ¥190). The **Uesugi Matsuri,** at the end of April and beginning of May, features a large-scale battle re-enactment.

The JR Ōu Line connects Yonezawa to Yamagata (50min., 1 per hr., ¥820) and Fukushima (45min., 1 per hr., ¥740). The **tourist information center** is in the station. (☎24-2965. Open daily 8am-6pm.) **Bike rental,** also in the station, is a good way to reach the castle grounds. (¥200 per hr.) The **post office** is across from the station and has an **international ATM. Postal code:** 992.

Across from the station is the historic **Hotel Otowaya** ❸ (ホテル音羽屋). Breakfast in the foyer is a great chance to soak up atmosphere. Western-style rooms have A/C, TV, and bath. (☎22-0124. Rooms from ¥5300 per person.) The reliable **Hotel Alpha One** ❸ is just down the road (☎21-7111. ¥5300 per person).

Yonezawa beef is famous for its marbled fat and rich flavor. Although the meat is quite expensive in town, it's worth the splurge if you're a hapless carnivore. Whether you want an old-fashioned steak, *shabu-shabu*, or *sukiyaki*, **Niku no Daikanbara** ❸ (肉の大河原), a few blocks north of the station in an old wooden house with rustic *tatami* rooms, serves several versions of Yonezawa's signature dish. (☎23-4502; fax 23-2983. Open daily 11am-10pm.) After your meal, head to the new **Machi-no-Hiroba** city plaza, midway between the station and the castle, lined with street stalls and performers. The plaza is festive in the evenings, and it's a great place to interact with locals and practice your Japanese.

ZAŌ ONSEN (蔵王温泉)   ☎023

Twenty kilometers north of Yamagata, urban sprawl gives way to a dramatic landscape of jagged mountains and fiery volcanoes. In winter, the mountains are covered in a thick blanket of white powder, and offer exciting skiing. In summer, the forests come to life in a verdant sea of green, and there are scenic hikes between mountain peaks. In any season, you can soak away your cares at **Zaō Onsen,** a hot spring resort town at the mountain base, part of Zaō Quasi-National Park.

In Zaō Onsen, you can literally see the steaming spring water flowing alongside the streets. There are various *onsen* near the town center, including the two tremendous outdoor baths of **Zaō Onsen Dai-rotemburo.** (Open daily from 9am. ¥450.) The **Zaō Sanroku Ropeway** (every 15min. 8am-5pm, ¥1200), 10min. southeast of the bus terminal, takes visitors to **Juhyō Kōgen,** home to Zaō's famous "snow monsters" (conifer trees frozen solid by the winds). From there, take another ropeway (every 15min. 8am-5pm, ¥1200) to **Zaō Jizō Sanchō Station,** the trailhead for a 1hr. hike over **Jizō-san** and **Kumano-dake,** which takes you to **Okama crater lake.**

In winter, Zaō transforms from a sleepy *onsen* town into the hub of one of the country's most popular skiing destinations. Zaō-san offers 14 slopes, 11 trails, and over 40 lifts. Extensive networks of shuttles take ski bunnies to the trails. One-day ski passes start at ¥4300, and discounted night skiing is available at some sites.

Zaō Quasi-National Park is an easy daytrip from Yamagata. **Buses** from Yamagata Station run to Zaō Onsen (40min., 1 per hr., ¥840). In winter, direct buses shuttle skiers from Tōkyō. Near the bus terminal, a small **tourist information center** provides hiking and skiing maps. (☎694-9328. Open daily 8am-5pm.) **Postal code:** 990.

There are close to 100 places to stay in the area, but during ski season, it's mandatory that you arrange stays prior to arriving. **Country Inn BeeHive** ❸ is a small hotel near the ropeway to Jizō. In addition to homecooked meals, a private TV, and A/C, you can enjoy a steam in one of the 24hr. private *onsen*. (☎694-2100. Check-in from 3pm. Check-out 11am. ¥8000-12,000 per night.) In summer, when the area is relatively untrafficked, you might daytrip from Yamagata, as Zaō is expensive. The majority of restaurants in town are unremarkable, but you shouldn't leave without trying *tamma konnyaku*, a jellied yam cake simmered in soy sauce.

YAMADERA (山寺)　　☎0236

Yamadera is one of Northern Honshū's most sacred sites. The temple dates back to 860, when Zen priests founded the original **Risshaku-ji** (立石寺). During the Edo Period, wandering poet Matsuo Bashō lavished praise on its tranquility with this *haiku:* "In the utter silence of a temple, a cicada's voice alone penetrates the rocks." Unfortunately, the crowds make it difficult to find the serenity that so impressed Bashō. Regardless, the 40 temples of the complex are stunning; even with the camera-fiends, it's impossible to not be awed by the lofty cedars and rocky mountainsides that serve as backdrop to Yamadera's contemplative aesthetic.

Before heading up to the temple complex, check out the **Bashō Kinenkan,** a small museum that details the poet's journey through Tōhoku. (About 10min. from the side of the station opposite the temple complex. Open Tu-Su 9am-4pm. ¥400.) From the station, maneuver through the maze of souvenir shops and cafes to the flight of steps farthest to the right. The first building at the top of the stairs is the **Konponchū-dō** (根本中堂), the main temple, which houses the "Flame of Belief," brought from Enryaku-ji in Kyōto and kept continuously burning for over 1000 years. After Enryaku-ji burned down, the flame from Yamadera was used to relight the parent-temple's flame. (Open 9am-4:30pm. ¥200.) The path to the left leads to **Hihōkan,** Yamadera's treasure hall, where you can see a sizeable collection of Buddhist statues. (Open daily 9am-4:30pm. ¥200.) Nearby is **San-mon gate,** the base of the 1000-step climb to Okuno-in, at the top of the mountain. (Open daily 9am-4:30pm. ¥500.)

Past San-mon, it takes about 40min. to reach the top, along a path littered with minor temples, statues, and lanterns. At **Niōmon gate,** the halfway point of the climb, you can detour to **Godaidō,** a simple veranda on the cliff's edge, which allows sweeping views of the nearby mountains. At the summit you'll find the **Buddha Hall** and the temple **Okuno-in.** On the way back down, turn right at San-mon and exit through a manicured garden featuring *bonsai* trees and a tadpole pond.

Yamadera can be reached via the JR Senzan Line from Yamagata (15min., 1 per hr., ¥230) or Sendai (50min., 1 per hr., ¥880). The train station is across the river from the steps up to the temple complex. The **tourist information office** (☎95-2816) is by the bridge. **Postal code: 999.**

Even at a slow pace, it only takes a few hours to see all the temples, so it's possible to visit Yamadera as a daytrip from Yamagata. There are, however, two choices between the train station and the temple

THE LOCAL LEGEND

WANDERING UP NORTH/ HE PERFECTED THE *HAIKU*/MATSUO BASHŌ

Traveling can be tough, especially in Tōhoku, where English is about as prevalent as the pairs of clean socks in your rucksack. When the hardships of the road get you down, know that the path you're treading was laid long ago.

Born in 1644, famed *haiku* poet Matsuo Bashō began his life in service to the Tōdō clan. He started his literary training with Tōdō son Yoshitada; after Yoshitada's death, he headed to Kyōto, where he mastered the classics.

Much of Bashō's life, however, was determined by wanderlust, and the poet is most rememberd for his three lengthy journeys through Japan. His second journey, through Tōhoku, resulted in the travelogue *The Narrow Road to the Deep North,* revered for its ability to essentialize the places the poet visited. The work blends *haiku* poetry with prose, and is considered Bashō's masterwork.

Without clear destination or purpose, Bashō's travel gave him ample opportunity for introspection. He wrote, "To talk casually about an iris flower is one of the pleasures of the wandering journey." To anyone who knows the joys and trials of travel, Bashō's works are inspiration to keep moving: "With a hat on my head and straw sandals on my feet, I met on the road the end of the year."

complex. **Pension Yamadera** ❸ (ペンション山寺) has luxurious *tatami* rooms in an old wooden building with a ground-floor restaurant. (☎95-2240. 2 meals included. ¥8000.) **Yamadera Hotel** ❹ (山寺ホテル) is an equally impressive old building with similar rooms. (☎95-2216; fax 95-2217. 2 meals included. ¥8500.)

TENDŌ (天童)   ☎0236

Checkmate. Japan's chess capital is Tendō, which churns out nearly all of the country's *shōgi* (Japanese chess) pieces. Carving and painting chess pieces from wood was once a way for *samurai* to make ends meet. Now it's the basis of the town's economy and identity. Tendō's center extends north from the station, and all of the sights can be reached easily by foot. Your first stop should be the **Tendō Shōgi Museum,** in the station, which collects chess paraphernalia. (Open Su-Tu and Th-Sa 9am-5:30pm. ¥300.) Next, exit the station and head north 15min. to **Eishundō,** where local craftsmen carve *shōgi* pieces before your eyes. (Open daily 9am-5:30pm. ¥500.) The interesting **Hiroshige Art Museum,** nearby, holds the 19th-century master's woodblocks. (Open Su-M and W-Sa 9:30am- 6pm.) For a touch of the absurd, finish your day with the ■**Tendō Mingei-kan,** 10min. north of the station, which exhibits 30,000 folkcraft items from *samurai* armor to handmade purses. (Open daily 8:30am-6pm.) Each year, at the late-April **Sakura Matsuri,** locals in *samurai* armor participate in a human chess match directed by *shōgi* masters. If you can't be in Tendō for the *matsuri*, you can still view the **chessboard,** at the top of Maizuri Mountain, 20min. north of the station.

An easy daytrip from Yamagata, Tendō can be reached by **train** (20min., 1 per hr., ¥230) or **bus** (40min., 1 per hr., ¥440). A small **tourist information center** on the second floor of the train station has maps.

SENDAI (仙台)   ☎022

With its towering architecture and expansive boulevards, Sendai is sure to humble. How could it not? "The gateway to the North" has 1 million inhabitants who enjoy quality shopping and nearby *onsen* retreats, not to mention a resonating nightlife that could wake Date Masumane from his grave halfway across town. To the traveler, Sendai is a "comfort zone" of sorts—a hub that provides easy access to wonders such as Matsushima, an endless shopping mall, an all-star game of hostels, and a debaucherous party center that exists only on the TV screens of the rest of Tōhoku. Yet, even while considering all of the city's benefits, one can't help but realize that Sendai lacks that *je ne sais quoi* that its counterparts—Tōkyō, Fukuoka, Ōsaka—surely emit. Sendai shouldn't be dwelled upon—and perhaps instead just valued as a nice weekend stopover.

ON THE WEB   Sendai: www.city.sendai.jp

▛ TRANSPORTATION

INTERCITY TRANSPORTATION

Flights: There are various domestic and international flights nearby at **Sendai Airport** (Sendai Kūkō; 仙台空港), 3-8-1, Honchō, Aoba-ku. To get there, take either bus #2 or 15 from the train station's west terminal (40min., every 15min., ¥910). Domestic flights to: **Fukuoka** (2hr., 5 per day, ¥33,300); **Narita,** Tōkyō (about 1hr.; 2 per day; ¥15,000, round-trip ¥30,000); **Ōsaka** (1½hr., 12 per day, ¥23,400); **Sapporo** (70min., 11 per day, ¥24,000). International flights to **Beijing** (4hr., 2 per week) and **Seoul** (2½hr., 1 per day).

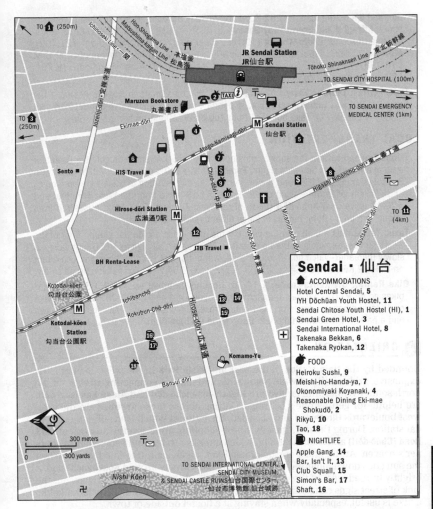

Sendai · 仙台

♠ ACCOMMODATIONS
Hotel Central Sendai, **5**
IYH Dōchūan Youth Hostel, **11**
Sendai Chitose Youth Hostel (HI), **1**
Sendai Green Hotel, **3**
Sendai International Hotel, **8**
Takenaka Bekkan, **6**
Takenaka Ryokan, **12**

● FOOD
Heiroku Sushi, **9**
Meishi-no-Handa-ya, **7**
Okonomiyaki Koyanaki, **4**
Reasonable Dining Eki-mae
Shokudō, **2**
Rikyū, **10**
Tao, **18**

■ NIGHTLIFE
Apple Gang, **14**
Bar, Isn't It, **13**
Club Squall, **15**
Simon's Bar, **17**
Shaft, **16**

Trains: Sendai Station, 1-1-1, Chūō, Aoba-ku (information ☎ 223-3313), is the central hub for most transportation within and out of Sendai. It has two terminals—the east and west—the latter of which is the larger one facing the city center. Open 5:30am-midnight. **Shinkansen** run to **Morioka** (1hr., 2-3 per hr., ¥5780) in the north and **Tōkyō** (about 2hr; every 15min.; ¥10,080, add ¥510-710 for a reservation). Local trains are hardly worth the lower prices; to **Tōkyō** (7hr. with 4 transfers, 1 per hr., ¥5780) and **Morioka** (3½hr., 1 per hr., ¥3280). Buy tickets at the JR office (www.jreast.co.jp) on the 2nd fl. of the station. Open daily 5:30am-10:30pm.

Buses: JR buses run to **Niigata** (4hr., 6 per day, ¥4500) and **Shinjuku,** Tōkyō (5½hr., 6 per day, ¥6210). Tickets are sold at the JR office (see above), and buses depart from the east bus terminal. **Tōhoku Expressway Buses** (東北急行バス), 1-1-7, Honchō, Aoba-ku, has buses to **Tōkyō Station** (5½-7½hr., 3 per day, ¥6210); board in front of the ticket office. From the bus station, turn right onto Ekimae-dōri, turn left onto Hirose-dōri and it's on the right. (☎262-7031. Open daily 9:30am-10:30pm.) Just across the street, **Miyagi Kōtsū Expressway Buses** (宮城交通高速バス), 1-6-31, Chūō, Aoba-ku, has buses to: **Kyōto/Ōsaka** (10½hr.; 1 per day; ¥11,930, round-trip ¥21,400); **Morioka** (2¾hr., 1 per hr., ¥2850/¥5000); **Nagoya** (10hr., 1 overnight per day, ¥10,190/¥18,340). Buses stop in front of the ticket office on Hirose-dōri. (☎261-5333; www.miyakou.co.jp.) Open daily 9am-6pm.

Port/Ferries: Taiheiyō Ferry (太平洋フェリー) runs boats to **Nagoya** (21hr., 1 per day, ¥5200) and **Tomakomai** (15hr., 1 per day, ¥6600). Ships serve **Sendai Port** (仙台港 ; ☎263-9877). Take bus #34 from Aoba-dōri (40min., 5 per day, ¥490).

LOCAL TRANSPORTATION

Public Transportation: The subway runs north to south, 5:45am-midnight. It is useful for visiting a handful of Sendai's sights. Fares start at ¥200. Local buses within downtown Sendai (starting at ¥100) and the outskirts of the city (starting at ¥170) are both quick and efficient *when there is no traffic.* Buses #1-19 leave from the **West Terminal** and #20-36 leave from **Aoba-dōri** (north of the West Terminal Exit). Most buses run from about 7am until 10pm, but exact times differ based on the route.

Taxis: Taxi-stands are all over the city, but the main ones are on the ground floor of the west and east terminals of the train station. Meters start as high as ¥650, but increase slowly thereafter—value lies in longer trips. When it's past your bedtime, you can count on **Dai-ichi Kōtsū Taxi** (第一交通タクシー ; ☎ 254-2221) to get you home safely.

Bike Rental: BH Renta-Lease, 2-14-20, Honchō, Aoba-ku (☎288-0505). Standard bikes go for ¥1700 per day and jazzy sports bikes cost an extra ¥500. Walk northwest on Higashi-nibanchō-dōri, turn right onto Hirose-dōri, make your first left, and it's two and a half blocks down on the left. Open M-Sa 9:45am-6pm.

✴ ORIENTATION

Bounded by the **train station** in the east and **Nishi Park** in the west, Sendai is an expansive, gridded city of wide boulevards and narrow connecting streets. Of the north-south avenues, the largest are **Higashi-nibanchō-dōri** and **Atago Kamisugi-dōri,** are helpful for getting one's bearings. Cutting across these avenues are the east-west boulevards **Hirose-dōri** and **Aoba-dōri,** the latter of which leads directly to Sendai station. During the day, the city's best shopping areas are the arcades of **CLIS Road (Chūō-dōri)** and **Ichibanchō-dōri,** which intersect to mark the epicenter of shopper's heaven. At the grid's north is **Jozenji-dōri,** an elegant, tree-lined street. When the sun goes down, nightlife emerges in the backstreets around **Kokubunchō-dōri,** a brightly lit road west of the city center. Overall, it's easy to find your way, but the lack of street signs can make it tricky in some areas. Although the city is walkable, a bike is useful, especially when staying at a hostel outside of town.

🛈 PRACTICAL INFORMATION

Tourist Offices:

Tourist Information Center (仙台市総合観光案内所 ; ☎222-4069; annai@stcb.or.jp), on the 2nd fl. of the train station, is loaded with free maps and informative brochures and always has at least 1 English speaker on-duty. The ladies cannot book your accommodation but will help you find one. Open daily 8:30am-8pm; 8am-5pm Dec. 31-Jan. 3.

The Sendai International Center (仙台国際センター ; ☎265-2471; www.sira.or.jp) offers resources for both travelers and foreign residents.

The Exchange Corner (交流コーナー). Head west on Hirose-dōri until Nishi Kōen. Turn left onto Nishi-Kōen-dōri, and right onto Aoba-dōri. The center is on the right, past the bridge. Free Internet access (30min. max.), English CNN, major English newspapers, a poster board of announcements, and an English-speaking staff. International ATM to the right of the entrance. Lockers ¥100. Open daily 9am-8pm. Closed Dec. 29-Jan. 3 and 1-2 to-be-determined days every month.

Tours: Although there are no English tours in Sendai, there is the **Loople**, which shuttles you around to Sendai's sights at your own pace.

Budget Travel: HIS Travel, 2-10-6, Honchō, Aoba-ku (☎711-6572), only deals with international destinations. Exit the station onto Aoba-dōri, and turn right onto Atago Kamisugi-dōri. The agency is just past Hirose-dōri on the right. Open M-F 10am-7pm, Sa 10am-6pm. **JTB Travel,** 3-6-1, Ichi-banchō, Aoba-ku (☎221-4422; fax 265-3860). From the station, walk down Aoba-dōri, turn right on Higashi-nibanchō-dōri, and it's 2 blocks down on the left. The wait can be long, but there are always English-speaking agents. Open summer M-F 10am-8pm, Sa-Su 10am-6pm; winter M-F 10am-7pm.

Currency Exchange: Changing money can be quite a task in Sendai. To change cash and traveler's checks during the day, head to the nearest bank or post office (see below). **Shichi-jū-shichi Bank** (七十七銀行), 1-10-1 Chūō, Aoba-ku (☎221-1681), in front of the train station, exchanges currencies and cashes traveler's checks. Open M-F 9am-3pm. At night and on the weekends, the reception desks of hotels like **Sendai International Hotel** will change up to $300 in cash or traveler's checks for non-guests.

ATM: The **Main Post Office**, the **Ekinai Post Office**, and the **Sendai International Center** have them. AmEx/MC/V/C.

Luggage Storage: The **train station** has both parcel storage (¥410 per day; open 6am-11pm) and different sized lockers (¥200-300 for the 1st 6hr., ¥100-200 for each subsequent 6hr. period). Located through the exit on the right of the ground floor of the west terminal. Some subway stations also have lockers.

Lost Property: With the parcel storage (see above).

English-Language Bookstore: Maruzen (丸善), 1-3-1, Chūō, Aoba-ku (☎264-0151), is the most comprehensive. From the train station exit, make a right and look for the purple sign a couple of blocks down on the right. Open daily 10am-8pm. **E Beans,** 4-1-1, Chūō, Aoba-ku (☎265-5656), also has an English section, which includes more novels, on its 5th fl. Head away from the station on Minami-machi-dōri, make the first left, and it's 2 blocks down on the left. Open daily 10am-8pm.

Disabled Services: Sendai City Association for Handi-capped People (Sendai-shi Shintai Shōgaisha Fukushi Kyōkai; 仙台市身体障害者福祉協会), 12-2, Itsutsu-bashi Ni-chōme, Aoba-ku (☎266-0292), can help find handicap accessible establishments.

Market: Sendai Morning Market Place (仙台朝市) sells fresh meat, fish, and produce. Take Minami-machi-dōri from the station and make the 2nd left after Atago-Kamisugi-dōri.It's on the 1st little street, behind E Beans. Open M-Sa 9am-5pm.

Laundromat: There's a good laundry adjacent to **Chitose-ya Youth Hostel. Komano-yū** bathhouse also has self-serve laundry (¥300, dryer ¥100). When all else fails, **Coin Laundry** (コインランドリー), 3-8-43, Miyamichi Aoba-ku, will get the job done. ¥2000 per 30 min., dryer ¥100 per 20min. Open daily 9am-10pm. Most accommodations offer some type of laundry service.

Public Baths: Enthusiasts can pick up a map of all the city's baths at the tourist office in Sendai Station. **Koma-no-yu** (駒の湯), Kokubun-chō, Aoba-ku (☎221-2859), is one of the nicer options (¥360). From the station, head all the way down Hirose-dōri, turn left onto Bansui-dōri and make your first left—it's on the right. Open 2-11pm.

Emergency: Police ☎110. Fire or ambulance ☎119.

English Hotline: ☎224-1919.

Pharmacy: Ōyakkyoku (大井薬局), 1-11-7 Honchō, Aoba-ku (☎ 265-4726) is good for everyday medicines. 2 doors down from Sento.

Hospital/Medical Services: Sendai City Hospital (Sendai-shi Shiritsu Byōin; 仙台市市立病院) is located at 3-1 Shimizukōji, Wakabayashi-ku (☎266-7111), directly south of the train station. Exit left from the station's west exit and head straight on

Atago-Kamisugi-dōri—it'll be on the left. The **Sendai Emergency Medical Care Center** (仙台市急患センター), 64-12, Funa-chō, Wakabayashi-ku (☎266-6561). The center is a few minutes north (on foot) from Kawara-machi Station. Open 24hr.

Internet Access: Internet access (30min. max.) is free at **Netto U Plaza** (ネットU), on the 5th fl. of Maruzen (see above), and at the **Sendai International Center.** Another option is the **Media Cafe,** 2-6-4, Chūō, Aoba-ku (☎726-7890). Head north from the station on Atago-Kamisugi-dōri, turn left onto CLIS Rd. (Chūō-dōri); it's upstairs on the right. Free drinks, *manga*, games, and personal laptop access to a LAN line. ¥250 for the 1st 30min., ¥90 for every subsequent 15min. Open 24hr.

Post Office: Central Post Office (仙台中央郵便局), 1-7, Kitame-machi, Aoba-ku (☎267-8077). Head south on Higashi-nibanchō-dōri and it's on the right, after you pass Kitame-machi-dōri. Changes money and has an international ATM (available M-F 7am-11pm, Sa 9am-9pm, Su 9am-7pm). Open M-F 9am-6pm, Sa-Su 10am-6pm. **Sendai Ekinai Post Office** (仙台市駅内郵便局 ; ☎227-2923) is on the ground level of the train station and also has an international ATM (available M-F 7am-11pm, Sa 7am-7pm, Su 9-5pm). Open M-F 9am-6pm Sa-Su 10am-6pm. **Postal Code:** 980.

▌ ACCOMMODATIONS

Although Sendai is dotted with ryokan and mid-to-high-end hotels, the city has little in terms of budget quarters. Hotels sit in clusters, so if one place is full, it should be easy to find another option nearby. Be sure to call ahead, especially beginning in July when half of Japan goes on holiday. The information center in the train station provides more details on rooms in Sendai.

▩ **Sendai Chitose Youth Hostel (HI)** (仙台千登勢ユースホステル), 6-3-8 Odawara, Aoba-ku (☎222-6329; www.ryokanchitoseya.co.jp). Exit the train station's west terminal, turn right onto Ekimae-dōri, and follow the avenue all the way down to Jozenji-dōri. At what seems like the end of both roads, turn right and follow the road to its end—then turn left. Take the 4th right (you should see a convenience store on the left) and then make your 3rd left—look for the hostel's sign on the right. Alternatively, take bus #19 to Miya-machi 2-chōme, turn right at the 1st convenience store, and then make your 3rd left. With *tatami*-style rooms and a friendly staff, Chitose is a quiet ryokan with a hostel's price. Super cozy, safe, and right off the center of town. Breakfast ¥600. Lockers ¥100 deposit. Beer vending machine ¥400. Sheets included. Laundry ¥200-300 per load, dryer ¥100 per 10min. Internet ¥100 for 30min. Bike rental ¥1000 per day. Reception 7am-10:30pm. Check-in 4pm. Check-out 10am. Curfew 10:30pm; request a door key to stay out late. Reservations recommended. Dorms ¥4000. Singles ¥5000; doubles ¥9000. ¥1000 discount with HI card. Foreigner's discount 10% (if no HI card). Closed Dec. 30-Jan. 6, and 3 to-be-determined days in the spring. MC/V. ❷

▩ **Dōchūan Youth Hostel (HI)** (道中庵ユースホステル), 31, Kita-yashiki, Onoda, Taihaku-ku (☎247-0511; fax 247-0759). Take the subway to Tomizawa Station (12min., ¥290) and ask for a mini-map at the subway information desk on the ground level. Turn right off the escalators and follow the road for 15min. After crossing a highway, make a right and look for the signs. Once an old farmhouse, now a hosteler's playground. Far from town, but an impressive Japanese-style, budget accommodation. Shared bathrooms. No smoking. Breakfast ¥600. Dinner ¥1000. Lockers ¥100. Laundry ¥200; dryer ¥100 per 15min. Bike rental ¥800 per day. Check-in 4pm. Check-out 10am. Reservations recommended. Dorms ¥3400; singles ¥5000; doubles ¥8200; triples ¥11,400. Discount up to ¥600 with HI card. Closed June 5-20 and Nov. 5-20. ❶

Sendai Green Hotel (仙台グリーンホテル), 2-5-6, Nishiki-chō, Aoba-ku (☎221-7070; fax 224-2015). Turn right out of the train station onto Ekimae-dōri and go 2 blocks past Jozenji-dōri (15min. walk). Ideally located. Attracts a young crowd with low-priced, bare-bones accommodation. The clean Western-style rooms can be cramped, but have baths. Breakfast ¥1000. Laundry ¥100; dryer ¥200. Reception 24hr. Singles ¥4100-5500; doubles ¥8200-11,000; triples ¥18,000. Credit cards accepted. ❷

Takenaka Ryokan (竹中旅館), 2-9-23, Chūō, Aoba-ku (☎225-6771; fax 264-7060). Right next to Hirose-dōri Subway Station. Despite its run-down exterior, Takenaka is city central with spacious rooms for groups and individuals. Shared bath. Breakfast ¥700. Free laundry, but no dryer. Reception 6:30am-10:30pm. Check-in 2pm. Check-out 10am. Reservations recommended. Singles ¥4200; doubles ¥6000; triples ¥9000. Group rooms ¥3000 per person. Credit cards accepted. An alternate location is nearby: **Takenaka Bekkan** (竹中別館), Aoba-ku Honchō 1-4-15 (☎261-2721). ❷

Hotel Central Sendai (ホテルセントラル仙台), 4-2-6, Chūō, Aoba-ku (☎711-4111; info@hotel-central.co.jp). Exit Sendai Station south on Atago-Kamisugi-dōri. Turn left on Yanagi-machi-dōri. A block up on the right. All rooms have bath. Internet ¥300 to hook up your computer. Laundry ¥300 per load. Reception 24hr. Check-in 2pm. Check-out 11am. Singles ¥6800-8000; doubles ¥12,000. Credit cards accepted. ❸

Sendai International Hotel (仙台国際ホテル), 4-6-1, Chūō, Aoba-ku (☎268-1112; www.tobu-skh.co.jp). On the left 2 blocks past Hotel Central Sendai. With a handful of restaurants offering world cuisines and unmatchable service, it's the best luxury option for the ex-budget traveler. English-speaking staff. Fitness room and pool ¥2500. Internet ¥250 for 15min. Parking available. Reception 24hr. Check-in before 1pm. Check-out by noon. Singles ¥11,500; doubles ¥26,000. Credit cards accepted. ❹

🍴 FOOD

The city's cosmopolitan character an eclectic selection of international cuisines at varying prices. For a host of good lunch options, head to **Ichibanchō** or **CLIS Road (Chūō-dōri)** where shouts of "Irasshaimase!" (welcome!) will lure you into one of the infinite *soba* or food stands. For dinner, wander the **Kokubanchō** area and choose from *rāmen*, Asian fusion, and other ethnic varieties. No matter where you go, watch out for table fees, which can be as high as ¥400, regardless of what you order. While convenience stores and food markets abound, the **Sendai Morning Market Place** (仙台朝市) sells the freshest groceries, meats, and fish. No trip to Sendai is complete without a sampling of its famous *gyūtan* (牛たん ; cow's tongue), which is surely as appetizing as it sounds!

Tao, 2-12-4, Kokubun-chō, Aoba-ku (☎227-3700). Go down Kokubun-chō from Hirose-dōri, make the 4th left; it's downstairs. A mix of meat, fish, and veggie dishes, many garlic-based. The filet steak (¥1500), garlic toast (¥300), and mango pudding (¥380) are specialties. Deals for groups of 3 or more. Open daily 5pm-midnight. ❸

Rikyū (利久), 2-2-16, Chūō, Aoba-ku (☎716-9233). Head up CLIS Rd., make your 2nd left at Atago-Kamisugi-dōri, and it's on the left. Known for preparing the best *gyūtan* in Sendai, this bustling little joint is sure to satisfy the tongue. The *gyūtan* set (¥1000-1300), which comes with soup and Japanese cucumber, is the only way to go. Lines are not uncommon. Open daily 11:30am-2:30pm and 5-11pm. Credit cards accepted. ❷

Heiroku Sushi (平録寿司), 2-2-26 Chūō, Aoba-ku (☎267-7766). From Sendai Station, take Atago-kamisugi-dōri north, turn left onto CLIS Rd., and this *kaitenzushi-ya* is on the left 1½blocks up. A sushi-lover's dream come true, Heiroku's tuna, eel, *bonito*, and eggplant-*nigiri* are a mere ¥100 per plate! Grab a tea and guard your territory; you're about to fill up on sushi for under ¥1000. Open daily 11am-10pm. ❶

Reasonable Dining Eki-mae Shokudō (駅前食堂), 1-2-3 Chūō, Aoba-ku (☎6324-7203). To the right on the ground floor of the station's west terminal exit. A quick, affordable option that serves a killer omelette rice. Lunch ¥680. Dinner ¥780. Take-out available. Open 11am-11pm. ❶

THE HIDDEN DEAL

OK, OH NO..!, ME? A QUI.

Escape from the herd on CLIS Rd. and enter a temple of food at **Okonomiyaki Koyanaki** (お好み 焼き小柳), where you can indulge in one of Japan's ritualistic food specialties. *Okonomiyaki*, originally just a way of topping off a night before the popularization of left-overs, consist of veggies, fish, meat, and batter, and can be catered to your specific taste buds. Creating an *okonomiyaki* is a hands-on, interactive endeavor where salarymen, college kids, and other locals cook their own versions of what has become a national favorite.

As for you and your *okonomiyaki*, there's no better place to find yourself than at **Koyanaki**. Providing all of the necessary utensils, ingredients, and inspiration, the restaurant has been a secret lunchspot for almost 30 years. Although the dearth of English-speaking staff makes it sink-or-swim, the learning curve to cook them is fast, and even if your pancake appears drab next to the masterpiece of a nearby diner, once it's in your mouth, it all tastes the same. *Sendai-eki-mae. ☎ 262-8367. Exit the station to the right and turn left onto Hapina Nakakechō, which turns into CLIS Rd. a block up. Look for a Japanese sign halfway up Hapina Nakakechō on the 3rd fl. Open daily noon-11pm, last order 10pm.*

Meshi-no-Handa-ya (めしのはんだや), 8-30 Chūō, Aoba-ku (☎ 227-2917). Look for the 2nd little alleyway on the left as you walk down the 1st block of CLIS Rd. from Atago-Kamisugi-dōri. A super-cheap cafeteria-style eatery overflowing with local workers. Assemble your own meal for as little as ¥300. Open 7:30am-9pm. ❶

🔆 SIGHTS

Although by no means a cultural or historical center, Sendai has a few sights worth working into your daily itinerary. **Zuihoden Mausoleum** (瑞鳳 殿), 23-2, Otamayashida, Aoba-ku, is the ancestral tomb of the great 16-17th-century lord and Date-clan founder, Date Masamune. Although the view and natural surroundings are resplendent, it's a bit of a trek from the center of town. Take bus #11 or 12 from Sendai Station, continue up the road, and turn left to reach the entrance. (☎ 262-6250. Open Feb.-Nov. 9am-4:30pm; Dec.-Jan. 9am-4pm. ¥550.) About 15min. away on foot, across the street from the International Center, is **Sendai City Museum** (仙 台市博物館) San-no-maruato, Kawauchi, Aoba-ku. Displaying armor suits from the days of the Date-clan and art from the city area, the museum is just right for a rainy day. (Open Tu-Su 9am-4:45pm. Closed Dec. 29-Jan. 4 and days proceeding national holidays. ¥400, students ¥200.) If it's nice out, continue up the hill from the museum and explore the old **Site of Sendai Castle** (仙台城跡), Tenshudai, Aoba-ku. While all that remain today are a few original stone walls, you can absorb a 3-D video of the historic castle at **Aoba Castle Museum** (青葉城資料展示館), right nearby. (☎ 227-7077. Open daily 9am-4:30pm. Castle free. Museum ¥700, students ¥500.) Sendai's modern face is undoubtedly **Sendai Mediateque,** 2-1, Kasuga-machi, Aoba-ku, an information center which houses the city library, a multimedia library, and a studio theater. From the station, take Aoba-dōri to Higashi-dōri and turn right. Make a left at Jozenji-dōri and Mediateque is on the right side of the street near the park's beginning. Despite Mediateque's various resources, most visitors just come to check out its sleek architecture. (☎ 713-3171. Open daily 9am-10pm. Closed Dec. 29-Jan. 3 and once a month for maintenance. Free.)

The practical way to tour the city is the **Loople** trolley bus, which shuttles you around at your own pace (departs from the station every 30min. from 9-4pm, daypass ¥600). The route has 11 stops, including all of the sights above. It takes about 1hr. non-stop to complete. Maps are available at the information center.

To shop the day away, join the masses on **CLIS Road** (Creative Life in Shopping Road) and its counterpart, **Ichibanchō-dōri**. Here, you'll find vast department stores (like **Daiei**) to lose yourself in, as well as tiny specialty stores (like a *kutsu-shita-ya*; sock store) that sell nothing but...socks. The best place for a long walk is **Jozenji-dōri**, which has a bit of everything—the shopping, the nature, the women.

🎵 🎤 ENTERTAINMENT AND NIGHTLIFE

Whatever Sendai lacks in history and culture, it makes up for with its bumping nightlife—eight days a week. A modern-day jungle, the center of the city's action is **Kokubunchō-dōri**, where starting in the early evening, *izakaya* tame college crowds, karaoke-professionals sing like Tarzan, and hostess girls seek out their prey. While strolling the streets, pay special attention to hidden signs, which often indicate great bars on the upper floors of easily overlooked buildings. For a more relaxed scene, head to the area in front of the train station where you're less likely to end up doing something you'll regret the next morning.

Shaft, 3, Kokubunchō-dōri, Yoshiyokaya B/D 4 fl. (☎722-5651; www.clubshaft.com). From the intersection of Kokubunchō-dōri and Hirose-dōri, head north up Kokubunchō; it's 3 blocks up on the right. Inspired by the movie, Club Shaft is a tribute to the 70s and to the club of pals who like to throw party after party. A good mix of Japanese and *gaijin*. Check the online schedule for upcoming events. Live band Tu. Drinks ¥500. Cover ¥1200 with a drink. Open M-Th 7pm-2am, Sa 9pm-4am, Su 7pm-2am.

Simon's Bar, Taishin Bldg. 9-1 (☎223-8840). With Shaft to your right, make the 1st left, and it's just on the right. Slip into the small, but comfy, Simon's for a break from Kokubunchō's crazy fluorescence. Jazz-fusion lightens the mood set by the interior's dim lighting, dark-stained tables, and talkative younger crowd. Beer ¥400, drinks from ¥500. No cover. Open Su-Th 7pm-2am, F-Sa 7pm-4am.

Bar, Isn't It, Date One Bldg. 3rd fl., 3-9-13, Ichibanchō (☎262-0901). From the intersection of Aoba-dōri and Ichibanchō, head north through the arcade of Ichibanchō and it's 2½ blocks up on the left. The typical *gaijin* hangout, where DJs spin a variety of house, techno, rock, and hip-hop. Things pick up past midnight. Beer ¥500. Cover ¥2000 F-Sa. Open Su-Th 6pm-midnight, F-Sa 6pm-5am. Credit cards accepted.

Club Squall, 3-9-5, Ichiban-chō, Aoba-ku (☎223-3606). Behind Bar, Isn't It. If the crowds eagerly waiting to get into this "underground" hotspot didn't spill out onto the street, we'd never know it existed. Inside, 20-somethings get it on to music of featured DJs and occasional live bands (starting 8pm). Beer ¥500. 19+. Lockers ¥100. Cover ¥1500 with 2 drinks. Open Su-Th 9pm-3am, F-Sa 9pm-5am.

Apple Gang, 3-4-3, Ichiban-chō, Aoba-ku (☎222-1155). Head west on CLIS Rd. from Higashi-dōri, and Apple Gang is on the right, just past Ichibanchō. Some of the cheapest karaoke around. ¥960 per person per hr., up to 6 people ¥2000 per hr., up to 8 people ¥3000 per hr. Beer and drinks from ¥450. Open daily 10am-5am.

NEAR SENDAI

MATSUSHIMA BAY   ☎022

Designated one of Japan's three most beautiful sights in 1952, Matsushima is cherished for both its stunning 250-island archipelago and its wealth of cultural and historical sights. To take in the best views of the harbor, consider one of two short boat cruises. One stays in **Matsushima Bay** (50min., every hr. on the hr., ¥1400; tickets available at Sightseeing Information Building) while touring the various islands, and the other ventures over to **Shiogama** (50min., every 30min., about ¥1400; tickets available at Sightseeing Information Building), a famous fishing port of sushi bars and Shintō shrines. The latter ends in Shiogama.

Explore the small town of Matsushima starting with the bay (exit left from the train station). Strolling along the water, you'll come across the entrance to **Zuigan-ji** (瑞巌寺), the most famous temple in Tōhoku. Rebuilt in 1609 after the original from AD 828 was destroyed, the temple showcases an entrance gate that bridges two different worlds. (Open daily 8am-4pm. ¥700.) If you bear left out of the temple and head down toward the water, you'll encounter **Godaidō** (五大堂), Matsushima's sacred worship hall, only opened to the public once every 33 years. Next showing: 2006. (Free.) Just beside Godaidō is a long red bridge leading to the cozy island of **Fukūra-jima** (福浦島). Inhabited by swans and their relatives, the island is a botanical garden ideal for sea-gazing and walking. (Open daily 8am-5pm. ¥200.) To get to the **Date Masamune Wax Museum** from Fukura-jima's red bridge, take the road that leads back to Rte. 45 and look to the right. The museum is popular for its impressive wax sculptures, which are used to tell an artist's version of the port town's history. (☎354-4131. Open daily summer 8:30am-5pm; winter 9am-4:30pm. ¥1000, junior high and high school students ¥600, elementary students ¥500.) To take a break from it all, back track on the main road toward Matsushima-kaigan-eki, then look for **Karantei** (観らん亭) on the left as the road begins to curve right. The picturesque teahouse offers fresh and foamy green tea (¥300) and hot chocolate (¥400), as well as a waterfront view close enough to see the water's ripples. (Open daily 8:30am-5pm. ¥200.) Those who enjoyed Fukūra-jima won't want to finish the day without visiting **Oshima** (お島), about 7min. southeast of the teahouse. Reached by dirt paths and a classic wooden bridge, Ōshima is known for its Buddhist stone inscriptions and a tablet etched with the great poet Bashō's words. (Always open. Free.)

From Sendai, take either the JR Seiseki Line to **Matsushima-kaigan-eki** (30-45min., 2 per hr., ¥400), or the JR Tōhoku Line to **Matsushima-eki.** (25min., 2-4 per hr., ¥400). The former option leaves you south of the town center, while the latter option leaves you to the north. Although getting around to all of the town's sights is easy enough on foot, **Aihara Shōten** (相原商店), 10 Aza-nami-uchi-hama, rents bikes. (Open daily 8am-8pm. ¥200 per hr.) The **tourist office** (松島海岸駅前案内所) 7-1 Nami-uchi-hama, nearby has a multilingual staff and plenty of reading material. (☎354-2263. Directly to the right of Matsushima-kaigan-eki's exit. Open daily 9:30am-4:30pm.) Japanese speakers might find the bayside **Central Sightseeing Office** (松島観光協会), 98-1 Aza-chōnai, more comprehensive. (☎354-2618. Open daily 8:30am-5pm, until 4pm in the winter.) There are no international ATMs, but **Shichi-jū-shichi Bank** (七十七銀行) changes cash and traveler's checks. It's about a 10min. walk east from Matsushima-eki. (Open M-F 9am-3pm.) Just across the street, next to Takagi-machi Station, is the **Matsushima post office** (松島郵便局), 2-22-30, Higashi Takagi-machi. (☎354-3040. Open M-F 9am-4pm.) **Postal code:** 981.

Value-wise, the best accommodation is **Folklore ❷** (フォルクロロ), Matsushima-chō, Matsushima Aza-san-jū-kari 17. From the train station exit, turn right and follow the road up a steep hill. Go straight through the intersection; it's to the left. (☎353-3535; www.eki-net.com/hotel. Curfew 11pm. Check-in 3pm. Check-out 10am. Singles ¥6000; doubles ¥12,000; triples ¥17,000. Credit cards accepted.) To splurge, book traditional Japanese accommodation at **Sakura-gawa Ryokan ❹** (桜川旅館), 12-1 Takagi. Take Rte. 45 north from Matsushima-kaigan-eki until you get to Matsushima Bridge. Cross the footbridge a few kilometers down, bear left, turn right when the road ends, and follow the signs. (☎354-2513. Breakfast included. Free laundry. Check-in 3pm. Check-out 4pm. Reception 6am-midnight. ¥8000 per person.) For cheaper options, return to Sendai or inquire about what the nearby town of **Naruse** (鳴瀬; 6 stops down on the Seiseki Line) has to offer. For food, join fish-lovers at the **Matsushima Seafood Market ❶**

Matsushima Bay and Oshika Hantō·
松島湾と牡鹿半島

(松島お魚市場), 4-10, Aza-funendō, which has yummy sea creatures you've never heard of on the first floor, and slurp-alicious *rāmen* (¥600) on the second floor. (Open daily 8am-5pm.)

DEWA-SANZAN (出羽三山)　　☎0235

> How cool it is, a pale crescent shining above the dark hollow of Mount Haguro. How many columns of clouds had risen and crumbled, I wonder before the silent moon rose over Mount Gas-san. Forbidden to betray the holy secrets of Mount Yudono, I drenched my sleeves in a flood of reticent tears.
> — Matsuo Bashō

The three mountains of Dewa-Sanzan are among the holiest in Japan. In the 6th century, an imperial prince fled to the region after the death of his father. Pursuing a vision of a three-legged crow, the prince arrived at Haguro-san (Black Wing Mountain), where he lived until his death at age 90. During this time, he slowly developed Shugendō, a blend of Buddhism and Shintō. The followers of this faith became known as the *yamabashi* (ones who sleep in the mountains), and garnered fame for their mystic powers and virtuous asceticism. The sect continued to flourish, and even today you can see *yamabashi* in their white robes and black hats, carrying conch shells said to stir the mountain gods when sounded.

A traditional pilgrimage to Dewa-Sanzan takes 2-3 days, and starting at Mount Haguro, where the three gods of the mountains are enshrined, and continuing via Mount Gas-san to Mount Yudono—Haguro is said to represent birth, Gas-san death, and Yudono rebirth. Although it's possible to hike all three mountains in a long day, it's best to take your time, enjoy the scenery, and seize the opportunity to overnight in one of the temples. In summer, you'll see white-robed pilgrims on the mountain trails, as well as the occasional Tōkyō salaryman who has thrown a white smock over his business pants.

◪ TRANSPORTATION

Three bus lines from in Tsuruoka lead to the mountain tops. If you're planning on hiking from Haguro to Yudono, take a bus to the trailhead in Haguro-machi, and head back to Tsuruoka via another line when you finish. If you want to visit all the

AT A GLANCE

AREA: Dewa-Sanzan is directly east of Tsuruoka, comprising three mountains, well-connected by hiking trails.

GATEWAYS: Buses to each of the mountaintops originate from Tsuruoka (p. 298). The village of Haguro-machi, beneath the summit of the mountain, is the traditional starting point of the pilgrimage, so you'll find temple lodgings there.

HIGHLIGHTS: The principal attractions are the mountaintop shrines, though the trails to the summits pass pristine alpine meadows and old-growth cedar forests.

CAMPING: Camping is not allowed.

WHEN TO GO: There is heavy snowfall in winter (Mt. Gas-san is covered in snow as late as the end of June), so it's best to visit between July and late September.

mountains, you'll have to keep heading back to Tsuruoka—there are no buses between the mountains (with the exception of a summer line between Haguro and Gas-san). All three lines depart from bus stand #2, in front of JR Tsuruoka Station.

The first bus line runs directly to **Haguro Summit** (55min., 1 per hr., ¥990), but also stops at **Haguro-machi** (35min., ¥680) where you can pick up the trailhead to the summit. This bus also has onward services to **Gas-san Hachigōme** (8th Station) from July to September. Alternatively, you can take one of three morning buses from Tsuruoka directly to Gas-san Hachigōme (50min., ¥1240). There's also a bus line between Tsuruoka and the peak of **Yudono-san** (50min., 5 per day, ¥1330) via **Ōami** (30min., ¥780). From the Yudono-san Hotel at the peak of the mountain, there are occasional buses in summer that run directly to **Yamagata** (1½hr., ¥1750).

■✻ ⁊ ORIENTATION AND PRACTICAL INFORMATION

East of Tsuruoka, the village of **Haguro-machi** is the starting point of the pilgrimage. From there, the trail heads to the shrine at the top of **Mount Haguro**, and then continues to **Mount Gas-san** and **Mount Yudono**. The descent down Mount Yudono brings you to **Yudono Jinja**, the finish line of the pilgrimage. The road from there heads back to Tsuruoka via Ōami, a tiny village with a few old Buddhist temples. Before starting the hike, consult with Tsuruoka's **tourist information center** (☎/fax 25-7678; open daily 9:30am-5:30 pm), or visit the **Haguro Center** (☎62-2260; open 24hr.) in Haguro-machi. If you're interested in arranging a pilgrimage that incorporates *yamabashi* rituals, including waterfall climbing and fire leaping, inquire about the three-day course organized by the **Ideha Cultural Museum**, in the Tōge District of Haguro-machi. (☎62-4727. ¥26,000.)

⁊ ⌂ ACCOMMODATIONS AND FOOD

The three main areas for accommodation are the Tōge district of Haguro-machi, the summit of Haguro-san, and around Yudono Jinja. At some point during your trip to Dewa-Sanzan, spend at least one night in a **shukubō** (temple lodge), usually run by a *yamabashi*. The temple lodges serve exceptional *shōjin-ryōri*, traditional Buddhist vegetarian food, which features local mountain vegetables . During the day, sample this cuisine by visiting either a *shukubō* or a cafe on the top of Haguro and Yudono mountains.

Over 30 *shukubō* operate in Haguro-machi, so you should have no problems finding a place to sleep. Rates are typically ¥7000-8000 per night, including two vegetarian meals. If you have problems finding a bed, the **Haguro Center** in town can help. **Saikan** ❸ (斎館), perched atop of Haguro-san, offers temple lodging with spectacular views. Phone ahead—it's often booked solid in summer. (☎62-2357; fax 62-2352. ¥7000 per person.) If you need to unwind before moving on, the **Yudono-san Hotel** ❹ (湯殿山ホテル), next to the bus terminal at Yudono Jinja, has comfortable Western-style rooms. (☎54-6231. ¥8500 per person includes 2 meals.)

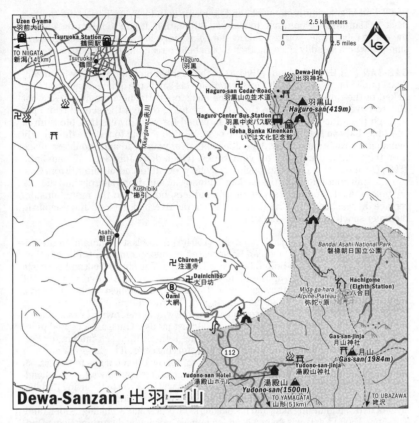

Dewa-Sanzan · 出羽三山

👁 🗺 SIGHTS AND HIKING

HAGURO-SAN (羽黒山). The pilgrimage through Dewa-Sanzan starts at Haguro-machi, at the base of Haguro-san (419m). From the village bus stop, walk through vermilion-lacquered **Zuishinmon,** the second largest *torii* in Japan, and the entrance to the sacred precincts. The 2,466 stone steps (1.7km; 50min.) wind their way through a serene cedar forest before reaching the summit. Along the way, look for the 33 lotus leaves, gourds, and *sake* cups engraved on the steps. Enroute to the top, you'll come across the **Gojyū-no-tō,** a beautifully preserved wooden pagoda that dates back to the 10th century, last reconstructed in the 1300s. About halfway up, you'll pass a small teahouse, a great place to catch your breath and admire the views. (Open Apr.-Nov. daily 8:30am-5pm.) At the top of the staircase, one more *tōri* ushers you into the temple complex. There are a number of buildings at the summit, but the main attraction is **Sanshin Gossaiden,** a massive temple dating from 1818 with the country's largest thatched roof. In front of the hall is **Kagami-ike,** a tranquil lily-pond said to reflect the spirits of the mountain gods, primarily known for the vast treasure of antique hand mirrors found in its depths in 1950. Before women were admitted to Dewa-Sanzan, men tossed mirrors into the waters in honor of their female relatives. Today, you can see the extraordinary collection in the nearby **History Museum.** (Open daily 8:30am-5:00pm. ¥200.) After meandering through the temple complex, the path joins the tourist drag, where you'll find vegetarian restaurants and souvenir stands. From here, take the bus back to Tsuruoka, or continue to Gas-san 8th Station. If you're intent on walking the entire pilgrimage, you can follow the 20km ridge line hike from Haguro-san's summit, which steadily rises another 1000m before reaching the peak of Gas-san.

GAS-SAN (月山). Gas-san (1984m) is the highest mountain in Dewa-Sanzan. Since public buses only reach the 8th station, Gas-san is the quietest and least trafficked of the three mountains. From the bus stop at Hachi-gōme, it takes about 2hr. to cover the last 5km on the ridge line hike, though the scenic trail cuts through the Mida-ga-hara meadows, renowned for wildflowers that blossom in late June. **Gas-san Jinja** sits on top of the peak. Bow your head to receive the priestly benediction, rub a small snowflake-like paper over your head and shoulders, place it on the fountain, and take off your shoes. (Open daily July-Sept. 15 6am-5pm. ¥500.) Once rested and at ease, begin the 2½hr. descent to Yudono Jinja. From Gassan, the trail continues past the peak of Yudono-san and drops sharply into the valley below. At this point, a series of iron ladders, bolted into the mountainside, replace the washed-out path. At the bottom of the riverbed, Yudono Jinja squats in the inner sanctum of Dewa-Sanzan.

YUDONO-SAN (湯殿山). Yudono-san (1504m) is the last mountain on the pilgrimage to Dewa-Sanzan, and can be accessed by descending the trail from Gassan or by the Yudono-san-bound bus from Tsuruoka. The shrine **Yudono Jinja** casts a holy aura from midway up the mountain. In the olden days, pilgrims were not allowed to speak of what they saw there, Dewa-Sanzan's holiest spot. It's about a 10min. walk down the road to the bus stop the Tsuruoka-bound shuttle passes. If you have spare time, it's worth stopping along the way at the town of **Ōami,** famous for its two "living Buddhas," mummified Buddhist monks. Once an accepted practice, but rejected by Buddhist doctrine since the 19th-century, self-mummification was the ascetic confluence of meditating and starving oneself to the point of death before being buried alive. From Ōami Bus Stop, follow the red signs to **Dainichibō,** which has an impressive collection of artifacts, including Tokugawa Ieyasu's handprint. After a tour of the temple grounds, the priests will lead you to the living Buddha, a macabre form in bright orange robes. His skeletal, withered body is covered in a thin layer of dark, shimmering skin, and his bulging skull is absolutely chilling. (Open daily 8am-5pm. ¥500.) Nearby is **Chūren-ji,** which houses an equally disturbing living Buddha, although temple records indicate that the monk was a convicted murderer who reformed and became a powerful priest. (Open daily 8am-5pm. ¥500.)

🔲 FESTIVALS

The biggest festival at Dewa-Sanzan is the **Hassaku Matsuri** (Aug. 24-31), involving elaborate fire rituals performed by *yamabashi* to ensure a bountiful harvest. On New Year's Eve, the **Shōrei-sai** showcases acrobatic dancing and more fire rituals.

TSURUOKA (鶴岡)   ☎0235

Tsuruoka is a gateway to the nearby mountains of Dewa-Sanzan. Although most travelers pass quickly through the city, Tsuruoka has a long history as a castle town and the major cultural center of the region. If you're waiting for a bus connection, it's worth visiting some of the surrounding sights. From the station, head about 2km southwest through the modern downtown to **Tsuruoka Kōen,** which houses the modest remains of Tsuruoka's castle amidst a lush city park. (Free.) Although it's easily accesible by foot, the frequent Yunohama Onsen-bound bus from the train station also passes by the park (10 min., ¥240). On the southwest corner of Tsuruoka Kōen is the **Chidō Hakubutsukan,** an inviting museum on the area's history and culture, including exhibits of Sakai family heirlooms, and adjacent to several Meiji-era buildings. (Open Tu-Su 9am-4:30pm. ¥700.) On the south side of Tsuruoka Kōen you'll find the **Chidō-kan**, a Confucian school for early 19th-century young *samurai*. (Open Su and Tu-Sa 9am-5pm. Free.) On your way back to the station, pass the Chidō Hakubutsukan and look for the **Tsuruoka Catholic Church Tenshudō**, a Western-style building founded by French missionaries in 1903. (Open daily 8am-6:30pm. Free.) Trek 7km west of town to **Zenpo-ji**, a 10th-century Zen Buddhist pagoda that honors the Dragon King. Just past the temple is one of the region's most bizarre attractions, **jinmengyo**, carp that, viewed from above, appear to have human faces. To reach the temple, take the frequent Yunohama Onsen-bound bus to Zenpo-ji Bus Stop (30min., ¥580). Tsuruoka also hosts the **Tenjin Matsuri** (Masked Face Festival; May 25), when locals don masks and parade through the streets.

Tsuruoka is on the **JR Uetsu Line**, which starts in Niigata (7 per day, 2hr., ¥3890) and travels north to Akita (1¾hr., ¥3530) via Sakata (35min., ¥650). The station is at the northeast corner of the city center. Buses run to Sendai (3hr., 7 per day, ¥2550), and from June to early November, to Yamagata (2¼hr., 4 per day, ¥2150). All buses make a stop at the JR terminal, but the **bus station** is a 5min. walk west of the train station. Local buses, which include all routes to Dewa-Sanzan, leave from the bus stand in front of the train station. For more information, see p. 295. An **overnight bus** to Tōkyō departs from the Tōkyō Daiichi Hotel (9hr., 9pm, ¥7540). The **tourist information office,** just outside the station, is the best place to pick up pamplets and information on Dewa-Sanzan. (☎/fax 25-7678. Open daily 9:30am-5:30pm.) About 5min. east of the station, a small **post office** has **international ATMs.**

There are hotels around the station, though it's hard to beat **Petit Hotel Tsuruoka ❸**, next to the station. This quaint hotel breaks the business model by offering bright, homey rooms, and the friendly staff will make dinner if you order in advance. (☎25-1011. Western- and Japanese-style rooms. ¥6000 per person.) A few blocks east of the station is the **Nara Ryokan ❷** (奈良旅館), a bargain with comfortable *tatami* rooms. (☎22-1202. ¥4200 per person.) Though there are numerous *izakaya* in the downtown area, the cheapest eats are on the restaurant floor in the shopping center just southeast of the station. Here, you'll find **Hanaguru ❷** (花ぐる ; ☎23-0833), which serves up some truly innovative (and remarkably green) *ocha soba*. *Unagi* sets with *soba*, *miso* soup, and pickled vegetables are ¥880.

SAKATA (酒田)   ☎0234

Sakata is a launch pad for the summits of Dewa-Sanzan. Although it's dreary and relatively uninteresting, just south of the city is the ▨**Domon Ken Kinenkan**, a

THE BIG SPLURGE

BUNGEE BANZAI

It's hard being an adrenaline junky in a foam-padded, Playskool wonderland. In a country where living on the edge consists of jaywalking and eating *fugu*, the opportunity to partake in extreme sports is rare. However, if you're near Dewa Sanzan and need a fix, spend time with the staff of the Japan Outdoor System. Reckless living will never feel so good.

A single jump costs ¥5775 (life insurance policy included), but for another ¥2000, the on-site photographer will shoot a roll of film during the plunge, evidence of your momentary lapse of reason. If you're feeling truly wild, tell your jump sensei "Mizu o sawaritai desu!" and watch as the slack on your bungee cord is lengthened, allowing you to dunk your arms into the river at the lowest point of your dive.

If you don't speak Japanese, there are English instructions and waivers available, and fortunately, the charades needed to convey proper bungee jump technique are pretty universal. As you stand on the edge of the bridge questioning your sanity, just remember, you're in Japan. *(The JOS bungee jump facility is in Asahi Village next door to the Gassan Asahi Hakubutsu Mura. ☎53-3777; www.bungy.co.jp. Open daily 9am-5:30pm. Take the Yudono-san-bound bus from stand #2 in front of Tsuruoka Station. 5 buses per day, ¥890.)*

world-class museum devoted to the art of photographer Ken Domon, famous for his neo-realist chronicles of post-war Japan. The museum also houses his "Pilgrimage through Old Temples," a collection of somber Buddhist images. The building is on the edge of a secluded carp pond, and on a clear day you can see the top of Dewa Fuji from the museum grounds. The **Domon Ken Kinenkan** is about 4km outside the city center, easily reachable by bicycle, which you can rent for free at the **tourist information center** inside the train station. (☎24-2459. Open daily 9am-5pm.) Or, take the Jūrizuka-bound bus, which leaves the train station and passes Domon Ken Kinenkan-mae Stop (20min., 1 per hr., ¥340). Head to the city center for the **Homma-ke Kyū-hontei,** a model of preservation and home to a fine collection of artwork. (Open daily 9am-4:30pm. ¥600.) Nearby is the Edo-period mansion **Abumiya House.** (Open daily 9am-4:30pm. Closed M Dec.-Mar. ¥310.)

Sakata is on the **JR Uetsu Line,** which runs south to Niigata (7 per day, ¥4620, 2¼hr.) via Tsuruoka (¥650, 35 min.) and north to Akita (¥1890, 1¾hr.) via Kisakata (¥650, 40 min.). There are daily **buses** to Sendai (¥2750, 3¾hr.) via Tsuruoka (¥820, 50min.) as well as an **overnight bus** to Tōkyō (9hr., departs at 9:30pm, ¥7870).

If you end up staying in Sakata, **Hotel Alpha One ❸,** right next to the train station, offers typical business hotel rooms. As an added bonus, the hotel stocks an assortment of videos; you can rent films for ¥300 and watch them in your room. (☎22-6111. ¥5000 per person.) There's a **Lawson** around the corner from the Hotel Alpha One, as well as several *izakaya* on the main street leading out from the station. A popular lunch and early dinner spot is **Somaro ❸,** a few blocks east of Hiyoriyama Kōen. Watch live *maiko* dancing and sample classic Japanese dishes. (☎21-2310. Courses from ¥2000. Show cover ¥1000. Open Su-Tu and Th-Sa 10am-6pm.)

NEAR SAKATA

TOBISHIMA (飛島)   ☎0234

Isolation amid clear waters, wildflowers, and a sparse, undeveloped beachfront define Tobishima, a tiny island off the Japan Sea coast. The island boasts scuba diving, bird watching, cycling, and spelunking. Ferries connect **Sakata-ko** to Tobishima. (☎22-3911. 1½hr., 1-2 per day, ¥2040.) Call ahead to confirm the schedule and reserve a seat. There are number of inns—the standard rate is ¥7000 per night with two meals included. The island's best accommodation deal is the **Youth Hostel Sawaguchi Ryokan ❶** (ユースホステル沢口旅館), north of the ferry pier, about a 5min. walk. Arrange bike rental, scuba trips, and fishing expeditions at the front desk. During the high-season, call ahead to reserve a bed before coming over to the island. (☎95-2246. June 1-Sept. 30 dorms ¥2200, off-season ¥2000.)

KISAKATA (象潟)   ☎0184

Kisakata, a laid-back beach town on the Japan Sea coast, is a convenient base for travelers hoping to conquer Tōhoku's second highest peak, **Chōkai-san** (2236m). The summit of the mountain was formed by two separate volcanic eruptions, and the top of Chōkai-san is covered in a thin layer of glacial ice year-round. Even if you're not planning to climb Chōkai-san, Kisakata is a pleasant place to stop for a night if you're heading to or from Akita, especially since **Kisakata Beach** is usually filled with locals during the warm, summer months. It's also worth checking out **Kanman-ji,** just north of the town center, a temple built by priests from Kyōto's Enryaku-ji and visited by Bashō. (Open daily 8:15am-5:15pm.)

Kisakata is on the **JR Uetsu Line,** which runs south to Sakata (40 min., 7 per day, ¥650) and north to Akita (1¼hr., ¥1280). There is a **tourist information center** in the train station. Before tackling Chōkai-san, pick up hiking maps from the center. (☎43-2174. Open daily 9am-5pm.) Take the shuttle bus from Kisakata Station to Hakodate (5th Station), where the 4½hr. ascent begins. Shuttle buses depart

Kisakata Station (mid-July to mid-Aug. 6 and 8am, last ride to Kisakata leaves Hakodate at 4:20pm). If you get stuck on the mountain, there is a **campsite** located in Reiho Park at the third stage of the Chōkai Blue Line route.

The best accommodation option is the **Kisakata Youth Hostel** ❶ (象潟ユースホステル; ☎43-3154), a steal at ¥2500 for a dorm bed. From the station, follow the main street a few blocks to an intersection with a hostel sign, and turn left. Look for it behind a supermarket. Next door is a **campsite** ❶. (Open May-Oct. Rental equipment available. ¥500 per site, ¥400 per person.) Cheap eats can be found at the small shops near Kisakata Beach, but for a more substantial meal, head to the hostel sign and you'll find **Masaen** ❷ (まさえん). Masked by a Chinese temple facade, it dishes out heaps of *rāmen* and bargain *teishoku* sets for ¥800.

HIRAIZUMI (平泉) ☎0191

If there were another Kyōto, a cultural center where monks and *geisha* peacefully co-exist, it would be Hiraizumi. Somewhere along the line, this simple-man's town absorbed some of Kyōto's magnificence into its Heian gardens and Buddhist temples. Although it's not as sight-filled as it was in the days of the Fujiwara, it retains enough of its architectural gems to attract the (mostly older Japanese) northbound traveler for a couple of days. In recent years, the town has worked to bring into harmony its divergent goals of cultural preservation and modernization, with spotless roads and sidewalks navigating the path through historical grounds.

ON THE WEB	Hiraizumi: www.town.iwate.jp

TRANSPORTATION AND PRACTICAL INFORMATION. The easiest way to reach Hiraizumi is to take a **shinkansen** or local train from Sendai to Ichinoseki (*shinkansen* 40min., local 1½hr.; 1-2 per hr.; ¥3410/¥1620), then switch to a local line for Hiraizumi (10-15min., 1-2 per hr., ¥190). Although Sendai-Hiraizumi direct tickets (¥1890) are sold at Sendai Station, breaking the trip into two parts saves money and allows for a nice stop-over in Ichinoseki. **Buses** run from Sendai to Ichinoseki (board in front of Sendai Station West Terminal; 80min., 5 per day, ¥1500) and from Ichinoseki to Hiraizumi (20min., 2-3 per hr., ¥310). For info on Ichinoseki, visit the **Ichinoseki Tourist Center** (一ノ関観光案内所), in front of the train station. (☎23-2350; www.city.ichinoseki.iwate.jp. Open daily Mar.-Oct. 9am-5:30pm; Nov.-Feb. 9am-5pm.)

All types of transport end up at **Hiraizumi Station** (平泉駅), at the east end of town. There are storage lockers (¥300-500) in the station. To the right of the exit is the **Hiraizumi Tourist Office** (平泉町観光協会), 61-7, Aza-izumi, which stocks English pamphlets, and allows 10min. of free **Internet** use. (☎46-2110; fax 46-2117. Open daily 8:30am-5pm.) While the town is walkable, the surrounding sights difficult to reach by foot. Next to the station is a **Renta-Cycle** (レンタサイクル), a lifesaver if you're pressed for time (or just lazy). In an emergency, call ☎110 for **police,** ☎119 for **fire** or **ambulance.** For money exchange, go to the **Bank of Iwate** (岩手銀行; open M-F 9am-3pm), two blocks up from the station on the main street, or cross the street to the **post office,** 137-5, Aza-shirayama (☎46-2150) which transfers and exchanges money and has an **international ATM.** (Open M-F 9am-4pm; ATM open M-F 8:45am-6pm, Sa 9am-5pm, Su 9am-3pm. AmEx/V/C.) **Postal code:** 029.

ACCOMMODATIONS AND FOOD. Only in northern Japan could you stay at a hostel as Buddhist as **Mōtsūji Youth Hostel (HI)** ❶ (毛越寺ユースホステル). Located on the temple grounds, the hostel is a prime location for sight-seers. From the station, exit onto the main road and walk for about 10min. It's at the end of the road within Mōtsū-ji. (☎46-2331. Japanese and Western-style rooms. Breakfast ¥600. Dorms ¥3600; doubles ¥7000; members ¥2800.) For more privacy but fewer memories, **Shirayama Ryokan** ❸ (志羅山旅館), 139-8, Shirayama, has *tatami* rooms big enough to fit the whole family. From the station, turn right at the first light and make your first left. (☎46-2883. 2 meals included. ¥7500 per person.)

The best lunch spot in town is **Izu-sobaya** ❶ (泉そば屋), 75, Aza-izumiya, with its cheap, flavorful *soba* and *udon* dishes (¥550). (☎46-2038. Open daily 9am-5pm. Closed the 2nd and 4th W of the month.) Korean barbecue joint **Sōru Restaurant** ❷ (ソウル食堂), 116-11, Aza-shirayama, reigns supreme at dinner with its tender sirloin and pork. Cook your own combo of meets and veggies for half the price of the *yaki-niku* spots in the cities. Plates of meat ¥500-700. From the station, head toward Mōtsū-ji—it's a few blocks down on the left. (☎46-5199. Open daily 5pm-midnight.) The town also has some convenience stores and **supermarkets** on the main road. **Sūpā Maruge** (スーパーまるげ), 2-3, Aza-shirayama, one block from the train station, has bread and fruit. (☎23-2355. Open M-Tu and Th-Su 7am-8pm.)

⬛ SIGHTS. Hiraizumi's sights are scattered, often beyond walking distance. To get to many of them, you'll want a two-wheeler, available at Rent-a-Cycle. Alternatively, befriend some older Japanese tourists and share a taxi from the station.

Of the town's many attractions, three simply cannot be missed. The first is **Chūson-ji** (中尊寺), accessible either by local bus from the train station (2 per day) or on foot from Mōtsū-ji; turn right down the park wall and follow the signs. Established in the mid-9th century as a center for Tendai Buddhism, Chūson-ji once housed over 400 temples and pagodas, which were destroyed in the 14th and 15th-century wars. Today, visitors enjoy walking the complex's tree-lined path, discovering the staggering views of the valley, outdoor *nō* theater, and orchidaceous **Konjikidō**. (Golden Hall; 金色堂 ; ☎-6-2211. Open daily Apr.-Oct. 8am-5pm; Nov.-Mar. 8am-4:30pm. Free.) Closer to town, at the end of the main road is **Mōtsū-ji** (毛越寺). Also built in the mid-800s, in its 12th-century glory days, its 40 pagodas and 500 monasteries made it the largest complex in Tōhoku. The expansive garden, a peaceful place to lose yourself, looks much as it would have in the Heian Period. (☎46-2331. Open daily Apr.-Oct. 8am-5pm; Nov.-Mar. 8am-4:30pm. ¥500.) Temple-lovers will be amazed by the unusual **Takkoku no Iwaya** (達谷岩谷), a cave temple. Restored in 1961, the original structure dates back to the 9th century, when *samurai* Sakanoue Tamuramaro built it to honor the warrior god. (Take a 15min. bus from the train station. 2 per day. ¥300.) At the end of the day, relax at **Yūkyū-no-yu** (悠久の湯), 1-1, Aza-osawa, an *onsen* that gives its bathers free, unlimited Internet access—when they're not in the pool. (☎34-1300. M-F ¥500 for 3hr., Sa-Su ¥800 for 3hr. Open daily 10am-9pm, closed 2nd and 4th Su of the month.)

❀ FESTIVALS. Hiraizumi's most elaborate festival is the **Spring Fujiwara Festival** (May), when actors dress up as the legendary Yoshitsune and Benkei, and parade from Mōtsū-ji to Chūson-ji. Flower lovers, work the Iris garden displays at Mōtsū-ji (over 30,000 flowers from June 20-July 10) and the Chrysanthemum Viewing at Chūson-ji (Oct. 20-Nov. 15) into your itinerary.

TŌNO VALLEY (遠野)　　　　　☎0198

Below the misty mountains of Iwate Prefecture, off-the-beaten-path **Tōno** (遠野) is known for folk tales, watermill villages, and endless rice fields. Plagued by famine and various natural disasters, the region floundered as a castle town and market place in the feudal era. Yet today, the valley takes pride in its farming traditions and works hard to promote and preserve its precious shrines, temples, and natural surroundings. To take it in properly, visitors should spend at least a couple of days among the rice paddies, away from the rather drab town. Don't let the small-town facade fool you—Tōno's not so easy to get around. Technically, it's Japan's 14th largest city. Practically, it's a maze of long, hilly roads.

▣ TRANSPORTATION. Take the Tōhoku Line to Hanamaki from: Hiraizumi (45min., 1-3 per hr., ¥820) or Morioka (39min., 1 per hr., ¥650), then transfer to the Kamaishi Line to Tōno (70min., 1 per hr., ¥740), or take a *shinkansen* to Shin-Hanamaki—from Morioka (13min., 1 per hr., ¥840) and Sendai (70min., 1 per hr., ¥2520) and then take the Kamaimishi Line to Tōno (54min., 1 per hr., ¥740).

▨ PRACTICAL INFORMATION. The **tourist office,** 5-13, Shinkoku-chō, a few doors down on the right from the train station, has English brochures and maps. (☎62-2111. Open daily summer 8am-6pm; winter 8:30am-5:30pm.) There are storage lockers outside the tourist office and to the left of the train station (¥300-500), but the cheapest storage facility is **Nihon Tsūun** (日本通運), 5-8, Shinkoku-chō, in a brown building across from the station exit. (Open daily 8:30am-5:30pm. ¥200 per bag per day.) There's free **Internet access** at the public library on the opposite side of town, near the Municipal Museum. (☎62-2340. Open Tu-Su 9am-5pm.) The **post office** (遠野郵便局), 6-10, Chūō-dōri, beats any bank when it comes to **currency exchange.** They take traveler's checks and have an **international ATM.** Exiting the station, go two blocks down Fudabadōri, turn left, and look for the red 〒 on your right. (☎62-2831. Open M-F 9am-4pm. ATM open M-F 8:45am-7pm and Sa-Su 9am-5pm. AmEx/Cirrus/V.) **Postal code:** 028.

▨▢ ACCOMMODATIONS AND FOOD. YH Tōno Youth Hostel (HI) ❶ (遠野ユースホステル), 13-39-5, Tsuchibuchi, Tsuchibuchi-chō, is a great base for exploring the sights. Run by fun former city-slickers, the hostel pampers its guests with spotless facilities (including a *manga* library), and service parallel to what a Francophone candlestick might whip up in an enchanted castle. From the station, take the Sakanoshita-bound (坂ノ下) bus to Nitagai (似田貝 ; 15min., 1 every 2hr., ¥290) and walk for 10min., following the signs. (☎62-8736; www1.odn.ne.jp/tono-yh/index-e.htm. Bike rental ¥800 per day, ¥500 per half-day. Dorms ¥3100; singles ¥3600; doubles ¥4300. Nonmembers add ¥600. Credit cards accepted.) At quiet **Minshuku Rindō** ❶ (民宿りんどう), 2-34, Daiku-chō, 10min. west of the station, the staff speaks little English as the guests are mostly Japanese. Make a right out of the station and walk down to Daiku-chō-dōri and turn left. It's two blocks down on the right, at the end of a little walkway. (☎62-5726. Check-in 4pm. Check-out 10am. ¥4000 per person. ¥6300 with breakfast and dinner.) For a good deal on Western-style rooms, JR's **Tōno Folklore** ❷ (遠野フォクロア), 5-7, Shinkoku-chō, is next to the train station. (☎62-0700; www.eki-net.com. Breakfast included. Check-in 3pm. Check-out 10am. 11pm curfew. ¥6000 per person. Credit cards accepted.)

Tōno is known for its original dishes, *hittsumi* (ひっつみ) and Tōno *rāmen*. You can sample such hometown specialities at a number of lunch spots on Fudaba-dōri. **Umenoya** ❶ (食堂うめのや), Ekimae-dōri, two blocks up from the station on the left, serves it all—*rāmen* (¥400), Tōno *rāmen* (¥650), and *hittsumi* lunch set (¥950)—the ambitious can try all the originals in one sitting. (Open 11:30am-8pm. Closed 2 days each month, to-be-determined.)

▨ SIGHTS. To see Tōno without a car, take the all-inclusive **JR Bus Tour** or rent a bike from the tourist office (¥1000; return by 5pm) or the youth hostel. The JR Tour is pricey, and it leaves out some key sights, but it's up to you how you want your bottom to feel at the end of the day. (Morning tour ¥5000. 10:30am departure from tourist office. Afternoon tour ¥4400. Noon departure.) The tourist office's helpful English brochure suggests three biking routes, color-coded green, blue, and red. The historical **green route** (18km) includes Fukusen-ji (福泉寺), some old castle sights, and royal tombstones. The **blue route** (26km) covers many of the places mentioned in Yanagita's *Legends of Tōno*. The highlights include the water mill (水車), Suikōen (水光園), and Denshōen (伝承園). The **red route** stretches 24km west, past the Tōno Municipal Museum, Gohyaku Ryokan (old Buddhist rock-carvings), and Minshuku Magariya (a historic thatched-roof house). Although all the routes are worthwhile, you might want

NORTHERN HONSHŪ

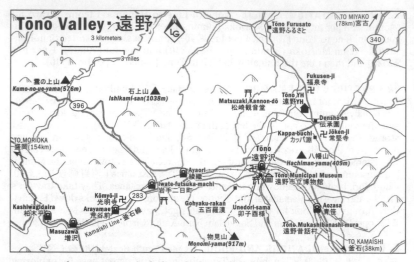

Tōno Valley ･ 遠野

to put together your own, including the best of all three, plus the places the guides miss. One exciting attraction the routes miss is the village **Furusato** (ふるさと), 5-89-1, Kamitsukimōshi, Tsukimōshi-chō. In a secluded part of the valley, the village has many old thatched-roof houses where enthusiastic locals educate you about Tōno's past. (From the station, take Rte. 340 north. Follow the signs. ☎ 64-2300. Open daily 9am-5pm. Closed Dec. 28-Jan. 4. ¥500.)

■ **FESTIVALS.** Tōno holds many festivals, some bright and colorful, others just plain shocking. In the **Tōno Festival,** hundreds of performers in glowing red costumes and gold hats dance in the streets to traditional music (Sept. 14-15). The **Men Walking Nude to Iwataki Shrine Festival** is a short pilgrimage that dares the boldest of men to let it hang out. Unfortunately for all, the festival is on February 28.

MORIOKA (盛岡) AND AROUND ☎019

Once the 16th-century castle town of Lord Nobunao, Morioka has sold its medieval garb and become Iwate Prefecture's urban center. Today, the city is known as the home of literary stars Miyazawa Kenji and Ishikawa Takuboku and as a haven for noodle-lovers. The most curious of travelers might keep busy here for a day, but passers-through will likely leave Morioka reminded that it is, both truthfully and metaphorically, a castle town without a castle.

| **ON THE WEB** | Morioka: www.city.morioka.jp |

▛ TRANSPORTATION

Trains: All trains run through **Morioka Station** (盛岡駅), 1-48, Ekimae-dōri, at the southwestern end of town. ☎ 622-3456. Open daily 5:30am-10:45pm. The **shinkansen** provides the most efficient transport to: **Aomori** (1¾hr., 1 per hr., ¥6260); **Hakodate** (2hr., 8 per day, ¥11,190); **Sendai** (40min., 1 per hr., ¥1620); **Tōkyō** (2½hr., 1 per hr., ¥13,840). Local trains to **Sendai** are cheaper but take longer (3hr., 1 per hr., ¥3260).

Buses: Bus info (☎ 022-256-6646) is outside on the 1st fl. of the train station's east terminal. Open daily 7:55am-8:35pm. Long distance buses arrive and depart from the west terminal to **Sendai** (2½hr., 1 per hr., ¥2850, round-trip ¥5000) and **Aomori**

(3hr., 6 per day, ¥3160). Overnight buses to **Tōkyō** (7hr., ¥7850, round-trip ¥14,130) and **Yokohama** (8hr., ¥8950/16,110) stop at the station's east terminal or the bus center.

Public Transportation: The city's local buses stop in front of the train station and at the city's **bus center** (盛岡バスセンター), 1-9-22, Naka-no-hashi-dōri, on the northeastern side of town. Buses run daily 6am-11pm. Tickets from ¥100.

Taxis: There's a taxi stand at the station's east terminal, and they are easy enough to catch around town. Call the taxi info center if you're stranded. ☎622-5240. Open 24hr.

Bike Rental: Sasaki Bicycle, 10-10-2, Ekimae-dōri, rents bikes for ¥200 per hr., or ¥1000 per day. (☎624-2692.) Open daily 8:30am-6pm.

▪ ORIENTATION

The easiest way to handle Morioka is to divide it into three districts. First, there's the train station area in the southwest, mainly restaurants and upscale hotels. Across the Kitakami-gawa river (北上川) lies the bustling city center, which spreads across the Ōdōri (大通 り) shopping arcade. Noodle shops, Asian cuisine eateries, and *izakaya* fill this area. Activity converges on the cross-street, **Elgakan-dōri** (映画館通). At night, the north end comes alive with sketchy characters. To the east, tucked in at the end of the arcade, bordering the **Nakatsu-gawa river** (中津川), is the castle grounds district, with its museums, administrative buildings, and banks. Morioka is small enough that you can walk almost everywhere.

▪ PRACTICAL INFORMATION

Tourist Offices:

City Tourist Office (盛岡観光協会), 1-1-10, Naka-no-hashi-dōri 2F, is on the northeastern side of town in a modern building. Take the shopping arcade street down to the Nakatsu-gawa river, and the office is just over the bridge on the right (in Plaza Odette). **Free Internet** (30min. max.). ☎621-8800. Open daily 9am-8pm. Closed 2nd Tu of the month.

Northern Tōhoku Sightseeing Center (北東北観光案内 所), on the 2nd fl. of the train station. Free English maps and pamphlets with information on the entire Tōhoku region. Closer than the city tourist office. English-speaking staff. ☎625-2090; fax 625-2091. Open daily 9am-5:30pm.

Iwate International Plaza (岩手県立国際交流プラザ), 2-4-20, Osawakawara. Mostly for foreign residents, but helpful for travelers. Free **Internet** (if you register) and multi-lingual newspapers. From the station, head over Kaiun-bashi bridge and make your 1st right. Make a right at Kumagai Ryokan, and the plaza's a few blocks down on the left. ☎654-8900. Open Tu-F 10am-9pm, Sa-Su 10am-5pm. Closed on days after national holidays and Dec. 29-Jan. 3.

THE LOCAL LEGEND

THE FOLKORE OF TŌNO

As you traipse through the sunken valleys of Iwate Prefecture, it would be wise to keep out of the abandonded houses locals refer to as *mayoi-ga*, which literally translates into "a house found when one loses her way." According to local folk tradition, these mysterious mountain huts harbor the power to bestow endless fortune upon he who procures an object within the *mayoi-ga*. Too bogus for your taste? Just ask any local how Tōno's wealthiest have come upon their riches, and perhaps you will hear about the woman who acquired a red tea cup, and upon using it to cook, found that she had an endless supply of rice.

Capturing the spirit of Tōno's folklore, *The Legends of Tōno* was published in 1934 by the godfather of Japanese folkore and mythology, Kunio Yanagita. Opening up a portal into the world of ancient mysticism, Yanagita introduced Japan to Tōno's legends by recording the words of the oldest story-tellers in the land. The entertaining and illuminating tales address everything from love and denial to deceit and murder. Regardless of your beliefs, to get a peek into the culture of Tōno, dabble in the region's oral tradition.

The Legends of Tōno is available at the tourist info office, the Municipal Museum, and other local bookstores. The tourist office carries a hardcover English version (¥2000).

Budget Travel: HIS Travel, 2-6-8, Ōdōri, 2F (☎626-4461), is along the main arcade, a block up from the Comics and Internet Cafe. Open M-F 10am-7pm, Sa 10am-6pm.

Currency Exchange: Shichi-jū-shichi Bank (七十七銀行), 3-3-10, Ōdōri (☎624-1177), changes American dollars and traveler's checks for a fee. Head over Kaiun-bashi Bridge, continue onto Ōdōri, and the bank is on the left corner 2 blocks up. The **Central Post Office** and its **Eki-mae** location also make exchanges.

ATM: International ATMs are scarce. Try the Central and Eki-mae Post Offices or the **Daily Yamazaki** convenience store, Ekimae-dōri, 2 blocks up from the station.

Luggage Storage: On the 1st fl. of the station, to the left. Lockers ¥300-600.

Emergency: Police ☎110. Fire or ambulance ☎119.

Pharmacy: Kusuri-no-Kenkōdō (くすりの健康堂), 1-10-17, Ōdōri, 2 blocks up from HIS, on the left. ☎652-1752. Open M-F 10am-8pm, Sa-Su 10am-7pm. For prescriptions, go to **Komachi Yakkyoku** (こまち薬局), 9-10, Ekimae-dōri, in front of the station. ☎652-7581. Open M-F 8:30am-6:30pm, Sa 8:30am-3pm.

Hospital: Ikadaigaku Fuzoku Byōin (医科大学附属病院), 19-1, Uchimaru (☎651-5111), a few blocks toward Nakatsu-gawa river from the Central Post Office. The **emergency center** (kyūmeikyūkyū sentā; 救命救急センター), open 24hr., is in the back.

Internet Access: Connect for free at the **Iwate International Plaza** of the **City Tourist Office** (see above), or pay at **Comics & Internet Cafe** (コミック＆インターネットカフェ), 3-2-2, Ōdōri. ¥280 for 1st 30min., ¥470 per hr. Marked by an orange sign a block from Shichi-jū-shichi Bank. ☎654-9800. Open daily 11am-midnight.

Post Office: Central Post Office (盛岡中央郵便局), 1-13-45, Chūō-dōri (☎624-5353). North of the arcade; from Ōdōri, make the 2nd left after HIS and walk 10min. The office has an **international ATM.** Open daily 9am-7pm. Currency and traveler's checks exchange 9am-6pm. ATM open M-F 7am-11pm, Sa 9am-9pm, Su 9am-7pm. A few blocks from the train station, the **Eki-mae branch,** 10-12, Ekimae-dōri, has the same services. ☎651-1805. Open M-F 9am-6pm. **Postal Code:** 020.

ACCOMMODATIONS

Since Morioka's one and only youth hostel is far from the city center, most travelers opt to stay at cheap ryokan around the station area. The cheap places tend to make you think that WWII is still going on. Below are the more appealing options.

Morioka Youth Hostel (HI) (盛岡ユースホステル), 1-9-41, Takamatsu (☎662-2220). From Morioka Station, take a bus to Takamatsu-no-Ikeguchi (15min., ¥210), and from this stop, walk toward the post office on the corner. Turn left at the post office and continue down the road (5min.). Although thrown out in the city's northwestern burbs, MYH is the cheapest accommodation in town. Breakfast ¥600. Check-in 3pm. Check-out 10am. Curfew 10pm. Dorms ¥2900; nonmembers add ¥600. ❶

Taishōkan (大正館 ; ☎622-4436). From the station, cross Kaiun-bashi bridge and make the far right turn. Follow the street left. It's a few blocks down (10min. on foot). If you can ignore the slightly run-down exterior, settle into one of the town's best bargains. Well-kept rooms, worn-in feel, and amicable staff. Breakfast ¥1000. Dinner ¥1000. Free self-serve laundry. Check-in 3pm. Check-out 10am. ¥3500 per person. ❶

Kumagai Ryokan (熊ヶ井旅館), 3-2-5, Ōsawakawara (☎651-3020; fax 626-0096). In a folkloric wooden building next to Taishōkan, Kumagai offers the best value of its kind with cozy rooms and a well-decorated interior. Breakfast ¥800. Dinner ¥1500. Free parking. Check-in 4pm. Check-out 10am. Reservations recommended. Singles ¥4500; doubles ¥8000; triples ¥10,000. Credit cards accepted. ❷

Morioka·盛岡

▲ ACCOMMODATIONS

Kumagai Ryokan, **10**
Morioka New City Hotel, **11**
Morioka Youth Hostel (HI), **1**
Taishōkan, **9**

🍎 FOOD

Azuma-ya, **12**
Kōjan, **5**
Picca Pecca, **7**
Sanmaruku Cafe, **6**
Shokudōen, **4**

NIGHTLIFE

Faces, **3**
Jirocho, **8**
Tippertary Irish Pub, **2**

Morioka New City Hotel (盛岡ニューシティホテル), 13-10, Ekimae-dōri (☎654-5161; www.moriokacityhotel.co.jp). From the train station, turn left before Kaiun-bashi bridge and walk along the river—it's on the left corner. Very convenient. Small rooms with bath, TV, fridge. Breakfast ¥840. Reception 24hr. Check-in 4pm. Check-out 11am. Singles from ¥5400; doubles from ¥7800; triples ¥18,000. Credit cards accepted. ❸

⬛ FOOD

The noodle-capital of Japan, Morioka attracts visitors with its specialized *rāmen* and *soba* dishes. If you're not in the mood to sample the creative local cuisine, just wander up and down Ōdōri or the station area, and you're likely to find something tasty or cheap, if not both.

▨ **Picca Pecca**, 2-7-21, Ōdōri, Sorento Bldg. (☎651-2061). Right across from HIS travel. With light reggae to keep the beat, Picca serves Asian fusion by day (until 3pm), coffee by evening (until 5pm), and cocktails by night. Don't miss the lunch appetizers, like the beef omelette rice (¥700). Entrees from ¥400. Mixed drinks over ¥500. All you can drink plus 6 food dishes for ¥3000. Open Su-Th 11am-midnight, F-Sa 11-2am. ❷

Shokudōen (食道園), 1-8-2, Ōdōri (☎651-4590). Walk up the shopping arcade from the station, turn left onto Eigakan-dōri, and make your 1st right—it's at the end of the alley on the left. Any local will direct *reimen* virgins to Shokudōen to introduce them to this hometown dish. Choose the spicyness level that's right for you, and you can't go wrong (¥850). Open M-F 8:30am-3:30pm and 5-10pm, until midnight on weekends. ❷

Kōjan (香醤), 2-4-18, Ōdōri (☎626-2336). Turn left onto Eigakan-dōri from the shopping arcade, and then make your 2nd left just before Lawson—it's just on the left. Often the after-hours worker's last stop before heading home, Kōjan has arguably the best *jaja-men* noodle (¥450-650) in the city. Squeeze in and take a seat, because it fills up fast. Beer ¥350. Open daily 11am-3am, closed every other Su. ❶

Sanmaruku Cafe (サンマルクカフェ), 2-6-7, Ōdōri Fuchisawa Bldg. (☎606-1309). With 3 fl. of spacious seating and a live pianist, there's an unsupposing elegance you won't find at the other cafes on Ōdōri. Light sandwiches ¥280. Coffee from ¥180. Pastries from ¥100. Live piano daily 12:30-8:30pm. Open daily 7:30am-9:30pm. ❶

Azuma-ya (東家), 1-8-3, Naka-no-hashi-dōri (☎622-2252). Just in front of the train station, on the corner bldg.'s 2nd fl. One of the best *wanko-soba* places in town. Not the site of the Wanko-soba Festival, but the perfect arena for you to go head to head with a friend. Reservations recommended. Open daily 11am-midnight. ❹

⬢ SIGHTS

All that's really necessary to see Morioka's few noteworthy sights is a nice day and a decent pair of walking shoes. Although bikes are available for rent, they're unnecessary. For a basic tour of the city, walk the length of the Ōdōri shopping arcade (大通商店街) until you encounter **Sakurayama Shrine** (桜山神社) on your right. Head up the stairs and through the shrine to arrive on the grounds of what was once the magnificent **Morioka Castle** (盛岡城跡). The castle, constructed by Nabunao, Lord of Nambu, over 36 years in the 17th century, was destroyed during the Meiji Restoration. Only a granite wall remains today, but the grounds make for a nice afternoon stroll. Exit Sakurayama Shrine to the right and cross the Nakano-hashi Bridge (中ノ橋), and you'll find the **Bank of Iwate** (岩手銀行), a striking red-brick building. It was designed in 1911 by Kasai Manji, famous for designing Tōkyō Station. The nest left leads to **Gozaku** (ござ九), an Edo-period merchant building. Peek into the shops to see Morioka's famous iron kettles and colorful textiles. Continue up this road past the first bridge, to elaborately decorated **Kamino-hashi bridge** (上の橋). Look for the fist-shaped bronze railing ornaments. Circle back to the station side of Nakatsu-gawa river, turn right after **City Hall** and pass through the civic center. Two and a half blocks down on the right is the **rock-splitting cherry tree**. It's unclear if the tree really broke the rock in two, but biologists guess it's 300-400 years old. In April, check out its beads of pink petals.

Hedonists in a hurry might pass over Morioka for the nearby **Tsunagi** (繋) *onsen* district. Easily reached by bus (30min., 1 per hr., ¥620; depart from east terminal of train station; last bus M-F 7:15pm, Su 5:30pm), Tsunagi is a paradise of 21 *onsen*. **Aishinkan Inn** (愛真館) has the most baths, with an indoor/outdoor selection of hot springs. (Open daily 7-9am and 11am-6pm. ¥800 per person.)

🎵 ENTERTAINMENT

Every day, beginning in early afternoon, movie-goers "shop" the theaters on **Eigakan-dōri** (映画館通り) to catch showings of everything from Hollywood blockbusters to Japanese indies. Tickets are pricey (around ¥1500 each), but there are discounts for students and occasional deals. English-speakers will be delighted to find that imported films are usually spared dubbing and subtitled in Japanese instead. **The Forum** (フォーラム), 1-11-8, Ōdōri (☎622-4703), one of the largest theaters, shows English-language films, including the sporadic indie. From the arcade, walk down Eigakan-dōri, and it's downstairs on the left. (Tickets ¥1600.)

NIGHTLIFE

Although Morioka's night scene caters primarily to locals, the city has a handful of bars and clubs to excite the country-ridden traveler. When the sun goes down, most city residents hit up the area of town north of Ōdōri and the arcade, while others will sneak off to their favorite hangouts on the south side.

Faces, 2-4-22, Eigakan-dōri, 3rd Fl. (☎ 653-7606). Upstairs from Tippertary Irish Pub. The dance joint where everyone goes on weekends. Spins everything from rap to techno. Beer ¥500. Reggae on Tu. Salsa on Th. Cover ¥2000 on F (with 3 drinks), and ¥2000 on Sa (with 2 drinks). Open Su-Th 5:30pm-1am, F-Sa 9pm-3am.

Tippertary Irish Pub, Eigakan-dōri (☎ 652-6070). Heading away from the station on the arcade, turn left on Eigakan-dōri. It's 2 blocks down on the left. Trying too hard to be Irish, a melting pot of Japanese and *gaijin.* Good, but expensive beer. ½ pint of Guinness ¥450. Open M-Th 5pm-3am, F 5pm-4am, Sa 3pm-4am, Su 3pm-3am.

Jirocho, 2-4-5, Saien 2nd Fl. (☎ 653-4433). Turn right onto Eigakan-dōri heading away from the station. Make a 2nd right onto a side street—it's on the left. A stylish younger crowd plays darts and watches soccer in an upscale bar. Karaoke ¥200 per song. Beer ¥400. Mixed drinks from ¥500. No cover. Open M-W 7pm-2:30am, Th-Sa 7pm-3am.

FESTIVALS

Tōhoku is often praised for its exciting summer festivals, one of which is the thunderous **Morioka Sansa Ōdōri** (さんさ踊り). Held August 1-3, 20,000 dancers, 600 flute-players, and 5000 drummers to create a sensational display. In mid-March, the city holds the thrilling (and filling) **Wanko-soba Festival** (see p. 309).

KAKUNODATE (角館)　　☎ 0187

Kakunodate, sometimes called "Little Kyōto," is one of the prettiest towns in Tōhoku. Although the major sights can be covered in an afternoon stroll, it's worth spending the night since the town boasts a number of comfortable ryokan and great restaurants. Although the Edo-period merchants' quarters have been replaced by an unappealing downtown, about a 15min. walk northwest of the train station, the *samurai* district has been preserved. You'll know when you enter the district, which is strangely reminiscent of an American suburb. You can enter the fenced-in grounds of a

ON THE MENU

SHALL WE SLURP?

Though it's common practice to slurp up a storm when eating noodles in Japan, no city makes more noise over its noodle dishes than Morioka. Why is that? Well, because when it comes to food, Moriokans take things very seriously...*competitively.* Every Mar., the hungry and the slurping of the nation gather in the noodle capital of Japan for a *wanko-soba* contest, which is nothing short of outrageous. Downing bowl after bowl of chilled *soba*, 8-10 wacky-*wanko* competitors put their appetites on the line in hopes of outlasting their opponents and reaching the mind-blowing all-time record of 559 bowls. As for the regular crowd, they tend to stick to these local favorites:

Wanko-soba (わんこそば): Small bowls of *soba* noodles served continuously until the customer can no longer bear to continue. Usually purchased full course including sashimi, mixed meat, and vegetable sides. (From about ¥2500 per person.)

Jaja-men (じゃじゃ麺): A bowl of *udon*-like noodles served with *miso* paste and veggies on top. Mix the dish before trying it, and add more *miso* as you go along in order to keep things tasty.

Rei-men (冷麺): A soup-filled bowl of cold, transparent *rāmen* noodles. The dish is toppled with veggies, melon (other fruits) and a hard-boiled egg. There are usually 3 levels of spiciness—*karasa*—to choose from.

few of the *samurai* houses for free, and the majority of the district is open to tourists daily 9am-5pm. The most interesting is the **Aoyagi-ke,** which now contains an eclectic mix of museums. (¥500.) Farther up the street is **Ishiguro-ke,** one of the district's oldest houses. (¥300; ¥720 with admission to the Art Museum and Denshōkan.) At the center is **Denshōkan,** which displays the treasures of the Satake clan, and trains *kabazaika* artists. *Kabazaika*, the practice of coating objects with a thin layer of cherry bark, dates back to the feudal era when poor *samurai* turned to the craft for supplemental income. *Kabazaika* souvenirs run about ¥300 at any of the shops—it's *the* quintessential souvenir of Kakunodate.

At the end of the street, you'll spot the neo-Gothic architecture of **Hirafuku Memorial Art Museum,** which displays local artists' work. (¥300.) On the way back, head west toward the river where you can walk under a canopy of **cherry trees** brought from Kyōto over 300 years ago. If you have extra time, a rewarding half-day can be spent visiting the **Suzuki Shuzōten** (☎ 56-2121; info@hideyoshi.co.jp), a 300-year-old *sake* brewery famous for its award-winning Hideyoshi brand. If you call ahead, you can arrange a tour and sampling. Take the JR Tazawa-ko-bound train towards Omagi to Ugo Nagano Station. Suzuki Shuzōten is 3min. west of the station on foot.

Kakunodate is connected by **shinkansen** to Akita (45min., 15 per day, ¥2430), Tazawa-ko (15min., ¥1050), and Morioka (50min., ¥2260). The slower, cheaper, JR Tazawa-ko Line, runs to Morioka (50min., 7 per day, ¥1110) via Tazawa-ko (22min., ¥320). A bus service runs to Tazawa-ko (45min., Apr.-Dec. 5 per day, ¥850) and Akita (1½hr., ¥1330). The train station is south of the town center, and the bus terminal is about a 10min. walk farther north. The **tourist information office** next to the train station has a good English map detailing the *samurai* quarter. (☎ 54-2700. Open daily 9am-5pm.) There's **bike rental** (¥300 per hr.) at Hanaba Taxi on the road into town. Ten minutes north, the **post office** has an **international ATM. Postal code:** 014.

Although there are a few business hotels near the station, walk 15min. towards the *samurai* district for delightful ryokan and minshuku. One of the most popular *gaijin* places is **Minshuku Hyakusui-en ❸** in a black *kura* west of the post office. The English-speaking owner is famously hospitable. (☎ 55-5715. ¥7000; with 2 meals ¥9800.) If you're looking for a cheaper sleep, there are many ryokan, mostly along the road to the *samurai* district. (Around ¥5000 per night.)

If you haven't arranged meals at your accommodation, there are some wonderful little places near the *samurai* district. At the entrance to the main street of the *samurai* quarter is a **noodle house ❷,** where you can lounge on comfortable *tatami* mats in a wood-trimmed dining hall. The homemade noodles (¥1000) are simply divine, especially with sesame dipping sauce. (Open daily 11am-9pm.) Just a few blocks north in an old wooden *samurai* house is another small **noodle restaurant ❷** that specializes in *inaniwa udon (*¥1000), a thin, slippery noodle served in a light soup of vegetables and mushrooms. (Open daily 11am-9pm.)

TAZAWA-KO (田沢湖)   ☎ 0187

At 423.4m, Tazawa-ko is the deepest lake in Japan. Numerous legends speculate about what lies beneath the emerald green waters, and even today there is an aura of mystery. Though principally a scenic attraction, in summer you can hike, cycle, swim or boat around the lake. In winter, relax at Nyūtō Onsen after a long day on the ski slopes. From April to November, there are 40min. cruises around the lake. Tours leave from Shirahama, a short walk from Tazawa-kohan Bus Terminal (4 per day, ¥1170). One of the area's most rewarding hikes is to the summit of **Akita Komaga-take** (1637m). In summer, take a bus from Tazawa-ko Station to Hachigome (1hr., usually 5 per day, ¥810). From there, it's a 1hr. hike to the top. For an all-day trek, follow the 4hr. trail to the top of Nyūtō-zan; it's 5km down to **Nyūtō Onsen,** a hidden hot spring. Six rustic inns offer a variety of hot springs and delicious country cooking. Soak away your aches, then catch the bus back to Tazawa-ko to take a gander at the **Tatsuko Statue.**

According to legend, a girl named Tatsuko was instructed by a goddess to drink water from the lake in order to gain perpetual beauty. Upon drinking, however, she became a dragon and sank into the lake. Take a bath or dine divinely at **Heart Herb**, on the northeast shore. (☎43-0130. ¥500 admission includes bath. Bath only ¥400. Open daily 9am-5pm. Bath open 11am-9pm.)

The nearest train station is **Tazawa-ko**, in Tazawa-ko-han, on the JR Akita **shinkansen** line. Trains serve Akita (1hr., 15 per day, ¥3280) via Kakunodate (45min., ¥2940) and Morioka (35min., ¥1980). The **JR Tazawa-ko Line** connects to Kakunodate (22min., 7 per day, ¥320) and Morioka (1hr., 16 per day, ¥740). A **bus** runs from Tazawa-ko Station to Akita (2hr., Apr.-Dec. 5 per day, ¥1680) via Kakunodate (45min., ¥850). A local bus runs to Tazawa-ko Haruyama (15min.; 33 per day, 12 in winter; ¥350). Another runs to Nyūtō Onsen (45min., 9 per day, ¥740). Most accommodations rent **bicycles** and **mopeds**. The **Fo-lake Tourist Information Center** in Tazawa-ko Station has camping and hiking maps and books lodgings. (☎43-2111. Open daily 8:30am-6:30pm.)

Tazawa-ko Youth Hostel (HI) ❶ (田沢湖ユースホステル), on the main street in Tazawa Haruyama, near Kōen-Iriguchi Bus Stop, has friendly staff and delectable food. (☎43-1281. Dorms ¥2900.) Otherwise, several **minshuku** dot the shore. (Around ¥6000 per night with 2 meals.) **cafe+inn THAT SOUNDS GOOD! ❹** is worth the price. Book well in advance—it's popular. The English-speaking owner (who will pick you up at the terminal) organizes jazz shows and daytrips. (☎/fax 43-0127; sanzoku@hana.or.jp. ¥8500, ¥10,000 with 2 meals.) At Nyūtō Onsen are a **campsite** and ryokan. Sites charge ¥500 per person. Pick up a camping guide at the station information office.

The cafes near the lake shore are mostly overpriced noodle houses. One gem is **ORAE ❶**, a popular spot for locals and tourists where you can enjoy a microbrew (¥470) while munching on *izakaya*-style snacks. In summer, if the weather's nice, the outdoor seating is very atmospheric. (Open daily 11am-9pm.)

AKITA (秋田) ☎018

Akita is the largest city on the western coast of Tōhoku, a rapidly developing commercial and industrial center with an extremely modern downtown. Although few travelers spend time in Akita, it's a good place for an overnight stop on the way to Kakunodate or Tazawa-ko. The city has a boisterous entertainment district and a unique, regional cuisine. And yes, it's also where those cute, fluffy dogs originated.

ON THE WEB	Akita City: www.city.akita.akita.jp

Ꞓ TRANSPORTATION. All trains arrive at the unbelievably modern **JR Akita Station**, on the eastern edge of the city. The JR Akita **shinkansen** runs through Kakunodate (45min., 15 per day, ¥2940) and Tazawa-ko (1hr., ¥3280), terminating in Morioka. Infrequent **local trains** along the JR Tazawa-ko Line connect Akita to Kakunodate (1½hr., 7 per day, ¥1280) and Tazawa-ko (2hr., ¥1620). From Niigata, the JR Uetsu Line runs via Sakata and Tsuruoka (3¾hr., 3 per day, ¥7020). There're also **inter-city buses** via Kakunodate (1½hr., 6 per day, ¥1330) or Tazawa-ko (2hr., ¥1680). **Overnight buses** run to Tōkyō, Shinjuku Station (9hr., 9 and 10pm, ¥9450). The terminal is in front of the train station. A small **airport** is about 40min. south of the city by bus (every 15min., ¥849).

In the city itself, an extensive network of buses radiates from the terminal to the residential districts, but the majority are of little interest to the passing traveler. If you need your own wheels, **Eki Renta-Car** (☎33-9308), **Nippon Renta-Car** (☎32-5789), and **Toyota Renta-Car** (☎33-0100) are all near the station.

⑦ PRACTICAL INFORMATION. The **tourist information office** on the second floor of the train station has a good English walking map. (☎ 32-7941. Open daily 9am–7pm.) **Akita Bank** and **Hokuto Bank** on Chū-dōri that **exchange** foreign **currency**. The **post office** on Chū-dōri also has **international ATM** access. The **police station** (☎ 35-1111) is just west of the castle park, and there is Red Cross **hospital** (☎ 34-3361) at 1-4-36, Naka-dōri. In an emergency, call ☎ 110 for **police**, ☎ 119 for **fire** or **ambulance**. **Internet access** is available at a small kiosk on the second floor of the Topico department store, next to the train station. (¥200 for 30min.) **Postal code:** 010.

⑥⚫ ACCOMMODATIONS AND FOOD. Akita isn't that well equipped for overnight stays. There are two ryokan near the station as well as the usual business hotels, but none of the hostels and capsule hotels you'd expect in a city this size. Just southwest of the station, at **Ryokan Chikuba-sō ❷** (旅館竹馬荘), you'll be able to relax in spacious *tatami* rooms. (☎ 32-6446. Meals ¥2000. ¥5000 per person.) A few blocks south is **Kohama Ryokan ❷** (小浜旅館), a friendly, family-run place. (☎ 32-5739; fax 32-5845. ¥5000 per person.) Western-style rooms are available at the **Hotel Metropolitan Akita ❹** (ホテルメトロポリタン秋田), a smart, modern business hotel in the train station, offering TV and private baths. (☎ 31-2222. ¥8500 per person.) The **Hotel Hawaii Eki-mae-ten ❸** (ホテルハワイ駅前店) an older business hotel, is decorated to look like a bad 70s movie. A few blocks west of the train station, it's perfectly adequate. (☎ 83-1111. ¥5200 per person.) In terms of luxury, you can't do better then the new **Akita View Hotel ❹** (秋田ビューホテル), across the street from Hotel Hawaii. Perks include restaurants, a luxurious indoor swimming pool, and a gym with state-of-the art equipment. (☎ 32-1111. Gym ¥3500 per day. From ¥9500 per person.)

Akita is known for its cuisine, and most restaurants have at least one regional specialty on the menu. Look for *kiritanpo*, kneaded rice roasted over charcoals and stir-fried in soy sauce-flavored chicken soup with green onions, Japanese parsley, and *maitake* mushrooms. *Shottsuru*, a strong-tasting stew of fermented fish mixed with green onions, tofu, and spices, is also popular. The most famous restaurant in Akita for *kiritanpo* and *shottsuru* is **Hamanoya ❹**, in the center of the Kawabata nightlife area, in the lobby of Hotel Metropolitan. (☎ 62-6611. Open daily 11:30am–10pm.) If Haminoya is too pricey, try **Suginoya's ❸** (杉のや) regional specialities and delicious *wappameshi* and *chirashi* sets (around ¥1500). It's on the third floor of JR Akita Station in the restaurant arcade. (☎ 35-8903. Open daily 10am–9pm.) For cheap eats, the publicly run **Akita Citizen's Market** (Akita Shimin-ichiba; 秋田市民市場), a few blocks southwest of the train station, sells fresh foods, clothing, flowers, and snacks. (☎ 83-1855. Open M-Sa 6am–5pm.)

⑥ SIGHTS. Just north of the city center is **Senshū-kōen**, a public park that houses the remains of Akita's second castle, built in 1604 by the Satake clan and destroyed by the forces of the Meiji Restoration. Although only the turret and the moat remain, the park is popular, especially in spring when the azaleas and cherry trees blossom. (Open dusk-dawn. Free.) At the park's southern edge is the **Hirano Masak-ichi Art Museum** (平野政吉美術館), easily identified by its sloping, palace-style roofs. The museum showcases the collection of Masakichi, who was a merchant in Akita, and Tsuguji Fujita, a modern Japanese artist, as well as a few works by European artists including Cezanne, Van Gogh, and Picasso. (☎ 33-5809. Open Tu-Su 10am-6pm, 10am-5pm in winter. ¥410.) If you won't be in town for the Kantō Matsuri, be sure to check out the **Kantō Festival Center** (Nebushi Ryūshikan; ねぶし流し館), west of the park across the river, for videos of the famous *kantō* pole dancing. The friendly staff will let you try to carry the 10m, 60kg poles. (Open daily

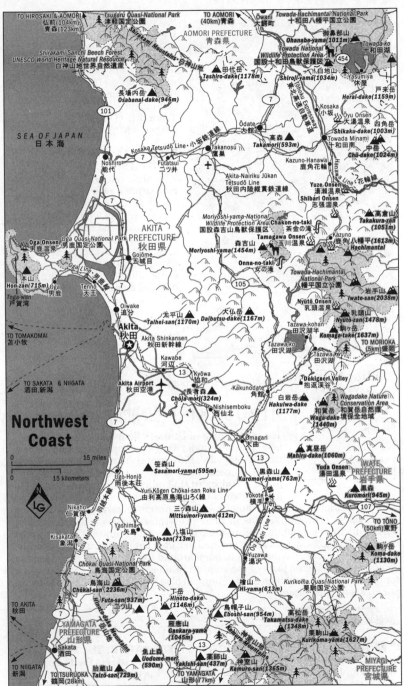

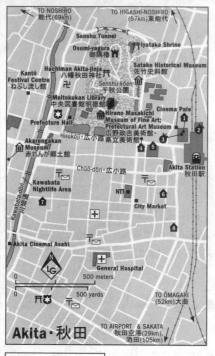

Akita · 秋田

■ ACCOMMODATIONS
Akita View Hotel, **5**
Ryokan Chikuba-sō, **6**
Hotel Hawaii, **4, 7**
Hotel Metropollitan Akita, **1**
Kohama Ryokan, **8**
🍴 FOOD
Hamanoya, **3**
Suginoya's, **2**

9:30am-4:30pm. ¥100). From the festival center, turn right and walk 500m to the **Akarengakan,** a brick building erected in 1912 as the headquarters of Akita Bank. It's extremely well preserved, and there are some wood-cuttings by self-taught local legend Katsuhira Tokushi. (Open daily 9:30am-4:30pm. ¥200.)

🎭🎪 **ENTERTAINMENT AND FESTIVALS.** In the mood for a wild night out? Head to the **Kawabata nightlife area,** southwest of the castle on the opposite bank. This crazy street is a party just about any hour of the night. With 1000 bars, restaurants, and clubs, something's bound to appeal. August 4-7, Akita hosts the **Kantō Matsuri.** The event starts in the evening when over 150 men carry 10m poles hung with lanterns. The beat is kept by *taiko* drummers, and although the *kantō*-bearers are skilled, it's not uncommon to see the poles crash down into the crowd. The entire city shuts down to partake in the festivities. If you're planning to participate, arrange a room well ahead of time.

HIROSAKI (弘前) ☎0172

The castle town of Hirosaki flourished both politically and culturally under Tsugaru clan rule in the 17th century. In the late 1800s, however, after the Meiji Restoration, Hirosaki lost out to Aomori in the contest to be prefectural capital. Today a rather unremarkable downtown is complemented by the well-preserved Edo-era district of *samurai* homes and an enormous park centered around the remains of Hirosaki-jō, one of the most famous castles in Japan. History buffs will find a number of Buddhist temples and Meiji-era buildings to explore. Hirosaki's sights can be covered in a day, but the restaurants and live-music halls should convince you to stick around for the night. On a clear day you can see the sacred peak of the volcano Iwaki-san—ask at the tourist office for information on dayhikes there. They can also help you plan a daytrip to the popular spa Aoni Onsen.

ON THE WEB Hirosaki: www.city.hirosaki.aomori.jp

🚆🚌 **TRANSPORTATION AND PRACTICAL INFORMATION.** The **JR Hirosaki Station** is on the eastern edge of the city. Hirosaki is connected via the **JR Ōu** line to Akita (2hr., 1 per hr., ¥3870) and Aomori (50min., 1 per hr., ¥650). A few minutes west of the station, behind the Daiei department store, is the **Hirosaki Bus Terminal.**

Long-distance buses serve Sendai (4½hr., 3 per day, ¥5090) and from April to late October, Towada-ko (2¼hr., 3 per day, ¥2350). A **tourist loop bus** heads to Tsugaru Neputamura, near the entrance to the castle park (15min., every 10min., ¥100). For rental wheels, try **Eki Rent-a-car** (☎35-0074), just south of the station. (From ¥5500 per day.) **Chūō-dōri**, flanked by banks and office buildings, runs northwest. To the south, **Dotemachi** has most of the shops and restaurants. There are two **tourist information centers**, one in the train station (☎32-0524; open daily 8:45am-6pm, 5pm in the winter) and the main **Sightseeing Information Center** (☎37-5501; fax 39-6394), at the castle's southern entrance. The main **post office**, which has an **international ATM**, is 15min. north of the station. **Postal code: 036.**

⌘ ACCOMMODATIONS. An overnight stay in Hirosaki can be uneconomical, but don't pass up on █Blossom Hotel ❹ (ブロッサムホテル), half a block south of the station. Breaking the standard business hotel mold with brightly decorated rooms, Blossom has TV, A/C, queen-sized beds, and refrigerators. The price includes a lovely breakfast in the adjacent cafe. (☎32-4151; fax 34-5423. ¥7700 per person.) If you're on a budget, head to **Hirosaki Youth Hostel (HI)** ❶ (弘前ユースホ ステル), 11, Mori-machi, a convenient few blocks south of the castle park. Since there's no curfew, this can be a fun place to stay in summer. (☎/fax 33-7066. Dorms ¥2950.) Although there are a number of ryokan around the castle, **Kobori Ryokan** ❹ (小堀旅館), 89, Hon-chō, stands above the rest, offering *tatami* rooms in a beautiful old wooden building. (☎32-5111. 2 meals included. From ¥9000 per person.) For the spiritually inclined, there's temple lodging at **Minshuku Henshō-ji** ❸ (民宿遍照寺) in the Shin-Teramachi district, about 10min. south of the castle park. (☎32-8714. 2 meals included. Reservations required. ¥6000 per night.) Closer to the station, **Business Ryokan Akira** ❸ (ビジネス旅館明), 1-10-120, Ōmachi, is 5min. south of the station. Fairly simple as ryokan go, it's clean and comfy. (☎33-1101; fax 33-5035. 2 meals included. ¥6500.) The **City Hirosaki Hotel** ❹ (シテイ弘前ホテル), across from the train station, offers classy Western rooms with A/C and TV. Bars, restaurants, and a swimming pool are icing on the cake. (☎37-1091. ¥5700-¥10,000 per person, depending on season.)

⌘ FOOD. On top of great food, a few of Hirosaki's restaurants also have live music. The town is also the largest apple producer in Japan, so be on the look out for apple juices, wines, and pastries. A few blocks east of the main tourist information center, three-storied █Hokusaikan ❷ (北菜館) pays homage to everyone's favorite fermented beverage. You can toss back a few rounds in the downstairs Irish pub, the second floor Western-style bar, or the *izakaya* upstairs. Choose from over 240 international beers, including unique local microbrews, while testing the wide variety of pub food. Beers run about ¥500. (Open daily 11am-10pm. ¥350 table charge.) Behind the Hi Rosa department store, the small, atmospheric restaurant **Anzu** ❹ (杏), 1-44, Oyakata-machi, offers traditional Japanese fare and *jamisen* music. The set courses (¥3000) are exquisitely presented. (☎32-6684. Open M-Sa 5-11pm.) Below the Blossom Hotel, south of the station, **Be Side** ❶ is a European-style cafe with a relaxed dining hall and outdoor seating in summer. It's a perfect place for a cup of coffee and a pastry, and they have exceptional ¥550 pasta entrees. (☎32-4141. Open daily 11am-11pm.) One block south, look for the sign for **Chinese King** ❷ and head up to the second floor for a no-frills Chinese restaurant with an wide selection of noodle dishes. (☎35-5776. Open daily 11am-10pm.) **Kagi-no-hana** ❸ (かぎのはな), 43-6 Shin Kaji-machi, is a few blocks southeast of the tourist information center, in the basement of the black concrete building. The entrance is to the left. The house speciality, *jappa jiru*, is a savory stew cooked in *miso* broth with alpine vegetables and codfish. There's an impressive selection of regional *sake*. *Teishoku* courses start at ¥1600. (☎36-1152. Open daily 11am-10pm.) Across from Nakasan department store, **Manchan** ❷

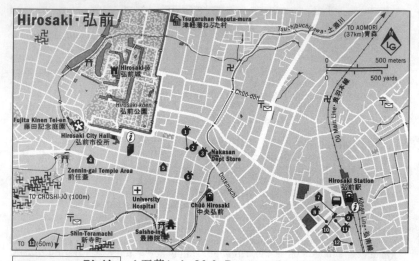

Hirosaki・弘前

Hirosaki・弘前

🏠 ACCOMMODATIONS
Blossom Hotel, **10**
Business Ryokan Akira, **12**
City Hirosaki Hotel, **7**
Hirosaki Youth Hostel (HI), **4**
Kobori Ryokan, **5**
Minshuku Henshō-ji, **13**

🍴 FOOD
Anzu, **1**
Be Side, **9**
Chinese King, **11**
Hokusaikan, **2**
Kagi-no-hana, **6**
Livehouse Yamauta, **8**
Manchan, **3**

(万茶ン), 36-6, Dote-machi, the oldest cafe in Tōhoku, is renowned for its relaxed atmosphere and exquisite Hokkaidō cheesecake. (☎35-4663. Open daily 11am-10pm.) **Livehouse Yamauta ❸** (ライブハウス山唄), 1-2-7, Omachi, is a few blocks west of the train station. A great place to hear traditional music—the owner's son is the current national *tsugaru jamisen* (three-stringed traditional guitar) champion. There are two sets nightly; if you order a meal or a beer, you can listen for free. (☎36-1835. Open daily 5-11pm.)

🔵 **SIGHTS.** The original, five-storied **Hirosaki-jō** (弘前城) was constructed in 1611, but the castle was destroyed by lightning only 16 years later. The rebuilders replaced it with the current three-storied structure. Today a small **museum** of *samurai* weapons occupies one of the restored towers. (Open daily 9am-5pm Apr.-Nov. ¥200.) The turrets, gates and moats have been turned into an exquisite **public park**, especially striking in spring when the 3000 cherry trees are in bloom. The park can be reached from the station by taking the 15min. **tourist loop bus** to the Tsugaru Neputa Mura near the entrance. (Open dawn till dusk. Free.) Nearby the castle, the **Tsugaru Neputa Mura** (津軽ぬぷた村) museum displays the floats that are paraded through the streets during Hirosaki's Neputa Matsuri. Attached to the museum is the famous **Yokien Garden,** which features soaring pine trees and tranquil ponds. (Open daily 9am-5pm, 4pm in the winter. ¥500.) Just north of the museum, you'll find the **Historical Preservation District** and a few old *samurai* houses from the Umeda and Iwata families. (Open on irregular days, dawn to dusk. Free.) Recently restored **Saishō-in** (最勝院), 15min. south of the park, was built by the feudal lord Nobuyoshi in 1667. It took nearly 10 years to complete the five-storied pagoda, which is awash in beautiful reds and greens. (Open daily 9am-4pm. Free.) About 20min. west of the castle, the temples of **Zenrin-gai** (禅林街) are one of Hirosaki's most resplendent sights. The main approach, lined on both sides by temples, eventually leads to **Chōshi-jō,** a magnificent Edo temple that houses nearly 50 statues of Zen disciples. (Open daily 8am-5pm. ¥300.)

August 1-7, Hirosaki hosts the **Neputa Matsuri,** when hand-painted fan-shaped floats are paraded down the streets in a huge procession of dancers and drummers. This is one of the most popular festivals in Tōhoku, so book accommodation ahead of time if you're planning to partake in the festivities.

AOMORI (青森) ☎017

Perched on Mutsu Bay in the very north of Honshū is Aomori—a typical Japanese city gone *too* typical. After suffering serious blows during World War II, the city recovered only to suffer yet again—this time from a lack of character. Even its praised surroundings are often too expensive and time-consuming to access. To be fair, it makes a decent launch-pad for getting to otherwise unreachable rural destinations, and it has a few museums that could help kill a day if necessary. The only time the city merits a visit on its own is in early August, at the balls-out **Nebuta Matsuri** (ねぶた祭)—one of Japan's rowdiest celebrations (p. 321).

ON THE WEB	Aomori City: www.city.aomori.aomori.jp

▐ TRANSPORTATION. Aomori Station (青森駅), 1-1-1, Yanagawa (☎722-7781), at the western end of town, has a JR ticket counter. (Open daily 5:30am-10:20pm.) **Trains** connect Aomori to the south with a *shinkansen* or a local/express train combo. Most southbound trains start with a leg to Hachinohe with an express train on the Tōhoku Honsen Line (1hr., 1 per hr., ¥3030). From Hachinohe, switch to a *shinkansen* or express train to reach your destination. Tickets for the full journey are sold to: Morioka (1¾hr., 1 per hr., ¥6260 yen); Sendai (2¼hr., 1 per hr., ¥10,670); Tōkyō (3¾hr., 1 per day, ¥16,890). Aomori is connected to the north via Hakodate (2hr., 1 per hr., ¥5340) and Sapporo (6¼hr., 1 per hr., ¥13,200). JR **buses** operate from in front of the tourist center; the ticket office is inside (☎773-5722; open daily 6:40am-5:30pm). Buses run to: Morioka (3hr., 6 per day, ¥3160); Sendai (5hr., 4 per day, ¥5700; reservations recommended); Tōkyō (9½hr., 1 per day, ¥10,190). **Tōhoku Dōsoku Buses** (☎773-5006), go to Ikebukuro in Tōkyō (10hr., 1 per day, ¥10,000). Catch a city bus from the train station (35min., frequency depends on number of flights, ¥560) to **Aomori Airport** (青森空港), 1-5, Ōtani-aza-kotani (☎739-2140). Flights run to: Chitose (45min., 2 per day); Fukuoka (2hr., 1 per day Su-M and Th-F); Nagoya (1¼hr., 2 per day); Ōsaka (1½hr., 2 per day); Tōkyō (1¼hr., 8 per day). **Aomori Port** (青森港), 2-11-1, Ōkidate, at the northwestern end of town, has ferries to **Hakodate** (3½hr., 9 per day, from ¥1850) and **Muroran** (6½hr., 1 per day, ¥3460). Buy tickets on the boat. The high-speed ferry no longer exists.

Both **Shiei Buses** (市営バス) and **JR Buses** run approximately 6:30am-10pm (fares from ¥150). JR has two routes, one along the eastern side of the coast, and one running southwest toward Aomori Public University (青森公立大学). Board JR Buses in front of the tourist office. Shiei Buses cover parts of the city that the JR routes don't reach. Board at the covered green platform in front of the train station. **Miyago Kankō Taxi** (三八五観光タクシー ; ☎743-0385) is open 24hr.

◰ ORIENTATION. Aomori's center is easily navigable. The city is bordered in the north by **Mutsu Bay** (陸奥湾) and the **Aomori Bay Bridge** (青森ベイブリッジ), and in the west by the train station. **Shinmachi-dōri** (新町通り), the main shopping street, shoots directly east from the station, crossing **Yanagimachi-dōri** (柳町通り) and reaches **Tsutsumi-gawa river** (堤川) in the east. Most establishments are near the station and along Shinmachi-dōri, but nightlife is east of Yanagimachi-dōri.

▐ PRACTICAL INFORMATION. The Aomori **tourist office** (青森市観光案内所), 1-3-29, Yasukata (☎723-4670; fax 777-8639), lends a helpful hand with its English maps and brochures. The friendly staff speaks some English and provides info on accommodations The office also has info on the *free* **Aomori Welcome Card**, which provides various discounts at area hotels, buses, *onsen*, and more. Although the card is geared toward high-end establishments, its bus discounts are valuable for longer routes. There are **storage lockers** in a special storage room on the first floor of the train station. (Open 5:30am-midnight. ¥300-500.) From the station, it's on the 1st block to your right. Open daily 5am-6:30pm. The ▨**Auga Building** 4F., 1-3-7, Shinmachi, has the only **public Internet access** in Aomori City—and it's free! Usually no wait. (☎721-8000. Open daily 10am-9pm. Closed once a month, day to-be-determined.) **Shinsen Market** (新鮮市場), a fish and fresh foods market, is in the basement. **Murakami Pharmacy** (村上薬局), 1-9-22, Shinmachi, just 2 blocks from the train station on the left, has basic medicines. (☎722-7246. Open daily 8am-10pm.) **City Hospital** (shimin byōin; 市民病院), 1-14-20, Katta, is to the southeast of town center, beyond Heiwa Park. From the station, walk 12 blocks down Shinmachi-dōri and turn right on Heiwa Kōen-dōri. It's a few blocks after the park. (☎734-2171. Open 24hr.) In an emergency, call ☎ 110 for **police**, ☎119 for **fire** or **ambulance**. The **Central Post Office** (青森中央郵便局), 1-7-24, Tsutsumi-machi, exchanges currency and traveler's checks. It also has an international ATM. (☎775-1629. Open to take mail 24hr.) Closer to the station area is **Pa Lu Lu Plaza Aomori-nai Post Office** (ぱるるプラザ青森内郵便局), 1-2-14, Yanagawa (☎775-7331), a branch in the Pa Lu Lu Building. It also has an international ATM. Open M-F 9am-5pm. ATM open M-F 9am-7pm, Sa-Su 9am-5pm. **Postal Code:** 030.

⌀ ACCOMMODATIONS. Despite its wide selection of average ryokan, luxury hotels, and ugly and uglier business hotels, Aomori's accommodations fill up rather quickly. Most accommodations cluster in front of the station area, and the nicest places to stay are on Shinmachi-dōri itself. Making reservations is always a good idea, and it's absolutely necessary in early August during the Nebuta Festival. From Aomori Station, take a Moya-bound bus (雲谷) to Moya-kōgen (雲谷高原); the hostel **Aomori Moyakōgen Youth Hostel (HI) ❶** (青森雲谷高原), 9-5, Yamabuki, is a 1min. walk away. Though a good 35min. out of town, it's almost perfect with spotless rooms, an English-speaking owner, nearby *onsen*, and Guinness beer. Check out the surrounding sights. (☎764-2888; FZJ05604@nifty.ne.jp. Tea time 9-11pm. Breakfast ¥500. Dinner ¥1000. Check-in 3-9pm. Check-out 10am. Closed mid-Nov.-mid-Dec. and mid-Jan.-early-Feb. Reservations recommended. Dorms ¥3200, members ¥3000.) **Daini Ryokan ❶** (大二旅館), 1-7-8, Furukawa, is a bare-bones ryokan that defies housing economics with rock-bottom prices, run by a woman who likes to give foreigners discounts. Turn right out of the station, make your next left onto Niko-niko-dōri, make the second right, and it's to the left. (☎7222-3037 or 221-5138. Reception until 11pm. Check-in 3pm. Check-out 10am. Reservations recommended. ¥3000 per person.) Hook a left around the backside of the tourist office and **Michinoku Business Hotel ❷** (みちのくビジネスホテル), 1-2-15, Yasukata, is one block up on the left (2min. on foot). The cheapest of the bland business hotels, it's convenient and has clean, compact rooms. (☎722-5173; fax 723-1735. Laundry ¥400 per load. Reception 24 hr. Check-in 3pm. Checkout 10am. Singles ¥4000, with bath ¥5000; doubles ¥7600/¥9000; triples ¥12,000.) From the station, head up Shinmachi; the **Aomori Grand Hotel ❸** (青森グランドホテル), 1-1-23, Shinmachi, is on the second block up on the left. It might be expensive, but you get your money's worth with its perfect location. (☎723-1011; www.agh.co.jp. Breakfast ¥1500. Dinner ¥3400. Parking available. Reception 24 hr. Check-in 2pm. Check-out 11am. Reservations recommended. Singles ¥5775-8000; doubles ¥12,000-16,000; large Japanese-style rooms ¥20,000 for two guests, add ¥3000 per additional person. Credit cards accepted.)

The Far North ·
青森県

HOKKAIDŌ
北海道

TO HAKODATE
函館へ(35km)

七ッ岳
Nanan-dake(957m)

大千軒岳
Daisengen-dake(1072m)

OSHIMA
渡島支庁

Matsumae
松前町

岩部岳
Iwabe-dake(794m)

Fukushima
福島町

白神岳
Shirakami-dake(352m)

Tsugaro Kaikyō
津軽海峡

PACIFIC OCEAN
太平洋

Ōma-zaki
大間崎

Ōma
大間町

Sai
佐井村

Hotokegaura
仏ヶ浦

大尽山
Ozukushi-yama(828m)

Ōma
大間町

釜臥山
Kamabuse-yama(879m)

燧岳
Hiuchi-dake(781m)

中岳
Chū-dake(672m)

Yogen Onsen
薬研温泉

桑畑山
Kuwabata-yama(400m)

Shimokita-Hantō Quasi-National Park
下北半島国定公園

Mutsu
むつ市

Seikan Tunnel
生遠トンネル

Tappi-misaki
竜飛岬

SEA OF JAPAN
日本海

Tsugaro Hantō
津軽半島

Kanita
蟹田村

Ōminato-wan
大湊湾

Wakinosawa
脇野沢村

Mutsu-wan
陸奥湾

Noheji-wan
野辺地湾

15 kilometers

15 miles

大倉岳
Ōkura-dake(677m)

Kanagi
金木町

Aomori-wan
青森湾

Asamushi Onsen
浅虫温泉

Aomori
青森市

Noheji
野辺地町

Ōminato Line
大湊線

Tsugaru Quasi-National Park
津軽国定公園

Gonō Line 五能線

Namioka
浪岡町

Higashi-dake(684m)
東岳

Ogawara-ko
小川原湖

Misawa
三沢市

Towada-Hachimantai National Park
十和田八幡平国立公園

Hakkōda Ski Area
八甲田スキー場

八幡岳
Hachiman-dake(1020m)

Tōhoku Line 東北本線

Hyaku-zawa Ski Area
岩木山百沢スキー場

岩木山
Iwaki-san(1625m)

Hirosaki
弘前市

Kuroishi
黒石市

Towada
十和田市

Towada-ko Onsen
十和田湖温泉

Tsuta Onsen
蔦温泉

Towada National
Wildlife Protection Area
国定十和田鳥獣保護区

Hachinohe
八戸町

AOMORI
PREFECTURE
青森県

Ōwani
大鰐町

Oirase-gawa · 奥入瀬川

Towada-ko
十和田湖

Nagawa
名川町

名久井岳
Nakui-dake(615m)

Futatumori(1086m)
二ツ森

Komaga-take(1158m)
駒ヶ岳

AKITA PREFECTURE
秋田県

Yasumiya
やすみや

Hachinohe Expressway
八戸高速自動車道

Hachinohe-Expressway

長場内岳
Osabanai-dake(946m)

Ōdate
大館市

Ōyu Onsen
大湯温泉

中岳
Chū-dake(1024m)

IWATE PREFECTURE
岩手県

Ninohe
二戸市

FOOD. Aomori is a port town in one of the world's leading fish-eating countries. Enjoy the daily catch at tucked-away sushi and *sashimi* bars, or head directly to **Shinsen Ichiba** (新鮮市場 ; inside the Agua Building), said to be the best market in town. More conventional options—*rāmen*, *donburi*, curry rice, and *okonomiyaki*—are along the first few blocks of Shinmachi-dōri. Going up Shinmachi-dōri from the station, make your last left before Yanagimachi-dōri, and then make the first right—■**Tempura Tsutsumi ❷** (天ぷら堤), 2-7-4, Shinmachi, is halfway up the block on the right. Sample delicious and crispy *tempura* in a broth with *soba* noodles (*tempura soba*; ¥600), on top of rice (*tendon*; ¥1000), or as a set meal platter (*tempura teishoku*; ¥1600). (☎ 723-7506. Open daily 11:30am-2pm

NORTHERN HONSHŪ

Aomori・青森

🏠 **ACCOMMODATIONS**
Aomori Grand Hotel, **2**
Aomori Moyakōgen
    Youth Hostel (HI), **9**
Daini Ryokan, **8**
Michinoku Business Hotel, **1**

🍎 **FOOD**
Bistro Palmer, **4**
Ippachi Sushi, **3**
Tempura Tsutsumi, **7**

🍸 **NIGHTLIFE**
End of the World Bar, **6**
Remixx, **5**

and 5-10pm.) Try catching the local dialect at **Ippachi Sushi ❷** (一八寿し), 1-10-11, Shinmachi, a savory sushi bar. Courses around ¥1500-2000. From the station, walk up the street parallel and to the left of Shinmachi-dōri; it's on the left before Yanagimachi-dōri. (☎ 22-2639. Open M-Sa 11:30am-10pm, Su 11:30am-9pm.) On the main shopping street, 2 blocks from the train station, **Bistro Palmer ❷** (ビストロ パルメ), 1-8-2, Shinmachi, has upscale, yet casual feel due to the affordable, tasty lunch specials (¥650; changes daily) and long wine list (¥450 per glass). Some English is spoken. (☎ 723-2999. Open Tu-Su 11:30am-2pm and 5-10pm.)

🎴 **SIGHTS.** The best way to get acquainted with Aomori is to take a short walk along its glamorous bay. From the station the first sight is the **Bay Bridge** (ベイブ リッジ), which dominates the scene with its sleek suspension design. Constructed in 1984, the bridge spans 2km across the city. Farther east is the **ASPAM** (Aomori Prefectural Center for Industry and Tourism), 1-1-40, Yasukata, pyramid-building, which promotes cultural awareness across the greater Aomori region and has a lookout tower on its top floor. The center has various video and computer resources, but they're mostly in Japanese and aren't worth the time. Whether you visit ASPAM or not, get a glance of it at night when its green glow lights up the sky. (☎ 735-5311. Open daily 9am-6pm. Observation tower ¥800.)

About 45min. out of town is **Shōwa Daibutsu** (昭和大仏), a giant bronze Buddha over 27m tall. It was constructed in 1984. If you've never seen one before, it's worth the long bus ride, especially since there's a beautiful five-story white cedar pagoda nearby. (458, Yamazaki, Kuwabara. Take a city bus from the station. ☎726-2312. Open Apr.-Oct. 8am-5:30pm; Nov.-Mar. 9am-4:30pm. ¥400.)

An exceptional display of *ukiyo-e* (Japanese wood-block prints; 浮世絵) are the highlight of **Munakata Shikō Museum** (棟方志功記念館), 2-1-28, Matsubara, about 2km southeast of the city center and reachable by bus. Paying tribute to the famous Aomori-based artist Shikō Munakata, the permanent exhibitions house collections of his oil-paintings, *ukiyo-e*, and calligraphy drawings. (Take a city bus from the station toward either Kobata Danchi or Nakatsutsui, and get off at the Munakata Shiko Kinenkan-dōri Stop. ☎777-4567. Open Tu-Su 9:30am-4:30pm; last admission at 4pm. Closed Dec. 27-Jan. 4. ¥300, college students ¥150.)

About 1km northwest of Aomori Station is the impressive **Michinoku Traditional Wooden Boat Museum** (みちのく北方漁船博物館), 2-2-1, Okidate, sure to captivate anyone interested in historical boats and fishing practices. Inside you'll find about 130 wooden ships and sailboats that have been recognized as Important Folk Properties. (☎761-2311; www.mtwbm.com/english/index.html. Take a city bus from the station toward Nita Junkansen and get off at Okidate Shobo Bunshomae. Open daily Apr.-Sept. 8:30am-6pm; Oct.-Nov. 9am-4:30pm. Call ahead during off-season months. ¥200, students ¥100.)

🅽 **NIGHTLIFE.** Though far from happening, Aomori does have the standard bars and clubs. Things generally get going east of **Yanagimachi-dōri** (柳町通り) around 9pm. The best bars are in the nooks and crannies, and sometimes on the upper floors of buildings. More optimistic than it sounds, **End of the World Bar**, 2-7-11, Yasukata, is a small, but occasionally rowdy, drinking spot for foreigners and Japanese. Go all the way up the street 2 blocks north and parallel to Shinmachi. It's on the right just before Yanagimachi-dōri. Note the creative Southwestern US decor. (☎776-6745. Beer ¥500. Pizza ¥700. Open M-Sa 6pm-1am.) The only hip-hop club in town that features guest DJs from Tōkyō, **Remixx**, 2-16-13, Yasukata, 4F, is across from End of the World Bar—look for the sign. After midnight, there's hot and heavy dancing and straight smooth-talk in the outside hallway. (☎723-8380. Drinks ¥500-700. Cover M-F ¥500, Sa ¥2000 includes 2 drinks. Open M-Sa 9pm-5am.)

🅵 **FESTIVALS.** Exquisitely patterned floats, dazzling firework exhibitions, and the sound of floor-shattering bass drums—these are but a few ingredients in Aomori's explosive summer festival, the **Nebuta Matsuri** (ねぶた祭), held annually August 1-7. Acclaimed as one of Tōhoku's most exciting celebrations, the Nebuta Festival was created during the Taishō Era (1912-1916) and is now the pride of Aomori. The festival's artistic centerpiece, *nebuta*, are large paper dolls representing mythical figures. The Nebuta Matsuri is a raucous, and at times debaucherous, party that has everyone in the streets. Every year the festival attracts more than 3½ million visitors to, so book reservations as early as January of the same year. For more information, call the festival information office (☎723-7211).

TOWADA-KO (十和田湖)　　　　☎0176

At the northern end of Towada-Hachimantai National Park is the volcanic lake Towada-ko. With crystal-clear waters over 300m deep, Towada-ko is often regarded one of the top sights in Tōhoku. Flowing out from Towada-ko is Oriase

Stream, a gorgeous mountain brook flanked by a gentle hiking trail with scenic views of the surrounding park. The area is easily reached from Aomori and Morioka, and is a pleasant, secluded destination. The **Lake Towada Information Center** (☎75-2425; open daily 8am-5pm) in Yasumiya north of the JR terminal, has hiking maps and books accommodations. They also have a guide to local campsites.

AT A GLANCE

HIGHLIGHTS: Unspoiled natural beauty, lakeside hiking, and lake cruises.

GATEWAYS: The main tourist center is **Yasumiya**, where you can find accommodation. Smaller centers include **Utarube** on the southeastern shore and **Nenoguchi** in the east.

CLIMATE: In winter, heavy snowfall. Other seasons are temperate. In summer, frequent rain and cool evenings.

CAMPING: Campsites ring the lake.

WHEN TO GO: Fall foliage is famous. Summer brings warm weather, and spring features blossoming wildflowers.

TRANSPORTATION AND PRACTICAL INFORMATION. The nearest station to Towada-ko is **Towada-Minami**, on the **JR Hanawa Line**. Coming from Tōkyō or Aomori, you'll first pass through Morioka where you can pick up the Hanawa Line (1hr., 7-8 per day, ¥1800). Since the station is about 1hr. from Towada-ko, you will have to transfer to a Yasumiya-bound shuttle bus (4-5 per day, ¥1130). Yasumiya has two **bus terminals**, but all JR buses end at the northern terminal. Six trains per day come from Aomori (3hr., ¥3000) and Morioka (2¼hr., ¥2350). A night bus from Towada-ko heads to Tōkyō, Ikebukuro Station (9½hr., 9pm, ¥10,090). JR buses only run late April-early August, and although railpasses are valid on these lines, passholders must book in advance at a JR green ticket window. Once in the area, you can move between the different towns via the JR Aomori Bus, though there are only 6 buses per day. You can travel between Yasumiya and Nenokuchi via the **sightseeing boat** (1-2 per hr., 8am-4pm, ¥1320 each way, 1 hr). There are no local car rental agencies, but you can rent in Aomori or Morioka and drive to the park. Several accommodations rent out **bicycles** and **mopeds**.

ACCOMMODATIONS AND FOOD. The best lakeside options are the two youth hostels. **Hakubutsukan Youth Hostel (HI) ❶** (博物館ユースホステル), within Towada-ko Grand Hotel in Yasumiya, is a bargain with its on-site *onsen*. (☎75-2002. Dorms ¥3200.) In a much quieter and more secluded location just outside Yasumiya on the bus route towards Towada Minami Station is **Towada Youth Hostel (HI) ❶** (十和田ユースホステル). (☎75-2603. Dorms ¥2000.) If you want even more privacy, avoid the resorts and try one of the many **minshuku ❷** on the road away from the lake. (Around ¥4000 per person, with 2 meals ¥6000.) If you're planning on **camping ❶**, sites charge around ¥500 per person. Pick up a camping guide from the tourist information office in Yasumiya. Most restaurants here are pricey snack shacks—consider stopping in the **convenience store** in town center. **Yamagoya ❷** (山五屋) across from Towada Kankō Hotel has a good set menu for ¥1000, and there's karaoke in the evenings. (Open daily 11am-10pm.)

SIGHTS AND OUTDOORS. The region's main attraction is the 14km **Oirase Valley Nature Trail**, which closely follows the Oirase-gawa river (奥入瀬川). The trail begins beside the stream in Nenokichi on the northeastern shore of the lake and runs as far as Yakeyama, though hikers often stop after 9km in Ishigedo and take the bus back to Yasumiya (1hr., ¥1100). The downside is that the highway runs uncomfortably close to the trail at several points, though the roar of the waterfalls muffles the sound of the cars. Located in Yasumiya, the famous **Maidens by the Lake** is the symbol most often associated with Towada-ko. The statue of two naked women touching hands was cast in 1953 by the poet and sculptor Takamura

Kōtarō, a Tōhoku native, who modeled the figures after his wife, painter Takamura Chieko. She suffered from schizophrenia and died in 1938. The small town of **Shingō** (新郷), 20km east of Towada-ko along Rte. 454, claims that Jesus once walked its streets. A museum explains how the Savior died there at the age of 106. (Open M-Tu and Th-Su 9am-5pm; look for the English sign.) Nearby are the **Ōishigami Pyramids,** rock piles which some claim were built millennia before the larger Egyptian ones.

OSOREZAN (恐山)

One of Japan's most sacred places, the temple at Osorezan is said to be an essential stop-over for dead spirits, whether they're headed for heaven or hell. According to local belief, Japanese must visit Osorezan to communicate with lost loved ones and to bless them by building mounds of volcanic rocks and leaving bouquets of flowers along the abandoned beach. (¥700.) If that's not eerie enough for you, come during the **1Grand Festival** (July 20-24) when a group of local blind women attempts to talk with the dead through a prayer called *kuchiyose* (口寄せ).

Behind Osorezan's ritualistic traditions lies the brilliance of the sheer beauty of the surrounding mountains and lakes. The temple grounds are at the side of a dormant volcano that can only be reached by a winding bus trip through a haunting forest. The views inside the grounds are especially fabulous. You can't see the top of the volcano, but you can bathe in its waters at the on-site *onsen*. (Take your own towel, and let cold water run into the pool for 20min. before entering.)

The easiest way to get to Osorezan is by a JR express train and bus combination that transfers at Shimokita. Only one direct train runs from Aomori to Shimokita (1 per day at 9:10am, ¥1890). For the same price, go to Shimokita and transfer at Noheji; trains leave Aomori at 6:10am, 7:09am, 12:13pm. At Shimokita, look for the Osorezan-bound bus (40min., ¥750) in front of the station—buses are timed to meet arriving trains. On the way back, buses leave for Shimokita at 10:40am, 12:30, 3:30, and 5:28pm.; ¥750.

NORTHERN HONSHŪ

CENTRAL HONSHŪ

Although Central Honshū is often dismissed as unexciting, the area boasts both mountain and seashore, culture and history, cities and villages, encompassing the historic cradle of land southwest of Tōkyō and northeast of Kyōto. In the center stand the magnificent Japan Alps, featuring unparalleled scenery, popular hikes, and adrenaline sports. To the east lie Nagano, home to Zenkō-ji, and Matsumoto with its grand castle. Farther south are the undisrupted villages of the Kiso Valley, as well as fast-paced Nagoya. Heading up the west side of the Alps, you'll encounter small town tradition, from Inuyama's cormorant fishing to Gujō Hachiman's festival. But the best of Central Honshū is farther north, with Takayama's museums, temples, and sights and larger Kanazawa's culture and history. An unmistakable heritage is preserved in the farmhouses of Gokayama and Shirakawa-gō, while the Noto-hantō peninsula has rugged coasts and the sparkling Sea of Japan.

The area is served by major JR and *shinkansen* lines, in addition to long-distance buses and local buses, trains, and subways. While it's best to move slowly between the numerous towns, absorbing their individual attractions and characteristics, zipping between the large cities of Nagoya, Kanazawa, Takayama, and Nagano is an efficient way of traveling. The districts of Central Honshū may not compare in popularity or fame with the well-touristed sights of other parts of Japan, but the region boasts a variety and depth of sights unparalleled elsewhere.

HIGHLIGHTS OF CENTRAL HONSHŪ

SPLENDID SKIING. Schuss down Japan's most famous slopes at **Shiga Kōgen** (p. 331), **Hakuba** (p. 339), or **Happō-O-Ne** (p. 340).

THE TATEYAMA-KUROBE ALPINE ROUTE. Traipse across the Japan Alps using every form of transportation you can imagine (p. 357).

KANAZAWA DREAMING. Find the traditional Japan you thought only existed in your imagination in this city by the sea (p. 359).

NAGANO (長野)   ☎026

Small Nagano, 200km northwest of Tōkyō and the capital of Nagano Prefecture, rose to international prominence during the 1998 Winter Olympics. Although some remnants of the Games remain—state-of-the-art athletic arenas, towering hotels, and improved transportation—Nagano nevertheless has retained a rustic charm. The city's cultural center, Zenkō-ji, attracts millions of tourists and Buddhist pilgrims every year; otherwise, the hamlet offers little in the way of sightseeing or entertainment options. Nagano does, however, function as an important transportation center, with several *shinkansen* lines running between Nagano and Japan's major cities. The Shinshū region (the area around Nagano and Matsumoto), home to many natural sights and recreation centers, is easily reached from Nagano.

▐ TRANSPORTATION

Trains: JR Nagano Station. The Nagano *shinkansen* "Asama" runs between **Tōkyō** and Nagano Stations (1¾hr., every 20-30min., ¥7460). From Shin-Ōsaka Station, the JR Tōkaidō *shinkansen* runs to Nagano (65min., every 10min., ¥6180). The JR limited express "Shinano" connects **Matsumoto** and Nagoya (2hr., every 10min., ¥5870).

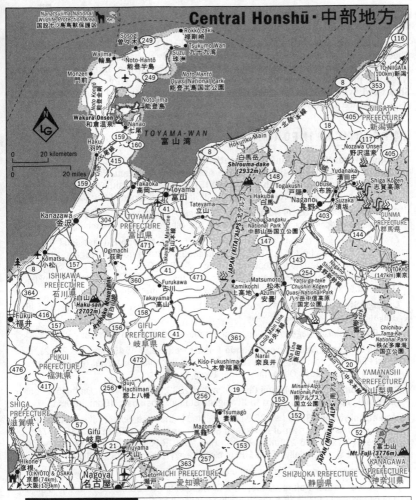

Central Honshū・中部地方

ON THE WEB   Nagano city: www.city.nagano.nagano.jp

Buses: Nagano Bus Terminal. Highway buses by **Seibu Kawa Nakajima Bus Company** (☎295-8050) run between **Tōkyō Shinjuku** and Nagano (2¾hr., 6 per day, ¥4000). The **Keiō Nagaden Bus Company** (☎224-7400) runs highway buses between **Tōkyō Ikebukuro** and Nagano (3¾hr., 8 per day, ¥4000). Reservations required.

Public Transportation: The **Nagano Dentetsu Line** runs to **Suzaka, Obuse,** and **Yudanaka;** the Shinano Line services **Niigata;** and the Chūō Line connects Nagano with **Matsumoto** and **Nagoya.** In addition, Nagaden Buses run around Nagano city.

Taxis: Nagano Taxi, ☎227-2222. **Utsunomiya Taxi,** ☎232-8181.

Car Rental: Eki Rent-a-Car, ☎227-8500. Just outside JR Nagano Station's Zenkō-ji Exit. From ¥5500.

ORIENTATION

Diagonally across from JR Nagano Station's Zenkō-ji Exit lies the city's main drag, **Chūō-dōri**, which runs north 2km towards Zenkō-ji. About halfway between the station and Zenkō-ji, **Gondō Arcade**, a bustling thoroughfare and the center of Nagano's nightlife, intersects Chūō-dōri perpendicularly. Closer to the station, **Shōwa-dōri**, which runs east-west, also intersects Chūō-dōri and leads to the Prefectural Office on its west and the City Office on its east.

PRACTICAL INFORMATION

Tourist Office: Nagano Tourist Information Center (☎226-5626). Inside JR Nagano Station. Open daily 9am-6pm. Or try the **Association of Nagano Prefecture for Promoting International Exchange (ANPIE)**, 692-2, Habashimo (☎235-7186; www.avis.ne.jp/~anpie). Nagano Prefectural Office 2nd fl. Open M-F 8:30am-5:15pm.

Currency Exchange: Hachi-jyū-ni Ginkō (82 Bank), is Nagano Prefecture's main bank. Its several branches, located throughout the city, all provide foreign exchange services.

ATM: Two in-town locations accept international cards. **Nagano Eki-mae Post Office,** 1355-5, Suehiro-chō (☎227-0983), is diagonally across from JR Nagano Station, Zenkō-ji Exit, to the left of West Plaza. Open M-F 9am-9pm, Sa 9am-7pm, Su 9am-5pm.) **Daily Yamazaki Convenience Store** is to the right of Nagano Station's Zenkō-ji Exit, next to Midori department store. Open M-F 8am-9pm, Sa-Su 9am-5pm.

Luggage Storage: Coin lockers are available by both the East and Zenkō-ji Exits of JR Nagano Station (¥300-600).

Lost Property: In JR Nagano Station, near the tourist office. Open daily 9am-5:30pm.

English-Language Bookstore: Heiandō Bookstore (☎224-4545; fax 226-2552), in West Plaza Nagano, offers a good selection of English books, magazines, and children's books on the 4th floor. Open daily 10am-10pm.

Cultural Center: 1-22-6, Minami Chitose (☎224-2233; fax 228-5733). On the 5th floor of Midori department store next to JR Nagano Station. Open daily 10am-6:30pm.

Market: Tōkyū Food Show (☎226-8181), located in the basement of Tōkyū department store, which is to the right of JR Nagano Station's Zenkō-ji Exit. Open daily 10am-7pm. **Monzen Plaza,** 1485-1, Shinden-chō, 1km from JR Nagano Station on Chūō-dōri (☎267-5511). Open daily 10am-10pm, closed every 1st and 3rd W of the month.

Emergency: Police ☎110. Fire or ambulance ☎119.

Police: Prefectural Police Office, 692-2, Habashita (☎233-0110). There is also a **police box** right outside JR Nagano Station's Zenkō-ji Exit.

Crisis Lines: Foreign Advisory Service, ☎232-3413.

Pharmacy: Drug Terashima, 1437-1, Kita Ishidō-chō (☎267-5518). Located 7min. from Nagano Station on Chūō-dōri. Open daily 10am-9pm.

Hospital/Medical Services: Nagano Sekijūji Byōin, 5-22-1, Wakasato (☎226-4131), is Nagano's main hospital.

Internet Access: Boo Foo Woo, Daito Bldg. 2nd fl. (☎226-0850). Located 1km from Nagano Station on Chūō-dōri. Free drinks and twice hourly McDonald's delivery service from 11:15am-6:15pm. Open 24hr. ¥390 for 1hr., ¥570 for 1½hr., ¥750 for 2hr.

Post Office: Nagano Central Post Office, 1085-4, Minami-Agata (☎226-2077). 5min. from the Prefectural Office towards Chūō-dōri. Open M-F 9am-7pm, Sa 9am-5pm, Su 9am-12:30pm. **Nagano Eki-mae (Station) Post Office,** 1355-5, Suehiro-chō (☎227-

0983), located diagonally across from JR Nagano Station to the left of West Plaza Nagano. Open M-F 9am-5:30pm. **Postal Code:** 380.

🔪 ACCOMMODATIONS

Nagano's accommodation options cluster around the JR station, and along Chūō-dōri, leading to Zenkō-ji. They range from cheap business hotels to classy upscale choices; ryokan and minshuku, however, are hard to come by in these parts.

Hotel New Nagano, 828, Minami Chitose-machi (☎ 227-7200; www.avis.ne.jp/~hotel-nn). Turn right out of JR Nagano Station's Zenkō-ji Exit, at the corner with Tōkyū department store; it's a 2min. walk. This seemingly upscale hotel provides surprisingly clean, fairly spacious rooms for affordable prices. Breakfast ¥1000. Coin laundry available. Check-in 3pm. Check-out 10am. Singles ¥5500; twins and doubles ¥11,000. ❸

Nagano Station Hotel, 1359, Suehiro-chō (☎ 226-1295; fax 226-1056). Head straight out of JR Nagano Station's Zenkō-ji Exit; it's a convenient 2min. walk. Provides larger and better furnished rooms than most business hotels. Big, relaxing bath, comfortable Japanese- and Western-style rooms, and low prices. Check-in 3pm. Check-out 10am. Singles ¥6000; twins ¥12,000; doubles ¥10,000. ❸

Zenkō-ji Kyojuin Youth Hostel (HI), 479, Motoyoshi-chō (☎ 232-2768; fax 232-2767). Take a Zenkō-ji-bound bus to Zenkō-ji-mae (10min., every 10min., ¥150), or walk down Chūō-dōri towards Zenkō-ji (30min.), go through Nakamise-dōri, turn right before entering Zenkō-ji, then take the first right. Right by Nagano's main attraction. A very, very old Japanese temple full of *fun'iki* (atmosphere) and historic charm. Check-in 3pm. Check-out 10am. ¥2900; nonmembers ¥3900. Reservations recommended. ❶

Nagano Central Hotel, 1358, Suehiro-chō (☎ 224-4111; fax 227-2513). Conveniently located a straight 2min. by foot from JR Nagano Station's Zenkō-ji Exit. This elegant-hotel provides well furnished, comfortable, and spacious rooms for fewer yen than you'd expect. Check-in 3pm. Check-out 10am. Singles ¥7000; twins ¥10,000. ❸

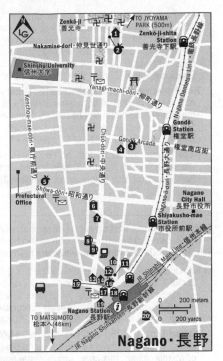

Nagano・長野

🔺 ACCOMMODATIONS
Hotel New Nagano, **10**
Hotel Metropolitan Nagano, **19**
Hotel Sankei-en, **7**
Hotel Yama, **4**
Nagano Central Hotel, **13**
Nagano Station Hotel, **14**
Zenkō-ji Kyojuin
  Youth Hostel (HI), **1**

🍴 FOOD
Kanshin Miwa, **2**
Rāmen TenTen, **3**
Sakura-ya, **16**
Soba Kura, **5**

🏢 SHOPPING
Midori Department Store, **18**
Monzen Plaza, **6**
West Plaza Nagano, **17**
Tōkyū Department Store, **11**

🌙 NIGHTLIFE
High Five, **15**
Liberty, **8**
Nagano Club Junk Box, **9**
Winds, **12**
Winds East, **20**

Hotel Sankei-en, 1477, Shinden-chō (☎228-3399; http://jcha.yadojozu.ne.jp/ 2020107). From JR Nagano Station, walk along Chūō-dōri towards Zenkō-ji. It's on your left, about 1km from the station. Alternatively, take a Zenkō-ji-bound bus to Shōwa-dōri (4min., every 10min., ¥100). Cheap and neat rooms, with a huge bath and open-air *onsen;* the lighting in the rooms tends to be dim. Breakfast ¥700. Check-in 4pm. Check-out 10am. Curfew 1am. Singles ¥3900-4500; twins ¥3800-4200 per person. ❷

Hotel Metropolitan Nagano, 1346, Minami Ishidō-chō (☎291-7000; www.metron.co.jp). To the left of JR Nagano Station's Zenkō-ji Exit. An upscale choice adjacent to the station, this hotel has beautifully furnished, elegant, and comfortable rooms, complete with a full set of amenities. Breakfast ¥1500. Check-in 2pm. Check-out 11am. Singles ¥8000; twins ¥16,000; doubles ¥17,000. 10% service charge added. ❹

Hotel Yama, 2273, Gondō-chō (☎235-1634; fax 234-8325). A 12min. walk down Chūō-dōri from JR Nagano Station toward Zenkō-ji. Turn right before the Gondō Arcade. Business hotel with simple rooms. Check-in 3pm. Check-out 10am. Singles ¥5000. ❷

🍴 FOOD

Most of Nagano's restaurants, which span diverse genres, are along **Chūō-dōri**, leading to Zenkō-ji. The fifth floor of Nagano Station's **Midori** department store and the 7th floor of the **Tōkyū department store** also promise cheap but fulfilling options.

🍴 **Kanshin Miwa,** 486, Motoyoshi-chō (☎235-2620). Located on Nakayose St., in front of Zenkō-ji. Take the Zenkō-ji-bound bus to Zenkō-ji Daimon (10min., every 10min., ¥100). An extremely trendy sweets shop, Miwa offers cute, colorful tarts, cookies, and Japanese delicacies (¥300-700) that are fascinating to look at and even better to eat. *Soba* and green-tea-twisted soft ice cream (¥250) are amazing. Open daily 9am-5pm. ❶

Rāmen TenTen, 2258-5, Gondō-chō (☎234-6911). In the Gondō Arcade, which intersects Chūō-dōri halfway between Nagano Station and Zenkō-ji. Among Nagano's oodles of noodle shops, this cozy, simple restaurant gets especially high praise for its tasty soup and *rāmen*. TenTen rāmen ¥600. Open Tu-Th 11:30am-2pm and 6:30pm-midnight, F-Sa 11:30am-2pm and 6:30pm-2am, Su 11:30am-3pm and 6:30pm-2am. ❷

Sakura-ya, Suehara-chō 1358 (☎223-1011). In an alley between Hotel Ikemon and Hotel Sunrise Nagano, opposite JR Nagano Station's Zenkō-ji Exit. Frequented by businessmen for delicious and fulfilling no-frills food. Home-style meals include broiled fish (¥650), rāmen (¥540), pork cutlet sets (¥650), and about 15 different ¥100 appetizers. Menu pictures are helpful. Open M-F 11:30am-3:30pm and 5:30-11:30pm, Sa 11:30am-3:30pm and 5:30-10:30pm, Su 11:30am-3:30pm and 5:30-10pm. ❷

Curry Station (☎224-9130). One of the several restaurants on the 5th fl. of Midori department store. This casual, tiny (only 2 counters), largely self-service restaurant serves curry just like the curry Mom made for you (or would have, if she'd been Japanese). Shout out your order and help yourself to a glass of water. Beef, chicken, or vegetable curry ¥500. Chicken cutlet curry ¥700. Open daily 11am-9pm. ❷

Pasta Bella (☎224-2286). Also among the restaurants in Midori, Pasta Bella's appeal comes from the sheer variety of its Italian dishes. From lasagna to spaghetti to pizza (¥730-980), you're bound to find something appealing. The unique soup spaghetti is particularly tasty (¥850). Open 11am-9pm. ❷

Hida (☎224-0021). Down an alley left of Tōkyū department store. Serves hearty Japanese meals in a traditional setting. *Kaisen don* (seafood over rice; ¥1350), *tempura don* (¥1200), and *soba* (¥580) are tasty choices. Traditional lunch sets, which change daily, are offered noon-2pm, an excellent deal at ¥780. Open daily noon-9pm. ❸

Soba Kura, Minami Ken-chō (☎235-3189). Diagonally across from the Prefectural Offices. Serves Nagano's specialty, buckwheat noodles (¥700), and much more. Delicious set dishes (¥650-1300) include *soba* and *tempura*. Local crowds stop by in the evenings for beer and *sake* (¥400). Open daily 11am-2pm and 6-11pm. ❸

◎ SIGHTS

ZENKŌ-JI (善光寺). This 1300-year-old temple's claim to fame is that it supposedly housed the first-ever Buddha image in Japan, in AD 552. Zenkō-ji's immense popularity stems from its liberal reception of Buddhists from all sects (and even women!), and it has long been respected as a destination for religious pilgrimages.

Whether you trek up Chūō-dōri (中央通り) towards Zenkō-ji, or take the Zenkō-ji-bound bus, upon arriving at the temple, you'll first walk through **Niō-mon Gate** (仁王門). You'll be plunged into the bustling Nakamise Rd., lined with souvenir gift shops, ryokan, and snack stalls. On the right is the **Roku Jizo** (六地蔵), a line of six large statues, representing the guardians of the six worlds of hell, starvation, beasts, carnage, human beings, and heavenly beings that one's soul must pass through. The 200m road leads to the striking wooden **San-mon** (三門), which marks Zenkō-ji's main entrance. From here, the featured **Hondō** (本堂) stands prominently ahead of you, 30m high, 24m wide, and 54m deep. Inside this hall is the Amida triad, and a ticket gets you entrance into the **Okaidan** basement. It was here in the absolute darkness—maintained today—that the original image of Buddha rested and believers came seeking eternal salvation. Using your hands, navigate the dark by following the tunnel on the right until you feel a metallic object, which many believed to be the key to paradise. In the outer sanctuary is a statue of Binzuru, Buddha's follower and physician, which believers touch to cure their impurities. Farther inside is the worshipers' space, filled with golden decorations.

Many believers visit Zenkō-ji for the 5:30am morning service, at which priests lead hundreds of followers in prayer and celebration. This is followed by the *Ojuzu Chōdai* ceremony, in which pilgrims are blessed by the Buddha's holy ojuzu beads. *(Zenkō-ji is 2km north of JR Nagano Station's Zenkō-ji Exit along Chūō-dōri. Zenkō-ji-bound buses run regularly from Terminal #1, near the station's Zenkō-ji Exit (10min., every 10min., ¥100). 491, Motoyoshi-chō. ☎234-3595; fax 235-2151. Open daily 5:30am-4:30pm. Okaidan entrance ¥500, college and high school students ¥250, under 15 ¥100.)*

NAGANO PREFECTURAL SHINANO ART MUSEUM (NAGANO KEN SHINANO BIJUTSUKAN; 長野県信濃美術館) AND HIGASHIYAMA KAII GALLERY (HIGASHIYAMA KAII KAN; 東山魁夷館). Located in Jōyama Park, just 5min. from Zenkō-ji, this smallish museum features works by local artists, while the gallery focuses on famous painter Higashiyama Kaii, whose artwork generally depicts Nagano's breathtaking scenery. While the sculptures, scroll- and screen-paintings, and pictures displayed are obviously the work of talented artists, Higashiyama's paintings, which adorn the gallery's walls, are incomparable. His use of color, strokes, and depth is captivating. *(1-4-4, Hako Shimizu. ☎232-0052; fax 232-0050. Open Su-Tu and Th-Sa 9am-5pm. ¥500, college and high school students ¥250, under 15 ¥100.)*

M-WAVE. The speed skating rink used in the 1998 Olympics, this state-of-the-art athletic facility has been transformed into an arena housing memories, souvenirs, and equipment from the Games. Among the items on display are Japanese team uniforms from the Nagano Olympics, Olympic medals, the Olympic torch, and the skates of Japanese speed skater Hiroyasu Shimizu. In addition, M-WAVE features a 3-D Olympic theater and a bobsled simulator complete with sounds and vibrations. *(195, Kita-Nagaike. From JR Nagano Station's East Exit, take the Yashima- or Suzuka-bound bus to the M-WAVE entrance (15min., every 30min., ¥260). ☎222-3300; fax 222-3222. Open Su-M and W-Sa 10am-4pm. ¥700, under 12 ¥350.)*

⚲ SHOPPING

Shops selling souvenirs and specialty foods can be found lining **Nakamise-dōri** (仲見世通り), the 200m path to Zenkō-ji. Worth a look is **Kaze no Yakata** (風の館), 486, Motoyoshi-chō, which sells handmade souvenirs featuring colorful, intricately woven paper balls and dolls. *(☎235-2620. Open M-F 10am-6pm, Sa-Su 9am-6pm.)*

🆕 NIGHTLIFE

Nagano's nightlife is concentrated either near JR Nagano Station or along **Gondō Arcade;** both places get fairly boisterous on weekend nights. For more information, stop by the **Night Life Information Center** (Night Spot Annai-jō; ナイトスポット案内所), where you can pick up discount tickets and browse message boards. The center is on the road parallel to Chūō-dōri, to its east, past Shōwa-dōri on the first floor of Sun Marutan Corpo. (☎234-6387. Open M-Sa 6pm-midnight.)

🆕 **Liberty,** 1434-1, Kita Ishidō-chō (☎090-8596-7603). On the small alley running perpendicular to Chūō-dōri, to the right of Again department store. With its cozy interior, friendly people, and fun atmosphere, this American-style bar is a good place to kick back and make new friends. Beer and cocktails ¥450-800. Open daily 6pm-midnight.

High Five, 1350, Suehiro-chō (☎090-1806-5815; fax 090-2464-9804). Located down a narrow alley opposite JR Nagano Station's Zenkō-ji Exit, between Hotel Ikemon and Hotel Sunroute Nagano. A happening dance club playing hip-hop and house. Packed with young people on weekends, it's a great choice for those who love to shake it. Drinks from ¥500. Cover ¥1000-1500. Open daily 9pm-midnight.

Winds and Winds East, 1-28-3, Minami Chitose-chō and 1020-1, Kurita (☎224-1681 and 225-6464). Winds is in the basement of Hotel Sunroute, across from the JR station's Zenkō-ji Exit; Winds East is on the 3rd floor of the Stella Bldg., opposite the station's East Exit. Bar and restaurant, both places serve Italian food (¥1000) and get crowded on weekends. Cocktails ¥500. Beer from ¥600. Open daily 11am-midnight.

Nagano Club Junk Box, 1429-1, Kita Ishidō-chō (☎267-9120; www.junkbox.co.jp). On the 7th fl. of Again department store, 5min. from Nagano Station on Chūō-dōri. A boisterous nightclub. Live music by aspiring and established bands. Fun place to dance. Drinks ¥600. Cover ¥300 plus band cover (about ¥1000). Open daily 6pm-midnight.

AROUND NAGANO

Once you've exhausted Nagano's sights, move on to the surrounding towns for ski slopes, *onsen*, small attractions, and nature in spades, all a short train ride away.

🏠 ACCOMMODATIONS

Though it's possible to visit any of these towns as daytrips from Nagano, the youth hostels around the region provide cheap stays convenient to the slopes and sights.

Koshasanroku Miyukino Mori (HI), 3782-12, Kami Kijima. (☎/fax 0269-82-4551). From JR Iiyama Station, take a Nukazuka-bound bus to Skii-jō Iriguchi; it's a 20min. walk. Breakfast ¥600. Dinner ¥1000. ¥3200; nonmembers ¥4200. ❶

Nojiriko Miyagawa Ryokan (HI), 261-2, Nojiri (☎026-258-2501). From JR Kurohime Station, take a Nojiriko-bound bus and get off at the end terminal. Breakfast ¥600. Dinner ¥1000. ¥2900; nonmembers ¥3900. ❶

Obuse No Kaze (HI): See Obuse (p. 331). ❶

Togakushi Kogen Yokokura (HI): See Togakushi (p. 333). ❶

Togari Kanzanso (HI), Iiyama-shi Otagoka (☎0269-65-2094; fax 65-2195). A 20min. walk from JR Togari Nozawa Onsen Station. Breakfast ¥600. Dinner ¥1000. ¥2900; nonmembers ¥3900. ❶

SUZAKA (須坂)   ☎026

Suzaka's charm comes from the wooden buildings and black-and-white storehouses that line the streets. One such merchant's house has been reconstructed into the charming **Gonshō No Yakata, Tanaka Honken Museum** (豪商の館・田中本家博物館), 476, Koku-chō, a 15min. hike southeast of Suzaka Station. Its five buildings display Edo-era dolls, gorgeous bridal wear, pottery, paintings, lacquerware, and calligraphy. A Japanese garden on the grounds rounds out the sightseeing. (☎248-8008; www.valley.ne.jp/~tanaka-m. Open Su-M and W-Sa Apr.-Nov. 9am-5pm; Dec.-Mar. 9:30am-4:30pm. ¥600, high and middle school students ¥300, under 12 ¥150.) **Yamada Onsen** (山田温泉), promising numerous natural spas and slopes for skiing and snowboarding in winter, is a 20min. drive from Suzaka. Suzaka is accessible by the Nagano Dentetsu Line from Nagano (20min., every 20min., ¥520; or, by limited express, 15min., every hr., ¥620). The **tourist office**, 1528-1, Suzaka, is opposite the station on the second floor of Silky Plaza Building. (☎248-3489 or 248-9005; www.city.suzaka.nagano.jp. Open daily 8:30am-5pm.)

OBUSE (小布施)　　　　　　　　　☎026

The town of Obuse, 20km northeast of Nagano, has atmospheric Edo-era houses lining its streets. The **Hokusai Museum** (Hokusai-kan; 北斎館), 485, Obuse, its main attraction, boasts woodblock prints by master Hokusai Katsushika and two festive floats. The traditional art displays are unique in style and color. Head straight up the road opposite Obuse Station, take the second right; the museum is a 5min. walk to your left. (☎247-5206; www.hokusai-kan.com. Open daily 9am-5pm. ¥500, under 18 ¥300.) Down a narrow road opposite the museum is **Takai Kōzan Memorial Hall** (Takai Kōzan Kinenkan; 高井鴻山記念館), 805-1, Obuse, the home of artist and philosopher Takai Kōzan. Although Kōzan is best known for his *Yokai-ga*, works depicting ghosts and goblins, through which he expressed the irony and sadness of the Meiji Era, his artistic talents were diverse. An accomplished calligrapher, his handwriting is said to inspire others—check out the long scrolls. Kozan was also a patron of Hokusai; though their works look quite different, the two were close friends. (☎247-4049. Open daily 9am-5pm. ¥200, under 12 ¥100.) One kilometer east of Obuse Station, the quaint temple of **Ganshōin** (岩松院) is best reached by the shuttle bus from Obuse Station, which tours the town's sights (15min., every hr., daypass ¥300). The temple's stunning ceiling painting has an area equivalent to 21 *tatami* mats. (☎247-5504. Open Apr.-Nov. daily 9am-4:30pm; Dec.-Mar. Su-Tu and Th-Sa 9:30am-3:30pm.)

From Nagano Station, take the Nagano Dentetsu Line to Obuse Station (30min., every 20min., ¥650; limited express: 20min., every hr., ¥750). The **tourist office**, 1458-1, Obuse, is on the first corner, up the road perpendicular to Obuse Station. (☎247-2028; fax 247-2153. Open M-F 8:30am-5pm.) On the road leading to Hokusai Museum is the friendly and helpful **Guide Center**, 789, Obuse-chō. (☎247-5050; fax 247-5700. Open daily 9am-6pm.) In an emergency, call ☎110 for **police**, ☎119 for **fire** or **ambulance**. The **post office**, 1132-1, Nakamachi, is on the same road, closer to the station. (☎247-2049. Open M-F 9am-5pm.) The Guide Center runs a small hotel, ▩**Guest House Obuse ❸**, 780, Obuse-chō, with luxurious rooms and friendly owners. (☎247-5050; www.icon.pref.nagano.jp/usr/araobuse. Breakfast ¥800. Check-in 2-5:30pm. Check-out 11am. Singles ¥7000; twins ¥12,000.) **Obuse No Kaze (HI) ❶**, 475-2, Obuse-chō, next to the museum, is a welcoming youth hostel. It hosts events like hiking, apple-picking, chestnut-gathering, and *soba*-making. (☎247-4489; http://homepage2.nifty.com/obusenokaze. Check-in 4-10pm. Check-out 10am. Breakfast ¥600. Dinner ¥1000. ¥3200, nonmembers ¥4200.) For tea and cake, head to **Obuse Do San Poo Loh ❶** (小布施堂傘風楼), 500, Obuse-chō, between Hokusai-kan and the Takai Kozan Memorial Hall. They serve up tasty treats and chestnut confections, like *kuri* crepes and ice cream. (☎247-5433. Open daily 9-11am and 3-6pm.)

YUDANAKA AND SHIGA KŌGEN (湯田中・志賀高原)　☎0269

Quiet Yudanaka has many hot springs, the most famous of which is the **Shibu Onsen Kyo** (渋温泉郷), a cluster of nine *onsen* districts in a 2.5km radius. Each—Shin Yudanaka, Hoshikawa, Yudanaka, Honami, Andai, Shibu, Kakuma, Kanbayashi, and Jigokudani—contains different minerals and has a distinct water composition. If you're low on time, **Yudanaka Onsen** (a 5min. walk from Yudanaka Station) and **Shibu Onsen** (a 10min. bus ride, ¥160) are the most prominent. **Jigokudani Onsen** (Hell's Valley) are famous for the wild snow monkeys (Japanese long-tailed monkeys) who escape Nagano's cold winters by bathing in the *onsen*. Take the Nagaden bus to Kanbayashi (15min., every hr., ¥220); it's a 30min. uphill walk through the woods.

Although Yudanaka's ski resort, **Gorin Kōgen,** is decent, it's worth taking the 30min. trip to **Shiga Kōgen.** Located in Jōshinetsu Kōgen National Park, the area has beautiful lakes and marshes during the spring and some of Japan—and the world's—best skiing at its 21 resorts during the winter. The slalom events of the 1998 Olympics were held on the slopes of Oku Shiga and Mt. Yokote—the farthest but the best of the bunch. On the summit of Mt. Yokote is **Yokote Sanchō Hyutte,** a bakery with unbeatable home-baked bread. (☎34-2430. Open daily 9am-2:30pm.)

To get to Yudanaka, take the Nagano Dentetsu Line to the end (1hr., every hr., ¥1130; or, by limited express, 45min., every hr., ¥1230). Be sure to check where the train is bound before boarding, as most stop at Shinshū Nakano. To continue from Yudanaka to Shiga Kōgen, hop on a Oku-Shiga-bound bus (30min., every hr., ¥1050). The **Yudanaka Tourist Office,** 3352-1, Heion, is located behind the station, to your right. (☎33-1106 or 33-2138. Open daily 9am-5pm.) The **Shiga Kōgen Tourist Office,** Shiga Kōgen Hasuike, has some English speakers who can help travelers navigate the slopes. (☎34-2404; fax 34-2344. Open daily 9am-5pm.)

There are plenty of places to sleep, both near Yudanaka Station and in the Shiga Kōgen area, although many are upscale hotels and ryokan. Cheaper stays are available at **Lodge Nagasaka ❶,** where simple *tatami*-style rooms await, located 15min. by car or 35min. walking from Yudanaka Station. (☎33-6317. Check-in 3pm. Check-out 10am. ¥3000, with 2 meals ¥6500.) Another reasonable option is **Uotoshi Ryokan ❷,** a member of the Japanese Inn Group, which provides comfortable *tatami* rooms, a convenient 7min. from Yudanaka Station after you cross the Yomase River. (☎33-1215; fax 33-0074. ¥4000, with 2 meals ¥8000.) As area dining options are fairly limited, it's a smart idea to order meals where you're staying.

NOZAWA ONSEN (野沢温泉)   ☎0269

When you hear the sound of water trickling, you've reached Nozawa Onsen, a tightly knit village 50km northeast of Nagano. The 5000 villagers own and maintain a popular ski resort and 13 public hot baths. All 13 of the **Soto Yu** are free, and it's enjoyable to spend a day strolling from one to the next (all open daily 6am-11pm); just be sure to follow proper bathing etiquette (see p. 95 for a refresher course). The best of the bunch is **Oyu Bathhouse** (大湯), near the center of the village, along with **Ogama Hot Springs** (Ogama Onsen; 麻釜温泉). The water temperatures in these baths reach over 90°C (194°F), and locals boil vegetables and eggs in them while chit-chatting.

Nozawa Onsen's other main attraction is its excellent ski slopes—in fact, proud locals refer to the area as the birthplace of skiing in Japan. In addition to the slopes which hosted the biathlon events of the 1998 Nagano Olympics, look for the **Japan Museum of Skiing** (Nihon Skii Hakubutsukan; 日本スキー博物館). Inside are gazillions of old wooden skis, bindings, pictures of Austrian Hannes Schneider (who spread the two-pole technique in Japan during the 1930s), and books, medals, and diplomas from past Olympics. The small museum is located at the base of Hikage slope, a 20min. uphill walk from Nozawa Onsen village. (☎85-3418. Open F-Su Apr.-Nov. 10am-4pm; Dec.-Mar. 10:30am-3pm. Open daily Apr. 25-May 5, July 11-Aug. 31, and Dec. 26-Jan. 12. ¥300, under 15 ¥150.)

To get to Nozawa Onsen, take the Iiyama Line from JR Nagano Station to Togari Nozawa Onsen (55min., every hr., ¥740), then transfer to a Nozawa Onsen-bound bus, which departs right outside the station (20min., every hr., ¥300). Alternatively, take the Shinshū Bus from JR Nagano East Exit, which runs directly to Nozawa

Onsen (1¾hr., every 1-2hr., ¥1300). Ask the Nagano Station tourist office which will get you there faster, as both train and bus run infrequently. Once you arrive, there's a **tourist office** in Nozawa Onsen, down a slope from Oyu Onsen. (☎85-3111. Open daily 8:30am-5:30pm.) In an emergency, call ☎110 for **police**, ☎119 for **fire** or **ambulance**. The **post office** is at 9615, Tomisato. (☎85-2003. Open M-F 9am-5pm.)

Accommodations in this area tend to be pricey; inquire at the **Ryokan Information Center**, Nozawa Onsen Mura, opposite the bus terminal, for reservation details. (☎85-2056; fax 85-3149. Open daily 8:30am-5:30pm.) Some cheaper options are **Suehiroya Ryokan ❸**, Kawahara Yu, whose well-maintained *tatami* rooms are in the center of town (☎85-2175, fax 85-3979; ¥8000) and **Yamadaya Ryokan ❸**, Nozawa Onsen Mura, an atmospheric place where dinner's served in your room (☎85-2059, fax 85-3897; ¥8000). Closer to Togari Nozawa Onsen Station is **New Kanzan ❷**, Ōta Goni Shukuhaku Gai, a cheaper but accordingly inconvenient stay. Contrary to what its Western exterior suggests, the inn offers comfortable *tatami* rooms. It's a 15min. walk from the station—turn left out of the station, take the first right onto a major road, then take the fourth left. (☎65-2044; fax 65-2195. ¥3000, with 2 meals ¥6000.) Diner-like restaurants line the streets of Nozawa Onsen and cluster around the slopes. Pick up some *onsen manjū*, sweet red bean-filled dumplings, or Nozawa's specialty *nozawana*, bitter green vegetables, at a souvenir shop.

TOGAKUSHI (戸隠) ☎026

Blessed with fantastic nature, famous *soba*, and friendly birds of more than 100 species, Togakushi lies 20km northwest of Nagano and makes a good daytrip. At the foot of Mt. Togakushi, the town's main sight is **Togakushi Shrine**, Togakushi Mura, which includes the Hōkōsha, Chūsha, and Okusha shrines (Hōkōsha: ☎254-2012; Chūsha/Okusha: ☎254-2001). According to tradition, the proper order is to visit Hōkōsha first, then Chūsha, and finally Okusha. **Hōkōsha** is the oldest of the three, and stands atop more than 200 stone stairs. It's decorated with beautiful carvings of dragons and swans, and is most easily reached by getting off the bus at Hōkōsha Miyamae. A 2km walk north leads you to **Chūsha**, at the center of town, where the streets are lined with ryokan, *soba* restaurants, and souvenir shops. The three Japanese cedar trees are said to be over 800 years old. For those who don't feel like walking, the Chūsha Miya-mae bus stop is most convenient. Another ☎2km north, along a serene road with more

NO WORK, ALL PLAY

GO CLIMB A TREE

The villagers have been waiting for years; travelers from around Japan and abroad come in flocks to attend; you, too, can witness the dramatic festival held every six years for the past 1200 years—the **Onbashira Festival**, held at Suwa Taisha in Suwa City, Nagano.

In early April, the **Yamadashi** portion of the festival begins. Trunks from 200-year-old Japanese firs are cut and brought from the forest. The largest are 16m tall, 1m in diameter, and weigh 12 tons. Then comes the climatic event of the festivities, the *Kiotoshi*. This perilous tradition involves young men sitting on the *onbashira* (trunks) and sliding down 30-40° slopes.

The trunks are put to pasture until early May when, during the **Satobiki Festival**, they are taken to the Suwa shrine. The excitement builds as men move the 12-ton logs over 10km, singing as they go. The trunks finally reach the shrine and are erected as *Tate Onbashira*. As they're pulled up, two young men sit on them, rising to the top of the 16m *Onbashira*, where they perform for the crowd.

This unique celebration will be held in 2004. In 1998, over 1.78 million visitors attended, making it one of Japan's three largest festivals. *(For details, contact the Suwa Tourist Office at ☎52-4141. Take the JR Chūō Line to Kami Suwa Station (30min., ¥570). Transfer to a bus (40min., ¥690) to Kamishamae Stop.)*

cedars lining the sides, leads you to **Okusha.** According to Shintō legend, neighboring Mt. Togakushi was created by god Ameno Tajikara Onomikoto, who opened the rock door leading to the cave where Sun Goddess Amaterasu hid herself; the shrine commemorates this event annually. The closest bus stop is Okusha Iriguchi, but after that, a 45min. walk awaits.

At the entrance to the road to Okusha, near the bus stop, is **Togakushi Minzoku Museum** (Togakushi Minzoku Kan; 戸隠民俗館), Togakushi Mura, three buildings whose highlight is an exhibition on ninja warriors. (☎254-2395. Open mid-Apr. to late Nov. daily 9am-5pm. ¥500.) The **Soba Museum** (Soba Hakubutsu Kan; そば博物館), Togakushi Mura, is reached by taking the bus to Soba Hakubutsukan-mae stop. This unique and yummy museum explains the history of Japanese buckwheat noodles, displays of old dishware and equipment, and introduces *soba* culture as it exists throughout the world. You can take classes where local pros help you make your own noodles (available 10am-3pm; reservations required; ¥3000), or, for ¥600, you can save the labor and simply eat some freshly made *soba*. (☎254-3773. Open mid-Apr. to Nov. Su-Tu and Th-Sa 9am-4:30pm. ¥250.)

Kawa Nakajima Bus Company runs buses from Nagano Station to Togakushi, which leave from the terminal in front of West Plaza Nagano and Heiandō Bookstore (1hr.; every hr.; Hōkōsha ¥1110, Chūsha ¥1160, Okusha ¥1280). They approach Togakushi through the scenic Birdline Highway; the Chūsha stop is at the center of the town and where the shops are , while the Okusha stop is more convenient for visiting Togakushi Okusha shrine. Pick up maps at the tourist office in Nagano, as the **tourist office** in Togakushi only takes calls and doesn't speak English. (☎254-2326; fax 254-3711. Open daily 9am-5pm.)

The cheapest accommodation option is the cozy **Togakushi Kōgen Yokokura Youth Hostel (HI) ❶**, 3347, Otagoka. The friendly owner offers *tatami* dorms. Get off at Chūsha, and it's a 3min. walk to the ski slopes, away from Chūsha temple. (☎254-2030; fax 254-2540. Breakfast ¥600. Dinner ¥1000. ¥2900; nonmembers ¥3900.) Other options are expensive, ranging from ¥8000 to ¥15,000, but if you're willing to pay, ryokan are numerous. The town is known for its handmade *soba;* more than 30 *soba* restaurants surround Chūsha shrine. **Iwatoya ❷**, 3357, Chūsha, is very popular, serving noodles and *tsuyu* (¥700) whose taste the owners claim hasn't changed since the restaurant's beginnings. Turn left out of Chūsha shrine; it's a 3min. walk. (☎254-2038. Open daily 8:30am-6pm; holidays and Aug. 8am-7:30pm.)

MATSUMOTO (松本)　　　　　　☎0263

With a magnificent castle set against the stunning Japan Alps, Matsumoto runs the risk of being passed over as just another quaint, clichéd mountain town. But while this second-largest city in Nagano Prefecture, 50km south of the capital, retains a traditional feel, the scattered black-and-white merchant houses give way to a developed city center. Numerous trendy stores and cafes give the city a fashionable, even classy, feel, proving that an old dog can learn new tricks. With history, tradition, and contemporary culture concentrated within its bounds, Matsumoto promises to be a worthwhile stop before heading for the hills.

ON THE WEB　　Matsumoto: www.city.matsumoto.nagano.jp/www_cbox

▐ TRANSPORTATION

Flights: Matsumoto Airport (☎58-2517), 8km southwest of the city. Domestic flights to and from **Fukuoka, Hiroshima, Ōsaka,** and **Sapporo.** Buses run between the airport and JR Matsumoto Station, timed to flight arrivals and departures (25min., ¥540).

Matsumoto · 松本

ACCOMMODATIONS
Ace Inn Matsumoto, **15**
Hamilton Inn, **1**
Hotel New Station, **10**
Matsumoto City Hotel, **19**
Matsumoto Green Hotel, **17**
Matsumoto Tourist Hotel, **20**
Super Hotel Matsumoto, **6**

FOOD
Donguri, **12**
Minoya, **3**
Nomugi, **5**
Sanmura Ya, **18**
Traffic Diner, **9**

SHOPPING
ESPA dept store, **16**
Midori dept store, **13**
Parco dept store, **8**

NIGHTLIFE
Bacchus, **7**
Eonta, **2**
Heaven, **4**
Vamonos, **11**
Zeku, **14**

Matsumoto Castle 松本城
Japan Folklore Museum 日本民俗資料館
NTT Bldg.
Yonashira Shrine
TO ③ (120m)
TO KYŪ KAICHI SCHOOL (3.5km)
NAKA-MACHI 中町
143
Isecho-dōri
Kōen-dōri
Daimyō-machi-dōri
Honmachi-dōri
Matsumoto City Museum of Art 松本市美術館
Eki-mae-dōri
Matsumoto Station JR
Nippon Rent-A-Car
TIC
TO (400m) & ⑰
0 200 meters
0 200 yards

Trains: JR Matsumoto Station. The JR Shinonoi Line runs between Matsumoto and **Nagano** (express: 60min., ¥2770; local: 90min., ¥1110). From the Tōkyō area, the Azusa express runs from **Tōkyō** and **Shinjuku** Stations (2½-3hr., every hr., ¥6200). The Shinano express connects **Nagoya** and Matsumoto (2¼hr., every hr., ¥5360). The local JR Oito line services neighboring regions, including **Hakuba.**

Buses: Matsumoto Dentetsu Bus Terminal, ☎ 35-7400. **Alpico and Matsuden** runs long-distance buses between Matsumoto and major cities. To: **Nagoya** (3½hr., 4 per day, ¥3460); **Ōsaka** (5½hr., 2 per day, ¥5710); **Tōkyō Shinjuku** (4hr., 13 per day, ¥3400).

Public Transportation: The **Town Sneaker** excursion bus runs between Matsumoto Station and major tourist sights (every 30min.; ¥100, daypass ¥300).

Taxis: Matsumoto Taxi, ☎ 33-1141.

Car and Bicycle Rental: Nippon Rent-A-Car, 1-3, Fukase (☎ 33-1324). Right outside JR Matsumoto Station. Cars from ¥5500 per day. Bikes ¥300 per hr. or ¥1500 per day.

ORIENTATION AND PRACTICAL INFORMATION

The major road running east of JR Matsumoto Station is **Eki-mae-dōri.** It intersects with **Daimyō-machi-dōri** running north-south, which has **Matsumoto Castle** at its northern end. The **Chūō** and **Fukashi** districts to the northeast and southeast of the station are the busiest, with bunches of restaurants, hotels, and bars. The **Naka-machi** district, near the station, is lined with traditional merchant houses.

Tourist Office: A small tourist office, 1-1-1, Fukashi (☎32-2814), with English-speaking staff, is outside JR Matsumoto Station's Central Exit, and can provide maps and book accommodations. Open daily Apr.-Oct. 9:30am-6pm; Nov.-Mar. 9am-5:30pm.

Tours: Goodwill Guide Group runs free tours of Matsumoto Castle and the Japan Folklore Museum mid-Apr. to mid-Nov. 10am-4pm. Contact Mr. Masahiko Saito (☎32-7140; daily 8am-noon) or the Matsumoto Castle Office (☎32-2902; daily 8am-5pm).

Currency Exchange: Nagano Prefecture's main bank, **Hachijūni Bank**, has offices throughout the city and exchanges money. Other banks are numerous and easily found.

ATM: The ATMs in Matsumoto Central Post Office (see below) accept international credit cards including AmEx/MC/V. Open M-F 8:45am-9pm, Sa-Su 9am-7pm.

Luggage Storage: Coin lockers outside JR Matsumoto Station's Central Exit (¥300-500).

Lost Property: There's a customer service and lost property office outside the ticket booth of JR Matsumoto Station. Open daily 8:40am-6:30pm.

English-Language Bookstore: Parco Book Center, 1-10-30, Chūō (☎38-2113), in the basement of Parco department store, has a limited selection of English books and magazines. Open daily 10am-8pm.

Emergency: Police ☎110. Fire or ambulance ☎119.

Internet Access: The restaurant/bar **People's** (☎37-5011) provides Internet access for ¥200 per hr. A 15min. walk south of Matsumoto Station. Open daily 6pm-1am.

Post Office: Matsumoto Central Post Office, 7-5, Chūō (☎35-0078), is on Honmachi-dōri, 15min. from the JR station. Open M-F 9am-7pm, Sa 9am-5pm, Su 9am-12:30pm. **Matsumoto Eki Mae Post Office,** 1-6-15, Chūō. Take a left out of the JR station and turn right at Matsumoto Super Hotel. Open M-F 9am-5pm. **Postal Code:** 390.

⌂ ACCOMMODATIONS

In addition to serving as an essential gateway to the Japan Alps, Matsumoto is a prospering business city; consequently, most rooms around Matsumoto Station are in dreary business hotels. You won't have trouble finding a bed near the station or castle, within walking distance of the major sights, but there are more comfortable ryokan to be had a bit farther from the city.

Matsumoto City Hotel, 2-3-16, Fukashi (☎32-5025). Head straight out of the JR station, turn right at the post office, and walk 7min. A no-frills business hotel. Drab rooms made up for by the friendly owners. Check-in 3pm. Check-out 10am. Singles ¥3500. ❷

Super Hotel Matsumoto, 1-1-7, Chūō (☎37-9000). Turn left from the JR station and walk 5min. New hotel with great rooms and semi-double beds. Breakfast free. Check-out 10am. Singles ¥4800; twins ¥3500 per person; triples ¥2600 per person. ❷

Hamilton Inn, 4-9-3, Ōte (☎32-2888; fax 32-2555). Head straight out of the JR station up Eki-mae-dōri, turn left at the post office, continue straight 7min., and turn right after the NTT bldg. Near the castle and Naka-machi, this value hotel has simple rooms with semi-double beds. Check-in 3pm. Check-out 10am. Singles ¥6000; twins ¥11,000. ❸

Matsumoto Tourist Hotel, 2-4-24, Fukashi (☎33-9000). Head straight up Eki-mae-dōri, and turn right at the post office; it's a 5min. walk. Clean hotel with free lobby Internet access. Check-in 3pm. Check-out 10am. Singles ¥5300; twins and doubles ¥9990. ❸

Fukashisō (並柳), 2-11-21, Namiyanagi (☎28-6500; www.mcci.or.jp/www/fukasiso). Though it's 4km south of Matsumoto Station, this classic ryokan's location is made up for by the atmospheric Japanese garden. *Onsen* available 24hr. Check-in 4pm. Check-out 10am. Singles ¥6000, with 2 meals ¥8000. ❸

Hotel New Station, 1-1-11, Chūō (☎35-3850; fax 35-3851). A 3min. walk after a left out of the JR station. Fairly new business hotel with comfy rooms. Breakfast ¥800. Check-in 3pm. Check-out 10am. Singles ¥5800; doubles ¥9800; triples ¥12,400. ❸

Ace Inn Matsumoto, 1-1-3, Fukashi (☎35-1188). Adjacent to the JR station, this slightly more upscale business hotel provides well-maintained, good-sized rooms in its sharp-looking building. Check-in 3pm. Check-out 10am. Singles ¥6700. ❸

Asama Onsen Youth Hostel (HI), 1-7-15, Asama Onsen (☎46-1335). From the bus terminal in ESPA department store, take either the #6 bus to Shita Asama (20min., ¥240) or the #7 bus to Dai-Ichi Kōkō-mae (20min., ¥280). Proximity to popular Asama Onsen may make up for unappealing metal bunk beds and distance from the city. Check-in 3pm. Check-out 10am. Curfew 9pm. Dorms ¥3200. ❶

Matsumoto Green Hotel, 1-5-14, Fukashi (☎35-1277; www.mcci.or.jp/www/green-h/). Turn right out of the JR station and walk 5min. Among the business hotels around the station, this is a less classy choice. Western- and Japanese-style rooms—one of the few business hotels with *tatami*. Breakfast ¥800. Check-in 3pm. Check-out 10am. Singles ¥6000; semi-doubles ¥8000; twins ¥12,000; Japanese-style rooms ¥10,000. ❸

◪ FOOD

Like most other towns in Nagano, Matsumoto's specialty is Shinshū *soba*, and restaurants serving the fresh, homemade noodles can be found in the **Naka-machi** district. A wide variety of dining options crowd the alleys and streets around **JR Matsumoto Station.** Some cheap choices can be found in **Midori** department store, connected to the station, and the first floor and basement of **ESPA** department store have groceries and ready-made foods (open daily 11am-8pm).

Donguri, 1-4-5, Chūō (☎35-9505). A 5min. walk from the JR station, located on Kōen-dōri, a diagonal left from the station. Ample Western meals—often with a Japanese twist. Great place for a casual bite. Seafood *paella* (¥800) and tuna with tomato sauce spaghetti (¥650) are particularly tasty. Open Su-W and F-Sa 11am-9pm. ❷

Minoya, 2-7-3, Ōte (☎33-4319). Head straight out of the JR station onto Eki-mae-dōri, take the 2nd left, and walk 10min. This family-run store has served delicious, nostalgic Japanese sweets for over 100 years. Their specialty is *dango* (sticky rice balls) covered with red bean paste or sweet sauce (¥200). Open daily 11am-5pm. ❶

Nomugi, 2-9-11, Chūō (☎36-3753). Walk straight down Eki-mae-dōri from the JR station, take the 5th left, and it's a 3min. walk. Renowned for handmade Shinshū *soba*. Frequented by locals, who line up out the door, and flocked to by tourists—all in search of *zaru soba* (cold noodles; ¥1000). Open Su-M and W-Sa from 11:30am until the noodles are gone. Closed every 2nd W of the month. ❸

Sanmura Ya, 1-4-1, Fukashi (☎39-3599). Turn right from the JR station and take the 2nd left after Tokyu Inn hotel; it's a 3min. walk. Casual noodle joint. The *rāmen* (¥600) has been featured in local magazines. Open Su-Tu and Th-Sa 11am-9pm. ❷

Traffic Diner, 2-3-21, Chūō (☎37-5517). From JR Matsumoto Station, head straight to Parco department store until you reach a T-intersection, then turn left. A cafe-style bar, this stylish space has sofas and huge glass windows. A relaxing place to sit and talk—ideal for a date. Good cocktails ¥700. Light meals ¥800. Open daily 11am-11pm. ❷

Ciao, 4-15-B, Ryōjima (☎27-6608; fax 27-6609). A 25-30min. hike south of Matsumoto Station, this cute ice cream bar serves delicious desserts. Unique, often seasonal, flavors include pumpkin, cherry, and avocado (¥300). Open Tu-Su 10am-9pm. ❶

◪ SIGHTS

MATSUMOTO CASTLE (MATSUMOTO-JŌ; 松本城). Matsumoto's main attraction, and rightly so, this magnificent castle stands in the center of the city. The Ogasawara clan played a major role in the construction and fortification of the castle during the late 1500s. Inside the grounds, the principal sight is the five-turreted main tower, built in 1595. Enter the castle to see the vast array of weapons, with which people have attacked castles—bombs and rifles included—on the lower floors. Steep ladders and stairs lead you to the sixth floor, where you can look over the city. *(4-1, Marunouchi. Head straight up Eki-mae-dōri from the JR station, then turn left at Matsumoto Central Post Office onto Daimyō-machi-dōri; it's a 15min. walk. Alternatively, take the Town Sneaker bus 5min. to Matsumoto Jō Kuromon. ☎ 32-2902. Open daily 8:30am-5pm. Combined admission with Japan Folklore Museum ¥520, under 15 ¥250.)*

THE JAPAN FOLKLORE MUSEUM (NIHON MINZOKU SHIRYŌKAN; 日本民俗資料館). Outside Matsumoto Castle, this appealing museum proffers exhibits of battle guns and matchlocks used to protect Matsumoto Castle and attack others, as well as displays relating to Japanese folklore, culture, and the history of Matsumoto. Noteworthy exhibitions include Tanabata dolls, agricultural tools, pottery, antique clocks, and armor. *(4-1, Marunouchi, adjacent to Matsumoto Castle. ☎ 32-0133; fax 32-8974. Open daily 8:30am-5pm. Combined admission with castle ¥520, under 15 ¥250.)*

KYŪ KAICHI SCHOOL (KYŪ KAICHI GAKKO; 旧開智学校). This white building with stained glass and blue roof tiles, one of Japan's first elementary schools, appears incongruously Western in contrast to the town's very Japanese castle. Built in 1873 and used until 1963, it's been designated an Important Cultural Property. The school was restored and transformed into a museum displaying former school books, flags, banners, and other scholastic artifacts. *(2-4-12, Kaichi. Head north from Matsumoto Castle for 10min.; 25min. north of Matsumoto Station. ☎ 32-5725; fax 32-5729. Open Mar.-Nov. daily 8:30am-5pm; Dec.-Feb. Tu-Su 8:30am-5pm. ¥310, under 15 ¥150.)*

NAKA-MACHI (中町). The streets of Naka-machi are lined with traditional whitewashed merchant houses, many of which have been restored and converted into cafes, art galleries, and fashionable restaurants. A walk through the area lets you steep in the historic and pleasant atmosphere. *(Near Matsumoto Station.)*

JAPAN UKIYO-E MUSEUM (NIHON UKIYO-E HAKUBUTSU KAN; 日本浮世絵博物館). This oddly modern-looking museum houses over 100,000 important woodblock prints, screens, and paintings, collected by the Sakai family over several generations. The current displays include around 80 works, from widely known pieces to hidden gems. *(3km west of Matsumoto Station. Take the Matsumoto Dentetsu local train to Ōniwa (5min., every 15min., ¥170), take a left outside Ōniwa Station and continue straight for 3min., take another left at the main road, and keep straight for 300m. Go under the overpass, then continue straight for 100m. An easier way is to hop in a taxi from Matsumoto Station (15min., about ¥2100). ☎ 47-4440. Open Tu-Su 10am-4:30pm. ¥1000.)*

MATSUMOTO CITY MUSEUM OF ART (MATSUMOTO-SHI BIJUTSUKAN; 松本市美術館). Newly opened in 2002, this stylish museum mainly displays works by local artists, including renowned Yayoi Kusama. The common theme is Matsumoto itself, with works often depicting the stunning scenery that surrounds the city. Scrolls containing calligraphy by Shinzan Kamijo are displayed in the memorial exhibition room. Don't be put off by the hideous, multicolored flower sculptures towering over the entrance: worthwhile exhibits await you inside. *(4-2-22, Chūō. ☎ 39-7400; fax 39-3400. The Town Sneaker connects Matsumoto Station and the museum; get off after 15min. at the Matsumoto-shi Bijutsukan stop. Alternatively, walk straight out of Matsumoto Station onto Eki-mae-dōri and continue for 20min. Open Tu-Su 9am-5pm. ¥800, college and high school students ¥500, 70+ and under 15 free.)*

📷 NIGHTLIFE

Matsumoto is a fashionable city filled with young people, so, of course, there's an active after-hours scene. You can find casual *izakaya* and hip bars scattered around Matsumoto Station in the Chūō district; many are open late.

Vamonos, 1-4-13, Chūō (☎36-4878). Head out of the JR station onto Eki-mae-dōri and turn left at the KFC; then walk 2min. Mexican restaurant by day, bar by night. Generous meals (¥850) and Mexican liquors (¥650). Open M-Sa noon-3pm and 6pm-midnight.

Heaven, 2-10-5, Chūō (☎33-2020). Walk straight out of the JR station, turn left onto Honmachi-dōri, then take a right before the bridge. A comfortable, chic bar, the glowing interior contrasts with the faded exterior walls. The place to be for a classy atmosphere with colorful cocktails (¥850). Open Su-W and F-Sa 7pm-2am.

Cave, 1-7-10, Honjō (☎32-2522). Head out of the JR station, turn left at the post office, and cross the river to the Honjō district. Aptly enough, this snug, tiny bar is enclosed by stones and enhanced by plants and bamboo. Friendly owner serves Asian dishes (¥800) to a chill crowd. Cocktails and beer ¥500. Open M-Sa 6pm-midnight.

Eonta, 4-9-7, Ōte (☎33-0505). Head out of the JR station onto Eki-mae-dōri, turn left at the 7th light, walk 10min., and take the 3rd left after the bridge. A laid-back jazz bar where more than 1000 CDs and records line the shelves. A great place to sit back, relax, and enjoy the music. Drinks ¥700-850. Open Su-Tu and Th-Sa 4pm-midnight.

Bacchus, 1-8-26, Chūō (☎39-3268). Turn left out of the JR station and enter a small alley opposite New Station Hotel to find this casual shot bar. Located on the 2nd fl., this relatively new nightspot has a cozy and welcoming atmosphere, with a friendly bartender greeting you as you enter. All drinks ¥500. Open daily 7pm-3am.

Zeku, 2-2-1, Fukashi (☎38-1917). A 7min. walk from the JR station along Eki-mae-dōri. If you're looking for crazy dancing, blasting music, and flowing alcohol, this club is the place to be. Talented DJs guarantee good tunes. Cover ¥1000. Open F-Sa 10pm-2am.

⬛ FESTIVALS

In early August townsfolk let loose at the **Matsumoto Natsu Matsuri** with festive floats and fireworks. Next comes the mid-August **Tagaki Nō Matsuri,** during which classical *nō* is performed outside Matsumoto Castle by torchlight. November 3 brings the **Matsumoto Oshiro Matsuri,** celebrating the castle with flower shows, extravagant costumes, and festive floats. The **Ebisu Matsuri,** on November 19 and 20, concludes the year with merchant stalls overflowing the city streets.

AROUND MATSUMOTO

HAKUBA (白馬)   ☎0261

A popular alpine resort, Hakuba claims attractions from hiking, mountaineering, and biking in the summer to skiing and snowboarding in the winter. Prominent events, including the ski jump of the 1998 Olympics, have been held here, and snow frosts the mountains even during the summer. The mountaintop park **Tsugaike Shizen-en** (栂池 自然園 ; 1880m), boasts high-altitude flowers and striking autumn leaves. A 3hr. hike circles the park; for those who approach via ropeway (the least hiking-intensive way), the sights are stunning. From Hakuba Station, take a Tsugaike Kogen-bound bus to the end (25min., every hr., ¥500) and transfer to the Tsugaike gondola (20min.) and ropeway (9min.) to reach the park. (¥300. Round-trip ticket for 2 ropeways ¥3300, includes park admission. The Hakuba tourist office sells discount tickets for ¥2900, under 12 ¥1550, until Nov. 3; buy tickets in advance.)

An arduous, but popular, two-day hike, **Shirouma Dake** (白馬岳) is another way to approach Tsugaike Shizen-en. Climbing Shirouma Dake (2932m) takes 6hr. and requires preparation—ask for info at the tourist office. Two huts, **Son-ei Shirouma Jiri Sō** and **Shirouma Jiri Koya,** provide lodgings along the way, and two more, **Shirouma Dake Sancho Shukusha** (☎75-3360) and **Sonei Chōjyō Shukusha,** sit at the mountain's peak. If you bed down at one of the huts, you can continue on the 3½hr. hike to **Shirouma Ōike** (白馬大池) the next day, descend to Tsugaike Shizen-en (2½hr.), and return to Hakuba Station via ropeway (see above). Buses run from Hakuba Station to the trailhead, at Sarukura (30min., June-Sept. every hr., ¥960).

Winter transforms the **Happō-O-Ne** (八方尾根) area into a buzzing ski resort. The hike to Happō-O-Ne is easier than the one to Shirouma, but it's equally popular. To hit the trails, take the bus from Hakuba Station to Happō (5min., every 30-60min., ¥180) and walk 8-10min. to the cable car station. One cable car and two chairlift rides later, you'll be at the start of the 1hr. **Happō-O-Ne Shizen Kenkyūro** (八方尾根自然研究路) which ends at Happō-Ike (八方池). Hardcore hikers can continue to Karamatsu Dake Sanso Hut (3hr.), and from there hike to the peak of **Karamatsu Dake** in 30min. (Round-trip ticket for cable car and 2 chairlifts ¥2600. Discount tickets ¥2260, under 12 ¥1320; available at Hakuba Station tourist office.)

For guided adventures, try **Evergreen Outdoor Center** (☎72-5150; tours@evergreen-outdoors.com), where experienced instructors lead activities from bike tours (¥4500, under 12 ¥3500) and kayak and canoe tours (half-day ¥5000, under 12 ¥4000, under 6 ¥500; full-day ¥8500, under 12 ¥7500) to rock climbing (¥4500, ages 8-12 ¥3500) and paragliding (half-day ¥4500, full-day ¥8000).

To get to Hakuba from Matsumoto, take the JR Ōito Line (local: 105min., every 45-60min., ¥1110; express: 60min., 3-4 per day, ¥2770). From Nagano, take the bus from Nagano Station (65min., every hr., ¥1400). The **tourist office**, Hakuba Eki-mae, is to the right of Hakuba Station. (☎72-2279. Open daily 8:30am-5:15pm. Extended summer and winter hours.) More than 500 minshuku, ryokan, and hotels crowd the area. A no-frills option is **Resort House Windy ❶**, at the base of Happō-O-Ne ski slope in a snug cottage. (☎72-5382. 1 person ¥3300, with bath ¥3980; 2+ people ¥2980 per person.) **Shoseikan ❶**, Hakuba Eki-mae, a small house with simple *tatami* rooms, is 2min. up the road opposite Hakuba Station. (☎72-2169. Check-in 4pm. Check-out 10am. ¥3000.) **Minshuku ❷** (白峰荘), 6133-1, Kitajō, a 3min. walk from the station, offers standard *tatami*. (☎72-2613. ¥3500, ¥6000 with 2 meals.) A more upscale Western choice is **Hotel Hakuba ❸**, 5470-1, Kitajō. Turn left out of the station, take the first right, then go straight. (☎72-8122; fax 72-8120. Check-in 3pm. Check-out 10am. ¥7000 per room.) Reach the **Hakuba No Sato Youth Hostel (HI) ❶**, Tsugaike Kogen, by taking the Tsugaike Kogen-bound bus to the last stop. (☎83-3011. Breakfast ¥600. Dinner ¥1000. ¥2900-3200; nonmembers ¥3900-4200.)

Dining options around Hakuba Station are fairly limited. **Emu ❷**, 6375, Kitajō 6375, serves inexpensive set dinners, including *rāmen* (¥470) and pork cutlet (¥650). Cook your own *okonomiyaki* (¥600-800) at the tables. (☎72-4305. Open daily 11:30am-9pm.) Cafes and rest houses can be found near the ski slopes.

ŌMACHI (大町) ☎0261

Small Ōmachi bustles with travelers, as it's the start point for the **Tateyama-Kurobe Alpine Route** (p. 357). It was once on the famous **Salt Road** (Shio No Michi; 塩の道), a 120km path along which salt was carried from the Sea of Japan to Matsumoto and other cities. Ōmachi now has the **Salt Museum** (Shio no Michi Hakubutsukan; 塩の道博物館), the restored home of a former salt merchant. It has travel items, storehouses, and other artifacts pertaining to sodium chloride. Make a right from Shinano Ōmachi Station and walk 5min. (☎22-4018. Open May-Oct. daily 8:30am-4:30pm; Nov.-Apr. Su-Tu and Th-Sa 9am-4:30pm. ¥500.) The JR Ōito Line runs between Matsumoto and Shinano Ōmachi (1hr., every hr., ¥620) and continues to Hakuba (40min., every hr., ¥570). The **tourist office**, 3177, Ōmachi, is near Shinano Ōmachi Station. (☎22-0190. Open daily 9am-5pm.) **Hakuba Sanroku Onsen Youth Hostel (HI) ❶**, 10594, Ō-Aza Daira, Kizaki Ko Onsen, is the cheapest, a 15min. walk north towards Kizaki Lake from Shinano Kizaki station on the Ōito Line. (☎22-1820; fax 22-1977. Breakfast ¥600. Dinner ¥1000. ¥2900; nonmembers ¥3900.)

KAMIKOCHI (上高地) ☎ 0263

The popular alpine resort of Kamikochi attracts thousands of visitors every summer. Nestled in the northern Japan Alps, Kamikochi's fantastic views should be enjoyed between late April and early November, as the area shuts down during the harsh winter. These towering mountains were dubbed the "Japan Alps" by foreigners during the late 1800s. Later, British missionary Reverend Walter Weston daringly hiked from mountain to mountain, raising interest in mountaineering among the Japanese; a festival is held in his memory on the first weekend of June. The sights are inarguably some of Japan's best and travelers come accordingly—the area gets unbelievably crowded from late July through September.

🖅🏃 TRANSPORTATION AND PRACTICAL INFORMATION. From **Matsumoto**, take the Matsumoto Dentetsu Line to Shin-Shimashima Station (30min., every 45min., ¥680) and transfer to the Alpico Bus to Kamikochi (70min., every hr., ¥2050). Alternatively, a direct bus services Kamikochi from mid-April to mid-November, departing from the Matsumoto Bus Terminal (100min., 2 per day, ¥2500). If approaching by car, note that private vehicles are prohibited past Kama Tunnel: park at one of the 14 lots nearby (¥500 per day) and switch to a shuttle bus (¥1000) or taxi (about ¥4500). From **Takayama**, take a bus to Hirayu Onsen (55min., every hr., ¥1530) and transfer to the Kamikochi shuttle bus (30min., every 30min., ¥1050). A bus runs seasonally between Takayama and Kamikochi (85min., late Apr. to mid-Nov. 2 per day, ¥2000). Upon arriving at Kamikochi, reserve a return ticket at the bus terminal's window #2, as seats fill quickly. Private vehicles are banned past Hirayu Onsen, so park at the Akandana lot (¥500 per day).

A **tourist office** at the bus terminal provides hiking maps and books accommodations. The staff's English is limited, so it may be easier to use tourist offices in Matsumoto and Takayama. (☎95-2405. Open late Apr. to mid-Nov. daily 9am-5pm.) The **Kamikochi Visitor Center,** 10min. north of the bus terminal, has pictures and displays of Kamikochi's flora and fauna. The friendly staff organizes guided walking tours of the area. (☎95-2606; www1.neweb.ne.jp/wa/kamikochi/index2.html. Open late Apr. to mid-Nov. daily 8am-5pm. Tours 8am and 1pm. ¥300.)

🏃🏠 ACCOMMODATIONS AND FOOD. Accommodations in Kamikochi are expensive and fill up quickly during the peak season. Make reservations well in advance; the tourist offices in Matsumoto and Takayama can help. Of the seven lodges and four ryokan in the area, **Kamikochi Nishi Itoya Sansō ❸** (上高地西糸屋山荘), offers the most reasonable deal. Located 7min. south of Kappa Bridge, to the west of Azumi River, the wooden lodge is convenient and attractive. (☎95-2206. 2 meals included. Bunkbeds ¥7700; standard rooms ¥11,000.) Farther north, **Kamikochi Myojinkan Ryokan ❹** (上高地明神館旅館) is also a decent deal. It's some 40min. north of Kappa Bridge by foot, and offers views of the mountains from their bath. (☎95-2036; www.myojinkan.co.jp. Check-in 3-4pm. Check-out 8:30am. Open Apr. 27 to early Nov. Bunkbeds ¥8000; standard rooms with 2 meals from ¥10,000.) An alternative to overpriced lodges is camping; the **Konashi Daira Camp Site ❶** (Konashi Daira Kyanpujō; 小梨平キャンプ場) is just north of Kappa Bridge, east of the Azumi River. (☎95-2231. ¥400 per person; rental tents ¥2000.)

Restaurants in Kamikochi are equally pricey and limited. Your best bet is to take your meals at your lodge or to bring food with you. **Kamonji Goya ❸** (嘉門次小屋), a 1hr. walk north from Kappa Bridge and the bus terminal, west of the Azumi River by Myojin Bridge, is well known as a restaurant. It's quite hidden as an affordable place to sleep, however, offering *tatami*-style dorms. Try the famed *teishoku* (¥1600), which include local specialties like *iwana* fish and *sansai soba*. Simple and less expensive *soba* (¥800) or *iwana* (¥1200) sets are also available. (Dorms: ☎95-2418. Food: ☎95-2039. Dorms with 2 meals ¥7000. Restaurant open M-F 6:30am-4pm, Sa-Su 5:30am-4pm.) Many hotels and lodges around Kappa Bridge have classy cafes inside, offering basic meals, cake, and coffee (¥500-1000).

◪ **HIKING.** The Kamikochi area is home to two popular dayhikes. The first, a leisurely, largely flat loop hike, takes about 3hr. to complete. Heading north from Kamikochi Bus Terminal, your first stop should be **Kappa Bridge** (Kappa Bashi; 河童橋), Kamikochi's most famous sight. After crossing the suspension bridge and admiring the clear waters, you can continue up either the east or west side of the Azumi River to the **Myojin Bridge** (Myojin Bashi; 明神橋), catching panoramas of nearby mountains and rivers along the way. Turn around after crossing Myojin Bridge, perhaps stopping by serene **Myojin Lake,** and walk back toward the bus terminal. The second option is to head south after Kappa Bridge. Along the west side of the Azumi River, 15min. from the bridge, are the **Weston Park** and **Monument,** followed by the **Tashiro Bridge** (Tashiro Bashi; 田代橋), which you can cross. The **Kamikochi Nature Exploration Path** (Kamikochi Shizen Kenkyuro; 上高地自然研究路) begins here. The two marked paths are the **Azumi River Course,** with views of the water, and the **Rinkan Course,** which leads through the forest. The two converge after 20-30min. at **Tashiro Lake** (Tashiro Ike; 田代池). From there, another 20min. hike south leads to scenic **Taishō Lake** (Taishō Ike; 大正池), where sparkling waters reflect the mountains and woods. The hike takes 1-1½hr. each way.

Several longer hikes and climbs are possible around Kamikochi. As always with such expeditions, prepare in advance and pack warm clothing (the weather fluctuates severely on the mountaintops, reaching freezing temperatures even during the summer). The most popular of these are climbs to Yarigatake and Hotakadake. The **Yarigatake** (3180m) climb starts past Tokusawa and takes 5-6hr. From there, an intense three-day trip, following the alpine ridge south, brings you to the summit of **Hotaka-dake** (3190m), Japan's third highest mountain. Mountain huts along the way provide basic accommodation and food (around ¥8000).

KISO VALLEY (木曽谷)

With the Japan Alps towering on both sides, the Kiso Valley is a quiet region that was once an important post road, connecting Edo—now Tōkyō—with Kyōto. Consequently, the area prospered as towns found business providing food and accommodations to weary travelers. The tiny towns suffered an economic blow when new highways and the Chuō Line were built, both of which provided easy access between formerly unbridged towns. However, residents took advantage of their history during the 1960s, restoring old buildings and working to preserve a flavor of traditional Japan. Their efforts proved successful, as the area has became a famous tourist site, home to well-preserved sights and an Edo-period atmosphere.

◪ **HIKING**

Perhaps the best way to experience the Kiso area is to make like a mailsack and hike the post road. The 3hr. walk between Magome (p. 343) and Tsumago (p. 343) is quite popular. From Magome, continue up the main road to a narrow path leading into the forest. From there, the road leads into a steep hike up to Magome Tōge Pass and then continues through the quiet woods toward Tsumago. There are several signposts along the way. The hike can be done in either direction; starting from Tsumago is more difficult as there are more uphill climbs. Luggage forwarding (¥500 per piece) is available through the Magome and Tsumago tourist offices from July 20-August 31, as well as on Saturdays, Sundays, and national holidays from April 1-July 20 and September 1-November 23. Drop-offs for the morning service are accepted until 11:30am; for the afternoon service, the cut-off is 1pm.

MAGOME (馬籠)　　　　　　　　　　☎0264

The southernmost town on the Nakasendō Highway, Magome is a quiet hamlet. Its main street lies on a steep slope and is lined with traditional houses, shops, and cafes. While Tsumago and Narai are famous for their preserved historic buildings, Magome is better known as the birthplace of poet and novelist Shimazaki Tōson (1872-1943). Consequently, its main attraction is the **Tōson Memorial Museum** (Tōson Kinenkan; 藤村記念館), 4256-1, Kamizaka, halfway up the main road. Built on the site of Tōson's home, the mostly-in-Japanese museum displays books, scrolls, and pictures. (☎59-2047; fax 59-2231. Open daily Apr.-Oct. 8:30am-5pm; Nov.-Mar. 8:30am-4:30pm. ¥500, under 15 ¥250.) The graves of Tōson and his family rest in **Eisho-ji,** a temple off the main road, marked by arrows.

The closest train station is **Nakatsugawa,** on the Chuō Line, which can be reached from Matsumoto or Nagoya. (Matsumoto express: 85min., every 1-2hr., ¥4180. Nagoya local: 1½hr., every hr., ¥1280; Central Liner: 1hr., every hr., ¥1590; Shinano Express: 45min., every 1-2 hr., ¥2980.) From Nakatsugawa Station, buses run to Magome (30min., every hr., ¥540). From Nagoya's Meitetsu Bus Terminal, a bus runs to Magome (100min., 4 per day, ¥1830). A **tourist office** halfway up the main road, next to the Tōson Memorial Museum, provides maps and reserves beds. (☎59-2336. Open daily 8:30am-5pm.) In an emergency, call ☎110 for **police,** ☎119 for **fire** or **ambulance.**

Lodging options include bushels of minshuku and ryokan. While the tourist office is probably your best bet for finding accommodations, you won't go wrong with friendly **Minshuku Shirokiya ❸.** (☎59-2048. 2 meals included. ¥7000.) **Minshuku Iroribata ❸** has well-maintained *tatami* rooms in wooden building. (☎59-2026. 2 meals included. ¥8000.) Both are on the main road. Eat at **Shoku Dokoro Masuya ❷,** whose specialty is *jidori* (free-range) chicken. The owner makes delicious *jidori wappa meshi* (¥750), rice cooked with salt flavors and topped with *jidori* chicken. (☎59-2133. Open daily Apr.-Oct. 9am-4:30pm; Nov.-Mar. 10:30am-4pm.)

TSUMAGO (妻籠)　　　　　　　　　　☎0264

Tsumago's well-preserved buildings make the intimate town a highlight of the Kiso Valley. The once-prosperous post town crumbled after the development of modern roads and railway tracks; in 1968, however, the villagers restored the traditional village, transforming it into a cultural treasure. No telephone poles or lines stain the picturesque scene, and it's been named a Protected Area for the Preservation of Traditional Buildings. Tsumago tends to be more prominent and to attract greater crowds than similarly-preserved Narai (p. 344), so those seeking a quieter and more authentic visit should consider going there instead. In addition to the buildings, Tsumago's main attraction is the **Nagiso Machi Museum** (Nagiso Machi Hakubutsukan; 南木曽町博物館), a three-unit complex. The **Rekishi Shiryō-kan** (歴史資料館) has over 200 exhibits of earthenware and tools from the Nagiso area, dating back to the Jōmon Period, as well as displays on the history of Nagiso. The **Tsumago Juku Honjin** (妻籠宿本陣) is the house of prominent Shimazaki Tōson, restored to its original state, while the **Wakihonjin Okuya** (脇本陣奥谷) is a castle-like house built with *hinoki* (cypress wood), the felling of which was strictly regulated until 1877. (☎57-3322. Open daily 9am-5pm. ¥700 for all 3.)

To get to Tsumago, take the Chuō Nishi Line from **Matsumoto** to Nagiso Station (150min., every 1-2 hr., ¥1350). From **Nagoya,** take the Chuō Honsen Line to Nakatsugawa (70min., every hr., ¥1280), and transfer to the Chuō Nishi Line to Nagiso

(30min., every 2hr., ¥590). From Nagiso Station, a bus runs to Tsumago (10min., every hr., ¥270). Buses also run between Tsumago and Magome (35min., 5 per day, ¥650). Halfway down Tsumago's main road is the **tourist office**, 2159-2, Azuma, whose staff can provide you with maps and book a bed at one of the town's minshuku or ryokan. (☎59-3123. Open daily 9am-5pm.) Average prices are ¥7000-8000 for minshuku and ¥9000 and up for ryokan. **Minshuku Daikichi ❸** offers comfortable *tatami* rooms 5min. from the Tsumago bus station. (☎57-2595. 2 meals included. ¥800.) **Minshuku Maruya ❸** (☎57-3117; 2 meals included; ¥8000) and **Minshuku Shitabata ❸** (☎57-2090; 2 meals included; ¥7500) also provide friendly stays.

KISO-HIRASAWA (木曽平沢) ☎0264

A tiny village known for gorgeous lacquerware, Kiso-Hirasawa is where the medals for the 1998 Nagano Olympics were painted. Its main attraction is the **Kiso Lacquerware Museum** (Kiso Shikkikan; 木曽漆器館), 2324-150, Hirasawa, a wooden building hosting informative exhibits of modern and ancient pottery. In addition to massive antique pots, intricately designed boxes, and gold-plated dishware, the museum also displays tools and equipment used in lacquerware production. Turn left out of Kiso-Hirasawa Station, then follow the road to the large bridge; across the bridge, the museum is to your right. (☎34-1140. Open daily Apr.-Nov. 9am-4:30pm; Dec.-Mar. 9am-4pm. ¥200, under 15 ¥100.) Find artists selling and displaying their work 10min. after turning right out of Kiso-Hirasawa Station, in the center of the village. Although Kiso-Hirasawa's sole attraction is its lacquerware, it's worth a quick visit. A recommended route combines a visit to Kiso-Hirasawa with one to Narai, as the towns are connected by a well-marked 30min. walk along the Narai River.

NARAI (奈良井) ☎0264

An important post town on the former Nakasendō Highway, the picturesque town of Narai was located halfway between Kyōto and Edo (Tōkyō). As the last town before the arduous and dangerous Torii Tōge Pass, Narai earned its keep as a resting place for travelers preparing for the road ahead. Narai's streets haven't changed much in the intervening centuries, with traditional two-story wooden houses still lining its streets. The old buildings are unique in that the second story hangs completely over the first, with the eaves sloping down steeply.

The traditional houses extend about 1km along the main road, starting as you exit left out of Narai Station. Five wells dating from the Edo Period remain in the area; later additions are the souvenir shops peddling handmade chopsticks, bowls, straw hats, and baskets. Other sights include quiet temples hidden to the side of the main road, and the impressive **Kiso Bridge** (Kiso No Ōhashi; 木曽の大橋)—a wooden bridge marked by a high circular arc over the Narai River. The traditional houses, once ryokan where travelers stayed, are now smaller minshuku, *soba* places, and coffee shops. The most famous is **Nakamura Tei** (中村邸), a lacquerware shop transformed into a timeless museum. (☎34-2655. Free.) If you crave more background on Narai and the post road, the **Kamidonya Museum** (Kamidonya Shiryokan; 上問屋資料館) has displays in Japanese. (☎34-3101. Open Jan.-Mar. and May-Oct. Tu-Su 8:30am-5pm; Mar.-Apr. and Nov.-Dec. Tu-Su 9am-4pm. ¥300.)

To get to Narai, take the local Chuō Nishi Line from **Matsumoto** (45min., every 2 hr., ¥570). Express trains do not stop here. From **Nagoya**, the Chuō Line runs through Nakatsugawa to Narai (100min., every 2hr., ¥1350). One legacy of Narai's hospitable history is the many minshuku and ryokan lining its main road. **Minshuku Ikariya ❹** provides pleasant stays in a historic wooden building (☎34-3202; 2 meals included; ¥8500), as does **Minshuku Iseya ❸** (☎34-3051; 2 meals included; ¥8000).

Both are on the main road. Because Narai's lodgings are maintained by local families, some may choose not to accept visitors at certain times, especially during the off season. **Kanameya ❷**, 482, Narai, serves curry (¥650), *soba* (¥780), and *udon* (¥680) in a wooden house. (☎34-3329. Open Apr.-Nov. Su-Tu and Th-Sa 10:30am-9pm.) Tiny, cozy **Echigoya ❸** serves local *soba* (¥800) and specialty *gohei mochi* (sweet rice dumplings; ¥500) at its two tables. (☎34-3048. Open daily 9am-5:30pm.)

KISO-FUKUSHIMA (木曽福島) ☎0264

Another post road town, Kiso-Fukushima retains some old buildings and temples, but is more modernized than the other stops in Kiso Valley. There's little to see or do here, apart from climbing nearby **Mt. Ontake** (Ontake San; 御嶽山 ; 3067m), an active volcano. Kiso-Fukushima can be a useful place to spend the night; beds and restaurants are numerous. The **Kiso Ryōjōan Youth Hostel (HI) ❶**, 634, Shinkai, is the cheapest. Take the Obara-bound bus to the last stop (25min., ¥510) and walk 5min. (☎23-7716; www.oct.zaq.ne.jp/afabz707/an/index.html. Breakfast ¥400. Dinner ¥1000. ¥2900; nonmembers ¥3900. Closed M and Tu during off-season.) From Matsumoto, take the Chuō Nishi Line, local or express, to Kiso-Fukushima (local: 2hr., every 2hr., ¥1150; express: 1½hr., every 1-2hr., ¥2680). From Nagoya, take the Chuō Honsen Line to Kiso-Fukushima (express: 2hr., every hr., ¥3390).

TAKAYAMA (高山) ☎0577

Nestled deep in the Japan Alps, attractive Takayama claims a wealth of sights, museums, temples, and shrines. Walking through the streets lined with traditional houses, you'll quickly get a feel for the culture rooted in the city. Takayama was established as a castle town, and served as an important administrative office under Tokugawa rule. Although souvenir shops detract from the atmosphere of today's Takayama, the city is still unique in its cultural richness.

| ON THE WEB | Takayama: www.hida.jp |

▬ TRANSPORTATION

Trains: JR Takayama Station, ☎32-0099. The JR Takayama Line runs from **Toyama** in the north (express: 1½hr., ¥2770; local: 3hr., every 30-60min., ¥1620) via Takayama down to **Nagoya** (express: 2½hr., 10 per day, ¥5360). Express trains run to **Gifu** (3½hr., ¥4300), **Kyōto** (4½hr., ¥8380), and **Ōsaka** (5hr., ¥9010). From **Tōkyō**, the combined cost on *shinkansen* and express trains is ¥13,000.

Buses: Hida Takayama Bus Terminal (☎32-1160) is located to your left when JR Takayama Station is behind you. Numerous long-distance highway buses connect Takayama to: **Kanazawa** (3¼hr., 2 per day, ¥3300); **Kyōto** (4¾hr., 2 per day, ¥5500); **Matsumoto** (2¼hr., 4 per day, ¥3100); **Nagoya** (2¾hr., 9 per day, ¥2900); **Ōsaka** (4¾hr., 2 per day, ¥5500); **Tōkyō Shinjuku** (5½hr., 4 per day, ¥6500). Buses also run to sights around Takayama. Direct buses between Takayama and **Hirayu Onsen** run 3 times a day (1hr., ¥1500) and continue to **Shirakawa-gō** (1¾hr., ¥2400).

Public Transportation: All of Takayama's sights, except Hida Folk Village, are within walking distance of each other. A local bus runs via Takayama Jinya (8min., ¥100) to Hida Folk Village (15min., ¥250) every 30min.

Taxis: Hato Taxi, ☎32-0246. **Shinkyō Taxi,** ☎32-1700. **Yamato Taxi,** ☎32-2323. There's also a taxi pool in front of the JR station.

Car Rental: Eki Rent-A-Car (☎33-3522) is to your right as you exit the JR station. **Nissan Rent-A-Car** (☎35-3923) is 5min. west of the station. Both from ¥5500 per day.

Bike Rental: More than 400 rental shops are scattered through Takayama. **Hara Cycle** (☎32-1657) is on Kokubunji-dōri. ¥300 per hr., ¥1300 per day. The parking lot (☎33-3522) outside **JR Takayama Station** also rents bikes. ¥300 per hr., ¥1300 per day. Youth hostel guests (see **Accommodations**) can rent from the hostel for lower prices.

▓ ORIENTATION

While Takayama is relatively small, the city is packed with things to do, see, eat, and buy. With the exception of the Hida Folk Village, all the sights are near the city center, around the **Sanmachi Suji** district, 10min. east of the JR station. **Kokubunji-dōri,** running east-west, is the main road, lined with restaurants and shops. From the station, the road crosses the **Miya River,** intersecting the three streets of Sanmachi Suji and continues toward the **Teramachi** district and **Shiroyama Park.**

❔ PRACTICAL INFORMATION

Tourist Office: Hida Tourist Information Center, Shōwa-machi 1 Takayama Eki-mae (☎32-5238). English speakers. Open daily Apr.-Oct. 8:30am-6:30pm; Nov.-Mar. 8:30am-5pm. Book beds at the **General Accommodations Reservation Center** (Sōgō Shukuhaku Yoyaku Center; 総合宿泊予約センター), 1-64, Hatsuda-chō (☎33-1181; fax 33-9606), 5min. from the station, on Kokubunji-dōri. Open M-Sa 9am-6pm.

Currency Exchange: Hokuriku Bank and **Jūroku Bank** change money.

ATM: The ATMs inside the **Central Post Office** (see below) accept international cards. ATM available M-F 8am-9pm, Sa-Su 9am-7pm.

Luggage Storage: Coin lockers are available inside the JR station (¥300), although the souvenir shop just outside the station also holds luggage (¥200).

Emergency: Police ☎110. **Fire** or **ambulance** ☎119.

Internet Access: The tourist information center offers free Internet access, as does the Takayama Municipal Office. Open M-F 9am-5pm.

Post Office: Takayama Central Post Office, 5-95-1, Nadamachi (☎32-0059), is a 5min. walk east of the JR station. Open M-F 9am-7pm. **Postal Code:** 506.

▐ ACCOMMODATIONS

Accommodation options in Takayama are diverse and plentiful. Prices tend to be high, but most places are near the train station and Takayama's main sights.

Takayama Central Hotel (高山セントラルホテル), 1-5-2, Hanaoka-chō (☎35-1881; fax 34-4040). From the JR station, head left, then take a right at the 1st traffic light, onto Kokubunji-dōri. Take the 1st left and it's a 1min. walk. Clean, mid-range business hotel, with comfortable Western- and Japanese-style rooms. Check-in 4pm. Check-out 10am. Singles ¥5500; twins ¥11,000; Japanese rooms ¥15,000. ❸

Hida Takayama Washington Hotel Plaza (飛騨高山ワシントンホテルプラザ), 6-59, Hanasato-chō (☎35-1881; fax 35-3755). Directly across from the JR station's Central Exit. A spotless, attractive hotel with courteous service. Its proximity to the station is

Festival Floats Exhibition Hall
高山屋台会館

Kitayama Kōen
北山公園

Theater of Karkuri

Sakurayama Nikkō-kan

Yoshijima Residence
吉島家住華宅

Lacquerware Exhibition Hall
春慶会館

Kusakabe Folk Art Museum
日下部民芸館

Enakogawa・江名子川

Takayama City Hall
高山市役所

TO TOYAMA (89km)
富山へ

SANMAJI-SJI

Miyagawa・宮川

San-no-machi・三之町
Ichino-machi・一之町
Ni-no-machi・二之町

Takayama Betsuin-Ji
高山別院寺宝館

Miyagawa Market
宮川朝市

Hachiga Art Gallery
八賀民俗美術館

Hida Kokubun-ji
飛騨国分寺

Oita Wild Bird Museum
老田野鳥館

Kokubunji-dōri・国分寺道

Hirata Folk Art Museum 平田記念館

OLD RESIDENTIAL AREA

Takayama Museum of Local History
高山市郷土館

Honmachi-dōri

(158)

JR Takayama Station

Hirokōji-dōri

TO 17 (166km)

Takayama Jinya
高山陣屋

Shiroyama Kōen
城山公園

■ **Jinya Mae Market**
陣屋前朝市

Shorenji
照蓮寺

TO NAGOYA (166km)
名古屋へ

Takayama・高山

0 100 yards
0 100 meters

---

unbeatable, and the experience is slightly upscale. Parking ¥1000. Check-in 2pm. Check-out 10am. Singles ¥5800; twins ¥13,000; triples ¥18,000. ❸

International Ryokan Rickshaw Inn (インターナショナル旅館人カイン), 54, Suehiro-chō (☎32-2890; fax 32-2469). From the JR station, go to Kokubunji-dōri and take the 5th left; it's a 7min. walk. Stylish inn run by English speakers. Comfortable for foreigners. Laundry ¥200. Parking ¥1000. Check-in 4pm. Check-out 10am. Dorms ¥3200; singles ¥4200, with bath ¥6000; twins ¥9800. ❶

Takayama・高山

🏠 **ACCOMMODATIONS**
Hida Takayama Washington Hotel Plaza, **15**
International Ryokan Rickshaw Inn, **7**
Minshuku Yajima, **17**
Orion Plaza Hotel, **10**
Ryokan Kaminaka, **9**
Takayama Central Hotel, **5**
Tomareru Otera, **6**

🍴 FOOD
Ajikura, **16**
Ban, **1**
Chaya Sanban Machi, **14**
Hiro Sushi, **12**
Kyōya, **2**
Robata Yaki Sumishō, **8**
Suzuya, **11**
Unashin, **13**

🍸 NIGHTLIFE
Bagus, **4**
Red Hill Pub, **3**

Orion Plaza Hotel (オリオンプラザホテル), 6-51, Hanasato-chō (☎34-5677; fax 34-5\676). Turn left out of the JR station; it's a 3min. walk, on the right before Kokubunji-dōri. The cheapest business hotel near the station, its drab rooms reflect its low prices. Check-in 4pm. Check-out 10am. Singles ¥3300-3800; twins ¥7500. ❶

Hida Takayama Tenshō-ji Youth Hostel (HI) (飛騨高山天照寺ユースホステル), Tensho-ji Machi 83 (☎32-6345; fax 32-6392). In the Hiyashiyama and Teramachi district, a 20min. walk from the JR station. Peaceful, greenery-surrounded temple. Strict routine enforced, with curfew and early morning calls. Breakfast ¥500. Check-in 4pm. Checkout 10am. Curfew 10pm. ¥3200; nonmembers ¥4200. ❶

Minshuku Yajima (民宿矢嶋), 1-143, Shōwa-machi (☎32-4115; fax 34-2832). Behind the JR station; a 5min. walk. Facilities more like a small ryokan than a minshuku. Comfortable *tatami* rooms for reasonable prices, and an *irori* (Japanese-style hearth). Check-in 4pm. Check-out 10am. ¥5000, with 2 meals ¥7000. ❷

Tomareru Otera (泊まれるお寺), 49, Hirosue-chō (☎32-0519). From the JR station, head onto Kokubunji-dōri, then take the 5th left. A night at this old temple is one with absolutely no frills. Large *tatami* dorm rooms at a low price and central location. Check-in 4pm. Check-out 10am. Dorms ¥3000. ❶

Ryokan Kaminaka (旅館かみなか), 1-5, Hanaoka-chō (☎32-0451; fax 32-4478). From the JR station, head to Kokubunji-dōri; it's on the corner of the 1st left. An upscale choice with tasteful rooms, a relaxing bath, a serene inner garden, and meals featuring local specialties. Check-in 3pm. Check-out 10am. 2 meals included. ¥11,000. ❹

▸ FOOD

Takayama is a great place to eat, offering numerous local specialties. You'll detect the sweet scent of *mitarashi dango*, grilled *mochi* rice battered with soy paste, wafting wherever you go. Hida *soba*, buckwheat noodles topped with green vegetables, and *sansai ryōri*, dishes featuring wild plants and vegetables, are tasty regional choices. While carnivores will drool over the rich Hida beef, vegetarians will be delighted at the range of creative non-meat options. Tents selling fruit, pickled vegetables, and local crafts crowd the two daily morning markets. The **Miyagawa Asa Ichi** is the larger one, lining both sides of a narrow street running parallel to the river, while the smaller **Jinya Mae Asa Ichi** is confined to the open space in front of Takayama Jinya. (Both open Apr.-Oct. 6am-noon; Nov.-Mar. 7-11am).

Ajikura (味蔵), 4-147, Hanasato-chō (☎37-1129; fax 37-1143). Turn right out of the JR Station and walk 1min. A casual, sharp restaurant; sample Hida beef barbecue-style without busting your wallet. Dinner set ¥1900 per person, with salad, rice, soup, dessert, and the meat. Open Su-M and W-Sa 11am-2pm and 5-10pm. AmEx/MC/V. ❸

Kyōya (京や ; ☎34-7660). Located along Ni-no-machi road, 5min. north of Kokubunji-dōri. An attractive restaurant serving *sansai* plates and rich vegetable *nimono* (simmered dishes). Their *nabe* (stew), which holds over 10 different types of mushrooms, is extremely popular (¥1300). Extensive menu of local specialties. Great place for vegetarians. Open Su-M and W-Sa 11am-10pm. ❸

Unashin (うな信 ; ☎32-0846). From the JR station, head along Kokubunji-dōri and turn right after the bridge. It's a 3min. walk to your right. This small restaurant has specialized in *unagi* (eel) for over 45 years. Mouthwatering *una-don* with salad, soup, and pickled vegetables ¥1600. Open Su-Tu and Th-Sa 11am-2pm and 4:30-9pm. ❸

Chaya Sanban Machi (茶屋三番街), 84, Kami San-no-machi (☎32-0417). After crossing the river on Kokubunji-dōri, turn right, heading south, onto San-no-machi. It's on your left after a 3min. walk. A traditional teahouse with a 100-year history; open-kettle *irori* and dark beams. Menu items match the atmosphere; specialty sweets include *zenzai* (¥650) and *shiratama* (¥500). Open Su-W and F-Sa 10am-4pm. ❶

Daikokuya (大黒屋), 2, Tenshōji-machi (☎35-1227). 20min. north of the JR station, in the Teramachi district. Despite its distance from the center of town, this *soba* and *udon* spot attracts crowds with delicious homemade noodles and broth. The favorite is simple *zaru soba* (cold noodles; ¥700). Open daily 10am-10pm. ❷

Suzuya (すずや), 24, Hanakawa-chō (☎32-2484). 7min. from the JR station on Kokubunji-dōri. A popular place renowed for local specialties (¥1000); a great stop for traditional foods. Casual atmosphere and English menu. Open daily 11am-8pm. ❷

Ban (ばん), 1-35, Ōshinmachi (☎34-7999). A 15min. walk from the JR station. Turn left after crossing the Miya River and continue north. For a taste of Takayama *rāmen,* a less well-known local specialty, slurp some at this authentic spot. Soups from standard soy (¥500) to *miso* (¥700) and *tonkotsu* (pork; ¥500). Open daily 10am-4pm. ❶

Robata Yaki Sumishō (ろばた焼き炭庄), 11-4, Asuka-chō (☎34-6848). Along Kokubunji-dōri, to the left from the JR station, across the river. A bitsy, bustling *izakaya* serving more than 70 varieties of vegetables, meat, and fish (¥250-900), with local *sake* (¥500). To see chefs at work, sit at the counter. Open daily 5pm-11pm. ❸

Hiro Sushi (廣すし), 2-10, Hanakawa-chō (☎34-3977). From the JR station, head onto Kokubunji-dōri and take the 6th right. Although sushi is the big deal, the place also prides itself on broiled fish (¥700) and cooked appetizers. Delicious sushi sets ¥1000-3000. *Kaisen-don* ¥1200. Open Su-Tu and Th-Sa 11:30am-1:30pm, 5:30pm-11pm. ❷

🅖 SIGHTS

TAKAYAMA JINYA (高山陣屋). An administrative building during the Edo period, Takayama Jinya retains much of its original 1615 architecture. It's the largest and oldest structure of its kind remaining in Japan. Walking through the endless rooms and corridors, you'll see offices, residences, bathrooms, and kitchens used by officials and their servants. The numerous entrances and different styles of *tatami* mats reveal the strict caste system in place until the Meiji Restoration, while the torture chamber attests to the inequities of the time. The adjacent storage building functions as a museum, with displays of swords, guns, armor, and maps. *(1-5, Hachiken-machi. Follow Kokubunji-dōri to the Miyagawa River and turn right before the bridge; it's a 10min. walk south. ☎32-0643; fax 32-0612. Open Mar.-Oct. 8:45am-5pm; Nov.-Feb. 8:45am-4:30pm. Free English tours upon request. ¥420, under 18 free.)*

FESTIVAL FLOATS EXHIBITION HALL (TAKAYAMA YATAI KAIKAN; 高山屋台会館 **).** Four of the multi-tiered floats used during the spring festival in Takayama are the attractions here, so if you can't be here during the festival, this is the next best thing. Marionettes, also part of the festival, are also displayed. The neighboring **Sakurayama Nikko-kan** has intricate reconstructions of old temples, gates, and pagodas. *(178, Sakura-machi. From the JR station, walk along Kokubunji-dōri across the bridge to the Sanmachi Suji district. It's 10min. north from there. ☎32-5100; www.hida-hachiman.org. Open daily 8:30am-5pm. Both museums ¥820, high school students ¥510, under 15 ¥410.)*

SANMACHI SUJI OLD RESIDENTIAL AREA (SANMACHI SUJI FURUI MACHI NAMI; 三町筋古い町並み **).** Three parallel streets, **Ichi-no-machi, Ni-no-machi,** and **San-no-machi,** compose the district known as Sanmachi Suji. Museums, breweries, and souvenir shops line the busy streets. The southern half of San-no-machi features traditional wooden houses, with rickshaws adding to the historic feel.

HIDA KOKUBUN-JI (飛騨国分寺). This large 8th-century temple has grounds handsomely decorated with a magnificent three-story pagoda, a huge dark bell, and a 1200-year-old gingko tree. *(To your left on Kokubunji-dōri coming from the JR station, to your right coming from Sanmachi Suji. ☎32-1395. Open daily 9am-4pm.)*

TAKAYAMA MUSEUM OF LOCAL HISTORY (TAKAYAMA-SHI KYODOKAN; 高山市 郷土館 **).** This museum boasts a vast variety of exhibits relating to local culture. Elaborate and colorful firefighting gear, displays from previous festivals, old *samurai* armor, and countless tools and household items adorn the interior of the traditional building. Two attractive Japanese gardens complete the picture. *(75, Kami Ichi-no-machi. From the JR station, head onto Kokubunji-dōri, cross the river, and take the 4th right; the museum is a 5min. walk to your left. ☎32-1205; fax 35-1970. Open Apr.-Oct. daily 8:30am-5pm; Nov.-Mar. Tu-Su 8:30am-5pm. ¥300, under 15 ¥150.)*

KUSAKABE FOLK ART MUSEUM (KUSAKABE MINGEIKAN; 日下部民藝館 **).** The former residence of the rich Kusakabe merchant family, the building is a good example of traditional Edo architecture, with strong beams and pillars of Japanese cypress. An Important Cultural Asset, the small museum displays over 5000 items, including lacquerware, baskets, shelves, and tools. Enjoy free tea and rice cakes in the inner resting place. *(1-52, Ōshinmachi. Follow Ichi-no-machi northward for 5min. from Kokubunji-dōri. ☎32-0072; fax 36-0288. Open daily 8:30am-5pm. ¥500, under 15 ¥300.)*

YOSHIJIMA RESIDENCE (YOSHIJIMA-KE JŪTAKU; 吉島家住宅 **).** Walking through this old merchant house gives you a good look at traditional Japanese architecture, including lattice windows and high ceilings. The careful attention to detail used in constructing the house is apparent in its simple beauty. *(On Ichi-no-machi-dōri north of Kokubunji-dōri. Next to the Kusakabe Folk Art Museum. ☎32-0038. Open daily Mar.-Nov. 9am-5pm; Dec.-Feb. 9am-4:30pm. ¥500, under 15 ¥300.)*

THEATER OF KARAKURI (SHISHI KAIKAN; 獅子会館 **).** The museum displays over 800 festive lion masks, many elaborately designed with expressive features. See the instruments played during the lion mask dances, as well as a demonstration of the puppets. *(53-1, Sakura-machi. A 7min. walk north of the Sanmachi Suji district, by the Festival Floats Exhibition Hall. ☎32-0881; www.toyoadv.com/kan. Shows every 30min. Open daily Apr. 21-Oct. 20 8:30am-5:30pm; Oct. 21-Apr. 20 9am-5pm. ¥600, under 15 ¥400.)*

HIDA FOLK VILLAGE (HIDA MINZOKU MURA; 飛騨民俗村 **).** Unless you're planning a visit to the Shirakawa-gō or Gokayama region, where you can see similar sights in their original locations, this open-air museum should be high on your list. Featuring various styles of traditional Japanese houses, most of which have been transplanted from around the prefecture, the park is a compact display of rare architecture. The village is divided into two sections; one admission gets you into both. **Hida-no-Sato** is the larger and more interesting of the two. Strolling through the park counter-clockwise around the central pond, you'll find 12 traditional houses. Duck inside to explore the interior design and household items and tools. Local craftsmen demonstrate their skills at lacquerware and wood carving. The smaller **Hida Folklore Museum** is a 5min. walk downhill from Hida-no-Sato, and is composed of four buildings with displays of rural life and crafts. *(1-590, Kami Oka-moto-chō. A 20-30min. walk west of the JR station. Alternatively, take the Hida-no-Sato-bound bus from gate #2 at the Takayama Bus Terminal (10min., every 30min., ¥250). ☎34-4711; www.hidanosato.org. Open daily 8:30am-5pm. ¥700, under 15 ¥200.)*

MAIN WORLD SHRINE. This magnificent shrine's brilliant gold roof is striking against the natural green mountains and blue sky. The headquarters of the Sukyu Mahikari sect of the Shintō religion is worth visiting just to check out the amazing architecture, which includes well-executed imitations of Mexico's Quetzalcoatl Fountain and a set of Islamic-inspired fountains. *(1km west of Hida Folk Village.)*

LACQUERWARE EXHIBITION HALL (SHUNKEI KAIKAN; 春慶会館 **).** Wooden craftwork, shelves, boxes, trays, and sculptures—if you can lacquer it, it's here, done in the traditional Shunkei technique, indigenous to the Hida region. The explanation of the production process is quite informative. *(1, Kanda-chō. From the JR* *station, head up along Kokubunji-dōri, and turn left at the last traffic light before the river. The museum's a 5min. walk to your left. ☎32-3373; fax 32-3374. Open daily Apr.-Oct. 8am-5:30pm; Nov.-Mar. 9am-5pm. ¥300, high and middle school students ¥200, under 12 free.)*

TERAMACHI (寺町) AND SHIROYAMA PARK (SHIROYAMA KŌEN; 城山公園).

East of central Takayama lies a cluster of temples and shrines collectively called the Teramachi district. A stroll through the area, with stops to pop in the various religious structures, is a relaxing way to enjoy an afternoon. Clearly marked paths lead you toward Shiroyama Park, a pleasant flower-speckled patch of green. Near the top of the mountain lie the remains of once-magnificent Takayama Castle.

HIRATA FOLK ART MUSEUM (HIRATA KINENKAN; 平田記念館).

This small merchant house is an unremarkable museum displaying everyday items from the region. Exhibits include crafts, lacquerware, lamps, and clothing. *(Kami Ni-no-machi 39. From Kokubunji-dōri in the Sanmachi Suji district, head east along Ni-no-machi-dōri. It's on your right. ☎33-1354. Open daily 9am-5pm. ¥300, under 15 ¥150.)*

⌐ ⌐ SHOPPING AND CRAFTS

Many traditional crafts are Takayama specialties. Shunkei-style lacquerware is particularly attractive and famous, and it's sold both in souvenir shops lining San-machi Suji and in the Lacquerware Exhibition Hall. The traditional Yamada-yaki style and more extravagant Shibukusa-yaki style of pottery are also Takayama's own, along with intricate wooden carvings known as *ichii ittobori*.

NIGHTLIFE

Nightlife in Takayama tends to be unexciting, with restaurants closing early and most of the area saying goodnight well before the witching hour. The sliver of nightlife that exists is centered around Kokubunji-dōri and the Miya River.

Red Hill Pub (☎33-8139). A 10min. walk from the JR station. Follow Kokubunji-dōri north. The local hangout spot, this happening bar attracts crowds with its trendy ambience and great variety of beers (¥500) and Middle Eastern foods (¥700). Though locals pack the place, there are foreigners around also. Open Tu-Su 7pm-midnight.

Bagus (☎36-4341). From the JR station, head onto Kokubunji-dōri and take the 3rd left, then 1st left; it's behind Hida Kokubun-ji. A friendly reggae bar, popular for its great drinks (¥600) and still better music. Open M-Sa 7pm-2am.

FESTIVALS

Known as one of Japan's three most beautiful festivals, the Takayama Festival consists of the **Sanno Festival** in the spring and the **Hachiman Festival** in the autumn. The spring festival is associated with Hie Shrine, and is held in early April, featuring ritual ceremonies, a massive parade of residents in traditional costume and extravagant floats and marionettes. The autumn festival is associated with Sakurayama Hachimangu Shrine and is held in early October. The festivities are similar to those of the spring festival, with parades, floats, and puppets, although the procession carrying the *mikoshi* (portable shrine) is unique to the autumn.

AROUND TAKAYAMA　(高山周辺)

SHIRAKAWA-GŌ　(白川郷) AND
OGIMACHI (荻町)　　　　　☎05769

The Shirakawa-gō region is famous for its large collection of *gasshō-zukuri* houses, traditional thatched-roof farmhouses with a structure resembling a pair of praying hands. The steepness of the truss-like structure of the roofs allows adequate space inside, and prevents snow from piling up and damaging the houses. All *gasshō-zukuri* have pin connections and cross-bracing which impart an amazing structural efficiency. Ogimachi is where these fascinating and historic structures are clustered, and the village is home to townsfolk who still live, work and farm in the traditional manner. Recent hype about the area, however, has transformed the village from an authentic cultural treasure to a popular tourist attraction, and the tour buses and souvenir shops detract from the overall atmosphere and appeal.

❚❷ TRANSPORTATION AND PRACTICAL INFORMATION. Transport to and from the region is infrequent and complicated, so check bus and train schedules at a tourist office. From **Takayama,** it's easiest to take a direct bus (run by Nohi) to Shirakawa-gō (100min.; 3 per day; ¥2400, round-trip ¥4300). Alternatively, take the Nohi bus to **Makido** (1hr., 3 per day, ¥1930) and transfer to the JR bus to Ogimachi (1hr., 3 per day, ¥1430). From **Kanazawa,** the Nagoya Tetsudo Bus runs to Ogimachi (3½hr., 2 per day, ¥2680). Otherwise, take the JR Hokuriku Line to **Takaoka** and transfer to a bus (2½hr., 4 per day, ¥2350). The same bus company provides transport between **Nagoya** and Ogimachi (6hr., 1 per day, ¥4760), as does the JR bus (4hr., 1 per day, ¥4760). Once you've made it to Ogimachi, the main sights are within walking distance, but if you're looking to visit nearby **Gokayama,** bus service is infrequent and expensive. There's a **tourist information center** near the center of Ogimachi, right by the Gasshō-Shūraku bus stop. The friendly staff can help you find lodgings, and provide maps and brochures. (☎6-1013. Open Su-Tu and Th-Sa 8:30am-5pm.) In an emergency, call ☎110 for **police,** ☎119 for **fire** or **ambulance.**

❚❒ ACCOMMODATIONS AND FOOD. There are plenty of minshuku and ryokan in Shirakawa-gō, many of which are traditional *gasshō-zukuri* houses. Work through the tourist office in either Ogimachi or Takayama (p. 345) to make reservations. A stay in a minshuku will run you ¥6000-8000 and a ryokan ¥8000-10,000; both options will include two meals. Dining options are clustered along the main road in Ogimachi, but the quality tends not to justify the inflated prices—you're best off taking meals at your minshuku or ryokan. **Irori ❷** serves *soba* (¥700), *gyudon* (beef bowl; ¥800), fried tofu sets (¥1500), and *iwana* sets (¥1500) in an old *gasshō-zukuri,* complete with a raised hearth. The restaurant is 3min. north along the main road from the tourist office and main bus stop. (☎6-1737. Open daily 11am-5pm.) Across from the tourist office is **Shiraogi ❷,** a restaurant often flooded with tour groups. Specialties include local tofu and *iwana* fish dishes. The green tea or milk-flavored soft ice cream (¥300) may be the best choice, however. (☎6-1832. *Soba* ¥800. Set meals from ¥2000. Open daily 11am-5:30pm.)

❒ SIGHTS. Your first destination after arriving at the Gasshō-Shūraku bus stop should be the **Wada-ke Residence** (Wada-ke Jūtaku; 和田家住宅), 997, Sanetsu, a 2min. walk south along the main road on your left. This traditional *gasshō-zukuri* house functions as a museum, with household treasures, daily items, and lacquerware on display. (☎6-1058. Open daily 9am-5pm. ¥300, under 12 ¥150.) Continuing down along the main road, away from the tourist office and bus terminal, you'll see the **Myōzen-ji Temple Museum** (Myōzen-ji Kuri Kyōdōkan; 明善寺庫裡郷土館). Inside, you'll find remnants from when priests and monks occupied the space. As in most *gasshō-zukuri* buildings, you can see the open-slit floorboards, designed to allow steam from the *irori* to heat the entire house during the cold winter. (☎6-1009. Open daily Apr.-Nov. 8:30am-5pm; Dec.-Mar. 9am-4pm. ¥300, under 12 ¥150.)

Another 5min. southward brings you to the **Shirakawa Hachiman Shrine** (Shirakawa Hachiman Jinja; 白川八幡神社), the village's fascinating main shrine complex. Next door is the **Doburoku Festival Exhibition Hall** (Doburoku Matsuri no Yakata; どぶろく祭りの館), displaying *shishimai* and dolls in an attempt to recreate the annual **Doburoku Festival.** Held October 13-16, the festival is centered around the production of *doburoku*, a local, milky-colored *sake*. The museum walks you step-by-step through the brewing process, concluding with a small sample of the end result. (☎6-1655. Open Apr.-Nov. daily 9am-4pm. ¥300, under 12 ¥150.) At the end of the main street to your right is the **Gasshō-Zukuri Museum of Daily Life** (Gasshō Zukuri Seikatsu Shiryōkan; 合掌作り生活資料館), a small collection of random household items, from handcrafts to tools. (☎6-1093. Open daily Apr.-Nov. 8am-6pm; Dec. 9am-6pm. Free.) After the museum, continue down the road away from the village 20m or so, then turn around—you'll find an unobstructed, postcard view of three *gasshō-zukuri* houses.

Although most sights line the main road, it's worth venturing over to the smaller side road running parallel to the main street, just to the east. While the main road is the center of tourist sights, the back road is the center of village life, featuring many private *gasshō-zukuri* homes. On the west of the Shō River, across a bridge, the **Gasshō-zukuri Open-Air Folklore Park** (Yagai Hakubutsukan Gasshō-zukuri Minka-en; 野外博物館合掌作り民家園) has a well-maintained collection of 25 traditional houses. Demonstrations of handicrafts, woodworking, and ceramics are held inside some houses, and a teahouse offers free tea. Quiet and rather abandoned, the museum pales in comparison to the real village just across the river. (☎6-1231. Open Apr.-July and Sept.-Nov. daily 8:40am-5pm; Aug. daily 8am-5:30pm; Dec.-Mar. Su-W and F-Sa 9am-4pm. ¥500, under 12 ¥250.)

A great end to your Shirakawa-gō visit is the 15min. hike up to the fantastic **Ogi-machi Lookout Site** (Ogimachi Tenbōdai; 荻町展望台). From the tourist office and bus terminal, head north on the main road for 10min., then follow the small tree-lined road up the hill. The lookout has panoramic views of neighboring mountains and the Shō River, as well as an unbeatable view of the *gasshō-zukuri* houses.

GOKAYAMA (五箇山) ☎0763

With two sights enrolled on the World Heritage List, quaint Gokayama has much to be proud of. The two *gasshō-zukuri* villages for which the area is famous are filled with life, not by the noisy tourists who crowd nearby Shirakawa-gō and Ogimachi, but by villagers who live there. Untainted by tourism, Gokayama offers a quieter and more enjoyable atmosphere in which to view these unique buildings.

▐▐ **TRANSPORTATION AND PRACTICAL INFORMATION.** Getting to and from Gokayama is difficult due to infrequent bus services. From Takaoka Station, the Kaetsuno Tetsudō Bus runs to the region, stopping at various points of interest in the area (2hr., 4 per day, ¥3760). Gokayma's sights, though worthwhile, are far apart, and transport can be a hassle. The best option is to rent a car in Takayama (p. 345) and then take the scenic drive through the mountains to Gokayama. Once you arrive, there's a **tourist information center** in the northern part of Gokayama, next to Gokayama Washi No Sato. (☎66-2468. Open daily 9am-5pm.) In an emergency, call ☎110 for **police,** ☎119 for **fire** or **ambulance.**

▮▐ **ACCOMMODATIONS AND FOOD.** The best option is to stay in one of the small minshuku in the Suganuma or Aikura *gasshō-zukuri* villages. A night in one of these World Heritage treasures costs ¥8000-10,000 per night, with two meals included. The Gokayama and Takayama (p. 345) tourist offices can make reservations for you. **Kokumin Shukusha Gokayamasō ❸** (国民宿舎五箇山荘) has modern Japanese-style rooms and an open-air bath. (☎66-2316; www.vill.taira.toyama.jp/sansou. Check-in 4pm. Check-out 10am. ¥7000.) **Etchū Gokayama Youth Hostel (HI) ❶** (越中五箇山ユースホステル) offers cheap beds in a *gasshō-zukuri* house. (☎67-3331. Check-in 4pm. Check-out 10am. ¥3200; nonmembers ¥4200.)

▣ **SIGHTS.** From Takaoka, your first sight is the **Aikura Gasshō-Zukuri Village** (Aikura Gasshō-Zukuri Shuraku; 相蔵合掌作り集落). As locals still live and work in the small village, the place retains a traditional air untarnished by modernization. Inscribed on the World Heritage List in 1955, this protected treasure offers a living image of an older Japan. A small museum, the **Aikura Minzokukan** (相蔵民族館), is hidden near the back of the village, featuring household items, tools, and lacquerware. (☎66-2732. Open daily 8:30am-5pm. ¥200, high school students ¥100, under 15 ¥50.) Farther south is the **Suganuma Gasshō-Zukuri Village** (Suganuma Gasshō-Zukuri Shuraku; 菅沼合掌作り集落), a similar, although smaller and quieter, World Heritage sight. The cluster of 14 thatched-roof houses is a tightly knit community, where earthen- and wood-walled storehouses can also be seen. Two small museums, the **Enshō No Yakata Museum** (塩硝の館) and the **Gokayama Minzokukan** (五箇山民族館), allow a look inside the houses and have displays of traditional crafts and tools (Enshō No Yakata ☎67-3652, Gokayama Minzokukan ☎67-3262. Open daily 9am-4pm. ¥210 for 1, ¥300 for both; under 15 ¥100/ ¥150.) Near the center of Gokayama is the 350-year-old **Murakami Residence** (Murakami-ke; 村上家), another fine example of, you guessed it, *gasshō-zukuri* architecture. (☎66-2711. Open daily 8:30am-5pm, closed 2nd and 4th W of the month. ¥300, under 15 ¥150.) Across the river is the quirky **Ryūkei Hut** (Ryūkei Goya; 流刑小屋), a wooden shack where exiled prisoners were kept hostage. If you have the automotive independence to get there, the largest and best example of a *gasshō-zukuri* house is the **Iwase Residence** (Iwase-Ke; 岩瀬家). A five-story Edo-period building, this enormous structure once housed over 35 people. Get a Japanese explanation over a cup of tea, then climb the steep ladders upstairs to explore the many stories. Walking across the open-slit floors is quite a thrill, and old tools and artifacts lie along the sides. (☎67-3338. Open daily 8am-5pm. ¥300, under 15 ¥150.)

Gokayama Washi no Sato (五箇山和紙の里) sells paper lanterns, letter sets, dolls, fans, and other *washi* paper items. The real fun is the workshop nextdoor, where you can make *washi*. It only takes 10min. and you leave with a beautiful handmade souvenir. (☎66-2403; fax 66-2250. Open daily 9am-4pm. ¥500.)

FURUKAWA (古川)　　　　　☎0577

A pleasant daytrip from Takayama, Furukawa offers quaint roads lined with old wooden houses and white-walled storehouses. The former castle town is by a river and is surrounded by towering mountains. The compact area boasts museums and attractive temples, but is best known for the boisterous spring Furukawa Festival.

▮▐ **TRANSPORTATION AND PRACTICAL INFORMATION.** From **Takayama**, Furukawa is three stops north on the JR Takayama Line (15min., every hr., ¥230). Buses depart from Takayama Bus Terminal (30min., 1 per hr., ¥590). Infrequent trains also chug in from **Toyama** (1hr., every 1-2hr., ¥1450). The small **Kida-Hida Tour-**

ist **Information Center** is outside JR Hida-Furukawa Station. The staff don't speak English, but have maps and pamphlets. For more info, inquire at the Takayama tourist office (p. 345) before setting out. (☎73-3180. Open daily 9am-5:30pm.)

▐▌▐▌ ACCOMMODATIONS AND FOOD. Furukawa is best seen as a daytrip from Takayama, as accommodation options are few. If you do stay the night, try the **Hida Furukawa Youth Hostel** ❶ (HI; 飛騨古川ユースホステル), a comfortable stay surrounded by mountains and rice paddies. To get there, take the Takayama Honsen to Hida Hosoe Station, two stops north of Hida Furukawa (10min., every hr., ¥230), and walk 15min. toward Shinrin Kōen. If you call in advance and arrive after 6pm, they'll pick you up at the station. (☎75-2979; www.d2.dion.ne.jp/hidafyh. Check-in 4pm. Check-out 10am. Breakfast ¥500. Dinner ¥1000. Closed Mar. 30-Apr. 10. ¥3100; nonmembers ¥4100.) Across from JR Hida-Furukawa Station is **Ōmuraya Ryokan** ❷ (大村屋旅館). Though geographically more convenient, the owners speak no English and the ryokan is geared towards Japanese guests. (☎73-2787. Check-in 4pm. Check-out 10am. ¥4500, with 2 meals ¥8000.)

There are restaurants near Furukawa's main sights and closer to the station, most serving local dishes. Head straight out of the station, take the second right, and continue past the second light to find **Takumi** ❷ (匠), 2-18, Honmachi, a cute noodle shop serving Hida *soba* (¥600) and *rāmen* (¥650), as well as handmade sweets. (☎73-2917. Open Su-Tu and Th-Sa 10:30am-5pm.) For local *sansai* dishes, try **Matsuya** ❸ (まつや), 11-24, Kanamori Machi, whose wild vegetable lunch sets, prepared according to old recipes, are a fantastic deal (¥2000). Head out of the station and take the first right. (☎73-2929. Open Su-W and F-Sa 11am-5pm.)

◪ SIGHTS. All of Furukawa's sights are within walking distance of the station. The most popular way to visit Furukawa is to first head to the **Shirakabe Dozō** (白壁土蔵) district, a 5min. walk southwest of Hida-Furukawa Station. With the **Seto River** (Seto Gawa; 瀬戸川) running alongside traditional white-walled earthen storage houses, this district is a pleasant stroll that will take you back to Edo times. Enormous carp swim through the small river, opening their mouths in anticipation of food. At the end of the line of merchant houses, turn right to find **Honkō-ji** (本光寺), a temple whose sheer size, intricate carvings, and beautiful decorations are impressive, as is the large dark bell adjacent to the main building. From the temple, turn around and follow Ichi-no-machi, a road lined with shops, *sake* breweries, and traditional houses. **Mishimaya** (三嶋屋) is a famous candle-making shop that has specialized in traditional methods for over 200 years. Inside, watch the skilled craftsmen melt and mold the wax or color the finished products with a dark red finish. The 17th-generation master will proudly explain the history of the shop, with a special emphasis on how the shop only makes the most traditional of all Japanese candles. (☎73-4109. Open Su-Tu and Th-Sa 9am-6pm. Free.) Farther down the road, massive leaf balls hang above the entrances of two *sake* breweries, the **Watanabe Brewery** (渡辺酒造店) and the **Kama Brewery** (蒲酒造店).

A 2min. walk from the breweries leads you to the central square, where there are two museums. The **Hida Furukawa Festival Museum** (Hida Furukawa Matsuri Kaikan; 飛騨古川まつり会館), 14-5, Ichi-no-machi, has displays of the floats used during the annual festival. Puppet shows bring the festival marionettes to life and a 3-D showing of the Furukawa Matsuri is a great substitute for those unable to attend the actual festival. (☎73-3511; fax 73-6660. Open daily Mar.-Nov. 9am-5pm; Dec.-Feb. 9am-4:30pm. ¥800, high school students ¥700, under 15 ¥400.) Across the square is the **Hida No Takumi Cultural Museum** (Hida No Takumi Bunka-kan; 飛騨の匠文化館), 10-1, Ichi-no-machi, a small museum dedicated to prominent local *takumi*-style wooden architecture. The building is an excellent example of this style, with amazing wooden beams and craftswork, built without a single nail.

(☎73-3321. Open Apr.-Nov. daily 9am-5pm; Dec.-Feb. Su-M and W-Sa 9am-4:30pm; Mar. Su-M and W-Sa 9am-5pm. ¥200, under 15 ¥100. Joint ticket to both museums ¥900, high school students ¥810, under 15 ¥450.)

◘ **FESTIVALS.** The main festival is the **Furukawa Matsuri,** an extravagant event held annually on April 19 and 20. Nine ornamented multi-tiered floats parade down the roads during the day, but the highlight is the Okoshi Daiko, held after dark. At midnight, hundreds of rowdy young men, scantily clad in loincloths, proceed through the town and compete fiercely to place small drums atop a stage. The festival is overwhelming both in terms of the tremendous energy of the participants, and because of the sheer mass of nearly naked men squashed together, and is appropriately nicknamed the Hadaka Matsuri (Naked Festival). On October 16 is the **Kitsune Hi Matsuri** (Fox Fire Festival). Quieter than the Furukawa Matsuri, it features townsmen in fox costumes proceeding through town with lanterns. The slightly spiritual event concludes when the parade reaches the Okura Inari Shrine and enacts a wedding ceremony, whereupon a huge bonfire is started. The festival is traditionally believed to bring good luck to the village and bless its people.

TOYAMA (富山)　　　☎076

The modern, industrial city of Toyama has few sights, and there's little reason to stay here when the more interesting vistas of Kanazawa and Takayama are so close by. Toyama is, however, an important transportation hub, squatting at the intersection of the JR Hokuriku and Takayama lines. A critical access point for the northern Japan Alps and the cities of the Japan Sea coast, Toyama provides a link to Tateyama Station, the start or end point for the Tateyama-Kurobe Alpine Route.

▣ **TRANSPORTATION.** The **JR Hokuriku Line** runs from Niigata (express: 3 hr., ¥6620) through Naoetsu (express: 80min., ¥4280) to Toyama, then continues west through Takaoka (local: 15min., ¥320) to Kanazawa (express: 40min., ¥2610; local: 60min., ¥950); Nagoya (express: 3½hr., ¥7770); Kyōto (express: 3½hr., ¥7250); and Ōsaka (express: 4hr., ¥7890). To access the Takayama area, take the **JR Takayama Line** through Hida-Furukawa (local: 2½hr., ¥1450) to Takayama (express: 1½hr., ¥2770; local: 3hr., ¥1620). The **Toyama-Tateyama Line** runs to Tateyama (30min., every 30min., ¥1170), where the Tateyama-Kurobe Alpine Route begins (p. 375).

◪ **PRACTICAL INFORMATION.** The **tourist information center,** 1-1-1, Sakurama-chi, outside JR Toyama Station's Central Exit, has English maps and pamphlets and can book beds after 2pm. They also have info on the Tateyama-Kurobe Alpine Route. (☎432-9715. Open daily 8:30am-8pm.) The **ATMs** inside the post office accept international cards. (Available M-F 7am-11pm, Sa 9am-9pm, Su 9am-7pm.) The **Hokuriku Bank** will advance money on credit cards if you show a passport. (Open M-F 9am-3pm.) In an emergency, call ☎110 for **police,** ☎119 for **fire** or **ambulance.** There's a **police box** outside JR Toyama Station's Central Exit. For Internet access, head from the North Exit of JR Toyama Station to **Internet Cafe Captain,** on the second floor of the Urban Place building. (☎431-7419. Open daily 10am-9pm. Closed every 2nd and 4th M of the month. ¥300 per hr.) **Toyama Central Post Office,** 6-6, Sakurabashi-dōri, is a 5min. walk to the left from the station. (☎432-3920; fax 432-3975. Open M-F 9am-7pm, Sa 9am-5pm, Su 9am-12:30pm.) **Postal code:** 930.

◪ **ACCOMMODATIONS.** Business hotels surround JR Toyama Station, the best of which is **Toyoko Inn Jr Toyama Eki-Mae ❸,** 1-4-5, Sakuramachi. Across from JR Toyama Station's Central Exit, this value hotel offers spacious, brightly lit rooms with Internet access and semi-double beds. (☎405-1045; www.toyoko-inn.com. Breakfast free. Check-in 4pm. Check-out 10am. Singles ¥5300-5800; twins ¥8800; doubles ¥7800.) A slightly more upscale choice is the **Toyama Chitetsu Hotel ❸**, 1-1-1, Sakuramachi, adjacent to JR Toyama Station's Central Exit. (☎443-6611; fax 442-8153. Breakfast ¥1200. Dinner ¥2000. Check-in 3pm. Check-out 11am. Singles ¥6500; twins ¥13,000; doubles ¥12,000.) **Hotel Alpha One ❸**, 1-1-1, Shintō-chō, diagonally across from JR Toyama Station's Central Exit is an economy business hotel. Good location is complemented by additional bonuses, among them free Internet access, a fridge, an iron, a TV and VCR, and an ice machine. (☎433-6000. Check-in 4pm. Check-out 10am. Singles ¥5200-5500; twins ¥10,000; triples ¥16,800.)

◪ SIGHTS. The single sight near the city is the **Toyama Municipal Folkcraft Village** (Toyama-shi Minzoku Mingei Mura; 富山市民俗民芸村), 1118-1, An'yobo, a complex of eight museums, each displaying a selected genre of traditional artifacts. Choices include the Museum of Medicine Peddlers, the Thatched Roof Folk Art Museum, the Enzan Municipal Tea Ceremony House, the Museum of Folklore, the Folk Art Museum, the Museum of Ceramic Art, and the Memorial Art Gallery for Takamura Gyūjin. (☎433-8270; fax 433-8370. Open Tu-Su 9am-4:30pm. ¥630 for all 8, ¥110 for 1; under 15 ¥320/¥50.) The museum village is at the base of Kuresan Kōen Hill Park, inside which lies **Chōkei-ji** (長慶寺). The temple's most remarkable feature is the **Gohyaku Rakan** (五百羅漢), 500 tiny statues of Buddha's disciples. To reach the sights, take the Kureha Rōjin Center-bound #14 bus from the JR station to Toyama-shi Minzoku Mingei Mura Shita (10min., every 1-2hr., ¥250).

TATEYAMA-KUROBE ALPINE ROUTE
(立山黒部アルペンルート)

A memorable way of traveling from the Japan Sea coast to the Shinshu region of Nagano Prefecture is via the grand Tateyama-Kurobe Alpine Route. The journey crosses the northern Japan Alps, moving travelers in small segments by various forms of transportation. Using buses, ropeways, cable cars, trolley buses, and trains, the 90km route offers scenery, hikes, and a one-of-a-kind experience. Some break the route at Murodō to cut costs, turning back towards Toyama; the true value of the route, however, is in the views at Kurobe Dam and the experience of completing it all, so if you're going to do it, go all the way. The entire route takes 6-7hr., and can be traveled heading east from Toyama and Tateyama, or west from Nagano and Shinano Ōmachi. While it may not be worth the cost just for the heck of it, the price is close to that for the train from the coast to Nagano, so it's a worthy way to cap off a trip if you're traveling that direction anyway.

🛈 PRACTICAL INFORMATION

Information facilities are limited along the route, so get pamphlets and maps in Toyama (p. 356) or Shinano Ōmachi (p. 340). A **tourist office** at the Murodō bus terminal provides basic assistance. (☎076-465-5771. Open daily 9am-5pm.) For **hiking information**, call ☎076-442-2020. In an **emergency**, call ☎076-465-5778.

🛏 ACCOMMODATIONS

There are hotels and lodges throughout the route and along some of the hiking routes, as well as a few campsites. Reservations are strongly advised. At Tateyama Station, try **Mochida Kan ❸** (もちだ館; ☎076-482-1890; singles ¥7000) or **Tateyama**

AT A GLANCE

CLIMATE: Cool year-round, with extraordinarily harsh winters and chilly summers. Spring temperatures are -5-10°C (23-50°F). Summer temperatures rise to 7-15°C (45-60°F). Autumn comes quickly: by early Oct., temperatures near freezing.

HIGHLIGHTS: Mountains, hiking, the Kurobe Dam.

GATEWAYS: Tateyama (near Toyama, p. 369) and Shinano Ōmachi (p. 340).

FEES: Only transportation fees. The entire route from Toyama to Shinano Ōmachi costs ¥10,320. Most convenient is to buy a package ticket which covers all transportation, either at Tateyama or Ogisawa Station.

WHEN TO GO: The best time to go is spring, early summer, or fall. During July and August, the route is crowded with tourist groups. Due to harsh winters, the route is only open April 20-November 30.

Kan ❸ (立山館 ; ☎076-482-1229; singles ¥8000). **Hotel Tateyama ❺** (ホテル立山) is at Murodō Daira station. (☎076-465-3333. Open Apr. 10-Nov. 29. ¥17,000-27,000.) At the Midaghara bus stop between Bijodaira and Murodō lies **Midagahara Hotel ❺** (弥陀ヶ原ホテル ; ☎076-442-2222. Open Apr. 10-Nov. 29. ¥17,000-27,000.)

🎿 THE ROUTE

TOYAMA (富山) **TO TATEYAMA** (立山). The route begins officially at Tateyama. Access the town by the Toyama Chihō Tetsudō Line, which runs from Toyama via a pleasant rural landscape to Tateyama (50min., every hr., ¥1170).

TATEYAMA (立山) **TO BIJODAIRA** (美女平). From the second floor of Tateyama Station, hop on a **cable car** to ascend over 500m of mountain. As the car climbs, you can enjoy scenic views of nearby forests and rare wild trees (7min., ¥700).

BIJODAIRA (美女平) **TO MURODŌ** (室堂). At Bijodaira, transfer to a **Kōgen Bus** (55min., ¥1660), which travels uphill through mountain scenery and across the **Midagahara** plateau. Easily one of the best parts of the route, this leg lets you watch the scenery change from green trees and shrubbery to snow-covered plains. Highlights include the enormous **Tateyama Sugi Tree** and the **Shomyo Waterfall,** one of Japan's largest. If you're traveling between May and early June, the bus will pass through a 20m-high tunnel of towering snow just before arriving at Murodō. Although Murodō Bus Terminal is crowded with tour groups and blaring megaphones, there are short hikes nearby if you're ready to stretch your legs. A 20min. hike northwest is **Jigokudani Onsen,** the highest altitude *onsen* in Japan, while a 10min. hike north leads to **Mikuriga Pond.**

MURODŌ (室堂) **TO DAIKANBŌ** (大観峰). The next leg of the journey is an **underground trolley bus,** which runs directly beneath Mt. Tateyama. Japan's highest altitude trolley bus trip is a dark, unexciting one through a small tunnel (10min., ¥2100), but to make up for it, the view across Kurobe Pond (Kurobe Ko) at Daikanbō, with snow-covered mountains in the background, is simply gorgeous.

DAIKANBŌ (大観峰) **TO KUROBE DAIRA** (黒部平). From Daikanbō, transfer to the Tateyama **ropeway,** which descends a quick, steep 500m. The one-of-a-kind ropeway has no poles along its entire span, and the views as you move across the mountains are spectacular (7min., ¥1260).

KUROBE DAIRA (黒部平) **TO KUROBE KO** (黒部湖). A short **underground cable car** journey through a steep tunnel brings you to **Kurobe Dam** (5min., ¥840).

KUROBE KO (黒部湖) TO KUROBE DAM (黒部ダム). At Kurobe Ko Station, a pedestrian path crosses the massive dam. On one side is emerald-green **Kurobe Pond** (Kurobe Ko) while on the other is the stunning **Kurobe Dam**, spurting millions of gallons of water. Climb to the old lookout point for an aerial view or descend to the new lookout point for a closer look. A 30min. **boat cruise** ferries travelers across the pond. (☎0261-22-0804. ¥930, under 12 ¥470.) For your next connection, walk to Kurobe Dam Station via the long tunnel at the end of the walkway.

KUROBE DAM (黒部ダム) TO ŌGISAWA (扇沢). Another dark **underground trolley bus** ride whisks you to Ōgisawa Station, crossing the Toyama/Nagano prefectural boundary to the end of the alpine route (16min., ¥1260).

ŌGISAWA (扇沢) TO SHINANO ŌMACHI (信濃大町). From Ogisawa Station, frequent buses run to Shinano Ōmachi Station (40min., ¥1330), where you can catch connecting local and express trains to Matsumoto. Buses also run irregularly between Ōgisawa and JR Nagano Station (100min., 6 per day, ¥2300).

KANAZAWA (金沢)   ☎076

When travelers dream about Japan, Kanazawa is the city they see. The sprawling streets are jam-packed with sights and shops, while Kenroku-en garden and Kanazawa Castle Park add a natural touch to the otherwise urban setting. The Asano and Sai rivers flow along the east and west sides of the city, framing this ideal destination. The city's history is intertwined with that of the Maeda clan, the second most influential family in feudal Japan, who ruled the city for 300 years between the 16th and 18th centuries. Under the Maedas' leadership, Kanazawa grew into an extraordinarily prosperous region, and it retains its feudal legacy with well-preserved *samurai* residences. Art and culture are highly regarded, as apparent from the city's production of traditional silks, lacquerware, and pottery.

ON THE WEB	Kanazawa: www.city.kanazawa.ishikawa.jp

✈ INTERCITY TRANSPORTATION

Flights: Komatsu Airport, ☎121-9803. 30km southwest of the city, the airport is serviced by JAL, ANA, and JAS. Flights to: **Fukuoka** (1¼hr., 3 per day, ¥28,000); **Kagoshima** (1¼hr., 1 per day, ¥30,000); **Okinawa** (2hr., 1 per day, ¥34,500); **Sapporo** (1½hr., 1 per day, ¥31,000); **Sendai** (1hr., 1 per day, ¥23,000); **Tōkyō** (1hr., 11 per day, ¥18,500); **Seoul, Korea** (1½hr.; 3 per week M, W, F; ¥41,200). A shuttle bus runs between Kanazawa and the airport (40-55min., every 30-60min., ¥1100).

Trains: JR Kanazawa Station, ☎261-1700. The fastest way to get to Kanazawa from **Tōkyō** is to take the Joetsu *shinkansen* to Echigo Yuzawa Station, transferring there to a limited express to Kanazawa (4hr., ¥12,700). Alternatively, take a sleeper train from Tōkyō's Ueno Station around 11pm, arriving early the next morning (7½hr., 2 per night, ¥10,690). The JR Hokuriku Line runs from **Toyama** (local: 2hr., ¥950) and **Takaoka** (local: 90min., ¥740) in the northeast, continuing through Kanazawa and south to **Fukui** (local: 1½hr., ¥1280); **Kyōto** (express: 2½hr., ¥6200); **Maibara** (express: 2hr., ¥5040); **Nagoya** (express: 3hr., ¥6620); and **Ōsaka** (express: 3hr., ¥6930). The JR Nanao Line services **Noto-hantō** and **Wajima** (2¼hr., every 30-60min.).

Buses: Kanazawa Hokutetsu Bus Terminal, ☎233-2050. Long-distance buses depart from the East Exit of JR Kanazawa Station, to: **Kyōto** (4hr., 5 per day, ¥4060); **Matsumoto** (5hr., 2 per day, ¥4000); **Nagoya** (4hr., 10 per day, ¥4060); **Niigata** (4¾hr., 2 per day, ¥4580); **Sendai** (8½hr., 1 per day, ¥8970); **Tōkyō** (7½hr., 6 per day, ¥7840); **Toyama** (3¼hr., 2 per day, ¥3300); **Yokohama** (8¼hr., 1 per day, ¥8250). The Hokutetsu Bus to **Wajima** and **Noto-hantō** also uses this terminal (2hr., ¥2200).

▛ LOCAL TRANSPORTATION

Kanazawa ·

⌂ ACCOMMODATIONS
APA Hotel Kanazawa Chūō, 24
Garden Hotel Kanazawa, 2
Hotel Econo Kanazawa Asper, 27
Kanazawa Youth Hostel (HI), 6
Katamachi Tour Hotel, 17
Matsui Youth Hostel (HI), 32
Murataya Ryokan, 25
R&B Kanazawa Eki Nishi Guchi, 1
Tōyoko Inn Kanazawa Kōrinbō, 7

🏛 MUSEUMS
Honda Museum, 30
Ishikawa Prefectural Museum of Art, 26
Ishikawa Prefectural History Museum, 33
Ishikawa Prefectural Museum of Traditional Products and Crafts, 18
Kaga Yūzen Traditional Industry Hall, 8
Kanazawa Phonograph Museum, 5
Nakamura Memorial Museum, 31

✴ FOOD
Calra, 10
Idobata, 15
Kōsuiten Rāmen, 20
Peperoncino, 16
Shanghai Chusha Yien, 21
Shiki no Table, 9
Sushi Genbei, 4
Yotteki-Ya, 14

🍷 NIGHTLIFE
Bar Spoon, 28
I No Ichiban, 29
Live House Kento's, 23
Offshore, 12
Polé Polé, 19

🛍 SHOPPING
Daiei Dept. Store & Supermarket, 3
Kōrinbō 109 Dept. Store, 13
Kōrinbō Daiwa Dept. Store, 11
Labbro Dept. Store, 22

Public Transportation: Kanazawa is served by an extensive, reliable bus network. Local buses depart from outside JR Kanazawa Station's East Exit, with fares starting at ¥200. To get to **Kōrinbō** and **Katamachi**, take bus #20, 21, or 30 from boarding area #6, 7, or 8 (10min., ¥200). To access **Kenroku-en**, take #10 or 11 from boarding area #3 to Kenroku-en Shita stop (10min., ¥200). A daypass for all local buses (¥900) is available on board or at the Hokutetsu Kankō Bus Company office, outside the East Exit.

Taxis: Ishikawa Kōtsū, ☎231-4131. Ishikawa Kintetsu Taxi, ☎221-3265. Hokuriku Kōtsū, ☎241-6111.

Car Rental: Toyota Rent-a-Lease Ishikawa (☎224-0100), **Nisshin Rent-a Car** (☎232-4123), and **Nippon Rent-a-Car Service** (☎263-0919) are all located outside JR Kanazawa Station's West Exit. From ¥5000 per day.

Bike Rental: Hokutetsu Rent-a-Cycle (☎264-0919) is at the JR station's West Exit. ¥300 for 2hr., ¥1000 per day. Open daily 9am-6pm. **JR Kanazawa Eki Rent-a-Cycle** (☎261-1721) is in the station. ¥600 for 4hr., ¥1000 per day. Open daily 9am-6pm.

✴ ORIENTATION

One of the largest cities on the Sea of Japan coast, Kanazawa comprises a collection of varied districts. While there are hotels around the JR station, the city's true center is around the **Kōrinbō** and **Katamachi** districts, 10min. southeast of the station by bus. **Hyakuman-goku-dōri** runs from the train station to the **Kōrinbō intersection**, where the Kōrinbō 109 and Daiwa department stores stand, then continues east toward Kenroku-en. Sights and museums cluster around **Kenroku-en** and the **Kanazawa Castle Park**. A shopping arcade extends from the Kōrinbō intersection to the **Katamachi intersection,** lined with restaurants, cafes, and shops. South of Katamachi, across the **Sai River,** are the **Teramachi** temples, while the **Nagamachi** district's *samurai* houses are a 5min. walk west of the Kōrinbō intersection. East of the city lie the mountains of the **Higashiyama** district, popular for hiking.

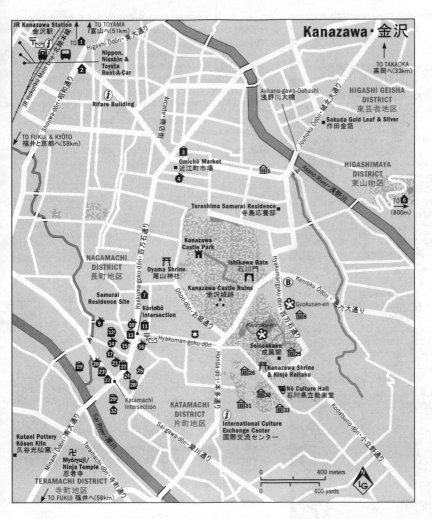

Kanazawa・金沢

✂ PRACTICAL INFORMATION

Tourist Office: The excellent **Kanazawa Tourist Information Center**, Hiro-oka Machi 1 (☎231-6200), is inside JR Kanazawa Station, by the entrance to Hyakubangai Station department store. English-speaking staff always available. Open daily 9am-7pm. For advice on living in Kanazawa, head to the **Ishikawa Foundation for International Exchange**, 1-5-3, Honmachi (☎262-5931; fax 263-5931), on the 3rd and 4th fl. of the Rifare Bldg., 5min. straight out of JR Kanazawa Station's East Exit. Friendly staff, English newspapers, magazines, and TV news. Open M-Sa 9am-6pm, Su 9am-5pm.

THE HIDDEN DEAL

ALL THAT GLITTERS

As you browse through Kanazawa's shops, gold-decorated plates, boxes, and accessories may catch your eye. Most of Kanazawa's, and a large percentage of Japan's, gold leaf production takes place at the **Sakuda Gold and Silver Leaf Company** (Sakuda Kinpaku; 作田金箔工芸), in the Higashiyama district.

At first, the shop resembles any other souvenir store, with gold-rimmed cups and jewelry boxes lining its shelves. Venture inside, however, and you'll be led to the workshop behind the shop. The souvenirs outside are brilliant, but the real attraction is the demonstration of the gold-leaf making process. Craftsman pick up amazingly thin sheets of gold, then blow, cut, and place it. The delicacy of the work is mind-boggling.

After exiting the workshop, you'll be served tea with flakes of gold, said to be good for health and beauty. Upstairs are a collection of gold-leaf paintings, and two bathrooms, worth over ¥30,000,000, with gold and platinum tiles, walls, and decorations. For ¥500, you can coat chopsticks with gold leaf. *(1-3-27, Higashiyama.* ☎*251-6777; www.success21.com/goldleaf. From JR Kanazawa Station, take a bus from Gate #4 to Higashiyama Stop (10min., ¥200). It's a 2min. walk. Open daily 9am-6pm. Workshop closed noon-1pm. Reservations required for chopstick gilding (9:30am, 1:15, 3pm), which takes 60-90min.)*

Tours: Kanazawa Goodwill Guide Network offers free guided tours in English. Make reservations through the tourist office or at ☎239-2353. Available daily 8am-9pm. Volunteer guide group **Maido-San** (☎232-5555; fax 232-1170) works through the Kanazawa Tourist Bureau. They provide free tours, can accommodate travelers' needs, and have some English speakers. Make reservations 1 week ahead. Available daily 9am-5pm.

Currency Exchange: Hokuriku Bank can change money, as can other national banks.

ATM: Post office ATMs (see below) accept international cards. Station ATM available M-F 8am-9pm, Sa 9am-9pm, Su 9am-7pm; Kōrinbō ATM available M-F 7am-11pm, Sa 9am-9pm, Su 9am-7pm. International ATMs can also be found on the 1st fl. of **Daiei** department store (open M-F 10am-6pm, Sa-Su 10am-5pm), the 1st fl. of **Labbro** department store (open Su-Tu and Th-Sa 10am-6pm) and the 7th fl. of **Daiwa** department store (open Su-Tu and Th-Sa 10am-6pm).

Alternatives to Tourism: The **International Culture Exchange Center** (☎223-9575) inside the Shakyo Center by Kenroku-en offers language courses. The **Kanazawa International Exchange Foundation** (☎220-2522; www.kief.jp), on the 2nd fl. of the Rifare Bldg., below the Ishikawa Foundation for International Exchange (see above), provides cultural experiences through volunteer work and homestays. Open M-Su 9am-5pm.

Luggage Storage: Coin lockers inside **JR Kanazawa Station** (¥300-500) or outside **APA Hotel Kanazawa** (see **Accommodations**) near Kōrinbō intersection (¥200).

Lost Property: Lost and Found in the JR station. Open daily 9am-6pm.

English-Language Bookstore: The **Meitetsu Book Center,** 1-5-3, Honmachi, on the 2nd floor of the Rifare Bldg., has English books and magazines. Open daily 10am-8pm.

Emergency: Police ☎110. Fire or ambulance ☎119.

Police: The **Prefectural Police Office,** 2-1-1, Hirosaka (☎62-1161), is located inside the Prefectural Government Building.

Hospital/Medical Services: Kanazawa's main hospital is **Kanazawa University Hospital,** 13-1, Takaramachi (☎262-8151), 1km southeast of Kenroku-en.

Internet Access: The **Ishikawa Foundation for International Exchange** (see above) provides free Internet access in its library. 30min. max. **Kanazawa Biz Cafe,** 2-2-9, Katamachi (☎233-1008), in the shopping arcade by Kōrinbō, offers free Internet access with any food (¥600) or drink (¥350) purchase. Open daily 11am-9pm.

Post Office: There's a post office **branch** in Hyakubangai department store inside the JR station, Hiro-oka Machi 1 (☎224-3822). Open M-F 9am-7pm. The **Kōrinbō Post Office,** 1-1-32 (☎221-1724), is a 2min. walk toward Kenroku-en from Kōrinbō 109 department store and the main intersection. Open M-F 9am-6pm. **Postal Code:** 920.

ACCOMMODATIONS

Kanazawa has many options around JR Kanazawa Station, although staying near Kōrinbō and Katamachi provides better access to sights, restaurants, and bars.

Tōyoko Inn Kanazawa Kōrinbō (東横イン金沢香林坊), 1-2-35, Kōrinbō (☎265-1045; www.toyoko-inn.co.jp). Take the bus from the JR station to the Kōrinbō stop. From the main intersection and Kōrinbō 109, walk toward Kenroku-en and take the 1st left. A clean, comfy business hotel with bright rooms. Semi-double beds, free Internet, and free Japanese breakfast. Laundry ¥200. Parking ¥800. Check-in 4pm. Check-out 10am. Reservations recommended. Singles ¥4800; twins ¥8800; doubles ¥7800. ❷

R&B Kanazawa Eki Nishi Guchi (R&B 金沢駅西口), 1-3-31, Hiro-oka (☎224-8080; www.washingtonhotel.co.jp). A 3min. walk from the JR station's West Exit. One of the best values near the station. Business hotel with attractive wooden interior. Semi-double beds. Free Western breakfast. Check-in 4pm. Check-out 10am. Singles ¥5000. ❷

Hotel Econo Kanazawa Asper (ホテルエコノ金沢アスパー), 2-24-13, Katamachi (☎234-0001; www.greens.co.jp). From the Kōrinbō bus stop, go down the arcade to the Katamachi intersection and turn right. It's a 2min. walk. Centrally located business hotel. Free Internet and free breakfast. Laundry ¥100. Parking ¥1000. Reception 24hr. Check-in 3pm. Check-out 10am. Singles ¥4200; twins ¥7000; triples ¥10,000. ❷

APA Hotel Kanazawa Chūō (APA ホテル金沢中央), 1-5-24, Katamachi (☎235-2111; www.apahotel.com). From the Kōrinbō bus stop, continue down the shopping arcade away from Kanazawa Station. The hotel is to your left. Opened in July 2003, this upscale choice has a grand interior and modern exterior. Open-air bath and spa facilities, free Internet access, and attractive rooms. Check-in 3pm. Check-out 11am. Singles ¥7000-8000; twins ¥13,000-16,000; semi-doubles ¥10,000; doubles ¥11,000. ❸

Matsui Youth Hostel (HI) (松井ユースホステル), 1-9-3, Katamachi (☎221-0275). From the Kōrinbō intersection, go down Hyakuman-goku-dōri to the Katamachi intersection, turn left, walk 5min. on Chūō-dōri, and it's down a road to the right. The more convenient of Kanazawa's 2 hostels. Welcoming dorms. In the city center, though the 10pm curfew limits nights out. No meals. Check-in 4pm. Check-out 10am. Curfew 10pm. Closed Dec. 30-Jan. 2. Dorms ¥3100, nonmembers ¥4100; singles ¥4200. ❶

Kanazawa Youth Hostel (HI) (金沢ユースホステル), 37, Suehiro-chō (☎252-3414). From the JR station, take a Utatsuyama Kōen-bound bus to Youth Hostel Mae (25min., ¥370); it's across the road. A distance from the city, Kanazawa's hilltop hostel offers Japanese dorms. The downsides are the location and the strict rules. Breakfast ¥600. Dinner ¥1000. Kitchen. Bike rental. Reception 4-10pm. Check-in 4pm. Check-out 10am. Curfew 10pm. Dorms ¥2900, nonmembers ¥3900; singles ¥3900. ❶

Katamachi Tour Hotel (片町ツアーホテル), 2-5-18, Katamachi (☎223-3636). From the Kōrinbō intersection, walk away from the JR station toward the shopping arcade. Turn right and it's a 1min. walk to the left. Standard business hotel; the selling point is location. Check-in 4pm. Check-out 10am. Singles ¥4800; twins ¥8800. ❷

Garden Hotel Kanazawa (ガーデンホテル金沢), 2-16-16, Honmachi (☎263-3333; www.gardenhotel-kanazawa.co.jp). Across from JR Kanazawa Station's East Exit. An upscale hotel. Prices reflect the spacious rooms, elegant lobby, and courteous service. Check-in 3pm. Check-out 10am. Singles ¥6930; twins and doubles ¥13,200. ❸

Murataya Ryokan (村田屋旅館), 1-5-2, Katamachi (☎263-0455). From the Kōrinbō bus stop, head down Hyakuman-goku-dōri towards Katamachi, turning left at the 2nd alley. Turn left again at the 1st intersection and it's a short walk. A friendly ryokan in the heart of town. Your best choice for Japanese-style accommodations. Easy access to sights. Check-in 4pm. Check-out 10am. ¥4500, with 2 meals ¥6300. ❷

🌜 FOOD

Kaga dishes, Kanazawa's elegant, traditional cuisine, incorporating local seafood and vegetables, are served at older, more upscale area restaurants. International restaurants cluster in the Kōrinbō and Katamachi districts. The fourth floor of **Kōrinbō 109** department store hosts inexpensive restaurants. For the catch of the day or fresh produce, head to the **Omichō Ichiba** (p. 367), a market known as "Kanazawa's kitchen." The basement of **Daiei** department store, 2-1, Obari-chō (☎223-7111), at the intersection of Hyakuman Goku-dōri and the road from JR Kanazawa Station's East Exit, has groceries. (Open daily 10am-9pm.)

Idobata (井十八太), 2-7-2, Katamachi (☎233-2274). From the Kōrinbō intersection, head down the road left of Kōrinbō 109 department store. To your left at the small T-intersection. A casual, friendly *izakaya*. Inexpensive dishes (¥380-780) make it affordable to try a variety of foods. Cocktails ¥400. Beer ¥350. Open M-Sa 5pm-midnight. ❷

Peperoncino (ペペロンチーノ), 1-3-27, Katamachi (☎232-5253). At the Kōrinbō intersection, diagonally across from Kōrinbō 109. A cute Italian restaurant serving over 30 types of spaghetti (¥700), pizza (¥800), and omelettes (¥600). The dishes are tasty, though portions tend to be small. Open M-Sa 11am-11pm, Su 11am-9pm. ❷

Shanghai Chusha Yien (上海酒家豫園), 2-5-6, Katamachi (☎232-1580). From the Kōrinbō intersection, go down the street left of Kōrinbō 109. Turn left at the T-intersection; it's a 3min. walk. Waitresses in Chinese dresses add to the ambience. Authentic Shanghainese food (¥750 per dish). Open daily 11am-2pm and 5pm-3am. ❸

Calra (カルラ), 2-1-1, Kōrinbō (☎220-5072). In the basement of Kōrinbō 109 department store. Amazing bakery stocked with fresh pastries, sandwiches, rolls with sausage or ham, cream-filled breads, and pizza (¥100-180). Open daily 9am-7pm. ❶

Shiki no Table (四季のテーブル), 2-8-1, Katamachi (☎265-6155). In the Nagamachi district. Head down the street left of Kōrinbō 109, turn right at the T-intersection, and take the 2nd left. It's on your right after a 5min. walk. For Kaga dishes, try this elegant restaurant, which prides itself on fish fresh from the ocean and well-balanced homemade dishes. Full sets from ¥1600. Open Su-Tu and Th-Sa 9:30am-10:30pm. ❸

Sushi Genbei (鮨源平), Omichō Ichiba (☎261-4349). Inside Omicho Ichiba. From the Musashi entrance, take the 2nd right; it's a 5min. walk to your left. This tiny sushi bar (10-12 seats) serves only the best and freshest. With over 70 different kinds (¥200-1200 per piece), it's a sure treat. Sets from ¥2000. Open M-Sa 10:30am-7pm. ❸

Kōsuiten Rāmen (壺水天ラーメン), 2-25-19, Katamachi (☎264-8278). From the Kōrinbō intersection, head toward the arcade to the Katamachi intersection and turn right; it's a 5min. walk. This *rāmen* cafe serves flavored noodles (¥650-800) in a cozy interior. Open incredibly late—great news for hungry clubbers. Open daily 11am-5am. ❷

Yotteki-Ya (よってき屋), 2-6-1, Katamachi (☎222-6001). At the entrance to Kikura Machi-dōri. Head down the street left of Kōrinbō 109 and turn left at the T-intersection. It's the 3rd right, then walk 5min. A stylish spot to make *okonomiyaki* and *monjya-yaki* (Japanese pancakes). Terrific menu; good prices. Open daily 11am-4am. ❷

SIGHTS

AROUND KENROKU-EN (兼六園周辺)

KENROKU-EN (兼六園). You'll immediately understand why Kenroku-en been named one of Japan's top three gardens. Kenroku-en is easily Kanazawa's best attraction, luring visitors from all around Japan. Because of the garden's immense popularity, its grounds get crowded with tourist groups. An early-morning or late-afternoon stroll through the garden's sights will help you avoid crowds. The garden's name evokes the six features of perfection—antiquity, artifice, seclusion, spaciousness, abundant water, and sweeping views—necessary to any true Japanese garden. Features of the landscape include the **Kasumiga Ike,** a large clouded lake, spatially and symbolically the center of Kenroku-en; Japan's first **fountain,** built in 1861; and **Kotoji Tōrō,** a tremendously famous two-legged stone lantern. The sprawling grounds boast several ponds, cherry and plum trees, artistically pruned old pines, and stone pathways and bridges. *(1-1, Marunouchi. North of Kōrinbō and the center of Kanazawa. Take the bus to Kenroku-en Shita stop, or walk 5min. up Hyakuman Gokud-dōri from the Kōrinbō intersection, away from Kōrinbō 109. ☎ 234-3800; fax 234-5292. Open daily Mar. 1-Oct. 15 7am-6pm; Oct. 16-Feb. 28 8am-4:30pm. ¥300, under 12 ¥100.)*

GYOKUSEN-EN (玉泉園). Smaller and less grand than Kenroku-en, this charming two-level garden offers an enjoyable, tranquil atmosphere. Sip green tea in the tearoom looking out on the green paths and water. This garden shouldn't replace a visit to Kenroku-en, but could be a nice accent to your visit. *(1-1, Marunouchi. 2min. south of Kenroku-en Shita bus stop. ☎ 221-0181. Open Apr.-Nov. daily 9am-4pm. ¥500.)*

SEISONKAKU (成巽閣). An elegant two-story residence constructed in 1863, this building is an architect's delight. Playful decorations, including turtles and fish on the sliding screens, adorn the mansion. In a break from traditional architecture of the time, the windows are constructed of glass imported from the Netherlands. The rooms' bold colors give the place a glamorous feel. *(1-2, Kenroku. Located near Kenroku-en, adjacent to Kanazawa Shrine and across the road from the Ishikawa Prefectural Museum of Art. ☎ 221-0580. Open 9am-5pm, closed W. ¥600; under 15 ¥300.)*

KANAZAWA SHRINE (金沢神社) AND KINJŌ REITAKU (金城霊沢). Quiet and hidden behind trees and shrubbery, Kanazawa Shrine is often missed by the roaming tourist hordes, but the brilliantly colored structure and reverent atmosphere are worth a visit. Near the shrine is Kinjō Reitaku, the spring from which Kanazawa derives its name. *(Right by Kenroku-en, across the road from the Ishikawa Prefectural Museum of Art. ☎ 261-0502. Open daily 8am-5pm. Free.)*

THE ISHIKAWA PREFECTURAL MUSEUM OF TRADITIONAL PRODUCTS AND CRAFTS (ISHIKAWA KENRITSU DENTŌ SANGYŌ KŌGEIKAN; 石川県立伝統産業工芸館). This impressive small museum displays dyed silk, religious items, tools, lacquerware, musical instruments, and other crafts. The variety and quality of the artwork, as well as the attention obviously lavished on the displays, attests to Kanazawa's regard for the arts. *(By Kenroku-en, next to Seisokukan and Kanzawa Shrine. ☎ 262-2020. Open daily 9am-5pm. Closed every 3rd Th Apr.-Nov.; every Th Dec.-Mar. ¥250.)*

ISHIKAWA PREFECTURAL HISTORY MUSEUM (ISHIKAWA KENRITSU REKISHI HAKUBUTSUKAN; 石川県立歴史博物館). An old brick building, once used as a military storehouse, holds displays explaining the history of Kanazawa and its surroundings. The third exhibition room is particularly noteworthy, with reconstructions of old merchant houses and streets. *(3-1, Dewa-machi. West of Kenroku-en, it's a 15min. walk east of Kōrinbō intersection and a 5min. walk south from Kenroku-en Shita bus stop. ☎ 262-3236. Open daily 9am-5pm. ¥250, college students ¥200, under 18 free.)*

ISHIKAWA PREFECTURAL MUSEUM OF ART (ISHIKAWA KENRITSU BIJUTSUKAN; 石川県立美術館). Stunning works of art, including intricate carvings, paintings, magnificent calligraphy scrolls, and lacquered plates and statues, fill this important museum. The collection is a good mix of the traditional and the contemporary. Brilliant special exhibits sometimes outdo the permanent displays. *(2-1, Dewa-machi. West of Kenroku-en. A 10min. walk east of Kōrinbō intersection and 8min. south of Kenroku-en Shita bus stop. ☎231-7580; www.ishibi.pref.ishikawa.jp. Open daily 9:30am-5pm. ¥350, college students ¥280, under 18 free. Additional fee for special exhibitions.)*

HONDA MUSEUM (HONDA ZŌHINKAN; 本多蔵品館). This museum displays items collected by the Honda family. The old warrior uniforms and military equipment are fascinating, while cups, burners, and other daily items shine light onto the lives of traditional families. As chief retainers of the Maeda clan, the Honda family was of considerable rank; their possessions hold great historical value. *(3-1, Dewa-machi. West of Kenroku-en, it's a 15min. walk east of Kōrinbō intersection and 5min. south of Kenroku-en Shita bus stop. ☎261-0500. Open Mar.-Oct. Su-W and F-Sa 9am-5pm. ¥500.)*

NAKAMURA MEMORIAL MUSEUM (NAKAMURA KINEN BIJUTSUKAN; 中村記念美術館). The restored residence of wealthy *sake* brewer Nakamura Eizan features tea ceremony utensils, traditional pottery, amazing calligraphy, and other important crafts. The highlight of a visit is the free cup of delicious green tea. *(2-1, Dewa-machi. Behind the Ishikawa Prefectural Art Museum. ☎221-0751; www.city.kanazawa.ishikawa.jp/bunho/nakamura. Open Su-M and W-Sa 9:30am-5pm. ¥300, under 15 ¥150.)*

OYAMA SHRINE (OYAMA JINJA; 尾山神社). While the shrine itself is unremarkable, the Shin-mon gate leading to the grounds is unique. The three-storied tower is ornamented with stained glass, while the ceiling is decorated with Japanese flowers. Merging Japanese, Chinese, and European architecture, the gate is unlike any other in Japan. The shrine, built in 1873, is dedicated to Lord Maeda Toshiie and his wife, who were significant in the development of Kanazawa. *(1-1-1, Oyama-machi. A 5min. walk from the Kōrinbō intersection on Hyakuman Goku-dōri towards the JR station, the shrine is located by Kanazawa Castle Park. ☎231-7210; fax 231-4685. Free.)*

ISHIKAWA GATE (ISHIKAWA MON; 石川門) AND KANAZAWA CASTLE PARK (KANAZAWA JŌ KŌEN; 金沢城公園). One of very few structures that survived a devastating 1881 fire, famous Ishikawa Gate marks the southern entrance to Kanazawa Castle Park. Surrounding the gate are stone walls which once protected Kanazawa Castle; other picturesque walls, as well as the castle itself, were reconstructed in 2001. *(Northwest of Kenroku-en, the Ishikawa Gate is a 5min. walk from the garden. ☎234-3800; www.pref.ishikawa.jp/kouen/map/park/kanazawa. Open daily Mar. 1-Oct. 15 7am-6pm; Oct. 16-Feb. 28 8am-4:30pm. ¥300, under 18 ¥100.)*

ISHIKAWA MODERN LITERATURE MUSEUM (ISHIKAWA KINDAI BUNGAKUKAN; 石川近代文学館). Kanazawa, once home to several prominent authors, has a rich literary background. This red-brick museum is in European style, and houses exhibits including old materials and works of Tokuda Shūsei, Izumi Kyoka, and Murō Saisei. Some knowledge of Japanese literature—or of the Japanese language, at least—is probably necessary for a full appreciation of the collection. *(2-2-5, Hirosaka. From the Kōrinbō intersection, walk north on Hyakuman-goku-dōri. The museum is a near Oyama Shrine. ☎262-5464; http://kinbun.com. Open daily 9:30am-5pm. ¥400, high and middle school students ¥100, under 12 free.)*

KAGA YŪZEN TRADITIONAL INDUSTRY HALL (KAGA YŪZEN DENTŌ SANGYŌ KAIKAN; 加賀友禅伝統産業会館). Peer at gorgeous Kaga Yūzen-style printed materials, and watch the dyeing process up-close at this popular museum. From modern works to valuable traditional items, a wide range of prints are on display. You can slip on a printed *kimono* or try your hand at dyeing and printmaking for a fee. *(Next to Gyokusen-en and Kenroku-en. ☎224-5511; www.kagayuzen.or.jp/kaikan. Open Mar. 21-Nov. 20 daily 9am-5pm; Nov. 21-Mar. 20 Su-Tu and Th-Sa 9am-5pm. ¥300.)*

NAGAMACHI DISTRICT (長町周辺)
NAGAMACHI SAMURAI RESIDENCE SITE (NAGAMACHI BUKEYASHIKI ATO; 長町武家屋敷跡).

A 5min. walk west of the central Kōrinbō district lands you worlds away from the modern city, depositing you in an area of preserved *samurai* residences. The cobbled roads are lined with dark yellow and grey earthen walls topped by ceramic roofs, and a stream trickles alongside the street. For a walking tour of area sights.

TERAMACHI DISTRICT (寺町周辺)
TERAMACHI TEMPLES (TERAMACHI JI-INGUN; 寺町寺院郡).

South of the city center, across the Sai River, lies a cluster of buildings known as the Teramachi temples. All of Kanazawa's religious buildings were moved to three districts surrounding the city—Teramachi, Shorin-no, and Utatsuyama—as a defensive tactic, and now more than 50 temples and shrines fill the narrow backstreets here.

MYŌRYŪ-JI TEMPLE (MYŌRYŪJI; 妙立寺).

Not your standard religious site, Myōryū-ji was nicknamed Ninja Temple (Ninja Dera; 忍者寺) because of the assassins who lived inside and constructed a fortress rife with trick doors, secret chambers and staircases, underground passages and tunnels, and other defensive trickery. Book a tour in advance (Japanese only) to see the interior and discover that, while the temple looks two stories high, there are seven levels hidden inside. From the observatory where the ninjas once kept guard, you can look across the city and its surrounding mountains and rivers. *(1-2-12, Nomachi. From the Kōrinbō intersection, head down towards the shopping arcade and the Katamachi intersection and continue straight across the bridge. The temple is a 5min. walk from the river on your left.* ☎241-2877; www.myoryuji.or.jp. *Open daily 9am-4:30pm. Tours every 30min. Reservations required. ¥800.)*

KUTANI POTTERY KŌSEN KILN (KUTANI KŌSEN GAMA; 九谷光仙窯).

Founded in 1868, the Kōsen kiln is the only working kiln in Kanazawa city. Staffers demonstrate the entire process of making indigenous Kutani pottery, from potting to designing to firing to painting. *(From Myōryū-ji, return to the main road and continue away from the city. Take the 1st right, then the 3rd left; the kiln is to your right after a 7min. walk.* ☎241-0902. *Open daily 9am-noon and 1pm-5pm. Free.)*

AROUND OMICHŌ ICHIBA (近江町市場)
OMICHŌ MARKET (OMICHŌ ICHIBA; 近江町市場).

A marketplace of narrow streets packed with stalls selling fruits, vegetables, and fish fresh from the Sea of Japan. The place is noisy with vendors yelling to customers, neighbors chattering to one another, and the sheer mass of people and shops,

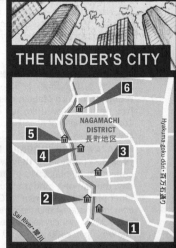

THE INSIDER'S CITY

NAGAMACHI

The *samurai* residences lining the roads of the Nagamachi district offer a glimpse into days of yore.

1 **Maeda Tosanokami-ke Museum** (前田土佐守家資料館) holds armor and paintings. (☎233-1561. ¥300.)

2 The **Shinise Kinenkan** (老舗記念館) collects medical items from Chinese herbs to ceremonial paper cords. (Free.)

3 **Saihitsu-an** (彩筆庵) explains the traditional Yuzen dying technique, demonstrating the process in a restored *samurai* house. (☎264-2811. ¥500.)

4 A typical high-ranking *samurai* residence, **Nomura-ke** (野村家) has elaborate rooms and a garden. (☎231-6531. ¥500.)

5 Another *samurai* residence, **Kyū Takeda-ke Ato** (旧武田家跡) shows "longhouse" style, in which rooms are split.

6 The **Ashigaru Shiryokan** (足軽資料館), a lower-class *samurai* house, provides a basis for class comparisons.

especially just before dinnertime. Known as "Kanazawa's kitchen," it's a great place to buy high-quality ingredients or to try outrageously fresh fish at a sushi counter. *(From Kōrinbō intersection, head back along Hyakuman Goku-dōri for 10min. The market extends for a few blocks from the corner across from Meitetsu M'za department store. From the JR station, head straight out of the East Exit. The market is a 10min. walk, at the Musashigatsu-ji intersection.)*

TERASHIMA KURANDO SAMURAI RESIDENCE (TERASHIMA KURANDO TEI ATO; 寺島蔵人邸跡). The residence of the Terashima family, middle-class retainers to Lord Maeda, has high ceilings and sweeping *tatami* mats. The beamfree design allowed sufficient space for indoor sword practice. *(10-3, Otemachi. A 10min. walk north of Kenroku-en. ☎224-2789; www.city.kanazawa.ishikawa.jp/bunho/terashima. Open daily 9:30am-5pm. ¥300, 65+ ¥200, under 18 free.)*

KANAZAWA PHONOGRAPH MUSEUM (KANAZAWA CHIKUONKI KAN; 金沢蓄音機館). You thought they went out with the dinosaurs, but this quirky specialist collection displays 540 phonographs and over 20,000 SP records. Three times a day, the one-of-a-kind museum holds demonstrations of Thomas Edison's wax cylinder phonograph. *(From the Omichō Market and Meitetsu M'za department store, head away from the JR station and the Kōrinbō district—the museum is on your left after a 10min. walk. ☎232-3066; www.city.kanazawa.ishikawa.jp/bunho/chikuonki. Tours 11am, 2, 4pm. Open daily 10am-5:30pm. ¥300, 65+ ¥200, under 18 free.)*

🎵 🎭 ENTERTAINMENT AND NIGHTLIFE

History courses through Kanazawa's sights and museums, but is particularly present in traditional *nō* theater. Performances are held approximately weekly at the **Nō Culture Hall** (Nōrakudō; 能楽堂), and you might be able to watch a practice for free. Inquire at the tourist office for details. (☎264-2598. Hall open Tu-Su 9am-5pm. Free.) Kanazawa's night scene is exciting and diverse. The majority of Kanazawa's clubs and bars cluster in the Kōrinbō and Katamachi districts, along the main road and in smaller alleys behind. Several multi-story buildings dedicated solely to various incarnations of drinking and dancing spring to life after 7pm.

I No Ichiban (居乃一 BAN), 1-9-20, Katamachi (☎261-0001). Follow the directions for Murataya Ryokan (p. 364); the entrance is on the 1st fl. of the Sekano Bldg. This fashionable *izakaya* merges West and East, pumping hip-hop in a Japanese setting. From the bar, you can see the chefs in the kitchen; the entrance has a bamboo grove. Young, modern vibe; a comfy place for drinks (¥650). Open M-Sa 6pm-3am, Su 6pm-midnight.

Polé Polé (ポレポレ), 2-31-30, Katamachi (☎260-1138). From the Kōrinbō or Katamachi district, walk toward the river and turn right before the bridge; the bar is behind the Legion Indonesian restaurant to your right. This rambunctious spot attracts both Japanese and foreigners. Expect extremely loud reggae music, very few lights, and a carpet of monkey nut shells. 45+ kinds of cocktails and beer (¥700). Open daily 8pm-5am.

Offshore (オフショア), 2-9-13, Katamachi (☎224-5120). From the Kōrinbō intersection, head away from Kenroku-en; it's a short walk on your right. A funky Australian bar decorated with beach paraphernalia. Rooftop seating during the summer. Relaxed and enjoyable atmosphere. Drinks from ¥700. Beer from ¥550. Open daily 6pm-2am.

Bar Spoon, 1-5-3, Katamachi (☎262-5514). From the Kōrinbō intersection, walk down the shopping arcade to the Katamachi intersection and turn left. Take the 1st left, and it'll be to your left. Stylish bar, attracting a slightly older, elegant crowd. Over 50 unique cocktails are served (¥800). Cover ¥1500. Open Tu-Sa 6pm-3am, Su 6pm-2am.

Live House Kento's, 2-21-30, Katamachi (☎263-3180). From the Kōrinbō intersection, walk down the arcade to the Katamachi intersection, turn right and walk 2min. Chill atmosphere. Live music nightly, usually oldies. Cover Tu-Th and Su ¥3000, F-Sa ¥4000; includes entree and unlimited drinks. Open M-Sa 10:30pm-2am, Su 7:30pm-midnight.

◘ FESTIVALS AND EVENTS

Kanazawa's year begins with **Kagatobi Dezomeshiki**, January 6, when local firemen, minimally clothed, venture out into the cold, climbing ladders and drinking *sake*, to show off traditional firefighting skills. **Dekumawashi**, held February 10-16 in nearby Oguchi, features the traditional puppet theater form *jōruri*. A festive event featuring traditional dance and music on the banks of the Asano River, **Asano River Enyūkai** arrives in early April. But Kanazawa's most extravagant festival is the **Hyakumangoku Matsuri**, June 13-15. A parade of residents in 16th-century garb commemorates the first time Kanazawa surpassed 1,000,000 *goku* (or 150,000 tons) in rice production. A special *nō* performance (Takigi Nō) features lighted torches on the Sai River. Elaborate events are also held at Kenroku-en.

NOTO-HANTŌ (能登半島)

The scenic peninsula of Noto-hantō, poking into the Sea of Japan north of Kanazawa and Toyama, boasts unspoiled nature and sparkling beaches. The rural landscape and coasts are best explored by car or bicycle, as transportation is infrequent and difficult to navigate. But thanks to these inconveniences, the area is relatively free of tourist crowds and the traditional lifestyle of Noto's seaside people has been preserved. The largely uninhabited interior of the peninsula is studded with mountains, while the coasts offer the best sights and attractions. One recommended approach is to head up the rugged west coast, pass through Wajima on the way to the peninsula's tip, and return down the calmer east coast.

AT A GLANCE	
CLIMATE: Harsh winters, mild summers.	**GATEWAYS:** Kanazawa (p. 359), Takaoka, and Toyama (p. 356).
HIGHLIGHTS: Beaches, coastline.	
CAMPING: Several campsites are available, but camping is not necessary.	**WHEN TO GO:** The peninsula gets crowded during July and August, so the best time to go is during the spring or fall.

▚ TRANSPORTATION

Flights: Noto Airport (☎076-225-1337; http://noto-airport.net). Flights are available from Japan's newest airport to Haneda Airport in Tōkyō (1hr., 2 per day, ¥20,500). Buses run between the airport and Wajima (30min., 1 per hr., ¥570).

Trains: The JR Nanao Line runs between **Kanazawa** and **Wakura Onsen** (local: 1¾hr., 8 per day, ¥1460; express: 70min., 1 per day, ¥2190; limited express: 55min., 6 per day, ¥2730). From there, transfer to the private Noto Tetsudō Line to reach **Anamizu** (45min., every 1-2hr., ¥1770) or continue farther north to **Tako-jima** (2½hr., every 1-2hr., ¥3420). As train lines only run along the east coast, those heading to **Wajima** need to transfer at Anamizu to the Noto Chūō Bus (30min., 15 per day, ¥740).

Buses: The Hokutetsu Kankō Company (☎076-237-5115) services Noto-hantō from Kanazawa. To: **Maura** via **Sosogi** (2¾hr., 3 per day 1:35-6pm, ¥2510); **Monzen** (2½hr., 4 per day 11am-4:30pm, ¥2100); **Suzu** (2¾hr., 2 per day 11am-2:30pm, ¥2600); **Wajima** (2hr., 11 per day 7:35am-10:20pm, ¥2200).

Public Transportation: Trains serving Noto-hantō run only along the eastern coast, making local **buses** the main internal method of transport. The Hokuriku Tetsudō Company runs from **Wajima** to: **Anamizu** (30min., every 1-2hr., ¥740); **Monzen** (45min., every 1-2hr., ¥740); **Sosogi** (40min., every 1-2hr., ¥760); and **Wakura Onsen** (1¼hr., every 2hr., ¥1200). Buses also connect **Monzen** and **Anamizu** (40min., 9 per day, ¥670).

Taxis: Ishikawa Taxi ☎076-22-2285.

Car Rental: Renting a car in Kanazawa (p. 360) is a great way to explore Noto-hantō.

Bike Rental: Touring Noto-hantō by bike is a viable option, as the terrain is largely flat and the roads are scenic. Be aware, however, that the peninsula is larger than it may initially appear. For rental cycles, look in Kanazawa (p. 360) or Wakura (p. 374).

■ ◪ ORIENTATION AND PRACTICAL INFORMATION

Noto-hantō is characterized by a mountainous and hilly interior region, a rugged west coast, and a quieter indented east coast. Most of the peninsula's few sights are clustered along the western coast, particularly in Wajima.

Maps: Available at tourist offices in Kanazawa (p. 361), Wakura (p. 374), and Nanao.

Tours: Guided tour buses are available through the Hokuriku Tetsudō Company (☎076-239-0123). They are more convenient than the infrequent public bus system, but lack flexibility and come with preset Japanese commentary. Tours last 4-8hr. Most stop by Wajima, Ganmon, Chirihama, and other sights, and include lunch. ¥6300-8000.

Emergency: Police ☎110. Fire or ambulance ☎119.

◪ ◪ ACCOMMODATIONS AND CAMPING

There are three hostels in Noto-hantō and a plethora of minshuku and ryokan. Camping is certainly the cheapest option, but is by no means necessary.

Noto Isaribi Youth Hostel (HI) (能登漁火ユースホステル), 51-6, Ogi (☎0768-74-0150; www.suzu.or.jp/pub/isaribi/index.html). Take the Noto Railway Line to Tsukumo Wan Ogi Station, and it's a 20min. walk. Breakfast ¥600. Dinner ¥1000. Check-in 4pm. Check-out 10am. Members ¥3100; nonmembers ¥4200. ❶

Sosogi Kajiyama Youth Hostel (HI) (曽々木梶山ユースホステル), 4-1, Sosogi Kibu (☎0768-32-1145). From Wajima Bus Terminal, take a Ushitsu-bound bus to Sosogi Guchi (45min., ¥1350). Breakfast ¥600. Dinner ¥1000. Check-in 4pm. Check-out 10am. Closed Aug. 13-18, Dec. 30-Jan. 3. ¥2900; nonmembers ¥3900. ❶

Noto Minazukiwan Youth Hostel (HI) (能登皆月湾ユースホステル), Aza Minazuki (☎0768-46-2022). From Monzen Station, take a Isozu-bound bus to Nanaura Nōkyō-mae stop (40min., ¥1200). Breakfast ¥600. Check-in 4pm. Check-out 10am. Closed Dec. 29-Jan. 7 and M-W Oct. 1-Mar. 31. ¥2750; nonmembers ¥3750. ❶

HAKUI (羽咋)   ☎0767

Known for the scenic **Chirihama Coast** (千里浜海岸), whose magnificent white beach extends southwest of the town, Hakui attracts visitors with both terrestrial and aquatic sights. Cars and motorcycles can cruise on the sandy beaches on the wonderful oceanside **Chirihama Nagisa Driveway** (千里浜なぎさドライブウェイ). Several kilometers north lies **Keta Taisha** (気多大社), Teraya-machi. The oldest shrine in Noto-hantō, it's said to have been founded in the 8th century. Hundreds of heart-shaped *ema* boards, each with a hopeful wish written on it, adorn the gates and trees of the wooden buildings, known for their association with the god of love. From Hakui Station, take the Noto Seibu bus to Ichinomiya stop (10min., ¥280) and walk 5min. (☎22-0602; www.keta.or.jp. Operates 8:30am-4:30pm. ¥100.) Farther north is **Myōjō-ji** (妙成寺), Takiya-machi Yo no Ichibanchi, an important temple of the Nichiren sect of Buddhism. A five-story pagoda towers over the complex. From Hakui Station, take the Seibu bus to Takiya-guchi stop (20min., ¥370) and it's a 15min. walk. (☎27-1226; fax 27-

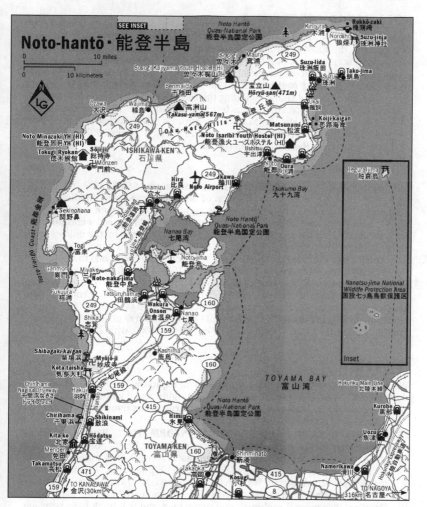

Noto-hantō · 能登半島

0 ─────── 10 miles

0 ─────── 10 kilometers

SEE INSET

Inset

1227. Open daily Mar.-Oct. 8am-5pm; Nov.-Feb. 8am-4:30pm. ¥500, under 15 ¥300.)
Slightly out of the way, south toward Kanazawa, is **Kita-ke** (喜多家), Kitakawa Jiri, the
residence of the prominent Kita family, whose influence once extended over ten villages. The elegant structures, built in local farmhouse style, are complemented by a
garden and museum. The proud Kita family still lives on the grounds. Take the JR
Nanao Line to Menden Station and walk 20min. (☎28-2546; fax 28-3199. Open daily
8am-5pm. ¥700, middle school students ¥400, under 12 ¥300.) From Kanazawa, the JR
Nanao Line runs via Tsubata to Hakui Station (70min., every hr., ¥820). Simple **Hakui
Green Hotel ❷** (羽咋グリーンホテル) is 3min. from the station. (☎22-5151. Check-in
3pm. Check-out 10am. Singles ¥5000.)

NOTO KONGŌ (能登金剛)   ☎0767

Jagged rock formations protrude from the 16km coastline between Fukūra and Sekinohana, the most prominent feature of the Noto Kongō coast. The most famous and scenic spot along here is **Ganmon** (巌門), where a large cave, 15m high, 6m wide, and 60m deep, resembles a towering gate. Though you'll see plenty without it, a **sightseeing boat tour** (Noto Kongō Yūransen; 能登金剛遊覧船) will give you a closer look at sights including the **Lion Rock** and Japan's oldest wooden **lighthouse.** (☎48-1233. Open daily 8am-4pm. Closed Nov. 15-Mar. 31. ¥800, under 12 ¥400). From **Kanazawa**, take the Noto Seibu Express bus to **Togina** (1¾hr., ¥1880), then transfer to the local Noto Seibu bus to Ganmon stop (10min., ¥250). There are also local buses from **Hakui** to Togina (55min., ¥1090).

MONZEN (門前)   ☎0768

Although small Monzen barely has any notable sights, the **Sōji-ji** (総持寺), a training center for Zen monks, is a collection of beautiful time-faded buildings and a gorgeous inner garden. Upon entering through the towering gate, cross the red bridge, turn right, and follow the path countless Buddhist monks and pilgrims have tread. Walking the wooden corridors, you'll be amazed by the golden ornaments, calligraphy scrolls, and carvings. After following the counter-clockwise tour, you'll enter the serene garden. Take the local Noto Seibu bus to Sōji-ji stop (5min., ¥160) from Monzen. (☎42-0005; fax 42-1515. Open daily 8am-5pm. ¥400, high school students ¥300, middle school ¥200, under 12 ¥150.) To get to Monzen from **Kanazawa,** take the Noto Seibu Express bus (2½hr., ¥2100). From the **Noto Kongō** area, there are local buses from Togina to Monzen (45min., ¥890). Accommodation options are limited, but the simple **Tokugi Ryokan ❷** near Monzen is comfortable. (☎42-0010. Check-in 4pm. Check-out 10am. ¥5000, with 2 meals ¥7000.)

WAJIMA (輪島)   ☎0768

Wajima is a transportation hub and great base for exploring Noto-hantō. A lacquerware mecca, Wajima has neat museums, ocean sights, and a vibrant morning market. The downside is Wajima's increasing popularity draws numerous tourists.

⟦🖃⟧ TRANSPORTATION AND PRACTICAL INFORMATION. Wajima is a transportation center for the entire peninsula, but especially for its northern half. No trains run to Wajima, but the **Wajima Bus Terminal** receives lots of traffic. The community bus, **Noranke,** has four lines (8 per day, ¥100). Local buses run between Wajima and Monzen, Anamizu, Wakura Onsen, Sosogi, Maura and Noto Airport (p. 369). The **tourist information center,** 20-1-131, Kawai-machi, right beside the Wajima Bus Terminal, has maps, brochures, and timetables, and will book beds between 9am and 6pm. (☎22-1503; www.wajima-city.co.jp. Open daily 7am-10pm.) In an emergency, call ☎110 for **police,** ☎119 for **fire** or **ambulance.** The **post office,** 15-13-10, Kawai-machi, is along the main road, a 7min. walk northeast of the bus terminal. Inside the post office are **international ATMs.** (☎ 22-0392. Open M-F 9am-7pm. ATMs available M-F 8:45am-7pm, Sa-Su 9am-5pm.) **Postal code:** 928.

⟦🖂⟧ ACCOMMODATIONS AND FOOD. Lodgings in Wajima tend to be in small minshuku or pricey ryokan. Across from Wajima bus terminal is **Minshuku Mangetsu ❷** (民宿満月), which has a relaxing *onsen* and comfy *tatami* rooms. Its location is unbeatable for those using public transport. (☎22-4487. Check-in 4pm. Check-out 10am. ¥4500, with 2 meals ¥7000.) A similar choice is **Minshuku Hakutōen ❷** (民宿白塔園), a 3min. walk from the Wajima Bus Terminal. (☎22-4487. Check-in 4pm. Check-out 10am. ¥4000, with 2 meals ¥6800.) **Wajima Station**

Hotel ❷ (輪島ステーションホテル), to the right as you exit the terminal, has a drab exterior, but is one of the area's few Western hotels. (☎22-0177; fax 22-1855. Check-in 3pm. Check-out 10am. Coin laundry. Singles ¥5000; twins ¥11,000; triples ¥13,500.) Farther from the terminal is **Pension Croissant ❷** (ペンションクロワッサ ン), by the Morning Market. (☎22-1767; fax 22-1797. ¥3500; with 2 meals ¥7000.)

Dining options are few; most people eat where they're staying. For delicious seafood, try **Sushi Shinpuku ❸** (寿司処伸福), a casual spot where the friendly chef serves fresh-caught fish for great prices. The best deal is *asaichi don* (¥2000), a voluminous bowl of rice with more than 12 types of *sashimi*. From the terminal, take Urushi Course Noranke bus to Yayoi Machi stop. (☎22-8133. Open Su-Tu and Th-Sa 11:30am-2pm and 4:30-11:30pm.) **Wajima Yabu Honten ❷** (輪島やぶ本店) serves homemade *soba*, made with a generations-old recipe. (On the same road as the market. ☎22-2266. Open Su-M and W-Sa 11am-3pm and 5-10:30pm.)

🖼 **SIGHTS.** Wajima's main sights can be covered by foot or community bus. The **Ishikawa Wajima Urushi Art Museum** (Ishikawa Wajima Shitsugei Bijutsukan; 石川輪 島漆芸美術館), 11, Shijūkari, has a fabulous collection of lacquerware in its four quiet galleries. A fascinating exhibit shows the step-by-step process of lacquerware production. Take the Umi Course of the Noranke bus to Shitsugei Bijutsukan stop (10min., ¥100) from the bus terminal. (☎22-9788; fax 22-9789. Open daily 9am-5pm. ¥600, college and high school students ¥300, under 15 ¥150.) Go across town to the **Kiriko Museum** (Kiriko Kaikan; キリコ会館) for the elaborate 15m floats used in the Noto-hantō Festival. Unlike those elsewhere in Japan, these floats feature vertical sheets decorated with calligraphy and vibrant paintings. Take a Sosogi-bound bus to Inachū Kaikan-mae stop (6min., ¥100). (☎22-7100; www.jeims.co.jp/inachu. Open daily 8am-5pm. ¥500, high school students ¥400, under 15 ¥350.) Walking back to the station, you'll find **Jūzō Shrine** (Jūzō Jinja; 重蔵 神社), a wooden building with slanted roofs, where the Wajima Festival is held every year. Near the center of town is the **Lacquerware Hall and Museum** (Shikki Kaikan; 漆器会館), 24-55, Kawai-chō, where artists display their crafts, allowing visitors to compare different styles. (☎22-2155; www.wajimanuri.or.jp. Open daily 9am-5:30pm. ¥200, high school students ¥150, under 15 ¥100.)

A fun daytrip is **Hegura-jima** (舳倉島), 50km north of the city. A popular bird-watching spot, the island has several shrines, a lighthouse, and great oceanside walks. (Hegura Ferry Company, ☎22-4381. Ferries depart for the 90min. trip Mar.-Oct. 9am and return at 3pm; Nov.-Feb. 9am/2pm. One-way ¥1900, under 12 ¥950.)

⬛ **MARKETS.** Arguably Wajima's main attraction, the **morning market** (Asa Ichi; 朝市) is said to date back more than 1000 years. Every morning, local ladies and fishermen line the streets, setting up tents or sitting on straw mats, yelling to passersby and selling fresh fish, vegetables, flowers, homemade crafts, and other goodies. From Wajima Bus Terminal, turn left, towards the ocean, then turn left on the second to last road before the water. (22-7653. Open daily 8am-noon. Closed the 10th and 25th of the month). If you miss the morning market, there's a quieter and less tourist-oriented **evening market** (Yū Ichi; 夕市), held on the grounds of Sumiyoshi Shrine. (Open daily 3:30pm-sunset. Closed the 10th and 25th of the month.)

SOSOGI (曽々木) ☎0768

Passing through the rural village of Sosogi, you'll notice the oddly shaped **Senmaida** (千枚田), one thousand rice paddies organized in declining slopes towards the sea. The attractive green fields, quiet roads, and blue ocean make for pleasant walking. The main sight is the Tokikuni Residences, impressive buildings belonging to the former Tokikuni family, which split during the 16th century. The **Kami Tokikuni Ke** (上時国家) is the more elaborate of the two, with a steep slope leading up to the wooden mansion. Inside, explore the elegant house while peering at important collections and household items. (☎32-0171. Open daily Apr.-Nov. 8:30am-6pm; Dec.-Mar. 8:30am-5pm. ¥420, high school students ¥360, under 15 ¥240. Joint admission to both houses ¥500/¥300.) In contrast, the **Shimo Tokikuni Ke** (下時国家) features traditional farmhouse architecture and a gorgeous inner garden. (☎32-0075; fax 32-0901. Open daily Apr.-Nov. 8:30am-5pm; Dec.-Mar. 8:30am-4pm. ¥250, under 15 free.) From Sosogi-guchi, take the Oku Noto Kankō Kaihatsu bus to Kami Tokikuni stop (2min., ¥100) or walk 10min. southeast.

From Wajima, take the Oku Noto Kanko Kaihatsu Bus, Ushitsu-bound, to the Sosogi-guchi stop (35min., every 1-2hr., ¥740). Coming from Ushitsu, it's 40min. (¥850); from Anamizu, 30min. (¥710). There's a youth hostel 8min. from the Sosogi-guchi bus stop (see p. 370). **Minshuku Yokoiwaya ❷** (民宿横岩屋) has *tatami* rooms and seafood dinners. From the Sosogi-guchi bus stop, head 3min. down the road. (☎32-0603. Check-in 4pm. Check-out 10am. ¥5000, with 2 meals ¥7000.)

ROKKŌ-ZAKI (禄剛崎)   ☎0768

The northernmost tip of Noto-hantō is marked by a white lighthouse, worth visiting for the magnificent ocean view. The fishing village of **Noroshi** has hikes along the coast but little else to offer. Transportation is infrequent and inconvenient. From Wajima, first take a Ushitsu-bound bus to Sosogi-guchi (35min., every 1-2hr., ¥740), then hope for a connecting Noto Kankō Kaihatsu Bus to Noroshi stop (50min., every 2hr., ¥860). There are also buses from Suzu station on the Noto Testudo Line (45min., 5-6 per day, ¥730). From Kanazawa, an express bus runs directly to Rokkō-Zaki (2½hr., ¥2530). There are two campsites, the **Yamabushi-yama Campground ❶** (☎88-2737), just east of Noroshi, atop a hill, and the less convenient **Kinoura Campsite ❶** (☎86-2038), 8km west of town. A comfortable in-town stay is the gallery-like **Garō Minshuku Terai ❷**. (☎86-3304. Check-in 4pm. Check-out 10am. ¥5000, with 2 meals ¥6500.)

TSUKUMO WAN (九十九湾)   ☎0768

A scenic bay where you can enjoy the quieter beaches of Noto-hantō's east coast, Tsukumo Wan is characterized by an indented coast and many off-shore islands. "Tsukumo Wan" means "99 Indented Bay," referring to the countless coves. A **glass-bottom boat** tour (Tsukumo-wan Yūransen; 九十九湾遊覧船) is a fun way to see the area. (☎74-0261. Open Apr.-Nov. 8am-5:30pm; Dec.-Mar. 9am-4pm. ¥1000.) The local Noto Tetsudō Line runs by Tsukumo-Wan. The closest station is Tsukumo-Wan Ogi, 5min. from the bay. For an inexpensive stay, try comfortable **Tsukumo Wan No Minshuku ❷** (九十九湾の民宿). The inn is a short walk north of the bay. (☎72-0495. Check-in 3pm. Check-out 10am. ¥4500, with 2 meals ¥6500.)

WAKURA ONSEN (和倉温泉)   ☎0767

A famous hot spring resort, Wakura Onsen attracts crowds. If you're not staying in a ryokan or minshuku with its own *onsen*, the best public bath is **Sōyu** (総湯), where the numerous relaxing baths are complemented by a foot bath and sauna. Weary travelers appreciate the free resting rooms with reclining chairs meant for napping. The *onsen* is a 10min. walk northwest of Wakura Onsen Station. (☎62-2221. Open M-Sa 7am-10pm. Closed every 25th of the month. ¥480, under 12 ¥180.)

Wakura Onsen is the last stop serviced by the JR Nanao Line, making access relatively easy. From Kanazawa, **trains** run once every 1-2hr. to Wakura Onsen (local: 2hr., ¥1280; express: 55min., ¥2730). Coming from Wajima, take the Noto Chuō bus to Anamizu (30min., every 1-2hr., ¥740), transfer to the local Noto Tetsudō Line (40min., every 1-2hr., ¥1770). The **tourist office**, 2-13-1, Wakura-machi, 5min. west of Wakura Onsen Station, has few resources, but can provide maps. (☎62-1555;

www.wakura.or.jp. Open daily 9am-5pm.) As Wakura Onsen is a popular tourist destination, there are lots of beds, although most are pricey. The cheapest options are tiny minshuku, which charge around ¥8000 with meals included; larger ryokan charge an exorbitant ¥15,000-20,000. **Yunokuni ❷** (ゆのくに) is a cozy minshuku with an *onsen*. (☎62-2450. Check-in 4pm. Check-out 10am. 2 meals included. ¥7000.) Another budget choice is **Okudaya ❷** (奥田屋), an agreeable, albeit unattractively modern, minshuku that prides itself on delicious seafood. (☎62-2062. Check-in 4pm. Check-out 10am. 2 meals included. ¥6000.) **Hotel Kiyomizu ❹** (ホテ ルきよみず) is more upscale, with tastefully decorated rooms. (☎62-3400. Check-in 3pm. Check-out 10am. 2 meals included. ¥12,000.) While Wakura dining options are limited, **Nobu Sushi ❸** (信寿し) serves scrumptious sets (¥2000-2500), topped by ocean-fresh fish. It's 1min. from the bus terminal. (☎62-2019. Open daily 11:30am-2pm and 5pm-midnight. Closed every 3rd W of the month.)

NOTO-JIMA (能登島)   ☎0767

The pleasant island of Noto-jima, connected to the mainland at two points, boasts better nature and beaches and more sights than touristy Wakura Onsen, 10km to its south. Noto-jima's main sight is **Noto-jima Aquarium** (Notojima Suizoku-kan; 能登 島水族館), an amusement-park-*cum*-aquarium with dolphin shows, a penguin pool, an otter-watching center, and tanks where you can touch shrimp, fish, and crab. Recreational activities include a cycle monorail (¥400), auto monorail (¥300), go-carts (¥500), a water coaster (¥300), and a fishing zone (¥200). Near the northern coast of Noto-jima, the aquarium is best accessed by bus. (☎84-1271; www3.nsknet.or.jp/~aquarium. Open daily Mar. 20-Nov. 30 9am-5pm; Dec. 1-Mar. 19 9am-4:30pm. ¥1320, under 15 ¥400.) The remaining sights are related to the island's reputation for the production of glassware. **Noto-jima Glass Art Museum** (Noto-jima Gurasu Bijutsukan; 能登島グラス美術館) 125-10, Koda, is an eclectic, jagged-edged facility displaying colorful glass art. From Wakura Onsen take a Rinkai Kōen-bound bus (25min., ¥540) and get off at Bijutsukan-Mae stop. (☎84-1175; fax 84-1129. Open daily Apr.-Oct. 9am-5pm; Nov.-Mar. 9am-4:30pm. ¥800, under 15 free.) Just downhill from the museum is the **Noto-jima Glass Workshop and Gallery** (Noto-jima Gurasu Kōbō; 能登島グラス工房), 122-13, Koda, where craftsmen bend glass into beautiful shapes. Next door is a gallery where you can pick up souvenirs. (☎84-1180; fax 84-1380. Open daily 9am-5pm.) From Wakura Onsen, hourly buses run to Noto-jima. From Nanao, take the Noto-jima Kōtsū Bus (50min., ¥750).

FUKUI (福井)   ☎0776

Heavily bombarded during World War II, then damaged by an earthquake in 1948, the capital of Fukui Prefecture is unattractive and uninteresting. The modern city does, however, proffer facilities and accommodations useful when visiting nearby Eihei-ji and Tojinbō, and to its credit, Fukui comes to life during the **Mikuni Festival** (May 19-21), when enormous warriors parade the streets.

Fukui can be reached by **JR Hokuriku Honsen** from Kanazawa (1hr., ¥1280) and Toyama (1½hr., ¥2210), which runs roughly every 30-45min. The same line continues south to Tsuruga (45min., ¥950), a transport hub for Nagoya (¥2940) and Ōsaka (¥3260). **Fukui City Sightseeing Information**, 1-1-1, Chūō, provides English maps and brochures. It's right of the Fukui Station's Central Exit. (☎20-5348. Open daily 8:30am-5pm.) The **Fukui International Activities Plaza** (Fukui Ken Kokusai Kōryu Kaikan; 福井県国際交流会館), 3-1-1, Hoei, has pamphlets, magazines, and free Internet (30min. max.). From Fukui Station's Central Exit, turn left and continue to Osensui-dōri. Turn left and walk 5min. (☎28-8800; www2.interbroad.or.jp/fia-net. Open W, F, Sa-Su 9am-6pm; Tu and Th 9am-8pm.) In an emergency, call ☎110 for **police**, ☎119 for **fire** or **ambulance**.

GIVING BACK

BEING BUDDHIST

Buddhism—quintessential symbol of the exotic East. Bald-headed monks clad in robes and wooden sandals, kneeling in prayer and meditation, living in temples deep in the woods. This may seem out of your realm of reality. But if you'd like to see the way monks really live, Eihei-ji is an opportunity to do just that.

The temple's unique overnight or 4-day-3-night trainee program is called *sanrōsha*. Participants observe the Buddhist monks' daily schedule, starting with a cleansing bath at 3pm, in which you purify your body and prepare your mind and soul. A strictly vegetarian meal is served at 5pm. The real religious experience starts with a 30min. *zazen* meditation session. Afterwards, you watch a short video explaining the monks' rituals and routines in Eihei-ji temple. An early bedtime of 9pm is necessary so you can get up again for the 3am *zazen* meditation, followed by a prayer session at 5am. After a comprehensive tour of Eihei-ji's buildings and facilities, a simple breakfast is served at 8:30am, and the overnight program ends.

Although you might emerge starving and sleep deprived, the one-of-a-kind opportunity may be your most memorable experience in Japan. (Reservations required at least 1 month in advance. ☎0575-63-3631; fax 63-3640. Overnight ¥8000; 4-day-3-night program ¥9000.)

The **Central Post Office,** 3-1, Ōte, is 3min. east of Fukui Station; go straight on Chuō Ōdōri and turn right at the light. (☎24-0042. Open M-F 9am-7pm, Sa 9a-5pm, Su 9am-12:30pm; international **ATM** available M-F 7am-11pm, Sa 9am-9pm, Su 9am-7pm.) The **Ōte Post Office,** 2-3-20, Ōte, is a 5min. walk out of Fukui Station's Central Exit. (☎23-7879. Open M-F 9am-5pm; international ATM M-F 9am-5:30pm, Sa: 9am-12:30pm.) **Postal code:** 910.

Hotels and ryokan surround the station. In addition, **Fukui Ken Seinenkan Youth Hostel (HI)** ❶ (福井県 青年会館), 3-11-17, Ōte, is by Chuō Kōen, a 10min. walk northwest of Fukui Station. From Fukui Station's Central Exit, walk on Chuō Ōdōri for 5min. Turn right before the bus terminal and the intersection; the hostel is a 5min. walk. Neat rooms and convenience make up for the aged exterior. (☎22-5625. Check-in 4pm. Check-out 10am. ¥3200.) **City Hotel Fukui** ❸ (シティーホテル福井), 1-1-17, Hinode, outside the East Exit of Fukui Station, offers comfy rooms and fax, copy, and laundry services. (☎23-5300. Check-in 3pm. Check-out 11am. Singles ¥4900-5800; twins ¥9000; doubles ¥8000.) For a Japanese-style stay, try small **Yamauchi Ryokan** ❸ (山内旅館), 5min. northwest of Fukui Station. (☎23-4881. Check-in 3pm. Check-out 10am. ¥5000, with 2 meals ¥7300). An economical, modern option is **Fukui Palace Inn** ❷ (福井パレスイン), 1-12-17, Junka, a business hotel. Head straight out of Fukui Station's Central Exit on Chuō Ōdōri, then turn right on Phoenix-dōri. Walk 5min.; it's on the left. (☎23-3801. Check-in 3pm. Check-out 10am. Singles ¥4300; twins ¥9000; Japanese-style rooms ¥9000.)

DAYTRIPS FROM FUKUI

EIHEI-JI (永平寺). A center of Zen Buddhism 20km northeast of Fukui, Eihei-ji's influence extends through Japan and across the world. The impressive temple, surrounded by a serene cedar forest, was founded by Dōgen in 1244, and is currently headquarters for the Sōtō sect of Zen Buddhism. Souvenir shops have proliferated along the road leading uphill to the 70-odd buildings that compose the complex. But contrary to what the shops suggest, Eihei-ji is an active religious community. As you walk between the seven main halls—*Butsuden* (Buddha Hall), *Hattō* (Dharma Hall), *Sōdō* (Priests Hall), *tosu* (toilet), *yokushitsu* (bath), *daikuin* (kitchen), and *San-mon* (gate)—you'll get a feel not only for the temple's beauty, but also for the daily activity of the 200 monks who live there. With atmospheric wooden buildings, some decorated in gold and vibrant colors, Eihei-ji is a truly spiritual temple with a strong sense of community. A training program (p. 376) is available for those who wish to experience the life of the monks more intimately. (☎0575-63-3631; fax 63-3640. Open daily 5am-5pm. ¥400.)

Take the Keifuku Dentetsu Eihei-ji Line from Fukui Station to Eihei-ji (35min., every 30min., ¥720). Most trains are direct, but some stop at Higashi Furuichi, in which case you need to transfer. From the station, the temple complex is a 5min. walk; turn right and walk up the main approach to Eihei-ji. The temple often closes for 5-10 days for religious services; check with the tourist office in Fukui. To stay near the temple, try **Eihei-ji Monzen Yamaguchi Sō (HI) ❶** (永平寺門前山口荘), right by the main road to the temple. (☎0575-63-3123; fax 63-3122. Breakfast ¥600. Dinner ¥1000. Check-in 4pm. Check-out 10am. ¥2900; nonmembers ¥3900.)

TŌJINBŌ (東尋坊). An easy and enjoyable daytrip from Fukui is Tōjinbō, famous for its rugged 50m cliffs, dramatically spread along 1km of coastline. A 30min. trip on a **sightseeing boat** (Tōjinbō Kankō Yūransen; 東尋坊観光遊覧船) allows visitors to view the sculpted rocks from a completely different angle, looking up at the cliffs. (☎81-3808. Open daily 8am-6pm. ¥1110, under 12 ¥550.) A less expensive—and less exciting—choice is to ascend **Tōjinbō Tower** (東尋坊タワー). From its observatory you can scan the coastline and endless horizon. (☎81-3700. Open Apr.-Oct. 8:30am-5:30pm; Nov.-Mar. 8:30am-4:30pm. ¥500, under 15 ¥300.)

A 45min. walk north from Tōjinbō is uninhabited **Oshima** (雄島), connected to the mainland by a 224m bridge. Near the bridge is small **Ōminato Shrine** (Ōminato Jinja; 大湊神社), from which you can depart on a 3km walk around the island. Oshima boasts plentiful nature, and it's perfect for an afternoon stroll. In summer, **Mikuni Sunset Beach** (三国サンセットビーチ) attracts locals and visitors with sparkling waters and white sand. In addition to swimming and sunbathing, you can try surfing and windsurfing, with rentals and lessons available. From Mikuni Station, take a Tōjinbō-bound bus to Shuku stop (5min., every hr., ¥230).

To reach Tōjinbō from Fukui, take the Keifuku Line from near the East Exit of Mikuni Station (45min., every hr.), then transfer to a Tōjinbō-bound bus (10min., every hr., ¥270). A direct bus runs from Fukui Station (60min., 3 per day, ¥1110). From the Tōjinbō Bus Station, follow the trail of souvenir shops to the jagged rocks and ocean. The **Mikuni Tourist Office** is a 2min. walk from the bus station away from the ocean. (☎82-5515; www.mikuni.org. Open daily 8:30am-9pm.) Strolling along the main road leading to the jagged cliffs, you'll find more souvenir shops and small restaurants serving seafood (¥1000-1500) and finger food (¥500).

NAGOYA (名古屋)   ☎052

Nagoya has been something of a middleman ever since its Edo-period founding. The Tokugawa shōgunate wanted to use it as a buffer to shield Edo against attacks from the Kansai region because the Imperial family still held power over Kyōto and Ōsaka. North of the city, Nagoya Castle is a reminder of the Edo Period, but this edifice was reconstructed within the last 50 years, as was the rest of the city after everything was flattened by bombing late in WWII. Modern-day Nagoya is a transportation hub, a point on the map from which subway, train, ferry, and bus routes snake out to every corner of Japan. If you're traveling in Honshū, you'll probably end up passing through. But if you stay, you might be pleasantly surprised by Nagoya's relaxed residents and varied attractions.

ON THE WEB   Nagoya: www.ncvb.or.jp

CENTRAL HONSHŪ

✈ INTERCITY TRANSPORTATION

Flights: Nagoya Airport (domestic flight info ☎0568-28-5633, international ☎0568-29-0765). Take the **Meitetsu Airport Bus** from Nagoya Station's *Shinkansen* Exit (32min., every 20min., ¥870) and Hirokōji Exit (28min., every 30min., ¥870), the Meitetsu bus center (28min.; every 10min.; ¥870, round-trip ¥1740), or the Oasis 21 bus terminal in Sakae (36min., every 30min., ¥730). Domestic flights all over Japan; international flights to China and Southeast Asia, as well as several to the Americas and Europe.

Trains: Nagoya Station is a major stop on the Tōkaidō *shinkansen* line and connects to subways, buses, and private rail lines. *Shinkansen* platforms are on the Taikodōri side of the station. To: **Tōkyō** (Kodama 3hr., ¥10,580; Hikari 2hr., ¥10,580; Nozomi 1¾hr., ¥11,340); **Kyōto** (Kodama and Hikari 55min., ¥5440; Nozomi 40min., ¥5900); **Shin-Ōsaka** (Kodama 1¼hr., ¥6180; Hikari 1hr., ¥6180; Nozomi 50min., ¥6640); **Hiroshima** (Hikari 2¾hr., ¥13,430; Nozomi 2¼hr., ¥14,550); **Hakata** (Hikari 4¼hr., ¥17,530; Nozomi 3¼hr., ¥18,860). The **Kintetsu Line** (☎581-4718; www.nagoya-kyousei.com) has windows in the south wing of the Sakura-dōri side of Nagoya Station. 1 train per hr. to: **Kyōto** (local ¥2190, limited express ¥1560), **Nara** (¥2520/¥1850).

Buses: Meitetsu and JR run day and overnight expressway buses from the 4th fl. of the Meitetsu Bus center and from the JR stop on the ground floor of Nagoya Station. Routes to Kyōto and Ōsaka run more frequently than others. To: **Hiroshima** (8¾hr., ¥8400, round-trip ¥15,100); **Kyōto** (2½hr., ¥4000); **Matsuyama** (9¼hr., ¥10,000/¥18,000); **Ōsaka** (3hr., ¥4600); **Takamatsu** (7¼hr., ¥7130/¥12,230); **Tokushima** (6hr., ¥6600/¥11,800); **Tōkyō Shinjuku** (6hr., ¥5100); **Yokohama** (6½hr., ¥5750).

Ferries: The **Taiheiyo Ferry** departs from Ferry-futo Port and connects to Sendai and Tomakomai (☎582-8611; www.taiheiyo-ferry.co.jp). Take a Meitetsu bus from the Meitetsu bus center, 3rd fl., platform #8 (1 per day at 6:30pm). At other times, take the Meijo Subway Line to Tsukiji-guchi, and then a #1 city bus toward Kantsukichi.

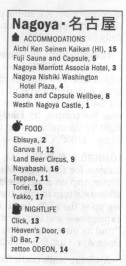

Nagoya・名古屋

🏠 ACCOMMODATIONS
Aichi Ken Seinen Kaikan (HI), **15**
Fuji Sauna and Capsule, **5**
Nagoya Marriott Associa Hotel, **3**
Nagoya Nishiki Washington
Hotel Plaza, **4**
Suana and Capsule Wellbee, **8**
Westin Nagoya Castle, **1**

🍎 FOOD
Ebisuya, **2**
Garuva II, **12**
Land Beer Circus, **9**
Nayabashi, **16**
Teppan, **11**
Toriei, **10**
Yakko, **17**

🌙 NIGHTLIFE
Click, **13**
Heaven's Door, **6**
iD Bar, **7**
zetton ODEON, **14**

▣ LOCAL TRANSPORTATION

Subway: Nagoya has 4 subway lines that cover most of the city. The red **Sakura Line** and yellow **Higashiyama Line** pass through Nagoya Station and run parallel through Sakae before crossing and heading to the southeast and northeast respectively. The blue **Tsurumai Line** and purple **Meijo Line** run north-to-south. Subway fares ¥200-320; **single day pass** ¥740, elementary school students ¥370. Another pass gives you access to city buses (¥850, elementary school students ¥430). Ticket prices for the 8th of each month drop to ¥620. These cheaper tickets are sold starting on the 1st of that month.

Trains: The local Meitetsu Line runs through Nagoya Station but isn't a great option for transportation within the city, as the subway system is so quick and extensive.

Buses: The Nagoya bus system is confusing and best used only for specific routes. **City buses** charge ¥200 within the city; day passes (without subway access) are ¥600, elementary school students ¥300. The private companies **Meitetsu** and **Kintetsu** charge based on distance, but if you get off at a city bus stop the charge is ¥200.

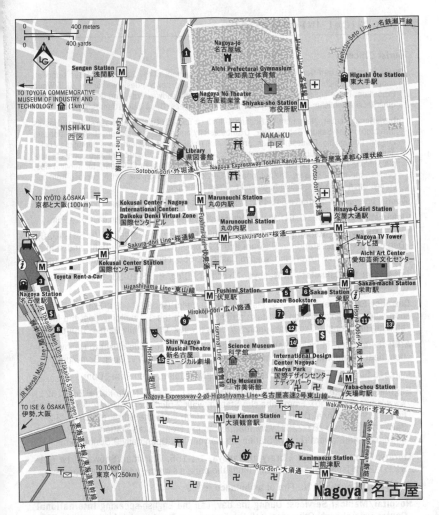

Nagoya · 名古屋

Taxis: Dentaku, ☎881-9493. Tsubame Cruise, ☎471-4181. Base fare ¥610.

Car Rental: Toyota Rent-a-Car, Nakamura-ku Meieki 4-5-26, ☎541-0100. From Nagoya Station, exit on the Sakura-dōri side and walk 2 blocks down Sakura-dōri. Toyota is on the right. Open daily 8am-8pm.

ORIENTATION

Nagoya Station lies west of most of the action. Sakura-dōri runs perpendicular to the station and through the heart of the city. This area is dominated by businesses closer to the station but becomes more commercial as you move through Nishiki and Sakae. The four subway lines snake out of the station into residential areas.

🛈 PRACTICAL INFORMATION

Tourist Offices:

Oasis 21 Information Center (☎963-5252). In the basement of the Sakae-machi Bus Terminal, connected to Sakae Station. Distributes the *Goodwill Guide*, newly redesigned for the 2005 World Exposition. These highly detailed maps include numbered subway exits, and list restaurants and other local establishments with English-speaking employees. Open daily 10am-8pm.

International Center, Nakamura-ku Nagono 1-47-1 (☎581-0100; www.nic-nagoya.or.jp). Has its own stop on the Sakura Subway Line. Distributes city maps, offers free counseling in Japanese, English, Portuguese, Chinese, Korean, and Spanish (available at different times during the week), and compiles information on restaurants, bars, and tourist sights. Volunteer board connects people seeking language exchange. Check out their monthly "Nagoya Calendar" for survival tips, events, and movie listings. The Information Service Corner is on the 3rd fl., across from the library. Open Tu-Sa 9am-8:30pm, Su and holidays 9am-5pm.

Tourist Information Center (☎541-4301). In Nagoya Station. Open daily 9am-7pm.

Information Desk (☎323-0161). In the North Exit of Kanayama Station. Open daily 9am-7pm.

Tours: Nagoya Sightseeing Bus Tours, Nagoya Bus Terminal Bldg. 2F (☎561-4036). Depart the city bus station at 9:30am and 1:20pm. Tours run about 3½hr. and stop at Atsuta Jingu, the TV Tower, and Nagoya Castle. ¥3650, children ¥2050. Japanese only.

Consulate: US Consulate in Nagoya, Nishiki SIS Bldg. 6F, 3-10-33, Nishiki, Naka-ku (☎203-4011).

Currency Exchange: UFJ, 1-2-4, Meieki, Nakamura-ku (☎582-1443). Exit the Sakura-dōri side of Nagoya station and take a right. UFJ is in the 1st building past the Melsa building on the right. Exchanges money 7 days a week. Open daily 9am-4:30pm.

ATM: There's an ATM inside Meitetsu department store on the side closer to Nagoya Station, near the information desk on the ground floor. Cirrus/MC/V. Open 9am-7pm.

Luggage Storage: There are coin lockers in Nagoya Station open 9am-10pm.

English-Language Bookstore: Kinokuniya, 3-18-1, Sakae, Naka-ku (☎265-2621; www.kinokuniya.co.jp). From Yaba-chō Station, walk 2 blocks back toward Nagoya Station; the International Design Center is on your right; go to the 6th fl. **Maruzen,** 3-2-7, Sakae, Naka-ku (☎261-2251; www.maruzen.co.jp). From Sakae Station, walk 3 blocks on Hirokōji-dōri toward Nagoya Station; it's on your left. Open daily 9:50am-8pm.

Library: Tsuruma Central Library of Nagoya, 1-1-155, Tsurumai, Shōwa-ku (☎741-3131). From Tsurumai Station, walk along the park; it's on the edge by the expressway.

Emergency: Police ☎110. **Fire** or **ambulance** ☎119.

Hospital/Medical Services: During the day, call the English-speaking **International Center** (see above). Otherwise, call the **Emergency Treatment Info Center** (☎263-1133; Japanese only). Imazu Geka and Kato Medical Clinic have English-speaking staff.

Fax Office: There are three 24hr. **Kinko's** stores. One is near the #4 Exit of Fushimi Station (☎231-9211)—walk 2 blocks along Hirokōji-dōri and turn right. Another is near Nagoya Station (☎541-9800)—take a right out of the Sakura-dōri side of the station, pass the Melsa Building, Meitetsu Grand Hotel, and Meitetsu Seven Building, and take a left at the light. It's on the right after 2 blocks. The 3rd is in Sakae next to the Fuji Park Hotel (☎951-8826)—go out the #2 Exit and walk toward Sakura-dōri; it's on your right.

Internet Access: Chikō Raku (☎587-2528). From Nagoya Station, exit the Sakura-dōri side and turn right. Pass the Melsa and Kintetsu Buildings and cross at the 1st light; it's in the basement of the Meitetsu Lejac Bldg. ¥480 per hr. Open 24hr. **Media Cafe Popeye,** 3-6-15, Nishiki, Naka-ku (☎955-0059). Across from the Television Tower. Offers billiards, darts, foot baths, showers, and free drinks. ¥100 for 30min., ¥90 per 15min. thereafter. Open 24hr. Also try the **International Center** (see above). ¥500 per hr.

Post Office: Nagoya Central Post Office, 1-1-1, Meieki, Nakamura-ku (☎564-2103). Exit Nagoya Station on the Sakura-dōri side, take a left, and it's a few blocks on your left. Open M-F 9am-7pm, Sa 9am-5pm, Su 9am-12:30pm. After-hours area open 24hr. Postal ATMs open M-Sa 12:05am-11:55pm, Su 12:05am-8pm. Postal Code: 450.

🏠 ACCOMMODATIONS

The area around Nagoya Station is packed with options, and there's even a hotel in the station. The Sakae district also has its fair share of accommodations. The two hostels are cheapest, but early curfews preclude any late-night shenanigans.

Nagoya Nishiki Washington Hotel Plaza, 3-12-22, Nishiki-dōri, Naka-ku (☎962-7111). From Sakae Station, walk 3 blocks on Nishiki-dōri toward Nagoya Station. Turn right, then left, and it's on the right. The cheaper of the 2 Washingtons. In an exciting district. Check-in 2pm. Check-out 10am. Singles ¥5455; twins and doubles ¥11,256. ❸

Aichi Ken Seinen Kaikan (HI), 1-18-8, Sakae, Naka-ku (☎221-6001). From Fushimi Station, walk 3 blocks toward Nagoya Station, turn left, pass 2 lights. On-site restaurant. Check-in 3-8pm. Check-out 10am. Lockout 10am-3pm. Curfew 11pm-7am. Dorms ¥2850; Japanese single ¥3650 for 1, or ¥2850 per person; with toilet ¥3950/¥3650; Western single with bath ¥4250, twin ¥3950. Nonmembers add ¥300-600. ❶

Nagoya Sakae Tōkyū Inn, 3-1-8, Sakae, Naka-ku (☎251-0109; www.tokyuhotels.co.jp). From Fushimi Station's eastern exit, walk 2 blocks on Hirokōji-dōri away from Nagoya Station; look right. Good location in the middle of Sakae. Starbucks on 1st fl. Breakfast at Shangri-La ¥950 (children ¥500). Internet ¥1000 per night in some rooms. Check-in 3pm. Check-out 10am. Singles ¥8500; twins ¥14,000; doubles ¥18,000. ❹

Fuji Sauna and Capsule, 3-22-31, Nishiki, Naka-ku (☎962-5711; www.fto.co.jp). From Fushimi Station, head down Hirokōji-dōri. Turn left before the Maruzen bookstore block; it's on the right. Sauna, bath, and relaxation room free. Massage available. In-house restaurant. Check-in 4pm. Check-out 10am. Curfew 3am. ¥3800. ❷

Sauna and Capsule Wellbee, 1-25-2, Meiekiminami, Naka-ku (☎586-2641). From Nagoya Station, exit on the Sakura-dōri side, take a right, and pass the Kintetsu and Melsa buildings. Look for the Meitetsu Lejac Bldg. after the 1st stoplight; Wellbee is on the 4th fl. Expansive lounge and bath areas. Massages. Internet ¥100 per 15min. In-house restaurants. Check-in noon. Check-out noon. ¥4100. ❷

Nagoya Marriott Associa, 1-1-4, Meieki, Nakamura-ku (☎584-1113; www.associa.com/nma). In one of the JR towers, attached to Nagoya Station. Head to the Sakura-dōri side, turn right, and go to the 15th fl. Restaurants, bars, and lounges, plus fitness center and auditorium; you may never have to leave the station. LAN Internet in all rooms. Check-in 1pm. Check-out noon. Singles ¥17,000; doubles ¥24,000. ❺

The Westin Nagoya Castle, 3-19, Hinokuchi-chō, Nishi-ku (☎521-2121; www.castle.co.jp). From Nagoya Station's JR Highway Bus terminal, take the shuttle (15min., every hr. 10am-5:30pm). Some rooms have a view of the castle, lit beautifully at night. Short walk from 2 subway lines. Shuttle to Nagoya Station every 30min. 10am-5:30pm. Check-in 1pm. Check-out 12pm. Singles ¥13,000 (no view); twins ¥24,000. ❹

Nagoya Youth Hostel (HI), 1-50, Tashiro-chō, Aza Kameiri, Chikusa-ku (☎781-9845). From Higashiyama Kōen Station, take Exit #3, walk along the park a few minutes, then follow signs right and past the zoo entrance. Far from the city center and a hike from the station, but you can't beat the prices. Single-sex floors. Breakfast ¥600, 7:30am-8:30am. Lunch ¥550. Dinner ¥850, 6pm-7:30pm. Sheets ¥200 for 3 nights. Robe (*yukata*) ¥100 for 3 nights. Laundry free. Bath 6-9:30pm. Check-in 3-9:30pm. Check-out 6:30-10am. Curfew 10pm. Reservations suggested. ¥2000, under 16 ¥1500. ❶

Ryokan Marutame, 2-6-17, Tachibana, Naka-ku (☎321-7130; www.jin.ne.jp/marutame). From Higashi Betsuin Station (on the Meijo Line), take Exit #4, cross the street, pass Higashi Betsuin temple, and turn right; it's on the left. Run by a pleasant family. Breakfast

ON THE MENU

THE REIGN OF REGIONAL BEER HAS BEGUN

In Japan, 1994 is referred to as the first year of the reign of "regional beer." Traditionally, the "Big Four" beer companies (Asahi, Kirin, Sapporo, and Suntory) dominated the Japanese market due to strict regulations. These are the ones you'll see everywhere—on tap, in bottles, in cans, in vending machines. Until 1994, in order to have a brewing license, Japanese brewers had to brew at least 2 million liters per year. When this requirement was lowered to 60,000 liters, the dam that had been holding back Japanese craft breweries unleashed a flood of delicious beers. Since 1994, over 300 "regional breweries" have been established, ranging from local brew pubs to full-scale regional breweries. The types of beer range just as much, from German-style dunkels and bocks to English ales and Czech pilsners.

Of course you'll never be far from the standard Japanese light lagers, either, as they are sold in grocery stores, bars, and vending machines nearly everywhere. These golden, highly carbonated brews are perfect for the hot and humid Japanese summer. Make sure to pour for your drinking partners first, admire the foamy head, toast with "Kanpai!" and then scream "Oishi!" after a huge gulp.

For further intoxicating info, check out www.bento.com/r-beer.asp or Michael Jackson's *Great Beer Guide.*

¥500. Dinner ¥500. Check-in 3pm. Check-out 10am. Curfew 11pm. Reservations suggested. Singles ¥4800; doubles ¥8400; triples ¥10,800. AmEx/M/V. ❷

🍴 FOOD

Nagoya has a wide variety of restaurants—you should be able to find nearly any type of food you desire. The local specialties are *kochin tori*, a kind of fried chicken; *hitsumabushi*, a variation on *unagi-don* (eel); and *kishimen*, a wide flat noodle in clear broth. Sakae and Nishiki are loaded with good restaurants; you'll find the fashionable ones along Hirokōji-dōri. Good steals are in the back streets around the Osu shopping area (*shōtengai*).

🏮 **Yakko,** 2-30-1, Osu, Naka-ku (☎231-0021). Osu Kannon Station. From the road from the entrance gate to the Kannon, walk 2 blocks into the *shōtengai*; Yakko will be on your right. An *unagi* joint, serving huge wooden bowls of *unagi-don* (small ¥800, large ¥1500). The local specialty is *hitsumabushi* (¥2200): scoop *unagi-don* into a bowl; top it with *nori* (seaweed), spring onions and *wasabi*; then pour broth over it. Crowded at mealtimes, come early for quiet. Open M-Sa 11:30am-2pm and 4pm-9pm. ❸

🏮 **Garuva II,** Grand Bldg. 7F, 3-9-22, Sakae, Naka-ku (☎261-6648; www.ganet.gr.jp/garuva2). Sakae Station. From the front of the International Design Center, go 1 block toward Hirokōji-dōri and turn left. All dim lamplight and incense. The waiter will lead you to a table under a tent and give you a shaker to call for assistance. Curry-enhanced Garuva *udon* (¥600) is their trademark. Thai curry ¥900; octopus *kimchi* ¥600; Ho Chi Min light *udon* ¥600. English menus available. Bar has no counter but you can lounge on beanbags. Open M-Th 6pm-3am, F-Sa 6pm-5am. JCB/MC/V. ❸

Teppan, 4-14-21, Sakae, Naka-ku (☎241-4288). Sakae Station. From the east side of Sakae Station, walk 2 blocks south from Hirokōji-dōri along Hisaya-ōdōri and take a left. It's in the basement on the left. This *okonomiyaki* joint also serves up *teppanyaki*-style dishes. *Okonomiyaki* ¥750. *Teppanyaki* plates ¥500-750. Open daily 5pm-midnight. ❸

Land Beer Circus, 1-4-30, Sakae, Naka-ku (☎223-9191). Fushimi Station. From the station walk 2 blocks back toward Nagoya Station on Hirokoji-dōri and take a left at the Hilton. It's on the left, across from the Hilton. Land Beer is brewed in Nagoya, and the Circus shows it off. Try 1 of 5 European-style beers (glass ¥480, mug ¥580, pitcher ¥1800, sample of 3 ¥800). Set meals

¥1200, but you can also pick out sausages and sauerkraut (¥680) or other snacks. The *miso* fondue (¥980) reflects the European-Japanese fusion. Open M-Sa 11:30am-2pm and 5pm-10:30pm, last order 9:45pm. ❸

Ebisuya, 3-20-7, Sakae, Naka-ku (☎961-3412). A couple of locations in main areas of Nagoya, so you won't have to look far for a tasty bowl of *kishimen*, flat noodles in soy-based sauce with fried tofu and fish flakes and parsley sprinkled on top. *Kishimen* and basic *soba* ¥650. Set meals like *tempura teishoku* for around ¥1250. ❷

Toriei (鳥栄), 3-8-3, Sakae, Naka-ku (☎241-5552). Across from Maruei. Look for the window full of chicken statues. Serves up great *kochin tori*, lightly fried chicken. Lunch specials (from ¥750) come with soup, rice, and other selections. Dinner meals from ¥3100. Don't order chicken *sashimi* unless you actually mean to. Open M-Tu and Th-Sa 11:30am-2:30pm and 4:30-9pm; Su 11:30am-2:30pm and 4:30-8:50pm. ❷

Nayabashi (納屋橋), Osu Banshōji-dōri. (☎241-1662). Kamimaezu Station. Nayabashi is four blocks off Otsu-dōri towards Osu Kannon along Banshōji-dōri. Look on the corner. This little pastry shop serves up dough filled with sweetened red-bean paste, whether in dumpling form (*manjū*), deep-fried (*agemambo*), or grilled (*paiman*). ❶

▣ SIGHTS

The sights in Nagoya are few and far between, but the subway system helps prevent the blisters, making all but a few of the sights easily accessible. You can cover most of them in a day with the handy subway pass.

▉TOYOTA COMMEMORATIVE MUSEUM OF INDUSTRY AND TECHNOLOGY. This museum traces the rise of the Toyota company from the production of textiles and the evolution of looms to the current focus on the automobile industry. It's housed in old factory buildings, so display spaces are expansive. The Textile Machinery Pavilion has several different kinds of working looms. At the Automobile Pavilion, there are displays on different aspects of car construction and on the physics of cars; dozens of engines and car skeletons show how the parts operate. After making your way through, drop by Technoland, a room full of hands-on activities demonstrating various physical laws. Highlights include the human hamster wheel, a tremendous scale that uses an engine to measure your weight, and a wind tunnel. *(From Nagoya Station take the #11 city bus to the "Commemorative Museum of Industry and Technology" stop. Continue down the street past the stoplight, and the museum will be on your right. 4-1-35, Shin-machi, Nishi-ku, Noritake. ☎551-6115; www.tcmit.org. Open Tu-Su 9:30am-5pm. ¥500, junior and senior high school students ¥300, primary school ¥200.)*

NAGOYA CASTLE. The castle was originally constructed in 1612 and used as a buffer between the Edo-based shōgunate and the Imperial Family in Kansai. The castle was destroyed by bombing late in WWII but has been reconstructed; only three towers, three gates, and some paintings survive from the original. The reconstruction on the whole is rather modernized. In the Ninomaru Gardens, the dry pond and some scraggly stones make a nice walking area. *(Take the Meijo Line to Shiyakusho Station. 1-1, Hommaru, Naka-ku. ☎231-1700; www.nagoyajo.naka.nagoya.jp. Open daily 9am-4:30pm. ¥500, elementary school students ¥100.)*

NAGOYA NŌ THEATER. When there are no *nō* rehearsals or performances, you can walk in free of charge and look at the exquisite stage, built in 1997, as well as a few exhibits on *nō* costuming and acting. *(In the vicinity of Nagoya Castle, a 10min. walk from Shiyakusho Station on the Meijo Subway Line. 1-1-1, San-no-maru, Naka-ku. ☎231-0088. Open daily 10am-4pm. Performance tickets ¥2000-5000.)*

TOKUGAWA ART MUSEUM. This museum displays the Owari clan's treasures, containing impressive displays on the life of an important *daimyō* family—*nō* theater and tea ceremony artifacts are displayed, while weapons and armor show the role of Nagoya in the defense of Edo. By far the most important item is

IN RECENT NEWS

NATURE'S WISDOM

Shintō and Buddhism have always stressed the importance of nature in people's daily lives. But as Japan modernized in the 19th and 20th centuries, fostering economic growth and competing with Western powers became national priorities, often at the expense of the environment. Nagoya is a typical modern city. Laid out on a grid, the city's spotty park areas and tree-lined avenues are dominated by urban sprawl.

For the **2005 World Exposition,** however, Nagoya will become the focus of the world. The exposition's theme is "Nature's Wisdom," and the center of the convention will be Aichi Prefecture's Satoyama, a forested mountain and protected ecosystem. Rather than throwing up new buildings around Nagoya, the idea is to create communities than can live within the environment.

The exposition is searching for ways to realize this vision. Space, the final frontier, will be considered for its potential to help alleviate environmental problems; to symbolize this, there will be live broadcasts from a space station to the exposition. Japan's recycling program will strengthened—ideally, into one that will develop beyond the exposition. Some buildings will be made purely from recycled bottles. The event seeks to be a guide for future progress—progress that doesn't come at the expense of nature.

the 12th-century illustrated handscroll of *The Tale of Genji.* The original scrolls survive in fragments too delicate for permanent display, but a replica is available for viewing. For two weeks in November, selections from the actual fragments are shown; in 2005 all the fragments will be shown. *(Take a city bus from the #7 stop at the Eki-mae bus terminal for Jiyūgaoka or Idaka Shakō to the Shindeki stop. Walk down Tokugawa Art Museum St., turn left and follow the street to the entrance, on the right. 1017, Tokugawa-chō, Higashi-ku. ☎ 935-6262; www.cjn.or.jp/tokugawa. Open Tu-Su 10am-5pm. Closed national holidays. ¥1200, high school and university students ¥700, children 7-14 ¥500.)*

IDCN DESIGN MUSEUM. On the 4th floor of the Design Center Building and itself an impressive piece of architecture, this small display describes the evolution of modern design and illustrates its effects on consumer products. Leaving this museum through the Loft department store on the lower levels will make you realize how accurately the museum pegs the relationship between design and product. *(3-18-1, Sakae, Naka-ku. ☎ 265-2100; www.idcnagoy.co.jp. Open 11am-8pm. ¥300, high school students and above ¥200, junior high school students or below free.)*

NAGOYA/BOSTON MUSEUM OF FINE ARTS. The sister-museum of the MFA in Boston displays rotating exhibits from the MFA's collection, a long-term exhibit and a regular semi-annual exhibit. The art is international for the most part, but one corner focuses on Japanese artists and art forms. *(Outside the South Exit of Kanayama Station. 1-1-1, Kanayama-chō, Naka-ku. ☎ 265-2100; www.nagoya-boston.or.jp. Open Tu-F 10am-7pm, Sa-Su 10am-5pm. Long-term exhibit ¥400, college and high school students ¥300, junior and high school students free; all exhibits ¥1200/¥900/¥500.)*

ATSUTA JINGU. One of Japan's more important shrines, Atsuta Jingu houses the huge sword Kusanagi, one of the three sacred treasures of Japan. Three brown wooden *torī* lead visitors through the woods and to the main building. Pigeons and roosters wander around, the latter announcing imaginary dawns every now and then. Off the main path, the **Atsuta Jingu Museum,** 1-1-1, Atsuta Jingu (☎ 671-4151), contains a small collection of donated items. The most impressive object, a 6ft. sword, is right through the main doors; viewing it doesn't require an entrance fee. *(Open daily 9am-4:30pm. Closed last W and Th of every month. ¥300, children ¥150.)*

SHIROTORI GARDEN. The design of the artificial stream and waterfall is inspired by the Kiso River. In the garden, the biggest in Aichi Prefecture, visitors can while away the afternoon watching fat, lazy carp. The Seiu-tei is a handsome ceremonial tea room. *(A 10min. walk from Atsuta Jingu. 2-5, Nishi-machi, Astuta, Astuta-ku. ☎ 681-8928. Open Tu-Sa 9am-4:30pm; closed 3rd W of every month. ¥200, age 12 or under ¥50.)*

NAGOYA PORT. South of the city on the other branch of the Meijo Line is Nagoya Port. The **Port of Nagoya Public Aquarium** is not enormous but has a popular dolphin show (at least 3 per day). The aquarium also has a good whale collection, including a recently acquired orca. Tickets are pricey, but before 1pm you can buy a combination ticket that covers the three other port area attractions. *(1-3, Minato-machi, Minato-ku. ☎654-7000; www.nagoyaaqua.or.jp. Open Apr. 1-July 20 Tu-Su 9:30am-5:30pm; July 21-Aug. 31 Tu-Su 9:30am-8pm; Dec. 1-Mar. 31 Tu-Su 9:30am-5pm. ¥2000, junior high and elementary students ¥1000, children 4 or older ¥500; combination ticket ¥2400, children ¥1200).* The **Maritime Museum** in the Port Building *(open Tu-Su 9:30am-5pm)*, the **Observation Tower** *(open M-F 9:30am-9pm; closed 3rd M of each month)*, and the **Fuji Antarctic Museum** *(open Tu-Su 9:30am-5pm)* are nearby. All emphasize the development of the port; the Fuji Antarctic Museum is the most impressive, commemorating the Japanese ship *Icebreaker*. *(1 museum ¥300, children ¥200; all 3: ¥700/¥400.)*

⌐ SHOPPING

Sakae is the center of the shopping district in Nagoya. The **Maruei Shopping Center** on Hirokōji-dōri is a huge department store, but the street itself has tons of specialty shops. If you're looking for older or cheaper stuff, try the shopping streets around **Osu Kannon**, which are filled with toy stores, discount stores, and restaurants, and become the center of antique sales on the 18th and 28th of the month.

◪ NIGHTLIFE

Nagoya has an excellent nightlife scene, focused mostly in Sakae and Nishiki. The subway stops running around midnight, but many places are open until 5am or later, only an hour before the subway reopens.

■ **Heaven's Door,** City Point Bldg. B1, 3-23-10, Nishiki, Naka-ku (☎971-7080). Sakae Station. From the station walk 2 blocks toward Nagoya Station on Nishiki-dōri; take a left after Otsu-dōri. It's in the basement. No need to knock, and we bet you never thought the stairway to heaven would go down. Best music in Nagoya—all vinyl and no cover. Loud classic rock mixed as meticulously as the drinks. Bar food from ¥400. Beer from ¥500. Open Tu-Su 6pm-4am, food served until 3am.

zetton ODEON, 3-12-23, Sakae, Naka-ku (toll-free ☎0120-590-855; www.zetton.co.jp). Sakae Station. From the front of the International Design Center, go 1 block toward Nagoya Station; it's on your right. Great Happy Hour (half-price drinks) daily 5-7pm in a hip bar. Sweet margaritas—try the Milky Veil for a Japanese twist on the icy dessert. Pastas from ¥850. Open M-F 11:30am-midnight, Sa-Su 11:30am-3am.

iD Bar, Mitsukoshi Bldg., 3-1-15, Sakae, Naka-ku (☎251-0382; www.idx-net.com/iD). Sakae Station. From Maruzen Bookstore on Hirokōji-dōri, walk 1 block toward Nagoya Station and take a left; it's on the right. Everything costs ¥500—from beer, to burgers, to a cheese plate, to gin and tonics. Packed on the weekends; lots of dancing, probably induced by the lewd cartoons on the walls. Be prepared to show your passport or naturalization papers—the name is no joke. Open Su-Th 7pm-1:30am, F-Sa 7pm-3:30am.

Click, Higashi Sakae Building 3F, 4-11-6, Sakae, Naka-ku (☎242-3253). Sakae Station. From the station, walk 1 block away from Nagoya Station on Hirokōji-dōri and take a right, then your 3rd left. It's on the 2nd block to the right. Cozy 3rd-floor bar with hip-hop, reggae, R&B, and soul. You can hear the music from the 1st floor if you're in the right area. The DJs here play iD Bar some Sa. Open M-F 8pm-3am, Sa-Su 8pm-5am.

GIFU (岐阜)　　☎058

Seriously damaged in a massive 1891 earthquake and devastated by World War II bombings, Gifu still shows signs of the century's wear and tear. The city offers little to the time-pressed traveler, save cormorant fishing and famous handicrafts. A small castle sits atop Mt. Kinka with several decent museums and a temple nearby.

🖙🔁 TRANSPORTATION AND PRACTICAL INFORMATION. From Nagoya, take the Meitetsu Nagoya Line from Shin-Nagoya Station to Shin-Gifu Station (35min., every 10-15min., ¥540). Gifu has two train stations, Meitetsu Shin-Gifu Station and JR Gifu Station, 5min. apart by foot. From Meitetsu Shin-Gifu Station, head to the intersection with Parco department store, then turn left and continue; JR Gifu Station is to the left. The **tourist office**, Gifu Eki Kōnai, is on the second floor of JR Gifu Station, by the Nagara Exit. The staff speak a little English, and have maps and an accommodations list. (☎262-4415. Open Mar.-Nov. 9am-7pm; Dec.-Feb. 9am-6pm.) In an emergency, call ☎110 for **police**, ☎119 for **fire** or **ambulance. NetStation Io** in NTT Multimedia Gallery, 8-1, Kin-chō, provides free **Internet access**. It's 3min. from JR Gifu Station on Kinka Bashi-dōri. (☎0120-10-2950. 10min. max. Open M-Sa 10am-6pm.) The **post office**, 1, Tetsumei-dōri, is 15min. from Gifu Station; head up Nagara Bashi-dōri and turn left at Melsa department store. It's 2min. to your right. (☎262-4300. Open M-F 9am-5pm.) **Postal code:** 500.

🖙🖸 ACCOMMODATIONS AND FOOD. Lodging options cluster around the stations with a few near Gifu Kōen. **Weekly Mansion Shō ❶**, 1-14, Kinen-chō, is convenient and rents furnished rooms. Though it's geared toward long-term visitors, short stays—even a single night—are welcome. Rooms have microwaves, toaster ovens, and coin laundry. Head out of JR Gifu Station onto Nagara Bashi-dōri for 8-10min., turn right at the third light, and it's a 2min. walk to your right. (☎262-6540; fax 262-6542. Check-in 4-9pm. Check-out 8-10am. Singles ¥3000-3500; twins ¥5000.) Another good deal is **Tōyoko Inn Shin-Gifu ❷**, 5-9, Motomachi, 3min. behind Meitetsu Shin-Gifu Station. Rooms have semi-double beds and free LAN Internet access. (☎264-1045; fax 264-3045. Breakfast included. Check-in 4pm. Check-out 10am. Singles ¥4800-5800; doubles and twins ¥7800.) **Yamaguchi-Ya Ryokan ❷**, 2-9 Tamamiyamachi, has nice *tatami* rooms. Walk straight up Nagara Bashi-dōri from JR Gifu Station, turn left at the light, toward Parco; it's down the second alley to your right. (☎263-0984. Check-in 4pm. Check-out 10am. ¥4000, with 2 meals ¥6000).

The **Gifu Melsa Gurume Kan ❷**, at the intersection of Nagara Bashi-dōri and Gifu Tōzai-dōri, has a collection of restaurants. (Open daily 10am-9pm.) **Okonomi Daigaku Poran ❷**, 1-20, Hinode-chō, has loads of ingredients; you can cook your own pancakes (¥500-800). From JR Gifu Station, head up Kinka Bashi-dōri, take the first right after Takashimaya department store; it's on your right. (☎264-1386. Open daily 11am-10:30pm.) **Ichōya ❶**, behind Meitetsu Shin-Gifu Station and Loft department store, is a *rāmen* spot with six different kinds of *gyōza*, including a popular cheese *gyōza* (¥450). (☎263-3449. Open Su-M and W-Sa 5pm-1am.)

🖸 SIGHTS. Cormorant fishing, or **ukai**, is held on the Nagara River, north of Gifu's stations. Prices are higher than in Inuyama, however, and the eating and drinking festivities are shorter. Enjoy a free show from Nagara Bridge, or if you're up for a ride, make reservations at the office next to the bridge. Take the #11 bus (25min., every 15min., ¥200) from Gifu or Shin-Gifu Station to Nagara Bashi Station. (☎262-0104; fax 264-2061. Fishing May 11-Oct. 15. Boats depart 6:45pm. ¥3300, under 12 ¥2900.) The other attraction is **Mt. Kinka** (Kinka-zan; 金華山) in Gifu Park (Gifu Kōen; 岐阜公園), which can be reached by #11 bus to Gifu Kōen Rekishi Hakubutsukan-mae (20min., every 15min., ¥200). **Gifu Castle** (Gifu-jō; 岐阜城), atop the mountain, can be reached by the Kinkazan Ropeway (5min.; every 15min.; ¥600, under 12 ¥280, round-trip ¥1050/¥520), or by a 1hr. hike up the shrubbery-packed mountain road. The small castle, 7min. from the ropeway station, is a too-perfect reconstruction of the original; its best feature is the view from its top balcony. (☎263-4853. Open daily Mar. 16-Oct. 15 9am-5:30pm; Oct. 16-Mar. 15 9am-4:30pm. ¥200, under 16 ¥100. Discount tickets available at info center at JR Gifu station bus terminal.) While you're up there, check out the bushy tails at the tiny **squirrel village** (¥200).

Down in the park are several museums. The largest is the **Gifu City History Museum** (Gifu-shi Rekishi Hakubutsukan; 岐阜市歴史博物館), 2-18-1, Ōmiya-chō, with displays of history and culture and exhibitions on cormorant fishing. (☎265-0010. Open Tu-Su 9am-5pm. ¥500, under 15 ¥250.) Admission also gets you into the annex, the **Kato Eizo Toichi Memorial Art Museum** (Kato Eizo Toichi Kinen Bijutsukan; 加藤栄三・東一記念美術館), 1-46, Ōmiya-chō, a hall displaying works by local brothers Eizo and Toichi Kato. (☎264-6410. Open Tu-Su 9am-5pm.) The entomophobic should steer clear of the quirky **Nawa Insect Museum** (Nawa Konchū Hakubutsukan; 名和昆虫博物館), 2-18, Ōmiya-chō, which displays over 18,000 different types and 300,000 different specimens. (☎263-0038; fax 264-0394. Open daily 10am-5pm. ¥500, under 15 ¥400.)

A 5min. walk from Gifu Park away from the Nagara River, is externally unimpressive **Shōhō-ji** (正法寺); inside the temple, however, is Japan's largest lacquered Buddha. Nearly 14m tall, the statue took 38 years to complete. (Open daily 9am-4pm. ¥150, under 12 ¥100.) Gifu's specialty, handmade **paper parasols** and **lanterns**, can be found in the alleys off Nagara Bashi-dōri and Gifu Tōzai-dōri. **Sakida Honten,** 27, Kanōnaka Hiroe, is 10min. south of JR Gifu Station, and specializes in paper crafts—if you're lucky, you might see the workmen. (☎72-3865. Open M-Sa 7am-noon and 2-5pm.)

GUJŌ HACHIMAN (郡上八幡)　　　　☎0575

North of Gifu lies quiet Gujō Hachiman, known across Japan for its **Gujō Odori Festival** (郡上おどり祭), held from mid-July to early-September. The lively festival features nightly dancing by residents in *yukata;* visitors are welcome to join in. The festival peaks August 13-16, with fireworks, dance competitions, and incessant dancing. The main sight is **Gujō Hachiman Castle** (Gujō Hachiman Jō; 郡上八幡城), a 1933 reconstruction. While picturesque, the new exterior detracts from its historic importance. (☎67-1819. 20min. north of train station. Open daily Mar.-May and Sept.-Oct. 9am-5pm; June-Aug. 8am-6pm; Nov.-Feb. 9am-4:30pm. ¥300, under 12 ¥150.) The **Gujō Hachiman Art Museum** (Gujō Hachiman Mingei Bijutsukan; 郡上八幡民芸美術館) has modern art and traditional artifacts. It's on your way to the castle and town center. (☎65-2329. 10min. from train station. Open Oct.-June Su-W and F-Sa 9am-5pm; July-Sept. daily 9am-6pm. ¥350, under 12 ¥200.)

To get to Gujō Hachiman, take the JR Takayama Line from Gifu to Mino Ota (40min., every 15min.) and transfer to the Nagaragawa Line to Gujō Hachiman Station (75min., every 30min.). The two trips will run you ¥1680. Alternatively, the Kosoku Gifu Bus or Shiro Tori Bus runs from the bus terminal near Meitetsu Shin-Gifu Station to Gujō Hachiman Joshita Plaza (80min., 4 per day, ¥1480). The **tourist office** is near the river at the center of town, inside the Gujō Hachiman Kyuchōsha Kinenkan building. (☎67-0002. Open daily 8:30am-5pm.) In an emergency, call ☎110 for **police,** ☎119 for **fire** or **ambulance.** The cheapest bed is the **Gujō Tōsen-ji Youth Hostel (HI) ❶**, 417, Ozaki-chō, a comfortable, newish place by Tōsen-ji. (☎67-0290; fax 67-0549. Breakfast ¥500. Dinner ¥800. Check-in 4pm. Check-out 10am. Closed Aug. 11-16 and Dec. 29-Jan. 5. ¥3200; nonmembers ¥4200.) The **Hachiman Cycling Terminal ❸**, 5km from town, is part of an association offering cyclists affordable stays. Although the rooms and facilities are basic, they'll lend you a bike for free. From Gujō Hachiman Station, take a Honchō terminal-bound bus to the last stop, then transfer to the Meihō bus to Chuō Bashi; it's a short walk from the bus stop. (☎62-2139. ¥5800 per person.) An upscale choice closer to the town center is **Tabata Onsen Yunomoto Kan ❹**, an attractive ryokan. (☎63-2888. Check-in 4pm. Check-out 10am. ¥9000.) During the festival, and especially during the main days in August, vacancies are scarce.

INUYAMA (犬山)   ☎0568

It's hard living in the shadow of a city like Nagoya, but Inuyama competes by tendering experiences outside urbanity's realm. Though it's a mere half-hour from the city, the cormorant fishing and river rafting seem worlds away. Nearby open-air museum parks Meiji Mura and Little World do that theme one better, transporting visitors through time and across the globe. The most prominent sight, however, is Inuyama Castle, complemented by serene Uraku-en garden and attractive Jo-An teahouse. An easy daytrip from Nagoya or Gifu, Inuyama merits a longer visit.

ON THE WEB	Inuyama: www.city.inuyama.aichi.jp/inuyama

▐▬ ▐? TRANSPORTATION AND PRACTICAL INFORMATION

Inuyama is served by the Meitetsu Line, which runs from Nagoya through Inuyama to Gifu. From Nagoya Station, take the subway's Higashiyama Line to Fushimi, then transfer to the Tsurumai Line, heading toward Kami Otai. Some trains run directly to Inuyama; if yours doesn't, transfer to the Meitetsu Inuyama Line to Inuyama (30min., every 5-10min., ¥700). If you're coming from Shin-Gifu, again take the Meitetsu Line to Inuyama (30min., every 15min., ¥440). Inuyama Station is located in the center of the city, while Inuyama Yūen Station, one stop from Inuyama Station, is closer to Inuyama Castle and cormorant fishing. (From Inuyama: 4min., ¥160. From Nagoya: 35min., ¥750. From Shin-Gifu: 25min., ¥440.)

The **tourist office**, 14, Fujimi-chō, in Inuyama Station, provides English maps and brochures. (☎61-6000; fax 62-6155. Open daily 9am-5pm.) The **Inuyama Sightseeing Center Freude** has helpful English speakers. Take a right at the first light outside the station's East Exit. (☎61-1000. Open daily 9am-7pm.) In an emergency, call ☎110 for **police**, ☎119 for **fire** or **ambulance**. **Post offices** are near the East and West Exits of Inuyama Station. (Open M-F 9am-5pm.) **Postal code: 484.**

▐▌ ▐ ACCOMMODATIONS AND FOOD

Although accommodations tend to be quite expensive, there's no need to worry—the ▨**Inuyama International Youth Hostel (HI)** ❷, 162-1, Himuro, is cheap, extraordinarily comfortable, and attractive. With courteous staff, free laundry, and a stone bath, it's easily the area's best stay. The closest station is Inuyama Yūen; from there it's a 20-30min. walk. Turn right out of the station, cross back over the tracks, and follow the river to the Himuro traffic light, where a sign points uphill. A taxi from the station costs ¥700-800. (☎61-1111; fax 61-2770. Check-in 4pm. Check-out 10am. Curfew 10pm. Breakfast ¥800. Dinner ¥1500. Singles ¥3700; twins ¥3200. Japanese rooms ¥2900 per person. Reservations recommended.) Closer to Inuyama Yūen Station and Inuyama Castle, **Kawamiya Ryokan** ❸ has rooms facing the Kiso River. Head right from Inuyama Yūen Station, turn left before the Inuyama bridge, and walk 3min. (☎61-0448. Check-in 4pm. Check-out 10am. ¥7500.) **Inuyama City Hotel** ❸ is near Inuyama Station's West Exit. Straight out of the station, take a right at the first light. (☎61-1600. Check-in 3pm. Check-out 10am. Singles ¥6500; twins ¥11,000; doubles ¥10,000.)

Dining options around Inuyama Castle and Inuyama Yūen Station are severely limited; instead, head to Inuyama Station. Look for cheap eats (*rāmen, yakisoba, okonomiyaki*, sandwiches), as well as a good supermarket, in the basement of **Itōyōkadō department store** ❶, just outside the East Exit of Inuyama Station. (Open daily 10am-8pm.) A 5min. walk straight from the West Exit is **Yoshino Sushi** ❷, a small sushi bar. (☎61-0782. Sushi ¥800-1500. Open daily 11am-2pm and 4:30-8pm.)

🔵 SIGHTS

INUYAMA CASTLE (INUYAMA-JŌ; 犬山城 **).** The symbolic center of Inuyama, three-tiered Inuyama Castle claims to be the oldest in Japan. Constructed in 1537, its ownership was exchanged among various families through its long history, but it was eventually given to the Naruse family, making it Japan's only privately owned national treasure. The castle is atop a hill, overlooking a small grounds. Inside are maps, books, *samurai* armor, and guns, but the highlight is the view at the top of four flights of extremely steep stairs. *(65-2, Aza Kita Koken. From Inuyama Yūen Station, turn left at the Kiso River, to the right of the station, then follow the river 10min., until a sign directs you leftwards. From Inuyama Station's West Exit, go straight for 10min. to the Honmachi intersection, turn right, and go straight for 15min. ☎ 61-1711; fax 61-5611. Open daily 9am-5pm. Guided tours in English upon request. ¥400, under 15 ¥100.)*

URAKU-EN AND JO-AN TEAHOUSE (有楽苑・国宝茶室如庵 **).** This serene garden is home to Jo-An Teahouse, a national treasure. The master of tea ceremony, Oda Uraku, younger brother to warlord Oda Nobunaga, built Jo-An in 1618. Walk through the garden's stone paths and greenery, then sip a cup of tea (¥500) amid the traditional houses. *(On the grounds of Meitetsu Inuyama Hotel, a 5min. walk toward the Kiso River from the castle. ☎ 61-4608. Open Mar.-Nov. 9am-5pm; Dec.-Feb. 9am-4pm. ¥1000. Combined admission with castle ¥1100. Discount tickets available at castle ticket office.)*

INUYAMA ARTIFACTS MUSEUM (INUYAMA-SHI BUNKA SHIRYOKAN; 犬山市文化資料館 **) AND KARAKURI EXHIBITION ROOM (KARAKURI TENJIKAN;** からくり展示館 **).** This small museum near Inuyama Castle displays two of the thirteen extravagant floats used during the annual Inuyama Festival, as well as miniature models, mechanical puppets, and other cultural treasures. The exhibitions are limited, but the price is right. *(Kita Koken 8. A 2min. walk south of Inuyama Castle. ☎ 62-4802. Open daily 9am-5pm. Combined admission for both museums ¥100, under 15 free.)*

CORMORANT FISHING (UKAI; 鵜飼 **).** By the Kiso River awaits an opportunity to watch *ukai*, the technique of fishing with graceful cormorant birds, up close. Eating and drinking atop a wooden boat, you'll enjoy traditional methods performed by skillful fishermen by firelight. *Ukai* is done near Inuyama Bridge, next to Inuyama Yūen Station, nightly from June through September. Reserve a ticket at the office down by the dock, or through the tourist office in Inuyama. It's also possible to watch for free from the bridge, though partaking of the full on-board experience is recommended. *(2, Shirayama Daira. Turn right out of Inuyama Yūen Station, cross over the railway tracks and follow the river 2min. to find the office. ☎ 61-0057; fax 61-6126. Open June 1-Sept. 30. Boats depart at 7:45pm from June-Aug. and at 7:15pm in Sept. Board starting at 6pm. June and Sept. ¥2500, under 12 ¥1250; July-Aug. ¥2800, under 12 ¥1400.)*

KISO RIVER RAPIDS (NIHON RHEIN KUDARI; 日本ライン下り **).** For an adrenaline-soaked experience, try shooting the Kiso River Rapids on a slender wooden boat. Led by a traditionally dressed guide, the 1hr. trip down 13km of Kiso-Gawa is a thrilling way to interact with nature. *(The Meitetsu Hiromi Line runs from Inuyama to Nihon Rhein Imawatari Station (10min., every 15min., ¥730), where buses shuttle you to the dock. Alternatively, a shuttle bus runs from the ticket office near Inuyama Yūen Station (30min., every 30min., free). ☎ 28-2727. Reservations required. ¥3400, under 12 ¥1700.)*

MEIJI MURA (明治村 **).** With 67 Meiji-era buildings in this massive outdoor museum, Meiji Mura easily has some of Japan's greatest architectural exhibits. Don't miss the former home of Natsume Sōseki, author and face on the ¥1000 bill; Frank Lloyd Wright's Imperial Hotel; and the Nijubashi Lamp, which once lit the grounds of the Imperial Palace. Transport A steam locomotive (¥500) and a Kyōto streetcar (¥300), as well as modern electric buses (¥600), will shuttle you around. The restaurants and tearooms allow you to fully experience—or at least imagine— life over 100 years ago in Japan. *(1, Uchiyama. Take the Meiji Mura-bound bus from Inuyama*

Station East Exit (20 min.; M-F every 30min., Sa-Su every 15min.; ¥410). ☎ 67-0314; fax 67-0358. Open Mar.-Oct. daily 9:30am-5pm; Nov. daily 9:30am-4pm; Dec.-Feb. Tu-Su 9:30am-4pm. ¥1600, high school students ¥1000, under 15 ¥600, 65+ ¥1200.)

LITTLE WORLD (リトルワールド). An open-air museum, Little World gathers traditional houses from around the globe. Wander into Ainu huts from Hokkaidō, landlord residences from Peru, Yao houses from Thailand, farmhouses from France, and homesteads from South Africa. There are 33 buildings from 22 countriesl and an exhibition hall with over 700 cultural artifacts. Dress up in traditional garb from different countries, including Taiwan, Indonesia, Germany, France, Italy, and India. Top off your visit at one of the eight ethnic restaurants. *(90-48, Imai Narusawa. Take the Little World-bound bus from Inuyama Station East Exit (20min.; M-F every 30min., Sa-Su every 15min.; ¥480).* ☎ 62-5611. Open daily Mar.-Nov. 9:30am-5pm; Dec.-Feb. 9:30am-4pm. ¥1600, high school students ¥1000, under 15 ¥ 600, 65+ ¥1200.)

🔲 FESTIVAL

The **Inuyama Festival** is held at Haritsuna Shrine in Inuyama, on the first weekend of April. It features thirteen three-story festive floats, atop which puppet shows are performed, accompanied by Japanese flute and drums. At night, 365 paper lanterns on the floats are lit, and the floats are paraded through cherry blossom trees.

SETO (瀬戸)   ☎ 0561

It's said that Japanese pottery production began here during the 8th century, and the Japanese term for ceramics is still *Seto-mono*, or "Objects of Seto." The pottery industry developed in the 13th century, when Chinese methods were introduced, but dwindled during the 14th-century wars. After a lengthy dormant period, modern ceramic technology was introduced in the early 19th century by Tamikichi Kato, and Seto again prospers as Japan's primary producer of breakable objects.

On the second weekend of September is the **Seto Pottery Festival,** when ceramic-selling vendors cram the streets. The largest outside market of its type, the festival attracts scads of visitors nationwide. Pottery shops and galleries are scattered around the town's sights. **Seto Ceramics and Glass Art Center** (Setoshi Shinseiki Kōgeikan; 瀬戸市新世紀工芸館) has five galleries of intricate ceramic and glass works. In the cozy cafe downstairs, choose a unique handmade cup in which to have your beverage (¥250-350). From the tourist office, turn right as you exit the shopping arcade; it's the green building 2min. up the hill to your right. (☎ 97-1001. Open Su-Tu and Th-Sa 10am-6pm. Free.) A 10-15min. walk east leads you to **Hosen-ji** (宝泉寺), a 700-year-old temple with a two-story pagoda, while fun **Kamagaki no Komichi Road** (釜垣の小径) has pottery tools and products embedded in it. Back toward the station, take your first left and go up the road for 15min. to find **Kamagami Shrine** (Kamagami Jinja; 釜神社), where Tamikichi Kato, who introduced porcelain to Seto, is enshrined. His statue is atop a steep flight of stone steps.

From Nagoya Station, take the subway Higashiyama Line two stops to Sakae (5min., every 5-10min., ¥200), walk 5min. through the underground path to Meitetsu Railway's Sakae Machi Station. From there, the Meitetsu Seto Line runs to Owari Seto, closest to the center of Seto (local: 37min., subexpress: 33min.; express: 30min.; every 5-10min.; ¥470). The helpful **tourist office,** 1-7-1, Suehiro Machi, is 10min. awat. From Owari Seto Station, walk to the first traffic light, cross the bridge; it's at the shopping arcade entrance. The office organizes free tours of Seto's sights in Japanese and English; call and reserve a spot one week in advance. (☎ 85-27301; www.city.seto.aichi.jp/setomono/kankou. Open Tu-Su 9am-5pm.)

TOYOTA (豊田)   ☎ 0565

Aichi Prefecture's second largest city was once famous as the birthplace of the Tokugawa family, who established the Tokugawa shōgunate in 1603 and unified Japan after 150 years of civil war. In recent years, Toyota has turned from autocrats to automobiles and is associated with internationally famous Toyota Motors, headquartered in Toyota city. Nearly one-sixth of Toyota's 350,000 residents work for the company. Check out the ⊠**Toyota Exhibition Hall** (Toyota Kaikan; トヨタ会館), 1, Toyota-chō, and **tours** of Toyota's factory and assembly line. The exhibition hall is a fascinating, and, happily, free establishment, with scores of hands-on activities. Close-up views of F1 racing cars, the newest Toyota line, engines, and car parts will bring out anyone's dormant engineer. The entire hall is trilingual, with Japanese, English, and Chinese translations of everything, including films. (Open daily 9am-4:30pm. Free.) Get the real scoop on a guided tour of the factories. (Japanese ☎29-3355, English ☎23-3922; www.toyota.co.jp/company/factory. Reservations required 2 weeks to 3 months in advance. Tours depart from exhibition hall. Tours available 9am-noon and 1-4:30pm.)

The closest station to Toyota's headquarters and the exhibition hall is Mikawa Toyota. From Nagoya, take the subway's Higashiyama Line one stop to Fushimi, then transfer to the subway's Tsurumai Line and continue to Akaike. If you're lucky, you'll catch a train running directly through Akaike to Toyota-shi; if not, transfer to the Meitetsu Toyota Line and go to Toyota-shi Station (45min., every 10min., ¥790). At Toyota-shi, turn right out of the station and cross the elevated walkway to Shin-Toyota Station. The Aichi Kanjō Line connects Shin-Toyota Station with Mikawa Toyota Station, two stops away (5min., every 30min., ¥220). Take a left out of the station and continue for 5min. to a large road at a T-intersection. Turn left there and go straight for 15min.; the Exhibition Hall is to your left.

KANSAI (関西)

The central pivot on which the island of Honshū turns, Kansai shelters a dense agglomeration of sights and images powerfully associated with traditional Japan. It is true that the region's seven prefectures have accumulated no small amount of urban-technological glitz, from Kōbe's artificial islands to Ōsaka's neon-lit nightlife to Kyōto's space-age train station. But the notion of Kansai as the country's core, preserving its religious essence and aesthetic spirit, remains strong. Many first-timers to Japan happily spend their days among the countless shrines and temples of Kyōto and while away their nights in the old-timey Gion entertainment district. It is here, among *geisha* and *kabuki* actors, that visitors most easily find the strikingly painted face that Japan presents to the rest of the world. The lakeside beaches of Shiga Prefecture lie just west of Kyōto; to the east is the grand castle Himeji-jō; and in the south, the sacred deer of Nara graze unflappably among awestruck tourists. The coastline of the Kii Peninsula offers stunning scenery all the way from Wakayama in the west to Shima-hantō in the east, where the Shintō shrines at Ise stand undisturbed among the forests of Ise-shima National Park.

HIGHLIGHTS OF KANSAI

KABUKI IN KYŌTO. The smell of the face-paint, the roar of the crowd—the dramatic art of *kabuki* thrives yearlong in Kyōto's historic **Minamiza theater** (p. 417).

BEHIND THE MUSIC. Ōsaka, Kansai's party hub, also houses a **Human Rights Museum** that examines discrimination and environmental issues in Japan (p. 440).

ELEVATED STATES. Stay in *shukubō* (temple lodgings) and live among monks in **Kōya-san,** the mountain home of Shingon Buddhism (p. 467).

COWS ARE HAPPIER WHEN PAMPERED. And they taste better, too! Kōbe's fine-living bovines yield **Japan's tenderest beef.** Grab a bite, or several, while in town (p. 463).

KYŌTO (京都)   ☎075

Simply put, Kyōto is a perpetual embarrassment of riches. Japan's capital for more than 1100 years, it has a legacy of over 1600 temples, hundreds of shrines, and countless national treasures large and small. Just as a lotus blossom encompasses the universe, so too does Kyōto encompass an infinite number of smaller worlds, each exquisite in its detail—from the rock clusters of a Zen garden to the red lanterns of the Gion entertainment district, and from the clack of family looms in the Nishijin neighborhood to the tangled roots of a temple's ancient camphor trees.

Dreamy-eyed historical romantics, though, should beware. Given that Kyōto's name evokes images of moonlit boating parties and snowy cherry blossoms, the first glimpse of the city from the gargantuan glass-paned train station inevitably disappoints. You'll have ample opportunity to lose yourself in the stark, suggestive minimalism of famous gardens, but you're just as likely to get lost in the unending downtown clutter of flashy boutiques and arcades. While the city can endlessly develop upward, its outward growth is happily checked by the surrounding mountains. Its most lovely temples and shrines remain surrounded by aging cryptomerias, valleys of maples, and thin-stalked forests of bamboo, havens from the jam-packed intersections of the shopping districts.

First settled in the 5th century by the Korean Hata clan, Kyōto became the new imperial capital in 794 after the Emperor Kammu decided to leave Nara, where Buddhist priests were wielding their power a little too freely. Near the end of the

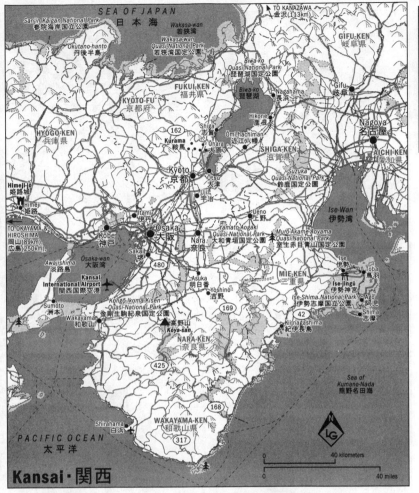

Kansai · 関西

Ashikaga shōgunate in the late 15th century, a secession dispute led to the disastrous Onin Wars, which damaged almost all the temples you see today. In the wake of this devastation, a commander of obscure origins named Toyotomi Hideyoshi rose to the shōgunate. His successor, Tokugawa Ieyasu, soon betrayed the Toyotomi regime and set up his own government. Meanwhile, the merchant class grew increasingly wealthy and fueled the development of the "floating world" of *kabuki* theater and *geisha*. By moving the imperial court to Tōkyō, the Meiji Restoration initially had devastating economic effects on Kyōto but also gave the city incentive to modernize. Spared bombing because of its architectural heritage, Kyōto survived World War II comparatively well, but Kyōtoites themselves razed many traditional wooden buildings to prevent fires in case of attacks. In the years since, Kyōto has become one of Japan's undisputed cultural and educational capitals.

ON THE WEB Kyōto City: www.city.kyoto.jp

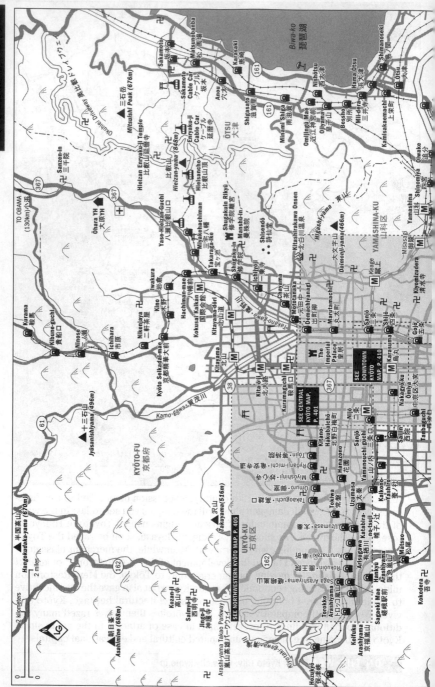

Kyōto and Surrounding Areas
京都と囲まれた地域

⊠ INTERCITY TRANSPORTATION

BY PLANE

Domestic and international flights depart from **Kansai Airport** (☎072-455-2500). Limousine buses to Kyōto leave from the ground floor; regional trains to Kyōto depart from the second floor. Limousine buses to the airport stop in front of Hotel Keihan, facing the south side of Kyōto Station (1¾hr., every 40min. 6am-8pm, ¥2300). The **Kansai Tourist Information Center** (☎072-456-6025) has English-speaking staff. Open daily 9am-9pm. Domestic flights depart from **Itami Airport** (☎066-856-6781). Limousine buses run to Kyōto, stopping in front of the Avanti Bldg. that faces the south side of Kyōto Station (55min., every 20min. 6am-7:15pm, ¥1280).

BY TRAIN

At **Kyōto Station,** *shinkansen* trains and the Kintetsu Line leave from the south side. The **Tōkaidō-Sanyō Line** goes to: **Shin-Kōbe, Shin-Ōsaka** (45min., every 30min., ¥540), **Tōkyō** (3hr., every hr., ¥13,220). To get to **Nara,** take the **JR Nara Line** (40min.-1¼hr., every 15min., ¥690) or the **Kintetsu Line** (45min., every hr., ¥610; limited express 35min., every 30min., ¥1110). Departing from **Karasuma Station,** the **Hankyu line** runs to **Umeda Station** in **Ōsaka** (1¼hr., every 30min., ¥390).

The **Train Information Desk** on the first floor can provide limited help in English and distributes the railway timetable, available in English. Open daily 8am-9pm. The **Kyōto City Tourist Information Center** on the second floor usually has an English-speaking staff member. Otherwise, the **JNTO Tourist Information Center** in Kyōto Tower provides timetables, fares, tickets, station maps, and a detailed map of the Kansai train system. Lockers are available (small ¥300, large ¥400), and there's manned locker service near the *shinkansen* boarding area. (¥410 per piece per day; after 6 days ¥820 per day. Open 9am-9pm.) For lost luggage, go to the information desk on the south side of the station; English is spoken.

BY BUS

JR Highway buses go to Tōkyō from the JR bus stop in front of the north side of the station. Four **JR Highway Dream Buses** depart 10-11:10pm and arrive at Tōkyō Station or Shinjuku Station the following morning (8hr.; ¥8180, round-trip ¥15,640). **JR's daytime bus** leaves 1min. before the hour 7am-3pm (7hr.; ¥5700, round-trip ¥9200). For bus schedules, visit the JNTO tourist information center. All JR tickets must be bought in advance at the Bus Ticket Center (see below). **Keihan Bus** and **KB Bus** (☎661-8200) run a slightly less expensive overnight bus to Shinjuku Station in Tōkyō (7hr.; departs 10:50pm; ¥8180, round-trip ¥14,400). Buy tickets in advance at the Keihan Hotel, facing the south side of Kyōto Station.

⊟ LOCAL TRANSPORTATION

BY BUS

Local buses are easy to use with a copy of the *Kyōto City Bus Sightseeing Map,* available at **JNTO Tourist Information Center** in Kyōto Tower. The central **bus terminal** and **Bus Ticket Center** (☎341-0489; open daily 7:30am-8pm) are on the north side of Kyōto Station facing Karasuma-dōri. Normal intercity buses are pale green with a dark green stripe and will take you to most of Kyōto's tourist destinations, usually for ¥220. The tan buses with a maroon stripe serve a limited number of inner-city stops as well as the suburban neighborhoods, including Ohara to the northeast and Arashiyama to the west. On local buses, enter through the rear door and pay at the plastic box up front when you get off. On suburban buses, take a ticket when you enter and pay up front when you get off. Most buses have a change machine.

BY SUBWAY

There are two local subway lines, the north-to-south **Karazuma Line** and the east-to-west **Tōzai Line**. Five additional private train companies run lines within Kyōto. Ticket machines in the stations have bilingual transport maps. Find the fare to your destination, insert money, and choose the corresponding amount. Keep your ticket to deposit at the turnstile on your way out. Frequent-use buses and trains generally run 5:30am-11pm; less frequent or suburban buses run 6:30am-9pm.

PASSES AND PREPAID CARDS

Passes and prepaid cards are sold at the following locations: the Kyōto City Tourist Information Center on the second floor of Kyōto Station; the city bus and subway information center in the station basement; the Bus Ticket Center; and several central subway stations. For inner-city buses, you can buy a **one-day bus pass** (¥500). A **prepaid card** (¥2000; no time limit) will give you a little extra for your money; you can also use it on suburban buses, paying the difference on your way out. If you're hitting several sights quickly, the combination **bus-and-subway pass** may make sense (1-day ¥1200, 2-day ¥2000). **Trafica prepaid cards** can also be used on buses and subways with no time limit; buy them in amounts of ¥1000 and ¥3000.

BY TAXI

MK Taxi (☎075-662-1139) employs some English-speaking drivers and provides cheap service (¥580 first 2km, ¥80 each additional 400m; rates 20% higher 11pm-5am). Look for the heart logo on their cabs. You can also hire their drivers for city tours (¥1000 per hr.); call in advance or visit their office facing the south side of Kyōto Station. Other taxis line up at stands on both sides of Kyōto Station.

BIKE RENTAL

Kyōto's roads are easily biked, and cycling is one of the best ways to discover the city's back alleys and hidden neighborhoods. The police, however, can be strict about impounding illegally-parked bikes; avoid parking around major train or subway stations and opt for a side street instead. Ask the JNTO Tourist Information Center for a list of rental locations. **Muji** (☎361-1111) is on the first floor of the Platz Kintetsu department store just north of Kyōto Tower on Karasuma-dōri. (¥1000 per day, deposit ¥3000. Open M-W and F-Su 8am-6pm.) The friendly owner of **Tour Club** hostel rents bikes to guests and visitors. (¥630 per day, deposit ¥3000.)

■ ORIENTATION

Protected by pine-covered mountains to the west, north, and east, Kyōto is divided by the Kamo River, which flows south through the eastern half of the city. **Karasuma-dōri** (からすま道り) is the central artery, running from the glass-and-steel behemoth of Kyōto Station in the south to the rectangular garden of the Imperial Palace in the north. Banks and larger buildings are situated between these two areas. Downtown Kyōto is roughly the square area between Karasuma-dōri and **Kawaramachi-dōri** (河原町道り), bordered by **Oike-dōri** to the north and **Shijo-dōri** (四条道り) to the south—this is the city's shopping, dining, and entertainment district, and the Shijo-Kawaramachi intersection is the city's busiest. Directly to the east of the Kamo River is the famed entertainment district of **Gion** (祇園), and beyond that, at the foot of the eastern mountains, lie the most famous temples.

Kyōto is easy to navigate, having retained the grid system originally borrowed from a Chinese model. The horizontal streets from Jujo-dōri (10th Street) south of the station to Ichijo-dōri (1st Street;) in the north are numbered. Kyōto addresses combine the two intersecting streets that are closest to the building, and often add a further level of precision by stating if the building is situated north (agaru), south (sagaru), east (higashi), or west (nishi) of those streets.

The local population may have a reputation for elitism, but relative to other Japanese cities, Kyōto is fairly cosmopolitan and welcoming to foreigners. Several publications will give you a better sense of the city's offerings. *Kansai Time Out* publishes fun articles and music/movie/restaurant reviews (¥300), the *Kyōto Visitor's Guide* has good listings and a current events section (free), and the *Kyōto Journal* is an excellent literary/cultural review about contemporary Japan (¥900).

🔃 PRACTICAL INFORMATION

TOURIST AND FINANCIAL SERVICES

Tourist Offices:

JNTO Tourist Information Center (☎371-5649). Kyōto Tower Bldg. east side facing Kyōto Station; enter from Karasuma-dōri. **Welcome Inn** reservation service M-F 9am-noon and 1-4:30pm. Free map, map of walking tours, map of train station and local bus routes, and Kyōto Visitor's Guide available. Information on cultural events, special exhibitions, volunteer guide program, and home-visit program. Help with lost-and-found. Open M-F 9am-5pm, Sa 9am-noon.

Kyōto City Tourist Information Office (☎343-6655). Kyōto Station Bldg., 2nd fl. Fewer resources than JNTO's Tourist Information Center, but conveniently located. English-speaking employees can help with hotels. City bus daypasses and free maps available. Two computer kiosks with information on sights, cultural events, walking tours, and excursions. Open daily 8:30am-7pm.

Kyōto Prefectural International Center (☎342-0088). Kyōto Station Bldg., 9th fl.; enter through Isetan department store. International TV, magazines, and newspapers; postings for Japanese language and craft lessons. Small English book and video collection. Internet access ¥100 per 15min. Open daily 10am-6pm; closed 2nd and 4th Tu each month.

Kyōto International Community House (☎752-3010). One block north of Keage Station (street slopes downward). Large modern building, 3 floors. Message corner for informal language exchanges, private lessons, accommodations, items for sale. Library, exhibition room, study, and conference rooms. Arranges home-visit program. Fax, word processing, and printing (¥20 per page) available. Open Tu-Su 9am-9pm; if M is a holiday, then open M and closed Tu.

Tours:

Johnnie Hillwalker's Johnnie Kyōto Walking Tours (☎622-6803, mobile ☎090-1890-0096; http://wab.kyoto-inet.or.jp/people/h-s-love). Hits Higashi Hongan-ji, Sho-Seien Garden, and traditional workshops, with a stop for tea. Open Mar. 3-Nov. 28 M, W, F. Gather 10am in front of Kyōto Station, just in front of the Bus Ticket Center. 5hr. ¥2000 per person. Cash only.

Sunrise Tours (☎341-1413). Bus tours around Kyōto and excursions to Nara, Ōsaka, Himeji, and Miyama. Schedule and list of pick-up locations available from JNTO Tourist Information Center. Reserve in advance. M-Sa 10am-6pm. ¥5300-26,000; includes entrance fees.

Acoustiguide Audio Tours. Available from several hotels, including Hotel Granvia, around Kyōto Station. Tours in Kyōto West, Central, and East. ¥1500 for 1 day, ¥1000 each additional day. Brochure available at JNTO Tourist Information Center.

Geisha Walking Tours (☎0905-169-1654; www.kyotosightsandnights.com). Run by Peter MacIntosh, *geisha* and *maiko* expert and long-time Kyōto resident. Walking tours in two *geisha* districts. Reserve in advance. Morning ¥4000, evening ¥3000. Cash only.

Travel Agencies: A'cross Travel, Royal Plaza Bldg., 2nd fl. (☎255-3559). 1 block east of Karasuma-dōri, 3 blocks north of Shijo-dōri. **No. 1 Travel,** Kyogoku-Toho Bldg., 3rd fl. (☎251-6970). 1 block west of Kawaramachi-dōri, 1 block north of Shijo-dōri.

Consulates: The British Council, Karasuma Chūō Bldg., 8th fl., Karasuma-dōri (☎229-7151). 1½ blocks north of Shijo-dōri. Free Internet access on 2 computers. Open M-F 10am-8pm, Sa 10am-5pm.

Japan Foundation, Sampo Japan Universe Kyōto Bldg., 8th fl., Karasuma-dōri (☎221-1312). 1½ blocks north of Shijo-dōri. Screens classic Japanese films W 2pm (free). Foreigners only. M-F 9:30am-5:30pm.

Currency Exchange and Banks: Banks cluster along the Karasuma-dōri and Shijo-dōri intersection. Normal hours M-F 9am-3pm. The **Central Post Office** just east of Kyōto Station exchanges traveler's checks. So does the **World Currency Shop,** on the 8th fl.

of Kyōto Station. Open M-F 11am-5pm. To exchange traveler's checks on weekends, visit the **Kyōto Handicraft Center,** (☎761-5080), on Marutamachi-dōri to the east of the intersection with Higashioji-dōri. Open daily 10am-6pm.

International ATMs: On the B1 level of the Kyōto Tower Hotel, facing Kyōto Station (open daily 10am-7pm); in the **All Card Plaza,** on the west side of Teramachi Arcade, north of Shijo-dōri (see **Downtown Kyōto** map; open daily 9am-8pm); and at the **Citibank** on Shijo-dōri, ½ a block west from Karasuma-dōri (open 24hr.).

LOCAL SERVICES

English bookstores:

Maruzen, Kawaramachi-dōri (☎241-2161). 3 blocks north of Shijo-dōri. Non-Japanese newspapers, magazines, best-sellers, and language guides on 8th fl. English-language maps of Kyōto. Open daily 10am-9pm.

Fismy Book Center, Avanti Bldg., 6th fl. (☎671-8987). South of Kyōto Station. Assorted English-language paperbacks and books on Japanese culture and language. Open daily 10am-9pm.

Asahiya, Platz Kintetsu department store, 5th fl., Karasuma-dōri. Just north of the Tourist Information Center. Travel guides, paperbacks, and a small selection of maps. Open daily 10am-8pm.

Ticket agencies: Concert, theater, exhibition tickets available at Takashimaya department store, 7th fl. Shijo-dōri and Kawaramachi-dōri intersection. Open 10am-8pm.

Laundromats: Several laundromats surround Kyōto Station—ask at the Kyōto City Tourist Information Center for a map. **Jabujaburando** is on the northeast corner of Shichijo-dōri and Horikawa-dōri. **Aya** is a block east of Kyōto Station, just off of Shiokoji-dōri.

EMERGENCY AND COMMUNICATIONS

Emergency: Police ☎110. **Fire** or **ambulance** ☎119. For a less urgent health problem, call JNTO or the **AMDA International Medical Information Center Kansai** (☎066-636-2333). Open M-F 9am-5pm. KICH provides a *Medical Handbook for foreigners residing in Kyōto,* which lists addresses and phone numbers for a variety of clinics.

Police: Kyōto Prefectural Police (☎414-0110). Open M-F 9am-5:45pm.

Hotlines: Japan Help Line (☎021-046-1997). Travel questions, emergency assistance. 24hr. **Travel-Phone** (☎371-5649). Questions on tourism in Kyōto. 9am-5pm daily.

Hospitals (some assistance in English): Sakabe International Clinic (☎231-1624), Gokomachi-dōri, south of Nijo-dōri. **Japan Baptist Hospital** (☎781-5191), in Sakyo-ku, north of Mikage and east of Shirakawa.

Internet access:

Campus Plaza, Nishinotoin-Shiokoji-Sagaru, Shimogyo-ku (☎353-9111). From Kyōto Station North Exit, turn west and follow the street behind the post office 1 block; Campus Plaza is on your right before APA Hotel. Free Internet access for up to 1hr., 15 terminals. Open Tu-Su 9am-9:30pm.

Dot Comic (☎212-3030). Close to the Museum of Kyōto on Sanjo-dōri, east of Karasuma; across from the Post Office, in the Juko Bldg., 3rd fl. ¥200 every 30min. Open daily 10am-midnight.

Kinko's (☎213-6802). On Karasuma-dōri 2 blocks north of Shijo-dōri. Internet ¥200 per 10min. Fax and copying services also available. Open 24hr.

Post Office: Central Post Office (☎365-2471). Near the north side of Kyōto Station. Currency exchange, *Poste Restante,* 24hr. service counter for posting international mail and buying stamps. Open M-F 9am-7pm, Sa 9am-5pm, Su 9am-12:30pm.

▐ ACCOMMODATIONS

CENTRAL KYŌTO

Sun Hotel Kyōto (サンホテル京都 ; ☎241-3351; www.sun-hotel.co.jp). Subway: Kyōto Shiyakusho-mae, change lines at Karasuma Oike. On Kawaramachi-dōri, 1 block south of Sanjo-dōri, 2nd fl. Take bus #17 from Kyōto Station to Kawaramachi Sanjo.

Small rooms, but well-lit and nicely appointed. Busy central location. Reception 24hr. Breakfast ¥1000. Singles ¥7000-8000, doubles ¥12,200. AmEx/MC/V. ❸

Ryokan Yuhara (旅館ゆはら), Kiyamachi-dōri, Shomen-agaru (☎/fax 371-9583). Take bus #17 or 205 to Kawaramachi-Shomen, turn east onto Shomen, and cross the river; it's on the right. Peaceful location on Takase River. Sweet English-speaking proprietress. Check-in 3pm. Check-out 11pm. Singles ¥4000, doubles ¥8000. AmEx/MC/V. ❷

Ryokan Matsubaya (旅館松葉家), Nishi-iru, Higashinoto-in, Kamijuzuya-machi (☎351-3727; www.matsubayainn.com). From Kyōto

Central Kyōto · 中央京都

🛏 ACCOMMODATIONS
J-Hoppers, 26
Kyōto Dai-ni Tower Hotel, 24
Myōren-ji, 1
Ryokan Matsubaya, 17
Ryokan Shimizu, 20
Ryokan Yuhara, 18
Shoho-In Shukubō, 13
Tour Club, 19

🍴 FOOD
Asian Wind, 10
Ball n' Chain, 7
Cafe Peace, 8
Didi's, 4
Eating House Hi-Lite, 9
Ebisuwa Supermarket, 22
Honyarado, 6
Izumiya Supermarket, 2
Musashi Sushi, 25

Second House Spaghetti and Cake, 21
Speakeasy, 3
Taqueria Pachanga, 5

🛍 SHOPPING
Kikuya Antique Kimonos, 15
Kungyoko-dō, 16
Kyōto Craft Center, 12
Platz Kintetsu Dept. Store, 23

🌙 NIGHTLIFE
CK Cafe, 14
Metro, 11

Station, walk down Karasuma past JNTO Tourist Information Center; stay to the right. Past Higashi Hongan-ji, take 3rd right. Garden-view rooms pricier. Check-in 3pm. Check-out 11pm. Japanese breakfast ¥1000, Western à la carte. Singles ¥4700-5200, doubles ¥9400-10,400. AmEx/MC/V. ❷

Ryokan Shimizu (旅館しみず), 644, Wakamiya-agaru, Shichijo-dōri (☎371-5538; www5.ocn.ne.jp/~yado432). From Kyōto Station, walk down Karasuma, turn left on Shichijo, and take the first right on the west side of the temple. Classy new ryokan on peaceful side street. Japanese breakfast ¥1000. Singles ¥5500; doubles ¥10,000; triples ¥15,000; Mar., Apr., and Nov. add ¥500. Cash only. ❸

Tour Club (ツアークラブ), 362, Momiji-chō, Kitakoji-agaru, Higashinakasuji-dōri (☎353-6968; www.kyotojp.com). From Kyōto Station, head down Karasuma past JNTO Tourist Information Center, and turn left on Shichijo-dōri; it's on the 2nd block to your left. Clean and new. *Kimono* available. Info on sights and transportation in Kyōto and around. Shared kitchen. Bike rental ¥630 per day, ¥3000 deposit. Internet access ¥50 per 5min.; wireless service available. Currency exchange (USD and EUR). Dorm curfew 11:30pm. Reserve up to 6mo. in advance. Dorms ¥2300; discounts after 4th and 10th night. Twins ¥7400, triples ¥8900; private bath and toilet. ❶

Shoho-In Shukubō (正法院), Omiya Matsubara, Nishi-iru (☎881-7768; for reservations in English, call Ms. Kato, ☎090-3947-4520). From Kyōto Station, take bus #206 to Omiya Matsubara. Lovely 200-year-old temple lodgings in 3 large rooms overlooking garden. Shared bathrooms. Owner will teach longer-staying guests to write their names in *kanji* calligraphy. ¥4500 per person, ¥5000 to add breakfast. Cash only. ❸

J-Hoppers Kyōto Guest House, Nakagoryo-chō, Higashikujo (☎/fax 681-2282; http://j-hoppers.com). From Kyōto Station south exit, turn left onto Hachijo-dōri, then right onto Takeda-kaido on the left side of the Avanti Bldg. Walk 4 blocks to Kujo-dōri, turn left, and the guesthouse is on your right. Common shower; clean shared kitchen. Printer available for digital cameras. Bike rental ¥100 per hr., ¥500 per day. Reception 7am-midnight. No curfew, but you need a key after midnight. Internet ¥5 every min. Dorms ¥2500, singles and doubles ¥3000 per person. AmEx/DC/MC/V. ❶

Kyōto Dai-ni Tower Hotel (京都第２タワーホテル), Higashinotoin-dōri, Shichijo-sagaru, Shimogyo (☎361-3261; www.kyoto-tower.co.jp). From Kyōto Station north exit, head to the right past Hotel Granvia. You'll see Kyōto Century Hotel across the street; Kyōto Dai-ni is to the left. Chain hotel, small clean rooms. Buffet breakfast ¥1500. Singles ¥6000-7000; doubles ¥13,000-14,000; triples ¥18000. AmEx/MC/V. ❸

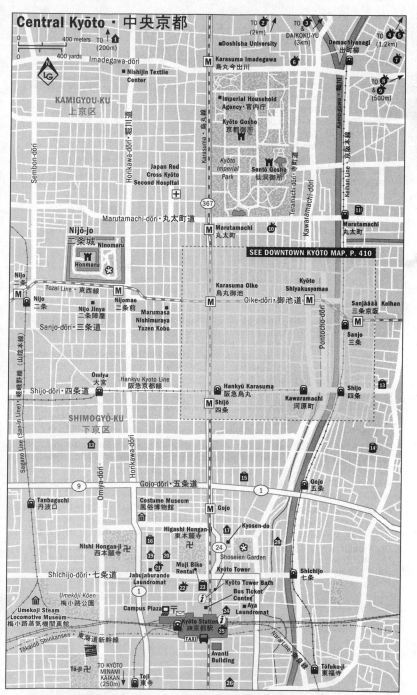

Central Kyōto · 中央京都

KANSAI

KANSAI

EASTERN KYŌTO

Higashiyama Youth Hostel (HI) (東山ユースホステル ; ☎761-8135; www.biwa.ne.jp/~kyoto-yh). Subway: Tōzai Line to Higashiyama Station. High-quality hostel, well-maintained, clean, and cozy. Common bath. Internet ¥100 per 15min. Bike rental ¥800 per day, deposit ¥1000. Coin laundry. Curfew 10:30pm. Dorms for members/nonmembers ¥3200/4000, with breakfast ¥3700/4200, with dinner ¥4000/¥4500, with both ¥3900/4300 (yes, it's less, not a misprint); private rooms with meals ¥5000/5500, plus bathroom ¥5600/6000. ❶

Hotel Hean no Mori (☎762-3130; fax 761-1333). From Kyōto Station,

Eastern Kyōto · 東京都

🏠 ACCOMMODATIONS

Higashiyama Pension, **21**	Kyōto Traveler's Inn, **18**
Higashiyama Youth Hostel (HI), **20**	Ōto Ryokan, **27**
	Three Sisters Annex, **16**
Hotel Hean no Mori, **17**	Three Sisters Inn Main, **14**
ISE Dorm, **8**	

🍴 FOOD

Asian Wind, **15**	Okutan, **19**
Ball n' Chain, **2**	Omen, **5**
Buttercups, **6**	Rakushō, **23**
Cafe Peace, **3**	Second House Cake
Caravan, **7**	Works, **10**
Eating House Hi-Lite, **4**	Senmonten, **22**
Honyarado, **1**	Yuba-sen, **25**
Kikyo, **28**	Zac Baran, **25**
Okonomiyaki Rogu, **13**	

🍸 NIGHTLIFE

CK Cafe, **24**	
Metro, **9**	

🛍 SHOPPING

Huran, **12**	
Kyōto Handicraft Center, **11**	
Kyōto Tojiki Kaikan, **26**	

take bus #5 to Higashi Tenn-chō. Classy hotel, views of Kurodani Temple and Kyōto Tower. Spacious well-lit rooms. Beautiful Japanese bath with garden view. Lunch 11:30am-2pm. Dinner 5:30-9:30pm. Singles ¥9000; doubles ¥14,000-25,000. AmEx/DC/MC/V. ❹

Three Sisters Inn, Main (Ryokan Surii Shisutāsu; 旅館スリーシスタース ; ☎761-6336; fax 761-6338). From Kyōto Station platform D2, take bus #206 to Kumano Jinja-mae. Walk north (in the bus's direction) and turn right onto Kasugakita-dōri; it's 5 blocks down on your left. Ryokan run by 3 charming elderly sisters. Spacious rooms overlook quiet street. Free breakfast. Singles ¥8900; doubles ¥13,000-18,900; triples ¥21,000-22,500. Cash or traveler's checks preferred, but credit cards accepted. ❹

Three Sisters Inn, Annex (☎761-6333; fax 761-6335). Slightly cheaper than Main, but still comfortable. Some rooms have private bathrooms. Breakfast ¥700-1200. Curfew 11:30. Do not use the Main phone/fax numbers to make a reservation at the Annex. Singles ¥4900-5900, with bath ¥9400; doubles ¥9800, with bath ¥13,800. ❷

ISE Dorm (☎751-7439; fax 771-0566). Follow directions to Three Sisters Inn (Main, see above). Take the small street running north to the left of the inn, and follow it 2½ blocks. Private rooms, most with tiny kitchens. College-y atmosphere; many long-term English teachers live here. Coin shower ¥100. Towels ¥100-300. Coin laundry. Check-in 2-9pm. Singles ¥2800, doubles ¥3950, triples ¥5500, quads ¥7000. ❶

Higashiyama Pension (東山ペンション ; ☎882-1181). Subway: Tōzai Line, Higashiyama Station. Small, dim rooms, but cozy. Peaceful spot along Shirakawa River. Breakfast ¥800. Curfew 11:30pm. Singles ¥4400, with private shower ¥6000. MC/V. ❷

Ōto Ryokan (☎541-7803; http://dns1.dhp.co.jp/users/ohto). From Kyōto Station, take bus #206 or 208 (platform D2) to Nanajo Keihan-mae. Western-style breakfast ¥300-500, Japanese-style ¥1000. Singles ¥4000-4500, with bath ¥5500; doubles ¥7000-7500, with bath ¥8000-9000. AmEx/MC/V. ❷

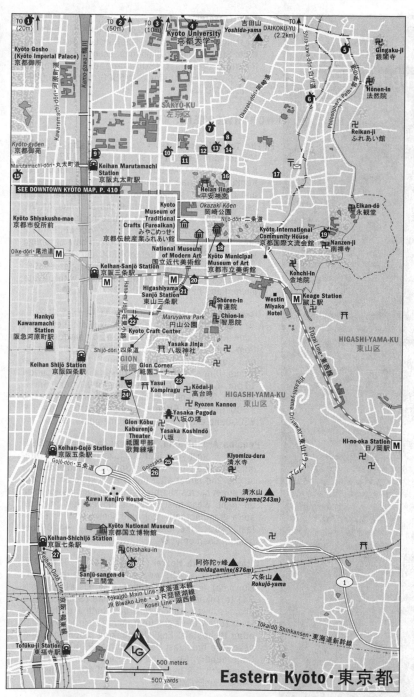

Eastern Kyōto・東京都

THE HIDDEN DEAL

MYŌREN-JI SHUKUBO

Sleep next door to a copy of the Lotus Sutra handwritten by the Emperor Fushimi. Rouse yourself at dawn to the beat of drums calling monks to prayer. **Myōren-ji Shukubo 3**, Omiya-Higashi-iru, Teranuchi-dōri, Kamigyo-ku (☎451-3527; fax 451-3597), provides spacious lodgings inside the temple Myōren-ji. Guests stay in three tatami rooms, and while there are no meals or bathing facilities, the experience of living inside a working temple is well worth the schlep to the nearby public bathhouse (the *shukubo* subsidizes a free visit).

Whatever your religious persuasion may be, Myōren-ji is a fascinating and welcoming place to learn more about daily life in a Kichiren sect temple dating back to the 13th century. While the temple has seen more than its fair share of fires and reconstructions, today it houses a number of important sutras and a rare skirt-shaped Buddhist belfry.

From Kyōto Station, take bus #9 to Horikawa Teranōchi. Head west on Teranōchi, enter the temple gate on the 2nd block on your right, and follow the paved path past the main temple building. Myōrenji Shukubo will be facing you at the end of the path. The owner speaks English. The daily prayer service begins at 6:30am and involves drums—be sure to take this into consideration. Curfew 10pm. Check-out 9am. ¥3800 per person. Cash only.

Kyōto Traveler's Inn (トラベラーズイン京都 ; ☎771-0225; www.kid97.co.jp/traveler.html). Subway: Higashiyama Station (Tōzai Line), or take bus #5 from Kyōto Station to Bijutsukan-mae. Economy hotel; good location. Breakfast ¥800. Japanese-style rooms ¥5000 per person; singles ¥5500; twins ¥10,000. AmEx/V/MC. ❸

NORTHWESTERN KYŌTO

🏠 **The Tani House** (谷ハウス), 8, Daitoku-ji-chō, Murasakino (☎211-5637, fax 252-3277). From Kyōto Station, take bus #206 from A3 platform to Kenkun Jinja-mae (30min.). Head west on Kita-oji and take your 1st right onto Funaoka Higashi; you'll see a small sign in English at the 3rd alley on the right. Inside a traditional house near Daitoku-ji. 30min. bike ride from city center, but unbeatable price. Nice old proprietress has taken care of foreign guests for 30 years. Internet ¥300 per 30min. Bike rental ¥500 per day. Dorms ¥1700, singles ¥4000, doubles ¥4200-4600, 4-person suite with private kitchen and bathroom ¥6000. DC/MC/V. ❶

Utano Youth Hostel (HI) (宇多野ユースホステル ; ☎462-2288; utano-yh@mbox.kyoto-inet.or.jp). From Kyōto Station, take bus #26 (platform B4); from Sanjo-Keihan, take bus #10 or 59. Single-sex 8-bed dorms, 2 twin rooms, and 2 Japanese-style rooms. Dinner ¥850, buffet breakfast ¥500. Curfew 11pm. Coin laundry. Internet ¥100 per 15min. Kitchen. Bike rental 1st hr. ¥200, then ¥100 per hr.; ¥600 per day. Sheets ¥150. ¥2500, under 19 ¥2000; no extra charge for nonmembers. ❶

Pension Arashiyama, 67, Miyanomoto-chō (☎881-2294). From Kyōto Station, take bus #11 to Oita-guchi. Walk a block west on Sanjo-dōri and take a left on the 2nd street after the grocery store on the left. The street curves sharply to the left; the pension is on the right. Western-style rooms; flowers and frills create a grandmotherly feel. Hall showers/toilet. Breakfast ¥800. Bike rental ¥300 per day. ¥4200 per person. Cash only. ❷

Kitayama Youth Hostel (HI) (北山ユースホステル ; ☎492-5345; www4.freeweb.ne.jp/travel/kitayama). From Kyōto Station, take bus #6 (platform B4) to Takagamine Genkohan-mae (35min.); from Kitaoji subway station, take bus North 1 to the same stop. Follow the signs from there (5min.). Older than other HI hostels. English-speaking proprietor. Japanese-style breakfast ¥525. Internet ¥100 for 30min. Coin laundry. No kitchen. Curfew 10pm. Single-sex rooms with 4-8 beds. Members ¥2940, nonmembers ¥4440. AmEx/MC/V. ❶

KANSAI

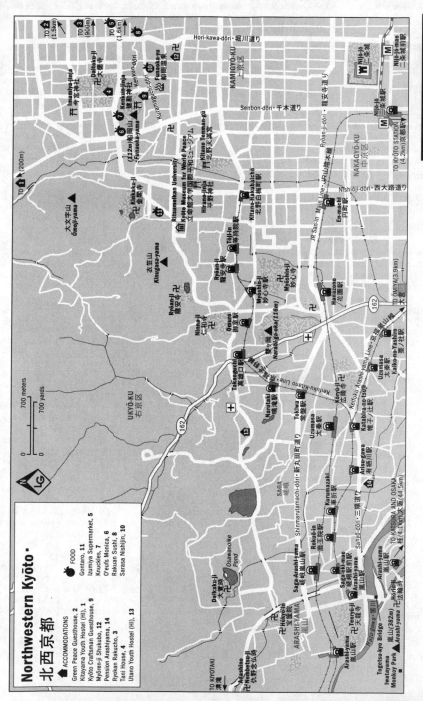

Northwestern Kyōto・北西京都

▲ ACCOMMODATIONS

Green Peace Guesthouse, 2
Kitayama Youth Hostel (HI), 1
Kyōto Craftsman Guesthouse, 9
Myōren-ji Shukubo, 12
Pension Arashiyama, 14
Ryokan Rakucho, 3
Tani House, 4
Utano Youth Hostel (HI), 13

🍴 FOOD

Gontaro, 11
Izumiya Supermarket, 5
Knuckles, 7
O'eufs Monica, 6
Rakuan Sushi, 8
Sarasa Nishijin, 10

A peek into Japan's caffeine culture.

While green tea may be the Japan's default beverage, served almost as soon as you sit down at an office, in meetings, and at homes, coffee is the drink of leisure, of calm moments away from offices, meetings, and even homes. Both respite from the rigors of tourism and destinations in themselves, *kissaten* (coffeeshops) and cafes become part of even a transient's daily life in Japan.

Japan is the world's third largest coffee importer, after the US and Germany, a fact with deep historical roots. From the earliest days of contact with the Portuguese and Dutch in Nagasaki and later, in Kōbe, coffee has been known, if not always loved. The first Japanese sippers, guests of these foreigners, thought it might be medicine and praised its medicinal properties (even as we learn today that coffee protects the body from blood clots as it stimulates). But they didn't much like the taste. Sugar wasn't yet a regular substance in the Japanese diet and milk was almost unknown as an accompaniment. It wasn't Starbucks coffee they were drinking in any case—or for that matter, Nishimura's or Inoda's, two famous local Kansai roasters.

Coffee's popularity began as a catalyst for social life. In 1888, the first public coffeehouse was established by one Tei Ei Kei, a well-traveled young Chinese man who spent time at Yale. His Koffie Kan was like an English men's club, outfitted with billiard tables, baths, changing rooms, writing desks, and a lending library. All but the coffee was free, and the long hours men lounged, absorbed in the amenities, ate into his profits. Success of this kind bankrupted him and he slunk off to Washington, presumably to help establish Seattle as the coffee town it is today, though the connection needs more research.

By the turn of the Meiji Period into the Taishō, the coffee boom in Japan had taken off. In Japan's "roaring twenties" a female presence was noted, either as women customers—or as *jokyū*, decorating the premises with their beauty, in *bijin kissa* (coffeeshops with famously beautiful waitresses). By this time, the clubby, masculine English-style coffeehouse had met the influence of the newer French-style cafe, where artists, writers, and philosophers gathered and where daring, liberated, and intellectual women could be seen.

Famous cafes and *kissaten* of the era clustered in the Ginza in Tōkyō. Also popular were themed coffeeshops, Viennese-style houses, jazz *kissa* where recordings or live musicians could be heard, and *meikyoku kissa*, the classical music coffee shops where the sanctity and quiet of a concert hall prevailed. Then there were places where less elevated senses were served, especially after the war, places such as "no-pants" cafes, where waitresses walked over mirrored floors in skirts and not much more.

Let's not forget the brown gold that gave all these places their raison d'être. Japanese coffee is on the whole darker, richer, and stronger than conventional American coffees. The blends (or *"burendo"* as you will request in a *kissaten*) are served hot or iced—if iced, accompanied by a pitcher of sugar syrup and one of heavy cream, which you will pour to taste, watching the cream descend in little waves through the ice cubes, before you stir. Most people drink blends, but connoisseurs are moving towards "straight" single-bean coffees, much as scotch drinkers have fetishized single-malt scotches. My sources say a good blend demonstrates far more connoisseurship than a single-bean coffee, but here we are playing java one-upsmanship. Coffee is expensive—from about ¥280 (less at chains like Doutor) per cup to ¥1000 or more at connoisseur coffeeshops of the extreme type (How about trying my Yemen '92 beans? Or: We roast to order, call 24hr. ahead before you plan to sip the Yrgacheffe), where you're paying for the space, the calm, the service, and often the decor. You are renting a seat and you can stay, usually, as long as you like. Real estate being expensive, shops being small, and turnover being slow, it's no wonder they have to charge more.

The most "high end" popular coffees keep changing. We are now seeing the decline of Buruman (Jamaican Blue Mountain, over 70% of the crop annually purchased by Japanese buyers) and Kona from Hawaii. New coffee ventures are vying for trend-leader—among them Mandheling, Kilimanjaro, and Cuban coffees, made with exquisite care by the dramatic syphon system or painstaking drip method, one cup at a time. In some shops, the menu of coffees is as long as a wine list in a good French restaurant. Watch for Cambian coffee: it will be the Next Big Thing.

Merry White is a professor of anthropology at Boston University. Her most recent book is Perfectly Japanese: Making Families in an Era of Upheaval.

Kyōto Craftsman Guesthouse (Kyōto Shokunin No Uchi; 京都職人の家; ☎/fax 751-5185; www1.neweb.ne.jp/wa/kyoto888). Look online for the map; it's tucked among tiny little streets, with a tiny English sign. Looking for a more personal welcome? This guesthouse offers 1 Japanese-style room in a pleasant home, across the street from the family *kimono* and *obi*-weaving factory. Breakfast ¥300 (*onigiri*, *miso* soup, tea). No bath; 3min. walk from Funaoka Onsen. ¥4610-5000 per person. ❷

Ryokan Rakuchō (旅館洛頂; ☎721-2174; www.rakucho-ryokan.com). From Kyōto Station, take the Karasuma Line to Kitaoji, walk east on Kitaoji over the river, and turn left onto Shimogamonaka-dōri. Or, take bus #205 from Kyōto Station (A2 platform) to Furitsudaigaku-mae. Japanese-style rooms overlooking garden. Welcoming and helpful proprietress. No breakfast. Coin laundry. Kitchen available. Singles ¥5000; doubles ¥8000-8800; triples ¥12,000. MC/V. ❷

Green Peace Guesthouse (☎791-9890; www.kyoto.zaq.ne.jp/greenpeace). Karasuma Line to Matsugasaki; take Exit 2, turn right onto Kitayama, and take a left just before Notre Dame Women's College. Common room with TV. Backpackers, expats, and 4 cats. Internet ¥100 per 30min. Dorms ¥1200-1600 per day, ¥26,000 per month; singles ¥2000-2400/¥42,000; doubles ¥2285-3000/¥46,000. Cash only. ❶

◪ FOOD

You can find a cheap meal at any hour in the **Kyōto University** area, particularly along Imadegawa and Higashioji-dōri. Restaurants also crowd the **Shijo-Kawaramachi** area and, west of the Kamo River, the narrow streets of **Pontochō** and **Kiyamachi**. On the latter two streets, the north end caters more to locals (i.e., more authentic, subdued-chic restaurants, usually with no English menu), while south-end options are touristy and flashy but ultimately more accessible.

There are only a few cheap supermarket and grocery options in the central Kyōto area. One is the **Sakae supermarket** smack in the middle of the Teramachi Arcade. (Open daily 9am-9pm.) A huge four-floor **Izumiya supermarket** is on Kitaoji-dōri, east of Shimogamo-higashi-dōri before you cross the river, on the south side of the street. (☎721-2101. Open daily 10am-8pm.) Near Kyōto Station, just behind the New Hankyu Hotel, there's a smaller grocery store, **Ebisuwa**. (Open daily 10am-8pm.) In a grocery emergency, you can always try the overpriced food markets in department stores. For better deals and more selection, head to the fringes.

KYŌTO STATION (京都駅)

Kyōto Station can provide a multitude of eating options in a pinch, but few of them offer much in the way of ambience. The **Porta underground mall** has both Western and Japanese cafes. A more expensive option is **Eat Paradise**, an entire floor of restaurants on the 11th level of the JR Isetan department store inside the station, where meals run ¥1500-4000. You can always grab something to go from the ubiquitous *bentō* stands, but the B2 level of JR Isetan has classier *bentō* as well as a mind-boggling array of deli options and bakery fare for just a few extra yen.

Musashi Sushi (むさし寿司; ☎662-0634). Branch on the 1st fl. of Kyōto Station (*shinkansen* side). Follow the signs from the subway to "South Exit," walk up the stairs on the left, and curve around to the right; it's across from the McDonald's. Sit down and select plates of sushi from the conveyor belt in front of you. Almost always crowded. ¥120 per plate (2 pieces). Open daily 11am-10pm. ❶

Second House Spaghetti and Cake (☎342-2555). On Shichijo-dōri, 2 blocks east of Horikawa-dōri. In a Meiji-era pillared grey building (once a bank), with pine tables and exposed ceiling beams. Good deals, fresh food. Lunch set of pasta or pizza, salad, bread, and juice/coffee ¥850-1100. Open daily 10am-11pm. ❷

ON THE MENU

KYŌTO'S BEST COFFEE

At risk of creating a rush, I offer a few favorite Kyōto *kissaten*. I won't give everything away; we coffee lovers protect our sources. **Ryūgetsudo** is a *meikyoku kissa*, a classical music coffee-house. Buy something to eat at the bakery; at the entrance to the "concert hall," you'll be instructed to use scissors to open the bags. This should alert you to the fastidiousness with which silence is observed. The music room's speakers face lines of chairs and sofas. Write a request in the ledger; then when your number's up, they play your choice: Waitresses in felt-bottomed shoes offer drinks in cups without saucers (no clinking) with wooden spoons (no clanking) to stir. *(Across from Demachiyanagi Eiden Station, in northeast Kyōto.)*

Parisian cafes have nothing on open-air **BonBon.** You can sit outdoors in almost any weather, as the canopied deck has heat poles. About ten outdoor tables with wicker chairs, and for winter, lap blankets, greet you. Students inside or out spend hours over the cheap, delicious coffees and teas, and nibble at salads or gorge on the much-too-much for much-too-little specials at lunchtime. *(At the junction of the Kamo River and Imadegawa on the northwest side.)*

The coffee is excellent, the views quiet and leafy: it is **Café Sagan** on the Philosopher's Path. The owner-master says it is a "space for communication," but it

CENTRAL KYŌTO

🏠 **Cafe Peace** (カフェピース ; ☎707-6856). On the northwest corner of Imadegawa and Higashioji, 3rd fl. Cute organic vegetarian cafe with a conscience. View of busy university intersection. Cool lounge area with low tables and a floor covered with loose polished stones—like walking on a very small and perfect beach. Soy burgers ¥750, Indian chickpea curry ¥780, tofu salad ¥500. Dumplings and other "meat" products use a bean-and-wheat substitute. Lunch set ¥780. Open M-Sa 11:30am-midnight. ●

Taqueria Pachanga (タケリアパチャンが ; ☎712-7891). Small sunny-yellow restaurant next to Didi's (see below). Go for the classic taco, or try fun variations like garlic mushroom, Brazilian sausage, or avocado and salmon (¥280). Mexican rice ¥680, salads ¥600, *huevos rancheros* ¥500. Lunch set ¥680, includes 2 tacos, small salad, and a drink; ¥880 for 3 tacos. Open M and W-Su 11:30am-10pm. ●

Didi's (☎791-8226). On Higashioji-dōri, a few blocks north of Mototanaka Station on the east side of the street. Indian curries (¥880), homemade desserts and yogurt. Decorated with traditional puppets. Illustrated menu with English. Weekday vegetarian lunch ¥750. Open M-Tu and Th-Su 11am-10pm. ●

Eating House Hi-Lite (☎721-1997). On Imadegawa-dōri, just east of Higashioji-dōri. The first of the small diners and cafes that line Imadegawa-dōri just north of Kyōto University. Not much atmosphere. Decent-sized fried chicken lunch with salad (¥570). Chicken with cheese (¥530). Open M-Sa 11am-11:30pm, Su 11am-10:30pm. ●

Asian Wind (☎211-9388). Off Maruta-machi, just south of the Imperial Palace, on Tominokoji-dōri. Small Thai restaurant, bright and cheerful. Some communal benches, bright tablecloths, fountain in back. No English menu; just tell them what kind of curry you want. Excellent curries come with rice, spring roll, salad, and lychee juice (¥850). Open M-Sa noon-2:30pm and 5:30-10pm. Cash only. ●

Senmonten (泉門天 ; ☎531-2733). From Shijo-dōri, walk 2 blocks north on Yamato-oji-dōri (1st block west of Higashioji-dōri); it's on your right. Popular joint specializing in *gyōza* (Chinese pot-sticker dumplings). Good for a snack in Gion. Long lines during busy mealtimes. 10 for ¥460. Open daily for take-out from 1pm, dinner 6pm-midnight. ●

Honyarado (ほんらや洞 ; ☎222-1574). On Imadegawa, 1 block east of Imperial Park, north side. Typical student cafe near Doshisha University. Cheap and wholesome meals. Lunch set with salad and bread/rice

(¥600; noon-5:30pm). Vegetable/chicken curry rice (¥600). Dinner set (¥700). Open daily 11am-10:30pm. Cash only. ●

DOWNTOWN KYŌTO

Tagoto (田毎 ; ☎221-3030). Subway: Hankyu-Kawaramachi. On Sanjo-dōri in the covered arcade, just east of Shinkyoguko Arcade—look for the photos of noodles outside. This *soba* and *udon* restaurant is one of the oldest and best in the city. Traditional interior with paper screens and muted colors. Lunch ¥880-1000. Dinner ¥950-1500. *Kaiseki bento* ¥2000-3000. Open daily 11am-3pm, 6-10pm. ●

Yamatomi (山とみ ; ☎221-3268). Subway: Hankyu-Kawaramachi. On the south end of Pontochō. One of the few restaurants along this street that is both classy and accessible to travelers. *Teppinage* consists of meat and vegetables that you fry yourself in a pot of oil (¥2800 per person; 2 orders minimum). *Yosenabe*, a hearty soup of chicken, prawns, and vegetables, is offered Nov.-Mar. During the summer months, ask to sit out on the veranda overlooking the Kamo River. Open Tu-Su noon-2pm and 4-11pm. ●

Biotei (びお亭 ; ☎255-0086). On Sanjo, 1 street east of Karasuma, 2nd fl. Diagonally across from the post office; near the Museum of Kyōto. Organic restaurant catering to a slightly older crowd. Wood interior, cozy little bar, jazz music. English menu. Try the chicken simmered in tea with mustard (¥680). Fish dishes ¥450-650. Tofu salad ¥500. A selection of differently prepared seaweeds. Lunch set ¥800. Dinner set ¥1200. Open Tu-W and F 11:30am-2pm and 5-8:30pm, Th 11:30-2pm, Sa 5-8:30pm. ●

Kerala (ケララ ; ☎251-0141). On Kawaramachi a few blocks north of Sanjo-dōri, 2nd fl. Decent Indian food in a central location. Tandoori plates ¥1200-1800, curries ¥1300-1800, *naan* ¥400. Open daily 11:30am-2pm and 5-9pm. ●

Fufutei (風風亭 ; ☎252-0113). On Kiyamachi, just north of Takoyakushi. *Shabu-shabu* chain restaurant; cook thinly sliced meats, vegetables, and noodles yourself in a pot of boiling water. Pork/beef *shabu-shabu* ¥1480, all-you-can-eat ¥1980. *Chanko* (tofu-veggie stew favored by *sumō* wrestlers) ¥1990. Open daily 5pm-midnight. DC/MC/V. ●

Tori-Dori (とりどり ; ☎211-5055). On Kiyamachi-dōri, on the west side of the creek, 2 blocks north of Shijo-dōri. Trendy spot for a drink or dinner, popular with 20- and 30-somethings. Slick dark interior, noisy. Brown wood exterior decorated with big paintings of vegetables. Cocktails ¥500-650. Chicken

is also a contemplative space, where the service is attentive without being obtrusive. Placement on the Philosopher's Path secures the difference. People must walk to get here, and they are already in a relaxed mood. They've come to see cherry trees, maples, or the quiet and peace of any season. *(Just south of Ginkaku-ji.)*

Café Tsukiji is full of the flavor of the past. Red velvet sofas, mahogany tables, and lots of glass and mirrors are just right for imagining novelists and artists consorting here, arguing and working off hangovers. Open your eyes, and you'll see nice Kyōto ladies, laden with shopping bags, sampling classic Taishō-period cafe dishes. *(Just inside the 1st right turning as you walk up Kawaramachi from Shijo-dōri.)*

Modernity is not Post- in Kyōto's coffeelands. Many shops have a flair for the form-following-function style; they're inhabited by the young and often serve very good Euro-style coffees. **Prinz** is a gallery-coffeehouse, elegant bare walls touched with the art. On the minimalist garden patio cement squares alternate with grass squares. *(Off Shirakawa-dōri near Kyōto's Arts University.)*

I'm reluctant to reveal the whereabouts of my secret heaven, so I'll only hint at it and tell you you'll love it if you find it. It's on a hilltop on the east side of Kyōto, standing alone. You can get delicious coffees in handmade cups, fine cappuccino, and truly superb fresh scones; if you do find it, promise not to mistreat it; I want it to be there when I return!
- *Merry White is an anthropologist studying Japanese coffeehouse culture.*

KANSAI

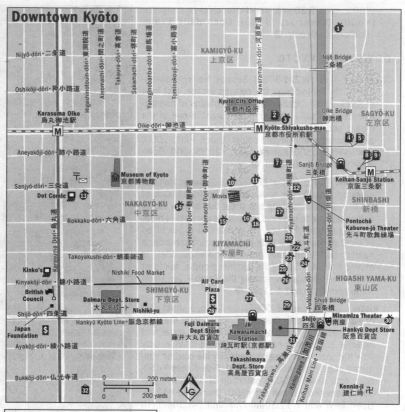

Downtown Kyōto

¥600. *Oden* ¥350-450. Pasta of the day ¥680. Open M-Th 5-11pm, F-Sa 5pm-3am. AmEx/DC/MC/V. ❷

The 844 Store Cafe (☎241-2120). Tiny cafe on a side street parallel to Kiyamachi-dōri, 3 streets from Shijo-dōri. Round tables, African carvings, and a large tree trunk covered with Christmas lights. Organic vegetarian foods. Tofu burger ¥600, cheese and *natto* (fermented soybean) omelette ¥750, penne with tomato ¥900. Draft beer (¥500), organic *sake*, Belgian beers. Open M and W-Su 5:30-11pm. ❷

Kane-yo (かねよ ; ☎669-2020). From Kawaramachi, head west on the 1st street south of Sanjo-dōri. No English sign—look for the plastic models out front and the old charcoal stove in the front window. View of waterfall in the back gives this *unagi* (eel) restaurant a very open feel. Big grill area in front. Run by cute elderly ladies. *Unagi* with rice, medium or large ¥1470/2200. Open daily 11:30am-8:30pm. ❸

Hill of Tara (☎213-3330). In the Millennium Oike Building on Oike-dōri just to the east of Kawaramachi. Irish pub with an older crowd. Fish and chips ¥1200. Salmon with a tasty warm mustard dressing over salad ¥1200. Irish soda bread ¥500. Live Irish music on many weekends starts 9pm. Open Su-Th 5pm-midnight, F-Sa 5pm-1am. ❸

Takasebune (高瀬舟 ; ☎361-0694). From Shijo-dōri, head south on the 1st tiny street east of Hankyu department store; it's at the end on the right, past the love hotels. Dodge the crowds in this tiny, classy *tempura* joint. Watch the cook fry it up fresh. *Tempura* sets in three sizes (¥800/1500/2000). *Sashimi* and *tempura* ¥3000. English menu available. Open daily 11am-3pm and 4:30-9:30pm. Cash only. ❸

Sarasa (さらさ ; ☎212-2310). On Tominokoji-dōri between Karasuma and Kawaramachi, just south of Sanjo-dōri, 2nd fl. No English sign; look for bike rentals on 1st fl. Student cafe. *Okonomiyaki* ¥700, salads ¥630, sandwiches ¥840. Lunch set from ¥740. Flyers for events around city. Open daily noon-midnight. Cash only. ❷

Mr. Young Men (☎225-4591). Subway: Hankyu Kawara-machi. In the Teramachi Arcade off Shijo, 2 blocks west of Kawaramachi. A long-established *okonomiyaki* joint with an '80s feel. Try the classic *okonomiyaki*, or jazz it up with toppings like asparagus and lemon, shrimp and *bonito* flakes, or the "French" sauce. Open daily 11:30am-10pm.

Sancho. Off of Shijo-dōri; head north on the 1st alley west of Kawara-machi, keep to your right, and Sancho will be on the left, on the 2nd floor. Popular salad restaurant. Smallish salads ¥650-850, with a side of meat ¥950-1150. Nothing too exotic—expect plain lettuce salads with tomato. Open daily 11:30am-9pm. ❷

Ikka (一花; ☎541-7878). On the south side of Shijo-dōri, 1 block east of Minamiza Theater. Conveyor-belt sushi. Slightly classier version of Musashi Sushi—serves *unagi* (eel) and has a bigger shrimp selection. Plates ¥120-480. Open daily 11:30am-9:30pm. ❶

Sushi No Musashi (寿しのむさし ; ☎222-0634). On Kawara-machi, at the intersection with Sanjo. Older downtown branch of the sushi restaurant in Kyōto Station. Also sells takeaway *bento* boxes. Open daily 11am-10pm. ❶

EASTERN KYŌTO

🏯**Rakushō** (洛匠 ; ☎561-6892). Teahouse near Kodai-ji (p. 417). *Koi* pond, little stone bridges, lush garden, and a waterfall. *Tatami* room in rear overlooks small garden. Expensive, but realizes idyllic visions of the prototypical Kyōto teahouse. Orange juice ¥500. Green tea with Japanese cake ¥800. Open daily 9:30am-5:30pm. ❷

Omen (おめん). Heading back down Philosopher's Path from Ginkaku-ji (p. 419), take the 1st right after the parking lot. Take a break from temple-hopping in this fun, lively restaurant. Low tables, *tatami* mats. English menu. *Omen* are noodles to be dipped in sauce, with veggies (¥1000, large ¥1200). Open M-W and F-Su 11am-10pm. AmEx. ❸

Speakeasy (スピークイージー ; ☎781-2110). Fun American-style greasy-spoon with spooky cowboy mannequin in the window. CNN, English newspapers, jukebox. *The* place for bacon and eggs; Western-style breakfasts served until 6pm (¥400-550). Burgers ¥650-750, homemade pizza ¥750-900, enchiladas ¥750. Open daily 9am-2am. ❷

Yuba-sen (ゆば泉). On Gojozaka-dōri, just south of Kiyomizuzaka. Specializes in *yuba*, the skin that forms on soymilk during the tofu-making process. It's bland, creamy, slightly sinewy in texture, and really rich in protein. In the workshop out back, watch them pull long, thin sheets from huge vats. Heaven for the tofu enthusiast. Snack of *hiashi-yuba*: *yuba* slabs served with soy sauce, ginger, and a side of dried *yuba* flakes (¥500). Full meal set ¥1800. Open daily 10am-5pm. ❸

Zac Baran (☎751-9748). On the north side of Marutamachi-dōri, a few blocks east of Higashioji-dōri. Dim interior, jazzy ambience. Serves spaghettis. Workers out for a night on the town wait here until dawn to catch a train home. Open noon-5am. ❶

ON THE MENU

VEGGIE HEAVEN

What better place to try *shōjin ryōri* (vegetarian temple cuisine) than in Japan's temple city par excellence? Pilgrims of all persuasions flock to enjoy *yodofu* (tofu cooked in a pot at the table), *fu* (wheat gluten), and vegetable *tempura* on Kyōto's most beautiful temple grounds. Be warned: asceticism these days ain't cheap. **Okutan** (☎771-8709) is in the Nanzen-ji complex. Arrive before 1pm to avoid the lines at Kyōto's favorite *fucha ryōri* (Zen vegetarian cuisine) spot. The dining room opens onto a lush garden; there is also outdoor seating under bright parasols. The *yodofu* (¥3000) meal comes with *fu*, *dengaku dofu* (skewered slices of grilled tofu slathered in *miso* paste), vegetable *tempura*, rice, and pickles. Open M-W, F-Su 11am-6pm. **Kikyo** (☎531-0210) is in Chishaku-in across the street from the Kyōto National Museum on Higashioji-dōri. Enter through the main gate; the restaurant is on your right. Kikyo's *shōjin ryōri* centers around *konnyaku*, a root vegetable used in traditional Japanese cuisine. The *konnyaku* lunch set (¥1500) comes with *konjac* in its baked and pickled forms, along with vegetable *tempura*, soup, and pickles. The *kaede-gozen* (¥2000) comes with *konnyaku*, mushrooms, a soybean dish called *shiguredaki*, vegetable tempura, rice, and soup. *Soba* and *udon* (¥600-1200) are also served. Open daily 11am-5pm.

Blues Cafe Ball n' Chain (ボールアンドチェイン ; ☎721-4863). Cute hole-in-the-wall on a side street near Kyōto University. Blues music and posters, and a harmonica-playing owner who particularly loves customers from Chicago and New Orleans. Toasted sandwich ¥400, soup and bread ¥500, set lunch or spaghetti ¥700. Homemade cake and coffee/tea ¥500 (2-5pm). English menu. Open Tu-Su 11am-midnight. ❶

Second House Cake Works (☎751-1907). Right above Zac Baran (see above). Tasty cakes and creme brulee in the ¥350 range. Cheap sandwiches to go from ¥400. Cheery and brightly-lit; also sells jewelry. Open daily 10am-8pm. ❶

Okonomiyaki Rogu (お好み焼きろぐ ; ☎751-5235). Off Marutamachi, on Yoshida-hon-dōri—just before you reach the pedestrian bridge, heading east. Cheap *okonomiyaki* in a little log-cabin-like restaurant, cooked on big frying plates right in front of you (¥600-1200). Lunch set includes *okonomiyaki*, rice, and *miso* (11am-2pm, ¥750). *Teppanyaki* side or full meal ¥350-1900. Open Tu-Sa 11am-11pm, Su 5-11pm. ❷

Caravan (☎751-1365). On Yoshida-hon-dōri; follow directions to Okonomiyaki Rogu (see above). Small food stand for the impoverished student. Probably one of the cheapest places in town for a decent-sized meal of *yakisoba* (fried noodles), *tempura*, or *okonomiyaki* (¥500). Open daily 6pm-1am. Cash only. ❶

Buttercups (☎751-9537). On Shirakawa-dōri, just north of the intersection with Shirakawa River. Mexican rice, sandwiches, Indonesian fried rice. Internet access ¥250 per 30min. English menu. Open M and W-Su noon-9:30pm. ❷

Mikōan (彌光庵 ; ☎751-5045). On Kawabata-dōri, 3 blocks south of Marutamachi-dōri. Vegetarian restaurant. Peruse their book collection while you eat. Several cats. Lunch platter ¥800, dinner ¥1000. Open M-F noon-8pm, Sa 11am-11pm, Su 11am-10pm. ❷

NORTHWESTERN KYŌTO

▨ **Sarasa Nishijin** (ささらにしじん ; ☎432-5075). On Karasuma-dōri, a few blocks east of Funaoka-higashi-dōri. Cafe, bar, and gift shop in an old bath house—the bright green mosaic tiles are perfectly preserved. Funky music, fun menu. Noodle dishes ¥790-840, tacos ¥890, fried rice ¥680-740. Fairly large portions. Lunch sets ¥740/840, dinner set ¥890. Open M-F noon-10:30pm, Sa-Su noon-11pm. ❷

O'eufs Monica (ウフモニカ ; ☎441-9100). On the southeast corner of the intersection of Kitaoji-dōri and Senbon-dōri. On the 2nd fl., just above the Monica French pastry shop. Cheerful sunny-yellow walls and polished stainless steel chairs. Omelettes ¥650-1100. Pasta ¥680-850. Elaborate yummy desserts and sundaes (¥950); too-perfect-to-eat pastries from the shop downstairs (¥300-420). Open daily 11am-9:30pm. ❷

Knuckles (ナックルズ ; ☎441-5849). On Kitaoji-dōri, a few blocks west of Daitoku-ji. Cheery little American-style sandwich shop with bright pillows and paintings. Lunch boxes ¥850-950. Cake ¥400. Sandwiches (including, predictably, the "Knuckle Sandwich") also available à la carte. Open Tu-Su 11am-10pm. ❷

Gontaro (権たろ ; ☎463-1039). On Kitsuji-dōri, several blocks south of Kinkaku-ji; look for the blue curtains over the gate. Noodle restaurant chain. Classy place for a midday meal. Cold *soba* ¥700, hot *soba* or *udon* ¥700-1250. Open daily 11am-10pm. ❷

Rakuan Sushi (洛庵 ; ☎411-9400). On the northeast corner of the Shimei-dōri and Horikawa intersection. Convenient location near Daitoku-ji; sushi both on and off conveyor belt. *Maki* ¥200-400. Larger plates ¥800-1300. Open daily 11:30am-10pm. ❷

◎ SIGHTS

CENTRAL KYŌTO

NIJŌ-JŌ (二条城). This 400-year-old palace was the official residence of Shōgun Ieyasu. Its showiness outweighed its functionality as a fortress, but today it serves as a classic example of decadent Momoyama-period architecture. Restored in the late 19th century, the castle served as the banquet hall during Hirohito's coronation. At the Ninomaru Palace entrance, there's an English-language guide to the chambers inside. These are connected by a corridor called Uguisu-bari, or the "nightingale floor"; the wooden planks squeak underfoot, alerting guards to trespassers. Take a few minutes to explore the Ninomaru garden, designed by 17th-century tea master and architect Kobori Enshu, and the Chinese-style Shinsen-in garden. *(Open daily 9am-5pm; closed Dec. 26-Jan. 4. ¥600, students ¥350.)*

KYŌTO IMPERIAL PALACE (京都御所). Today's Imperial Palace is a renovated version of the 14th-century original. The guided tour begins in the Cherry Blossom, Crane, and Tiger rooms, and continues to the central gate Kenrei-mon, the enthronement building **Shishin-den,** and the Oike-niwa garden designed by Kobori Enshu. To visit and tour the Kyōto Imperial Palace or any of the adjoining palaces—Sento Gosho inside the Imperial Park, Katsura to the southeast, and Shugakuin to the northeast—you must apply in advance to the Imperial Household Agency, located in the northeast region of the Imperial Park. Tours are in English or provide information sheets in English. You must be 18 or older to enter Sento, Katsura, and Shugakuin; in the Kyōto Imperial Palace, persons under 18 must be accompanied by an adult. *(Subway: Karasuma Line to Imadegawa. Walk 2 blocks south to reach the entrance nearest the Imperial Household Agency. ☎211-1215. Agency open M-F 8:45am-noon and 1-4pm; occasionally Sa Apr.-May and Oct.-Nov. Kyōto Palace tour 50min.; 10am, 2pm. Sento 1hr.; 11am, 1:30pm. Katsura 1hr.; 10, 11am, 2, 3pm. Shugakuin 1¼hr.; 9, 10, 11am, 1:30, 3pm. Free.)*

NISHI HONGAN-JI (西本願寺). Built in the 13th century to house the ashes of radical monk Shinran, founder of Jōdō Shinshu ("True Pure Land") Buddhism, this temple one of Kyōto's wealthiest today. Sending out missionaries in the 19th century brought the sect into greater contact with the Western world, as evidenced by the small organ in Amida Hall. This hall also contains elaborate Kano-school wall paintings. The most elaborate Momoyama-period interiors, however, are inside the Shoin, open only twice a month to guided tours. For information on these tours, ask in the building to the left of the Founder's Hall (which, incidentally, is closed for a 10-year roof restoration project). The Karamon gate on the south side of the temple also features some flamboyant carvings and is known as the "Sunset gate," because it is said that visitors could admire it from dawn to dusk without noticing the passage of time. *(Open daily 6am-5pm. Free.)*

HIGASHI HONGAN-JI (東本願寺 **).** Alarmed by the growing power of the Jōdō Shinshu sect at Nishi (East) Hongan-ji, Ieyasu sponsored a splinter group in 1602 based in Higashi (West) Hongan-ji. Devastated by fire in the mid-19th century, this temple received little funding for reconstruction, as Emperor Meiji favored Shintōism over Buddhism. Female devotees cut their hair to form 53 long ropes used to raise the heavy beams; a long coil is displayed in a glass case between the two halls. The Amida Hall contains the *shurmidan*, an altar symbolizing Mount Sumeru, the central mountain in Buddhist cosmology. *(Open daily 6am-4:30pm. Free.)*

KYŌTO STATION (KYŌTO EKI; 京都駅 **).** Designed by Hara Hiroshi for a national competition, the station is a sweeping steel-and-glass structure whose sheer size boggles the mind. Take the escalators to the 12th-floor Sky Garden to enjoy views of the city and station. To indulge in a bit of heady materialism, explore the posh Isetan department store or the stylish young-thing shops in the Cube.

SOUTH OF KYŌTO STATION

▓TŌ-JI (東寺 **).** Founded by Kōbō Daishi in 794 after the imperial capital moved from Nara to Kyōto, Tō-ji is the proud home of Japan's tallest pagoda and best Shingon Buddhist sculptures. The Kondō building dates from the Momoyama Period and contains a gilded statue of Yakushi, the Buddha of healing, as well as two attending *bosatsu* or bodhisattvas, Nikkō and Gakkō. Around Yakushi's throne are gathered the Twelve Sacred Generals. The Kodō building, with its striking red pillars, contains statues from China arranged in a mandala, a three-dimensional representation of the Buddhist universe. On the 21st of each month, locals and tourists rummage through goods at the **Tō-ji flea market;** there is also a smaller **antique market** on the first Sunday of every month. *(☎691-3325. Open 9am-4:30pm daily. Markets open 7am-4pm. Temple free; Kondō and Kodō ¥800, students ¥700.)*

DAIGO-JI (醍醐寺 **).** One of Kyōto's largest temples, Daigo-ji belongs to the Shingon sect and was built as early as 874 to house two Kannon statues. The temple is divided into the lower **Shimo-daigo** area and the **Kami-daigo** at the top of Mt. Daigo, 3km up along a narrow mountain trail. Shimo-daigo's centerpiece is the lovely subtemple **Sanpo-in,** where Hideyoshi held elaborate receptions. The Omote Shoin, the central building, features Momoyama-style architecture and a thatched roof. The garden of Sanpo-in, with its large pond, narrow paths, and stone bridges, was the site of Hideyoshi's famous cherry-blossom viewing parties. Beyond Sanpo-in, through groves of maples, lies one of Kyōto's oldest five-story pagodas. The trek up to Kami-daigo takes about 1hr. from there. *(Take Tōzai Subway Line to Daigo, last stop. Take Exit 2 and turn right. At the 1st light, turn right and follow the winding road past the cemetery and bamboo grove, and finally under a small overpass. ☎571-0002. Open daily Mar.-Oct. 9am-5pm; Nov.-Feb. 9am-4pm. Grounds free; Sanpo-in ¥600.)*

TŌFUKU-JI (東福寺 **).** One of Kyōto's largest Rinzai Zen temples, Tōfuku-ji was founded in 1236 by a Heian statesman who wanted Kyōto to have a temple rivaling Nara's Tōdai-ji and Kofuku-ji. While Tōfuku-ji's massive buildings are certainly impressive, the real gems are the ▓**gardens.** Crossing the maple-filled valley below the airy Tsuten-kyo bridge, you'll arrive at the garden of Kaisando, which combines a raked-gravel garden with a lily pond surrounded by carefully pruned azalea bushes. The four small but stunning gardens surrounding the Hodō, or Abbot's Hall, are best seen in or just after the rain, when the moss and azaleas are an intense green. The smallest eastern garden is composed of pillars in a gravel bed, representing the Great Bear constellation. Four rock clusters and five sacred moss-covered mounds comprise the southern garden. The western and northern garden use azalea and moss, respectively, in a checkerboard pattern. In a pinch, skip the bridge in favor of the gardens. *(Take any of the Keihan Subway Lines to Tōfuku-ji. From Kyōto Station, walk 20min. or take the JR Nara Line 1 stop. ☎561-0087. Open daily 9am-4pm. Tsuten-kyo bridge and Kaisando garden ¥400; 4 gardens of the Hodō ¥400.)*

FUSHIMI INARI TAISHA (伏見稲荷大社). Among the thousands of Inari shrines (dedicated to the god of harvests) throughout Japan, Fushimi is the oldest, dating back to 816, and also one of the most frequently photographed. The 4km path winding into Mount Inari is lined with giant, closely-packed crimson *torii* (gates). Today, farmers still visit the shrine, but they're joined by business owners who purchase individual *torii* for large sums as offerings to the gods. Look for the fox statues, emblematic of Inari shrines. The kitschy tourist stands sell a variety of fox-related goods, from tacky plush toys to tasty *inarizushi*, sweet-salty tofu pouches of rice, believed to be the fox's favorite food. *(From Kyōto Station, take JR Nara Line to Inari; or, from any Keihan station, take the train to Fushimi Inari Station.)*

EASTERN KYŌTO

SANJŪSANGEN-DŌ (三十三間堂). Housing 1000 gold-plated, full-size statues of Kannon and one larger-than-life version, Sanjusangen-dō has the biggest collection of bodhisattvas you'll ever see in one place. Built in the 12th century by Emperor Go-Shirakawa, the temple and its statues were restored after a 1249 fire. The corridor in the rear provides information in English on the building's construction and its major ceremonies. Edo-period archers once practiced and competed by shooting down the long west corridor. Today their bows rest in the hall's glass case. On January 15, a brief archery display commemorates this aspect of the temple's history. *(Open daily Apr.-Nov. 15 8am-5pm, Nov.16-Mar. 9am-4pm. ¥600.)*

YASAKA (八坂) KONSHINDŌ AND PAVILION. Dedicated to people who rely on their hands to make a living, this neighborhood temple attracts few tourists but is of tremendous importance to the local community. Atop the red gate sit three monkey statues in see-no-evil, hear-no-evil, and speak-no-evil postures. Inside, a large statue of a seated monkey is covered in strings of round red monkey-dolls, left as charms. The street leading north from Yasaka Konshindō will take you to **Yasaka No To pagoda,** a five-story landmark dating from 1436. *(Walk down Ishibei-koji from the Kodai-ji end, then turn left and walk 1½ blocks.)*

KIYOMIZU-DERA (清水寺). The image of this temple's wooden main hall jutting out over the forest is one of Kyōto's defining images. If you can brave the swarms of camera-laden pilgrims making the same upward trek, the view from the top of the temple is worth the jostling. Founded in 788 by the priest Enchin, Kiyomizu-dera conceals a sacred Kannon statue that makes a brief appearance only once every 33 years. Down the long flight of stairs beyond the Hondō is the Otawa waterfall, where you can take a sip of the temple's famed **kiyomizu** ("clear water"). On the grounds is the independently run Jishu Shrine, a love shrine dedicated to the "cupid of Japan" and frequented mostly by gaggles of giggling schoolgirls and lusty young couples. Past the entrance gate and kitschy vendors lie the two "love stones" set 10m apart from each other. To gain success in love, you must walk, eyes closed and murmuring the name of your beloved, from one stone to the other. *(Southeast of Yasaka Pagoda, down Kiyomizuzaka. ☎551-1234. Open daily 9am-6pm. ¥600.)*

KAWAI KANJIRŌ HOUSE (KAWAI KANJIRŌ HAKUBUTSUKAN; 河井寛次郎博物 館). Once the home of Kawai Kanjirō, a master potter from the first half of the 20th century, this house now displays his pottery, the stepped *noborigama* kiln he used, and some woodcarvings he made later in life. Kanjirō was one of the principal exponents of the *mingei* ("folk art") movement which revived traditional crafts to counter the tide of industrialization. He also helped found the Japan Folk Craft Museum in Tōkyō. *(North of Kyōto National Museum. Open Tu-Su 10am-5pm. ¥900.)*

SANNENZAKA (三円坂). The cobblestone street of Sannenzaka ("Three Year Slope") is lined with some of Kyōto's last *machiya*, or traditional wooden townhomes. While many have been rebuilt in the past 100 years, they're still characteristic of the long narrow houses used by merchants for centuries. Built in the

TEAHOUSES, TEMPLES, AND TOFU BYPRODUCTS

TIME: 5hr.

DISTANCE: 1¼ mi.

WHEN TO GO: mid-morning

STARTING POINT: Walk from Choraku-ji to Maruyama Park

FINISH POINT: Kiyomizu-dera

For a healthy dose of eastern Kyōto's cultural and culinary offerings, hit the Higashiyama district at about 9am with a good breakfast inside you. This leisurely route oozes tradition and local flavor. Work your way through shrines, temples, teahouses, and neighborhoods—and remember, we're *meandering*, not *marching*, and definitely not *galloping*. Think Zen. Ja?

1 MARUYAMA PARK AND YASAKA SHRINE (P. 417). If the cherry trees are blooming, so much the better, but in any season the park's ponds and footpaths merit a stroll. Pray at the shrine to the god of healing for a cure to your Japanophilia. Note the Buddhist gate on this Shintō shrine—an ancient injunction for the modern world to put aside its denominational differences, perhaps?

2 RAKUSHŌ (P. 411). Don't miss this quintessential Kyōto teahouse. Sip green tea, gaze out over the garden, and murmur appreciatively. Nibble on cake. Look at the garden. Sip more tea.

3 KODAI-JI (P. 417). Explore the ponds and pavilion in this Rinzai Zen temple. Lusting after some traditional Japanese lacquering? The Tamaya (Sanctuary) building is covered in it.

4 ISHIBEI-KOJI (P. 417). Every day in Kyōto is a winding road; this quiet little lane winds its own charming way past classy ryokan and teahouses.

5 YASAKA KONSHINDŌ AND YASAKA PAGODA (P. 415). Carpenters, basket-weavers, and Faberge-egg-makers take note: this temple serves those who rely on their hands to earn a living. Strings of monkey-dolls hang everywhere, and the cute factor is irresistible—you and everyone you know *must* have one. You should also take a gander at Yasaka pagoda nearby, a Kyōto symbol.

6 SANNENZAKA (P. 415). A trot down the cobblestones here affords you a look at Kyōto's last *machiya*, or traditional wooden houses. These long narrow structures developed in response to an old housing tax based on the size of the facade. Crafty, those feudal-era merchant families.

7 YUBA-SEN (P. 411). Hungry? Vegetarian? Either way, you'll have a good time packing in the protein at this restaurant specializing in *yuba*, the skin that forms on soymilk as it morphs into tofu. Peek into the workshop out back to watch them skim the stuff off the top of steaming vats.

8 KIYOMIZU-DERA (P. 415). Finally, clamber up the hill to one of Kyōto's trademark temples. Take a sip of purifying water from the Otawa waterfall. See how you fare with the "Love Stones" at the Jishu Shrine—if you make it from one stone to the other, eyes closed and murmuring the name of your current crush, then your wishes may be on their way to fulfillment.

unagi-no-nedoko ("eels' nests") style, these houses evolved out of necessity: an old housing tax was levied according to the width of the house's entrance. The narrow wooden window slats had a twofold purpose: to cool the house and to allow merchants to peek out at passing *samurai* and priests without being seen. The lowest class, merchants were forbidden from looking down on their social betters.

KŌDAI-JI (高台事). Now belonging to the Rinzai Zen Buddhist sect, this temple was built in 838 and converted into a nunnery in 1598 when the widow of Shōgun Toyotomi Hideyoshi became a nun. A Momoyama-style roofed bridge, pavilion, and sloped-roof "Reclining Dragon Corridor" span Kōdai-ji's ponds and lead to the Kaisan-dō (Founder's Hall). The Tamaya (Sanctuary) is well-known for the rich raised lacquering that covers the walls, furniture, and cabinets. *(North of Ninenzaka and Sannenzaka. ☎ 561-9966. Open daily 9am-4:30pm. ¥600.)*

ISHIBEI-KOJI (石塀小寺). Some of Kyōto's wealthiest estates once stood on this small winding lane, before they were sold or abandoned after World War II. Today the lane is home to a number of classy, understated ryokan and teahouses. *(Leaving Kodai-ji by the main stairway, turn left onto the street running parallel to the temple, and take your first right onto Ishibei-koji.)*

MARUYAMA PARK (丸山公園) AND YASAKA JINJA (八坂神社). The park is flooded with visitors in April during the cherry-blossom season, but tourists pass through it year-round on the way to Yasaka Shrine. Once known as Gion-san, the shrine remains the spiritual heart of Gion today. Suffering from a hard-hitting plague in the 9th century, Kyōtoites prayed to the god of medicine here. To honor that event, the Gion Matsuri parade starts at Yasaka Shrine each July. The shrine has two interesting architectural features: the Buddhist-style main gate facing Shijo-dōri, reflecting the pre-Meiji fusion of Buddhism and Shintōism; and the Emado building up to the left from the Shijo entrance, which is raised on pillars and thus displays an even older, pre-Buddhist native architecture. *(From Kodai-ji, go north until you reach Rakusyou on the right, a teahouse with a pond and waterfall. Head right to reach Maruyama Park, and turn left to get to Yasaka Shrine.)*

GION (祇園). The name "Gion" inevitably evokes images of the pleasure-seeking "floating world" of Japan's past. Those images are far from gone: streets of dark wooden *ochaya* (teahouses) lit by red lanterns, *maiko* (apprentice *geisha*) on the way to their appointments, evening throngs gathered on Shijo-dōri under the imposing roof of the Minamiza *kabuki* theater. Highrises have replaced many of the area's traditional houses, and today's *geisha* are less likely to blacken their teeth in accordance with ancient standards of beauty, but Gion maintains its traditional atmosphere, thanks to special government protection and rigid architectural guidelines. Originally part of a pilgrimage path leading up to Kiyomizu-dera, Gion was revitalized by the merchant class after the end of the 16th-century civil wars. **Hanami-koji** is the quintessential Gion street, lined with wooden teahouses like the famous **Ichiriki** on the corner of Shijo-dōri and Hanami-koji. In the mid-19th century, political opponents of the Tokugawa shōgunate met here to plot the overthrow of the regime. Down the street on the left, you'll find the **Gion Kobu Kaburen-jō Theater** (p. 422), which hosts traditional dance performances and the annual **Miyako Ōdori** (Cherry Blossom Dance; p. 426) in April. At dusk, head over to **Pontochō** just as the restaurants are lighting their lamps for dinnertime. Formerly a red-light district, this small alley has evolved into a pricey and popular area for food and nightlife. *(Take the Keihan Line to Keihan-Shijo Station.)*

MINAMIZA (南座). Founded in 1615, Minamiza is Japan's oldest theater and the birthplace of *kabuki* (p. 100). In the early 17th century, a female shrine attendant named Okuni began performing dances in the area and spawned a number of different *onna* (women's) *kabuki* troupes. The shōgunate banned these groups because of their links to prostitution and replaced them with male troupes. Unfor-

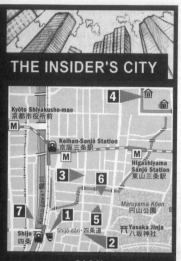

THE INSIDER'S CITY

Kyōto Shiyakusho-mae
京都市役所前

Keihan-Sanjō Station
京阪三条駅

Higashiyama
Sanjō Station
東山三条駅

Maruyama Kōen
円山公園

Shijō-dōri · 四条道

Yasaka Jinja
八坂神社

Shijo
四条

Kamo-gawa · 鴨川

GION

The birth of Gion as an entertainment district coincided with the rise of a wealthy merchant class in the 16th century. Today, the streets preserve their traditional feel while offering a host of sights and shopping options.

1 **The Minamiza Theater.** *Kabuki* acts play year-round at Japan's oldest theater (p. 417).

2 **Ichiriki.** Famous traditional teahouse, site of Tokugawa-era intrigues (p. 417).

3 **Hanami-koji.** Quintessential Gion street (p. 417).

4 **Kyōto Museum of Traditional Crafts (Fureaikan).** Elegant market selling high-quality fabrics, fans, and pottery (p. 421).

5 **Shimbashi-dōri.** Quiet street of expensive teahouses near the Shirakawa River.

6 **Shinmonzen-dōri.** Street lined with expensive antique and print dealers.

7 **Pontochō.** Catch dinner here, and perhaps a glimpse of a *geisha* or *maiko* (p. 417).

tunately, the beauty of the adolescent actors also aroused the off-stage passions of priests and *samurai*. The stage then became the sole territory of adult male performers, who developed the flamboyant, exaggerated style of modern *kabuki*. Today, Minamiza puts on plays throughout the year and attracts the country's top performers. *(Across the street from Keihan-Shijo Station.* ☎*561-1155. Open daily 10am-6pm.)*

CHION-IN (知恩院). Founded in the late 12th century by the priest Honen, Chion-in is a busy working temple and the main complex of the popular Jōdō ("Pure Land") sect of Buddhism. The Ohojo houses a well-known *shoin* (priest's study) and has gilded doors painted by the Kano school. The temple also features a large collection of "miraculous" curios, including a rock that bore cucumbers and a sliding door painted with a cat whose eyes follow passersby. *(From the north end of Maruyama Park, follow the long flight of stone steps up to Chion-in.* ☎*531-2111. Open daily Mar.-Nov. 9am-4:10pm; Dec.-Feb. 9am-3:40pm. ¥400.)*

SHŌREN-IN (書蓮院). Less busy than Chion-in, Shōren-in is a pleasant, shady Tendai Zen temple famous for the ancient sprawling camphor trees near the entrance and in the garden. It once served as a lodging for priests from Enryaku-ji when they visited the imperial family in Kyōto. Many of its buildings were reconstructed in the 19th century. The path starting in the garden leads around to a partly-hidden waterfall and bamboo forest. *(*☎*561-2345. Open daily 9am-5pm. ¥500.)*

PHILOSOPHER'S PATH. Leading from Eikan-dō up to Ginkaku-ji along a shady canal, this path was a favorite morning stroll for early 20th-century philosopher Nishida Kitaro. It's now lined with small boutiques, some kitschier than others. *(From Kyōto Station or Sanjo-Keihan, take bus #5 to Ginkaku-ji-mae.)*

KONCHI-IN (金地院). Part of the Rinzai Zen Buddhist sect's central complex, Konchi-in is one of the bigger subtemples. The Akechi-mon gate reflects the Chinese-style favored by Momoyama architects. Through the gate is the small Benten-Ike, a water-lily pond. The dry garden, Tsurukame no Niwa, is one of the few that can be historically attributed to architect Enshu Kobori. The placement of the rocks and tree is an example of the classic *tsurukame* ("crane-and-tortoise") designs of the period. *(From Keage Station, take Exit 1 and walk down the hill; turn right at the first brick archway and walk 2min. until you see Konchi-in on your left.* ☎*771-3511. Open daily Mar.-Nov. 8:30am-5pm, Dec.-Feb. 8:30am-4:30pm. ¥400; English pamphlet ¥100.)*

NANZEN-JI (南禅寺). Past Konchi-in, the path leads to Sanmon, the main gate of the Nanzen-ji complex. Head up to the gate's second story to see Kano-school murals and several Buddha and bodhisattva statues. Continuing along the path beyond Sammon (the main gate), turn left onto the main road after the second building; it will take you to Hojo, the Abbot's Quarters, renowned for its "leaping tiger" garden. Retrace your steps from the Hojo, and you'll see a brick aqueduct (still functioning), beyond which lies the Nanzen-in subtemple. The two-pond garden here dates from the Kamakura Period; the northern pond is shaped like a dragon, the southern like the character for "heart." A statue honors the Emperor Kameyama, who built a palace on these grounds before turning it into a temple in 1291. (☎ 771-0365. Open 8:30am-4:30pm. Sammon ¥500. Hojo ¥500. Nanzen-in ¥300.)

EIKAN-DŌ/ZENRIN-JI (永観堂). The main temple of the Jōdō Shu (Pure Land) Buddhist sect, Zenrin-ji is often called Eikan-dō after the 11th-century priest Eikan. According to legend, Eikan saw the Buddha statue here come to life and step down from the altar. This event is commemorated by the gilded statue of the "Backwards-Looking Amida Buddha" inside the Amida-dō. Set among the hills and woods of Higashiyama, this peaceful temple draws visitors in the fall eager to see the lovely maples. (North of Nanzen-ji. ☎ 761-0007. Open daily 9am-4pm. ¥500.)

HŌNEN-IN (法然院). Hōnen, founder of the Jōdō Buddhist sect, certainly has larger and more grandiose temples to his credit, but this rustic eponymous temple has a refreshing simplicity. Hōnen-in is well-known for its camellias, which bloom in early spring, as well as the elegant *ikebana* displays framing its altars. The 25 flowers strewn around the altar in the main hall represent the 25 bodhisattvas. (From Eikan-dō, follow Philosopher's Path north. Open daily 7am-4pm. Free.)

GINKAKU-JI (銀閣寺). Originally the private villa of shōgun Ashikaga Yoshimasa, Ginkaku-ji was transformed into a Rinzai Zen temple upon his death. The main attraction, Yoshimasa's pavilion, is a simple two-story wooden structure with bell-shaped windows that is said to shine silver under moonlight. The temple grounds also contain Dojin-sai, a small *tatami* room used for Japan's earliest tea ceremonies. The temple today is perpetually swamped with tourists; head over early in the morning or just before closing to dodge the crowds. (Follow Philosopher's Path north from Hōnen-in to reach Ginkaku-ji. ☎ 771-5725. Open daily 8:30am-5pm. ¥500.)

HEIAN JINGŪ (平安神宮). Built in 1895 to mark Kyōto's 1100th anniversary, Heian Jingū was dedicated to Kammu and Komei, the first and last emperors to claim Kyōto as their capital. **Jidai Matsuri** ("Festival of the Ages") takes place here each October (p. 426). The orange-trimmed main building, Daigoku-den, was based on a model of the original Imperial Palace. Behind it, the Honden houses the spirit of the two emperors. The real attraction, however, is the large garden replicating Heian-period gardening styles. (From Higashiyama Station, take a left on Sanjo-dōri, then another left at the 1st large intersection; the shrine is at the end of the road. Open daily 8:30am-5:30pm. Grounds free, garden ¥600.)

SHUGAKU-IN RIKYŪ (修学院利休). Shugaku-in Imperial Villa was designed by the former Emperor Gomizuno in 1655 after his abdication. He might have had a hard time with the business of ruling the kingdom—he ascended the throne at the age of 15 and was soon forced to marry the shōgun's daughter—but he did have a knack for gardening, amply demonstrated on the villa grounds. When the princess Akenomiya inherited the villa from her father 10 years later, it was converted into her private residence and later into her personal nunnery. The villa is actually composed of a lower, middle, and upper villa. The middle villa's Kyakuden guest house is known for its elegantly-designed "Shelves of Mist" and charming painted panels depicting Gion Matsuri. The real draw, however, is the **Rin-un-tei pavilion** at the top of the upper villa, which offers a panoramic view of the garden and surrounding hillsides. The free tours are in Japanese only, but the helpful pamphlet is available in English. *(Take the Eidan Eizan line to Shugaku-in and walk east; or, take bus #5 from Kyōto Station to the Shugaku-in Rikyū-michi stop. Admission by application to the Imperial Household Agency only; see Imperial Palace, p. 413.)*

MANSHU-IN (曼殊院). Founded in a different location in the 8th century, Manshu-in moved to its present spot during the Edo Period when Prince Ryosho, son of the Emperor Tomohito, was head abbot. The temple is known for its *shoin* (study) rooms, designed in an architectural style popular among the upper classes. The dry garden features a "crane and tortoise" design. *(From Shugaku-in, head south until you reach the Otowa River. Follow it to the east until you see the Kansai Seminar House on a side street to the right; just beyond that is Manshu-in. ☎ 781-5010. Open daily 9am-5pm. ¥500.)*

SHISEN-DŌ (詩仙堂). Known also as the "House of the Poet-Hermits," Shisendō was the retreat of Jozan Ishikawa, a 17th-century *samurai*, Chinese scholar, and landscape architect. Converted into a temple after his death, it is presided over today by Soto Zen monks. The priest's quarters, study, main room, sanctuary, and small second-floor moon-viewing room all have a simple beauty. The garden is composed of raked gravel punctuated by azalea bushes. In the corner of the garden is the world's last remaining *sozu*, a bamboo pipe that fills with water, tips, and creates a loud sound intended to frighten away deer and other wild animals. *(South of Manshu-in; near the larger Tanukidani Fudoin temple. Look for the little stone stairway and bamboo gate to Shisen-dō. ☎ 781-2954. Open daily 9am-5pm. ¥500.)*

NORTHWESTERN KYŌTO

DAITOKU-JI (大徳寺) AND DAISEN-IN (大仙院). Founded by Zen master Daito Kokushi, this complex is the head temple of the Rinzai Zen Buddhist sect. Following the destruction of the original temple in the Onin Wars, Toyotomi Hideyoshi funded its reconstruction in the late 15th century. The principal temple is not regularly open to the public; most visitors head for the subtemple Daisen-in. The more famous garden, a small allegorical Chinese landscape, is at the temple's eastern corner; on the other side is a stark garden composed of a gravel rectangle and two cones of sand. Are they sinking into the surrounding Sea of Nothingness or are they rising? Did they inspire Madonna's late-'80s fashions? *(Take Karasuma Line to Kitaoji Station. Open daily 9am-5pm. ¥400.)*

KITANO TENMAN-GŪ (北野天満宮). Originally built to house the spirit of the thunder god, this shrine was re-dedicated in the 10th century to Sugawara-no-Michizane, a poet and statesman who died during his unjust exile in Kyūshū. His angry spirit stirred up a series of storms and epidemics, and to appease him, the Japanese government gave his spirit a shrine and several honorary governmental promotions. Scholars and students regard Sugawara as their patron saint, and the charms stack up here every winter before "examination hell." The shrine also features some large stone cows, relics from the pre-Sugawara days. Rubbing an ailing body part on one of the carved bovines is said to relieve pains and maladies. The **Kitano Tenman-gū flea market** takes place on the 25th of every month; stalls are generally open 8am-6pm. *(Take Kitano Line to Kitanohakubacho Station. Free.)*

KINKAKU-JI (金閣寺). Originally the retirement home of Shōgun Ashikaga Yoshimitsu, Kinkaku-ji was converted into a Rinzai Zen temple after his death. The **Golden Pavilion** survived centuries of warfare only to be torched by an obsessed monk in 1955; the reconstruction, however, is exact. The first floor, ungilded and modeled on the palace style, served as a reception hall; the second floor, built in the *samurai* house style, held the Hall of Roaring Waves where the Shōgun welcomed special guests; and the third hall, in a Zen-temple style, was a private floor for tea ceremonies with close friends. Plagued by crowds of tourists, Kinkaku-ji today is unfortunately anything but tranquil. *(From Kyōto Station, take bus #101; from Shijo Karasuma, take bus #12 or 101. ☎ 461-0013. Open daily 9am-5pm. ¥400.)*

RYŌAN-JI. Founded in 1450 by Muromachi military leader Hosokana Katsumoto, Ryōan-ji is affiliated with the Myoshinji school of the Rinzai Zen sect. It boasts one of Japan's most famous and enigmatic Zen gardens: a raked gravel pit with 15 stones in small clusters, surrounded by an oil-stained mud wall with a shingle roof. Interpretations abound, from the boringly obvious (islands in the sea) to the completely inexplicable (tigers crossing a river). In any case, squint with the hordes, attain or feign understanding and contentment, and move on to admire the peaceful lily pond, Kyoyochi. *(Take bus #59 from Kinkaku-ji to Ryoan-ji. ☎463-2216. Open daily Mar.-Nov. 8am-5pm; Dec.-Feb. 8:30am-4:30pm. ¥400.)*

NINNA-JI (仁味寺). Drawing fewer crowds, this temple is a refreshingly tranquil place after the bustle of Ryoan-ji. Established in 888 by Emperor Uda, Ninna-ji now belongs to the Omuro School of the Shingon sect and is renowned for its Omura School of Flower Arranging. Like virtually every Kyōto temple, Ninna-ji was damaged during the Onin Wars and rebuilt 180 years later under Tokugawa Iemitsu. The series of buildings to the left after the main gate comprise the **Omuro Gosho,** which contains a large garden with a waterfall and the **Shinden.** This latter building houses some exquisitely detailed murals of cherry blossoms, peacocks, aristocratic boating parties, and scenes from the Aoi (hollyhock) festival. To the north is the Kondo (Main Hall) and to the east stands a five-story pagoda. *(Take bus #59 from Kinkaku-ji to Ninna-ji. Open 9:30am-4:30pm. ¥500.)*

MYŌSHIN-JI (妙心寺). Within this vast Rinzai Zen temple complex, the oldest and most interesting subtemple is Taizo-in. Its beautiful garden is composed of a thatched pavilion, low shrubs, a babbling stream, and a dry garden of black and white sand. The temple also features an Ashikaga-period black-and-white painting by Josetsu entitled "Catching Catfish with a Gourd," which imbues a fisherman's quotidian activity with intense vitality. *(From Kyōto Station, take the San-in (Sagano) line to Hanazono and walk 5min. northwest along Shinmarutamachi-dōri; or, take bus #10 from Sanjo-Keihan to Myoshiji-kita-mon-mae. Open daily 9am-5pm. Grounds free; Taizo-in ¥400.)*

KŌRYŪ-JI (広隆寺). Particularly attractive to art-lovers, the Shingon temple Kōryū-ji is fabled to have been constructed by Prince Shotoku in the 7th century. The **Kodō** (Lecture Hall) dates back to 1165 and is Kyōto's oldest structure. The temple's real treasure, however, is the new **Reihokan** building, which houses some fine Buddhist sculptures. The collection includes a painted wooden bust of Prince Shotoku at age 16, huge wooden statues of Kannon dating from the Nara Period, and the centerpiece: a small, fragile-looking wooden statue of Miroku Bosatsu (the Future Buddha) dating from the Asuka Period (552-645). Despite the statue's venerable age, it's the most living object in the room—leaning forward intently, he seems prepared to rise any minute with an answer for the salvation of humanity. *(Take Arashiyama Line to Uzumasa Station. ☎861-1461. Open daily 9am-5pm. ¥700.)*

▥ MUSEUMS

▧ KYŌTO MUSEUM OF TRADITIONAL CRAFTS (FUREAIKAN; ふれあい館).
This elegant new museum contains thoughtfully presented displays on Kyōto's ongoing craft traditions, from landscape gardening to stenciled *yuzen* dyeing and lacquerware. Works by local artists abound, and diagrams trace the often painstaking production processes. Detailed English explanations accompany the exhibits. Weekend workshops allow visitors to try their hand at stenciling designs onto fabric. *(Eastern Kyōto. In the basement of the Kyōto International Exhibition Hall. ☎762-2670. Free. Workshops Sa-Su 9:30am-4pm; handkerchief ¥600, T-shirt ¥1500, fan ¥800.)*

KYŌTO NATIONAL MUSEUM (KYŌTO KOKURITSU HAKUBUTSUKAN; 京都国立 博物館 **).** This medium-sized museum provides a good overview of Japanese art, from the earliest Jōmon pots and Yayoi bronze bells to Zen paintings and ceramics. English texts explain the background of the pieces. Objects from the permanent collection rotate through the boxy modern building; the brick Victorian building houses special exhibitions. From mid-January to mid-March 2004, there will be a special exhibition of costumes and art from *Star Wars Episodes I and II*. *(Eastern Kyōto.* ☎ *541-1151. Permanent collection open Tu-Su 9:30am-5pm. ¥420, students ¥130. Special exhibitions open Tu-Th 9:30am-6pm, Sa-Su 9:30am-8pm. ¥1300, students ¥900.)*

MUSEUM OF KYŌTO (KYŌTO BUNKA HAKUBUTSUKAN; 京都文化博物館 **).** Charts, diagrams, and models of Kyōto through the ages dominate this historical museum. With few actual artifacts, the displays are ultimately weak on content for English speakers. Guided tours are available daily; call ahead for times. Volunteer guides explain the Chinese origins of the city plan and the housing tax that led citizens to build *machiya* houses such as those seen along Sannenzaka (p. 415). Be sure to catch the full-sized costume of an aristocratic Heian woman, with 12 layers of clothing. *(Central Kyōto. From Karasuma-Oike subway station, head south and turn left onto Sanjo-dōri; it's 1 block east of Karasuma-dōri.* ☎ *222-0888. Open Tu-Su 10am-7:30pm.)*

KYŌTO MUNICIPAL MUSEUM OF ART (京都市立美術館 **).** Despite a lack of English translations, this museum's collection of post-Meiji screen paintings and large canvases may be of interest to art enthusiasts. "Okoku Konoshina" (Winter Moon) is a highlight—a multi-paneled screen painting of a fox in a stark, snowy forest. *(Eastern Kyōto.* ☎ *771-4107. Open Tu-Su 9am-5pm. ¥900.)*

NATIONAL MUSEUM OF MODERN ART KYŌTO (京都国立近代美術館 **).** Kyōto's modern art museum houses a small collection of works by Picasso, Mondrian, and Redon, a large number of Ansel Adams photographs, and several Western-influenced paintings of daily life in Kyōto at the turn of the century. *(Eastern Kyōto.* ☎ *761-9900. Open Tu-Su 9:30am-5pm; Apr.-Oct. open Tu-Th 9:30am-5pm, F 9:30am-8pm, Sa-Su 9:30am-5pm. ¥420, students ¥130. Special exhibitions ¥830, students ¥450.)*

🔳 🏳 ENTERTAINMENT AND CRAFTS

THEATER

Minamiza Theater (☎561-1115**).** See p. 417 for background info. Plays run throughout the year; the Kaomize performances in Dec. feature Japan's most famous actors. Shows are long, so you may want to catch just 1 act. Open daily 10am-6pm.

Gion Kaikan (☎561-0160**).** Theater hosting various dance and drama performances. Onshukai *geisha* dances Oct. 1-10 (¥4000); Gion Ōdori Nov. 1-10 (¥3000).

Gion Kōbu Kaburen-jō (☎605-0074; tickets ☎541-3391**).** Site of the annual Miyako Ōdori festival (p. 426). Performances daily 12:30, 2, 3:30, and 4:50pm. Unreserved seat ¥1900, reserved ¥3800, with tea ceremony ¥4300. Open Apr. 1-30 noon-7pm.

Gion Corner Theater (☎561-1119**).** Good introductory survey of traditional arts. *Geisha* and *maiko* perform *bunraku* (puppet shows), music, *kyogen* (comedies), tea ceremonies, *ikebana* flower arrangement, and dances. English program available. Open Mar.-Nov., performances daily at 7:40 and 8:40pm. ¥2800.

TEA CEREMONIES

🔲 Taiho-an Teahouse (☎077-423-3334**).** In Uji (p. 430).

Shikunshi Japanese Tea Stage (☎771-7111**).** Westin Miyako Hotel, 3rd fl. Classy, convenient place for a tea ceremony. *Matcha* and 1 sweet ¥1000. Open daily 10am-7pm.

ARTS AND CRAFTS

Kyōto International Community House (p. 398). Offers various Japanese craft workshops, including *origami*, calligraphy, *ikebana* (flower arranging), and using an abacus. Look in the message board room for current class offerings and dates. Free.

Marumasu Nishimuraya Yuzen Kobo (☎211-3273). On Oike and Ogawa; walk west from Karasuma-Oike subway station. *Yuzen* dyeing (traditional stencil-dyeing) workshop in an old wooden *machiya* townhouse. Make items from a coaster to a tablecloth (¥500-3000). Takes about 1hr. Call in advance to reserve. Open daily 9am-5pm.

Kyosen-dō (☎371-4151). 1 block east of Higashi Hongan-ji. Paint a traditional fan in their studio, and they'll bind it up and deliver it to a Japanese address within a month. ¥2200, including postage. No English spoken. Open 9am-5pm.

◪ BATHS

The public bath *(sento)* is not only the perfect place to unwind at the end of a long day, but also a chance to experience an integral part of Japanese daily life. While the number of *sento* in Japan is decreasing as more and more homes install their own bathrooms, the public bath remains popular among Japanese of all ages, and it's a prime place to catch up on neighborhood gossip. Many provide towels for rent, soap, shampoo, and razors. You can also buy small handy towels at the ¥100 stores. Note that hot baths can be *incredibly* hot. The key is to sit in the corner near the cold water valves and not to move once you're in the water. For directions to the nearest neighborhood bath, just ask at your hotel or hostel.

■ **Funaoka-yu** (船岡温泉). Kuramaguchi-dōri, just east of Funaoka Higashi-dōri. One of Kyōto's best traditional *onsen*-style baths. While one side has been recently renovated, the other side maintains the original, elaborately carved wooden panels and colored tiles. Both have outdoor pools and jacuzzis with foot jets. Plus, the water is not as excruciatingly hot as in other places. Open M and W-Su 3pm-1am. ¥340.

Nishiki-yu (錦湯 ; ☎221-6479). Sakaimachi-dōri, just south of Nishiki market. A small old-fashioned bath with wood-ceiling changing rooms and a great atmosphere in the heart of downtown. The green bubbling herb bath will make you feel like you're steeping in a giant cup of green tea. Open Tu-Su 4pm-midnight. ¥440.

Kyōto Tower Bath (京都タワー ; ☎361-3215). Inside Kyōto Tower, B3; take stairs to the left of Kyōto Tower Hotel entrance. Large and modern (if impersonal) *sento*. Open daily 7am-8:30pm. ¥750, but the TIC next door has coupons for ¥150 off.

Daikoku-yu (大黒湯). South of Shugakuin Station. Pass Speakeasy and turn left; it's just before the railroad tracks. Typical neighborhood bath with sauna, jacuzzi, cold bath, really hot bath, electric bath (believed to be therapeutic). Near Kyōto University International Dormitory, so crowd is more mixed. Open Tu-Su 4:30-11:30pm. ¥360.

◪ SHOPPING

While Kyōto's department stores aren't as huge as those of other major cities, there are a number of biggies (**Daimaru, Hankyu,** and **Takashimaya**) that line Shijo-dōri between Karasuma and Kawara-machi. Be sure to check out the season's latest *kimono*—they are always gorgeous (if wholly unaffordable) affairs. Fashion mavens should be sure to hit the Kyōto Station area. **JR Isetan** is perhaps the city's most sophisticated department store. In the basement of the Station, the Porta and the Cube malls have some fun and trendy boutiques. Just north of the JNTO Tourist Information Center, **Platz Kintetsu** has a selection ranging from The Gap to Muji. For mall rats, the arcades of **Teramachi** and **Shinkyogoku** between Karasuma and

Kawaramachi have a number of less-expensive clothing shops and tourist boutiques. In recent years, **Kitayama-dōri** in the north, just east of the Kitayama Bridge over the Kamo River, has gone yuppie with its fashionable cafes and boutiques.

As for finding the perfect gifts for friends back home, the Japanese know a thing or two about *omiyage* (the obligatory souvenir). Kyōto's craftsman heritage makes it arguably the best place in Japan to buy handcrafted items. The **Fureaikan Kyōto Museum of Traditional Crafts** (p. 421) is the best place to educate yourself about crafts such as *yuzen* dyeing, textile weaving, embroidery, lacquerware, and fan-making; it also houses a high-quality boutique.

In addition to the listings below, Kyōto has a number of fascinating markets for the souvenir-hungry. **Tō-ji** (p. 414) hosts two big monthly markets, great for antique-hunters. **Kitano Tenman-gū** (p. 420) hosts a market devoted mostly to crafts and second-hand *kimono*, with some boardwalk-type games. The **Nishiki market** features expensive exotic food products, though not necessarily ready-to-eat; Kyōto restaurateurs buy special ingredients here. (Open daily 7am-6pm.)

■ **Kungyoku-do** (薫玉堂 ; ☎371-0162). On Horikawa-dōri, across from Nishi Hongan-ji's central gate (east side). The authority on incense for centuries, this beautiful 3-story boutique maintains a baffling array. Helpful staff burns samples; many scents labeled in English. Open daily 9am-7pm. Closed the 1st and 3rd Su of each month.

■ **House of Kajinoha** (Morita Japanese Paper Co.; ☎341-1419). On Higashionto-in, 2 blocks east of Karasuma, and Bukkoji-dōri, 2 blocks south of Shijo-dōri. Perhaps Kyōto's best selection of handprinted and handmade papers, notebooks, and cards. Open M-F 9:30am-5:30pm, Sa 9:30am-4:30pm.

Yamato Mingei Ten (やまと民芸店 ; ☎ 221-2641). On Kawaramachi, just north of Maruzen Bookstore. Convenient location, 2 floors of Japanese goods. One of the best places to pick up inexpensive, nicely-made souvenirs, including *washi* paper (for letters and cards), fabrics, pottery, and sandals. Open M and W-Su 10am-6pm.

Kyōto Tojiki Kaikan (Pottery Center). On Gojo-zaka, west of Kiyomizu-dera. The biggest of the pottery shops lining the trek up to Kiyomizu-dera that sells the local *kiyomizu-yaki* pottery. These shops are expensive; count on at least ¥1000 for a very small glass, more for bowls. For cheaper pottery, scour the flea markets. Open daily 9:30am-5pm.

Kyōto Handicraft Center (京都ハンぢクラフトセンター ; ☎761-5080). Above Heian Shrine, on Marutamachi, just east of Higashioji-dōri. Popular place for souvenir-hunting, with 7 floors of crafts. Touristy signs proclaim tax-free purchases over ¥10,001. Offers classes on cloisonné (gold enameling), woodblock printing, and doll-making (1hr., 1 every hr. 1-4pm, ¥1500). Change traveler's checks here, even on Su. Open daily Mar.-Nov. 10am-6pm; Dec.-Feb. 10am-5:30pm; Apr. and Oct. 10am-7pm.

Kyōto Craft Center (京都クラフトセンター ; ☎561-9660). Shijo-dōri, Gion. Smaller but more upscale selection of printed and woven fabric goods, fans, and pottery. Open M-Tu and Th-Su 11am-7pm.

Nishijin Textile Center (☎451-9231). On Imadegawa and Horikawa. Nishijin has been weaving gorgeous silk brocades since the 16th century. Check out traditional looms and techniques (like the near-microscopic "fingernail weaving") in their display room and 3rd-fl. museum. Extensive boutique on 2nd fl. Several *kimono* shows throughout the year (free). The *geisha*-obsessed can get dolled up in *kimono* and wig for ¥8800; available 9am-3:30pm; reserve in advance. Open daily 9am-5pm. Free.

Huran (ふらん ; ☎761-1020). On Katsugakita, 1 block north of Marutamachi-dōri, just east of Yoshida Hon-dōri. Silk-screened and stenciled designs on paper and fabric. Workshop in rear. Offers some stunning simple designs of objects from nature, made luxurious by the use of gold paint on solid-color paper.

Kikuya Antique Kimonos (キクヤ ; ☎351-0033). 1 street north of Gojo, between Karasuma and Kawaramachi. If you miss the Tō-ji or Tenman-gū flea markets, look here for inexpensive vintage *kimono* (from ¥2000, *obi* belts ¥1000). Open M-Sa 9am-7pm.

▓ NIGHTLIFE

Kyōto has a decent nightlife scene, though not one as all-pervasive as Ōsaka's. Kiyamachi is the place to be for students and 20- or 30-somethings—it's pretty thumpin' after 10pm. In the summer, people congregate to chat, smoke, and play guitar along the Kamo River on the west side near Shijo-dōri. In Gion, you'll find a number of bars on Hanami-koji north of Shijo-dōri.

▓ ING (イ ン グ ; ☎255-5087). Kyōto Royal Bldg., 2nd fl., on the west side of Kiyamachi, halfway between Shijo and Sanjo-dōri. Intimate bar popular among both foreigners and locals. Cheap food and drinks; friendly, likable staff. Beer ¥450-500, cocktails ¥550-600, food ¥300-700 (curry rice, pizza, gyōza, soba, tortilla chips, salads). Open daily 6pm-midnight, but customarily closes later on weekends, earlier on weekdays.

Metro (☎752-4765; www.metro.ne.jp). On the Keihan train line, Marutamachi stop; take Exit 2. Competes with Sekai World for the title of Kyōto's most popular nightclub. Mix of DJs and live acts; program varies from hip-hop and ska to Latin nights and Bob Marley tributes. 4th F of each month is Diamond Night, featuring a drag show. Check calendar online or in Kansai Time Out. Cover weekdays ¥1000 (including 1 drink), weekends ¥2000-3000. Drinks ¥500. Open Su-Th 10pm-3am, F-Sa 10pm-5am.

Club Sekai World (☎213-4119; www.world-kyoto.com). On Kiyamachi just north of Shijo-dōri in Imagium Bldg. Bar World on ground fl., lounge 2nd fl., Club World on 3rd. Hip-hop, soul, disco, techno. Check ahead for prices and times. Kansai Time Out lists special events. Cover ¥2000-3000; door tickets generally more expensive and less likely to include a drink. At Bar World, beer ¥350, wine ¥400, cocktails from ¥500.

Pig and Whistle Pub (ピ ッ グ ＆ ホ イ ッ ス ル ; ☎761-6022). Northeast corner of Sanjo-dōri and Kawabata intersection. Archetypal British pub. Decent-priced pub grub: pizza (¥670), hamburgers (¥650). Drinks ¥700-800. Dish and drink set combo ¥1000 before 7:30pm. Daily Happy Hour 6-8pm (¥100 off all cocktails and pints/bottles). Open M-W 6pm-1am, Th-Sa 6pm-2am, Su 5pm-midnight.

Cock-a-hoop (コ ッ ク・ア・フ ー プ ; ☎231-4939). On east side of Kiyamachi, 1 block down from Oike-dōri, 7th fl. Chill Latin ambience, salsa-type music. Drinks ¥600, food ¥500 (south-of-the-border appetizers). Open M-Tu and Th-Su 6pm-2am.

Live Spot Rag (☎225-7273). Below Cock-a-hoop, 5th fl. Student crowd. Music varies nightly; schedule posted downstairs. Drinks ¥600-1000. Live music 7:30-10:30pm, cover ¥2500-3000 (includes 1 drink). Open Su-Th 6pm-3am, F-Sa 6pm-4:30am.

Orizzante (ト ッ プ ラ ウ ン ジ オ リ ゾ ン テ ; ☎254-2534). Kyōto Hotel Okura, 17th fl., on the northeast corner of Karasuma-dōri and Oike-dōri intersection. Expensive drinks, but great view of the cityscape. Cocktails ¥1100-1400. Open 11:30am-11pm.

Bar, Isn't It? (☎221-5399). Off Kawara-machi (to the east), 2 blocks south of Sanjo-dōri. The sign leading to the bar (it's in the basement) warns that police will be summoned in the case of fights and that they card (20+). Basement bar with young, sociable air. Mixed crowd, primarily Japanese with some tourists.

Jumbo Karaoke Hiroba (ジ ャ ン ボ カ ラ オ ケ 広 場 ; ☎761-3939). In basement below Pig and Whistle. One of the cheapest karaoke places in town. Offers private rooms, not a bar—a good place to hone your skills with only the derision of your closest friends. ¥680 per hr., including 1 drink. Fried snacks from ¥300. Open daily 11am-6am.

A-Bar (☎213-2129). Just above The 844 Store Cafe, on the 1st tiny side street parallel to Kiyamachi (the west side), 3 streets up from Shijo-dōri. Look for the sign with the @ symbol. Small, cheap izakaya jam-packed with students and 20-somethings. Log interior, bright South American blankets, bench seating. Cocktails ¥500, fried foods ¥300-450, grilled meats ¥400, salads ¥350-450. Open 5pm-midnight.

Rub-a-dub (ラブアダブ ; ☎256-3122). On the east side of Kiyamachi, just south of Sanjo-dōri. Famous for its jerk chicken (¥600). Spicy fried rice ¥600. Coconut chicken curry ¥650. Cocktails ¥600, pina coladas ¥600, beer ¥400-600. Tiny basement hole-in-the-wall with limited seating and a corrugated metal shack against the wall for, um, atmosphere. Open Su-Th 7pm-2am, F-Sa 7pm-4am.

Backgammon (☎223-0416). Dimly lit bar, lots of industrial-looking steel. Small upstairs alcove accessible by ladder; benches back-lit with red light and covered with graffiti. Beer ¥500, cocktails ¥700. Open daily 8pm-5am.

CK Cafe (☎533-6180). In the Dai 8 Parl Bldg. basement, south Gion. On the small side, but the TIC sometimes distributes flyers with a 50% entry discount. Hip-hop, '80s, Latin, house, trance. Food and drink ¥500. Open F-Sa and holidays 9pm-late.

◙ FESTIVALS AND EVENTS

January 15: Toshi-ya (traditional archery contest), at Sanjusangen-dō. Participants in traditional attire shoot at a target from the rear of the 118m-long hall.

April 1-30: Miyako Ōdori, at Gion Kobu Kaburen-jō (see p. 422). Cherry blossom dance, performed by Gion's *geisha* and *maiko*.

3rd week in April: Kabuki Appreciation, Minamiza theater. Lectures by *kabuki* experts, followed by short scenes from classic *kabuki* works. In Japanese. Arrive early for a good seat. 11am or 2pm. Ask at JNTO Tourist Information Center or call ☎561-1155.

April 29: Kyokusui no Utage. An ancient poetry-writing game held in the afternoon at Jonan-gū. The winner is the poet who can write a 31-syllable *tanka* poem before a cup of *sake* floats down the stream in front of them.

May 1-24: Kamogawa Ōdori. Dances by *geisha* of the Pontochō Kaburen-jō Theater. Daily at 12:30, 2:20, and 4:10pm. Reserved seat ¥3800, with tea ceremony ¥4300.

May 15: Aoi Matsuri (Hollyhock Festival), at Shimogamo and Kamigamo Shrines. Originally a Shintō ceremony to prevent storms and pray for good crops.

3rd Sunday of May: Mifune Matsuri (Boat Festival), in Arashiyama on the Oi River. Reproduces the Emperor's boating trips during the Heian Period.

June 1-2: Takigi Nō. Torch-lit performance by several *nō* schools at Heian Shrine.

July: Gion Matsuri, at Yasaka Shrine. One of Kyōto's most famous festivals, Gion Matsuri is held throughout July. Principal parade takes place July 16 and 17, when a procession of enormous wooden floats pass through the Gion district. Dates from the Heian Period, when it was a Shintō ceremony to halt epidemics and calm evil spirits of the dead.

August 16: Daimonji Bonfire, on Mount Nyoigadake. At the end of the Obon festival (Aug. 13-15), the spirits of ancestors are welcomed back to earth. A bonfire in the shape of the character "big" is lit to bid farewell to their souls.

October 22: Jidai Matsuri (Festival of Eras), Heian Shrine. Commemorates founding of Kyōto in 794. Procession of 2000 people in costumes from the Heian to Meiji Periods.

October 22: Kurama no Himatsuri, a fire festival in the nearby mountain village of Kurama. At the end, village men carry long burning torches up to the Yuki shrine.

2nd Sunday in November: Arashiyama Momiji Matsuri (Maple Festival), held on the Togetsukyo Bridge in Arashiyama to celebrate the autumn leaves. Followed by traditional dancing and *kyogen* (p. 100) theater performances.

◪ DAYTRIPS FROM KYŌTO

KURAMA

Take Eiden Eizan Line from Demachiyanagi Station to Kurama, last station. 30min., every 30min., ¥410. Make sure train is labeled for Kurama; track splits for Mt. Hiei.

Kurama offers one of the Kyōto region's best and most accessible hikes, in a peaceful rural setting spotted with single-road villages. Partway through the uphill climb, you'll come to **Kurama-dera**, a temple founded in 770 by the priest Gantei. After centuries under the Tendai sect, Kurama-dera founded its own Kurama-Kokyo sect in 1949. The Main Hall, rebuilt in concrete in 1971, houses a statue of Bishamon-ten from Nara. Look also for the large flat rock upon which Mao-son, the spirit of the earth, descended from Venus millions of years ago. Pick up the English pamphlet that describes the main temple sights and the path that leads onward to Kibune. Near Kurama-dera is the **Yuki Shrine**, designed to protect the city from malevolent spirits thought to come from the northeast.

This hike is best followed by a soak at the **Kurama Onsen**, if you can afford the hefty price. Their indoor bath is private and intimate, surrounded by a garden and offering a panoramic view of the pine forests beyond. If you'd rather bypass relaxation for more exertion, continue past Kurama-dera temple, up to the peak of the mountain, and then down on the other side to the small valley town of Kibune—home to expensive ryokan and restaurants. From there, catch a train back to Kyōto from the Kibune Guchi Station (a 20min. walk south from the town).

HIEI-ZAN (MOUNT HIEI; 比叡山) AND ENRYAKU-JI(延暦寺)

The cheapest and easiest way to get to Enryaku-ji is by JR bus from Kyōto Station or Sanjo-Keihan (1hr., ¥800), and you get great views over Lake Biwa on the way up. If you're looking for a route that's more complicated and more expensive, but also more fun, take bus #17 or 18 from Kyōto Station (¥390) to Yase-yuen Station, or the Eiden Eizan train line from Demachiyanagi (¥260) to the same station. From there, follow the path over the river and up to the left to reach the Hiei cable car (¥840). After the cable car and another ropeway, you need to either take a bus (¥160) or hike (20min.) to Enryaku-ji. If hiking, take the path lined with pictures leading down to the left. Just before you reach the Daikodo building and the small bell-tower, you'll see the temple entrance and bus stop. Open daily Apr.-Nov. 8:30am-4:30pm; Dec.-Mar. 9am-4pm.

Nestled in the forests of Mount Hiei, northeast of Kyōto, **Enryaku-ji** (☎ 578-0001) is an enormous Tendai complex founded by the monk Saichō in 788 to protect the new capital from the evil spirits of the northeast. In the following centuries it gained a powerful reputation, and by the turn of the 16th century it had accumulated over 3000 buildings.

GIVING BACK

LOOKING FOR A FEW GOOD MEN IN GION

Every year, the Gion Festival (p. 228) seeks 10 male *gaijin* (foreigner) volunteers to pull the traditional Gion floats through the streets during the July 17 parade. Originally a Shintō ceremony designed to shield Kyōtoites from plague, the festival today gives particularly selfless foreigners a unique opportunity to participate in and contribute to a local event.

No ability to speak Japanese is required, and for 3hr. of toil, you can earn the admiration of millions. Volunteers wear a broad conical hat called a *kasa*, a collarless tunic called a *happi*, and slitted short-shorts. The Japanese media is apparently intrigued by the image of sweaty foreigners in traditional garb pulling large wooden carts, so chances are you'll get your picture in a paper.

To sign up, e-mail coordinator Yasuyuki Niimi at niimi@kpic.or.jp (or fax 075-342-5050) by the end of April. Include your name, nationality, age, phone, e-mail, and home address. You must attend the obligatory orientation meeting for all participants at Yasaka Shrine two weeks before the parade. The parade is always held July 17, rain or shine, 7am-2pm. If you sign up, you are responsible for showing up. Skipping out will likely derail the whole arrangement, so in the name of diplomacy do not flake.

Most of these (along with their inhabitants) were destroyed by the warlord Nobunaga in 1571, but his successor Hideyoshi helped rebuild the temple. Today the complex still boasts 130 temples on its extensive grounds. Through the main entrance and beyond the Toto parking lot, the newly-built **Kokuho-den museum** (¥450) houses many of Enryaku-ji's statues and manuscripts. Up the hill past the museum is the **Daiko-dō** (Lecture Hall), containing portraits of Enryaku-ji's prominent priests. Beyond that you'll find the temple bell, perpetually rung by curious tourists who are then embarrassed by the loud noise it makes. Down the stairs and to the left is the weather-beaten **Konpon Chū-dō**, Enryaku-ji's most unusually designed building, with a vast sunken altar and three screen lanterns that have burned continuously for the past 1200 years.

After the Konpon Chū-dō, retrace your steps back to Daiko-dō, and take the middle of the three branching paths; you'll pass by the red Amida-dō and its pagoda. About 1km down this path is Saitō. One of the first buildings you'll pass is the gate-surrounded **Jodo-in**, which serves as Saichō's mausoleum. Continuing along the path, you'll arrive at the red, white-trimmed **Shaka-dō** (Sakyamuni Buddha Hall), the oldest surviving temple on Mount Hiei. At the main bus stop in front of the main temple entrance, you can purchase a **day-pass ticket** (¥900) for the shuttle buses that circulate through Enryaku-ji, connecting the areas of Tōtō (east pagoda), Saitō (west pagoda), and Yokawa (which most tourists skip as its central hall has been reconstructed in concrete). If you're not in a hurry, it's cheaper to walk.

OHARA (大原) AND SANZEN-IN (三千院)

Take bus #17 or 18 from Kyōto Station (¥580), or #16 or 17 from Keihan Sanjo (¥490).

Nestled in the valley region of Ohara, Sanzen-in offers a bit less grandeur than mountaintop Enryaku-ji, but the maple-lined riverside walk to Sanzen-in is peaceful and shady. A branch of Enryaku-ji, **Sanzen-in** (☎744-2531) was founded by Saicho in the valley created by Mt. Hiei and the Takano River. The temple grounds are situated along the hill of Gyozan ("Fish Mountain"). The first building, **Kyaku-den** (Reception Hall) houses various treasures from the temple, including some *ikebana* diagrams. After passing through the Imperial Hall, you'll come to the detached 12th-century **Ojo-Gokuraku-in**, the oldest temple building, which contains a sculpted cedar Amida Buddha attended by two bodhisattvas, Kannon and Seishi. The mossy garden **Yusei-en** surrounds the Main Hall and contains a large pond bordered by tall cedars and filled with sluggish carp.

ARASHIYAMA (嵐山)

Take the JR San-in (Sagano) Line from Kyōto Station to Saga Arashiyama (¥230); or bus #11 from Shijo Karasuma to Arashiyama (¥240); or the Keifuku Arashiyama Line from Shijo Omiya (¥230), which takes you a few blocks closer to the Togetsu-kyo bridge.

This region of mountains and forests is a popular suburban getaway for hordes of local tourists and school groups, especially on weekends. Accordingly, the areas around the train stations and the Togetsu-kyo bridge tend to have a cheap, resort-like air, with legions of ice-cream stands, souvenir kiosks, and *geisha*-for-a-day makeup studios. If you're looking for a change of scene away from the city center, however, the temple walk in the north of Arashiyama yields a memorable stroll through bamboo forests, winding streets lined with gift shops, and some unique little temples. In the northern streets just west of Daikaku-ji, you'll see some of Kyōto's few remaining traditional thatch-roof houses.

The **Sagano Sight-seeing Tram** (the "Romantic Train"; ☎861-7444) takes a scenic route along the Katsura River and through surrounding forests. Trams run from the Saga Tram Station to the JR Saga-Arashiyama station and back, with multiple stops along the way (Mar.-Dec. 29, every hr. 8:30am-6pm, ¥600).

The **Togetsu-kyo** ("moon-crossing") **Bridge** is the definitive Arashiyama landmark, so be sure to stop by. From the bridge and the riverbanks nearby, you may get a distant view of cormorant fishing from July to mid-September. This ancient method of fishing uses trained cormorants with metal rings around their throats that prevent them from swallowing their catch. Boatmen use torches to lure the fish to the water's surface. To get a much closer view, go out on a boat (☎861-0223; ¥1700). Schedules vary, so ask for information at the JNTO Tourist Information Center. Boats board on the north side of the Togetsu-kyo Bridge, at either end.

The main attraction across the bridge is the **Iwatayama Monkey Park** (☎861-1616). After appreciating pristine gardens and roped-off temple altars, there's something refreshingly intimate in seeing a mother monkey groom her baby less than an arm's length away. A 20min. hike up the small mountain brings you to a bird's-eye view of the city and about 50 of Kyōto's prehensile-tailed friends. Neither monkeys nor visitors seem bothered by the absence of barriers, although signs warn you not to feed or make eye contact with the other species. Inside a small observatory, you can buy apple wedges to feed them. (Open daily 9am-5pm. ¥500.)

Among Arashiyama's temples, a few merit a visit. **Tenryu-ji** (☎881-1235) is a well-known Rinzai Zen temple established by the Ashikaga shōgunate in 1339. The Cloud Dragon painting on the ceiling of the Hatto is the temple's most famous artistic treasure, and the Sogenchi Garden designed by the monk Muso Soseki is one of Japan's oldest. From Tenryu-ji, continue down the bamboo path, which turns right at Okochi Sanso, the villa of legendary *samurai*-movie actor Okochi Denjiro. Continue north past a series of small temples—each has an entrance fee of at least ¥300, so you're better off taking a quick peek through the main gate. **Adashino Nembetsu-ji** (☎861-2221), however, is worth the admission price. To many Kyōtoites, this temple connotes death, as it's been a burial area for centuries. More than 8000 gravestone images of Buddha have been gathered from the surrounding bamboo forests and collected here. Since gravestones were usually reserved for the wealthy class, each one here probably represents a number of commoners. A memorial service is held on August 23 and 24, and 1000 candles are lighted for the spirits of ancestors. (Open Mar.-Nov. 9am-4:30pm; Dec.-Feb. 9:30am-4pm. ¥500.)

Originally part of Emperor Saga's country villa, **Daikaku-ji** was converted into a Shingon temple in 876 after his death. To the east of the temple lies the Osawa-no-Ike pond, a popular boating-party spot for Emperor Saga's court. (Open daily 9am-4:30pm. ¥700; Daikaku-ji and Gio-ji combined ticket ¥800.)

TAKAO

From Kyōto Station, take a JR bus from the JR3 platform to the Takao stop—ask the driver to tell you where to get off for Jingo-ji, as the stop isn't clearly marked. 50min., 1 per hr., ¥500. Or, take a Kyōto city bus #8 from Shijo-Karasuma. 40min., ¥500.

Combining a visit to Takao's most fascinating temple with a hike along the local trail makes for a perfect outdoorsy getaway. From the bus stop, head down the steps on the same side of the street. At the bottom is the river, festooned with paper lamps and featuring a couple of restaurants. On the other side of the bridge are two paths. The one leading up to the left is the start of the **Kiyotaki hiking trail.** It takes roughly an hour to reach the town of Kiyotaki (which also has a bus stop) via this trail, and about another hour to get down to Torokko Hozukyo Station.

Returning to the beginning of the trail, the steps on the right lead up several flights to **Jingo-ji** (☎861-1769). Founded in the late 8th century, the temple served as a refuge for those disillusioned by the politics at Nara (a problem that soon led Emperor Kammu to move his court to Kyōto). After the entrance booth, walk straight until you reach the Godaidō and Bishamondō buildings; to the right up the stairs is the Kondō (Main Hall), trimmed with vermilion paint and bits of gold. It houses a healing Buddha statue thought to be over 1200 years old. Behind the Kondō along the left path is the grave of Wake no Kiyomaru, the courtier who founded the Jingo-ji. (Open 9am-4pm. ¥400.) Back down the steps from the Kondō, continue to the right down the woodsy path until you reach a clearing that offers a stunning view of the surrounding forest and valley. Here you can buy small clay disks, write your wishes on them, and hurl them out into the valley below.

UJI (宇治) ☎077

From Kyōto Station, take the JR Nara line to Uji. Pick up English maps and pamphlets at the Uji city tourist office just outside the station. ☎423-3334. Open daily 9am-5pm.

A developed industrial little city along the Uji River, Uji boasts an impressive resumé. Once a home away from home for Heian aristocrats, it is also the location of the famous Heian-period temple Byōdō-in, the site of Japan's first tea cultivation industry, and the setting for the last third of Lady Murasaki's *The Tale of Genji*. Uji merits a half-day trip to see the temple, stroll along the river east of the Uji Bridge, and attend a tea ceremony at the Taihoan teahouse.

Byodo-in (☎421-2861) was converted in 1502 from a Fujiwara family villa. Its most famous building, **Phoenix Hall,** was built a year later to house a statue of Amitabha Tathagata. Now imprinted on the ¥10 coin, the hall is said to resemble a phoenix with its wings spread and is also topped with two bronze phoenix statues. The excellent new **Hoshokan museum** features a computer-generated reconstruction of the hall's original brightly-painted interior. Also on display are the temple's original bronze bell and phoenix statues, and the 52 bodhisattvas that once floated on individual clouds in a frieze surrounding the statue of Amitabha Tathagata. Having seen the computer-generated interior, it may seem redundant to plunk down ¥500 to see the faded walls of the reality. The gilded statue of Amitabha Tathagata seated before a gold-plate flame, however, is an impressive sight. (Open daily Mar.-Nov. garden 8:30am-5:30pm, museum 9am-5pm, Phoenix Hall 9:10am-4:10pm; Dec.-Feb. garden 9am-4:30pm, museum 9am-4pm, Phoenix Hall 9:30am-3:30pm. Temple grounds and museum ¥600, Phoenix Hall ¥500.)

Known for tea cultivation, Uji is also home to the ◙**Taihoan Teahouse** (☎423-3334), along the river east of the Uji Bridge and just behind Byōdō-in. Buy a ticket next door at the Uji City Tourist Information Center. This pleasant municipal teahouse performs one of the cheapest tea ceremonies in the Kyōto area, without sacrificing quality. (Open daily 10am-4pm. *Matcha* tea and 1 sweet ¥500.)

ŌSAKA (大阪) ☎06

Work hard, play hard is the name of the game in Ōsaka, Kansai's largest city and one of Japan's most active business centers. If suits are *de rigueur* by day, anything goes after nightfall, as Ōsaka's youngest and hippest elbow their way through buzzing arcades, ferris-wheel-topped *depāto*, and bass-pounding hip-hop clubs. What Kyōto is to the intellectual, Ōsaka is to the hedonist—unbeatable for the diversity and quality of its restaurants, its vibrant expat-friendly nightlife, and its ever-changing parade of fads and fashions. Admittedly, Ōsaka lacks the visual refinement of its neighboring cities. After the devastating firebombings of World War II and the subsequent era of rapid urban development, Ōsaka has few buildings left from the prosperous Edo Period. Beyond the city's architectural gaffes, however, its interesting museums and good-natured kitsch merit a few days' visit.

ON THE WEB   Ōsaka City: www.city.osaka.jp/english

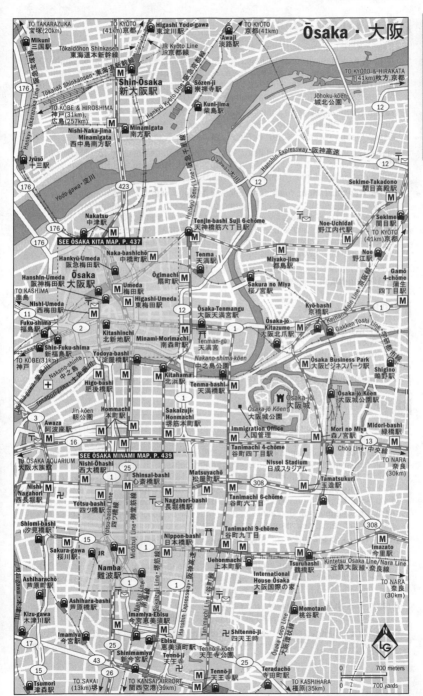

KANSAI

⌷ TRANSPORTATION

Flights: KATE limo buses to **Kansai International Airport** depart from Ōsaka Station in front of New Hankyu Hotel (50min., 5:30am-9:45pm, ¥1300) and from Namba OCAT (45min., 6am-8pm, ¥880). Limo buses to **Ōsaka International Airport** depart from Shin-Ōsaka Station, Ōsaka Station in front of New Hankyu Hotel and the Maru Building, Namba OCAT, and Tennō-ji (6am-9pm, ¥490-620).

Trains: *Shinkansen* serve Shin-Ōsaka Station. Tōkaidō Line links Ōsaka Station in Umeda with **Biwako, Kyōto, Kōbe,** and **Nagoya.** For **Nara,** take JR Yamatoji Line from Ōsaka Station (50min., ¥280) or Kintetsu Line from Namba (express: 30min., ¥1040).

Buses: The tourist offices listed below have information on buses to Tōkyō. For a JR bus, book in advance at the Bus Office in Ōsaka Station. **Kintetsu** and **Hankyu** reservations can by made by phone. (Around 8hr.; ¥5000-8610, round-trip ¥10,000-15,190.)

Public Transportation: You'll soon become familiar with Ōsaka's many subway lines, since the biggest sights are fairly spread out. Pick up a subway map from the information centers. Look at the subway network map at your station, find the price that corresponds to your destination, and insert the appropriate amount to select the correct ticket. Keep your ticket until the end of the ride; you'll need it to exit the station. There are a variety of subway and bus passes available.

Taxis: Two major Ōsaka cab companies have English-speaking drivers: **MK Taxi** (☎6554-2310) and **Nihon Taxi** (☎6928-5151).

⛌ ORIENTATION

Ōsaka is divided into the **Kita** (north) and **Minami** (south) areas, separated by **Chūō-dōri.** Ōsaka Station, surrounded by department stores and restaurant-filled alleys, is the heart of Kita, while Minami is the shopping and entertainment hub. The city's best sights lie outside both these areas. To the east is **Ōsaka Castle,** and below that **Tennō-ji.** To the west are **Ōsaka-wan** and the excellent Ōsaka Aquarium.

❷ PRACTICAL INFORMATION

Tourist Office: The tourist information center in **JR Namba Station** is the nicest and easiest to find (☎6643-2125; www.tourism.city.osaka.jp). Ask for a free map, the monthly guide to cultural and sporting activities, and just about anything else. They can help book accommodations. The other information centers, in **Tenno-ji Station** (☎6774-3077), Umeda's **JR Ōsaka Station** (☎6345-2189), **Shin-Ōsaka Station** (☎6305-3311), and **Universal City** (☎064-804-3824) offer identical services. All open daily 8am-8pm. Longer-term visitors can visit **Ōsaka International House,** several blocks north of Shitenno-ji off Uemachi-suji-dōri. They have info on language lessons, as well as bulletin boards, newspapers, and a library. Pick up a copy of *Enjoy Ōsaka.*

Tours: Ōsaka Systemized Good-Will Guides organize volunteer guides for sights and shopping. Call in advance ☎072-721-1636 or ☎6635-3143. For Japanese-speakers, the **Ōsaka Sightseeing Bus "Rainbow"** gives themed tours of the city. ¥3250-10,320. Buy advance tickets at the Umeda Sightseeing Bus Information Center at JR Ōsaka Station. (☎311-2995.) Open daily 8:30am-6pm.

Budget Travel: A'cross Travel (☎6345-0240; www.across-travel.com), on Yosubashi-suji, south of JR Kitashinchi Station, 5th fl. Open M-F 10am-7pm, Sa 10am-5pm.

Currency Exchange: World Currency Exchange Shop (☎6486-2234). Yodobashi Umeda Bldg., 3rd fl. Changes money and traveler's checks. Open daily 10am-8:30pm.

ATM: The ATM in **Sumitomo Bank,** Hankyu Station, B1. Open daily 6am-11:30pm. MC/V. The **Central Post Office** (see below) has an international ATM, as does **Citibank** on Midosuji-dōri between Namba and Shinnsaibashi Stations.

English-Language Bookstore: Books Kinokuniya on the 1st fl. of Hankyu Umeda Station. Open daily from 10am-9pm. ☎6372-5821.

Ticket Agencies: PIA, on the M2 fl. of JR Tennō-ji Station (☎6771-3988), sells tickets to a variety of cultural events in Ōsaka and Takarazuka. Very limited English.

Emergency: Police ☎110. **Fire** or **ambulance** ☎119.

Hospital/Medical Services: The **AMDA International Medical Information Center** (☎6636-2333) provides information about medical services in the region. English is spoken 9am-5pm. The **Ōsaka University Hospital** (Tokutei Kinō Byōin; ☎6879-5111) accepts walk-in patients daily 8:30am-11:30am.

Internet Access: The best deal in town is **Optic@fe** (☎6359-1510), on the 1st fl. of the Yodo Umeda Building. ¥100 for 30min. Open daily 9:30am-9pm. More convenient and much more expensive is **Kinko's** (☎6442-3700) in JR Ōsaka Station. ¥200 for 10min. Open 7am-10:30pm.

Post Office: The **Central Post Office** is just west of JR Ōsaka Station. Mail service daily 8am-midnight. Cash service open M-F 8am-9pm, Sa-Su 9am-5pm. **Postal Code:** 530.

▟ ACCOMMODATIONS

▓ **Ōsaka International Youth Hostel (HI),** 1-5, Hagoromo-kōen-chō (☎072-265-8539). Take Nankai Main Line to Hagoromo Station, or JR Hanwa Line to Higashihagoromo. Take the West Exit, turn left, and follow the south road, keeping straight as it turns right. Pass the intersection with the supermarket and follow the arrows (12min.). Clean, bright single-sex dorms with unit bath, TV, and A/C. Lovely common bath overlooks garden. Breakfast ¥600. Dinner ¥1050. Free bike rental; Internet access ¥100 for 15min. Coin laundry. Curfew 11pm. Dorms ¥3150; Japanese-style dorm ¥3600; twins ¥4300 per person. Nonmembers ¥600 extra. MC/V. ❷

Ōsaka Shiritsu Nagai Youth Hostel (HI) (☎699-5631; fax 699-5644). Take Midosuji Subway Line to Nagai Stop. Take Exit 1 and walk into the park, curving to the left toward the huge concrete stadium. The hostel is built into the stadium on its far side—follow the signs in the

IN RECENT NEWS

ŌSAKA'S FIRST LADY

Despite record-low voter turnout, election day 2000 in Ōsaka will go down in the books as an important first. Ota Fusae won in a landslide victory to become Japan's first female governor. The former Ministry of International Trade and Industry official was backed by the Liberal Democrats Party and beat out two rivals.

Since her election, three more female governors have already been elected in Japanese prefectures, a strong indication that this shift in leadership is more than a blip in Japan's political history. Liberal policy-makers are encouraged by these largely progressive female governors, who have sought to better voice the concerns of women and working class citizens than their predecessors. Ms. Ota has said that she hopes to reawaken the political interest of the voter base.

And to stir up a few fusty traditions. Ms. Ota made international news when the Japanese Sumō Association forbade her from presenting an annual championship award, since women are not allowed to step into the sumō ring. For the past three years she has petitioned unsuccessfully to have the rule changed. But perhaps fourth time's a charm? At press time, Ms. Ota was planning to run in the next election as well, so the Sumō Association may be in for it...

park. Clean and friendly. Breakfast ¥420. Internet and coin laundry available. Kitchen ¥50. Sheets ¥200 for 3 nights. Curfew 11pm. Dorms ¥2500; private rooms ¥3000 per person; family rooms ¥3500 per person. ❶

Hotel Kinki (☎321-9117; http://hotelkinki.com/eng). A 7min. walk from JR Ōsaka Station. Don't be put off by the love hotel look—this is an outstanding tourist hotel with small, clean rooms. Check-in 3pm. Japanese-style singles ¥4500; Western-style ¥5000; twins ¥6400. ¥1000 discount for checking in 9-11pm. AmEx/DC/MC/V. ❷

Hotel Awina (☎772-1441; www.awina-osaka.com). A 3min. walk from Uenomachi Station. Large business hotel with mostly Western-style rooms. Bath, fridge, and TV in all rooms. Internet access available. Breakfast buffet ¥1200. Check-in 4pm. Check-out 10am. Curfew 12pm. Singles ¥7800; twins ¥15,400. ❸

Business Hotel Resort Juri, 1-9-7, Seninichi-mae (☎213-8590; www.1ocn.ne.jp/~h-juri). On Seninichimae-dōri a few blocks east of Namba Subway Station. Decent business hotel. Great location in central Minami. All rooms have bath, satellite TV, fridge, and A/C. Breakfast ¥400. Check-in 3pm. Check-out 10am. Singles ¥5500-6000; twins ¥11,000-12,000; doubles ¥9000. AmEx/DC/MC/V. ❸

Sunroute Umeda (☎373-1111; www.hotelsunroute.co.jp/umeda). Exit Umeda Station, walk left to the end of the street, and take a right; it's across the street (5min.). Cheerful, upscale business hotel. Breakfast ¥1200. Check-in 3pm. Check-out 10am. Singles ¥8400-8900; twins ¥15,000-21,000; doubles ¥13,000. AmEx/MC/V. ❹

Hotel Green Plaza (☎374-1515). A 7min. walk from Ōsaka Station. Popular wedding venue, offering Western-style rooms with large single beds and bath. Breakfast in the cute French cafe downstairs ¥800. Check-in 3pm. Check-out 10am. Singles ¥6800; twins ¥9800-13,500. AmEx/DC/MC/V. ❸

Osakafu Hattori Ryokuchi Youth Hostel (HI), 1-3, Hattoriryokuchi (☎862-0600; youthhostel@osakaymcca.or.jp). Take Midosuji Subway Line north to Ryokuchi-kōen. Take the West Exit and follow the signs through the park. Smaller rooms than Nagai Hostel, but perfectly adequate. Sheets included. Helpful English-speaking staff. Breakfast ¥390. Dinner ¥870. Curfew 10pm. Dorms ¥2500 for 19+; under 19 ¥2000. Cash only. ❶

Hotel Apio Ōsaka (☎941-5860; www.apio-osaka.or.jp). On 5th fl., just south of Morinomiya Subway Station, southeast of Ōsaka-jō Kōen. Sleek, spacious, modern rooms, Japanese- or Western-style. Curfew 11pm. Singles ¥4800; twins ¥7200. ❷

Ebisu-so Ryokan (☎643-4861). A 12min. walk from Namba Station. One of Ōsaka's only affordable ryokan, although the rooms don't really merit the price. Singles ¥5500; doubles ¥10,000. AmEx/MC/V. ❸

Capsule Inn Namba (☎633-2666; fax 633-5568). A 3min. walk from Namba Station. Convenient location makes it popular with tourists. Men and women both welcome. Capsules ¥2500; singles ¥4980; doubles ¥7270. MC/V. ❶

Hotel Kikuei (☎633-5656; www.kikuei.com). Sakaisuji-dōri, north Den-Den Town; 7min. walk from Namba Station. Good-sized rooms with bath; non-smoking available. Breakfast ¥400. Curfew 1am. Singles ¥6000; twins/doubles ¥9000. AmEx/DC/MC/V. ❸

🍴 FOOD

Ōsaka's breadth of culinary choices is enough to overwhelm anyone. In addition to having the highest rate of *fugu* (blowfish, see p. 503) consumption in Japan, the city is known for *okonomiyaki* (savory pancake), *takoyaki* (octopus balls), and *kitsune udon* (noodles with fried tofu). Home to Japan's largest Korean community, Ōsaka boasts a huge covered market full of Korean barbecues and food stalls. Browse endless rows of cafes, sushi joints, pastry stands, and international restaurants in food courts like **Hankyu San Bangai,** beneath Hankyu Station. Other collections of cafes and restaurants can be found in **Kappa Yokocho Koshonomachi**, an affordable street-level arcade, and the multi-story **Shinjuku Gochisō**, across from Tennō-ji Station on the south side.

Freshness Burger (☎ 798-7031). Across from Phoenix Bldg., west side. Burgers ranging from classic beef to *teriyaki* chicken, to the novel (if sloppy) lasagna burger (¥260-350). Try the yummy sweet-potato fries. Open M-F 8am-3am, Sa 8am-10pm. ❶

Daikichi (☎ 6773-4123). Take Sennichimae Line to Tsuruhashi. From exit 7, turn left and take another left at the corner. Daikichi is 3 blocks down. Friendly Korean barbecue with huge portions and delicious entrees. Korean hot-pots ¥750-850, soups from ¥500. For a treat, try the *samgetan*, a chicken stuffed with rice, dates, ginseng and pine-nuts (¥1800). Open M-W and F-Su noon-11:30pm. ❷

Little Little Forest (☎ 258-5166). In Amerika Mura, Big Step Bldg., 2nd fl. Cute, classy organic vegetarian restaurant. Sells pottery. Lunch set ¥850. Open daily 11am-8pm. ❷

Fugetsu (☎ 367-8002). In Amerika Mura, 3rd fl. The best sit-down prices for *okonomiyaki* (¥550-800) and *yakisoba* (fried noodles; ¥580-1100) in town. Great view over Umeda. Vegetarian options and English menu. Open daily 11am-9:30pm. ❶

Higashiyama Sushi (☎ 359-7333). South side of Hankyu San Bangai; look for the yellow plexiglass walls. Trendy *kaiten-zushi* (conveyor belt sushi) restaurant with oh-so-cool marble interior. Artfully presented sushi (including Ōsaka's trademark *hako-zushi*, sushi pressed into wooden boxes) sails on the conveyor belt to your seat. Sushi from belt ¥200-300; from menu ¥400-800. Open daily 11:30am-9pm. ❷

The Don Shop, 2-4-11, Umeda (☎ 6341-5138). Kappa Yokocho Koshonomachi, north side. *Shabu-shabu* beef ¥1980, pork ¥1450. Jazz organ on premises for live jazz every evening, 7pm-midnight. Lunch sets ¥790-1280. Open daily 5pm-5am. ❷

Court Lodge, Konishi Bldg., 1st fl., 1-4-7, Sonezaki Shinchi (☎ 6342-5253). Sri-Lankan hole-in-the-wall. Cheap lunch and dinner sets. Chicken/beef/mutton curry ¥500, plus salad and *dahl* ¥650. Tasty pineapple *lassi*. Open M-Sa 11am-3pm and 5-11pm. ❷

Mannen (☎ 6315-5121). Across from Bar, Isn't It. Cozy wood interior with rustic pig motifs, open very late. *Rāmen* from ¥600. Open Su-Th noon-5am, F-Sa noon-6am. ❶

Cafe Org (☎ 6312-0529). Near Mannen. Spacious, warmly-lit organic cafe, a black sheep in this rowdy neighborhood. Pasta dinners ¥900-1500. Lovely rustic sandwiches on whole-grain ¥390-480. Organic juices ¥450-550. Open daily 11am-11pm. ❷

Taikyuya (☎ 772-7777). Just east of Daikichi. Home-style Korean cooking. Lunch specials ¥900/1500. Barbecue dinner ¥3800. Open M-Tu and Th-Su 11am-8:30pm. ❸

Yamachan (☎ 072-622-5308). Just east of the Hoop Mall, south of Tennō-ji Station. *Takoyaki* place popular with locals, with a sit-down restaurant in the corner. Give the octopus balls a moment to cool—the centers are piping hot. ❷

La Bamba (☎ 213-9612). West Dōtombori, on 2nd fl. Mexican restaurant. Tacos a la Parilla ¥1000, enchiladas ¥1300. Take-out available. Open daily 4pm-midnight. ❸

Kani Dōraku (☎ 211-8975). Under the giant mechanical crab on Dōtombori. Ōsaka's unrivaled crab specialist. Huge dinners run ¥4500-8000. Cheaper options: rice bowls with crab (¥1000), salads (¥1200), *tempura* (¥1400). Open daily 11am-11pm. ❸

Zuboraya (☎ 211-0181). Blowfish? Why not! This well-known place is a must if you want to partake of this potentially deadly delicacy. English menu. A full meal is about ¥3000; get a smaller serving if you just want a been-there-done-that experience. Blowfish *sashimi* with green tea noodles ¥1000. Open daily 11am-11pm. ❸

Kuidaore (☎ 211-5300). Across from Kani Dōraku; look for the mechanical drum-beating clown. *Takoyaki* gratin (¥680), *kitsune udon* (¥580), *sukiyaki* (¥1980). Top it all off with a clown sundae (¥800). Open 11am-10pm. ❷

Africa (☎213-4622). Just south of America Mura. Vaguely African-themed subterranean restaurant serving nouveau-European food. Small portions and a ¥300 bread charge, but it's interesting and trendy. Pizza ¥780-1100, pasta from ¥800, meat and seafood ¥1200-1500. Open Su-Th 6pm-midnight, F-Sa 6pm-5am. ❷

◎ ⌐ SIGHTS AND SHOPPING

ŌSAKA-JŌ AND SURROUNDINGS

ŌSAKA-JŌ (大阪城) AND CASTLE MUSEUM. Ōsaka-jō is the ostentatious triumph of Toyotomi Hideyoshi, the late 16th-century warlord who united Japan. Born to a poor rural family, Hideyoshi entered into the warlord Nobunaga's service, rose through the ranks, and succeeded him after his death. He built Ōsaka-jō in 1583 on the site of the old Ōsaka Hongan Temple. His successor Tokugawa Ieyasu turned against the Toyotomi family and burned the castle to the ground during the Summer War of 1615. In a series of resurrections, it was rebuilt by the Tokugawa in 1620, razed by lightning soon after, rebuilt again just before the Meiji Restoration, then burned again by Meiji forces. Today's castle dates from the 1930s. The *donjon* miraculously survived the WWII bombings, only to be gutted and modernized in 1997. Because of this, visitors rarely find the Castle Museum worth the price, since the lovely exterior can be seen for free. Inside are panels on the castle's origins, the Summer War, and the life of Hideyoshi—fun for history buffs. The top floor does offer a panorama of the park and surrounding area. On the grounds outside, English labels provide information on the walls, turrets, and gates. Look for the Octopus Stone and the aptly named Kimono Sleeve Stone in the castle walls; at 100 tons, these stones are the biggest in the castle. *(Castle Museum, 1-1, Ōsaka-jō. Take the Chūō Subway Line to Morinomiya Station. ☎941-3044; http://www.tourism.city.osaka.jp/ en/castle. Open daily 9am-5pm. ¥600, children free.)*

ŌSAKA HISTORY MUSEUM (ŌSAKA REKISHI HAKUBUTSUKAN; 大阪歴史博物館). This multi-floored new museum is inside a lozenge-shaped skyscraper near Ōsaka-jō. Starting from the top floor, work your way through a reconstruction of Nawari Court, dating from when Ōsaka was the nation's capital in the mid-7th and 8th centuries, and related archaeology. Move on to the Edo Period exhibit, including a wonderfully detailed wood-carving parade float, and an exhibit on Ōsaka through the roaring twenties and the modern period. *(Connected to the NHK Bldg., just next to the Tanimachi 4-chōme stops on the Tanimachi and Chūō subway lines. Leave by Exit 9 and take the elevator to the 10th floor. ☎6946-5728; www.mus-his.city.osaka.jp. Open M, W-Th, and Sa-Su 9:30am-5pm, F 9:30am-8pm. ¥600, high school students ¥360, elementary free.)*

ŌSAKA INTERNATIONAL PEACE CENTER (ŌSAKA KOKUSAI HEIWA SENTĀ; 大阪国際平和センター). There are perhaps happier ways to spend a Sunday afternoon in the park, but Peace Ōsaka gives a detailed educational account of the horrors perpetrated by and against Japan before and during WWII. There are firsthand accounts of events such as the Rape of Nanking and the firebombing that devastated Ōsaka; the latter puts Umeda's current development into dramatic perspective. *(On the south edge of Ōsaka-jō Park. ☎6947-7208. Open Tu-Su 9:30am-5pm. ¥250.)*

KITA (北) AND UMEDA (梅田) AREAS

UMEDA SKY BUILDING. From the highest point in Ōsaka, you can see all the way to Awaji-jima. Two giant glass towers are joined 170m up by the platform of the **Floating Garden Observatory,** perforated by a large circular opening. You'll love or hate its Lego-like appeal—Ōsakans themselves are torn on the building's architec-

Ōsaka Kita ·
大阪北（梅田）

tural value. In the basement of this architectural giant, **Takimi-koji** is a world apart. This reconstruction of a narrow-alleyed 1920s neighborhood contains a number of Japanese restaurants. There are cinemas on the third and fourth floors; Cine Libre Umeda often shows foreign and art films. *(1-1-18, Ōyodonaka. Open daily 10am-10:30pm. Buy tickets on the 3rd fl. of the East Tower. ¥700.)*

MUSEUM OF ORIENTAL CERAMICS (ŌSAKA SHITRITSU TŌYŌ TŌJI BIJUTSUKAN; 大阪市立東洋陶磁美術館).

With a world-class collection of Chinese, Japanese, Korean, and Vietnamese ceramics, this museum gives a detailed history of the art form and its techniques. There are lovely examples of Korean celadon glaze and some striking pieces of Edo-period *arita*-ware, white porcelain with bold bright geometric patterns. *(From Yodobashi Subway Station, head north into Nakanoshima Park, take the 1st right, and pass the City Office; it's just beyond the neo-Baroque Public Hall. ☎ 6223-0055; www.moco.or.jp. Open Tu-Su 9:30am-5pm. ¥500.)*

Ōsaka Kita ·
大阪北（梅田）

🏠 ACCOMMODATIONS
Hotel Green Plaza, **3**
Hotel Kinki, **5**
Sunroute Umeda, **1**

🍎 FOOD
Cafe Org, **9**
Court Lodge, **11**
The Don Shop, **2**
Freshness Burger, **15**
Fugetsu, **6**
Hankyu San Bangai, **7**
Higashiyama Sushi, **8**
Kappa Yokocho
  Koshonomachi, **2**
Takimi-Koji Alley, **4**

🍸 NIGHTLIFE
Canopy, **14**
Captain Kangaroo, **13**
Karma Bar & Cafe, **12**
Sam & Dave Umeda, **16**
Tocca a Te, **10**

HEP FIVE. Each year, this youth-oriented mall behind Hankyu Umeda Station draws more visitors than Tōkyō Disneyland. The large red ferris wheel on top provides a good view over Umeda. The interior is a teeny-bopper's dream come true, with dozens of stores devoted to fashion. *(An 8min. walk from Umeda Station. ☎6313-0501. Open daily 11am-11pm. Tickets and entrance for ferris wheel on 7th fl. ¥500.)*

NAKANOSHIMA KŌEN (中之島公園). If you want to spend any time outdoors, come here instead of Tennō-ji Kōen. It's free and quite lovely, filled with bower after bower of roses and rose trees. Little wonder that it's so popular for wedding photos. *(Take the subway to Kitahama Station. ☎312-8121.)*

TENNŌ-JI (天王寺) AREA

SHITENNŌ-JI (四天王寺). Built by Prince Shotoku in 593, the original temple is one of Japan's oldest, although nearly everything here has been rebuilt. You can ascend the pagoda for an obscured view of the temple grounds. The pagoda's unattractive stairwell unfortunately diminishes the experience. Inside the treasure house, several statues of Prince Shotoku and related memorabilia (scrolls and swords he used) are on display. *(From Tennō-ji Station, walk north on Tanimachi-suji for 10min. After two diagonal intersections, follow the small alley to the right to the main temple grounds. ☎6771-0066. Open daily Apr.-Sept. 8:30am-4:30pm, Oct.-Mar. 8:30am-4pm. Treasure house closed M. Temple grounds free; treasure house, pagoda and other buildings ¥200.)*

TENNŌ-JI KŌEN (天王寺公園). Nice but not outstanding, this park provides an interesting stroll past homeless shanties and karaoke stands where you can sing your favorites at bargain prices. The **Municipal Museum** has permanent exhibitions on a variety of Japanese (and occasionally Chinese and Korean) arts, as well as notable special exhibitions. The **zoo** is known for its hippos, polar bears, pandas, and rhinos—a great place to take children. *(☎6771-8401. Open Tu-Su 9:30am-5pm. Park entrance ¥150; zoo ¥500; museum ¥300, students ¥200.)*

SHINSEKAI (新世界). Shinsekai means "New World," but its name belies its age. A stopover for Edo-period travelers on their way to Sumiyoshi Taisha, this area was transformed into an entertainment district in the early 20th century. Damaged in WWII firebombings, it was rebuilt in 1956 but quickly lost its appeal. Today, *pachinko* parlors compete for the patronage of old men in the shadow of Tsutenkaku Tower, an Eiffel wannabe. The view of this somewhat seedy neighborhood isn't necessarily worth the admission price. *(To the west of Tennō-ji Kōen. Open daily 10am-6:30pm. ¥600.)* At the southern end of the area, **Festivalgate Amusement Park** has several rides, including a rollercoaster and large swing ride. *(☎6635-1000. Open daily 10am-9:30pm. Entrance free, pay individually for rides.)*

MINAMI (南)

DEN-DEN TOWN. Deriving its name from the word *denki* (electricity), this area sustains dozens of shops devoted to intricate gadgets, from computers to cell phones to cameras to watches. Some shops are Duty Free, so bring your passport for a tax exemption. *(Take Sakaisuji Subway Line to Ebisucho Station. The North Exit puts you in the heart of Den Den Town. Most shops open daily 10am-7pm, some closed W.)*

KUROMON ICHIBA. A bustling market has occupied this area since the 1820s, when merchants began gathering here to trade fish. Today, the stalls along this shopping street sell seafood to sushi restaurant owners and anyone else. If you're eating on the go, it's a good place to pick up a *bentō* box or a few skewers of chicken. Otherwise, it's a unique shopping experience. *(Most stalls closed Su.)*

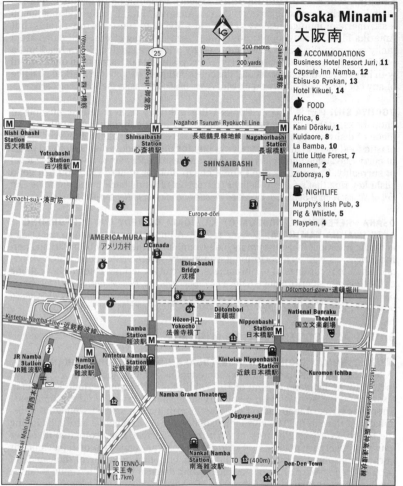

Ōsaka Minami · 大阪南

ACCOMMODATIONS
Business Hotel Resort Juri, **11**
Capsule Inn Namba, **12**
Ebisu-so Ryokan, **13**
Hotel Kikuei, **14**

FOOD
Africa, **6**
Kani Dōraku, **1**
Kuidaore, **8**
La Bamba, **10**
Little Little Forest, **7**
Mannen, **2**
Zuboraya, **9**

NIGHTLIFE
Murphy's Irish Pub, **3**
Pig & Whistle, **5**
Playpen, **4**

DŌTOMBORI (道頓堀). Just south of Dōtombori-gawa, this street is home to an unending array of restaurants and a riotous clash of architectural styles. A Tudor half-timber building shares the block with a giant plastic squid, while Kani Dōraku's iconic wiggling mechanical crab bathes in the light of the marquees. The bridge Ebisu-bashi is the place to view the madding crowds against the backdrop of building-tall advertisements. *(Take the Midori-suji Line to Namba Station.)*

HŌZEN-JI YOKOCHŌ (法善寺横丁). A tiny temple decorated with bright paper lanterns gives its name to this neighborhood sandwiched between Dōtombori and Sennichimae-dōri. It's a little slice of old Ōsaka, with nostalgic eateries lining the narrow alleyways. Two recent fires, one in April 2003, have caused damage in the area, but reconstruction is underway. *(A short walk south of Dōtombori Arcade.)*

AMERIKA MURA AND EUROPE-DŌRI. Ōsaka's variation on Chinatowns and Little Italies is the ever-popular trend-ghetto, Amerika Mura. It's doubtful that penniless American immigrants ever eked out a living in these narrow streets, but Amerika Mura's teenybopper boutiques, used clothing stores, and cafes are a tacky paean to the US of A, symbolized by a large spangled clown head and a building topped by a Statue of Liberty. Nearby Europe-dōri attracts an older crowd with its expensive restaurants and upscale boutiques, despite the marked absence of any cobblestoned old-world charm. *(West of Midō-suji along the Dōtombori Canal.)*

DŌGUYA-SUJI (道具屋筋). Cooks will think they're in paradise: bushels of chopsticks, stacks of lacquerware, and every imaginable kitchen appliance or piece of dishware can be found along this street. The highlight, however, is the plastic food models that restaurateurs buy for their window displays. Rigid pools of curry rice aligned vertically take this Japanese display art to a whole new level of surreality. The models don't come cheap, but for a mere ¥650 you can get a sushi key-ring that's sure to delight (or disgust) friends back home. *(Near the East Exit of Nankai Namba Station, in a covered arcade extending from Nansan-dōri.)*

ŌSAKA PREFECTURAL MUSEUM OF KAMIGATA COMEDY AND PERFORMING ARTS (WAHHA KAMIGATA; ワッハ上方). A multi-floored tribute to the Ōsaka comedic tradition, this museum includes exhibits on the history of traditional performances, as well as a performing arts library where visitors can watch videos and listen to recordings of performances. You can sometimes catch a show at one of the museum's performance halls. *(12-7, Sennichi-mae, Namba. 5min. walk from Namba Station. ☎6631-0884. Open Su-Tu and Th-Sa 11am-6pm. Last admission 5:30pm. Handicapped accessible. ¥250, college and high school students ¥250, junior high and younger ¥120.)*

SOUTH AND SOUTHWEST OF MINAMI

■**ŌSAKA HUMAN RIGHTS MUSEUM (ŌSAKA JINKEN HAKUBUTSUKAN; 大阪 人権博物館).** This excellent museum contains exhibits about minority groups, including the indigenous Ainu of Hokkaidō, the Okinawans, ethnic Koreans in Ōsaka, and the *burakumin*, a socially subordinate group of ethnic Japanese. There is extensive material on ongoing discrimination against women, the disabled, and the elderly. The museum also looks at environmental issues, including the tragic, infuriating history of *minamata* disease, a neurological disorder caused by mercury poisoning. During the post-war years, two of Japan's major corporations dumped mercury in the ocean, crippling or killing of thousands of people. The famous picture of a mother gazing down at her afflicted child is one of the most moving images you'll ever see. *(Take the JR Loop Line to Ashihara-bashi Station, and walk south 3 blocks. ☎6561-5891; www.liberty.or.jp. Open Tu-Su 10am-5pm. ¥250.)*

SUMIYOSHI TAISHA (住吉大社). If you're going to see anything religious in Ōsaka, it should be this shrine. Dedicated to the three Sumiyoshi sea gods, this has been for centuries a place of prayer for seamen. The 400-year-old bright orange, highly arched Ori Hashi bridge is the defining landmark, but be sure to check out the four central buildings. Constructed in the Sumiyoshi Zukuri style with cypress-thatched roofs and high copper exterior beams, they represent Japan's oldest shrine architecture. Over 100 ceremonies and festivals take place here each year, especially in the summer. One of the most astounding is the mid-June rice-planting ceremony, Otaue Shinji, in which *samurai* reenactors beat large drums and "battle" in the fields while dancers entertain the crowd. *(Take Nankai Dentetsu Subway Line from Nankai Namba Station to Sumiyoshi Taisha Station. ☎6672-0753. Open daily 6am-6pm.)*

ŌSAKA BAY (ŌSAKA WAN; 大阪湾) AREA

ŌSAKA AQUARIUM (KAIYUKAN; 海遊館). Designed around the theme of the Pacific Rim volcano belt, this aquarium easily merits half a day. Starting at the top, work your way down from the water's surface to the lower half of the large tanks. Watch sea otters clean their faces on the surface and then dive torpedo-like to the bottom. The centerpiece is the enormous Pacific Ocean tank, which houses a whale shark and spotted eagle rays, although penguin-feeding time is a favorite with the children. The two final exhibits are equally stunning. The jellyfish tanks house gorgeous orange Lion's Mane jellies with long wispy tentacles. The "Japan's Deep" exhibit has nightmarishly large spider crabs, found in the darkest regions of the sea. *(Take Chūō Subway Line to Ōsaka-ko; from exit 1, walk toward the ferris wheel. ☎ 6576-5501; www.kaiyukan.com. Open daily 10am-8pm. ¥2000, under 16 ¥900, under 6 ¥400. The ¥2500 Kaiyu Kippu Pass gets you admission, 1 day unlimited subway use, and a 10% reduction on the Tempozan Giant Wheel. Purchase at any subway station from kiosk near ticket machines.)*

OTHER ATTRACTIONS. The rest of Ōsaka Bay is pretty skippable. The **Tempozan Giant Wheel** claims to be the largest in the world, but views from the top aren't as spectacular as you'd hope. *(☎ 6576-6222. Open daily 10am-9:30pm. ¥700.)* Other than that, there's the generic **Tempozan Market**, with a KFC and Claire's Boutique, and the **boardwalk**, lined with industrial structures.

OTHER AREAS

◙ OPEN-AIR MUSEUM OF OLD JAPANESE FARMHOUSES (NIHON MINKA SHŪRAKU HAKUBUTSUKAN; 日本民家集落博物館). An outdoor museum with eight Edo-period thatched-roof farmhouses is perhaps the last thing you'd expect to find in the overdeveloped buzz of Ōsaka—precisely what makes this sight such a gem. These original farmhouses have been moved from all over Japan, allowing the visitor to compare different architectural styles and functions. Fascinating English pamphlets explain the construction and purpose of the houses. All the interiors are open for touring. Many seem quite large until you consider than some housed 43 family members. There is also a rural *kabuki* stage, a startling contrast to the big theaters of cosmopolitan Ōsaka. *(Take the Midosuji Subway Line north to Ryokuchi-Kōen. Follow the signs from the station, about a 15min. walk. ☎ 862-3137. Open Mar.-Oct. Tu-Su 10am-5pm; Nov.-Feb. Tu-Su 10am-4pm. ¥500.)*

UNIVERSAL STUDIOS JAPAN. This theme park offers all the Universal Studio classics—*Back to the Future*, *JAWS*, *Jurassic Park*, and *Waterworld*. The California-themed restaurants include a drive-in, a Beverly Hills *boulangerie*, and the bizarre Discovery Restaurant where you can eat a dinosaur-shaped steak. *(Take JR Yumesaki Line to Universal City Station. ☎ 064-790-7000; www.usj.co.jp. Open daily, hours vary but generally 9am-8pm. ¥5500, children ¥3700, seniors ¥4800.)*

▣ NIGHTLIFE

Ōsaka nightlife is anything but boring. The monthly *Kansai Time Out* lists special events at the clubs below and many others.

KITA (北)

▣ Tocca a Te, 2-2-15, Sonezaki-shinchi *(☎ 6365-5808)*. Take the subway to Higashi Umeda Station. A "bar and creative space" with M night salsa and other themed events. Popular with both Japanese and *gaijin*. Warm wood interior with a European flair. Handmade pizza ¥600. Happy Hour 6-8pm. Open M-Th 6pm-late, F-Sa 6pm-later.

Sam and Dave Umeda (☎6365-1688). A 2min. walk from Higashi-Umeda Station. Slick dark interior with dancing space and Christmas lights. Theme nights include "no panties required" and "staff wearing only cling wrap." Happy Hour daily 7-9pm. M night free billiards, Th no cover. Cover ¥2000 for men with 2 drinks, ¥1000 for women with 1 drink. Food ¥500-700, beer ¥500, cocktails ¥700.

Captain Kangaroo, Okawa Bldg., 1st fl., 1-5-20, Sonezaki-shinchi (☎6346-0367). A happening place with a huge dragon mural on the wall, this popular *gaijin* bar is a prime place for people-watching. Happy hour 5:30-7pm (drafts ¥300, cocktails ¥400). Beer ¥500-600, food ¥300-700. No Cover. Open M-Sa 5:30pm-5am.

Karma Bar and Cafe, Kasai Bldg., 1st fl., 1-5-18, Sonezaki-shinchi (☎6344-6181; www.club-karma.com). Trendy, pricey place with all-night techno. Website lists upcoming events (in Japanese). Advance tickets ¥2000, including 1 drink; ¥2500 at the door.

Canopy, 1-11-20, Sonezaki-shinchi (☎6341-0339). Kitashinchi Station. Great place to kick back and look cool. Potted palms as ceiling drapery provide great atmosphere. Beer ¥650-700, cocktails ¥800-900, sandwiches and burgers ¥1200. Happy Hour 5-8:30pm, midnight happy hour midnight-2am. Open M-Sa 5pm-6am, Su 5pm-midnight.

MINAMI (南)

▨ **Playpen**, 2-8-12, Shinsai-bashi (☎6214-8789). From Shinsai-bashi Subway Station, take exit 6; you'll see Daimaru department store across the way. Enter the covered walkway, head 2 blocks to the right, and take a left; Playpen is on the 2nd block. Popular basement bar. Bright red staircase leads down to a cool black bar with red booths. Large-screen TV. Beer ¥600, cocktails ¥700. Open daily 7pm-late.

Murphy's Irish Pub (☎6282-0677). Midosuji Line to Shinsaibashi Station. From exit 6, take a right and you'll see a Swatch Shop on the corner. Take a left there and you'll see the Lead Plaza Building; go to the 6th fl. Perennial favorite for English crowd. Free Internet and Playstation, and occasional live music. Fish and chips ¥750. Happy hour midnight-2am, pints and cocktails ¥500. Open daily 5pm-3am.

Pig and Whistle, 2-5, Sonezaki (☎6361-3198). Ohatsu Tenjin Biru, B1, near Umeda Station. Alternate location in Across Bldg., 2nd fl., north of Holiday Inn on Midosuji (☎6213-6911). Pub popular with English teachers. Fish 'n chips ¥750, pint of Guinness ¥800. Open Su-Th 5pm-midnight, F-Sa 5pm-1am.

🎵 ENTERTAINMENT

Ōsaka has a rich show-business tradition in multiple genres. Check out the **Ōsaka Prefectural Museum of Kamigata Comedy and Performing Arts** (p. 440) for a historical perspective, but don't stop there—experience Japanese entertainment firsthand at one of the city's many excellent theaters. Tickets can be expensive, usually over ¥4000, but if you have any interest in Japanese art, it will be money well spent. Without a reservation, however, you'll be out of luck.

Torii Hall, Kamigata Bldg., 1-7-11, Sennichimae (☎6211-2506). Near Nihonbashi Station. A venue for Ōsaka's up-and-coming young entertainers and traditional *rakugo* (p. 100) comedians. Hours and prices vary according to event; consult *Kansai Time Out* or call ahead for schedules and tickets. Reservations required.

Ōsaka Shochiku-za, 1-9-19, Dōtombori (☎6214-2211; www.shochiku.or.jp). A 1min. walk from Namba Station on the Midosuji Line. In the early 1900s, this theater made headlines as the first Western-style theater in Japan. Filling 10 full stories, 8 of them above ground, Shochiku-za concentrates on traditional *kabuki* plays. Renovated in the mid-'90s, it's truly state-of-the-art. Usually 2 shows per day; call or visit the website (Japanese only) for schedules and ticket reservations.

National Bunraku Theater of Japan, 1-12-10, Nippon-bashi (☎6212-2531; reservations ☎6212-1122). A short walk from Namba Station on the Midosuji Line. Ōsaka is famous for the art of *bunraku*, in which black-clad puppeteers manipulate almost-life-sized puppets as a narrator tells a story while playing the three-stringed *shamisen*. Consult *Kansai Time Out* to see if there's a show on. If there is, don't miss it, as this is *the* place to see *bunraku*. About 5 shows per year, each running 2-3 weeks.

🔊 HIKING

The tourist office has a photocopy of *Hiking Spots in Ōsaka*, with a list of hiking areas and info on how to reach them. The easiest spot to access is the **Minō Quasi-National Park.** From Umeda Station, take the Hankyu Takarazuka Line to Ishibashi Station, change to the Hankyu Minō Line to Minō Station, and follow the signs. A 2-3hr. walk through maple forests brings you to **Ryoan-ji** and the 33m **Minō Waterfall.**

🔁 DAYTRIP FROM ŌSAKA

TAKARAZUKA

From Umeda Station, take Takarazuka Line to Takarazuka Station (35-40min.). Takarazuka Grand Theater is white with a red roof, 5min. on foot from the station. http://kageki.han-kyu.co.jp. Shows M-Tu and Th-Su 11am, 1, and 3pm. Tickets ¥3500-7500; call PIA ☎6363-9999, Lawson Tickets ☎6387-1772, CN Agency ☎6776-1199 (all in Japanese). Osamu Tezuka Manga Museum: ☎079-781-2970, www.city.takarazuka.hyogo.jp/tezuka/index.htm; open M-Tu and Th-Su 9am-5pm. Tessai Museum: Open Tu-Su 10am-4:30pm.;¥300.

Northwest of Ōsaka, Takarazuka was just another little spa town until Hankyu railway tycoon Ichizo Kobayashi got the clever idea to turn it into an entertainment center in 1914. He created the Takarazuka Revue, an all-female cabaret with women playing the parts of both male and female characters. The Revue has been a hit ever since, and today it puts on shows ranging from dance revues to Broadway plays, and even a musical version of the *Tale of Genji*. Throngs of adolescent girls dream of being selected for the competitive and rigorous two-year training process and eventually starring in a show at the **Takarazuka Grand Theater.** About a block past the Grand Theater is the plastic-y but fun **Osamu Tezuka Manga Museum,** dedicated to the famous cartoonist Osamu Tezuka, best known for his boy superhero Astro Boy ("Tetsuwan Atom"). A theater downstairs screens his animated works. On your way back from the show, take the Hankyu Takarazuka Line to Kiyoshi Kōjin Station to see the temple **Kiyoshi Kōjin Seichō-ji,** built in 893 and dedicated to the gods of the hearth and fire. It's worth a visit on the 27th and 28th of each month, when a market and ceremonies attract large crowds. Within the temple grounds, the **Tessai Museum** is dedicated to Tomioka Tessai, a modern Japanese artist renowned for his take on classic Ming-style painting.

NARA (奈良)   ☎0742

Sitting squarely in Yamato, the heartland of Japan, Nara is considered the cradle of Japanese civilization. As the imperial state's growing complexity began to demand greater administrative control, the Japanese abandoned their custom of moving their capital with the death of each emperor and settled their government at Nara. This newfound stability sparked a wave of architectural and artistic creativity that culminated with the building of the monumental Buddha of Tōdai-ji, which has remained for 1300 years the largest bronze statue in the world. The wave produced seven other UNESCO world heritage sites and scores of shrines and temples meant to adorn the capital for perpetuity. Nara's stint as the Japanese capital,

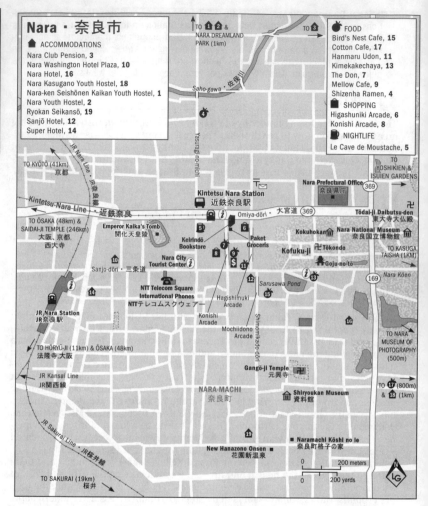

Nara · 奈良市

ACCOMMODATIONS
Nara Club Pension, **3**
Nara Washington Hotel Plaza, **10**
Nara Hotel, **16**
Nara Kasugano Youth Hostel, **18**
Nara-ken Seishōnen Kaikan Youth Hostel, **1**
Nara Youth Hostel, **2**
Ryokan Seikansō, **19**
Sanjō Hotel, **12**
Super Hotel, **14**

FOOD
Bird's Nest Cafe, **15**
Cotton Cafe, **17**
Hanmaru Udon, **11**
Kimekakechaya, **13**
The Don, **7**
Mellow Cafe, **9**
Shizenha Ramen, **4**

SHOPPING
Higashuniki Arcade, **6**
Konishi Arcade, **8**

NIGHTLIFE
Le Cave de Moustache, **5**

however, lasted a paltry 75 years, and its boom days came to an end when the court and its dynamism moved to Kyōto. A provincial city of low buildings, well-tended gardens and quiet tree-lined streets, modern Nara provides few distractions from the monuments of its ancient past.

ON THE WEB   Nara City: www.city.nara.nara.jp

⬛ TRANSPORTATION

Trains: JR Nara Station (JR Nara Eki; JR 奈良駅; ☎22-7700), on the western edge of downtown, connects Nara with the JR network through **Ōsaka** (¥760), **Nagoya** (¥2190, limited express ¥3750) and **Tōkyō** (*shinkansen* 2½hr., ¥13,220) via **Kyōto** (1¼hr.,

¥740). **Kansai International Airport** can be reached via Tenno-ji (1hr., ¥2210). **Kintetsu Nara Station** (Kintetsu Nara Eki; 近鉄奈良駅 ; ☎26-6355), at the northern edge of downtown, services the private Kintetsu regional line and offers transport to **Ōsaka** (local train 35min., ¥540), **Kyōto** (local train 45min., ¥610; limited express 30min., ¥1110), and **Kansai International Airport** via Namba (1hr., ¥1430).

Buses: Nara Kōtsu bus service (奈良交通 ; ☎22-5110; www.narakotsu.co.jp) operates from the Nara line house across from Kintetsu Nara Station (office open 9am-7pm). Overnight buses depart from Kintetsu Nara Station for **Tōkyō** (10:30pm, arrive Tōkyō Shinjuku 6:20am; ¥8400) and **Yokohama** (10:40pm, arrive 7:45am; ¥8970). Arrange limo bus service to **Kansai International Airport** at the line house (1½hr., every hr., ¥1800).

Local Buses: Nara Kōtsu (奈良交通 ; ☎22-5110; www.narakotsu.co.jp) also runs local and regional buses. The main terminals are in front of the 2 rail stations—the numbered bays correspond to the various lines. Buses #1 and 2 circulate downtown, reaching most of the city's sights, and cost a flat ¥180. Other lines connect downtown Nara with outlying suburbs, and use a variable fare system—take a numbered ticket when you board. The number corresponds to a fare chart above the driver; when you get off, pay the amount shown in the corresponding space. Bus stops contain posted timetables, and buses run reliably every 30min. 8am-5pm, becoming scarcer after hours. Apart from its local service, **Nara Kōtsu** (☎22-5263) offers special routes during the tourist season. The **World Heritage Loop Line Bus** operates daily Mar. 20-June 8 and Oct. 1-Nov. 30; otherwise only on weekends and holidays. The ¥800 ticket includes unlimited use not only of the loop bus, but also the local bus network as far as Yakushi-ji Temple and Kasuga Grand Shrine. Another option is the **Nara-machi Bus** (¥100), which departs from the train stations and cruises the Nara-machi district.

Taxis: Fares start around ¥650. **Kainara Taxi, ☎**0120-227-001.

Bike Rental: Kintetsu Sunflower (☎24-3528), near the Nara City tourist center, rents bikes for ¥300 per hr. and ¥900 per day weekdays, ¥350/¥1000 weekends. Open daily 9am-5pm. Guests at the **Nara-ken Seishōnen Kaikan** hostel get a daily flat rate of ¥500.

ORIENTATION

Nara has maintained the Chinese grid pattern upon which it was founded, making navigation fairly simple. Unfortunately, it has also maintained the Japanese tradition of assigning street names to only the most important thoroughfares, making following directions more than a little confusing. The **JR Kansai and Nara Lines** run along the western edge of downtown, while the slopes of **Mt. Wakakusa** (Wakakusa-san; 若草山) mark the eastern boundary of Nara. South of downtown lies the historic **Nara-machi** area, while northern Nara peters out into bland suburbs beyond the Dreamland amusement park. **Sanjō-dōri** (三条通り), running east-west from JR Nara Station, is the most important shopping and service area, with dozens of restaurants and stores in the streets extending north and south from its edges. Maps are essential for getting around—pick up the *Nara Sight Seeing Map* and the *Strolling Around Nara* map from your hotel or a tourist office.

PRACTICAL INFORMATION

Tourist Office: Nara City Tourist Center (奈良市観光センター ; ☎22-3900), at the corner of Sanjo-dōri and Yasuragi-no-michi, is the largest of the 4 major city infocenters. Helpful staff suggest walking tours and dispense maps. English speaker available 9am-5pm. Open daily 9am-9pm. Similar info centers are at **Kintetsu Nara Station** (☎24-4858), **JR Nara Station** (☎22-9821) and **Sarusawa Pond** (Saruwasa-ike; 猿沢池 ; ☎26-1991). All have English-speaking staff and are open daily 9am-5pm. For practical information on living in Nara, visit the **Nara International Foundation (NIFS) lounge**

(☎27-2463) on the 6th floor of the Kintetsu Station Building. Apart from offering advice to visitors and resident foreigners, they maintain an English-language reading room and offer Internet access (¥100 for 15min.). Open Tu-Sa 10am-6pm. The English-language www.info-nara.com website is another good resource.

Walking Tours: 3 groups provide free walking tours to foreign tourists. They all offer roughly the same service—a Japanese translator and guide takes you through whatever sights interest you in exchange for an opportunity to practice his English. The tours are free, but you should pay the guide's travel expenses and buy him lunch. Call a day ahead (3 days for SGG guides) and leave contact information. **YMCA Goodwill Guides** (☎45-5920) offers guides with formal English training; **Nara Student Guides** (☎26-5595), based out of the Sarusawa Pond Info Center, is staffed by young, enthusiastic students; and the mandate of **SGG Guides** (☎22-5595) is slightly broader, offering interpreter services for projects as well as walking tours.

Bus Tours: The **Nara Kōtsū** bus service (☎22-5263) offers bus tours of the area, from a 4hr. excursion to Tōdai-ji, Kasuga Grand Shrine, Kōfuku-ji, and Mt. Wakakusa (4 per day Mar. 20-Nov. 30, 2 per day Dec. 1-Mar. 19; ¥3910) to a 7½hr. expedition through Todai-ji, Gangō-ji, Kasuga Grand Shrine, Hōryū-ji, Yakushi-ji, and past the Suzaku-Mon (9:15 and 10:15am mid-Mar. to mid-May and mid-Sept. to Dec.; 9:15am only in the off-season; ¥6940). Free English info tape. Lunch available for fee on long tours.

Budget Travel: The Travel Information Satellite (☎22-7744), at the NIFS lounge (see above), across from the information desk, helps travelers purchase airline tickets and can arrange local hotel discounts. Open daily 10:30am-6:30pm.

Banks: Banks abound along Sanjō-dōri, most featuring English signs towards their currency exchange desks. **Nanto Bank** (Nanto Ginkō; 南都銀行 ; ☎22-1573; www.nanto-bank.co.jp), between the Higashimuki and Konishi shopping arcades, exchanges money, cashes traveler's checks, and offers Visa cash advances. Open M-F 9am-3pm.

ATM: International ATMs can be found in the Kintetsu line building and in the post office branch just north of Kintetsu Station (see below).

Luggage Storage: Both train stations have lockers; price varies with size. 3 day max.

English-Language Bookstore: Keirindō (Keirindō Shoten; 啓林堂書店 ; ☎20-8001), next to Paket supermarket down the Konishi arcade. Open daily 9am-9pm.

Emergency: Police ☎110. **Fire** or **ambulance** ☎119.

Police: To contact the police, it's often easiest to simply go directly to the nearest **police box** (kōban; 交番). The main police station can also be reached at ☎33-0110.

Hospital/Medical Services: Nara National Hospital (Kokuritsu Nara Byōin; 国立奈良病院 ; ☎24-1251). Open 24hr.

Internet Access: Nara lacks a proper Internet cafe, but access can be found at the **NIFS lounge** (see above) or the **Bird's Nest Cafe** (see **Food**). At the Suien Cafe in the **Hotel Asyl Nara** (☎22-2577), 1 block behind and to the left of the main tourist center, ¥525 buys you a drink and 2hr. of Internet. Open daily 8am-10:30pm.

Post Office: A **branch post office** is just across the street from Kintetsu Nara Station in the arcade farthest to the right. Postal services and international ATM. Open M-F 9am-5pm for mail, M-F 9am-7pm, Sa-Su 9am-5pm for ATM use. **Postal Code: 630.**

◤ ACCOMMODATIONS

With no fewer than three hostels, Nara is much friendlier to budget travelers than most Japanese cities. Unfortunately, the hostels are all some distance from the train stations, and the downtown area is dominated by expensive business and luxury hotels. A travel agent can frequently get you discounts at business hotels.

The peaceful residential neighborhoods north and south of downtown feature quiet pensions and old-style ryokan that let tourists soak up local atmosphere. All establishments listed have some English-speaking staff unless otherwise noted.

Nara Youth Hostel (HI) (奈良ユースホステル ; ☎22-1334; www.jyp.gr.jp/nara/index.html). About 1 block northeast of the Seishōnen (see below). From either station, take the #108, 109, 110, 115, or 130 bus to Shiekyūjō-mae and walk about 100m straight ahead. Quite modern. TV and couch in each dorm. Staff can help with travel info, faxes, and discount Dreamland tickets. Breakfast ¥600. Dinner ¥1000. Communal baths: bathing available 3-10pm, morning showers 7-9am. Free lockers (¥100 deposit). Laundry ¥150, dry ¥100. Check-in 3-9pm. Check-out 10am. Lockout 10am-3pm. Curfew 10pm. 6- or 12-bed dorms members ¥2400; nonmembers ¥3000. 4-bed *tatami* rooms ¥3000/¥4000 per person. Japanese citizens pay more. AmEx/MC/V. ❶

Nara Seishōnen Kaikan Youth Hostel (HI) (奈良青少年会館ユースホステル ; ☎22-5540). A 30min. uphill walk north of downtown. Take bus #12, 13, 131, or 140 from either station to the Ikuei-gakuen stop, follow the bus to the 1st traffic lights, and follow signs from there. Friendly staff make up for a concrete slab of a building. No showers. Communal baths 6-9pm. Breakfast ¥330. Dinner ¥900. Free lockers (¥100 deposit). Laundry ¥150, dry ¥100. Check-in 4-8pm. Check-out 8:30am. Curfew 10:30pm. 6-bed dorms ¥2650; private *tatami* room ¥3850 per person. Cash only. ❶

Ryokan Seikansō (旅館静観荘 ; ☎22-2670; sekanso@chive.ocn.ne.jp). In the heart of Nara-machi. From Sanjō-dōri, turn down the Mochiidono shopping arcade and keep going straight. An old-fashioned Japanese inn, half of which once served as a *geisha* house. Slightly worn rooms overlook a courtyard that always seems to be in bloom. Traditional *tatami* rooms named for the shape of their carved windows. Shared Japanese-style bath. Western breakfast ¥450. Japanese breakfast ¥700. ¥4000 per person. ❷

Nara Club Pension (Nara Kurabu; 奈良倶楽部 ; ☎22-3450; www.naraclub.com). Just north of the Shosoin Treasure Repository, next to Gokoin Temple. Facing Tegaimon gate, turn left. Go straight 2 blocks and turn right–it will be 300m farther. 7min. from Tōdai-ji. A tiny reading room features an equally tiny couch. Occasionally guests fall asleep to the sound of neighboring monks reading *sutras*. Breakfast included. Dinner ¥3500. Check-in from 3pm. Check-out 10am. Bike rental half-day ¥500, full-day ¥1000. Weekday singles ¥8500; doubles ¥15,000; triples ¥21,000; quads ¥28000. Weekends ¥9500/¥17,000/¥24,000/¥32,000. Golden Week, O-bon and New Year's: singles unavailable, ¥19,000/¥27,000/¥36,000. Book online for a discount. ❹

Nara Kasugano Youth Hostel (HI) (奈良かすが野ユースホステル ; ☎23-5667; www6.airnet.ne.jp/kasugano/index.htm). South of Nara Park. Take the #1 or 2 bus to Wariishi-chō and follow the signs to Shin-yakushi-ji; the hostel is opposite the temple on the same block. Set in an elegant, traditional Japanese house, guests are housed in small dorms at the top of an impossibly narrow and steep staircase. The owner speaks no English. Breakfast ¥500. Dinner ¥1000; off-season ¥2000. Shared rooms ¥3200; singles ¥4700; doubles ¥4200. Nonmembers ¥4200/¥5700/¥4700. Cash only. ❶

Nara Hotel (奈良ホテル ; ☎26-3300; www.narahotel.com). Where the Emperor stays when he comes to Nara. One of the first Western-style hotels in Japan, the Meiji-era hotel is just inside Nara Park. High-ceilinged old wing and modern new wing. Breakfast ¥2200. Check-in from 3pm. Check-out 11am. Concierge can arrange airport buses and other transport. Rooms from ample singles (¥14,000) and roomy doubles (from ¥22,000) to the fit-for-an-Emperor Imperial suite (¥300,000). Add 15% tax and service fee. ❹

Super Hotel (スーパーホテル ; ☎20-9000; www.superhotel.co.jp). Just across the street from JR Nara Station. A modern budget hotel in an extremely convenient location. If you can cram 3 people into the rooms, it rivals the hostels for price. Breakfast (coffee and pastries) included. Check-in 3-11pm. Check-out 10am. Singles ¥4800; doubles ¥7140; triples ¥8190. Add 5% tax. Stay for a week and receive 10% cash back. ❷

Nara Washington Hotel Plaza (奈良ワシントンホテル ; ☎27-0410; http://what.com). Right downtown on Sanjō-dōri. A modern, spic-and-span business hotel with all the usual amenities. June-Sept. and Dec.-Feb. singles from ¥6900; doubles from ¥12,000. Mar.-May and Oct.-Nov. ¥7800/¥14,000. ❸

Sanjō Hotel (三条ホテル ; ☎23-6661). Downtown on Sanjō-dōri. A Western-style facade fronts a Japanese-style hotel, with *tatami* rooms and futon beds. Excellent location near sights and restaurants. Check-in 4-8pm. Check-out 11am. Curfew 11pm. Singles ¥5775; doubles ¥10,500. Prices rise significantly for Golden Week, O-bon, and New Year's. ❸

🗗 FOOD

The problem with food in Nara is that there's so much and it's so good. Restaurants and cafes—Japanese and foreign—cluster along every street, beckon from every basement, call from every awning. Sanjō-dōri and its arcades host the most restaurants, but every side street has its own culinary scene. Persimmon-wrapped sushi is a local delicacy. Locals prize *tororo*, a pasty bowl of mixed rice, soy sauce, seaweed, barley, and grated yam. As the original Japanese capital, Nara also serves its own variety of *kaiseki*, the meal associated with the tea ceremony. If you want to prepare your own meals, **Paket,** in the Konishi arcade next to Kintetsu Nara Station, is a fully-stocked grocery store. (Open daily 9am-9pm.) After 8pm, *bentō* lunch boxes and sandwiches are half-price.

🈂 **Bird's Nest Cafe** (☎26-5536). At the end of the Mochiidono arcade on the 2nd fl. of a narrow house. One of the most relaxing spots in Nara. The ever-helpful English-speaking owner serves up vegan delights in a laid-back setting. A full lunch, with dessert, runs ¥900. Comfortable couches and free Internet access. Open M-Tu and F-Su 11am-9pm. ❷

Hanmaru Udon (はんまるうどん), on Sanjo-dōri. Cheapest place in Nara. Plain *udon* noodles start at ¥100/¥200/¥300 for small/medium/large servings. Extras include raw egg, scallions, and bits of fried pork. Open daily 11am-6pm. ❶

Kimekakechaya (☎22-0920). Set on the north side of Sarusawa Pond. This unpretentious *udon* house serves simple, tasty dishes with an unbeatable view. *Tamago udon* (¥500) is tasty and, if you learn to say it, it'll help you avoid the point-and-pray ordering technique—there is no English menu. Open daily 10am-6pm. ❶

The Don, in the Higashuniki arcade. A popular noodle joint that serves the best of Japanese fast food—rice bowls, noodles, and hearty soups. Prices start at ¥350 and don't go much higher than ¥600. Open daily 11am-8:30pm. ❶

Sanshu (三秀), overlooking Isuien Garden at the western edges of Nara Park. Local *tororo* dishes served in *tatami* rooms. The garden view is a feast for the eyes, while the menu offers two for the stomach—*mugitoro gozen* (plain *tororo*; ¥1200) or *unatoro gozen* (*tororo* with eel, ¥2500). Open M and W-Su 11:30am-2pm. ❸

Mellow Cafe (☎27-9099). In the wood-toned unit off of the Konishi arcade. Open, faux Hispano-French cafe. Serves pasta, sandwiches, pizza, and other Euro-favorites (¥850-1000). After 9pm, the lights dim and Mellow Cafe becomes Mellow Bar, a chill place to nurse your beer (¥500-700) or cocktail (¥700-800). Open daily 11am-11:30pm. ❷

Cotton Cafe (☎22-5282). On the main street south of Nara Park. A cozy diner-style restaurant. English menu makes ordering easy. Snug interior can get packed on busy days. Most dishes mix the Western and the Japanese (¥650-800). Open daily 8am-6:30pm. ❷

Shizenha Rāmen (自然派らーめん ; ☎20-1113). The acme of Japanese fast food, on the main north-south road north of downtown. Serves up its hearty fare well into the night. *Rāmen* meals start at ¥490 and don't top ¥1000. Open daily 11am-midnight. ❷

🔍 SIGHTS

While Nara is a major tourist city, it is a major *Japanese* tourist city—there are relatively few Western visitors, and thus a relatively undeveloped English-language infrastructure. Arranging for a volunteer guide through one of the free guide services (see **Practical Information**) is a good idea. That said, major sights provide foreigners with English-language guidebooks, and the maps available from tourist centers give clear directions, so independent visits are also feasible.

NARA PARK (奈良公園)

THE PARK. Built on enclosed wasteland in 1880, Nara Park rivals downtown Nara in size—2km long on its east-west axis (from downtown proper to the slopes of Mt. Wakakusa), it stretches 4km north-south. It also rivals downtown Nara in population—apart from the innumerable tourists, over 1000 Japanese deer fearlessly roam the park's leafy expanse. Legend has it that one of Nara's Shintō deities arrived from the Kantō region riding on a giant white stag and the local deer have been considered sacred ever since. In the pre-Meiji era, the killing of a deer, deliberately or not, was a capital crime. Nowadays, the deer seldom die of hunger—vendors sell deer crackers (shika senbei; ¥150) for tourists to give the animals. Apart from being a sight in its own right, Nara Park also contains most of the city's major attractions. The cedar- and moss-lined paths leading between the various legendary temples make a nice segue from one sanctum sanctorum to the next.

KŌFUKU-JI (興福寺). Commissioned in AD 669 by the consort to the Fujiwara potentate Kamatari, Kōfuku-ji was originally constructed near modern Kyōto. With the establishment of Nara as Japan's first permanent capital, Kōfuku-ji was dismantled and moved—lock, stock, and barrel—from its former site to its present one at the eastern edge of Sanjō-dōri. Perhaps the move was not an auspicious one, for, as the power of the Fujiwara waned in the 12th century, Kōfuku-ji fell victim to the warring factions of medieval Japan. Many of the current buildings, including the two pagodas, are medieval or later reconstructions. The highlight of the temple grounds is the **Gojū-no-to** (five-storied pagoda; 五重の塔), the second tallest in Japan, rising over 50m into the air. The **Kokuhōkan** (national treasure hall; 国宝館) features elaborate Buddhist sculpture, including the renowned Asura statue, with its spindly arms and four faces, and a monumental Buddha head. The

THE LOCAL LEGEND

MONKEY BUSINESS

While the Nara-era imperial court was going gaga over Chinese Buddhism, Nara-machi hoi polloi were intrigued by their own inic spirituality. While their ▮ers crafted giant Buddhas and speckled the hills with temple ▮nd monasteries, the comm▮ers adopted practices from Daoism and Chinese folk traditions.

Two days in the Chinese lunar calendar are named for Koshin-san, a six-armed, sword-wielding deity of vengeance. According to tradition, within each of us dwell three spectral worms, which act as Koshin-san's personal informants. On his two feast days, they emerge from our sleeping bodies to rat us out for our crimes, sins, and dirty tricks of the last six months. If Koshin-san doesn't like what he hears, he descends to earth to kill the hapless human.

The crafty Nara-machites invented several means of blunting Koshin-san's wrath. On▮ was to try to prevent the sp▮ral worms from emerging by re▮ng to sleep on Koshin-san's feast day, instead praying, socializing, and devouring copious amounts of konnyaku, a jelly-like potato-based pesticide for those pesky spectral worms. Another possibility was the decoy strategy: the round red-and-white silk figures you see hanging from all the eves in Nara-machi are migawarizaru, or "substitute monkeys," there to be taken by Koshin-san should he descend for their masters.

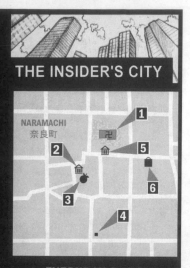

THE INSIDER'S CITY

NARAMACHI
奈良町

EVERYDAY NARA

Now that Tōdai-ji and Kasuga Grand Shrine have given you a taste of the high culture of historic Japan, a stroll through Naramachi will give you an idea of how everyday Narans used to live—as well as spare you exorbitant entry fees. Remember, you may pay for salvation, but the sidewalk is free.

1 Say goodbye to high Buddhism at **Gangō-ji** (☎ 23-1377). One of the eight UNESCO world heritage sites in Nara, and dating back to AD 718, the structure displays the 13th-century Chiko Mandala. Open daily 9am-4:30pm. ¥400.

2 Say hello to the flotsam and jetsam of 500 years of daily Japanese history at the **Shiryō-kan Museum** (☎ 22-5509), while sifting through remnants of the Edo and Meiji periods. Reminisce about the days when most Japanese knew *kanji* as well as you do, and store signs were shaped like the wares inside. Open Tu-Su 10am-4pm. Free.

Tōkondō (eastern golden hall; 東金堂) displays the altar of Kofuku-ji, with an enshrined Buddha surrounded by two bodhisattvas, four Deva Kings, and twelve Celestial Generals. *(At the western edge of Nara Park, on Sanjo-dōri. Kōfuku-ji is visible from the road. ☎ 22-7755. Temple grounds always open. Free. Tōkondō open daily 9am-5pm. ¥300 includes English booklet. Kokuhōkan open daily 9am-4:30pm. ¥500 includes English booklet.)*

YOSHIKIEN (吉城園) **AND ISUIEN** (衣水園) **GARDENS.** These two gardens are serene places to repose, safe from the shameless deer. Both date from the Meiji Era, the heyday of garden construction. Stone paths meander past teahouses, flower beds, and rainy cedar trees. The centerpiece of each garden is a small pond, perfect for quiet contemplation. Yoshikien is more intimate, with fewer visitors to spoil the seclusion, while Isuien has an infrastructure to match its reputation—a restaurant (Sanshū, see **Food**) and a small pottery museum. *(From Sanjō-dōri, walk toward the park. Don't take the underpass; cross the street and turn left. Continue to the next major intersection, then go 100m and turn right. Yoshikien: ☎ 22-5911. Open Apr.-June and Aug.-Dec. M and W-Su 9am-5pm. ¥250. Isuien: ☎ 22-2173. Open M and W-Su 10am-4:30pm. Closed late Dec.-early Jan. ¥600, including museum admission.)*

NARA NATIONAL MUSEUM (NARA KOKURITSU HAKUBUTSUKAN; 奈良国立博物館 **).** Set in Nara Park, the Meiji-era neo-Classical facade of the National Museum hardly matches the Nara-period Buddhist sculptures within. The permanent collection consists of a treasure trove of Buddhist sculpture from the pre-Nara periods to medieval Kamakura art. If you can catch one, helpful guides will show you around and happily explain the difference between a Buddha and a bodhisattva for the chance to practice their English. A modern annex puts on special exhibitions (additional fee). The grounds, speckled with streams and foliage, are worth a gander even if you give the exhibits a pass. *(At the western edge of Nara Park, off Sanjo-dōri. ☎ 23-5962; www.narahaku.go.jp. Open Tu-Su 9:30am-5pm. Extended hours on F, May to mid-Nov. 9:30am-7pm. ¥420, students ¥130. Surcharge for special exhibitions.)*

KASUGA GRAND SHRINE (KASUGA TAISHA; 春日 大社 **).** While Nara is best know as the cradle of Japanese Buddhism, it is also an important Shintō site. Four major Shintō deities are worshiped in the shrine—two native to the region, and war and thunder gods from Kantō. Unlike Buddhist temples, however, there are no altars or statues in Shintō shrines—since the gods being worshiped are insubstantial, the halls are empty save for a closed chapel or mirror. Another difference visitors will note is the newness of the shrine—while Buddhist temples maintain the original conditions as much as possible, Shintō shrines are ceremoniously rebuilt every 20 years. Kasuga is best known for its collection of stone and metal lanterns, numbering in the thousands. While they are always on display, they are only used twice a year for elaborate festivals. *(Follow Sanjō-dōri into Nara Park and go straight for about 1.5km.* ☎ *22-7788. Open daily 9am-4pm. Free.)*

TŌDAI-JI COMPLEX (東大寺)

Sprawls through the northern third of Nara Park. Sights open daily Apr.-Sept. 7:30am-5:30pm; Oct. 7:30am-5pm; Nov.-Feb. 8am-4:30pm; Mar. 8am-5pm unless noted.

The Tōdai-ji temple complex includes dozens of temples, pagodas, gates, and treasure halls. The complex has a noble pedigree—it was founded by Emperor Shomu, after the official introduction of Buddhism to Japan, as the headquarters and mother church for all of Japanese Buddhism. Named a UNESCO world heritage site, Tōdai-ji draws visitors from all over the world.

DAIBUTSU-DEN (HALL OF THE GREAT BUDDHA; 大仏殿). The Daibutsu-den is the largest wooden structure in the world. Originally built in the 8th century, the hall has burned down and risen from the ashes several times. The current version, built in 1709 is only two-thirds the size of the original. The hall houses Nara's premier attraction, the **Monumental Buddha** (Daibutsu), an enormous seated figure, over 16m tall and weighing nearly 450 tons. Fourteen adults can stand on his upturned left palm. The statue, now blackened, is covered entirely with gold. The gilding technology of the day involved mixing mercury with gold to get the desired effect—on a project of such a large scale, dozens of craftsmen perished from the toxic fumes. Like the hall itself, the current Buddha was restored in the Edo Period, previous Buddhas having been lost to fire and earthquake. Behind the statue, a line forms behind a pillar. The pillar contains a hole said to be the size of the Buddha's nostril—those who fit through are guaranteed enlightenment. Unless you're 14 and unusually spry, *Let's Go* does not recommend giving it a try. *(From Sanjō-dōri, go straight into Nara Park past the National Museum. Following the signs, take the first major left and go straight through Nandaimon gate.* ☎ *22-5511. ¥500.)*

KAIDAN-IN (ORDINATION HALL; 戒壇院). As a means of fighting heresy and heterodoxy, which had already begun to creep into Japanese Buddhism in the Nara Period, the Chinese missionary cleric Ganjin established an ordination hall to school monks

3 Take a break from sightseeing to munch on a soybean-enhanced lunch while sitting on *tatami* mats at renowned specialty tofu restaurant **Kondō**. The set lunch will run you ¥1810. Open daily 11am-2:30pm. Be sure to check out the intriguing **monkey-shaped fountain** across the street before continuing on.

4 March through **Kōshi no ie** (☎ 22-4820), an immaculately restored Nara-era merchant house. The facade was purpose built for narrowness to dodge medieval taxes (which were assessed based on the building's frontage), but the house has a surprising depth, and includes a picturesque garden and a host of innovative features. Open Tu-Su 9am-5pm. Free.

5 Gawk at $20,000 pottery from the Nara area, and other contemporary one-of-a-kind local crafts at the extensive and modern **Konjaku craft museum** (☎ 27-0033). Open daily 9am-5pm. Free.

6 Sift through community-made crafts, clothes, and other trinkets at the budget-friendly **Naramachi Monogatori-kan** (☎ 26-3476). Locals from the area use the hall to display their own amateur crafts, as well as holding occasional *ikebana* (flower arranging) displays. Open Tu-Su 10am-5pm. Free.

and nuns. It churned out 440 of them in rapid order, including the retired Emperor Shōmu. The current site is still the original, but the buildings have been rebuilt following serious fires in 1180, 1446, and 1567. The hall is relatively untouristed and features particularly striking clay Deva Kings, dating back to the 8th century. *(Facing Daibutsuden, turn left. Kaidanin is a short, signposted walk away. ¥500.)*

NIGATSU-DŌ AND SANGATSU-DŌ (FEBRUARY AND MARCH HALLS). Along the east side of the Tōdai-ji complex, Nigatsu-dō and Sangatsu-dō stand perched on the slopes of Mt. Wakakusa and overlook Nara Park. The buildings are Nara-period originals, with Sangatsu-dō, completed in 729, taking the honors as the oldest building in Nara. In February, Nigatsu-do hosts the Omizutori ceremony, but is open the rest of the year. A climb up its steep staircase grants gorgeous views of the area. Sangatsu-dō holds a three-eyed Nara-period bodhisattva notable for the detail on its crown, which includes more than 20,000 gemstones. *(Facing Daibutsuden, turn right. The 2 halls are a 5min. walk. Nigatsu-dō free; Sangatsu-dō ¥500.)*

NANDAI-MON (GREAT SOUTH GATE; 南大門). Suitably magnificent to be the entryway to the great Buddha, the Nandai-mon marks the main entrance to the Tōdai-ji complex. Rebuilt in the 13th century, the gate illustrates many features of traditional Japanese architecture—the pillars are all made from a single giant tree trunk, and no metal is used for joints. The entryway is flanked by two giant protector demons (Niō) standing over 7m tall. One, with an open mouth, is thought to be saying "Ah," the other, with pursed lips, "N"—the first and last letters of both the Japanese *kana* alphabet and Sanskrit. Coincidence? Possibly. *(Always open. Free.)*

OTHER SIGHTS

NARA MUSEUM OF PHOTOGRAPHY (NARA-SHI SHASHIN BIJUTSUKAN; 奈良市 写真美術館). Housed in a sleek minimalist building, the Museum of Photography can't be mistaken for anything ancient. The airy, light-filled space enhances master photographer Takichi Irie's stunning nature images. A high-definition video theater displays films of prints not on display. The grounds, all stone and water, are worth a look as well. *(Just south of Nara Park. Head directly south from Tôdai-ji for about 1.5km and turn left at the Wariishi Tram Stop. From there, follow the signs.* ☎ *22-9811; fax 22-9722. Open Tu-Su 9:30am-5pm. ¥500; students ¥200.)*

NARA-MACHI. While Imperial courtiers were busy intriguing against each other and constructing Buddhist monuments, the traders and merchants of Nara-machi were making a killing on the traffic brought in by Nara's capital status. Some of the feeling of those olden days of glory capitalism still remains in this tidy little neighborhood, where Nara-period storehouses and residences still survive amid the power lines and parking lots. The area's quaint charm is easy to absorb, and wandering Nara-machi is a pleasant break from the monumentalism of Nara's temples; see p. 450 for a guide. *(Just south of downtown, off the Michiido arcade and Shimikado.)*

🎵 🎭 ENTERTAINMENT AND NIGHTLIFE

As a city based on the serene and placid teachings of the Buddha, Nara is not the place to go for high-octane excitement. Nevertheless, after a full day of flower-watching and temple-viewing, there are a few entertainment options to be had. One option is to play like the Japanese kids do—dozens of **arcades** dot the downtown core, most open until midnight. Another is to while away the time playing *pachinko* at any of the dozens of parlors around the city. To splash around, head to **Nara Dreamland Park,** north of the city, for waterslides, rollercoasters and other assorted chaos. (☎ 23-1111. Open daily 10am-5pm. Pay per ride.) All of the **cinemas** downtown play Hollywood films, along with the newest pan-Asian movies (subtitled in Japanese, of course). There is no real club scene in Nara, and few bars or cafes stay open past nine, so nightlife choices aren't extensive.

Gentry Jazz Spot (☎26-2622). Near the front of the Shimo-mikado arcade. A cozy, minimalist place with slight European pretensions. Relaxing place to kick back and sample a lengthy drink menu (cocktails ¥600-700). Live music once a week, F or Sa, 8:30pm. ¥1000 cover music nights. Open daily 5:30-11:30pm.

Rumors (☎26-4327). A 3rd-floor bar on Sanjō-dōri and the local expat hangout. A self-described "English Public House in Nara," Rumors attracts many of the resident foreigners with a comfortable, English-speaking atmosphere. Lots of wood panelling. Occasional theme nights and the longest hours in Nara make it a good place to end the evening. Drinks ¥600-900. Open Su-Th 6:30pm-2am, F-Sa. 6:30pm-3am.

The Bronx Shot Bar (☎27-2139). Upstairs on Sanjō-dōri, just before Sarusawa Pond. More East Village (elegant, trendy) than any other New York locale. A patio overlooks the street, granting ample people-watching opportunities. Happy hour 6-8pm (most drinks ¥500). Drinks ¥700-900 thereafter. Open Su-Th 6pm-midnight, F-Sa 6pm-1am.

Le Cave de Moustache. In a basement by the train station. Serves up fancy French wines by the glass until 2am (from ¥900). The relaxed, intimate atmosphere makes it a charming alternative to the pub scene. But a warning to skinflints—those dried figs aren't free (¥600). Open daily 5:30pm-midnight.

FESTIVALS AND EVENTS

As befits the erstwhile-capital and former headquarters of Japanese Buddhism, Nara boasts an impressive schedule of annual events, many dating back over a thousand years. While some favor the stately grace of the outdoor nō dances, few can resist the excitement of the frenzied fire rites, which in the past have led to the fiery demise of more than one temple building.

Yama-yaki (Grass-Burning Festival). The Su before the 2nd M of Jan. (Jan. 11 in 2004). Monks of Kōfuku-ji set fire to the slopes of Mt. Wakakusa. The festivities start at 6pm.

Onioi (Ogre Festival). Feb. 3. More pyrotechnics as torch-brandishing ogres attempt to storm Hōryū-ji and Kōfuku-ji. 2 Shintō gods intervene to cast them out for another year. In celebration, the monks scatter sacred soybeans for the audience to fight over.

Omizutori (Water-Drawing Festival). Mar. 1-14. A Buddhist rite to hasten the coming of spring. Over 1000 years old, it originated with the prophetic dream of a Nara-period monk. During the 2 weeks, the monks of Todai-ji chant sutras for the forgiveness of sins and general peace. On the final night, priests light huge torches and run around the balcony of Nigatsu-dō while crowds on the meadow below look on.

Tagiki Nō (nō performances). Mid-May. An outdoor, all-night performance of select nō plays in the Kofuku-ji compound.

Shika-no-Tsunokiri (Deer-Antler-Cutting Ceremony). Early Oct. A 300-year-old event, where Japanese gauchos wrangle their prey into submission and Shintō priests ceremoniously shorten the antlers. A Nippon rodeo.

Shōsōin treasures exhibition. Late Oct.-early Nov. The only time when the Nara-period artifacts of Tōdai-ji's Shōsōin (treasure repository) are on display. Because of the volume of artifacts, only a fraction are shown in any given year—every year's exhibition is themed and extensively curated, giving viewers an in-depth look at ancient Nara.

On-Matsuri (Costume Parade). Dec. 15-18. A procession of hundreds in 9th-19th century ceremonial outfits makes its way through Nara Park to Kasuga Grand Shrine.

KANSAI

⚡ DAYTRIPS FROM NARA

HŌRYŪ-JI (法隆寺) AND CHŪGŪ-JI (中宮寺)

Trains and buses run to Hōryū-ji from Nara. JR trains to Hōryū-ji Station cost ¥210 and take 10min. From Hōryū-ji station, a bus runs to the temple (7min., ¥170). Buses #52, 97, and 98 run directly to Hōryū-ji from JR Nara and Kintetsu Nara stations (1hr., ¥740). A useful visitor's center stands in front of Hōryū-ji, with English guides available first-come, first-served. (☎0745-74-6800; www.town.ikaruga.jp/icenter. Open 9am-2pm.) Hōryū-ji: ☎0745-75-2555; www.horyuji.or.jp. Open Feb. 22-Nov. 3 8am-5pm; Nov. 4-Feb. 21 8am-4:30pm. ¥1000. Chūgū-ji: ☎0745-175-2806. Open daily 9am-5pm. ¥500.

Designated a UNESCO world heritage site for its antiquity (Hōryū-ji was a temple site before the founding of Nara), Hōryū-ji contains some of Japan's oldest Buddhist art. It has also been declared the world's oldest intact wooden building. But a mere recitation of its distinctions fails to capture the magnificence of the temple—the compound is huge, the constructions towering, and the images beatific.

Visitors receive a three-part ticket, with separate fields for entry to the Saīn Garan (West Precinct; 西院伽藍), Daihōzōin (the Gallery of Temple Treasures), and the Tōin Garan (East Precinct; 東院伽藍). Don't lose the ticket or you may be denied admission to further areas. The **Saīn Garan** section holds the oldest buildings, dating from the pre-Nara Asuka Period. The most striking single edifice is the Goju-no-to (Five-story Pagoda). On each side, doors open in on scenes from the life of the Buddha rendered in clay miniature. The neighboring **Kondō** (Main Hall) is the oldest of Hōryū-ji's components, and contains a triad of the Shaka Buddha (historical Buddha), one of the Yakushi Nyorai (healing Buddha), and a single statue of the Amida Buddha (Heavenly Buddha). The statues of the Guardians of the Four Directions are notable for their simplicity and composure—in later centuries, the guardians would become ferocious warriors as intricate in their design as the Buddha himself. Above, canopies depict a Buddhist Paradise, known as "the land to the West of China"—Uzbekistan. These are the only reproductions in the Kondō—the original murals survived WWII only to be destroyed in a 1949 fire.

Filing past the outer wall of the precinct, visitors arrive at the **Daihōzōin.** It houses the majority of the temple's artwork, a collection 1400 years in the making. Notable among these is the Yumechigai Kannon (Dream-Changing Kannon), a bodhisattva figure endowed with the power to convert nightmares into pleasant dreams. Also worth a look is the Tamamushi altar, once the color of the metallic blue *tamamushi* beetle, but now faded to an uncertain black. The sides depict events from the life of Buddha, including his suicidal leap from a cliff to feed a starving lioness and her cubs with his body. In the second section of the building stands the Kudara Kannon. Particularly slender and fluid, it has been suggested that the statue shows Korean influence in its posture and demeanor. Whatever the case, it is certainly one of the greatest works of Japanese Buddhist art.

The **Eastern Precinct** is the smallest of the main areas of Horyu-ji, only added in 739 in memory of Prince Shōtoku, the patron of early Japanese Buddhism. Its clay walls enclose the octagonal Yume-dono (Dream Hall; 夢殿), which contains a strikingly-well preserved 7th-century statue, the Kuze Kannon. Unfortunately, the statue is only on display for part of the year, from April 11-May 18 and again October 22-November 22, for the ritual worship of the statue. At other times, representative images of several ancient monks and screens with scenes of the life of Shōtoku are worth a look. From the Eastern Precinct, either retrace your steps to the main entrance, or follow the signs to Chūgū-ji temple.

Dwarfed by monumental Hōryū-ji, **Chūgū-ji** is often overlooked by the crowds that throng its famous neighbor. This neglect makes the gardens and central room a quiet place to rest in relative tranquility. The building was originally erected on another site, but following the death of Prince Shōtoku's mother the Empress Ana-hobe no Hashibito, it was moved to its present location and dedicated to her memory. It is more notable for its contents than its architecture—it houses the Nyoirin Kannon Buddha and the fragments of the Tenjukoku Mandala tapestry. The Nyoi-rin Kannon is carved with the particular soft curves of the pre-Nara Asuka style, as it sits in a position of intense concentration, pondering the salvation of mankind. The Mandala was commissioned to mourn the death of Prince Shōtoku and depicts the prince reposing in a Buddhist paradise. The original has suffered through hard times, and its fragments had to be pieced together in the Kamakura Period. A reproduction is currently on display.

TŌSHŌDAI-JI (唐招提寺)

To get to Tōshōdai-ji, take bus #52, 97, or 98 from Nara, any of which will bring you to Tōshōdai-ji stop, directly in front of the temple (15min., ¥240). ☎0742-33-6001. Open daily 8:30am-5pm. ¥500. ¥100 to enter Shin Hozo when treasures are on display.

Founded in 759 AD by the Chinese missionary monk Ganjin, who went blind during 11 unsuccessful attempts to cross to Japan before he reached its shores and became one of its greatest religious figures, Tōshōdai-ji was granted to him as a reward for his committed service in Nara. The **Kondō** (Main Hall) is unfortunately closed for renovations, set to be completed in 2010. The white scaffolding covering the hall also mars the otherwise remarkable beauty of the gardens. Some of Tōshōdai-ji's statues are now on display in the Nara National Museum (p. 450). Visitors are still able to tour the Kodō (lecture hall), but it contains little of note. On March 21-May 19 and September 15-November 3, the treasures of the temple are displayed in the modern Shin Hozo (New Treasure Hall). They consist mostly of statues and fragments, with a few Buddhist instruments. On June 6, the day of Ganjin's death, his statue is displayed in the Miei-do. It is the oldest piece of representational art in Japan, vividly capturing the weariness of a man who devoted his entire life to bringing Buddhism to Japan.

YAKUSHI-JI (薬師寺)

South of Tōshōdai-ji along a well-marked path (8min. by foot). ☎0742-33-6001; www.nara-yakushiji.com. Open daily 8:30am-5pm. ¥500; treasure display ¥500.

Originally commissioned by Emperor Temmu for the recovery of his wife, the temple took so long to complete that, by the time of its dedication, Temmu had died. His then-healthy wife, the Empress Jito, dedicated it to the Buddha of Healing (*Yakushi Nyorai*) in his name. First constructed in Asuka, the temple was moved to its current location at the beginning of the Nara Period. Although its Asuka-period origins make it one of the oldest temples in the Nara area, wars, fires, earthquakes, and storms have leveled most of the original buildings, leaving only the East Pagoda intact. Some of the current buildings were restored as late as 1980 and have their original bright colors and gilding intact.

The centerpiece of *Yakushi-ji* is the 7th-century Yakushi triad, composed of the Buddha of Healing with the bodhisattvas Nikkō (sunlight) and Gakkō (moonlight). The hall showcasing the triad is cut so that visitors can see the rear of the Buddha's pedestal, notable for its Indian-style crouching demons and Mediterranean grape motif. The presence of these images in Nara-period Japan has yet to be explained. The temple also contains a rare screen portrait of Kichijo-ten, the Buddhist goddess of peace. For a peace goddess she looks remarkably stern, but so are the rules for viewing her—she is only on display (with other temple treasures) on January 1-15 and October 8-November 10.

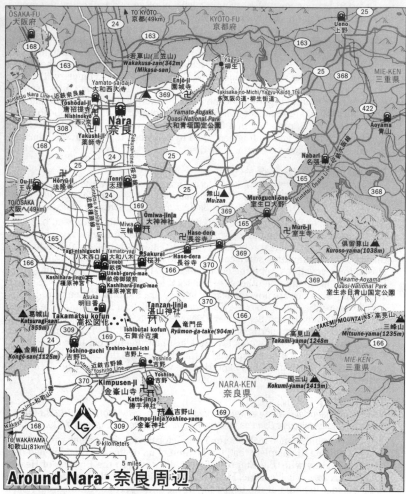

Around Nara · 奈良周辺

SOUTH OF NARA

While Nara was the first permanent capital of Japan, it in no way marked the beginning of Japanese culture, religion, or architecture. The area to the south of Nara includes the Asuka region, the near-mythical site of the ancient court. With such an illustrious history, it is no surprise that the mountaintops and forests of this region conceal some of Japan's most striking temples and shrines, as well as myriad tombs and archaeological sites. A warning to those who would explore remote Asuka, though—it may seem possible to visit a number of sights in one day, but in practice only one or two can be can viewed properly in a day.

ŌMIWA-JINJA (OMIWA SHRINE; 大神神社). Built to revere Miwa mountain, Ōmiwa-jinja sits at the foot of its titulary god. Apart from the size and beauty of this shrine, a few other things make it notable—the *torii* at the beginning and end of the elaborate entryway are the highest in Japan. On summer weekends, a flea market extends from the front of the shrine to the train station. *(10min. east of the Miwa stop on the JR Sakurai Line (¥320), about 15min. south of Nara. ☎0744-42-6633. Free.)*

TANZAN-JINJA (談山神社). It's a bit of a journey to Tanzan-jinja, but the location, a mountainside setting in a particularly verdant evergreen forest, makes the trip worthwhile. Including travel time there and back, budget at least half a day for this unique shrine, as few visitors escape the temptation of the backwoods paths behind the shrine that afford dramatic views of the valley below. The history of the shrine is intimately tied to the Fujiwara clan, an aristocratic house that virtually ruled Japan from the 8th to the 12th centuries. The temple site was selected by the Joue, the eldest son of the Fujiwara patriarch Kamatari, to enshrine the body of his deified father. One of the major shrine festivals, mid-October Kemari (ball kicking), commemorates the Fujiwara's game-side, intriguing against the then-dominant Soga clan. The shrine's most striking feature, a graceful 17m 13-story pagoda, contains a roof for each Soga male killed during the successful coup. *(To reach Tanzan-jinja, take a train on the JR Sakurai Line to Sakurai (¥320, 30min.). The shrine is a another 40min. on bus #4 (¥440). ☎0744-49-0001. Open daily 9am-4:30pm. ¥500.)*

MURŌ-JI (室生時). Murō-ji shares many similarities with Tanzan-jinja—a remote location, a long journey, and a scenic setting with hiking opportunities. One major difference is the temple creed—while Tanzan-Jinja is a Shintō shrine to a deified nobleman, Murō-ji is a Shingon-sect Buddhist temple enshrining an image of the *Shaka Nyorai*, the historical Buddha. It is said that the beautiful rhododendron gardens were the miraculous result of one monk's attainment of enlightenment through dedicated worship of the figure. In any case, the altar deserves a look—Buddha and his haloed bodhisattvas tower over a series of guardians and celestial beings. The 9th-century style of the sculptures makes a marked contrast to the Nara-period art of most of the region's other temples. The midget five-story pagoda, the shortest in Japan, is also worth a glance. One other notable fact is that, unlike most Shingon temples, Murō-ji freely admits women. *(Take the Kintetsu Line to Murōguchi-Ono (¥470, 40min.). From the station, buses #43, 44, 45, and 46 head for the temple (¥400, 20 min.). ☎0745-93-2003. Open Feb.-Nov. 8am-5pm; Dec.-Jan. 8:30am-4pm. ¥500.)*

HASE-DERA (長谷寺). Built in the Asuka Period, Hase-dera has grown into a Buddhist center of renown and influence—it claims 2 million worshippers, 3000 affiliated temples, and a reputation for its intricate theology. The temple consists of over a dozen buildings linked together by covered stairways and corridors— fully viewing the temple involves quite an investment of time and legwork. The main image of the temple hall is the *Juichimen Kanon* (the 11-headed Buddha), who saves all in the world. Also notable are the child-Buddha images that line the upper walkway, each one a little work of art. Apart from the religious attractions, many tourists come to Hase-dera to view the famous peony gardens, whose flowers are lovingly tended to by the monks. The best season for peonies is the late spring, while autumn also attracts guests for the strikingly colorful foliage. *(From Nara, take the Kintetsu Line to Hase-dera Station (¥420, 30min.). From there it's a 20min. uphill slog to the temple gates—take the main road downhill, turn right, and follow the crowds. ☎0774-47-7001. Open Apr.-Sept. 8:30am-5pm; Oct.-Mar. 9am-4:30pm. ¥500.)*

THE MUSEUM, ARCHAEOLOGICAL INSTITUTE. The region south of Nara includes Asuka, the ancient capital, and was the birthplace of Japanese civilization. As a result, the area has produced important archaeological finds and discoveries. Many of the artifacts unearthed are on display in the museum in Kashihara. Unlike the temples, which trace their history from the Asuka Period, the museum showcases pre-Asuka artifacts dating as far back as the Jōmon/Yayoi Period, the truly ooga-booga phase of Japanese history. Although much of the curation is in

Japanese only, there are English-language pamphlets and labels. *(Take the Kintetsu Line to Unebigoryo-mae (20min., ¥400). From the station, walk 1 block directly forward and take your 1st left. Following the curve of the street should bring you right to the museum. ☎0744-24-1185. Open Tu-Su 9am-5pm. ¥400; students ¥300. Extra charge during special exhibitions.)*

KASHIHARA-JINGU (橿原神官). Set in park-like gardens, Kashihara-jingu aims to capture the spirit of the Grand Shrine at Ise (p. 470). While the grand spaces of Kashihara do evoke a certain majesty, the shrine itself is a relatively recent innovation, built during the Meiji Era to commemorate Jimmu, the mythical first emperor of Japan. Such a date suggests its consecration had less to do with holy rites than with the post-Restoration veneration of Shintō engineered by nativist authorities. In any case, the tree-lined avenues and reflecting pool make the shrine a nice place to meditate or eat lunch. *(5min. from Kashihara-jingu-mae Station on Kintetsu Line (18min., ¥380). From the station, take the main road. ☎0744-22-3271. Grounds free; treasure museum ¥300. Grounds open 24hr.; museum daily 10am-5:30pm.)*

ASUKA (飛鳥)   ☎0744

The town of Asuka bears the name of the ancient capital and its outskirts are strewn with the remains of the ancient court—*kofun* tombs are a dime a dozen, and royal mausoleums speckle the hillsides. The closest sight is the **Takamatsuzuka kofun,** about 10min. from the station. While the tomb itself is off-limits, a small museum houses the frescoes preserved from the inner walls. (☎54-3340. Open daily 9am-5pm. ¥250; students ¥130.) Another *kofun* worth investigating is the **Ishibutai burial mound.** Visitors are allowed inside to poke around. (Open daily 8:30am-5pm. ¥250.) **Asuka-dera,** another temple in the area, houses Japan's oldest extant Buddha image. (☎54-2126. Open daily 9am-5:15pm. ¥300.) To reach Asuka, take the Kintetsu Line south from Nara (¥690, 50min.). An **information center** just in front of the station can give you a map and some guidance (☎54-3624. Open daily 8:30am-4:30pm.) The minor sights in the area requires a lot of walking. For those who prefer to pedal, rows and rows of bicycle shops near the station offer rentals.

YOSHINO (吉野)   ☎07463

In isolated hill country to the south of Nara, Yoshino has had a long and illustrious run in Japanese history. During the Nambokuchi Era, when northern and southern emperors ruled simultaneously, each calling the other usurper, Yoshino was the site of the southern court. It was made such by Go-Daigo, an emperor who tried to wrest power from the Kamakura emperors and rule in fact as well as in name. His Kemmu Restoration lasted all of five years before he was forced to flee Kyōto for Yoshino and take refuge in the hills. Refusing to leave behind the comforts of the court, especially his beloved cherry blossoms, Go-Daigo introduced the flowering trees to Yoshino, now Japan's premier **cherry-blossom viewing** site. Blossoms are on display for most of April, when crowds throng the narrow streets and crane their necks for a better look at the 30,000 cherry trees blanketing the hillsides.

Outside of cherry blossom season, little is plentiful in Yoshino except for rain—the hills in this area are the rainiest spots in Japan, a country not known for aridity. The remoteness of Yoshino also makes the voyage a little unappealing—it begins with an ¥840 ticket for 1½hr. train ride to the end of the Kintetsu Yoshino spur (since it's not a JR track, even railpass holders have to pay). From the station, it's either a 45min. hike up to the township or a 5min. cable car ride (¥350, round-trip ¥600). At the top, the main street continues on to the left, along a ridge affording gorgeous views of the **Yoshino Valley** (吉野谷). The front gate of the temple **Kinpusen-ji** (金釜山寺) rises at a fork in the road. The gate opens into an equally well-appointed main hall that houses a number of imposing Buddhist statues. (☎2-8371. Open daily 8am-4:45pm. Admission to main hall ¥400.) Behind Kinpusen-ji, you'll find the town's **tourist information center,** which provides useful English maps and brochures of the area (☎2-8014. Open daily 9am-5pm.) Roads behind Kinpusen-ji lead to other temples and shrines. Once you pass through Yoshino village, you reach the paths leading up to **Omie-san** and **Odai-ga-hara,** a hill and an alpine plateau famous for their lush vegetation and gorgeous views. Omie-san, however, is also the site of a renowned pilgrimage trail dating back to ancient times. The corresponding ancient mentality causes parts of the trail to be closed to women. These are considerable hikes, and it would be wise to bring rain gear.

It is possible to stay in Yoshino inexpensively—a local temple, the **Kozoin,** operates a **hostel ❶** in its buildings. To reach Kozoin, take the second left past the information center (about 500m away) and continue another 200m—the temple will be on the left, with the youth hostel sign obscured by a stone lantern. (☎2-3014. ¥3200; nonmembers ¥4200. Breakfast ¥600. Dinner ¥1000. Closed Dec.-Jan.) Most of the restaurants in the area cater mainly to tourists during cherry blossom season—**Shizukatei ❷,** at the juncture of the main road and the hostel path, is reliably open year-round (☎2-3157. Open M and W-Su 9am-8pm. Udon meals ¥600-800.)

KŌBE (神戸) ☎078

Kōbe broke onto the world stage with its foreign shipping and residence in 1867, when it transformed from a sleepy provincial port into one of the busiest trade centers in Japan. The early introduction to the West engendered a refreshing xenophilia, such that modern Kōbe features a synagogue, Jain temple, and mosque, as well as the usual profusion of shrines and temples. Its restaurants serve Southeast Asian, Indian, and Western cuisines, and foreigners and Japanese mingle easily at bars and nightclubs. Hit hard by the 1995 Great Hanshin Earthquake, Kōbe bounced back with alacrity and now bears few signs of that tragedy.

ON THE WEB Kōbe City: www.city.kobe.jp

⬛ TRANSPORTATION

Airport Access: The cheapest way to get to **Kansai International Airport** is by train through Ōsaka Station (1½hr., ¥1660). Save time and the hassle of changing trains by taking a limousine bus from the south side of Sannomiya Station (at least 1 per hr.; 40min. and ¥1020 to Ōsaka Itami airport; 1¼hr. and ¥1800 to Kansai International). The fastest way to travel is by jetfoil—the **Kōbe City Air Terminal (KCAT)** is on Port Island. Bus fare to or from Sannomiya is included in the ¥2400 price for the 30min. trip.

Trains: Downtown Kōbe is serviced by two JR train stations. **Shin-Kōbe** (Shin Kōbe Eki; 新神戸駅 ; ☎242-3383) is at the northeastern end of the downtown core and provides *shinkansen* service to **Tōkyō** (3½hr., ¥13,760); **Fukuoka** (3½hr., ¥13,760); **Hiroshima** (2½hr., ¥9230); **Nagoya** (2hr., ¥7140); **Kyōto** (50min., ¥2730); and **Himeji** (45min., ¥2630). **Sannomiya Station** (Sannomiya Eki; 三ノ宮駅 ; ☎242-3383), right in the middle of downtown, serves local trains and regional expresses. To: **Tōkyō** (7½hr., ¥9030); **Fukuoka** (7½hr., ¥9030); **Hiroshima** (6hr., ¥5250); **Nagoya** (4hr., ¥3250); **Kyōto** (2½hr., ¥1050); **Himeji** (1½hr., ¥950); **Ōsaka** (25min., ¥390).

Ferries: As a major port, Kōbe sees a fair amount of ferry traffic. Two terminals serve individual passengers—one at **Naka Pier** (中突堤旅客ターミナル) in the Merikan portside development, and the other on **Rokkō Island** (六甲船客ターミナル). Information on ferry departures can be obtained from the Sannomiya infocenter (☎322-5673) or at www.kobe-ferry.com. Ferry routes operate independently, with different phone numbers for different boats. These are the most direct ferry routes to: **Beppu** (☎391-6601;

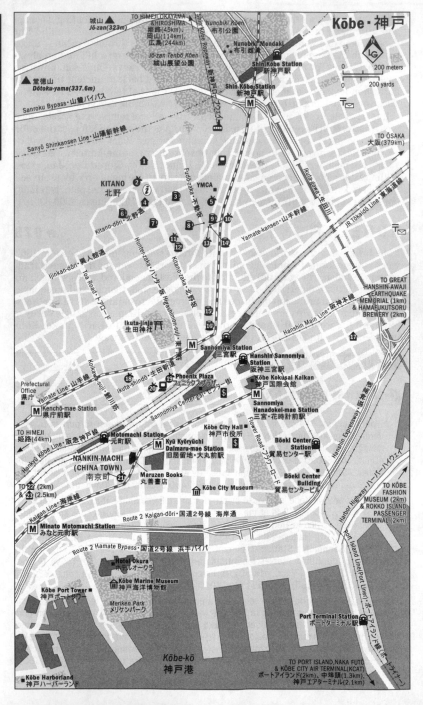

Kōbe・神戸

Kōbe · 神戸

♠ **ACCOMMODATIONS**
Kōbe Kitano Youth Hostel, **1**
Kōbe Sannomiyia Union Hostel, **17**
Kōbe Tarumi Youth Hostel, **22**
Maiko Villa Kōbe, **23**
Petit Hotel Arcons, **4**

🍴 **FOOD**
Around the Asia, **19**
Café Berthier, **18**
Candy's Kitchen, **13**
La Gargotte, **10**
Nailey's Cafe, **5**
Panpara, **2**
Pearl Cafe, **11**
Rokumeisou, **21**
Yum Jamu, **20**

🎷 **NIGHTLIFE**
Cafe Spark, **15**
Dai Dai, **14**
Holly's Live House, **9**
King of King's, **3**
Kōbe Honky Tonk, **8**
Restaurant and Live Sone, **7**
Ryan's Pub, **16**
Sunflower/Seed, **6**
The Lockup, **12**

11½hr., 1 per day, ¥7400) via **Matsuyama** (7¾hr., ¥5200); **Nihama** (☎06-6612-1811; 9¾hr., 1 per day, ¥3660); **Ōita** (☎857-9525; 10¼hr., 2 per day, ¥7400) via **Imabari** (5¼hr., ¥4300); **Naha** (☎06-6341-8071; 65hr., 3 per day, ¥17,300) via **Miyazaki** (18¾hr., ¥8380); and **Naze, Amami-Oshima** (31hr., ¥13,200). Direct service to **Shimoji** (☎857-1211; 12½hr.; 2 on Su, 1 per day M-Sa; ¥6200); **Takamatsu** (☎327-3111; 3¾hr., 5 per day, ¥1790); **Shodo-shima** (☎391-6601; 3hr., 1 per day, ¥3000); and **Tenshin, China** (☎321-5791; 50hr., F noon, ¥20,000).

Public Transportation: The JR Kōbe Line runs parallel to the shorefront through downtown. If you are staying outside the downtown area, **trains** from Sannomiya to Maiko or Tarumi Stations take approximately 20min. and cost ¥270. The Portliner, a **monorail** from Sannomiya, goes directly to Port Island (¥240). To get to Rokkō Island, travel first to Sumiyoshi Station (¥170, 5min.), then take the Rokkō Liner monorail (¥240). The Ikuta Line of the **subway** links the Sannomiya area with Shin-Kōbe (1 stop, ¥200). A kitschy retro **tourist bus** shuttles gawkers from sight to sight in a downtown loop. Bus stops are ubiquitous and clearly marked in English. Daypasses grant discounts to certain tourist attractions; both passes and single tickets are bought on the bus. (Single ride ¥250, full-day ¥650. Bus operates M-F 9:30am-4pm, Sa-Su and holidays 9:30am-5pm.)

Taxis: Mainichi Kōtsū, ☎691-0055.

🚖 ORIENTATION

Kōbe began on a thin strip of land between the mountains and the sea. Since then, the Japanese have leveled some of the mountains and filled in some of the sea, creating a flat, smooth city. **Sannomiya Station** marks the heart of the city, with the uptown **Old Foreign Settlement** and **Nankin-Machi** (Chinatown; 南京町) to the south, before the waterfront areas of **Harborland** and **Meriken Park** and the artificial **Port** and **Rokkō Islands**. To the north stretches **Kitano** (北野), a hip area of former foreign colonization intruding into the northern hills. Farther east, **Shin-Kōbe** is trendy and green, with upscale shopping as well as a mountain nature reserve.

🚻 PRACTICAL INFORMATION

The **major train stations** also function as service centers for the wandering tourist. Drop your bags off at the **coin lockers** (starting at ¥300 per day), call home from the international pay phones, pick up some band-aids at any of the dozens of pharmacies (look for the *hiragana* Kusuri signs) before heading out to your hotel.

Tourist Office: The main information center (☎322-0220) just south of Sannomiya Station has useful maps and some English-speaking staff. Open daily 9am-7pm. Look for stands in Shin-Kōbe Station and on the hilltop in **Kitano**. Both open daily 9am-6pm.

Tours: A student club, **Kōbe Student Guide**, offers free tours of attractions in Kōbe, Ōsaka, and Himeji, giving its members a chance to practice their English. Tourists are expected to pay the guide's transport and admission costs as well as treat him to lunch. Contact the group at least a day ahead of time (ksg-ml@ml-b8.infoseek.co.jp).

Budget Travel: Japan Travel Agencies (☎241-1881; www6.nta.co.jp/sannomiya) have an office in Sannomiya station. Arranges hotel stays and airline, maritime, and train trips. Open M-F 10am-7pm, Sa-Su 10am-6pm.

Banks: There are many in the Sannomiya and Kitano areas. **Nakashin Bank** (☎222-3525), at the 1st intersection of Tor Road north of Sannomiya, exchanges dollars and euros and handles other routine banking services. Open M-F 9am-7pm.

ATM: International ATMs can only be found at post offices (see below).

English-Language Bookstore: Maruzen (丸善 ; ☎391-6003), near Chinatown, has an entire floor dedicated to foreign books and magazines. Open daily 10am-7pm.

Emergency: Police ☎ 110. **Fire** or **ambulance** ☎ 119.

Police: The main police station (☎341-7441) is in southern Kitano.

Hospital/Medical Services: Contact staff at your hotel or call the tourist information service to find an English-speaking specialist. Otherwise, one option is to call **Kōbe University Hospital** (Kōbe Daigaku Bōyōin; 神戸大学病院 ; ☎341-7451). 24hr. service.

Internet Access: Internet cafes line the street on Sannomiya Station's north side. Most offer free drinks, a comic book library, and a choice of spacious booths or narrow cubicles. **Popeye Media Cafe** (☎325-8877), halfway between Motomachi and Sannomiya stations, is one of the best. ¥50 for 1st 30min., then ¥100 per 15min. Open 24hr.

Post Office: Nearly every block in the downtown area has a branch post office. One is in the **Kōbe Kokusan Kaikan** building just south of Sannomiya Station. Open M-F 9am-5pm for mail; M-F 9am-7pm and Sa-Su 9am-5pm for **ATM** use. **Postal Code:** 650.

▐ ACCOMMODATIONS

With the bustle of its land and sea traffic, Kōbe attracts its fair share of visitors and has lodging options for a variety of budgets and tastes. The areas around Shin Kōbe and Sannomiya stations are thronged with upscale and mid-range business hotels, while budget travelers can choose between rival hostels. Look to the waterfront, Port Island, and Harbor Island if you're interested in nothing but the best.

Kōbe Tarumi Youth Hostel (HI) (神戸たるみユースホステル ; ☎707-2133). 6 stops west of Sannomiya on the JR Kōbe line. Take a local train to Tarumi Station, west of Sannomiya, and follow the main road between the tracks and waterfront west for 10min. Requires a bit of travel but imposes no curfew. Groups can opt for private *tatami* rooms. Laundry facilities. Check-in 3-9pm. Check-out 10am. Dorms ¥2800, nonmembers ¥3800; private rooms ¥3500/4500. ❶

Maiko Villa Kōbe (シーサイドホテル舞子ビラ神戸 ; ☎706-3711; www.maikovilla.co.jp). Head 7 stations west on the JR Kōbe Line and follow the signs. Slightly out of the way, but all twins and deluxe twins have gorgeous ocean views. Set on a hilltop; from the bottom of the driveway, a diagonal elevator whisks you to the lobby. Check-in from 3pm. Check-out 11am. Annex singles ¥6400. Doubles single-occupancy ¥7500, double-occupancy ¥11,000. Twins ¥12,000/15,000 and ¥18,000 for triple-occupancy. Deluxe twins ¥16,000/20,000/24,000. Prices rise ¥1500 on holidays, during Golden Week, and from July 20-Aug. 20. 10% service charge. AmEx/MC/V. ❸

Petit Hotel Arcons (☎231-1538). A comfortable budget alternative in the Kitano area. The fading paint job is more than made up for by comfort and charm. Check-in from 2pm. Check-out 10am. Singles ¥6200; doubles ¥10000. MC/V. ❸

Kōbe Sannomiya Union Hotel (☎242-3000; fax 242-0220). East of Sannomiya Station. The cheapest business hotel in the area. Standard amenities. Check-in 2-10pm. Check-out 11am. Singles ¥7200; doubles single-occupancy ¥8300, double occupancy ¥9900; twins ¥8800/11,000; suites ¥11,000/12,100. AmEx/MC/V. ❸

Kōbe Kitano Youth Hostel (HI) (神戸北野ユース
ホステル ; ☎221-4712; www.kobe-kitano.net). Up
a steep hill behind the information center in Kitano.
Conveniently placed in the chic Kitano district, but
the steep, 300m climb from the nearest road and a
10pm lockout that precludes late-night pubbing are
drawbacks. Neat 4- and 6-person dorms. Laundry
available. Check-in 3-9pm. Check-out 10am. ¥3200,
nonmembers ¥4200. ●

🍴 FOOD

Kōbe's diversity comes out nowhere as deliciously
as in its food. Apart from the legendary **Kōbe beef,**
the city is known for the quality of its international
fare, with countless excellent restaurants representing dozens of national cuisines. **Kitano** avenues
are filled with trendy and tasty eateries, often
stacked on top of one another, with pricier dining
in the uphill **Ijikan** district.

Yum Jamu, on the 3rd fl. near Tor Rd. Serves up vegetarian pan-Asian meals in an Indochine-type setting.
Lunch specials (¥1000) keep even carnivores happy,
as some seafood dishes are available. All ingredients
additive-free and organic. An English menu makes it
easy to decide—the many delicious choices make it
hard. Open daily 11:30am-2pm and 5-10pm. ●

Cafe Berthier (☎331-6505). On Tor Rd., 500m up from
the tracks. Scrumptious French meals in an oddly Victorian restaurant. Lunch specials are by far the best
value, with salad, bread, coffee, and an entree for
¥1000-1800. Dinners average ¥2500. Lunch served
until 3pm. Open M-F 10am-11:30pm, Sa-Su and holidays 9am-11:30pm. ●

Rokumeisou (鹿鳴荘 ; ☎391-7635). In the heart of
Chinatown. Helps out tourists with an English-language
menu. A sure bet are the *shumai* dumplings (¥600),
but the more exotic shark-fin soup (¥1200) can also be
tempting. Open M and W-F 11:15am-3pm and 4:15-
9:30pm, Sa-Su and holidays 11:15am-9:15pm. ●

Pearl Cafe, just inside the Ijikan district on Kitano-
zaka. Fronts a nice terrace made for people-watching.
Coffee (¥400). Cake (¥500-600). Open daily
11:30am-10pm. ●

Nailey's Cafe (☎231-2008). Near the YMCA just off of
Flower Rd. A hip, contemporary cuisine restaurant without a
national theme. Serves tasty sandwich and pasta-based
dishes. Lunch meals ¥1000. Drink purchase comes with
30min. of Internet time, meal with 1hr. Open Su-Th
11:30am-midnight, F-Sa 11:30am-2am. ●

Around the Asia (☎391-8895). Downstairs across
from the tracks near Ikuta-dōri. Specializes in Indonesian food. Reasonably priced dinners hover between

ON THE MENU

WHERE'S THE BEEF?

Alberta beef may be big in Canada, and Texas beef all the rage
stateside, but in Japan, quality
steak has one name—Kōbe. While
quality cattle in North America are
ranged out to make them strong
and lean, the Japanese take a different approach. On Kōbe's cattle
farms, the animals lead a life of
high, if forced, leisure. They are fat-
tened on a diet of the finest grains
and the secret ingredient, beer,
which is also massaged into their
hides with giant brushes. Reports
of cattle suspended in slings to
save their legs from having to bear
their weight may not be exaggerated—these hefty heifers can be
twice the size of normal cows.

The effects of this pampered lifestyle are readily apparent—not
only do the cows display a jaded,
demoralized worldview and reluc-
tance to take responsibility for
their lives, but their meat is visibly
different from that of their rugged
American cousins. Instead of lingering in a few veins along the
edges, the fat in Kōbe beef is
speckled throughout the cuts,
appearing in blocks, speckles,
and veins inside the meat. The
creamy stripes are the hallmark of
Kōbe beef—sometimes called
"beef fois gras"—and the finest
specimens fetch thousands of dollars per kg. Fortunately for the less
affluent, Kōbe beef can be
acquired at more terrestrial
prices—while it's still expensive,
Sandaya, in Kitano, serves Kōbe
beef at ¥3000-5000 per plate.

¥1200 and ¥1800 and include mammoth portions of *nasi goreng* (fried rice). Seating in intimate, *batik*-shrouded booths. Open M-F 5pm-midnight, Sa-Su 11:30am-3pm and 5pm-midnight. ❸

Candy's Kitchen (☎252-7378), just off of Flower Rd. Caters to 2 different sets—dog lovers and their dogs. Kōbe's canine fans can bring in their pets, pooch sweaters and all, and clip their leashes to loops set in the floor. While Patches nibbles on ground beef, you can indulge in a Japanese-style hamburger (¥1200, set meal ¥2000). The walls are plastered with signed pet pictures—befriend Candy and maybe she'll let you put up a portrait of Patches. Open M-Tu and Th-Su 11am-11pm. ❸

La Gargotte (☎262-7076), just off of Flower Rd. Jammed every night with hip young Kōbeans who come for the delicious French-Italian food. Lunch specials (¥1200-1800) are the best deal, but the ¥2000 dinners more than satisfy. Come early, as La Gargotte sees a brisk business. Open Tu-Su 11:30am-10pm. ❸

Panpara (☎222-9919). Tucked away off the main street behind the info center in the Ijikan district, but worth the effort it takes to find. A combination import store/cafe, Panpara offers up some of the cheapest, tasty meals in Kitano. The only drawback is its short hours. Indian curries ¥650. Open Su-F noon-6pm. ❷

ⓖ SIGHTS

Kōbe is a relatively modern town, only blooming after the opening of its port to foreign commerce in 1868, and, as such, it lacks the venerable temples and shrines of some of Japan's older cities. The vitality of the city does help it maintain a number of interesting museums and recreational sites, and the downtown streets make for good people-watching.

THE GREAT HANSHIN-AWAJI EARTHQUAKE MEMORIAL (人と防災未来センター). At 5:46am on January 17th, 1995, Kōbe was struck by an earthquake of 6.8 magnitude on the Richter scale. Some buildings fractured and toppled, others collapsed as their foundations sank into liquefied soil. Even the superhighways, the pride of Japanese engineering, broke under the strain of the twisting, jostling earth. The sun rose on a wrecked and ruined Kōbe, with fires set by falling power lines spreading into the suburbs and waterfront. The earthquake killed over five thousand people and left tens of thousands homeless. The elaborate **Great Hanshin-Awaji Earthquake Memorial Museum** drives home the devastation felt by the citizens of Kōbe on that day through video presentations, survivors' testimony, and careful documentation of the destruction and reconstruction of Kōbe. A sister museum linked by a second-floor bridge holds exhibits pertaining to disaster prevention and preparedness. *(The museums are in a new development along the water front, approximately 15min. south of JR Nada station. From the south exit of that station, follow the main road towards the water. The museums are the twin square buildings dominating their stretch of road.* ☎262-5050; www.dri.ne.jp. *Open Tu-Th and Su 10am-6pm, F-Sa 10am-8pm. Individual museum ¥500, students ¥400; double ticket ¥800/640.)*

KŌBE CITY MUSEUM (KŌBE SHIRITSU HAKUBUTSUKAN; 神戸市立博物館). In the downtown core south of Sannomiya station, the **Kōbe City Museum** is the city's best known and most well-established museum. The permanent collection focuses on the effects of Kōbe's opening to foreign influence and the rapid modernization of the late 19th and early 20th centuries, while top floors display traveling collections from other major world museums. In the permanent collection, particularly interesting are the Namban (southern barbarian) works. The result of the introduction of Christianity and Western civilization by the Portuguese and Dutch in the 16th century, these works by Japanese artists combine both native and foreign elements *(☎391-0035. Open Tu-Su 10am-5pm. Permanent collection ¥200; students ¥150. Extra charge for special exhibitions.)*

NANKIN-MACHI (CHINATOWN; 南京町). A few blocks west of the City Museum, Kōbe's Chinatown lacks the size of those in New York, San Francisco, or Vancouver, but the atmosphere is lively and the **Choan-mon** (East Gate) is impressively lit after dark. On weekends and holidays, the throngs truly do evoke the masses of China, and the area makes for a decent couple of hours of sightseeing.

MERIKEN PARK (メリケン園). On the waterfront farther south is the new development of Meriken Park. A pleasant area of promenades and shops, the entrance is marked by a giant wire-and-mesh fish. Inside the **Kōbe Maritime Museum,** an entertaining collection of exhibits cover maritime transport and engineering and explain how Port and Rokkō Islands were reclaimed from the sea. (☎391-6751; fax 332-4739. Open Tu-Su 10am-5pm. ¥600. ¥100 discount with foreign passport.) Nearby, the **Kōbe Port Tower (** 神戸ポートタワー) mars the cityscape with its red 180m-high structure, a relic from an age of unsatisfactory architecture. *(Open Tu-Su 10am-5pm. ¥500, joint ticket with the Maritime Museum ¥900.)* Visitors can ascend the tower, but **Kōbe City Hall** is equally tall and climbing it is free.

PORT ISLAND. The two artificial islands in Kōbe Bay are not only engineering marvels but also suitable places to stroll and shop. Both contain parks and squares, and each contains an eccentric museum on a consumer culture topic. On Port Island, the vaguely coffee-cup shaped **UCC Coffee Museum** gives out a free serving of their famous blend with every ticket. The exhibits follow the production process, from the coffee bushes to the fine porcelain with which the steaming liquid is drunk. It seeks to bring the producers and consumers of coffee closer together in a commitment to coffee culture, based on good wages and working standards. *(To reach the museum, take the Portliner monorail from Sannomiya Station to Minami-Kōen stop (¥240). ☎302-8880. Open Tu-Su 10am-5pm. ¥210.)*

ROKKŌ ISLAND (六甲). No particular philosophy stands behind Rokkō Island's lavish **Kōbe Fashion Museum** (神戸ファッション美術館), just a love of couture. Displays run the gamut from Victorian court dress to traditional peasant wear to vintage styles by modern fashion houses, all housed in a bizarrely shaped hall. *(Take the Rokkoliner from JR Sumiyoshi Station to Island Center Station (¥240). ☎858-0050; fax 858-0058; www.fashionmuseum.or.jp. Open M-Tu and Th-Su 10am-6pm. ¥500.)*

NADA DISTRICT. On the way back from Rokkō Island, it's worth stopping off in the Nada district, known for its long tradition of **sake brewing.** From the monorail station, go straight along the waterway— very soon you'll reach maps and signposts leading

THE LOCAL STORY

CROSSING CULTURES

After marrying a Japanese woman, John Montgomery moved from the United States to Japan, where he has lived for 24 years.

On Japan: I think it's a very orderly country and the people in general are very gentle, so it's an easy country to live in. The normal response in Japan to most anything is pretty peaceful. To get uptight about something, particularly physically, like you might find people doing in the West, especially in cities as big as Tokyo, is very unusual here.

On being an expatriate: I'm spoiled because I'm a foreigner, so I'm excused for almost anything I do....If you're an apologetic foreigner or a self-effacing kind that looks at yourself as the person who's done something wrong, the Japanese will think you're cute and love you for it, and you'll never have a lot of problems. But I've been here so long that I can get around easily...I get the best of both worlds.

On his marriage: I think I was naïve. I thought crossing cultures in this day and age and for somebody as open-minded as me would be no problem, but I found that when it's matters of the heart and getting along on a daily basis, it can be very trying at times. It's obviously nobody's fault, but it's challenging because expectations are very different and the Japanese don't see talking things out necessarily as the way to do things.

KANSAI

the way to the dozen or so breweries open to the public. The easiest to reach is **Hamafukutsuru Brewery** (浜服鶴), a couple of blocks east of the first information post. A self-guided path leads past English-language descriptions of the *sake* brewing process—afterwards, tourists can sample up to three varieties of *sake*. *(The breweries are accessed from Minami-Uozaki Station on the same line as the fashion museum (¥240). ☎ 4111-0492. Open daily 10am-5pm. Free.)*

KITANO (北野) **AND SHIN-KŌBE** (新神戸). The main draw for the many Japanese who come here are the **Ijikan** (literally "foreigners' houses") standing on the hillsides of northern Kitano. They give the neighborhood a historic feel, and are a good backdrop for the chic cafes and wedding halls that dot the area, but the clapboard and shingle houses themselves will seem familiar to most Westerners. Visitors should know that few of the buildings are originals—most were rebuilt after the 1995 earthquake. Info centers carry maps listing the many Ijikan and indicating whether or not they charge admission (prices range from ¥300-700). At the northeastern end of Kitano, by Shin-Kōbe station, the **Shin-Kōbe Ropeway** (新神戸ロープウェー) leads up through forests and grants marvelous views of the city and bay. *(☎ 271-1160. Open M-F 10am-5pm, Sa 10am-8:30pm, Su 10am-7:30pm. ¥550, round-trip ¥1000.)* At the top, the **Nunobiki Herb Park** (Nunobiki Haabu-en; 布引ハーブ園) displays innumerable herbs and flowering plants, both outdoors and in elaborate greenhouses. A favorite spot for Japanese couples, it's particularly lovely around sunset. If you don't feel like riding the cable car, the walk up takes 30min. and the walk down 15min. *(☎ 271-1131. Park closes 30min. before the ropeway. ¥200.)*

🎵 NIGHTLIFE

Kōbe has a fair amount going on for a city its size. Cafes and restaurants stay open well into the night, and evenings out often start over dinner before segueing into pubbing and clubbing. As with food, the abundance of options makes deciding where to go the only hard part of an evening out.

Restaurant and Live Sone, 1-24-10, Nakayamate-dōri. (☎ 221-2055; fax 221-7009), on Kitano-zaka. Kōbe's premier jazz spot. Run by the Sone family, it has a reputation as classy and comfy. Attracts an impressive array of acts, Japanese and international. Drinks ¥700-1200. Cover ¥700-1000. Open M-Sa 5pm-12:30am, Su 5pm-midnight.

The Lockup (☎ 241-6505). An elaborate "entertainment complex" with an emphasis on eating and drinking. The entrance is on the basement level. Guests are handcuffed and led to their table by a hostess in a police uniform in a mad laboratory/S&M dungeon/ gothic cathedral/prison atmosphere. Hidden triggers on the ground emit screams. Drinks served in lightbulbs and beakers ¥700. No cover. Open daily 5pm-1am.

Dai Dai (☎ 230-9858), just off Flower Rd. Chill, hip bar with couches ideal for lounging. Small space; intimate atmosphere. Drinks ¥600. Cover ¥300. Open daily 8pm-5am.

Holly's Live House, 2-4-10, Kanō-machi (☎ 251-5147). In an alley near the YMCA. Classic American bar atmosphere. Live '50s and '60s oldies and jazz acts. Mellow mood. Drinks ¥450-600. Live charge ¥300, table charge ¥300. Open daily 6pm-midnight.

King of Kings, 2-3-16, Kitano-chō (☎ 241-2338). in the Ijikan district of Kitano, a 15min. walk from Sannomiya Shin-Kōbe. Drink in a genuine Ijikan! They've kept the furniture from the heady days of British Empire, and you can't help but feel nostalgic for the Raj and Hong Kong. Toast the Queen with English beer (¥850) and plot the capture of Mandalay. Open daily 5pm-1am.

Ryan's Pub (☎ 391-6902; www.ryansirishpub.com). Just outside Sannomiya Station, above a McDonald's. The local *gaijin* bar, Ryan's has a comfortable Irish pub atmosphere. Even on weekdays, the place fills up with foreigners and the Japanese who love them. Drinks begin at ¥400. Open Su-Th 5pm-midnight, F 5pm-1am, Sa 5pm-2am.

Cafe Spark 4-10-1, Kanō-machi (☎331-5290). Chic cafe-bar overlooking bustling Flower Rd. Trendy atmosphere—minimalist colorful. Enjoy your concoctions among a friendly staff and crowd. Drinks start at ¥500. Open M-Sa 2pm-1am, Su 2-10pm.

Sunflower/Seed (☎242-1545), in upper Kitano. Sunflower is a chill-out bar with low lights and an easy mood, while Seed is the crash-boom-bang dance club upstairs. A full evening will see some migration between the two. Drinks start at ¥500. Sunflower open M and W-Su 7pm-5am; Seed M-Tu and Th-Su 7pm-5am.

Kōbe Honky Tonk (☎241-2161), on a cross street between Kitano and Flower Rds. Marked by a psychedelic Confederate flag. Narrow bar with an intimate space that hosts live music and jam sessions on weekends. Drinks ¥600-800. Open daily 6pm-midnight.

◗ FESTIVAL

One event not to be missed is the annual **Luminarie,** held in mid-December. Inspired by Italian lamp design, the event commemorates Kōbe's spectacular revival after the Great Hanshin Earthquake. The streets around City Hall are lit up by lanterns on metal arches, producing a dazzling effect. The Luminarie is quite popular, so plan your accommodations ahead and expect to fight throngs.

WAKAYAMA (和歌山)

The southwestern part of the Kii peninsula (the biggest peninsula in Japan), extending below Ōsaka and Nara prefectures, is known for its majestic mountains and seasides. The soul of Wakayama Prefecture is at Kōya-san, a large Shingon Buddhist temple complex high on a mountain plateau. Transportation is expensive, slow and infrequent in this area, so if you're short on cash and time, just make a beeline for Kōya-san—the long train ride is gorgeous, rolling by mountain after mountain of untouched pine forest. Grab the JNTO pamphlet *Shirahama and Wakayama Prefecture* from the Ōsaka Tourist Office before heading out, as it has maps of Kōya-san and Shirahama, as well as detailed transportation info.

KŌYA-SAN (高野山)   ☎0736

On a tall plateau in the midst of lush forests sits Kōya-san, birthplace and mecca of the Shingon Buddhist sect, founded here by the monk Kūkai (known as Kōbō Daishi after his death) in 816. Even Kōya-san's geography is a multi-layered symbol—a plateau surrounded by eight mountains, each of which represents a petal of the lotus blossom, a representation of the universe in Shingon Buddhism.

◖ TRANSPORTATION. From Ōsaka's **Nankai Namba Station,** take the Kōya Line (1¼-1¾hr.; regular ¥850, express ¥1610) to **Gokurakubashi,** where you transfer to the **Kōya-san Cable Car** (5min., ¥380)—you can buy a ticket including the cable car at Nankai Namba. From **Wakayama,** take the JR Wakayama Line to Hashimoto, switch to the Nankai Kōya Line, and then catch the cable car from Gokurakubashi.
    From the cable car station, take a **bus** through the winding road to get to town, as there is no sidewalk or shoulder. (¥210 and up, depending on your stop.) You can buy a **daypass** at the cable car station for ¥800, although unless you're in a big hurry you're better off walking, as the distances are not enormous (at most, it's 25min. from the town center to Okunoin).

⁊ PRACTICAL INFORMATION. The **tourist information center** can help book temple lodgings. The staff speaks limited English, but you can grab a map and brochure. (☎56-2616; www.shukubo.jp. Open daily 8:30am-5pm.) In an emergency, call ☎110 for **police,** ☎119 for **fire** or **ambulance. Postal code:** 640-8435.

⚞ ⬔ ACCOMMODATIONS AND FOOD. An integral part of visiting Kōya-san is staying in a *shukubō* (temple lodging) overnight, getting up early for a before-breakfast prayer service, and eating *shōjin ryōri* (Buddhist vegetarian cuisine) for breakfast and dinner. Altogether, about 55 temples offer accommodation on Kōya-san, and the tourist office can help you make reservations. Most *shukubō* will charge about ¥9000 for lodging and two meals; the following are the most popular, least expensive, and most comfortable with hosting foreigners travelers.

Haryō-in ❸ is a pleasant and clean *shukubō*. The halls are a bit clinical-looking, but the rooms are nice, and the fresh flowers are a classy touch. Priests and staff speak English and French. All in all, considering the very tasty dinner and breakfast, this is an excellent value for the budget traveler. (☎56-2702. ¥6500 including two meals.) Across the street, the master of **Rengejō-in ❹** speaks fluent English and often holds morning prayer services in English in his temple, which offers pristine gardens and spacious rooms. (☎56-2233; fax 56-4743. ¥9000-15,000 per person.) Just west of the Reihōkan Museum lies **Henjoson-in ❺**, another excellent choice with friendly monks, perfect raked gardens, huge wooden baths overlooking a garden, and a bar and gift shop. Ask to speak to Shimamoto. (☎56-2434, fax 56-3641. ¥6300 per person; ¥9000-12,000 with dinner and breakfast.)

Even if you don't have the resources to stay over in a *shukubō*, you can still partake of their vegetarian *shōjin-ryōri* for lunch or dinner. Set courses are offered for ¥2500, ¥3500, and ¥5000—reserve a place several days in advance through the tourist office. For a cheaper lunch, restaurants and coffee shops cluster near the tourist office—you can get a bowl of *soba* noodles for around ¥600.

From the tourist office in town, walk north and keep following the road past the intersection on the left; the **⬔Kōya Youth Hostel (HI) ❶** is beyond the Kōya Town Office. All rooms are *tatami*-style, lovely, and well-maintained by the friendly owners, but only four are available, so reserve up to three months ahead. There's no curfew, and the hostel offers Internet access, coin laundry, free bike rental—it even has its own little temple in the back. (☎/fax 56-3889. Breakfast ¥600, dinner ¥1000. ¥3200, nonmembers ¥3800; Japanese pay slightly more.)

⬕ SIGHTS. Kōya-san is divided into two major sightseeing areas: the temple complex Garan to the west, with the famous Daitō (Great Pagoda); and Okunoin in the east, which includes an ancient cemetery and the mausoleum of Kōbō Daishi.

The largest temple on Kōya-san and currently the headquarters for the Shingon sect, **Kongōbu-ji** was originally built in 1593 in memory of Toyotomi Hideyoshi's mother, but the current buildings date from the mid-19th century. This temple features a number of exquisite rooms, of which the first is the Ohiroma room with graceful cranes painted on Kanō-school panels. Then comes Yanagi-no-ma, painted with willow designs, where Toyotomi Hidetsugu, adopted son of Hideyoshi, committed *seppuku*, though not entirely by choice—his adoptive father, after having fathered a biological son, strenuously requested that he disembowel himself. Jodan-no-ma, a reception room with pure gold-leaf walls, is minimalist decadence at its best. All the buildings of Kongōbu-ji are cypress-roofed, and be sure to look for the lovely wood dragon carvings on main gate. The enormous Banryutei rock garden out back, with more than 140 granite chunks from Shikoku, represents two dragons in a sea of clouds. The garden is so vast that it seems to extend into the horizon. (☎56-2011. Open 8:30am-4:10pm. ¥500.)

If you continue along the path after Kongōbu-ji, you'll see the gravel path leading west through a wooded area to **Garan** (伽藍). This is the central monastic complex at the heart of Kōya-san, and one of the oldest areas on the mountain. The pagoda **Daitō**, one of Kōbō Daishi's pet projects, was built shortly after the founding of Kōya-san to represent the ideal universe of the Shingon sect. The vermilion-trimmed, two-storied structure is in very good shape, as it was rebuilt in the 1930s and recently repainted. Inside, the blue-haired golden Dainichi Nyorai cosmic Buddha is surrounded by four other gold Buddha statues and a forest of crimson pillars painted with bodhisattvas, each seated upon a psychedelic-colored lotus. To the west of Daitō, the **Miedō** was the original residence of Kōbō Daishi and now houses his portrait. Every year in mid-April, all the monks of Kōya-san attend a ceremony here to honor his death and to offer him a change of robes. Slightly to the south between Daitō and Miedō facing the main street, the **Kondō** originally served as a lecture hall in which Kōbō Daishi delivered his sermons. In its 7th incarnation after several fires, the current building dates from 1932 and is still used for important ceremonies in the Kōya-san community. The Reihōkan Museum houses many of the statues, paintings and scriptures belonging to Kongōbu-ji and other Kōya-san temples, including carved triptychs brought back from China by Kōbō Daishi and his written vow to devote his life to Buddhism. The building design is meant to be modeled on Uji's Byōdō-in temple. (☎56-2254. Open 8:30am-4:10pm. ¥500.)

The immense cemetery area of **Okunoin** (奥の院) is a 20min. walk northeast from the tourist information center in the middle of town. The cemetery path extends about 2km from the entrance to the tomb of Kōbō Daishi. Shaded by cryptomerias, the 200,000 tombs include those of Hōnen (founder of the Jōdo Shin sect), Shinran (founder of the Jōdo sect), Oda Nobunaga, Toyotomi Hideyoshi, a fistful of Edo-period emperors, and even some famous *kabuki* actors. Age and moss have melded them into a muted congregation at the foot of towering, cathedral-like trees. In the modern area of the cemetery south of the Tamagawa River, you'll see quite a hodgepodge of creative tombstones and markers, including a number of company logos (look out for the huge rocket-shaped monument and the granite coffee cup). To reach the path leading to Kōbō Daishi's mausoleum, you'll need to cross the **Mimyo no Hashi** bridge, before which a line of bronze Jizō figures sit at attention in their bright bibs. Visitors used the ladles provided to douse the statues in water in honor of the dead, and put strips of wood with the names of the deceased near the statues or in the Tamagawa stream next to the Mimyo-no-hashi. In the **Torodo (Hall of Lamps)**, the central religious image is a small sandalwood statue of Kōbō Daishi holding a five-prong *vajra*. Another building to the right of the main Hall of Lamps, called the Memorial Hall of Lamps, was constructed to make room for additional lamps and scriptures. Torodō was constructed by Daishi's disciple Shinzen in memory of the master, and today is lit with hundreds of eternal flames donated by worshippers from all over Japan. The effect is magical at dawn or twilight. Nestled behind Torodō at some distance from the blaze of the eternal lamps, **Kōbō Daishi's mausoleum** is protected by a rough-hewn gate. In accordance with his own prophecy, Daishi assumed a meditative posture and entered into eternal meditation at the age of 62. His disciples placed him, still cross-legged, in a cave designated his tomb, and built the current structure around it. The entire mausoleum seems to whisper "hush" as the master sleeps until the coming of Miroku Nyori.

SHIRAHAMA ☎0739

White-sanded Shirahama was one of Japan's most popular spa resort towns until international travel became popular and affordable, and newlyweds deserted domestic beaches for Hawaii. Shirahama has upped the number of attractions in an attempt to win back tourists, but the best reason to come here remains the exquisite **Shirarahama Beach**, crowded in July and August. The best outdoor bath, **Sakino-yu**, used to be frequented by royalty; now it's completely free. About 500m south down the coastal road, you'll smell the sulphur before seeing the bath, but the water itself is pure. (☎43-3016. Open Sept.-June daily 8am-5pm, July-Aug. daily 8am-6:30pm; closed every 4th W.) A little over 1km south of the beach is **Shirahama Park Sogen-no-yu** (look for the fat pigtailed man making the peace sign in a wooden bathtub), with a dizzying array of different baths. (☎82-2615. Open May-Oct. daily 7am-11pm, Nov.-Apr. daily 7am-10pm. ¥1000.)

Spectacular rock formations jut over the Pacific. About 1½km south of the beach, the thin, flat layers of **Senjojiki** have been dubbed "*tatami* rock." The dramatic jagged cliffs of **Sandanbeki**, 500m past Senjojiki, make for a great photo op. **Engetsu** is a rocky island 1½km north of the beach; the hole in the rock at water level has earned it the nickname of "eyeglass" island.

From Ōsaka, take the JR limited express Super Kuroshio or Ocean Arrow from Tennō-ji or Shin-Ōsaka (110min., ¥4600). From Kōya-san, the express train is also worth the extra yen (local ¥3330; express ¥4310). **Shirahama Station** is a few kilometers from the beach, so hop on a Meiko bus in front of the station (every 30min., ¥330-380). If you're staying in the youth hostel in Kii-Tanabe, three stations north of Shirahama, keep in mind that local trains run about every hour to and from Shirahama (¥190). You may be better off taking the Meiko bus (30min., ¥500.) The sights near the beach aren't that far, but if you want to get around quickly, rent a bike at Shirahama Station (¥300 for 2hr., ¥1000 per day).

By far the best place to stay is the **Ōgigahama Youth Hostel (HI) ❶**, 35-1, Shin-Yasiki-machi, Kii-Tanabe. You'll share a carpeted room with a futon and TV. The kitchen is well-appointed, and the staff can give you good advice about the region. It's a 3min. walk from a **Sakae supermarket** and several coffee shops and bakeries. (☎/fax 22-3433; www.aikis.or.jp/~to-hi/index.html. Doubles ¥2500.) **Ōgigahama Beach**, 5min. away from the hostel, is a bit less touristy and crowded than Shirahama's. From the train station, walk out straight and continue for 10min. as the road bends slightly. When you see the Denmark bakery, turn left at the light (it's the fourth light from the station), walk a block, and take your first right.

SHIMA-HANTŌ

The eastern part of the Kii Peninsula, a forest-covered and inlet-riddled chunk of land sticking out bravely into the Pacific, is Shima-hantō. This entire region has been designated Ise-shima National Park for its forests and the pine-covered islands dotting the bay, but little has been done for the benefit of visitors. Streams of Japanese tourists flow constantly through the shrine Ise Jingu, one of the most ancient and venerated in all Japan. Travelers to the peninsula will probably want to base themselves in Ise. Hundreds of oyster rafts bob in the placid bay at nearby Toba, modest hometown of the Mikimoto cultivated pearl empire. South of Toba, the tiny, woodsy islands of Ago-wan are ideal for a sunset cruise.

ISE-SHI   ☎ 0596

Ise Jingū, one of the oldest shrines in Japan (dating to the 4th century), draws over 6 million people each year. Western visitors may not be particularly struck by its pre-Buddhist iconography and architecture—consisting of simple, unpainted buildings with thatched roofs and high crossbeams called *chigi*—but the unending flow of pilgrims is itself an amazing sight. In harmony with nature and veiled in mystery, the shrine honors Amaterasu Omi-kami, the Sun Goddess. Since the 7th century, it has been ritually rebuilt every 20 years and the *kami* transferred in an evening ceremony to their new home. The next rebuilding will take place in October 2013. The shrine consists of two different areas several kilometers apart: smaller Geku, not far from the two train stations; and the more famous Naiku, accessible by bus from either station or from Geku. In both areas, the most sacred buildings are hidden behind high wooden gates and open only to the Imperial Family, but you can see the gold-tipped crossbeams above the gates.

Naiku, the larger shrine, houses the sacred mirror that is Amaterasu's symbol. After crossing the Uji Bridge, a path on the right leads to a place in the river where pilgrims purify themselves. Continuing along the road, you'll come to the Main Sanctuary, built in the form of a traditional rice storehouse. Pilgrims with special

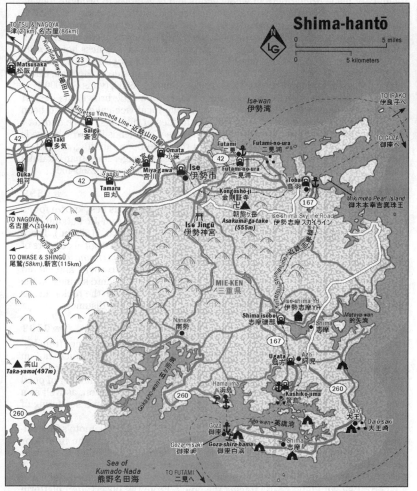

Shima-hantō

requests can pay to enter one of the external gates, led by officiating priests, to bow and pray. Exiting Naiku, you'll see the Oharai-machi area to the right, a reconstructed Edo-style neighborhood. Visitors to the shrine come here to have dessert, lunch, or dinner and to shop in the boutiques. The restaurants are very atmospheric and reasonably priced (Ise *udon* ¥400-600).

Geku shares most of Naiku's characteristics: thatched roofs, unvarnished cypress walls, tall crossbeams, and round logs called *katsuogi* along the ridge of the roof. Geku honors Toyōke Omi-kami, the *kami* of clothes, food, and housing. Twice a day, Ise Jingu's priests leave offerings, which Toyōke relays to Amaterasu.

If you decide to stay in Ise, there are a few reasonable options. From Uji-Yamada Station, head right, follow the curving main road, and take the first big road to the right across the train tracks. **Hoshidekan** ❷ is several blocks down to the right. A lovingly decorated interior features calligraphic scrolls and carved screens. Relax in the traditional garden to the sound of two water zithers. Meals are largely macrobiotic, or made primarily from whole grains and vegetables to promote longevity; the 83-year-old owner also runs a macrobiotic shop next door. (☎28-2377; http://hoshidekan.cool.ne.jp/hoshidekan. Breakfast ¥800, dinner from ¥1000. Singles ¥4800; doubles ¥8500; triples ¥12,000. Amex/MC/V.) A few blocks closer to Uji-Yamada Station is **Ise City Hotel ❸**, a comfortable if generic business hotel. (☎28-2111; www.greens.co.jp. Breakfast ¥1050. Singles ¥6200; twins ¥12,000.) The **Ise City Hotel Annex ❸**, just north of the main hotel on the right side of the road, offers slightly larger and brighter rooms with a fridge. (Singles ¥6600; twins ¥14,000.)

Halfway down the main street past the entrance to a little bridge, the dessert shop **Akafuku Honten ❶** sells *akafuku mochi*, the local rice-cake and red bean paste treat that's extremely popular with the hordes of pilgrims. Three *akafuku mochi* with tea cost ¥230. To the left down the street that leads from the bridge is a square with more shops. Turn left around the little open building, and a few doors down is a traditionally decorated shop with even longer lines than Akafuku Honten. This one sells green tea- or orange-flavored snow-cones (¥350-400).

FUTAMI   ☎0599

A few stops between Ise-shi and Toba on the JR Line, Futami is best known for its **Wedded Rocks** *(meoto-iwa)* just off shore, a 15min. walk from JR Futaminoura Station. Alternatively, you can take a bus from Ise Jingu to Futami (30min.). These two rocks represent the union of Izanagi and Izanami, the mythological creators of Japan. They are joined together by a long straw rope called a *shimenawa*, similar to the belt worn by highest-ranking sumo wrestlers. The two rocks and sacred rope form an unconventional *torii*, like the gates in front of Shintō shrines. In the early hours of summer days, you can watch the sun rise between the rocks, and as the morning mist dissipates, Mt. Fuji is sometimes visible in the distance.

TOBA   ☎0599

This thriving fishing village is a few stops down the JR and Kintetsu Lines from Ise-Shi. There is very little to see here besides **Mikimoto Pearl Island**—if you're not up for paying the ¥1500 island admission fee (including museum, observation area, and display room), there's no point in coming to Toba. There are a number of pearl shops in the imaginatively-named Pearl Building next to the station, as well as a number of restaurants on the third floor. Other than that, it's just a scattering of rather dismal shops and buildings along the waterfront.

A 5min. walk from Toba Station is the birthplace of Kokichi Mikimoto's first cultured pearl. Mikimoto Pearl Island has an interesting museum. The first floor explains the process of pearl-making in scientific detail, from seeding to harvesting and grading. The second floor has exhibits about pearls throughout world history and some of Mikimoto's pearl creations, including a pearl-studded globe and a Liberty Bell with blue pearls tracing the crack. From the observation platform you can watch the *ama* (female divers) make an appearance in their traditional white garb before they plunge into the waters. They no longer search for oysters—now it's seaweed and abalone—but you can pretend. (☎25-2028. Open Jan.-Mar. 20, June-July 20, Sept., and Nov. 21-30 8:30am-5pm; Mar. 21-May 31, July 21-Aug. 31, Oct.-Nov. 20 8:30-5:30; Dec. 9am-4:30pm. ¥1500.)

AGO-WAN   ☎0599

Ago-wan, the scenic bay at the bottom of Shima-hantō, consists of small woodsy islands with oyster rafts bobbing among them in the calm waters. Take the Kintetsu Line to **Kashiko-jima,** the last stop. There's very little of interest on Kashiko-jima except for a few pearl shops, and you can't really appreciate the islands from the wharf—Ago-wan is best explored by ferry or cruise. The wharf, a 1min. walk from the station, is the launching place for a number of boats. The cheapest and perhaps best option is the ferry to Goza, which threads past the islands to reach the long thin extension of the mainland. Near Goza, Shirarahama Beach (p. 469) is a beautiful and popular white sand beach. (☎43-1023. About 5 per day. One-way ¥600) The ticket office is on the right side of the street just before the wharf. The **Kashikojima Espana Cruise** is a decidely campy venue. (☎25-3147. Boats leave every 30min. 9:30am-4:30pm. 50min. cruise ¥1500.) **Ago-wan Shima Meguri** is a regular sight-seeing boat (☎43-1048. Every 30min. 9:30am-3:30pm. 1hr. tour ¥1400.)

SHIGA (滋賀)

East of Kyōto beyond the Higashiyama mountains is **Biwa-ko,** Japan's largest lake, and the surrounding Shiga Prefecture. **Ōtsu** and **Hikone** are Shiga's two major cities, on Biwa's southern and eastern shores, respectively. They're joined by a host of small former castle and merchant towns scattered on all sides of the lake. While many of Shiga's attractions can't compete with the grandeur of Kyōto, they do make worthwhile half- or full-daytrips. Edo-period Hikone Castle, the shady canal of Omi-Hachiman, and the accessible beaches of Omi-Maiko are especially noteworthy. Before you head out, pick up a copy of JNTO's *Lake Biwa, Otsu and Hikone* guide, which has detailed maps of those areas.

From Kyōto Station, the JR Biwa-ko line runs to: **Ōtsu** (¥190); **Omi-Hachiman** (¥650); **Hikone** (¥1100); **Nagahama** (¥1280). The JR Kosei line serves: **Hiei-zan Sakamoto** (¥320); **Katata** (¥400); **Omi-Maiko** (¥650). Cruises on Lake Biwa—some of which stop on the lake's islands—can be a good way to see the area, but expensive fares (from ¥3000) make the rail lines a more reasonable method of sightseeing.

ON THE WEB | Shiga prefecture: www.pref.shiga.jp

ŌTSU (大津)   ☎077

The capital of Japan for a brief five years during the 7th century, Ōtsu today remains the capital of Shiga and an important regional transportation hub. It's most notable for the long, winsome Nagisa Park boardwalk, running 5km along the lakefront, a few popular festivals, and a smattering of charming old temples. Near Ōtsu Port, **Biwa-ko Hana Funsui Fountain** (びわこ花噴水), a very, very long computer-controlled fountain, takes a variety of formations and lights up at night in a variety of colors. The comparatively young **Omi-Jingu** (近江神宮), which dates back to the 1930s, is dedicated to Emperor Tenji, who was responsible for moving the nation's capital to Ōtsu. It houses, of all things, a **clock museum,** since Tenji allegedly created Japan's first waterclock. (Shrine open 24hr. Free. Museum open 9am-4:30pm. ¥200.) Nestled at the foot of Mt. Nagara, **Mii-dera** (三井寺) was founded in 686 in memory of the oldest son of Emperor Tenji. It's home to one of Japan's most famous bells, "The Evening Bell of Mii-dera," and is also famous for its cherry blossoms. (Open daily 8am-4:30pm. ¥450.)

Every August 8, **fireworks** explode over Biwa-ko, starting at 7:30pm. October, on the two days preceding the national Sports Holiday, heralds the **Ōtsu Matsuri** festival. Similar in spirit to Kyōto's Gion Festival, the event features floats on parade on the second day, from 9:30am-5:30pm.

From Kyōto Station, take the JR Tōkaidō Main Line to Ōtsu (about 15min., ¥190). The friendly, English-speaking staff at the **tourist office** in the JR Ōtsu Station have maps, pamphlets, and plenty of knowledge about other regions around Biwa-ko. (☎077-522-3830. Open daily 8:40am-5:25pm.)

SAKAMOTO (坂本)   ☎077

This village above Ōtsu has a tranquil (blunt folk might say boring) atmosphere, largely because it is home to 50 *satobo*, stone-walled retirement temples for older Buddhist monks associated with Enryaku-ji. You're best off taking a quick stroll down the main street before heading to Hiei-zan via the Sakamoto cable car.

From either of Sakamoto's two stations, turn west onto the main road and follow it beyond Omiya Bridge (about 10min. from Keihan Sakamoto Station) to reach **Hiyoshi-taisha** (日吉大社). You'll come to a famous maple-viewing spot, known for its *mikoshi* (portable shrines), and see Hiyoshi-taisha's enshrined deities, protecting Mt. Hiei. (Open daily 9am-4:30pm. ¥300.) Every April 13-14, the shrine hosts the **Sannosai Festival,** with a boat procession of the *mikoshi* shrines.

Saikyō-ji (西教寺) is a 20min. walk from Keihan Sakamoto Station, or a short ride on bus #31, 32, or 34 to Saikyo-ji stop. The temple features 25 stone Buddhas with musical instruments. (☎578-0013. Open daily 9am-4:30pm. ¥400. Zen meditation sessions 1hr. each, daily 9am-5pm. Call ahead for reservations and to make sure the English-speaking priest will be there. Donation requested.)

Sakamoto is accessible from Hama-Ōtsu via the Keihan Line or JR Kosei Line. To the east of the two train stations and just north of Hiyoshi-toshogu (follow the signs), Sakamoto **cable cars** run to Hiei-zan near Enryaku-ji (11min.; every 30min. 8am-6pm; ¥840, round-trip ¥1570). In Sakamoto, the **Saikyō-ji Youth Hostel (HI)** 1 is just north of Saikyō-ji. (☎0578-0013; fax 578-3418. Breakfast ¥500. Dinner ¥800. Dorms ¥2500; nonmembers ¥3500. Closed the 2nd week of Aug.)

KATATA (堅田)   ☎077

From Katata Station on the JR Kosei Line, take the Town Circuit bus to the Demachi Stop and walk east towards Biwa-ko to reach **Ukimi-dō** (Floating Pavilion; 浮御堂). Elevated on stilts over the lake, this small Zen temple appears to hover delicately above the blue waters at the end of the dock. Inside, 1000 small gold statues of Amida Buddha are perfectly aligned along the walls. From the dock, you can spot Hira-san, the Suzuka mountain range, and Okishima. (☎572-0455. Open daily 8am-5pm. ¥300.) Katata itself is a grungy little town with little to recommend it.

OMI-MAIKO (近江舞子)   ☎077

On a hot day in Kyōto, Omi-Maiko is the most convenient place to travel for a cooling swim. The long white beach, **Omatsuzaki** (雄松崎), one of Shiga's eight scenic beauties, is conveniently near the Omi-Maiko Train Station.

The train ride passes a number of terraced rice fields at the foot of Hira-san. From Kyōto Station, take the JR Kosei Line to Omi-Maiko (¥650). Overnight stays are reasonable at **Trek-Station Maiko Hut** ❷. The post-grad proprietors lead hikes around Hira-san (dayhike, including rope-lift and lunch ¥8900) and can give advice on hiking routes. Call from the station for pickup. (☎596-8190; www.trekstation.co.jp. Continental breakfast ¥500. Japanese breakfast ¥800. Check-in 3pm. Check-out 10am. Flexible midnight curfew. Bike rental ¥200 per hr., ¥1000 per day. Japanese dorms ¥3500 per person; Western dorms ¥4500 per person; add ¥1000 per room for 2- or 3-person private rooms. Reserve 3 days in advance.)

HIKONE (彦根)   ☎074

Hikone is the largest town on the east side of Biwa-ko, 1hr. from Kyōto Station by train. If you can't get to Himeji, ■**Hikone-jō** (彦根城) is a worthy nearby alternative. With its variegated peaked roofs and brilliant white exterior, Hikone-jō's *donjon* is a gem of an Edo-period castle. Completed in 1622, the exterior castle walls are ingeniously composed of larger boulders with small stones fitted between them to prevent earthquake damage. Through the Tenbin-Yagura battle tower is the *donjon*. Note the unusual interior ceiling beams—rather than hacking the wood into regular four-sided beams, the castle's architects used the natural curves of the tree trunks. The third floor offers a good view of Biwa-ko, although screens in front of the windows make picture-taking impossible.

Between the interior and exterior moats to the east lies the stunning garden **Genkyū-en** (玄宮園), built in 1677, with small bridges, a thatched-roof teahouse, and a splendid view of the *donjon* perched triumphantly on the hill above. Back near the castle entrance, the **Hikone Castle Museum** curates a collection of armor, calligraphy, and *nō* costumes. (Castle ☎922-2742; museum ☎922-6100. Open daily 8:30am-5pm. Castle and garden ¥500; museum ¥500; castle, garden, and museum ¥900.)

Extending southwest from the Kyobashi Bridge, **Yume Kyobashi Castle Road** is a merchant-lined street recently reconstructed to resemble its white-walled, lattice-doored Edo-period predecessor, complete with teahouses and upscale craft shops. The ye olde worlde effect is spoiled slightly by the traffic on the wide pavement and by giant green plastic ice cream cones in front of various shops. **Ryoan-ji** (竜安寺) is a 20min. walk northeast of JR Hikone Station. A Rinzai Zen temple founded by *daimyō* Ii Naotaka, it is known primarily for its dry gravel-raked garden with 48 stones. (Open daily Mar.-Nov. 9am-5pm; Dec.-Feb. 9am-4pm. ¥400.) To the north, Matsubara beach (松原) is good for a swim on a hot day. A small **tourist office** in front of the station provides maps of the city's major sights. (☎922-2954.)

NAGAHAMA (長濱)　　　　　　　　　　　　☎074

Nagahama is a small castle town north of Hikone, known primarily for the Kurokabe Square glass galleries, old *machiya* (traditional townhouse) merchant homes, and the castle. Behind (west of) the train station near the harbor, **Nagahama Castle Historical Museum** is a small-scale castle. It doesn't have the quite the same appeal as Hikone-jō, but it was built by 16th-century warlord Toyotomi Hideyoshi and the museum contains a number of Hideyoshi-related artifacts. (Open daily 9am-5pm. ¥400.) One of the historic centers of the city, **Hokkoku-dōri** (北国道リ) was once a thriving merchant neighborhood. Today the wooden *machiya* houses hold boutiques and little restaurants good for a midday meal. On Hokkoku-dōri is the **Kurokabe Square glass gallery,** which sells a variety of glass objects popular with tourists. Nagahama is also famed for its **Hikiyama-matsuri,** held each April 15 with 13 floats and *kabuki* performances by young boys. A small **tourist booth** in front of the station has English maps and brochures.

OMI-HACHIMAN (近江八幡)　　　　　　　　☎074

An appealing little town on the eastern side of Biwa-ko, Omi-hachiman is known for the shady Hachiman-bori canal, lined with old merchant homes. The rice fields around the town are riddled with small streams and inlets, where it's possible to take out a hand-rowed houseboat. Farther north are a number of beaches accesseible by bus from the station. The tourist kiosk near the station hands out English-language maps. In the center of the old commercial neighborhood, the **Nishikawa family residence** (西川家住宅), the Edo-period home of the town's wealthiest merchant family, is open to the public. (☎832-7048. Open Tu-Su 9am-5pm.)

Several companies offer **boat tours** of the surrounding reed beds and rice fields. Omi Hachiman Wasen Kanko is closest to town center. (☎832-2564. Tours daily Apr.-Oct. 10am-3pm. ¥2100 per person; min. 4 people per boat.) Nearby at ◪**Omi-Hachiman Youth Hostel (HI) ❶,** perks include bike and canoe rental, several pianos, and special menus of Omi beef and *shabu-shabu* (¥1500-4500; order in advance). Take the Kōmeiji-bound bus #6 (3 per hour until 8:40pm, ¥400) from Omi-Hachiman Station to Youth Hostel Mae. (☎832-2938; fax 832-7593. Breakfast ¥500. Dinner ¥1000. ¥3000; nonmembers ¥4000.)

HIMEJI
☎ 0792

For the minor provincial township that Himeji so evidently is, it boasts an impressive number of significant sights. Striking Himeji-jō, Japan's most beautiful original castle, is a daytrip essential for anyone passing through eastern Kansai, while the elaborate and immaculate Kokōen gardens and the surprisingly well-endowed Himeji City Art Museum tempt you to stay a little longer. If you run out of time the first day, make a return trip to see the fusion Indian pagodas in Nagoyama Cemetery park. But don't let the sun set on you in Himeji—the town has few budget accommodations and little in the way of fine dining or nightlife.

ON THE WEB	Himeji: www.city.himeji.hyogo.jp

☰ TRANSPORTATION. Although Himeji sits on the *shinkansen* trunk line, it makes little sense to visit it as anything other than a daytrip from Kōbe or Ōsaka, in which case it's simpler and faster to take the regular service. Trains leave Himeji continually to: **Okayama** (1hr., ¥1450); **Kurashiki** (1½hr., ¥1890); **Ōsaka** (1hr., ¥1450); and **Kōbe** (40min., ¥950). Most sights in Himeji can be easily toured on foot, but the free **bike rental** offered by the information center is tempting (☎ 85-3792; return bikes by 5:30pm). A quaint **bus** loops around the castle on weekends and holidays. (Departs from the station. Operates 9am-5pm. Single ride ¥100, daypass ¥400). The daypass includes a 20% discount on admission to Himeji-jō, Kokōen garden, the Museum of Art, and the Museum of Literature.

⬛🔢 ORIENTATION AND PRACTICAL INFORMATION. The main street in Himeji, **Ōtemae-dōri,** runs between JR Himeji Station and Himeji-jō. Most sights and services can be found along this stretch of road. In front of the castle, another major road runs east-west, crossing the **Ibo River** and leading to Nagoyama cemetary. The station contains the usual services—**luggage lockers,** a Travel Information Satellite **travel agency** (☎ 25-0401; open M-Sa 10am-6:30pm, Su 10-6pm), and a **tourist information center** (☎ 85-3792; open daily 9am-5pm; English-speaking staff on duty 10am-3pm). A **police box** just outside the station provides 24hr. assistance. In an emergency, call ☎ 110 for **police,** ☎ 119 for **fire** or **ambulance. Comic Buster,** west of the castle, provides **Internet access** for ¥390 per hr. and includes free drinks. (☎ 98-2552. Open daily 10am-3am.) The main **post office,** one block southeast of the castle, across from Otemae park, contains an **ATM** and can **exchange currency** as well as providing postal services. (Open for mail and currency exchange M-F 9am-7pm, Sa 9am-5pm, Su 9am-12:30pm. ATM open M-F 8am-9pm, Sa-Su 9am-7pm.)

🔢⬛ ACCOMMODATIONS AND FOOD. There is no reason to stay in Himeji—all of the sights close by 6pm, and the city offers little else. Furthermore, the only budget accommodation, the **Seinen no Ie Youth Hostel (HI) ❶,** is far enough out of the way and difficult enough to find for the info center to issue a special explanatory map. To reach the hostel, take bus #37 and get off at the Chūō Kōen Guchi stop. Turn left at the next intersection (a cafe marks the spot), cross the river, head under two pedestrian overpasses, and pass a playground to turn left again at the hostel sign. Follow the signs approximately another 300m from there. Now do this with your heavy pack. On the bright side, the hostel is quite inexpensive. (☎ 93-2716. Kitchen available. Bath without shower available 5-9pm only. Sheet charge ¥200. Check-in 3-9pm. Check-out 10am. Closed every 2nd and 4th M of the month and at year-end. Dorms ¥700; Japanese-style rooms ¥1000.) For those with other tastes, **Hotel Sungarden ❹,** behind the station, offers the usual business amenities (☎ 22-2231; www.gardenhotels.co.jp. Check-in from noon. Check-out noon. Singles ¥9000; doubles ¥17,000.) **Hotel Himeji Plaza ❸,** behind Hotel Sungarden, is a mid-priced option. (☎ 81-9098; h-plaza@memenet.or.jp. Check-in from 3pm. Check-out 10am. Singles ¥4935, with bath ¥6510; doubles with bath ¥9450.)

For a light lunch by the castle, the **Menme Udon ❶** shop has hearty soups between ¥400-850. (☎25-0118. Open M-Tu and Th-Su 11:30am-7pm.) **Conservo Deli ❶** serves up baked goods and sandwiches on the main drag. (☎25-0245. ¥300-700. Open daily 8am-8pm.) A more elegant alternative is pan-Asian restaurant **Len ❸**, tucked away in a shopping arcade. Dishes start at ¥750 for lunch, but expect to spend more for dinner. (☎25-5505. Open M-Tu and Th-Su 11:30am-midnight.)

■ **SIGHTS.** Dating from 1580, ▨**Himeji-jō** is widely considered to be the finest original castle in Japan. Seeing its immense white form looming over the city, visitors will be hardpressed to argue otherwise. Also known as the Castle of the White Egret for its striking color and grace, the castle was recognized in 1993 as a UNESCO World Heritage Site. One reason Himeji-jō is so well-preserved has to do with the circumstances of its construction—built in the wave of fortification following the unification of Japan by Toyotomi Hideyoshi, Himeji-jō has never actually seen bat-

Himeji · 姫路

🏠 ACCOMMODATIONS
Hotel Himeji Plaza, **5**
Hotel Sungarden, **4**
🍴 FOOD
Conservo Deli, **3**
Len, **2**
Menme Udon, **1**

tle. A visit to the castle begins with a trek around the spiraling **outer wall,** designed to force besiegers to cover the most ground possible. Former kill zones, the inside corners of the walls now contain cherry trees which stand out against the stark white walls. The most awe-inspiring part of the castle, of course, is the immense **donjon** with its many towers and gables sweeping down like frozen waves. The interior of the castle is a bit less thrilling than the views outside would suggest—the rooms are mostly bare, and visitors must ascend many, many steps. If you arrive early enough in the day, you may be able to snag an English-speaking guide for a 90min. tour, available on a first-come, first-served basis. The wealth of English explanatory signs, however, make a self-guided tour nearly as informative. (☎85-1146. Open daily Sept.-May 9am-4pm; June-Aug. 9am-5pm.)

Spectacular ▨**Kokōen,** just to the west of the castle, is as recent as the castle is old—it was constructed in 1992, to celebrate the town's centennial. Built on the former site of the lord's residence and *samurai* barracks, the garden consists of nine separate areas blocked off by wall remnants. Each micro-garden has its own theme, put together by a Japanese garden specialist from Kyōto University. A teahouse on the grounds features *kimono*-clad beauties serving traditional powdered green tea (¥500 with sweet). While this may seem like a good place to picnic, eating and drinking on the grounds are strictly forbidden. Violators are fed to the carp. (☎89-4120. Open daily Sept.-May 9am-5pm; June-Aug. 9am-6pm. ¥300.)

Northeast of the castle, the red-brick **Himeji City Museum of Art** houses a surprisingly distinguished collection. One hall in the former armory is reserved for traveling exhibits, while the other displays the city's Rodins, Munchs, and Magrittes, as well as an assortment of 19th- and 20th-century Japanese art. (☎22-2288; www.city.himeji.hyogo.jp/art. Open Tu-Su Sept.-May 10am-5pm; June-Aug. 10am-6pm. ¥500.) North of the castle sits the cubed glass **Hyōgo Prefecture Museum of His-**

tory. While it covers the history of the region from its early traces through the barbarous middle ages into the present, the museum tends to dwell, perhaps understandably, on castle-related issues. Cast models of all surviving Japanese castles let you compare and contrast. (☎88-9011. Open Tu-Su 10am-5pm. ¥200, students ¥150.) Set on a hill top in northwestern Himeji, the park-like **Nagoyama Cemetery** is worth a visit for a stroll through the peaceful grounds and the view from the hilltop. Apart from the gravestones, which can be quite ornate, the peak features a set of pagodas and charnelhouses (vaults for the dead) set around a pond and garden. The park is a symbol of Indian-Japanese friendship through Buddhism, and the pagodas have a decidedly subcontinental feel. The central pagoda serves as an active temple, and its images and icons, inside and out, are an attempt at fusing Japanese and Indian religious traditions. (Open daily 9am-4:30pm. ¥300.)

Northeast of Himeji proper, the **Engyō-ji temple complex** on Shosha-san affords glorious views of the sunset and the countryside. Dating from the 10th century, the extensive grounds surprise with their abundance of spectacular buildings and their woodsy setting. The main hall, dating from 970 but rebuilt in 1932, is dedicated to the Buddhist Goddess of Mercy and contains a dream-inspired altar of the goddess standing on a cherry tree. Unfortunately, it can only be viewed on January 18. If you miss the date, let the **Daiko-dō**, a 1000-year old temple hall with guardian statues, console you. It is possible to stay at Engyō-ji; one night with two meals will set you back ¥7350. To get to Shosha-san, take bus #6 or 8 from the station and ride to the last stop (30min., ¥260). From there, pay ¥500 one-way or ¥900 round-trip to take the cable car to the temple—the views are worth the price. (Cable car operates Apr. 1-Oct. 10 M-F 8:30am-6pm, Sa-Su 8:30am-7pm; Oct. 11-Nov. 30 M-F 8:30am-5pm, Sa-Su 8:30am-6pm; Dec. 1-Feb. 28 daily 8:30am-5pm; Mar. 1-Mar. 31 daily 8:30am-6pm. Temple ☎66-3327. Accommodations inquiries ☎66-3240; kaikan@shosha.or.jp. Temple open daily 9am-5pm. ¥300.)

原爆死没者慰霊碑
(広島平和都市記念碑)
Cenotaph for the A-bomb Victims
(Memorial Monument
for Hiroshima City of Peace)

WESTERN HONSHŪ

Hiroshima, of course, is one of the most iconic cities in the world. The site of the first atomic bomb explosion in history, it has become for many synonymous with the horrors of war and science's destructive side. Razed in an instant, Hiroshima has spent the past half century in a spectacular rise from the ashes. Today it's a modern, cultured metropolis, and a popular destination for travelers

In the shadows of better-known regions like Tōkyō and Kantō, the rest of Western Honshū, mostly industrial cities and rural towns, doesn't get too many visitors. Just because it doesn't scream for attention doesn't mean there's nothing there to see—in terms of beautiful scenery, rustic historic villages, and excellent art museums, Western Honshū holds its own. If glamour is your goal, don't bother stopping by, but if you're searching for the heartland of a nation, Western Honshū belongs on your itinerary.

HIGHLIGHTS OF WESTERN HONSHŪ

A CRY FOR PEACE. The incredibly moving sights of **Hiroshima Peace Park** (p. 487) are food for thought—and then some.

A DIVINE SUNSET. Watch the sun set over the "floating" gate off the hauntingly beautiful sacred island of **Miya-jima** (p. 494).

SANDS OF TIME. Slide down Japan's only sand dunes in **Tottori** (p. 524). Much more fun than you'd imagine—promise!

HIROSHIMA （広島） ☎082

Hiroshima can be rendered in Japanese in two ways. In *kanji*, it's written 広 (*hiro*) and 島 (*shima*), meaning "broad islands" (the city is built on a series of low, flat islands in the Ota-gawa Delta). This Hiroshima is one of bustling shopping arcades, a raging nightlife, and long walks along tree-lined boulevards. Hiroshima can also be written phonetically: ヒロシマ. This Hiroshima was born one August day in 1945. It is the nuclear Hiroshima, that incinerated bit of land where all was devastation, gray waste. It refers to the city whose vaporized citizens left only dark shadows on concrete backgrounds, and the hapless survivors on whose bodies the black rain—a mixture of radioactive dust, soot, debris and water—fell. Mercifully, the nightmare ended, the city was rebuilt and this Hiroshima has faded into the background—Broad Island Hiroshima is most anywhere you look.

But not everywhere. Hiroshima remembers, and there are hints of that other city everywhere—in the street names, the phoenix trees, the survivor buildings, and the art galleries. And, of course, when one enters Hiroshima Peace Park and tours the Peace Museum, nothing can dilute the impact of seeing the remnants of nuclear Hiroshima. It is quite possible to enjoy yourself thoroughly in the restaurants and gardens of Broad Island, but the relics of that other Hiroshima will leave you weak-kneed and trembling.

▐ TRANSPORTATION

Flights: All Japanese airlines fly to **Hiroshima Airport** (広島空港 ; ☎0848-86-8131; www.hij.airport.jp), 40km southwest of the city. Domestic flights to: **Okinawa** (2hr., 1 per day, ¥26,800); **Sapporo** (2hr., 2 per day, ¥35,400); **Sendai** (1½hr., 2 per day, ¥31,800); **Tōkyō** (1½hr., 1-2 per hr., ¥23,700). International flights to: **Harbin** (3½hr., Th and Sa, ¥76,500/round-trip ¥135,80); **Hong Kong** (2½hr., M-Tu and Th-Sa,

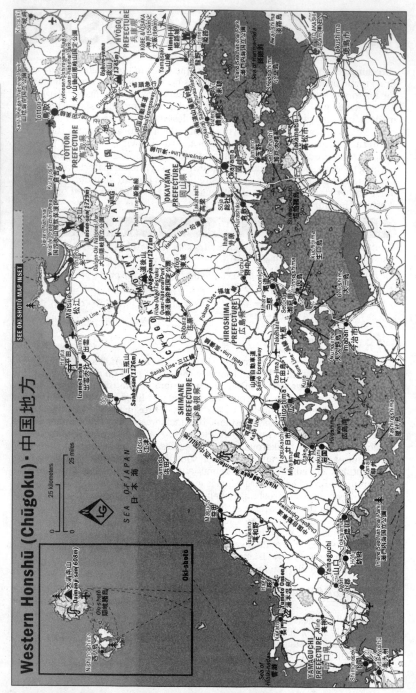

WESTERN HONSHŪ

Western Honshū (Chūgoku) · 中国地方

Oki-shotō

Okifushi
Nishino-shima
西ノ島

Daimanji-san (608m)
大満寺山

Oki-shotō
隠岐諸島

Sea of
Hibiki-nada
響灘

SEE OKI-SHOTŌ MAP INSET

N

0   25 kilometers
0   25 miles

SEA OF JAPAN
日本海

Kirosaki

Sanin Kaigan National Park
山陰海岸国立公園

Hyōnosen/Ushiroyama/Nagisan
Quasi-National Park
氷ノ山後山那岐山国定公園

TO KOBE & ŌSAKA
神戸 (55km)へ
大阪 (90km)へ

HYŌGO
PREFECTURE
兵庫県

Ushiro-yama
(1345m)

Himeji-jō
姫路城

Himeji
姫路

TO AKASHI
明石へ

TO NARUTO
鳴門へ

Awaji-shima
淡路島

Inland Sea (Seto-naikai) National Park
瀬戸内海国立公園

Tokushima
徳島市

Tottori
鳥取

TOTTORI
PREFECTURE
鳥取県

Chūzan Line 智頭急行

Chizu
智頭

CHŪGOKU MOUNTAIN RANGE · 中国山地

Daisen National
Wildlife Protection Area
大山隠岐国立公園
国設大山鳥獣保護区

Daisen (1729m)
大山

Daisen-san
Ōyama
大山

Daisen-Oki National Park
大山隠岐国立公園

Dōgo-yama (1271m)
道後山

Hiba-Dōgo-Tatsuyama
Quasi-National Park
比婆道後帝釈峡国定公園

Okayama
岡山市

OKAYAMA
PREFECTURE
岡山県

Yanai

Setouchi-shi
瀬戸内市

Takamatsu
高松市

Shōdo-shima
小豆島

Sea of Harima-nada

Bizen
備前

Takamatsu
高松市

Seto-Ōhashi
瀬戸大橋

Kurashiki
倉敷

Sōja
総社

Takahashi
高梁

Niimi
新見

Shinjō
新庄

Kurayoshi
倉吉

Matsue
松江

Izumo
出雲

Izumo-taisha
出雲大社

Hirata
平田

Kisuki Line · 木次線

Odo
大田

Sanbe-san (1126m)
三瓶山

Hakubi Line · 伯備線

Fuchū
府中

Ihara
井原

Kasaoka
笠岡

Fukuen Line · 福塩線

Fukuyama
福山

Onomichi
尾道

Mihara
三原

HIROSHIMA
PREFECTURE
広島県

Geibi Line · 芸備線

Miyoshi
三次

Shōbara
庄原

Sankō Line · 三江線

Gōtsu
江津

Hamada
浜田

Masuda
益田

Tsuwano
津和野

Yamato Onsen
山陰本線

Yamaguchi
山口

Hōfu
防府

YAMAGUCHI
PREFECTURE
山口県

Shimonoseki
下関

Kita-Kyūshū
北九州

Mine
美祢

Nagato
長門

Ogōri
小郡

Chūgoku Expressway
中国自動車道

Sanyō Expressway
山陽自動車道

Eta-jima
江田島

Etajima
江田島

Kure
呉

Kure Line · 呉線

Takehara
竹原

Tadanoumi
忠海

Hiroshima
広島市

Miyajima
宮島

Miyajima-guchi
宮島口

Hatsukaichi
廿日市

Ōtake
大竹

Iwakuni
岩国

Nishi-Chūgoku Mountains
西中国山地

Chūgoku Sanchi
Quasi-National Park
西中国山地国定公園

Hiroshima-wan
広島湾

Okunoshima
大久野島

Ikuchi-jima
生口島

Ōmi-shima
大三島

Imabari
今治市

Inland Sea (Seto-naikai) National Park
瀬戸内海国立公園

Kashirogashima
笠戸島

| ON THE WEB | Hiroshima City: www.city.hiroshima.jp/index-E.html |

¥91,000/¥144,300); **Honolulu** (11hr., Tu and Th, ¥165,600/¥308,500); **Seoul** (1¾hr., daily, ¥33,200/¥58100); **Shanghai** (1hr., M-Tu and Th-Sa, ¥57,400/¥103,000); **Singapore** (7hr.; M, W and F-Sa; ¥156,300/¥244,700). The **Shareo Center**, in the underground plaza downtown, has extensive information about flights to and from Hiroshima. (☎546-3111. Open daily 10am-9pm.)

Trains: Hiroshima is a major hub on the JR network. From **Hiroshima Station**, trains depart for (shinkansen listed first): **Fukuyama** (45min., ¥4300; 2hr., ¥1890); **Hakate** (2¼hr., ¥8190; 5hr., ¥4940); **Kōbe** (2½hr., ¥9230; 7hr., ¥5250); **Kyōto** (3hr., ¥10,280; 8¼hr., ¥6300); **Nagoya** (3¾hr., ¥12,920; 9½hr., ¥8190); **Okayama** (2hr., ¥7560; 5½hr., ¥4310); **Ōsaka** (2½hr., ¥9340; 7¼hr., ¥5460); **Shimonoseki** (1¼hr., ¥5670; 3hr., ¥3260); **Tōkyō** (4¼hr., ¥17,540; 11hr., ¥11,340).

Buses: Airport buses (¥1300) run from the rear of the train station to Hiroshima Airport every 15min. There are 2 major bus hubs in Hiroshima: at the back of the train station and downtown, on the 3rd fl. of Sogo department store. The first is in a **Swallow Travel** stand (☎263-4633; open daily 8:30am-6:30pm). To: **Nagoya** (8¾hr., 1 per day, ¥8400, round-trip ¥15,100); **Ōsaka** (5-9hr., 2 per day, ¥5000-5700/ ¥9000-11,000); **Takamatsu Shikoku** (3½hr., 2 per day, ¥4000/¥7000); **Tōkyō** (12hr., 1 per day, ¥12,060/¥22,000). The above buses also stop at the bus center at Sogo department store (☎225-3133). To: **Foucault** (4¼hr., 4-6 per day, ¥4000/ ¥7000); **Fukuyama** (2¾hr., 5 per day, ¥2300/¥4100); **Kōbe** (8hr., 2-3 per day, ¥5600/¥9000); **Kyōto** (10hr., 1 per day, ¥6620/¥11,720); **Okayama** (3hr., 5 per day, ¥2800/¥5000); **Ōsaka** (8¼hr., 2-3 per day, ¥5600/¥9000); **Shimonoseki** (3½hr., 6 per day, ¥3000/¥5400); **Tottori** (5hr., 5 per day, ¥4400) and **Yonago** (4hr., 5 per day, ¥3800).

Ferries: Hiroshima is an active port on the Inland Sea, and you can get here and away by ferry as well as the usual terrestrial alternatives. **Hiroshima Port** is the terminus for tram lines #1, 3, and 5 (¥150 from the city center or train station). The Ferry Terminal (☎251-5191) connects Hiroshima with: **Beppu** (3hr., 2 per day, ¥8500); **Imabari** (2hr., 5 per day, ¥4450); **Matsuyama** (by Super Jet Boat 1¼hr., 1 per hr. on the half hr., ¥5800; by Cruise Ferry 2¾hr., 10 per day, ¥2500).

Local Transportation: A swift and efficient **tramline** (☎231-5171) connects the city center with the principal port, the Miya-jima ferry, and other points in and around the city. Fares are ¥150 on the City Lines, ¥100 extra on the Hakushima extension, and variable on the Miyaguchi Line past Hirodennishi-Hiroshima Station. Buy commuter cards with a 10% discount at the tram terminals around the city (the easiest to find is in front of the station). 1-day **tram cards**, sold on board trams, grant unlimited tram travel, ¥600; there's a similar ¥840 card for trams and the ferry to Miya-jima, and **2-day cards** covering the tram network, Miya-jima ferry service, and the Miya-jima ropeway cable car, ¥2000. On sale at information desks, larger tram stations, and luxury hotels.

▟◢ ORIENTATION

Hiroshima has a compact downtown, and the main sights can easily be toured by foot. The train station sits on the mainland at the eastern edge of the downtown core. The massive bridge Ekimae-ohashi crosses the **Enkogawa river** and feeds into the Eki-mae-dōri traffic artery, which cuts southwest through town on its way to Funari ward. The east-west streets that intersect with **Ekimae-dōri** lead into the city center and the important parts of Hiroshima—Jonan-dōri, the northernmost, heads to Hiroshima Castle and Chūō Kōen; **Aioi-dōri** cuts through the commercial heart of the city to the northern

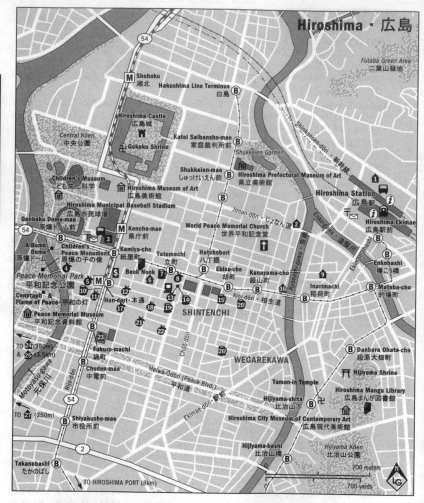

Hiroshima · 広島

end of Peace Memorial Park and the A-bomb Dome; and **Heiwa-Ōdōri** (Peace Boulevard) leads from **Hiyajima Kōen** in the east through a swank section of luxury hotels and office buildings over the Heiwa-ohashi bridge to the heart of Peace Memorial Park. The main shopping/eating district, **Hondōri**, is between Aioi-dōri and Heiwa-Ōdōri, as is the night-life neighborhood of Shitenchi. **Rijo-dōri** and **Chūō-dōri** are the main north-south streets in town. The free *Guide to Downtown Hiroshima* and *Welcome to Hiroshima* maps, available at the tourist centers, make navigating in the city quite simple.

🛈 PRACTICAL INFORMATION

Tourist Office: The main tourist information center is in the **Hiroshima City Tourist Association** building at the north end of Peace Park, across from the A-bomb Dome. It has

Hiroshima · 広島

🛏 ACCOMMODATIONS

ANA Hotel Hiroshima, **23**
Aster Plaza International
  Youth House, **27**
Hiroshima Kokusai
  Hotel, **6**
Hotel Granvia, **1**
Kikkawa Hotel Flex, **2**
Kyōbashi Ryokan, **9**
Minshuku Ikedaya, **24**
Regalo Hotel, **16**
World Friendship Center, **25**

🍴 FOOD

Andersen, **12**
E.1 Restaurant Cafe, **8**
Ikkyu, **17**
Ikkyu Chinese Dining, **11**
Namche Bazaar, **18**
Nanak Nanak, **21**
New York New York, **22**
OX, **5**
Poco a Poco, **4**
Shukran, **13**

🎶 NIGHTLIFE

Blue Grosso, **7**
Henry's Bar, **15**
Living Bar Aulea, **19**

🛍 SHOPPING

Sogo Department Store, **3**

Marble, **14**
Mingus, **20**
Sam's Bar, **10**
Twister's Cafe, **26**

extensive information on the city, scores of pamphlets and brochures, and a courteous, multilingual staff. (☎247-6738; www.tourism.city.hiroshima.jp. Open Oct.-Mar. 8:30am-5pm; Apr.-Jul. and Aug.16-Sept. 9:30am-6pm; Aug. 1-15 9:30am-7pm.) There are smaller **tourist information centers** by the south and *shinkansen* exits of the main train station. The English-speaking can assist with accommodations. (☎261-6738. Open daily 9am-5:30pm.) Another resource of some value is the **International Conference Center**, at the heart of the Peace Park near the museums, which has a foreign periodicals reading area and scads of local information and can arrange homestays. (☎247-9715. Open May-Nov. daily 9am-7pm, Dec.-Apr. daily 10am-6pm.)

Budget Travel: The **Travel Information Satellite** (☎261-8300; fax 262-0353), in Hiroshima station, is an oddly named full-on travel agency that arranges hotels, air travel, and package tours. (Open M-F 10am-7pm, Sa-Su 10am-6pm.)

Tours:

    Bus: Hiroshima Bus (☎506-2821; www.hirobus.co.jp) runs tours from the rear of the main train station. Daily trips leave at 9, 10am and 1pm., and last 3½-7½hr. ¥3500-6500

    Boat: River cruises (☎240-5955) depart from a landing by Aioi-bashi bridge near the peace park. Six per day; adults ¥1000, children ¥500.

Bank: Banks and ATMs are easily found in Hiroshima.

Luggage Storage: Hiroshima Station has a range of coin lockers from ¥300 per day.

English-Language Bookstore: Kinokuniya (☎225-3232) on the 7th floor of Sogo department store, has a broad selection of books in English. Open daily 10am-8pm. **Peek-A-Book Nook** (☎244-8145; www.outsider.co.jp/booknook), a comfortable bookstore/cafe, buys, sells, and trades used English-language books. Visitors can sit down and watch a video over a free cup of coffee. Open M-F noon-11pm, Sa 1-6pm.

Laundromat: The **Ocean Coin Laundry** (☎232-4582), west of Peace Park, can't guarantee your whites will be whiter, but they will come out white. ¥300 to wash, dryer ¥100 per 10min. Open daily 7am-midnight.

Emergency: Police ☎110. **Fire** or **ambulance** ☎119.

Police: In an emergency, find a police box (*kōban*) at which to file your report. You can also contact the main police station in Moto-machi at ☎221-0110.

Hospital: Hiroshima Municipal Hospital (Shimin Byōin; 市民病院) provides standard medical services. ☎221-2291.

Internet Access: Popeye Media Cafe, near the Hon-dōri arcade, has superfast connections and offers free drinks and reading material. First 30min. ¥230, ¥70 per 15min. thereafter. Open 24hr.

WESTERN HONSHŪ

Post Office: The **main post office** downtown has short business hours. (Mail M-F 9am-7pm, Sa-9am-3pm. Cash corner M-F 7am-11pm, Sa 9am-9pm, Su 9am-7pm.) **Higashi Post Office,** near the south exit of the train station, may be more convenient. (Open for mail M-Sa 9am-7pm, Su 9am-12:30pm. **ATM** open M-Sa 24hr., Su midnight-8pm.)

ACCOMMODATIONS

Hiroshima abounds with hotels in all shapes and sizes. The hostel has rock-bottom prices, but at the cost of convenience and a relatively early curfew. There are a few inexpensive—but good—alternatives, however, as well as business hotels from the very comfortable to the decadently luxurious. Downtown is the most convenient and charming place to spend the night, but if you have a heavy pack, station-side options are plentiful.

World Friendship Center (ワルドフレンドシップセンター; ☎503-3191; http:// ha7.seikyou.ne.jp/home/wfc/indexE.html) Take trams #2 or 3 to Koami-chō Stop. Get off, cross the rail bridge and turn left. Keep going until you cross Heiwa-Ōdōri as it comes over the river. Take the 4th little street to your right—there's a sign. A non-profit peace organization with 3 rooms available to travelers. Housed in a Japanese residence, the center has a homey feel. Started by a Quaker peace activist in the '60s, the center can, with at least 4 days advance notice, arrange meetings with A-bomb survivors and English-language tours of Peace Park. The operation is small and interest high, so call at least a week ahead. ¥3500 per person. ❷

Kyōbashi Ryokan (京橋旅館; ☎261-7608; fax 261-7668). Near the train station and Inari-machi Tram Stop. Combines convenience and comfort. Spacious *tatami* rooms, The friendly staff look after their guests. Check-in 4-11pm. Check-out 11am. Singles ¥3800, with bath ¥4300; doubles ¥7000/¥8000. ❷

Aster Plaza International Youth House (☎247-8700; fax 246-5808), in the Aster Plaza building a few blocks south of Peace Park, has Western-style accommodation at reasonable rates. Rooms with phone, private bath, and TV. Has an international public phone plus a fax and photocopy service. A favorite of student groups, it can fill up, so plan ahead. Curfew midnight. Check-in after 3pm. Check-out 10am. ¥3620 per person. ❷

Hiroshima Youth Hostel (HI) (広島ユースホステル ; ☎221-5343; www.ttec.jp/ ~hyh). Take any bus from station platform #11 up to Ushitashinmachi-chōme Bus Stop (¥240). Take the opposite cross street—look for the signs. The low price is the only happy result of its remote location at the northern fringes of the city, 600m uphill. Efficiently run, but a little motel-like with its outdoor pool. 10pm curfew. Apr.-June and Oct.-Nov. ¥2270; July-Sept. and Dec.-Mar. ¥2440. ❶

Kikkawa Hotel Flex (☎223-1000), 5min. from the station over Ekinshikoka-bashi and Kamiyanagi-bashi bridges. A new business hotel in a stylish building. Well tended, spacious rooms with micro-fridges and more sundry amenities. Doubles are solid value. Check-in after 3pm. Check-out 11am. Singles ¥6000; doubles ¥9000. AmEx/MC/V. ❸

Minshuku Ikedaya (☎231-3329). West of Peace Park. Provides spic-and-span *tatami* rooms close to the sights downtown. Fairly sedate neighborhood. Check-in after 3pm. Check-out 10am. Shared bath. Singles ¥4200; doubles ¥7350; triples ¥11,025. V. ❷

Hotel Granvia (☎262-1111; www.hgh.co.jp). Right on the *shinkansen* side of Hiroshima Station. Features a cavernous lobby, helpful staff, rapid elevators, and purple prose in its brochure sufficient for any guest short of J.P. Morgan. Check-in 1pm. Check-out noon. Singles ¥9300, doubles ¥16,500. Service charge and tax extra. Amex/MC/V. ❹

ANA Hotel Hiroshima (☎241-1111; www.anah-hiroshima.co.jp). A downtown alternative to the Granvia. Rooms come with leather-upholstered furniture, free broadband Internet access, and the bragging rights that come with staying at such a place. Check-in noon. Check-out 11am. Singles start at ¥9000; doubles at ¥18,500. Service charge and tax extra. AmEx/MC/Visa. ❹

Hiroshima Kokusai Hotel (広島国際ホテル ; ☎248-2323; fax 248-2622). In the city center, 30sec. from Hon-dōri. Atmospheric for a business hotel, with unusual architecture and a rococo interior; it evokes a fetching old-timey feel. According to the brochure "the bright placid rooms have enjoyed popularity from overseas guests." They're also comfortable. Check-in after 2pm. Check-out 11am. Singles start at ¥7000; doubles at ¥10,200. 10% service charge. AmEx/MC/V. ❹

Regalo Hotel (☎224-6300; fax 224-6301). Along the river front, just north of Inari-ohashi bridge. Musters a convincingly Italian feel. Guests relax in the house cafe or on the comfortable couches scattered around the lobby. Check-in from 3pm. Check-out 11am. Breakfast included. Singles ¥6500; doubles ¥9500. Amex/MC/V. ❸

◨ FOOD

Hiroshima has some of the best eating this side of Kōbe, with a slick mix of Japanese and international cuisines sure to please even the most discerning diners. Most restaurants price in the middle range, with lunch specials tending to be the best deal. The cheapest eating to be had is at the outlets of the **Sukiya** chain, conveniently open 24hr. Their *gyudon* bowls start at ¥280.

▨ **Poco a Poco** (☎247-6060). Near the river. Offers great views from its 2nd and 3rd floors. A tasty Italian restaurant, sometimes playing 50s movies downstairs while Italian and Brazilian Bossa Nova plays above. The ¥1300 pasta lunch and ¥1500 pasta dinner are art—tasty art. Open M-Sa 11am-11pm, Su 11am-10pm. ❸

Shukran (シュクラン ; ☎541-6447). Just off the Hon-dōri shopping arcade. Straight from the Chinese end of the Silk Road—dumplings, omlettes, and wontons all feature prominently. The 3rd. fl. location makes for excellent people-watching. Entrees ¥900-1200. Open daily 11:30am-2:30pm and 5-11pm. ❷

Ikkyu (一級 ; ☎541-6019). Just south of Hon-dōri, in the east end. A lively *kaitenzushi* joint where everything is ¥100. This popular place gets crowded most evenings—plan accordingly. Open M-F 11:30am-2:30pm and 5:30-10pm, Sa-Su 11:30am-10pm.❶

Namche Bazaar (☎246-1355). On an upper floor on a side street in Hon-machi. Take the uninspiring elevator to an indoor Zen garden, vast Mongol tent, and window-side terrace. The Buddha's watchful gaze encourages karmically proper mealtime behavior. Many vegetarian choices, all between ¥500 and ¥1200. Quite popular, so consider calling ahead. Open daily 11:30am-10pm. ❷

Nanak Nanak (ナーナック; ☎243-7900). The Hiroshima branch of the cheerfully over-the-top restaurant serves up spiced-to-order curries straight from India. Fights may break out over the Kashmir set: *lassi*, choice of curry, *naan* bread, and sides (¥1500). Open M-F 11am-3pm and 5:30-10pm, Sa-Su 11am-10pm. ❸

Ikkyu Chinese Dining (☎240-4419). Not to be confused with the sushi place nearby (see above), this Ikkyu has daily lunch specials that draw the salarymen in droves. Specials feature several courses, including *shumai*, soup, and other delights (¥800-1200). Open M-Sa 11:30am-2:30pm and 5-11pm, Su 11:30am-2:30pm and 5-10pm. ❷

Andersen, (☎247-2403). On the main drag of Hon-dōri. So authentically Scandinavian that the 6th fl. is the honorary consulate of Denmark. Eat deliciously fresh sandwiches (from ¥400) while sipping your coffee of choice. Open daily 8am-10pm. ❶

THE FIRST ATOMIC BOMB

It was 1945. The European war had closed with the fall of Berlin, but in Asia the war between the Anglo-Saxon powers and the Empire of Japan continued. For practical purposes, Japan was already defeated—its navy rusting at the bottom of the Pacific, its airforce reduced to teenagers and college students flying *kamikaze* missions into warships, and its cities bombed day and night. But the Atlantic Declaration of the Allies made it clear that the US and Britain were after unconditional surrender. Aware of their situation, Japanese leaders were nevertheless reluctant to accept these terms, fearing for the Emperor—a living god to the Japanese. Then in the spring, the Soviets entered the Pacific War, invading Japanese-held Manchuria and Korea, and moving towards China's big cities. The US wanted to defeat Japan without allowing the Soviets substantial gain in territory, so the Truman administration decided to use nuclear weapons.

The targets were carefully mulled over. Tōkyō was eliminated since it was already so devastated by conventional and incendiary bombing that an atom bomb attack would, in the words of an American general, merely "pile bodies on top of bodies and rubble on top of rubble." Kyōto was eliminated in the third round of selection because of its cultural significance. Three cities remained—Kokura, Nagasaki and Hiroshima. All were large urban areas with strategic significance, and none had suffered bomb attacks up to this point. Many reasons are put forth as possible motivations for choosing untouched cities—that such a target would demonstrate the full power of the bomb, terrifying the Japanese into submission (and cowing the Soviets); that the effects of the bombs could be compared through the amounts of damage each city suffered; that the attacks would hasten war's end, preventing the millions of casualties that would result from an invasion. Likely some combination of these factors weighed into the American decision, but the die was cast and the bombs were shipped to Saipan, the American base for the Japan campaign. Kokura's bomb sank en route. Hiroshima and Nagasaki were less fortunate.

On August 6th 1945, the Enola Gay, a US Air Force B-29 bomber, took off from Saipan air field towards Japan. A weather crew confirmed clear skies over Hiroshima, and the plane cruised over the city. When it reached the T-shaped Aioi-bashi Bridge, it released its payload, the uranium bomb known as "Little Boy." As it fell, the change in air pressure detonated the bomb, triggering an atomic explosion above the city center.

An atomic bomb explodes in three waves. First, the most intense radiation flashes outwards in a heat blast. Flammable materials are incinerated, water scalds and boils, and human flesh burns, nearly instantaneously. This is followed by the explosive force—within one second, Little Boy exploded with the force of 15,000 tons of dynamite, killing 80,000 people and destroying 70,000 buildings. The fires burned whatever suburbs were left around the city. However, it is the third phase of a atomic explosion that makes it substantially different from a typical bomb. The whole city was covered in radioactive particles, concentrated so intensely that it penetrated concrete walls and undermined the foundations of stone buildings. The day of the bombing, the radioactive soot and dust particles in the atmosphere caused a torrent of scalding black rain. Though the radiation intensity dropped after the first 24 hours, it remained at lethal levels for weeks. A year after the bombing, another 60,000 people had died of wounds, burns, and radiation sickness. The death toll is currently estimated at 200,000.

"Hiroshima" evokes a special horror, but its terrible fate was hardly atypical. Before the blast, it was one of the few cities not leveled by firebombing. Tōkyō was so ravaged that in one night 200,000 people burned to death. The entire Pacific War was a bloodbath. In Asia, the Japanese committed many atrocities—Koreans were enslaved for the war effort, the women forced into brothels for the use of Japanese soldiers and the men made to work in mines and factories, many in Hiroshima. In China, civilian victims of the Japanese number in the millions, including 300,000 in the Rape of Nanking.

Prior to WWII, Hiroshima was a collection of stone and plaster Edo-era shops and houses, interspersed with a few more modern structure. The wooden buildings were destroyed by the heat, but buildings with reinforced concrete construction, though gutted, remained standing—the most notable example is the A-bomb dome. A few other structures survived the blast—the tourist information center in Peace Park, the Andersen bakery and shop, and part of Fukuyama department store contain pre-bomb elements. Some survivor buildings have stories—the Bank of Japan in the southern part of downtown lost all its workers but was in operation two days later. In the Fukuromachi Elementary School, survivors of the attack wrote still-preserved notes to their classmates and teachers on the walls. (☎247-9241. Open daily 9am-5pm. Free).

- Jakub Wrzesniewski

E.1 Restaurant Cafe (☎246-6630). Just off Hon-dōri. Delicious European cuisine in a chic, minimalist setting. The basement has a posh bar good for chilling and watching beautiful people. Lunch sets are a handy deal at ¥1500. Open daily 11am-midnight. ❸

OX (☎249-9388). At the river end of the Hon-dōri area. Serves up curries to taste in an elegant atmosphere. Attention is paid to every detail—the rice is steamed with cranberries, and comes with dried coconut as a garnish. 3-course lunch meal with dessert ¥1500. Open daily 11:30am-2:30pm and 5-10pm. ❸

New York New York (ニューヨークニューヨーク ; ☎541-7000). Just off Hon-dōri Arcade, near the Parco building. A stylish eatery channeling bits of Manhattan and Greenwich Village. The place to go for inexpensive, tasty food (including cheeseburgers; lunches ¥800-¥1200) or, after dark, for a casual drink. Movie scenes and underground animation are projected onto a screen at the rear of the main area. Open Su-Th 11:30am-midnight, F-Sa 11:30am-2am. ❷

⊙ SIGHTS

The sights of Hiroshima, of course, revolve primarily around the atomic catastrophe that befell the city in the final days of WWII. Every visitor must see the Peace Park and the Atomic Dome and tour the Peace Memorial Museum—these are sites of importance to everyone with even a passing interest in human history. However, visitors should be prepared for a moving and somber experience; even on a warm and sunny day, Hiroshima exacts an emotional toll, and the feeling of desolation can last well into the evening.

Those spending more time in Hiroshima will also get to experience a different, side. Few appreciate how swiftly and how elegantly the city was rebuilt. Modern Hiroshima has a few excellent museums, broad green boulevards perfect for strolling, and a couple of charming traditional gardens in which to while away a much lighter summertime afternoon.

THE PEACE PARK AND AROUND

The northern section of the central island, as well as the river banks east of it, have been converted into a memorial park for the atom bomb victims. The Peace Park is a pleasant green place, cheerful in summer, but it is made somber by the dozens of memorial statues that dot the area. Highlights are listed in detail below.

HIROSHIMA PEACE MEMORIAL MUSEUM. Stretching across the park center, the museum records for posterity the story of the world's first atomic attack. The films *Hiroshima: A Mother's Prayer* and *Hiroshima and Nagasaki*, screened five times daily (4 per day Jan.-Mar.), introduce visitors to the story of Hiroshima. The museum itself houses exhibits on Hiroshima before the bombing, the Manhattan Project and the invention of nuclear weapons, WWII in Asia, and Hiroshima's place in the Japanese war as well as the main collection of artifacts and information about the A-bomb attack and its aftermath. Artifacts from the blast site have been collected to illustrate the effects of the bombing on even the most solid objects, and photographs—some very graphic—show the horrendous damage the weapon inflicted on human beings. The exit corridor contains disturbing drawings of the attack by those who lived through it, as well as photographs and messages from world leaders on their visits to the museum. (☎542-7941; www.pcf.city.hiroshima.jp. Open Apr.-July 9am-6pm, Aug. 1-Aug.15 8:30am-7pm, Aug. 16-Nov. 8:30am-6pm, Dec.-Mar. 8am-5pm. ¥50.)

PHOENIX TREES. After the attack and the rain of black, radioactive ooze that followed, most Hiroshimans despaired of their city's soil ever sustaining life again. However, nature proved more resilient than expected, and within weeks buds appeared on the blasted trees and grasses began to grow in the open areas. Trees within 200m of ground zero survived, and they have become symbol of the reconstruction of Hiroshima. Dubbed "phoenix trees," these carefully tended veterans stand throughout the city, the most prominent concentrations being along Peace Boulevard, around the edges of Peace Memorial Park, and around Hiroshima-jō.

▨STATUE OF THE MOTHER AND CHILD IN THE STORM. The title tells the story—a mother, huddled, running attempts to shield her child with her own body in a tableau of the moment before their incineration. The image mirrors that of many other disaster monuments, and is curiously moving in its universalism. *(To the south of the Peace Memorial Museum.)*

CENOTAPH FOR THE A-BOMB VICTIMS. The centerpiece of the monument, based on traditional Japanese funerary designs, the stone chest rests in the middle of a flat pool and contains the names of all the known Japanese victims, a roll of some 100,000 people. Behind the Cenotaph is the **Flame of Peace,** a torch above the water meant to burn so long as atomic weapons threaten the world. Once the last bomb is destroyed, the flame is to be extinguished. *(To the north of the museum, just beyond the recreation of Aioi-bashi.)*

CHILDREN'S PEACE MONUMENT. The monument sits inside a fountain, where a little girl rendered in bronze holds aloft an oversized *origami* crane. The monument was inspired by the story of Sadako Sasaki, a Hiroshima 12-year old who developed leukemia from the background radiation caused by the bomb. Her story is known in the outside world through Eleanor Coerr's children's book *Sadako and the Thousand Paper Cranes*—Sadako believed that if she folded 1000 paper cranes, a traditional Japanese symbol of health and recovery, she would beat the leukemia. Despite her best efforts, she succumbed to the illness before reaching that mark, but her friends continued to fold cranes in her memory. Behind the monument, in a series of plexi-glass cases, those paper cranes, now numbering several thousand and growing, are on display. Submissions are still being accepted—if you are interested in folding cranes, inquire at the tourist info center. *(Just across the footpath from the Flame of Peace.)*

A-BOMB DOME. Originally the Industrial Promotion Hall, the A-bomb Dome was the ferro-concrete building closest to the hypocenter of the nuclear blast and its ruins, with the fragile frame of the dome intact, symbolize the destruction of the city. The ruins have been left largely as they were after the blast. As a memento of the first destruction of a city by nuclear weapons, the dome was designated a UNESCO World Heritage site in 1996. It has become the most recognizable symbol of Hiroshima, and school children often leave brightly colored *origami* cranes by its north face. *(Across the footbridge from the Children's Peace Monument.)*

MONUMENT IN MEMORY OF THE KOREAN VICTIMS OF THE A-BOMB. Korea had fallen under Japanese domination in 1905, and as the Japanese war effort faltered, and Japanese men were needed for the armed forces, ship loads of Korean men were taken from their homes on the peninsula to work in Japanese war industries. Hiroshima had significant military industries and it is estimated that at the time of the A-bomb attack some 200,000 Koreans were residing in Hiroshima—collaborators, translators, comfort women, but mostly industrial slaves. It is estimated that 10%—20,000 people—were killed in the attack or died of resulting injuries and radiation poisoning. Exact numbers are sketchy since little attention was paid to the Korean victims in any of the prayers or services following the explosion. They are not included in the Cenotaph in the center of the park. No monument existed to those thousands of souls until 1973, when the Hiroshima's Korean community, at its own expense, commissioned this monument, with a trilingual obelisk explaining the story. *(Opposite the Flame of Peace, across the river.)*

BEYOND THE PARK

NORTH OF PEACE PARK. Immediately north of Peace Memorial Park, the **Hiroshima Municipal Baseball Stadium** (Go Carp!) marks the southern end of Chūō Kōen (Central Park), an expanse of memorial-free greenery containing a number of municipal and city institutions. *(Info line ☎ 223-2141. Tickets start at ¥1500.)* The **Children's Museum,** home of the Laboratory of Doctor Scitech and a sizeable planetarium, is at the center of the park. *(☎ 222-5346. Open Tu-Su 9am-5pm. General exhibits free; planetarium shows ¥440, children ¥170.)* Across Jodan-dōri, Yuka garden is a slightly more grown-up attraction—the garden, modelled on traditional Chinese gardens and only recently completed, offers an island of serenity in the middle of the big city. *(Open Apr.-Sept. daily 7am-6pm; Oct.-March daily 9am-6pm. Free.)* Slightly farther east along Jodan-dōri, across the street from Hiroshima-jō, stands the sizeable **Hiroshima Museum of Art.** It specializes in late 19th and early 20th century French painting, including works by Matisse, Renoir, and Monet, as well as several by Picasso and Van Gogh. The museum also owns a number of Western-style works by Japanese artists. While the elegant, marble-accented museum is cool and airy on a hot summer day, the steep admission cost makes it an iffy value. *(☎ 223-2530. www.mighty.co.jp/museum. Open daily 9am-5pm. ¥1000, students ¥500.)*

HIROSHIMA PREFECTURAL MUSEUM OF ART. Just north of Sakae-bashi bridge on the central island, the museum and surrounding Shukkien Garden are the most interesting and attractive of the non-A-bomb related sights of Hiroshima. Set in a striking modern building, it contains a permanent exhibition of local and Hiroshima-related art pieces as well as hosting special exhibitions from around the world. One of its most notable pieces is Salvador Dali's *Dreams of Venus.* *(☎ 221-6246; www1.hpam-unet.ocn.ne.jp. Open Tu-F and Su 9am-5pm, Sa 9am-7pm. ¥500, students ¥300. Additional charge for special exhibitions.)* **Shukkein Garden,** originally built in the early 17th century for the local *daimyō* Asano Nagakira, contains a miniaturized version of the scenery around Xihu in Hangzhou province, China. With a number of bridges crisscrossing its central ponds, and a variety of different green areas—from rice fields, to stands of conifers, to the plum orchard—it's very pleasant and charming. *(☎ 221-3620. Open Apr.-Sept. 9am-6pm. Oct.-Mar. 9am-5pm. ¥250, students ¥120. A combined ticket for the museum and garden can be purchased at the ticket counter in the museum for ¥600.)*

WORLD PEACE MEMORIAL CHURCH. Hiroshima was one of the centers of Portuguese Jesuit evangelism in the 16th century, and a small Catholic community has survived since those times. The original Hiroshima Cathedral survived the atomic blast, but its foundation was compromised by irradiation and the remains were leveled. Father Hugo Lassalle, the parish priest and an A-bomb survivor, committed himself to the reconstruction effort and the modern cathedral exists mainly due to his tireless fund raising. Built in 1953, it suffers a little from the architectural brutalism then fashionable, but its dedication to world peace and unique history make a visit a memorable and moving experience. *(4-42, Naka-ku. ☎ 730-0016; www.noborichō-catholic.com. English Mass held every Sun. at 8am.)*

HIROSHIMA-JŌ. The original castle was incinerated by the A- bomb, but this reinforced concrete reconstruction faithfully reproduces the original. The castle is set in a park-like grounds which also holds the picturesque Gokoku Shrine. The compound is surrounded by a moat, originally formed by diverting river water through culverts and canals. The castle is relatively impressive; inside is a museum where the artifact labels and even the animatronics are bilingual. *(☎ 221-7512; fax 221-7519. Open daily Apr.-Sept. 9am-5:30pm; Oct.-Mar. 9am-4:30pm. ¥320.)*

HIJIYAMA HILL AREA. On the southeast island of Hiroshima, south of the station and east of downtown, Hijiyama Hill has been made the centerpiece of a park. It includes a number of sights, but most are fairly minor. If you haven't already seen some of the grander shrines and temples in Japan, the two inside the park, **Hijiyama Shrine** and the temple **Tamon-in**, may be worth a look. Otherwise, the main attraction is the **Hiroshima City Museum of Contemporary Art.** Devoted to post-war, particularly avant-garde, art, most of the collection dates from the '60s or onwards. The collection is extensive, including a number of chrome sculptures arranged on the museum grounds and two series of paintings—one by Japanese, the other by foreigners—commissioned on the theme "Hiroshima." In addition to the permanent collection, special exhibitions, including the annual Hiroshima Art Competition, cycle through the museum. (☎264-1121. www.hcmca.cf.city.hiroshima.jp. Open Tu-Su 10am-5pm. ¥500, students ¥300. Additional fee for special exhibitions.) Behind the museum is the **Hiroshima Manga Library,** which houses thousands of comic books. It may surprise foreigners that the clientele is truly universal. In addition to boys and young men, families, single females, and even older people frequent the library. Alas, the collection is almost entirely in Japanese. (☎261-0330; www.mighty.ne.jp/hiroshima.city.lib. Open Tu-F 9am-7pm, Sa-Su 9am-5pm.)

♫ ▣ ENTERTAINMENT AND NIGHTLIFE

Hiroshima is a lively city and offers any number of entertainment options. The downtown brims with cinemas, playing both Asian films and a steady stream of Hollywood blockbusters. There's no shortage of places for a good time out—it's estimated that Hiroshima has 4000+ drinking establishments. A good resource to help you get the options straight is the website www.gethiroshima.com/en.

A few general rules of thumb to keep in mind when headed out for the evening—the cafes and bars in Hon-dōri tend to be mellow, hip, and cool places to get a drink. The main nightlife areas are slightly east of Hon-dōri—Shintenchi to the north, and Nagarekawa farther south. Generally, the farther south, the sketchier the scene. The 10th floor **Quattro Club,** in Hon-dōri, is a major venue for out of town acts, with live shows in various styles every weekend. Expect to pay upwards of ¥2500. Call their info line at ☎249-8334 for listings.

Living Bar Aulea (☎545-8600), in the 2nd fl. of the ASD bldg. in Hon-dōri, is a chic hangout for artsy types. The patio, hanging over a busy pedestrian street, makes a prime people-watching spot. Mellow music and light sets a comfortable mood. Food starts at ¥500, beer ¥500, and drinks ¥700. Open M-Sa 6pm-3am, Su 6pm-1am.

Sam's Bar (☎241-0047), on the 2nd fl. of an office building on Rijo-dōri downtown is rather difficult to miss—just look for the Texan flag and neon Budweiser signs. This cheerful bit of Americana has undeniable charm, with a honky-tonk-cum-Irish-pub aesthetic and a vibe straight from Cheers. The sign outside lists prices, but only for Bud—¥500 by the glass and ¥800 by the mug. Open M-Sa 6pm-12:30am.

Mingus (☎244-6060), along the main drag in Shintenchi, is a jazz bar owned and run by a bassist who occasionally plays his own sets. It's decidedly upscale—elegant decor, first-class music, finely made drinks. Costs reflect this; cover charges (including table charge and drink) can reach ¥4000. Open M-Sa 7pm-12:30am.

Blue Grosso (☎504-4333), on the 3rd fl. along a side street in Hon-dōri, serves up drinks with European style in a space that blends together Tuscan wine cellar with Alpine forest. Drinks from ¥600. Open daily 5:30pm-3am.

Twister's Cafe (☎243-0466), on the 3rd fl. of a club in Nagarekawa, is a raucous dance club catering to those who want to rage on until the dawning of the light. ¥1000 cover charge includes 1 drink. Open F-Sa from 6pm to 6am and Su-Th 6pm-4am.

Marble (☎545-7175), in Hon-dōri just above Shukran restaurant. A trendy, modernist watering hole, all chrome and concrete. The space is small, making for a cozy, intimate environment. Drinks start at ¥600. Open daily 11am-2am.

Henry's Bar (☎541-1051), in the basement of the Apple 2 building, has an old-fashioned, fedora-and-suspenders feel. 15% discount for those willing to sit at the bar—otherwise, drinks clock in at ¥800. Happy hour 7-9pm features ¥500 drinks. Open M-Th 7pm-3am, F-Sa 7pm-4am, Su 7pm-2am.

WESTERN HONSHŪ

ONOMICHI (尾道)　　　　☎0848

With its dilapidated shopping arcades and mini-mall style terminal-side development, Onomichi looks at first glance like a bland little port town. Away from the port, however, hugging the hillside that forms the towns northern edge, is a charm-

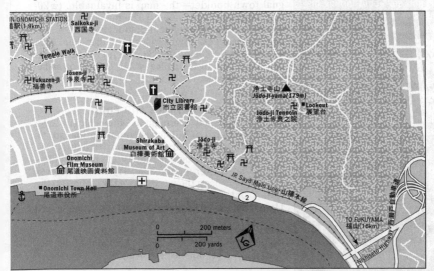

THE LOCAL LEGEND

MISSING MOMMY

The story of Kosan-ji is intimately linked to that of its founder, arms magnate and doting son Kanemoto Kozo. After making a fortune manufacturing steel tubes for the Imperial Army during the various Asian wars of the early 20th century, he built his mother a sumptuous country ▮▮ n their hometown of Set-oda. When she died, he was so struck by grief that he built a temple in her honor, buying a priesthood out of Kyōto and appropriating the name of a minor-league temple in northern Japan. Perhaps seeing the writing on the wall (it was 1936), he left arms manufacturing for the equa ▮ crative field of religious tourism. He took his priesthood seriously, growing out his hair and changing his name to Kosanji Kozo, and set about turning his mother's memorial temple into a religious tourist attraction.

In designing the temple, originality was not a priority–the temple buildings are primarily miniaturized versions of the most f▮ous bits of temple architecture i▮pan, from Kyōto, Nikkō, and Byodō-in. To increase the allure of the temple, aviaries of exotic birds were added, and a museum was tacked on. The resulting attraction draws crowds from all over Japan, raking in a steady income that, because of its religious function, can't b▮ axed by the government. Arms may be a good place to start, but the smart money is in religion.

ing precinct of temples, temples, and more temples. The city is famous for its temple walk, a day-long tour of these Buddhist sanctuaries. The full course is a bit of an endurance test—the less than pious may want to skip out some of the less interesting houses of worship and visit a few non-religious sights instead.

ON THE WEB www.city.onomichi.hiroshima.jp

TRANSPORTATION. Onomichi is served by two train stations—**Onomichi Station,** right at the center of town, next to the ferry terminal, and **Shin-Onomichi Station,** about 25min. out of town. It makes little sense to arrive at Shin-Onomichi; if you're traveling by *shinkansen*, it is more convenient to switch either at Mihara or Fukuyama and avoid the trouble of finding a bus into town. From Onomichi station, regular **trains** run to Fukuyama (38min., ¥400); Hiroshima (1½hr., ¥1450); Mihara (25min., ¥230); Okayama (1¼hr., ¥1280). Onomichi also serves as the gateway to Ikuchi-shima in the Inland Sea. **Buses** make the 1hr. run from platform #7 in front of Onomichi Station and cost ¥1300 one-way. **Passenger ferries,** which depart from the terminal across the street from Onomichi Station, are a quicker and cheaper way of making the trip (40min., ¥690).

PRACTICAL INFORMATION. The tourist information center is in the Teatro Shell building to the right of the station exit. Be sure to pick up the bilingual town booklet—the map is invaluable. (☎20-0005. Open daily 9am-6pm.) The main **post office** is one block east of Onomichi Station, and offers mail and **ATM** services. (Mail services M-F 9am-7pm. ATM available M-F 8:45am-9pm, Sa 9am-7pm.) In an emergency, call ☎110 for **police,** ☎119 for **fire** or **ambulance. Postal code:** 722.

ACCOMMODATIONS AND FOOD. There is little reason to stay overnight in Onomichi. The town suffers a dearth of budget accommodation, so it's wisest to make a day-trip from Hiroshima or Okayama. The cheapest places are the business hotels that cluster station-side. Try **Dai-Ichi Hotel ❸** (大一ホテル), on the west side of the station on the waterfront. (☎23-4567. Check-in 3pm. Check-out 11am. Singles ¥5500; doubles ¥10,000.) Ultra-modern **Green Hill Hotel Onomichi ❸,** behind the ferry terminal, is the town's plushest hotels. (☎24-0100; www.hotwire.co.jp/gho. Check-in 2pm. Check-out 11am. Singles from ¥7500; doubles ¥13,000.)

For a town its size, Onomichi has surprisingly good food options. **Bistro Vin Bière ❷**, on the second floor of the strip mall across from the ferry terminal, is a good place for Western food. Tasty French and Italian dishes cost ¥800-1800, and the view of the sea from the patio makes a pleasant backdrop. (☎22-5001. Open daily 11:30am-3pm and 5-10:30pm.) Next to the bottom station of the Senkōji ropeway, **Common ❷** is a convenient stop on the temple walk. This chic-but-comfortable dessert cafe specializes in waffles, Belgian and otherwise, topped with any combination of treats. Prices hover ¥700-1000. (☎37-2905. Open M and W-Su 9am-7pm.) For Japanese food, try the popular **Shuka-en ❶** (朱華園), a *rāmen* restaurant across the main street from the cable car station that always draws crowds seeking its hearty soups. Bowls start at ¥500. (☎37-2077. Open M-W and F-Su 11am-8pm.)

◪ **SIGHTS.** The best place to start a tour of Onomichi is Nagaeguchi Bus Stop, at the base of the Senkoji ropeway. Walking takes 20min.; a ¥140 bus ride from the station takes 5min. Take the ropeway up to **Senkō-ji Kōen** (千光寺公園), which in spring becomes a wonderland of flowers and cherry blossoms. Out of season, gorgeous views of the Inland Sea make an acceptable consolation prize. (☎22-4900. Ropeway daily 9am-5pm, ¥280, round-trip ¥440.) Inside its namesake park, **Senkō-ji** (千光寺) looms over the city from its hillside perch. Legend sets the founding of the temple at 806, and the forested surrounds add a touch of the primeval to any visit. Also in the park is the **Onomichi Path of Literature** (文学小路), a tribute to the various authors and poets who made Onomichi their home. The path wends down the hill and makes a pleasant stroll past stones inscribed with their works. It ends at the base of the hill with the **Nakamura Kenkichi Residence** (中村憲吉家) and the **Commemorative Library of Literature.** While the architecture is appealing, the language barrier limits its appeal. The steps down from the literary sights end at **Tennei-ji** (天寧寺), whose three-storied pagoda is worth a look. The original was five stories high, but when it was reconstructed in 1692 after a fire, there weren't enough funds to bring it back to full height. Farther along the trail (follow the markers) you'll come across medieval **Fukuzen-ji** (福善寺). The temple building is unexceptional, but the gate, carved with dragons and birds, is quite marvelous.

Twenty meters on, the trail fronts a second, smaller hill, home to several temples. The most important is **Saikoku-ji** (西國寺), one of the region's largest Shingon temples. Although it has a picturesque three-storied pagoda, the real draw is the **Niōmon gate** (仁王門). In addition to the traditional two Deva kings flanking the entry way, there are giant wooden sandals hanging from it, which symbolize that this is a traveler's temple—praying here will ensure a good journey.

Jōdo-ji (浄土寺) anchors the far end of our truncated temple walk. The temple has a particularly illustrious history. Said to have been founded by Prince Shōtoku, the first imperial benefactor of Buddhism in Japan, it was later patronized by the Ashikaga shōgun, and its grounds contain a tea house brought in from one of Toyotomi Hideyoshi's castles. Apart from its historical pedigree, the temple attracts with bright colors and fantastical embellishments. The gold shining off the two-storied pagoda is a particularly impressive sight.

IKUCHI-JIMA (生口島)　　　　　　　☎08452

One of the most fascinating islands in the Inland Sea, Ikuchi-jima is well worth a side trip. The recession hit the region quite hard, and today the main city, Setoda, is a bit of a ghost town. The hotels have a deserted feel, and the streets are empty even by day. The island has its share of natural beauty—attractive beaches, and hills are lined with citrus groves—but the real draw is the cultural sights.

Entry to the main sight, **Kōsan-ji,** is through Chūmon gate, past several disgruntled peacocks. The extravagance begins at the 5-Tiered Pagoda, whose copper-plated roofs were Kōzō's innovation. Beyond lies **Kōyōmon gate,** which takes Buddhist art into a carnivalesque realm. The designs, shape, and scale are taken from a gate in Kyōto, but the color scheme is unique. Inside is a 10m statue of the Goddess of Mercy, based on the central sculpture of Nara's Hōryū-ji. Then there's the **Senbutsudō** (Cave of a Thousand Buddhas), a tunnel that leads past murals of Buddhist heavens and hells. The passage, which sometimes looks like a cavern and often like a bunker, is lined with the promised 1000 Buddhas. (Open daily 9am-5pm. ¥1000 includes admission to Colle Della Speranza and the Art Museum.)

Apart from the temple, the grounds contain the **Colle Della Speranza,** an abstract sculpture park on a hill overlooking the temple and the island below. The entire hilltop is sheathed in white marble, a dazzling sight on sunny days. The hill also contains **Caffé Cuore ❸,** a chic cafe with great views and tasty pizza (¥1200). The same ticket gets you into **Kōsanji Art Museum,** across from the temple entrance. After the giddy excess of the temple and the Colle, the museum may seem a bit dry. In a quiet corner (follow the signs and you'll find it) is **Chōseikaku,** the estate Kōzō built for his mother. The interior is lavishly decorated, with ceiling murals in two rooms, and there's a large Zen garden. Admission is ¥300 extra. The complex is several blocks away from the ferry terminal, down a shop-lined street. (☎ 7-0800. www.kousanji.or.jp. Open daily 9am-5pm. ¥1000.)

The Ikuo Hirayama Museum of Art is behind the art museum. Hirayama was in Hiroshima as a junior high school student when the A-bomb was dropped, and suffered years of radiation sickness as a result. The bombing inspired him to take up art to spread a message of peace. He has crossed the silk road several times, following the footsteps of early Buddhist missionaries. Much of his work, on display here, is inspired by the monuments of ancient civilizations he has visited in Asia and the Middle East. (☎ 7-3800. Open daily 9am-5pm. ¥600, students ¥400.)

The island **info center** in front of the Ikuo Hirayama Museum hands out literature and rents **bikes.** (☎ 7-0051. Open daily 9am-5pm. Bikes ¥500 per day) The **post office,** near Boogie Kitchen, has an **international ATM.** (Open for mail M-F 9am-5pm; for cash service M-F 8:45am-6pm, Sa 9am-5pm, Su 9am-1:30pm.) In an emergency, call ☎ 110 for **police,** ☎ 119 for **fire** or **ambulance.**

If you don't mind seclusion, it is possible to stay over in Setoda. The recession has seen the closure of all the business hotels, but the main hostel, the **Setoda Youth Hostel (HI) ❶,** has survived. To reach it from Kōsan-ji, head towards the dock. Take the first left, then the second right. On this street are signs leading the rest of the way—the hostel is a brightly painted block on a hillside, behind an orchard. The friendly owner speaks English, and will happily point out areas of interest. (☎ 7-0224. Check-in 3pm. Check-out 10am. ¥2700, nonmembers ¥3700. **Boogie Kitchen ❶,** at the base of the hill, is a pleasant backpacker hangout. The food is organic and hearty, and relatively inexpensive at ¥500-900. (☎ 7-2723. Open daily 11am-2pm and 5-8pm.)

MIYA-JIMA (宮島) ☎ 082

ON THE WEB	Miya-jima: www.miyajima.or.jp

Miya-jima is not just an island, nor just a tourist attraction—it is in fact a god. This explains Itsukushima-jinja, the Shintō shrine that serves as the islands main draw— since the island itself is the object of worship, the shrine floats on a set of piers offshore. Before the Meiji Restoration, commoners, whose footsteps would profane the island, were prohibited from landing; instead, they arrived at the shrine by boat, cruising through the floating *torii*.

How times have changed. Now, ferries ship thousands of tourists onto the island, where they pack the shrine and village, rubber-necking the main sights or jamming the nature trails around Misen-san, the principal hill and park of the island. While the island and its attractions are certainly impressive, they are best enjoyed at evening or early morning, when you are jostled by a minimum of daytrippers. In the right conditions, Miya-jima lives up to its reputation as one of the three best views in Japan—with the Otorii gate standing out among gently lapping waves, and the sun setting over Mise-san, it's unforgettable. If you arrive mid-afternoon, expect the crowds and the mud to be as memorable as the sights.

TRANSPORTATION AND PRACTICAL INFORMATION. There are a number of ways to get to Miya-jima. The simplest and cheapest, but not the fastest, is to take the #2 **tram** from anywhere in Hiroshima to Miyajima-gūchi Terminal (70min., ¥270 one way) and then cross to the island on one of the ferry lines (10min., constant departure, ¥170). One of the lines is operated by Japan Railways, so rail-pass holders can use the service for free. If you're also touring Hiroshima, the **trip cards** offered by the tram service might be a good idea (p. 479). A faster alternative is to take the **train** on the JR Sanyō Line from Hiroshima Station to Miyajima-gūchi Station, and from there take the **ferry** (30min., ¥400). The train, though faster, runs less frequently than the tram. Even faster is the **Miyajima Hydrofoil** from Hiroshima port, but even costlier as well—the 20min. ride costs ¥1460. Call ☎251-5191 for more information.

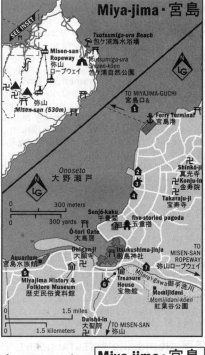

Miya-jima・宮島

Miya-jima・宮島

⛺ ACCOMMODATIONS
Hotel Kamefuku, **2**
Iwaso Ryokan, **7**
Kinsuikan, **4**
Kokuminshukusha, **5**
Hiroshima Miyajima-guchi
 Youth Hostel, **1**

🍎 FOOD
Fukuya, **3**   Tenshin, **6**

At the ferry terminal, an info booth hands out pamphlets and brochures. Most are in Japanese, but there's an English-language map. (☎944-2011; www.hiroshima-cdas.or.jp/miyajima. Open daily 8:30am-7pm.) At the terminal, you can rent **bikes**. (☎944-0035. ¥320 for 2hr., ¥1050 all day. Open daily 8am-6pm.)

ACCOMMODATIONS. The cheapest option is to **camp** at the northern end of the island. Simple sites are available in a park setting. (☎944-2903. ¥300 per person.) On Miya-jima proper, there are two types of accommodation available—very expensive ryokan, or very, VERY expensive ryokan. The closest budget option is on the mainland, **Hiroshima Miyajima-gūchi Youth Hostel ❷,** is conveniently close to the ferry terminal. The lodging is hostel-utilitarian, with spartan but comfortable dorms. From the tram terminal, head away from the water and turn left at the post office. From the train station, head toward the water and turn right at the post office. In either case, the hostel is the tall brick building, clearly marked. (☎956-1444. www.alles.or.jp/~mygmcyh. Breakfast ¥400. Dinner ¥700. Members ¥2600, nonmembers ¥3600.) The least expensive lodging on the island is the **Kokumin-shukusha Miya-jima Morinoyado ❷**, but it frequently fills up with people eager to take advantage of its reasonable prices. (☎944-0430; fax 944-2248. Breakfast ¥1000. Dinner ¥2000 and up. ¥4800 per person for Japanese or Western-style rooms.) For those looking to splurge, there are any number of choices. **Hotel Kamefuku ❹** is a large, elaborate modern hotel. Service is exquisite, and the rooms are lush and well-tended. The public baths are gorgeous and the cuisine is first-class. (☎44-2111; www5.ocn.ne.jp/~kamefuku. Rooms begin at ¥13,000, including 2 meals.) A more old-fashioned high-class hotel is **Kinsuikan ❹**. The amenities and facilities are the same as Kamefuku—excellent food, gorgeous baths, well-appointed rooms—but the atmosphere is more woodsy and intimate. (☎44-2131; www.kinsuikan.jp. ¥13,000, ¥15,000 with breakfast and dinner.) While these hotels are truly luxurious, the ultimate in extravagance is the **Iwaso Ryokan ❺**, secluded in the park at the foot of Mise-san. Traditional, elegantly furnished, and immaculately kept *tatami* rooms surround guests in comfort and style. Iwaso is known for the quality of its food and the hospitality of its *kimono*-clad staff. (☎44-2233; www.iwaso.com. Rooms start at ¥21,000 with 2 meals.)

⌂ FOOD. Since virtually all of the hotels provide high-class meals for their guests, the restaurant scene on Miya-jima is extremely weak. It is virtually impossible to find an eatery open after 5pm, and even during the lunch rush options tend to be limited to *udon* stands and the like. Miya-jima does have a local speciality that's inexpensive and easy to track down. *Anago* is a type of freshwater eel, traditionally served over rice in a dish known as *anagoburi*. **Fukuya ❸**, a simple storefront eatery on the waterfront, serves this dish for a reasonable ¥1350. (☎44-0127. Open daily 9am-5pm.) **Tenshin ❶**, by the Ikutsushima-jinja exit, is an unpretentious *udon* shop that serves standard fare at reasonable prices, starting around ¥500. (☎44-0246. Open daily 11am-4pm.)

◉ ♫ SIGHTS AND ENTERTAINMENT. The main reason to visit Miya-jima is the ancient shrine of **Itsukushima-jinja.** Although a sea god cult likely practiced here since the emergence of Japanese civilization in the 6th century AD, it wasn't until Taira-no-Kiyomori commissioned the construction of a grand shrine here that Itsukushima-jinja took on its present incarnation. Since the object of worship is the island itself, the shrine is set on a series of raised piers by the seaside. Despite this unconventional setting, Itsukushima-jinja is impressively large, with hundreds of meters of bright vermilion columns, a floating *nō* stage and a number of massive open chambers, all connected to the mainland by a series of delicate, arched bridges. Also, the shrine is famous for its *bugaku* dances, harkening back to the palaces of Heian-era Kyōto. The dances, exceedingly rare in modern Japan, are only preformed six times a year; inquire at the shrine for exact dates. Be warned, however, that they may not meet Western expectations of dance—while the costumes are elaborate and beautiful, the movements of the dancers are slow and set to traditional atonal Japanese music. The shrine is a 10min. walk from the ferry terminal; from the terminal head along the waterside towards the shrine. (☎44-2020; fax 44-0517. ¥300. Open Jan.-Feb. daily 6:30am-5:30pm; Mar.-Oct. daily 6:30am-6pm; mid-Oct.-Nov. daily 6:30am-5:30pm; Dec. daily 6:30am-5pm.)

Off of the main shrine complex are a number of minor sights. Climb the hill to the right of the shrine and you'll find a diminutive **five-storied pagoda,** standing red against the back drop of the mainland. Behind is **Senjokaku,** "the hall of a thousand *tatami*," part of a shrine complex begun (but not finished) by Toyotomi Hideyoshi in the 16th century. The name is hyperbolic, but gives a sense of the wide, Saskatchewan-like emptiness of the hall. (Open daily 9am-4pm, ¥100.) On your left as you exit the main shrine, the **treasure hall** houses various bits of historical flotsam and jetsam that ended up on Miya-jima. As far as "treasure" goes, this collection is a little thin, and you can safely afford to give it a pass. (Open daily 8am-5pm. ¥300. A combination ticket for the shrine and treasure hall is available for ¥500.) If you want a break from the Shintō vermilion that sheathes most of the island, amble on to **Daisho-in**, the main Buddhist temple. It competes in elaborateness with more-famous Itsuku-jinja, with a slight baroque finish and grounds with bridges, giant lanterns, and lily-ponds. For those who know about these things, this is a Shingon-sect temple.

The relative seclusion of the island has been good for the sacred deer of Miya-jima who scamper by the dozens around both the park area and the village harassing tourists. The best way of touring the forest is to climb **Misen-san**, the island's 530m peak. There are two options: for the gung-ho, a trail winds to the top and can be tackled at an easy pace in two or three hours. For everyone else, a cable car travels most of the length, dropping tourists off about 15min. from the summit. The bottom station is in **Momiji-dani** (Maple Valley), a park about 25min. from the boat terminal. If you don't feel like walking the distance, a free shuttle bus operates from the side of Iwaso Ryokan. At the top of the ropeway, monkeys join the deer in pestering tourists. You may be tempted to get close for a cute, postcard-picture with the simians, but that's a wish best left unfulfilled—closely related to humans, monkeys are unpredictable and can turn instantly vicious and violent. The views of the **Inland Sea** are gorgeous, but the path to the summit has a more singular distinction. Before a mountain-side temple is a fire that has been kept continuously burning for 1600 years; originally used as a Buddhist saint's cooking fire (note the charred pots around it), it is said to have magical properties (including enthralling tourists).

Apart from the religious sights and Misen-san, there are a few more workaday attractions around Miya-jima. The **Miya-jima Public Aquarium** features sea-lion, penguin, and piranha shows, as well as whales on display. (☎44-2010; www.netmarketweb.com/guide/miyajima. Open daily 8:30am-5:50pm. ¥1050.) Miya-jima also has a **History and Folklore Museum**, displaying various local artifacts including boats, farm implements, and other local tools too crass for the treasure hall. (☎44-2019; fax 44-0631. Open Tu-Su 8:30am-5pm. ¥260.)

■ **FESTIVALS.** Like many religious spots in Japan, Itsukushima-jinja keeps a busy calendar of festivals and special events.

Kangensai. 17th day of the 6th lunar month. Call the shrine for an exact date. Ceremonial boats arrive in procession at the shrine, and traditional, Heian-era music played accompanies them on their arrival.

Hanabi Matsuri (Firework Festival). Aug. 14. Underwater fireworks are set off around the Ōtorii gate, illuminating the night sky. This is an extremely popular event, the largest fireworks display in Western Honshū, so make arrangements well ahead of time. Fireworks shows occur at the spring and autumn festivals, Apr. 15 and Nov. 15 respectively.

Tamatori Matsuri. Mid-Aug. Incomprehensible to those unacquainted with Shintō (and to many so acquainted), in this festival men in loincloths fight over a sacred ball suspended over the water.

Kaki Matsuri (Oyster festival). 2nd weekend of Feb. A food festival in which you can sample the local delicacy at its freshest.

Jin-Nō (Sacred Nō Plays). Apr. 16-18. The floating nō stage sees some use as the plays it was originally built to showcase are reprised on its surface. This has been going on since the stages construction in 1568.

Chinkasai (Fire Prevention Festival). Dec. 31. The festival is oddly named—dozens of youths fighting one another for sacred pine torches (thought to bring good luck) seems more likely to start a fire than prevent one.

IWAKUNI (岩国)   ☎ 0827

The seat of the Kikkawa clan of feudal lords, Iwakuni was their administrative and military capital, briefly (1608-1615) boasting a mountain castle of its own. Modern Iwakuni is based solidly on the presence of an American air force base. The tourist appeal is concentrated around its most famous attraction, the Kintai-kyo, a graceful, five-arched bridge spanning the Nishiki-gawa river. It has been named by the hierarchy-loving Japanese one of the top three bridges of Japan. Iwakuni is an easy destination, less than an hour from Hiroshima, and is compact enough to make a lazy day trip.

ON THE WEB	Iwakuni: www.city.iwakuni.yamaguchi.jp

🖳🔋 TRANSPORTATION AND PRACTICAL INFORMATION. Kintai-kyō is equidistant from the town's two **train** stations, **Shin-Iwakuni** (*shinkansen* 17min., ¥1520) and the local **JR Sanyō Line B** (44min., ¥740). From the station, JR and **local buses** run the 10min. course to Kintai-kyo (approx. ¥240). Pass holders can use JR buses for free. It's easy to confuse buses or routes, so be sure to ask before boarding. **Tourist information booths** can be found at both stations as well as the downtown, but only the one at Iwakuni local station is open regularly (☎21-6050; open Tu-Su 9am-5pm), while the others only operate on holidays and weekends.

🛌🍴 ACCOMMODATIONS AND FOOD. The **Iwakuni Youth Hostel (HI)** ❶ (岩国 ユースホステル) is exceptionally well placed. On the nicer side of Kintai-kyo, it is in a low building set just at the point that an Edo-period neighborhood gives way to a forested park. Apart from this picture-perfect environment, the hostel is pretty standard material—slightly institutional dorms above a slightly ratty common area. (☎43-1092, fax 0927-43-0123. Check-in 3pm. Check-out 10am. Breakfast ¥500, dinner ¥1000. ¥2700, ¥3200 nonmembers.) Otherwise, options are limited to business hotels. The **Iwakuni Kinsui Hotel** ❸ (岩国金水ホテル), next to Iwakuni Station, has mid-range prices and standard amenities. (☎22-2311. fax 24-1403. Check-in 2pm. Check-out 11am. Singles begin at ¥6500, doubles ¥7500.) The **Iwakuni Kokusai Hotel** ❸ (岩国国際ホステル), near Kintai-kyō, about 500m upstream from the bus stop, is a slightly more upscale version of the modern business hotel, with well-appointed Japanese style rooms. (☎43-1111; fax 0821-41-2483. Check-in 3pm. Check-out 10am. Breakfast ¥1000. Per person rates begin at ¥7500.)

Udon noodle places and informal Japanese eateries cluster in the bridge area. One of the nicer ones is **Hirasei** ❷, in the back of an antique shop a couple of blocks away from the bridge. With the bridge to your back, take the street to your left and head straight three blocks; it will be on your right. It serves the local specialty, *Iwakuni-zushi*, a block of vinagered rice covered by bits of raw fish and pickled vegetables. A fixed-price *zushi* lunch comes to a reasonable ¥840. (☎41-0236. Open daily 11am-2pm and 5-7pm.) Another option is to pack a lunch and eat in the pleasant and picturesque Kikka Kōen. The **Andersen Outlet** ❶, right next to Iwakuni Station, sells delicious sandwiches and baked goods from around ¥300. (☎21-2242. Open daily 7am-8pm.)

📷🎏 SIGHTS AND ENTERTAINMENT. Kintai-kyo is the centerpiece for the town's tourist district, and its surrounding scenery has been preserved with great care. The bridge itself is a bit of a marvel—it arches not once, not twice, but five times in crossing the wide Nishikiga-kawa river. It was built in 1673, when local *daimyō* Kikkawa Hiroyoshi set his brain trust on the problem of bridging the river's floodplain; the steep arches represent cutting edge 17th-century civil engineering. It is a testament to its designers that it took Typhoon Kezia in 1950 to bring it down—what remains is a 1953 reconstruction. In the Edo Period, the bridge was *samurai*-only, and there is still a ¥220 toll for crossing the bridge. You can pick up a combination ticket at the toll booth, covering the bridge, the ropeway, and entry to the castle for ¥840, saving you ¥180. To get a good (free!) view of the bridge, cross **Kinjo-kyō,** which runs parallel to Kintai-kyō.

Across the bridge lies the expansive **Kikko-kōen,** whose broad green spaces spill into Edo-era houses and alleyways on either side. The entire area was once the estate of the Kikkawa *samurai* clan, who did absolutely everything in Iwakuni. On the northern side of the park (on your right with your back to the bridge), you'll find the imposing gate **Kagayake-mon,** once the entryway to the Kikkawa compound. The residence itself is two blocks farther north, and has been converted into the **Kikkawa Historical Museum,** displaying the historical relics of the Kikkawa clan. You may find yourself more drawn to the Zen rock garden than the lovingly-preserved artifacts. (☎41-1010; fax 41-3100. Open M-Tu and Th-Su 9am-5pm. ¥500, students ¥300.) Across the park from the residence, near the foot of the mountain lies the **Kikkawa Lords' Graveyard,** with paired mounds for each lord and his wife set in a mazelike series of white enclosures. At the park's far end, the **Iwakuni Historical Art Museum** houses various examples of traditional Japanese art, include a battalion's worth of *samurai* weapons and armor. (☎41-0506. Open Dec.-Feb. M-Tu and Th-Su 9am-5pm; March-June and Sept.-Nov. M-Tu and Th-Su 9am-5pm; July-Aug. M-Tu and Th-Su 9am-4pm. ¥500, students ¥300.) Next to the cablecar station, the **White Snake Viewing Facility** displays Iwakuni white snakes, a species unique to the area. The snakes inhabit the river valleys, where warmer-than-normal temperatures are thought to have promoted albinism. Harmless, they are considered a symbol of good luck. (☎22-8634. Open daily 9am-5pm. Viewing free. Leaflet ¥100.)

The cable car leads up **Iwakuni-jō.** As an alternative, a 30min. hike leads up to the castle from beside the youth hostel, for those who want a workout. The castle is 7min. from the top cable car station. (¥320, round-trip ¥540 unless you bought the combination ticket.) The original stood for only seven years, 1608-1615, falling victim not to warfare but to the "one domain, one castle" policy enforced by the Tokugawa. The current structure dates from the 1960s, with only the foundations of the original visible; it can't compete with the grander castles in Himeji and Ōsaka. (Open daily 9am-5pm, ¥260.)

■ **FESTIVALS.** A few special events are of more than passing note. April 29 **Kintai-kyō** comes alive with its own festival, as a procession in Edo-era costume crosses and recrosses for tourists and their cameras. May 5, the local American airbase puts on its annual **air show.** On the first Saturday of August, the bridge is illuminated by **fireworks** in an impressive combination of pyrotechnics and quaint Edo-period civil engineering. During the summer months, men in boats fish with cormorant every night—for ¥3500 you can have a go too.

YAMAGUCHI (山 口)　　　　☎083

During the Sengoku Period (1467-1568), Yamaguchi was riding high. The conflict had cut Kyōto off from this stretch of Honshū, and Yamaguchi became a refuge for courtiers fleeing the conflict in other parts of Japan. When Catholic priest Francis Xavier preached here in the mid-16th-century, it was a veritable second capital, its bustle and culture rivaling the cities in Kantō and Kansai. Unification was a great bane for the city—now, Yamaguchi is little more than the administrative capital of its prefecture, a sleepy provincial town offering tourists few reasons to linger.

ON THE WEB Yamaguchi: www.city.yamaguchi.yamaguchi.jp

Central
Yamaguchi·
中央山口

⌂ ACCOMMODATIONS
La Francesca, **2**
Sun Route Yamaguchi, **3**
Yamaguchi Youth Hostel, **1**

Five-Storeyed Pagoda
Rurikō-ji 五重塔
瑠璃光寺

Kōzan Kōen
香山公園

Tōshun-ji
洞春寺

香山 ▲
Kō-zan

Yamaguchi
Dai-jingū
山口大神宮

Yamaguchi
Prefectural Office
山口県庁

Yamaguchi
History Museum
山口市歴史民俗資料館

TO JŌEI-JI (1.5km),
SESSHŪTEI (1.5km)
& ⌂ (8km)
常栄寺

9

Yamaguchi Prefectural
Museum
山口県立山口博物館

Ekimae-dōri · 駅前通り

Kameyama Kōen
亀山公園

St. Francis Xavier
Memorial Chapel
ザビエル記念聖堂

TO ⌂ (50m)

Ichinosaka River · 一の坂川

Yamaguchi Prefectural
Art Museum
山口県立美術館

Yamaguchi
City Hall
山口市役所

TO CHUYA NAKAHARA
MEMORIAL MUSEUM 🏛 (1.2km)

Arcade · アーケード

3

Ekimae-dōri · 駅前通り

4

Local Court
地方裁判所

5

6

JR Yamaguchi Line · 山口線

Yamaguchi Station
山口駅

Fushino River · 椹野川

0   200 meters
0   200 yards

🍴 FOOD
Cafe Appasionato, **4**
Sazanami, **5**
Shiva, **6**

⎗ TRANSPORTATION. Yamaguchi sits on the Yamaguchi Line, connecting the main Sanyō Line in Ogori with the north coast of Masuda. Trains from Yamaguchi Station (☎924-3581) depart southward for Ogori (30min., ¥250) and north for Masuda (1½hr., ¥1450). Weekends and holidays, a steam engine runs the route from Ogori to Tsuwano along this line, stopping at Yamaguchi. Make sure to reserve a seat well in advance. Renting a bike near the station is a good way to see the town. (¥320 for 2 hr., ¥840 for the day. Return by 5pm).

🛈 PRACTICAL INFORMATION. The **tourist information center** is on the second floor of the station building. (☎933-0090. Open daily 9am-6pm.) The sizeable **Central Post Office** has an **international ATM.** (Open M-F 9am-7pm, Sa 9am-5pm, Su 9am-12:30pm. ATM open M-F 7am-11pm, Sa 9am-9pm, Su 9am-7pm.) In an emergency, call ☎110 for **police,** ☎119 for **fire** or **ambulance.**

Yamaguchi is set on two axes—one runs along the train tracks to Yuda Onsen, containing most of the commercial and service centers of the city, and another extends straight ahead from the station along **Ekimae-dōri,** where most of the sights and administrative buildings are. Another important artery is **Route 9,** in the north of town, which connects the city with Joe-ji temple, 4km and a tunnel away.

🛏🍴 ACCOMMODATIONS AND FOOD. Yamaguchi Youth Hostel (HI) ❶(山口ユースホステル) is a considerable distance (8km) out of town. It's best reached by bus, either from Yamaguchi Station or Miyako Station, two stops east on the Yamaguchi Line. Ask at the info center for bus information. The remote location compensates for itself with the peace and quiet of the setting. Friendly, English-speaking owners maintain the charming ivy-draped house with a cozy common room and spic-and-span dorms. (☎928-0057. Breakfast ¥500. Check-in after 3pm. Check-out 10am. ¥2600, nonmembers ¥3600.) **La Francesca ❺**, at the base of Kameyama, is a favorite spot for wedding parties. An airy lobby leads to a restaurant and court-yard in this lovely villa-style hotel, with rooms gorgeously done in a combination of Tuscan rustic and Euro-chic. The staff are as friendly as they are well-dressed. (☎934-1888. Check-in after 4pm. Check-out 10am. Rooms start at ¥15,000 per person.) **Sun Route Yamaguchi ❸** (サンルート山口), right at the center of town, is in one of Yamaguchi's only skyscrapers, impossible to miss. It provides all the usual amenities in a remarkably convenient location. (☎923-3610. Check-in after 4pm. Check-out 10am. Singles from ¥6000, doubles from ¥12,000.)

There are a few good places to grab a bite. **Shiva ❸**, on the street straight ahead from the station, serves up tasty curries. The ¥800 lunch specials are only available on weekdays. Otherwise you'll pay upwards of ¥1200. **Cafe Appasionato ❶** is a good place to go if you're tired of exotic food and are jonesin' for some more comfort-able grub. The cafe atmosphere is a bit generic, but the sandwiches and baked goods are cheap (¥420-450) and delicious. (☎922-1243. Open M-Sa 8am-8pm, Su 9am-8pm.) **La Francesca ❸** has lunch specials, diabolically tempting at ¥1200-2500, but dinner starts at ¥2200 and rises fast. Due to the popularity of the hotel for func-tions, it may be unexpectedly closed. (☎934-1888. Open daily 11am-10pm.) **Sazan-ami ❸**(さざなみ), in the commercial area in front of the station, is an unpretentious noodle house that serves heaping portions of *rāmen*. Depending on how extravagant you like your soup, prices range ¥800-1500. (☎922-0893.)

⑤ SIGHTS. The station-front street **Ekimae-dōri** (駅前通) leads up to **Kameyama Kōen** (亀山園), marking the center of town. The park itself is pleasant enough, as are the views from the top of the hill. On the far side of the hill is the **St. Francis Xavier Memorial Chapel** (Yamaguchi Sabieru Kinen Seidō; 山口サビエル記念聖堂) that was originally built in 1952 to mark the 400th anniversary of St. Francis Xavier's arrival in Yamaguchi. The Jesuit missionary arrived in Japan in the mid-16th-century, intent on converting first the Emperor, then the Imperial Court, and finally bringing the whole of the nation to Christ. Things didn't work out that way, but the six months he spent in Yamaguchi did bear fruit—the Catholic community here, though ravaged by persecution under the Tokugawa Shogunate, dates from his mission. The original chapel was done in a classic European style, but it burned down in 1991. The new church is quite a departure—bright white and angular, from the outside it looks a little like an architectural blasphemy. The inte-rior is equally unusual, but far more successful—the acoustics amplify and expand the organ music, and light, tinted by stained glass windows, casts soft pools of color on the immaculate white walls. Beneath the church is a museum recounting the missions undertaken by St. Francis Xavier. (☎920-1549; www.urban.ne.jp/home/xavier. Open daily 9am-5pm. Museum admission ¥300.)

Also on the park grounds, along Ekimae-dōri, are two local museums, **Yamaguchi Prefectural Art Museum** (Yamaguchi Kenritsu Bijutsukan; 山口県立美術館) and **Yamaguchi Prefectural Museum** (Yamaguchi Kenritsu Hakubutsukan; 山口県立博物館). There is very little reason to go here—the art museum's collection is tiny and dull, and the Prefectural Museum is a Japanese-only experience. (Art museum: ☎924-7001; fax 924-7080. Open Tu-Su 9am-5pm. ¥190. Prefectural museum: ☎922-2094; fax 922-0353. Open Tu-Su 9am-4:30pm. ¥130, students ¥80.) Farther north, about 500m past Rte. 9, is **Kōzan Kōen** (香山公園), a broad, open park containing the graves of the local Mori lords. Abutting the park is the Buddhist temple **Rurikō-ji** (瑠璃光寺), well known for its five-tiered pagoda. The early 15th-century tem-ple is brilliantly set on a tranquil lake. Yamaguchi boasts another classical Japa-nese sight of note, the Zen garden of **Jōei-ji** (常栄寺). Designed by master

WESTERN HONSHŪ

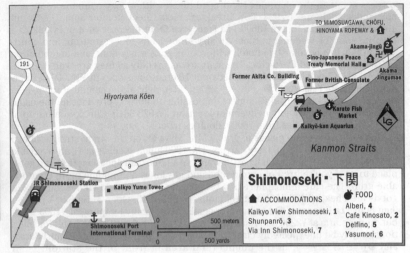

landscape architect and painter Sesshu, the garden bears the name of that great monk—**Sesshūtei** (雪舟庭). The centerpiece is a sizeable pond bedecked with small inlands where turtles sun themselves. A miniaturized mountain in the back of the garden is a nice touch. (☎922-2272. Open daily 8am-5pm. ¥300.) The one drawback to this garden is its rather inconvenient location about 3km northeast of town on Rte. 9. Buses don't make the trip reliably, so a bicycle is a good way of getting here. Take Rte. 9 out of town, go through the tunnel, and follow the signs.

A little out of the way in the Yuda Onsen part of Yamaguchi is the **Chūya Nakahara Memorial Museum** (Nakahara Chūya Kinenkan; 中原中也記掩館). Chūya Nakahara was a turn-of-the-century Japanese poet credited with introducing Rimbaud into the Japanese poetic consciousness. He lived a truly bohemian life, often drunk and penniless, forever pursuing his first love even as she traded up to his more successful friends (and ended up marrying a banker). The poetry may seem inaccessible to foreigners, the museum makes every effort to help English speakers. Upstairs you can hear the poetry sung at the touch of a button. Apart from the literary appeal, the musuem is worth seeing for its architecture. (☎932-6430. Open May-Oct. Tu-Su 9am-6pm; Nov.-Apr. Tu-Su 9am-5pm. ¥300, students ¥200.)

SHIMONOSEKI (下関) ☎0832

Shimonoseki, at the western tip of Honshū, has always been a gateway city. In ages past, it served as the embarkation point for Kyūshū, only 700m away at the Kanmon Strait. During WWII, Shimonoseki was a major port, ferrying personnel and cargo between Japan and Korea. As a result, it was pulverized by allied bombing, leaving little to attract visitors. For most, this will simply be a stepping stone to Kyūshū or Korea, but for those who have an afternoon to kill here, the *samurai* district of Chōfu is worth a visit.

ON THE WEB   Shimonoseki: www.city.shimonoseki.yamaguchi.jp

⎙ TRANSPORTATION. Shimonoseki Station (下関駅) sits right in the middle of town, and is the one to use if you're visiting. **Shin-Shimonoseki,** two stops out of town, services the *shinkansen* trains. From Shin-Shimonoseki, trains depart for points on Honshū and Kyūshū, including: Hakata (30min., ¥3130); Hiroshima (2hr., ¥5670);

Ōsaka (4hr., ¥12,920); Tōkyō (7hr., ¥20,060). Trains from Shimonoseki Station depart to smaller towns in the area, including: Kokura (15min., ¥270); Moji (15min., ¥220); Nagasaki (2hr., ¥1280); Ogori (1hr. 40min., ¥1110).

Shimonoseki is better known for its international ferry service, which can whisk you overnight to mainland Asia. The boats leave **Shimonoseki International Ferry Terminal** (下関港国際ターミナル), on the water a few minutes straight out of the train station. The ticket offices are on the second floor. (Open daily 8:30am-4:30pm.) **Kampu Ferry** (☎24-3000; fax 24-3006) offers daily service to Pusan, South Korea. (14hr.; 1 per day at 7pm; *tatami* mat area ¥8500, students ¥6800; bed ¥12,000-18,000.) **Orient Ferry** (☎32-6615; fax 32-6616) offers service to Qingdao, China. (25hr.; 2 per week; *tatami* mat area ¥19,000; bed ¥40,000. Additional fee ¥600 per person.) Since Shimonoseki is one of the least expensive ports of entry into Japan, immigration controls are particularly strict—expect to have your documents scrutinized. Inconveniently enough, you cannot change Chinese or Korean currency here, and if you need visas or other documents to travel to South Korea or China, there is no consulate at which to obtain them. Plan accordingly.

■▮ **ORIENTATION AND PRACTICAL INFORMATION.** Shimonoseki extends along the Kanmon Strait from the train station. The area by the station contains little more than a shopping mall and the ferry terminal. The city gets more interesting further east along the main thoroughfare. The *samurai* quarter of Chōfu is quite a while away, requiring a 20min. bus ride. There are **tourist information centers** at both stations, Shin-Shimonoseki (☎56-3422; open daily 9am-7pm) and Shimonoseki (☎32-8383; open daily 9am-7pm). They have a number of useful English pamphlets about the area and a helpful staff. The station-side **post office** has an **ATM** for foreign cash withdrawals. (Open M-F 9am-7pm, Sa 9am-5pm, Su 9am-12:30pm. ATM open M-F 8:45am-9pm, Sa 9am-7pm, Su 9am-7pm.) In an emergency, call ☎110 for **police**, ☎119 for **fire** or **ambulance**.

▮▮ **ACCOMMODATIONS AND FOOD.** Although there's no reason to stay in Shimonoseki longer than you have to, if you find yourself stuck here between ferries or trains, you have a number of choices on where to crash. Unfortunately, the cheapest option, the local youth hostel, is closed for renovations, expected to reopen in April or May of 2004. The newly opened **Kaikyō View Shimonoseki ❸** (海峡ビュー下関), sits on the slopes of Hinoyama. Housed in an attractive mod-

ON THE MENU

AND OH, THEM BLOWFISH BLOW

Japan is a country of odd culinary tastes, but in Shimonoseki, the local delicacy can kill. The *fugu*, or globefish, the city mascot, is inescapable—it's on phone booths and manhole covers, billboard and brochures, and has the place of honor in the city aquarium. The spiky little fish has the city eating out of its fin.

The appeal lies in the risk—the globefish defends itself with a deadly toxin. While only a few organs contain it in lethal doses, if any are nicked by an inexperienced chef, *sashimi* turns deadly. The risk is miniscule, but the stakes are high, and every year a few diners succumb.

At **Kitagawa,** behind Karato Fish Market, *fugu* runs ¥2000. (☎32-3212. Open daily 11am-9:30pm.) At swanker **Hanase** in the Grand Hotel, feasts for two start at ¥15,000. (☎31-5000. Open daily 7am-10pm.)

If you're not ready to dance with death, Shimonoseki has another local seafood specialty. While Japan abides by the worldwide ban on whaling, it procures a small catch for scientific purposes. Some of these whales end up on the food market, and Shimonoseki is one of the few cities where it's available in restaurants. Due to the small catch, it's difficult to track the whale from ocean to kitchen—ask the tourist information center for restaurants that might serve the whale *du jour*.

ern building, it's the best accommodation value. Ocean front rooms have a bracing view of the Kanmon Strait. (☎29-0117; www.kv-shimonoseki.com. Check-in after 3pm. Check-out 10am. Japanese-style rooms, with toilet but without bath, single ¥7000; double ¥13,000. Rooms with bath, single ¥7500; double ¥14,000. Western-style rooms, with bath, single ¥7000, double ¥13,000.) **Shunpanrō ❺** (春版楼), near the Karato Fish Market, sets the standard for quality hotels in Shimonoseki. With lavish suites and a reputation for great food, this hotel attracts an elite clientele—just count the luxury cars out front. (☎23-7181; www.shunpanro.com. Check-in after 3pm. Check-out 10am. ¥25,000 per person. 3 meals included.) **Via Inn Shimonoseki ❸** (ヴィアイン下関), right in front of the station, offers similar rates, although it's the better bargain for pairs. (☎22-6111; www.viainn.co.jp. Check-in after 3pm. Check-out 10am. Singles ¥5700, doubles ¥9600.)

It should be no surprise that Shimonoseki, straddling two bodies of water, specializes in seafood. There are a number of local fish specialties found only in the Shimonoseki area. Since it is the most convenient port of entry from Korea, a Koreatown has sprung up, adding a touch of variety to the local cuisine. **Delfino ❸**, right on the water next to the Shimonoseki Grand Hotel, is an extravagant fusion restaurant. Most meals are a combination of Italian seafood and Japanese flavors. As for the dolphins, they're literal—they dance and cavort in a tank to entertain during dinner. (☎29-4303. Dinner around ¥2500. Open daily 11am-9pm.) **Cafe Kinosato ❷** (桂のさと), in Chōfu, lights up the end of a quiet, residential street. A peaceful family-run cafe, Kinosato offers a light menu in a serene setting. While the inside is stylish and comfortable, outdoor seats are preferable, especially in summer. Light meals are ¥500-1000, and there's a wide desert selection. (☎41-0200. Open M-Tu and Th-Su 10am-7pm.) Just north of the station in the block of Korean shops and restaurants, **Yasumori ❸** (やすもり) serves Korean-style *yakiniku*. Fresh slices of meat and vegetables are cooked up right at your table. Vegetarians might not be comfortable. Meals run ¥1600-3000. (☎22-6542. Open daily 11am-midnight.) **Alberi,** in the shopping area up from Karato Fish Market, boasts a stylish interior and attracts a younger crowd. The food is a combination of French and Italian. Specials, which run in deliciously at ¥1690, are the way to go. (☎31-1016. Open daily 11am-2pm and 5pm-midnight.)

◪ SIGHTS. Fortunately, the town's linear layout makes sightseeing simple—get on any bus from bay #1, by the station, get off when you reach your attraction, and catch a bus going the opposite direction to get back. If you're pressed for time, head to Hinoyama Hill for the view, or to the Edo-era neighborhood in Chōfu.

The nearest worthwhile sight close to the station is the **Kaikyō Yume Tower** (海峡 ゆめタワー), just past Shimonoseki Sea Mall. Diminutive as skyscrapers go, it still offers a good view of the straits from its spherical observation deck. At night, when it lights up, the view gets more interesting. (☎31-5600. Open daily 9:30am-9:30pm. ¥600.) Further along, around Karato Bus Stop, lie the vestiges of Meiji-era Shimonoseki. The **Former British Consulate** (旧下関英国領事館) has been preserved in its 19th-century brick building, and is now a museum. (☎31-1238. Open Tu-Su 9am-5pm. Free.) Nearby, the former **Akita Co. Building** is now a tourist center. One of Japan's earliest ferro-concrete buildings, it has a rooftop Zen garden. (☎31-4141. Open daily 9am-5pm. Free.) The conveniently close **Shimonoseki Nabechō Post Office** is a relic of the same bygone era, but rather than opt for memorialization, it's a working post office. (Open M-F 9am-5pm.) The seaside **Karato Fish Market** (唐戸市場) is also an attraction of sorts, especially during mornings when it's thronged with fish and those who buy and sell them. Next to the market, somewhat ironically, is the **Shimonoseki Kaikyō-kan Aquarium** (海峡館). The town mascot, the *fugu*, gets a specially designed tank to itself, but it has to compete with the dolphin shows for viewers. (☎28-1100. Open 9:30am-5:30pm. ¥1800.)

Farther along the waterside is the colorful shrine, **Akama-jingū** (赤間神宮). Important enough to merit its own bus stop, Akama-jingū commemorates the child-emperor Antoku, who was spirited away by the Taira clan during the Heike War. He perished when the Taira were defeated by the Minamoto at the battle of Dannōra in the straits below the shrine. Once dedicated to the dead warriors of the Taira clan, Akama-jingū contains the graves of their best men. There's a statue of monk Hōichi Miminashi, known in Lafcadio Hearn's ghost stories as Earless Hōichi. Next door, in front of Shunpanrō Hotel, is the **Sino-Japanese Peace Treaty Memorial Hall** (日清講和記家館), where the Treaty of Shimonoseki, ending the Sino-Japanese war, was signed (1895). It now holds artifacts from the summit and wax dummies of the summiteers. (☎31-4697. Open daily 9am-5pm. Free.)

The next stop of interest is **Mimosusogawa** (みもすそ川), just past the Kanmonbashi Bridge, which links Honshū and Kyūshū. Next to the bridge is the Kanmon Tunnel, it allows visitors to walk the 750m from Honshū to Kyūshū. It takes about 20min. each way. (☎32-2811. Open 6am-10pm. Free.) Nearby, the **Hinoyama Ropeway** (火の山のロープウェイ) offers gorgeous views of the strait as it climbs to Hinoyama Park. (☎31-1352. Open 9am-5pm. One-way ¥200, round-trip ¥400.)

Chōfu (長府) is served by Jōka-machi Bus Stop—be sure to ask the driver where it is, as getting stranded in the suburbs of Shimonoseki is no fun. A useful map can be found in the *Strait Walker*, the free guidebook given out by the tourist info center. At the southern end of Chōfu are two worthy sights—the **Shimonoseki City Art Museum** and **Chōfu Garden** (長府庭園). The art museum displays an interesting collection of mostly modern works by Japanese artists. (☎45-4131. Open Tu-Su 9am-5pm. ¥200, students ¥100.) The garden is elaborate, expansive, and lovingly tended. The scenery is varied, with hundreds of meters of paths through groves, open spaces, and along streams and ponds. The garden is on a careful calendar, so *something* is always blooming. (☎46-4120. Open daily 9am-5pm. ¥200.)

On the far side of Chōfu, through a maze of canals and Edo-period houses, is **Kōzan-ji** (功山寺), a 14th-century Zen temple. The sternly ungilded building is quite grand and the grounds are expansive. The slightly dull **Chōfu Museum** (長府博物館) shares its grounds. (☎45-0555. Open Tu-Su 9am-5pm. ¥200, students ¥100.) Nearby, the former residence of the Mori lords who ruled the region has been preserved and opened to the public. The Zen garden is perfect for serene contemplation of gravel. (☎45-8090. Open Tu-Su 9am-5pm. ¥200.)

■ **FESTIVALS.** If you're in Shimonoseki in late April, try to catch the **Sentei Matsuri,** April 23-25. After the defeat of the Taira at Dannōra, the noble ladies were sold into prostitution by the Minamoto conquerors. They were allowed a moment of respite only on the day of the battle, when they could return to Shimonoseki to mourn for their fallen, and for the child-emperor Antoku, at Akama-jingu. For this festival, elaborately costumed young women reenact the rituals of the Taira ladies.

HAGI (萩)   ☎0838

Perched on the bleak Sanin coast, Hagi has had an illustrious run these past 400 years. Founded as a fortification site by warlord Mori Terumoto, the city became a provincial capital in the Edo Period, rapidly expanding to fill up its island between the Hashimoto and Matsumoto rivers. As a castle town, it attracted artisans and *samurai* affiliated with the Mori clan, filling up the old districts of the city with compounds. The interesting times continued into the 19th-century—as the hometown of Yoshida Shōin, one of the most prominent *sonno-jōi* (revere the Emperor, expel the Barbarian) ideologues, Hagi was a hotbed of unrest in the run up to the Meiji Restoration. Since the 1860s, however, Hagi has slid into an appealing provincial listlessness. Its relative obscurity saved it from allied bombing in

WESTERN HONSHŪ

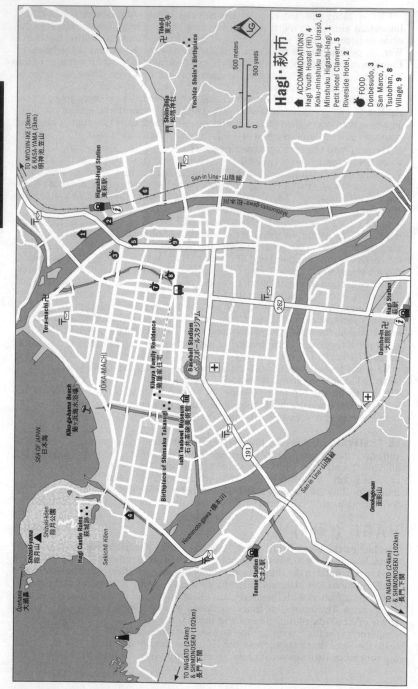

Hagi・萩市

▲ ACCOMMODATIONS
Hagi Youth Hostel (HI), **4**
Koku-minshuku Hagi Urasō, **6**
Minshuku Higashi-Hagi, **1**
Petit Hotel Clanvert, **5**
Riverside Hotel, **2**

● FOOD
Donbesudo, **3**
San Marco, **7**
Tsubohan, **8**
Village, **9**

卍 Tōkō-ji 東光寺

Yoshida Shōin's Birthplace

卉 Shōin-Jinja 松陰神社

TO MYOJIN-IKE (3km)
& KASA-YAMA 笠山
明神池・笠山

Higashi-Hagi Station 東萩駅

San-in Line・山陰線

Matsumoto-gawa・松本川

Tera-machi 寺町

Baseball Stadium ベースボールスタジアム

262

Daisho-in 卍 大照院

Hagi Station 萩駅

Kikuya Family Residence 菊屋家住宅

JŌKA-MACHI

Kiku-ga-hama Beach 菊ヶ浜海水浴場

Birthplace of Shinsaku Takasu

Ishi Teabowl Museum 石井茶碗美術館

SEA OF JAPAN 日本海

191

Shizuki-yama 指月山

Shizuki-kōen 指月公園

Hagi Castle Ruins 萩城跡

Sekicho Kōen

Hashimoto-gawa・橋本川

San-in Line・山陰線

Ozehana 大瀬鼻

Omokage-san 面影山

TO NAGATO (24km)
& SHIMONOSEKI (102km)
長門・下関

Tamae Station 玉江駅

TO NAGATO (24km)
& SHIMONOSEKI (102km)
長門・下関

500 meters
500 yards

WWII, so the historic districts preserve an undeniable authenticity—the temples are a regional highlight. Much of the modern city is a rusting hulk of failing shops and locked up factories.

ON THE WEB   Hagi: www.city.hagi.yamaguchi.jp

⬅ TRANSPORTATION. Hagi is served by three train stations, **Tamae** (玉江駅), **Hagi** (萩), and **Higashi-Hagi** (東萩駅). Tamae is conveniently close to the castle park and the old part of town. Hagi is convenient to nothing and is best avoided. Higashi-Hagi is in the center of the modern city. The San-in Rail Line serves Hagi city, only connecting conveniently to Shimonoseki (on the Sanyō Line, 2hr., ¥1890) and Matsue (3hr.; ¥3890). Travelers may prefer the bus service. The bus center (☎22-3816) is at the town center and runs to: Hiroshima (9 per day, one-way ¥3300, round-trip ¥5900); Ōsaka (1 per day; 8:35am; ¥9480/¥17,030); Tōkyō (1 per day; 6:45pm; ¥14,250/¥25,650).

⬛ PRACTICAL INFORMATION. Hagi has two **tourist information centers**, at Hagi (☎25-1750) and Higashi-Hagi (☎25-3145) Stations. The staff speak no English, but they can sell you the useful *Hagi Sightseeing Guide* (¥200). Both are open daily 9am-5pm. The **main post office** is on the central drag, near the bus terminal. It offers mail and ATM service. (Open M-F 9am-7pm. ATM open M-F 8:45am-7pm, Sa-Su 9am-7pm.) In an emergency, call ☎110 for **police**, ☎119 for **fire** or **ambulance**. Hagi is rather spread out, so the optimum way to tour it is by bicycle. Fortunately, rent-a-cycle stands are quite easy to find. Generally speaking, the rates of the town stands are slightly better than those near the station, but you shouldn't pay more than ¥700 per day no matter where you rent. Most of Hagi is built on an island made by the forking of the Hashimoto and Matsumoto rivers. The western and central portions are made up of old *samurai* estates and are good places for strolling. The island's eastern part is the core of the modern city. The east bank of the Matsumoto river contains Higashi-Hagi Station and inexpensive hotels.

⬛⬛ ACCOMMODATIONS AND FOOD. Hagi has a good range of budget accommodations, but the business hotels are hurting. Tourist traffic has ebbed in recent years, so there should be no difficulty finding rooms in most seasons. The main accommodation areas are Shizuki-Kōen and Higashi-Hagi station.

Hagi Youth Hostel (HI) ❶ (萩ユースホステル), by Shizuki Kōen, is in a somewhat charmless modern building, but the location and bike rentals (¥500 per day) make it an appealing choice. Guests are lodged in tidy dorm rooms. (☎22-0733; fax 22-3558. Check-in after 4pm. Check-out 10am. ¥2800, nonmembers ¥3000.) **Kokuminshuku Hagi Urasō ❸** (国民宿萩浦荘), on the station side of the Matsumoto-gawa, is affordable, and the riverside setting is fairly nice. Unfortunately, the vintage concrete low-rise has an institutional feel. (☎22-2511; fax 026-0143. *Tatami* rooms. 2 meals included. ¥7350 per person.) Family-run **Minshuku Higashi-Hagi ❷** (民宿東萩), a little north of Higashi-Hagi Station, takes the prize for best value in Hagi. The friendly staff speak some English and go out of their way to ensure that guests feel welcome and at home. Beware that the family atmosphere extends into the realm of rules—there's an 11pm curfew. (☎22-7884. Check-in after 4pm. Check-out 9am. ¥4000 per person, with 2 meals ¥7000.) **Petit Hotel Clanvert ❸** (プチホテルクランベール), located just across the river from Higashi-Hagi Station, is a modern hotel with European pretensions, convincingly appropriating chalet and BandB elements. With the downturn in tourism in Hagi, you might get a discounted rate. (☎25-8711; fax 25-8735. Check-in after 3pm. Check-out 10am. ¥6700, with 2 meals ¥10,300.) **Riverside Hotel ❷** (リバーサイドホテル), across the street from Higashi-Hagi Station, offers standard, business-style rooms at very low rates. The building has a bit of a desolate feel, but you can't argue with the price. (☎22-1195. Check-in after 4pm. Check-out 10am. Singles ¥4500; doubles ¥8000.)

While Hagi doesn't offer the same range as the more cosmopolitan cities of Hiroshima and Kōbe, there are a few eating options that might appeal to a hungry traveler. The local specialty is *uni* (sea urchin; an acquired taste). For more delicate fare, try any of the tea houses in the *samurai* district—there's one on almost every block. **Village ❷** is a jazz bar that's definitely worth visiting. The atmosphere is friendly and relaxed, and on weekends live bands are occasionally lured out of the larger cities to play here. Meals start at ¥600, drinks at ¥400. (☎25-6596. Open M and W-Su 10am-11pm.) **Tsubohan ❸** (つぼ半), near the bus station, is a classic Japanese restaurant specializing in urchins. Grab a bowl of *uni*-topped rice for ¥1600. The environment is low key, so it's tempting to linger. (Open daily 10am-7pm.) **San Marco ❷**, in the modern part of town, is an unpretentious eatery serving up all sorts of Italian-inspired dishes. Meals cost ¥800-1600. (☎25-4677. Open daily 11am-9pm.) **Donbesudo ❶**, on the ground floor of an office building in the modern part of town, is a brand new noodle joint. Simple *udon* and *rāmen* dishes are start at ¥360 in a pleasant modern interior. (☎25-9377. Open daily 10am-9pm.)

🅢 **SIGHTS.** Hagi's main draw is the old *samurai* district, Jōka-machi (城下 町), east of Shizuki Kōen and the ruins of Hagi Castle. Jōka-machi, and neighboring Tera-machi (寺町 ; temple district) have a great deal of charm in their Edo-period flavor and quiet back streets, but the appeal has more to do with atmosphere than with specific sights. Although the *Hagi Sightseeing Guide* lists dozens of sights in the area, most of them amount to little more than an explanatory tablet (in Japanese) next to a historical gate or entryway. Few permit visitors—although one that does is the **Kikuya Family Residence** (菊屋家住宅). Merchants rather than *samurai*, the Kikuya used their wealth and their political connections to assemble quite an estate. The buildings and the Zen garden are open to the public, with various historical curiosities exhibited. (☎25-8282. Open daily 9am-5pm. ¥500.) Enthusiasts of the Meiji Restoration may find the **Birthplace of Shinsaku Takasugi** (高杉晋作誕生地) interesting. As a young *samurai*, Takasugi agitated for the restoration of imperial rule, and a number of his pictures and documents are on display. (☎22-3078. Open Apr.-Oct. 8am-5pm; Nov.-Mar. 9am-4pm. ¥100, students ¥50.) **The Ishii Teabowl Museum** (石井茶碗博術館) provides an expensive lesson in traditional Japanese ceramics, with an emphasis on locally produced *hagi-yaki*. (☎22-1211. Open Tu-Su 9am-noon and 1-4:45pm. ¥1000, students ¥300.)

Going west from Jōka-machi, one reaches the **Horiuchi district.** This area is composed primarily of Edo-period compounds, but its main draw is the local pottery, *hagi-yaki*. Known as one of the finest styles of pottery in Japan, *hagi-yaki* was inspired by Korean pottery brought over by Toyotomi Hideyoshi's army after their abortive invasion of Korea. Dozens of shops are scattered throughout the district, offering similar prices and similar wares. Note that each piece has a notch cut from its base. This is a tradition from the Edo Period, when only *samurai* were allowed to buy ceramics. While commoners could not buy proper pieces, if an item were "damaged" by notching its base, it could be sold on the open market.

Just north of Horiuchi, **Shinzuki Kōen** (指月公園) begins. Based on the ruins of Hagi castle, the park also contains a shrine and a teahouse. Admission is charged to the park grounds, but the same ticket is good for the Mori House. (Open daily 8am-4:30pm. ¥210.) **Mori House,** just south of the park, is not the actual residence of the Mori clan, but rather boarding chambers for the lower *samurai*. The rooms, tidy but small, make one realize that most *samurai* didn't lead the sort of opulent lifestyles for which the *daimyō* were famous. Out of the spartan atmosphere of the lower *samurai* row houses came the spirit that would lead to the

Meiji Restoration. (Open daily 9am-5pm.) To the west of the park by the seaside is **Sekichō Kōen** (石彫公園), a sculpture park with various modern pieces. Entry is free and unlimited, and the park itself is a relaxing spot to lunch or just to wander. The area behind Higashi-Hagi Station is the site of a number of Hagi's better-known attractions. **Shōin-jinja** (松陰神社), the largest shrine in the area, is dedicated to the memory of Yoshida Shōin. Shōin was a major ideologue during the run up to the Meiji Restoration, propagating his ideas as a teacher while under house arrest and agitating for direct imperial rule at all other times. His plot to assassinate a shogunate official came to light in 1860, and he was executed at the age of 29. He is considered one of the lights of the Meiji Restoration, a national martyr, and Shōin Jinja honors him. The shrine also contains the **Shoka Sonjuku**, a tiny schoolhouse where he taught while under house arrest, and a Japanese-language museum charting his career. (Open daily 9am-5pm. ¥100.)

Further east is the impressive temple complex of **Tōkōji** (東光寺). Founded in the late 17th-century, it was a funerary temple for the Mori lords who used to rule this region. Apart from the graceful buildings, rendered in Zen style with some Chinese trappings, the graveyard, a spooky collection of hundreds of moss-covered stone memorial lanterns, is worth a look. This temple houses only half of the Mori lords, the 3rd, 5th, 7th, 9th, and 11th. (☎ 26-1052. Open daily 8:30am-5pm. ¥200.)

Before heading to that temple, it's worth visiting **Yoshida Shōin's birthplace** (吉田 松陰誕生地). On top of Dangoiwa hill, although his childhood home has survived only in the form of paving stones, a statue of Shōin and an anonymous follower have been erected to commemorate the site. Nearby, bringing the circle of life to a close, is his gravestone. **Daishōin** (大松陰) is the counterpart to Tōkō-ji, a funerary temple for the 2nd, 4th, 6th, 8th, and 10th Mori lords. Somewhat simpler than Tōkō-ji, Daishōin retains a rustic charm that makes a nice break from the tourist crowds that swarm its rival. The burial arrangements were identical for both sets of lords—here, too, is a mossy graveyard with carefully arranged stone memorial lanterns. An interesting difference is that it's not just the lords who are buried Daishōin—eight of Mori Hidenari's (the second Mori lord) retainers chose to follow him into the grave, committing *seppuku* on hearing of their master's death. As a reward for the ultimate loyalty, they are entombed in the temple with their master. (☎ 22-2124. Open daily 8am-5pm. ¥200.)

Kasa-yama (笠山), 4km northeast of town, sits on a promontory that offers great views of the sea of Japan. The mountain is actually a volcanic cone, and at the summit you can see the collapsed crater, as well as marvel at the views of the sea. At the foot of the hill is the unusual **Myōjin Ike** (明神池). This small pond is connected with the sea, and thus supports both fresh and salt water varieties of fish, as well as making a nice backdrop for a photograph. Catch a northbound bus from Higashi-Hagi Station. (15min., ¥240.)

TSUWANO (津和野)   ☎ 0856

Wedged tightly in a mountain valley in Western Honshū's tip, remote Tsuwano is surrounded by natural beauty. The little town, however, has hit tough economic times, and it might be difficult to find a good open restaurant on weekdays. Tsuwano draws few visitors from the metropolises of Kantō and Kansai, but if you happen to be in the area, the town offers several fine museums.

☐ ⑦ TRANSPORTATION AND PRACTICAL INFORMATION. Tsuwano lies on the JR Yamaguchi Line, which links the Sanyō Line at Ogōri with the San-in Line at Matsuda. From Ogōri, local trains head to Tsuwano (2hr., ¥1110). In summer, the always-popular steam engine follows the JR Line from Ogōri to Tsuwano (¥1650). Seats are often booked well in advance.

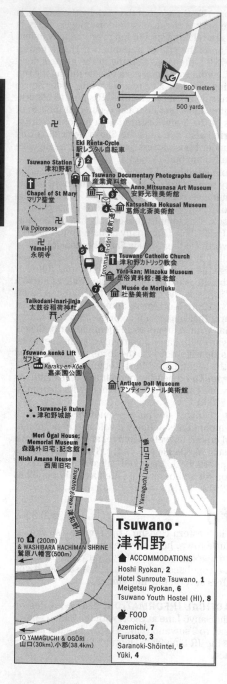

Tsuwano · 津和野

▲ ACCOMMODATIONS

Hoshi Ryokan, 2
Hotel Sunroute Tsuwano, 1
Meigetsu Ryokan, 6
Tsuwano Youth Hostel (HI), 8

🍴 FOOD

Azemichi, 7
Furusato, 3
Saranoki-Shōintei, 5
Yūki, 4

The village is ideally explored by bike; the area in front of the station teems with **rent-a-cycle stands**, which charge ¥500 for the first 2hr. and ¥100 per 1hr., or ¥800 per day. **Eki Rent-a-Cycle** (☎72-3112) is closest to the station. (Open daily 8am-7pm.) As village of some 6000 inhabitants, Tsuwano offers little in the way of services. The town's **information center** (☎72-1771) shares a building with the Tsuwano Documentary Photography Gallery and sells a useful guide for ¥200. In an emergency call ☎110 for **police**, ☎119 for **fire** or **ambulance**. (Open daily 9am-5pm.) The **post office** has an **international ATM**. (Open for mail M-F 9am-5pm; ATM M-F 8:45am-6pm, Sa 9am-5pm, Su 9am-1pm.)

🏠🍴 ACCOMMODATIONS AND FOOD. It's easy to find a place to stay—the greater question is whether or not you want to spend the night here, since you can easily complete your visit in a day, and there are few evening diversions. **Hoshi Ryokan ❸**, by the train station, is perfect for the road-weary. Cozy *tatami* rooms have the usual amenities—TV, green tea, and A/C. (☎72-0136. Check-in 4pm. Check-out 10am. 2 meals included. ¥6000 per person.) **Meigetsu Ryokan ❹** is in the center of town. From the station, go straight along the main street to the post office and follow the road left. Take the next left. The elegant Meigetsu is known for its cooking. *Tatami* rooms are larger and more luxuriously furnished than at most places. (☎72-0685; fax 72-0637. Check-in 3:30pm. Check-out 10am. 2 meals included. ¥10,000 per person.) **Hotel Sunroute Tsuwano ❹** offers the town's only Western-style accommodations. Turn left away from the station and take a right at the bridge; the hotel is 70m farther. Clean rooms come with every convenience, including movie channels. (☎72-3232; fax 72-2805. Check-in 3pm. Check-out 10am. Singles

from ¥8300, doubles ¥11,000.) Take any southbound bus to the Youth Hostel-mae stop in front of the **Tsuwano Youth Hostel (HI) ❶**, at the southern edge of town, 30min. from the station. It's cheaper than the minshuku, but you'll have a hard time finding breakfast. Dorm rooms are clean and comfortable, but the decor is dated. (☎72-0373. Check-in 3pm. Check-out 10am. ¥2900, nonmembers ¥3900.)
    Tsuwano has a fair number of eateries. Hours are unreliable—many places close on weekdays. If you arrive during a tourist ebb, expect to wander a bit in search of grub. Tsuwano has two specialties: *uzume-meishi*, a rice soup with mountain vegetables and mushrooms, and the ubiquitous carp. Across from the post office, **Furusato ❸** serves up the local specialties in a traditional white-washed house. It's the best place in Tsuwano to try *uzume-meishi*. (☎72-0403. Open daily 11am-3pm.) On the main street past the post office, **Yūki ❸** is a pricey restaurant housed in a wood-toned building. A stream flowing through the dining area is filled with carp you can order for your table. (☎72-0162. Open M-Tu and Th-Su 10am-7pm.) **Azemichi ❷** is an unpretentious *rāmen* restaurant at the bend of the street that runs in front of the station. The exotic fare sets this place apart: *chōgekikara* (hellishly spicy) *rāmen*, and the ¥700-¥1200 wild boar *don*. (☎72-1884. Open daily 9:30am-5pm.) **Saranoki-Shōintei ❸**, across from the Catholic church, specializes in *kaiseki-ryōri*, which traditionally accompanies the tea ceremony. The dining area overlooks a charming garden. (☎72-1661. Open daily 10am-4pm.)

◙ **SIGHTS.** Immediately to the right of the station exit are two museums that deserve a look. The **Tsuwano Documentary Photographs Gallery** displays the works of photojournalist Kuwahara Shisei, including his coverage of the fall of Communism, repression in North Korea, and voyages to other perilous corners of the globe. (☎72-3171. Open daily 9am-5pm. ¥200.) Across the street in an Edo-style hall the **Anno Art Museum** houses the work of local artist Anno Mitsumasa. It's interesting to see how a Japanese artist depicts the West—most works are set in America or Europe. The museum has a tiny planetarium. (☎72-4155; fax 72-4157. Open daily 9am-5pm. Closed some W. ¥600.) Between two temples behind the station, a path wends through a damp and luminous forest to **Maria-Seidō**, the Chapel of St. Mary, built in 1948 by a German missionary in memory of the Christians who died in the Meiji Era's violent ultra-nationalist phase. You can return by Tsuwano's Via Dolorosa, on the other side of the Chapel. Lined with stations of the cross, it terminates at **Yōmei-ji**. The temple has a pleasant Zen garden, and is home to the grave of novelist Mori Ōgai. (☎72-1717. Open 8:30am-5pm. ¥300.)
    South of the station along the Tsuwano River is the Edo-era neighborhood of **Tonomachi**. White-washed houses with wooden finishes and grates line the quiet roads. The atmosphere is only slightly marred by power lines. Along the streets, the best has been made of the drainage ditches, which have been converted into iris farms and carp hatcheries. In times past, the carp were an edible hedge against bad harvests or warfare. A number of the traditional houses in the area have been converted into souvenir shops. Tsuwano is a good place to pick up local *sake*, paper crafts, and the bean-paste treat *genjin-machi*.
    A number of museums fill you in on the town's past. The **Katsushika Hokusai Museum**, at the north end of Tonomachi by the post office, houses a collection of prints, paintings, and drawings by the Edo-era master and his followers. (☎72-1850. Open 9:30am-5pm. ¥500.) Farther south, the Catholic church follows the Jesuit tradition of mixing local cultural elements with traditional European forms. The interior is a *tatami* room, but the stone building features a gothic spire, stained glass windows, and an organ that would be at home in Barcelona. While the church dates from 1931, the Catholic community is descended from the original 16th-century wave of converts. Across the street is the **Minzoku Museum**, for-

WESTERN HONSHŪ

merly a *samurai* school, now dedicated to "folk art." (☎72-1000. Open daily 8:30am-5pm. ¥200.) Across the river, just before the train tracks is **Musée de Mori-juku**, a traditional farmhouse converted into a gallery for local contemporary artists. On the 2nd floor are the museum's treasures—the only set of Goya etchings in Western Honshū. (☎72-3200. Open daily 9am-5pm. ¥500.)

Heading farther south, cross the railroad tracks and keep going to the **Antique Doll Museum**, which displays dolls from all over Europe. (☎72-3110. Open M-W and F-Su 9:30am-5:30pm. ¥800.) Beyond are the graceful **Mori Ogai Memorial Museum** and the preserved residence of the Meiji-era novelist, where you can wander the grounds. (☎72-3210; fax ☎72-3307. Open daily 9am-5pm. ¥100.) The lovely museum building houses the personal effects of this canonical author, best known for *Vita Sexualis* and *Wild Geese*. (Open Tu-Su 9am-5pm. ¥500.) Nearby, the home of Nishi Amane, a Meiji Restoration bigwig, can be viewed from the outside.

Across the river at the north end of Karaku-en lies **Taikodani-Inari-Jinja**, famous for its multitude of *torii* (over 1000), which almost form a tunnel up the hillside. The complex is one of the largest Inari shrines in Japan, and the beauty of the vermilion, black, and gold buildings can't be denied. Farther south is the **Tsuwano Kankō lift**, which whisks you up to the mountain ridge around Tsuwano. (☎72-0376. Open Dec.-Feb. daily 10am-5pm, Mar.-July and Sept.-Nov. 10am-4pm, Aug. daily 9am-5pm. Round-trip ¥450.) From the top, a path leads to the medieval ruins of **Tsuwano-jō**. Only the castle's foundations remain, but the view makes the trip memorable. For a workout, a path leads up from the side of Taikodani-Inari-Jinja.

◾ **FESTIVALS.** During the **Washibara Hachimangū Taisai** (2nd Su in Apr.), archers gather in Washibara Shrine to compete for glory. On **Otome-Tōge** (May 3, 10am), a Catholic holiday, a procession walks from the Church to the chapel of Saint Mary, culminating in an open-air Mass on the hillside. The **Sagi Mai Matsuri** (July 20, 24, 27) is a festival featuring the Heron Dance, a religious dance performed at Yasaka Shrine by devotees dressed as birds. The third Saturday in October is a **culinary festival**, celebrating the region's *sake*, *jizake*, and the locally grown variety of sweet potato, *imoni*—it's a good chance to sample these specialties. The **Yakko Procession** takes place on the Sunday closest to November 23 when locals dressed as Edo-era footmen parade through the streets to Shōrinzan Tenman-gū.

MATSUE (松江) ☎0852

Apart from Hiroshima, Matsue is the most appealing and energetic city in Western Honshū. Wedged on the coast of the Ōhashi River between two coastal lagoons, Shinki-ko and Nakanoumi-ko, Matsue's compact size and many waterways make it a pleasant city to explore. The city attracts not just with impressive sights—an original castle, a clutch of fine museums, and the literary legacy of Lafcadio Hearn—but also with its chic neighborhoods, fine restaurants, and mellow vibe.

ON THE WEB Matsue: www.city.matsue.shimane.jp

🖺 **TRANSPORTATION.** You can reach Matsue by plane, bus or train. There are two airports in striking distance of the city: **Yonago** (☎0570-029-222 or ☎0859-313211; www.yonago-air.com) and **Izumo** (☎0852-59-2828; www.san-in-tabi.net). Izumo is closer to Matsue and has a regular bus service (¥850). From Yonago, take the bus to the train station (¥570) and switch to the local line to Matsue. Ichibata Bus Corporation runs long-distance buses from stop #9 outside Matsue Station to: **Hiroshima** (3¼hr., 14 per day, ¥4000); **Ōsaka** (4¾hr., 8 per day, ¥5100); **Tōkyō** (4 per day, 5hr., ¥5400). The closest *shinkansen* stop is **Okayama** (4hr. or more, ¥5610).

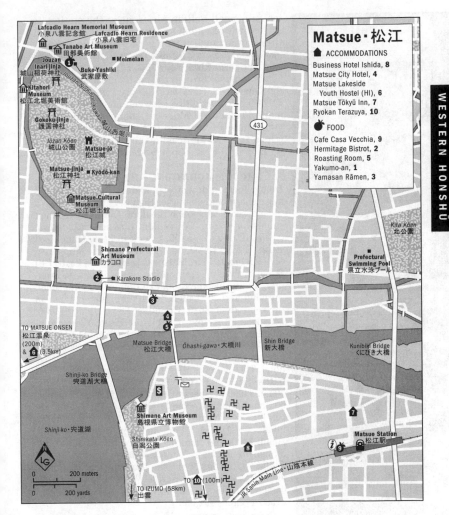

Matsue・松江

⌂ ACCOMMODATIONS

Business Hotel Ishida, **8**
Matsue City Hotel, **4**
Matsue Lakeside
　Youth Hostel (HI), **6**
Matsue Tōkyū Inn, **7**
Ryokan Terazuya, **10**

● FOOD

Cafe Casa Vecchia, **9**
Hermitage Bistrot, **2**
Roasting Room, **5**
Yakumo-an, **1**
Yamasan Rāmen, **3**

■ **ORIENTATION.** Matsue is split by the Ōhashi-gawa River. Although the south side contains a fair number of services as well as the train station, the true heart of the city is on the north side. There, over the Matsue bridge and along both sides of the Kyōbashi River, a lively downtown with funky shops and restaurants competes for attention with the attractions of the castle area and the *samurai* district further north. Farther west, past the city hall, is the Matsue Onsen Stop of the Ichibata Electric Railway, which connects Matsue to Izumo Taisha.

◪ **PRACTICAL INFORMATION.** A fair-sized town, Matsue provides a number of services. There is a **travel information satellite service** in the train station. (☎23-3320. Open M-F 10am-6pm, Sa-Su 10am-5pm.) The **tourist information cen-**

THE LOCAL LEGEND

MATSUE'S ADOPTED SON

By the time the Tuttle Company published his essays on life in Japan, Western author Lafcadio Hearn had been declared "as Japanese as the *haiku*." The road to Japan, however, was neither straight nor easy. His family moved from Greece to Ireland just in time to fall apart. He was left with his aunt, and spent his childhood in Dublin. His aunt had him educated in France and England, but when the money ran out, he was left to make his own way.

Penniless, he went to earn his fortune in New York, but failed, and headed to Cincinnati, where he learned to proofread. He made a life for himself working on the *Cincinnati Enquirer and Commercial*, and became a journalist. Later, in New Orleans, he began writing for *Harper's Magazine*. He continued writing for them when he left for Martinique.

Hearn left the West Indies in 1890 to travel to Japan for *Harper's*. He taught English in Matsue, where he developed a passion for Japanese culture. He married the daughter of a *samurai* family and in 1895 became a Japanese citizen, taking the name Yakumo Koizumi. Through his work, he contributed more than any other writer to the Western understanding of Japan.

Hearn's best-known books on Japan include: *Japan: An Attempt at Interpretation* (1904), *In Ghostly Japan* (1899), and *Kwaidan* (1904).

ter, in a small building in front of the station, is staffed with English speakers. If you call ahead, they can arrange a free goodwill guide service. (☎21-4034; fax ☎27-2598. Open daily 9am-6pm.) The **Horikawa River Boat Tour** runs an interesting 50min. course through the castle moat and around the downtown. (☎27-0417. Every 15min. 9am-5pm. ¥1200.) The **post office** between Matsuejō and Shimane Prefectural Museum changes money, provides mail service, and has an **international ATM**. (Open for mail and cash exchange M-F 9am-5pm; ATM open M-F 9am-5pm, Sa-Su 9am-12:30pm.)

⌨ ☐ ACCOMMODATIONS AND FOOD. Conveniently located downtown, **Matsue City Hotel ❷** has more charm and character than most of its rivals—a tile mosaic greets you at the door, and tidy, well-kept rooms lie within. Convenient downtown location. (☎25-4100; fax 25-5100. Check-in 3pm. Check-out 10am. Singles ¥5000, doubles ¥9000.) One stop down on the Ichibata Line, **Matsue Lakeside Youth Hostel (HI) ❶** has a pleasant staff and standard facilities. From the Tiffany Museum Stop, exit opposite the museum. Turn left and go straight for 10min.; the hostel is on the right. (☎36-8620. Breakfast ¥600. Dinner ¥1000. Check-in after 4pm. Check-out 10am. ¥2800, nonmembers ¥3800.) Closer by, **Business Hotel Ishida ❷** (ビジネスホテル石田), next to the tracks 150m past the station, is more a minshuku than a business hotel. The plain but neat *tatami* rooms have shared baths. (☎21-5931. Check-in after 3pm. Check-out 10am. ¥4000 per person.) Opposite Matsue Tenmangū, the charming **Ryokan Terazuya ❷** (旅館寺津屋) is run by a remarkably friendly staff and serves tasty meals. (☎21-3484. Check-in after 4pm. Check-out 10am. ¥4000 per person, ¥7000 with breakfast and dinner.) If all else fails, **Matsue Tōkyū Inn ❸** (松江東急イン), across from the station, has standard amenities in its nondescript Western rooms. (☎27-0109. Check-in after 2pm. Check-out 11am. Singles ¥7000; doubles ¥12,000.)

Cafes, restaurants, and inexpensive eateries abound in Matsue. The downtown area is particularly rife with dining possibilities. **EGL Darts and Bar ❷** is one pleasant hang out. Try your luck with the local pool sharks. Drinks ¥500 and up. (☎27-7666. Open M-Sa 5pm-3am, Su noon-1am.) On the main pedestrian street downtown, one of the nicest chains in town, **Yamasan Rāmen ❶** is convenient and cheap, serving heaping bowls of tasty *rāmen* for ¥550-700. (Open M-Sa 11:30am-2pm and 5-10pm.) The **Roasting Room ❶**, in a quaint brick building on the riverside, is a good place to pick up a mug of joe. The old-timey setting might tempt you into staying for one of the massive ¥600 sandwiches. (☎25-

0585. Open daily 8am-10pm.) Uniquely set in a former Bank of Japan building, **Hermitage Bistrot ❸** is one of the showiest restaurants in town, serving a high-brow blend of French and Italian cuisines, with a delicious Japanese twist. (☎20-7000. Lunch ¥1000-2800, dinner ¥2500-4000. Open 11am-9pm.) An old-fashioned noodle house in an enclosed garden across from the castle moat, **Yakumo-an ❶** serves *warigo soba* noodles for ¥600. (☎22-2400. Open daily 9am-4:30pm.) At the western end of the station-front square is **Cafe Casa Vecchia ❷**, a classy European-style place. The desserts are sweet and fluffy (cake set ¥680). (☎24-4347. Open daily 11am-midnight.)

ⓒ SIGHTS

Matsue-jō, in the northern part of the city, is the center of the *samurai* quarter and houses the city's interesting sights. The black-and-white **donjon** is smaller than others in the area, but it's the 1611 original. (☎21-4030. Open Apr.-Sept. 8:30am-6:30pm, Oct.-Mar. 8:30am-5pm. ¥500.) The castle sits in a woodsy park, which it shares with picturesque **Jozan Inari Shrine,** in the northern corner, and the colonnaded **Kyōdō-kan,** built for a Meiji-era Imperial visit that fell through. The display is less interesting than the architecture. (Open daily 8:30am-5pm.)

The **Shimane Art Museum** is across from the bend in the railroad tracks. The striking modern building sweeps along the shoreline, and there's a sculpture garden. The permanent collection has a Monet and several Rodins, and there are frequently special exhibitions. (☎55-4700; www2.pref.shimane.jp/sam. Open Tu-Su Oct.-Feb. 10am-6:30pm, Mar.-Sept. 10am-30min. after sunset. Permanent exhibition ¥300, students ¥200. Special exhibition ¥1000/¥600. Both exhibitions ¥1150/¥700.) If you have time, head to **Karakoro Art Studio** (カラコロ) in the downtown center southeast of the castle. Housed in a former Bank of Japan building, the studio assembles arts and crafts in a number of ateliers spread through the building and in the outdoor plaza. Impressively lit at night, the studio is worth a look even if you won't be buying any crafts, and the cafe and restaurant are tempting places to loiter. (☎20-7000; fax 20-7070. Shops open daily 9:30am-6:30pm. Free.)

South of the castle, **Shimane Prefectural Museum** (☎22-5750; www2.pref.shimane.jp/koda), houses historical and archaeological artifacts. Ask for the remarkably complete English booklet, which charts the history of the area. Especially interesting is the history of nearby Izumo Taisha, which has been a cult site since the emergence of Japanese civilization. (Open Tu-Su 9am-5pm. ¥200, students ¥100.) To the north, **Shiomi Nawate**, the main street of *samurai* houses, runs along the north edge of the moat. Most of the houses are museums, restaurants, or tourist stores. At the bend in the river, the **Kitahori Museum** (Matsue Kitahori Bijutsukan; 松江北堀美術館), in a boxy modern building, displays a range of French *art nouveau* pieces. (☎31-6811; http://homepage2.nifty.com/kitahori. Open Tu-Su 9am-5pm. ¥1000.)

Farther along Shiomi Nawate are the sites related to Lafcadio Hearn, one of the most respected Western writers in Meiji-era Japan (p. 514). He loved the country so much that he took Japanese citizenship and raised a family here. He lived in Matsue for less than a year, but the town influenced much of his writing, and he's become a favorite son. The fascinating **Lafcadio Hearn Memorial Museum** houses his personal effects, and bilingual videos trace his journey to Japan. (☎21-2147. Open daily Apr.-Sept. 8:30am-6:30pm, Oct.-March 8:30am-5pm. ¥250.) Nearby, the **Lafcadio Hearn Residence** is preserved as it was during his sojourn there. He could afford decent digs—the house was a former *samurai* residence. Although it's picturesque, there's little to be learned here. (Open daily 9am-5pm. ¥200.)

One door down is the **Tanabe Art Museum,** which sits in a closed, *samurai*-style compound in the middle of a broad rock garden. The collection inside, primarily tea-ceremony accessories, is a bit of a letdown. (☎26-2211. Open Tu-Su 9am-5pm.

(vertical text in right margin) WESTERN HONSHŪ

¥500.) A little farther on is the **Buku Yashiki Samurai Residence,** the largest Edo-period residence in Matsue, which has been extremely well preserved. Tour *tatami* rooms festooned with the daily objects of premodern Japanese life. (☎ 22-2243. Open Apr.-Sept. 8:30am-6:30pm, Oct.-March 8:30am-5pm. ¥250.)

Follow the signs to **Meimei-an,** a tea house on a hill near the *samurai* area. Built in 1779 by a retainer to *daimyō* Matsudaira Fumai, the diminutive house conforms to exacting tea-ceremony requirements. It was moved to its current site in 1928 and now sits in a well-raked garden. Access is prohibited, but it's so small that essentially all of it is visible from outside. (Open daily 9am-5pm. ¥200.)

▶ DAYTRIP FROM MATSUE

IZUMO TAISHA

Take the private Ichibata Line from Matsue Onsen Station in the northern part of Matsue (1hr., ¥790; you may have to change trains) to Izumo Taisha. If you're heading there and back, get the LandR Free Kippu, a special all-day train pass (¥1200).

The second most important Shintō shrine in Japan after Ise (p. 470), Izumo Taisha has been a center of Japanese religious life ever since the emergence of civilization here in the Yayoi Period. The shrine is mentioned in the oldest Japanese chronicles, the *Kojiki* and *Nihon Shoki*, and serves a central role in Shintōism. Myth says the sun goddess Amaterasu founded it. The current buildings, though magnificent, are much more recent—most date back to the 19th century. The main shrine was built in 1744. Each October, the 8 million Shintō gods gather at Izumo Taisha for the annual Kamiari-sae festival. Not to be outdone, the Imperial family also pays an annual visit—which you can witness if you're here May 14-16. Not all pilgrims are brought by piety—singletons flock to worship the resident god, Ōkuninushi, patron of harmonious partnerships. These lonely romantics perform a slight variation on the traditional Shintō clapping prayer—rather than clapping twice, as is normal, they clap four times, twice for themselves and twice for their future partner. The modern treasure house, **Shinkoden,** displays the shrine's collection of historical artifacts, none of which are very memorable, though the exhibit has a certain charm. One of the more interesting displays is a tiny model of the shrine in its 13th-century heyday. (Open daily 8am-4:30pm ¥150.) At the opposite end of the compound, past a bunker-like modern structure, is the **Oracle Hall.** Visually the most impressive of the shrine's buildings, the entryway is capped with a giant traditional twist of straw rope (*shimenawa*). You can see where visitors have jammed in ¥1 and ¥5 coins for good luck. Shintō rites are constantly being performed, so even casual visitors can catch a glimpse of Shintō in action.

From the station, pass through a village of *soba* stands, hotels, and souvenir stores to reach the shrine. The outer edge of the grounds is marked by a massive grey gate as the path winds from the village streets into a park of graceful trees and modern statues. Following the main path leads to the **Haiden** (prayer hall). The building's mossy peak reaches 24m into the air. Although it's off-limits to casual visitors, you can lean in from the main gate for a good look at the decorations and carvings adorning the hall. Behind the Haiden is the **Honden** (sanctuary). A low wall enforces the prohibition, but you can get a look at the building from outside. Farther back, behind the sanctuary, is the old treasure house **(Shōkokan).** Since the treasures were moved to another building, the Shōkokan has housed statues of Ōkuninushi as Daikoku, one of his manifestations, along with his son Ebisu. Both are jovial deities; Daikoku holds a hammer and stands on three rice bales, while Ebisu usually has a fish tucked under one arm. (Open daily 8am-4:30pm. ¥50.)

TAKAHASHI (高橋) ☎ 0866

Takahashi is set in a remote inland river valley and has the sleepy feeling of a town
seldom visited. Nevertheless, the town's sights, including the largest mountain
castle in Japan and a picturesque Zen garden, are worth a day of touring.

ON THE WEB	Takahashi: www.city.takahashi.okayama.jp

▐▌🚹 TRANSPORTATION AND PRACTICAL INFORMATION. Set off the main
JR line, Takahashi requires some effort to reach. **Trains** run to and from Okayama
(1hr., ¥820) and Kurashiki (40 min., ¥570). **Takahashi Station** is at the center of
town, with a **taxi stand** and a **police box** outside. The tourist information booth is
shut down, but **maps** of the city are available in a green tray in the station's central
stand. A route extends westward of the station towards the Takahashi-gawa river,
but more useful is the perpendicular cross-street that runs to the canal zone and
the town's sights. In an emergency, call ☎ 110 for **police,** ☎ 119 for **fire** or **ambulance.**

▐▌🏠 ACCOMMODATIONS AND FOOD. There is no reason to stay in Takahashi. After 5pm, when all the sights are closed, there is nothing to do or see. If you
have a reason to overnight in Takahashi, there are a few options. The most economical and readily accessible to foreigners is the **Takahashi Youth Hostel (HI)** ❶
(高橋ユースホステル) near the rail bridge over the canal. A standard hostel
with dorm rooms and a convenient location. However, it closes periodically and
without a schedule, so don't make this your only option. (☎ 22-3149. Members
¥2700, nonmembers ¥3700.) You can get to **Midori Ryokan** ❷ (みどり旅館) by taking the first left on the main street fronting the station. A comfortable place, it has
tatami rooms available for ¥4200. (☎ 22-2537.)

There are few food choices in Takahashi. A number of restaurants cluster
around the station—one, **Victoria Udon House** ❶ (ビクトリア), offers soups for
¥300-800. (☎ 22-3263. Open Tu-Su 10am-9pm.) **Chateau Caferest** ❷ serves a blend of
Euro-food with a down-home American atmosphere. Tasty lunches ¥800-900.
(☎ 22-1008. Open M-Sa 7:30am-8pm, Su 7:30am-5pm.)

◪ SIGHTS. The most significant sight, **Bichū-Matsuyama-jō** (美中松山城), is far
from the center of town. Built prior to the rise of urban power, the castle was
designed for maximum remoteness and invisibility. It sits on Matsuyama, a strenuous 1½hr. hike from the station. A taxi ride (¥1200) is a good idea, especially for a
group. Even with some vehicular assistance, it's a 30min. uphill hike to reach the
highest castle in Japan. This distance was a defensive measure—enemies worn
down by travel would be easier to defeat in battle. The castle was built in the 13th
century, at the height of Japan's chaotic and bloody civil wars and is said to be the
inspiration for Akira Kurosawa's dark masterpiece *Throne of Blood.* Walking
down from the castle, you'll encounter bilingual signs leading to the town's other
major attractions. The first you'll reach is the **Warrior's House Museum,** an Edo-era
samurai house. The inside is outfitted with antiques and dummies representing
the *samurai* family and their servants, while a hall out back displays armor and
weapons from the age of *samurai* warfare. (☎ 22-1480. Open daily 9am-5pm.
¥300.) A block farther, you'll reach **Raikyu-ji** (頼久寺) with its beautiful Zen garden. Walk through the temple's *tatami* rooms to view different sections of the
elaborate garden, with its exquisitely composed space of shrubs, stones, rivers,
and flower beds. The "borrowed scenery" of the mountain Atago-san adds to the
effect. The lasting appeal of this 400-year-old garden is a testament to the mastery
of its designer, the famous Kobori Enshu. (☎ 22-3516. Open daily 9am-5pm. ¥300.)
Slightly farther along, the **Local History Museum** (Kyōshi Shiryōkan; 郷土資料館)
is housed in a unique bit of Meiji-period East-West hybrid architecture. Originally
a schoolhouse from the turn of the century, its wood-shingled facade resembles a

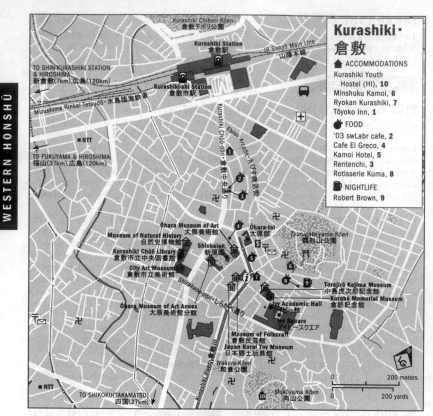

Kurashiki·
倉敷

🏠 ACCOMMODATIONS
Kurashiki Youth
  Hostel (HI), **10**
Minshuku Kamoi, **6**
Ryokan Kurashiki, **7**
Tōyoko Inn, **1**

🍎 FOOD
'03 swLabr cafe, **2**
Cafe El Greco, **4**
Kamoi Hotel, **5**
Rentenchi, **3**
Rotisserie Kuma, **8**

🍸 NIGHTLIFE
Robert Brown, **9**

little house on the prairie... except for the temple-style Japanese entryway. Inside find a jumbled mix of peasant bric-a-brac, worth 30min. in rainy weather. (☎22-1479. Open daily 9am-5pm. ¥300.) About 10min. walk east of the station, the twin temples **Shoren-ji** (松蓮寺) and **Yakushiin** (薬師院) aren't exceptional, but their hillside location allows nice views of the city. (Open 9am-5pm. Free.)

KURASHIKI (倉敷)   ☎086

A sister city to Okayama, Kurashiki sits slightly off the main railroad junction and has a more leisurely feel. The town derives almost all of its fame from a stretch of Edo-era white-and-black merchant houses—the rest it gets from the world-class Ōhara Museum of Art. While these attractions merit a look-see, do as the Japanese do and make Kurashiki a daytrip from a more active city. Once the museums and cafes close up at around 5pm, Kurashiki becomes a sleepy place.

ON THE WEB   Kurashiki: www.city.kurashiki.okayama.jp

⌨️ TRANSPORTATION AND PRACTICAL INFORMATION. *Shinkansen* stop in **Shin-Kurashiki Station,** two stops from **JR Kurashiki Station** (10min., ¥190), but arrivals are infrequent and it's more convenient to travel via **Okayama** (15min., ¥320). There are regional connections from JR Kurashiki Station (☎422-0453) to: Uno (1½hr., ¥820), Fukuyama (1¼hr., ¥740), and Takahashi (1½hr., ¥990).

Kurashiki is compact and walkable. From the station front, **Kurashiki Chūō-dōri** is the main north-south road, intersected by **Shirakabe-dōri** south of downtown. The station, the Ebisu arcade leads to the **Bikan district** (canal district) around which the city's sights cluster. East of the canal zone, the **Hon-machi** area contains the nicer restaurants and nightlife. The most helpful **tourist office** is in the train station (☎426-8681; open daily 9am-5pm), while there's another at the main bend in the canal (☎422-0542; open daily 9am-5pm). In an emergency, call ☎110 for **police,** ☎119 for **fire** or **ambulance.** Other services include: **Goodwill Guide Tours** (☎422-0542; open daily 9am-5pm); **currency exchange** at **Chūgoku Bank** (中国銀行), at the intersection of the Ebisu arcade and the canal area (☎424-2233; open M-F 9am-3pm); an **international ATM** at the branch **post office** across from Chūgoku Bank (open M-F 9am-5pm, ATM available M-F 9am-7pm, Sa-Su 9am-5pm.)

⌨️ ACCOMMODATIONS. A 10min. bus ride to Shimin Kaikan Bus Stop (¥190) followed by a 30min. uphill slog, or an ¥810 taxi ride, woodsy **Kurashiki Youth Hostel (HI) ❶** (倉敷ユースホステル) would be ideal if not for its inconvenient location. The hostel has 4-bunk dorms; groups rarely share with strangers. (☎422-7355; www.jyh.gr.jp/kurashiki. Dinner ¥850. Check-in after 2pm. Check-out 10am. Doors lock at 10pm. ¥2800, nonmembers ¥3800.) Find tidy and comfortable *tatami* at old-fashioned and friendly **Minshuku Kamoi ❸** (カモ井), a block from the canal district. (☎422-4898. Check-in after 3pm. Check-out 9am. 2 meals included. ¥6000 per person.) The height of traditional luxury is **Ryokan Kurashiki ❺** (旅館倉敷). This Edo-period ryokan houses guests in spacious *tatami* rooms along the Kurashiki canal. (☎422-0730. Meals included. From ¥20,000 per person. AmEx/MC/V.) **Tōyoko Inn ❸** (東横インイン), on the main road, is a Western-style hotel for the digital age. There's free Internet access in the business corner, and each room has a complimentary LAN hookup for laptops. (☎430-1045; www.toyoko-inn.co.jp. Check-in 4pm. Check-out 10am. Singles ¥4800; doubles ¥7300. AmEx/MC/V.)

⌨️ FOOD. Although there are a number of restaurants in Kurashiki, be aware that most close early, and guests in traditional accommodations are usually expected to eat at their ryokan or minshuku. **The Kamoi Hotel ❷** (カモ井), on the canal street, serves sushi, *tempura*, and other Japanese staples in sets for ¥800-1600. (☎422-0606. Open M-Tu and Th-Su 10am-6:30pm.) On the main street, **Rentenchi ❷** (煉天地) serves up tasty Italian food in a relaxed environment. The littleback clams are well worth the ¥1100. (☎421-7858. Open daily 11am-3pm and 5-10pm.) Trendy, new, and oddly-named, **'03 swLabr cafe ❶** is in a green clapboard building. It features decadent deserts (¥500-800) to match its cushy couches. After hours, it turns into a bar where Kurashiki's hipsters hang out. (☎434-3099. Cafe open M-W and F-Su 11:30am-8pm; bar open M-W and F-Su 8pm-3am.) For drinks and cakes (¥400-600), try **Cafe El Greco ❶**. Seating is at common tables, and it gets packed during the lunch rush. (☎422-0297. Open Tu-Su 10am-5pm.) An upscale option in the historic Hon-machi quarter, **Rotisserie Kuma ❹** serves French fare in a candle-lit setting. (☎424-2915. Dinners ¥2500-3500. Open M-Tu and Th-Su 6-10pm.) **Robert Brown ❷** (ローベルトブラーン), also in Hon-machi, is an immaculate live jazz bar. Sip your highballs and cocktails (¥500-800) while listening to Billie Holiday covers. (☎424-8043. Live cover ¥500. Open daily noon-11pm.)

🔘 **SIGHTS.** The **Bikan district's** stretch of Edo-era white-and-black **merchant's houses** along the picturesque Kurashiki-kawa canal are the major attraction. Strolling along the canal with its houses unmarred by power lines or garish neon signs, visitors experience an odd feeling of nostalgia for a time they themselves never experienced. Although the Bikan district is fairly narrow, the feeling can be extended by strolling to the Hon-machi area, slightly farther west. While the canal with its swans and carp may be missing, the 17th-century buildings there have a charm of their own. To supplement the already considerable appeal of the canal zone, a number of museums have been installed in the area.

By far the most significant of the city's museums, the **Ōhara Museum of Art** (Ōhara Bijutsukan; 大原美術館) is a world-class institution. Built by the textile magnate Magosaburo Ōhara to memorialize Torajiro Kojima, his best friend and a local painter and art collector, it houses a collection impressive enough to mark its main gate with two of Rodin's masterpieces, the stark *St. John the Baptist* on the left and to the right the *Burghers of Calais*. Rather than cash in on the Edo-era charm of the Bikan area, the museum's main building, the best-known in Kurashiki, stands out, fronting the canal with a neo-classical sandstone facade. The faux-Greek temple is merely the first of a series of galleries that house an impressive collection of western art, including one of Monet's waterlilies as well as works by Gauguin, Toulouse-Lautrec, and El Greco. An elaborate annex houses Western-style works by Japanese artists from the late 1800s to the present. A craft gallery contains traditional works by well-known masters, and a small Asian gallery contains ancient Buddhist art from continental Asia and Japan. (1-1-15, Chūō, Kurashiki 710. ☎422-0005; fax 427-3677. Open Tu-Su 9am-5pm. ¥1000, students ¥600.)

The city has numerous other museums. The **Kurashiki Museum of Folk Craft** (Kurashiki Mingeikan; 倉敷民芸館) contains a mostly Japanese collection of industrial art, but a few foreign pieces can be identified. The location, inside a number of linked Edo-era storehouses (*kura*), rivals the exhibits for interest. (1-4-11, Chūō, 710. Farther down the canal from the Ōhara Museum. ☎422-1637. Open Tu-Su 9am-5pm. ¥700; college students ¥400; elementary students ¥300.) The top that holds the world record for the longest single spin is only one of the attractions at the **Japanese Rural Toy Museum** (Nihon Kyōshi Gangukan; 日本郷土玩具館). Traditional crafts from around Japan are displayed, including wood-carved toys, fish flags, kites, and dolls. A well-stocked gift shops lets you take away new versions of the toys on display. (Next door to the Kurashiki Museum. ☎422-8058; fax 422-8028. Open daily 9am-5pm. ¥500.) The **Kurashiki Museum of Natural History** (Shizenshi Hakubutsukan; 自然史博物館) hosts mammoth bones, as well as collections of plants and animals, making a nice break from the fine arts-and-history focus of the rest of the city. (2-6-1, Chūō, 710. Outside the Bikan Canal zone, across Shirakabe-dōri. ☎425-6037. Open Tu-Su 9am-5pm. ¥100.) The Japanese art at the **Kurashiki City Art Museum** (Shiritsu Bijutsukan; 市立美術館) can't really compete with the collections at the Ōhara, but the building is an interesting bit of brutalism. (2-6-1, Chūō, Kurashiki 710. Next to the Museum of Natural History. ☎425-6034; www.city.kurashiki.okayama.jp/kcam/index.html. Open Tu-Su 9am-5pm. ¥200.)

Rather than being demolished, the obsolete Meiji-era brick buildings southeast of the canal zone were renovated and opened as **Ivy Square** in 1974, with several museums, a hotel, restaurants, and gift shops. The most significant on-site museum is the **Torajiro Kojima Museum,** a satellite of the Ōhara museum, containing works by Kojima as well as halls full of his European and Oriental acquisitions. (☎426-1010. Open Tu-Su 9am-5pm. ¥350, students ¥200.) **Kurabo Memorial Hall,** in one of the former cotton mills, traces the history of Kurashiki as a textile town. Its Academic Hall follows Western art through the ages in a series of reproductions of great masterpieces. (☎422-0010. Open daily 9am-5pm. ¥350; students ¥200.)

Okayama · 岡山

ACCOMMODATIONS
Hotel Excel Okayama, **3**
Hotel Granvia Okayama, **7**
The International Center (HI), **2**
Okayama-ken Seinenkaikan
    Youth Hostel (HI), **1**

FOOD
Hakodate Ichiban, **6**
Les Maroilles, **5**
Quiet Village, **4**

OKAYAMA (岡山) ☎ 086

Okayama, better loved by freight transporters than budget travelers, is best known as the most important railway interchange between Ōsaka and Shimonoseki. As such, it was an obvious target for bombing during WWII and the air raids destroyed the city's historical sights. While modern Okayama is a vibrant provincial industrial center, it is not a big draw in other respects.

ON THE WEB   Okayama City: www.city.okayama.okayama.jp

TRANSPORTATION. Okayama sits on the trunk of the JR Sanyō Line, right at its junction with the Seto Ohashi bridge to Shikoku. It is a significant gateway to the smaller island. **JR Okayama Station** (☎ 221-2445) services *shinkansen* and regular **trains** to: Himeji (*shinkansen* 40min., local 1¼hr.; ¥3640/¥1450); Hiroshima (2hr./4hr., ¥5860/¥2940); Kōbe (2hr./3½hr., ¥5440/¥2520); Ōsaka (2hr./4hr., ¥5860/¥2920) and Shimonoseki (3½hr./8hr., ¥10,580/¥6090). Local trains also serve Ueno (40min., ¥570), Kurashiki (20min., ¥320), Fukuyama (1¼hr., ¥950), Takahashi (1hr., ¥820), and Takamatsu (2hr., ¥1470). Rent

THE LOCAL LEGEND

OKAYAMA'S HERO

Once upon a time there lived an old couple. Although they were virtuous, they did not have the thing they most wanted: children. One day as the old man was out fishing in the river, he saw a giant peach drifting downstream. He hadn't caught any fish, so he took the peach home instead. When he and his wife cut the fruit open, they found a baby boy inside.

The kindly couple took him in, raising him as their own. At an early age, the strong, smart lad decided to seek adventure, setting out to defeat a monstrous three-eyed ogre that had been terrorizing residents of a nearby island. The old woman prepared some special cakes for the trip, which Momotaro shared with a pheasant, a monkey, and a dog he met along the way. The animals joined him on his journey, and eventually the ragtag crew overthrew the ogre and stole his treasure. The people were saved and Momotaro went to share his wealth with his family.

Momotaro means "peach boy," and he's a beloved figure throughout Japan. His story is associated with determination and cooperation succeeding over brute power. Okayama, whose tourist industry had been faltering, now uses its association with Momotaro to good effect—he's a city mascot. His statue stands downtown and at the station, and if you look down, you'll see him on the manhole covers as well.

bikes at **JR Rent-a-Cycle** in Okayama Station. (Open daily 7:30am-7:30pm. Last rental 5:30pm. ¥600 per day.)

■ ✶ 🔏 **ORIENTATION AND PRACTICAL INFORMA-TION.** From the front of the station, the main drag, **Momotarō-ōdōri** (桃太郎大道り), unfurls towards the castle, which marks the center of what is euphemistically known as the Okayama Culture Zone. The main north-south street, **Shiroshita Suji Ave.**, leads to most of the town's museums. A tram connects the station with the castle area (¥150).

The **tourist office** is in the train station. (☎222-2912. Open daily 9am-6pm.) The **Okayama International Center** (Okayama Kokusai Kōryū Sentā; 岡山国際交流セ ンター) offers expat info and free **Internet** on top of the obligatory travel propaganda. (☎256-2000; somu@opief.or.jp. Open Tu-Su 9am-9pm.) In an emergency, call ☎110 for **police,** ☎119 for **fire** or **ambulance.** Other services include: **currency exchange** and **international ATM** access at the **Central Post Office** (open M-F 9am-7pm, Sa 9am-5pm, Su 9am-12:30pm; ATM available M-F 8am-9pm, Sa-Su 9am-7pm); **luggage storage** at the station (☎221-0272; open M-F 10am-7pm, Sa-Su 10am-6pm); **Maruzen** bookstore, beneath the Concert Hall, with English-language books on its second floor (open daily 10am-8pm); local **police** (☎234-0110); English-speaking **Okayama University Hospital** (Okayama Daigaku Igakubu Byōin; 岡山大学医学部附属病院), 2-5-1 Shikata-chō, 700 (☎223-7151); and **Internet access** at **Megalo,** a new 24hr. cafe downtown (¥230 per 30min. and ¥60 per 15min. thereafter).

🛏 🍴 **ACCOMMODATIONS AND FOOD.** Try the **International Center (HI) ❸** for inexpensive guestroom service close to the station. The rooms are nice, though the neighborhood is uninviting. (Check-in 4-9pm. Check-out 10am. Singles ¥5600; doubles ¥8000; triples ¥10,500.) Spiffy, shared *tatami* rooms can be yours at the **Okayama-ken Seinenkaikan Youth Hostel (HI) ❷** (岡山県青性会館ユースホステル). It's 10min. from the station by bus #5 or 15—turn right after the pedestrian bridge. (☎252-0651; http://member.nifty.ne.jp/okayama-yh. Bike rental ¥300 per day. Members ¥2800, nonmembers ¥3800.) Downtown, **Hotel Excel Okayama ❷** (ホテルエクセル岡山) has all the business amenities. (☎224-0505; fax 224-2625. Check-in/out noon. Singles ¥4800; doubles ¥9600; triples ¥15,000.) **Hotel Granvia Okayama ❹** (ホテルグラ ンヴィア岡山) is next to the station. From the impressive lobby, staff will whisk you to a plush room. (☎234-7000; reservations ☎233-3444. Check-in 1pm. Check-out noon. Singles from ¥8500; doubles from ¥17,000.)

For a bite to eat, try the underground mall in front of the train station, **Orange Street**, which brims with inexpensive Japanese eateries. Among them is **Hakodate Ichiban ❷** (函館一番), a conveyor sushi place that serves up fish so fresh it's almost moving. A healthy appetite will run you ¥1000. (☎801-3075. Open daily 11am-10pm.) Another good place to look is the alleyways behind the Okayama Concert Hall—a surprising variety of stylish restaurants have sprung up there. **Quiet Village ❷** is one of them, featuring Japanese-style curries (¥700-880) in a friendly setting. Shared benches make for a village that's anything but quiet. (☎231-4100. Open Tu-Su 11:30am-8:30pm.) Nearby, **Les Maroilles ❹** is a good bet if you aim to impress. (☎221-9877. Light dinners ¥2800, full dinners ¥5000-8000. Reservations recommended. Open Tu-Su 11am-2:30pm and 5:30-9:30pm.)

◨ SIGHTS.

Okayama's sights of interest are concentrated downtown. Consider getting the **combined ticket deal,** which give you access to multiple sights at a reduced price. A ticket to Korakuen and the Okayama Prefectural Museum within it costs ¥440, one for Korakuen and Okayama-jō goes for ¥520, and the gardens, castle and Hayashibara Art Museum will run you ¥670.

In a building that looks like a cross between a farmhouse and a New England church, **⬛Yumeji Art Museum** (Yumeji Kyōshi Bijutsukan; 夢二郷士美術館) is the most fascinating sight in Okayama. It exhibits the work of early 20th-century artist Yumeji Takehisa, who neither aped European avant-garde nor clung to tradition, fusing French elements with the Art Nouveau aesthetic to create a Japanese Romanticism. (☎271-1000; www.city.okayama.okayama.jp/museum/yumeji. Open Tu-Su 9am-5pm. ¥700, students ¥500.)

Looming **Okayama-jō** (岡山城) got the nickname "Crow Castle" from its black trimmings, but this bird can't compare with Himeji's White Egret. From a distance it's an awesome sight, but inspection reveals a ferro-concrete reproduction; only one original turret survived WWII. It's thoroughly unimpressive. (☎225-2096. www.city.okayama.okayama.jp/keizai/kankou/ujo. Open daily 9am-5pm. ¥300.) One of Japan's "big three" gardens, **Okayama Korakuen** (岡山後楽園) was built in 1700 on an island in the Ashigawa River, the playground of various *daimyō* (feudal lords) until its 1884 nationalization. Unfortunately, what makes the garden special to Japanese is what makes it tedious to Westerners, especially of the suburban variety—Korakuen is known for its expansive lawn. The fringes of the garden contain slightly more appealing groves and ponds. The perfunctory **Okayama Prefectural Museum** (Okayama Kenritsu Hakubutsukan; 岡山県立博物間) is nearby. (On the north side of the castle across the Tsukimbashi Bridge. ☎272-1148; www.okayama-korakuen.jp. Open Apr.-Sept. 7:30am-6pm; Oct.-Mar. 8am-5pm. ¥350. Museum: ☎272-1149; www.pref.okayama.jp/kyoiku/kenhaku/hakubu.htm. Open Apr.-Sept. 9am-6pm; Oct.-Mar. 9:30am-5pm. ¥200.)

Of the town's remaining museums, the **Hayashibara Museum of Art** (Hayashibara Bijutsukan; 林原美術館) is the most worth seeing. It houses the donated collection of the magnate Ichiro Hayashibara, an avid buyer of traditional Asian art. (To the southwest of the castle moat, across Ujo Michi Ave. ☎223-1733; fax 226-3089. Open daily 9am-5pm. ¥300.) The **Okayama Orient Museum** (Oriento Hakubutsukan; オリエント博物館) contains artifacts tracing the history of the Near East from ancient times to the present, including a Roman mosaic. (Close to Okayama-jō along Shiroshita Suji Ave. north. ☎232-3636; www.city.okayama.okayama.jp/orientmusuem. Open Tu-Su 9am-5pm. ¥300, students ¥200.) Surprisingly solid, the **Okayama Prefectural Museum of Art** (Okayama Kenristu Bijutsukan; 岡山県立美術館) features modern European works, as well as paintings by the American-inspired Yasuo Kuniyoshi. A traditional section provides the cranes and calligraphy. (Just north of the Orient Museum. ☎225-4800. Open Tu-Su 9am-5pm. ¥300, students ¥200.)

WESTERN HONSHŪ

▣ FESTIVAL. One of Okayama's few claims to fame is its role in hosting the annual **Saidaiji Eyō festival.** The Kibi plain area, known as the Kibi Kingdom, was a center of religion, art, and culture before the ascendancy of Nara and then Kyōto; the Saidaiji Eyō harkens back to these olden times. Better known in the rest of Japan as the Hadaka or Naked Festival, the event takes place at **Kannon-in** near Okayama. Hundreds of men take part in purification rites, then donning traditional loincloths for a battle royale. As they mill around the main temple hall, a priest casts two sacred sticks *(shingi)* into the crowd and the men duke it out to see who gets them and wins good luck for the next year. Group cooperation is the norm, and competitors form alliances to gain advantage over the others. To make things interesting, priests douse the combatants with frigid well water from time to time. The festival takes place at midnight on the third Saturday of February.

TOTTORI (鳥取)   ☎0857

A maze of industrial parks, shopping arcades, and semi-congested traffic routes, Tottori has little appeal for tourists. Unless you're the regional representative for Sato-brand broom bristles, there's just one reason to visit Tottori—the **dunes.** Covering 6 sq. km of seaside, the dunes reach dozens of meters in height. The crowds are dwarfed by the towering sands, and a visit has a slightly surreal quality. The tourist infrastructure is omnipresent, from the dune-chuting teenagers to the rental dromedaries (¥1800 for 1 person, ¥3000 for 2.) The only dunes in Japan, they have a certain power over the Japanese imagination. They were the inspiration for Abe Kobo's novel *Woman of the Dunes,* and the film version of the book was shot on location here. The dunes are a ways out of town center—take a bus from platform 3 out to either Sakyū Kaikan or Sakyū Center (about 30min., ¥360). Sakyū Kaikan is next to the dunes, while Sakyū Center is at the top of a hill overlooking them. The two are connected by chairlift (6:30am-4:50pm; ¥200, round-trip ¥300).

Tottori is well off the beaten track. The closest *shinkansen* stop is **Okayama,** connected to Tottori on the Chizu Line (4hr., 3 per day, ¥2710). **Matsue** is 90min. and ¥1200 away. Tottori is served by planes as well—see Matsue (p. 512). The train station contains the **tourist information center.** (☎22-3318. Open daily 9am-7pm). The main service center is in front of the station. In an emergency, call ☎110 for **police,** ☎119 for **fire** or **ambulance.** The **post office,** nearby the station, contains an international **ATM.** (Open for mail service M-F 9am-7pm, Sa 9am-5pm, Su 9am-12:30pm. ATM open M-F7am-11pm, Sa 9am-9pm, Su 9am-7pm).

Business hotels are the rule in Tottori. One of the cheapest and easiest to find is **Green Hotel Morris ❷**—entering the area just north of the train station, you'll see the sign soon enough. The hotel is quite standard, with the usual amenities. (☎22-2331. Check-out 10am. Singles from ¥5000, doubles from ¥7000.) On the south side of the train station, visible from the exit, is **Tōyoko Inn ❸** (東横イン). Rooms come with a few perks such as a free morning pastry and Internet access. (☎36-1045; fax 36-1046. Check-in after 4pm. Check-out 10am. Singles ¥5200, doubles ¥7200.) On the north side of the station (the one with the fountain), the arcades contain a number of dining options. For those with a taste for Japanese fast food, **Maneki ❶** serves up large portions of steaming noodle soups for ¥480-780. (☎26-3636. Open daily 11am-9pm.) A Western alternative is **Caffe Piache ❶,** one block farther east, which offers tasty, fresh sandwiches. Snacks, large enough to satisfy, run ¥480-500. (☎39-7333. Open Tu-Sa 11:30am-10pm, Su 10am-10pm.)

SHIKOKU (四国)

The smallest of Japan's four main islands, Shikoku is also the one least frequented by foreign visitors. Historically, however, it developed as a giant tourist attraction centered around the Shikoku Pilgrimage. Passing through 88 temples founded by Buddhist priest Kōbō Daishi in the 9th century, this route still attracts thousands every year, though today's pilgrims have the benefit of cars and bus tours.

Shikoku literally means "four countries," a reference to the four prefectures whose old names—Awa (Tokushima), Sanuki (Kagawa), Tosa (Kōchi), and Iyo (Ehime)—often pop up with regard to local culture and food. The island is linked to Honshū by three bridges, the most famous of which is the 8-mi. Setō Ohashi. Its relative isolation today belies the cosmopolitan features of its history: Kōbō Daishi planted Buddhism here after studying in China, and the legendary John Mung, from Ashizuri Misaki, played a major role in 19th-century US-Japanese relations.

Much of Shikoku is difficult to access but rewards the intrepid traveler with stunning natural scenery. Two of Japan's most beautiful rivers, the Yoshino and Shimanto, flow through the green mountains in the interior. Kōchi Prefecture spans the entire southern coast, and the two capes, Ashizuri Misaki and Muroto Misaki, are points on the pilgrimage route. Beaches dot the Kōchi shoreline and the southeastern coast of Tokushima Prefecture; Okinohama, Ikumi, and Kaifu are some of Japan's most exciting surfing destinations.

HIGHLIGHTS OF SHIKOKU

STEP BY STEP. Climb some portion of Kompira-san's 1368 steps leading up to the Sake Museum, the theater Kanamaruza, and the famous mountaintop shrines (p. 546).

A RIVER RUNS THROUGH IT. The soul expands among the water-carved vistas of Iya Valley and Ōboke Gorge. Rough it in a tent, or soak in luxurious outdoor *onsen* (p. 549).

DO AS THE DŌGOANS DO. The resort town of Dōgo next to Matsuyama is loaded with bathhouses and saunas. You should emerge supremely relaxed and pruney (p. 573).

AWAJI-SHIMA (淡路島)

Awaji-shima, the largest island in the Seto Inland Bay besides Shikoku itself, is connected to Honshū by the Akashi Kaikyō Bridge, the world's longest suspension bridge. The beaches open to swarms of tourists during the vacation months, but for the rest of the year, the island is inhabited mostly by friendly locals who retain traces of the Kansai dialect, as a result of the island's connection with Kōbe. On the whole, the beaches on the east coast are a little rockier than those on the west coast, where you can wade far out into the sea. Still, some of the most popular beaches, such as Ohama Beach near Sumoto, are on the east coast.

The bus system within Awaji-shima is divided into three veins. **Expressway Buses** run from Kōbe through Awaji-shima to Tokushima, stopping at: Awaji, Higashiura, Hokudan, Tsuna-Ichinomiya, Sumoto, Seidan-Mihara, and Minami-Awaji-shima. Buses run from **Maiko** to: **Awaji Dreamstage** via **Higashiura** (¥500, 25min.) and **Sumoto bus center** via **Tsuna** (1hr., ¥1500); from **Ōsaka** to: **Sumoto bus center** via **Tsuna** (2hr., ¥2300); from **Shin-Kōbe Station** to: **Awaji Dreamstage** via **Oishi Port** (1hr., ¥900), **Higashiura** (¥500, 25min.), **Sumoto bus center** via **Tsuna** (1¼hr., ¥1800).

Awaji-shima buses also run along Rte. 28 in the southeast and Rte. 31 in the northwest, stopping more frequently than the Expressway Bus. Although these routes offer comprehensive coverage of the island, buses are expensive and infrequent. Only attempt to circle the island if you have a car or bicycle.

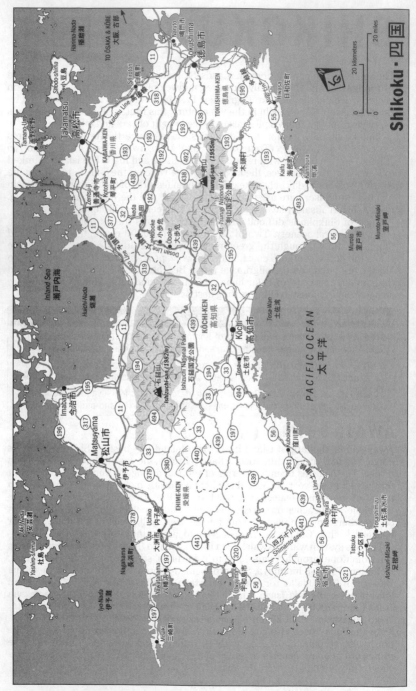

There are **tourist information centers** (usually at bus terminals) in most villages, including **Tsuna** (☎ 0799-62-5558; www.tsuna-cho.jp/kankou-k), **Hokudan** (☎ 0799-82-1144; www.awaji-is.or.jp/hokudan), and **Seidan** (☎ 0799-36-4079; www.seidan-unet.ocn.ne.jp). Employees at the island's **main tourist center in Awaji bus terminal** (☎ 0799-25-5820; www.awaji-navi.jp) can help you find transportation and accommodations, although it's always best to have a reservation, especially during the crowded summer season. There are campgrounds on both coasts of the island. The **Myōjin Campground ❶** is in the middle of the west coast, 20min. by bus or car from the Tsuna interchange. (☎ 0799-85-1122. Open year-round. ¥300 per person.)

MAIKO ☎ 078

Engineering buffs should not miss Maiko, which has several sights devoted to the world's biggest suspension bridge. If heading to Awaji-shima from Honshu, you'll probably pass through Maiko, a few stops on the JR Sanyo Line from Kōbe—be sure to take the local train rather than the express towards Himeji. The **Akashi Kaikyo Bridge Exhibition Center**, 4-114, Higashi-Maiko-chō, Tarumi-ku, Kōbe, is a highly scientific museum that details the construction of the Akashi Kaikyo Bridge and other famous bridges in Japan. The numbers and scientific facts have been translated into an English handout, but the displays themselves are in Japanese. (☎ 784-3339. Open Tu-Su 9:30am-5pm. ¥200, elementary and junior high school students ¥100.) The **Maiko Marine Promenade**, 2051, Higashi-Maiko-chō, Tarumi-ku, Kōbe, a glass-bottom walkway running under the bridge eight floors above the river, offers striking views of ships on the strait. (☎ 785-5090. Open daily 9:30am-6pm; closed 2nd Tu of each month. ¥500, elementary school students ¥250.) The **Sun Yat-sen Memorial Hall** is a museum dedicated to the Chinese intellectual and his connections to Kōbe and to Wu Jintang, the man who built the hall in 1915. All exhibits are in Japanese. (☎ 783-7172. Open Tu-Su 10am-5pm. ¥400, students ¥250.)

SUMOTO (洲本市) ☎ 0799

Tucked into the southeast corner of Awaji-shima, Sumoto is the island's only legally defined full-size city and gets packed with Japanese tourists in July and August. **Ohama Beach**, a 5min. walk from the main bus terminals, is one of the most popular beaches in Awaji-shima. (Open for swimming July-Aug.)

Besides the beach, the biggest attraction is the **Awaji-shima Museum**, 1-1-27, Yamate. From the bus terminal, walk toward the beach, turn right at the light, then take a right at the second light; it's on the left. The museum contains exhibits on *ningyō jōruri* (puppet drama) and the mythical and actual history of Awaji-shima; a collection of art by Gyokusei Jikihara, a local artist and *haiku* poet; and *haiku* by Shiki, Kyoshi, and Seisensui. Few exhibits are translated. (☎ 24-3331. Open Tu-Su 9am-5pm. ¥400, high school and university students ¥250, junior high and elementary ¥100.) Down the street from the museum is **Sumoto Foot Springs**, where you can bathe your feet with locals from dawn to dusk. The water is naturally cold, but a boiler keeps one of the pools at a steamy 99°F. (Free.)

From Kōbe and Maiko, you can take the Expressway Bus to Sumoto. If you're already on Awaji-shima, most buses heading south pass by Sumoto. There are two **bus terminals**, one for local and another for long-distance buses. The **Sumoto Tourist Information Center** (☎ 22-0742; http://kanko.awaji-is.or.jp/sumoto) in the long-distance bus terminal offers free bike rentals 9:30am-3:30pm. Sumoto has the island's only public Internet connection, and luckily it's free: the Port Building has an **internet salon**, 1-11-1, Kaigan-dōri, 2nd fl. After filling out a small form, you can use one of their computers for up to an hour. (☎ 26-0666. Open Tu-Su 9am-7pm.)

A short walk from the beach are several minshuku and ryokan, as well as a hotel or two. Across the street from Ohama Beach, **Hotel Arex ❹**, Kaigan-dōri, Ohama (☎ 22-5207; www.hotel-arex.co.jp) offers spacious Western (from

¥12,000) and Japanese rooms (from ¥15,000), but check the prices as they fluctuate. The minshuku and ryokan offer lower rates, and all the ryokan have their own *onsen*. A few minutes from the beach toward the bus terminal is **Hotel Kinei ❸**, 1-6-1, Kaigan-dōri (☎22-0155), a small family-run minshuku. (Check in 4pm. Check out 10am. Breakfast ¥900. ¥6000 per person.) **Ryokan Nabe-tō ❸** (旅館なべ藤), 2-5-26, Kaigan-dōri, is a little more upscale. From the bus terminal, walk towards the beach, turn right at the light, then take the first right; the ryokan is on the left. (☎22-0061. ¥7000 per person, with meals ¥13,000.) For some typical regional food, head to **Miketsukuni ❹** (御食国), 1-1-8, Shioya, a block away from the bus terminal. Awaji beef steak sets start at ¥6600, but you can fill up on their popular Japanese beef *yaki* set for ¥2800. (☎26-1133. Open daily 11:30am-2:30pm and 5-9pm.)

HIGASHIURA (東浦) ☎0799

The town of Higashiura is renowned for its carnations, but these are eclipsed by the stunning lotus flowers that supposedly sprouted from 2000-year-old seeds and now grow at the top of the **Mizumido** (Water Temple). This is the main hall of the strikingly modern temple **Honpuku-ji**, 1309, Higashiura-chō, one of three buildings on Awaji-shima designed by famous architect Ando Tadao (p. 105). Unfinished concrete walls encircle the pond, and a stairway splitting the water leads into the temple area below. The temple is aligned perfectly so that the setting sun illuminates the main area and backlights the temple's central image—the Bhaisajyaguru, or the Yakushi Buddha. To reach the temple from the Higashiura Bus Terminal, take a right on Rte. 28, walk past two stoplights, and then take a left at the police box on the corner. The Mizumido is at the top of the hill behind older temple buildings. (☎74-3624. Open daily 10am-5pm. ¥300, children ¥150.)

To get to Higashiura from Maiko Station, take the Maiko Expressway Bus directly to Higashiura Bus Terminal (15min., every 30min., ¥600). Inside, the friendly employees at the **Higashiura Tourist Center** (☎74-4101) distribute maps and help visitors find accommodations and sights.

The **Awaji Island Westin ❺**, 2, Higashiura-chō, Yumebutai, is another famous Ando design with bay views and balconies in every room. It's expensive, but Awaji-shima is meant for relaxation. (☎74-1111; www.westin-awaji.com. Twin and king rooms from ¥25,000.) For a less pricey place to stay, check out **Okuraso ❷** (大倉荘), 421, Higashiura-chō, Kariya, a family-run minshuku on Rte. 28 south of Higashiura Bus Terminal. After the restaurant Yan, take a left. (☎74-3131. Singles ¥4000.) **Yan ❶** (やん ; ☎74-5123) is the family's *udon* restaurant. *Udon* from ¥500, special lunch set from ¥1000, dinner set from ¥2000.

TOKUSHIMA (徳島) ☎088

Centered on Hyōtan Island, Tokushima is famous for hosting the Awa Ōdori dance festival in August and for being on the first leg of Shikoku's 88-temple pilgrimage—the first 23 temples are in Tokushima Prefecture. *Hyōtan* means "pumpkin," but the island looks more like a squash. Walking through the city, you'll see endless references to Awa Ōdori in the form of statues, mosaics, sculptures, and paintings depicting the colorful dancers. On August 12-15, the town swells with over a million visitors who come to watch dance troupes parade through the streets. The festival dates back to the time of Hachisuka Ieyasu, a *daimyō* appointed to oversee Tokushima Prefecture when it was still called Awa.

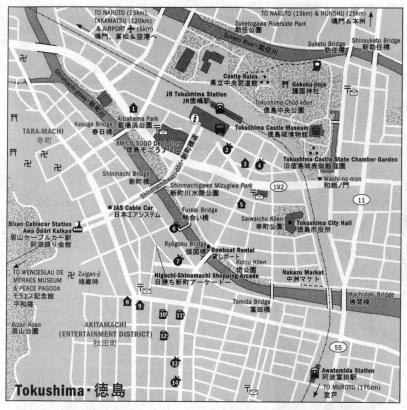

Tokushima · 徳島

TRANSPORTATION

Airport: Tokushima Airport (☎ 699-2831; www.tokushima-airport.co.jp). Airport buses leave from bus platform #2 in Tokushima Station (25min., every hr.). Flights go to: **Tōkyō** (1hr.; 6 per day; JAS ¥18,850, SKY ¥12,900); **Nagoya** (1hr., 2 per day); **Fukuoka** (1¾hr., 2 per day); **Sapporo** (2hr., 1 per day).

Trains: The **Tokushima Line** connects Tokushima to **Naruto** (¥350) and **Takamatsu** (¥1410, limited express fee ¥1150).

Buses: The bus terminal is to the left as you exit Tokushima Station. To: **Okayama** (2½hr.; 5 per day 8:10am-6:10pm; ¥3300, children ¥1650); **Nagoya** (6hr.; 11:30pm; ¥6600, round-trip ¥11,800); **Ikeda** (45min., 4 per day 7:30am-5:30pm, ¥2500); **Matsuyama** (3¼hr., 4 per day 7:30am-5:30pm, ¥7800); **Kōbe** (1¾hr.; every hr. 7am-7pm; ¥3200, round-trip ¥5760); **Ōsaka** (2½hr.; every 30min. 6:30am-7:40pm; ¥3600, round-trip ¥6480); **Kyōto** (2¾hr.; 6 per day; ¥4100, round-trip ¥7380).

Tokushima · 徳島

🏠 **ACCOMMODATIONS**
3 Met Plaza, **9**
Hotel Marston Green, **5**
Takimi Ryokan, **1**
Tokushima Ekimae
  Daiichi Hotel, **3**
Tokushima Washington
  Hotel Plaza, **8**

🍎 **FOOD**
Akachōchin, **14**
Akaoni, **13**
Big Brothers, **4**
Indigo, **6**
R's Cafe, **2**
Yamashige, **7**

🎵 **NIGHTLIFE**
jazz cabin 88, **12**
Mogura-Tei, **10**
Underground, **11**

THE LOCAL LEGEND

KOBO DAISHI

Kobo Daishi (774-835), often called the father of Japanese culture, is known for introducing a form of Buddhism from China in the 9th century. He's most famous in Shikoku, as he was born close to Zentsū-ji in Kagawa Prefecture and studied in temples all over the island. Expected to take a role in the local government, he become disillusioned with Confucianism aftern studying in Nara, and turned to Buddhism. He found enlightenment at 19 while meditating in a cave on the Muroto Misaki coast, and took the name Kū[   ]sky and sea"). Today a statue of him stands on the site.

In 804, he joined a scholarly envoy to Tang China, hoping to study at Chang'an, the world's most cosmopolitan city. After two years, he ended his studies and brought Shingon Buddhism back to Japan. In addition to the new religion, he brought back tea, technology, medicine, and *sutras*, enabling Japan to develop her own variation on Chinese culture. He is also credited with the creation of *hiragana* and *katakana*.

Kūkai's followers were the first to make the 88 Temple Shikoku Pilgrimage, a commemoration of the 23 Buddhist saints. Pilgrims began following the trail in the 10th century, but the numbers picked up in the Edo Period as travel became easier.

The standard route begins at M[ ]Kōya near Kyōto, the site of Kūkai's mausoleum. From there

Ferries: The **Tokushima Ferry** departs every 2hr. from **Tokushima Port**. Take Tokushima city bus #4 from platform #6. To: **Wakayama Port** (2½hr.); **Kansai International Airport** (3½hr.); **Namba**. ¥1730; elementary school students ¥870.

Local Transportation: The **city buses** are the only form of public transportation, but most everything is within a 10-15min. walk. City buses (¥200) leave from the platform to the right when you exit Tokushima Station. The other platform is for long-distance **Tokushima buses;** some of these stop within city limits.

Taxis: Tomida Taxi (☎622-5158). **Bizan Taxi** (☎622-8103). Base fee ¥540.

Car Rental: Toyota Rent-a-Car, 1-18, Nakano-chō (☎652-0100).

Bike Rental: Tokushima City Tourism Association has free bike rentals in the basement outside Tokushima Station. Application form and ID or ¥3000 deposit required. Rentals must be made before 3:30pm. Open daily 9am-4:30pm.

✴ ORIENTATION

Two rivers define the sides of Hyōtan Island; the fat end of the island borders the ocean. Two mountains flank Tokushima Station. To the north is Shiro-yama, an undersized mountain on the Tokushima Castle grounds. To the south, the taller Bizan has a ropeway that makes ascending the mountain a 6min. breeze. Most everything in Tokushima is within walking distance, but the buses can be handy for traveling to the more remote sights and to other parts of Shikoku. The Akitamachi district (see **Nightlife**) is a 3-block square that lies to the south of the station across the river, and its most prominent landmark is the ACTY 21 building.

🛈 PRACTICAL INFORMATION

Tourist Offices: Tourist information center, outside Tokushima Station to the right of the bus terminal. (Open daily 9am-8pm. ☎622-8556). **TOPIA (Tokushima Prefectural International Exchange Association),** Clement Plaza, 6th fl. Take elevator from inside station. Maps and info on regional activities and sights. English-language books and periodicals. Two computers, photocopier, and fax machine available for small fee.

Currency Exchange: UFJ Bank, Shinmachi-dōri, a few min. from the station past Sogo.

ATM: There is an **international ATM** on the 2nd fl. of Clement Plaza, on the Clement Hotel side. Open M-F 8:45am-8pm, Sa-Su 9am-6pm.

English-Language Bookstore: Kinokuniya (☎602-1611), Sogo department store, 8th fl., Shinmachi-dōri, 1 block from Tokushima Station. Open daily 10am-7pm.

Library: Tokushima Municipal Library, Tokushima-chō (☎654-4421).

Emergency: Police ☎110. **Fire** or **ambulance** ☎119.

Police: Tokushima East Police Station, ☎624-0110.

24hr. Pharmacy: Lawson, a few minutes from the station. Exiting the station, walk to the left, keeping the Tokushima City department store on your left, then take your 1st right; Lawson will be on the left. The Akitamachi district also has many convenience stores.

Medical Services: TOPIA (see **Tourist Offices,** above) helps travelers find medical care. **Tokushima Municipal Hospital** (☎622-5121) is a public hospital. **Tokushima Municipal Clinic,** Saiwai-chō 3-chōme (☎622-3576), offers daily after-hours care.

Internet Access: TOPIA, Clement Plaza, 6th fl., allows free Internet use for 10-50min. **Naisu,** 4-59, Terashima-honchō (☎652-0320), is on the 2nd fl. of the shopping arcade to the right of Tokushima Station as you exit. ¥100 initial fee, ¥300 for 1st 30min., then ¥100 per 15min. Free drinks. Open daily 11am-9pm. **Freedom,** 2-8, Nakano-chō (☎623-9266), 3 blocks from ACTY 21 Bldg., on the street perpendicular to Akitamachi. (Open M-Sa noon-6pm and 8pm-midnight). ¥400 per hr. Coffee and tea available.

Post Office: Tokushima Central Post Office, 1-2, Yaoya-chō (☎622-7010), 5min. from Tokushima Station. Head diagonally to the left from the station, follow the street to the stoplight, and take a left; the post office will be on your right. Open M-F 9am-7pm, Sa 9am-5pm, Su 9am-12:30pm. After-hours services are available.

ACCOMMODATIONS

There are plenty of reasonably priced accommodations in Tokushima throughout the year, except during Awa Ōdori in the second week of August. Hotels usually start booking as far in advance as April, and by the beginning of summer many are completely full. Business hotels are scattered around the station and on the banks of the river. Unfortunately, the cheapest place to stay is the hostel, a 30min. bus ride from Tokushima Station (¥320).

Tokushima Ekimae Daiichi Hotel (徳島駅前第一ホテル), 2-21, Ichiban-chō (☎655-5005; www.tokushima-daiichihotel.co.jp). From Tokushima Station, walk to the right, keeping Tokushima City department store on your left. Take the 1st right, then a left; the hotel is to the left. Quality business hotel.

the path goes across the Inland Sea to Shikoku and then clockwise around the island, starting in Tokushima Prefecture, through Kōchi, Ehime, and finally to Kagawa Prefecture. Pilgrims wear special clothing—white clothes, symbolizing death, a sedge hat, and a large staff said to cotainKobo Daishi's soul. Pilgrims pay someone at each temple to inscribe record books with the name of the temple. M▉y temples offer accommodation, ▉ut there are often minshuku or hostels nearby.

Not all the temples are Shingon, but they are connected by devotion to Kobo Daishi, usually in the form of his statue. Despite its religious nature, many, especially those traveling on foot, find the trip as much a physical pilgrimage as a spiritual one.

A great story of enlightenment on the Shikoku Pilgrimage is that of Saburo Emon, a rich man who lived in Iyo (current Ehime Prefecture). Emon hit Kodo Daishi and refused to help him as he begged at his door. But over the next week, Emon's eight sons died and he suddenly realized his sins. He began following Kūkai to beg forgiveness. Emon did 20 laps ▉nd Shikoku, but Kūkai stayed o▉▉ep ahead of him. He collapsed in the middle of the 21st lap. As he was breathing his last, Kūkai arived to absolve him of his sins and grant a wish. Emon asked to be reborn as Lord of Iyo. The saint wrote a message on a stone and put it in Emon's hand. Soon after, the Lord of Iyo's son born with a clenched fist. Inside the fist was a stone inscribed "Emon Saburo Reborn". The 51st temple, near Matsuyama, is called Ishite-ji (Stone Hand Temple) in his honor.

Breakfast ¥600, coffee and bread ¥300. Parking ¥1000 per night. Check-in 3pm. Check-out 10am. Singles M-F ¥5953, Sa-Su ¥4953, extra person ¥2000. Credit cards accepted. 2nd location across river. ❷

Takimi Ryokan (瀧見旅館), 2-10-1, Aiba-chō (☎652-3012). From Tokushima Station, walk to the left through the covered shopping mall, cross the street, and take a left. Then take your 2nd right, and Takimi will be on the right. Although the name says ryokan, don't expect *tatami* rooms—all rooms include a bath and bed. ¥4500 per person. Check-in 3pm. Check-out 10am. Curfew midnight. ❷

Hotel Marston Green (ホテルマーストングリーン), 1-12, Ryōgoku-honchō (☎654-1777). Exiting Tokushima Station, walk across the bus station and to the left, taking the diagonal street. Turn right at the light; the hotel is on the left of the 2nd block. Fitness room, pool, men's sauna. Cafe serves coffee and cake. Check-in 3pm. Check-out 10am. Curfew 1am. Singles ¥5700; doubles ¥9000; twins ¥11,000. ❸

3 Met Plaza (サミットプラザ), 1-8, Ōmichi (☎22-1177). 15min. walk from Tokushima Station. Cross Shinmachibashi and take a left down the Shinmachi arcade. When the street forks, head right. Continue straight across the street at the corner; it's on the left. Capsule hotel; men only. If staying more than 1 night, store your stuff in your locker or behind the counter. Reception 24hr. Check-in 4pm. Check-out 10am. Standard capsule ¥3500, private capsule with private locker and small desk area ¥4500. ❷

Tokushima Youth Hostel (HI) (徳島ユースホステル ; ☎663-1505). Take bus from Tokushima Station to Omiko Tennis Center; it's the last stop (30min.; last bus 6pm weekdays, 5pm weekends; ¥320). Far from the station, but nice location on tree-lined coast. Breakfast ¥600. Dinner ¥1000. Check-in 4pm. Check-out 10am. Lockout 10am-4pm. Curfew 10pm. ¥2800, nonmembers ¥3800. ❶

Tokushima Washington Hotel Plaza (徳島ワシントンホテルプラザ), 1-61-1, Ōmichi (☎653-7111). From Tokushima Station, cross Shinmachi-bashi and go left through Shinmachi Shopping Arcade. Head right at the fork; as you exit the arcade, it's across the street to your right. Excellent service from this Japanese hotel chain. Prime location across from the Akitamachi district. One cafe, 3 restaurants (Japanese, Chinese, steakhouse). Check-in 2pm. Check-out 10am. Singles ; ¥7360, twins ¥15,152. ❸

⬛ FOOD

Big Brothers, Fukuya Bldg., 1st. fl., 1-12-2, Terashima-honchō-higashi (☎624-0340). From Tokushima Station, walk to the left, keeping the Tokushima City department store to your left. Take your 2nd right; Big Brothers will be on the left. Sandwich shop run by an American and a Canadian (the Big Brothers). Mean sandwiches for nice prices, including turkey, meatball, and vegetarian, served hot or cold. Pita or half-loaf ¥400-490, whole loaf ¥780-970. Open Su-M and W-Th 11am-9pm, F-Sa 11am-10pm. ❷

Akachōchin (あかちょうちん), Joyful Bldg., 1st fl., 2-23, Akitamachi (☎22-2908). From the ACTY 21 building, walk to the light; Akachōchin will be on your right a little farther along the block. This restaurant may be a little far down Akitamachi but definitely merits a visit. *Yakitori* (fried chicken) ¥350. Set meals from ¥650. Sushi from ¥300. Try their tofu and potato originals. Open daily 5:30pm-midnight. ❷

Yamashige (山しげ), 9, Ginza (☎623-4889). Walk down the Shinmachi shopping arcade, take a left at the fork, and then take your 1st left. Yamashige will be on the 1st block on the left. Great *udon* place: plain *udon* ¥350, *tempura udon* ¥600, "stamina" *udon* with *tempura* and beef ¥900. Illustrated menus. Open daily 11am-5:30pm. ❶

R's Cafe, Dai-ni Bantō Bldg., 2nd fl., 3-30, Ichiban-chō (☎623-4787; www.rscafe.com). From Tokushima Station, walk along the left side of Tokushima City department store. Take the 1st right; it's across from the Lawson. Pizza, pilaf, pasta, and sandwiches from ¥500. Illustrated menu. Good selection of cocktails and desserts. For 30min. free Internet use on house computer, just ask (first come first served). Open daily 3pm-3am. ❷

Indigo, 2-8, Senba-chō (☎655-4110). From Tokushima Station, cross Shinmachi-bashi and take a left walking along the river. Indigo will be on the right as soon as you reach the small pedestrian bridge. This riverside restaurant's specialty is American lobster: lunch (¥3800), dinner items a la carte (¥1900). "Light lunches" (from ¥800) have fairly large portions and include a salad bar. Open daily 11am-2:30pm. ❹

Akaoni (赤鬼), Kirinsiguramu Bldg., 1st fl., 2, Akitamachi (☎652-5077). Walk down Akitamachi from ACTY 21; it's just past the stoplight on the right. Don't be scared by the "Red Demon" outside this friendly *izakaya*. Illustrated menu. Plenty of standards like *yakitori* (fried chicken) and *yaki-onigiri* (fried rice balls). If you're daring, go for the *irikasu* (¥450)—cow stomach and intestines, a local specialty. Open daily 5pm-3am. ❸

🎥 SIGHTS

AWA ŌDORI KAIKAN AND BIZAN

2-20, Shinmachi-bashi. Walk south from Tokushima Station, follow the palms along Shinma-chi-dōri across the river, and you'll eventually come to the Kaikan. ☎611-1612. *www.awaodori-kaikan.jp. Combination ticket ¥1500, museum and ropeway ¥1100.*

AWA ŌDORI KAIKAN. This building introduces visitors to the history and practice of the Awa Ōdori festival. The first floor is a large souvenir store that sells regional products such as sugar and indigo-dyed fabric, in addition to Awa Ōdori equipment and costumes. The **Awa Odori Hall** (second floor) puts on daily performances in which a dance team explains the hypnotic motions of the dance and invites visitors onstage to try it for themselves. The **Awa Ōdori Museum** (third floor) displays paintings depicting the festival's evolution. It also has videos of the modern-day performance and the first vinyl recording of Awa Ōdori music, which brought fame to the small-town dance. A fun activity is the Dance-Dance-Revolution-style game that teaches you the moves. *(Performances M-F 2, 3, 4pm; Sa-Su 11am, 2, 3, 4pm; evening shows 8pm. Closed 2nd and 4th W of each month. ¥500, 8pm show ¥700. Museum open daily 9am-5pm. Closed 2nd and 4th W of each month. ¥300.)*

BIZAN ROPEWAY AND HIKING ROUTES. The fifth floor of Awa Ōdori Kaikan accesses a ropeway to the top of Bizan, where you can visit the **Tokushima Pagoda** and **Moraes Museum.** On a clear day the view from the top is incredible, stretching as far as Awaji-shima and Honshu. If you want to skip the ropeway completely, a hiking path up the mountain begins behind the shrine to the left of Awa Ōdori Kaikan (30 min.). The first part has stairs, but the second half is a steep, rocky climb. A sign at the top shows a series of hiking paths around Bizan. *(Ropeway open Apr.-Aug. M-F 9am-6pm, Sa-Su 9am-9pm; Sept. Su-F 9am-6pm, Sa 9am-9pm; Oct. Su-F 9am-5:30pm, Sa 9am-9pm; Nov.-Mar. daily 9am-5:30pm. Open until 10pm during Awa Ōdori performances. ¥600, round-trip ¥1000; elementary school students ¥300, round-trip ¥500.)*

MORAES MUSEUM. This museum is dedicated to the life and writings of Wenceslau de Moraes, a Portuguese sailor and the Consulate General of Kōbe who lived near the foot of Bizan for 16 years after his retirement in 1913. You can read a short biography of Moraes in English, but the displays are in Japanese and many of the items themselves are in Portuguese. *(At the top of Bizan. ☎622-4010. Open daily Apr.-Sept. 9:30am-6pm, Oct.-Mar. 9:30am-5pm. Closed 2nd and 4th W of each month. ¥200, high school and university students ¥150, elementary and junior high ¥100.)*

OTHER SIGHTS

TOKUSHIMA CHŪŌ-KŌEN. This pleasant park is graced by an iris garden, an old train, and a statue of Hachisuka Ieyasu. Tokushima Castle once stood on these grounds, but all that remains are the walls and moats. Climb the stairs to the top of **Shiro Yama** (Castle Mountain; really more of a hill) to get a reasonably good view of Tokushima and Bizan. The **Tokushima Castle Museum** details

NO WORK, ALL PLAY

DANCE DANCE EVOLUTION

There are dance festivals all over Japan in the first two weeks of August, but nowhere do the crowds dance harder than in Tokushima. The Awa Ōdori festival (Aug. 12-15) draws over 1.3 million visitors each year. The tradition dates back to 1587 when Hachisuka Ieyasu opened the newly-completed castle to throngs of dancing celebrants. This dance became an annual event and is now one of the largest dance festivals in the world, rivaling Rio de Janeiro's Carnaval in size.

Since its inception, the festival has become much more ritualized. Groups (called *ren*) of 50-100 men and women carefully coordinate their movements to music. The dancers wear *yukata* (summer *kimono*) and play *shamisen* (a stringed instrument), drums, flutes, and *kane* (similar to bells).

If you're in Tokushima for Awa Ōdori, make hotel reservations in advance. The **Tokushima International Association** assembles a group for Aug. 12; call ahead (☎622-6066). **TOPIA** (☎656-3303) also arranges a *ren* (¥1000 to rent a costume). For lessons, look for **Nikawa-ren** (☎622-4010) at City Hall and Higashi Shinmachi shopping arcade. Dancing begins around 6pm, so by 3pm the "watching fools" begin lining up. Just remember: everyone is a fool, whether dancing or watching, so why not be a dancing fool?

life in and around Tokushima Castle during the heyday of Hachisuka Ieyasu, who ruled Tokushima as a *daimyō* during the Edo Period. Most of the exhibits are in Japanese, but the scale model of Tokushima Castle is a fine piece of work, and the museum also displays an impressive letter of thanks from Tokugawa Ieyasu to Hachisuka. Nearby, the **State Chamber Garden** is a pleasant little space filled with ponds and stone paths running throughout. *(From Tokushima Station, walk east along the train tracks, and cross one of the bridges; the park is straight ahead. Museum: 1-8, Shironōchi, Tokushima-chō. ☎656-2525. Open Tu-Su 9:30am-5pm. ¥300, students ¥200. Includes entrance to State Chamber Garden. Garden open Tu-Su 9:30am-5pm. ¥50, children 6-11 ¥30.)*

ZUIGAN-JI (瑞巌寺 **).** The highlight of this temple is the red-and-gold, three-tiered building housing a Kannon statue. Below this is the source of the stream that feeds the pond in the garden outside the main building. Visitors can participate in *zazen* meditation sessions, but are not allowed to participate in the tea ceremony without prior experience and familiarity with the techniques. *(Walk 4min. southeast around the base of Bizan from Awa Ōdori Kaikan. ☎652-5968. Open daily summer 5:30am-6pm; winter 7am-4:30pm. ¥300. Zazen meditation Th 7-8:30pm.)*

ASTY TOKUSHIMA TAIKENKAN. ASTY allows visitors to get a close look at the Awa Ōdori Festival. The highlight is the 360° Travel Theater showing a 20min. video on Awa Ōdori that flies viewers around Tokushima Prefecture. The show relies on a cheesy premise (three friends reuniting at Awa Ōdori after 10 years) to convey the festival's excitement and show off the theater's technology, but it's an impressive experience nonetheless. After the video, you can learn dance moves or play the drums and gongs. The other exhibits are virtual tours of Tokushima, centered around outdoor activities. There are also *ningyō joruri* performances (robot puppeteers on weekdays, humans on weekends) where you can experiment with handling the dolls. *(Yamashiro-chō, Higashihamaboji. ☎0886-24-5111. Open daily 9am-5pm. Closed 3rd Tu of each month. ¥910, students ¥700, children ¥500.)*

AWA JUROBEI YASHIKI. For a better look at *ningyō jōruri* (puppet drama) and *bunraku* (shadow puppetry), hop on a bus to this charming 18th-century house. It once belonged to the famous *samurai* Jurobei, whose life was fictionalized in the puppet play *Awa no Naruto* by Chikamatsu. The museum inside contains the best display of puppets in Tokushima, from monkeys to ladies to old bearded men. Some English text describes the life of Jurobei and Chikamatsu's play. The puppet play theater hosts daily performances of the most famous scene from *Awa no Naruto*. In case you can't make it to a regular performance, you have the option of arranging a private one for ¥15,000. *(Kawauchi-chō, Miyajima-honchō-ura. Take the city bus to Tomiyoshi Danchi (富吉団地) and get off at the Awa Jurobei Yashiki-mae Bus Stop (20min.). ☎665-2202. Open daily 8:30am-5pm. ¥400; junior high, high school, and university students ¥300; elementary ¥200. Performances Apr.-Aug. M-F 10:30am, Sa 3pm, Su 10:30am and 3pm; Sept.-Nov. Sa 3pm, Su 10:30am and 3pm; Dec.-Mar. Sa-Su 3pm.)*

SHINMACHI RIVER. Walking south from Tokushima Station, you'll eventually come to the Shinmachi River that divides the station area from Akitamachi. The river has wooden boardwalks lined with sculptures, fountains, and benches, ideal for an evening stroll. You can rent **boats** to take between Ryogoku Bridge and Kasuga Bridge. *(☎652-3617. Open Mar. 21-Nov. 30 daily 10am-6pm; Dec. 1-Mar. 20 Sa-Su 10am-6pm. Cycle-boats ¥500 per 20min, rowboats ¥500 per 30min.)*

NIGHTLIFE

The lively Akitamachi district is the heart of Tokushima's nightlife, with late-night *izakaya*, reggae and house clubs, snack bars, karaoke bars, and salons. Taxies line the streets after 10pm, even on weekdays. Most clubs really get going only on the weekend, but you should be able to find entertainment any night of the week.

Mogura-Tei, Itsuki Bldg., B1, 1, Sakae-machi (☎625-8086). Walk south on Sakae-machi; Mogura-Tei is on the 1st block on the right, in the basement. Look for the big 300 sign. This *izakaya* has the best prices in Akitamachi: everything is ¥300. Tasty solutions to late-night cravings: beer, mixed drinks, *tempura, yakitori.* Open daily 6pm-5am.

Underground, ACTY Ijinkan (異人館) Bldg., B1, 1-50, Akitamachi (☎624-0340). From the ACTY 21 Bldg., walk down Akitamachi; look for "Underground" written on the white wall before the stairs going down. Friendly bar with music and darts. On weekends it holds joint events with other restaurants and bars, featuring DJs who spin mostly house music. Cover Su-Th free, F-Sa ¥1000-2000. Open daily 9pm-4am.

jazz cabin 88, Genmon Bldg., 3rd fl., 1, Sakae-machi (☎655-7888). On the 2nd block of Sakae-machi, look for the sign on the right. Intimate jazz bar run by pianist Yoshihide Nakamura, who performs live with friends. Sit down after your 88-temple pilgrimage to enjoy a cold glass from their extensive whiskey selection. Open daily 8pm-2am.

DAYTRIPS FROM TOKUSHIMA

NARUTO

From Tokushima Station take a Tokushima Bus (8:15am and every hr. 9am-4pm, 1-1½hr.) from platform #1 to Naruto. The bus makes stops at Naruto Kanko Port and Naruto Kōen.

On the peninsula that connects Awaji-shima to Shikoku is **Naruto National Park,** home of the famous **Naruto whirlpools** that can become over 20m in diameter, depending on the tides. Many Japanese-language pamphlets at tourist information centers list times when the whirlpools are at their largest. One of the best places to view the pools is **Uzo no Michi** (渦の道), Naruto-chō, Naruto, Kōen-uchi (☎683-6266), a glass-bottom walkway running underneath the Ōnaruto Bridge, 45m above the water. Open Tu-Su Apr.-Sept. 9am-6pm, entrance until 5:30pm; Oct.-Mar. 9am-5pm, entrance until 4:30pm. ¥500, junior high and high school students ¥400, elementary ¥250; combined ticket with EDDY ¥880. The **Naruto Bridge Memorial Museum** (☎687-1330) features exhibits on Naruto, including a video of the whirlpools and other natural sights in the area. Virtual tours include a bike ride across the bridge, virtual fishing, and a submarine ride. Open Tu-Su 9am-5pm. ¥600, junior high and high school students ¥400, elementary ¥250. Check out the whirlpools from the top of a hill in the park; an escalator leads up to the **observation point**. (☎ 687-1221; www.narutokanko.co.jp. Open daily 8:30am-7pm. ¥300, children ¥100.) Boats, of course, will get you closest to the vortices. **Kankokisen** (☎ 687-0101; www.uzusio.com) runs two boats, **Wonder Naruto** (every 40min.; ¥1530, elementary school students ¥770) and **Aqua Eddy** (every 30min.; ¥2200, elementary school students ¥1100); the latter also offers underwater views. To reach the boats, take the bus to Naruto and get off at Naruto Kanko Port. **Uzushio Kisen** also runs boats. (☎ 687-0613; www.uzushio-kisen.com. Every 30min. ¥1500, elementary school students ¥750.) Take a bus to Naruto Kōen, then take the shuttle to the port.

SOUTHEAST COAST

HIWASA (日和佐) ☎ 0884

The main attraction in Hiwasa is **Yakuō-ji,** the 23rd temple on the Shikoku pilgrimage, perched on a mountainside a few blocks northeast of the JR station. The main building is up two flights of stairs, littered with one-yen coins left by visitors. To the right of the main building, another set of stairs leads to an enormous pagoda with an excellent view of the Hiwasa coastline. In the basement, you'll see a dark altar and a display of scrolls. (Basement entry ¥100.) You can probably skip reconstructed **Hiwasa Castle,** a 20min. walk from the station on top of a hill. More museum than castle, it offers nature photography, shells, and a view of the city. (☎ 77-1370. ¥200, students and children ¥100.)

Sea turtles paddle to Hiwasa to lay their eggs on the beach. You won't see them just lounging around; if you're interested, your best bet is the **Hiwasa Chelonian Museum** (Hiwasa-chō, Ohama Kaigan) on the beachside, which keeps a tank full of hatchlings. The English pamphlet gives a good outline of the exhibits, and the turtle video is worth a look. Near the exit, you'll see full-grown turtles being hosed down. (☎ 77-1110. Open Tu-Su 9am-5pm. ¥600, junior high and high school students ¥500, elementary ¥300.) When the turtles are in residence, beach areas are fenced off to protect the eggs, so head farther south for swimming or surfing.

Hiwasa is on the JR Mugi Line, an easy daytrip from **Tokushima** (1 per hr. 6:15am-9pm; local 2¼hr., ¥1060; limited express 1¼hr., ¥2210). The line continues to **Kaifu** (¥540), where you can transfer to the private line to **Shishikui** (¥780) and **Kannoura** (¥810). To the right of Hiwasa Station as you exit is a **tourist information center**. (☎ 77-1875. Bicycle rental ¥100 per day. Open Tu-Su 10am-5pm.) There's no real reason to stay overnight at the grubby **Hiwasa Youth Hostel (HI) ❶**, but if you must, walk straight from the station and take your first left, then third right; it's on the left. (☎ 77-0755. Breakfast ¥600. Dinner ¥1000. Check-in 4pm. Check-out 10am.)

KAIFU (海部) ☎ 0884

Kaifu is a famous surf town, and for good reason. The Kaifu River hits the coastline at the edge of town and creates an astounding break when all the elements are in place. After a heavy rain, a sandbar forms, helping to form tube waves that grow to 2.5m and attract professional surfers like Kelly Slater. Legendary board shaper Allan Byrne has a surfshop, **Byrning Spears**, 1-27, Okūra Ichiudani, Kaifu-chō, on Rte. 55 one block west of the station. If you're lucky, Byrne himself might be at work when you visit. (☎ 73-3495; www.byrningspearsjapan.com. Board rental ¥3000 for 3hr. or ¥5000 per day. Open Su-W and F-Sa 9am-7pm. MC/V.) To get to the **surfpoint,** take a right off Rte. 55 just before the bridge crossing the Kaifu River as you head east. Drive straight and you'll see it where the river hits the ocean; there's a small parking lot to the right. (Construction is being done in the port area and there are plans for more parking lot areas.) When the waves are good, you might be crowded out by the experts who come to ride the legendary Kaifu barrels, but it's worth a try. If you catch one, it'll be the ride of a lifetime.

Kaifu is the last stop on the JR Mugi Line from **Tokushima** (2hr., about 1 per hr. 6:45am to 8:21pm, ¥1580), but a private train line continues two more stops to **Shishikui** (7min., 1 per hr. 6:46am to 8:56pm, ¥240) and **Kannoura** (¥270). There's no tourist office, save the **town office,** across Rte. 55 from the station and a few minutes down the road to the left. In an emergency, call ☎110 for **police,** ☎119 for **fire** or **ambulance.** You'll be able to withdraw money from the post office **ATM** at the **Kaifu Post Office** (☎73-0050). From the station, walk across Rte. 55 and take a left at the next big cross street. The post office is ahead on the right. There aren't many places to stay in Kaifu, but it's close to Kannoura's campground and Ikumi's inexpensive beach hotels. In town, there are two ryokan on the same street as the post office. **Ikumoto ❷** (生本 ; ☎73-1350) has rooms from ¥3500 (with meals from ¥7000). Right across the street, **Minami ❸** (みなみ) has better rooms from ¥7000. (☎73-1373. 2 meals included. Check-in 5pm. Check-out 10am. Curfew 11pm.)

KANNOURA (甲浦)　　　　　　☎0887

SHIKOKU

Kannoura doesn't attract surfers, but **Shirahama Beach** is a wonderful swimming beach, sheltered from bigger waves by two arms of mountainous coast. Depending on the tides, the water can stay waist-high up to 100m out. The beachside has snack booths and a public bathroom with showers and hoses. There's a **campground ❶** next to the parking lot. (¥1200.) For a nicer stay, the **White Beach Hotel ❸,** 88-8, Shirahama, offers rooms that couldn't be much closer to the water. (☎29-3344. Check-in 3pm. Check-out 10am. Curfew 11pm. Weekdays from ¥6000; weekends from ¥8000. Rates higher Apr. 26-May 4, July 19-Aug. 23, and Dec. 29-Jan. 4.)

Kannoura is the last stop on private **train** line that starts at Kaifu (¥270). From the station, walk the 500m to the beach, or take the infrequent **bus.** The bus line continues from Kannoura seaside to Kōchi; the entire run takes 3½hr. Kannoura Eki (Kannoura Station) is one stop from the Kannoura seaside stop. The station rents bikes for ¥200 per day. (¥1000 deposit. Day rental lasts 10am-3pm.)

IKUMI BEACH (生見)　　　　　　☎0887

For surfing action, head to Ikumi Beach, one bus stop from Kannoura. Although the beach can get crowded when the breaks are good, it's still worth checking out, as the surf is friendly for beginners but still provides big waves. The two-stoplight town offers several waterfront hotels and minshuku, and there are a number of restaurants and bars. The best option is ▧**Michishio ❷** (みちしお), 575-17, Ikumi, a beachside minshuku with free showers and parking, across from the **Three F** (スリーエフ) convenience store. The rooms have coin-operated A/C, but the ocean breeze might be sufficient. You can rent surfing equipment—body boards (women only) and short surf boards are ¥2000 per half-day or ¥3000 per day; long surfboards are ¥3000/¥5000. (☎29-3471. Check-out 10am. Curfew 11pm or midnight. ¥3500 per person, with meals ¥5000.) The pink building behind Michishio is **Seaside Pension Yukai ❸,** 575-11, None-tani, Ikumi-aza. The Japanese- and Western-style rooms have bathrooms and showers. The attached restaurant has a patio and serves up tasty eats. (☎24-3131. Curfew midnight. From ¥5000 per person.) For everything from jalepeño hot dogs (¥300) and beer (¥500) to surfboard rentals, head to **Eccentric Surf Shop,** 575-1, Ikumi. A rental boogie board set includes fins for ¥3000 per day or a surfboard for ¥4000. The shop can meet all your beach-going needs, from sunscreen to surfboard wax. (☎29-2382. Open sunrise to sunset.)

MUROTO-MISAKI (室戸岬)　　　　　☎0887

The main attraction at Muroto-misaki is **Homutsumisaki-ji,** also known as Higashi-dera. It's the 24th of the 88 temples and a tough hike from the coast up to the top. The temple sports a small pagoda and is rather worn down compared to the Ashizuri-misaki temple. From the back of the grounds you'll be able to see 100-year-old **Muroto Point Lighthouse,** and at night you can watch its huge beam spin. The lighthouse is open to the public three times a year. (Free. Open May 12, July 21, and the Su closest to Nov. 1. 10am-3pm.) You'll get a great view of the rugged coastline during the climb to the temple, but you can also walk along the **Ransho Promenade.** There are several sights between Muroto-Misaki and Kannoura. The first is the enormous white statue of Buddhist monk **Kōbō Daishi,** on the location where he is said to have attained enlightenment. (☎22-0506. Open daily 8am-6pm. ¥300.) A little north of that is the **Meiotoiwa,** two finger-like projections of rock linked by giant twisted ropes, forming a makeshift shrine. The rocks are a little precarious, and construction in the area may prevent tourists from getting too close.

You'll have to hop on a bus from either Kōchi or Kannoura to get to Muroto-misaki. The bus stops in front of the statue of **Nakaoka Shintarō,** one of Sakamoto Ryoma's fellow activists. The **tourist information center,** 6, Muroto-misaki-chō, is a few minutes from the bus stop. (☎22-0574. Open daily 8:30am-5pm.) **Hotsumisaki-ji Youth Hostel (HI) ❶,** 4058-1, Muroto-misaki-chō, is an excellent hostel. The only problem is that it's at the top of the hill next to the temple—a 20-30min. trudge from the bus stop. Japanese and Western rooms are available, with attached toilets and shared baths and showers. (☎23-0024. Breakfast ¥600. Dinner ¥1000. Check-in 3pm. Check-out 10am. Curfew 8pm. ¥3200.) If you don't feel like hiking, look for **Murotoso ❷,** an inexpensive, grubby minshuku with large Japanese-style rooms. The upside is that it's right across from the tourist information center, a quick walk from the bus stop. (☎22-0409. Check-in noon. Check-out 10am. Curfew 11pm-midnight. ¥3500 per person, with 2 meals ¥6000.)

TAKAMATSU (高松)   ☎087

Perched on Shikoku's northern coast, the capital of Kagawa Prefecture is a pleasant, modern city set against sweeping views of the Inland Sea. Once a Tokugawa castle town, Takamatsu now serves as an administrative center for all of Shikoku and a worthy point of entry into the island's interior wonders.

ON THE WEB   Takamatsu: www.city.takamatsu.kagawa.jp

✈ INTERCITY TRANSPORTATION

Flights: Buses to **Takamatsu Airport** leave from JR Takamatsu Station #1 platform (30min., at least 2 per hr. 6:45am-7:30pm, ¥740). JAL flies to **Fukuoka** (1¼hr., 1 per day, ¥20,000), **Kagoshima** (1½hr., 1 per day, ¥24,500), **Sendai** (1¼hr., 1 per day, ¥30,500), **Sapporo,** and **Tōkyō** (1¼hr., 6 per day, ¥25,000). ANA has flights to **Naha** (2hr., 1 per day, ¥28,900), **Sapporo,** and **Tōkyō** (1¼hr., 6 per day, ¥25,000).

Trains: JR Takamatsu Station is in the north of the city across from the port. The JR Kōtoku Line runs southeast to Tokushima. The JR Yosan Line runs west and breaks off at Tadotsu, becoming the JR Dosan Line which runs south to Kōchi. To: **Awa Ikeda** (¥1410, limited express ¥2560); **Kotohira** (¥830/1340); **Matsuyama** (¥3400/5500); **Ōboke** (¥1750/2900); **Okayama** (¥1470/2620); **Tokushima** (¥1410/2560); **Uwajima** (¥5080/7390); **Zentsū-ji** (¥740/1250).

Buses: The terminal is outside the JR station. To: **Hiroshima** (3¼hr.; 8am and 5:30pm; ¥4000; round-trip ¥7000); **Kansai Airport** (3½hr., 7 per day 4:20am-2:05pm, ¥5000); **Kōbe** (2½hr., 18 per day 6:15am-7:15pm, ¥3600/6480); **Kyōto** (3½hr., 6 per day 6:30am-5:30pm); **Matsuyama** (2½hr., 12 per day 7:50am-7:50pm, ¥4000/7200); **Nagoya** (7¼hr, 10:30pm, ¥9070/16,310); **Ōsaka** (3½hr., 46 per day 5:30am-8pm, ¥3600/6000); **Tōkyō** (9½hr., 9:47pm, ¥10,000/18,200); **Tōkyō Shinjuku** (10hr., 9:10pm, ¥10,000/18,200); **Yokohama** (9½hr., 9:30pm, ¥9500/17,100).

Takamatsu · 高松市

▲ ACCOMMODATIONS

ANA Hotel Clement
Takamatsu, **1**
Golden Time, **13**
New Gekkōen, **3**

Takamatsu Terminal Hotel, **5**
Takamatsu Washington
Hotel Plaza, **10**
Urban Hotel Takamatsu, **2**

🍎 FOOD

Ichidai, **4**
King's Yard, **18**
Macous Bagel Cafe, **7**

Queensberry @ Cafe, **17**
Sanbiki no Kobuta, **16**
SWAD, **15**
Tenkatsu, **6**

📕 NIGHTLIFE

baba boom, **9**
Delta Market, **11**
Jammingway's Cafe, **14**

Piccadilly, **12**
Sea Dragon, **8**

Ferries: Sunport Takamatsu refers to the development around the port, as well as the port itself, which connects Takamatsu to Inland Sea islands, Kōbe, and Ōsaka. Myriad companies and different departure points make things confusing, so confirm your plans at the Information Plaza outside JR Takamatsu Station. To: **Kōbe:** (2¼hr., 2 per day, round-trip ¥5800); **Megijima** (20min., at least 6 per day); **Naoshima** (1hr., 6 per day, ¥510); **Ogijima**: (40min., at least 6 per day); **Ōsaka** (3¼hr., 2 per day, round-trip ¥5800); **Shōdo-shima** (1hr., at least 1 per hr., ¥510); **Uno** (1hr., 2 per hr., ¥390).

⬔ LOCAL TRANSPORTATION

Public Transportation: The **Kotoden Line** runs from a station next to Tamamo Kōen, a few blocks from JR Takamatsu Station. It makes stops at Katahara-machi, at Kawara-machi, and a few blocks east of Ritsurin Kōen, before heading to Kotohira. To: **Kawara-chō** (3min., every 20min., ¥180); **Yashima** (change at Kawara; 14min. from Kawara, every 20min., ¥310); **Kotohira** (1hr., every 30min., ¥610). Takamatsu has a local **bus** system, but you're better off using the extensive Kotoden Line or the bike rental system.

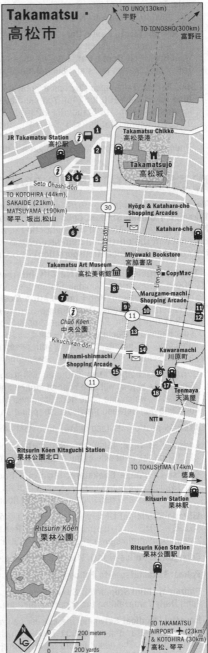

Takamatsu · 高松市

TO UNO(130km) 宇野
TO TONOSHO(300km) 高野荘

JR Takamatsu Station 高松駅
Takamatsu Chikkō 高松築港
Takamatsujō 高松城
Seto Ōhashi-dōri
TO KOTOHIRA (44km), SAKAIDE (21km), MATSUYAMA (190km) 琴平・坂出・松山
Hyōgo & Katahara-chō Shopping Arcades
Katahara-chō
Miyawaki Bookstore 宮脇書店
Takamatsu Art Museum 高松美術館
CopyMac
Marugame-machi Shopping Arcade
Chūō Kōen 中央公園
Kikuchikan-dōri
Kawaramachi 川原町
Minami-shinmachi Shopping Arcade
Tenmaya 天満屋
NTT
Ritsurin Kōen Kitaguchi Station 栗林公園北口
TO TOKUSHIMA (74km) 徳島
Ritsurin Station 栗林駅
Ritsurin Kōen 栗林公園
Ritsurin Kōen Station 栗林公園駅
TO TAKAMATSU AIRPORT (23km) & KOTOHIRA (30km) 高松・琴平

0   200 meters
0   200 yards

SHIKOKU

Taxis: Taxis are plentiful, especially around the station and the shopping arcades, but if you need to call one, try **Hinode** (☎831-7411) or **Ōkawa Taxi** (☎851-3356).

Car Rental: Toyota Rent-a-Car, 10-21, Nishinomaru-chō (☎851-0100). Walk south from the taxi stand at Takamatsu Station, take the second left, and it'll be on the right. Open 8am-8pm. **Orix Rent-a-Car,** 5-1, Nishinomaru-chō (☎851-3850). Walk south from the Takamatsu Station taxi stand and take a right at the Mini-stop; it's on the left.

Bike Rental: Takamatsu City has a great bike rental system. The high-quality ▧ **light-blue bikes** are ¥100 for 24hr. You can keep them up to 3 days and pay on return. 4 locations: Takamatsu Station (☎-821-0400), Kotoden Kanara-machi Station (☎837-1775), Ritsurin Station (☎835-0789), and Kajiya-machi, off the shopping arcade where it switches from Marugame to the Minami Shinmachi arcade (☎822-3943). Open daily 7am-10pm. Register to get a rental card. Return bikes to any location.

◢✳◪ ORIENTATION AND PRACTICAL INFORMATION

Takamatsu starts in the north at the **Sunport, JR Takamatsu Station,** and **Kotoden Takamatsu Chikkō Station.** **Chūō-dōri** runs down the middle of the city to **Ritsurin Kōen** in the south. Most of the sights lie between Ritsurin Kōen and the transportation hubs in the north in a 2km stretch, so walking is practical. You can also take the *kotoden* (see **Local Transportation**) to or from Katahara-chō or Kawara-chō.

Tourist Office: The **Takamatsu City Information Plaza,** 1-16, Hamano-chō (☎851-2009), is outside Takamatsu Station's south exit. Open daily 9am-6pm. In the same office, the **Ryokan/Hotel Information Desk** (☎822-7173) can help non-Japanese-speakers book beds. Open 9am-8:30pm. A good source of info is **I-PAL Kagawa** (☎837-5901), the Kagawa International Exchange Center, 1-11-63, Banchō. Pick up your Kagawa Prefecture Welcome card, which gets you discounts at some stores, museums, and restaurants, by flashing your passport. The library shows English CNN and has a great selection of international newspapers and periodicals. Open Tu-Su 9am-6pm.

Currency Exchange: Most big hotels will exchange money for guests. The Central Post Office (see below) will also change money and is closer to the station than most of the big banks, which line Chūō-dōri. Branches of Sumitomo, UFJ, and Chuo Matsui are all on Chūō-dōri between the Hyōgo shopping arcade and Bijutsukan-dōri.

ATM: All post offices (see below) have ATMs that work with most international cards.

Luggage Storage: Takamatsu Station has coin lockers and baggage storage (☎851-1337) on the right side of the station as you exit. 1 day ¥310. Open M-Sa 8am-5pm.

English-Language Bookstore: Miyawaki Bookstore, 4-8, Marugame-machi (☎851-3733), is to the left of the City Museum of Art (see **Sights**) and has a good selection of English books and periodicals on the 5th floor. Open daily 9am-10pm.

Library: Municipal Library, 1-2-20, Showa-chō (☎861-4501). Open Tu-F 9:30am-7pm, Sa-Su 9:30am-5pm. **Kagawa Prefectural Library** (☎868-0567; www.library.pref.kagawa.jp). Open Tu-F 9:30am-7pm, Sa-Su 9:30am-5pm.

Emergency: Police ☎110. **Fire** or **ambulance** ☎119.

Police: Takamatsu Kita Police Station ☎811-0110.

Pharmacy: Mini-Stop and a **Sunkus** are close to the station; there are several **Lawson** and **Daily Yamazaki** on the shopping arcades.

Hospital/Medical Services: The closest central public hospital is **Takamatsu Sekijūji Hospital,** 4-1-3, Banchō (☎831-7101), which is 1 block west of the southwest corner of Chūō Kōen. The hospitals are on a rotating on-call system Su, nights, and holidays. Call ☎822-0199 (Japanese only). **Takamatsu Night Emergency Clinic** (☎839-2299) is on the 1st floor of the Takamatsu Health Center. Open daily 7:30pm-11:30pm.

Fax Office: Send faxes from the **Tourist Information Plaza** (see above). The "Business Salon" on the 1st floor of the **ANA Hotel Clement Takamatsu** (see **Accommodations**) also has fax and copy services. Domestic faxes ¥200 per page plus price of call. International faxes ¥300 per page plus price of call. There are also 2 **Copy Macs.** One is at 7-8, Imārata-chō (☎802-0313), just off of Lion-dōri on Bijutsukan-dōri. Open M-F 9am-9pm and Sa-Su 10am-9pm. The other, 13-12, Tamachi (☎802-0313), is on the Tamachi arcade. Open M-F 8am-8pm, Sa-Su 10am-8pm.

Internet Access: If you're close to the station, head to the "Business Salon" on the 1st floor of the **ANA Hotel Clement Takamatsu** (see **Accommodations**). ¥200 for 20min. Open daily 9am-7pm. **Queensberry @ Cafe** (see **Food**) lets you surf for ¥100 per hr. with food or drink order—a minimum cost of ¥350 for the 1st hour (cost of *gelato* + Internet) of the slowish connection. **I-PAL Kagawa** (see above) has free Internet, but you may have to wait. Max. 30 min.

Post Office: Takamatsu Central Post Office, 1-15, Uchi-machi (☎851-5705). On the block just before the start of the Marugame Shopping arcade. Open 24hr. ATM service available M-F 7am-12pm, Sa 9am-9pm, Su 9am-7pm. **Kawara Post Office,** 2-11-4, Kawara-chō (☎861-9367). 1 block east of the shopping arcade on Kikuchikan-dōri. Open M-F 9am-5pm. ATM available M-F 8am-5pm, Sa-Su 9am-5pm. **Postal Code:** 760.

⌐ ACCOMMODATIONS

Takamatsu offers a range of places to stay. The cheapest option is the capsule hotel off the shopping arcade, but it's only for men—and no tattoos or drunks!

Takamatsu Terminal Hotel (高松ターミナルホテル), 10-17, Nishinomaru-chō (☎822-3731; www.webterminal.co.jp). From the taxi platform outside Takamatsu Station, it's a quick walk south; the hotel will be on the right of the 3rd block. A quick walk from the station and a good value. Free Internet access in the lobby. All rooms equipped with ethernet jacks and computer cables. Check-in 4pm. Check-out 10am. Curfew 2am. Singles from ¥5800; twins from ¥10,000; doubles from ¥11,000. ❸

New Gekkōen (ニュー月光園), 12-9, Nishinomaru-chō (☎822-3890). From Takamatsu Station Information Plaza, head straight south. Reasonably priced business hotel close to the station. Average-sized rooms have A/C. Cafe attached to the 1st floor. Check-out 10am. Curfew 12pm. Singles ¥4000, with bath ¥5000. ❷

Takamatsu Washington Hotel Plaza (ワシントンホテルプラザ), 1-2-3, Kawara-chō (☎822-7111). Kotoden Kawara Station. On Rte. 11 between the Marugame shopping arcade and Lion-dōri, closer to Lion-dōri. Walk out of the station down Kikuchikan-dōri and take a right at the shopping arcade; at the next stoplight, cross the street, take a right, and it's on your left. Front desk on 2nd fl. Excellent location in the middle of the shopping and nightlife districts. Variety of hotel restaurants. Reception 24hr. Check-in 2pm. Check-out 10am. Singles from ¥6300; twins and doubles from ¥13,500. ❸

Golden Time (ゴールデンタイム), 2-1-7, Kawara-chō (☎833-1234, toll-free 0120-45-1232). Walk south on the arcade and take the 2nd left after Rte. 11 (where Minami-Shinmachi arcade starts). It's on the right. Front desk on the 5th floor. This men-only capsule is a cheap place to crash in the center of nightlife activity. Some capsules pump negative ions. We're puzzled, too. Rice breakfast ¥680, bread ¥600. Reception 24hr. Check-in 4pm. Check-out 10am. ¥3000, negative-ion capsule ¥3300. ❶

ANA Hotel Clement Takamatsu, 1-1, Hamano-chō (☎811-1111; www.ana-clement.com). From Takamatsu Station, take the South Exit and you'll see the building in front of you across the plaza. This is about as close to the station as you can get, and you'll pay for it. Luxurious rooms. A number of hotel restaurants, including the Beer Terrace during the summer (all you can eat and drink ¥3800). Check-in 1pm. Check-out noon. Singles from ¥10,500; twins from ¥21,000; doubles from ¥18,000. ❹

Urban Hotel Takamatsu (アーバンホテル高松), 2-23, Nishinomaru-chō (☎821-1011). Directly across the street from the Takamatsu Station taxi stand. One of the closest hotels to the station. Standard business hotel rooms. Check-in 4pm. Check-out 10am. Curfew midnight. Singles from ¥5000; twins from ¥10,000; doubles from ¥8500; triples from ¥12,000. Japanese-style room for 3 ¥4500 per person. ❷

▣ FOOD

Takamatsu is a prime location to try the region's famous *sanuki udon*. There are plenty of places in Takamatsu proper, but one of the best and most fun, **Waraya,** is in Yashima (p. 545). Takamatsu also offers good seafood, frequently served raw.

SWAD, 2-3, Tamachi, Okabiru, 1st fl. (☎863-4282). A block off a giant shopping arcade right near Chūō-dōri. Indian restaurant. Lunch sets include curry, rice, and salad (from ¥500). Dinner sets (from ¥1350). The Chef's Special approaches gluttony with 2 curries, *naan*, rice, salad, chicken, *kebab*, and drink (¥880). The elephant-ear sized *naan* is delicious. Open daily 11:30am-2:30pm and 5-10:30pm. ❷

Sanbiki no Kobuta (三びきの子ぶた〆), 1-4, Tokiwa-chō (☎861-5353). On the corner of the 1st block of Tokiwa arcade, across from Kawara Station. This deli-esque shop serves up cheap sandwiches and a huge variety of desserts, from crepes and *gelato* (from ¥200) to pastries and parfaits (from ¥350). The egg salad sandwich (¥200) is recommended. Tuna and *teriyaki* sandwiches ¥280. Open daily 10am-7pm. ❶

Ichidai (一代), 12-3, Nishinomaru-chō (☎822-9001). From Takamatsu Station, walk straight south from the taxi stop, take a right 1 block before Seto-Ōhashi-dōri, walk 1 block; it's on the corner. This lunchtime noodle restaurant serves long, thick *sanuki udon* and *zaru udon* (¥340). Go at the right time, and you might see noodles being made on-site. Open M-F 7:30am-4pm, Sa-Su 7:30am-2pm. ❶

King's Yard, 2-3-35, Tokiwa-chō (☎837-2660). Kotoden Katahara Station. Exit the station and walk left 1 block south of the Tokiwa arcade. Take a right, and it's on the left of the 2nd block. This friendly Jamaican restaurant serves authentic dishes—jerk chicken or fish ¥750—and bumps authentic Jamaican beats. One-coin lunch (¥500) available 11:30am until the food is gone. Wash it down with a Red Stripe (¥700), Hemp Seed beer (¥800) or straight off the tap (¥500). Open M-Sa 11:30am-2pm and 6pm-1am. ❷

Tenkatsu (天勝), Hyōgo-chō, Nishizume (☎821-5380). From Takamatsu Station, walk south on Chūō-dōri and take a right on the Hyōgo arcade. It's on the left after the covered arcade ends. The highlight of this historic restaurant (from 1866) is the aquarium—you can see dinner swimming around before it's served up. Small sushi sets from ¥870, meals cost a good bit more. *Tempura* sets from ¥1300; huge courses ¥4000-5000 per person. Regional favorite *anago* in rolls for ¥250. Picture menu and plastic replicas of set meals. Open M-F 11am-2pm and 4-10pm, Sa-Su 11am-9pm. AmEx/MC/V. ❸

Queensberry @ Cafe, 1-10-4, Tokiwa-chō (☎812-0680; www.queensberry.co.jp). Directly across from Kawara-chō Station. Typical Japanese cafe-style eats, from cake and *gelato* (¥250) to hot dogs and curry. Several computers have not-so-fast Internet connections. Internet ¥100 per hr. with order. Open 8am-11pm. ❶

Macous Bagel Cafe, 1-9-11, Banchô (☎822-3558). From the front of I-PAL, walk left 1 block and Macous will be on the corner to your right. The only thing they left back in Manhattan is the holes in the bagels. Tasty sandwiches (around ¥400) include classics like salmon and pastrami and new inventions like *teriyaki* chicken and Korean BBQ. Coffee ¥250; cappuccino ¥280. Delivery 9am-9pm. Open daily 8am-8:30pm. ❶

◎ SIGHTS

RITSURIN KŌEN. Japan's largest garden, weighing in at 75 hectares, lies 2km south of the main station. With tree-covered Mt. Shiun as the backdrop, Ritsurin Kōen is a great place for walking or picnicking, as long as you can avoid the megaphone-wielding tour guides. The garden was born more than 350 years ago as part of the villa of the Matsudaira family, which also built Takamatsu Castle, but today's garden dates from many different periods.

The East Gate is off Chūō-dōri and puts you between the North and South gardens, near the museum and shop buildings. The **Ritsurin Zoo** is next to the East Gate, but you'll probably want to save your money for tea in the garden. *(Open daily 9am-6pm. ¥500.)* You can also enter through the North Gate, a few hundred meters from JR Ritsurin Kōen North Gate Station. Information desks at the gates have English maps and pamphlets, but signs throughout the park also provide English explanations of key points. Two suggested routes, taking about an hour, cover both gardens, but there are plenty of other pathways through the gardens, so take the routes more as a suggestion than a strict path.

The route through the older **South Garden** begins at the **Tsurukame Matsu,** a contorted pine tree above a large rock formation, said to resemble a crane taking flight from the back of a turtle. The most famous view is of **Engetsu-kyo Bridge,** looking from the southeastern corner of the garden. From there you can also see the Edo-period **Kikugetsu-tei Tea Hall.** The **North Garden** centers around two ponds, one filled with lotuses and the other a former duck hunting site, now blessed with a small iris garden. *(☎833-7411. Open daily. Hours vary by month, but always include 7am-5pm.)* Between the two gardens is the **Center for the Encouragement of Commerce and Industry,** which sells various lacquerware and ceramic pieces and hosts artists on weekends. *(Open daily 8:30am-5pm; demonstrations Sa-Su and festival days 10am-4pm).* The quieter and more interesting (though untranslated) **Sanuki Folkcraft Museum** is nearby. *(Open Su-Tu and Th-Sa 8:45am-4pm, W 8:45am-3pm.)*

TAKAMATSU CASTLE GROUNDS (TAMAMO KŌEN). The park here is just a small bit of the remains of Takamatsu Castle, built by original ruler Lord Ikoma and then controlled by a long line of Matsudaira rulers. Most of the original buildings have been destroyed—there's a small shrine where the castle once stood and several watchtowers are still standing, but many other buildings are reconstructions. The **Hiun-kaku,** used for housing Very Famous People, is the largest building on the grounds and was lavishly constructed by the 12th generation of the Matsudaira family in 1917. Now a highway separates the castle from the ocean, but long ago, ships were able to sail directly into the moats. *(2-1, Tamamo-chō. Directly to the east of JR Takamatsu Station across Chūō-dōri. ☎851-1521. Unfortunately, visitors can't enter the buildings. Open daily. Hours vary by month, but always include 7am-5pm. ¥200, 16 or younger ¥100.)*

KAGAWA HISTORY MUSEUM (香川県歴史博物館 **).** The museum has well curated displays of the prefecture's history. The permanent display replays Kagawa's history from the earliest days of man up through WWII. If you don't have time to visit the rest of Kagawa, this is a perfect opportunity to get a feel for it. Display models of cultural objects, such as Yayoi-period huts and Kobo Daishi's scrolls, are prominent. The third floor houses rotating exhibits that focus on specific pieces of art or historical figures. Not much is translated, but the English audio tour is worthwhile. *(5-5, Tamamo-chō. Around the corner from the castle. ☎822-0002. Open Tu-Th and Sa-Su 9am-5pm, F 9am-7:30pm. Last entrance 30min. before close.)*

TAKAMATSU CITY MUSEUM OF ART. This museum feels a little out of place—it's surrounded by restaurants and little boutique stores from the neighboring shopping arcade—but it puts together nice collections of contemporary and traditional art. The glass-ceilinged lobby has gray marble walls and contains modern sculptures. The two permanent collections on the first floor are in high contrast—one focuses on art post-WWII, including works by Warhol, Dalí, Duchamp, and Ernst; the other shows items related to Kagawa Prefecture, including lacquerware, pottery, and ironworking by local artists. The second floor hosts rotating special exhibitions. *(10-4, Konya-machi. ☎823-1711. Open Tu-F 9:30am-7pm, Sa-Su 9:30am-5pm. ¥200, students ¥150. Special exhibition prices vary.)*

⌐ SHOPPING

Takamatsu has some of Japan's longest covered shopping arcades, so there's no shortage of places to shop. The name-changing main shopping arcade starts as **Marugame**, becoming **Minami-Shinmachi**, and then **Tamachi** as you go south. Another arcade crosses Chūō-dōri a couple blocks south of the castle, intersecting the start of the main shopping arcade and **Lion-dōri**, home to restaurants and food stalls. The nightlife district runs through the areas between the main shopping arcade and Ferry-dōri, one street east of Lion-dōri. The enormous **Tenmaya** (天満屋) department store is off Ferry-dōri in the same complex as Kotoden Kawara-chō Station.

☒ NIGHTLIFE

There are plenty of late-night eats, pubs, and snack bars in Takamatsu, but few dance clubs—the city's close enough to Kōbe and Ōsaka that people go there to get down. Even bar owners admit that Takamatsu is more about noodles than nightlife. But don't let that put you off: many bars have special events (live music or guest DJs) on weekends. An especially hip-feeling part of town is east across the Kotoden tracks in Fukuda-chō—there's a cluster of nice, non-sketchy *izakaya*, tea shops, bars, and cafes.

Sea Dragon, 4-5, Kajiya-machi, B1 (☎821-6738). Walking south on Marugame arcade, go 2 blocks past Bijutsukan-dōri (the Museum of Art's street) and take a right. It's on the left in the basement, a bit hidden. This sea-themed *izakaya* serves a variety of foods with its drinks, from pizza and pasta (from ¥750) to *sashimi* (¥650) and Korean beef (¥950). Import beers and cocktails ¥600. Open Su-Th 6pm-midnight, F-Sa 6pm-2am.

Jammingway's Cafe, 2-10-10, Kawara-machi (☎837-3669). From Ferry-dōri, walk 1 block west on the Tokiwa arcade. Take a right; it's on the left of the 1st block after the light. Serves snacks and drinks weekdays with no tax or table charge. Draft beer ¥500. Cocktails ¥600-700. Variety of tunes to drink to. Most weekends offer a DJ event, usually at 9pm. Event cover ¥1000-2000, with 1-2 drinks. Open daily 11am-3pm.

baba boom, 7-8, Marugame-machi, Quattro Torri, B1 (☎823-8681). On the Marugame arcade, 1 block before Rte. 11; in the basement. Bar with an expansive floor area. Fills up on the weekends for live shows and DJs. Lots of reggae, but there's usually a mix. Cocktails in huge glasses ¥700. Cover charge varies with event. Open M-Sa 6pm-1am.

Piccadilly, 9-5, Fukuda-machi (☎822-0091). From the intersection of Rte. 11 (runs north along Chūō-dōri) and Ferry St., walk 1 block north and take a right. Cross the train tracks; it's on the right. This hip, art deco cafe is open late and serves sweet mixed drinks and snacks. Smoothies, alcoholic and non-alcoholic, start from ¥500. Eats like pizza and pastas from ¥780. Cheese fondue ¥980. Wide variety of dumplings from ¥1150. Open M-Th 5:30pm-1am, F-Sa 5:30pm-2am, S 5:30pm-midnight.

Delta Market, 6-5, Fukuda-machi (☎823-0375). Follow the directions for Piccadilly, but turn left instead of right. Look for the huge neon sign. Sold as a "deli," but besides a couple neon orange deli-style bench seats, it's a bar—don't expect deli food. Open late every night, with a funky atmosphere. Main dishes from ¥800. Beer ¥500; cocktails ¥700. Open M-F 6pm-3am, Sa 6pm-midnight. Closed 1st and 3rd M of the month.

⚡ DAYTRIP FROM TAKAMATSU

YASHIMA

From Takamatsu, you can take the JR Line to Yashima Station, but the kotoden line (¥310) is a better option, since it's closer to the Yashima Cable line, which carries you up from the base of the plateau (5min.; every 20min.; ¥700, round-trip ¥1300, children ¥350/¥650). The station for the Cable Line is a few minutes north of Kotoden Yashima Station. You can hike up to the top along Henro-michi (Pilgrim Rd.). Take a left 2 blocks before the kotoden station and follow the road up to the top—the hike up takes 45-60min.

Towards the end of the 12th century, the power of the Taira (Heike) clan was waning. In 1185, they camped out on the beaches beneath the cliffs of the Yashima plateau. As the soldiers expected an attack by water, the cliffs should have provided an excellent defense, but the Minamoto were daring and led their horses straight down the cliffside from the top of the plateau, decimating the Taira forces and putting an end to the legendary Japanese family rivalry. Currently the plateau is a bit of a ghost town, but it still has enough to offer a good daytrip.

You can walk between the sights on the top of the plateau, but you can also rent a bike at the first building on the left from the Cable Station. (Open 10am-5pm. ¥500.) **Yashima-ji,** 500m from the Cable Station at the top of the plateau, is the major sight. It's the 84th temple on the 88-temple circuit, so you'll probably see a lot of tired pilgrims. The main hall of the temple dates back to the Muromachi Period and has been restored twice since, once in the 17th century and then again between 1957 and 1959. It's a little weathered, but still beautiful with its intricate woodwork and bright colors. To the right of the main hall are two huge statues of badgers, a tunnel of *torii,* and a small temple dedicated to the Yashima Taburō Badger, one of the three famous badgers in Japanese history. Also on the temple grounds is the **Yashima Temple Museum,** which has an interesting display of relics from the battle between the Heike and the Genji. (Museum open daily 9am-5pm. ¥500, elementary and junior high students ¥300.) The **Pool of Blood,** a small pond where the victorious Genji warriors supposedly washed their sword blades, is a short walk from the temple grounds. The road between Yashima-ji and the Pool of Blood leads to a parking lot, north of which you'll find a great view of the Inland Sea. A 2.3km trail leads to the northernmost tip of the peninsula.

The best reason to visit Yashima is ⚡**Shikoku Mura,** at the base of the plateau, a quick walk east through several parking lots from the Cable Station. The open-air museum collects 30-some buildings from all over Shikoku and from all different periods of history. A winding path along the base of the plateau will take you back to 13th-century vine bridges from Iya, an Edo-period sugarcane press and tea hall, and Meiji-era lighthouse keepers' houses. The included **Shikoku Mura Museum of Art** was designed by Tadao Ando and is characteristic of his style—an unfinished concrete building incorporated into its natural environment through a garden and several ponds. The museum has local sculpture and pottery alongside Chagall, Renoir, Matisse and Picasso. The garden behind the museum is full of roses. (91, Naka-machi, Yashima. ☎843-3111; www.shikokumura.or.jp. Open daily Apr.-Oct. 8:30am-5pm; Nov.-Mar. 8:30am-4:30pm. ¥800, high school students ¥500, junior high ¥400, elementary ¥300. Museum ¥500, children ¥300.)

Yashima is best as a daytrip, but if you want to sleep close to the plateau, try **Sasaya Ryokan ❷** (ささや旅館), 68-2, Naka-machi, Yashima. It's on the right, one block before the Cable Station as you approach from the *kotoden* station. (☎841-9533. 2 meals included. Rooms from ¥5000 per person.) For food, make sure you stop by ⚡**Waraya ❷,** a popular *udon* restaurant down the steps from the parking lot outside the Shikoku Mura exit, in a building that wouldn't be out of place in

SHIKOKU

Shikoku Mura. If you go in a group, get the *kazoku udon* (¥2300), an enormous wooden bowl of noodles, enough to feed four, over which you can chopstick-battle for the last strand. (☎843-3115. Open daily 10am-7pm.)

KOTOHIRA (琴平)   ☎0877

Easily accessible as a daytrip from Takamatsu, Kotohira is home to one of Japan's oldest tourist attractions, Kotohira-gū, known affectionately as Kompira-san. This mountain shrine has been a popular pilgrimage site since the Edo Period, when pilgrimages were one of the few forms of travel permitted under the feudal system. Hot springs, sake breweries, and noodle joints have sprouted up around the famous 1368 steps. Mercifully, the main temple buildings are only 785 steps from the bottom. Although Kotohira-gū is rather far inland, it is known as a mariner's shrine, and a light shining from the temple can be seen as far as the Inland Sea.

🖾🖬 TRANSPORTATION AND PRACTICAL INFORMATION. Kotohira JR Station (☎73-4171) is a couple of blocks from the Kanakura River on the side opposite Kompira-san. The Dosan Line connects Kotohira with the rest of Kagawa Prefecture and runs south through Tokushima Prefecture to Kōchi. To: **Awa Ikeda** (1 per 2hr.; ¥640; limited express 40-50min., ¥1150); **Hiroshima** (¥4080, limited express ¥7060, transfer at Okayama); **Kōchi** (1 per 2hr., ¥2030; limited express 1¾hr., ¥3810); **Okayama** (1 per hr.; 1¾hr., ¥1300; limited express 1hr., ¥2450); **Takamatsu** (1 per hr.; 1hr., ¥840; limited express 35min., ¥1350); **Tokushima** (¥2030, limited express ¥3690, transfer at Takamatsu). At the **Kotoden Station** on the edge of the Kanakura River, the **Kotoden Line,** slightly cheaper than the JR Line, connects Kotohira to Takamatsu (¥610, children ¥310) with stops at smaller towns in between.

From JR Kotohira Station, the **Kotohira Tourist Information Center,** 316, Kotohira-chō, is left of the first block towards Kompira-san before the Kotoden Station. (Bike rental 10am-7pm; ¥100 per hr., ¥500 per day.) Pick up a free Kagawa Prefecture Welcome Card for discounts at museums and hotels. (☎75-3500; www.town.kotohira.kagawa.jp. Open daily 9:30am-8pm.) **Postal code:** 860.

🖬 ACCOMMODATIONS. There are a good number of ryokan and hotels along Kanakura River and on the streets approaching Kompira-san, but most are very expensive. Nearby Takamatsu has a wider range of reasonably priced accommodations. The cheapest place in Kotohira is **Kotobuki Ryokan** ❷ (ことぶく旅館), Shinmachi, Ichinohasi-Aze. From the JR station, walk to Kanakura River and take a left. Past two pedestrian bridges, Kotobuki will be on the corner to the left at the next automobile bridge. Next to the Shinmachi shopping arcade, this clean hotel is run by a welcoming family. (☎73-3872. Check-in 4pm. Check-out 9am. Curfew midnight. ¥4000 per person, with meals ¥6000.) An older, more weathered option is **Fuji Ryokan** ❸ (富士旅館), Sangū-dōri. From the JR station walk across the Kanamura and take a left. Fuji Ryokan will be on the left, behind the Tako Zushi restaurant—look for the giant octopus on top of Tako Zushi. (☎75-2245. Check-in 3pm. Check-out 9:30am. Curfew 11pm. 2 meals included. ¥7000 per person.)

If you're looking for luxury, head for **Kotosankaku** ❺ (琴参閣). From the JR Station, walk straight across the river and take a right at the T-junction. Kotosankaku will be on the left. This huge two-building luxury hotel features hot springs, free for guests and available to visitors for a fee. (☎75-1000; www1.ocn.ne.jp/~koto3. Reservations necessary. Rates vary. Japanese-style rooms from ¥17,000; Western-style from ¥13,000; weekends add ¥4000. Hot springs free for guests 5am-1am, open to visitors 10:30am-3:30pm for ¥1200.) For easy access to Kompira-san, stay at **Sakuranosho** ❸ (桜の抄), 977-1, Kotohira-chō. Head up the first 22 steps at Kompira-san, take a left, and it's on your right. This reasonably priced hotel offers van service to the JR station. After climbing Kompira-san, relax in the hotel's hot springs and enjoy the view of the mountain. (☎75-3218; www.hananoyu.co.jp. Sin-

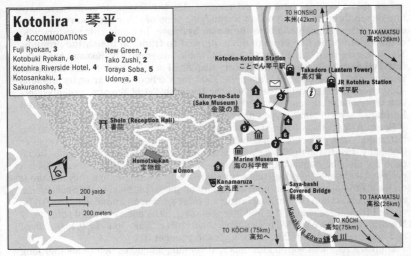

Kotohira · 琴平

🏠 ACCOMMODATIONS

Fuji Ryokan, 3
Kotobuki Ryokan, 6
Kotohira Riverside Hotel, 4
Kotosankaku, 1
Sakuranosho, 9

🍴 FOOD

New Green, 7
Tako Zushi, 2
Toraya Soba, 5
Udonya, 8

TO HONSHŪ
本州(42km)

TO TAKAMATSU
高松(26km)

Kotoden-Kotohira Station
ことでん琴平駅

Takadoro (Lantern Tower)
高灯籠

JR Kotohira Station
琴平駅

Kinryo-no-Sato
(Sake Museum)
金陵の里

Shoin (Reception Hall)
書院

Homotsu-kan
宝物館

Ōmon

Marine Museum
海の科学館

Kanamaruza
金丸座

Saya-bashi
Covered Bridge
鞘橋

0   200 yards
0   200 meters

TO TAKAMATSU
高松(26km)

TO KŌCHI (75km)
高知へ

TO KŌCHI
高知(75km)

Kanakura gawa 鎌倉川

SHIKOKU

gles from ¥6000; twins ¥6000 per person; Japanese-style rooms from ¥10,000. For 2 meals, add ¥4000 weekdays, ¥2000 weekends.) The **Kotohira Riverside Hotel** ❸ (琴 平リバーサイドホテル), 246-1, Kotohira-chō, is a business hotel on the Kanakura River. Walk to the river from the JR Station and take a left; at the first pedestrian bridge, it's on the left. (☎75-1800. Check-in 2pm. Check-out 10am. Curfew midnight. Singles from ¥7000; twins from ¥13,000; weekends add ¥500.)

📷 **FOOD.** *Udon* restaurants line the street approaching Kompira-san—in this neighborhood, you can't throw a rock without hitting a noodle. There are also lots of restaurants along the shopping arcade and near the river. For some tasty noodles, check out **Toraya Soba** ❶ (虎屋そば), 814, Kotohira-chō, to the right just before the steps. Look for an old-fashioned building with tigers carved into the woodwork. (☎75-3131. Cold *zaru udon* ¥450. Open daily 8:30am-5pm). For sushi, head over to **Tako Zushi** ❷ (たこ寿司), Sangū-dōri; you'll know it by the huge octopus on top of the building. (☎75-2245. 8-piece *nigiri* plates ¥800, cucumber rolls ¥450. Noodles from ¥400. Open daily 9am-5pm.) For a hearty set meal, head to **New Green** ❸ (ニューグリーン), a little restaurant on the left corner of the block after Ichinohashi Bridge. (☎73-3451. Noodles from ¥450. Full-size burger ¥800. Add ¥300 for soup and rice; ¥400 for soup and bread. Open M-W and F-Su 8am-9pm.) For a quieter noodle restaurant off the beaten track, try **Udonya** ❶ (う どんや), 177-2, Kotohira-chō. Head down the Shinmachi shopping arcade, take a right down the alley before the ACT Kotohira building, and Udonya will be on the left of the first block. (☎75-3907. *Udon* from ¥300. Open Tu-Su 10am-6pm.)

🎭 🎵 **SIGHTS AND ENTERTAINMENT.** ■**Kompira-san** is the reason people have been traveling over land and sea to Kotohira for the past 400 years. The shrine lies up on the mountain, and locals love to count the steps to the top—785 to the main shrine, 1368 to the last shrine building at the highest accessible point. For those weak in the legs, you can pay to have yourself carried up and down the first 365 steps to the **Ōmon,** the "big gate" at the entrance to the shrine. The ascent costs ¥5000, the descent ¥3000, and a round trip ¥6500. But since walking up the steps is half the fun, grab a bottle of Pocari Sweat and a walking stick from one of the souvenir shops that line the steps to the Ōmon, and take the climb slow and steady.

Two fierce-looking statues stand guard inside the Ōmon, an impressive two-tiered gate through which you get a satisfying view of the stairs you've just conquered. After the gate you pass the **Gonin Byakusyo,** five souvenir vendors who commemorate the five farmers once allowed to trade on the shrine grounds. Shortly up the path to the right are two missable museums. The **Homotsu-kan** is the first building you'll see. It's a two-story display of scroll paintings and armor, all untranslated. (Open daily 8:30am-5pm. ¥500, high school and university students ¥200, children free.) Just to the right is the **Takahashi Yuichi Museum,** a small collection of sea paintings and areas around Kotohira by Takahashi, who considered Kotohira a second home. (Open daily 8:30am-5pm. ¥500, children ¥200.)

Back on the path, you'll come to a break in the steps, with a horse stable to the left and a giant propeller donated by the Okayama-based Nakashima Propeller Company. Just to the right is a statue of a dog carrying a purse in its mouth. In the past, people who couldn't afford to make the pilgrimage (Japan's always been a pricey place) sent their dogs out with a purse and a note, hoping they'd make it one way or another. After another quick hop up the steps, head to the **Shoin** on the right. A path around the building borders a quiet garden and pond, designed to be viewed from the inside of the building. Amazing 18th-century painted screens by Maruyama Okyo are labeled in English. (Open daily 8:30am-5pm. ¥500, high school and university students ¥200, junior high and younger free.)

There's a rest area with bathrooms and vending machines before another long flight of steps to the intricately carved **Asahi-sha,** dedicated to Amaterasu, the Shintō goddess of light. Once you make it up the next 156 steps, you'll see the **Hongu main shrine building,** with a giant horse statue outside. Looking over the edge of the cliff from here, you'll see the huge light that shines from Kompira-san, supposedly visible to sailors on the Inland Sea. Left of the main hall is a boat covered by solar panels and paintings of ships. This is the **Ema-dō,** where pilgrims bring votive pictures of their aquatic conveyances for blessings. Those with more energy can hike the remaining 500 steps through jungle foliage to the **Oku-sha,** the highest temple building. Two faces are carved into the cliffside, one a *tengu* demon with a huge nose. If you know some Japanese, you might pick up some interesting facts by tailing one of the Japanese tour groups that charge up the mountain led by megaphones and flags. *Let's Go,* however, does not recommend mooching.

On your way down from Kompira-san, take a right at the 22nd step and the **Maritime Museum** will be on your left, inside a building that looks like a giant sail. The museum is entirely in Japanese, but you don't need text to appreciate the ship models and videos. The highlight is the rooftop Bridge Deck, taken from an actual ship, that looks out over Kotohira. (☎73-3748. Open daily 9am-5pm. ¥400, junior high and high school students ¥300, elementary and younger ¥200.) Head up the hill past the museum to reach ◧**Kanamaruza,** 1241, Kotohira-chō, Otsu. Dim lanterns lend Japan's oldest permanent theater a sacred atmosphere. Built in 1835 and restored in 1976, it's a typical *kabuki* theater with secret lifts, a bridge stretching from the main stage into the audience, and a revolving stage. Wander backstage to see dressing rooms and the massive revolving device that allows rapid scene changes. Plays go up occasionally, but tickets are difficult to get. (☎73-3846. Open daily 9am-5pm. ¥300, junior high students ¥200, elementary ¥100.)

Continuing down the stairs, the **Kinryo Sake Museum** is on the left on the block before the first cross street. It's housed in an original Meiji-era storage facilities of the Kinryo Sake Company. The displays are in Japanese, but explanations of the company's history and the *sake* brewing process are in English. After you walk through the exhibits of Meiji-style mannequins making *sake,* you can try three different types for ¥100 each and sit out in the brick courtyard under an 800-year-old camphor tree. (☎73-4133. Open daily 9am-5pm. ¥310, junior high and high school students ¥260, elementary and younger free.)

ŌBOKE (大歩危) AND IYA (祖谷) ☎0883

The Ōboke and Koboke Gorges and Iya Valley are some of the few areas in the world where the full extent of nature's enormity lies just outside human comprehension. The Yoshino River connects Ōboke, Koboke, Nishi-Iya, and Higashi-Iya, boring west from Tokushima and turning southward at Ikeda, sending tributaries every which way and extending into Shikoku's mountainous heart. Highways are cut into sheer cliffs, over nearly vertical drops down to a rocky riverbed.

The region served famously as a refuge for the Heike Clan after its defeat by the Minamoto at the battle of Yashima, near Takamatsu. Marks of Heike culture remain in the thatched farmhouses that speckle the area. Because of the train line and a pair of bus routes, the area has acquired some tourist trappings. The real gems are the campgrounds hidden in the heart of the mountains, which you can reach by cycling or driving up some steep hills.

AT A GLANCE

HIGHLIGHTS: Yoshino River, Kazura Bashi's famous vine bridges and the Heike Yashiki, Mt. Tsurugi, bathing in outdoor *onsen*.

CAMPING: Allowed in campgrounds. Reasonably priced (¥3000-4000).

GATEWAYS: Ikeda—access via Tokushima Interchange, JR Dosan Line, or buses from Kōbe and Ōsaka.

WHEN TO GO: Early summer—cooler and less crowded than midsummer. Many campgrounds close in winter.

SHIKOKU

⊏ TRANSPORTATION

The JR Dosan Line runs through the interior of Shikoku all the way from Takamatsu to Kōchi, with stops at Awa Ikeda, Awakawaguchi, Iyaguchi, Koboke, and Ōboke Stations. Rte. 32 follows the Dosan Line for its entire length. Iya Highway, also known as Old Scenic Rte. 32, traces a tributary of the Yoshino River past the Pissing Boy Statue and Iya Onsen. Cars are the best way to get around the area, but an infrequent bus system stops at major sights.

Train: The **JR Dosan Line** starts at Takamatsu and runs through Awa Ikeda, Iyaguchi, Koboke, and Ōboke Stations on the way to Kōchi.

Intercity Buses: Shikoku Kōtsū buses run to and from Ikeda Station (☎72-1231). To **Kōbe** (3hr.; 3 per day 8am-6:30pm; ¥4100, round-trip ¥7380) and **Ōsaka** (4-6hr., 5 per day 9am-7:30pm; ¥4500/¥8100).

Local Buses: Shikoku Kōtsū runs 2 local lines from Ikeda Station. One runs down Rte. 32 to Ōboke, through Kazura-bashi, and east 2 more stops (4 per day, 2¼hr.). The 2nd runs down Iya Highway to Deai (4 per day) or Kazura-bashi (3 per day, 1¼hr.).

Car Rental: Rent at Tokushima (40min. from Ikeda on the Tokushima Expressway; p. 528), Takamatsu (2hr. on Rte. 32; p. 538), or Kōchi (1½hr. on Rte. 32 and the Kōchi Expressway; p. 553).

⁊ PRACTICAL INFORMATION

Don't count on Internet or international phones while in Ōboke and Iya. Before you head out on your camping trip or daytrip, stock up on supplies in Ikeda.

Tourist Office: Most tourist locations have maps, but the **Awa Ikeda Tourist Information Office** is right outside Awa Ikeda Station and has great maps in Japanese and English. They can also help arrange trips to the interior. (☎72-5865. Open 9am-5pm.)

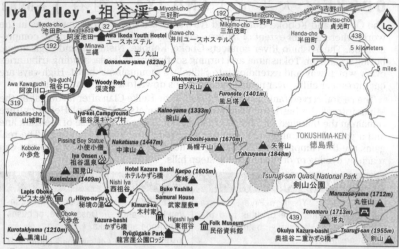

Iya Valley · 祖谷渓

Tours: Bonnet Bus tours are among Japan's most famous tours. Their old-style buses hit the main tourist sites in Ōboke and Iya. 1 tour daily, 11am-4:20pm. ¥5200, children ¥4700. Lunch at Manaka restaurant included.

Gear: Ikeda has larger supermarkets and convenience stores that you won't find farther south. Bringing your own tent is wise, but many campgrounds have bungalows.

Emergency: Police ☎110. **Fire** or **ambulance** ☎119.

🏠🏕 ACCOMMODATIONS AND CAMPING

For places so isolated, Ōboke and Iya offer a surprising number of accommodations born from the tourist boom. There are luxurious hot springs on the side of the gorges, but campgrounds remain the cheapest option.

🏠 **Ryugugake Park** (龍宮崖公園 ; ☎88-2893). A 20min. drive east of Kazura Bashi on Scenic Rte. 32. The car entrance is just past the pedestrian bridge over the river. Nothing short of an incredible deal. Great view of a tributary of the Yoshino River from a walking bridge. Climb down the path to the river and wade through it, surrounded by huge craggy rocks. Check-in 5pm. Check-out 10am. Cabins fit up to 6 people, ¥4000 per person. Fully equipped kitchens included, barbecue pits ¥500. ❷

🏠 **Hikyo no Yu Onsen** (秘境の湯), 401, Inouchi, Yamamura, Nishi-iya (☎87-2300; www.hotel-hikyounoyu.co.jp). From Awa Ikeda or Ōboke, take a bus right to this luxury hotel (4 per day, 9am-5:10pm from Ikeda). Easy access to Iya's most beautiful sights. Great hot spring surrounded by mountains. 2 meals included. Hot springs free for guests, open 10am-11pm; visitors ¥1000, open 10am-9pm. Check-in 3pm. Check-out 11am. Singles and twins from ¥17,000; Japanese-style rooms from ¥19,000. ❺

Awa Ikeda (HI), Ikeda-chō, Masako, Nishi-iya (☎72-5277). Owners pick up guests from Awa Ikeda Station at 6pm. If you're arriving late, call. The drive up the mountain takes 10min., but the view is worth it. They'll return you to the station if you ask. Parking free. Breakfast ¥500. Dinner ¥1000. Check-in 4-8pm. Check-out 10am. Curfew 10pm. Reservations required. Japanese-style rooms ¥3000 for members; non-members ¥4000. ❶

Hotel Kazura Bashi (ホテルかずら橋), Zentoku, Yamamura, Nishi-iya (☎87-2171). Take the bus from Ikeda/Ōboke. On main highway just before Kazura Bashi itself. Hot springs open to guests 8am-11pm, visitors 9am-9pm. Check-in 3pm. Check-out 10am. Curfew 11pm. Japanese-style rooms ¥15,000 per person, weekends ¥16,000. ❺

Shinoku Iya (新奥祖谷), Zentoku, Yamamura-aza, Nishi-iya (☎87-2203). As close as you can get to sleeping on Kazura Bashi—this hotel/restaurant is next to the bridge. Restaurant on 1st fl. Check-in 5pm. Japanese-style rooms ¥6500 per person. ❸

Iya Onsen (祖谷温泉), 367-2, Ikeda-chō (☎75-2311; www.iyaonsen.co.jp). Easily accessible from Ikeda or Ōboke via the bus that runs down the Iya Kaido. On the side of Scenic Rte. 32, the perfect spot to soak in hot springs while taking in the scenery of the Yoshino River (guests free; visitors ¥1500; open 8am-5pm). A cable car runs down to the river (guests free; visitors ¥1500), where you can bathe in the lukewarm sulphurous spring water. 2 meals included. Check-in 2pm. Check-out 10am. Curfew 9pm. Singles ¥18,000, 2 people ¥16,000 per person, 3 people ¥15,000 per person. ❺

Iya-kei Campground (祖谷渓キャンプ村), 525-1, Matsumoto, Matsuo-aza, Ikeda-chō (☎75-2044; www.awaikeda.jp). Off Scenic Rte. 32, about 3km north of Iya Onsen and 7km south of Iyaguchi. On the Iyakei Gorge. Plenty of options for different sorts of campers. Showers ¥100. Open Apr. 1-Nov. 30. ¥310 per day with your own tent. Bungalows fit 5 people, ¥3150 per person for 4pm-9am; add ¥2100 for 10am-4pm. Nature preservation fee ¥420, junior high and high school students ¥210. ❶

Iyashi Onsen (いやし温泉), 28, Sugeoi, Yamamura, Higashi-iya (☎88-2975). Deep into Higashi-iya on Scenic Rte. 32, Iyashi is a 45min. drive from the Kazura Bashi and 1½hr. from the Ikeda Interchange. A bus runs down Rte. 32 to the Sugeoi Bus Stop, where the hotel will pick you up. This brand new hot springs hotel contrasts with the small farming houses that surround it. The luxury and isolation may be worth the trip and the hefty prices. Check-in 3pm. Check-out 10am. Curfew 10pm. Make reservations 2 weeks in advance. Japanese-style rooms for 2 ¥25,000; Western-style rooms ¥9000 per person; bungalows ¥7000; weekends add ¥1000. ❹

Okuiya Kazurabashi Campground (奥祖谷かずら橋; ☎88-2640). On the other side of the Kazura Bashi, a car ride from Ōboke or Ikeda or a 30min. walk from Nagoro (the last stop on the bus line) down Rte. 439. Carry your pack across one of the bridges or use the unique pulley device to pull your stuff across. Basic campground, but it's on a little river, and a waterfall

IN RECENT NEWS

HOW GREEN IS MY VALLEY

Tightly intertwined with government policies responsible for Japan's current economic despair is the fate of Shikoku's Iya Valley. Locked away in one of Japan's three "hidden regions," Iya is marked by deep gorges, sparkling rivers, and, notably, an absence of people. The region's most famous attractions are its vine bridges, which served as "cross and slash" getaways for the Minamoto and Taira clans 900 years ago.

Yet, as those who live among its fading beauty will explain, Iya's future is in danger as the government continues to endorse construction projects aimed only at stimulating the troubled economy. The result of this policy has been the unleashing of a monster who viciously covers treasured areas with concrete slabs. Reform has been discussed, but the issue hasn't been prioritized, and a solution seems far down the road.

Even with this in mind, however, visitors should not skip over the region that awards avid hikers with bubbling *onsen* (hot springs) and flowing waterfalls. One can only hope that a trekker's sense of sadness may spur him to help in the struggle to preserve the remaining gems of Iya Valley. To read more about the issues concerning Iya and the destruction of cultural and natural areas in Japan, check out *Dogs and Demons: Tales from the Dark Side of Modern Japan,* by Alex Kerr.

GIVING BACK

CHIIORI

In his book *Lost Japan*, Alex Kerr writes about the mountains of Iya and the preservation of ancient Japanese culture. The book was the first written by a non-native Japanese to win the equivalent of a Pulitzer Prize in Japan. Kerr is also renowned for developing Chiiori, an old farmhouse he bought 30 years ago, into a working cultural preservation project. Long-term residents maintain the house, while others chip in money or work weekends.

The house itself is 200-300 years old, with a thatched roof and rafters and floorboards made from beautiful dark polished wood. The *irori*, an indoor open hearth, fills the house with a smoky fragrance. Fresh vegetables lie in the kitchen for meals, all cooked on site. Unlike many tourist attractions in similar houses, Chiiori has an airy, lived-in feel.

With an eye to preserving ancient arts, Chiiori also houses artists in residence such as lantern makers and musicians who hold seminars on weekends. Visitors are welcome; fees vary.

A schedule of events is posted on the website (www.chiiori.org). Only on volunteer weekends can visitors stay at the house for a reasonable rate (¥3000). It's not certain Chiiori will house visitors in 2004, so if you're interested, contact them via their website or by calling ☎+81-883-88-5290. The house is looking for long-term caretakers and volunteer staff.

creates a perfect wading pool. 7km from Mt. Tsurugi. Open Apr. 1-Dec. 1. ¥300 per 24hr. Bridge crossing fee ¥500, children ¥300. ❶

🍴 FOOD

Most of the noodle shops and restaurants in Ōboke and Iya are clustered around the tourist attractions. Campers should stock up on supplies before heading out. Left of Rte. 32 just before Iyaguchi Station, **Woody Rest ❷** (渓流館), Iya Rte. 32 (☎86-1858), advertises "Good Grub," but it's Japanese-style grub with set meals from ¥1100; options include hamburger, *tonkatsu* (fried pork cutlet), fried shrimp, and eel. The Iya *soba* set is ¥700, or you can order a la carte: *udon* and *soba* from ¥400, curries from ¥650. The friendly owners speak some English. On the path before the entrance to Kazura Bashi, **Shinoku Iya** (新奥祖谷), Zentoku, Yamamura-aza, Nishi-iya (☎87-2203), sells snacks out front. Try *dengaku*, a combo of *yamaimo* (yam-like vegetable), tofu, and *konnyaku* (konjac, another root vegetable product) on a stick (¥300); or *amego*, fish roasted on a stick (¥500). Inside you can order standard noodle fare and set meals. ❷

👁 🏔 SIGHTS AND OUTDOORS

ŌBOKE GORGE. Ōboke's sights center around the gorge itself, which becomes increasingly magnificent as you head south. The Yoshino River cuts south from Ikeda, veering away from the westward path it takes from Tokushima. Shortly after you pass the signs for Koboke Station along Rte. 32, you'll see **Restaurant Ōboke-kyō Manaka** (レストラン大歩危峡まんなか), Yamashiro-chō, Ōboke, which runs a spectacular 30min. boat ride along 2km of the Yoshino River. Buses run from Ikeda, or you can walk 20min. north from Ōboke Station on Rte. 32. The meeting place for the MontBell Outdoor Challenge programs is in the parking lot. (☎84-1211. Departures every 30min. 9am-5pm. ¥1050, children ¥525.) A few minutes down the road is **Lapis Ōboke Stone Museum** (ラピス大歩危石の博物館), Yamashiro-chō, Miyoshi, which has geological exhibits and a beautiful display of minerals and gems. An English pamphlet points out some highlights, including a Martian meteorite and the oldest stone in Tokushima Prefecture. The Rte. 32 bus stops here. (☎84-1489. Open Tu-Su 9am-5pm. ¥500, children ¥300.)

NISHI-IYA. Crossing the Ōboke Bridge on Rte. 32, you'll enter Nishi-Iya, the 400-year-old mountain refuge of the Heike clan. Set against the tree-covered Iya mountains, the farmers' houses and bridges reflect a culture and architectural style that took root here after the battle of Yashima. The **Heike Yashiki**

(平家屋敷), Migashi-Nishioka, Yamamura, is an old thatched-roofed farmer's house converted into a cluttered museum of old books, guns, swords, kitchen utensils, and other household goods. The house dates back only to the Edo Period but retains some Heike characteristics. (☎84-1408. Open 8am-6pm. ¥500, children ¥300.) Continuing toward eastern Iya, you'll come to the **Kazura Bashi** (かずら橋), Zentoku, Yamason, vine bridges that the Heike built to cross dangerous gorges and then cut down to delay their enemies. Now the bridges are reinforced with well-hidden cables. After crossing, take a quick walk to the left and you'll come to the hissing **Biwa Waterfall**, named for the instrument that the Heike played to mourn their fate. (Open dawn to dusk. ¥500, children ¥400.) A detour up the **Iya Kaido** (Old Scenic Rte. 32) takes you past **Iya Onsen** (p. 551), where you can bathe in a spring by the river or in the *onsen* off the roadside. Just a few minutes farther is the **Peeing Boy Statue**, a regional icon. He sits atop a cliff 200m from the river.

HIGASHI-IYA. Rte. 439 runs all the way from Otoyo to Mt. Tsurugi and links to Scenic Rte. 32 shortly after Ryugugake Park. It's the road to the interior of eastern Shikoku. About 7km before Mt. Tsurugi, the bridge **Oku Iya Kazura Bashi** is on the right side of the road. Oku Iya Kazura Bashi is considered the female counterpart to the larger, wider, male Kazura Bashi in Nishi-Iya; together they are known as the "couple bridges." There's a small waterfall and wading area as well. (☎88-2640. Open Apr. 1-Nov. 30 dawn to dusk.) At 1955m, **Mt. Tsurugi** (☎62-2772; www9.ocn.ne.jp/~tsurugi) is the second tallest mountain in Shikoku and offers plenty of climbing opportunities for outdoorsy types. At the base of the mountain is **Tsurugi Shrine**, which isn't much to look at but marks the start of the 4000m climb to the peak (40-50min.). If you don't want to walk, you can go part of the way by taking the lift (15min.). From the drop-off point, three paths of different length lead to the peak: 960m, 1200m, and 1980m. The 1200m route will take you past the one shrine building at the mountaintop. No need to worry about being stranded at the top—there is a restaurant and a hotel if you get too tired to make the trip back down. The **Tsurugi-san Chōjō Butte ❷** offers rooms for ¥4300, ¥7000 to add two meals. (☎088-623-4533. Open Apr. 28-Nov. 23.)

KŌCHI (高知)　　　☎088

Lying slightly inland off the Pacific, Kōchi is the capital and pivot point of Kōchi Prefecture, lying between Ashizuri-misaki and Muroto-misaki, the capes at either end of the prefecture. The region is often referred to as Tosa, especially in relation to the local cuisine, *tosa ryōri*—centered around tremendous plates of sliced fish—and the *tosa* fighting dogs, based in nearby Katsurahama. You may pass through Kōchi on the Shikoku Pilgrimage, en route to Godai-san to see Chikurin-ji. If you're in town in August, check out the Yosakoi dancing festival, just as unique and exciting as Awa Ōdori, though not so widely hyped. There's also no shortage of nightlife, as the locals stay out later than elsewhere in Shikoku.

⊠ INTERCITY TRANSPORTATION

Flights: Kōchi Airport, 58, Otsu, Hisaeda (☎864-1525; www.shikoku.ne.jp/kochi-ap/kochi-at/index.htm), is in Nankoku, a few kilometers from Kōchi Station. Flights to Fuku-oka, Hiroshima, Itami, Nagoya, Okinawa, and Tōkyō. Buses run to and from Kōchi Station, stopping at Harimaya Bashi (30min., every 20min. 6:30am-6:30pm, ¥700).

Trains: The JR Dosan Line connects Kōchi with northern Shikoku. To: **Awa Ikeda** (local 2½hr., ¥1580; limited express 1hr., ¥2730); **Kotohira** (local 2¼hr., ¥2030; limited express 1½hr., ¥3810; transfer at Awa Ikeda); **Ōboke** (local 2hr., ¥1240; limited express 50min., ¥2390); **Okayama** (7 per day; local 3½hr., ¥3180; limited express 2½hr., ¥5280); **Takamatsu** (local ¥2660; limited express 2¼hr., 5 per day, ¥4760); **Tokushima** (local 4¼hr., ¥3080; limited express 3¼hr., ¥5180).

Buses: Long-distance and city buses depart from the terminal to the right of Kōchi Station. To: **Matsuyama** (2½hr.; 6 per day 9am-6pm; ¥3500, round-trip ¥6000); **Nagoya** (10hr.; 8:10pm; ¥9070, round-trip ¥16,310); **Okayama** (2½hr.; 9 per day 7am-6:50pm; ¥3500, round-trip ¥6300); **Ōsaka** (5hr.; 2 per day 7:40am-3:40pm; ¥6000, round-trip ¥10,800); **Takamatsu** (2hr.; every hr. 7:10am-7:40pm; ¥3300, round-trip ¥6000), **Tokushima** (2¾hr.; 4 per day 8am-5:30pm; ¥3500, round-trip ¥6300), **Tōkyō** (11½hr.; 1 per day; ¥10,000, round-trip ¥18,000).

⌨ LOCAL TRANSPORTATION

Tram: 2 street tram lines cross Kōchi, one north-south, from Kōchi Station and across the rivers, the other east-west, intersecting the 1st track at Dencha-dōri. You can transfer between the lines at no cost by asking for a *norikae* ticket. Most rides within the city cost ¥180, but range ¥100-500.

Taxis: Kōchi Ekimae Kanko, ☎0120-17-0512. **Kōnan Hire,** ☎833-1000.

Car Rental: Toyota Rent-a-Car, 4-15, Ekimae-chō (☎823-0100). Across the street from Kōchi Station on the right. Open daily 8am-8pm. **Nissan Rent-a-Car,** 2-1-12, Kita-hon-chō (☎883-4485), across the street from Kōchi Station on the left.

Bike Rental: New Cycle Creation Kagiyama, 4-11, Aioi-chō (☎882-1585). Walk left from Kōchi Station; turn right before Los Inn. It's on the right at the 3rd block. ¥600 for 1st 4hr., ¥100 every hr. thereafter; ¥1200 per day. Open daily 9:30am-7:30pm.

✚ ORIENTATION

You'll probably pull into JR Kōchi Station, in the very north of the city. Most of Kōchi lies between **Enokuchi River,** which runs east-west just south of the station, and **Dencha-dōri. Kōchi Castle** marks the western limit of the city proper and is surrounded by offices, the international center, and the city and prefectural libraries. The **Obiya-machi** shopping arcade runs from Harimaya-bashi-dōri to Kōchi castle and is the easiest way to get across town. Almost everything is within walking distance, but riding the antique-looking tram is fun and helps get you to some sights.

❼ PRACTICAL INFORMATION

Tourist Office: Tourist Information Center, 2-7-1, Kita-honchō (☎82-1634; www6.ocn.ne.jp/~k-yado21). Inside Kōchi Station near exit. Distributes maps. Can handle most English inquiries. Linked to Nikanren hotel group and can arrange a place to stay. Open daily 9am-5pm. **Kōchi International Association,** 4-1-37, Hon-machi (☎875-0022; www.kochi-f.co.jp/kia). Across from Kōchi Castle, on the left as you approach via Obiya-machi. Focuses on exchange programs, but will help tourists. English and Chinese. Small English-language library. Open M-Sa 8:30am-5pm.

Tours: There are 2 half-day and 1 full-day bus tours that depart from the terminal at Kōchi Station. Runs Mar.-May and July 20-Nov. 30. ¥2450-5350. The **Kōchi Systematized Goodwill Guide Club** (☎833-4198, y.k@sage.ocn.ne.jp) arranges tours of Kōchi Castle and other attractions. Call at least 1 week in advance.

Currency Exchange: There are several banks on Dencha-dōri close to the intersection with Harimaya-bashi-dōri, including **UFJ, Kōchi Bank,** and **Bank of Shikoku.** Most change money weekdays. The post office (see below) also changes money.

ATM: All post offices (see below) have international ATMs. AmEx/V.

Luggage Storage: There are coin lockers near the Kōchi Station exit.

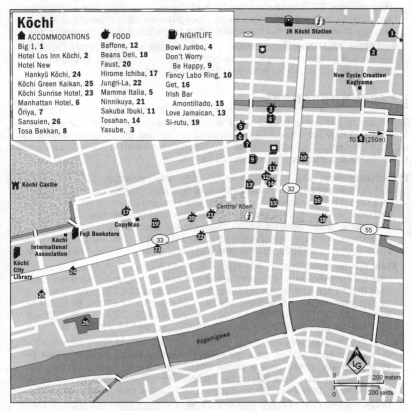

Kōchi

♠ ACCOMMODATIONS	♥ FOOD	♠ NIGHTLIFE
Big 1, **1**	Baffone, **12**	Bowl Jumbo, **4**
Hotel Los Inn Kōchi, **2**	Beans Deli, **18**	Don't Worry
Hotel New	Faust, **20**	Be Happy, **9**
Hankyū Kōchi, **24**	Hirome Ichiba, **17**	Fancy Labo Ring, **10**
Kōchi Green Kaikan, **25**	Jungri-La, **22**	Get, **16**
Kōchi Sunrise Hotel, **23**	Mamma Italia, **5**	Irish Bar
Manhattan Hotel, **6**	Ninnikuya, **21**	Amontillado, **15**
Ōriya, **7**	Sakuba Ibuki, **11**	Love Jamaican, **13**
Sansuien, **26**	Tosahan, **14**	Si-rutu, **19**
Tosa Bekkan, **8**	Yasube, **3**	

English-Language Bookstore: Fuji Bookstore, 4-1-46, Hon-machi (☎873-3570). After the Obiya-machi arcade, walk 3 blocks and Fuji is on the corner on the left. Small English-language section. Open M-F 9:30am-8:30pm, Su 10am-7pm.

Library: Kōchi City Library, 5-1-30, Honchō (☎875-9018). Past the city offices, Obiya-machi becomes a street; it's on the left. Open Tu-F 9:30am-7pm, Sa-Su 10am-5pm.

Market: Sunday Market along Ōtesuji-dōri, where locals sell foods and crafts.

Emergency: Police ☎110. **Fire** or **ambulance** ☎119.

Police: Kōchi Police, 1-9-20, Kita-honchō (☎822-0110). Opposite Kōchi Station.

24hr. Pharmacy: Lawson stores on Harimaya-bashi-dōri and Dencha-dōri.

Hospital/Medical Services: Kōchi Prefectural Emergency Medical Information Center (☎825-1299; http://plaza26.mbn.or.jp/~kyukyuiryo). Japanese phone line. Website has English listings. Open 24hr.

Fax Office: Copy Mac, 2-1-22, Obiya-machi (☎802-2030; fax 802-2031). Toward the end of Obiya-machi on the left as you approach Kōchi Castle. Faxes ¥100 per page. Open daily 8am-8pm.

Internet Access: Hot Station (ほっとステーション), 1-3-1, Beruepokku Bldg., 5th fl., Ōtesuji (☎820-6741). From Kōchi Station, cross Enoguchi River and take a right on Ōtesuji-dōri; it's in the building to the right, 5th fl., not on the corner. Lots of connections available. ¥100 membership fee, then ¥100 per 15min. If you have a laptop and LAN card you can surf for free. Free drinks. Open 24hr. The Kōchi International Association (see **Tourist Offices**) has a computer with a connection that you can use for free.

Post Office: Kōchi Central Post Office, 1-10-18, Kita-honchō (☎822-7809). Exiting the station, walk a block to the right and the post office will be on the right. Open 24hr. ATM open M-F 9am-11pm, Sa-Su 9am-5pm. **Postal Code:** 780.

ACCOMMODATIONS

There are no dirt cheap hostels in or around Kōchi, but you won't have to pay more than ¥4000 for a room. Accommodations across the river are nearer to sights, shopping, and nightlife. The tourist information booth at Kōchi Station can reserve beds at a number of clean and friendly hotels.

Manhattan Hotel, 5-16, Nijudai-chō (☎821-2111; www.manhattan.co.jp). From Kōchi Station, walk along Harimaya-bashi-dōri. Turn right after crossing the Enokuchi River. Take the 1st left after Bowl Jumbo, then the 2nd right, and it's on the left. Perhaps the best value in Kōchi, this sparkling and fashionable hotel one-ups other basic choices. 13th-floor restaurant boasts a ¥2800 all-you-can-eat. Doubles and twins have in-room saunas. Free Internet in lobby. Parking ¥500. Breakfast ¥800. Check-in 2pm. Check-out 10am. Singles from ¥6000; doubles from ¥8000; twins from ¥13,500. AmEx/MC/V. ❸

Kōchi Sunrise Hotel, 2-2-31, Hon-chō, (☎822-1281; www.inforyoma.or.jp/sunrise). From the Harimaya-bashi-dōri and Dencha-dōri intersection, walk toward the castle along Dencha-dōri, and Sunrise will be on the left, 2 blocks after Chūō-kōen. Good pricing and great amenities. Free Internet in lobby; use in room for ¥1000. Bike use free. Breakfast from ¥1100. Lunch from ¥2000. Dinner from ¥3500. Check-in 3pm. Check-out 10am. Singles from ¥5300, twins from ¥9600, doubles from ¥11,000. ❸

Ōriya, 1-6-21, Ōtesuji (☎821-0100, toll-free ☎0120-074-351; www.kochi-f.co.jp/ooriya). From Kōchi Station, cross the Enokuchi River, take a right, and then take the 1st left after Bowl Jumbo. Ōriya is on the right corner of the 4th block. This comfy, ryokan-esque hotel has a restaurant on the 1st floor. Western- and Japanese-style rooms. Check-in 4pm. Check-out 10am. Curfew 1am. Singles from ¥6000; twins from ¥12,000; triples from ¥15,000. AmEx/MC/V. ❸

Tosa Bekkan, 1-11-34, Sakurai-chō (☎883-5685). Exiting Kōchi Station, head to the left, take a right before Los Inn, and cross Enokuchi River. Take the 1st left, 3rd right, and 1st left; it's on the left. Away from town center. Coin laundry machines outside the building. Check-in noon. Check-out 10am. Japanese-style rooms ¥4200 per person. ❷

Hotel Los Inn Kōchi (ホテルロスイン高知), 2-4-8, Kita-honchō (☎884-1110). From Kōchi Station, cross the street and walk 2 blocks left. It's on the right on the corner. The name refers to Los Angeles, but the lobby decor recalls the L.A. of decades past—brown leather sofas and glass column chandeliers. Perfect for a business trip or sightseeing. Management speaks some English and Spanish. Check-in 4pm. Check-out 10am. Singles ¥5775; twins or Japanese-style rooms ¥10,500. ❸

Sansuien (三翠園), 1-3-35, Takajō-chō (☎822-0131; www.sansuien.co.jp). From Kōchi Station, walk or take a tram down Harimaya-bashi-dōri, bearing right at Dencha-dōri. At Kencho-mae Tram Stop, head 2 blocks left; it's on the next corner. Dinner served in your room overlooking garden. Hot springs free for guests; ¥900 for visitors, open 10am-4pm. Check-in 2pm. Check-out 10am. Singles ¥7500, with breakfast ¥9000; twins and Japanese-style rooms from ¥15,000, 2 meals included. ❸

Kōchi Green Kaikan, 5-6-11, Hon-chō (☎825-2701). Take the tram down Dencha-dōri, get off at Kencho-mae, walk 1 block away from the castle, and it's on your right. Only a few blocks from Obiya-machi and Kōchi Castle. Breakfast ¥700. Dinner ¥1800. Check-in 3pm. Check-out 10am. Curfew midnight. Singles from ¥5565; twins from ¥5250 per person; Japanese-style doubles from ¥5145 per person. ❸

Big 1, 3-9-45, Kita-honchō (☎883-9603). Exiting Kōchi Station, walk 3 blocks to the left; it's on the corner on the left. Male-only capsule hotel. Sauna with several large baths, lounge area with 2 TVs, and a restaurant. Breakfast ¥500. Parking free. Reception 24hr. ¥3700 for a capsule 4pm-noon. If you just want to use the sauna, packages (from ¥1000) allow you to crash on the floor of a big room with blankets and pillows. ❷

Hotel New Hankyu Kōchi (高知新阪急ホテル), 4-2-50, Hon-machi (☎873-1145; http://hotel.kochi-newhankyu.co.jp). On Dencha-dōri, Hotel New Hankyu offers access to shopping and nightlife, as well as nice in-house restaurants: Japanese, Chinese, *teppanyaki* (cooked in front of you), and Western. Fitness room, pool, and sauna for guests. Breakfast ¥1600. Lunch ¥2000. Dinner ¥5000. Check-in 1pm. Check-out 11am. Singles from ¥9500; twins from ¥18,500; doubles from ¥22,000. ❹

🍴 FOOD

You'll find plenty of cheap places to eat all over Kōchi—restaurants over shopping streets, hole-in-the-wall basement places, and big food courts. Among the many street stalls, a good choice is **Yasube** outside Bowl Jumbo which offers *rāmen*, *gyoza* (dumplings), and beer for ¥500 apiece. (Open Su and Tu-Th 7pm-3am, F-Sa 7pm-3:30am.) Keep an eye out for *tamago-yaki* (玉子焼き), a delicious, puffy, spherical pastry; a good-sized bag is ¥500. At the very end of Obiya-machi, **Hirome Ichiba** is a crowd of food booths and small boutique-type stores. You'll find *udon* and *soba* from ¥100 and *unagi* (eel) from ¥450 just about everywhere, but there are many alternatives if you aren't quite sure what you want. (☎822-5287; www.hirome.co.jp. Open daily 8am-10pm.)

Mamma Italia, 4-4, Nijudai-machi (☎873-3131). From Kōchi Station, walk across Harimaya-bashi and take a right. Take your 1st left and 2nd right, and Mamma's on the right. The owner and chef speaks English; English menu. Specializes in dinner-plate-sized pizzas from ¥1000; pastas from ¥1000; salads from ¥500. Seafood pizza with tuna, octopus, shrimp, clams, and mussels ¥1250. AmEx/DC/JCB/MC. ❸

Sakuba Ibuki, 1-1-3, Ōtesuji (☎871-2288). This noodle joint is perfect for late-night eats after some drinks. The specialty is *ebichin*, shrimp topped with a crumbly covering (¥650), but *rāmen*, served in near-boiling soup, is a better deal (¥600). The Fukuoka-style bowl has delicious traces of ginger. Look for the *takoyaki* (octopus balls) stand outside; ¥450 per tray. Open Su-Th 3pm-2am, F-Sa 3pm-4am. ❷

Baffone, Sansui Bldg, 1st fl., 1-2-10, Obiya-machi (☎822-3884). From the look and feel of the place, you'd expect Hemingway or Monet to stroll in any second, sit down next to you, and order a chicken foccaccia panini with a bottle of wine. Perfect starting point for a long night out. Bass Ale on tap ¥900 a pint, Carlsberg ¥800, Guinness ¥800. Mostly Italian food: standard antipastos from ¥900, risotto from ¥850, pastas from ¥800. Small panini from ¥500, with chicken, salmon, cheese, mushroom, or prosciutto. Open M-F 5pm-midnight, Sa-Su noon-midnight. Closed 3rd W of every month. ❸

Jungri-La, 1-4-26, 2F, Hon-chō (☎873-9966). A block past Chūō-kōen away from Harimaya-bashi-dōri on the opposite side of Dencha-dōri—look for huge neon signs. This tackily decorated pirate-themed *izakaya* comes off like an MGM sound studio, but the food is a good deal. Steak *gyōza* ¥380, hot dog and fries ¥500, club sandwich and fries ¥650. International beers from ¥500 per bottle, cocktails ¥500. Open Su-Th 5pm-11pm, F-Sa 5pm-midnight. AmEx/MC/V. ❷

Tosahan, 1-2-2, Obiya-machi (☎-875-0090). From Harimaya-bashi-dōri, walk 2 blocks toward Kōchi Castle on Obiya-machi; it's on the right. Serves the local cuisine, *tosa ryori*, with a flare for *tataki katsuo*, or thick strips of tender fish lightly seared; meal sets from ¥1300, sushi from ¥800. Large groups can get massive trays of sliced fish (¥4000-6000 per person). Open daily 11:30am-10pm. AmEx/MC/V. ❸

Faust (ファウスト). Walk up the Obiya-machi arcade, take a left after Daimaru department store, and walk 1 block to the street parallel to Obiya-machi; it's on the 1st block after Chūō-kōen. Jazzy cafe with 3 floors, including an upstairs gallery area. Small breakfast sets of toast and coffee from ¥350. Lunch sets from ¥690—the NY set has pastrami on a bagel; the Peter Pan set has *teriyaki* chicken in a pita. Curry breads (¥180) are a great cheap snack. Open daily 9am-9:30pm. ❶

Beans Deli, 1-5-18, Harimaya-chō (☎882-8182). Cross Harimaya-bashi and pass the Obiya-machi arcade, take a left when you see the water-lined avenue, and walk the remaining block to Dencha-dōri. It's toward the end on the left. Great for early morning coffee and toast, this airy little cafe lies on the park walkway before Dencha-dōri. After noon, opt for a lunch set (¥750)—usually a bagel sandwich, hashed potatoes, and dessert. The BBQ chicken bagel is delicious. Open Su-Tu and Th-Sa 8am-6pm. ❷

Ninnikuya, 1-2-25, Hon-chō, 2nd fl. (☎826-0200). On the 1st block walking down Obiya-machi from Chūō-kōen. All about garlic (ninniku). Slices of garlic cover chicken, steak, pasta, other vegetables, and more garlic. Italian tinge to many dishes. Lunchtime buffet M-F ¥1000, Sa-Su ¥1200; dinner set meals from ¥1380. Open M-Th 11:30am-3:00pm and 5:30-11pm, F-Su 11:30am-3:30pm and 5:30pm-midnight. ❸

🅖 SIGHTS

■ **MAKINO BOTANICAL GARDENS.** The gardens double as a museum honoring Dr. Tomitaro Makino, a Kōchi-ken native and vigorous pioneer of the botanical sciences—he named over one-third of all plant specimens in Japan. Established in 1957 after his death, the gardens were completely refurbished in 1999, when the **Makino Museum of Plants and People** was added. The museum and Exhibition Hall are both beautiful spiral-shaped buildings constructed out of wood and unfinished concrete. The Exhibition Hall holds rotating exhibits of artists who take plants as their subjects. It also contains a biographical exhibit commemorating Makino's work. Most displays are translated and well-designed. You can grab a *bentō*-style lunch at **Arbre Restaurant** (¥1000), but a picnic is a better idea. Entering the gardens from the main gate puts you closer to the museums; use the south gate if you want to get to the picnic areas or greenhouse first. *(4200-6, Godai-san. Head down the main steps of Chikurin-ji, and you'll be across from the south gate. ☎882-2601; www.i-kochi.or.jp/hp/ makino. Open Tu-Su 9am-5pm. ¥500, high school students and younger free.)*

GODAI-SAN. This mountain-based park provides a great view of Kōchi Port and is home to the 31st temple on the 88-Temple Pilgrimage. Begin by enjoying the vista from the **Godai Tembo Service Center**, where there is also a restaurant and souvenir store. Head up the stairs to the lookout platform, where you can watch ships in Kōchi's harbor. *(About 2km south of the Kōchi Museum of Art. Unfortunately, no bus lines run to the mountain, and a cab from Kōchi Station costs ¥1800-1900. Your best bet may be to catch a cab from the Kōchi Museum of Art, which is much closer to the park than the station.)*

CHIKURIN-JI. The 31st temple on Kobo Daishi's legendary pilgrimage, Chikurin-ji dates back to 724 when Emperor Shomu ordered that a temple be built in the image of one in China. Kobo Daishi stopped by during the 9th century and helped work on repairs. In addition to the main temple building, there is a five-story red pagoda, drawing house, and garden. *(From Godai-san, approach Chikurin-ji from a set of stairs in the woods behind the main temple building. Grounds free. Drawing house and garden open 8:30am-5pm; ¥400, high school students ¥200, junior high ¥150, elementary ¥150.)*

KŌCHI MUSEUM OF ART. Surrounded by a shallow artificial pond, this strikingly modern building features a Japanese-style garden on an island in front of the museum. The museum divides its permanent collection into three main categories: Marc Chagall, Kōchi artists, and contemporary artists. Rotating exhibits usually have audio tours and some English translation; for 2004, the museum has planned exhibits of works by Frida Kahlo (Jan. 4-Feb. 22) and Wilhelm Lehmburck (Feb. 29-Apr. 4). Get a copy of the museum newsletter, as it lists other museum activities, including film screenings, dance productions, and cultural events. *(353-2, Takasu. ☎866-8000. From Kōchi Station, take the tram and switch at Harimaya-bashi to an eastbound tram. Get off at the Kenritsu Bijutsukan-dōri (Museum Road) Tram Stop, and the museum is a 5min. walk to the north. Open Tu-Su and 1st M of each month 9am-5pm. ¥350, university students ¥250, high school students and younger free.)*

KŌCHI CASTLE. Lying to the west of the city, the castle itself isn't mindblowing, but the grounds have been arranged into a beautiful park. The buildings that remain survived the Meiji Reformation, when many politicians tried to erase Japan's feudal past by destroying its most visible icons. Fortunately, the *donjon*, the main gate, the main hall, and several other buildings still stand today. As you pass through the Ōte-mon, the huge main gate, you'll see a statue of Itagaki Taisuke, a Meiji-era leader of the Freedom and People's Rights Movement. The *donjon* building has several interesting displays, including a model of the castle surrounded by scaffolding while under construction. The top floor offers a breezy 360° view of Kōchi and the surrounding hills and mountains. On Sundays you can join a free Japanese or English tour in front of the Itagaki statue. Call ahead for guides on other days. *(1-2-1, Marunouchi. From Kōchi Station, cross Enoguchi River and take a right down either Ōtesuji-dōri or Obiya-machi; both lead to the castle grounds. ☎780-0850. Open daily 9am-4:30pm. ¥400, high school students and younger free.)*

KYU-YAMANOUCHI-KE. Located almost directly on the grounds of the Sansuien hot springs hotel, this old building houses several untranslated displays of painted screens, blueprints for the building, and a tattered palanquin. *(1-3-35, Takajō. Walk 3 blocks south from the Kōchi Castle park area. ☎873-1429. Open 7am-5pm. Free.)*

█ ▐◙ SHOPPING AND NIGHTLIFE

Obiya-machi is the center of Kōchi's shopping area. The Daimaru department store lies at the beginning, and close to the end is Hirome Ichiba. Nearby is Obisandōri, a little shopping street that follows Obiya-machi from Chūō-kōen. These areas offer a mix of restaurants, boutiques, bars, chain stores, and outlets. Every Sunday, one lane of Ōtesuji-dōri shuts down and the locals come out to show off their wares at Sunday Market—fresh vegetables, fruit, tea, rice, *kimono*, and knives. The shopping arcades also teem with people on weekends.

Kōchi's nightlife is clustered around the shopping areas but also extends farther north to Ōtesuji-dōri. Options include bowling alleys, *izakaya*, bars, and dance clubs. Things start around 9pm and end early the following morning—you can usually find somewhere to go until 5 or 6am.

Si-rutu, 2-1-29, Obiya-machi, 4th fl. (☎825-0789). In the building between Obiya-machi and Obiya-machi Park, at the end of Obisan-dōri, 4th fl. Walk down Obiya-machi and turn left after the Daiei. Bar/club with a hip industrial-antique feel; corrugated steel and a caged DJ juxtaposed with stained-glass lamps. Hip-hop Sa; funk, house, or Latin other nights. No cover most nights; event cover usually ¥1000 including 1 drink. Cocktails from ¥600, beer from ¥500. Open Su and Tu-Th 8pm-4am, F-Sa 9pm 'til the party ends.

Love Jamaican, Sunshine Fujimoto Bldg., 3rd fl., 1-5-5, Obiya-machi (☎872-0447). From the start of Obiya-machi, walk 3 blocks toward the castle, head right at the fork, and take a left; it's on the left. This place bumps reggae and hip-hop all week long. Good selection of strong mixed drinks. Beer ¥600-700, cocktails ¥700. Cover for events is usually ¥2000 including 1 drink. Open Tu-Su 10pm-7 or 8am.

Don't Worry Be Happy, 1-4-14, Ōtesuji, 2nd fl. (☎871-6378). Walk 3 blocks down Ōtesuji-dōri toward the castle, and this bar is on the 2nd fl. of the corner building on the left. Run by a former Hard Rock Cafe Ōsaka Most-Valuable-Employee, this bar draws

(vertical text in right margin) SHIKOKU

from a wide variety of pop cultures in its decor. Great place to relax. Freshly squeezed orange and grapefruit juice for use in Salty Dogs, screwdrivers, and other citrus drinks. Beer and cocktails ¥600. Open Su-Th 9pm-3am, F-Sa 9pm-5am.

Irish Bar Amontillado, 1-1-17, Obiya-machi (☎875-0599). You can't go wrong with Guinness and Kilkenny's on tap—pint ¥900, half-pint ¥500. Mix for a Black and Tan at ¥700. English menu makes ordering drinks easier after a few rounds. Excellent whiskey selection (from ¥600) backs up the beers. Open daily 11am-1am.

Get, First Bldg., 4th fl., 1-7-16, Harimaya-chō (☎884-2999). From Kōchi Station, cross the Enokuchi River and take a left on Obiyamachi-dōri, then the 1st right, and another left. The dance hall will be on your left. Break out your polyester: this is the place for some serious late-night discoing. Things get going around midnight or 1am and last as long as the crowds do. Expect Earth, Wind, and Fire's "Fantasy" (their most requested song), K.C. and the Sunshine Band, and ABBA. Cover ¥2000, includes 1 drink. Free cigarettes. Open daily 9pm 'til the cock crows.

Fancy Labo Ring, Ohoi Bldg., 4th fl., 2-3-7, Haryimaya (☎882-7007). Off the corner of Ōtesuji-dōri and Harimaya-bashi-dōri, you'll see the Coca-cola sign in the 4th-fl. window and signs outside. Huge TV screen plays eclectic music videos when there isn't live jazz or rock. Entrance ¥500, drinks ¥250-700. Arrange all-you-can-drink sessions for 10+ people at ¥2500 every 2hr. Cover for live events varies with the band. Open 8pm-3am.

Bowl Jumbo, 2-1, Judai-chō (☎823-4171). From Kōchi Station, walk across Enokuchi River on Harimaya-bashi-dōri; you'll see the giant bowling pin on top to the right. *The place to be* almost any time during the week. Weekend nights draw crowds; on F and Sa you may have to wait up to an hour for a lane. Shoes ¥200; frames ¥500, student discount ¥340. Open Su-Th 10am-11pm, F-Sa 10am-midnight.

⊠ DAYTRIP FROM KŌCHI

KATSURAHAMA

Hop on a bus from Kōchi Station (40min., every hr. 9am-4:30pm, ¥610). Buses also run from Harimaya-bashi (35min., ¥560) and Kōchi Castle (45min., ¥630). Returning from Katsurahama, if you miss the last bus to Kōchi Station, you can catch a bus to Kōchi Castle (7am-9:43pm), which makes a stop at Harimaya-bashi.

If you've exhausted all the sites in Kōchi, head to Katsurahama, 40min. away by bus. A walkway running along the beach connects all of the main sights, so it isn't difficult to navigate Katsurahama on foot once you've arrived. The Katsurahama Bus Stop has a tourist information center and is close to the parking lot, surrounded by souvenir stores and the **Tosa Tōken Center** (☎842-3315), home to the famous wrestling dogs of Tosa. Dogs are bred and trained to compete in *sumō*-esque tournaments. The dogs only fight once or twice a day, so it's good to call in advance; ¥2000 buys a seat at the melee and a 15min. demonstration of Yosakoi dancing, which features little clappers. Afterwards, grab some fresh juice made from tasty regional fruits such as the *konatsu*. Shaped like an orange but yellow like a lemon, it yields a refreshing, pulpy glass (¥500).

Near the beach, a short walk from the bus stop, is a **statue of Sakamoto Ryoma,** modeled after the famous photograph of the Meiji-era political activist standing on this beach—you'll see painted reproductions of this picture all over Kōchi. The beach is too rocky for good swimming, but it's good strolling turf. A few minutes farther down the path is the tiny **Katsurahama Aquarium,** 778, Urado, which puts on dolphin shows three times a day. (☎841-2437. Open daily 8:30am-5:30pm. ¥1100, junior high and high school students ¥600, elementary school ¥500, younger ¥300.)

The path up the hill leads to the **Sakamoto Ryoma Memorial Museum,** 830, Urado-shiroyama, dedicated to the local legend who worked to bring about the Meiji Restoration. The museum has a good collection of documents and artifacts relating to his life—political writings, the gun he used to fend off an assasination attempt, and his letters requesting safe harbor in Kyōto. Little is translated beyond the pamphlet, so it's missable unless you have a strong interest in Meiji politics. (☎841-0001. Open daily 9am-5pm. ¥400, students 18 or under free.)

WESTERN KŌCHI-KEN

KUBOKAWA (窪川) ☎0880

Kubokawa is the gateway to the southwestern half of Kōchi Prefecture, famous for its beaches and for Ashizuri Misaki, one of the prefecture's two Pacific capes. While Kubokawa isn't the most exciting city, it's home to the 37th of the 88 temples, **Iwamoto-ji**. The lantern-lit streets are lined with family-run restaurants and stores, especially around the temple and ryokan.

The JR Dosan Line stops at Kubokawa, which is about as far south as the line goes. Trains run frequently from **Kōchi** (local 2hr., limited express 1hr.; 1 per hr. 6am-9pm; ¥1410, limited express additional ¥1150). You can also drive from Kōchi; Kubokawa is right off of Rte. 56. From Kubokawa, the JR Yodo Line runs west through **Taisho-chō** and **Towa-mura** and then to **Uwajima** (2hr., 7 per day 6:28am-7:48pm, ¥1780) on the west coast, with a stop in Ekawasaki (50min.). The private Kubokawa-Sukumo Line runs from Kubokawa through **Nakamura** (local 1½hr., limited express 30min.; 1 per hr. 6am-10:46pm; ¥1060) on its way to **Sukumo** (local 2hr., limited express 1hr.; ¥1550). Its separate station is next to the JR station. **Bus lines** are all local, though one runs to the beach at **Okitsu** (40min., 4 per day 6:40am-5:40pm). Otherwise, everything is within walking distance.

There's no easily accessible proper tourist office, but the staff in both train offices have maps. In an emergency, call ☎110 for **police**, ☎119 for **fire** or **ambulance**. The only **International ATM** is in the **post office**, Kubokawa-chō, Mogushi-machi. From the JR Station exit, walk to the left. After crossing a small bridge, you'll come to a 5-way intersection and see the post office on the right. The post office also **exchanges money**. (☎22-0635. Open M-F 9am-7pm. ATM open M-F 8:45am-7pm and Sa 9am-5pm.) **Postal code:** 786.

Iwamoto-ji (HI) ❶ (岩本寺), 3-13, Shigekushi-machi, Kubokawa-chō, Takaoka-gun, is the optimal place to stay—a clean temple hostel only 10min. from the main train station. From the JR station, turn left down the street as you exit and take a right when the road ends. The temple will be on the left. All rooms are Japanese-style shared *tatami*. (☎22-0376. Breakfast ¥600. Dinner ¥1000. Check-in 3-6pm, until 7pm without dinner. Check-out 9am. Curfew 9pm. Members ¥3200; nonmembers ¥4200.) If you want a ryokan, head to **Mima** ❸ (美馬), 3-4, Hon-machi, Kubokawa-chō, Takaoka-gun, which looks like a florist shop from the front. From the station, walk to the left, then take the first right and a quick left. Walk over the bridge and it's on the left. If you don't stay at Mima, stop in for a meal. Find space at the counter amid collections of cups, dishes, and plants, or grab a *tatami* room. *Udon* and *soba* start from ¥600; regional favorite *katsuo tataki* (seared bonito fish) is ¥1800. (☎22-1101. Restaurant open daily 11am-2pm and 5-10pm. Check-in 4pm. Check-out 10am. Curfew 11:30pm. Singles ¥8000; Japanese-style room ¥10,000 per person.) For a beachside location, try **Okitsu Seishōnen Ryokō Mura** ❶ (興津青少年旅行村), a campground half an hour away. Bare wooden bungalows, which include futons, run ¥12,600 for four people (additional people ¥2000 each); pitch your own tent for ¥920. For something a little fancier, get a 6-person trailer house (¥18,360, additional people ¥2550 each). You can rent just about anything—from tents (¥2340) to barbecue equipment (¥520)—from the campground. (☎25-0632. Coin showers.) For groceries, head down the main street past the post office. After a few blocks, you'll see the store **Days** and an unlabeled **Plaza** supermarket on your right. (☎22-1950. Open daily 9am-8pm.)

NAKAMURA (中村)　　　　　　　☎0880

Nakamura, on a strip of land between the Shimanto Gawa River and a smaller tributary, is a good staging point for river trips. Of the 47 causeway bridges that cross the Shimanto, four are located just north of Nakamura. These bridges have no side railings and are one lane wide, designed to be submerged in high water, so be careful crossing. The largest is **Sada Causeway Bridge**, 6km from the station.

Before he founded Nakamura, Nirifusa Ichijo was chased out of Kyōto by the Onin War. Living in exile and longing for his former home, he modeled his new town on the ancient capital, copying many of the place names. If you're in town on July 16, catch the **Daimonji Okuribi** festival, one of the many ways Nakamura lives up to its "Little Kyōto" nickname. As in the Kyōto equivalent, a fire is lit on the hillside in the shape of the Japanese character 大 ("big").

Nakamura is on the Kubokawa-Sukumo Line, right at the Shimanto Gawa. The station is a little southeast of the city center, but all the necessities are within walking distance. **Trains** run from **Sukumo** (local 35min., limited express 15min.; 1-2 per hr. 6:47am-11:25pm; ¥610, limited express fee ¥300) and **Kubokawa** (local 1hr., limited express 45min.; 1-2 per hr. 5:24am-10:33pm; ¥1060, limited express fee ¥400). The **bus station** is across the parking lot and to the left of the train station. Buses head to **Sukumo** (1hr., 6 per day 8am-5:35pm, ¥1100), **Ashizuri** (1¾hr., 9 per day 8:30am-7:10pm, ¥1930), and **Kōchi**, stopping at the Kōchi Prefectural Transportation and Business Office (2½hr., 2 per day at 7am and 1:20pm, ¥2700) and Kōchi Airport (3hr., 2 per day at 7am and 1:20pm, ¥3300). The local bus system, the **"Machi-Bus,"** is on-call for pick-ups and drop-offs at 30-some spots around the city. (☎34-1269. Runs 8am-11am, noon-2:30pm, and 4:30-6pm. ¥200.) Renting a car is a good idea if you plan to explore southwestern Kōchi Prefecture. **Toyota Rent-a-Car**, 8-2, Ekimae-chō, is to the left of the train station. (☎35-6200. Open 8am-8pm.)

The **Nakamura Tourist Information Office** is across from the station and to the right as you exit. They have maps of the city and can help you arrange a place to stay. (☎35-4171. Open 8:30am-5pm. Bicycle rental ¥600 for 5hr., ¥1000 for the day.) In an emergency, call ☎110 for **police,** ☎119 for **fire** or ambulance. For Internet access, head to **Hyper Convenience US. Mart,** 18-1, Ekimae-chō. From the station, walk one block straight ahead and then take a right—it's across from Shikoku Bank. Internet is ¥100 for 15min. and all of the snacks in the store cost ¥100. If you've got time to kill, try the billiards or arcade games. (☎31-0207. Open 24hr.) The **Nakamura Post Office**, 3-28, Ekimae-chō, is three blocks from the station. Walk straight out, cross Rte. 439, and take the first right; it's on the right. (☎34-4856. Open M-F 9-5pm. **International ATM** open M-F 9am-5:30pm and Sa 9am-12:30pm.) **Postal code:** 787.

Close to the station are two reasonably priced, clean, neat, and altogether very similar minshuku. **Sakura ❷** (民宿さくら), 9-5, Ekimae-chō, is directly left of the station—head left as you exit, and it's on the right very shortly. (☎34-3062. ¥3500 per person, with meals ¥5500. Check-in 2pm. Check-out 10am.) **Minshuku Tosa ❷**, 5-13, Ekimae-chō, is on the first block on the right, straight out of the station. (☎34-2929. ¥3500 per person, with meals ¥6000. Check-in 3pm. Check-out 9:30am.)

SHIMANTO GAWA AREA (四万十川)　　　☎0880

While not as dramatic as the steep cliffs and jagged boulders of the Yoshino Gawa, the Shimanto Gawa River has majestic elegance. The mountains on either side drop down before the river and rice paddies, grassy fields, or rocky shores gently slope the rest of the way to the bank. In June and July, hydrangea and other flowers line the roadside. You'll see a variety of different bridges—picturesque red railroad bridges, suspension bridges, and the famous causeway bridges without guardrails. The Shimanto is promoted as the last free flowing river in Japan, but its 196km length actually does contain one dam. Many campgrounds and hot springs are available in the towns along the river's banks, as are lots of opportunities for biking, kayaking, and hiking. (Note that Japanese establishments often call kayaking "canoeing"—call ahead to check which you're getting if it matters to you.)

The JR Yodo Line follows the river from Kubokawa to Ekawasaki, a jumping-off point for outdoor activities as the river turns south. For access to the full length of the river, however, you'll need to drive along Rte. 381 between Kubokawa and Ekawasaki and then on Rte. 441 between Ekawasaki and Nakamura. Renting a car in Kōchi (p. 554) will put you within a 2-3hr. drive of most sights. The **Michi no Eki Shimanto Taishō** (道の駅四万十), a few kilometers before the intersection of Rte. 439 and Rte. 381, is a great place to gather information. Pamphlets and computer resources are available (no e-mail checking). There's a restaurant and bathroom, and a balcony that overlooks the river. (Open 9am-5pm.)

Far and above the best option for staying the night and canoeing is ▨**Shimanto Gawa (HI) ❶** (四万十川ユースホステル), 493-2, Nakaba, Nishi-Tosa-mura, a beautiful foliage-covered hostel. To get to the hostel from Ekawasaki, hop on the 4:45pm bus (¥300) to Kuchiyanai, where the staff will pick you up, or grab the 4:25pm bus from Nakamura (¥850). Both arrive around 5:15pm. Weekdays, the boating package includes lessons from 9:30am-noon, then freedom to explore the river until 4pm (¥5500). There's a 12km tour (9:30am-3:30pm; ¥8000) on weekends. (☎54-1352; www.netwave.or.jp/~shimanto/index.htm. Breakfast ¥600. Dinner ¥1000. Bike rental ¥1000 per day. Check-in 4pm. Check-out 10am. Curfew 10:30pm. 3-bed dorms ¥3150; nonmembers ¥4150.) About 5min. from the Michi no Eki is **Riverpark Todoroki Campground ❶** (リバーパーク轟 ; ☎27-0111), a bare-bones site near the river. Bring your own tent and ¥100 coins for showers. (¥500 per person, high school students and younger ¥200.) Fifteen minutes from the Michi no Eki, north on Rte. 439, is **Welcome ❶** (ウェル花夢), 546, Taishō-chō Eshi, a campground with tent sites, luxurious two-floor cabins, and a mini-convenience store at reception (open 9am-5pm). Follow signs from Rte. 439. (☎27-1211. Sites from ¥3000; cabins ¥15,000 for 4 people. Electricity charge. Coin shower, washers, and dryers in common building. Check-in 3pm. Check-out 1pm for sites, 10am for cabins.) If you're limited to public transportation, head straight for Ekawasaki Station via Kubokawa. A 3min. bus ride from the station (20min. by foot) is **Canoe-kan ❶** (カヌー館), 1111-11, Nishi-Tosa-mura Mochii, a "canoeing memorial" and campsite. Three bus lines head to the Canoe-kan, but infrequently and on similar schedules. Campers have their choice of bungalows and pitch sites. Kayaking packages (¥3000-6500) include rentals and lessons. (☎52-2121; www.canoekan.com. Bungalows ¥3000 for 1 person, ¥2800 per person for 2-4. Sites ¥350 per person.)

For tasty eats, look near the picturesque red Tsudabashi (津大橋), which cuts across the Shimanto Gawa between the Canoe-kan and the youth hostel. **Iwaki Shokudō ❷** (いわき食堂) is to the right of the bridge before you cross. Slurp up a bowl of Shimanto *udon* stock full of stuff straight from the river—shrimp, *nori* (seaweed), and wild plants—and even a little fruit (¥500) or try the river shrimp (¥1000) and *amego* (fish; ¥1500) set meals. (☎52-1172. Open daily 8am-8pm.)

ASHIZURI MISAKI (足摺岬)   ☎0880

Ashizuri Misaki is the more dramatic of Shikoku's two capes, with tall cliffs keeping watch over waters that have shaped awesome rock formations like ▨**Hakusan Cave,** the largest cave mouth in Japan. About 2.5km of walkways lace the area, covered by bushes overhead, and run around the coastline. Staircases at several points lead to the path—the closest to the cave is right across from the hostel.

The requisite seashore statue is of **John Mung,** whose story is chronicled at **John Mung House,** to the right of the bus stop. After a shipwreck, Mung was taken in by the captain of the American ship that rescued his Japanese shipmates. He spent time in the US before returning to Japan and acting as a go-between for the shōgun. (Open Su-W and F-Sa 9am-4pm.) A short walk from the statue is a **lookout**

SHIKOKU

point, from which you can see a lighthouse, as well as the top of the two-story pagoda and part of the roof of the **Kongōfuku-ji** main building. The sparklingly clean temple is the 38th on the 88-temple tour. The grounds are filled with statues—Kobo Daishi and a giant turtle make appearances—and small ponds.

Buses run to Ashizuri Misaki from **Sukumo** (2½hr., 4 per day 9:50am-3:50pm, ¥2680) via **Nakamura** (1¾hr., 9 per day 7:15am-5:21pm, ¥1930). The bus station has a **Ryokan Information Center** (☎88-0472) which distributes maps and books accommodations. For other inquiries, head to John Mung House (see above).

The best option for housing is **Ashizuri Youth Hostel (HI) ❶**, 1351-3, Ashizuri, right off the main street, shortly past John Mung House. There are single-sex *tatami* rooms and a shared bath on the first floor. The hostel provides easy access to the sights—Konfuku-ji is just down the street, and a staircase to the walkway is across the street. Eat here or bring your own food, as there are few restaurants. (☎88-0324. Breakfast ¥600. Dinner ¥1000. Check-in 3-7:30pm. Check-out 10am. Curfew 10:30pm. Members ¥2900; nonmembers ¥3900.) Nearby are several large hotels and a reasonably priced minshuku, **Minshuku Ashizuri Hassen ❷** (民宿足摺八扇), directly across from the John Mung House. Most rooms have a nice view of the coast. (☎88-0941. Check-in 3pm. Check-out 9am. Curfew 10pm. ¥4500 per person, with meals ¥6500.) If you're making the 88-temple run, you may be able to arrange a stay at Kongōfuku-ji (☎88-0038), but they've discontinued their youth hostel.

While there aren't many swimming beaches on the cape, **Okinohama,** north off of Rte. 55 isn't far, and it's a long beach with great waves. Swimming is best in July and August, but you can go in June or September if you don't mind a little chill and big waves. Take a bus from Ashizuri to Wada Bunki. Walk 200m down the road and take a right at the Okino Beach sign. The beach is about 100m from there. In the parking lot right before the treeline, you can rest at **Umihiko's Playground ❶**, 2930-77, Tosashimizu Ōki, and grab some *okonomiyaki* or *yakisoba* for ¥500. Surf equipment is sold here, if you've forgotten your board, and rentals are planned for the future. (☎82-8823; www7.ocn.ne.jp/~umihiko. Open daily 9:30am-6pm.)

OGATA (大方)   ☎0880

The **Ogata-chō Fishing and Shipowners Association** (☎43-1058; www.gallery.ne.jp/~kujira) organizes whale-watching boats from locations around Ogata harbor. From May to August you're likely to see Bryde's whales and dolphins. Trips start at 8am; plan to be on the boat for about 4hr. Of the departure locations, Irino Fishing Harbor (入野漁港) and Kamikawa-guchi Harbor (上川口港) are the most accessible: Irino is 20min. west along the shore from Irino Station. Kamikawa-guchi is 10min. south of Kamikawa-guchi Station, two stops from Irino Tosa Station. (Boats run late Mar.-Oct. ¥5000, elementary students ¥3500, children ¥1000.)

Tosa Irino Station takes you to the center of Ogata. You can go to either end of the train line—**Sukumo** or **Kubokawa**—for ¥850, or **Nakamura** for ¥240, so Ogata is an easy daytrip. There's no tourist office, but the **city office** is right by the station—just walk left as you exit and it'll be on the left. (☎43-1203. Open Su-F 8:30am-5pm.)

TATSUKUSHI (竜串)   ☎0880

Tatsukushi's attractions revolve around the sea-life, coral, and rock formations in the waters off shore. The coastline is also called the Minokoshi coastline, which means "left unseen," because famed monk Kōbō Daishi supposedly never bothered to visit this area of Shikoku. Unless you have a strong interest in marine biology, you may want to follow his lead, as most sights in this isolated town are aging.

The bus that runs along Rte. 321 drops you off at the roadside souvenir shop and restaurant, 500m from the **Ashizuri Kaiteikan** (足摺海底館), a retro-looking underwater observatory from which you can watch fish eat algae. (☎85-0201; www.a-sea.net. Open 9am-5pm. ¥900, children ¥450.) Near the walkway to the Kaiteikan is the dock for **glass-bottom boats** (☎85-1155), which sail over the coral formations. Visibility varies, so inquire the day you go. No boats go out when the waves are big. (☎85-1155. Rides last around 30min. Departures 8am-4:30pm.) A little bit east of the Kaiteikan building is the **Ashizuri Ocean Museum** (足摺海洋館), a small aquarium with a cylindrical two-story tank. (☎85-0635; www.gallery.ne.jp/~manbow. Open daily 9am-5pm. Closed 3rd Th of the month. ¥700, under 18 free.) Your last stop on the Tatsukushi tour is the **Coral Museum,** in a Chinese-style building a few minutes east on Rte. 321 from the aquarium. This old building gets toasty in the summer and houses unimpressive displays of international coral. The more interesting coral statues include the Nagoya Castle replica and the giant coral tiger. (☎85-0231. Open daily 8am-5pm. ¥300, junior high school students ¥200, elementary school students ¥150.) Tatsukushi is right on the coast off Rte. 321, so you'll need a bus from Sukumo or Ashizuri-misaki to get there. **Buses** stop in front of the Tatsukushi Kaiteikan four times a day, sometimes more often on weekends.

SUKUMO (宿毛)   ☎0880

Sukumo is a jumping-off point for Okinoshima and interesting diving and outdoor activities. It's the last stop on the private train line that starts in **Kubokawa** (local 1¾hr., limited express 1hr.; 1 per hr. 5:55am-8:50pm; ¥1550, limited express fee ¥600) and runs through **Nakamura** (local 35min., limited express 20min.; 1-2 per hr. 5:55am-10:33pm; ¥610, limited express fee ¥310). The **Sukumo Tourist Information Center** is in Sukumo Station. They have plenty of maps, pamphlets for local tourist sights, and accommodation information. (☎63-0801; www.city.sukumo.kochi.jp. Open 8am-6pm.) In an emergency, call ☎110 for **police,** ☎119 for **fire** or ambulance. The **Sukumo Post Office,** 2-42, Saiwai-chō, is a hike from the station towards the main area of town—exit the front of the station and take a left, going under the train tracks. The post office is on the right after the next stoplight. (☎63-4173. Open M-F 9am-5pm. **ATM** available M-F 9am-5:30pm, Sa 9am-12:30pm.)

The place to stay closest to the station is **Hotel Matsuya ❷** (ホテルマツヤ), a standard business hotel. Exit the front of the station, walk down the street to the left to the stoplight, then take a left. It's on the right. Higher-end rooms have Internet connections, but you need your own computer. (☎63-1991. Check-in 3pm. Check-out 10am. Curfew midnight. Singles from ¥4800; twins and doubles from ¥9000.) If you're just in town between buses or trains, head to **Shōgen Udon ❶** (将元うどん), across from the station, for a tasty bowl of noodles. (☎0880-63-3363. *Udon* from ¥220. Toppings ¥50-100. Curry *udon* ¥380. Open daily 11am-7pm.)

MATSUYAMA (松山)   ☎089

Matsuyama abounds with throwbacks to a rich mythical and literary history. The streetcar line, one relic of a past age, runs around castle-topped Katsuyama Hill and all the way to *onsen*-town Dōgo. During the Shōwa Era, authors Masaoka Shiki and Natsume Sōseki brought the area literary fame. Sōseki's *Botchan* has a particularly strong presence in the city; the book's title is now plastered on everything from sweets and trains to information booths and beer. Although the book's protagonist expresses an often dim view of then-rural Matsuyama, the modern-day city is one of Shikoku's friendliest and most attractive. It's easy to hop across the water to Kyūshū, but once you've slipped into the city's hot springs, it's a good bet you won't be heading elsewhere anytime soon.

SHIKOKU

☒ INTERCITY TRANSPORTATION

Flights: Matsuyama Airport is a short bus ride from Shieki Station platform #4 or JR Matsuyama Station. Flights to **Fukuoka, Hiroshima, Nishi, Itami** (Ōsaka)**, Kagoshima, Kansai, Komatsu, Miyazaki, Nagoya, Sapporo, Sendai, Tōkyō Haneda,** and **Seoul.**

Trains: JR Matsuyama Station lies to the city's west and the Yosan Line runs from **Takamatsu** through **Tadotsu** to Matsuyama and then on to **Uwajima.** There's a JR info desk in addition to the station tourist information center to assist you with travel inquiries. Open 7am-11pm. To: **Takamatsu** (limited express: 1½hr., 8 per day 6:15am-5:23pm, ¥5500); **Okayama** (limited express: 2¾hr., 9 per day 5:09am-5:23pm, ¥6120); **Uwajima** (limited express: 80min., 1 per hr. 6:49am-11:10pm, ¥2900).

Buses: Long-distance buses stop at Shieki Station and sometimes also at JR Matsuyama Station. Buses run to Shikoku's prefectural capitals and to major cities on Honshū. Buy tickets at the Iyotetsu Ticket Center on the 1st fl., next to Takashimaya department store. To: **Kōbe** (4hr.; 8:10am and 5pm; ¥6200, round-trip ¥12,500); **Kōchi** (2½hr., 5 per day 8am-7pm, ¥3500/¥6300); **Kyōto** (5½hr., 7:30am and 2:30pm, ¥7000/¥12,500); **Okayama** (3hr., 6 per day 7:40am-6pm, ¥4300/¥7800); **Ōsaka** (5¼hr., 4 per day 7:10am-11pm, ¥6700/¥12,000); **Takamatsu** (2½hr., 12 per day 7:50am-7:50pm, ¥4000/¥7200); **Tokushima** (3¼hr., 4 per day 8am-5:40pm, ¥4300/¥7800); **Tōkyō** (12½hr., 7:10pm, ¥12,000/¥21,400).

Ferries: Matsuyama Tourist Port (Matsuyama Kankō-kō). Take a bus from Shieki Station platform #6 (30min., 1 per hr. 7:02am-6:57pm) which stops by JR Matsuyama Station or take an Iyotetsu train from Shieki Station track #2 to Takahama and get off at the terminal station, then take the bus from the station to the port (whole shebang ¥550). Multiple companies travel to multiple destinations, so check your information before shipping out. To: **Beppu** (4¼hr.; 11:50am and 2:15pm; ¥4800, children ¥2400); **Hiroshima** (Super-Jet 1¼hr., 1 per hr. 6am-9pm, ¥5800/¥2900; ferry 2¾hr., 10 per day 6:35am-7:55pm, ¥2500/¥1250); **Imabari** (2¾hr., noon and 8:30pm, ¥1000); **Kita-Kyūshū** (2½hr., 7:50am and 3:10pm, ¥7500/¥3750); **Kōbe** (9hr., noon-10:40pm, ¥5200); **Ōita** (3½hr., 7:50pm, ¥2600); **Ōsaka** (10hr., 10:40pm, ¥5200).

▭ LOCAL TRANSPORTATION

Streetcar: The excellent streetcar system has 5 lines. Lines 1 and 2 run laps around the castle, stopping at the stations. Line 3 goes from Shieki Station to Dōgo, Line 5 from the JR Station to Dōgo, and Line 6 from Hon-machi to Dōgo. There is no Line 4. Fare ¥150; pay when you get off. You can purchase a ¥1000 swipe card with a ¥1100 credit on it on-board. Swipe it when you get off—it also works on Iyotetsu buses and trains. Transfer lines at Kami-ichiman, Minami-horibata, Nishi-horibata, or Hon-machi 6-chōme; just ask the driver for a *norikae*-transfer ticket. 19th-century **Botchan Trains** also run on the streetcar lines. Fare ¥300. 2 lines from Dōgo, one terminating at Shieki Station, the other running through the JR Station and terminating at Komachi Station.

Bus: There is a city bus system, but streetcars cover the main area pretty well. Bus #53 to the airport (20min., every 15min., ¥400) leaves from Shieki platform #4. To reach Dōgo, the streetcar is cheapest, but bus #52 also runs to Oku Dōgo (15min., 2 per hr.).

Taxis: Iyotetsu Taxi, ☎921-3166. **Kintetsu Taxi,** ☎924-6111. **Yoshifuji,** ☎921-6161.

Car Rental: Nissan Rent-a-Car, 1-11-7-2, Ōte-chō (☎931-4123; http://nissan-rent-acar.com). **Nippon Rent-a-Car,** 2-5-10, Ōte-chō (☎933-4066).

Bike Rental: Tōkyō Dai-Ichi Hotel Matsuyama, 6-16, Minami, Horibata-chō (☎947-4411), across the street from the southern entrance to Shiroyama Kōen, rents bicycles for ¥300 for 3hr. or ¥500 per day. **EPIC** (see **Practical Information,** below) lends foreigners bikes for free (visitors up to 2 wk.; students 1 yr.).

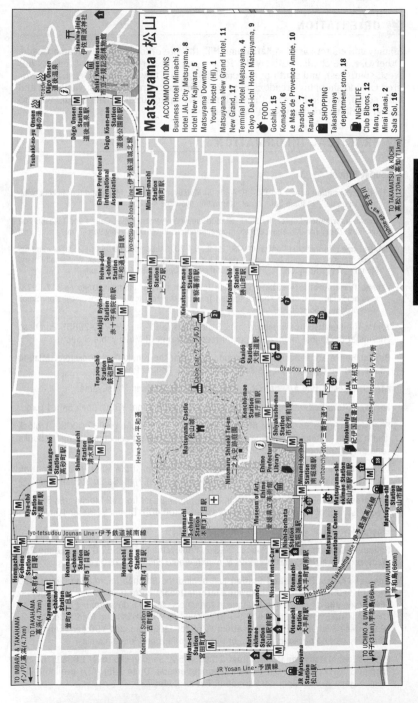

Matsuyama・松山

ACCOMMODATIONS
Business Hotel Mimachi, **3**
Hotel JAL City Matsuyama, **8**
Hotel New Kajiwara, **5**
Matsuyama Downtown
 Youth Hostel (HI), **1**
Matsuyama New Grand Hotel, **11**
New Grand, **17**
Terminal Hotel Matsuyama, **4**
Tokyo Dai-ichi Hotel Matsuyama, **9**

FOOD
Goshiki, **15**
Komadori, **6**
Le Mas de Provence Amitie, **10**
Paradiso, **7**
Raruki, **14**

SHOPPING
Takashimaya
 department store, **18**

NIGHTLIFE
Club Bibros, **12**
Maru, **13**
Mirai Kanai, **2**
Sala Sol, **16**

◢ ORIENTATION

Matsuyama centers around **Katsuyama Hill,** the site of looming Matsuyama Castle. Otherwise, the city is relatively flat for several miles around. Most of the city lies west, southwest, and south of the castle; **Dōgo** is a few kilometers east. The covered Ōkaidō shopping arcade is near the southeast corner of Katsuyama Hill and runs south, connecting with the Gintengai shopping arcade, which runs west to Shieki Station—good news if it starts raining.

⁊ PRACTICAL INFORMATION

Tourist Office:

Tourist Information center (☎931-3914), in JR Matsuyama Station. Maps and tour tickets available. Open daily 8:30am-5pm; hotel information available 4-8:30pm.

Botchan Information Center, by Shieki Station, between Iyotetsu Ticket Center and Takashimaya on 1st fl. Maps and info about Iyotetsudo train and bus lines. Open daily 9am-7pm.

Matsuyama International Center, COMS, 1st fl., 6-4-20, Sanban-chō (☎943-2025). For more rigorous inquiries or English-language questions. Counseling, free guide services, and small library. Monthly *What's Going On?* highlights cultural events. Open Tu-Su 9am-5:30pm.

Ehime Prefectural International Association (EPIC), 733, Ichiman, Dōgo (☎917-5678; www.epic.or.jp). Left of the Kenmin Center. Take the streetcar to the Minami-machi stop. Small library. Open M-Sa 8:30am-5pm.

Tours: The **Iyotetsu bus company** runs 3 city tours (all 2-3hr., ¥1700-2980). Purchase tickets at the tourist information center (see above) in JR Matsuyama Station.

Banks: Banks are clustered near Ōkaidō and near the Kinokuniya bookstore. **Mizuho Bank** and **Iyo Bank** are on the same street as the Central Post Office.

ATM: The **post office** ATMs are the only international ATMs in Matsuyama.

Luggage Storage: Stations have lockers. Matsuyama Station: ¥300, open 5am-11pm.

English-Language Bookstore: Kinokuniya, 5-7-1, Chifune-chō (☎932-0005). 1 block north of the Gintengai shopping arcade, at the end. Decent selection of English books and periodicals on the 4th fl. Open daily 10am-8pm.

Library: Ehime Prefectural Library (☎941-1441). Just past the Museum of Art as you enter Shiroyama Park from the south. Open Tu-F 9:40am-7pm, Sa-Su 9:40am-6pm.

Laundromat: Coin laundry on the main street running east from JR Matsuyama Station. Look just right of Hotel New Kajiwara. Washers ¥300-400. Dryers ¥100 for 10min.

Emergency: Police ☎ 110. **Fire** or **ambulance** ☎ 119.

Police: Matsuyama Higashi Police, 2-13-2, Katsuyama-chō (☎952-0110). **Ehime Prefectural Police Headquarters,** 2-2, Minamihoribata-chō (☎0120-31-9110).

Internet Access: Broadband Station just behind the Botchan Information Center (see above). Free. Max. 30min. **Matsuyama International Center** (see above). ¥100 per hr. **EPIC** (see above) offers free Internet to foreigners. The Ōkaidō shopping arcade hosts two 24hr. options: **Hot Station,** 2-5-7 3F, Ōkaidō (☎934-8814) and **Media Bomb,** 2-2-6 3F, Ōkaidō (☎987-6231). Both about ¥250 for 1st 30min. and ¥90 per 15min. after that. Discounted packages of 3, 6, or 9hr. Free drinks and lots of comics.

Post Office: Matsuyama Central Post Office, 3-5-2, Sanban-chō (☎941-0381). On the corner 3 blocks west of the Ōkaidō shopping arcade. Open 24hr. ATM available M-F 7am-11pm, Sa 9am-9pm, Su 9am-5pm. **Postal Code:** 790.

▌ ACCOMMODATIONS

Matsuyama's expensive hotels have great views of the castle, but there are plenty of affordable rooms all over the city. The main areas for lodgings are around the station and Ōkaidō, but there are hotels all along the streetcar lines. Another option is to stay in Dōgo (p. 573), only a short streetcar ride away.

▧ Matsuyama Downtown Youth Hostel (HI), 3-8-3, Ōkaidō (☎986-8880). Take streetcar to Ōkaidō and walk toward castle ropeway; it's on the 2nd fl. across from the ropeway. Easy castle access, and 5min. from nightlife and streetcar. Cafe and reception 2nd fl. Free laundry (no dryers), fridges, stoves in room. Rooms fit 2-4; families and couples fine. Breakfast ¥500. Check-in 4-11pm. Members ¥3200; nonmembers ¥4200. ❶

Matsuyama New Grand Hotel (松山ニューグランドホテル), 3-4-10, Niban-chō (☎933-3960). Take the streetcar to Ōkaidō and walk south on the Ōkaidō arcade. Take the 2nd right and 3rd left; the hotel is on your left. Quick walk from shopping and nightlife; great value for location. Sauna on the 1st fl., open 4pm-midnight. Breakfast ¥680. Check-in 3pm. Check-out 10am. Old building singles from ¥4000; twins ¥7000; doubles ¥6500; triples ¥9000. New building rooms about ¥1000 more. AmEx/MC/V. ❷

Business Hotel Mimachi (ビジネスホテル美町), 9-6, Miyada-chō (☎921-6924). Exit JR Matsuyama Station and take the 1st left; Mimachi is on the right of the 1st block (1min.). Cheapest hotel in town. Check-in 3pm. Check-out 10am. Curfew 11pm. Japanese-style singles ¥2800; twins ¥6000; Western doubles with bath ¥6800. ❶

Tokyo Dai-ichi Hotel Matsuyama (東京第一ホテル松山), 6-16, Minami, Horibata-chō (☎947-4411; www.td-mat.co.jp). Across from the southern side of Shiroyama Park; closest streetcar stop is Minami Horibata. A hike from the stations, but close to the streetcar and you can rent a bicycle at the front desk. Breakfast ¥1220. Check-in 3pm. Check-out 11am. Singles from ¥6900; deluxe (fits 2) ¥11,000; twins ¥12,000; doubles ¥13,000. Deals for 88-temple pilgrims. AmEx/MC/V. ❸

New Grand (ニューグランド), Matsuyama Shieki-mae (☎945-7089). Across from Shieki Station. Take the elevators inside the New Grand Building, to the left of the Homerun *pachinko* parlor, to the 9th fl. One of the rare unisex capsule hotels. Cheap, but you get what you pay for. Check-in 3pm. Check-out 10am. Capsules ¥2600. ❶

Terminal Hotel Matsuyama (ターミナルホテル松山), 9-1, Miyada-chō (☎947-5388). Left of the bus terminals in front of the station. Reasonable rates and reliable, if standard, rooms. Check-in 4pm. Check-out 10am. Curfew 2am. Singles ¥5500; doubles ¥9000; twins ¥10,000. AmEx/MC/V. ❸

Hotel JAL City Matsuyama (ホテル JAL シティ松山), 1-10-10, Ōte-machi (☎913-2580; http://matsuyama.jalcity.co.jp). Take the streetcar to Nishihoribata; it's on the corner. Luxurious hotel southwest of Katsuyama Hill with castle views and comfy rooms. 3 restaurants, including gourmet La Terrazza (lunch sets ¥980). Check-in 2pm. Check-out 11am. Singles from ¥7400; twins ¥15,500; doubles ¥15,000. AmEx/MC/V. ❸

Hotel New Kajiwara (ホテルニューカジワラ), 2-9-10, Ōte-machi (☎941-0402). From the station, walk east down the main street; it's on the left of the 1st block. Standard hotel next to a coin laundry. Breakfast from ¥800. Lunch from ¥700. Dinner from ¥1000. Check-in 3pm. Check-out 10am. Curfew midnight. Singles from ¥4700; twins and doubles ¥8000. Japanese-style rooms for 2 from ¥7000, with bath ¥10,000. ❷

▐ FOOD

Natsume Sōseki's famous novel supplies the name for one of Matsuyama's best-known treats, the *botchan dango*, a toothpick of three soft sweets. *Taruto*, an originally Portuguese jellyroll-like treat, is another famous local dessert. But

SHIKOKU

before you spoil your dinner, indulge in a wide variety of eats along the shopping arcades and in the nightlife districts. *Izakaya* and ethnic restaurants are plentiful. A fun local meal is *goshiki sōmen* (五色そうめん), a five-colored noodle dish.

Le Mas de Provence Amitie, 6-23, Minami, Horibata-chō (☎998-2811). Close to the corner where the streetcar goes south, next to the Minami Horibata stop; 2 buildings left of the Dai-ichi Hotel. Funky restaurant/bar filled with statues, paper-covered lights, and hardwood floors. Authentic French dishes around ¥1200. Salads from ¥750. Quiche of the day ¥650. Wide variety of wines (average ¥3000 per bottle). English and French menus available. Open daily 11:30am-5pm and 5:30-10pm. ❷

Komadori (こまどり), Metropolis Bldg., 4th fl., Ōkaidō (☎45-7135). From Ōkaidō streetcar stop, walk south on the shopping arcade; it's upstairs on the right. Best selection of tea on the shopping arcade in an exquisite, museum-like atmosphere. Teas range from gunpowder (¥600) to jasmine (¥550) to Ti Kuan Yi (¥1000). Good selection of cakes; cake sets from ¥850. Open Su-Th 11:30am-9pm, F-Sa 11:30am-11pm. ❷

Goshiki, 3, Sanban-chō (☎933-3838). Walk south down Ōkaidō shopping arcade and take the 3rd right; it's on the left just before the Central Post Office. Serves up thin *sōmen* noodles, including the local 3-colored variety (¥750). Summer brings *ryōmen*, noodles under piles of ham, *yamaimo* (yam-like vegetable), mushrooms, cucumbers, and egg, with a slice of watermelon (¥850). Souvenir boxes of colored noodles up front. Open daily 11am-9pm, last orders 8:30pm. AmEx. ❷

Paradiso, 1-11-9, Niban-chō (☎941-5077). Walk south on the Ōkaidō arcade and take your 1st left; this restaurant/bar has 2 buildings on the corners of the 3rd and 4th blocks. One is a standard restaurant and the other a counter where you can watch pizzas cook. Great pizza selection (¥800-1000); menu has pictures. Calzone (¥900) and calzoncino (¥550) are good snacks with various fillings. Usual Italian suspects (salad, pasta, tiramisu) also in the lineup. Open daily 6pm-3am. ❷

Raruki (ラルキー), 5-9, Kaen-chō (☎948-0885). Head 2 blocks south of the Minami Horibata streetcar stop, on the main street towards Shieki Station. Lunch specials: curry, salad, and *naan* or rice (¥680); add tandoori chicken (¥780). Dinner curries ¥980. Open Tu-F 11am-3pm and 5-10pm, Sa-Su 11:30am-3pm and 5-10pm. ❷

◔ SIGHTS

▧ MATSUYAMA CASTLE (MATSUYAMA-JŌ). One of Japan's great flat-topped mountain castles, Matsuyama Castle is also the center of the city, perched high on pine-covered Katsuyama Hill. There's been a castle on the site since 1627, but the current buildings date to 1854. The original five-story masterpiece was built by Yoshiakira Katoh, an orphaned *samurai* who fought his way to wealth and power under Hideyoshi Toyotomi and Tokugawa Ieyasu. The hill allows a spectacular view of the Inland Sea and the flat surrounding cityscape. There are several ways to the top. Walking up takes 30-40min. (descent 15-20min.). On the east side of the castle, up a few flights of stairs, is **Shinonome Jinja,** a 19th-century shrine, famous as a stage for *nō* plays. A pathway up to the castle starts just to the left of the main shrine building. Another path starts on the southwestern corner of the hill, just behind the Ninomaru Shiseki Teien. Alternatively, a **ropeway** can whisk you up the hill in minutes. (☎921-4873. Open 8:30am-5pm, later in summer. ¥260, round-trip ¥500.) Castle buildings are a short walk from the upper ropeway station. You'll pass through several gates and walk up more stairs before getting to the hill's flat top, scattered with castle buildings (some rebuilt as recently as the 1980s), and the *donjon*, the castle's highlight. Most signs at the gates, towers, and exhibits are in English, making the castle's history accessible. *(Atop Katsuyama Hill. ☎921-2540. Open daily 9am-5pm. Arrange tours at Matsuyama International Center. ¥500, children ¥150.)*

NINOMARU SHISEKI TEIEN. This garden on the southwest side of Katsuyama Hill was rebuilt in 1992, based on the ruins and plans of the original construction by the second lord of Matsuyama, Tadachika Gamō. The moats, high stone walls, fences, turrets, and gates speak to the defensive purpose of the original. At the entrance, a building contains a replica of the small garden and old pictures. The ponds, sidewalks, and the teahouses are noticeably new; an impressive original well provides ample contrast. *(5, Marunouchi. From the top of the castle, saunter down the staircase with very large steps and you'll end up behind the garden. Otherwise, take the streetcar to Shiyakusho-mae and walk north; the road heads left to the garden. ☎921-2000. Open Apr.-Aug. M-Sa 9am-4:30pm, Su 9am-7pm; Sept.-Mar. daily 9am-4:30pm. ¥100, students ¥50.)*

MUSEUM OF ART, EHIME. The permanent collection includes works by the requisite French artists—Monet, Bonnard, Cézanne—as well as pieces by Heihachiro Fukuda and many local artists. A glass bridge connects the museum's two brand-new buildings; the old building next door occasionally houses free exhibits put on by private organizations. *(Horinouchi. Take streetcar to Minami Horibata stop and cross the moat heading north; it's on the right. ☎932-0010; http://joho.ehime-iinet.or.jp/art. Open Tu-Su 9:40am-6pm. ¥500, high school and university students ¥400, elementary and junior high free.)* The museum also has an **Annex** (Bunkan; 分館) in a 1922 French villa just to the east of the main buildings, almost directly south of the castle. Exhibits change four times a year and usually focus on local artists. *(3-3-7, Ichiban-chō. Walk east, following the streetcar lines, and take a left just before the Meiji Life Insurance Bldg. Follow the street around to the building. ☎921-3711. Open Tu-Su 9:40am-6pm. ¥100, children ¥50.)*

SHIKI-DŌ. This replica of the house where Masaoka Shiki, father of the modern *haiku*, grew up is a testament to Matsuyama's literary history. Outside is a statue based on the famous picture of Shiki tying his shoes to leave Matsuyama for Tōkyō. Peruse the old pictures and handwriting samples inside. Little is translated; if you can read Japanese, ask for a "Shiki no Hurusato Matsuyama Sanpo" map, which marks the places in Matsuyama that inspired Shiki's poems. There are also *haiku* forms that can be dropped in boxes across the city to be read by poets and possibly published in the newspaper. The Shiki Kinen Museum in Dōgo (p. 574) is a more intensive commemoration of the writer. *(16-3, Suehiro-chō. From Shieki Station, walk to the left, then take your 1st left. Walk across the train tracks and take another left; it'll be straight ahead. ☎943-2274. Open daily 8:30am-4:40pm. ¥50, students ¥40, children ¥30.)*

🛒 SHOPPING

Shopping in Matsuyama runs along the two main arcades—**Ōkaidō** and **Gintengai.** Ōkaidō runs from directly south of the castle ropeway to intersect with Gintengai. Gintengai then runs west to Shieki Station and the nine-floor **Takashimaya** department store, topped with a ferris wheel (¥1000). From July to mid-August, Ōkaidō fills up on Saturdays for a festival proffering everything from crepes and soft ice cream to beetles and bags of small fish. Many locals show up in *yukata* (summer *kimono*). If you're looking for fashion, the road one block north of Gintengai is filled with hidden boutiques and little cafes.

🌙 NIGHTLIFE

Nightlife centers in Niban and Sanban-chō, mostly on the street three blocks east of the Ōkaidō arcade—towering buildings with neon signs advertise a bounty of hostess bars and *izakaya*. Ōkaidō is overrun with the overly hip on weekends, especially Saturday night. Restaurants and cafes on the arcade stay open late to the tunes of would-be Japanese idols playing the latest pop hits.

SHIKOKU

Maru, Sanbankan Bldg., 1st fl., 2-6, Sanban-chō (☎934-1291). Walk south on the Ōkaidō shopping arcade and take your 2nd left; the bar is on the right just before the 4th right. For the restaurant, take the 4th right; it's on the 2nd block on the right. Delicate reeds arc over the tables at this new-age *izakaya*. Cocktails, wines, and beers. Pizzas (¥650), pastas (¥750), and salads (¥600). For a different ambience, head to the bar and lounge on awesome leather couches. Open M-Sa 6pm-3am, Su 6pm-midnight.

Sala Sol, Ciel Bldg., 3rd fl., 2-3-5, Sanban-chō. Walk south down the Ōkaidō shopping arcade and take the 4th left; it's on the left. Nice, smallish bar with a native/expat crowd that gets excited enough to do some dancing. 500 draft beers and huge buckets of fries; good selection of other snacks as well. Open daily 7pm-late.

Club Bibros, Skytower, 7th fl., 2-10-1, Sanban-chō (☎948-0788; www3.to/bibros). One of the few pure dance clubs in Matsuyama. Crowd reaches 100 on a good night (F-Sa), but otherwise it's low-key. Hip-hop, reggae, house, techno. Cover usually ¥1000-2500, with 2 drinks. Open 9pm-3am. Usually open Tu-Sa.

Mirai Kanai, 2-5-1, Kiyo-machi (☎934-0108). Walk north on Ōkaidō and take a right just before the castle ropeway; it's on the left. Excellent place to kick back and hear some English. Chill music and a reasonably quiet crowd at night. Draft beer ¥500. Bar snacks ¥600. During the day, stop by for a cup of chai. Open daily noon-2am.

Fast, 2-4-14, Ōkaido (http://fast-wao.jp). Take the streetcar to Ōkaido; it's on the right corner at the start of the arcade. Bowling-karaoke-*pachinko* über-complex. The 2nd building a block down the arcade has billiards and darts. Prices vary by day and hour and are generally lower until 5pm. Karaoke daily noon-5am. Bowling M-Th noon-1am, F noon-2am, Sa 10am-3pm, Su 10am-1am. *Pachinko* daily 10am-11pm.

▶ DAYTRIP FROM MATSUYAMA

ISHIZUCHI-SAN (石鎚山). Matsuyama is a great base from which to make a one-day strike at the highest point on Shikoku, Ishizuchi-san (1982m). You may not see much while you're in the clouds, but regardless of the weather, you'll enjoy incredible views on the way to the mountain and on the way up.

From Matsuyama, there are two ways to the trails at the mountain's base. A **bus** runs from Shieki Station to Tsuchigoya, the start of a trail southeast of the summit (3hr., 3 per day, ¥3160, transfer at Kuma), but you'll have to catch an 8am trip; the last return is at 4:30pm. The bus usually runs weekends only, but runs daily April 1-7, July 1-10, and July 21-August 31. The other option is to take the **JR Yosan Line** east to Iyo Saijō (1hr., at least 1 per hr., round-trip ¥4600). From the front of Iyo Saijō Station, catch a bus (55min., 4 per day M-Sa 7:41am-4:13pm, ¥970) to a ropeway where you can catch a cable car (open 9am-5pm; ¥1000, round-trip ¥1900) to the start of the trail. From the station, the first stop on the trail is **Jōjū-sha** (成就 社) a small mountainside temple. The climb takes 20-25min. You can also take a lift (¥300, round-trip ¥450) to within 300m of Jōjū-sha. From Jōjū there's a short, relaxing descent before the climb to the top gets started.

From **Tsuchigoya** the climb is 3.3km and from **Jōjū** 4.3km. You can go up one way and down the other, but the Jōjū route is more accessible and lets you climb all three giant *kusuri*, black chains planted in the mountain to help climbers scale the steep, rocky cliffs. The Tsuchigoya route intersects the Jōjū route after the first chain. The third chain puts you right in front of the Okumiya **Chōjō-sha** (奥宮頂上 社), the summit shrine. There is also a standard, though extremely primitive, path to the top—follow the signs to the chains, or you'll end up taking the path.

You can stay overnight at the summit if you make reservations at the **Summit Mountain Villa ❹** (頂上山荘 ; ☎0897-55-4168; 2 meals included; ¥8500). **Tengu-dake,** the highest point on the mountain, is another 15min. up.

DŌGO (道後)   ☎089

Dōgo is worth a two-day visit—one to check out the sights and the other just to kick back and relax. A short streetcar ride from Matsuyama, Dōgo is one of Japan's oldest tourist attractions, as its Dōgo Onsen has attracted royalty since the 8th century. You, too, will leave squeaky clean. Dōgo Kōen, the site of Yuzuki-jō, lies south of the city and offers a great view of Katsuyama Hill and the Dōgo area.

🖙🛈 TRANSPORTATION AND PRACTICAL INFORMATION

The easiest way to get to Dōgo is on the streetcar from Matsuyama. Hop on a #3, 5, or 6 streetcar (15min., ¥150) from either JR Matsuyama Station or Shieki Station. There's a **Botchan Information**, 1-10-12, Dōgo (☎941-2234; open daily 9am-5pm) in the streetcar station and a larger **tourist information center**, 6-8, Yunomachi, Dōgo (☎943-8342; open daily 8am-10pm), right across the street, that doubles as an *onsen*/ryokan guide. The **Dōgo Post Office** is just off the shopping arcade—from the station, walk down the arcade and take the first left; it'll be on the right after 300m.

⌂ ACCOMMODATIONS

▨ Matsuyama Youth Hostel (HI), 22-3, Himezuka (☎933-6366; www5a.biglobe.ne.jp/~sinsenen). Head toward Isaniwa Jinja, take the road to the right of the shrine stairs, and follow it up the hill and to the right. Rooms for men, women, couples, and families. Free Internet, English papers, lounges. Tennis courts across from hostel. Scooter rental ¥2900 per day. Breakfast ¥525. Dinner ¥1050. Laundry available. Check-in 4pm-midnight. Check-out 6-10am. Curfew midnight. ¥3360 per person. ❶

Dōgo Business Hotel (道後ビジネスホテル), 2-25, Yuno-machi (☎943-2911). Across from the north entrance to Dōgo Kōen. Small, with attached cafe. Check-in 2pm. Check-out 10am. Curfew midnight. Singles ¥4500; twins and doubles ¥10,000. ❷

Funaya (ふなや), 1-33, Yuno-machi (☎943-2139; www.dogo-funaya.co.jp). From Dōgo Onsen Station, head toward Isaniwa Jinja; it's on your right. Luxurious ryokan with an *onsen* set over a babbling brook in the woods. 2 meals included. Check-in 3pm. Check-out 11am. ¥28,000 for 1; ¥21,000 per person for 2; ¥18,000 for 3. ❺

Dōgo Kan, 7-26, Tako-chō (☎941-7777; www.dogokan.co.jp). 2 blocks north of Tsubaki no Yu. Another extravagant ryokan. The Grand Baths may be worth the price. Free Internet. Check-in 3pm. Check-out 10am. ¥26,000 for 1; ¥21,000 per person for 2; ¥19,500 for 3. Western rooms ¥17,500/¥15,500. ❺

◖ FOOD

The best food options in Dōgo are probably the ryokan (if you're staying at one), which cook up extravagant meals with lots of fresh seafood.

cafe de namo (cafe de なも), 12-29, Yuno-machi (☎943-9721). From Dōgo Onsen Station, walk up the arcade; it's on the left side of the 1st block. Coffee shop in an odd round building with streetlight in front of the door. Inside are cool lamps and chairs. Coffee and teas ¥400. Pizza toast or mixed sandwich ¥500. Open Tu-Su 9am-10pm. ❷

Bakushukan (麦酒館), 20-13, Yuno-machi (☎945-6866). Across the street from the left side of Dōgo Onsen Honkan. Run by Dōgo Brewery, which produces 3 tasty brews—Sōseki Stout, Madonna Alt, and Botchan Kelsch (glass ¥450, mug ¥800). Various Ehime Prefecture specialties: *konnyaku, jako tempura,* and *iyo* cooked chicken, either *yaki* (¥400) or *don* (¥600). Set meals from ¥800. Botchan set ¥1500. ❷

SHIKOKU

◉ ◎ SIGHTS AND BATHS

DŌGO ONSEN HONKAN. The tiled roof of the Dōgo Onsen spreads like a bird's wings, and the crane perched on top commemorates the legendary bird whose wounded leg was magically cured in a pool of spring water. Though the water here might not heal all that ails you, it's certainly a refreshing way to get clean. The building dates back to 1894 and looks like a castle brought down from a mountaintop. Visitors can take guided tours of the royal bath **Yushinden** (¥210, children ¥100, Tama no Yu guests free; in Japanese). The bath is only filled when members of the royal family visit, but the gold-painted screens and luxurious rest rooms are impressive sights. *(5-6, Yuno-machi. From Dōgo Onsen Station, cross the street and follow the shopping arcade to the right; it ends in front of the onsen. Open daily 6am-11pm. ¥300-1240.)*

OTHER BATHS. The first hot spring you'll see at Dōgo may be the free **foot bath** a block from the station. Head down the street towards Isaniwa Jinja and it's on the left. If Dōgo Onsen is too crowded, there are plenty of other options. Most of the ryokan allow public use of their *onsen*. Good choices include the baths at **Funaya** (open noon-midnight; ¥1500; see p. 573), which has one outdoor bath on the fringes of Dōgo Kōen, and the **Grand Baths** at Dōgo Kan (open 11:30am-11:30pm; ¥1500). Head to **Tsubaki-no-yu** (椿の湯) if you just want to clean off. (Open 6:30am-11pm. Towels ¥50. ¥300.) For a serious meal and bath, try **Chaharu** (茶波瑠 ; ☎945-1321). Lunch runs ¥2500 and gives you access to the windowed and rooftop baths that overlook Dōgo. You'll be able to use them twice—before and after the meal.

SHIKI KINEN MUSEUM. Dedicated to Masaoka Shiki, Matsuyama's most famous literary son, this museum traces the chronology of his life in Matsuyama and Tōkyō. There are English explanations at the beginning of each museum segment, but none for the items on display. Take a look at the recreation of the house he shared with Sōseki, where he expounded important theories about *haiku* and *tanka*. *(1-30, Kōen. Walk in the direction of Isaniwa Jinja, take the 1st right, and turn left at Dōgo Kōen; the museum is straight ahead. ☎931-5566. Free English guides can be arranged; call 1 day in advance. Open Tu-Su 9am-5pm. ¥300.)*

SHRINES. Of the shrines in Dōgo, **Isaniwa Jinja** is the most striking. It's on a hill up a set of steep stairs a few minutes from Dōgo Onsen Station. Two aligned halls, in the Hachiman style, are connected by a gutter. **Yu Jinja** is on a smaller hill, up a road right of Dōgo Onsen Honkan. The 7th-century shrine is smaller and plainer than Isaniwa, but it enshrines the god who discovered Dōgo Onsen, so it's symbolically important. When the Great Nankai Earthquake stopped the flow of the *onsen* in 1941, people prayed here, and the water returned 38 days later.

ISHITE-JI. The 51st temple on the Shikoku Pilgrimage has extensive grounds on all sides of the Kamakura-period buildings. The **Niomon gate,** guarded by two kings, is the first on the grounds. Clouds of incense fill the open areas, and just in front is the temple's main attraction—the **three-tiered pagoda** said to contain a bone of the Buddha. The **main hall** sits up a small set of stairs to the left. To the right of the main area is another set of buildings, one housing the **treasure room** (¥200, children ¥100), a missable collection of masks, armor, scrolls, and statues. To the left of the main area is a golden **Burmese pagoda.** Once you've exhausted the main grounds, head through the tunnels to the left of the main building. Probably once an exciting attraction, it's now run-down and rather lame—the tunnels are lined with flashing lights and statues. Exiting, you'll see the giant statue of **Kobo Daishi** on a hill to the right. Cross the street and head up a small path to a **golden dome,** filled with dusty, spooky statues. *(2-9-21, Ishite. From Dōgo Onsen Station, take the #8 or 52 bus toward Oku Dōgo for 5min. and get off at Ishite-ji-mae. ☎977-0870; http://ishiteji.interlink.or.jp.)*

UWAJIMA (宇和島) ☎0895

In the southwest corner of Ehime Prefecture, the small port city of Uwajima was once the center of the Date family's power. Traces of the *daimyō* family are fading, but the castle, the family garden Tensha-en, and several museums recall that chapter of this city's history. The sights in Uwajima can be covered in half a day, but consider relaxing here for a few days and enjoying the delicious seafood.

▐ TRANSPORTATION. JR **Uwajima Station** is the last stop on both the Yosan Line, running from Taka-matsu, and the Yodo Line, running from Kubokawa in the east. To reach **Kōchi** by train, transfer in Kubokawa; to reach **Tokushima** or **Takamatsu**, take a train or bus via Matsuyama. To: **Uchiko** (at least 1 per hr. 5:40am-9pm; local 2hr., ¥1060; limited express 50min., ¥2210); **Matsuyama** (local 80min., ¥1750; limited express 3½hr., ¥2900); **Ekawasaki** (45min., 8 per day 6:40am-11:10pm, ¥740); **Kubokawa** (2hr., 6 per day 6:37am-6:23pm, ¥1780). A highway bus departs from **Uwajima Bus Center**, 1-3-20, Marunouchi (☎22-0226; open 8am-6:30pm), to **Ōsaka** (8½hr., 10pm, ¥8150) and **Kōbe** (7½hr., 10pm, ¥7650). The Matsuyama-Sukumo bus line stops at both Uwa-jima Bus Center and **Uwajima Eki-mae**. To: **Matsuyama** (2hr., 12 per day 7am-4:30pm); **Sukumo** (2hr., 15 per day 6:39am-7:10pm). A ferry runs from Uwajima to **Yawatahama** (local 1¼hr., limited express 30min.; 1 per hour 5:38am-10:53pm), and another ferry runs from Yawatahama to **Beppu** (2¾hr., 6 per day 12:20am-8:30pm, from ¥1770).

Local buses service Uwajima, but a **bike** is your best option. The Tourist Information Center across from the station rents them out for ¥100 per hour. Other-wise, call **Satsuki Taxi** (☎22-1500) or **Uwajima Taxi** (☎22-5454), or rent a **car** from **Toyota Rent-a-Car**, on the corner one block left of the station.

▐▌ ORIENTATION AND PRACTICAL INFORMA-TION. Uwajima lies between the hills to the south and the port. The JR station is in the northeast cor-ner; only a few blocks away is a shopping arcade that runs almost the full length of the city, parallel to the northeastern edge of Uwajima Castle. Nothing is too far, but a bike will help you reach the city's outskirts. The **Tourist Information Center**, 3-24, Nishiki-machi, is on the corner of the main street, across from JR Uwajima Station. The staff speaks English and rents bikes for ¥100 per hr. You can sign up for 1hr. of free Internet access. (☎22-3934. Open M-F 8:30am-5pm, Sa-Su 9am-5pm.) Coin lockers are available at Uwa-jima Station. **Iyo Bank** is on the shopping arcade, 3 blocks on the right from the main avenue (☎ 22-5700; open M-F 9am-5pm). In an emergency call ☎110 for

THE BIG SPLURGE

RUB-A-DUB-DUB

If you've only got one chance to visit Dōgō Onsen, go for the luxuri-ous ¥1240 Tama no Yu ticket. That's a lot of money for a dip, but the services included make it worth the price. Your private room will be just down the hall from the lounge where Sōseki used to relax with friends and wax literary. Attendants will escort you and your friends to the room and give you *yukata* and towels. A locking closet saves you the bother of dealing with coin lockers.

Let your rubber-ducky-loving inner child free, and go take a steep. Carved out of dark gray stone, the elegant Tama no Yu bath is much quieter than the cheaper alternative. After you bathe, attendants will bring tea and *botchan dango* (soft sweets) to the third-floor waiting room, where you can relax on *tatami* mats and gaze out the window. You can also explore the room dedicated to Sōseki down the hall.

You'll then be escorted to the Yushinden, the Imperial bath, filled only when members of the royal family visit. The tour is in Japanese, but the luxury is evident in the golden screens emblazoned with the trademark crane and the small garden just outside.

After the tour, lounge around in your *yukata* or float in the water for another 80min. You'll be able to check out the Kami no Yu if you're curious as to where the lowly commoners bathe.

police; ☎ 119 for fire or ambulance; if it's less serious, try **Uwajima City Hospital**, 1-1, Goten-machi (☎ 25-1111). A 24-hr. **Sunkus Pharmacy** is just off the shopping arcade. Walk one block toward the arcade from the Tourist Information Center and take a left at the light; it's five blocks up. **Uwajima Post Office**, 1-3-12, Marunouchi, is to the right of the castle. Walk down the main street from the station, take a left at the circular intersection, and cross the river. (☎ 22-0100. Open M-F 8am-7pm, Sa 8am-6pm, Su 9am-3pm). There's an **International ATM** in the same building. (ATM open M-F 8:45am-9pm, Sa-Su 9am-7pm.) **Postal code:** 798.

⌐ ACCOMMODATIONS. The cheapest option is the hostel, but it's a hike from the station. Most hotels cluster near the station, though there are a few around the port area and shopping arcade. A cab to your hotel will never cost more than ¥1000 (the price ceiling). **Business Hotel Shōchiku ❷** (ビジネスホテル松竹) offers cheap Japanese-style rooms. From the station, walk to the right, take a left at the light just before the Tourist Information Office, then take the first left; it's on the right. (☎ 22-1166. Check-in 5pm. Check-out 9:30am. Curfew 10pm. ¥4000 per night. ¥3000 per day.) To get to **◪Uwajima Youth Hostel (HI) ❶** (うわじまユースホステ ル), walk to the back of town and up the hill behind the shrine. There are two routes, a 1.2km road to the right and a steeper, curvier 0.8km route to the left. Though isolated, the hostel commands an awesome view of the town, and management is very friendly. Amenities including free bike rentals and laundry detergent, lounge areas, ping pong tables, and a grassy yard where you can cook. (☎ 22-7177; www2.odn.ne.jp/~cfm91130. Breakfast ¥630. Dinner ¥1050. Check-in 4pm-9:30pm. Check-out 6am-10am. Curfew 10:30pm. Members ¥3360 per night.)

Across from the station, **Uwajima Terminal Hotel ❷** (宇和島ターミナルホテル) has reliable standard rooms. (☎ 22-2280; www.sakawa.co.jp/terminal. Check-in 4pm. Check-out 10am. Singles from ¥4900, twins from ¥9700. AmEx.) The **Uwajima Grand Hotel ❺** (宇和島グランドホテル) offers slightly better rooms. Walk down the palm-lined main avenue and take a left after the Tourist Information Office; it's on the left on the corner of the next block. (☎ 24-3911. Check-in 2pm. Check-out 11am. Curfew 2am. Singles from ¥5500, twins from ¥10,500.) If you've got to be in the middle of the nightlife, head to the **Uwajima Dai-Ichi Hotel ❸** (宇和島第一ホテ ル), 1-3-9, Chūō-chō. Take a left at the two-lane covered intersection on the shopping arcade. Take the first right; the hotel is on the left. (☎ 25-0001. Check-in 3pm. Check-out 10am. Singles from ¥5200, twins from ¥10,500, doubles from ¥12,000.)

◪ FOOD. Uwajima is right on the sea, so there are plenty of places to eat delicious fresh fish. *Tai-meshi*, rice topped with pickled sea bream, is an expensive local specialty. If ordering sushi, be sure to request the seasonal fish. At the end of the main avenue on the right is the grocery store **Palty Fuji ❶**, 2-3-28, Ebisu-machi, which sells various *bentō* lunches, often discounted after 4pm. (☎ 22-6565. Open daily 9:30am-9pm.) Walk down the shopping arcade, and one block after the covered intersection, take a left; **◪Ja no Me ❸** (蛇の目), 5-20-1, Chūō-chō, is on the right. Tucked into a side street, this restaurant has a reputation for serious sushi. They have no English menu; sit at the counter so you can point at what you want. Prices average ¥400 for two pieces. Plan on spending at least ¥1500, or ¥2000-2500 to really fill up. (☎ 22-1354. Open W and F-Sa 11am-2pm and 4-10pm.) Walk down the avenue from the station and **Iyo no Sato ❷** (いよの里) will be on the right, just before the arcade. Try the delicious *Iyo no Sato udon*, filled with chicken, mushrooms, onions, and more (¥650). *Donburi* (rice bowls) are topped with *tamago* (egg; ¥500), *unagi* (eel; ¥1200), and other standards. (☎ 24-3069. Open Sa-Th 11am-10pm.) Walk down the arcade, and take a right one block after the covered intersection; **Kuraku ❷** (苦楽), 1-8-10, Chūō-chō, is on the left. Late-nighters park here for *rāmen* (¥500), *gyōza* (¥300), and cheap beer. (☎ 25-8844. Open daily 8pm-4am.) Two blocks from the end of the shopping arcade, **cafe de gateau Andorino ❶** (アンドリーノ), 2-8-4, Hon-machi, Oite, is on the right. This

Uwajima · 宇和島

🏠 ACCOMMODATIONS
Business Hotel Shōchiku, **5**
JYH Uwajima Youth Hostel, **14**
Uwajima Dai-Ichi Hotel, **8**
Uwajima Grand Hotel, **6**
Uwajima Terminal Hotel, **4**

🍴 FOOD
cafe de gateau Andorino, **13**
Iyo no Sato, **2**
Ja no Me, **9**
Kuraku, **10**
Palty Fuji, **1**
Wazu, **7**

🍶 NIGHTLIFE
Monkey Man, **11**
Red Boots, **12**
Texas, **3**

(Map labels: Warei Jinga, Taga Jinga, TO TŌGYŪ-JŌ (BULLFIGHT) (300m), JR Uwajima Station, Toyota Rent-a-Car, Iyo Bank, Kōri Gate, Kyōdōkan, Uwajima Bus Center, Uwajima-jo, TO (800m), Date Museum, Uwajima City Hospital, Tensha-en Garden, 200 meters, 200 yards)

SHIKOKU

jazzy French cafe serves up freshly ground coffees (¥400) and teas along with sandwiches (¥500) and set meals (¥800). Breakfast and lunch sets ¥700. They may even let you try out the house guitar. (☎22-8811. Open M-Sa 8am-9pm.) Walk down the shopping arcade and take a left when you see the au store; **Wazu ❷** (和厨) is on the second block on the left. This gourmet restaurant requires a reservation but returns the price of the phone call in shiny ¥10 coins. Once you've removed your shoes and seated yourself, you must pick at least three items from the menu. *Onigiri* (rice ball and seaweed; ¥450) and *miso* soup (¥350) are tasty choices, and the *wasabi* carpaccio (¥700) is delicious. Most items cost ¥750-1000. They can make sushi and fill most requests, even if it's not on the menu. Plan on spending at least ¥2500 per person to fill up and have a drink or two.

🅖 **SIGHTS.** The most infamous tourist attraction is **Taga Jinja**, a small shrine dedicated to fertility. Head down the main palm-lined avenue, and take a right at the circular intersection. Follow the road across the Suka River, take a left, and it will be on the right shortly. The shrine itself is rather small and unassuming, but the **Sex Museum** (Dekoboko Shindō; 凸凹神堂), 1340, Fujie, on site is about as subtle as the veiny, nine-foot wooden phallus to the left of the main shrine building. There is little in English, but this is one place where the displays couldn't be any clearer than they already are. The objects on display seem to be grouped by region, but the three-floor jumble jumps back and forth historically and geographically, from Kama Sutra to S&M equipment to ancient sexual mandalas. In a country that censors most of its pornography, the museum is surprisingly graphic, so steel yourself. (☎22-3444. Open daily 8am-5pm. ¥800. Adults only.)

Back in town, **Uwajima-jō** is worth a glance. Head back to the circular intersection and continue straight. After crossing a small river, walk a few blocks and look for the Kōri Gate (North Gate) on the right. This leads to a shady path with stone steps, up past a well and the old site of castle gates. The grounds are bare and pleasantly overgrown. Go up the three flights of stairs in the original Edo-period *donjon* for a clear view of the sea. (Open daily 9am-4pm. ¥200; elementary and junior high school students ¥100.) On your way down, stop by the **Shiroyama Kyodo-kan** (城山郷土館) to check out old photos of Uwajima and local festivals, and items donated by the Date family—pre-Meiji *daimyō* rulers of Uwajima—including pieces of houseware and some old palanquins. (Open Tu-Su 9am-4pm.)

The small **Date Museum** (伊達博物館), 9-14, Goten-machi, may be worth a visit. Follow the street around the castle and take a left on the street that runs along the south side of the castle. Take the fourth left; the museum is on the left. Objects on display include ceremonial palanquins, *nō* masks, clothes, and armor. (☎22-7776. Open Tu-Su 9am-4:30pm. ¥500, high school and university students ¥200, elementary and junior high school students free.) One block away is the Date family garden, **Tensha-en**, 9-9, Goten-machi, filled with big grassy areas, 22 varieties of bamboo, and a pond with a beautiful wisteria trellis. Though it's attractive, the garden's proximity to schools and streets disturbs the serenity. (☎25-2709. Open daily 8:30am-4:30pm. Dec.-Feb. closed M. ¥300, junior high students ¥100, younger ¥50.)

■ **NIGHTLIFE.** If you came to Uwajima for the nightlife, you must've been mistaken. There are, however, several friendly late-night bars. From the station, walk down the right side of the main palm-lined avenue; **Texas**, 2-1-4, Ebisu-machi, is on the block just before the arcade. Run by Boss Seiji, a metal-rock-blues-loving guy with a big laugh, Texas serves imported beers (from ¥500), including Heineken, Corona, and Budweiser. (☎22-2039. Open M and W-Su 6pm-3am. Credit cards accepted.) One block past the end of the arcade and to the right is **Red Boots** (レッドブーツ), 2-6-2, Hon-chō, Oite, another Texas-themed bar. This one plays oldies and classic rock, and has an impressive selection of whiskeys. (☎15-3506. Beer from ¥600, pastas ¥750, cheeses ¥500. Open Tu-Su 5pm-2am.) Take a left at the end of the shopping arcade and then the second right; **Monkey Man**, Benten Bldg., 1st fl., Hon-chō, Oite, is on the left—look for the giant monkey mural on the wall outside. This small reggae/hip-hop counter-bar occasionally hosts DJs but always plays loud beats. (☎23-3328. Drinks from ¥500. Open daily 8pm-4am.)

■ **FESTIVALS.** Uwajima is famous for its bullfights, called *tōgyū* (闘牛). Unlike Spanish bullfighting, *tōgyū* is a fight between two bulls, resembling a sumo match with half-ton bovines. The pampered bulls are led into the ring by their masters and forced to lock horns. Then instinct takes over as the bulls butt, push, and shove until one runs away or is injured. The fighting is very subtle, and each move has its own name. Mostly older people follow *tōgyū* closely, as the sport doesn't attract local youngsters; bouts can be slow, long, and tedious. Fights take place in the **Tōgyū-jō** on a hill east of the JR Station five times a year: January 2, the first Sunday of April, July 24, August 14, and the second Sunday of November. Bouts are held 12pm-3pm, and a free bus service runs from the JR Station to the stadium 10am-12pm. (☎25-3511. ¥3000, junior high school students and younger free.)

The July bullfight coincides with **Warei Taisai** and the **Ushioni Festival**, Warei Jinja's big festival on July 23-24. Warei Jinja is the shrine on the river, east of Taga Jinja. On the night of the 24th, Shintō priests bring the shrine's three *mikoshi*, which house the local gods, down for a swim in the river. The **Ushioni Festival** takes place during the day, when locals parade with giant bull floats called *ushioni* (demon bull), whose long necks make them look more like llamas.

KYŪSHŪ (九州)

Once connected to the Korean peninsula, and the site of the original Japanese kingdom and source of the Imperial lineage, Kyūshū has historically been the gateway to Japan. Kyūshū has received the brunt of cultural influxes—first Korean and Chinese refugees, then attempted Mongolian invasions, and finally proselytizing Europeans. In Nagasaki, Dutch and Chinese traders in Dejima were the only exceptions to the Tokugawa closed-country policy. Kyūshū's major cities—Fukuoka, Nagasaki, Kumamoto, and Kagoshima—are small in area and have few skyscrapers, allowing travelers to sense each city's essence. But Kyūshū's real treasures lie outside her cities. Her mountains account for 10% of all active volcanoes in the world; the subterranean plumbing forces steaming, mineral-rich water out of the ground, feeding the hot springs in Beppu and Yufuin. Aso-san, home to the world's biggest caldera, and Yaku-shima, a mystical forest, should not be missed. You'll need luck to get sunny weather—plan your trip around the rainy season, or alternatively, *during* the rainy season for a taste of organic Kyūshū. Railpasses are handy—the *shinkansen* runs to Hakata and Kokura, from where you can take the train down the eastern or western coasts.

HIGHLIGHTS OF KYŪSHŪ

RISING FROM DISASTER'S ASHES. Commemorate one of history's saddest stories and understand **Nagasaki's** (p. 596) urgent cry for peace at the **Nagasaki Atomic Bomb Museum** and **Peace Statue.**

ONSEN HOPPING. Exfoliate in the waters of **Beppu** (p. 605) on a sobering, purifying crawl of the city's hotness.

ARITA PLAYSKOOL. Relive the Playskool-OshKosh days as you make your own pottery in **Arita** (p. 593), or just buy someone else's masterpiece.

UNTAPPED LANDS. Hike through **Yaku-shima's** (p. 633) virgin forests and chameleon climates before the rest of the world discovers this island guarding the water exchange between the East China Sea and the Pacific Ocean.

KITA-KYŪSHŪ (北九州)　☎093

Created from the 1963 merger of five separate cities, Kita-Kyūshū is at the very tip of Kyūshū, just across the Kanmon Strait from Shimonoseki on the southern end of Honshū. Home to Japan's first national steel mill, Kita-Kyūshū was once an important international port. Major clean-up efforts have done wonders.

ON THE WEB　Kita-Kyūshū City: www.city.kitakyushu.jp/~english

⌨ TRANSPORTATION

Trains: Kokura Station is serviced by the JR Sanyō *shinkansen* line.

Buses: Highway buses stop at Tamaya department store outside JR Kokura Station's South Exit. To: **Kyōto** (8hr.; 10:05pm; ¥10,000, round-trip ¥17,800); **Nagoya** (9¾hr.; 10:05pm; ¥10,000/18,000); **Okayama** (7½hr.; 11:35pm; ¥6200/11,100); **Ōsaka** (8¼hr.; 10:40pm; ¥9500/16,800).

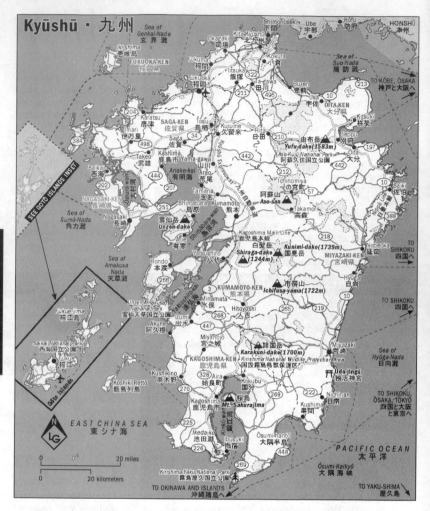

Kyūshū · 九州

Public Transportation: Buses run between major districts, but the areas themselves are easily navigable by foot. A **monorail** runs south straight out of JR Kokura Station through Kokura Kita-ku and Minami-ku.

Taxis: Central Taxi, ☎663-6663.

Car Rental: Budget Rent-a-Car, 1-2-35, Kokura, Kita-ku, Asano (☎512-0543; www.idex.co.jp/budget), is to the right of Kokura Station's North Exit. On the south side of Kokura Station is an **Eki Rent-a-Car** (☎531-1942).

⚡ PRACTICAL INFORMATION

Tourist Offices:

Tourist Information Center, 1-1-1, Asano (☎541-4189), is on the 1st fl. of the North Exit of JR Kokura Station, but the **Tourist Information Desk** on the 3rd. fl. of the South Exit is run by the same people and easier to get to. English-speaking staff can book beds. Open daily 9am-6pm.

Kita-Kyūshū International Association Kokura Information Desk, 3-8-1, Kokura, Kita-ku, Asano (☎551-0055; www.bcc-net.co.jp/kia), a 5min. walk to the big, yellow AIM building a few blocks north and then to the right from JR Kokura Station. The center is on the 2nd fl. of the shopping center. English CNN and newspapers. Open M-F 9am-5:30pm.

Kita-Kyūshū International Association (KIA) Office, 1-1-1, Yahatahigashi-ku, Hirano (☎662-0055; www.bcc-net.co.jp/kia). 10min. from Yahata Station, straight up the main road in a building on the left. Small library of English-language books and periodicals, but unless you are staying in the hostel nearby, stick to the Kokura Information Desk. Open Tu-Su 9am-5:30pm.

Currency Exchange: To exchange dollars and other currencies, head to **Tōkyō Mitsubishi Bank,** 1-6-16, Uomachi, Kokurakita-ku (☎521-7011). Open M-F 9am-3pm.

ATM: In Kita-Kyūshū post offices.

Luggage Storage: Coin lockers are in JR Kokura Station and the other JR stations.

English-Language Bookstore: Book Center Quest, 1-4-7, Bashaku (☎522-3914; www.honya-town.co.jp/bc-quest), on Komonji-dōri a block west of Uomachi shopping arcade. English-language books and periodicals. Open daily 10am-8pm.

Library: Kita-Kyūshū Central Public Library, 4-1, Jonai (☎571-1481), just south of Kokura-jō and City Hall. From JR Kokura Station, take the South Exit and walk straight, taking a right on Komonji-dōri. The library is on the left after you pass the City Hall.

Laundromat: There's a **24hr. coin laundry** to the right of Kokura Station as you exit the south side. It's at the end of the street, past the entertainment shops, and on the right.

Emergency: Police ☎110. Fire or ambulance ☎119.

Police: Kita-Kyūshū City Police Department, 5-1, Jonai, Kokurakita-ku (☎583-1110).

Medical Services: Emergency Medical Clinic, 1-7-1, Bashaku, Central Health and Welfare Office, 1st fl. (☎522-9999).

Fax Office: There are 2 **Kinko's stores.** Komemachi Store, 1-5-18, Kome-machi (☎513-6505). Walk straight out from the station and take a left 1 block after the large pink department store; Kinko's is on the left corner across from Washington Hotel. Open 24hr. Heiwa-dōri Store, 1-2-16, Sakai chō (☎513-8166). 1 block south of Heiwa-dōri Station on the corner. Computers, copiers, and fax at both locations. Open 24hr.

Internet Access: Cafe Centrino, Riverwalk Bldg., 1st fl., 1-1-1, Muro-machi, Kokura, Kita-ku (☎573-1616, www.cafe-centrino.jp), has **free Internet access** if you place an order. Open M-F 9:30am-9pm, Sa-Su 10am-9pm. **Manboo Internet Comic Cafe,** Zabo Bldg., 7th fl., 1-4-1, Uomachi (☎512-0010; www.manboo.co.jp). At the intersection of Uomachi arcade and Rte. 199. From the station's South Exit, go straight, and take a right 1 block after Tamaya department store; it's on the 2nd block, inside the arcade. ¥200 for 1st hr., then ¥100 per 15min; ¥780 for 3hr.; ¥1480 for 8hr. Open 24hr.

Post Office: Beppu Eki-mae Post Office, 3-8-1, Kyō-machi (☎511-4331), is directly to the left of JR Kokura Station's South Exit. Open M-F 9am-7pm, Sa 9am-3pm. ATM open M-F 8am-11pm, Sa 9am-9pm, Su 9am-7pm. **Postal Code:** 806.

▌ ACCOMMODATIONS

Tomoe Ryokan (ともえ旅館), 3-12-3, Tō-machi (☎521-5946). Exit the station's south side. Take a left after the pink department store and then the 2nd left just after a small park. It's on the right. Budget option close to Kokura Station. *Tatami* rooms with separate baths. Breakfast ¥500. Dinner ¥1000. Check-in 3pm. Check-out 9am. Lockout 9am-3pm, or pay ¥1000 to stay during the day. Curfew 1am. ¥3000. ❶

Kokura Washington Hotel Plaza (小倉ワシントンホテルプラザ), 1-9-8, Tanya-chō (☎531-3111). Take Kokura Station's South Exit and walk straight, taking a left 1 block after the pink department store; it's at the 1st light. Chain hotel, reliable service. Check-in 2pm. Check-out 10am. Singles ¥5000; doubles and twins ¥12,000. ❷

Nishitetsu Inn, 1-4-11, Kome-machi (☎511-5454; www.nnr.co.jp/nishitetsu_inn). Exit Kokura Station's south side and take a left after the large pink department store; it's on the right. Rates at this business hotel are better for 2. Check-in 3pm. Check-out 5pm. Singles from ¥6000; studio singles for two ¥9000; twins ¥11,500. ❸

Kita-Kyūshū Youth Hostel (HI) (☎681-8142). From Kokura Station, take an Itōzu Bus toward Tenjin, get off at Hobashira Cable-mae (30min., 2 per hr. 7:45am-9:45pm, ¥500), and walk past the Cable Car Station. Or, take the JR to Yahata Station, walk uphill past the International Center, cross the bridge, and bear left a few blocks before crossing the expressway; it's past Hobashira Cable Car Station. Breakfast ¥600. Dinner ¥900. Check-in 4:30pm. Check-out 10am. Lockout 10am-4:30pm. Curfew 10pm. Closed June 5-14. ¥2700; nonmembers ¥3700. ❶

Station Hotel Kokura, 1-1-1, Asano (☎541-7111; www.kosta.co.jp/hotel). Connected to Kokura Station on the left side as you head towards the South Exit. Luxurious business hotel. Fax, copy machines, and Internet available in business center. Check-in 1pm. Check-out 11am. Book online for a discount. Singles from ¥7800; doubles from ¥14,000; twins from ¥15,500; Japanese suites ¥42,500. ❹

🟦 FOOD

🔲 **Yakyū-dōri** (野球鳥 ; ☎521-6663), Kokurakita-ku. From Kokura Station, walk straight and take a left past the pink department store. It's on the right of the 1st block; look for the neon baseball player and diamond. A yakitori (fried chicken) joint that puns on Japan's adopted national pastime, baseball (yakyū). It's all delicious, served on a bed of astroturf cabbage. The beef (¥300) is recommended. Open daily 5pm-12am. ❷

Ocm Sandwich Factory, Kondo Bldg., 2nd fl., 3-6, Senbamachi (☎522-5973). Walk down Uomachi arcade and take a right at Doutor Coffee Shop, 1 block past McDonald's; it's on the 2nd block on the left. Thick, well-dressed deli-style sandwiches (from ¥280). Egg salad-hashbrown sandwich is delicious (¥350). Toppings such as hot-dog, hamburger, roast beef, chicken teriyaki, tuna. Open daily 10am-9pm. ❷

Shabu-kan (紗舞館), 1-5-31, Nishikaigan, Mojikō-eki, Kōnai (☎332-0144). Wonderful shabu-shabu restaurant inside Mojikō Station, oldest train station in Kyūshū. Hardwood counters and booths suit the old-style milieu. Sets include rice, veggies (from ¥900). Courses include drink, dessert, coffee (from ¥2400). Open daily 11am-8:30pm. ❷

Mojikō Retro Beer, Co., 6-9, Higashiminato-chō (☎321-6885). Across the pedestrian drawbridge and to the left on the Mojikō Marine Promenade. Regional brewery and restaurant. Great view over Kanmon Strait. Pale Ale, Weizen, Pilsner, and a seasonal selection brewed on site. Regular glass (¥450), large (¥550), pitcher (¥2000). Snacks from ¥500. Open daily 10am-10pm, last food order 9:15pm, last drink order 9:30pm.

Pizzeria, 1-3-23, Uomachi (☎513-0800). Kokura Station area. Go 2 blocks on Uomachi and take a left; it's on the left. Delicious pizzas from ¥1200. Italian courses from ¥2500. Open M-Sa 11:30am-2:30pm and 5:30-11pm, Su 11:30am-10pm. ❷

Cafe Centrino, Riverwalk Bldg., 1st fl., 1-1-1, Muromachi (☎573-1616). On the outside of the Riverwalk closer to the Murasaki River. Selection of coffees and coffee-based drinks from ¥250. Small sandwich and cake sets. Free Internet for customers. Open M-F 9:30am-9pm, Sa-Su 10am-9pm, last order 8:30pm. ❷

Ippei (一平 ; ☎527-4543). On the 1st block of Uomachi arcade on the left; you'll smell the rāmen as you pass by. Thick bowls of miso rāmen (¥600), Kyūshū rāmen (¥500), and chanpon (noodles with veggies; ¥700). Open daily 11am-11pm. ❷

◎ SIGHTS

Juxtaposed with the flamboyant new Riverwalk buildings in central Kokura is **Kokura-jō**, 2-1, Jonai, a reconstruction of the original 17th-century castle, famous for its un-gabled fifth layer. Inside the castle tower is a small museum of the history of Kokura including a great scale model of the castle town. (☎561-1210. Open daily Apr.-Oct. 9am-6pm, Nov.-Mar. 9am-5pm. ¥350, students 12-17 ¥200, children 4-11 ¥100.) For more traditional scenery, head across the street to the **Kokura-jō Japanese Garden**, 1-2, Jonai, Kokurakita-ku (☎582-2747; www.city.kitakyushu.jp/~k1201041), which has a beautiful sunken pond. (Open daily 9am-5pm. ¥300, junior high and high school students ¥150, elementary ¥100.)

If you have a few extra hours, **Retro World** in Mojikō is worth a look. The area was an important port until the mid-1920s. Many of the buildings were sold and moved, but within the last decade restorations and reconstructions have made Mojikō a small tourist area. Mojikō Station is a Renaissance-style building, the oldest station in Kyūshū. It's charmingly crumbly, and has a nice fountain in front. Across the street is the **Old Moji Mitsui Club**, a 1921 Art Deco building. The first floor has an expensive restaurant and nicely decorated rooms you can see for free. The second floor houses a small **museum** of Albert Einstein's visit to the building in 1922 and another dedicated to author Fumiko Hayashi. (Open daily 9am-10pm. 2nd fl. fee ¥100, junior high and elementary school students ¥50.) Across the pedestrian drawbridge (the only one in Japan) and to the right is the **Customs House**, reconstructed in 1994. (Open daily 9am-5pm. Free.) Nearby is **Mojikō Retro Tower View**; you can see the Kanmon Strait and the area around Mojikō from the 31st floor. Take a train from JR Kokura Station to JR Mojikō Station. (☎331-3103. Open daily 10am-10pm, entrance until 9:30pm.)

The **Kita-Kyūshū Municipal Museum of Art** (☎882-7777; www.city.kitakyushu.jp/~k5200020) is a small museum in Tobata-ku featuring modern Japanese and Western art. Take the #22 bus from Kokura Station or the #1 from the Uomachi Bus Stop to the Shichijō (七条) Bus Stop. A free shuttle runs to the museum every 10min. (Open Tu-Su 9:30am-5:30pm, last entrance 5pm. ¥150, university and high school students ¥100, junior high and elementary ¥50.) The new **Riverwalk Gallery**, Muromachi 1-chōme, will stimulate art lovers with its rotating exhibits of a wide range of art forms—from Osamu Tezuka's Astro Boy to M.C. Escher's prints. (☎861-0959. Open daily 10am-8pm. Admission varies by exhibit.)

If you need to entertain little ones, **Space World**, 4-1-1, Yahatahigashi-ku, is a small, animated space theme park built in connection with NASA—it even has a licensed Space Camp. Get the freepass if you plan on staying all day. It's a short walk from JR Spaceworld Station, one stop before Yahata from Kokura Station. (☎672-3600; www.spaceworld.co.jp. Opening days vary by season, but always 9am-9pm. ¥1000, child ¥500; freepass ¥3800, child ¥2800, family ¥12,000.)

⌐ SHOPPING

Shop at Kokura while in Kita-Kyūshū, specifically in the new **Riverwalk** alongside Murasaki River and across from Kokura-jō. The buildings are meant to blend with the surroundings, but the Riverwalk is like a massive four-piece modern sculpture—it couldn't stand out more. It houses fashion stores and boutiques; the **Riverwalk Gallery**, an annex of the Municipal Museum of Art on the fifth floor; and the **Kita-Kyūshū Performing Arts Center**, which hosts events throughout the year. (☎573-1500. Open daily 10am-9pm.) Rent **boats** outside. (Open Apr.-July 18 and Sept.-Oct. Sa 11am-7pm; July 19-Aug. 31 daily 11am-7pm. ¥500 for 30min.)

▣ NIGHTLIFE

Kokura is the largest ward of Kita-Kyūshū and has the most exciting nightlife. If you get stuck here overnight and need some watering holes, there are some bars and late night restaurants around the station and shopping arcade. Most of the nightlife spots are southeast of the station just on the other side of Komonji-dōri.

■ **Patico Tower,** Azabu 21 Bldg., 3rd fl., 8-16, Konya-machi (☎512-5222). Head down Heiwa-dōri from Kokura Station and take a left on Komonji-dōri. Take the 3rd right and 1st left; it's on the left. Friendly bar with free pool. Great food and drink specials. Happy Hour Su-F 9-11pm. Bagel sandwiches ¥500. Falafel ¥700. Open daily 9pm-5am.

Tropical Oasis Xehla, Yushin Bldg., 1st fl., 3-6-23, Kyōmachi (☎551-8683; http://es-web.net/xelha). From Kokura Station, take a left, then the 1st right, and a quick left; it's on the left. The perfect place to wet your throat, this jungle-themed oasis gets crowded even on weekdays. F-Sa dancing starts at midnight. Bass, Lowenbrau, and Asahi on tap (¥500). Exotic foods and cocktails. Open Su-Th 5pm-12am, F-Sa 5pm-2am.

Grass Roots, 1-5-14, Kokurakita-ku, Uomachi (☎512-7722). Walk 2 blocks along Uomachi arcade. Take a left, then the 1st right, and Grass Roots is on the left. Mixed music, funky decor. Get your drink on with beer from ¥500 and cocktails from ¥700. Happy Hour 6-9pm. Very friendly bartenders. Open daily 6pm-3am.

FUKUOKA (福岡)   ☎092

Many Japanese do not know the distinction between Fukuoka and Hakata, two names used almost interchangeably in conversation—Fukuoka refers to the official name of the city and Hakata to the local culture. Fukuoka seems to be another clean Japanese metropolis with all the traditional elements—a young fashionable area, a business corner, a Red Light District, huge department stores, new development on reclaimed land, and a historic portion. At the same time, travelers find comfort in the comparatively small size and low noise level of Fukuoka, the vivacity of Hakata's traditional culture, and the city's distinct culinary specialties. Fukuoka, the economic and cultural capital of Kyūshū, with a population of about 1.5 million, lacks the excess of bigger cities, but compensates for it in spirit. Folk culture is strong, evident in the famous Gion Yamakasa and Dontaku festivals (held in July and May, respectively). Closer to Pusan and Seoul in Korea than to its own nation's capital, Fukuoka's unique flavor is a fusion of past and present contact with continental Asia and the products of Fukuoka's local landscape.

Fukuoka · 福岡

🏠 ACCOMMODATIONS
Asahi Ryokan, **17**
Hotel Cabinas, **9**
Kashima Honkan, **1**
Skycourt Hakata (HI), **6**
Sumiyoshi Ryokan, **14**
Well Be, **8**

🍴 FOOD
Asian Cafe Ron-Dong, **3**
J Cafe, **15**
Karo no Uron, **5**
Marbre Blanc, **16**
Tetsu Nabe, **7**

▣ NIGHTLIFE
Blue Note Fukuoka, **10**
Crazy Cock, **4**
Fire Ball, **11**
Happy Cock, **12**
Mura Ichiban, **13**
Q's, **2**

ON THE WEB Fukuoka City: www.city.fukuoka.jp/index-e.html

▣ INTERCITY TRANSPORTATION

Flights: Fukuoka Airport (Fukuoka Kūkō; 福岡空港), 5min. from **Hakata Station** (¥250) and 11min. from **Tenjin Station** (¥250) by subway; get off at the Fukuoka Kūkō Station. Buses cost about the same, but take longer. Express buses run from the airport to Kokura, Saga, and Kurume (¥1000); a taxi into town runs ¥1500. Flights to all major cities in Japan and many in the Asia-Pacific Rim. JAL, ANA, and JAS operate flights to

Fukuoka・福岡

TO HIROSHIMA & OKAYAMA
広島(281km), 岡山(442km)

TO BAYSIDE PLACE (3km)

TO MOMOCHI (3.75km)

TO KEGO & KUROMON 薬院公園・黒門
TO 06 (200m)

Oyafuko-dōri

TO AIRPORT 福岡空港 (2km)
Hakata-Minami Line・博多南線
Kagoshima Main Line・鹿児島本線

TO NAGASAKI (154km)長崎へ

Shinkansen・新幹線

Chikushi Gate
Hakata Station 博多駅
Hakata Gate
Ko-Tsu-Center

US Consulate
Mikasa-gawa・御笠川

202

Kuramoto Intersection
Gion 祇園
Gofuku-machi 呉服町
M
Kūkō Line・空港線
Taihaku-dōri

Shōfuku-ji 聖福寺
Tōchō-ji 東長寺
Taihaku-dōri・大博通

FUKUOKA 福岡
Hakataekimae-dōri

Meiji-kōen 明治公園

200 meters
200 yards

Sumiyoshi-dōri・住吉通
SUMIYOSHI 住吉
Sumiyoshi-jinja 住吉神社
Sumiyoshi-bashi 住吉橋
TO 18 (100m)

Hakata Machiya Folk Museum 博多町屋ふるさと館
Hakata-jinja
Kushida-jinja 櫛田神社
Kushida-dōri 櫛田前町

Hakata Riverain 博多リバレイン
Fukuoka Asian Art Museum 福岡アジア美術館
Nakasu-Kawabata 中洲川端
Kawabata Shōtengai・川端商店街

CANAL CITY キャナルシティ

Nishitetsu Line・西鉄大牟田線

NAKATSU 中洲
Naka-gawa・中川

Former Historical Museum 元祖長浜屋
NISHI-NAKA-JIMA 西中島
NAKATSU 中洲
Nishi-naka-jima Bashi 西中島橋
Kōen-dōri-bashi 公園通橋
De-ai-bashi 出合橋
Haruyoshi-bashi 春吉橋
Kōkutai-dōri・国体道路

Meiji-dōri・明治通
Shōwa-dōri・昭和通

Tenjin Chūō-kōen 天神中央公園
Fukuoka City Hall 福岡市役所
Fukuoka Tenjin Station 西鉄福岡

Tenjin 天神
M

Cybac

Watanabe-dōri・渡辺通
Watanabe-dōri Iccho-me Intersection

Nishi-tetsu Ōmuta Line・西鉄大牟田線

Kego-jinja 警固神社
Kego-kōen 警固公園
Kinko's
Cybac

Tenjin Nishi-dōri・天神西通
Kōkutai-dōri・国体道路

202

KYŪSHŪ

Seoul (5 per day; ¥23,000-32,000) and **Taipei** (4 per day; ¥46,000-63,000). Domestic flights to: **Tōkyō Haneda** (45 per day; ¥17,300-30,500); **Kansai** (4 per day; ¥11,000-20,000); **Tōkyō Narita** (3 per day; ¥20,000-30,000). **Skymark** (☎ 736-3131; www.skymark.co.jp) offers domestic deals (as low as ¥8900 in advance, ¥18,000 on the spot). To: **Aomori, Kagoshima, Tokushima,** and **Tōkyō Haneda.** Call or visit the website.

Trains: The **Tōkaidō/Sanyō Shinkansen Line** runs from Tōkyō through Ōsaka (Shin-Ōsaka) and Hiroshima, ending at JR Hakata Station (☎ 471-8111). To: **Hiroshima** (every 2hr., 6am-9pm; Hikari 1hr., ¥9740 and Nozomi 1hr., ¥12,930); **Ōsaka** (every hr., 6am-9pm; Hikari 2hr., ¥15,210 and Nozomi 2hr., ¥15,390); **Tōkyō** (every hr., 6am-7pm; Hikari 5hr., ¥21,720 and Nozomi 4hr., ¥23,560). Use the **JR** and **Nishitetsu Train** systems within Kyūshū. JR runs down the island's east and west: the **Nippō Line** through Hakata, Beppu, Miyazaki, and Kago-shima; the **Kagoshima Line** through Hakata, Kumamoto, and Kago-shima. The **JR Nagasaki Line** runs west to Nagasaki.

Buses: Overnight buses (reservations ☎ 734-2727) depart from the **Tenjin Bus Center** (☎ 771-2961) and the 3rd fl. of **Kōtsū Center** at Hakata Station (☎ 431-1171). The buses depart from Tenjin, and stop at Hakata Station 10min. later. To **Ōsaka** (10hr., 9:05pm, ¥10,000) and **Tōkyō** (16hr., 7pm, ¥15,000). Other express buses depart from Kōtsū Center, then stop at Tenjin. To: **Hiroshima** (5hr., every hr., ¥4000); **Imari** (2hr., every hr., ¥2150); **Kagoshima** (4hr., 1-2 per hr., ¥5300); **Karatsu** (1½hr., 1-2 per hr., ¥1000); **Kumamoto** (2hr., 5 per hr., ¥2000); **Miyazaki** (4½hr., 1-2 per hr., ¥6000); **Nagasaki** (2½ hr., 4 per hr., ¥2500); **Ōita** (2½hr., 3-4 per hr., ¥3100).

Ferries: As the Japanese port closest to mainland Asia (the Korean peninsula is only 213km away), **Fukuoka Port International Terminal** (☎ 282-4871) is a bustling point of exchange. Accessible by bus from Hakata Station (take bus #11 or 19 from E Terminal across the street from Hakata Gate; ¥220) or Tenjin (take bus #55, 151, 152 or 209 from Terminal 2A in front of Tenjin Solaria Stage; ¥180). A 25min. walk from the Gofukuchō Subway Stop. Departure tax ¥400. **Beetle** (☎ 281-2315; www.beetle.jrkyushu.co.jp) ferry ships to **Pusan, Korea** (3hr., 4 per day; ¥13,000, round-trip ¥24,000). For travelers planning a few days in Korea, try the package deal of a return trip on Beetle and a 5-day Korean Railway Pass for ¥25,000 (7-day pass ¥27,000).

▐ LOCAL TRANSPORTATION

Ferries: West of the international port, **Bayside Place Hakata Futō** (☎ 272-3939) has restaurants, an aquarium, a skateboarding park, a public bath, and indoor snowboarding. Jetfoils to **Iki** (1hr., 3 per day, ¥4680) and **Tsushima** (2½hr., 2 per day, ¥5520-8950). Ferries to: **Genkaijima** (30min., 6 per day, ¥840); **Shikanoshima** (30min., 18 per day, ¥650); **Umi-no-nakamichi** (30min., 3 per day, ¥500).

Subway: 2 subway lines serve the central parts of the city (¥200-300). The **Kūkō Line** runs from the airport through Hakata, Nakasu-Kawabata, Tenjin, and Tō-jinmachi, to Meinohama. The **Hakozaki Line** links Nakasu-Kawabata with the residential areas of Kaizuka. The **one-day pass** (¥600) earns you a small discount at many sights.

Bus: Within the area enclosed by Hakata Station, Kuramoto Intersection, Tenjin, and Watanabe-dōri 1-chōme Intersection, **bus** fare is ¥100. The convenient "¥100 Junkan Bus" circulates around Hakata Station, Gofukuchō, Tenjin, and Canal City every 5min. daily 9:30am-8pm. A **one-day bus pass** is ¥600.

Riding the bus in Fukuoka and Kyūshū differs from the experience in much of Japan, particularly the Tōkyō area. Board from the back door and take a numbered ticket. Exit from the front door. Your fare corresponds to the price shown below your ticket number on the front electronic board. If you don't have exact change, the money machine in the front can break a ¥500 coin or ¥1000 bill.

■ ORIENTATION

The sections of the city, roughly from west to east, are shopping/entertainment, nightlife, and business. The **Naka River**, with the island of Nakasu in the middle, flows through the center of the city, placing **Hakata Station** on the east and **Fukuoka-Tenjin Station** on the west. Nakasu used to harbor, and to some extent still does, the city's red light district. Two main streets run parallel to the river: **Watanabe-dōri** strikes through Fukuoka-Tenjin Station and **Taihaku-dōri** originates from Hakata Station and heads northwest. Parallel and west of Watanabe-dōri is a road that attracts most popular restaurants, cafes, and bars: the northern half is the infamous **Oyafukō-dōri** ("the street that creates unhappy parents"); the less-exciting southern half is called **Tenjin Nishi-dōri**. Three major roads run east-west to form a grid-like frame: from north to south, **Shōwa-dōri**, **Meiji-dōri**, and **Kokutai-dōri**. While the bus and subway systems are convenient, central Fukuoka is quite walkable. Hakata Station to Fukuoka-Tenjin Station takes approximately 30min. on foot.

■ PRACTICAL INFORMATION

Tourist Offices:

Fukuoka City Tourist Information (☎431-3003). Hakata Station at the center of the ground fl. Run by the Municipal Office, it stocks English maps and pamphlets, and has English-speaking staff who can answer most questions. Pick up *Fukuoka on Foot* for guidance on reasonable walks, and the *Fukuoka Welcome Card* booklet for discounts at tourist sites (free). Open 8am-8pm.

Cultural Information Center (☎725-9100). On the 2nd fl. of ACROS Fukuoka in Tenjin. A quiet setting with extensive information on Fukuoka and other prefectures in Kyūshū. Open 10am-7pm. Closed Dec.29-Jan.3, and the 2nd and 4th M of each month.

Rainbow Plaza, on the 8th fl. of the shopping mall IMS. Members can use the computer for Internet access, put up messages on the bulletin board, and borrow books and videos from the library. Open 10am-8pm. Closed Dec.29-Jan.3. Membership is free.

Tours: The **Goodwill Guide Club** (☎725-9100) answers inquiries in English and offers free tours (arrange at least 2 days in advance). Open daily noon-6pm.

Budget Travel: H.I.S. (☎282-8001). On the 1st fl. of Canal City. Cheap fares, especially for international travel. Open M-Tu and Th-Sa 10am-7pm, Su 10:30am-6pm. Another budget agency is **Joy Road** (☎431-6215), run by JR on the ground fl. of Hakata Station. Open M-F 10am-8pm, Sa-Su 10am-6pm.

Consulates: US Consulate (☎751-9331), 2-5-26, Ohori, Chūō-ku. Open M-F 9am-4pm.

Currency Exchange: Few banks at the airport offer currency exchange services. In town, **Joy Road** in Hakata Station (see above), the **Hakata Post Office** (outside Hakata Station; open M-F 9am-4pm), and **Fukuoka Bank** (across the street from Hakata Gate; open M-F 9am-3pm) can exchange traveler's checks and cash.

ATM: 24hr. **Citibank ATMs** are on the 1st fl. of the airport's International Terminal and in Tenjin across from Nishitetsu Grand Hotel; a **Mitsui-Sumitomo Visa Cash Machine** is on the 1st fl. of Centraza Hotel, outside the Chikushi Gate of Hakata Station (available 6am-midnight); and a **Kyūshū VISA Card** machine is on the 1st fl. of Canal City.

Work Opportunities: Rainbow Plaza (see above) has job postings on its bulletin board. The monthly publication *Fukuoka Now* also has a listing of jobs in English.

Emergency: Police ☎110. Fire or ambulance ☎119.

Pharmacy: Matsumoto Kiyoshi, in the basement of Canal City. Open daily 10am-9pm.

Medical Services: Fukuoka Medical Clinic, on the 7th fl. of Fukuoka Bldg. in Tenjin, provides general and specialized service in English, German, French, Dutch, Chinese, and Japanese. Open M-F 8:30am-1pm and 2:30-6pm, Sa 8:30am-1pm.

Internet Access: Rainbow Plaza (see above) offers 30min. of free Internet. **Kinko's** has 6 branches in Fukuoka, one 1min. down Taihaku-dōri from Hakata Station, and another in Tenjin on Kokutai-dōri. Internet ¥200 for 10min. Open 24hr. **Cybac** has a branch on

ON THE MENU

OODLES OF NOODLES

The making, eating, and hunting of *rāmen* dominates the culinary culture of Fukuoka, and the quality of Hakata *rāmen* (*tonkotsu*, or pig-bone broth, *rāmen*) wins national fame. One note: no self-respecting Japanese would pass through Fukuoka without partaking of the region's *rāmen*, so expect long lines during peak hours.

For starters, pay a visit to **Rāmen Stadium** on the fifth floor of Canal City. Eight restaurants greet you, each offering a distinct regional *rāmen*—two from Kyūshū, three from Honshū, and three from Hokkaidō. Ballots collected in the box at the center of the floor determine monthly which *rāmen* eaters prefer. *(Open daily 11am-11pm. Purchase a food ticket from the machine before entering the restaurants. No English signs or menus.)*

Perhaps the most famous Fukuoka-born *rāmen* chain restaurant, **Ichiran** was the first members-only noodle fix in Japan, due to its overwhelming popularity. Fortunately, you no longer need to be a member to eat there. Sample Ichiran's famous red pepper sauce soup in the basement of Canal City *(open daily 10am-1am)*, two floors underground in a building across from Hakata Station *(open daily 10am-10pm)*, or in Tenjin on a street parallel to and east of Watanabe-dōri. *(24hr. Wait in line to enter, then fill out a form indicating how you want your rāmen made. English form available.)*

Tenjin Nishi-dōri and another 1min. northwest of Tenjin Subway Station. E-mail from a massage chair, use PlayStation2, read comics, watch DVDs, exploit the all-you-can-drink machines, and try the "relaxation room," for ¥480 per hr. Membership ¥200 with ID, required to use facilities. Internet without membership ¥300 for 30min. Open 24hr.

Post Office: Main office at Watanabe-dōri and Shōwa-dōri in Tenjin. Smaller branch outside Hakata Station. Open M-F 9am-7pm, Sa 9am-5pm, Su 9am-12:30pm. **Postal Code:** 806.

▗ ACCOMMODATIONS

Low-priced and mid-range accommodations cluster in the area between Hakata Station and Canal City. The most comfortable and low-cost stay will be at one of the ryokan, most of which are very conveniently located. The city also has its share of capsule hotels; try **Well Be ❶** (☎291-1009; ¥3800, tiered single ¥2800) or **Hotel Cabinas ❶** (☎436-8800; ¥3800/¥2800).

▨ **Sumiyoshi Ryokan** (旅館壽美吉 ; ☎291-0451). About an 8min. walk from the Hakata Gate of Hakata Station. Go down Hakataekimae-dōri for a few minutes until you hit a 5-street intersection. Take the 2nd left, cross 1 street, hang the next left, and the ryokan is 100m down on the left. The 7 homey *tatami* rooms are well-maintained by Mr. and Mrs. Nakamura. They speak minimal English, but will make your stay enjoyable. Shared bath. Breakfast ¥500. Dinner ¥1500. Dorms ¥3000; singles ¥3500; doubles ¥7000. ❶

Kashima Honkan (鹿島本館 ; ☎291-0746). 2min. from Gion Subway Station. Follow Kokutai-dōri south, take the 1st right, and it's on your right, about 100m down the road (don't be confused by the Yamamoto Ryokan next door). Built more than 80 years ago by a famous Kyōto carpenter, the impressive edifice will fit your image of a traditional inn. 25 rooms range from cozy to spacious. Most include TV and fridge. English spoken. Breakfast ¥700. Dinner ¥2000. Dorms ¥3500; singles ¥4500; doubles ¥7600. ❷

Asahi Ryokan (朝日旅館 ; ☎524-1200). 15min. walk from Hakata Station. Go about 10min. down Sumiyoshi-dōri, cross the Naka River on Yanagi Bridge, turn left after the river, and it's 250m down on your right. A self-described "business ryokan," Asahi lacks the family-run feeling, but is cheaper than anything but capsule hotels. Basic English spoken. Dorms ¥2500; singles ¥3000, with bath ¥3500; doubles ¥5000-5500. ❶

Skycourt Hakata (HI) (スカイコート博多 ; ☎262-4400; hakata@skycourt.co.jp). A 2min. walk from Gion Subway Station. Take the 1st left on Kokutai-dōri, it's on the right about 50m down the road. 159 rooms serve mainly as a business hotel. Singles ¥4000-5000. HI members get a ¥1000 discount. ❷

⚑ FOOD

Rāmen is central to the culinary culture of Fukuoka. If you get tired of noodles, however, Fukuoka has much more to offer.

▨ **Tetsu Nabe** (☎ 291-0890), off Kokutai-dōri, across from Skycourt Hotel. The most popular *gyōza* (fried dumplings) restaurant in town. Fukuoka businessmen and women stop by after work to enjoy the sizzling *gyōza* (¥450 for 8 dumplings) and a glass of beer (¥450). Order 2 portions per person—they're small. Open daily 5pm-12:30am. ❷

Asian Cafe Ron-Dong, off Oyafukō-dōri. Offers varied East and Southeast Asian dishes, embodying continental Asian influence. Mellow lighting, bamboo decor, and laid-back music. English drink menu. *Dim sum* set ¥500. Fried chicken Thai-style ¥500. Guinness ¥500. *Lassi* ¥800. Open M-F 11:30am-11pm, Sa 3pm-midnight, Su 11:30am-5pm. ❶

J Cafe (☎ 741-6900). 3rd fl. of a building on Kokutai-dōri, close to Tenjin Station. Modernized Japanese teahouse twists the traditional. Sounds of running water echo and spacious couches invite you to sink in. No English menu. *Mattcha* (green tea) ¥550. *Mattcha* cappuccino ¥600. Cocktails and dinner served. Open daily 11:30am-2am. ❷

Marbre Blanc (☎ 724-7699). Tucked away off Kokutai-dōri around Tenjin Station. Flips the best crepes in Fukuoka, if not all of Japan. Menu offers both sweet and savory, but the dessert crepes are real hits. Butter, sugar, maple syrup ¥450. Blueberry, chocolate, *nama* (whipped) cream ¥450. Marbre Blanc special (strawberry, banana, vanilla ice cream, chocolate) ¥600. No English menu. Open daily noon-9pm. ❶

Karo no Uron (かろのうろん). 2min. walk north of Canal City, on a corner; look for a big brown wooden sign. After 100 years, Karo no Uron remains the most famous *udon* noodle place in town. The noodles are cooked *al dente*. No English sign or menu. *Kake* (ordinary) *udon* ¥330. *Tempura udon* ¥700. Open M and W-Su 10:30am-7pm. ❷

Comparable in reputation is **Ippudo,** whose original shop is in Tenjin, just off Tenjin Nishi-dōri. If your tastebuds aren't yet accustomed to Hakata *rāmen*, sample the lighter *romaru* (¥550). Get a *mentaiko gohan* (¥300) here, topped with Hakata's other specialty, raw spicy cod roe. *(Open daily 11am-2am. English menu.)*

A list of popular *rāmen* places in Hakata would reach dozens of pages, and, in fact, a whole genre of Japanese books covers the best of the best in each region. To conclude your brief overview of Hakata *rāmen*, however, you should taste the *rāmen* dished out by Fukuoka's more than 200 *yatai* (street food vendors).

To say these mobile mini-kitchens lie at the heart of Hakata food culture is not an overstatement. Their menus range from ordinary *rāmen* and *yakitori* (chicken skewers) to Italian cuisine, and they serve the locals long after the tourists have gone home. Each *yatai* is a community centered on the *taishō*—master chef—who warms both heart and stomach. The *taishā* may not speak English and the *yatai* won't have an English menu, but travelers will be welcomed (if stared at) by the locals. A few tips on entering the *yatai* world: respect social space among other customers, don't go in large groups, don't stay too long, and, although *yatai* food tends to be quite cheap (¥400-600 for a bowl of *rāmen*), find a *yatai* with prices on the menu to avoid potential problems.

◉ ⌐ SIGHTS AND SHOPPING

Fukuoka's sights are separated into convenient clusters; two full days are enough to see what central Fukuoka has to offer. Pick up a free *Fukuoka Welcome Card* at a tourist information offices, or purchase a one-day subway pass for small discounts on some entrance fees. *Fukuoka on Foot* is a useful guide.

■ **HAKATA MACHIYA FOLK MUSEUM (HAKATA MACHIYA FURUSATOKAN; 博多町屋ふるさと館).** Although most labels are in Japanese, this fascinating museum takes you back to the Hakata of 100 years ago. Exhibits reveal daily life for Taishō- and Meiji-period merchants. *(6-10, Reisen-machi, Hakata-ku. Across the street from Kushida Jinja. ☎ 281-5050. Open daily 10am-6pm. Closed at New Year. ¥200.)*

MOMOCHI AREA (百道). Fukuoka's new seaside development lines the Hakata Bay coastal area northwest of Tenjin/Hakata Station and is home to some of Fukuoka's biggest attractions. It's a 10-15min. walk north of Nishijin or Tō-jinchō Subway Station. At 234m, **Fukuoka Tower** offers a 360-degree view of the city and nearby sea from the 5th floor. The tower is easily recognizable by the 8000 half-mirrors covering the outside. *(Open Apr.-Sept. 9:30am-10pm; Oct.-Mar. 9:30am-9pm. ¥800, with discount card or subway pass ¥620.)* The **Hawks Town** entertainment complex, built by retail giant Daiei, includes a mall with a Hard Rock Cafe and the **Fukuoka Dome** (☎ 852-1006), home to the Fukuoka Daiei Hawks baseball team. At the **Fukuoka City Museum** (Fukuoka-shi Hakubutsukan; 福岡市博物館), exhibitions detail the history of the Fukuoka area, as well as the folk culture of Hakata. The Golden Seal (kinin; 金印) is on display here; now considered a national treasure, the seal is believed to have been sent by the Chinese East Han Emperor, authorizing the rule of the king of Japan. Most displays have English texts. *(1-1, Momochihama 3-chō, Sawara-ku. ☎ 845-5011; http://museum.city.fukuoka.jp. Open Tu-Su 9:30am-5:30pm. ¥200.)* Sticking out into the bay along a man-made beach, **Marizon** (マリゾン) has international restaurants and cafes, and is the departure point for ferries to **Uminonakamichi** (海の中道), a seaside urban-getaway. Marine World aquarium (マリンワールド) hosts dolphin shows and displays huge sharks, and **Seaside Park** boast the biggest swimming pool in Western Japan. *(Marine World open daily 9:30am-5:30pm. ¥2100. Seaside Park open daily 9:30am-5:30pm. ¥400.)*

ŌHORI PARK (ŌHORI KŌEN; 大濠公園). Joggers and strollers dot the 2km loop around the Chinese-themed artificial lake, built in 1929. Most sights lie to the southeast of the park. Take the subway to Ōhori Kōen Station, or walk 30min. up Keiyaki-dōri from Tenjin Station. Modest but worthwhile, the **Fukuoka City Art Museum** (Fukuoka-shi Bijutsukan; 福岡市美術館) houses works of Eastern and Western artists, including Miro, Chagall, Warhol, Aoki, and Sakamoto. *(1-6, Ōhori Kōen, Chūō-ku. A 10min. walk towards Tenjin from Ōhori Kōen Station. ☎ 714-6051. Open Tu-Su 9:30am-5:30pm, closed around New Year. ¥200.)* The collections at the **Fukuoka Asian Art Museum** (Fukuoka Asia Bijutsukan; 福岡アジア美術館) cover a wide range of modern Asian art. *(7th and 8th fl., River Site, Hakata Riverain, 3-1 Shimokawabata-machi, Hakata-ku. Take the subway to Nakasu Kawabata Station. ☎ 771-8600; http://faam.city.fukuoka.jp. Open Su-Tu and Th-Sa 10am-8pm, closed around New Year. ¥200.)* **Fukuoka Castle** (福岡城) was built in 1608 by feudal lord Kuroda Nagamasa, but only a gate and turret remain today. *(15min. walk from Ōhori Kōen Station.)*

CANAL CITY (キャナルシティ). Canal City is a super-mall filled with shops, restaurants, cinemas, and hotels. Street performances and symphony orchestras frequently enliven the central fountain plaza. Be sure to check out **Rāmen Stadium, UNIQLO,** a popular, cheap clothing store, and **Club Sega,** featuring the latest arcade games. *(Almost halfway between Hakata and Tenjin Stations. Shops open 10am-8pm; restaurants open 11am-10pm.)*

TENJIN AREA (天神). This is the information, fashion, and nightlife center of Kyūshū. Delicious restaurants, soon-to-be fashionable clothing stores, and countless bars stand above a web of underground shopping arcades. The amalgamation of neon and concrete fills the nooks between department store giants Solaria, Mitsukoshi, Iwataya, and IMS. At night, Fukuoka's mobile mini-kitchens—*yatai*—light up the streets with red lanterns illuminating their tempting concoctions.

KUSHIDA JINJA (櫛田神社). The geographical and spiritual center of Fukuoka, this shrine was built in AD 757 and reconstructed in 1587 by Toyotomi Hideyoshi, one of the unifiers of early modern Japan. Be sure not to miss the *kazariyama* (decorated floats), the focal point of the Hakata Gion Yamakasa Festival. *(1-41, Kamikawabata-machi, Hakata-ku. 10min. walk north of Hakata Station.* ☎ *291-2591.)*

TŌCHŌ-JI (東長寺) **AND SHŌFUKU-JI** (聖福寺). Tōchō-ji hosts the biggest wooden Buddha statue in Japan (10m), an impressive Important Cultural Asset. *(2-4, Gokusho-machi, Hakata-ku. Down the street from the Folk Museum.* ☎ *291-4459.)* Just behind it is the less striking **Shōfuku-ji**, Japan's first Zen temple. It was built in 1195 by order of Minamoto Yoritomo, the first shōgun. *(6-1, Gokuso-machi, Higashi-ku. Down the street from the Folk Museum.* ☎ *291-0755.)*

▐ NIGHTLIFE

A night out in Fukuoka could never bore you—Kyūshū people are infamous for their drinking culture. You'll find a good mixture of both *izakaya* and Western bars and clubs. Pick up the free publications *Fukuoka Now* and *Rainbow* at any tourist information office to find out about special events.

Q's. A 3min. walk north of Tenjin Station. The biggest and hippest club on the island, with a capacity of 1000. M black music; Th eclectic mix; F hip-hop, R&B, reggae; Sa trance, hard house; Su trance, *parapara* (Japanese techno). M and Th 8pm-1am, F-Sa 8pm-4am, Su 8pm-3am. Cover M and Th ¥1000, ladies free; F-Sa ¥2000; Su ¥1500.

Blue Note Fukuoka (☎ 715-6666). A 3min. walk from Tenjin Fukuoka Station. A branch of the prestigious New York jazz club. Live music includes blues and R&B. Multi-course French dinner ¥2800. Glass of wine ¥900. Cocktails ¥800. Cover charge depends on the guest musician; starts at ¥3000 and climbs to ¥8000. Open daily 6-11pm.

Happy Cock, a 5min. walk west of Tenjin Fukuoka Station. **Crazy Cock,** on Oyafukō-dōri, is run by the same owner. Despite the suggestive names, these are not gay bars. Crowded on weekdays and bursting on weekends with *gaijin* and Japanese 20-somethings. Relatively cheap drinks. Happy Cock open F-Sa 7:30pm-4am, Su and Tu-Th 7:30pm-2:30am. When a guest DJ spins, ¥1000 cover (includes 2 drinks) and ¥3000 all-you-can-drink. On all other nights, entrance is free. Crazy Cock open F-Sa 9pm-4am. Cover ¥1000. Su and Tu-Th 9pm-3am. No cover.

Fire Ball, a 3min. walk west of Tenjin Fukuoka Station, caters to sports fanatics and beer drinkers. Features a sporting event every night on a big screen TV. Hamburger ¥999. Beer ¥450. Gin and tonic ¥499. No cover charge. Open daily 6pm-midnight.

Mura Ichiban, off Tenjin Nishi-dōri; look for the big orange sign. One of the many popular *izakaya* in town. Cocktails ¥500. Open daily 5:30pm-5am.

▐ DAYTRIPS FROM FUKUOKA

DAZAIFU (大宰府)

Dazaifu can be reached on Nishitetsu Trains from Nishitetsu Fukuoka (Tenjin) Station. Take either the local train direct to Dazaifu or take an express train to Futsukaichi Station and transfer (20-40min., ¥390). A tourist info center in the station and another near the entrance to Dazaifu Tenmangū have English maps. Both are open 8:30am-5pm. To see all the sights including the ones in the west, rent a bicycle from the station (¥200 per hr.).

Dazaifu was the capital of Kyūshū for six centuries beginning in AD 664. The town, a popular daytrip, boasts historical buildings and archaeological sites. The biggest attraction, however, is **Dazaifu Tenmangū Shrine,** built in memory of Sugawara no Michizane, who received a posthumous promotion to God of Learning. Hundreds of students flock to the shrine before school entrance examinations in January and February. Legend claims that after Sugawara no Michizane died, a container of his ashes was pulled around town by a bull as a mourning ceremony. The shrine was erected at the point where the bull terminated his parade and commemorates both the god and the bull's eminence. The plum tree next to the worship hall supposedly grew in Michizane's garden in Kyōto before accusations of political conspiracy exiled him to Dazaifu. When he had to leave his home in Kyōto, a divine force is said to have uprooted the tree, flying it to his new home prior to his arrival. Take a right out from the station, follow the touristy road with many archways to its end, and take a left.

A sharp contrast from the tourist frenzy of Tenmangū, nearby **Kōmyōzen-ji** is a peaceful 13th-century shrine. Before the end of the road to Tenmangū, take a right, and it's 100m down the road. Images of Buddha adorn the interior walls, and two beautiful Zen rock gardens decorate the outside. (Open 8am-5pm. Free.) The **Site of Dazaifu Government Office,** an archaeological site, and **Kanzeon-ji,** once the most significant Buddhist temple in Kyūshū, lie one train stop or a bike ride to the west of Kōmyōzen-ji, but don't prioritize these sights if you're in a rush. Completed in AD 746, Kanzeon-ji houses 16 Buddha images, some of them reaching 4 or 5m in height, and a bronze Bonshō bell, which is designated a National Treasure. **Kaidanin,** next to Kanzeon-ji, was one of the only three official ordination halls in Japan during the Heian Period.

On the way back to Fukuoka, ancient **Futsukaichi Onsen** is a popular place to rest. The baths are a 15min. walk or a quick bus ride from Nishitetsu Futsukaichi Station. Take the bus from Terminal 2, get off at the third stop, and walk 1min. (¥100). The three baths, **Baden House** (¥460); **Gozenyu** (¥200); and **Hakatayu** (¥100), crowd around each other. Don't necessarily choose the cheapest—you get what you pay for.

YOSHINOGARI HISTORICAL PARK (吉野ヶ里歴史公園)

Reach Yoshinogari Historical Park from Yoshinogari Kōen Station. To get to Yoshinogari Kōen Station from Fukuoka/Hakata, take the JR Kagoshima Line to Tosu (l25min., ¥820). Change to the local JR Nagasaki Line toward Hizen Yamaguchi/Nagasaki. Yoshinogari Kōen Station is 3 stops away (12min.). A community hall at the foot of the North Exit stairs provides free maps and can take luggage for ¥200 (9am-6pm). The 15min. walk from the station is marked by red arrow signs. Park admission ¥400. Open 9am-5pm.

Yoshinogari Historical Park hurls visitors back to the period of the first large-scale settlements in Japan. The largest prehistoric archaeological site in Japan, Yoshinogari was excavated only 13 years ago. Workers accidentally stumbled upon this portal into the past while conducting a land survey for the construction of an industrial park. Since its discovery, the site has attracted swarms of tourists, and has incited intellectual debate as to whether this was the site of a powerful empire during the Yayoi Period (300 BC-AD 300). Today's buildings are reconstructions based on archaeological and architectural hypotheses. The park consists of three major zones: Moat Encircled Village Zone, Ancient Field Zone, and Ancient Forest Zone. The latter two are designed as parks for leisure use, while the former (spanning an area comparable to six Fukuoka Domes) is where all the archaeological findings have taken place.

TAKEO ONSEN (武雄温泉)   ☎0954

Takeo and Ureshino have been known as the *onsen* centers in western Kyūshū for over a thousand years, dating as far back as AD 713, when the spring water's medicinal effects were first recorded. The two towns, similar in size, offer comparable tourist facilities. Takeo lies en route from Fukuoka to Arita, and only slightly off the course from Fukuoka to Nagasaki. Ureshino, however, is a 30min. bus ride from Takeo. Dip into the rejuvenating waters of Takeo and then call it a night.

Takeo Onsen is on the JR Saseho Line between Hizen Yamaguchi and Arita. From Hizen Yamaguchi the trip takes less than 20min. (¥550), from Yoshinogari 40min. (¥1080). There is a **tourist info center** inside the train station. (Open 9am-

5:30pm. No English spoken.) If you decide to walk to the youth hostel (see below), the map is highly recommended. **Coin lockers** are also in the train station. In an emergency, call ☎ 110 for **police**, ☎ 119 for **fire** and **ambulance**.

To reach the **onsen**, go out the North Exit of the station, take a right at the second traffic light, and follow the road until you see a big Chinese gate, which is the entrance (15min. walk). Besides the private baths (more than ¥2000 per hr.), there are three communal baths ranging from decent to luxurious. The cheapest (¥300; open 6:30am-11:30pm), built over 100 years ago, has a traditional feel, while the ¥400 (open 6:30am-9pm) and ¥600 (open 9am-11pm) baths are more modern, with the latter having a sauna. The water will surely revitalize your tired body.

An ideal route would depart Fukuoka early in the morning, stop off in Yoshinogari (p. 592) for a few hours, and arrive in Takeo in the late afternoon for an *onsen* immersion and overnight stay. Complications can arise in Takeo as the last bus (¥240) from the station to **Takeo Onsen Youth Hostel (HI) ❶** leaves at 5:09pm. If you miss it, call the hostel to see if the manager can pick you up. Otherwise, it's a 30min. walk (3km) to the hostel, complete with its own heartbreak hill. (☎ 22-2490. Check-in by 10pm. ¥2600 per person.) Accommodations in the center of town are expensive. Grab a bite at **Gyōza Kaikan ❷**, a Chinese restaurant specializing in fried dumplings (¥350). Go out the North Exit of the station, take the first left, and a smiling *gyōza* mascot will greet you on the right. (Open 11am-8:45pm.)

ARITA (有田)   ☎ 0995

One of the three famous pottery towns in the area, Arita offers an education on Japanese ceramics and Japanese countryside air before you city-hop from Fukuoka down to Nagasaki. While the two other pottery towns—Imari and Karatsu—produce work as impressive and artistically significant as Arita does, they have fewer attractive sights. The people of Arita have specialized in the production of porcelain for nearly 400 years, a tradition evident in the dozens of kilns and stores that line both sides of the nearly modernization-free main street. Wandering through the old narrow back-alleys and peeping into the antique kilns will give you a hint to why the brand Arita-yaki has attained global recognition.

E TRANSPORTATION. From Fukuoka, a direct express **train** line runs to Arita (1½hr., ¥2500). If you do not have a JR pass, local trains are a cheaper option (2-2½hr., ¥1770). Take the JR Kagoshima Line to Tosu, change to a different JR train heading to Saseho, Nagasaki, or Hizen Yamaguchi, and get off at Hizen Yamaguchi. Arita can be reached by the JR Saseho Line from Hizen Yamaguchi. To reach Nagasaki, go via Hizen Yamaguchi or Haiki. The Hizen Yamaguchi route will be more reliable and easier to figure out. (1½hr.; ¥1600, additional express fare ¥1520). An express **bus** connects Fukuoka and Arita (2hr., ¥2000).

⚡️ ORIENTATION AND PRACTICAL INFORMATION. Two parallel streets are of interest to visitors: Rte. 35, which the locals call Baipasu (bypass), and the main road, Yakimono-dōri. The main road slopes uphill from the station to the east. Accommodations gather around Arita Station and most sights are on the main road or not too far from it. English signs are unusual, but townspeople will be happy to direct you. Find a **tourist office** inside the train station (open 9am-5pm) and **currency exchange** at Saga Bank on Fudanotsuji Intersection, on the main road (open M-F 9am-3pm). There are **no international ATMs**. In an emergency, call ☎ 110 for **police**, ☎ 119 for **fire** or **ambulance**. The **police** are on Rte. 35 at Akamatsubara Intersection. Other services include: **Baba Clinic**, a bit east of the station on the main road; **Erena**, a **pharmacy**, two traffic lights south of the station, inside the supermarket complex (marked by an elephant sign); **bicycle rental** at **Ōkura** (open

10am-6pm), 30m outside of the station, on the right; **luggage storage,** also at Ōkura (¥300 per bag per day; free with bike rental); and a **post office,** on the main road near Akaechō Intersection, another two blocks east of the station. **Postal code:** 844.

▐▌▐▌ ACCOMMODATIONS AND FOOD. Only six housing options exist in Arita, because Japanese prefer staying in the *onsen* towns nearby, namely Takeo Onsen and Ureshino. As you walk out of the station, turn right at the first traffic light. **Minshuku Yamada ❷** (☎42-2080) is 10m before the traffic light on your left. Though not much English is spoken here, there is a small communal space upstairs, each room has a TV, and the energetic owner, Okano-san, will take care of you. (¥4200 per person, with 2 meals ¥7000.) Around the corner, you'll find **Minshuku Arita ❷** (☎43-2521), run by Okano-san's relatives, with similar rooms, and a pottery painting studio upstairs. (¥3500 per person, with 2 meals ¥5500.) Some Japanese restaurants and the only *konbini* (convenience store) in town—**Family Mart**—are plunked among the pottery-guru centers of the main road. Two reasonably priced sushi joints dish out the raw stuff in this area—**Kamei Zushi ❸,** 200m before the Town Office on the right side (sushi lunch with *godōfu,* a specialty of Arita, ¥1000), and **Kibun Zushi ❸,** two doors up the road from Imaemon ceramic studio (sushi lunch ¥1000). A Chinese restaurant, **Shanghai Hanten ❷,** a 15min. walk from the station on Baipasu towards the west, next to a gas station, serves *yakimeshi* (fried rice; ¥580), *gyōza* (fried dumplings ¥400), *kara age* (fried chicken; ¥1050), and *rāmen* (¥500) in huge portions. (Open M-Sa 11am-11pm, Su 11am-9:30pm.)

◪ SIGHTS. To visit even some of the sights, you might want to respect your legs and rent a bicycle. A sightseeing route can take 2-7hr., depending on your interest. Start at the **Kyūshū Ceramics Museum,** straight out of the station, two traffic lights down. With English texts on most items, the museum briefs you on the history of pottery, as well as on Kyūshū's stoneware. (Open Tu-Su 9am-4:30pm. Free.) The next logical stop is **Izumiyama Jisekijō,** where the first kaolin clay was found in 1616. This mine triggered, fostered, and sustained Arita's production of porcelainware for nearly 400 years. Although mining was terminated several years ago, the site demonstrates man's capacity to flatten mountains and alter nature's terrain. Izumiyama Jisekijō is 3km eastward on the main road from the station; bear left at the Family Mart as you go up the hill. Beside the former mine, **Arita Folklore Museum** consists of worn-down Japanese displays, and may be difficult for non-Japanese speakers to navigate. (Open daily 9am-4:30pm. ¥100, students ¥50.) Soon after the tree, take the first left and then another left to reach **Rokuroza,** where you can make your own pottery. (Open Su-W and F-Sa 9am-3pm. ¥1300-3900.) Continue down the main road until you hit Aritachō Kamikohira Intersection, where you should take a right. This back alley is called **Tonbai Hei,** deriving its name from the unique bricks that compose the wall, material which comes from the pottery kilns. Following down this back-alley, then hanging a right at the end of it, you will arrive at **Arita Ceramics Museum.** The displays here are not as impressive as at the Kyūshū Ceramics Museum, but a quick look will only take 10-15min. (Open Tu-Su 9am-4pm. ¥100, students ¥50.) Get back on the main road, proceed downhill, and immediately you will hit "Fudanotsuji Intersection." At the northeast corner of this intersection is **▩Aritakan,** where the world's only porcelain robot show takes place (shows 10am-4pm; ¥200). On the second floor, there's a coffee lounge where for just ¥100 you can pick your favorite porcelain cup from over 100 choices and drink coffee from it. (Open Su-M and W-Sa 9:30am-5pm.)

Fukagawa Museum and Shop lies 50m north of Fudanotsuji Intersection. Because the prices of Fukagawa products tend to be lower than those of other famous brands, this is a good place to purchase gifts. The founder of the Fukagawa ceramics brand initiated the first **Arita Annual Pottery Market** in 1903. Every year from

April 29 to May 5, hundreds of ceramic stalls line the main road. Across the main road, on the south side, you'll find **Tōzan Shrine,** known for its porcelain shrine archway. To the east of the shrine, on top of the hill, a monument is built for Lee Sampei, a Korean potter who was brought to Japan in 1598 and is considered the father of Arita-yaki. Returning towards the station, **Imaemon Kiln** is on the right. A few minutes down the road across from the post office, **Akaeza Studio** lets you paint on porcelain cups and plates for ¥1000. (Open Su-M and W-Sa 9:30am-4pm.)

Arita Porcelain Park, 4km south of the station, is shaped like a German palace and includes a museum, European garden, beer factory, restaurant, and kiln. (Open Su-M and W-Sa Mar.-Nov. 9am-5pm; Dec.-Feb. 10am-5pm. ¥1000.) Two kilometers southwest of the station are two renowned *kokuhō* potters, Kakiemon and Inoue Manji. After training your eyes for the day, you'll be able to appreciate the fine pieces—and prices—by these porcelain giants. (Both open daily 9am-5pm.)

GOTŌ ISLANDS (五島列島)

Seventy kilometers west of Nagasaki, the Gotō Islands speckle the waters of the East China Sea. Although the name means "Five Islands," there are actually around 1000 islands in the archipelago. The biggest and most popular is Fukue-jima, once a critical player in the Sino-Japanese trade. It's infested with tourists in the summer, but a day and night on Fukue-jima, among breathtaking cliff views and the best of Japan's beaches, is a pleasant get-away.

FUKUE-JIMA (福江島)   ☎0509

Although scenic viewpoints and beaches are bountiful on Fukue-jima, make sure to visit the beauties **Takahama Beach** and **Ōsezaki Cliff** before leaving. Cobalt waters tease the natural white sand on Takahama, a 45min. drive along the western coast from the village of Fukue. A couple of food stalls and cafes open during peak seasons. Ten kilometers south of Takahama, at the southwestern corner of the island, Ōsezaki Cliff looms over the East China Sea. The white lighthouse at the tip of the peninsula emits the brightest light in Japan, and each evening, Ōsezaki Cliff sees one of the latest sunsets in Japan. **Dōzaki Tenshudō** (open daily 9am-4pm; ¥300) at the northeastern corner of the island, was the first cathedral built in Fukue after the ban on Christianity was lifted in the 1870s. The Gothic building, made partly from Italian stone, houses documents and items about the *kakure kirishitan.* **Fukue-jō** (福江城), in the center of Fukue town, was the last castle built in the Edo Period and the only one equipped for defense against a sea attack. After a tour of the island, there's nothing quite like relaxing in a *rotemburo* (outside bath) at **Conkana Kingdom,** a 10min. drive from Fukue town. The "kingdom" is a resort complex of cottages, tennis courts, even restaurants, and a church. The spa is open to the public (open 7am-11pm; ¥500). Don't be alarmed if the bathwater looks filthy—high levels of iron give it a brown color.

Oriental Air Bridge (☎0120-848-909) flies to **Nagasaki** (30min., 3 per day, ¥10,000). A high-speed **jetfoil** runs to Fukue from **Nagasaki** (1hr., 3 per day, ¥6080) as does a slower **ferry** (4hr., 4 per day, ¥2400). The **tourist office** is in the ferry terminal. **Buses** tend to be expensive and inconvenient to tourist sights. Across from the ferry terminal, **Ikeda Rent-a-Car** (☎74-1133), under the green sign, has **scooters** (¥3000 per day) and small **cars** (¥5800 per day). There are only a few gas stations on the island (and some close on Sundays), so don't wait until the last minute to fill up. In an emergency, call ☎110 for **police,** ☎119 for **fire** or **ambulance.**

There are two budget places to stay on the island, an inn in the town of Fukue and a youth hostel 25km away. Small but clean **Tabi no Yado ❶** is a 7min. walk from the ferry terminal; take a right in front of the terminal, then the second left after the light, and it will be on the left, 50m down the road. (☎74-5641. Singles ¥3000; doubles ¥5000.) **Gotō Hiiraku Sunset Youth Hostel (HI) ❶** is on the other side of the island from Fukue; take a Hiiraku-bound bus from Fukue, get off at Hiiraku Chū-gakkō Stop (1hr.), and walk 20min. (☎84-3151. Closed Jan. 15-Feb. 28, May 15-June 30, Oct. 1-Dec. 28. ¥2700 per person.) There are a few restaurants, including *rāmen* shops, in downtown Fukue around the shopping streets. Also on the shopping arcade, **Hokka Hokka Tei ❶** (open 24hr.) serves cheap, quick takeout meals. Find a convenience store at the northwestern corner of the former Fukue-jō site.

NAGASAKI (長崎)   ☎095

In the morning and late afternoon, businessmen pack tiny trams built more than half a century ago. In the Yamate District, Western-style houses preserve an 18th-century colonial atmosphere. Defying Japan's secular habits, Christians in Nagasaki regularly attend church, a tradition of missionary days. The humble yet vivacious Chinatown sustains a Chinese presence that implanted itself centuries ago. Although the cataclysm of an A-bomb in 1945 annihilated many tangible markers of Nagasaki's textured history, the city refuses to forfeit its distinct roots, insisting that a physical and psychological shadow not cloud the air indefinitely. Owing to a conscious effort by Nagasaki's residents, the city has healed its wounds by encasing both its erased history as the only port in Japan to have traded with the outside world between 1639 and 1857, and its past as the last city in the world to be struck by an atomic bomb. From the dust and ashes of misdirected technology, Nagasaki has emerged stronger, as an exotic, international city.

> **ON THE WEB**   Nagasaki City: www1.city.nagasaki.nagasaki.jp/index.html

✈ INTERCITY TRANSPORTATION

Flights: The **Nagasaki Airport** is about a 1hr. bus ride from central Nagasaki. Buses shuttle between the airport and Ken'ei Bus Terminal, across from JR Nagasaki Station (4 per hr., ¥800). Flights to: **Nagoya** (4 per day, ¥20,000-24,300); **Ōsaka** (3 per day, ¥13,500-19,400); **Tōkyō Haneda** (12 per day, ¥23,500-29,700). Book flights through **JAL** (☎0120-255-971) or **ANA** (☎0120-029-222). **Oriental Air Bridge** (☎0120-848-909) flies to **Fukue** (3 per day, ¥10,000) and **Kamigotō** (2 per day, ¥7070).

Trains: JR trains run to: **Arita** (1½hr.; local ¥1500, express ¥3120); **Hakata** (2hr., ¥2730/¥4410); **Kumamoto** (2½hr., ¥3880/¥6170); **Nishi-Kagoshima** (5hr., ¥7040/¥10,300); **Saga** (1½hr., ¥2070/¥3440); **Shimabara City** (1½hr.; ¥1780/¥2080; change from JR to Shimabara Tetsudō at Isahaya Station).

Buses: To: **Fukuoka** (2½hr., ¥2500); **Karatsu** (4hr., ¥2400); **Kumamoto** (3hr., ¥3600), **Ōita** (4hr., ¥4500); **Ōsaka** (10hr., 9pm, ¥11,000); **Unzen** (2hr., ¥1900).

Ferries: Jetfoils and **ferries** depart from **Ōhato Port Terminal**, 500m south of Nagasaki Station. To: **Fukue** (jetfoil 1½hr., ¥6080; ferry 4hr., ¥2040); **Kamigotō** (ferry 1½hr., ¥5600); **Io-jima/Takashima** (Io-jima 30min., ¥600; Takashima 45min., ¥910); **Kagoshima** (4hr., 1 per day at 10am, ¥6500). 2 companies operate cruises around the Nagasaki Port, departing from Ōhata Port Terminal. **Marbella** offers a Harbor Cruise (1hr., ¥1200; available year-round); a Gunkanjima/Battleship Island Cruise (100min., ¥2980; available Mar.-Oct.); and a Sunset Cruise (1hr., ¥1500; July 20-Sept. 30). **Jelly Fish** operates 1 cruise (1hr. or 1¾hr., ¥1200/¥1600; Mar. 16-Nov. 30).

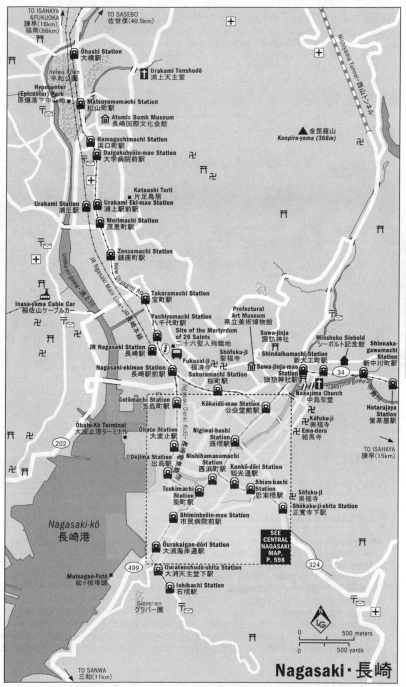

KYŪSHŪ

TO ISAHAYA
&FUKUOKA
諫早(16km),
福岡(86km)

TO SASEBO
佐世保(40.5km)

Nishiyama Tunnel 西山トンネル

Ōhashi Station
大橋駅

Urakami Tenshudō
浦上天主堂

Heiwa Kōen
平和公園

Hypocenter
(Epicenter) Park
原爆落下中心地

Matsuyamamachi Station
松山町駅

Atomic Bomb Museum
長崎国際文化会館

金毘羅山
Konpira-yama (366m)

Hamaguchimachi Station
浜口町駅

Daigakubyōin-mae Station
大学病院前駅

Kataashi Torii
片足鳥居

Urakami Station
浦上駅

Urakami Eki-mae Station
浦上駅前駅

Morimachi Station
茂里町駅

JR Nagasaki Main Line/JR 長崎本線

New Urakami Rd

Urakami-gawa 浦上川

Zenzamachi Station
銭座町駅

Inasa-yama Cable Car
稲佐山ケーブルカー

Takaramachi Station
宝町駅

Yachiyomachi Station
八千代町駅

Prefectural
Art Museum
県立美術館博物館

Suwa-jinja
諏訪神社

Minshuku Siebold
シーボルト記念館

Shinnaka-
gawamachi
Station
新中川町駅

Site of the Martyrdom
of 26 Saints
二十六聖人殉職地

Shōfuku-ji
聖福寺

Shindaikumachi Station
新大工町駅

JR Nagasaki Station
長崎駅

Fukusai-ji
福済寺

Suwa-jinja-mae
Station
諏訪神社前駅

Nagasaki-ekimae Station
長崎駅前駅

Sakuramachi Station
桜町駅

Nagasaki Denki Kidō 長崎電気軌道

Nakajima-gawa 中島川

Nakajima Church
中島聖堂

Hotarujaya
Station
蛍茶屋駅

Gotōmachi Station
五島町駅

Kōkaidō-mae Station
公会堂前駅

Kōfuku-ji
興福寺

Ema-dera
絵馬寺

Ōhato-Kō Terminal
大波止港ターミナル

Ōhato Station
大波止駅

Nigiwai-bashi
Station
賑橋駅

TO ISAHAYA
諫早(15km)

Dejima Station
出島駅

Nishihamanomachi
Station
西浜町駅

Kankō-dōri Station
観光通駅

Tsukimachi
Station
築町駅

Shian-bashi
Station
思案橋駅

Sōfuku-ji
崇福寺

Shōkaku-ji-shita Station
正覚寺下駅

Nagasaki-kō
長崎港

Shiminbyōin-mae Station
市民病院前駅

SEE
CENTRAL
NAGASAKI
MAP,
P. 598

Ōurakaigan-dōri Station
大浦海岸通駅

Matsugae-Futō
松ヶ枝埠頭

Ōuratenshudo-shita Station
大浦天主堂下駅

Ishibashi Station
石橋駅

Glover-en
グラバー園

N

0 — 500 meters
0 — 500 yards

TO SANWA
三和(11km)

Nagasaki・長崎

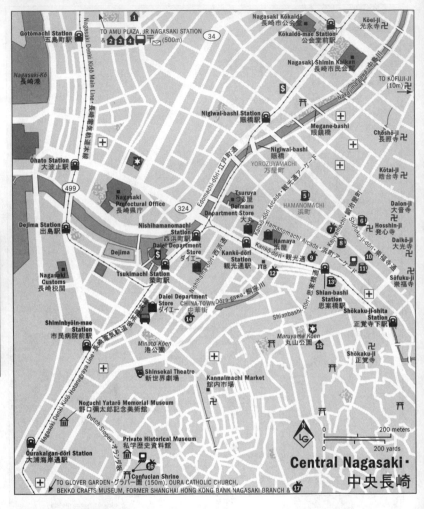

Central Nagasaki・
中央長崎

LOCAL TRANSPORTATION

Tram: A tourist attraction for its antiquity, the tram system covers most of the sights. There are four routes (#1, 3, 4, 5) and 51 stations, numbered 1 to 51. The map at each station is in English. Line #1 goes through the Urakami area—where the Atomic Bomb Museum and Peace Park are located—Nagasaki Station, Tsuki-machi, and Shian-bashi. Standard fare ¥100, daypass ¥500. Pass can be purchased at accommodation facilities and tourist information centers. Operates 6:15am-11:25pm.

Bus: The tram is much easier, but a bus might be necessary to board the ropeway to the peak of Inasayama; from Nagasaki Station take route #3 or 4 and get off at Ropeway-mae (¥150). An orange community bus makes a loop around Nagasaki Station, Chinatown, Shian-bashi, and Kōzen-ji. ¥100, one-day pass ¥300. Operates 10am-7pm.

Central Nagasaki
·中央長崎

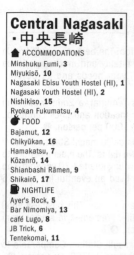

▲ ACCOMMODATIONS
Minshuku Fumi, **3**
Miyukisō, **10**
Nagasaki Ebisu Youth Hostel (HI), **1**
Nagasaki Youth Hostel (HI), **2**
Nishikiso, **15**
Ryokan Fukumatsu, **4**
🍴 FOOD
Bajamut, **12**
Chikyūkan, **16**
Hamakatsu, **7**
Kōzanrō, **14**
Shianbashi Rāmen, **9**
Shikairō, **17**
🌃 NIGHTLIFE
Ayer's Rock, **5**
Bar Nimomiya, **13**
café Lugo, **8**
JB Trick, **6**
Tentekomai, **11**

Ropeway: A ropeway runs from the bottom of Inasayama (Fuchi Jinja Station) to the mountain's peak, where there is a splendid panoramic view of the city. Operates Mar.-Nov. 9am-10pm; Dec.-Feb. 9am-9pm. Round-trip ¥1200. To get to Fuchi Jinja Station, take the bus (see above), or walk 1km from the Takara-machi Tram Stop. Another ropeway, **Skyway,** runs from the mid-point of the mountain to the top. Round-trip ¥500. Operates Mar.-Nov. 10am-10pm; Dec.-Feb. 10am-9pm.

⚡ 🔁 ORIENTATION AND PRACTICAL INFORMATION

Nagasaki is tucked on and between hills. Central Nagasaki can be split into three areas—**Urakami** in the north, **Yamate** in the south, and the **downtown area** around Nagasaki Station sandwiched between the two. **New Urakami Road,** which runs in front of Nagasaki Station, follows **Nagasaki Bay** and the **Urakami River,** connecting all three areas. The downtown area between Urakami and Yamate was the center of the old city and encases the narrow **Nakajima River.** The small **Chinatown** is in the Shinchi district at the edge of the old city area bordering Yamate.

Tourist Information: The **Nagasaki City Tourist Information Center** in the station provides maps, but has no English speakers. The **Prefectural Tourist Information Center,** across the road on the 2nd fl. of the bus terminal, stocks a pamphlets in abundance and responds to inquiries in English. **Chikyūkan** is a center for cultural exchange with Internet is available (see below) and a different international cuisine daily (see **Food**).

Travel Agency: Joy Road, Nagasaki Station (☎822-4813). Open M-F 10am-7pm, Sa-Su 10am-5:30pm. **JTB** (☎824-5159) is on Kankō-dōri near Shian-bashi. Open daily 10:30am-6:30pm.

Currency Exchange: Cash and traveler's checks can be exchanged at most banks (most open M-F 9am-3pm) downtown, and also at the Central Post Office (open M-F 9am-6pm). There are 2 **international ATMs. Saison Cash Dispenser** is on the 2nd fl. of Amu Plaza, next to the restaurant Royal Host. Open daily 7am-midnight. The other is on the left in the Central Post Office. Available M-F 7am-11pm, Sa 9am-9pm, Su 9am-7pm.

English-Language Bookstore: A bookstore on the 3rd floor of Amu Plaza, next to Nagasaki Station, has a small section of English books. Open daily 10am-9pm.

Emergency: Police ☎110. Fire and ambulance ☎119.

Pharmacy: On the 1st fl. of Amu Plaza. Open daily 10am-9pm.

Medical Services: Daigaku Byōin, a 5min. walk from Daigaku Byōin-mae Tram Stop, has extensive services, but minimal English-speaking staff.

Internet Access: Kinko's is on the 1st fl. of Amu Plaza. Open 24hr. ¥200 per 10 min. **Cybac,** near Shian-bashi Tram Stop. Open 24hr. 1st hr. ¥480, additional 15min. ¥90, members ¥200 per hr. with ID. **Chikyūkan,** near Dutch Slopes. 1st 5min. free, 1 drink for up to 30min., over 30min ¥100 per 10min.

Post Office: The Central Post Office is a 2min. walk from Nagasaki Station. Open M-Sa 9am-5pm, Su 9am-12:30pm. **Postal Code:** 850.

KYŪSHŪ

▐ ACCOMMODATIONS

Nishikiso (☎826-6371). 5min. from Shian-bashi Tram Stop. The best stay you'll find in all of Kyūshū. A quality Japanese inn with superb hospitality and much experience accommodating foreigners. Their service will meet all your needs and go beyond. ¥4000 per person, with bath ¥4500. ❷

Minshuku Fumi (☎822-4962). Behind the Ken'ei Bus Terminal, a 2min. walk from Nagasaki Station. Although the building is not new, its location and price cannot be matched. Warm-hearted owners. Communal bathroom. ¥3000 per person. ❶

Minshuku Siebold (☎822-5623). A 2min. walk from Shindaiku-machi Station on tram #3; take the 1st left off the tram, then bang 2 consecutive rights. The main incentive to stay here is the owner, Mr. Ueda, an English-speaking, young-hearted 70-year-old who experienced the 1945 disaster as a teenager and has lived an eventful life since. 5 rooms. Breakfast included. ¥3500 per person. ❷

Miyukisō (☎821-3487). 4min. walk from Shian-bashi Tram Station. This business hotel has 24 rooms. Plopped in the apex of Nagasaki nightlife. Western-style singles from ¥3500 per person; *tatami* singles from ¥4000 per person. ❷

Ryokan Fukumatsu (☎823-3769). 3min. walk from Nagasaki Station. Comparable to Minshuku Fumi. Minimal English spoken. Communal bathroom. ¥3500 per person. ❷

Nagasaki Youth Hostel (HI), 1-1-16, Tateyama (☎823-5032). 12min. walk from Nagasaki Station. The biggest and most popular of the 3 youth hostels in Nagasaki. As of Jan. 2003, it planned on temporarily closing April 2003. Call ahead to confirm it has re-opened. Washer and dryer available. Self-serve kitchen and table tennis. Check-in 3-10pm. Check-out 7-10am. ¥2800, elementary and junior high students ¥2500. ❶

Nagasaki Ebisu Youth Hostel (HI), 6-10, Ebisu-machi (☎824-3823). 5min. walk from Nagasaki Station. The owners run a tight ship. Breakfast ¥500. Dinner ¥1000. Dorms ¥2800 per person. ❶

▐ FOOD

Just as Fukuoka worships its *tonkotsu rāmen*, Nagasaki bows down to its own famous noodle dish—*chanpon*. Invented by Chen Heijun, a Chinese immigrant who was motivated by nostalgia for home food and by a yearning for more filling plates, the dish was born and raised in Nagasaki as a healthy and cheap alternative for Chinese students. *Chanpon* combines a mosaic of ingredients, including pork, chicken, squid, shrimp, oyster, cabbage, and bean sprouts.

Shikairō. At the bottom of Glover Garden. Although Shikairō moved from its original location to this building in 2000, this is the restaurant that introduced Nagasaki to *chanpon* in 1899. Taste and healthiness have remained the same, but inflation has raised prices: *chanpon* ¥950, spring rolls ¥300, *gyōza* (dumplings) ¥450. ❸

Kōzanrō. Situated by the north gate of Chinatown. Ranked the best *chanpon* restaurant in the area. Housed in 2 buildings, right across the road from each other. English menu available. *Chanpon* ¥700. Fried rice ¥600. *Gyōza* ¥500. ❷

Shianbashi Rāmen. Kankō-dōri. Serves a more Japanese-style *chanpon*. Popular among students and late-night eaters. *Chanpon* ¥650. *Rāmen* ¥480. Open 11:30am-4am. ❷

Hamakatsu. Kaji-ichi-dōri. Delicious *tonkatsu* (pork cutlet) with all-you-can-eat rice, *miso* soup, and cabbage. If the ordinary Japanese portion has left you starved, seize this opportunity to load up on carbohydrates. Japanese menu with pictures. Lunch menu around ¥1000. Dinner from ¥1400. Open daily 11am-10:30pm. ❸

Tentekomai. On the south side of Kankō-dōri. Serves *okonomiyaki* (pancake with meat and vegetables). If you sit at the counter, you can watch them being made in front of you. No English menu. They'll ask whether you want your pancake with *kyabetsu* (cabbage) or *negi* (scallions). *Buta* (pork) or *ika* (squid) *okonomiyaki* ¥600, *modan-yaki* (*okonomiyaki* with noodles) ¥750, *buta* or *ika yakisoba* (fried noodles) ¥700. Beer ¥500. Open Su-Th 5:30-11:30pm, F-Sa 5:30pm-3am. ❷

Chikyūkan (☎822-7966; www.h3.dion.ne.jp/~chikyu). Behind Confucian Shrine. Different international lunch daily. The chosen country might be Madagascar, Norway, Cambodia, or another to-be-determined place. Only 20 portions prepared. Check the website for the menu. Lunch ¥750. Open Su-Tu and Th-Sa noon 'til the food's gone. ❷

🔷 SIGHTS

Aside from **Inasayama,** which offers a grand view of the city, Nagasaki's sights can be grouped into three districts: **Urakami,** where the Peace Park and Atomic Bomb Museum are located; **Yamate,** the former foreign residential area; and the **downtown area** with miscellaneous sights. Two days should be sufficient to visit all three areas. In general, both the street signs for sights and the texts explaining displays are translated into English. A one-day passport to seven major sights is ¥1500; the package includes a one-day tram pass and is available at any of the seven sights.

URAKAMI. The Nagasaki Atomic Bomb Museum, Peace Statue, and Atomic Bomb Hypocenter all converge on one area of Urakami. Matsuyama-machi Tram Stop is the closest station. Walking from the tram station, you will first arrive at the **Hypocenter Park,** where a black triangular tower points to a space 500m above ground—the exact spot where the atomic bomb exploded at 11:02am on Aug. 9, 1945. The park also includes a display of the ground after the explosion, a surviving piece of Urakami Cathedral, and a statue with a time-stamp of 1945.08.09. Just up the stairs from the park, the **Nagasaki Atomic Bomb Museum** documents horrifying realities of the aftermath of the explosion, heart-wrenching stories from survivors, and the depressing current global situation of nuclear weapons. *(Open 8:30am-5:30pm. ¥200.)* On the second floor of the building, there's the less emotionally-charged and less impressive **Nagasaki City Museum** exhibiting the culture and history of the city—if time is a factor, you could skip it. *(Open 9am-5pm. ¥100.)* Up the hill, the 10m bronze **Peace Statue** rests solemnly with its right hand pointing to the sky (to symbolize the threat of nuclear bombs), left arm parallel to the ground (to wish for eternal world peace), and eyes half-closed (to express consolation for the victims of the bomb). Not totally irrelevant to the area's theme, **Urakami Cathedral** stands at the foot of the hills behind the Peace Statue. Symbolizing the strong Catholic spirit in Nagasaki, the cathedral was begun in 1873 by believers who had been deprived of freedom of faith for over 200 years. The cathedral was decimated by the atomic bomb, but was reconstructed in 1959. The last tourist site of interest in the Urakami area is **Sanno Shintō Shrine,** south of the Hypocenter, where an archway stands on one leg after the bomb blew away the other half. Although the remaining half miraculously stood on its own for some years, it has now been reinforced.

YAMATE AREA. After the country opened up in the latter half of the 19th and beginning of the 20th centuries, the Yamate area in the south end of Tram 5 was the foreigners' residential area. A 15min. walk from Ōra Tenshudō Shita Tram Stop, **Glover Garden,** which preserves a few 19th-century buildings, attracts Japanese tourists for its display of colonial, luxurious lifestyle. Although the garden may not trigger tremendous interest for international travelers, it provides a space to stroll while enjoying pleasant views of the harbor. *(Open daily 8am-6pm, in summer until 9:30pm. ¥600.)* In addition to Glover Garden, the Yamate area contains **Ōra Cathedral.** Designated a national treasure, it was built by French missionaries in 1865 and is now the oldest standing Gothic church in Japan. If you want to milk the one-day passport for everything, check out the **Former Hong Kong Shanghai Bank, Nagasaki Branch,** and **Bekko Crafts Museum.** Both museums lie on the waterfront road. The former bank captures the history of Sino-Japanese trade, in partic-

KYŪSHŪ

IN RECENT NEWS

GHOST TOWN IN THE BAY

The island of Hashima, located 18km off Nagasaki Bay, is known to only a fraction of Japanese. Soon, however, the island may become a tourist attraction, if chosen as a World Heritage Site. Gunkanjima got its nickname when during WWII, a US ship mistook it for a battleship and fired; the island's mines looked to the Americans like a military installation.

Coal had been the lifeblood of Hashima since the early 20th century, when the Japanese government forced many Korean and Chinese workers to mine coal here. After WWII, as demand for coal soared, the Hashima mines reached their peak under the management of Mitsubishi. In the '60s and early '70s, the island, smaller than three track fields, was the most densely populated area in Japan, and the entire population was involved in coal mining. In the '70s, the government switched to oil, and in 1974 the mine shut down. Sad story, but why is Hashima so special?

Given a luggage limit and a 3-month window in which to evacuate after the mine closed down, the harried inhabitants left behind many belongings. Thirty years since their hasty departure, it's as if people still live there. Old-fashioned items lie in the street, and a battered old shrine sits untended above the town. In the summer, a boat ferries tourists out to the island for a glimpse of a time now passed.

ular between Shanghai and Nagasaki, while the Bekko museum displays beautiful, yet inhumane, tortoise shell crafts. *(Both open 9am-5pm. ¥100 each.)* Walk on Ōra Kaigan-dōri towards the station and take a right before Shiminbyōin-mae Tram Stop to reach the **Dutch Slope.** The name stems from the period when the Japanese referred to all the foreigners in the area as "Hollanders." The **Confucian Shrine** is at the end of the slope as it loops back towards the bay. This religious piece of architecture, completed in 1893, is the only overseas Confucian shrine built by Chinese hands. *(Open 9am-5pm. ¥525.)* The **Chinese Historical Museum** behind the shrine holds artifacts provided by the Chinese government. *(Open 9am-5pm. ¥525.)*

DOWNTOWN. Tracing a clockwise circle from downtown Nagasaki Station, begin with the **Site of the Martyrdom of 26 Saints,** which commemorates Christians crucified in 1597 during the government's prohibition of Christianity. **Suwa Jinja,** by the Suwa Jinja-mae Tram Stop, is the spiritual center for many Nagasaki residents. Up the 193 steps, the shrine has English versions of *omikuji* (written oracles), for ¥200. To the south, the smile-inducing **Megane-bashi** ("Spectacles Bridge") arches over Nakashima-gawa. When the water of the river is high enough, the image reflected in the water paired with the bridge's double humps produces an illusion of spectacles. Besides this gimmick, the bridge draws fame as the first stone bridge with arches constructed in Japan, built in 1634 by a Chinese Buddhist monk. Two historic temples lie near the bridge. **Kōfuku-ji,** built in 1620 by a Chinese monk, is the oldest Chinese Tang Dynasty-style temple in Nagasaki. *(Open 8am-5pm. ¥200.)* **Sōfuku-ji** overshadows the significance of Kōfuku-ji with its national-treasure gates and main hall. *(Open 8am-5pm. ¥300.)* At the end of this downtown tour is **Dejima,** an artificial island built to isolate the Portuguese when xenophobia struck Japan in the early 17th century. The man-made construct has left its impression on Japanese history for its later role, however, as the only Japanese port open for overseas trade from mid-17th to mid-19th century. Although its humble size begs little respect, Dejima played a crucial role in the late 19th century's modernization and development. *(Open 9am-5pm. ¥300.)*

INASAYAMA. If the above three areas capture the historical influences of religious China, international trade, and the atomic bomb on Nagasaki, then Inasayama's sweeping view of the city highlights today's Nagasaki—proffering an aerial view of what it has developed into from its layered background. The twilight scene from the top of Inasayama is referred to as "the 10 million dollar view," coined in direct competition with Manhattan's "million dollar view." Hop on a ropeway at night to see the glittering lights of Nagasaki (see **Local Transportation**).

🎤 NIGHTLIFE

Nagasaki's entertainment district has traditionally been the Maruyama area, near Shian-bashi, where *geisha* softly pattered to work every night. The tradition has continued *sans geisha:* nightlife is concentrated on both sides of Kankō-dōri near Shian-bashi Tram Stop. If you're looking for clubs to dance the night away, hit **Ayer's Rock** or **Bajamut** (cover charge varies) in the Kajimachi district. They regularly invite house/hip-hop DJs from Tōkyō, Ōsaka, and Fukuoka, as well as from overseas. **JB Trick**, on the same street as Ayer's Rock, is a chill, soul-music bar that plays from a collection of over 3000 LPs, CDs, and DVDs. (Cafe open 3-7pm, bar open 7pm-3am. Beers and cocktails ¥500.) In the same district, **Café Lugo** is the café/bar/club that's been receiving swarms of partiers lately. The third Saturday of every month is a jazz/house club night. (Coffee ¥400. Cocktails ¥800. Light meal ¥1000. Open Su-Th 3pm-midnight, F-Sa 3pm-3am.) **Bar Ninomiya**, on the other side of Kankō-dōri, caters a dining and bar experience. Both traditional food and Western cocktails are served. (Beer ¥600. Dishes ¥1000. Open daily 6pm-midnight.)

SHIMABARA-HANTŌ (島原半島)

UNZEN (雲仙)　　　☎0957

If you step off the bus and smell rotten eggs and see white smoke rising everywhere, you know you're in Unzen. Home to Japan's first national park, Unzen is an *onsen* village fuming with sulphurous vapor. The eruption of Unzen Fugen-dake (雲仙普賢岳) in 1991 caused tremendous damage, but at 800m above sea level, the area has historically been a popular place to escape Kyūshū's summer heat. The astounding views on the hike around Fugen-dake and *jigoku meguri* (tour of hell) make Unzen worth a daytrip from Nagasaki.

🚍 TRANSPORTATION AND PRACTICAL INFORMATION. Reach Unzen by **bus** from **Fukuoka** (3hr., ¥2900), **Nagasaki** (2hr., ¥1900), or **Shimabara Port** (30min., ¥730). Buses run to **Nita Pass,** where you can take a ropeway or trek up to the summit of **Fugen-dake** (20min., 1 per hr., round-trip ¥740). Check the schedule for descending buses. Four roads create a rectangle around Unzen; the shorter sides lie to the north and south. The bus terminal is slightly north of the rectangle's northeastern corner, while the **tourist information center** lies on the southern edge. (Open daily 9am-5pm.) For more information about the plants and animals in the park, pick up brochures and watch a slideshow in the **visitors center** at the rectangle's southeastern corner. (Open daily Apr.-Oct. 9am-6pm; Nov.-Mar. 9am-5pm)

🏠 ACCOMMODATIONS AND FOOD. As a village economically dependent on tourism, Unzen is dominated by expensive hotels and ryokan. Newly-renovated **Minshuku Sekisō ❷**, 5min. on foot from the bus terminal, is a hidden deal overlooking a serene lake. Head west along the northern edge of the rectangle, take the second right and walk 200m. (¥3500 per person.) If Sekisō is full, the only other cheap options are on the other side of the village. **Minshuku Tokushimaya ❷** (☎73-3444; ¥3500 per person) and **Kokumin Shukusha Seiunsō ❷** (☎73-3273; ¥4500 per person) are next to each other, about a 20min. walk southwest of the bus terminal. The

perk about staying at either of these places is **Kojigoku (Little Hell) Onsen** next door. Most visitors have meals at their ryokan or minshuku, but **Restaurant Komatsu ❶** on the rectangle's east road offers Western and Japanese food (spaghetti ¥600, *udon* ¥400; open 10am-11pm.) There's a **supermarket** next door.

◙ SIGHTS. In Unzen itself, the famed *jigoku meguri* ("a tour of hell") turns out to be just a 30min. walk around bubbling hot springs. A good place to start is the **visitors center,** where you can pick up brochures; a path leads to hell from behind the center. **Daikyōkan Jigoku** (大叫喚地獄), the area's most active hot spring, derives its name from the human-like sounds it emits; supposedly these cries resonate in hell. The **Monument for Christian Martyrs** reminds visitors that the name "*jigoku meguri*" is not meaningless; during the ban on Christianity, the Tokugawa government sent more than 30 Christians to their deaths at these boiling springs.

If you want to pursue the hell motif in a more relaxing way, trek southwest for about 15min. from the visitors center to reach **Kojigoku** (Little Hell), an *onsen* renowned for its beautifying properties. For a less damning clean-up, **Yunosato Public Spa** is near the bus terminal. (Open 9am-11pm. ¥100.) **Shinyu Public Spa** lies by the southeastern corner of the rectangular area surrounding Unzen. (Open Su-Tu and Th-Sa 10am-11pm, ¥100.) Next to the visitors center is **Unzen Spa House,** a more modern facility with big wooden tubs both inside and outside and a sand bath. (Open daily 10am-7pm. Bath ¥800, sand bath ¥1000; combination ¥1500).

◪ HIKING. Dress appropriately in colder months—the weather on the mountains is harsher than in town. The journey to the peak of Fugen-dake, Unzen's main attraction, begins with a bus trip to **Nita Pass** (see **Transportation**). You can get hiking maps at a small booth inside the Nita Pass building before setting out. The 1-2hr. path that makes a clockwise loop through **Myōmi-dake** and provides access to **Kunimi-san** and **Fugen-dake.** At the peak, view **Heisei Shinzan,** a mountain created in 1992 as the result of a volcanic eruption. If the hike sounds strenuous, take a **ropeway** (3min., one-way ¥610) to Myōmi-dake (1333m), where you can walk 20min. to **Kunimi Wakare** or simply enjoy the pleasant view from the observatory.

SHIMABARA (島原) ☎0957

Travelers mainly visit Shimabara for ferry connections to Kumamoto. Two kinds of **ferries** run between the two cities: a faster one (30min., 6 per day, ¥650) and a slower one (1hr., 10 per day, ¥590). When entering Shimabara, get off the ferry at Port Stop instead of Shimabara Station. The last **bus** departs for **Kumamoto** at 8pm. Long-distance buses to **Fukuoka** (¥2900) and **Nagasaki** (¥1700) leave from the bus terminal. **Trains** go to **Nagasaki** via **Isahaya,** where you change from the Shimatetsu Line to JR (¥1780 plus express fare). Rent a bike from the **tourist info center** inside the port terminal (open daily 9:30am-5:30pm; ¥150 per hr.) or the youth hostel (¥600 per day). There are two main sights in Shimabara. The castle **Shimabara-jō** is accessible from the port by bicycle. Alternatively, buses and trains make the 3km trip to Shimabara Station, from where it's a few minutes walk. Supplement a trip to the castle by visiting the nearby 8.6m **Reclining Buddha** and the **carp swimming waterway.** On the other side of the port is **Mt. Unzen Disaster Memorial Hall,** a museum of high-tech and hands-on displays, including a huge dome-shaped screen that lets you experience the volcanic eruption and mudslides that hit the town several years ago. (Open 9am-5pm. ¥1000.) **Shimabara Youth Hostel (HI) ❶** is near the tourist information center. From the port terminal, go straight at the first intersection, cross the tracks, and take the first left. (¥2750 per person.)

ASO-SAN (阿蘇山)   ☎0967

The belly button of Kyūshū, Aso-san is the site of the world's biggest volcanic caldera. Aso-san usually refers to not only the five mountains (Aso Gokaku) in the middle, but also to the entire 18km-by-25km area enclosed by Gairin-zan (outer-ring mountains). This elliptical enclosure is divided into villages and towns; **Aso Town** takes up almost half of the area. Especially in spring and summer, when a lush grass carpets the area, this geologic wonder is not to be missed. Take the bus from Aso Station (35min., ¥540) to Aso-san Nishi-eki; during your ride you will probably stop at an observatory to take a quick initial peek at the mountain. Then pass **Komezuka,** a mountain shaped like an upside-down rice bowl. From Aso-san Nishi-eki, take a quick ride on the ropeway (¥410) to **Aso-san Kakō**—the summit—or walk on the road to the right of the ropeway station (15min.). At the top of the mountain, look down 100m into the magnificent water-filled crater.

> **! DON'T FORGET YOUR GAS MASK.** Depending on the concentration of poisonous gas emitted from the volcano, visitors may not be allowed to enter the observatory area at the summit. People with asthma are warned not to enter the summit area.

From the opposite (east) side of the caldera, the peak of Taka-dake is about a 2hr. hike. If you decide to walk down, a hike begins from a path just beyond the ski lifts and goes to the top of **Kijima-dake.** The 30min. ascent is mostly on stone steps. Be careful, as the wind sometimes picks up quickly here; if you feel yourself losing balance, crouch to lower your center of gravity. **Kusasenri,** just right after the first set of steps, is a beautiful grassland in spring and summer, where visitors can enjoy horseback riding. The **Aso Volcano Museum** across from Kusasenri is worth the admission price only if you are particularly interested in geology or if you had the bad luck to come on a day with high levels of gas emission—a simulcast monitor shows views from a camera stuck deep inside the crater.

A short stay in Aso should center around **JR Aso Station,** directly north of Aso Gokaku. Buses run between JR Aso Station and Aso-san Nishi Kakō, the gateway to the summit of Naka-dake (1 per hr., ¥540). The last bus descends at 5pm. Car rental is available at the **tourist info center** in the train station. (Open daily 9am-5pm. Rental cars ¥5000 for 12hr.) Next to the Aso Bus Terminal and Aso Train Station, **Kokumin Shukusha Aso ❷** offers basic but spacious Japanese-style rooms. (☎34-1882. ¥4900, ¥6300 with 2 meals.) One bus stop or a 15min. walk uphill from the train station is **Aso Youth Hostel (HI) ❶.** The hostel is run by an elderly couple who can give you comprehensive information about the region, including English hiking maps. (☎34-0804. Kitchen available. ¥2450.) The only drawback here is that there are no nearby restaurants. The owners may be able to drive you to **Ofukuro no Aji ❸,** a home-cooking restaurant on Rte. 57 that serves dishes using home-grown vegetables, but otherwise you'll need to buy food at the **Lawson** convenience store in front of the station, or trek down the hill to **East Restaurant ❸,** in front of the station, which serves both Japanese and Western goodies. If you want a homier place with more convenient food options, **Minshuku Aso no Fumoto ❷,** on Rte. 57, is a decent option. Take a right at the intersection in front of the bus terminal, and follow it for about 1km. (☎34-0194. ¥4200 per person, ¥6200 with 2 meals.)

BEPPU (別府)   ☎0977

The most important items to bring to Beppu are a large Ziploc bag, a towel that will fit in the Ziploc bag, a bottle of shampoo, and a bottle of body soap. Situated in a little nook on the eastern coast of Kyūshū, Beppu is one of Japan's most geother-

Aso & Central Highlands · 阿蘇

mically active regions, second only to Mt. Fuji, and you can use your bath kit at any of the several thousand hot springs. The area was undamaged by World War II, so the narrow back streets around Beppu Station whirl you back to times gone by. The town's strong association with bathing gives the area a vaguely sexual undertone, similar to Las Vegas or New Orleans, though the busy port and historic atmosphere draw the comparison closer to New Orleans.

ON THE WEB | Beppu City: www.city.beppu.oita.jp/51englishpage

◳ TRANSPORTATION

Flights: Ōita Airport is a short bus ride from Beppu Station or Kitahama Bus Stop. (40min.; 2 per hr. from Kitahama Stop and 6 per day from Beppu Station 7:50am-5:10pm; ¥1450, round-trip ¥2500). Flights from Ōita Airport go to **Nagoya, Okinawa, Ōsaka** (Itami and Kansai airports), **Seoul, Shanghai,** and **Tōkyō.**

Trains: The JR Nippon Line runs to **Hakata** (2¼hr.; at least 1 per hr. 4:04am-9:04pm; limited express ¥5250); **Kokura** (1¼hr.; at least 1 per hr.; ¥2420, limited express ¥3790); and **Ōita** (15min.; every 10-15min.; ¥200).

Buses: Long-distance buses stop across from the **Ōita Transportation Center,** 2-13-1, Kitahama (☎22-8101; open M-F 9am-5:30pm, Sa 9am-12:30pm, closed 2nd and 4th Sa) in front of Tokiwa department store, Ekimae-dōri, a quick walk from Beppu Station. Buy tickets there, or in Tokiwa. To: **Fukuoka** (2½hr.; at least 1 per hr. 5:40am-9pm; ¥3100, round-trip ¥5500); **Nagasaki** (3½hr., 7 buses daily 7:20am-6:20pm, ¥4500); and **Nagoya** (11½hr.; 1 per day at 8:15pm; ¥11,000, round-trip ¥19,800).

Ferries: The bus to **International Tourist Port** stops at **Beppu Station** (10min., ¥160), **Beppu Kōtsū Center,** and **Kansai-sen-mae.** The **Kansai-sen Ferry** goes to **Kōbe** (15hr., 4pm, ¥7400) and **Ōsaka** (16¾hr. or 11½hr.; the 4pm departure stops at Ōita and Kōbe, the 7pm goes direct; tickets from ¥7400). **Uwajima Ferry** goes to **Misaki** (2¼hr., 4 per day 2am-7:20pm, ¥1150) and **Yawatahama** (2½hr., 6 per day 5:35am-11:55pm, ¥1770). **Soleil Express** goes to **Hiroshima** (3hr., 2 per day at 4:20pm and 5:15pm, ¥8500) and **Matsuyama** (2¼hr., 1 per day at 11:50am, ¥4800).

Taxis: Kamenoi Taxi, ☎23-2221. **Kankō Taxi,** ☎22-3351. **Minato Taxi,** ☎23-5111.

Public Transportation: The **Kamenoi Bus System** in Beppu is extensive. Most buses run twice per hr. Bus passes are handy for a long day of sightseeing. The **Mini Free Pass** (¥900, children ¥450) is probably the best, usable on any Kamenoi Bus within city limits, which covers most tourist attractions. The **Ride Free Pass** (¥1600, children ¥800) includes further routes out to Yufuin and the African Safari. The **2 Days Free Pass** (adults ¥2400, children ¥1200) covers the same areas as the Wide Free Pass. The **3 Days Mini Passport** (¥7000, children ¥3500) is overkill, but allows for all routes and even sightseeing buses. Most routes start from the east or west side of Beppu Station.

Car Rental: Eki Rent-a-Car, 12-13, Ekimae-chō, (☎24-4428), outside JR Station East Exit. **Tattoo Rent-a-Car** and **Nissan Rent-a-Car** are outside International Tourist Port.

Bike Rental: Available at JR Station from the Green Yamaguchi (¥500 per 2hr.; if you purchase a train ticket 9am-5pm, bike rental ¥300 per 2hr.). If you're staying at the Kamenoi Hotel, you can rent a bike there for ¥500 per day.

ORIENTATION

Beppu occupies a broad zone between the mountains and the coast, but it's divided into several distinct areas. The JR Beppu Station area is the center of accommodations, entertainment, and shopping, easily explored on foot. **Khanat,** a 30min. drive north of the station, contains the Hells and other tourist sights as well as many small *onsen*. Farther northwest in the foothills is **Malbin,** a region of hot springs and thatched huts where *onsen* mineral salts are produced.

PRACTICAL INFORMATION

Tourist Office: There is a **tourist info center** at JR Beppu Station's East Exit, but the **Foreign Tourist Info Office** (☎23-1119; www.ctb.ne.jp/~Futō/001.html) is always staffed with English speakers. At the Beppu Station East Exit. Open M-Sa 9am-5pm.

Tours: Some of the best tours of Beppu are the Walking Tours organized by the curator of the small Hirano Museum (p. 611).

Currency Exchange: Mirai Shinkin, 1-31, Ekimae-honchō (☎25-7710), on Ekimae-dōri on the left, a few minutes from Beppu Station. Open M-F 9am-3pm.

ATM: The only ATMs in Beppu are in the post offices (see below).

Luggage Storage: Beppu Station, the **International Tourist Port,** and **Kannawa Bus** all offer useful coin lockers if you need to store your stuff for the day.

KYŪSHŪ

Beppu · 別府

⌂ ACCOMMODATIONS
Business Hotel Hayashi, **18**
Eki-mae Kōto Onsen, **19**
Beppu Youth Hostel (HI) **33**
Kamenoi Hotel, **32**
Kannawa-en, **10**
Nishitetsu Inn, **17**
Nogami Honkan, **24**

🍎 FOOD
Billiken, **20**
Cafe de Piacere, **29**
Chān, **22**
Kannawa Butaman
  Honpo, **14**
Junkyard, **26**
Takeya, **31**
Toyotsune, **16**
Zen, **21**

🍺 NIGHTLIFE
Black List 2, **23**
Copper Ravens, **26**
Hit Parade, **30**
Speak Easy, **25**

♨ 🚶 **ONSEN/JIGOKU/YU**
Chī no Ike Jigoku, **1**
Furō-sen, **28**
Hamawaki Onsen Area, **34**
Hyōtan Onsen, **9**
Jigoku Bura Onsen, **14**
Kamado Jigoku, **4**
Kinryu Jigoku, **6**
Mushi Yu, **8**
Oni ishi Bozu Jigoku, **3**
Oni ishi Jigoku, **2**
Oni ishi no Yu, **12**
Oniyama Jigoku
  (Devil's Mountain), **5**
Shiraike Jigoku, **7**
Takegawara Onsen, **27**
Umi Jigoku, **13**
Yu No Sato, **15**

Kamegawa
亀川

Nippon Line 日豊本線

Beppu Hihōkan
別府秘宝館

TO
♨15 (1.5km)

Beppu Daigaku
別府大学

700 meters
700 yards

Beppu-wan
別府湾

Beppu International
Tourist Port

Beppu Kōtsū Center

Laundry
洗濯機

Cosmopla
Shopping Centre
コスモピア

Tokiwa

Oita
Kōtsū

Soi Paseo

Hirano
Museum

B-Con
Plaza
Global Tower

Beppu Kōen
別府公園

200 yards
200 meters

SEE INSET MAP ABOVE

Beppu Station
別府駅

Trans-Kyushu Expressway · 東別府

TO OITA (12km)
大分へ

Higashi Beppu
東別府

KYŪSHŪ

English-Language Bookstore: Libro, 2-9-1, Kitahama (☎73-8090; www.libro.jp), in Tokiwa department store, 4th fl., Cosmopia, end of Ekimae-dōri. Open daily 10am-7pm.

Laundromat: Business Star Hotel, 1st fl., opposite the west side of JR Beppu Station.

Public Toilets, Showers, Baths: Public hot springs are in every nook and cranny, especially in the station and Kannawa areas. Turn off any main st. and keep your eye out for the characters 温泉. You'll be able to bathe for free in many places, or for as little as ¥100. Most hotels and ryokan also open their *onsen* to the public.

Emergency: Police ☎110. **Fire** or **ambulance** ☎119.

Police: Beppu Police Station, 9-13, Mochigahama-chō (☎21-2131).

24hr. Pharmacy: There's a **Family Mart** on the corner across from Beppu Station. There are several other 24hr. convenience stores on Ekimae-dōri.

Hospital: Nakamura Byōin (中村病院), 8-24, Akiba-chō (☎23-3212).

Internet Access: Internet around Beppu Station is scarce. The Foreign Tourist Information Office has free Internet which you can use for 10min. at a time.

Post Office: Beppu Post Office, 4-23, Mochigahama-chō (☎24-0500), 2 blocks south of International Tourist Port. Open 24hr. ATM M-F 8:45am-8pm, Sa-Su 9am-7pm. **Beppu Kitahama Post Office,** 2-9-1, Kitahama (☎21-6822), next to Cosmopia Bldg. Open M-F 9am-5pm. ATM M-F 9am-5:30pm, Sa-Su 9am-5pm. **Postal Code:** 874.

ACCOMMODATIONS

You can stay in nearly any part of town. The station area harbors all the budget options. Other areas, notably Kannawa and Myoban, offer secluded ryokan for travelers seeking something more scenic and luxurious. Many have their own *onsen* (hot spring bath), *rotemburo* (outdoor bath), or *kazokuburo* (family bath).

Kamenoi Hotel (亀の井ホテル), 5-17, Chūō-chō (☎22-3301; www.kamenoi.com). From the station, walk right and take a left at the end of the parking garage; it's on the 2nd block on the right. Kamenoi was the 1st American-style hotel in Beppu. Bike rental ¥500 per day. Free Internet in the lobby. Hotel *onsen*. Print the coupon from the website, or get it by eating in attached restaurant, Joyful. Check-in 2pm. Check-out 11am. Singles from ¥5800; twins from ¥9800; doubles from ¥8800. ❸

THE BIG SPLURGE

MASTERS OF THE *ONSEN* UNIVERSE

Most tourists who visit Beppu come for the baths. Even the locals make the (usually daily) rounds of the municipal baths, buying entrance tickets in sets of ten at a discounted rate. With this in mind, some jokesters in the city office designed the **Beppu Hatto Spaport** (別府八湯表泉家). A red book the size of a Japanese passport, it lists 88 Beppu *onsen*, à la Shikoku's 88 Temple Pilgrimage, with space for stamps from each one. Anyone who completes the pilgrimage receives a black towel with gold print declaring the bearer an "Onsen Master."

At the time of writing there were only three Onsen Masters, so you'll join an elite group of bathers when you complete the journey. The current recordholder took all of three days, but *Let's Go* suggests taking more time to savor the experience. You'll be getting a wonderful tour of Beppu's nooks and crannies, and since entrance fees bring the price of the towel to ¥34,890, you might as well make the most of it.

(A Spaport can be picked up for ¥50 at most hotels and some restaurants. Ask for the Spaport or about the Hachiju-hachi Kasho (八十八箇所) they'll know what you mean. Another good resource is the annually published Onsen-bon (温泉本). It's in Japanese, but coupons in the back allow free entrance to certain onsen; others coupons that will discount a normal onsen.)

Nogami Honkan (野上本館), 1-12-1, Kitahama (☎221-1334; www02.u-page.so-net.ne.jp/fb3/yasuko-n/). From the station, walk down Ekimae-dōri and take a right on Takegawara Alley—Nogami Honkan is on the left just a few blocks before Takegawara Onsen. These high quality *tatami* rooms are a real steal. Free Internet in lobby from 8am-9pm. Check-in 3pm. Check-out 10am. Curfew 2am. ¥4500 per person. ❷

Beppu Youth Hostel (HI), 20-28, Nakashima-chō (☎23-4116; www4.justnet.ne.jp/~beppuyh). A 25min. walk from the station. Hop a #16 or 17 bus from the station's east side to Yakyūjō-mae—from there it's a quick walk. The #8 bus from the west side puts you a block farther away. Get off at the stadium. Comfortable hostel with Western- and Japanese-style rooms. Great *onsen* and a small *rotemburo*. Breakfast ¥500. Dinner ¥1000. Laundry ¥200. Internet ¥100 for 15min. Check-in 3pm. Check-out 10am. Lock-out 10am-3pm. Curfew 10pm. ¥3200, nonmembers ¥4200. ❶

Eki-mae Kōto Onsen (駅前高等温泉), 13-14, Ekimae-chō (☎21-0541). From Beppu Station East Exit, Kōto Onsen will be on the right of the 2nd block. This legendary 24hr. *onsen* offers hot springs dips (¥300) and normal baths (¥100). Fills up during Japa-nese vacations. Reception 24hr. Check-in 4pm. Check-out 10am. Lockout 10am-4pm. *Tatami* dorms ¥1500 (only available 9pm-9am). Private rooms for 3 ¥2500. ❶

Business Hotel Hayashi, 3-5, Ekimae-honchō (☎24-2211). Across from station. Guests can use New Hayashi sauna (free) and main bldg. *onsen*. Men's *onsen* is a ■ **7th floor rooftop onsen** with a great view. Sorry ladies, women's *onsen* is on the 4th fl. Breakfast ¥500. Check-in 4pm. Check-out 10am. Singles from ¥3900; doubles from ¥6500. ❷

Nishitetsu Inn, 2-10-4, Kitahama (☎26-5151; www.nnr.co.jp/nishitetsu_inn). 1 block left of Ōita Bus Stop, across from Tokiwa department store. Solid business hotel. Free in-room Internet; bring your own computer. Nice *onsen* and *rotemburo*. Check-in 3pm. Check-out 10am, Su 11am. Singles from ¥5500; twins from ¥10,000. ❶

Kannawa-en, 6, Goko (☎66-2111). Between Yama Jigoku and Kamado Jigoku, a brief walk from Kannawa or Umi Jigoku-mae bus stops. Luxurious ryokan *avec onsen* and gardens. Baths cycle from clear to light blue every week. Visitors can use *onsen* for ¥800 Sa-Su 10am-2pm; only guests can use the *kazokuburo*. Check-in 3pm. Check-out 10am. Doubles ¥27,000 per person. ❺

Okamotoya Ryokan, 4, Myoban (☎66-3228). Take #5, 41, or 43 bus to Myoban Stop; it's on the right of Myoban Onsen Street. Fancy ryokan. Includes 2 meals, tax, and the lush *onsen* and *rotemburo*. Check-in 3pm. Check-out 11am. Curfew 12am. Reserve 1 month ahead for weekend stays. ¥13,000; weekends ¥15,000. ❹

◳ FOOD

The **Tokiwa department store**, 2-9-1, Kitahama (☎23-1111; open daily 10am-7pm), has a huge selection of *bentō* lunches and snacks in the basement food court.

Chān, 9-9, Ekimae-chō (☎23-7979). From the station, walk down Ekimae-dōri, take a right just before Business Hotel New Hayashi, and take the 2nd left; it's on the left. Spicy pan-Asian dishes; the green curry (¥700) is especially masochistic. A few doors down, sister restaurant **Zen** serves a more Japan-centric menu. Open daily until 1am. ❷

Cafe de Piacere, 6-23, Moto-machi (☎23-1182). From the station, walk down Ekimae-dōri and turn right on the Ginza arcade. It's on the right of the last block of the arcade. Cute espresso bar with drinks (from ¥350, ¥100 discount for takeout). Small selection of pastas and pizzas. Open M-Th 11am-1am, F-Sa 11am-3am, Su 11am-8pm. ❷

Kannawa Butaman Honpo (鉄輪豚まん本舗), 3, Ida (☎66-6390; www.irfnso.ne.jp/butaman). From Kannawa Bus Stop, walk east on the main street and take a left just before Jigoku Bura Onsen; it's on the right. Serves up slightly spicy Butaman dumplings (¥150). Open daily 9am-4pm. Closed 2nd M of the month. ❶

Billiken (ビリケン), 2-1-18, Kitahama (☎21-2088). Walk down Ekimae-dōri from the station; it's 2 blocks before the department store. *Teishoku* and *donburi* with easy-to-read menus. Sushi and *soba* sets (from ¥750). Lunch specials 11:30am-3pm. Rub the feet of the statue of Billiken, God of Things As They Ought to Be, outside the store. He came from America in 1908. Open W and F-Sa 11:30am-10pm, last order 9:30pm. ❷

Takeya, 15-7, Motomachi (☎23-1006). Across from Takegawara Onsen. Relax after your bath with coffees (from ¥350), *onigiri* (¥100), *miso* soup (¥150), curry (¥550), and a massage (¥1000 for 20min.). Open Tu-Su 10am-7pm (last order 6:30pm). ❶

Toyotsune, Fujino Bldg., 1st fl., Eki Bus Terminal-mae (☎23-7487). Across from JR Beppu Station. Specializes in *fugu* (blowfish) served as *sashimi* (¥2000) or *kara-age* (fried pieces; ¥1000). Extravagant *fugu* courses from ¥7000; if you need to save cash, the *Toyotsune teishoku* lunch is ¥700. Open F-W 11am-2pm and 5-10pm. ❷

Junkyard, 8-10, Motomachi (☎73-4422). Below Copper Ravens bar, 1 block off Ginza arcade. Look for Greek letters vaguely resembling "Junkyard" on the sign. Japanese variations on ethnic favorites like tacos (¥700), samosas (¥500), and nachos (¥400). 73 types of bourbon for your swigging pleasure (¥500-2200). Poke your head into **Copper Ravens** upstairs (p. 614) for dancing. Open Tu-Su 6pm-1am, last order 12am. ❷

🅖 SIGHTS

🔲 **HIRANO MUSEUM** (平野資料館), **BEPPU WALKING TOURS.** This museum on the history and culture of *onsen* is run by Yoshihiro Hirano, who also works in the city office. It houses a collection of old Beppu festival posters and decades worth of pictures of local beauties on the shore. The highlight, however, is Hirano's walking tours. The best are the three neighborhood tours: Takegawara, Kannawa, and Yamanote. These sometimes have English guides, but call a few days ahead to ensure one. *(11-7, Motomachi. From the station, walk down Ekimae-dōri and take a right at Takegawara Alley. It's on the right a block before Takegawara Onsen. ☎23-4748. Open M-F 2-6pm, Sa-Su 10am-6pm. Takegawara tour 2nd and 4th Su of each month. ¥1000 includes snack, lunch, and memorial picture. Meet 9:30am at Kitahama Park. Kannawa tour 3rd Su of each month. ¥700 includes snack and memorial picture, Meet 10am at Ōtani Park. Yamanote tour the 1st Su of each month. ¥1500 includes snack, lunch, memorial picture, and entrance to Global Tower and Chochokaku. Meet 10am in front of Global Tower. Museum entrance free.)*

🔲 **HYŌTAN ONSEN** (ひょうたん温泉). If you only have time for one *onsen* in Beppu, Hyōtan Onsen is a good place to cover all the bases. The expansive grounds have everything: waterfalls, *rotemburo*, pebble foot baths, sand baths (at two different temperatures), and steam baths (with both hot and warm steam). Private *kazokuburo* (family baths; ¥1000 per hr.) are also available. *(159-2, Kannawa. From Kannawa Bus Stop, walk east to get to Jigoku Bura Bus Stop, then take a right and Hyōtan Onsen will be on the right. ☎66-0527. Open daily 8am-9pm. ¥700; elementary school students ¥300; children ¥200; kazokuburo ¥1000 for 1hr.; yukata for the sand bath ¥200.)*

🔲 **MUSHI YU** (むし湯). "Steam bath" isn't a strong enough word for this intense experience. Guys, bring an extra pair of boxers, and ladies, a pair of shorts and t-shirt. Wash the lower half of your body in the normal *onsen* pool, which is itself very hot. Put on the boxers and t-shirts and, with towel in hand, crawl through a tunnel into the steam bath. The floor is covered with straw and the room isn't big enough to sit up in. Place the towel on one of the small rocks and use it as a pillow. Most people bake for about 8-10min., but even half that may feel like an eternity for claustrophobes. *(From Kannawa Bus Stop, walk east on the main street down*

KYŪSHŪ

FROM THE ROAD

CLEANING UP

I'd just returned, pink and freshly scrubbed, when a girl in my guesthouse gave me a quizzical look. "You went to a public bath? But, don't you find it all, well, really strange?" What? Is it so strange to lather up on a tiny slippery stool next to naked strangers who brush their teeth and spit with gusto in the drain before plunging into near-boiling, violet-hued, or electrically-charged water? Put that way, I guess it is a far cry from the more modest Midwest rubber-ducky bathtime of my childhood.

After surviving the first endless second between clenching my towel and choosing a stool, I realized that "modesty" is an irrelevant word in the bathhouse. Washing up isn't a chore to be done quickly and privately—cleanliness here is no less a ritual than rinsing your hands and mouth before visiting a temple. As for the nakedness, think of it as a uniform, part of a communal identity. Instead of donning a school uniform or a salaryman's suit, you're wearing, well, your skin.

Most bathhouses have a hot bath, a cold bath, and a medicinal bath (purplish or bluish), as well as a sauna and/or jacuzzi. Before jumping in, scrub and rinse at the showers (feel free to shave, brush your teeth, and shampoo). Always rinse off after using the sauna. The electrical bath is the pool in the corner that no one touches, but since you've come this far ...

- Annalise Nelson

the hill; it's on the left among a host of little shops. ☎ 67-3880. Open daily 6:30am-8pm, every 4th Th 6:30am-2pm. Steam bath ¥210, 2nd fl. relaxation room ¥400.)

TAKEGAWARA ONSEN (竹瓦温泉). One of Beppu's oldest hot springs, Takagawara Onsen is probably its most famous. Dating from 1879, the beautiful wood walls and tiled roof stand out among the neon signs of the bars and adult entertainment in the neighborhood. You can take a normal bath here, but the sand bath is the main draw. You need only a small towel to protect your delicates as the attendants cover you with dark, warm sand. Marinate for 10min., then wash off before dipping into the normal bath. All three baths—the sand room, and the men's and women's baths—are drawn from different sources and have unique qualities. Be prepared for a wait. *(16-23, Moto-machi. From the station walk down Ekimae-dōri and take a right at Takegawara Alley. On the left at the end of the alley. ☎ 23-1585. Open daily 6:30am-10:30pm, sand bath daily 8am-10:30pm, reception until 9:30pm. Sand bath closed the 3rd W of Mar., June, and Sept. Sand bath ¥780. Hot spring ¥100. Towel ¥210.)*

OTHER BEPPU STATION AREA ONSEN. The area east and south of Beppu Station is a maze of Edo-period alleys. There are *onsen* almost every other block, but several stand out. **Nagaishi Onsen** (永石温泉) is a one-bath hot spring in a wonderful Meiji-era wooden building. From the station, walk two blocks along Ekimae-dōri and take a right on Saihōji-dōri. The *onsen* is 7-10min. from there, on the lefthand corner three blocks after the second stoplight. *(Open daily 6:30am-10:30pm. ¥100.)* Diagonally across from the Kamenoi Hotel, **Furō-sen** (不老泉 ; "The Bath of Perennial Youth") doesn't seem to fulfill its promise, but it's one of the larger and cleaner of the municipal baths—worth a float. *(Open daily 6:30am-10:30pm. ¥100.)* **Ekimae Kōtō Onsen** (駅前高等温泉), 13-14, Ekimae-chō, is on Ekimae-dōri on the right of the second block as you walk from the station. *(☎ 21-0541. Open 24hr. Onsen ¥300, normal bath ¥100.)* For a free foot bath, head to **Kamiya Onsen** (紙屋温泉). From Nagaishi Onsen, walk one block back towards Ekimae-dōri and take a right; it's on the left. You can also drink from the stream that fills the footbath; the mineral water is famous for its health benefits. *(Open daily 1-11pm. ¥100.)*

YU NO SATO. Perched in the hilly Myōban Onsen area, Yu no Sato is a picturesque site filled with thatched huts where Yu no Hana ("flower of the water") mineral salts are produced. You can peek inside some of the huts; Japanese displays do a decent job of explaining the salt-making process. The great *rotemburo* offers a spectacular view of the expressway bridge, Beppu, and the surrounding mountains. The *kazokuburo* come in thatched huts of three different sizes. Pick up mineral salts for about ¥100 a pack at the souvenir store. *(6, Myōban Onsen. Take a #5, 41, or 43 bus and get off at Myōbo. Alternatively, Yu no Sato is a 15min. walk from Onsen Hoyō Land if you go there first—follow the street underneath the expressway and take a right at Myōban. Walk up the small street and take a right at the small coffee shop. Yu no Sato is on the left. ☎ 66-8166; www.d-b.ne.jp/yunosato/beppu.html. Open daily Apr.-Oct. 10am-10pm, reception until 9pm; Nov.-Mar. 10am-9pm, reception until 8pm; kazokuburo from 9am. ¥600; children ¥300; kazokuburo ¥1500, ¥2000, or ¥2500 per hr.)*

BEPPU ONSEN HOYŌ LAND (別府温泉保養ランド). At this *onsen*, you get dirty before you get clean again—the specialty here is mud baths. The thickest, hottest clay is not in the private mud baths but in the large, mixed *rotemburo*, where you can really slop around. There's a wicked hot steam room and a waterfall pool to soak in afterwards. You can stay overnight in the Japanese-style rooms; two meals and entrance to the mud baths are included in the rate. *(Myōban Konyajigoku. Take #5, 41, or 43 bus to Konyajigoku-mae; it's just across the street. ☎ 66-2221. Open daily 9am-8pm, indoor steam and mud baths close 7:30pm. ¥1050, elementary school students ¥570, children 2 and older ¥310. Rooms ¥7500 per person.)*

SUGINOI PALACE AND SUGINOI HOTEL (スギノイパレス). At the time of writing, Beppu's tackiest hot spring was receiving a traditional face lift. Its two legendary baths, one filled with giant Shintō icons and the other with Buddhist icons, were closing. The new Tanayu (Terrace Bath), opening in November 2003, will take advantage of Suginoi's position on the hills and offer views from *rotemburo*. Hot springs are just half the fun at Suginoi—inside there's bowling, batting cages, a theater for magic shows and dramas, and a water park. Guests who stay in one of the Suginoi Hotels can use the private hot springs and normal pools. *(1, Kankaiji. Take #8 bus from Beppu Station west side; 25-30min., ¥210. ☎ 24-1141; www.suginoi-hotel.com. Open daily 9am-10:30pm. ¥1400, children ¥700. Twin rooms ¥14,000 per person.)*

THE HELLS. The Hells *(Jigoku)* are Beppu's most notorious tourist attraction. They are a collection of nine areas where boiling or near-boiling water and steam gush up to the surface in a variety of viscosities, colors, and degrees of hotness. There are two groups—the larger group of seven is in Kannawa, north of the main Kannawa Bus Stop, and there are two isolated in the northeast. Don't mistake these for the warm *onsen* that draw from the same sources. As a sign at Kinryu Jigoku warns, "Do not fall in or you will be boiled!" *(559-1, Kannawa. ☎ 66-1577. All Hells open daily 8am-5pm. Individual tickets: ¥400, high school students ¥350, junior high and elementary school students ¥250. General admission booklet for all 9 Hells: ¥2000, high school students ¥1300, junior high school students ¥1000, elementary school students ¥900.)*

GLOBAL TOWER. The best way to get to know Beppu's layout is to head to the fourth floor observatory of the Global Tower, part of the B-Con Plaza Convention Center complex. On a clear day you'll be able to see all the way to Shikoku, but the city layout offers plenty to gawk at. *(12-1, Yamanote-chō. Exit the west side of Beppu Station and walk up the main street to Beppu Kōen. Cut across the park diagonally—B-Con Plaza is across from the northwest corner, and the Global Tower is just beyond. Alternatively, take a #8 bus from the west side of the station. ☎ 26-7111; www.b-con.or.jp/index.html. Open daily Mar.-Nov. 9am-9pm, Dec.-Feb. 9am-5pm. ¥300, junior high and elementary students ¥200.)*

BEPPU HIHŌKAN (別府秘宝館). It's unlikely you'll miss the Hihōkan or mistake its contents, as there's an old relief carving of busty, naked Indian women above the entrance. The displays in this sex museum range from anatomically correct wax sculptures of Raquel Welch and Snow White (being pleasured by one of the Dwarves, no less) to erotic *ukiyo-e* prints. These aren't limited to humans, either; whale genitalia are there for the gawking, as are several pictures of the animals performing the horizontal tango. The building is lit by dim pink fluorescent lights, giving it a red-light district feeling. If you have cash to drop, there are plenty of battery-run, vibrating souvenirs to consider bringing home. *(338-3, Kannawa Shibuyu. From Kannawa Bus Stop, walk west up the main street; it's on the left across from Oniyama Jigoku. ☎66-8790. Open daily 9am-10pm. ¥1000.)*

NIGHTLIFE

Nightlife in Beppu consists of an overwhelming number of soaps, snacks, and sordid strip shows. Fortunately, there are also bars that pander to the party lover.

Speak Easy, 12-1, Moto-machi (☎21-8116). Facing Takegawara Onsen, walk to the left and take the 3rd right. Speak Easy is on the right. This comfy jazz bar with counter seats or a cushion to lounge on is perfect for hipsters and hip-hopsters—you'll hear a range of good music. Draft beer ¥500. Cocktails ¥600. Run by the same people who own Copper Ravens just across the street. Open Su-M and W-Sa 8pm-4am.

Copper Ravens, 8-10, Moto-machi (☎25-5582). Across from Speak Easy; look for the giant neon sign. New dance club in old building, with a cool balcony. Red leather couches; counter and tables downstairs. Cover ¥1500 on Sa, including 1 drink. **Junkyard** downstairs serves ethnic eats (p. 611). Open Tu-Su 7pm-3am.

Black List 2, 9-2, Moto-machi (☎090-9720-0408). 3 blocks from Ekimae-dōri, on the left of Ginza arcade. Cooks up doughy octopus snacks for ¥500 'til the wee hours. Drinks from ¥500. Open Su-M, W-Sa 7pm-5am.

Hit Parade, Moto-machi, Takegawara Onsen-mae. (☎21-3166). Across from Takegawara Onsen. Post-prohibition-style live-house. Best for a group willing to boogie. Dames ¥3000, gents ¥3600. Ticket includes all you can eat and drink from limited menu. Make reservations on weekends. Open Tu-F and Su 6pm-1am, Sa 6pm-2am.

KUMAMOTO (熊本) ☎096

Known as the "City of Green and Water," Kumamoto became well-established as a castle town 500 years ago, during the Edo Period. This arrangement has continued until today—Kumamoto-jō boldly stands in the middle of the city, surrounded by the buzzing economic activity in the Kami-dōri and Shimo-dōri arcade area. The castle ranks as one of the three most visually and architecturally impressive in Japan, and the arcade area rivals Fukuoka's Tenjin district. A glimpse of Mt. Aso, the world's largest volcanic caldera, will leave an imprint on your visual memory.

ON THE WEB Kumamoto City: www.city.kumamoto.kumamoto.jp

TRANSPORTATION

Flights: Kumamoto Airport, 40min. from Kōtsū Center by bus (¥670), sends planes to **Hakata** (1½hr., ¥2070); **Naha** (2 per day, ¥18,000-20,000); **Nishi-Kagoshima** (2½hr., ¥5250); **Ōita** (2½hr., ¥4520); **Ōsaka** (10 per day, ¥10,000-17,000).

Trains: JR trains run from **Kumamoto Station** to **Aso** (1hr., ¥1080); **Hakata** (1½hr., ¥2070); **Nishi-Kagoshima** (2½hr., ¥5250); **Ōita** (2½hr., ¥4520).

Buses: Buses, the most affordable option for those without a JR pass, operate out of Kōtsū Center, headed for **Amakusa** (2½hr., ¥2330); **Aso** (1hr., ¥1220); **Fukuoka** (2hr., ¥2000); **Kagoshima** (3hr., ¥3600); **Kyōto** via **Ōsaka** (¥10,000); **Miyazaki** (3hr., ¥4500); **Nagasaki** (3hr., ¥3600); **Nagoya** (¥11,000).

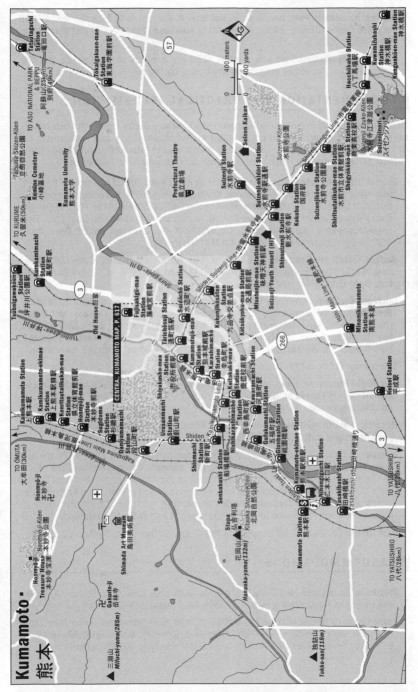

Kumamoto
熊本

Tatsuta Shizen-Kōen
立田自然公園

Kōmine Cemetery
小峰墓地

TO ASO NATIONAL PARK
& BEPPU
阿蘇山(25km)/別府(49km)

TO KURUME
久留米(50km)

TO OMUTA
大牟田(30km)

TO YATSUSHIRO
八代(28km)

TO YATSUSHIRO
八代(28km)

Honmyō-ji
本妙寺

Honmyō-ji-Kōen
本妙寺公園

Honmyō-ji
Treasure House
本妙寺宝庫

Gakurin-ji
岳林寺

▲ Mifuchi-yama(285m)
三渕山

Shimada Art Museum
島田美術館

Stupa
仏舎利塔

Kitaoka Shizen-Kōen
北岡自然公園

▲ Hanaoka-yama(132m)
花岡山

▲ Tokko-san(118m)
独鈷山

Tatsutaguchi Station
竜田口駅

Tōkaigakuen-mae Station
東海学園前駅

Kumamoto University
熊本大学

Kurokamimachi Station
黒髪町駅

Tsuboigawakōen Station
坪井川公園駅

Old House / 旧家

Prefectural Theatre
県立劇場

Seinen Kaikan
青年会館

Suizenji-Kōen
水前寺公園

Suizenji Station
水前寺駅

Suizenji-kōen Station
水前寺公園駅

Suizenji-ekidori Station
水前寺駅通駅

Shiden Kengun Line・市電健軍線

Kokubu Station
国府駅

Shinsuizenji Station
新水前寺駅

Suizenji Ezuko-Kōen
江津湖公園

Shogyōkōkō-mae Station
商業高校前駅

Suizenjinori
スイゼンジノリ

Hacchōbaba Station
八丁馬場駅

Kuwamizubashi Station
神水橋駅

Kengunkōen-mae Station
神水橋駅

Shiritsutaikukan-mae Station
水前寺市立体育館前駅

Shiritsutaikukan-mae Station
水前寺市立体育館前駅

Shiden Suizenji Line・市電水前寺線

Misotenjin-mae Station
味噌天神前駅

Kōtsukyoku-mae Station
交通局前駅

Suizenji Youth Hostel (HI)
新市街

Hōhi Main Line・豊肥本線

Minamikumamoto Station
南熊本駅

Heisei Station
平成駅

Fujisakigū-mae Station
藤崎宮前駅

Suidōchō Station
水道町駅

Kuhonjikōsatten
九品寺交差点駅

Karashimachō Station
辛島町駅

Kawaramachi Station
河原町駅

Gofukumachi Station
呉服町駅

Kumamoto-jō-mae Station
熊本城前駅

Kumamotojō-mae
熊本城前駅

Shiyakusho-mae
Station
市役所前駅

Torichōsuji Station
通町筋駅

Kamitōrichō Line・上通町線

Kamikumamoto Station
上熊本駅

Kamikumamoto-ekimae Station
上熊本駅前駅

Kenritsutaikukan-mae
県立体育館前駅

Honmyōji-mae
本妙寺前駅

Sugidomo
Station
杉塘駅

Daniyamamachi Station
段山町駅

Urasanmachi
Station
新山町駅

Shinmachi Station
新町駅

Shimada Art Museum

Shiden
Main Line
市電本線

Kagoshima Main Line・鹿児島本線

Senbabashi Station
船場橋駅

Shimmachi Station
新町駅

Nishikarashimachō
西辛島町駅

Kumamoto-ekimae Station
熊本駅前駅

Mihongiguchi Station
二本木口駅

Tasakibashi Station
田崎橋駅

Yasakibashi-dōri・田崎橋通り

Kumamoto Station
熊本駅

57

3

57

3

266

400 meters
400 yards
0

Ferries: Kumamoto Port, reachable by bus from JR Kumamoto Station (25min., ¥400) or Kōtsū Center (35min., ¥480), has ferries to **Amakusa** (1hr., ¥2600) and **Shimabara** (1hr., ¥590-650).

Public Transportation: Tram fare starts at ¥130 and depends on the distance. A 1-day pass (¥500; includes free access to some buses) can be purchased on any tram.

ORIENTATION AND PRACTICAL INFORMATION

Central Kumamoto is quite small: Kumamoto Castle, Kōtsū Center (the bus terminal), the shopping arcade streets (Kami-dōri and Shimo-dōri), and restaurants all fit within 1 sq. km. While the museums are also walking distance from this central square, the tram system helps visitors reach accommodations farther out.

Tourist Office: An **information center** inside JR Kumamoto Station can provide travelers with maps and answer basic questions. Open daily 9am-5:30pm. For an extensive collection of brochures, visit the **information center** (☎322-5060) on the 1st fl. of Sangyō Bunka Kaikan (Industry and Culture Center), next to the Karashima-chō Tram Stop. Free English-speaking volunteer guides are available with 2-3 days notice. Open daily 9:30am-6pm, closed every 2nd and 4th M of the month.

Budget Travel: Joy Road (☎322-8461), is in JR Kumamoto Station. Open M-F 10am-7pm, Sa-Su 10am-5:30pm. **STC** (☎327-2511) is on the 1st fl. of Sangyō Bunka Kaikan. Open daily 10am-7:30pm

Currency Exchange: Cash and traveler's checks can be exchanged at **Higo Bank Main Branch** (open M-F 9am-3pm), south of Karashima Kōen, or at the **Central Post Office** (open M-F 9am-6pm). **International ATMs** are in the basement of Kōtsū Center (open M-F 9am-9pm, Sa-Su 9am-5pm); in the post office at Kumamoto Station (open M-F 9am-5:30pm, Sa-Su 9am-5pm); and in the Central Post Office (open M-F 9am-9pm).

Emergency: Police ☎110. Fire or ambulance ☎119.

Late-Night Pharmacy: There are a few pharmacies in the Kami-dōri/Shimo-dōri arcade area, including **Takeya** on Shimo-dōri (open daily until 2am) and **Drug Eleven** on Sun Rd. Shinshigai (open daily 10am-11pm).

Hospital: Kokuritsu Kumamoto Byōin (☎353-6501) has English- and other foreign language-speaking staff. Open M-F 8:30am-5pm.

Internet Access: AU Shop, a 2min. walk from Karashima-chō Tram Stop (¥420 per hr.; open M-F 10am-10pm, Sa-Su 10am-6pm); **International Communication Area** (open M-F 9am-8pm, Sa-Su 9am-7pm, closed every 2nd and 4th Su) on the 2nd fl. of Kumamoto City. **International Center** has Internet access (¥50 for 5min.) and English magazines and books. The **Contemporary Art Museum** (p. 618) has 2 computers hooked up to the Internet for anyone to use for free. Open M and W-Su 10am-5:30pm.

Post Office: Central Post Office open M-F 9am-7pm, Sa 9am-5pm, Su 9am-12:30pm.

ACCOMMODATIONS

Minshuku Komatsusō (☎355-2634), a 3min. walk from Kumamoto Station. A convenient place to stay if coming by train. ¥3500, with breakfast ¥4200. ❷

Suisenji Youth Hostel (HI) (☎371-9193), a 3min. walk from Miso Tenjin Tram Stop or a 5min. walk from Suisenji Eki-dōri Tram Stop. A homey, *tatami* establishment with only 5 rooms, operated by a friendly and helpful manager. ¥2900 per person. ❶

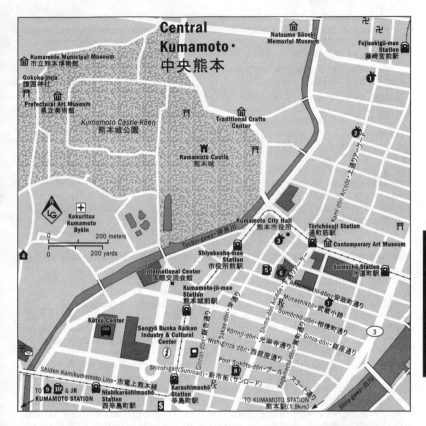

Seinen Kaikan (☎381-6221), a 10min. walk from Suisenji Eki-dōri Tram Stop. Hospital-like appearance, and slightly crowded, but there's a better chance of getting a room here than at Suisenji. ¥3000 per person. ❶

Minshuku Kajita (☎353-1546), a 5min. walk from either Urusan-machi or Shin-machi Tram Stops. A quality inn with 12 *tatami* rooms behind Kumamoto Castle, Kajita is experienced at accommodating foreigners. Doubles with shared bath ¥7000. ❸

⬛ FOOD

Komurasaki (☎325-8972; www.komurasaki.com), 5min. north of Kami-dōri, with a branch on Kami-dōri. Representing Kumamoto's regional *rāmen*, Komurasaki serves multiple variations of the pork-broth soup and garlic chip original. *Rāmen* ¥500. *Gyōza* ¥400. Open daily 11am-9:30pm. ❶

Central Kumamoto·中央熊本

🔺 ACCOMMODATIONS
Minshuku Kajita, 4
Minshuku Komatsusō, 9

⬛ FOOD
Cafe Restaurant Bu, 3
Komurasaki, 1, 2
Rāmen Jōkamachi, 6
Zealah, 7

⬛ NIGHTLIFE
Nijikaichaya, 8
Ekimae Jibiirukan, 10
Sharp, 5

Rāmen Jōkamachi, on the 8th fl. of Daiei department store on Shimo-dōri. Similar to Fukuoka's Rāmen Stadium, this newly-opened institution of higher noodles houses branches of 7 of Japan's top *rāmen* chains, inviting visitors to compare the regional varieties and vote on their favorites. Open daily 11am-9:30pm. ❷

Cafe Restaurant Bu, behind City Hall. Though strangely named, Bu offers a variety of dishes from Italian to *izakaya*-style food in a small, relaxed atmosphere. ❷

Zealah, on a sidestreet off Shimo-dōri. 6 totally different restaurants, including a beer hall, skewer place, *yakiniku* (Japanese BBQ) joint, and an Italian restaurant occupy the 2nd-7th fl. of this eclectic building. All the restaurants offer individual dishes for less than ¥1000, but the big attractions are the ¥2000 all-you-can-eat and the ¥3000 all-you-can-eat-and-drink options. Open daily 5:30pm-midnight. ❸

ⓒ SIGHTS

Kumamoto-jō (熊本城), at the center of the city, is one of the three largest and best-designed castles in Japan. Completed in 1607 by Lord Katō Kiyomasa, the towering castle flourished as the center of the Higo Province (present-day Kumamoto-ken) for over 200 years during the Tokugawa Period. What you see today, however, is mostly a reconstruction—much of the fortress was burned down during Japan's last civil war, in 1877—and the inside has been transformed into a museum exhibiting materials related to Kiyomasa, the Hosokawa Clan, and the civil war. (Open daily Apr.-Oct. 8:30am-5:30pm; Nov.-Mar. 8:30am-4:30pm. ¥500.) Also within the castle grounds lie the mildly interesting **Municipal Museum** (open Tu-Su 9am-4:30pm, closed national holidays; ¥300), **Traditional Crafts Center** (open Tu-Su 9am-4:30pm; ¥200), and **Prefectural Art Museum** (open Tu-Su 9:30am-4:30pm; ¥500). The **Contemporary Art Museum,** at the entrance of Kami-dōri Arcade, has a library of art books and a media gallery with computers and a ping-pong table for anyone to play with. (Open M and W-Su 10am-7:30pm.)

Pull out a ¥1000 note to take a look at the face of Natsume Sōseki, the Meiji Era's most famous novelist. During his four-year stay in Kumamoto, he moved six times—the fifth house he lived in has been turned into the **Natsume Sōseki Memorial Museum,** a 10min. walk northeast of the castle. (Open Tu-Su 9:30am-4:30pm. ¥200.) A 5min. walk west of the Municipal Museum, the **Shimada Museum** houses works by Miyamoto Musashi, best known to the Western world for the *Book of Five Rings,* which was considered to symbolize the principles underlying the Japanese post-war economic miracle. A legendary swordsman, he was also an accomplished portrait painter and calligrapher. (Open M-Tu and Th-Su 9am-5pm. ¥500.)

Suisenji Jōjuen, in the eastern part of the city, is a garden constructed more than 350 years ago. In the tearoom, you can enjoy a cup of green tea with the refined scenery. (Open daily Mar.-Nov. 7:30am-6pm; Dec.-Feb. 8:30am-5pm. ¥400.)

ⓒ NIGHTLIFE

Nijikaichaya, on a street off Shimo-dōri. Cafe by day; bar by night. Stop by in the afternoon to sip Chinese tea in a delicate teacup (¥500), but return later for cocktails (¥800) and sports on their 100-in. TV screen. Open daily 11am-6:30pm and 7pm-2am.

Ekimae Jibiirukan, across from JR Kumamoto Station. This prize-winning micro-brewery offers 5 craft beers, by the glass (¥500) or in a pitcher (¥2000). *Izakaya*-style food ¥300-600 for relatively small portions. Open M-Sa 4:30-11pm, Su 4:30-10:30pm.

Sharp, in a basement behind Daiei department store. If you want to check out the rowdy *gaijin* bar scene, head down here. 3hr. all-you-can-drink ¥2000 for men and ¥1500 for women. Beer ¥600. Cocktails ¥800. No cover. Open Su-Th 8pm-1am, F-Sa 8pm-4am.

KAGOSHIMA (鹿児島)   ☎099

Situated in Kyūshū's southernmost prefecture, Kagoshima is grounded in a distinct past and kept on its toes by volcano Sakurajima. Its proximity to continental Asia, has placed Kagoshima, historically known as Satsuma, at the fore in importing and implementing foreign ideas. This tendency fed the revolutionary movement of the Meiji Restoration, in which Satsuma played a defining role. These days, Kagoshima demonstrates the rare coexistence of an active volcano and a modern city, separated by only 4km of water. Despite the ashes, gases, and potential for eruption, residents respect Sakurajima as the city's symbol. Kagoshima serves as a gateway to increasingly popular Yaku-shima and the Okinawan Islands.

ON THE WEB	Kagoshima City: http://chukakunet.pref.kagoshima.jp

⌐ TRANSPORTATION

Flights: The **airport** is 1hr. by bus from Nishi-Kagoshima Station or Tenmonkan Stop (¥1200). **ANA** (☎0120-029-22) and **JAL** (☎0120-255-971) fly to: **Okinawa** (¥17,000-21,000); **Ōsaka** (¥12,500-20,300); **Tōkyō Haneda** (¥19,500-29,700). **JAC** (☎0120-511-283), operates flights to **Yaku-shima** (¥11,320). **Skymark Airlines** (☎223-2340) discounts fares to **Tōkyō Haneda** (¥8,900-18,000).

Trains: The train and bus hub is Nishi-Kagoshima Station. The Kyūshū *shinkansen*, which will run from Fukuoka to Kagoshima, is planned for completion in spring 2004. To: **Fukuoka** (local ¥5670, express ¥7770); **Ibusuki** (¥970); **Kirishima Hingu** (¥910/¥1510); **Kumamoto** (¥3570/¥5250); **Miyazaki** (¥2420/¥3790); **Nagasaki** (¥7040/¥10,300); **Ōita** (¥5880/¥9140).

Buses: Buses leave from Nishi-Kagoshima Station. Ask at the tourist info center for exact locations. To: **Fukuoka** (4hr., ¥5300); **Kōbe** (12hr., ¥11,500); **Kumamoto** (3hr., ¥3600); **Miyazaki** (2¾hr., ¥2700); **Ōita** (5½hr., ¥5500); **Ōsaka** (12hr., ¥12,000).

Ferries: Ferries depart from 1 of 3 wharves (North, South, or New): North serves Sakurajima, express to Okinawa (1 per week), and express ("Toppy") to Yaku-shima and Tanega-shima; South serves a slower ferry to Yaku-shima and Tanega-shima; New serves a slower ferry to southern islands, including Okinawa. A Nagasaki ferry departs from Kushinoki Port, 1hr. from Nishi-Kagoshima Station by JR and bus. To: **Nagasaki** (4hr., ¥6500); **Okinawa** (21-25hr., ¥13,200); **Sakurajima** (15min., ¥150); **Tanega-shima** (2½-4hr., ¥5370-6000); **Yaku-shima** (2½hr., ¥5200-7000).

Public Transportation: Two **tram** routes run from Kagoshima Station to Takamibaba—the midpoint between Tenmonkan and Nishi-Kagoshima Station—where they diverge into separate routes, both heading south. Fares from ¥160. The local **bus** system has been complicated by the proliferation of private bus companies.

✴ ⁊ ORIENTATION AND PRACTICAL INFORMATION

From Nishi-Kagoshima Station, the town's main artery extends 1.5km eastward to the **Tenmonkan** area, the center for shopping, entertainment, nightlife, and dining. At the Yamakataya department store intersection, the road continues straight as **Miami Road** (named for Kagoshima's sister city), which runs to the wharves, while a left turn follows the tramline toward Kagoshima Station.

Tourist Office: There's a **tourist info center** in front of Nishi-Kagoshima Station. English maps and booklets available. Open daily 8:30am-6pm.

Kagoshima · 鹿児島

0   200 meters
0   200 yards

TO KUMAMOTO & MIYAZAKI
熊本(125km)、宮崎(34km)

TO ISO-TEIEN & MIYAZAKI
磯庭園(0.7km)、宮崎(34km)

Kiiretsuchitorimochi Production Area
キイレツチトリモチ産地

Fukushō-Ji Ruins
福晶寺跡

Tagayama-Kōen
多賀山公園

TO SAKURAJIMA
桜島(4.5km)

St Francis Xavier's Memorial & Landing Site
ザビエル上陸記念碑

Gionnosu-ōhashi
祇園之洲大橋

Nanshū-Kōen
南洲公園

Kagoshima Station
Kagoshima Eki-mae Station
鹿児島駅前駅
鹿児島駅

TO OKINAWA
沖縄(319km)

Shiroyama Tunnel · 城山トンネル

Sakurajima Sanbashi-dōri Station
桜島桟橋通駅

Kagoshima City Aquarium
市立鹿児島水族館

Kita-futō Pier
北埠頭旅客ターミナル

Shiyakusho-mae Station
市役所前駅

Shiroyama-Kōen
城山公園

Asahi-dōri Station
旭通駅

TO IBUSUKI
指宿(38km)

Kagoshima-wan
鹿児島湾

Izuro-dōri Station
いづろ通駅

Flower Market
生花市場

Central Wholesale Market
中央卸売市場

Tenmonkan-dōri · 天文館通

Tenmonkan-dōri Station
天文館通駅

Tenmonkan-Kōen
天文館公園

Shiritsu Byōin-mae Station
市立病院前駅

Takamibaba Station
高見馬場駅

Perth-dōri · パース通

Kajiyachō Station
加治屋町駅

Shinyashiki Station
新屋敷駅

Okinawa Ferry Terminal
沖縄フェリーターミナル

Takami-bashi Station
高見橋駅

Nishi Kagoshima Eki-mae Station
西鹿児島駅前駅

Naples-dōri · ナポリ通

Natsukata-bashi
松方橋

Kiyotaki-gawa · 清滝川

Nishi Kagoshima Station
西鹿児島駅

Tenpōzan-bashi
天保山橋

Tenpōzan-ōhashi
天保山大橋

Tenpōzan Seeside Bridge
天保山シーサイドブリッジ

Miyako-dōri Station
都通駅

Takeno-bashi Station
武之橋駅

Kōtsūkyoku-mae Station
交通局前駅

Kōtsuki-gawa · 甲突川

Nakasu-dōri Station
中洲通駅

Tenpōzan-Kōen
天保山公園

Kagoshima Kokusai Jungle Park
鹿児島国際ジャングルパーク

Arata Hachiman Station
荒田八幡駅

Tabakosangyō-mae Station
たばこ産業前駅

Kagoshima Tropical Botanical Garden
鹿児島熱帯植物園

Shinden Station
神田駅

TO KUMAMOTO
熊本(139km)

Tōso Station
唐湊駅

Kishaba Station
騎射場駅

TO IBUSUKI
指宿(35km)

Bunka-Kōen
文化公園

Kamoike-Kōen
鴨池公園

Kamoike Dome
鴨池ドーム

SEE CENTRAL KAGOSHIMA MAP, P. 621

Central Kagoshima・中央鹿児島

Budget Travel: Joy Road (☎253-2201) is outside Nishi-Kagoshima Station. Open M-F 10am-7pm, Sa-Su 10am-5pm.

Currency Exchange and ATMs: Change cash and traveler's checks at **Kagoshima Bank** in front of Nishi-Kagoshima Station (open M-F 9am-3pm) or the **Main Post Office** (see below), which has **international ATMs** (M-F 7am-11pm, Sa 9am-9pm, Su 9am-7pm).

Luggage Storage: The tourist info center holds luggage. ¥200 per day. Available daily 8:30am-5:30pm.

Emergency: Police ☎110. Fire or ambulance ☎119.

Police: There's a police station in front of Nishi-Kagoshima Station.

Pharmacy: Tenmonkan Yakkyoku (green cross sign) is on the northern side of Tenmonkan Tram Stop. Open daily 9am-8pm.

Central Kagoshima
中央鹿児島

🏠 ACCOMMODATIONS
Gasthof Hotel, **10**
Hyūga Bekkan, **2**
Kagoshima Shiroyama
Youth Hostel (HI), **1**
Nakazono Ryokan, **3**
Suzuya Hotel, **14**

🍎 FOOD
Chill Out Café, **6**
Edokko Zushi (2 branches), **9,12**
Kurobuta, **8**
Tontoro Rāmen, **11**

🍷 NIGHTLIFE
Akatō, **4**
Doggy Park, **13**
Pannonica, **5**
Taiheiyō Biiru Kan, **7**

KYŪSHŪ

Hospital/Medical Services: Shiritsu Byōin (City Hospital), at the Shiritsu Byōin Tram Stop, is the biggest in town.

Internet Access: Internet cafes are a limited commodity. **Jiyū Kūkan,** a 3min. walk north from Tenmonkan Tram Stop, has private booths. Open 24hr. Membership ¥300, 1st hr. ¥480, ¥80 per 15min. thereafter. **At Run Up** is on the 3rd fl. of the Caparvo Bldg. ¥200 per 10min. Open daily noon-midnight.

Post Office: The **Kagoshima Main Post Office** is next to Nishi-Kagoshima Station. Open M-F 9am-7pm, Sa 9am-5pm, Su 9am-12:30pm. **Postal Code:** 890.

ACCOMMODATIONS

Kagoshima Shiroyama Youth Hostel (HI) (☎223-2648). From Nishi-Kagoshima Stations's bus stop #6 or 12, take a bus bound for Rte. 3 to Naka Sōmuta (10min.). Walk back 100m to an intersection, cross the street, and it's a 5min. walk uphill. With only 3 *tatami* guest rooms, it's a cozy stay. Cable TV. English spoken. Members ¥3100. ❶

Nakazono Ryokan (☎226-5125). 1min. from Shiyakusho-mae Tram Stop. The most popular inn among foreigners in Kagoshima because of the good location and English signs. No meals. ¥4000 per person. Credit cards accepted. ❷

Hyūga Bekkan (☎257-3509). A 7min. walk north of Nishi-Kagoshima Station. The place for Japanese-style stays in the station area. 10 *tatami* rooms with TV. Friendly managers. ¥3500 per person. ❷

Suzuya (☎258-2385). 1min. from Nishi-Kagoshima Station. Standard business hotel rooms within spitting distance of the station. Singles ¥3900-4500. ❷

Gasthof (☎252-1401). A 5min. walk from Nishi-Kagoshima Station. A slightly more luxurious stay, with the usual business hotel amenities. Singles ¥5300. ❸

FOOD

▨ Tontoro Rāmen. In the southern half of the Tenmonkan area. Dishes out *rāmen* like nothing you've ever tasted before. Long lines during lunch and dinner. *Rāmen* ¥550. *Chāshū* (pork chop) *rāmen* ¥700. Open daily 11:30am-1:30pm and 6:30pm-3:30am. ❷

Kurobuta. In the southern half of the Tenmonkan area. Serves quality *tonkatsu* (pork) in a traditional atmosphere. Although Kagoshima's specialty—*kurobuta* (black pig)—is expensive, regular meals are good and reasonably priced. Roast *katsu* set meal ¥1350. *Miso katsu* set meal ¥980. Open Tu-Su 11:30am-2pm and 6-11pm. ❸

Chill Out Café. In the northern half of the Tenmonkan area. Cafe by day, bar from dinnertime 'til the early morn. A cozy, white space. Pick drinks from the semi-English menu. Coffee ¥500. Pasta ¥800. Cocktails ¥800. Open daily noon-5am. ❷

Edokko Zushi. Main restaurant and a branch both in the southern half of Tenmonkan. Although most dishes are beyond the budget traveler's reach, the Jo-zushi set, served at lunch at the main restaurant and all day at the branch, is a good deal (¥1000). Open M-F 11:30am-midnight, Su 11:30am-10pm. ❸

SIGHTS

Most sights in Kagoshima pertain to the Meiji Restoration, as Kagoshima stood at the forefront of destroying the Tokugawa feudal system and opening Japan to the rest of the world. These sights cluster in central Kagoshima near Nishi-Kagoshima Station and the Tenmonkan area. All the sights, excluding Sakurajima, are connected by the **City View,** a bus route designed for tourists (¥180, day-pass ¥600).

MUSEUM OF THE MEIJI RESTORATION. Exhibits here describe the string of 19th-century events that directed Japan towards industrialization and modernization. Not much information is presented in English, but the 25min. robot show about the movement's main characters is entertaining. Outside the theater, antiquated inventions demonstrate the intellect of progressive 19th-century Satsuma. *(A 5min. walk from Nishi-Kagoshima Station. ☎239-7700. Open daily 9am-5pm. ¥300.)*

SAIGŌ TAKAMORI STATUE. Saigō-san, as most residents refer to him, was the charismatic leader of Satsuma and one of the Restoration's most prominent figures. Repeatedly exiled for his rebellious actions against the Tokugawa government, he persevered and succeeded in overthrowing the feudal system by force. He died at 49 during the last civil war, when he rebelled against the Meiji government he himself had helped found. The statue's big, too. *(About 10min. north of the Tenmonkan area, on Iso-dōri, across the street from Chūō Kōen.)*

MUSEUMS. Three museums cluster on Iso-dōri, near the statue and the Tsurumaru Castle site. The **Prefectural Museum of Natural Science,** at the Terukuni Shrine intersection, is not hugely interesting, but you can't beat the price. *(Open Tu-Su 9am-4:30pm. Free.)* On the opposite side of the statue, the **City Art Museum** exhibits works by Western impressionists and local Japanese artists. *(Open Tu-Su 9:30am-5:30pm. ¥200.)* As you walk away from the statue on Iso-dōri, the **Reimeikan Museum** is on the Tsurumaru Castle grounds. This museum is probably the most interesting of the three, with easy-to-understand displays on the history and culture of Kagoshima. *(Open Tu-Su 9am-4:30pm. Closed the 25th of each month. ¥300.)*

AROUND TERUKUNI SHRINE. Terukuni Shrine, with a huge archway, is dedicated to Saigō's mentor, Shimazu Nariakira, who aggressively imported ideas and technology from the rest of the world, taking the first steps toward the industrialization of Japan. The road to the right of the Reimeikan Museum leads to the **Shiroyama Observatory,** passing the **Loyal Retainers' Monument,** dedicated to the Satsuma souls lost in the construction of an embankment in Honshū, and **Saigō's Cave,** where Saigō Takamori committed suicide during a civil war. After a 20min. walk between tropical trees, an ideal view of Kagoshima with Sakurajima in the background awaits. *(Just beyond the Reimeikan Museum, on Iso-dōri.)*

SENGAN'EN. This garden-villa complex was constructed between 1658 and 1661 by the 19th Shimazu Lord. Garden attractions include Japan's first gas lanterns and a bamboo forest. Inside the building, intricate interior decoration demonstrates the strength and prosperity of the Shimazu Clan, which ruled Kagoshima for over 700 years. A walk along the stream brings you to a scenic view of the bay and Sakurajima. Next to Sengan'en, historical museum **Shōko Shu-seikan** preserves the roots of Japanese modernization. *(The northernmost stop on the City View. Open daily 8:30am-5:30pm. Garden ¥1000, garden and villa ¥1500. Fee includes museum admission.)*

▨ NIGHTLIFE

Taiheiyō Biiru Kan. Near the wharves. A happening beer hall that attracts herds of salarymen after work. Glass of beer around ¥500. The food's worth a taste, too, but you have to wonder why a beer hall would close at 9:30pm.

Pannonica. In the northern half of Tenmonkan area, on the 2nd fl. Classy jazz bar that routinely invites almost-famous artists. Wine and cocktails ¥700. Cover charge depends on act; it's free if there isn't live music. Open daily 6pm-2am.

Akatō. In the northern half of Tenmonkan area, next to Pannonica. A "kitchen-bar"— unwind while nibbling homey dishes and swigging beer. *Yakisoba* ¥600. *Edamame* ¥400. Beer ¥500. Open M-F 7pm-2:30am, Sa 7pm-3:30am, Su 7pm-1:30am.

KYŪSHŪ

Doggy Park. In the southern half of the Tenmonkan area. Frequently hosts DJ events with hip-hop, reggae, and techno beats. Cover varies. Open F-Sa 9pm until late.

DAYTRIPS FROM KAGOSHIMA

SAKURAJIMA (桜島)

Ferry runs 24hr. between Kagoshima's North Wharf and the Sakurajima Ferry Terminal on the western side of the mountain (15min., every 10-15min. during the day, ¥150). There's a tourist information booth at the terminal. Sightseeing bus (3hr., 2 per day at 9:30am and 3:30pm, ¥1700). A local bus also covers most sights (about 1 per hr.). Rainbow Sakurajima, 5min. south of the ferry terminal, rents bikes (¥400 per day). Sakurajima Rent-a-Car, in front of the ferry terminal, has bikes (¥300 per hr.), cars, and scooters.

Active volcano Sakurajima (1117m), Kagoshima's icon, is just a quick ferry trip away. Though it was once an island, the volcanic eruption of 1914 connected its southeastern edge to Ōsumi Peninsula. Having chalked up 76 minor eruptions in 2002, Sakurajima continues to be very much an active volcano, as the threatening smoke from **Minami-dake,** one of the three peaks, indicates. Because of the volcanic activity and steep, craggy slopes, hiking is prohibited. The highest point to which visitors are allowed is **Yunohira Observatory** (373m). Seven minutes south of the ferry terminal on foot is the **visitors center,** where displays and models explain the history of the volcano. (Open daily 9am-5pm. Free.)

KYŪSHŪ

Walk south for another 10min. to reach **Karasujima Observatory.** You'll need to rent a bicycle or take a bus to reach the other sights. A special **onsen** on the southern side, overlooking the bay, is inside **Furusato Kankō Hotel,** where the co-ed *rotemburo* (outdoor bath) houses a shrine. As it's a sacred place, you'll be given a white *yukata* (cotton *kimono*) to wear in the water. (Open W-Su 8am-8pm. ¥1000.) The other lookout point, **Arimura Observatory,** is 3km beyond Furusato. A less unique, but cheaper mud spa, **Shirahama Onsen** lies on the northern side. (Open 10am-9pm. ¥300.) **Kurokami Buried Archway,** on the island's eastern coast, demonstrates the amount of ash accumulated by the 1914 eruption; an originally 3m archway is submerged in 2m of ash. If you want to spend the night (and who doesn't want to curl up with an active volcano?), **Sakurajima Youth Hostel (HI)** ❶, a 5min. walk from the Ferry Terminal, is a big dormitory-like building that offers a cheap and friendly stay. (☎293-2150. Members ¥2650.)

SATSUMA HANTŌ (薩摩半島)

Buses for Chiran depart infrequently from the front of Nishi-Kagoshima Station or from Yamakataya Bus Center (1½hr., ¥920). Buses also make round-trips between Chiran and Ibusuki (1½hr., 3 per day, ¥930). Ibusuki and Kagoshima are connected by buses (¥850) and the JR Ibusuki Makurasaki Line (at least 1hr., ¥970). To reach Kaimon Dake, take the JR 1 stop farther to Kaimon Station (¥300), or take a bus from Ibusuki. If Yaku-shima's your ultimate destination, you can take the jetfoil ("Toppy") from Ibusuki (¥6000).

Satsuma Hantō, the sunny peninsula south of Kagoshima city, promises a daytrip jammed with historical and natural sights. The triangular loop between Kagoshima, Chiran, and Ibusuki, with an optional visit to Kaimon Dake, is best done counterclockwise, to avoid getting stranded in more remote Chiran.

Recently noted for the production of some of Japan's best tea leaves, the small town of **Chiran** offers two historic attractions. **Buke Yashiki** (*samurai* houses) from the rule of the Shimazu Clan have been preserved in the center of town, dominating a 700m street. The highlights of the houses are the gardens, each representing a different type of natural scenery. (Bukeyashiki Bus Stop. Open daily 9am-5pm.

¥500.) A 15min. walk southwest on the main road leads you to the **Peace Museum for Kamikaze Pilots.** During WWII, three years before the end of the war, a highly competitive air force training school was established in Chiran. As the war turned Japan to desperate measures, the military invented the Kamikaze Special Attack, in which the young pilots executed suicidal descents into enemy ships. The museum houses the pilots' farewell letters, written the night before their final takeoffs, as well as photos and personal artifacts. Although little of the collection is translated, the tears in the eyes of older Japanese visitors adequately convey the solemn sentiments. While the museum neglects to grapple with the morality of the attacks, it wraps the emotional response in an overwhelming desire for peace. (Open daily 9am-4:30pm. ¥500, with entry to Museum Chiran ¥600.)

At Kyūshū's southern tip, **Ibusuki** is a coastal town known for its sand bath, **Sunamushi Kaikan Saraku,** a 15min. walk or a quick bus ride (¥130) from JR Ibusuki Station. After changing into the provided *yukata*, walk out to the beach, where people with shovels await to bury you under the steaming sand. Afterward, wash yourself in the salty *onsen* bath, which draws ancient seawater from hundreds of meters underground. (*Onsen* bath ¥600. Sand and *onsen* bath ¥900. Open daily 8:30am-9pm. Closed M-F noon-1pm.) If you'd like to extend your stay, Ibusuki's **Yunosato Youth Hostel (HI) ❶,** a 10min. walk from the station, is convenient. (☎0993-22-5680. Breakfast ¥600. Dinner ¥1000. Members ¥2900; nonmembers ¥3900.)

At the very southern tip of the peninsula stands **Kaimon Dake** (924m), a mountain known as "Satsuma Fuji" for its aesthetically pleasing slopes. In spring, the area is carpeted with flowers, particularly in the park east of the mountain. A 2hr. hiking path leads to the peak from the JR station or the bus stop. On a clear day, the view extends beyond Sakurajima to Kirishima National Park and the southern islands.

KIRISHIMA NATIONAL PARK
(霧島国立公園)
☎0995

A beautiful highland resort, Kirishima National Park offers cool summer weather, scenic hiking courses, camping facilities, and relaxing *onsen*. And all this with a mythic twist: volcanic Kirishima Mountain is where, according to legend, Ninigi no Mikoto—distant ancestor of the Japanese Imperial Family—descended to earth. Conveniently on the border between Miyazaki and Kagoshima prefectures, it's worth slipping in if you're passing by.

◪ TRANSPORTATION. The park's drawback is the shortage of transportation options, both to other cities and within the park. From **Miyazaki,** Ebino Kōgen is the entry point. Take the bus from Miyako City Bus Terminal in front of Minami Miyazaki Station directly to Ebino Kōgen (¥2450) or connect at Kobayashi (¥1710) to an Ebino Kōgen Bus (¥690). If you have a JR pass, hop a train to Kobayashi Station (¥1600) then change to a bus for Ebino Kōgen. From **Kagoshima,** take the express bus from Nishi-Kagoshima Station to Kirishima Iwasaki Hotel in Kirishima Onsengō (1½hr., 7 per day, ¥1250; 1 per day continues to Ebino Kōgen, ¥1550) or take a train to Kirishima Jingū Station (¥910, express ¥1510) and wait for a bus to Kirishima Jingū-mae Bus Stop (15min., 1 per hr., ¥240.)

Transportation among the villages is trickier. While buses between Kirishima Jingū and Kirishima Iwasaki Hotel (Kirishima Onsengō) run frequently (20min., about 1 per hr., ¥390), Kirishima Iwasaki Hotel and Ebino Kōgen are only connected twice a day (¥330). On summer Sundays and holidays, a bus makes the 7km trip between Takachihogawara and Kirishima Jingū. If you want to check out the major sights quickly, try the **sightseeing loop bus** (3hr., 2 per day, roughly ¥2000).

KYŪSHŪ

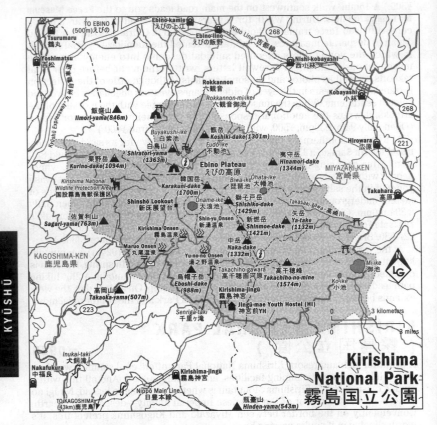

Kirishima National Park
霧島国立公園

🔲🔳 ORIENTATION AND PRACTICAL INFORMATION. Three villages in the national park serve as bases: Ebino Kōgen in the north, Kirishima Onsengō in the middle, and Kirishima Jingū in the southeast. But while **Kirishima Onsengō** is the most developed in terms of accommodation facilities and shops, budget travelers should use it simply as a transport hub, as its luxurious hotels target Japanese travelers. **Ebino Kōgen** and **Kirishima Jingū,** connected by a road via **Kirishima Onsengō** or a 4hr. hike across a string of four mountains, however, provide cheap stays. One navigational note: Kirishima Jingū village (and Kirishima Jingū-mae Bus Stop) is a 15min. drive from JR Kirishima Jingū Station.

There's a **tourist information center** in Kirishima Jingū near the bus stop. (Open Tu-Su 9am-5pm.) **Ebino Eco Museum Center,** next to the bus parking lot, has a free Japanese map and exhibits explaining the area's natural history. (Open daily 9am-5pm.) **Takachigowara Visitors Center** is at the opposite end of the four-mountain chain. (Open daily 9am-5pm.) In an emergency, call ☎110 for **police,** ☎119 for **fire** or **ambulance.** There are no exchange services or international ATMs in the park.

⑤ ⑥ ACCOMMODATIONS AND FOOD. The choice between Ebino Kōgen or Kirishima Jingū as a base depends on where you'd like to stay and what you'd like to eat. Ebino Kōgen has only a campground on its budget menu. Kirishima Jingū, however, has a host of budget sleeping options. **Ebino Kōgen Camping Ground ❶**, a 5min. walk from the Ebino Kōgen central parking lot, offers bare bungalows and rents tent space and tents. (☎0984-33-0800. Tent sites ¥500-810, ¥200 per person. Tent rentals summer only; ¥1220 per tent, ¥200 per person. Blanket ¥200. Bungalows ¥980-1650 per person.) **Takachihogawara Camping Ground ❶**, near the Takachihogawara Visitors Center, is a 7km walk from Kirishima Jingū. (☎57-1111. July-Aug. pitch site ¥1110; tent rental ¥2760. Sept.-June sites ¥100 per person; no tent rental.) If you want a solid roof over your head or a warmer environment in the winter, try quality **Kokumin Shukusha Ebino Kōgen Sō ❸** in Ebino Kōgen. (☎0984-33-0161. No meals. ¥6335 per person.) More economical **Kirishima Jingū-Mae Youth Hostel (HI) ❶** (☎57-1188) and **Minshuku Tozanguchi Onsen ❷** (☎57-0127) share an older building, 1min. by foot from the bus stop in Kirishima Jingū and have *onsen* baths. (Hostel ¥2500; minshuku ¥3500.) **Minshuku Takachiho ❷** is a 5min. walk west of the Kirishima Jingū tourist information center and boasts kind owners, Japanese and Western rooms, and an *onsen*. (☎57-0608. ¥4000.)

Ebino Kōgen's food choices are limited to cafeterias that serve fast food and set meals and close early. Bringing food from the convenience store in Kirishima Onsengō or a bigger city is recommended. In Kirishima Jingū, a few restaurants huddle near the central intersection; **Kasui'en ❷**, two doors from the post office, offers all-you-can-eat *yakiniku* (barbecue) for ¥975. (Open daily noon-11pm.)

⑥ ⑤ SIGHTS AND HIKING. The park offers hiking courses from short and easy to long and strenuous. A good place to find either is **Ebino Kōgen** (1200m). For a fairly easy 4km loop (less than 1hr.), take the path behind the Eco Museum Center past three crater lakes to Sai no Kawara, 1km northeast of the starting point.

Take on the area's tallest mountain, **Karakuni Dake** (1700m), from Sai no Kawara. The trek is steep and requires about 1½hr. A humongous crater, 900m in diameter and 300m deep, awaits challengers at the summit, which provides views of Sakurajima, Kaimondake (at Kyūshū's southern tip), and Mt. Aso on a clear day. Past climbers exaggerated about being able to see the Korean Peninsula from the peak, resulting in the name "Karakuni," which means "Korea" in Chinese characters. From Karakuni Dake, descend to stunning **Ōnami Ike** crater lake and return to Ebino Kōgen or continue along the volcanic chain southwards. The scenic trek through **Shishiko Dake** (1425m), **Shinmoe Dake** (1421m), and **Nakadake** (1345m) requires 4hr. to reach Takachihogawara. After descending to Takachihogawara, you may have to walk 7km down to Kirishima Jingū, as the bus only runs summer Sundays and holidays (around 4:30pm). If you haven't had enough of Takachihogawara after trekking the mountains, climb **Takachiho Mine** (1574m) to the east. About 1½hr. of effort rewards you with a sight of Ninigi no Makoto's divine sword pierced into the peak. In the village, there's another reminder of Ninigi no Mikoto at **Kirishima Shrine**, which is dedicated to him. A volcano destroyed the original 6th-century shrine in Takachihogawara; the present shrine was built in 1715.

Spice up your bath routine at **Sakura Sakura**, famous for its mud bath. While the tub water already contains mud particles, the fun part is dipping your hands in the bucket of mud and spreading it on your body. *(Walk 20min. uphill from the tourist information center or get off at the Yokodake Shimo Bus Stop. Open daily 6am-midnight. ¥500.)*

KYŪSHŪ

MIYAZAKI (宮崎)　　　☎0985

Aspiring young singers and guitarists greet visitors in front of Miyazaki's central station. The capital of Japan's most tropical prefecture (besides Okinawa), Miyazaki was once a favorite honeymoon destination, charming visitors with its tall palm trees, vivid flowers, and resort ambience. Its heyday has faded as young couples have begun to head overseas, but the now relatively uncrowded city still offers beaches, pleasant coastal roads, and deep blue water. Although the attractions in the city proper are unlikely to keep travelers more than a night or two, the Nichinan Kaigan coast, south of the city, is a guaranteed scenic getaway.

ON THE WEB	Miyazaki City: www.pref.miyazaki.jp/english

⨎ TRANSPORTATION

Flights: The airport is 25min. from Terminal 1 of Miyazaki Station by bus (¥400) or 10min. by train (¥340). **ANA** and **JAL** operate flights to: **Fukuoka** (¥6000-14,900); **Okinawa** (¥18,000-22,500); **Ōsaka** (¥10,500-17,600); **Tōkyō Haneda** (¥21,000-27,900). Budget competitor **Skynet Asia Airways** (☎61-7583) flies to **Tōkyō Haneda** (as low as ¥8500 if booked in advance).

Trains: The JR Nippō Line traces the east coast of Kyūshū, bending in at Miyazaki, toward Kirishima and Kagoshima. The JR Nichinan Line begins at Miyazaki and follows the east coast. To: **Fukuoka/Hakata** (¥9460); **Kirishima Jingū** (¥1430, express fee ¥920); **Kokura** (¥7960); **Nishi-Kagoshima** (¥2420/¥1370); **Nobeoka** (¥1600/¥920).

Buses: Long-distance buses depart Terminal 4 at Miyazaki Station for **Fukuoka/Hakata** (4hr., ¥6000) and **Kumamoto** (2¾hr., ¥4500). Buses for **Nishi-Kagoshima** (2¾hr. ¥2700) leave from a bus terminal across from Miyazaki Station. All these buses, as well as local buses, stop at Miyakō City Bus Terminal, across from Minami-Miyazaki Station.

Ferries: Miyazaki Port can be difficult to access. Only 1 bus runs there from Miyazaki Station (1 per day around 5:30pm, ¥240), so you may have to rely on a taxi (¥1200-1300). Ferries run to Kawasaki, Ōsaka, and Okinawa. **Kawasaki** (12hr., ¥12640) and **Ōsaka** (12hr., ¥8380) ferries depart 7-9pm. On M, W, and F, they depart from Hyūga Port, about 1hr. north of Miyazaki. No Su ferry. The **Okinawa ferry** (24hr., 3 ferries every 2 weeks, ¥14,200) stops at islands in between.

Public Transportation: Nearly all of Miyazaki is accessible by foot. Miyazaki Shrine requires a public bus from Terminal 1 of Miyazaki Station (¥210).

☀ ORIENTATION

Straight gridded roads outline the small central Miyazaki area, easily navigable on foot. The city's main intersection, **Tachibana-dōri San-chōme**, consists of Takachiho-dōri, originating from Miyazaki Station and heading westward, and of Tachibana-dōri, the busiest street in Miyazaki. Everything from the post office to bars fits into this district three blocks each way from these two backbone streets.

🛈 PRACTICAL INFORMATION

Tourist Office: There's a **tourist information center** inside Miyazaki Station. Open Mar.-Nov. 9am-7pm; Dec.-Feb. 9am-6:30pm. The **Prefectural International Center** in Higashi Bekkan, across the street from the Prefectural Office Bldg., is a multicultural lounge mostly for alien residents, but also for foreign travelers.

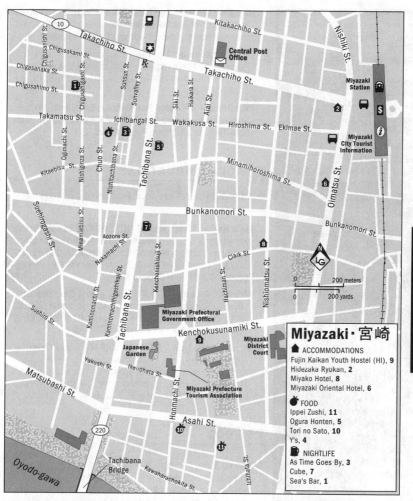

Miyazaki · 宮崎

▲ ACCOMMODATIONS
Fujin Kaikan Youth Hostel (HI), 9
Hidezaka Ryokan, 2
Miyako Hotel, 8
Miyazaki Oriental Hotel, 6

🍎 FOOD
Ippei Zushi, 11
Ogura Honten, 5
Tori no Sato, 10
Y's, 4

🍸 NIGHTLIFE
As Time Goes By, 3
Cube, 7
Sea's Bar, 1

Budget Travel: Joy Road (☎24-2626). Inside Miyazaki Station. Open M-Sa 10am-6:30pm, Su 10am-5:30pm.

Currency Exchange and ATMs: The **Central Post Office** (see below) can exchange both cash and traveler's checks. Available M-F 9am-6pm. International ATMs can be found in the **Central Post Office** (available M-F 7am-11pm, Sa 9am-9pm, Su 9am-7pm) and inside Miyazaki Station at the south end of the building (available daily 9:30am-11pm).

Emergency: Police ☎110. Fire or ambulance ☎119.

Police: *Kōban* (police box) at the Takachiho-Tachibana intersection's northwest corner.

Pharmacy: Drug Eleven is on Wakakusa-dōri, 1min. from Tachibana-dōri.

THE BIG SPLURGE

MOTORING MIYAZAKI

The inconvenient bus schedules and high fares down the southern coast of Miyazaki make it worthwhile to rent a car, especially if you can split the cost with another traveler. A cruise down the tropical road is a delightful liberation from days of reliance on public transportation. Beyond getting you to the sights in the Nichinan Kaigan section (p. 632), having your own vehicle will let you venture to the otherwise hardly-accessible southern cape, Toi Misaki, and to nearby Ko-jima.

The green hills and steep cliffs of **Toi Misaki** are home to wild horses, who have lived without human interference for over 300 years. Drive cautiously. *(Entrance fee ¥400. Visitor Center ¥500, students ¥300. Open Tu-Su 9am-5pm.)*

Ten kilometers north of Toi Misaki, tiny, monkey-inhabited **Ko-jima** lies just off the coast. *(Round-trip ferry ¥1000.)* Almost completely untouched by human hands, the Ko-jima monkeys are remarkably tame. The monkeys are also "cultured": they have learned to wash potatoes before eating them. To maintain the natural environment, no food is allowed on the island. *(Car rental shops cluster around Miyazaki Station. Budget ☎ 23-0543. A 2min. walk south of the station. Often has special deals. Smallest car ¥4500 for 6 hr., ¥5000 for 12hr. A full tank of gasoline runs ¥4000; a trip to Toi Misaki and back requires about half a tank.)*

Hospital/Medical Services: The **Prefectural Hospital,** 5min. north of the Takachiho-Tachibana intersection, has extensive services, though minimal English is spoken.

Internet Access: Tip Top is a 2min. walk from the Takachiho-Tachibana intersection. ¥500 for 30min; ¥100 additional 10min. Open M-Sa 9am-8pm, Su 11am-6:30pm.

Post Office: The **Central Post Office** is 5min. from Miyazaki Station on Takachiho-dōri. Open M-F 9am-7pm, Sa 9am-5pm, Su 9am-12:30pm. **Postal Code:** 880.

ACCOMMODATIONS

As Miyzaki is a resort area, budget options are very limited.

Fujin Kaikan Youth Hostel (HI) (☎ 24-5785). A 15min. walk from Miyazaki Station. 4 rooms, part of an office building. Bathtub is meticulously clean. Attached restaurant open 7:30am-8:30pm. Reservations suggested. ¥2600 per person. ❶

Hidezaka Ryokan (22-4900). Just across the street from Miyazaki Station. Prime location and reasonable price for its 11 *tatami* rooms. Cordial service in an older building. ¥3500 per person, with 2 meals ¥5700. ❷

Miyako Hotel (☎ 27-9991) and **Miyazaki Oriental Hotel** (☎ 27-3111). If the hostel is full, these 2 business hotels are within 5min. of the station. The Miyazaki Oriental is ever-so-slightly nicer. Miyako ¥3500; Miyazaki Oriental ¥3900. ❷

FOOD

Tori no Sato. Serves one of Miyazaki's specialties, *jidori* (free-range chicken). As the autographs on the walls testify, Japanese celebrities frequent this restaurant. Menu with pictures. Sautéed chicken thigh set ¥1000 (small) or ¥1400 (large). Raw chicken sushi ¥500. Beer ¥500. Open M-Sa 5pm-midnight, Su 5-11pm. ❸

Ippei Zushi. The granddaddy of Miyazaki's other specialty—lettuce sushi roll, a harmony of cooked shrimp, lettuce, and mayonnaise. The owner invented the roll as a solution to his friend's dislike for vegetables. Lettuce roll ¥950. *Moriawase* (combination) ¥900. *Kanijiru* (crab *miso* soup) ¥500. Open Su-M and W-Sa 11am-10pm. ❸

Ogura Honten. Tucked away in an alley. Home to specialty chicken *nanban* (fried chicken with tartar sauce). The 40-year-plus tradition has locked in a clientele of businessmen and office ladies. Chicken *nanban*, hamburger, or combination of both ("business lunch") ¥900. Open M-Sa 11am-3pm and 5-8:30pm, Su 11am-8:30pm. ❷

Y's. An *okonomiyaki* place in a small, clean basement; cooked in front you at the bar. Beer (¥400) served in a freezing mug hits the spot. No English menu. *Okonomiyaki* ¥650. *Yakisoba* (fried noodles) with toppings ¥650. Open M-Sa 6pm-3am. ❷

◎ SIGHTS

There are a few interesting tourist sights in Miyazaki City, but the main attractions of the tropical prefecture lie outside the city, scattered in the picturesque mountains and along coastal areas, all within daytrip range.

From downtown Miyazaki, the area of **Miyazaki Shrine** and **Heiwadai Kōen** is a quick ride away on bus #1 or one stop on the JR Nippō line from Miyazaki Station. The shrine is dedicated to the legendary first emperor of Japan—Jinmu Tennō—and his divine father. This location was the site of the capital before Jinmu Tennō's unification of Japan. Within the grounds, **Minka'en**, a set of reconstructions of Edo-era houses (open daily 10am-5pm; free), deserves a visit more than the **Prefectural Museum** (open Tu-Su 9am-4:30pm; ¥200) or the **Prefectural Art Museum** (open Tu-Su 10am-6pm; ¥300) across the street. **Heiwadai Kōen**, a park with a 37m tower at its center, is a 15min. walk northwest of the shrine block. The peace tower, constructed, ironically, in 1940 as Japan was expanding its East Asian empire, was named after the war and is negligible compared to such structures as the Peace Statue of Nagasaki. The tower is built of stones from all over the world and clapping your hands on the platform in front of the tower generates a strange echo. The four statues depict a warrior, fisherman, farmer, and architect. Behind the tower, **Haniwa Garden** holds numerous clay figurines of people and animals. Excavated from Saitobaru burial mounds in the suburbs of the city, *haniwa* were buried in 4th-century aristocratic tombs, probably as tomb guardians.

On the east side of the JR Nippō Line, you'll find a Science Park (Kagaku Gijutsukan) and a fascinating resort complex. The ▧**Science Park,** a 2min. walk from the east gate of Miyazaki Station, is marked by its life-size recreation of an H-1 rocket. It houses cutting-edge hands-on displays and the world's biggest planetarium. (¥520, with planetarium ¥730. Open Tu-Su 9am-4:30pm.) A coastal area about 8km northwest of Miyazaki Station is occupied by the deluxe **Seagaia** resort complex, which includes a world-class hotel, 27-hole golf course, tennis courts, a zoo, and the world's biggest water park—**Ocean Dome**. While Ocean Dome boasts an incredible man-made beach and the "seawater" is kept at 28°C with computerized waves, the park has been closing on and off due to management problems; check with the tourist information center. Buses (30min., ¥430) depart from Miyazaki Station and Miyako City. (Day-pass ¥4200. Viewing ¥1200. Open daily 10am-9pm.)

▧ NIGHTLIFE

▧ **As Time Goes By.** On Nishitachibana, near its intersection with Ichibangai. Deserves an afternoon visit for the "best coffee in town" or at night for its "Elvis" cocktail. Dimly lit, the interior is saturated with '50s and '60s Americana: think posters of John F. Kennedy, Marilyn Monroe, Frank Sinatra, and *Casablanca*. Owner often wears a pseudo-Elvis outfit. Coffee ¥400. Cocktails ¥700. Open daily 1:30-6pm and 8:30pm-2am.

Sea's Bar. At the corner of Chigusa-higashi and Chigusa-shimo. Emulates Miyazaki's tropical atmosphere with red walls, green lighting, and a sea turtle named Tom in a big tank. Try the tropical drinks—like the "Dolphin"—from the semi-English menu. Cocktails from ¥700. ¥300 bar charge, ¥500 for box seats. Open Su-M and W-Sa 8pm-1am.

Cube. On Tachibana, near its intersection with Bunka-no-mori. The place to be for clubbers on the weekends. Special events with popular DJs about every other weekend. For more info, check the flyers outside. Doors open at 9pm.

▶ DAYTRIP FROM MIYAZAKI

NICHINAN KAIGAN COAST

Buses depart for Aoshima from Miyazaki Station via Miyakō City bus terminal (45min., ¥670) and JR trains from Miyazaki Station (25min., ¥360). There's a tourist information booth at Aoshima Station (9am-6pm). A bus also runs from Miyakō City Bus Terminal to the Udo Jingū Stop in Nichinan (1½hr., ¥1440).

A tropical ambience of turquoise water and craggy cliffs dominates the coast that runs south of Miyazaki City through Aoshima and Nichinan to Toi Misaki. Because public transportation does not run conveniently along the coast and tends to be expensive, renting a car is the ideal option. If you want to rely on buses and trains, however, a day's ranging is limited to Aoshima, Nichinan, and Obi.

An oval tropical island, **Aoshima** protrudes out of the coast 15km south of Miyazaki City. Only 1.5km in circumference, this sandy isle attracts tourists with its picturesque scenery and warm water suitable for summer swims. The island is accessible by a footbridge or, during low tide, on **Oni no Sentakuita** ("Ogre's Washboard")—a layer of curious-looking bedrocks, a geological wonder that continues down the coast for about 100km. On the island itself, there's nothing but sand and a small shrine, **Aoshima Jinja,** the site of the legendary tales of Umi Sachihiko and Yama Sachihiko, ancestors of the imperial family. The Aoshima beach area is filled with hotels and minshuku, including a few *onsen.* **Aoshima Sankumāru** boasts an ocean-facing bath. (Open daily 10am-9pm. ¥1000.)

South of Aoshima, a set of sights crowd around Nichinan. Approaching them from the north, the first is **Cactus Herb Garden,** across from Saboten Harbu-en Bus Stop. The collection has reached 1.3 million cactus trees and 6000 herb grasses; the culinary menu offers steak, ice cream, and cactus wine. (Open daily 9am-5pm. ¥600.) Several minutes south by car or bus is **Sun Messe Nichinan,** a strange park of sun and tropical ocean motifs. The symbol of the park is the **Seven Moai Statues,** replicas of the real ones in the Easter Islands, constructed with special permission from tribal leaders of Easter. Each is 5.5m tall and weighs 18 metric tons. Get off the bus at the Moai Misaki Stop for a 10min walk. (Open Su-Tu and Th-Sa 9:30am-5pm. ¥700.) Several minutes south of Sun Messe Nichinan is **Udo Jingū,** a shrine in a scenic seaside cave, where people pray for good marriages and safe childbirths. Supposedly, this is where Jinmu Tennō's father was born; the round stones in the cave symbolize his mother's breasts. Candy made from water collected here is believed to aid lactation; you can buy some in the stalls inside or around the cave. Another superstitious practice is the throwing of *undama* (luck stones) into the indentation in the turtle-shaped rock. Wishes will be granted for successful throws (¥100 for 5 stones). It's a 10min. walk from the Udo Jingū Bus Stop.

YAKU-SHIMA (屋久島) ☎ 0997

Sixty kilometers from the southern tip of Kyūshū, two small islands—Yaku-shima, home to ancient virgin forests, and less-visited Tanega-shima, a launching point for Japanese space missions—mark the border between the East China Sea and the Pacific Ocean. Yaku-shima can be circled by car in less than 3hr., yet the highest point is just shy of 2000m, making the island a super-steep cone. This unique figure translates to a spectrum of climates, from the semi-tropical at sea level to the snowy and frigid near the summit. While it's said to rain 35 days a month on Yaku-shima, this World Natural Heritage Site hosts colossal millennia-old cedars and mammals found nowhere else. The news has gotten out to the Japanese, and the island's become a hot domestic destination, but most international travelers have yet to discover it—enjoy this natural highlight before the word spreads.

⌷ TRANSPORTATION. The Yaku-shima **airport** is equidistant from Miya-no-ura and Anbō (buses: 1 per hr., ¥410-490). Flights depart for Kagoshima airport (☎ 0120-511-283; ¥11,320). Two boats run between Yaku-shima and Kagoshima: the ferry and a speedier jetfoil ("Toppy"). The **ferry** operates between Kagoshima South Wharf and Miyanoura Port (4hr., 1 per day, ¥5200). **Toppy** runs from Kagoshima North Wharf alternately to Miyanoura and Anbō, Yaku-shima's two biggest towns (☎ 099-255-7888; 2½hr.; 5 per day; ¥7000, round-trip ¥12,300). Toppy also connects Ibusuki to Miyanoura (1 per day, ¥6000).

The **bus** is the only mode of public transportation available on the island, running from Nagata in the northwest, via Miyanoura, Anbō, and Onoaida, to Ōko no Taki in the southwest (Miyanoura to Anbō ¥600, to Ōko no Taki ¥1820). Other than the coastal loop road, a couple of roads lead up into the mountains: one from Miyanoura to Shiratani Unsuikyō and another from Anbō to Yakusugi Land. From March to November, buses trek up to Shiratani Unsuikyō (¥500) and Yakusugi Land (¥720) twice a day. A rental car, however, will maximize your travel options; **Suzuki Rent-a-Car** has competitive rates. (☎ 42-2734. ¥3000 for 6hr., ¥4800 for 24hr.). For bicycles and motorcycles, call **Terada Rent-a-Car** (☎ 42-0460).

◨◪ ORIENTATION AND PRACTICAL INFORMATION. Yaku-shima is a circular island with a road that traces the coast. The ports of **Miyanoura** (in the north) and **Anbō** (in the east), and the southern **Onoaida**, serve as hubs. There are **tourist offices** in the Miyanoura Ferry Terminal and in Anbō. (Both open daily 9am-7pm.) In an emergency, call ☎ 110 for **police**, ☎ 119 for **fire** or **ambulance**. The main **police station** is in Anbō near the tourist office. The **Miyanoura Post Office** is near the river bridge in the center of town and has an **international ATM**. (Open M-F 9am-5pm. ATM available M-F 8:45am-6pm, Sa 9am-5pm, Su 9am-3pm.) **Postal code: 891.**

⌂▯ ACCOMMODATIONS AND FOOD. Yaku-shima has a fair number of reasonably priced beds. In Miyanoura, **Minshuku Jōmon ❷**, 20min. from the ferry terminal, caters to budget travelers, with shared rooms, bunk beds, and free rice refills at meals. Call for a pickup from the terminal; if you're hoofing it, cross the big bridge, walk uphill, and hang a right after a gas station. (☎ 42-2955. 2 meals included. ¥3800.) **Minshuku Iwakawa ❶**, a 10min. walk from the ferry terminal, 3min. before the big bridge, is a basic, centrally located inn with a few private *tatami* rooms. (☎ 42-0747. No meals. ¥3000.) For **Minshuku Seikō Udoku ❷**, 15min. from the ferry terminal, hang a right at the corner of Iwakawa, and follow the road to the sign. The managers can provide you with information about hiking and sightseeing and will pick you up from the ferry terminal. (☎ 42-2070. ¥3500.)

In Anbō, **Minshuku Chiho ❷**, right outside the ferry terminal, is ideally located with clean *tatami* rooms. (☎46-3288. ¥4500 per person.) Cozy **Nature Boy ❷**, 10min. from the Anbō tourist information center, has only 5 rooms, close to the restaurants and shops at the center of town. (☎46-3465. ¥3500 per person.) In Hirauchi, friendly **Yaku-shima Youth Hostel (HI) ❶** is a 2min. walk from Hirauchi Iriguchi Bus Stop, 35min. from Anbō and 70min. from Miyanoura. Despite the inconvenient location, the hostel promises a wonderful stay that includes car, motorcycle, or bicycle rental. (☎47-3751; yakushima-yh@m6.dion.ne.jp. Breakfast ¥600. Dinner ¥1000. ¥2800 per person; 3 nights ¥7500.)

While a number of inexpensive restaurants line the main streets of Miyanoura and Anbō, none are more striking than the others. Eating in your accommodation is a good option, especially at Minshuku Jōmon, which was originally a restaurant. In Miyanoura, **Shimamusubi ❸**, a 5min. walk from the bridge towards Anbō, offers Western and Japanese food in a cabin-like building. In Anbō, **Rengaya ❷**, a 5min. walk from the harbor on the road leading to the center of town, serves *tonkatsu* (¥800), curry rice (¥600), and other popular dishes. (Open daily 10am-2pm and 6-10pm.) Miyanoura and Anbō each have a **supermarket:** Miyanoura's is on the main road a couple kilometers toward Anbō; Anbō's is opposite the ferry terminal.

◙◙ SIGHTS AND HIKING. Ideally, you'll have two full days or more on Yaku-shima: one to hike and visit Jōmon Saga and another to tour the rest of the island by car and trek in Yakusugi Land or Shiratani Unsuikyō Ravine. If you have more than two days, you can do an overnight hike in the mountains. Most of Yaku-shima's natural wonders are located in the thick high-altitude forests. You will probably encounter species unique to the island—monkeys (*yakuzaru*) and deer (*yakushika*)—either on the road or while hiking.

Estimated to be 7200 years old, the cedar **Jōmon Sugi**, Yaku-shima's most prominent symbol, has a trunk circumference of 16m and a height of 25m. Discovered in 1968, the legendary tree is at least a 5hr. hike (one-way) from the closest road. To see it requires either a dayhike starting around 4:30am or an overnight stay in a mountain hut. Limited accessibility has checked the number of tourists and the amount of environmental destruction, but also amplifies the novelty of the tree. It stands on the northern side of Yaku-shima's highest peak, **Miyanoura Dake** (1935m), accessible by two paths: the **Arakawa Forest Path** from the east and another route from **Shiratani Unsuikyō**. After the two paths converge, and before Jōmon Sugi, stands a tremendous cedar stump—**Wilson Kabu**. Its hollow stump area, 13.8m in circumference, can fit 30 adults. From Wilson, Jōmon Sugi is a 1½hr. hike.

If the journey to Jōmon Sugi is too intimidating, **Yakusugi Land** and **Shiratani Unsuikyō Ravine** offer a variety of trekking paths (30-150min.) through ancient forests. At an elevation around 1000m, the twisting and turning roots, layers of moss, and millennium-old trees create an ambience that mystifies tourists and inspired anime godfather Miyazaki Hayao to produce the mega-hit movie *Princess Mononoke*. (Buses operate Mar.-Nov. ¥300 entrance fee for each.) Seven kilometers beyond Yakusugi Land, **Kigen Sugi**, a 3000-year-old cedar, towers at the roadside.

Yaku-shima has two notable waterfalls, **Ōko no Taki** (88m) in the southwest and **Senpiro no Taki** (60m) in the south. While the former is within walking distance of the road, the latter requires a 30min. uphill drive from the loop and is not served by buses. **Nagata Inakahama Beach**, a 1km white-sand strip in the otherwise vacant northwest part of the island, is home to one of the few sea turtle nesting sites in Japan. From May to July, dozens of turtles come ashore to lay eggs at night. (Not accessible by public transportation.) A few kilometers west of Onoaida, on the southern edge of the island, **Hirauchi Kaichū Onsen** is an outdoor co-ed *onsen* formed by spring water bubbling from between seaside bedrocks. The rock pool only surfaces during the 2hr. period around low tide. (¥100.) **Yakushima Environmental and Culture Centre,** on the main street of Miyanoura, houses displays of Yaku-shima's natural highlights. The 30min. movie with multilingual subtitles on a 14m by 20m screen takes you on a helicopter tour of the island. Pay a visit if you missed some sights due to time constraints or weather, but don't make it your first stop, as it can ruin the fun of exploration. (Open Tu-Su 9am-5pm. ¥500.)

KYŪSHŪ

OKINAWA (沖縄)

Far to the south of Tōkyō, the Okinawan Islands (also known as the Ryūkyū Islands and Nansei-shotō) are a popular vacation destination for Japanese mainlanders, and there's a reason. Okinawa is a truly phenomenal experience, offering the rare opportunity to experience Japan while simultaneously enjoying all the benefits of vacationing in a tropical paradise. Situated between China and Japan, this 1000km stretch of islands gave birth to the Ryūkyū civilization, a distinctive fusion of Japanese and Chinese culture. Although the islands were annexed by Japan after the Meiji Restoration and the government attempted to integrate the Ryūkyū people into Japanese society, the native culture refused to give in, and lives on today. Bloody battles at the end of WWII took a terrible toll, however; nearly 250,000 Japanese died during the American invasion in 1945, many of them civilians who chose suicide rather than face the invaders. Physical scars from this conflict linger still at battle sites in the south of the main island, Okinawa-hontō, but also in society. Okinawa remains the nation's poorest region, and some Okinawans feel economically marginalized by and culturally separate from the "mainland" Japanese. The high concentration of American military bases on the islands since the Cold War hasn't helped much either, although it has created a unique blend of Japanese and American culture, especially on Okinawa-hontō.

Many foreigners take this history too much to heart, imagining Okinawa as an austere military complex and nothing more. They should think again. The horror of war gave birth to a culture of peace. Islanders say they wouldn't want to live anywhere else; the relaxed lifestyle and laid-back attitude of the people are just as appealing as the dramatic coastlines and rugged interiors. For outdoor enthusiasts there are moutains and valleys, rivers, corals reefs, and jungles to sate their appetites, while the artistically inclined will enjoy the traditional Ryūkyū art. Whatever your fancy, however, time spent in Okinawa is sure to challenge your preconceptions and impart much-needed relief from the frantic pace of the rest of the planet.

HIGHLIGHTS OF OKINAWA

TO BOLDLY GO... Trek through the uncharted wilderness of **Iriomote-jima** (p. 663).

NOTIONS OF EMPIRE. Admire the architecture of **Shuri-jō,** castle seat of the former Ryūkyū Kingdom (p. 645), or take in the ruins of nearby Nakagusuku (p. 646).

FULL FATHOM FIVE. Dive below the waves in search of rays at Manta Way (p. 663) or explore the underwater caves off Miyako-shotō (p. 658).

SHOPAHOLICA. Wend your way through the mazelike marketplace and shopping center of Naha's **Kokusai-dōri** (p. 645).

OKINAWA-HONTŌ (沖縄本島) ☎098

While local fishermen rise with the sun, fading neon lights signal the end of an all-night trance party. Wildflowers envelop white sand beaches with the scent of their exotic blooms while the Japanese desire for convenience transforms the landscape into a 24hr. strip mall. Yet despite the rapid pace of development on Okinawa-hontō, the residents of the island continue to fiercely protect their cultural heritage. Okinawa-hontō was the site of the heaviest fighting in the Pacific campaign of WWII, and much of the island was obliterated by Allied bombing. The bit-

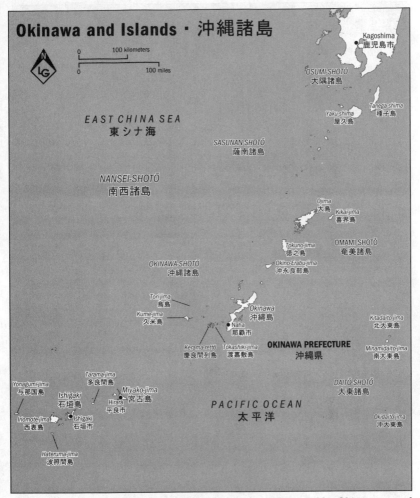

Okinawa and Islands · 沖縄諸島

100 kilometers

100 miles

EAST CHINA SEA
東シナ海

NANSEI-SHOTŌ
南西諸島

SASUNAN-SHOTŌ
薩南諸島

OKINAWA-SHOTŌ
沖縄諸島

Tori-jima
鳥島

Kume-jima
久米島

Kerama-rettō
慶良間列島

Tokashiki-jima
渡嘉敷島

Okinawa
沖縄島

Naha
那覇市

OKINAWA PREFECTURE
沖縄県

Yonagumi-jima
与那国島

Tarama-jima
多良間島

Miyako-jima
宮古島

Hirara
平良市

Ishigaki
石垣島

Iriomote-jima
西表島

Ishigaki
石垣市

Hateruma-jima
波照間島

PACIFIC OCEAN
太平洋

Kagoshima
鹿児島市

OSUMI-SHOTŌ
大隅諸島

Tanega-shima
種子島

Yaku-shima
屋久島

Ojima
大島

Kikai-jima
喜界島

Tokuno-jima
徳之島

OMAMI-SHOTŌ
奄美諸島

Okino-Erabu-jima
沖永良部島

Kitadaito-jima
北大東島

Minamidaito-jima
南大東島

DAITŌ-SHOTŌ
大東諸島

Okidaitō-jima
沖大東島

OKINAWA

ter memories of the war years still linger on in the minds of older Okinawans, and even today many of the islanders are wary of people they deem foreigners, including Japanese travelers visiting from the mainland.

Unfortunately, Okinawans have not been successful in keeping outsiders off of their main island. After the defeat of Japan in WWII, the United States held on to Okinawa-hontō until 1972, and even today 50,000 American soldiers are stationed there (p. 648). Developmental aid from the Japanese government has slowly transformed Okinawa-hontō into a holiday resort, and each week thousands of mainlanders descend on the island in convoys of bright blue tour buses. Not surprisingly, few traces of the native Ryūkyū culture remain.

Although most travelers use Okinawa-hontō as a gateway to more southerly destinations, you could easily spend a week exploring all that the island has to offer. History buffs will revel in the well-preserved wartime sites that adorn the southern

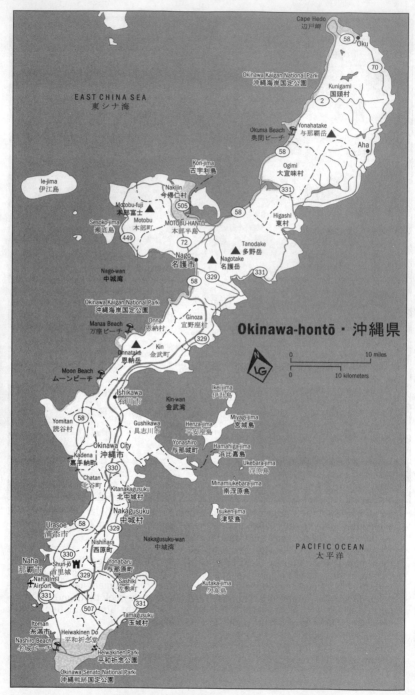

EAST CHINA SEA
東シナ海

Cape Hedo
辺戸岬

Oku

Okinawa Kaigan National Park
沖縄海岸国定公園

Kunigami
国頭村

Okuma Beach
奥間ビーチ

Yonahatake
与那覇岳

Aha

Ie-jima
伊江島

Kori-jima
古宇利島

Nakijin
今帰仁村

Ogimi
大宜味村

Higashi
東村

Motobu-fuji
本部富士

Motobu
本部町

MOTOBU-HANTŌ
本部半島

Sesoko-jima
瀬底島

Tanodake
多野岳

Nago
名護市

Nagotake
名護岳

Nago-wan
中城湾

Okinawa Kaigan National Park
沖縄海岸国定公園

Onna
恩納村

Ginoza
宜野座村

Manza Beach
万座ビーチ

Onnatake
恩納岳

Kin
金武町

Okinawa-hontō ・ 沖縄県

0   10 miles

0   10 kilometers

Moon Beach
ムーンビーチ

Ishikawa
石川市

Kin-wan
金武湾

Ikei-jima
伊計島

Yomitan
読谷村

Gushikawa
具志川市

Miyagi-jima
宮城島

Henza-jima
平安座島

Yonashiro
与那城町

Hamahiga-jima
浜比嘉島

Okinawa City
沖縄市

Ukebara-jima
浮原島

Kadena
嘉手納町

Chatan
北谷町

Kitanakagusuku
北中城村

Minamiukebara-jima
南浮原島

Tsuken-jima
津堅島

Nakagusuku
中城村

Urasoe
浦添市

Nakagusuku-wan
中城湾

PACIFIC OCEAN
太平洋

Nishihara
西原町

Naha
那覇市

Shuri-jō
首里城

Yonabaru
与那原町

Naha Intl
Airport
那覇空港

Sashiki
佐敷町

Kutaka-jima
久高島

Tamagusuku
玉城村

Itoman
糸満市

Heiwakinen Dō
平和祈念堂

Nashiro Beach
名城ビーチ

Heiwakinen Park
平和祈念公園

Okinawa Senato National Park
沖縄戦跡国定公園

OKINAWA

part of the island, while the wild north beckons the intrepid traveler with its palm-fringed beaches and relaxed pace of life. The capital city, Naha, charms with its international flavor and energetic nightlife, while nearby castle ruins offer a glimpse into a forgotten era. And, if you make an effort to meet the locals, you'll find yourself immersed in an extraordinary culture that draws its values from traditional Ryūkyū beliefs and imported American ideals.

▐▀ TRANSPORTATION

Buses: An airport bus line runs from the airport to the Naha Bus Terminal (¥200). On the City Line, enter through the front door and exit through the rear door. Bus fares on this line are always ¥200 regardless of how long you ride. On the Suburban Line, enter through the front door, and pick up a numbered ticket from the dispenser near the driver. Check your number against the electronic fare board at the front of the bus to see how much you will have to pay. When it's time to exit, put the exact amount into the fare box. If you need change, the bill changer accepts ¥1000 bills. The coin changer will also change ¥500, ¥100, and ¥50 coins.

Ferries: Four major ferry companies operate out of Naha. **Arimura Sangyō** (☎860-1980) runs a line from **Ōsaka** to **Taiwan** with stops in **Naha, Miyako,** and **Ishigaki. Marix Line** (☎862-8774) runs slow boats through the Satsunan Islands to Kagoshima. **RKK Line** (☎868-1126) ships to **Fukuoka, Kagoshima,** and **Ōsaka. Ōshima Unyu** (☎861-1886) connects **Tōkyō, Ōsaka, Kōbe, Miyazaki, Kagoshima,** and the **Satsunan Islands.** There are two main ferry terminals in Naha as well as some smaller ones, so verify the port of departure. Most ferries use **Naha Shin-ko,** which services **Fukuoka, Kagoshima, Kōbe, Ōsaka, Tōkyō, Miyako,** and **Ishigaki.** Take the #101 bus north to the terminal. Occasionally, ferries heading north to Hakata and Yoron-jima depart from **Naha-ko,** which is along the #24 bus route.

Taxis: You pay ¥450 the moment you step in the doors—from there the fare steadily creeps higher. For a 10min. ride, fare can be as high as ¥1000. If you need an English-speaking driver, try **Okito Kōtsu** (☎946-5656).

Car Rental: Assuming you're comfortable with driving on the left side of the road, a rental car is an efficient choice. The traffic in the center of the island can be frustrating, but the roads are well maintained, and most street signs are in English. The northern part of the island is virtually devoid of buses, but can be navigated easily by car. **Japaren** (ジャパレン ; ☎0120-41-3900), **Nippon Renta-Car** (日本レンタカー; ☎868-4554) and **Toyota Renta-Lease** (トヨタレンタリース沖縄 ; ☎857-0100) have offices at the Naha airport and the city center.

Bike/Moped Rental: Helmet Shop SEA, 3-15-50 Maki-shi (☎864-5116), west of Kokusai-dōri rents motorbikes and scooters from ¥1700 for 3hr. Also try **Sea Rental Bikes** (☎864-5116) near the Mitsukoshi department store, which rents motor scooters for ¥3300 per day and 250cc motorcycles for ¥10,000 per day.

Hitchhiking: Hitchhikers are known to stand along Rte. 58 and Rte. 333 to move north and south along the length of the island. However, the frequency of cars sharply decreases north of Nago and along the sparsely developed eastern coast. The American military presence has made many Okinawans wary of foreigners, which makes securing a lift difficult. Let's Go never recommends hitchhiking.

NAHA (那覇)   ☎098

You will inevitably stop in Naha, the prefectural capital, at some point during your trip to the Okinawan Islands. The city serves as the gateway for travelers heading to Okinawa and the southwest islands. Although it was completely leveled during

Naha・那覇

WWII, a fierce post-war modernization campaign resulted in the urban sprawl that characterizes much of the city. However, the city is home to impressive shopping and entertainment districts, most notably the 1.6km strip of eye candy that is **Kokusai-dōri.** The energetic pulse of this harbor city makes for an exciting night out, and there are several **Ryūkyū cultural sites** and **wartime memorials** just outside the city.

▐ TRANSPORTATION

Flights: All international and domestic flights arrive at **Naha International Airport,** 3km from the city. The following airlines have offices in the airport terminal as well as in Naha: **ANA** and **ANK** (☎0120-029222); **Asiana Airlines** (☎098-869-7701); **China Airlines** (☎098-863-1013); **JAL** (domestic ☎0120-25-5591, international ☎0120-25-5931);

ON THE WEB

www.city.naha.okinawa.jp/kanko/nahatabi/
english/index.htm

JAS (☎0120-51-1283); **Japan Asia Airlines** (☎0120-74-7801); and **JTA** and **Ryūkyū Air Commuter** (☎0120-10-0359). Call for seasonal pricing information.

Ferries: Four major ferry companies operate out of Naha. Arimura Sangyō, (☎860-1980) runs from **Ōsaka** to **Taiwan** with stops in **Naha, Miyako,** and **Ishigaki.** Marix Line (☎862-8774) runs slow boats through the **Satsunan Islands** to **Kagoshima.** RKK Line (☎868-1126) operates to **Ōsaka, Fukuoka,** and **Kagoshima.** Ōshima Unyu connects **Tōkyō, Ōsaka, Kōbe, Miyazaki, Kagoshima,** and the **Satsunan Islands.** There are two main terminals in Naha, so it's important to verify the port of departure when you buy your ticket. Most depart from Naha Shin-kō, which services **Fukuoka, Ishigaki, Kagoshima, Kōbe, Miyako, Ōsaka, and Tōkyō.** The ferry terminal is north of the city along the #101 bus route. Occasionally, ferries heading north to **Hakata** and **Yoron-jima** depart from Naha-kō, along the #24 bus route.

Buses: Although there are a number of different bus companies, buses with the same number cover the same route. As a general rule, routes #1-17 are categorized as the **Naha City Line,** whereas #20 and greater are the **Suburban Line.** When riding the Naha City Line, enter through the front door and exit through the rear door. Bus fares on this line are always ¥200. The main bus terminal is located two blocks southwest of the Palette Kumoji and the start of Kokusai-dōri. An **airport busline** runs from the airport to the Naha Bus Terminal for ¥200.

Monorail: Although the new monorail began running in August 2003, at the time of publication, the system was experiencing severe technical problems. The monorail connects the airport to Kokusai-dōri and outlying areas. Fares run ¥200-290.

Taxis: Street taxis are abundant in Naha, and they are a quick and efficient way to travel around the city. For a 10min. ride, the fare can be as high as ¥1000. If you need to arrange a cab ride, call the **Naha Private Taxi Business Cooperative** (☎857-0034).

Car Rental: The 3 major companies are located next to each other in the airport, making for easy price comparisons. **Japaren** (ジャパレン; ☎0120-41-3900), **Nippon Renta-car** (日本レンタカー; ☎098-868-4554), and **Toyota Renta-Lease** (トヨタレンタリース沖縄; ☎857-0100) have offices at the Naha airport and the city center.

Bike and Moped Rental: Helmet Shop SEA, 3-15-50 Maki-shi, (☎864-5116) west of Kokusai-dōri rents motorbikes and scooters from ¥1700 for 3hr. Also try **Sea Rental Bikes** (☎864-5116), near the Mitsukoshi department store, to rent motor scooters for ¥3300 per day and 250cc motorcycles for ¥10,000 per day.

ORIENTATION

Central Naha is strung along **Kokusai-dōri,** a shopping street filled with restaurants, bars, clubs, and touristy boutiques; most accommodations are nearby. Arrival at the port, bus station, or airport (3km from town) will put you near **Route 58,** which crosses Naha from the southwest and intersects Kokusai-dōri at the western edge of downtown. The famed **Tsuboya** pottery district is slightly south and east of central Naha, while **Shuri-jō** is about 3km to the northeast on Rte. 29.

PRACTICAL INFORMATION

Tourist Office: Although there are small branch tourist offices located all along Kokusai-dōri, the **main office** (☎868-4887) that stocks English maps of the city is a few doors down from Starbucks on Okiei-dōri. Open daily 9am-5pm. A **tourist information center** (☎857-6884) is located in Naha International Airport. Open daily from 9am-9pm.

Embassies and Consulates: Naha Immigration Office, 1 15-15 Higawa (☎852-4185), on Rte. 221 southeast of Kokusai-dōri. **The United States Consulate** is located near Naha in Urasoe City, 2564, Nishihara (☎876-4211).

Currency Exchange and Banks: In the Naha International Airport, the **Ryūkyū Bank** branch in the lobby exchanges foreign currency and traveler's checks. Open M-F, 9am-4pm. The airport's central information counter can change up to US$50. In Naha, most banks along Kokusai-dōri have foreign exchange desks. You can get a cash advance on a Visa card at **Ryūkyū** and **Okinawan** banks, or a Mastercard at **Kaihō** banks.

ATM: Your best option for withdrawing money from an international account is the **post office cash machine** in the arrival terminal of the Naha Airport. Open M-F 9am-9pm, and Sa-Su 9am-5pm. In Naha City, most of the minor post offices provide international ATM access, but many impose a ¥10,000 daily limit. For larger withdrawals, head to the **Naha Main Post Office** (see below).

English-Language Bookstore: On the 7th fl. of the Palette Kumoji Building, at the southwest end of Kokusai-dōri, **Bunkyō Tosho** has a modest English-language section. **Tower Records,** in the OPA Building on Kokusai-dōri, also has a small stock.

Police: Main police station, 1-2-9, Izumuzaki (☎836-0110). A small **prefectural police station** is located at the southwest end of Kokusai-dōri. When you reach the intersection before the Palette Kumoji building, turn left and head past the Prefectural Government Building. The station is on the right.

Emergency: Police ☎110. **Fire** or **ambulance** ☎119.

Hospital/Medical Services: Izumizaki Hospital, 1-3-8, Kumoji (☎853-3134), is located in Central Naha. If you need an English-speaking doctor, head to the **Adventist Medical Centre,** 4-11-1, Kohagura (☎946-2833), northeast of the city on Rte. 29.

Internet Access: The cheapest Internet access around is at the **Net C@fe** (☎941-2755), towards the northeast end of Kokusai-dōri, 1 block past the Mr. Donut (on the 2nd fl. of the shopping complex). ¥480 gets you 1hr. of access, and all the free tea and juice you want. Open daily 9am-7pm. **Technowork** (☎860-5757), is in the Fashion Bldg. on Kokusai-dōri. ¥500 for 30min. Open daily 9am-7pm.

Post Office: There are post offices every 500m along Kokusai-dōri. **Naha Central Post Office,** 3-3-8, Tsubogawa. Heading southwest on Kokusai-dōri, continue past the Palette Kumoji Bldg. and City Hall to the bus station. Follow Rte. 329 south about 10min. The post office is by the river next to Tsubogawa Station. **Postal Code:** 900.

ACCOMMODATIONS

Since most travelers to Okinawa will have to spend a night in Naha, there are a wide variety of quality accommodations centered around Kokusai-dōri. If you're heading to the city during Golden Week, August, or the New Year, phone ahead to reserve a spot. The information desk (☎857-6884) at the arrival terminal of Naha International Airport can phone ahead to help you find a place to sleep.

■ **Hakusei-sō** (拍清掃), 2-12-7, Nahashimatsuo (☎866-5757). Heading northeast on Kokusai-dōri, turn right down Ukishima-dōri, the tiny alley across the street from Seattle's Best Coffee. Keep following the street until you reach a large, paved area, and then bear right. Continue straight until you pass under the overhang, then look for the entrance to the ryokan, which is next door to the Baobob Cafe. Private *tatami* rooms are Naha's best-value accommodation. Laundry facilities (¥200 per wash, ¥100 per dry). Reception 9am-5pm. Check-out 10am. Single ¥2500, with bath ¥3000. ❶

▓ **Shinkinichi Ryokan** (新金一旅館), 2-12-7, Nahashimatsuo (☎866-5757). If there are no rooms available at Hakusei-sō, walk up 2 flights of stairs where you'll find Shinkinichi. Although the nearly identical *tatami* rooms are slightly more expensive, Shinkinichi owns several floors, so there's a better chance you'll be able to get a room. Reception 9am-5pm. Check-out 10am. Semi-private bath. Singles ¥3130. ❶

Okinawa International Youth Hostel (HI) (沖縄国際ユースホテル), 51, Ōnoyama, (☎857-0073; fax 859-3567). About 10min. south of the bus terminal on the other side of the Kokuba River. Follow Rte. 329 south, cross Meiji Bridge, and look for the hostel near Kokuwa Renta-car. Also on the airport bus line. A 20min. walk from Kokusai-dōri, with room for 200 people and the nicest cheap dorms you'll ever see. TV in each room. Laundry facilities and kitchen available. Arrange kayaking, biking, and scuba trips at reception. Check-in 3pm. Check-out 10am. Singles ¥3150. ❶

Capsule Inn Okinawa (カプセルイン沖縄), 2-4-3, Asato (☎867-6017). At the northeastern tip of Kokusai-dōri next to Quicksilver: look for a giant red capsule sign. On-site facilities include kitchen, laundry machines, showers, and a TV lounge. Capsule ¥3300. Upgrade to a "deluxe" pod for ¥1000 extra. ❶

Okinawa Guesthouse (沖縄ゲストハウス), 2-16-13, Nishi (☎9782-9696). From the bus terminal, head north on Rte. 390 for 5min. In a gritty alley behind Sango Sentā. The decor's not much to look at, but it's the cheapest sleep in Naha, the staff are about as relaxed as they come, and the place attracts really interesting backpackers. ¥1500. ❶

Sankyo Business Hotel (サンキョビジネスウホテル), 2-16, Makishi (☎867-5041; fax 867-7827.) A few blocks from the tourist office on Okie-dōri, next to Cozy convenience. Fewer amenities than your typical business hotel, but the rooms are clean and breakfast is free. Western-style rooms have TV, a private bath, and A/C. Check-out 10am. Singles ¥4000; subsequent nights ¥3500. ❷

Hotel Kokusai Plaza (ホテル国際プラザ), 1-4-10, Maki-shi (☎862-8481). On Kokusai-dōri at the intersection of Shobosho-dōri next to the Hotel New Okinawa. The plush Western-style rooms have been recently renovated, and it's smack dab in the middle of Kokusai-dōri. Impressive facilities include a bar, lounge, and restaurant. Breakfast buffet 7-10am (¥600). Lunch from 11:30am-3:00pm. Rooms have TV, private bath and A/C. Check-out 10am. Singles ¥6000; doubles ¥9600. ❸

Nansei Kanko Hotel (南西観光ホテル), 3-13-23, Makishi, (☎862-7144; www.cosmos.ne.jp/~ope/nansei.) At the far northeast end of Kokusai-dōri. This upmarket business hotel is as posh as they come in Naha. Stunning views. Manicured rooms with TV, private bath, and A/C. Check-out 10am. Singles ¥10,000; twins ¥15,000. ❹

▐ FOOD

For such a small city, Naha offers a wide palette of noteworthy restaurants. If you're new to Okinawan cuisine, Naha is a great place to score some *goya chanpuru* (p. 644) and a frosty mug of Orion lager. Since no self-respecting tourist would leave Okinawa without dining in an American steakhouse, the city offers about every conceivable variation on the theme, and a surprising number of international restaurants line Kokusai-dōri. Mitsukoshi's basement is home to a large food market where you can buy sushi *bentō* boxes, fresh produce, and other delicacies. Nearby, look for the entrance to **Heiwa-dōri shopping arcade,** an indoor market with discount stalls, souvenir stands, and produce and seafood vendors.

▓ **Helios Craft Beer Pub** (クラフトビアパブヘリオス ; ☎863-7227). On Kokusai-dōri next to Seattle's Best Coffee and across the street from the Ukishima-dōri turn-off. Beer snobs of the world unite! Helios sets the bar with skillfully crafted brews. A test-tube rack of all four is only ¥700. Cleanse your palate with inventive pub food, like *tako*

ON THE MENU

JAPANDELICIOUS

The Japanese maintain fierce loyalty to dishes from their own prefectures, but when they are traveling within the borders of their own country, they are quick to seek out regional specialties, and sample types of food that they can't find in their hometown. Since the Okinawan Islands are stepping stones between Japan and the Asian continent, Ryūkyū cuisine draws on traditional Japanese tenets of simplicity and presentation with its use of fresh, local produce and seafood, while incorporating the Chinese reverence for the pig in a variety of homestyle dishes.

Upon arriving in the islands, your first experience with Ryūkyū cuisine will undoubtedly be a hot, steaming bowl of Okinawan *soba*, the gastronomic symbol of the region. Unlike its mainland counterpart, Okinawan *soba* noodles are made of pure wheat flour instead of buckwheat, giving them a lighter texture and a flavor that blends well with tropical heat. Okinawan *soba* is prepared not from fish stock but by boiling pork ribs until the meat falls off the bone, making the broth extremely flavorful and the meat very tender. Be sure to try the Miyako-jima version of this dish, in which seaweed is mixed into the noodle dough.

The other staple food of the region is *goya chanpuru*, a homestyle dish of tofu, egg, and sauteed *goya* (a bitter cucumber native to the island chain). The

(octopus) *sashimi* on seaweed (¥700) or German-style sausage on a plate of shredded *daikon* radish (¥600). Open daily 11am-midnight. ❸.

Bambohe (バンボシュ ; ☎861-4129). From Kokusai-dōri, turn left down Okei-dōri and look for the bright yellow building on the left side, across the street from Starbucks. Step up to the trough, and get ready for a consumption marathon. You can choose from over 20 trays of raw meats and vegetables, then cook them to your liking at your own personal tabletop BBQ. Add the unlimited Okinawan *soba*, salads, ice cream, drinks, coffee, and rice, and you're talking about some serious eating. 90min. entry costs ¥980 for lunch and ¥1650 (men) or ¥1500 (women) for dinner. Open daily 11am-10pm. ❸

Taco-ya (Takosūya; タコスー屋; ☎862-6080). Centrally located on Kokusai-dōri, two doors down from the Kokusa-dōri Post Office. Look no further, because this tiny little restaurant serves the cheapest food in all of Naha. ¥150 per taco, and they're mighty tasty, too. Go now. Open daily from 11am-10pm. ❶

Grand Canyon Steakhouse (Uchina Sutēki Mura; うちなーステーキ村), 1-3-53, Makishi (☎867-0414). Located on Kokusai-dōri just south of the intersection with Okei-dōri, upstairs from the Maui Steakhouse. Forget everything you know about overseas Japanese steakhouses. Here, *hibachi* chefs in cowboy hats quickdraw *ginsu* knives from leather holsters while waitresses dressed as Native American princesses sing country-western songs in three-part harmony. The food's great, too. Steak, soup, salad, rice, and vegetables is ¥2000. Open daily 11am-10pm. ❸

Lucy's. From Kokusai-dōri, turn down Okei-dōri and walk a few blocks until you come to a large parking lot on your right. Tucked in the corner is Lucy's, a small concrete building that advertises hamburgers, hotdogs, and lemonade in huge painted lettering. A little slice of real Americana in Naha. Hamburgers and hotdogs ¥200 (or US$2). Fresh-squeezed lemonade for a buck. Open daily 11am-10pm. ❶

Nanak (Nanaku; ナーナック ; ☎861-2579). At the southwest end of Kokusai-dōri across the street from Kaiho Bank. Head into the basement when you see the sign outside. This branch of the chain Indian restaurant is run by a Bombay family living in Naha, and they haven't sacrificed the authenticity of the food. We're talking huge *thalis* and sizzling curries, set to the tune of Hindi pop classics. 20 different types of curries, including vegetarian (¥880). Great lunch sets only ¥680. Open daily 11am-9:30pm. ❷

☺ SIGHTS

Like other tourist streets around the world, **Kokusai-dōri** is a non-stop procession of frenzied consumption. Bars and clubs spill out onto the crowded streets while Japanese tourists strut their hottest threads to the tune of crossing signal anthems. By day or night, a stroll along Kokusai-dōri provides hours of entertainment—you could spend months exploring its intricate maze of sidestreets and alleys.

SHURI-JŌ. If you only have a limited amount of time in Naha, be sure to spend an hour or two at the ▓**Shuri Castle Ruins** (Shuri-jō Kōen; 首里城公園), the reconstructed Ryūkyū imperial residence, a World Heritage Site and artistic inspiration for the newly minted ¥2000 note. From Kokusai-dōri, buses #1, 13, or 14 will drop you off at the Shuri-jō Kōen Iriguchi Bus Stop, at the bottom of the castle mound. From the bus stop, take your first right and continue straight until you see the Visitor's Lobby. From there turn left, and at the top of the hill, you'll see photo-snapping tourists and women in Okinawan garb around the **Shurei-mon,** a gate that has become a much-revered Okinawan symbol. Continue past Shurei-mon to the **Kankai-mon,** an imposing tower that guards the pockmarked limestone walls. The **Seiden,** a massive palace at the focal point of a stately courtyard, stands past a few additional gates. Although the palace had to be completely rebuilt after WWII, every inch of detail was painstakingly restored, from the gold-leaf gilding on the exterior to the carved dragons presiding over the entrance. The red-lacquered interior holds a series of exhibits in Japanese and English that explain the rise and fall of the Ryūkyū empire, and the details of the 40-year restoration process. (☎866-2020; www.shurijo-park.go.jp. Open daily 9am-6pm, ¥800, students ¥600, children ¥300.)

TSUBOYA. At the eastern end of Heiwa-dōri, you'll find the pottery district, **Tsuboya.** A score of kilns still operate along the district's winding streets, and a visit to one of the workshops can be a good respite from the brutal sun. The new **Tsuboya Ceramics Museum,** at the entrance to the district, just past the end of the Heiwa-dōri arcade, can give you the scoop on the area's history, which dates back to 1682, with its collection of pottery and informative exhibits. (☎862-3761; www.naha-okn.ed.jp/tsuboya. Open Tu-Su 10am-6pm. ¥300, students ¥200, children ¥100.)

OTHER SIGHTS. After passing Shurei-mon, bear left instead of entering the castle grounds, and you'll pass a small pond that surrounds **Benzaiten-dō,** a temple reconstructed at the same time as Shuri-jō. East

unique dish is said to be an acquired taste, but goya chanpuru balances well with heavier pork dishes. It's usually served with mozuku, a thinly shredded seaweed is soaked in sweet vinegar, which cleanses the palate. Also keep an eye out for ikasumi-juri, a thick soup made of squid ink (it will turn your mouth an attractive black), as well as umi-budo, a grape-shaped seaweed, served on nigiri, that bursts open in the mouth and has a briny taste, like caviar.

Okinawa has the perfect climate for a double scoop of ice cream from Blue Seal, an American chain popularized on the islands due to the US military presence. Japanese flavors include matcha (green tea) and mango, but if you're really daring, go ahead and try an invigorating scoop of goya-flavored ice cream.

No regional cuisine would be complete without the local drink. Vending machine junkies, look for the yellow can of Sanpin-cha, a locally-brewed, refreshingly smooth ice-cold jasmine tea. If you were thinking of something a little stronger, Okinawa's frothy brew is a refreshing lager known as Orion, often served in local izakaya with a plate of pickled pig's ears. If you're in the mood for something with even more kick to it, Okinawa is the only place in Japan where you can find awamori, a distilled liquor made from black malted rice that has a flavor like a fire. Awamori also makes for some truly unforgettable hangovers—you've been warned. Be an adventurous gourmand. Eat heartily. Slurp your soba. And seriously man, easy on the awamori, okay?

of the temple are the modest remains of the temple **Enkaku-ji.** North of **Benzaiten-dō** is the **Okinawa Prefectural Museum,** which houses Ryūkyū artifacts. *(Open daily Tu-Su 9am-5pm. ¥200.)* On the western edge of the park are the remains of **Tama-udōn,** the mausoleum and burial grounds for the royal family from as early as 1501. *(Open daily 8:30am-6pm. ¥200.)*

⬛ NIGHTLIFE

Naha's nightlife is fueled by young Japanese tourists on vacation from the mainland, and by American servicemen on leave from the bases. Although it makes for a vibrant and energetic scene, club fees and drink prices in Naha rival those of Tōkyō, London, or any other major city. Still, there's an exciting mix of entertainment options in the city, and as long as you keep track of how much you're drinking, it is possible to dance the night away without going over budget.

> **Chakura (☎869-0283).** On central Kokusai-dōri. A funky livehouse run by Okinawan music legend Kina Shōkichi. Champloose, a band that has won the adoration of the entire city, plays here near nightly. Cover ¥2500-3000. Open 7pm-2am.

> **Soul Brother's Club.** Across the street from the Makishi Post Office on Kokusai-dōri, on the 6th floor of the building (look for a sign outside proclaiming "Black Harlem"). Surprisingly enough, this tiny club is a popular venue for local punk and ska bands and their youthful fans. The music is loud and raw. Cover ¥1700. Open daily 9pm-2am.

> **Kam's (☎863-3651).** On the 2nd fl. of the Soul Brother's Club bldg. A small piano bar that features a nightly line-up of jazz and blues artists. Cover ¥1000-2000.

> **Bump.** On Kokusai-dōri near the OPA Bldg. If you're into serious clubbing, Bump has alternating trance and hip-hop nights and attracts a fashionable crowd. Cover ¥2000-2500. Open 9pm-4am.

> **Be Green, (☎867-7578).** Aso on Kokusai-dōri across from the Hotel Yamanouchi (山の 内ホテル). A new hip-hop venue loaded with the latest in lighting and sound equipment. Slick dance floors, bi-level bars, and a private VIP lounge. The pulsing scene draws in a mix of foreign and Japanese tourists. Cover ¥1500-2500, ¥1000 extra for VIP access. Open 9pm-4am.

⬛ FESTIVALS AND EVENTS

Naha hosts an exciting number of festivals during the course of the year. In early May, colorful **dragon boats** race through the harbor as a prayer for the safety and properity of local fishermen. On August 10, **Naha's City Festival** reaches its climax during the Giant Tug of War when thousands of people compete in pulling the biggest handmade rope in the world (172m long and 1.5m in diameter) as recognized by the Guinness Book of World Records. In November, the **Shuri-jō Cultural Festival** is held on the grounds of the ancient Ryūkyū capital, featuring a variety of traditional performing arts and a royal procession. Finally, there's the **New Year** celebration from January 1-3, featuring traditional rituals and dances.

⬛ DAYTRIPS FROM NAHA

NAKAGUSUKU. The **Nakagusuku Castle Ruins** (Nakagusuku-jōseki; 中城城跡), just north of Naha, are probably the most impressive remains of the Ryūkyū kingdom left on the island. Constructed by in 1448, the castle lasted a mere 10 years before being demolished in a rebellion. Much of the original fortifications remains today, including six moss-covered stone citadels and the original limestone castle walls. The surrounding grounds make for a satisfying afternoon walk, and on a clear day you can see much of central Okinawa from the hilltop. To get to the castle ruins, take bus #23, 25, 31, 90, or 124 to Okinawa City, and get off at Futenma Junction (1hr., ¥1000). Transfer to the #58 bus, which passes directly by the entrance gate (15min., ¥200). No sign marks the castle, but you can't miss the tour buses in the parking lot outside. *(Castle open daily 8:30am-5pm. ¥300.)* After you finish touring the castle remains, walk 5min. east down the road to the **Nakamura-ke** (中村家), a prosperous family's farm- house from the early 1700s. The grounds feature rows of stone pig pens, and the thick groves of trees strategically placed to block typhoon winds. *(Grounds open daily 9:30am-5pm. ¥300 admission includes a hot cup of tea.)*

SOUTHERN OKINAWA

During the Battle of Okinwa, the Japanese made their final stand at the southern tip of the island as US forces swept down from their beachheads in Kadena and Chatan. Although this was one of the bloodiest chapters in the entire Pacific cam- paign, the darkest days for Okinawans were still to come. It was later discovered, after the Allied Forces took control of the island on June 21, 1945, that the hun- dreds of Japanese troops and civilians who had taken refuge in underground lime- stone caves had chosen to commit suicide rather than face capture. As Okinawans came to terms with the immeasurable loss of life that had befallen them, the mon- umental task of rebuilding their splintered island slowly began.

Although the scattered war monuments are constant reminders of Okinawa's tragic past, today the southern region of the island is a sprawling mass of apart- ment buildings, intercity throughways and industrial parks. Many of the war sites can be reached via public transportation from Naha. A number of companies offer Japanese-language package tours of the area, but for a few thousand yen more than the price of a full-day tour, you can rent a car in Naha and explore the area at your own pace. For a guided tour, contact **Naha Kōtsū**. (☎ 868-3750. About ¥4800.)

During the Battle of Okinawa, the main target of the US advance was the **Under- ground Naval Headquarters** (Kyū Kaigun Shireibugō; 旧海軍司令部壕), buried 20m deep in the soft limestone hills south of Naha. Before the headquarters fell to Allied Forces, about 175 men committed suicide by igniting their grenades to avoid capture. Take bus #33, 46, or 101 from the Naha bus terminal to Tomi- gusuku-kōen-mae (30min., about ¥250), and then walk 10min. uphill to the ticket gate. (Open daily 8:30am-5pm. ¥420.)

Mabuni Hill was the site of the final struggle for control of Okinawa-hontō. A park and the **Peace Memorial Hall** pay a somber tribute to the Japanese and Ameri- can troops who died during the Battle of Okinawa. The building houses various exhibits on the closing moments of the assault as well as a 16m lacquered Buddha statue, a symbol of the wish for future peace on the island. (Open daily 9am-5:30pm.) Nearby is the **Okinawa Peace Prefectural Museum,** which catalogues the horrors of WWII, and the remarkable post-war rebuilding campaign. (Open Tu-Su 9am-1:30pm. ¥100.) To get to Mabuni Hill, in the island's southeast, take bus #32, 34, 35, 89, or 100 to Itoman (40min., about ¥500), and then change to the #82 bus (20min., every hr., about ¥20), which passes directly by the park entrance.

Southern Okinawa is also home to **Gyokusendō** (玉泉洞), one of the longest and most impressive limestone caves in Asia. Unfortunately you have to pay admission to **Ryūkyū Okōku-mura** (琉球王国村) cultural theme park to reach the entrance to the cave. On the same grounds is the **Habu-kōen** (ハブ公園), a sideshow featuring the much-vilified habu pit viper (an indigenous poisonous snake). Pony up another ¥600 to watch the tourists squeal in terror as the snake handler actually gets within 50m of the serpentine beast. Bus #54 and 83 (30min., 2 per hr., about ¥500) connect the entire

IN RECENT NEWS

GAIJIN GO HOME

While proud of their post-war achievements, Okinawans have long resented the fact that they continue to host 26,000 of the 48,000 US military personnel stationed in Japan. Despite frequent requests by the prefectural government to legislatively remove the bases from Okinawa-hontō, the Diet continues to honor its part of the US-Japan security alliance, an important pillar of Japan's post-war foreign policy.

After the island returned to Japan in 1972, a movement grew up for the removal of all bases from the region. The protests were largely ignored; it took the high-profile rape of a 12-year-old Japanese girl by three US servicemen in 1995 to gain this issue global attention. The US officially apologized for the event and imposed stricter disciplinary measures for soldiers overseas, but refused to give up the Okinawa bases. Unfortunately, there have been subsequent rape cases, most recently the May 2003 rape of a 19 year-old woman by a Marine.

The US recently began a dramatic realignment of its forces, including the 100,000 troops stationed in Asia and the Pacific. Media have speculated that the US plans to move its Okinawan bases to Australia, but officials have not confirmed this. Meanwhile, the American presence in Okinawa is one political issue that the Japanese willingly and fervently discuss in the public arena.

complex, dubbed **Okinawa World** (おきなわワールド) to Naha Bus Terminal. (Open daily 9am-5:30pm. Park and cave admission ¥1200.)

To escape the heat of Naha's streets, take bus #53 (1hr., 1 per hr., about ¥500) from the bus terminal to the scenic beaches and clear waters of little **Ō-Jima** island.

CENTRAL OKINAWA

Central Okinawa is an eclectic area defined by its bizarre mix of traditional Ryūkyū culture and brazen Americana, containing a number of cultural hotspots as well as US military bases. Stretching from Naha to Ishikawa, central Okinawa is a sprawling urban jungle of overcrowded housing complexes, fast food restaurants, military complexes, and used car lots. First impressions of the area are unlikely to be good, especially if you've fled Tōkyō in search of solitude and seaside bliss. However, look beyond the concrete monolith and vending machine landscape of the main highways, and you're likely to find tastefully developed beachfronts, unique castle ruins, and some of the best diving in all of Japan.

RYŪKYŪ MURA (琉球村)　　　☎098

Ryūkyū Mura (Ryūkyū Village), 1130 Yamada, Onna Village, is a cultural theme park as informative about Okinawan rural life as "It's a Small World" is about geopolitics. Japanese tourists unload by the bus load to watch locals don traditional costumes and dance to the sound of ballads and clicking camera shutters. The complex houses about a dozen reconstructed wooden homes, which have all been converted into a strip mall of Okinawan delicacies. Watching old women in triangle hats drive oxen around a mock sugar cane mill is about as exciting as waiting for your instant *rāmen* noodles to soften, the price of admission is worth it just to see the enthusiastic looks on the faces of Japanese families that have traveled thousands of kilometers to experience their first Okinawan donut.

Ryūkyū Mura is on Rte. 58, north of Kadena Town and just south of the west coast resort strip. Bus #20 and 120 stop at the complex, about an hour south of Nago. Inside the park, you have the option of paying ¥460 for entry to the ◨**Habu Snake Show.** Watch as the habu engages in mortal combat against a mongoose in the Ring of Death, all for your viewing pleasure. Although the habu almost always gets its neck wrung, you'll feel warm inside knowing that the propietors of Ryūkyū Mura are keeping the island habu-free. (☎765-1234. Open daily 8:30am-5:30pm. ¥840, students ¥730, kids ¥420.)

OKINAWA CITY (沖縄市)   ☎098

At the heart of the Chanpuru Pop Culture Zone lies Okinawa City, often described as the throbbing heart of the island's international flare. If you venture beyond the gaudy facade of 24hr. steak houses, biker bars, and army surplus stores, you'll soon realize that the city is little more than a hedonistic stomping ground for American soldiers on leave from nearby **Kadena Air Base.** Kadena is the largest US Air Force base in the western Pacific, and houses nearly 20,000 military personnel in an area of 20½ sq. mi. If you've drunk your fill of Kirin Beer and are in dire need of a cold Bud, consider stopping in Okinawa City for the night. Otherwise, continue north to the less developed parts of the island.

Okinawa City is at the core of the urban sprawl that is central Okinawa. Although Nago, Naha, and Okinawa City are relatively close to one another, the virtual standstill of traffic that plagues Okinawa-hontō's central artery means that bus travel is dreadfully slow. From the Naha bus terminal, take bus #23, 25, 31, 90 or 124. Lines run every 15min. Expect to pay around ¥1000 for the 1hr. trip. From Nago, you'll need to take the #20 or 120 to Kadena, and then transfer to the #62 or 94. The trip takes about 1½hr. in total, and costs ¥1500. Okinawa City is centered on the **Goya Crossroads** where Rte. 333 intersects the main entrance road to Kadena Air Base. Heading west at the crossroads will bring you to the **Nakano-machi nightlife district,** whereas the main **shopping district** is on **Chūō Park Avenue,** to the left of Rte. 333 a few blocks north of Goya Crossroads. A small post office with an **international ATM** is located right around the corner from the hotel strip. Heading south on Rte. 333, make a left at the first street you come to after passing the Hotel Sunrise. The **post office** is just up the street on your left. **Postal code: 904.**

Accommodations in Okinawa City draw their lifeblood from the visiting families of servicemen, so don't expect to find any bargains. The **Hotel Sunrise ❸** (サンラ イズホテル), 2-1-46, Goya, offers standard Western rooms, and is the cheapest of the hotels on the eastern side of Rte. 333, south of the Goya Crossroads. Spotless rooms have an attached bathroom, TV, refrigerator, A/C, and queen-sized beds. (☎933-0171. Reception open 24hr. ¥5775.) Next door the (eerily similar) **Kyōto Kanko Hotel ❸** (京都観光ホテル), 2-1-51, Goya, offers equivalent rooms in newer building. Private rooms have attached bathroom, TV, refrigerator, A/C, and queen-sized bed. (☎933-1125. Reception open 24hr. ¥5900.)

There are few places to eat in Okinawa City, and very few notable. At the entrance to the Nakano-machi nightlife district is **Sun City,** an indoor market that's probably your best bet for cheap eats. While you're snacking on a hot dog, browse the used clothing racks for second-hand savings. A short cab ride (about ¥800) brings you to the **Mihama Complex** in Chatan Town, a Western-style entertainment complex of with cinemas, restaurants, bars, and shops, a popular weekend destination for servicemen with money to burn. The **Nakano-machi nightlife district** also has bars and clubs, but the majority of these establishments are hostess bars.

ISHIKAWA (石川) TO ONNA VILLAGE (恩納村)   ☎098

Ishikawa is the last major city before reaching Nago in the north. Although the city center is uninteresting, a beautiful stretch of **beaches** and **resorts** line the western coast, and submerged beneath the emerald waters are excellent dive sites. Buses #20 and 120, which run between Naha and Nago on Rte. 58, follow the windy, oceanside drive and pass by most of the major hotels. **Postal code: 904.**

The resorts lining Rte. 58 primarily cater to Japanese families, and are prohibitively expensive for the independent traveler. However, most hotels are open to the public, so you can lounge on the private beaches without paying exorbitant accommodation prices. Be sure to check out **Moon Beach** (ムーン ビーチ), which has all the exoticism of a hidden paradise—cobalt waters,

TIME: 4-5hr. driving time

DISTANCE: 50 mi.

SEASON: Year-round

Starting in Nago, head north along coastal highway Rte. 58, gazing out onto the calming waters of the East China Sea. Along the way, have some fun in the sun at **Okuma Beach** and skip stones off the northern edge of the island at **Cape Hedo.** When the road turns into Rte. 70, you've entered **Aha National Forest,** the largest nature preserve on the island. At the end of the park, merge onto Rte. 331, head through Higashi Village, and bypass Nago by taking Rte. 329. When you pass the city, merge onto Rte. 49. Crash for a peaceful night at **On the Beach LUE.** Spend the next morning beach-hopping **Sesoko-jima** and the **Ocean Expo Park,** and then throw some history into your roadtrip by following Rte. 505 to the **Nakijin Castle Ruins.** Finally, follow Rte. 72 and then Rte. 84 back to Nago, stopping for a few rounds of pineapple wine at the **Nago Pineapple Park.**

1 JAL PRIVATE RESORT OKUMA (JAL プライベートリゾートオクマ). Okuma Beach, a popular holiday resort for American soldiers and their families, is well-maintained and significantly quieter than Zampa Beach. Entry to the resort is ¥525, which grants you access to the private beach as well to as the facilities for yachting, canoeing, water-skiing and windsurfing. To get to the resort, follow Rte. 58 towards Cape Hedo. About halfway up the coast, follow the turn-off for JAL Private Resort Okuma. The complex is about 500m off Rte. 58.

2 CAPE HEDO (HEDO MISAKI; 辺戸岬). Past Okuma Beach, the ocean lightens to a turquoise hue, and the winding road passes through impressive mountain tunnels. This is cruisin' country, so roll down the windows, and scan the airwaves for some bass-thumping J-pop. At the northernmost tip of the peninsula, you'll come to Hedo Point, where you can watch surf crash on the high cliffs and gaze at distant Yoron-jima. Cape Hedo has tourist facilities (including a restroom, convenience store, and noodle shop), so sit down with a cup of *soba* (¥500) and enjoy the views.

3 AHA NATIONAL FOREST. Rounding the tip of the island and enter the village of Oku, Rte. 58 becomes Rural Rte. 70, your gateway into Aha National Forest and the most pristine scenery of the entire drive. On the east coast of Yanbaru, the highway cuts inward through a series of winding mountain passes, and the vegetation takes on a jungle-like appearance. Thick clouds of fog roll off the mountain tops and settle into the steamy valleys below, while calling birds and chirping insects add to the exotic atmosphere. Switch the dial to Wave 89.1, an armed forces radio station that transmits from Kadena Air Base, playing a good mix of classic rock, American top 40 and the worst morale-boosting ads you've ever heard.

ROAD TRIP

4 ▦ ON THE BEACH LUE (オン. ザ. ビーチ ルー) . You can finish the drive in one day, but On the Beach LUE is a perfect place to slow down and settle into the relaxed pace of tropical life. The private beachfront *tatami* rooms at the LUE are not to be missed. After Aha National Forest, follow Rte. 331 through Higashi Village (Higashi Mura; 東村) and merge onto the Rte. 329 Nago Bypass. Follow signs for Rte. 449, the highway along Motobu-hantō's western coast. On the Beach LUE is on the left side of the highway, minutes outside Nago. If you get to the bridge for Sesoko-jima, you've gone too far. In addition to the mind-blowing beaches, a restaurant in the lobby of the hotel serves Japanese dishes like *tempura* (¥1000) and Western "beach foods" like pork cutlet and fries (¥700). Rooms come with TV, radio, A/C, attached bathroom, outdoor patio, and all the sand and surf you can handle. (☎47-3535; www.luenet.com. Breakfast buffet ¥800. Singles ¥5250. Kitchen open 8am-9:30pm.)

5 SESOKO-JIMA (瀬底島). A few kilometers north of On the Beach LUE, you'll come to a massive suspension bridge that connects the tiny little island of Sesoko-jima to the mainland. On a clear day, you can see the peak of Motobu-hantō's **Yae-zan** from the top of the bridge. Although the main attraction of Sesoko-jima is the gorgeous **beaches** along the western shore, it's worth taking time to absorb the scenery. Along the road, you'll find dense sugar cane fields, tiny farming hamlets, and an assortment of carved stone mausoleums.

6 OCEAN EXPO PARK (OKINAWA KINEN-KŌEN; 沖縄記念公園). If you take the exit for Rte. 114 a few kilometers past Sesoka-jima, you'll come to Ocean Expo Park, the site of the 1975 International Ocean Exposition. Entrance to the **Okinawa Memorial Park** is free, but you'll have to pay separate fees for the individual exhibits. If you're being selective, the **Okinawa Churaumi Aquarium** is about as impressive as they come, and there are free sights on the grounds, including a manatee tank, a sea turtle pond, a dolphin show and nearby Emerald Beach. The aquarium itself is one of the world's largest, and has some mind-boggling exhibits. The 7500-ton **Kuroshio Sea Main Tank,** which houses schools of whale sharks and manta rays, is worth the price of admission alone. (☎48-3748. Open spring and autumn 9am-5:30pm, summer 9am-6:30pm, and winter 9am-5pm. ¥1800, high school students ¥1200, elementary and junior high ¥600.)

7 NAKIJIN CASTLE RUINS (NAKIJIN-JŌSEKI; 今帰仁城跡). After leaving the Ocean Expo Park, continue along Rte. 114 past the row of *fukugi* trees and merge onto Rte. 505. Follow the coast, and begin to look for signs for Nakijin Castle Ruins. Set deep in the Motobu-hantō's central mountain chain, the crumbling, moss-covered stone walls of Nakijin Castle are one of the few Ryūkyū cultural sites that survived the bombing of WWII. This World Heritage Site lends itself to scenic strolls around the 14th-century castle foundation, and the views of the nearby mountains and valleys are simply stunning. (Open 8:30am-6:30pm. ¥150.)

8 NAGO PINEAPPLE PARK (ナゴパイナップルパーク). After leaving Nakijin Castle, get back on Rte. 505 and follow the signs for Nago. Merge onto Rte. 72, and follow the signs for the city. Eventually, you'll enter Nago on Rte. 84, but before you return your rental, stop 3km outside the city at Nago Pineapple Park, where you can end your scenic drive with a "tropical delicious tour" of Motobu pineapple fields. Board the self-propelled Pineapple Pod, and you'll be whisked away on a magical mystery tour through the greenhouse. Although the Pod will lecture you in English on how yummy-tastic pineapples are for your body, it's hard to concentrate when you're trying to figure out how they get golf carts to navigate all the twists and turns.

After the ride, eat as much fresh pineapple as you can stomach. There is also homemade pineapple wine (think vodka with pineapple Kool-aid), but remember that you still have to *drive* that car back. Navigate the gauntlet of overpriced pineapple products, clutching your wallet for dear life. Nago Pineapple Park. You can't leave Okinawa without seeing it. (☎53-3659. Open daily 9am-5pm. ¥500.)

THE BIG SPLURGE

DIVERS DO IT DEEPER

There's a lot going on underneath those cool, blue ocean waves, but you'll never know unless you kick off the Hello Kitty® sandals. For a taste of adventure in Okinawa's sparkling seas, scrap your tight-fisted budget for a d████ book a dive trip at the ████a Misaki Diver's House in Onna Village near Ishikawa. The hostel is located near Cape Zampa and Manzamo Beach, two of Okinawa's hottest dive spots. Both feature 40-m drop-offs covered in brilliant soft coral █ nd there's a good chance of seeing ██ ge rays among the tropical fish. Swimming along the rocky ocean floor, keep an eye out for octopi—if you spot one that's legal size, the friendly staff at the Diver's House will serve you up the freshest *sashimi* you've ever tasted. Your first plunge will set you back ¥7500, but for an extra ¥2000 you can add a second dive. Equipment costs another ¥3000. For the uninitiated, the staff at the Diver's House also run PADI certification courses for ¥45,000.

*To get to the hostel, take the #120 or 20 bus to **Maribu Beach Resort** (マ ████ テ ル), at the intersection of Rtes. 6 ██ d 58. From here, walk south on Rte. 6 past the traffic light for about 10min. You'll see a road bearing to the right and a sign advertising the hostel. Follow this road for a few minutes; the ho████ is on top of a small hill overlooking ██ he ocean. (☎964-2497; www.maedamisaki.com.)*

white sands and palm trees with coconuts wrapped in safety nets. The cheapest place to stay near Ishikawa is ▧**Maeda Misaki Diver's House ❶** in Onna Village. Have buses #20 or 120 drop you off at the Maribu Beach Resort (マリブホテル) at the intersection of Rtes. 6 and 58. From here, walk south on Rte. 6 past the traffic light about 10min. You'll see a road bearing to the right and a sign. Follow the road for a few minutes, and you'll see the hostel on top of a small hill. You can also take a taxi from the intersection (about ¥450). The English-speaking staff arranges dive trips and offers certification courses. The hostel is a little travel worn, but it occupies a quiet location, has bike rentals (¥1000 per day), and offers nearby trails and views of Moon Beach. (☎964-2497; www.maedamisaki.com. Breakfast ¥600. Dinner ¥800. Full kitchen. Laundry available. Bike rental ¥1000 per day. Dorms ¥2000.)

NAGO (名護)   ☎098

Nago is a sleepy little city that serves as the gateway to the Motobu peninsula and the rugged mountains of Okinawa-hontō's northern region. Although Nago was in the spotlight in 2000 when the city hosted the G8 Summit, the relaxed pace of life quickly returned after the delegates departed. If you're planning on exploring the wild north, Nago is an excellent place for an overnight stop, especially since most bus lines terminate here. Nago lacks tourist sites other than the striking panoramas on the nearby Castle Hill.

If you're looking to kill time before hitting the road, there are a number of sights around the city center. Start at the **old banyan tree** (free), a perfect place to eat your *bentō* box while contemplating the path to enlightenment. A few blocks south of the banyan, the humble **Nago Museum** educates visitors about traditional Okinawan ways of life, especially agriculture. (☎53-1342. Open Tu-Su 10am-6pm. ¥150.) A few blocks east of the museum at **Orion Brewery** (☎52-2137) you can learn everything you ever wanted to know about the beer that's "Live, fresh and smooth-unique." Phone ahead for a free tour and tasting. From the brewery, the road leads northeast along the river to the long flight of stairs at the foot of **Nago Castle Hill.** The original castle is almost entirely gone, but the sweeping coastal views and the charming children's park at the left of the hilltop make the walk worth it. Ten kilometers southeast of Nago on Rte. 58, along the #20 and 120 bus routes, in the middle of Cape Busena, sits the **Underwater Observatory.** Climb down the 30m spiral staircase for a unique view of the coral reef. (☎52-3379. Daily 10am-6pm. ¥1000.)

Most **buses** from Naha eventually reach Nago, though it can take as long as 3hr. Lines #20 and 120 will drop you off at the Nago Bus Terminal, a few blocks north of the city center (¥1700). If you're planning on heading north, you'll most likely need a rental car, since public buses disappear as soon as you leave the city. The most affordable rental agency is the **Toyota Rent-a-Car** (トヨタレンタカー), in the Agarie District, off Rte. 58 between the Nago police station and A&W Restaurant. A compact car with insurance is ¥8250 per day.

Ohigashi-dōri is the main throughway—most sites are between the bus terminal in the north and the **banyan tree** in the south. At the center is the Nago Intersection. A small **tourist information center** at the southeast corner has free English maps. (☎53-7755; www.yanbaru.ne/jp/nago. Open 9am-5pm.) If you need **international ATM access,** head to the Nago Post Office. Go south on Ohigashi-dōri a few blocks past the banyan tree. At the museum, turn right—it's two blocks up on the left. In an emergency, call ☎110 for **police,** ☎119 for **fire** or ambulance. **Hōkoku Hospital,** ☎52-2719, is north of the city along Hwy. 71. A small coin-operated **laundromat** is on your left as you exit Hotel Ōkura. (☎52-1284. ¥4700.) **Postal code:** 905.

The cheapest hotel is **Business Hotel Shiroyama ❷** (ホテル城山), a block south of the banyan tree on the right side. Clean, comfortable rooms have a TV, bath, A/C, and refrigerator. (☎52-3111; singles ¥4000, doubles ¥6300.) **Hotel Ōkura ❷** (ホテ ルおおくら) next door has slightly larger doubles and equivalent amenities.

There's no shortage of places to eat in Nago, but if you ask any of the locals, they'll point you to **Shinzan Soba ❶** (新山そば), a noodle shop that's been in business for over 60 years. Like any neighborhood gem, it's a little tricky to find. Head north on Ohigashi-dōri past the banyan tree, and turn right down the alley at the pharmacy. Head left down the next alley and look for a tiny concrete building. Slide open the doors, take a ticket from the machine, and slurp your *soba* to the tune of this week's J-pop smash hit. (☎53-3354. Open for lunch and dinner.)

KERAMA ISLANDS (慶良間列島)

Thirty kilometers off shore of Okinawa-hontō, all vestiges of modern Japan seem to vanish as the high rises of Naha fade into the relatively uninhabited islands known collectively as the Keramas. These rural escapes offer a rare degree of solitude, and are a wonderful place to relax for a few days. Prior to 1960, the local economy was fueled by the whaling industry. Once the humpbacks got wise to the islanders' hunting routes, however, they changed their breeding paths and the whaling trade collapsed. When the whales returned 30 years later, the islanders were quick to learn from their past mistakes. Today, the Keramas are best known as a tourist destination for viewing migrating humpbacks, and prosperity is slowly transforming these once secluded destinations into holiday meccas.

ZAMAMI-JIMA (座間味島)   ☎098

Although the largest island, **Tokashiki-jima** (渡嘉敷島), is the most heavily touristed, **Zamami-jima** (座間味島) is the most unspoiled of the islands. If you're at all an outdoorsy type, this positively paradisical island is well worth a visit of several days, not for any man-made sights or attractions, but for its beaches, vegetation, and relaxed pace of life. If you don't have your own transportation, the only reachable sights are **Furuzamami Beach,** 1km east of town and **Ama Beach,** 1.6km west of town. Both are emptier then Okinawa-hontō's crowded shores, and the piles of coral that wash up on the shore add to the exotic atmosphere. If you have wheels, head north for sweeping views on your way to humpback whale lookout points. From January to April, you can spot migrating herds just off shore, especially with a good pair of binoculars. Although the northern area lacks notable sights, pristine tropical forests adorn the mountaintops, making for a serene afternoon cruise.

From Naha International Airport, you can fly Ryūkyū Air Commuter to Kerama Airport on Fukazaki-jima (15min., 3 per day, ¥13,000) and then take a small shuttle boat to Zamami, but frequent **ferry** connections make it difficult to justify the airfare. From Naha's Tomari Port, the high-speed Queen Zamami makes two trips to Zamami per day (1hr.; one-way ¥2750, return ¥5232). The slower but cheaper Zamami-maru makes one trip per day (2¼hr.; one-way ¥1860, return ¥3540). Both ferries are operated by the same company; call ☎866-7541.

Zamami is a one-traffic light town—it takes 5min. to walk from one end of the main street to the other. At the center is the Village Office, which has a post office with **international ATM** access and a small general store. (☎987-2277. Open daily 8:30am-5:30pm.) A tourist information center next to the ferry office has a free listing of the island's dive shops. Although a shuttle bus runs from the stand behind the TIC to Furuzamami and Ama Beach, it's not the best way to navigate the island. **Zamami Renta-Car** (☎987-3250), on the eastern edge of the village, rents compact cars for ¥8000 per day. Reservations are recommended. A small, unmarked shop on the road to the Village Office rents motor scooters (¥3000 per day) and bikes (¥1000 per day). In an emergency, call ☎110 for **police**, ☎119 for **fire** or **ambulance**.

Ama Beach Campground ❶ (Kyampujō; キャンプ場), 1.6km outside of town on the road to Ama Beach (about a 20min. walk), is in a flat, shady grove that opens up onto a private beachfront. (☎987-3259. ¥300 per person. Equipment rental ¥500.) Or, head over to the main street where you'll find a number of expensive minshuku. **Joy Joy ❹** (☎987-2445), on the northwestern edge of the village, has comfortable private rooms for around ¥10,000, but with two meals included, it's one of the island's better deals. If you don't arrange meals at your hotel, try some local dishes at **Morumiya ❷** (もるみ屋 ; ☎987-3555), also at the village's northwestern edge.

MIYAKO-JIMA (宮古島) ☎09807

A group of rural islands 300km southwest of Okinawa Hontō, Miyako-shotō is best known for its sun-drenched coasts and relaxed pace of life. The major island, Miyako-jima, has a flat interior covered with sugarcane fields. The relatively even ground makes Miyako-jima a perfect place to run and cycle, and in past years the island won notoriety as the site of the All-Japan Triathalon, a Strongman Challenge involving a 3km swim, a 136km bicycle race, and a 42km marathon.

Most travelers who arrive on the island use it to break the long trip from Naha to Yaeyama-shotō. Since there are no US bases on the island, however, the traditional culture is stronger, and the lack of tourists means the streets are free of souvenir stands. Add to the mix the islanders' laid-back attitude and inspiring stretches of beachfront, and very quickly Miyako-jima is the perfect decompression zone between Naha's urban edge and Yaeyama-shotō's rugged wilderness.

▐▛ INTERCITY TRANSPORTATION

Flights: All flights arrive at Miyako Airport, 3km from the Hirara city center. **JTA** (☎0120-25-5971) and **ANK** (☎0120-02-9222) have offices in the airport terminal as well as in Hirara. No bus line connects Miyako Airport to Hirara, and a taxi will cost as much as ¥1500. If you arrange scooter rental in the airport (¥3000), or a car rental (¥5000) from **Okinawa Rent-a-Car** (☎3-2774), they'll drive you to your accommodation, and then rent you a set of wheels for the day. **Toyota Rent-a-Car** (☎2-0100) and **Nippon Rent-a-Car** (☎2-0919) rent scooters and cars, with similar transfer services at equivalent prices.

Ferries: The **Hirara Ferry Terminal** is located on the northwest edge of the city off Rte. 390. Two major ferry companies operate out of Hirara. **Arimura Sangyō** (☎860-1980)

Miyako-shotō・宮古諸島

EAST CHINA SEA
東 シ ナ 海

Ikema-jima
池間島

Raza Cosmica
Tourist Home
ラザコスミカホーム

Ikema-Ōhashi
池間大橋

Nishi-henna-zaki
西平安名崎

Ōgami-jima
大神島

Shimajiri Mangrove Forest
島尻のマングローブ林

Sawada-no-hama
佐和田の浜

Tomb of Nakasone Toyumiya
仲宗根豊見親の墓

PACIFIC OCEAN
太平洋

Irabu-jima
伊良部島

230

Shimoji-
jima
下地島

204

Sunayama Beach
砂山ビーチ

Pisseogan-saki
平瀬尾神崎

IRABU-CHŌ
伊良部町

90

83

83

Hira-wan
平良湾

Painagama Beach
パイナガマビーチ

HIRARA-SHI
平良市

Yunapama Beach
ユナパマビーチ

Yoshino Beach
吉野海岸

Nagayama-wan
長山湾

192

194

Toguchi-no-hama
渡口の浜

Aragusuku Beach
新城海岸

Miyako YH
宮古YH

390   243

78

83

野原岳
Nohara-dake(109m)

78

GUSUKUBE-CHŌ
城辺町

200

Naka-no-Jima Beach
中の島ビーチ

Yonaha Mae-hama Beach
与那覇前浜ビーチ

SHIMOJI-CHŌ
下地町

190   201

198

199

Kurima-jima
米間島

197

197

UENO-SON
上野村

390

202

Higashi-
henna-zaki
東平安名崎

Kurima-Ōhashi
米間大橋

Hakuai Beach
博愛ビーチ

German Village
Theme Park
ドイツ村

OKINAWA

and **RKK Line** (☎868-1126) run 2-3 ferries per week to Naha' and Ishigaki-jima. Schedules change often, and should be confirmed. Overnight ferries to Naha take 11hr. Book in advance, especially during July and Aug. The trip to Ishigaki takes 6hr.

Taxis: The lack of public transportation on Miyako-jima means that taxis are abundant. To arrange a cab ride with an English-speaking driver, contact **Miyako Taxi** at ☎2-4123.

Hitchhiking: Islanders are more likely to offer a lift here than on Okinawa-hontō. From Hirara, Rte. 83 heads north to the beaches on Ikema Island. Heading southeast to Cape Higashahenna, take Rte. 78. *Let's Go* does not recommend hitchhiking.

HIRARA (平良)   ☎09807

The main population center of Miyako-jima and Miyako-shotō is Hirara, a large, slumbering town that sits idyllically on the northwest coast of the island. From Hirara, the major country roads radiate out through the sugarcane fields, connecting the town center to the island's pristine coastal beaches. Although notable sites are lacking around the town center, Hirara has a wide range of affordable accommodations, an impressive selection of unique bars and restaurants, and serves as a good base for exploring the perimeter of the island.

ON THE WEB   Hirara: www.city.hirara.okinawa.jp

⬛ TRANSPORTATION. A number of buses connect Hirara to the northern and southeastern tips of the island, but service is snail-paced. From **Yachiyo Bus Terminal,** a few blocks north of Hirara Post Office, buses #1, 2, 3, 4,7, and 8 head north to Ikema-jima. From **Miyako Kyoei Terminal** on Makuramu-dōri east of the post office, buses #10, 11, 12, 13, and 15 head south to Maehama and Henna-zaki. A **taxi** out to Miyako's northern or southeastern beaches costs from ¥1000-2000.

If you didn't arrange car rental at the Airport, **Okinawa Rent-a-Car** (☎3-2774), **Toyota Rent-a-Car** (☎2-0100), and **Nippon Renta-Car** (☎2-0919) have offices in Hirara. Unfortunately, they're pretty far outside the town center, so it's best to phone ahead and arrange for pick-up where you're staying. If you're primarily interested in a bike or scooter try **Honda Wing** on the eastern end of Nishizato-dōri.

⬛⬛ ORIENTATION AND PRACTICAL INFORMATION. Central Hirara is south of Rte. 369 and west of the harbor. **Nishizato-dōri** is the main throughway, and most of the town's restaurants and bars are located there. On the 4th floor of the ferry terminal is small **tourist information center,** which can help you find a room. (☎3-1881. Open M-F 9am-5:30pm, Sa 9am-noon.) If you're arriving at Miyako Airport, there is a also a small information desk in the arrival terminal that can phone ahead for you. (Open Su-M and W-Sa 9am-5:30pm.) In an emergency, call ☎110 for **police,** ☎119 for **fire** or **ambulance.** The main **post office** (☎3-1046), located in the northwest corner of the town at the intersection of Rte. 78 and 390, has international **ATM** access. Half a block east, the **public library,** has **free Internet access** in the lobby. (Open M-F 9am-5:30pm, Sa 9am-noon.) There is also a free Internet cafe in the waiting room of the ferry terminal that is occasionally open. **Postal code:** 906.

⬛ ACCOMMODATIONS. Since Hirara is the main base for exploring the island, there are a number of accommodations around Nishizato-dōri and close to the waterfront. Call ahead in summer, especially during the Triathlon. **Miyako Youth Hostel (HI) ❷** (宮古ユースホテル), about 1km south of the ferry terminal off of Rte. 390, provides standard dorm rooms with kitchen, shower, and laundry facilities. (☎3-7700. 2 meals included. ¥4000.) **Petite Hotel ❸** (プレミアホテル), sits near the waterfront at the western edge of Nishizato-dōri. It's refreshing to find a spot with so much character. Rustic rooms feature faux wood floors, turquoise leather couches, thick mattresses, and balconies overlooking either the waterfront or the city center. A/C, TV, and private bath are included. (☎73-8162; puremia@isis.ocn.ne.jp. ¥5000.) Behind Harimizu Shrine, **Hotel Kyowa ❸** (ホテル共和) has comfortable Western-style rooms with A/C, TV, and attached bath. Although it's slightly more expensive than the Petite Hotel, there is a restaurant, cocktail lounge, and sushi bar on the first floor. (☎3-2288; fax 3-2285. Singles ¥5500.) The classy **Hotel Atoll Emerald ❺** (ホテルアトールエメラルド宮古島) is Hirara's upscale lodging, flawlessly elegant rooms that overlook the harbor, just next to the ferry terminal. Top-notch facilities include a bar, restaurant, conference center, athletic room, and palm-fringed outdoor pool. All rooms have A/C, TV, bath, and patio. (☎3-9800; fax 3-0303. From ¥13,500 per person.)

⬛ FOOD. For a small island town, Hirara has a high number of bars and restaurants. Most are near the ferry terminal along the waterfront or off Nishizato-dōri. About 500m south of the terminal, across from Painagama Beach, the funky little cafe **A-Dish ❷** charms with mariner-themed decorations. The kitchen churns out inventive thin-crust pizzas and homemade pastas for under ¥1000. See **Nightlife** for the nightclub upstairs. (☎72-7114. Open Tu-Sa 6pm-midnight, Su 5pm-11pm.) Making your way down Nishizato-dōri, look for the bright yellow building that houses **Burney's Crepe ❶**. This adorable bistro serves sweet and savory crepes (¥400). Outdoor seating allows you to dine in true European fashion. (☎74-3461. Open daily noon-8pm.) Look for the orange うなぎ (*unagi*) sign across the street, and you'll be at **Taiyō ❷** (たいよう). This tiny restaurant specializes in *unagi* (grilled eel). For only ¥1000, you can get a set—*miso* soup, three grilled eel filets and rice. (☎2-9445. Open daily 11:30am-2:30pm and 6-11pm.) The *izakaya* **Chūzan ❷** (中山), on Rte. 369 a few blocks west of the post office, offers homestyle dishes. Just point and smile—no matter what comes, you'll enjoy it. (Open 5-11pm.) **Est Est ❷** makes the grade with huge pasta dishes and a broad wine selection. (Open daily 11:30am-2:30pm and 6-11pm.) Downstairs, quaint **Namiko ❷** (なみ古) serves a sushi dinner sets for around ¥1500. They also have one of the best selections of *awamori* (an Okinawan alcoholic drink) around. (Open daily 11:30am-2:30pm and 6-11pm.)

◙ SIGHTS. Most travelers use Hirara as a base for exploring the shoreline, but if you're looking to kill an hour or so, there are a few mildly interesting sights around the town center. Starting at the waterfront, head north from the ferry terminal until you pass the small **Harumizu Utaki** shrine, a small monument to two local gods. Up the hill is the **Miyako Traditional Arts and Crafts Center**, where local women demonstrate the weaving of *Miyako-jofu* fabric, considered one of the four finest fabrics in all Japan, and an Important Intangible Cultural Asset. (☎2-8022. Open daily 9am-5pm.) Going north on the same road, you'll come to the **Tomb of Nakasone Toyumiya**, a 15th-century mausoleum of hand-carved coral that pays tribute to the legendary Miyako hero who conquered Yaeyama-shotō and helped protect the island from invading forces. On the road behind the ferry terminal is the **Hakui Monument**. In 1876, Kaiser Wilhelm erected it to thank the town for rescuing the crew of a shipwrecked German vessel. **Painagama Beach,** 500m south of the terminal, is not nearly as attractive as the rest of the shoreline, but it's in easy walking distance of the town center and a pleasant spot for watching sunsets.

◪ NIGHTLIFE. From central Nishizato-dōri, head south four blocks, and you'll see **New York, New York** (ニュ—ヨ—クニュ—ヨ—ク) on your left after passing the parking lot. This restaurant may fail at its grafittied recreation of NYC, but there's always Orion on tap, and it's got great billiard tables. (Open daily 9pm-2am.) After dining at A-dish, head upstairs to **Bar Alchemist**, where you can sit out on the deck and watch the sun set over Paingama Beach while sipping an *awamori* cocktail (¥800). (☎4582-4278. Open daily 6pm-3am.) Next door to the Petite Hotel on Nishizato-dōri, tropical-themed **Bar Lula** is the center of the reggae scene—most nights feature great live music. Dreadlocked Chihiro at the bar speaks English and mixes a mean *mojito* for only ¥700. (Open daily 9pm-5am.)

DAYTRIPS FROM HIRARA

TO THE NORTH. Miyako-shotō is best know for its pristine shoreline. Immediately north of Hirara is **Sunyama Beach**, which has powdery white sand and a huge stone arch that beautifully frames the horizon. Continuing north, you'll come to **Ikema Island**, home to a number of virgin beaches and a picturesque lighthouse.

TO THE SOUTH. If you're looking for an amusing way to spend an afternoon, head to the **Ueno German Culture Village,** located south of Ueno directly on the beachfront. The reconstructed Bavarian village, complete with medieval castle, is an amusing sight, especially against the tropical Okinawan shoreline. (☎76-3771. Open daily from 9am-6pm. ¥700.) Farther south, you'll come to **Yoshino Beach** in Gusukube, which has an incredible variety of tropical fish about 50m offshore. It's a wildly popular snorkeling point. At the southeast tip of the island, a long strip of white sand known as **Maehama Beach** is sometimes called Japan's finest beach.

OKINAWA

TO THE WEST. Just 10min. west of Miyako-jima by high-speed ferry (every hour, ¥400) are the islands of Irabu-jima and Shimoji-jima, connected to each other via a series of bridges. These rural getaways offer secluded beachfronts away from the major tourist routes, but transportation on the island is difficult since there are no public buses. There are more than enough taxis waiting by the ferry port, however, to whisk you away for a small fee (around ¥1000 to the nearest beach).

DIVING. Miyako-shotō offers some of Japan's best scuba diving. If you want to tackle the famous underwater caves, trips can be arranged directly through your hotel or hostel. Popular Hirara operators include **Island Breeze** (☎ 2-3469), **OK Marine Club** (☎ 3-6677), and **Good Fellas Club** (☎ 3-5482).

YAEYAMA-SHOTŌ
(八重山諸島) ☎09808

Nearly 430km south of Okinawa-hontō lies Yaeyama-shotō, an island group consisting of Ishigaki-jima, Iriomote-jima, and several smaller islands. Although the Yaeyamas are a popular destination, they are regarded by mainlanders as existing in a different temporal dimension from the rest of the country. It's hard to believe that they're part of one of the world's most ultra-modern, post-industrial nations.

The Yaeyamas are a spectacular destination, especially if you've got a love for the outdoors and an adventurous spirit. The Yaeyamas are home to the most pristine and rugged wilderness in Japan, and the surrounding waters are often said to have the best scuba diving in all of Asia. The flawless shorelines of the islands are virtually deserted, and the group has the strongest imprint of traditional Ryūkyū culture in the entire prefecture. With opportunities for trekking, kayaking, and diving, Yaeyama-shotō provides explorations enough to last a week or more.

⊏ TRANSPORTATION

Flights: All flights arrive at **Ishigaki Airport,** a few kilometers from Ishigaki town center. **JTA** (☎ 0120-25-5971) and **ANK** (☎ 0120-02-9222) have offices in the airport terminal as well as in Hirara. Local **buses** connect the airport terminal to **Ishigaki** (10min., ¥200). If you are planning on exploring the island for a few days, consider investing in a **Free Pass** (¥1000), which allows free transportation between the airport, Ishigaki, Kabira Bay and Sukuji. A taxi ride to the town center will cost you around ¥1000.

Ferries: Boats from Miyako-jima, Naha, and Taiwan serve **Ishigaki Port Terminal,** 500m southeast of the bus terminal. Boats depart from the wharves opposite the bus terminal to Taketomi, Iriomote, and other islands. 2 long distance **ferry** companies run out of Ishigaki Harbor. **Arimura Sangyō** (☎ 860-1980) and **RKK Line** (☎ 868-1126) connec Naha with Ishigaki-jima via Miyako-jima (2-3 per week). Schedules change frequently—confirm in order to avoid missing your connection. Book overnight ferries to **Naha** (11hr.) in advance, especially in summer. The trip to Miyako-jima takes about 6hr. Ferries to the outlying Yaeyama Islands depart from the harbor wharves. The main companies operating lines are **Yaeyama Kanko Ferry** and **Anei Kanko,** both located along the harbor.

ISHIGAKI-JIMA (石垣島) ☎09808

Ishigaki-jima is virtually undeveloped outside of Ishigaki Town. The majority of the landscape is lush, verdant mountains and jagged, rocky coastline. Ishigaki-jima is home to exquisite white sand beaches whose turquoise waters conceal an elaborate network of coral reefs and a rainbow of tropical fish. Since travelers bound

Yaeyama-shotō · 八重山諸島

for the other islands arrive in Ishigaki first, you can arrange all your inter-island transportation there. A number of inexpensive accommodations, however, make Ishigaki an affordable overnight stay, so take a few days to explore.

TRANSPORTATION

Buses: A network of buses connects the town and airport to the beaches and resorts. The main **bus terminal** is northwest of the wharves in Ishigaki Harbor. 9 public buses connect the town to various coastal towns, but connections are infrequent and slow. A private company runs between the Ishigaki Bus Terminal and the tourist resorts in Kabira Bay. Single ticket ¥700; round-trip (5-day validity, purchase at the terminal) ¥1000.

Car Rental: Nippon (☎2-3629), **Nissan** (☎3-0024), and **Toyota** (☎2-0100) have agencies in town. Call to arrange for free pick-up from your lodgings. You can also try **Ishikawa Renta-Car** (☎8-8840), a few blocks west of the Ishigaki Grand Hotel. Prices are reasonable—depending on availability and season, expect to pay around ¥5000 per day.

Moped/Motorcycle Rental: Honda Wing (☎2-3255), 4 blocks west of Ishigaki Grand Hotel, south of the traffic light. Scooters ¥500 per hr. Motorcycles ¥4000 per day.

Hitchhiking: Starting in Ishigaki town, hitchhikers are known to catch lifts northeast by standing along Rte. 390 and northwest by standing along Rte. 79. Infrequent traffic along the coastal roads means that getting a lift back to town can sometimes be difficult. *Let's Go* does not recommend hitchhiking.

ISHIGAKI (石垣市)　　☎09808

At some point during your sojourn in the Yaeyamas, you'll probably spend at least a night in Ishigaki, the administrative center of Yaeyama-shotō. The town has no notable sights but offers many services and is the main transportation hub for Ishigaki-jima and the other Yaeyama Islands. Ishigaki also offers a wide breadth of accommodations, from affordable ryokan to upmarket minshuku, and a good variety of restaurants and bars to hit up before heading to more exotic locales.

■📱 **ORIENTATION AND PRACTICAL INFORMATION.** Ishigaki is centered around the harbor. Northwest of the ferry wharves is the **central bus terminal,** while the main town square—the Rte. 730 intersection—is directly north (look for the Ishigaki Grand Hotel). A few major streets run parallel to the waterfront, including two covered shopping arcades. The **Ishigaki City Tourism Association,** located in the civic building 5min. west of the bus terminal, across from the park, has city maps and an English guide to the island. (☎2-2809. Open Tu-Sa 8:30am-5pm.) Next door is the **public library,** which provides free **Internet access.** (Open Tu-F 10am-7pm and Sa-Su 10am-5pm.) If you buy a drink, you can also access the Internet at the **Ishigaki Net Cafe,** in the covered arcade upstairs from the market, where **Internet access** is free. (☎3-8684. Orion beer ¥450, whiskey ¥750. Open daily 11pm-3am.) The **Ishigaki Main Hospital** is 20min. north of the town center off of Rte. 369, but there is a small **clinic** located next to the post office. In an emergency, call ☎110 for **police,** ☎119 for **fire** or **ambulance.** The **post office,** two blocks north of the town square, has an **international ATM.** (☎2-3742. Open M-F 9am-5pm.) **Postal code:** 907.

▐ **ACCOMMODATIONS.** Since most travelers have to spend a night in town before heading to other destinations, there are a wide range of places to stay. From the ferry terminal, walk north along Rte. 390 for about 10min. When you see the Enos gas station, turn left and **Guesthouse Costa del Sol** ❶ (ゲストハウスコスタデルソル), 700, Tonoshiro, will be on your right. This newcomer to the Ishigaki hotel scene offers unbeatable rates. All rooms have A/C. Kitchen, laundry, shower, and Internet facilities are complimentary. (☎090-4532-5971. Dorms ¥1500.) Located directly behind Shinei Kōen, **Parkside Tomo** ❶ (パークサイドトモ), 6-4, Shinei-chō, although slightly more expensive then Costa del Sol, offers huge, private *tatami* rooms with fan, coin-operated A/C, and TV. There are kitchen, shower, and laundry facilities in the building. (☎8-8388. Singles ¥2000.) One block north of the covered arcades stands **Minshuku Rakutenya** ❶ (民宿樂天屋), 291, Ōkawa. Ren and Miyako, the extremely friendly English-speaking couple who run the intimate guesthouse, can help arrange activities. All rooms have a fan and coin-operated A/C. Kitchen, shower, and laundry facilities are available. (☎3-8713. ¥3000 per person.) Next door at **Minshuku Ishigaki-jima** ❸ (民宿石垣島), 6-4, Shinei-chō, the *tatami* rooms are fondly looked after by an attentive staff. All rooms have a fan and coin-operated A/C. Kitchen, shower and laundry facilities are available. (☎8-8388. 2 meals included. ¥6000 per person.) About half a kilometer southeast of the bus terminal, the über-modern **Hyper Hotel Ishigaki-jima** ❷ (ハイパーホテル石垣島), is a business hotel with automated check-in and futuristic toilets. All rooms have A/C, TV, bath, electric shoe shiner, and a queen-sized bed. (☎2-2000. Singles ¥4900, ¥1000 for each additional person.) A few blocks north of the ferry terminal, on the town square, is **Ishigaki Grand Hotel** ❹ (石垣グランドホテル), 1, Tomoshiro. In addition to stylish rooms, the Grand Hotel has a beautiful bath and sauna and a sophisticated sushi bar. Rooms come with A/C, TV, and attached bath. (☎2-6161. Singles ¥9000.)

◘ **FOOD.** Check out the **food markets** in the covered arcades, but don't miss out on Ishigaki's culinary culture! Just north of the markets, **KAPI Asian Kitchen** ❷ (アジアンキッチン), 199-102, Ōgawa, offers Vietnamese rice crepes (¥600), red-hot Thai curries (¥950), and a wide range of pan-Asian delicacies. (☎2-2026. Open daily 5:30-11pm.) From Honda Wing, head south until you reach the intersection, and on the left you'll see stylishly smart **Ajigoya** ❸ (あじ小屋), where guests dine on an extensive range of Western and Asian foods amidst ebony-paneled booths

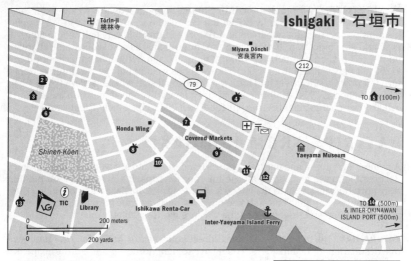

Ishigaki · 石垣市

Ishigaki · 石垣市

🏠 ACCOMMODATIONS
Guesthouse Costa del Sol, **5**
Hyper Hotel Ishigaki-jima, **14**
Ishigaki Grand Hotel, **12**
Minshuku Ishigaki-jima, **1**
Minshuku Rakutenya, **7**
Parkside Tomo, **3**

🍴 FOOD
Ajigoya, **11**
KAPI Asian Kitchen, **9**
La Vie, **13**
Misushi, **6**
Morinokokage, **4**
Tadaki, **8**

🍸 NIGHTLIFE
Asadoya, **10**
Pool Bar, **2**

OKINAWA

tended by a fashionable waitstaff. (☎8-5681. Open daily 5:30-11pm.) One block southwest of Shinen-kōen is **La Vie ❸** (レストランラーヴィ), 1-2-6, Hamizaki, cosmopolitan even by Tōkyō standards, offering truly delectable European dishes for under ¥1500. Live jazz some evenings. (☎3-3402. Open daily 11:30-2pm and 6-11pm.) Located 100m west of the post office, **Morinokokage ❶** (森のこかげ) 199, Ōgawa, has a wide selection of tapas-like dishes, including fried fish, braised tofu, and *kimchi* soup (around ¥500 each). (☎3-7933. Open daily 5-11pm.) At the northwestern corner of Shinei-kōen, simple, understated sushi bar **Misushi ❸** (三寿司), 10-28, Shinei-chō, offers some of the freshest fish around, with an attractive view of the Shinei-kōen grounds. (☎2-3708. Open daily 11:30am-1pm and 5:30-11pm.) Just past the Honda Wing dealer, look for the large, painted eel sign above **Tadaki ❸** (只喜), which charms with rustic-wooden fixtures and a vaulted A-frame ceiling. The *unagi* (eel) sets (¥1200) feature local eels braised over hot coals and marinated in rich sauces. (☎2-7779. Open daily 11:30am-1pm and 5:30-11pm.)

🔲 **SIGHTS.** It only takes a few hours to tick off all of Ishigaki's sites, but they are interesting, and the town is a pleasant place for a stroll. A 15min. walk northwest of the harbor is **Tōrin-ji** (桃林寺), a Zen temple built in 1614. A few blocks north of the post office is **Miyara Dōnchi** (宮良宮内), a red-tiled house from 1819. It contains a limestone rock garden and is the only *samurai*-style residence left in Okinawa-shotō. Just north of the harbor is the **Yaeyama Museum,** which has a modest exhibit on traditional Yaeyama lifestyles, and displays over 300 historical artifacts. (Open Tu-Su 9am-4:35pm. Closed national holidays. ¥100.) Two kilometers north of town on Rte. 79 is **Tōjin Grave** (唐人墓), an elaborate monument in memory of 400 Chinese laborers who died off the coast in 1852 en route to California.

NIGHTLIFE. Two blocks north of Shinen-kōen, across the street from the Enos gas station is the swanky ■**Pool Bar** (there's no sign, but it's there). Though it's a bit pricey, the glossy bartop and fixtures in this billiards hall seethe sharpness and sophistication. It attracts a mix of pool sharks and scenesters. There's bound to be good competition on any night. (Open daily 8pm-5am. Pool table ¥1200 per hr. Cocktails from ¥800.) Three blocks west of the Rte. 730 intersection, turn left down a side street and look out for a small sign where **Asadoya** (安里屋) makes its home. This small music bar has nightly live music performances. The ¥1000 cover charge includes free bar food. (☎8-6008. Open daily 10pm-2am.)

DAYTRIPS FROM ISHIGAKI

A number of cultural and natural sights around the island are worth exploring, and it's possible to use Ishigaki as a base for your daytrips. If you're reliant on public transportation, just head to the island's all-star attraction, **Kabira Bay,** by taking the resort shuttles or public buses. If you have your private transportation, however, a number of interesting sights along the way are worth visiting.

KABIRA BAY. North on Rte. 79, signs direct you towards **Kabira Bay,** the number one destination for mainlanders. You'll have to fight hordes of tourists during peak season, but Kabira Bay has some of the most spectacular scenery on the island. The emerald waters are dotted with tiny islets, and the shore is covered in white sand. The area's famous black pearls are available in jewelry shops all over the island. If the summer swarms become too much, **Sukuji Beach,** just a 15min. hike north, has similar scenery, *sans* tourists. At the southwestern edge of the beach is the **Sukuji Seaman's Club,** arranges a variety of marine activities including jetskiing, windsurfing, snorkeling, scuba diving, and deep sea fishing. A ride on a **glass-bottom boat** will let you see the pearl farms, but there are better ways to dispose of your hard-earned yen. (Tours depart from Sukuji Beach daily 9:15am-5pm. ¥1000.)

■**YONEHARA BEACH.** By far the most spectacular spot on the island is **Yonehara Beach,** 5km east of Kabira on Rte. 79. With a sturdy pair of sandals, you can walk along a huge expanse of dead coral that leads out into the sea. If you rent snorkel gear from the shops along the main road, you can explore the nearby reefs and drop-offs. Before diving in, consult the locals about the jellyfish, whose numbers vary with the season. For an overnight, try the small **campsite** nearby.

THE EASTERN COAST. At Ibaruma Bay, you have two options. North, you'll eventually hit **Hirakabu-zaki Tōdai,** a picturesque lighthouse overlooking the tiny island of Daichi Hanare-jima. Following Rte. 79 south, you come to **Tamatori-zaki Observation Platform,** an attractive lookout point surrounded by colorful gardens. Bus #9 (1hr., ¥750) from Ishigaki town runs to the base of the hill, but it comes out infrequently. Rounding the coast, stop at **Ryūgujo Cave,** a limestone cavern with impressive fossilized coral formations. (Open daily 9am-10pm. ¥1000.) Follow signs for **Banna-dake Forest Park,** where it's a short hike up to the top of **Banna-dake** (230m), which affords great views of the forest and Ishigaki town.

HIKING. Past Yonehara Beach, mountains dominate the landscape, and there are ample chances to hike. Lookout for the **Yaeyama tree,** a unique species of wild palm found only on these islands. There's a grove north of Yonehara, at the base of **Omoto-dake** (526m), the prefecture's highest point. The most challenging hike is a few kilometers north, at 282m high **Nosoko-dake.** It's a steep 45min. trek to the top of the dormant volcano, but the view of Hirakubo Peninsula is worth the effort.

DIVING. Most of the island's 50 dive sites are home to both hard and soft corals. For advanced divers, there are several caves and walls to explore. In addition to the usual tropical fish, there are opportunities to see eagle rays and blunthead sharks. If you're around in fall or winter, you have a good chance of seeing manta rays at the famous "Manta Way" between Kohama and Iriomote-jima. The more popular dive outfits are **Tom Sawyer** (☎3-4667), next to the Ishigaki Grand Hotel, and **Aquamarine** (☎2-0863), near the Hyper Hotel.

TAKETOMI-JIMA (竹富島)　　☎09808

If you came to Okinawa in search of Ryūkyū culture, hop on board a ferry to Take-tomi-jima. The islanders' laid-back attitude is infectious, and the village is an architectural gem. Most of the houses are built in traditional style, along dirt roads lined with coral walls and flower beds. *Shiisa* stone guardians stare down from the orange tiled-buildings, and the salty sea air mixes intoxicatingly with the seasonal bloom. An overnight stay is all that is needed to fully absorb the island's charm.

Yaeyama and Anei Kanko's **high-speed ferry** leave for Taketomi-jima from the wharves in Ishigaki town. (Every 30min. ¥580, round-trip ¥1100. Last ferry to Ishigaki 5pm.) When you arrive on the island, you'll be met by a number of stores offering **bicycle rentals.** Although the island is small enough to cover by foot, it's perfect for exploring by bike. (Standard rental prices ¥300 per hr. or ¥1500 per day.) If you choose to rent a bike, you will be driven from the harbor to Taketomi village, located at the center of the island. You can also take a 50min. romp around the island on a **buffalo-drawn cart** (¥1000). In an emergency, call ☎110 for **police,** ☎119 for **fire** or **ambulance.** There is a **post office** on the island, but since there's **no international ATM** access, get cash before setting out for Taketomi.

The main attractions of Taketomi-jima are strolling through the town center admiring the architecture and riding along the dusty roads to the island's two world-class beaches. Do not leave without spending a few hours on ▨**Kondoi Beach,** on the western shore. At lowtide, the ocean recedes and exposes about 1.5km of tidal pools full of brittle stars, sea cucumbers, and a few coral heads sheltering small schools of tropical fish, hermit crabs, sea anemones, and the occasional octopus. A shack on the beach serves snacks for under ¥500 and rents snorkel gear for ¥1500. Just south of Kondoi at **Kaiji Beach,** you'll find *hoshisuna* (star sand), the star-shaped skeletons of small sea creatures. If you have time to kill in the village before heading back to Ishigaki, **Kihōin Shūshūkan** is a small museum focusing on village life. (Open daily 9am-5pm. ¥300.) At **Taketomi Mingei-kan** you can watch *Minsā* sashes being woven. Men used to present the blue and white belts to women as a sign of love. There is also a small shrine nearby, **Nishitō Utaki,** which pays tribute to the 16th-century ruler of Yaeyama-shotō.

If you're staying overnight, there are a number of nearly identical ryokan in Taketomi Village, all of which provide two meals. Near town center is **Nohara-sō ❷** (野原荘 ; ¥5000). Opposite the post office is **Takana Ryokan ❸** (高那旅館 ; ☎5-2151), where singles are ¥7000 a night. Nearby, **Minshuku Izumiya ❷** (民宿泉屋) charges ¥5000 per night. Beachgoers have few food options aside from the small **convenience store** in town. At the southern edge of town and east of Kondoi Beach, **Kurukun ❷** (くるくん) has curry rice lunch sets for only ¥650.

IRIOMOTE-JIMA (西表島)　　☎09808

Lying 20km off the western coast of Ishigaki, Iriomote-jima is a desolate island of subtropical wilderness. The only inhabitants live along a small strip of coastline buttressed against the dark and lurking jungle. It is difficult to not be awed by this mysterious virgin terrain. Even today much of the rugged interior is impassible.

OKINAWA

Nearly 80% of Iriomote-jima is designated as part of the **Iriomote National Park,** and the island is home to one of the world's rarest animals, the *yamaneko* (Iriomote wildcat), as well as plants and insects you won't find anywhere else on the planet.

For most, the principal draw of the island is a boat trip up the murky **Urauchi-gawa,** a river that winds deep into the interior, but reward yourself by taking advantage of the opportunities to trek and kayak—the lush landscape rivals anything you'll find in nearby Southeast Asia. The waters surrounding Iriomote-jima are home to the best scuba diving in all of Japan, and at a number of sites you're almost assured an encounter with a manta ray. Iriomote-jima is a truly rewarding destination for the adventure traveler, so abandon your preconceptions, and get ready to match your outdoor prowess against one of the most untamed landscapes in all of East Asia. There's only a small info booth in Funaura, so get information from the Tourist Information Center of the Ishigaki ferry terminal.

▆ TRANSPORTATION. Yaeyama Kankō and **Anei Kankō** run ferries to Funaura (45min.;10 per day; ¥2000, round-trip ¥3800) and Ōhara (35min.; 10 per day; ¥1540, round-trip ¥2980). It's more convenient to take the Yaeyama ferries since they arrive directly in front of the accommodation strip, whereas Anei ferries arrive a few minutes north of town. Resort buses meet each ferry and offer free transfers. A public bus connects Funaura and Ōhara; expect to pay about ¥990 for the 1hr. trip, but the bus is unreliable. A **public bus** also connects Funaura with the mouth of the Urauchi-gawa (15min., ¥230). **Taxis** (☎5-6455) operate on the island, but fares are absurdly expensive. A small coastal road connects Funaura and Ōhara, but there are no roads leading to the interior. The few small towns scattered along the coastline are of little interest. The best way to explore the island is by arranging your own private transportation. Both youth hostels (below) rent **bikes, mopeds,** and **cars** for ¥1500, ¥3000, and ¥6000 per day respectively. **Iriomote Rent-a-Car** (☎5-5303), in Funaura, has similar rates. Since there's only one road on the island, hitchhikers say that it's easy to catch a ride in either direction, but the flow of traffic drastically decreases at night. *Let's Go* does not recommend hitchhiking.

🛈 PRACTICAL INFORMATION. A cartoony **map** of the island is free from the tourist information center in Ishigaki, and most hotels have some map. If you're going to trek the interior, buy an ordinance map at a bookstore *prior* to arriving. Otherwise, pick up a map at the trailhead. Bring all essentials, especially rain gear, with you. Most campsites rent out gear. If you're camping, make sure you have a ground sheet—the rain gets very heavy. Mosquitoes are bad in the rainy season, so bring repellent and coils. There are leeches in the interior, so carry either a lighter or salt with you. In summer, Iriomote-jima can be hit with serious typhoons, so check the local weather report prior to heading out. In an emergency call ☎110 for **police,** ☎119 for **fire** or **ambulance** ☎119. If you scrape yourself up, there are a few small clinics in Ōhara, Funaura, and Shirahama.

🛏🛖 ACCOMMODATIONS AND CAMPING. A number of campsites lie along the main road. Some travelers report that you can pitch your tent anywhere, but this is illegal and inadvisable. The nearest **campsite** is just a few kilometers east along the main road. You can also camp at the **Pension Hoshinosuna ❶** (ペンシオン 星の砂) on Hoshinosuna Beach. (☎5-6488. ¥300 per pitch. Equipment ¥625.) The majority of budget accommodations lie along the harbor in Funaura. The expensive hotels along the beaches cater mostly to Japanese package travelers. From the Yaemoni Kanko ferry port in Funaura, you'll first see the **Minshuku Kampira-sō ❶** (民宿かんぴら荘), the island's best bargain. (☎5-6526. ¥3500.) Next door is

Minshuku Uehara ❷ (民宿うえはら), slighly more expensive for the same amenities. (¥5000.) Continuing to the left, **Midori-sō Youth Hostel (HI) ❶** (みどり荘ユース ホテル) offers spotless dorm rooms with A/C for ¥3500. On the hill overlooking the port is **Iriomote-sō Youth Hostel (HI)❷** (西表荘ユ一スホテル) which has a dive center and a beautiful harbor view. (¥3950.)

Since most accommodations provide two meals, eating options are limited. The **supermarket** in Funaura has instant foods and fresh produce. 15km east of Funaura, you'll find **Takana ❸** (高那) perched next to a mangrove swamp, with great lunch sets. (☎5-5500. Sets under ¥1000. Open daily 11am-4pm.) Across from Urauchi-gawa Boat Tours is a small outdoor **cafe ❷**.

◪◩ SIGHTS AND HIKING. Before setting out, always inform your accommodations of your plans; should something go wrong, they'll know you need help. The all-star attraction is a boat trip up **Urauchi-gawa,** a murky-brown river that winds through dense mangrove forests. Tours depart from the river mouth, about 10km southwest of Funaura. It's a 30min. boat ride to the trailhead for **Mariudo-no-taki** and **Kanbire-no-taki,** then a relatively easy 45min. hike to the nearby falls, where you can cool off with a swim. Since a minimum of four people is required to set out, it's best to arrive in the morning so you can latch on to other groups. (Daily 9am-4pm. ¥1500.) A similar 90min. cruise operates along **Nakama-gawa,** Iriomote-jima's second longest river, departing from just north of Ōhara.

If you'd rather not head back down the Urauchi-gawa with the boat, you have the option of renting a **kayak** from the tour operator and paddling the 8km back to the river mouth. This trip, which costs about ¥8500 for the full day, lunch included, should be arranged prior to setting out. Feeling adventurous? The other option is to continue past Kanbire-no-taki to the trailhead for the 8hr., 15km **cross-island trek** to Ōhara. This is a serious hike that you absolutely should not attempt without first consulting locals. At the trail entrance, you will need to register with the police, who will not let you tackle the trail without a buddy. There are leeches in the summer—bring either salt or a good lighter. Keep an eye out for the huge, papery roots of *sakishima suōnoki* trees. It's only about 90min. from the Kaichu-doro Bridge, south of Funaura, to **Pinaisāra-no-taki,** the tallest waterfall in Okinawa.

◪ BEACHES AND DIVING. Since most visitors are eager to complete the river trip and make it back to Ishigaki by nightfall, the beaches on the island are relatively untouristed. **Haemita-no-hama,** south of Ōhara, is hailed as the island's most beautiful strip of sand. Near Funuara, **Hoshisuna-no-hama** has great snorkeling, and you should be able to find starsand. From Shirahama, at the western end of the coastal road, you can take a **ferry** (3 per day, ¥400) to deserted **Funauki Beach,** on a nearby islet. A nearby *onsen* is a good option in bad weather. (Open daily 11am-9pm. ¥1200.) Divers absolutely cannot leave without diving ▨**Manta Way,** between the eastern coast and Kohama-jima, where you're almost sure to see manta rays in winter and spring. Try **Mr. Sakana Diving Service** (☎5-6472) or **Diving Team Unarizaki** (☎5-6142), both in Uehara. A two-dive trip to the strait will set you back ¥12,000.

▨ ISLANDS AROUND IRIOMOTE-JIMA

Five kilometers north of Iriomote is miniscule **Hatoma-jima,** a 1km sq. island covered in tropical flowers. Close to the eastern coast of Iriomote is **Kohama-jima,** which has thick groves of banyan trees and a mountainous interior. Directly south of Iriomote is **Hateruma-jima,** the southernmost Japanese island, covered in farm villages and fields of sugar cane. Finally, there's **Kuro-shima,** south of Iriomote, where they raise bulls for *tōgyū* fights. All the islands are easily reached by ferry from the wharves in Ishigaki, and have a decent range of minshuku.

YONAGUNI-JIMA (与那国島)   ☎ 09808

One hundred kilometers west of Iriomote is **Yonaguni-jima,** the westernmost point in Japan, only 110km from Taiwan. Yonaguni is dotted with picturesque straw houses and intriguing rock formations. On a clear day, you can see Taiwan from **Urabu-dake** (231m), the island's highest point. **JTA** flies from Ishigaki (40min., 2 per day, ¥6400), and on Wednesday and Saturday the **Fukuyama ferry service** (☎ 7-2555) runs boats from Ishigaki (4hr., W and Sa, ¥3460). Schedules are liable to change.

HOKKAIDŌ
(北海道)

As you slip through the door into Hokkaidō—Japan's second largest island and the idyllic wild world for dreamers—don't bother taking off your boots, reaching for a tattered phrasebook, or searching for the elusive Last Samurai. In what many would call the country's playground, the scene is more natural, the story less cultural, and the weather and people cooler. The rhetoric on Hokkaidō is pervasive: Hokkaidō's an unspoiled frontier; an urban-dweller's getaway; an undiscovered animal kingdom; a meat market for single brown bears. What the manufactured slogans fail to convey is Hokkaidō's core. Beyond the dry weather, rainbow flower-fields, virgin mountains, and savory fish, this island feeds a free spirit infusing the countless motorcyclists who quit their jobs to hug the island's western coast for two months, the professional skiers and snowboarders from all over the world who train on Niseko's powdered slopes, and the scruffy backpackers who hike for three days in the golden mountains of Shiretoko National Park, then bathe like gods in the hot *onsen* waterfalls of Kamuiwakka Taki. While the island might be the youngest of Japan's main four, she's anything but the spoiled one—only ten percent of her land is inhabited, and she shelters five national parks.

Hokkaidō is cheaper than most other parts of Japan. However, although intercity transport is convenient, local transport can be costly and infrequent. When not relying on a JR Pass or Jūhachi Seishun Kippu, you'll want your own form of transport. If coming up from Honshū, you're most likely to enter through the port-city of Hakodate, where you can spend a day learning about 19th-century encounters between Japanese and Westerners. Move on to the blue waters and active volcanoes of Shikotsu-Tōya National Park. From there, head up to Sapporo where after sundown you can let loose in Susukino and trek into Hokkaidō's lesser-traveled regions during the day. The islands of Rishiri and Rebun lie to the north, and a series of parks and towns, including Daisetsu-zan and Shiretoko National Park, blanket the center of the island. Keep your eyes and ears peeled for opportunities to learn about the Ainu, Japan's quickly disappearing indigenous population.

HIGHLIGHTS OF HOKKAIDŌ

HIKE TO THE HEAVENS. Travel Von Trapp-style across the mountains of **Daisetsu-zan** (p. 702), **Akan** (p. 711), and **Shiretoko National Parks** (p. 715).

KALEIDOSCOPIC FLOWERS. Prance through the candyland of **Furano's** (p. 701) psychedelic flower fields.

NATURAL MAN. Gaze at Russia while contemplating isolationism on Japan's unsullied northern outcroppings, **Shiretoko National Park** (p. 715) and **Rishiri-Rebun-Sarobetsu National Park** (p. 721).

A WORLD-CLASS SWOOSH. Jump with the snow bunnies down lily-white moguls on **Niseko's** (p. 677) renowned slopes.

SEA OF JAPAN
日本海

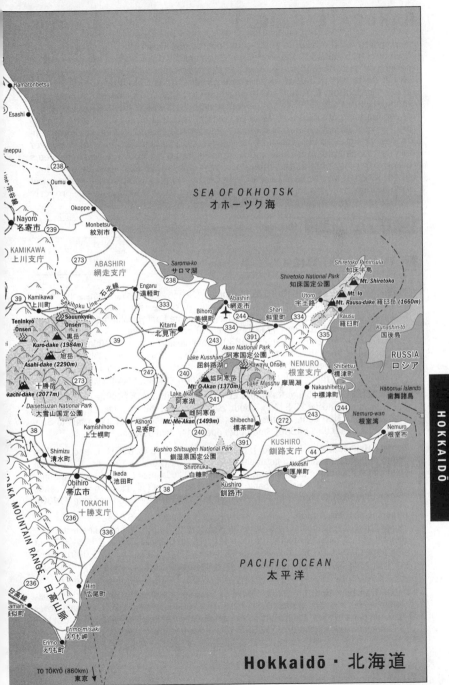

Hokkaidō · 北海道

HAKODATE (函館) ☎ 0138

As you step off the train in Hakodate Station, you won't find big bears holding "Welcome to Hokkaidō" signs or Ainu ice-fishing by the bay, but from the bite in the air you'll know that you've reached the *other* Japan. Snuggled between two bays at the border of Japan's wild frontier, Hakodate is a bustling port-city with a bit of cosmopolitan flare and sweet proximity to Hokkaidō's closest national park, Ōnuma. Historically, the city has assumed various roles—as an intelligence center for Japanese expansionists to monitor the northern peoples, as a key for 19th-century Western imperialists to unlock the Asian markets, and as a home to the rapidly decreasing Ainu population. While such historical faces are imprinted all over the city's fascinating museums and landmarks, today's younger generation seems to know the city best as the home of Glay—one of Japan's most beloved hair bands. Whether you're here to dabble in history, pop culture, or the vast natural surroundings, you'll want to put down your pack for a few days to get properly acquainted with your new friend, Hokkaidō.

ON THE WEB	Hakodate City: www.city.hakodate.hokkaido.jp

▐ TRANSPORTATION

Trains: The modern **Hakodate Train Station** (函館駅), 12-13, Wakamatsu-chō (☎23-2124), has a cafe and information/service counters on the 1st fl., and a handful of restaurants on the 2nd fl. Open 24hr. Reaching Hakodate from Honshū requires a transfer of trains at **Aomori Station** (青森駅) where JR's Hakuchō train snakes all the way up to Hakodate (2hr., about 1 per hr., ¥4830). From the north, take JR's **Hokuto** train from **Sapporo** (札幌 ; 3hr., 1 per hr., ¥8590) or **Tōya** (陶洞爺湖 ; 1½hr., 1 per hr., ¥5340). From **Niseko** (ニセコ) there are no direct trains, so you'll have to take a local train to Oshyanbe (長方部 ; 1¾hr., 6 per day, ¥1230), then transfer.

Buses: Local buses pull into **Hakodate Eki-mae Bus Station** (函館駅前バス駅), 21-1, Wakamatsu-chō (☎22-8111), about 20m in front of the train station. Open daily 8:30am-7pm. Next door, **Hokuto Kōtsū** (北都交通 ; ☎22-3265) has a bus to **Sapporo** (5hr., 6 per day, ¥4680). Info booth open daily 7am-9:30pm.

Ferries: Hakodate Port (函館港), 3-19-2, Minato-chō (☎42-6251), is about 3.5km north of the train station. To get there, take bus #101 (20min., 1 per hr., ¥250) from platform #3 in front of the train station; get off at Hokudai-mae (北大前). It's a 5min. walk from there. The main company, **Higashi Nihon Ferry** (東日本フェリ) sends ferries to **Aomori** (3¾hr.; every 2hr., 9-10 per day; from ¥1850, students from ¥1480).

Airport: Hakodate Airport (函館空港), 511, Takamatsu (☎57-8881), on the east side of town. Airport bus departs from the Harbor Hotel, to the right of the train station's central exit (20min., 2-3 per hr., ¥300). **JAL** flies to: **Chitose Airport** (千歳空港) in Sapporo (45min., 2 per day, ¥14,000); **Ōsaka** (2hr., 1 per day, ¥33,000); **Tōkyō** (1¼hr., 5 per day, ¥28,600). **ANA** flies to: **Okadama Airport** (丘珠空港) in Sapporo (6 per day, Y14,000); **Ōsaka** (2 per day, ¥33,000); **Tōkyō** (5 per day, ¥26,000).

Public Transportation: The 2 main forms of transport in Hakodate are **buses** (6:30am-10pm; ¥200-290) and **trams** (6:50am-10pm; ¥200-250). While the two usually cover different parts of town, the tram is more convenient where the two overlap. You can buy a 1-day tram/bus combo pass (¥1000) or a 1-day tram pass (¥600).

Taxis: The city's main taxi stop is in front of the train station's Central Exit (中央出口). **Fuji Taxi** (富士タクシー ; ☎43-2400) operates 24hr.

Goroyōkaku Kōen
五稜郭公園
Ruins of Goryōkaku Castle
五稜郭跡

Fukabouchō Station
深堀町駅

TO FERRY TERMINAL ⚓ (1.4km)
フェリーターミナル

Kashiwagichō Station
柏木町駅

Gorgōkaku Station
五稜郭駅

Suginamichō Station
杉並町駅

Gorgōkaku Kōen-mae Station
五稜郭公園前駅

Chūō Byōin-mae Station
中央病院前駅

Route 228・228号線

Chiyogadai Station
千代ヶ岱駅

TO HAKODATE CITY
HOSPITAL ✚ (1km)

TO 5

Horikawachō Station
堀川町駅

Hakodate Harbor
函館港

Shōwabashi Station
昭和橋駅

Chitosechō Station
千歳町駅

Shinkawachō Station
新川駅

Laundry

Hakodate Ekimae Station
函館駅前駅

Matsukazechō Station
松風町駅

Hakodate・函館

🏠 ACCOMMODATIONS
Hakodate International Hotel, 8
Hakodate Youth
　Guest House (III), 10
Minshuku Sudō, 7
Nice Day Inn, 9
Oyado Aozora Inn, 6

🍎 FOOD
Kantarō Zushi, 5
Omote Mon, 1

🍺 NIGHTLIFE
Beelong's, 2
Eiley's, 3
Topps, 4

Hakodate Station
函館駅

NTT

Hakodate City Hall
函館市役所

Shiyakusho-mae Station
市役所前駅

Tsugaru Kaikyō
津軽海峡

Uoichiba-dōri Station
魚市場通駅

Hakodate Dock-mae Station
函館どっく前駅

Ōmachi Station
大町駅

Hakodate City
Museum of
Northern Peoples
函館市北方民俗
博物館

Meijikan

Tūjigai Station
十字街駅

Suehirochō Station
末広町駅

Hōraichō Station
宝来町駅

Old British Consulate
旧イギリス領事館

Russian Orthodox
Church
ハリストス正教会

Aoyagichō Station
青柳駅

Motomachi Kōen
元町公園

Museum of
Photography

200 meters

200 yards

Foreigners'
Cemetery
外人墓地

Hakodate Kōen
函館公園

Yachigashira Station
谷地頭駅

函館山
Hakodate-yama (334m)

Tachimachi Cape

HOKKAIDŌ

Car Rental: Nissan Car Lease (日産カーリース), 22-15, Wakamatsu (☎27-4123), and **Mazda Rent-a-Lease** (マズダレンタリース), 22-7, Wakamatsu (☎27-4547), offer the best value. Rentals at both start at ¥4500 per day (add ¥2000 during summer months). To get to the side-by-side agencies, leave the train station's main exit, and turn left when you get to the 1st major street. Mazda is 2 blocks down on the left.

Bike Rental: Some accommodations rent bikes to guests, but the only rental shop is **BAY**, 11-15, Toyokawa-machi (☎27-5555), in Motomachi, where the set price is a hefty ¥1000 per day. To reach the shop, leave the station's West Exit (nishi-guchi; 西口), and walk along the street closest to the water. After going over a mini-walking bridge, you can't miss BAY's leaf-covered brick wall on your left. Open daily 9:30am-7pm.

■ ORIENTATION

Hakodate is positioned in between two back-to-back, U-shaped bays, which serve as eastern and western borders. The city itself has three main areas—around the station, Motomachi (元町), and Goryōkaku (五稜郭)—which are far apart, but each walkable in and of themselves. The center region is the station area, which contains most practical amenities but is otherwise pretty useless to the traveler. To the west of the station area is Motomachi—the old town—an area filled with historic landmarks, fascinating museums, and Mt. Hakodate. On the eastern side of town, Goryōkaku is the modern center for stores, food, and nightlife. Although a bike can be great to get around Hakodate, the easiest way to get from district to district is the efficient tram system, which sweeps across the heart of the city.

⁊ PRACTICAL INFORMATION

Tourist Office: The **tourist info office** (函館市観光案内所 ; ☎23-5440), Hakodate Station, to the left of the central exit, offers English pamphlets and maps on Hakodate, and Hokkaidō in general. English speakers are always on hand and the staff books accommodations for free. Open daily Apr.-Oct. 9am-7pm; Nov.-Mar. 9am-5pm.

Tours: There are no English tours of Hakodate, but **Hokuto Kōtsū** (北都交通 ; ☎57-7555; fax 57-7185) offers a 4¾hr. tour in Japanese. Highlights include the Old Public Hall, the Old British Consulate, Mt. Hakodate, Goryōkaku Tower, Trappistine Convent, and the Hakodate Milk Factory. ¥3500 per person. Optional lunch ¥1200. Operates Apr.28-Oct. 31. Reservations required.

Budget Travel: There are no budget agencies in town, but **JTB Travel**, 20-1, Wakamatsu (☎22-4185), finds cheaper plane tickets than the airlines offer. Open daily 10am-6pm. Closed every 2nd and 4th W of the month.

Currency Exchange and ATMs: At the central and station-front post offices (see below).

Luggage Storage: Lockers are in Hakodate Station to the right of the exit (¥300-700).

Lost Property: Consult the JR office on the 1st fl. of the train station.

Market: Morning market (asa-ichi; 朝市) runs every day from 5am through the late afternoon. Head out of the station's west exit and let your nose guide you to the fish.

Laundromat: Coin Laundry (コインランドリー) is the closest laundromat to the city center. Head straight out of the station, turn left onto the 1st main road, and then turn right onto a split street after 2 blocks. Make your 2nd left; it's on the right.

Public Baths: Yunokawa (湯の川), Hakodate's hot springs district, is east of the city center. To get there, hop on a #2 or 5 tram, or a #6 bus. The tourist office provides an info sheet on the area's various hotel and public *onsen* facilities.

Emergency: Police ☎110. Fire or ambulance ☎119.

Pharmacy: Kusuri-no-Kamei (くすりのカメイ), 18-1, Wakamatsu-chō (☎22-8100), carries the basic goods. Head out of the station's central exit and 2 blocks up the main road. Open daily 9:30am-7:30pm.

Hospital/Medical Services: Hakodate City Hospital (函館市病院), 1-10-1, Minato-chō (☎43-2000), is located about 3km north of the city center. Open 24hr.

Internet Access: NTT Building, 14-8, Shinonome-chō (☎22-8100), southeast of the station, offers 1hr. of free Internet. From the station's central exit, walk straight up to the 1st main intersection, continue for 2 blocks and then make a right—NTT is a white building 3 blocks down on the left. Open M-F 9am-5pm. **HotWeb Cafe,** 18-1, Wakamatsu-chō (☎26-3591). 3 blocks up from the train station and on the left. 1hr. free Internet is included with the purchase of 1 drink (¥300). Every additional 30min. ¥100. Open daily 10am-8pm. **@ Cafe St.,** (☎27-4826), in the train station—to the right just before the exit. You must buy 1 drink and pay ¥200 per hr. Open daily 6:30am-10pm. **FabColle** in Goryōkaku (p. 676) allows visitors to hook up their laptops to a fast LAN line.

Services: Nitsū Perikanbin (日通ペリカン便), 14-10, Wakamatsu-chō (☎23-8815). Packages to Tōkyō around ¥1500. To the right of the station's main exit, adjacent to the Harbor View Hotel. Open M-F 8am-6pm.

Post Office: Central Post Office (函館中央郵便局), 1-6, Shinkawa-chō (☎22-9124), is about a 15min. walk from the train station. Money exchange open daily 9am-4pm. ATM open daily 9am-7pm. Mailing window inside open 24hr. **Postal Code:** 040.

ACCOMMODATIONS

Hokkaidō's relatively low cost of living is perhaps most evident in the city's abundance of affordable, foreigner-friendly accommodations. Minshuku, inns, and ryokan can be found for as low as ¥2500, and the best of these choices can be found around the station. Reservations are a good idea throughout the year, and the tourist office will even book them for you if you're having trouble yourself.

▨ Oyado Aozora Inn (おやど青空), 22-4, Wakamatsu-chō (☎22-4978; www10.plala.or.jp/aozora-inn). Make your 1st left out of Hakodate Station onto a back street near the river—as you make your 2nd right, you can't miss the bright white inn on the left (2min.). Cozy inn run by a sweet middle-aged couple. Complimentary microwave and toaster available. Laundry available. Free Internet. Check-out 10am. Singles ¥3300; doubles ¥6000; triples ¥8400. ❶

Minshuku Sudō (民宿すどう), 12-21, Asahi-chō (☎22-5921 or 23-7358). From the station, take bus #1 to San Rifure (サンリフレ) then walk back a block; it will be on the left. A quicker route might be to take the tram to Shiyakusho-mae (市役所前), then walk a block past the stop and turn left. Walk all the way down until you see San Rifure on the right corner and go left. Shabby exterior and slightly run-down rooms, but the place is the cheapest in town and a bargain. Word on the street is that the nice old man here sometimes lends bikes out for free. Laundry available. Parking in back. ❶

Nice Day Inn (ナイスデイイン), 9-11, Ōte-machi (☎22-5919). Go down the street directly across from the International Hotel (see below); Nice Day is on the right. A good option for those who want to be close to Motomachi. Reception open based on arriving trains. English speakers on hand. Singles ¥3000 for foreigners, ¥3500 for Japanese. ❶

Hakodate Youth Guest House (HI) (函館ユースゲストハウス), 17-6, Hōrai-chō (☎26-7892; fax 26-0989). From the train station, take a bus to Hōrai-chō, walk in the direction of the park and make your 1st left—it's on the right. Slightly institutional from the outside, but pleasant common room and standard bedrooms. Location is less convenient than other better-priced options. Free coffee. Laundry ¥200; dryer ¥100. Reception 7am-10pm. Check-in 2-9pm. Check-out 10am. Curfew 11pm. July-Sept. ¥4200 per person; Oct.-June ¥3800 per person. ❷

Hakodate International Hotel (函館国際ホテル), 5-10, Ōtemachi (☎23-5151; fax 23-0239). Turn right out of the train station, and continue on the 2nd street up from the river—it's 7 blocks down on the right side (7min.). An upscale option with classy Western-style rooms, some of which overlook the water. Internet connections available. Laundry service. Breakfast ¥1100. Parking. Currency exchange at reception. Check-in 2pm. Check-out 11am. Singles M-Th ¥7000, F-Su ¥8500; doubles ¥14,000/¥17,000; add ¥1000 during July and Aug. Credit cards accepted. ❹

🍴 FOOD

Every day at 5am the fresh seafood culture of Hakodate starts with a splash at the Morning Market (see **Market,** p. 672)—if you're bold, go witness the fun and taste the fresh catch at the stands. Otherwise, Goryōkaku has the best food in town. Filled with a range of restaurants and *izakaya* serving up both local and foreign dishes, the area is well-known for its seafood, especially the squid and crab. Take a taste at **Kantarō Zushi** ❶ (函太郎寿司), 14-4, Ugaura-chō, on Rte. 28 between the mountain and Yunokawa. Hop on bus #6 or 96 from the station and get off at Ugaura-chō (宇賀浦町)—look for the sign across the street. This is Hakodate's best *kuru-kuru sushi* place. (☎48-8825. Plates from ¥120. Open daily 11am-10pm.) A dimly lit *izakaya* with fabulous food and the saltwater feel of an old fisherman's home, **Omote Mon** ❷ (おもて門), 11-8, Honchō, has a *gaijin*-friendly staff and an array of sushi, meat, and veggie dishes. Take the tram to the Goryōkaku Park stop and walk toward the park—the restaurant is a few blocks up on the left. (☎54-7082. No English menu. Most dishes ¥300-650. Beer ¥400. Open daily 5pm-midnight. Closed on the 2nd and 3rd M of the month.)

👁 SIGHTS

Hakodate is chock full of sights, and, fortunately, most of them are bundled together in the southern end of town. Begin near the station at the morning market, sweep through the old town and museums, and then top it off, quite literally, with the incredible view from the peak of Mt. Hakodate (函館山). Those with more time will want to check out Goryōkaku or a daytrip to Ōnuma National Park.

MOTOMACHI (元町)

■**HAKODATE CITY MUSEUM OF NORTHERN PEOPLES** (函館市北方民族資料館). The permanent exhibition of clothing and historic living tools should not be missed. The Ainu get the most attention of the indigenous groups, but the museum maintains integrity by including history about other tribes. *(21-7, Suehiro-chō. On the corner in front of the Suehiro-chō Tram Stop. ☎22-4128. English translations available. Open daily Apr.-Oct. 9am-7pm; Nov.-Mar. 9am-5pm. ¥300.)*

SUEHIRO-CHŌ (末広町). A smorgasbord of Western and Japanese buildings fill the old town. Start at Meijikan (明治館), the first in a row of Western-style brick buildings. Once the city's Central Post Office, Meijikan is now a souvenir shop with an interesting glass-blowing workshop. Satiate your taste for the past with a stop at the early 20th-century brick warehouses, dubbed the Hakodate History Plaza. *(From the Motomachi Tram Stop, take the West Exit and cross through the market.)*

HAKODATE'S OLD PUBLIC HALL (旧函館区公会堂). Built in 1909 to replace the public meeting hall that had burned down two years prior to that, the Old Public Hall now serves as a museum. The hilltop wooden mansion was intended to double as a residence, and it did when Emperor Taishō and the crown prince stayed here in 1911. *(11-13, Moto-machi. To the left of Suehiro-chō. ☎22-1001. English translations available. Open daily Apr.-Oct. 9am-7pm; Nov.-Mar. 9am-5pm. ¥300.)*

HAKODATE CITY MUSEUM OF PHOTOGRAPHY (函館市写真歴史観). Though there's little in the way of English explanation, the vivid pictures in this modest museum weave a story that any chimpanzee could follow. *(☎27-3333. Old Hokkaidō Agency, 2nd fl., in Motomachi Park. ¥200.)*

OLD BRITISH CONSULATE (旧イギリス領事間). The Consulate is in a white and blue building, which squats next to the Museum of Photography. Five years after the 1854 US-Japan Amity turned Hakodate into a major international port, the British too had a foot in the door with their very own consulate. The present building is the third consulate and was built in 1913 after the first two structures burned down. *(33-14, Motomachi. ☎27-8159. Down from the photo museum in a red and white building. Open daily Apr.-Oct. 9am-7pm; Nov.-Mar. 9am-5pm. ¥300.)*

RELIGIOUS LANDMARKS. East from the Old Public Hall is the **Roman Catholic Church,** completed in 1924 and showcasing an alter given to Japan by Pope Benedict XV. *(☎22-6877.)* Exiting uphill, you can't miss the classic Byzantine **Russian Orthodox Church.** The church is the symbol of Hakodate, which is ironic given its distinctly Eastern European look. *(☎23-7387. Open daily 0am-5pm. ¥200.)*

THE MOUNTAIN AND THE CAPE

MT. HAKODATE (函館山). The view from Mt. Hakodate. This volcano blew its cover about 2 million years ago and now serves as a tourist haven. The most popular route to the mountain's peak is the **ropeway,** a cable car located about ten minutes uphill from the Jūjigai streetcar stop. *(☎23-3105. Every 10min.; 3min. to the top. Operates daily 10am-9pm. ¥640, round-trip ¥1160.)* Alternatively, some good hiking trails encircle the 334m mountain. For more information, stop by the **Fureai Center** (ふれあいセンター ; 6-12, Aoyagi-chō), located up from the ropeway. *(☎22-6789. Road accessible Apr.-Aug. Closed 5-10pm.)*

TACHIMACHI CAPE (立待ち). This picturesque stretch of land makes a great stop on a clear day. Both the Japanese and the original Ainu name for the cape mean "to stand and wait," a commentary on the passive nature of fishing. *(South of the Mt. Hakodate Ropeway and toward the bay. Free.)*

GORYŌKAKU (五稜郭). Goryōkaku's main attraction is its pentagonal park that once served as a 19th-century fortress. In 1857, the fortress was constructed as a Western-style military shield designed to protect against a potential Russian threat from the north. The Russian threat turned out to be minimal and instead the fortress was instrumental in the civil war years after the Meiji Restoration (1868). Shōgunate rebels took Hakodate's castle as a stronghold, and fought hard for an independent Ezo (Hokkaidō) state, only to fall to the Meiji's imperial troops in May of 1869. The reforms of the 1970s demanded that all of the buildings within the fortress grounds be destroyed, and in 1914 Goryōkaku became a public park.

▣ NIGHTLIFE

Hakodate's nightlife takes center stage in Goryōkaku, where bars, *izakaya,* and karaoke joints pump the juices as soon as the sun sets. The area is quite walkable and cheap beer abounds, making for a great night on the town.

HOKKAIDŌ

Eiley's, 9-5, Honchō, 3rd fl. (☎54-4771), in the alley behind Tsubohachi. From the Goryōkaku-kōen-mae Tram Stop, walk to the corner, turn right, and make your 2nd left—Eiley's is 1½ blocks down on the left. An Irish pub with Guiness on tap. Locals and *gaijin* get rowdy on the weekends. Live music most Su 9pm. Beer ¥500. Pizza ¥800. Cover ¥1500 when there's live music. Open M-Sa 7pm-2am, Su 7pm-midnight.

Topps, 32-11, Honchō, 2nd fl. (☎56-0989). From the Goryōkaku-kōen Tram Stop, go 1½ blocks away from the park; it's on the left, around the corner from Marui Imai. A sports bar that's frequented by foreigners. 3 TVs entertain as you chow classic American food. Free popcorn. Beer ¥500. Pizza and pasta ¥800. Open Su and Tu-Sa 5pm-at least 1am.

Fab Colle, 31-17, Honchō (☎51-0888). A Beatles shrine full of original records, instruments, and paraphernalia. A Beatles tribute band rocks the house every 2nd and 4th Sa of the month. Free LAN connections with your own laptop. The mastermind behind the bar will happily play your favorite Beatles song or video. Beer ¥300. Fish 'n' chips ¥600. Cover ¥1000 after 7pm. Open M-Sa 11am-5pm and 7pm-midnight, Su 11am-5pm.

Beelong's, 32-11, Honchō, 2nd fl. (☎56-0989), next to Topps (see above). With beers on tap (¥500) and multiple foreign beers, Beelong's is the drinker's choice. Friendly aura welcomes locals and travelers. No cover. Open Su and Tu-Sa 5pm-at least 1am.

◘ FESTIVALS

Hakodate's highly anticipated **Port Festival** (函館港祭) is held annually in the first week of August. While the festival fills the streets with a host of games, arts performances, and craft vendors, let there be no mistake about what people truly come to see...human squid. In order to pay tribute to its official fish, the city has over 10,000 dancers do the Squid Dance—be sure to take your camera to embalm this scene forever. Less entertaining, but more dramatic, is the **Goryōkaku Festival** (五稜郭祭) during the third week of May. Set in the Pentagonal Park, the event commemorates those who died in the Hakodate War of 1869 with a recreation of the shōgunate forces' surrender—1000 actors participate in the massive display.

NEAR HAKODATE

ŌNUMA QUASI-NATIONAL PARK (大沼国定公園)   ☎0138

Thirty minutes from the bustle of Hakodate is the majestic Ōnuma Quasi-National Park (大沼国定公園), a perfect daytrip destination for the outdoor enthusiast or laid-back trail-trotter. The park attracts three million visitors per year and has been crowned as one of Japan's three most beautiful spots. While the name of the park, Ōnuma, translates colorlessly into "big swamp," visitors soon realize that the translation should read "stunning lake." Resting within a still-active volcano's crater, the glistening blue body of water contains over 100 baby islands and hosts climbing, camping, fishing, golfing, and *onsen* hopping. Come winter, Ōnuma's **Nanae Skii-jō** (七飯スキー場) reigns as the biggest ski area south of Niseko.

On the way to Ōnuma, try passing through **Konbu-kan** (昆布館), a state-of-the-art museum dedicated to *konbu* (kelp). The bizarre museum houses an exceptionally clear exhibit explaining the production process of the popular sea veggie and an IMAX cinema. (10 min., film showings every 20min.) Don't miss the *konbu* candy in the gift shop. (Aza Tōgeshita, Nanae-chō. On Rte. 5, 1km from Ōnuma tunnel. Take a park-bound car and get off at Konbukan-mae Stop (¥600); switch to a bus and get off at Ōnuma Park (¥220). ☎66-2000. Open daily 9am-5pm. Free.)

Inside the park, the English-speaking staff of the **tourist information office** provides info and the simple print-out map necessary to navigate the park. (85-15, Aza Ōmachō, Nanae-chō. ☎67-2170. Open daily Apr.-Nov. 8:30am-6pm; Dec.-Mar. 8:30am-

5pm. Closed Dec. 3-Jan. 5.) The map suggests four walking routes but the blue route (50min.) is the most scenic of the bunch. Two shops rent bikes: **Friendly Bear** (フレンドリーベア ; ☎67-2194), across the street from the tourist info office, has the best quality equipment (¥800 per hr.; open daily 8am-6pm), and **Tano Shōkai** (丹野商会) has the best daily rates (¥500 per day; open daily 8am-6pm). To get to the latter agency, exit left out of the tourist info office, turn right onto the main road, and turn right again at the light; it's the third house on the left. In an emergency, call ☎110 for **police,** ☎119 for **fire** or **ambulance.** A few doors down from Tano is the town's **Central Post Office,** 301-9, Aza Ōnuma, Nanae-chō (☎67-2860), which has an **international ATM.** (Open M-F 9am-5pm. ATM open M-F 9am-6pm, Su 9am-2pm). Many sightseers do Ōnuma come by tour bus, but there is another route. To get to Ōnuma by JR, hop either an express train (20min., 7 per day, ¥1500) or a local train (1hr., 6 per day, ¥530) from Hakodate Station. To see Konbu-kan, take a local bus from Hakodate Station (1hr.; 12:19, 4:51, 7:05pm; ¥710).

The affordable **Ōnuma Youth Hostel (HI) ❶** (大沼ユースホステル), Ikusa-gawa, Nanae-chō, offers Western beds and an ideal location. Reserve far in advance as it fills up quickly. The hostel is 2km from Ōnuma Station; take the main road in front and to the left of the tourist info office, and continue straight to the hostel's sign on the right. Alternatively, take a train from Ōnuma Station to Ikedaen-eki (池田園駅) and walk for 3min. (☎67-4126. Dinner ¥1000. Breakfast ¥600. Washer ¥100; dryer ¥200. Bike rental ¥500 per day. Cross-country ski rental ¥3000. Check-in 4pm. Check-out 9am. Members ¥2900, nonmembers ¥3900.) As nice as beds are, it's tough to pass up **Higashi Ōnuma Campground ❶** (東大沼キャンプ場), which is free and on the lake, providing a golden view of the volcano. The grounds are about 4.5km from Ōnuma Station. Take the road toward the youth hostel, but continue straight for an extra 2.5km—it's on the left. You can also take the train to Chōshi-guchi Eki (銚子口駅), then walk for 5min. You'll need your own tent, but the site has nice restrooms, sinks, and a grilling area.

If lunchtime finds you in town, refuel on Western dishes at **The Wald ❸** (ウァルド), next to the post office. This country kitchen serves hearty steaks, sandwiches, and burgers. The owner rents canoe and ice-fishing equipment on the side. (☎67-3877. Lunch sets about ¥1200. Open Su-W and F-Sa 11am-9pm.) For a more unique experience, go to **Yamagawa Bokujō ❷** (山川牧場), which serves Hokkaidō's roast beef, homemade milk, and ice cream. The treats are near central Ōnuma on the road to Nanae-jō. (889, Aza Ōnuma-chō. ☎67-2010. Lunch sets ¥800. Coffee milk ¥100. Ice cream ¥250. Open Apr.-Nov. Su-Tu and Th-Sa 10am-5pm.)

NISEKO (ニセコ)   ☎0136

Sleekly buckled boots, wrap-around goggles, and a need for speed that's too intense for the falling snowflakes—this is Niseko mounted on a billboard advertisement. If Japan's premier snowsport resort can make a a skier out of a one-legged sumo wrestler, then why not you? Niseko is sometimes neglected for its lack of accessibility and English services, but the ski town offers the opportunity to blend in with locals and experience small-town life.

◰ **TRANSPORTATION.** It is possible to get around Niseko without a car, but it's also very frustrating. JR trains pull into Niseko from: **Oshamambe** (1½hr., 7 per day, ¥1230); **Otaru** (2hr., 7 per day, ¥1410); **Sapporo** (2½hr., 8 per day, ¥2100). All trains go through Niseko Station (ニセコ駅) which is about 15min. from the slopes by car. Shuttle buses run frequently from the station to the slopes (about ¥500) in winter, but far less frequently in the summer. Throughout the year, **buses** go to Hon-dōri in Niseko from: **Lake Tōya Onsen** (洞爺湖温泉 ; 1¾hr., 4 per day, ¥1720) via Rusutsu (留寿都) and **Sapporo Station** (札幌駅 ; 3hr., 3 per day, ¥2100). From November to April a bus runs directly from Chitose Airport in Sapporo to the slopes at Annupuri.

▨ PRACTICAL INFORMATION. Niseko-gai Kankō Annai-jō (ニセコ街観光案内所) is about as close as you will get to an English info center in Niseko. **Niseko View Plaza** (ニセコビュープラザ), 77-10, Aza Moto-machi, Niseko-chō, Abuta-gun, provides helpful maps and info in Japanese. To get there from town, take Rte. 5 until you hit Rte. 66 at the juncture with the gas station. (☎43-2051. Free Internet access. Open daily July-Aug. 9am-7pm; Sept.-June 9am-6pm). The **tourist info center,** Niseko-chō Chūō-dōri, a booth just inside the entrance of Niseko Station, also caters to Japanese speakers. (☎44-2468. Open daily June-July 9am-7pm; Aug.-May 9am-6pm.) The super-helpful couple at Ryu's Inn (below) can provide info in English. **Niseko Town Community Library** (ニセコ町学習交流センター), 105, Hon-dōri, 10min. east of town and next to the town hall, offers free **Internet** access. (Open Su and Tu-Sa 10am-6pm. Closed on the 4th F of the month.) In an emergency, call ☎110 for **police,** ☎119 for **fire** or **ambulance.** The **Central Post Office,** 103, Aza Hon-dōri, Niseko-chō, 15min. uphill from the station in the refurbished part of town, has an **international ATM.** (☎44-2351. Open M-F 9am-5pm. ATM open M-F 8:45am-6pm, Sa 9am-5pm, Su 9am-2pm. After hours service Sa 8am-5pm, Su 9am-12:30pm.) **Postal code:** 048.

▨▧ ACCOMMODATIONS AND FOOD. Popular with Japanese and foreigners, ▨**Niseko Annupuri Youth Hostel (HI) ❶** (ニセコアンヌプリユースホステル), 479-4, Aza Niseko, Niseko-chō, is a fantastic cabin-esque hostel near the base of Mt. Annupuri. If you're down for a social environment and delicious home-cooked meals, this is the place for you. (☎58-2084. Dinner ¥1000. Breakfast ¥600. Washer ¥250; dryer ¥100 per 30min. Check-in 3pm. Check-out 10am. Curfew 11pm. Members and foreigners ¥3100, nonmembers ¥4100. Free pick-up from the station.) Those looking for a more relaxed experience should make reservations at the small bed and breakfast, ▨**Ryu's Inn ❶,** 744-2, Soga, Niseko-chō. Cushioned among flower beds and potato fields just 15min. from Mt. Annupuri, the cozy inn makes you feel as if you've just moved in with a local family. The affable owners will be happy to pick you up from your place of arrival, as well as cook dinners according to your budget. The owners also publish a semi-annual, bilingual guide to Niseko. (☎44-3265; www.niseko.gr.jp. Breakfast included. Laundry available. Bike rental ¥1500 per day. In-house concerts every third Sa of the month. Winter ¥4500 per person, summer ¥3500 per person.)

The local favorite, **Rise ❶** (ライズ), 65, Fujimi, Abuta-gun, Niseko-chō, is the place to grab a meal while in Niseko. Located right across the street from the town library, Rise has big portions of *rāmen* (¥560), *donburi* (from ¥580), and lunch sets (¥850-1000) that will satiate your appetite. (☎44-3561. Open daily 11:30am-2pm and 5-9:30pm.) Although you'll need a car to get to **Rum's Restaurant ❷,** Aza Soga, Niseko-chō, it's surely worth the drive. Filled with original sculptures by the owner, Rum's manages to be a museum, store, and eatery all at once. Coming from the slopes on Rte. 66, turn left at the 7-Eleven, then make your first right—Rum's will be on the left, just below and to the side of Niseko bridge. (☎44-1352. Entrees ¥800-1300. Open daily June-Oct. 11am-8:30pm; Nov.-May 11am-7:30pm.)

▨ OUTDOOR ACTIVITIES. Niseko's **winter season** kicks off in mid-October when snowfalls begin to grace the area's main three slopes: **Annupuri** (アンヌプリ), **Higashiyama** (東山), and **Hirafu** (比羅夫). While all three slopes are on Mt. Annu-puri and consist of comparable trails, each requires its own ticket. The more economical multiple ski pass provides access to all three slopes. One-day (8hr.) tickets are sold at the mountain's **gondola station** (www.niseko.ne.jp; specific mountain tickets ¥4300, multiple-pass ¥4500). Local convenience stores and pensions frequently have special deals with the ticket agencies and sell discount tickets. In addition to skiing and snowboarding, Niseko offers opportunities for snow-shoeing, ice-climbing, snowmobiling, and other off-beat ways to enjoy the snow. For equipment rental, tours, lessons, and English info on the outdoors, visit the **Niseko Adventure Center (NAC)**, 179-53, Yamada Kutchan Abuta-gun (☎23-2093; www.nac-web.com), or the **Niseko Outdoor Adventure Sports Club (NOASC)**, 170, Yamada, Kutchan-chō (www.noasc.com), both of which are near the ski slopes. The **Winter First Rental Company** (ウィンターファスト), 224-19, Azayu-no-sato, Rankoshi-chō, has the cheapest rentals of boots, skis, and poles. (☎58-2051. ¥3000 for the 1st day, ¥2000 for the 2nd. Delivery available.) For more information on skiing in Niseko and Japan in general, check out www.skijapanguide.com.

Though spring skiing lasts until early May, Niseko's short summer offers fabulous hiking, rafting, canoeing, and fishing. The easiest hike leads up **Mt. Annupuri** (1308m). Take the gondola (one-way ¥900) up 1000m, then hike the remaining 308m to the mountain's peak. A more challenging hike awaits at **Yōtei-zan** (羊蹄山 ; 1898m), east of Niseko town. To get to the mountain from Niseko Station, drive toward Sapporo on Rte. 66 until you enter Makkari Village (真狩村), and look for the sign that says Tōzan Entrance (登山口). It takes a solid 5hr. to get up the mountain, and 4hr. to get down, so plan to leave early in the morning unless you have reservations at the inn on top. The NAC and the NOAC also provide info on rafting, mountain biking, kayaking, and rainbow trout-fishing in **Shiribetsu-gawa River** (尻別川), one of Japan's finest.

SHIKOTSU-TŌYA NATIONAL PARK
(支笏洞爺国立公園)

Describing the astonishing lake and mountain views of Shikotsu-Tōya National Park (支笏洞爺国立公園) in words can never do it justice. Nevertheless, it's worth attempting the impossible to convince you not to pass up Sapporo's backyard of active volcanos, expert hiking, and lakeside sunrises. A mere 80km north of Sapporo, Shikotsu-Tōya is the type of region in which you could spend two, three, or even ten days as a wilderness man. The park is some 983 sq. km in area and made up of two fabulous lakes, both surrounded by heavenly ski moguls. Of the two lakes, **Tōya-ko** in the west is the smaller one, more touristed, but much easier to explore—its highlights are the baby volcano Shōwa Shin-zan and its papa, Usu-zan. **Shikotsu-ko,** the bigger lake in the east, is more barren and difficult to navigate, but offers better hiking—try **Tarumae-zan.** Both areas are great for canoeing and cycling—the best way to dig up info on these activities is to talk to hostel owners and the local rental shops.

Getting around the park is difficult, so you'll want to either hire yourself a car *before* heading out, or just plan on wandering like a *samurai* without his master. Keep in mind that public buses are infrequent, assuming they even exist in your desired destination. Hitchhiking is hard to do up here because most drivers are other tourists and not happy-go-lucky truck drivers. As always, *Let's Go* does not recommend hitchhiking. Finally, those with more time and cash might want to check out **Noboribetsu,** a popular *onsen* resort between the two lakes.

LAKE TŌYA (洞爺湖)   ☎0142

A donut-shaped caldera lake with Ōshima Island at its center, Lake Tōya thrives mid-summer when tourist buses dump packs of camera-toting oldies at Tōya-ko's luxurious hotels on the lake's southern side. Pass through here to enter and exit the park, but you'll find it more enjoyable to spend time further east, on the southern coast near Sōbetsu and the main volcano sights. Explore Sōbetsu by conquering its largest volcano, **Mt. Usu** (有珠山), and marinating in its views of the

HOKKAIDŌ

Mt. Yōtei (1898m) 羊蹄山
276 喜茂別町 Kimobetsu
230
TO SAPPORO 札幌(70km)
TO SAPPORO 札幌(36km)
Mt. Eniwa (1320m) 恵庭岳
Mt. Monbetsu (866m) モンベツ
Marukoma Onsen 丸駒温泉
Shikotsu-ko Onsen 支笏湖温泉
Shikotsu-ko 支笏湖
尻別岳 Mt. Shiribetsu (1107m)
留寿都村 Rusutsu
276
2
Mt. Fuppushi (1103m) 風不死岳
貫気別山 Mt. Nekikibetsu (993m)
大滝村 Ōtaki
樽前山 Mt. Tarumae (1041m)
洞爺村 Tōya
3
Tōya-ko 洞爺湖
ホロホロ山 Mt. Horohoro (1322m)
453
TO HAKODATE 函館(152km)
中島 Naka-jima
Tōya-ko Onsen 洞爺湖温泉
道央高速道路 Murojo-Main Line: 室蘭本線
36
Shiraoi Station 白老駅
白老町 Shiraoi
PACIFIC OCEAN 太平洋
4
昭和新山 Mt. Shōwa Shin (402m)
Tōya Station 洞爺駅
有珠山 Mt. Usu (737m)
丸山 Mt. Maru (622m)
伊達市 Date
Noboribetsu Onsen 登別温泉
倶多楽湖 Kuttara-ko
Date-Monbetsu Station 伊達紋別駅
Noboribetsu Station 登別駅
Mareppu Station 稀府駅
鷲別岳 Mt. Washibetsu (911m)
Horobetsu Station 幌別駅
Sakimori Station 防人駅
Shikotsu-Tōya National Park ·
支笏洞爺
国立公園
Uchiura-Wan 内浦湾
Higashi-Muroran 東室蘭駅
測量山 Mt. Sokuryō (200m)
Wanishi Station 輪西駅
Muroran 室蘭
TO HONSHŪ (120km) 本州
測量山
5 kilometers   10 kilometers
5 miles   10 miles
▲■ ACCOMMODATIONS
Toya-ko Youth Hostel (HI), 4
Mizubeno-sato Takarada Campsite, 3
Morappu Camp Site, 2
Poropinai Camp Site, 1

napping Shōwa Shin-zan, Lake Tōya, and even Mt. Yotei. Although every mountain in Japan has a ropeway, **Mt. Usu Ropeway** (有珠山ロープウエイ) is one worth its price. Walk to the end of the line of shops and turn right into the mini shop-center—boarding is on the second level. (☎75-2401. Round-trip ¥1450.)

▉☎ TRANSPORTATION AND PRACTICAL INFORMATION. Getting to Lake Tōya without your own transport is tough, as there are few direct connections. Nevertheless, there are **trains** on the Muroran Line from **Hakodate** (1½hr., ¥4830) and **Sapporo** (1¾hr., ¥5250) to JR Tōya-ko Station (洞爺湖駅), where you should catch a local bus to the main **bus station** (☎75-2736) at Tōya-ko Onsen (30min., every 30min., ¥320). To get to the line of fancy hotels, continue in the same direction for a couple hundred meters (15min. walk). To reach **Sōbetsu,** take a local public bus that cuts through the town and stops at the Youth Hostel (below) as well as at Usu-zan and Shōwa Shin-zan (15min., 9 per day, ¥330). **Buses** to Tōya go directly to the main bus stop at Tōya-ko Onsen and are a bit more convenient. They come from **Hakodate** (3½hr.; 1 per day May-Oct.; about ¥3000) and **Sapporo** (2¾hr., 1 per hr., around ¥2700). If you take a late train or bus to Tōya, you might miss some of the local connections. Although taxis are usually waiting at both the

HOKKAIDŌ

JR and main bus stations, they cost ¥4000 and ¥1000, respectively, for delivery to Sōbetsu. If you're stranded and need a taxi at any point, try either **Donan Hire** (☎75-2277) or **Mori Hire** (☎66-2366).

For tourist information, 184, Shōwa Shinzan, Sōbetsu-chō, your only real option is a brown wooden shack hidden among the shops in Sōbetsu town—it's on the side closer to the Ainu Museum. The one-man staff can offer help in Japanese, so you might choose a detailed English map/brochure. (☎73-2662. Open daily 9am-5pm.) In an emergency, call ☎110 for **police**, ☎119 for **fire** or ambulance.

▐▐ ACCOMMODATIONS AND FOOD. Even with the scattered minshuku in the area, the **Tōya-ko Youth Hostel (HI)** (洞爺湖ユースホステル), 103, Aza Sōbetsu Onsen, Sōbetsu-chō, Usu-gun, is the cheapest accommodation available. Fortunately, it has nice facilities and is as an ideal point of departure for hiking up Usu-zan (1hr.). Take the local bus from the Tōya-ko Onsen to the Shōwa-shin-mae Bus Stop and head up the cross street; it'll be on your right. The last bus leaves shortly after 7pm. (☎75-2283; fax 75-2481. Breakfast ¥600. Dinner ¥1000. Laundry ¥200. Free parking. Reception 3-10pm. Check-in 3pm. Check-out 10am. Curfew 11pm. Reservations recommended. Dorms ¥3000. Slightly nicer rooms ¥3500.) For camping, the campsite **Mizubeno-sato Takarada ❶** (水辺の里財田), 6, Tōya Aza, Takarada, has a picture-postcard location on the river's northern side. Although it's expensive for camping grounds, the price includes parking for your car or trailer. Take Rte. 132 around the lake and look out for the signs. (☎82-5111 or 82-5777. Open mid-July-Sept. From ¥1000.)

The main food options in Tōya are the meals served at the hostels or fancy hotels in the evening and, unfortunately, the dinky touristy shops in the towns of Sōbetsu and Tōya-ko Onsen by day. If you have a car, you might also stop at some of the *konbini* along the main road, Route 132.

◙ SIGHTS. After descending the mountainous stairway of Usu, prepare for another ascent to Mt. Usu's little baby and the talk of the town—**Shōwa Shin-zan** (昭和新山). For more on Masao Mimatsu, the man who bought this volcano, go down Shin-zan to the **Mimatsu Masao Museum** (三松正夫記念館), Aza Shōwa Shin-zan. Take a peek at Mimatsu's meticulous and awe-inspiring sketches of the famous volcanoes. Almost everything is in Japanese, but you can buy an informative English mini-book (¥500) on the events. (☎75-2365. Open Apr.-Dec. daily 8am-5pm. ¥300). Next

THE LOCAL LEGEND

MAN MEETS VOLCANO

In the town of Sōbetsu, where looming volcanoes and natural disasters remind residents on a daily basis of Mother Nature's awesome strength, it takes more than loud noise and spewing lava to make big news. One man achieved hero status by purchasing his own volcano to play with. Masao Mimatsu, the town postman during WWII and an amateur vulcanologist stumbled across the significance of Sōbetsu's wonders: Usu-zan and Shōwa Shin-zan. In 1944, Mimatsu plunged into his hobby-turned-passion when earthquakes on Usu-zan started a new era of volcanic activity and put the town of Sōbetsu on its toes. Working against government policy and in near secrecy until the war's end, the postman produced ground-breaking information. Without these records, the world would know little about Usu-zan's eruptions in the 1940s.

Despite these early accomplishments, Mimatsu desired greater access to the mountains, and in 1947 he used his own money to purchase the 3-year old Showa-shin-zan. Free to study in peace, the former postman rejected numerous lucrative offers for his tempestuous baby.

Now 26 years after Mimatsu's death, his legacy lives on through the rising fumes and blowing winds of Shin-zan. In accordance with his last wishes, the mountain remains free for all visitors to explore and enjoy.

door to the museum is the local **Ainu Museum** (アイヌ記念館), which houses fascinating pictures of Ainu rituals and hosts occasional outdoor dance performances. (Open late Apr.-late Oct. daily 8am-5pm. Free.)

A cartrip away is **Kudamono Mura** (Fruit Village; 果物村), Aza Takino-machi, Sōbetsu-chō, Usu-gun, a small collection of orchards where you can pick your own apples, grapes, cherries, and other fruits for as little as ¥1000 (all you can pick, price depends on the type of fruit). Established in 1987 to educate tourists about the region's longtime fruit-growing traditions, Kudamono Mura is especially fun if you're traveling with kids, or if you still cherish your inner child. Drive toward Sōbetsu from Tōya-ko Onsen, turn left when you get to National Route 453, and this main road will take you to the orchards. (☎66-2333. Hours vary with the orchard but most are open through the late afternoon.)

Flattened cars, shredded houses, and large gaseous clouds steaming from the earth—this is what you'll see at the nerve-chilling ◼**Nishiyama Crater Trail** (有珠山 西山散策路), a town-turned-museum just beside part of Mt. Usu. The area, which provides a realistic look into the awesome devastastion of volcanic eruptions, resembles something out of a Universal Studios theme park, only much more frightening. Plan on spending at least 1½hr. here, so you can walk all the way up the 800m trail and view the entire town from the crater-top lookout point. The last eruption was March 2000. To get here, drive along Route 230 (away from Sōbetsu and toward Sapporo) and make your first left after seeing the Hokkai Hotel (北海 ホテル) on your right—you'll see the parking lot at the end of the street. If you don't have your own car, you'll need to take a taxi, which runs about ¥800 each way. (Open 7am-6pm. Free.)

End or begin the day by taking an unforgettable bath in the Tōya-ko Onsen area, where there's a line of fancy hotels, each with its own enticing steamer. Among the bunch, the **Tōya-ko Park Hotel** (洞爺湖パークホテル) definitely has the most impressive facilities, which happen to be on the roof of its building. To get there, just walk east from the Tōya-ko Onsen Bus Stop, and it'll be on the left. (10min. walk. ☎75-2445. Baths ¥990.) As for Tōya's festivities, from April 28 to October 31 every year, Lake Tōya has its **Long Run Fireworks Display** (Tōya-ko longu run hanabi taikai; 洞爺湖ロングラン花火大会), which can be heard every single night, from every bed in town. Rather than fighting the noise, grab a picnic basket and bathe in multi-colored raindrops of light. (20min., around 8:45pm.)

LAKE SHIKOTSU (支笏湖) ☎0123

Japan's second deepest lake, Shikotsu-ko, has idyllic landscapes, rumbling volcanoes, and a caldera lake just like its friend Tōya. It scores advantage points over Tōya for its less-congested hiking trails . The area may be less developed and harbor fewer historical spots of interest, but, nevertheless, Shikotsu deserves a trip if you've got a car. The trails invite fabulous hiking; if the weather's good, trek up the mountains and get overhead views of the blue-on-blue caldera lake.

◪ **TRANSPORTATION AND PRACTICAL INFORMATION.** There are two direct buses from **Sapporo** (札幌 ; 1½hr., 4 per day, ¥1330; last bus 4:55pm) and **Shin-Chitose Airport** (新千歳空港 ; 1hr., 4-6 per day, ¥920; last bus 5:45pm) to Shikotsu-ko's central transportation hub, **Shikotsu-Kohan.** Not quite a town, Kohan is the area's base for navigation with the **Shikotsu-ko Onsen Hotel** (支笏湖温泉ホテ ル) at its center. From here, you'll need your own transport (or a taxi) to get from mountain to mountain, as there are no public buses or car rental agencies. For information on the surrounding area, stop by the **Shikotsu-ko Visitors Center** (支笏 港ビジターセンター), a big cabin-house to the left of Kohan as you face the lake. The staff will try their best to be helpful, but, unfortunately, none of them speak much English. However, there are topographical maps, nature displays, and an entertaining Shikotsu-ko video to help you out. (☎25-2404. Open Apr.-Nov. daily 9:30am-5:30pm; Dec.-Mar. Su-M and W-Sa 9:30am-4:30pm.) In an emergency, call ☎110 for **police,** ☎119 for **fire** or **ambulance.**

▚ ▐⃘ ACCOMMODATIONS AND FOOD. On the opposite side of Kohan awaits the budget accommodation of choice—the **Shikotsuko Youth Hostel (HI) ❶** (支笏湖 ユースホステル), behind the old hostel building, is a withered triangular house. While the hostel is a bit dull and institutional, it offers spacious and comfortable bunk-bed rooms. (☎25-2311. Check-in 3pm. Check-out 10am. Breakfast ¥600. Dinner ¥1000. Coin laundry ¥200. 10pm curfew. Bike rental ¥1400 per day. Members ¥3195, nonmembers ¥3820.) If you're looking for something cozier, wander through the tourist shops in Kohan and you'll find a bunch of B&Bs and minshuku to pick from—they run around ¥5000 a night and tend to fill up quickly. South of Kohan is **Morappu Camp Site ❶** (モラップキャンプ場), Shikotsu-ko's prettiest camping grounds, which let you camp right on the beach. To get here, take Kokudō 276 (国道 276 号) and keep your eyes peeled for the Morappu sign (20min. by car). Even those who aren't staying here can stop by and enjoy the site for a day. (☎25-2439. Open Apr.-Oct. Check-in 2pm. Check-out 11am. ¥500 per person to camp. ¥200 for the day.) For cheaper camping but inferior views and facilities, there's the **Poropinai Camp Site ❶** (ポロピナイ) at the very north of the lake and a good 30min. by car. From Kohan, take Rte. 453 north and follow the signs. (☎25-2755. ¥300.) **Shikotsuko Kyūkan ❸** (支笏湖休) offers a nicer option, 15min. south of the visitors center on foot. The slightly upscale accommodation has pretty large rooms and a great hill-top location overlooking Lake Tōya. Head down to the water behind the visitors center, cross the bright red steel bridge, and follow the path until you see the first trail going up hill. The hotel is at the top, nestled in the park. (☎25-2201; www.qkamra.or.jp.ll. Check-in 3pm. Check-out 10am. Curfew midnight. 2 meals included. Singles ¥8500; doubles ¥18,000.)

Kohan has nothing special in the food department, so you're best off window-shopping the small restaurants and food stands in town. Before heading out for your hikes, pick up a few snacks at one of the mini-marts.

▟ OUTDOOR ACTIVITIES. The volcano **Tarumae-zan** (樽前山 ; 1038m) is by far the favorite climb of most outdoorsmen who come to Shikotsu-ko. Forty minutes of easy hiking brings you to the peak of an active volcano. The visitors center (see below) offers explicit driving directions—from Kohan, circle southwest around the lake and follow the mountain's signs up to its 7th station; if you don't have a car, take a taxi (about ¥3500). From there, pick either the harder route directly up to the peak (about 1hr.), or opt for the easier, more roundabout route. Look for the signs to **Mt. Fuppushi** (風不死岳 ; 1½hr.). If you don't have time or transport for Tarumae-zan, consider nearby **Mt. Monbetsu** (紋別岳 ; 866m), a smaller peak that also has great views of Shikotsu-ko, as well as a panorama of the Pacific Ocean (1½hr. to the top). The entrance for the mountain is about a 7min. walk behind the Shikotsu-ko Youth Hostel in Kohan (see below). For something a bit more mysterious, head over to **Okotanpe-ko** (オコタンペ湖), a lake (572km above sea level; 5km of shore line) created by the lava ooze from nearby Mt. Eniwa. While personal transport is more time efficient, you can always hop one of the buses en-route to Sapporo (20min., 4 per day, ¥470) and get off at Okotan Bunkiten (オコタン分岐点)— the uphill path to the lake begins from there. True hikers in search of an all-afternoon workout might pass up the above options for **Mt. Eniwa** (恵庭岳), which takes a solid 3½hr. to climb and another 2½hr. to descend. From its peak there's a view of Shikotsu-ko as nice as any other, as well as a bird's-eye view of the lake Okotanpe-ko. Take one of the Sapporo-bound buses (10min., 4 per day, ¥340) and hop off early at Eniwa-dake Tozan Guchi (恵庭岳登山口).

Don't worry if you get lazy feet while in Kohan—there's a cure nearby and it's called **Marukoma Onsen** (丸駒温泉). For a less strenuous lake and mountain experience, jump on a motor boat (50min., every 1½hr., ¥1200) at the bay down from the Visitors Center, and head across the lake to Marukoma's multi-pool, indoor/outdoor *onsen*. (☎25-2301. Open daily 10am-3pm. ¥1000.)

■ **FESTIVALS.** If you're planning a trip to Shikotsu-ko in the fall or winter, aim for one of two outdoor festivals. In early February, the **Ice Festival** (Hyōtō Matsuri; 氷とう祭り) illuminates winter with its ice formations (Jan. 24-Feb. 15). In mid-October (around Oct. 12, date subject to weather), the **Red Leaves Festival** (紅葉祭 り) is a brilliant time when Mother Nature reveals herself in a fiery red costume.

SAPPORO (札幌)   ☎011

Something of a *gaijin* among the Japanese cities, Sapporo—the northern capital of Hokkaidō—is a spine-chilling wonderland of modern architecture and ice-strong character. If the city had its own Sanrio character, it would be a double-agent snowman, as smooth as the beer named in its honor. With little place in the books of traditional Japanese history, the nation's fifth-largest city has made its own history by hosting the Winter Olympic Games (1972), putting on the annual Yuki Matsuri (Snow Festival; p. 694), and brewing one of the world's greatest beers. Indeed, Sapporo is one of Japan's creations gone right and gone hip. The recipe seems simple: a spoonful of American city-planning, a scoop of Japanese industry, and a whole lot of nature, all tossed into a (Japanese-made) blender for 100 years. The product? Stylish cafes, sleek architecture, spacious parks, and a nightlife so energetic that doctors have considered prescribing Ritalin. *This* is modern day Sapporo, Japanese urbanity minus the concrete jungles and rusted steel frames that plague so many other major cities. Yet, despite the cheer, anyone who sticks around is bound to hear about the city's financial woes, for as the capital of Hokkaidō—where industry is scarce and business exists as an off-shoot from Tōkyō—Sapporo suffers from a lagging economy, and it isn't unusual for the stories of its local establishments to end abruptly at Chapter 11: Bankruptcy.

Sapporo・札幌

▲ ACCOMMODATIONS
Capsule Hotel Sapporo, **10**
Green Hotel, **14**
Ino's Place Backpacker's Hostel, **2**
New Budget Hotel, **8**
Sapporo House Youth Hostel (HI), **1**
Sapporo International
Youth Hostel (HI), **15**

🍴 FOOD
Asian Ishoku Enak, **3**
Cam・Cam, **5**
Daruma, **16**
Ebi-Ten, **4**
Hashiya, **7**
Kiraitō, **6**
Pasar Kaiten-zushi, **12**
Rāmen Gojōgen, **21**

🍸 NIGHTLIFE
Bar Locotonte, **17**
Booty Bar, **19**
Flore Cafe, **20**
Hendix's Art Cafe, **9**
Kento's, **13**
King Xmhu, **18**
Sally Bell, **11**

ON THE WEB Sapporo City: www.global.city.sapporo.jp

⊠ INTERCITY TRANSPORT

Flights: Two airports service Sapporo. **New Chitose Airport** (新千歳空港), Chitose-shi Bibi (☎23-0111) is about 40min. out of town and has domestic and international flights. To get to the airport, take a train from Sapporo Station (35min., every 15min. 8am-7pm,

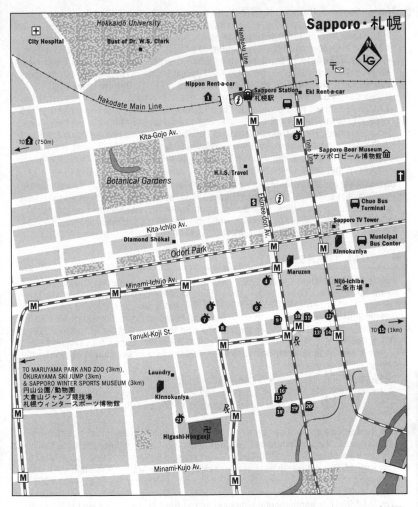

Sapporo・札幌

¥1040). Flights to: **Aomori** (青森 ; 45min., 2 per day, ¥20,000); **Fukuoka** (福岡 ; 2½hr., 3 per day, ¥46,000); **Hakodate** (函館 ; 40min., 4 per day, ¥15,000); **Hiroshima** (広島 ; 2hr., 1 per day, ¥41,000); **Kushiro** (釧路 ; 50min., 7 per day, ¥18,500); **Naha** (那覇 : 4½hr., 3 per day, ¥12, 000-14,000); **Ōsaka** (2hr., 9 per day, ¥37,000); **Sendai** (仙台 ; 1hr., 4 per day, ¥26,000); **Tokushima** (徳島 ; 2hr., 1 per day, ¥41,500); **Tōkyō** (東京 ; 1½hr., ¥30,000); **Wakkanai** (稚内 ; 50min., 1 per day, ¥19,500). Round-trip flights are significantly cheaper than one-way, and discount tickets are sometimes sold at agencies like H.I.S. **Okadama Airport** (丘珠空港), Higashi-ku, Okadama-chō (☎011-781-3612), which is reached by shuttle bus from the ANA agency in front of the South Exit (30min., usually leaves 1hr. before departing flights, ¥310; pick up schedule at tourist office). Domestic flights to: **Hakodate** (45min., 5 per day, ¥14,500); **Kushiro** (50min., 2 per day, ¥17,000); **Wakkanai** (1hr., 1 per day, ¥19,500).

Trains: Sapporo Station (札幌駅), North 6, West 3, Kita-ku (☎222-6131) is big and disorienting, so spot the North and South Exits (北口 / 南口) to get your bearings. Open daily 5:30am-midnight. JR trains run to: **Aomori** (about 7hr., midnight; ¥9240, for sleeper add ¥6300); **Asahikawa** (旭川 ; 1½hr., every 30min. 8am-8pm, ¥4170); **Hakodate** (5hr., 1 per day, ¥6820; express about 3hr., 11 per day, ¥8080); **Kushiro** (3¾hr., 7 per day, ¥8610; night train at 11pm, ¥8610, sleepers add ¥6300); **Muroran** (室蘭 ; 1¾hr., 5 per day, ¥4170); **Obihiro** (帯広 ; 2½-3hr., 6 per day; ¥6510); **Wakkanai** (about 5hr., 4 per day, ¥9660; night train at 11:02pm, ¥9660, for sleeper add ¥6300). Reservations add at least ¥510 to the price; necessary only around holidays. Buy tickets at the station's East and West Ticket Counters. For **JR train information** (☎222-7111; www.jrhokkaido.co.jp), head to the West Counter where there are usually English speakers. Walk down the central corridor from the South Exit and the counter is on the left, next to the Starbucks sign. Long lines may form, so be early.

Buses: There are 2 **bus terminals** (☎231-0500)—a central one at Ōdori, and one at the southeastern end of the train station. Open 7:30am-6pm. Consult a schedule to see from which station and platform your bus departs. Routes to: **Asahikawa** (2hr., 2 per hr., ¥2000); **Furano** (富良野 ; 2½hr., about 1 per hr., ¥2100); **Hakodate** (5hr., ¥4680); **Niseko** (ニセコ ; 3hr., 3 per day, ¥2100); **Otaru** (小樽 ; 1hr., 1 per hr., ¥590).

▐ LOCAL TRANSPORT

Public Transportation: The city has 3 main forms of transport—subway, local bus, and tram (or streetcar). Of the 3, the subway is most convenient with its 3 lines, the Nanboku (南北), Tōzai (東西), and Tōho (東豊). Rides start at ¥200, and it only takes about 2min. to get from stop to stop. The local buses and streetcars start from ¥200 and cover many of the subway's gaps. If you plan to use all 3 types of transport, get a **With You Card** (ウィズユーカード ; ¥1000) which allows for unlimited rides (there's also a subway-only card for ¥800). Buy the card in any subway station at the electronic ticket machine.

Taxis: The 2 main taxi stands in Sapporo are in front of the station's North and South Exits (北口 / 南口). Though taxis can be found all over town, call (☎561-1171) if you need a ride. Fares start at an expensive ¥600, and they're 20% higher after 11pm.

Car Rental: There are many agencies around Sapporo Station, most of which have similar rates. **Nippon Rent-a-car,** North 6, West 3, Kita-ku (☎746-0919), to the left as you walk out of Sapporo Station's North Exit, offers the most flexibility. ¥6800 for 1st day, ¥5500 per day thereafter. More expensive July-Aug. (add around ¥2000). If returning the car at other locations in Hokkaidō, additional fee of at least ¥3000. Open daily 24hr. **Eki Rent-a-car** (駅レンターカー), North 6, West 1, Kita-ku (☎241-0931), is another option, located across the street from the east side of Sapporo Station. Rates are same as above. Open daily 8am-8pm.

Bike: Diamond Shōkai (ダヤモンド商会), West 8, Ōdori, Chūō-ku (☎231-3533), charges the standard ¥1000 per day. The shop is just on the left as you cross Ōdori from the south. If you're desperate, shell out the cash at **Cycle Shop Nakamura** (サイクルショップ中村), North 4, East 1, Chūō-ku (☎272-1811), just on the north side of the station, where they charge a whopping ¥1000 per 3hr. Open daily 11am-8pm. Also, don't forget to check whether you can rent bikes from your accommodation—places like **NADA Inn** have rates as low as ¥500 per day.

✈ ORIENTATION

Unlike the typical Japanese city of jumbled, unnamed streets and alleys, Sapporo strikes visitors as an extraordinarily convenient and navigable city, defined by a simple grid layout, clear landmarks, and excellent public transportation. The city is divided into northern and southern halves by **Ōdōri Park** (大通公園), which cuts straight across from east to west, through the heart of town. In the northern half, **Sapporo Station** and **Hokkaidō University** hold their ground, while in the southern half you have expansive **Susukino** (すすきの), the city's infamous party and red light district. Connecting the two halves are three main boulevards that run directly from the station in the north to Susukino in the south; their intersection with Ōdōri Park marks the center of the city where shopping abounds.

Four Japanese characters serve as the tools with which you can decipher Sapporo's addresses: 北 (*kita;* north), 東 (*higashi;* east), 南 (*minami;* south), and 西 (*nishi;* west). By showing these four compass points in pairs of North (#) or South (#), and East (#) or West (#)—all central Sapporo addresses indicate on which city block a given establishment is located. Addresses with Ōdōri will not include a North/South cardinal point because this main road runs through the center park.

■ PRACTICAL INFORMATION

Tourist Office: The Sapporo International Communication Plaza Foundation (☎211-3670; www.plaza-sapporo.or.jp) runs 2 information counters, catering to English speakers. The **International Information Corner** (国際情報コーナー; ☎209-5030), is on the 1st fl. of Sapporo Station, inside and to the right from the South Entrance. Open daily 9am-5:30pm. **Plaza i** (プラザ i), Ōdōri West 2, (☎211-3678) is in the center of town by Ōdōri Park and near the Tōho Line's Ōdōri Exit. Book exchange on the 3rd fl. Open daily 9am-5:30pm. At both offices, you'll find English brochures, maps, and *What's On In Sapporo*, a free monthly newsletter produced by the Hokkaidō International Women's Association. While the staff can't book accommodations for you, they have a wealth of resources for helping you find a comfy bed. Weather board. Fax service ¥100.

Tours: With little time in Sapporo, the **Sapporo Sansaku Bus** (札幌散策バス) is your ticket to maximizing. The tour buses depart from Sapporo Station every 40min. and do a clockwise route around the city, stopping at sights such as the Ōkurayama Ski Jump. While each ride costs ¥200 per trip, you can save by buying an all-day pass for ¥750. Except for the names of the stops, everything is in Japanese. 1½hr., buses every 40min. 9am-5:40pm. Tour available Apr. 26-Nov. 3; tickets bought at the Plaza i or on the bus.

Budget Travel: For deals on overseas tickets, **H.I.S. Travel,** Chūō North 2, West 4 (☎222-3810) is the best option. From the station, head 3 blocks south, make a right; it will be on the left. Open M-F 10am-7pm, Sa 10am-6pm.

Currency Exchange: Available at the Central Post Office (see below), some other post office branches, and various banks that line the boulevards heading south from the train station. One bank with decent exchange rates is **Sumitomo Mitsui Bank** (住友三井銀行), Chūō North 1, West 4 (☎241-2351). Open M-F 9am-3pm. Late at night, try some of the upscale hotels near Ōdōri Park.

ATM: In the post offices as well as the **Cash Service Corner** (キャッシサービスコーナー), in the basement of the train station near the West Exit.

Luggage Storage: There's no storage window or booth, but there are decent-sized lockers (¥300-600) at the north end of the train station, just to the right of the exit.

Lost Property: There is a **lost and found** (遺失物; ☎222-6130) next to the east ticket gate in Sapporo Station. In the station, turn right just before the North Exit and make your 1st right—you'll see the ticket gate down on your right. (Open daily 6am-11:30pm).

English-Language Bookstore: Maruzen (丸善), 3rd fl., South 1, West 4 (☎241-7253), 2 blocks south of Ōdōri Park, has the best selection. If they don't have what you're looking for, try **Kinokuniya** (紀伊国屋), Ōdōri West 1, Chūō-ku (☎231-2131), which has a smaller section of English books on its 2nd fl. Open daily 10am-8pm.

Handicapped Services: The tourist offices have free English **Sapporo Barrier-Free Maps,** which indicate the wheelchair-accessible sights, bathrooms, telephones, and exits around town.

Market: Nijō-ichiba (二条市場), South 3, East 1-2 (☎222-5308), is pretty fishy—circa 60 stands sell all sorts of Hokkaidō delicacies. From the Ōdōri Subway Stop off the Tōho Line, walk a few blocks east, a few blocks south, and you can't miss it. If you have a flea-market fetish, pick up a list of them at either tourist office (see above).

Laundromat: Self-serve laundromats are all over, but most cuddle together in the south of town with comparable prices and facilities. ¥300 for wash; ¥100 per 8min. of super dry or 15min. of regular dry. **Coin Laundry** (コインランドリー), South 6, West 9 (☎811-4225). Open daily 7am-11pm. In the north, try **Coin Laundry Gobangai** (コインランドリー五番街), 9-4, Shinkotoni (☎764-9110). Open 8:30am-10:30pm. Closed Jan.

Weather: There are weather postings in both of the tourist offices, but a good reference is the Japan Weather Association's Weather Web Hokkaidō at **www.njwa.jp/eweather.**

Emergency: Police ☎110. Fire or ambulance ☎119.

Pharmacy: Sapporo Drug Store (札幌薬や), South 5, West 3, Chūō-ku (☎518-2212) is well-stocked and open late. At the main intersection of the Susukino Metro Stop, on the southern side of Rte. 36. South of town center is **Hashi Yakkyoku** (橋薬局), South 7, West 7, Chūō-ku (☎511-0029). Open daily 9am-10pm.

Hospital/Medical Services: Sapporo City General Hospital (札幌市立病院) North 11, West 14. (☎726-2211) is right next to Sōen Station in northwest Sapporo. The hospital has volunteer interpreters, but you should call to book them in advance.

Internet Access: Internet access can be expensive in Sapporo. A hidden spot for free access is the 3rd fl. of **Bic Camera** (ビックカメラ), in the southeast part of Sapporo Station. Open daily 10am-8pm. Although there are only 3 computers and you may have to wait, the connections are super-fast, and there's no time limit. **Cafe de Biz Cube,** on the 2nd fl. of White Cube Sapporo at North 9, West 2 (☎746-3389) also has free access, though there might be a wait. Open M-Sa 11am-11pm. Otherwise, Sapporo's streets ooze Internet cafes. Pick up a comprehensive list from the tourist office for addresses.

Work Opportunities: Try checking the classifieds, *Hello Work Sapporo* (ハローワーク札幌), at the **Job Placement Office** (札幌公共職業安定所), South 10, West 14, Chūō-ku (☎562-0101). Help hours for non-Japanese speakers Th 3-6pm.

Alternatives to Tourism: Kibbutz commune (☎0154-64-2821). ¥2000 per night with 2 meals. In the eastern countryside, close to Kushiro city.

Post Office: Central Post Office (札幌中央郵便局), North 6, East 1, Higashi-ku (☎748-2453). Make a right out of Sapporo Station's North Exit, and it's 2 blocks down on the corner of Rte. 5. True renaissance bank, handling mail, exchanging money (booths #4-10), and housing an **international ATM.** After hours and Poste Restante windows are around the corner from the main booths. Open 24hr. ATM open M-F 7am-11pm, Sa 9am-9pm, Su 9am-7pm. Other branches dot the town. **Postal Code:** 060.

▐ ACCOMMODATIONS

There are loads of places to stay all over Sapporo, but sleeping options fill up quickly in summer and during the Yuki Matsuri (Snow Festival) in winter. In a pinch, consider sliding into a capsule in Susukino (usually men only). The claustrophobic might prefer to call the tourist office to find more spacious quarters. Given the city's massive size, choose accommodations close to where you'd like to pass your waking time—daytrippers head north to the station area, shoppers stick to the city center, and night-hawks retreat to the southern end.

▨ **Sapporo Inn NADA,** South 5, West 9 (☎551-5882; www.sapporoinnnada.com). Take the Nanboku Line (南北線) to Susukino Station, and walk 5 blocks west on Rte. 36. Make a left at West 9, take your 2nd right after the 7-Eleven, and NADA is far down on the right of the block. Though a bit cramped, the inn is perfect for those who want to sleep cheap and hit the town at night for good food and drink. Relaxed and hospitable owners, comfortable dorm rooms, and unbeatable amenities. English CNN. Wireless cable modem signal. Breakfast ¥600. Laundry ¥250. Parking ¥600. Bike rental ¥500 per day. Reception 7:30am-11pm. Check-in noon. Check-out 10am. No curfew. Reservations suggested. Dorms ¥3500, singles ¥4000. MC/V with 5% surcharge. ❶

Sapporo House Youth Hostel (HI) (札幌ハウス), North 6, West 6, Kita-ku (☎726-4235). Turn right out of the station's South Exit and walk a few blocks and go right onto the street between West 6 and 7. The hostel is to the right after the overpass (5min. walk). Typical bare-bones hostel with a great location, Western-style and *tatami* rooms, but no special add-ons. Breakfast ¥500. Dinner ¥900. Laundry ¥300; dryer ¥100 per 15min. Check-in 3-9:30pm. Check-out 10am. Curfew 10pm. Lights-out 11pm. Reservations recommended. Dorms ¥2800; doubles ¥6400 (only available off-season). ❶

Ino's Place Backpacker's Hostel (バックパッカズホステル), 4-3-5-6, Higashi-Sapporo, Shiroishi-ku (☎832-1828; www.inos-place.com). Take the Tozai metro line toward Shin-Sapporo and get off at Shiroishi. From the top of the stairs at the metro exit, follow Nango St. back towards Lawson (in the Ōdōri Park direction) and turn right at the light just past Seico Market. Though out of the town center, Ino's is the real backpacker's choice, with full amenities and a pastoral lounge. Communal kitchen. Breakfast from ¥100. Laundry ¥300 (including dryer). Internet ¥100 per 10min. Parking ¥600 per day. Check-in 3-7pm. Check-out 10am. No curfew. Reservations recommended. Dorms ¥3400; singles ¥4800; add ¥200 heating charge Dec.-Apr. ❶

Sapporo International Youth Hostel (HI) (札幌国際ホステル), 5-35, Toyohira (☎825-3120; www.youthhostel.or.jp/kokusai). Take the Tōhō Line to Gakuen-mae, exit left and look for the hostel's sign on the opposite side of the street. It's through the plaza, 3min. away. Has spotless facilities and houses a mix of families, student groups, and couples. A bit out of town (40min. walk or 15min. bike ride). Breakfast ¥850. Laundry available. Reception 6am-midnight. Check-in 3-11pm. Check-out 10am. Curfew midnight. Reservations recommended. Dorms ¥3200; singles ¥3800. ❶

Green Hotel (グリーンホテル), South 4, West 2, Chūō-ku (☎511-4111). From the Susukino Metro Stop, walk east on Rte. 36; it's 2 blocks down on the right-hand corner. Western-style rooms and a convenient location 5 blocks from the city center. Breakfast ¥1300. Laundry service available. Reception 24hr. Parking ¥1500 per day. Check-in 2pm. Check-out 10am. Singles from ¥6500; doubles ¥8000; triples ¥18,000. AmEx/MC/V. ❸

New Budget Hotel (ホテルニューバジェット) South 3, West 6, Chūō-ku (☎261-4953; www.newbudget.com). Take the Nanboku Line to Susukino Metro Stop, go 3 blocks west on Rte. 36 and turn right; it's 2 blocks down on the right. Inexpensive, yet super clean rooms. Good location near tasty restaurants and cafes. Simple breakfast included. Laundry ¥200; dryer ¥100 per 30min. Internet available in room if you have your own computer. Parking ¥1000. Reception 24hr. Check-in 3pm. Check-out 10am. Singles ¥5200; doubles ¥16,800. ❸

Capsule Hotel Sapporo (カプセルホテル札幌), South 3, West 3, Chūō-ku (☎251-5571; http://capsule.cside.com). From Susukino Metro Stop (Nanboku Line), walk a block south away from the main crossway of Rte. 36 and make your 1st right onto a little side street—it's down on the left. A good last minute capsule option with great facilities, including a large bath and reading room. If you're staying out all night, take advantage of the daily special. Men only. Capsules include radio, alarm, and pay-TV. Lockers included. Laundry ¥300. Reception 24hr. Check-in 2pm. Check-out 10am. No curfew. Capsule ¥3200 from 3pm-10am, or ¥1200 from 6am-6pm the same day. ❶

◘ FOOD

The mean menu of trendy cafes and restaurants in Sapporo has it all, whether you're looking for the fast food world of Yoshinoya and Mos Burger or stylish Asian cooking. While most eateries string along Ekimae-dōri and in the Susukino area, the best restaurants are tucked away on the side streets, just a local's word away. For famous *rāmen*, try **Rāmen Alley** (South 5, West 3) in Susukino; if you're into all-you-can-eat and drink specials, check out the free *Hot Pepper* magazine (in Japanese only) at the tourist office for hidden deals. Finally, no visit to Sapporo is complete without a tasting of its speciality cuisines, Genghis Khan (lamb and veggies, self-cooked on a mini-stove) and Sapporo Rāmen.

■ **Daruma** (だるま), South 5, West 4, Chūō-ku (☎552-6013). From the Susukino Metro Station (Nanboku Line), walk south on Ekimae-dōri and turn right 1 block before Higashi Honganji-mae-dōri. Ode to the warrior! The best Genghis Khan for an affordable price. Come early as eager locals crowd the joint. Bar seating. No English, but that means fewer *gaijin* to cramp your style. Open M-F 5pm-3am, Su 4:30pm-1am. ❷

■ **Cam・Cam** (カムカム), South 2, West 7, Chūō-ku. (☎271-4449). A block north and across the street from New Budget Hotel. Whether it's late afternoon or early morning, Cam rocks the rasta feel and serves authentic Southeast Asian dishes. An originally decorated hut of drapes and English menu make the experience that much more enjoyable. Salads ¥350-700. Entrees ¥6000-7000. Dessert ¥200-400. Beer ¥450. Open M-F 5:30pm-1am, Sa 5:30pm-3am, Su 5:30pm-midnight. ❷

■ **Rāmen Gojōgen** (ラーメン五丈原), South 7, West 9 (☎561-3656). From Susukino Metro Station (Nanboku Line), walk south on Ekimae-dōri and turn right onto Higashi Honganji-mae-dōri when you see the temple on your right. Take the road to the end (20-25min.) and you'll see Gojōgen's sign after another larger temple on your left. Imagine how the locals feel now that word has gotten out on the best underground *rāmen* joint in Sapporo. Lines can be long—befriend the dude standing next to you or get too drunk to care. Soy, *miso*, pork *rāmen* ¥700. Open Su-M and W-Sa 4pm-4:30am. ❷

Hashiya (はしや), South 3, West 7, Chūō-ku. (☎272-0616). A block east from New Budget Hotel on the right—look for the dark wood entrance. Hashiya ("the chopsticks place") maintains quality while serving a variety of Japanese and Asian dishes. A sweet get-away for couples and groups seeking a soothing interior. *Age-harumaki* (揚げ春巻き ; fried spring rolls) are especially good (¥650). Open daily 5-11pm. AmEx/V. ❷

Ebi-Ten (えび天), South 2, West 4, Chūō-ku. (☎271-2867). From Ōdōri Metro Station (Nanboku Line), head south on Ekimae-dōri for a few blocks and turn right when you see Pivot on the right-hand corner. The restaurant is tucked in on the left, halfway down the block. Hidden on a side street off Ekimae-dōri, Ebi-Ten is a steal for delicious *tempura* and *sashimi* in a crowd of no one but Japanese citizens, Arudō Debito (p. 696) included. *Tempura-don* ¥650. Beer ¥480. Open daily 11:30am-10pm. ❷

Asian Ishoku Enak (アジアン異食) North 3, West 3, Chūō-ku (☎222-3004). A couple blocks from the station, across the street from Tōkyū department store. Best for a cheap lunch, Enak hits the 4 food groups with platters of Southeast and Japanese fusion. Come for the Indian-house ambience if nothing else. 2 set lunch specials per day (¥580-680 plus ¥100 for a drink). Entrees from ¥480. Asian teas and liquors from ¥380. Open daily 11am-11:30pm. AmEx/MC/V. ❶

Pasar Kaiten-zushi (ぱさーる), South 4, West 2, Chūō-ku (☎242-5567). On the main Route 36, 1½ blocks east of Susukino Metro Station. *Maguro* (tuna), *tekkamaki* (6-piece tuna roll), and squid plates for ¥100. Eel ¥200, salmon ¥150. Small, and unknown to most. Open M-Sa 5pm-4am, Su 5pm-1am. ❶

Kiraitō (喜來登), South 3, West 5, in the shopping arcade. For the well-seasoned *rāmen*-meisters who've been there and done that, get your taste of Sapporo's *miso rāmen* here. *Rāmen* ¥700; large ¥800. Open Su-W and F-Sa 11:30am-9:30pm. ❶

👁 SIGHTS

It's not uncommon that a first-time visitor greets Sapporo with a dumbfounded look. Where are the shrines? Where are the temples and the 5-story pagodas? Is this Japan? In a city where modernity rules the roost and history is a recent matter, Sapporo can't be everything to everyone. The city has plenty of sights, but they tend to break from tradition and masquerade as spacious green parks and gardens, sky-scraping architecture, and intoxicating museum tours. To enjoy sight-seeing here, take the district-by-district approach so you can tackle it all without back-tracking and losing time. Consider starting with sights around the city center—focusing on the Beer Museum and the TV Tower—then move on to the west where the Okurayama Ski Jump and the Winter Sports Museum await. If you have time, venture into the city's southwest district, specifically to see Jōzankei.

DOWNTOWN AND TO THE EAST

▧ SAPPORO BEER MUSEUM (サッポロビール博物館 **).** Beer connoisseurs will love every single one of their 90min. inside Sapporo's beloved beer factory. First explore the 120 year history of Hokkaidō's famous brew during a tour of the facilities, then enter the beer hall for all-you-can-drink bliss. *(North 7, East 9, Higashi-ku. East of town and most easily reached by public transport or bike. Take Factory Line city bus #88 from the station or Ōdōri and get off at the Sapporo Beer Garden Bus Stop. ☎ 731-4368; www.sapporobeer.jp. English guides are sometimes available, but you can always use the English audio guide. Open daily June-Aug. 8:40am-6pm, last entrance 4:40pm.; Sept.-May 9am-5pm, last entrance 3:40pm. Closed around New Year's holidays.)*

SAPPORO TV TOWER. At 147.2m high, Sapporo's great symbol might also be the budget Eiffel Tower of Japan—an ascending weave of steel that dates back to 1957. To get your money's worth, wait until evening and head up to the 90m platform for the view. *(Ōdōri, West 1, Chūō-ku. Take the Toho Line to Ōdōri Station and exit to the east. You can't miss the Tower, 3min. away. ☎ 241-1131. Open daily July-Sept. 9am-10pm; Oct.-June 9:30am-9pm and during the Snow Festival 9:30am-10pm. ¥700, children ¥300.)*

BOTANICAL GARDENS. With 4000 species, these are Japan's first botanical gardens, dating to 1886. Save this for a sunny day, and lose yourself on the winding paths. *(North 3, West 8, Chūō-ku. Southwest of the station. Turn right from the station's South Exit then left after a few blocks at the Keiō Plaza Hotel, on the right. The garden entrance is a few blocks down on the right. ☎ 221-0066. Open Tu-Su May-Sept. 9am-4pm; Oct. 9am-3:30pm; Nov.-Apr. 10am-5pm, greenhouses only. ¥400, children ¥280.)*

HOKKAIDŌ UNIVERSITY (北海道大学 **).** Just northwest of Sapporo Station, the University was established in 1876 as Sapporo Agricultural College. Its sprawling campus will keep your feet busy as you check out the historical buildings and statues. Before heading out, pick up a sightseeing guidebook (which has a map of the campus) from the tourist office; it'll be easier to keep your eyes peeled for **Furukawa Memorial Hall** and your nose closed for **Ginkgo Avenue**. *(North 9, West 5, Kita-ku. From the station, head straight out the North Exit.)*

HISTORICAL VILLAGE OF HOKKAIDŌ. Although cheesy for the historian, the Village does its best to zap visitors back 150 years to when Hokkaidō was settled by Japanese pioneers. The grounds are large enough to kill a few hours. *(53-2 Atsub-*

etsu-chō-konopporo, Atsubetsu-ku. ☎898-0456; *www.hmh.pref.hokkaido.jp. Open 9:30am-4:30pm. Last entrance 4pm. Closed M, New Year's holidays, and national holidays. ¥300; college students ¥100; high school, junior high, and elementary school students free.)*

TO THE WEST

ŌKURAYAMA SKI JUMP (大倉山ジャンプ競技場). A original classic from the '72 Olympic games, the ski jump is so high that you'll be terrified just looking at it from the ground below. Hop the chair lift for a behind-the-scenes look. Today, the jump is used for both competition and practice throughout the year; if you're lucky you'll catch one of the summer-night competitions. *(1274, Miyanomori, Chūō-ku. Take the Tōzai Subway Line to Maruyama, exit right, continue until you see the bus station on the right. Hop a city bus, West 14, to the jump entrance. 15min., every 30min., ¥200. ☎641-1972. Open daily July-Aug. 8:30am-9pm; Nov.-Mar. 9am-4pm; Apr.-Oct. 8:30am-6pm. Closed Apr. 1-15. Chair lift to the top ¥500.)*

SAPPORO WINTER SPORTS MUSEUM (札幌ウィンタースポーツ博物館). A full-hearted tribute to the Games of '72, the museum traces the results of virtually every winter sport with the help of entertaining visuals and movies and a few hands-on simulators you surely won't forget. Don't leave without taking your shot at the ski jumping record—all you have to do is strap in, throw on the virtual goggles, and speed down the ramp as fast as the last guy. *(1274, Miyanomori, Chūō-ku, at the base of the ski jump. ☎631-2000. Open daily May-Oct. 9am-6pm; Nov.-Apr. 9:30am-5pm. Closed last Tu of the month. ¥600.)*

MARUYAMA PARK AND ZOO (円山公園 / 動物園). Envisioned as the future center of Sapporo in the mid-1800s, Maruyama Kōen is now a beautiful green getaway full of peaceful walking trails. As one of the city's symbols, it's known for the **Hokkaidō Shrine Festival** (北海道神宮祭り ; June 14-16), and for its spring cherry blossoms. If you have time, check out over 220 animal species in the park's zoo, one of Japan's largest. *(Miyagaoka, Chūō-ku. Take the Tozai Subway Line to Maruyama, and it's about a 10min. walk from the station. Exit right onto Ōdōri and go straight, passing KFC on the right. Keep going and you'll see the trees and park entrance in front. To get to the zoo, bear left as you enter and stay on the road. ☎621-1426. Open daily 9am-5pm. ¥600.)*

TO THE SOUTH

JŌZANKEI HOT SPRING DISTRICT (定山渓). Jōzankei springs, founded by the monk Jozan about 130 years ago, is *the* rainy day choice in Sapporo. You won't be disappointed with its selection of *onsen* hotels. Buy an all-inclusive bathing and transport ticket (¥1700) at the Sapporo Station Bus Terminal. Bring your own towel or spend an extra ¥200. *(Minami-ku. From Sapporo Station Bus Terminal, take a Jotetsu Bus or a Donan Bus, platform #12, to the Jōzankei Stop. 70min., about 1 per hr., round-trip ¥1700 plus bathing fee. Tourist association ☎598-2012.)*

SAPPORO DOME. Built for the 2002 Soccer World Cup, the Dome looks more like a UFO than a multi-faceted concert venue, pro baseball stadium, and international soccer arena. It's aero-dynamic, hip, and guaranteed to knock the socks off any die-hard sports fan with its cutting-edge technology—namely, a hovering soccer stage and mobile artificial turf. Tours are in Japanese. *(1, Hitsuji-ga-oka, Toyohira-ku. Take the Toho Subway Line to its last stop in the south, Fukuzumi. Walk for 10min. ☎850-1020. Hours sporadic; call ahead or inquire at the tourist office. Tours require scheduling ahead of time. Observatory ¥500, tours ¥1000.)*

♪ ® ENTERTAINMENT AND NIGHTLIFE

All that Sapporo isn't by day emerges at night when the feisty district of Susukino rules in pure Tōkyō style. The area, which spreads throughout the blocks west of South 4 and between East 2 and West 7, is famous for its less-than-subtle mix of Redlight and traditional establishments and its ability to suck green out of drunk, homeward-bound businessmen. Not sure how you'll know when you've entered the sleaze? Using astute investigatory skills, you'll notice that the schoolgirl on the corner has no books and the nurse with the stethescope has high-heels on. Nevertheless, don't avoid Susukino because it drops Japanese conservatism. The area is not *only* an adult amusement park—it also provides a blacktop where all people can try their game once the sun goes down. Lines of hit *izakaya*, dance clubs, and live music pubs offer refuge from the street scene. Chat with the locals for the scoop on what's hot today.

Booty Bar, South 7, West 4, Chūō-ku (☎521-2336; www.booty-disco.com). On the east side of the same block as King Xhmu. Though its name is self-explanatory, Booty deserves at least a line or two of attention. 2 floors—an upstairs lounge and downstairs dance fl.—of hardcore weekend partying. Funk and soul on F, hip-hop and R&B on Sa. Good food ¥500. No cover. Open M-Th 9am-2am, Sa-Su 9am-4am.

Flore Cafe, South 7, West 3, Chūō-ku (☎552-9080; www.florecafe.com). From King Xmhu, head east a block and cross the main intersection. The club is on the right, after **Rad Bar,** a miss-able *gaijin* hangout. Flore Cafe is one of the few dance spots that draws a mostly Japanese crowd. Let loose to techno on the dance fl. or try to talk over the thumping beats in the adjacent lounge. Younger energy and rowdy on weekends, especially on International Night (check the website for events). Lockers ¥200. Beer and drinks ¥500. Usually no cover, but occasionally on weekends ¥1000. Open daily 8pm-6am.

Sally Bell (サリーベル), 3-3-33, South 3, 4th fl. (☎200-2445). On the eastern corner of the capsule hotel block (see above). Spray-painted walls, naked floors, and a liberated Japanese college crowd give Sally's an underground appeal. A great place to take friends or meet others for a late pre-game. ¥1333 all-you-can-drink special from 11pm-5:30am. Awesome food, especially the *hachimitsu* toast (cake bread; ¥550). ¥200 seat charge. Beer ¥330. No cover. Open daily 5pm-6am.

Hendix's Art Cafe, South 3, West 4, Chūō-ku (☎222-5533). Susukino Metro Stop (Nanboku Line). Across the street from the post office, on the northeast corner of the block. A new underground spot where friends don't let friends leave without taking advantage of the pre-gaming special—¥1000 all-you-can-drink beer and cocktails (60 types) midnight-5am. Also, be sure to check out the art on the walls and the menu of satisfying snacks. Cover ¥450. No cover. Open daily 5pm-5am.

Bar Locotonte, South 7, West 4, Chūō-ku (☎533-3728). From Booty Bar, head west and turn right at King Xmhu—it's just on the right, but it's an eye-spy game to find the sign. The archetypal after-hours place where everyone keeps promising they're going to leave, but no one actually does. A small dance fl. plays runner-up to social conversation on the outside deck. Cheap beer ¥300. Cocktails ¥400. Weekend cover ¥1000 worth of drink tickets. Open daily 8pm-5am.

Kento's, South 4, West 2, Chūō-ku (☎512-5459; kentos@aoki.gr.jp). From Susukino Metro Stop (Nanboku Line), head 2 blocks east on Rte. 36 and look for Aoki Bowling on the right (a flashy building). Kento's is inside, through the arcade and in the back. If you like '50s and '60s rock—Kento's amazes with its great live shows and uncanny recreation of the Chuck Berry era. Peep the authentic hair-wave of the dude at the door. 6 live shows per night starting at 7:30pm. Beer ¥550. Cover ¥1300. Open M-Sa 6pm-2am, Su 6pm-1am.

NO WORK, ALL PLAY

RELIVING SNOW DAYS

It's the dead of February and Sapporo is ice-bound. Outside in the streets, there are two million spellbound visitors. This is the magic of Sapporo's annual Yuki Matsuri, a showcase of snow and ice sculptures in the city's boulevards and parks. Started in 1950 by a group of high-schoolers and middle-schoolers, the Snow Festival symbolized optimism under the post-war American occupation of Japan. What was once "building sandcastles on snow days" turned quickly into a world-wide celebration when the Winter Olympics came to Sapporo in 1972. Now taken to a whole new level, the festival produces around 300 statues each year, the most mind-blowing of which are incredibly detailed and large enough to make your jaw drop.

The masterful creators travel from all corners of Japan to participate. Relying on detailed blueprints and often racing against the competition clock, the artists work in three main locations around the city: Ōdōri Park, Makomanai, and Susukino. For a taste of it all, start in Ōdōri Park to see the most artistic snow sculptures, head over to Makomanai to see the truly audacious, and finally, slide to the highly stylized ice sculptures in Susukino where parties glitter in the twilight. To enjoy the chills and thrills of the festival, book accommodations months in advance. (*More information at the Sapporo tourist offices.*)

King Xmhu, South 7, West 4, Chūō-ku (☎531-1388; www.king-xmhu.com). From Susuki-no Station (Namboku Line), walk south on Ekimae-dōri, and turn right when you see the old temple on your right about 5 or 6 blocks down. Walk down the street (Higashi Honganji-mae) and you can't miss Xmhu on the left corner at the end of the block. Supposedly designed by the Indiana Jones set architect, King Xmhu is a wonder of stone with a carved face etched onto the outside, and a cave full of booming music on the inside. Cheesy as it is, the club is worth a glance and perhaps a visit if they are hosting a live concert. Techno, trance, and hip-hop. Drinks from ¥500. Snack food ¥350-400. Cover ¥1000-4000. Open M-Th 9pm-3am, F-Sa 9pm-4am, Su 9pm-2am.

🎊 FESTIVALS

Many visitors are drawn by one of Sapporo's numerous celebrations—whether it's the dazzling **Yuki Matsuri** in early February or the **Yosakoi Soran Festival** in June. Also in June, the **Hokkaidō Shrine Festival** (北海道神社祭り) pays tribute to the Shintō gods and takes place in symbolic Maruyama Park (丸山公園 ; June 14-16). Last but not least is the visual spectacle that lights up the Toyohira River—the unforgettable **Fireworks Festival** (花火 お祭り) in late July or early August.

SHIRAOI (白老)   ☎0144

The little town of Shiraoi, only an hour from Sapporo and out in the sticks, is worth a visit only for its Ainu Village, 🏠**Poro Tokan** (ポロト館). Although the village is small and crawling with Japanese tourists, there's a lot to learn here about the endangered Ainu culture. Only some of those working at Poro Tokan are of actual Ainu blood; the rest are just enthusiastic Japanese helping out—although the staff won't speak Ainu to one another, some can speak a bit of the fading language. Within the village, plan on spending about 1½hr. so you can can witness a traditional dance (15min., every 15min. past the hour) and stick your head into a few of the old houses. You'll probably learn the most about this historic settlement by walking through the enclosed **museum** (www.ainu-museum.or.jp) and chatting openly with the locals who work there (unfortunately no English is spoken). For more English info than the leaflet provides, buy the bilingual guide *Ainu History and Culture* (¥500), available in the museum gift shop. (Open daily Apr.-Oct. 8:45am-5pm; Nov.-Mar. 8:45am-4:30pm. ¥750.) To get to the village from Shiraoi Station, it's about a 20min. walk. Exit the station, turn

THE FADING COLORS OF THE AINU

Japan's rapidly disappearing indigenous population

An old woman of average height stands draped in colorful garments. Despite her strongly Caucasian features, she speaks native Japanese, eats Japanese food, gestures with Japanese body language, and works every day on Japanese-owned land. This woman is a member of the Ainu, Hokkaidō's rapidly disappearing indigenous peoples who have faced centuries of oppression, exploitation, and discrimination at the hands of the Japanese. Today, as an older member of her community, this woman struggles to preserve and perpetuate a culture that has barely survived its haunting history. Though the exact time of the Ainu's arrival to Japan is uncertain (most say 5000-10,000 years ago), it's only been 150 years since the group had a strong presence in Northern Tōhoku, Hokkaidō, and the Kurile Islands. As hunters and gatherers, they lived modest lives that centered on the family, oral tradition, and a religious belief that god is present in everything—the animals, the rocks, the forests. The Ainu honored the animals they hunted and respected the land they cultivated (called *kotan*, a neighborhood of ten thatched-roof huts, a prayer altar, fishing boat dock, and a food-storage house).

The Ainu's ritual dances embody grace, their music and song speak of ancient wisdom, and their elaborately stitched robe-wear reflects inimitable craftsmanship. Yet even with a textured culture, the Ainu had no way of satisfying the land-hungry Japanese expansionists who began to advance north in the mid-15th and 16th centuries. The first major conflict between the indigenous tribes and the warlords from Honshū—the Battle of Koshamain (1457)—ended abruptly with a Japanese victory, and the event marked the beginning of the end for an outnumbered population. In the centuries to follow, the Ainu were systematically exploited through trade, forced to assimilate into Japanese culture, and pushed off the land they had inhabited for thousands of years. In 1868 the Japanese government capped off its oppressive policies toward the Ainu by making them Japanese commoners, a decision which prohibited the Ainu tongue—a unique and expressive language of the polysynthetic family—and prevented them from living according to their own traditions and beliefs. Soon after, the Ainu acquiesced to the assimilation policies of the Japanese government, and the remaining indigenous population was forced to live an existence devoid of cultural identity.

Recent times have brought the Ainu hope and increased prosperity, credited to the scattered population's hard fight to hold onto the remnants of their culture. Still bereft of land, the Ainu use the law to seek compensation for societal inequalities which are the products of deeply entrenched racial discrimination. Although it could be argued that today the Ainu are still exploited—this time more subtly, by a tourist industry that displays Ainu culture on a well-lit stage—local Ainu communities are able to use the proceeds from tourism to fund valuable projects. All is not lost for the Ainu, whose culture and language inspire passing *gaijin* as well as traveling Japanese. Throughout Hokkaidō, there are a handful of good museums where you can learn more about the indigenous peoples, numerous places that still bear original Ainu names, and even the authentic Ainu village of Nebutani (south of Shiraoi), where an old woman in colorful garments is known to reside.

Recommended Reading:

Our Land Was a Forest, by Kayano Shingero. The best book for assuming an Ainu perspective and learning about the cause. *Our Land* is a moving personal memoir by one of the community's most prominent leaders.

Unbeaten Tracks, by Isabella Bird. Published in 1879, the book is a collection of letters written during the tumultous Meiji years. Although Bird refers to the indigenous peoples as "complete savages," her interest was passion-driven and she produced a comprehensive account of the Ainu's lifestyle and practices.

Collected Stories of the Ainu Gods by Yukie Chin. Written by an Ainu girl in 1929, the collected stories look into the rich oral tradition of the Ainu.

Ainu Creed and Cult by Neil Gordon Munro (1863-1942). A fascinating account of Ainu beliefs, customs, ceremonies, religions, funerary practices, and festivities.

The Languages of Japan by Masabu Shibatani. Although the book is mainly an analysis of modern Japanese, it offers the most comprehensive linguistic description of Ainu available in English.

- Nick Topjian

THE LOCAL STORY

HOT ONSEN MEAN HOT LAWSUIT IN OTARU

Though you won't feel it bubbling furiously beneath the calm waters and placid streets here, the Otaru Onsen Case is making international headlines as it digs deep into the issue of a race-based national identity in Japan. The story begins with repeated incidents involving rowdy Russian shipmen at *onsen* in Otaru, which provoked three *onsen* to post "Japanese Only" signs in 1993.

Arudō Debito (formerly "David Aldwinckle" of the US), a nearly 20-year Hokkaidō resident and naturalized citizen of Japan, has accused the *onsen* of failing to uphold the Japanese constitution. Debito is not alone in his mission to challenge conceptions of race in Japan. Olaf Karthaus (of Germany) and Ken Sutherland (of the US), two of his friends and longtime Hokkaidō residents, have joined his battle, and since 2001 the three have been fighting the *onsen*'s discriminatory rules. A number of *onsen* have since taken their signs down, and in a lawsuit against the Yunohana *onsen*, the bathhouse was ordered to pay a fine of $25,000 to the three men. The decision is still awaiting appeals. We had the chance recently to chat with Debito-san and Mr. Karthaus about race and identity in Japan.

Arudō Debito is a tenured professor at the Hokkaidō Information University and Olaf Karthaus is an associate professor at the Chitose Institute of Science and Technol-

left at the first light and continue down the main street. Turn left before the Cosmo gas station and look for the giant bear head 100m down on your right. If you can survive the tourist shops in this building, you'll find the village on the other side.

Unless you have your own transport, Shiraoi is easiest done as a daytrip from Sapporo. Just hop on one of the few daily JR express trains from Sapporo station (1hr.; 5per day; one-way ¥2890, round-trip ¥3540) and be sure to buy a round-trip ticket if you don't have a JR pass—it will save you big-time. A cheaper option is to take a bus from Sapporo (2hr., 5 per day, ¥1500; leaves from the station bus terminal), which also has the advantage of dropping you off directly at the stop for Poro Tokan. Once you arrive at Shiraoi Station, stop by the **tourist office** (白老観光案内所), 2-3-4, Ōmachi, Shiraoi-chō, Shiraoi-gun, to the right of the exit. (☎82-2216; www.sanynet.ne.jp. Japanese pamphlets available. Open daily 8am-5pm.) In an emergency, call ☎110 for **police**, ☎119 for **fire** or **ambulance**.

OTARU (小樽)   ☎0134

Only 40km outside of Sapporo, Otaru is just what the doctor ordered for a case of the big-city blues, serving as a relaxing daytrip for some and a romantic getaway for others. The city is best known for its high-quality glass works, savory fresh fish, and historic canal area, all of which embody its rich history as a port-town and make for a pleasant day of mini-sights and strolls.

■■ TRANSPORTATION AND PRACTICAL INFORMATION. It's easiest to do Otaru either as a daytrip or on your way out of the big city. There are frequent connections between Otaru and Sapporo, and though JR **trains** (30-45min., 6 per hr, ¥660) are the fastest option, there are also **buses** that leave from Sapporo Station's South Terminal (1hr., 1-3 per hr., ¥590). If you decide to stop here en-route to Sapporo, you're best off taking the train from **Hakodate**, which requires you to switch trains at Oshamambe (to Otaru: 1 hr., 10 per day, from ¥2100; to Sapporo: 3hr., 7 per day, ¥2830), or **Niseko** (2hr., 9 per day, ¥1410).

Coming out of the turnstiles, take a left into the station's **tourist office** (観光案内所) where you'll find informative English guidebooks and good English maps of the town center. (☎29-1333; Open daily 9am-6pm). If there are too many people, consider heading down to the bigger **Unga Plaza Tourist Office** at the bottom of Chūō-dōri and next to the city museum. The info center is more spacious and stays open later, and even has **free Internet** access. (☎33-1661. Open daily 9am-9pm.) Store your stuff in small or large **lockers** (¥300-500) on the right as you exit the train's turnstiles. In an emergency, call ☎110 for **police,** ☎119 for **fire** or **ambulance.** For money matters, skip the banks and head for the **Central Post Office** (中央郵便局), 1-8-1, Ironai, which changes currency and has an **International ATM.** From the station, take Chūō-dōri (the main road in front), making a right when you hit Ironai St.—it's a couple of long blocks down on the right. (☎22-1228. Open M-F 9am-4pm for money exchange, 9am-7pm for mail and international ATM.) **Postal code:** 047.

⌐⌐ ACCOMMODATIONS AND FOOD. Otaru has a bunch of good budget accommodations, but as availability is iffy, you should make reservations ahead of time. Among the picks, **⛩The Otarunai Backpackers' Hostel ❶,** 4-15, Aioi, is the most loungy, with a hippie feel, upstairs garden, and two cute dogs. From the station, turn right onto Rte. 5 and take your third left after passing one of the post office branches. (☎23-2175; www.otaru-morinoki.com. Internet ¥100 per 20min. Reservations recommended. Dorms ¥3500; doubles ¥9000.) Though out of town and near Tengu-yama cable car, the **Otaru Youth Hostel (HI) ❶** (小樽ユースホステル) , 16-22, Mogani is another good option, especially for those who want to be near the ski slopes. From the station, take a bus (platform #9) to Mt. Tengu Ropeway (15min.; 3 per hr. at quarter after, 35 after, and 55 after the hr.; ¥200) and follow the signs as you get off. (☎34-1474. Members ¥3000, nonmembers ¥3600.) **Otaru Green Hotel ❶** (小樽グリーンホテル), 3-3-1, Inaho—not to be confused with the pricier New Green Hotel (ニューグリーンホテル)—is central and cheap, but has a dull '70s-throwback interior. They offer simple Western- and Japanese-style rooms. Walk straight out of the station; it's a few blocks up on the left. (☎33-0333. Reservations recommended. ¥3500 per person.) For a more homey minshuku, continue down the side street of Green's entrance, make the fifth left, and go up the little stairs in front. Here, **Satsukiso Inn ❶** (さつき民宿), 4-3-17, Inaho, has typical cozy *tatami* rooms for cheap. (☎32-4984. ¥3000.)

Though you'll have no trouble stumbling upon an eatery or twenty, try and save your appetite for a walk along **Sushi-ya Dōri** (寿司屋通り), an endless line of sushi restaurants, all of which will drain your wallet faster than you can sneeze *nigiri.* To minimize the damage, try **Shikama Sushi ❸** (しかま寿司), 1-1-9, Hama-zono, where sushi sets are somewhat affordable and you can order by the piece.

ogy. Learn more about the activists at www.debito.org, or check out Debito's book, *Japanese Only.*

LG: Why *onsen,* why now?

OK: Well, I think it's better to nip [the issue of racial discrimination in Japan] in the bud before it gets bigger. Today it's *onsen,* tomorrow it's supermarkets and restaurants.

AD: It's already *pachinko* parlors, bars, barbers, sports shops. There was a *rāmen* store in Susukino that refused foreigners during the World Cup. We're watching this balloon into something very important and it shows that there's a problem that needs to be addressed.

LG: How do you compare the discrimination here to that in other regions of the world?

OK: I think that racial discrimination in Japan is very blunt and very naïve. In Europe, of course, discrimination exists, but it's more subtle.

AD: It's not violent; it's more like institutionalized discrimination that's a function of the normal pigeon-holing that goes on in this society. In Japan, there's an attitude that says, "Of course certain subgroups—the *Burakumin,* ethnic Koreans—are going to be treated differently. They always have been."

LG: Your fearless activism has created a buzz in Japan and abroad. How have you been treated?

AD: In Japan, people listen, and that's one very positive aspect of Japanese society. Here, because there is a social control that makes sure that everyone stays calm and collected and composed at all times, if you speak your mind, people will listen. Because of that, you can actually take a mic and get your word out.

From Sushi-ya Dōri, turn onto the street across from the start of the shopping arcade—Shikama is just on the left. If you're set on eating sushi, but are swimming low in your budget, there's no shame in going for *kaiten-zushi* at **Asahi Beer ❶** (アサヒビール), in the train station across from the tourist office. It's not nearly as good, but keep reminding yourself that all the fish comes from the same bay; the cost of only ¥100-400 per plate should be ample comfort. (☎ 33-3400. Beer ¥230. Open 11am-9pm.) Finally, if you're still focused on the glass of Kitaichi, grab a set of *takoyaki* (octopus balls; ¥400) at **Kaidō-ya ❶** (海道屋), 4-19, Sakaimatsu, which is right along the shopping street. (Open 9am-5:30pm.)

◪ SIGHTS. Leaving the station area, shoot over to the bay where you can follow the city's canal and get a glimpse of the restored Meiji buildings. Since the canal is appealing only for a short section on the right of Chūō-dōri (中央通), don't bother going to the left. Instead, walk back to the base of Chūō-dōri, and learn about the town's people and commercial history at the **Otaru City Museum** (小樽市 博物館), 2-1-20, Ironai, which is full of antique maps, replicated cave murals, and statues. (☎ 33-2439. Around the corner from the tourist office. Open daily 9:30am-5pm. ¥100.) The **Kitai'ichi Glass Area** of town is a 15min. walk along the canal from the museum and to the right when facing the river. Take either the road that the museum is on or Ironai Street (which is up a block and parallel), and you'll see swarms of glass emporiums and gift shops. Inside, smoothly blown glass work ranges from ashtrays and ornaments to *sake* sets and flower vases—just what mom wants. Keep moving through the touristy haze and look for the small stairway to the left of Kitai'ichi Crystal-kan (きたいいちクリスタル館), Sakai-machi St., which leads to an obervatory overlooking the glass-artisans at work in the **Kitai'ichi Kengaku Kōjō** (きたいいち見学工場; open daily 9:30am-5pm. Free.) For a modest ¥1800, you can take the blowtorch into your own hands at **K's Blowing**, 2-17, Sakai-ichi, a smaller, more progressive factory on the left side of Sakai-ichi as you head back toward Chūō-dōri. Your little glass cup will take a day to cool off, but K's ships anywhere in Hokkaidō for ¥500 and anywhere in Japan for ¥1000. (☎ 31-5454. Open daily 10am-4:30pm. ¥1800.)

The coast of Shukutsu is worth a trip if you have time, as you can see the **Nishingoten**, 3-228, Shukutsu, an old fisherman's home and work studio built in 1897. The house is typical of Herring-era architecture, and the government has worked to maintain the mansion's traditional appeal. To get here, take a city bus (25min., ¥200) from Otaru Station to the last stop, Otaru Suiokukan (call for info ☎ 22-1038).

ASAHIKAWA (旭川)　　　　☎ 0166

Hokkaidō's second largest city, Asahikawa is kind of like your average beat-up truck—it's got the means to get you where you want to go, but not enough flair to make you love it for what it is. Like a strong-horse Toyota, it'll show you the way to Daisetsu-zan National Park in the east, Wakkanai and Rishiri-Rebun-Sarobetsu National Park in the north, and a splendid daytrip to Furano nearby, but don't anticipate the adrenaline rush that a red convertible with the top down might provide. Once a large Ainu settlement, Asahikawa quietly shed its colorful past during the transformational Meiji Era, only to become a major commercial center and transport hub of northern Hokkaidō. Today, visitors are likely to value the city most as a last chance to send postcards, dig up English info, and refill the wallet with yen before entering the city's more dramatic surroundings.

▐ TRANSPORTATION

Asahikawa also has a small **airport** (旭川空港), Higashi Ni-sen, Higashi-kagura-chō (☎ 83-3939), 16km south of town. To get to the airport, take a bus from in front of the station toward **Furano** (35min., 8 per day, ¥570). Flights to: **Kushiro** (40min., 1 per day, ¥12,300); **Ōsaka** (about 2hr., 1 per day, ¥39,300); **Tōkyō** (1¾hr., 6 per day, ¥24,000). You can book flights inside the train station's JR ticket office where there's a **Travel Center** (旅行センター ; ☎22-8180; open daily 9am-5:30pm). Most transport flows in and out of **Asahikawa Station** (旭川駅), 7, Miyashita-dōri, just south of the town center and beside the main shopping and eating areas. (☎25-6736. Open daily 5:30am-10pm.) There are **JR express trains** from: **Abashiri** (4hr., 5 per day, ¥7240); **Hakodate** (3hr., every 30min., ¥11,720); **Kushiro** (6hr., 6 per day, ¥7310); **Sapporo** (80min.; every 30min.; ¥4170, round-trip ¥4940); **Wakkanai** (4hr., 4 per day, ¥7560.) The **central bus station** (中央バスターミナル ; ☎25-3000) has a bus to **Sapporo** (2hr.; every 30min.; ¥2000, round-trip ¥3750). Buses connecting Asahikawa to northern and eastern Hokkaidō end up at the **Dōhoku Bus Station** (道北バスターミナル ; ☎23-4161; www.dohokubus.com), 8-chōme, Miyashita. Buses come from: **Kushiro** (6½hr.; 2 per day; ¥5300, round-trip ¥9600); **Obihiro** (3¾hr., 5 per day, ¥3150/¥6000); **Wakkanai** (4¾hr., 1 per day, ¥4350/¥7800). To get to **Daisetsu-zan National Park** (大雪山国立公園), you can either take a bus to its northern base, **Sōunkyō** (2hr., 7 per day, ¥1900), or its western base, **Teninkyō** (2hr., June 15-Oct. 14 3 per day, ¥1000). Both buses depart from platform #4 in front of the station. While getting around Asahikawa on foot is easy enough, **public buses** depart from the station area and can take you to the suburbs (7am-10pm, ¥140). For **taxis**, grab one from in front of the station or call **Personal Taxi** (個人タクシー ; ☎51-8510), the cheapest place in town. If you'd like a car for your explorations, **Eki Rent-a-car** (駅レンタカー), in the station next to the tourist office, is probably your best bet, since you can return the car at any of its affiliates all over Hokkaidō. (☎23-2498. Open daily 8am-8pm. Cars from ¥5500; July-Aug. ¥7500.)

🛈 PRACTICAL INFORMATION

Asahikawa is easy to navigate due to well-labeled streets and a predictable grid-layout. To get a nice English map, stop by the city **tourist information center** (旭川観光情報センター), in the station to the right as you exit the ticket stalls. The helpful English-speaking staff has info on sights in Asahikawa, as well as the surrounding parks. (☎22-6704; www.asahikawa-daisetsu.info. Open daily June-Sept. 8:30am-7pm; Oct.-May 9am-5:30pm.) In an emergency, call ☎110 for **police**, ☎119 for **fire** or **ambulance**. Though **Internet access** is sickly expensive, **Solution College** (ソリューションカレッジ), 3-jō-dōri, 8-chōme, on the 6th floor of a stationery store, will hook you up with a fast connection when **The Den** (see **Sights and Entertainment**) isn't open. Take Heiwa-dōri down six blocks, turn right onto 3-jō-dōri, and it's halfway down the block on the right. (☎29-3055. ¥700 for 1hr. Longer periods ¥500 per hr. Open M-Sa 10am-7pm.) The **Central Post Office** (旭川中央郵便局), 6-28-1, 6-jō, offers money exchange (booths #9-11) and mail services. (☎26-3431. Open M-F 9am-7pm, Sa 9am-5pm, Su 9am-12:30pm. Money exchange open M-F 9am-4pm. **ATM** open M-F 8:45am-7pm, Sa-Su 9am-7pm.) To get to the office, you'll need about 20min. (on foot) from the station—walk straight down Heiwa-dōri (平和通り) from in front of the station and turn left after 12 blocks—as you cross Daihyaku Seimei St. you'll see it a block down on the right. For an ATM, go to the branch in the train station (same hours as ATM above). **Postal code:** 070.

🏠🍴 ACCOMMODATIONS AND FOOD

While most accommodation in Asahikawa falls into the mid-range business hotel category, you can snag good bargains by making reservations ahead of time. Defying economics with its fabulous *tatami* rooms and spotless facilities is the ▨**Kamikawa Education Research Center** ❶ (Kamikawa Kyōiku Kenshū Sentā; 上川教育研修センター), 4-chōme, 6-jō-dōri, two blocks west of the Central Post Office. Though the center mainly plays host to visiting Japanese scholars, you can get by relying on a phrasebook and your best behavior. From the post office, just head west through Nishō Elementary School (日章小学校) and you'll see its stone, gray interior in front of you. (☎24-2501. All rooms *tatami*-style. Breakfast ¥600. Check-in 5pm. Check-out 10am. ¥2620 per person for singles. Reservations recommended.) The **Asahikawa Youth Hostel (HI)** ❶ (旭川ユースホステル), 1-jō 7-chōme, is another cheap option with clean rooms and a hospitable staff, yet its distant location will cost you some time and bus fees. From bus stop #11 in front of the station, take either bus #444 or #550 and get off at Inosawa Ski-jō (伊ノ沢場 前 ; 15min., every 30min., ¥300)—the hostel is across the street and a 2min. walk in the same direction. (☎61-2800. Breakfast ¥600. Dinner ¥1000. Dorms ¥3200; doubles ¥4500 per person.) A couple of minutes walk from the station is the **Fuji Business Hotel** ❷ (ビジネスホテル富士), 9, Miyashita-dōri, which has spacious singles, a nice dining area, and an unbeatable price. Turn right as you exit the station and look for the bright pink sign half a block down. (☎24-3251. Free laundry. Breakfast included. Dinner ¥800. Parking ¥500. Check-in 3pm. Check-out 10am. Singles ¥3800.) The **Green Hotel Bekkan** ❷ (グリーンホテル別館), 3F, 2-chōme, 1-jō-dōri, is a nice last-minute option with clean rooms and a prime location 5min. from the station. From the station, bear right out the exit and head straight up Midori-bashi-dōri (緑橋通) until you get to 7-Eleven—the hotel has a small entrance one block up and across the street. (☎26-1414. Check-in 3pm. Check-out 10am. Singles ¥4500; doubles ¥7930.)

Asahikawa is known for excellent *rāmen*. If you fancy a taste, head to the **Rāmen Village** (ラーメン村 ; ☎48-2153; www.ramenmura.com), where you can fill up on soy or *miso rāmen*. To get there, take a Dōhoku Bus from platform #18 in front of the Marui-imai department store (丸井今井デパート ; 15min., #66, 72, or 665). Get off at Nagayama (永山), 10-jō, 4-chōme. You'll find most cheap eateries and *izakaya* along Heiwa-dōri and around the 3-jō, 6-chōme area. While there are many lunch buffets around town, ⊠**Pako Hotel Viking Lunch** ❶, 1 jō-dōri, 7-chōme, on the 14th floor, is the best taste for value. Dishes included are *okonomiyaki*, *tempura*, and *tonkatsu*, and all are served in a pleasing cafe/restaurant that overlooks the city. (☎25-1022. Lunch 11am-2pm. ¥998 per person.) The silver medal for buffets goes to **Chinese Fuku-sai-kan** ❶, 4, 4-jō-dōri, 7-chōme, another all-you-can-eat lunch dive with a genuine Chinese twist. The lunch buffet consists of good veggie dishes, fried dumplings, and a few meat specialties. Go all the way down Heiwa-dōri and turn left onto 4-jō-dōri; it's at the end of the first block on the left. (☎27-8066. Buffet 11:30am-2:30pm, ¥850. Open daily 6am-10pm.)

👁 🎵 SIGHTS AND ENTERTAINMENT

Though it's tough to get excited about attractions in Asahikawa with Furano and Daisetsu-zan beckoning from nearby, it's worth flipping through the tourist office's English pamphlets. The most worthy sight is the **Otokoyama Sake Brewery and Museum** (男山酒造り資料館), 2-7, Nagayama, an internationally-recognized and award-winning *sake* producer 6km away from Asahikawa Station. Learn about the history of *sake*-brewing through woodblock prints, a collection of traditional tools, and a tasting session that will teach you to distinguish the good stuff from the not-so-good. Take a Dōhoku Bus from the Marui-imai department store (丸井今井デパート ; buses #67, 68, 70, 71, 667, 669; 20min.), get off at 2-7 Nagayama Stop and it's a 2min. walk. (☎ 47-7080; www.otokoyam.com. Open 9am-5pm. Free.)

When the sun drops, Asahikawa's nightlife gets going west of the shopping street, Heiwa-dōri, and around the 3-jō, 6-chōme area. One of the popular hangouts among foreign residents and travelers alike is **The Den**, 2-jō, 7-chōme, a *gaijin* bar with pool, darts, and extra hard rock. Head straight up Heiwa-dōri and turn left one block before 3 jō-dōri—it's halfway down the block on the left, on the fifth floor. (☎27-0999. Beer ¥500. Shots ¥400. Cocktails from ¥500. No cover. Open Su-

Wed 6pm-midnight, Th-Sa 6pm-5am.) A more relaxing pub completely void of the English scene is **Zero Cafe and Bar**, 4 jō-dōri, 7 chō-me, right on Heiwa-dōri, eight blocks up from the station where local Japanese residents find release after their hard day's nights. (☎ 25-2460. Beer ¥500. Cocktails ¥600. No cover. Open Su and Tu-Sa noon-4am.) If it's summer and the weather's good, there's an indoor/outdoor **beer garden** (ビアガーデン) on the fourth floor of the **New Hokkai Hotel** (ニュー 北海ホテル), 5-jō-dōri, 6-chōme, two blocks south of the Central Post Office. The garden is especially fun on weekends when larger Japanese crowds shout *kanpai* (cheers) into oblivion. (☎24-3111. Beer ¥600 or 6 beers for ¥3000. Light food from ¥350. No cover. Open daily May 23-Sept. 15 5-9pm; July-Sept. 5-10pm.)

FURANO (富良野)   ☎0167

It's no wonder that Furano, a small farming town in central Hokkaidō, is hailed as one of the island's most breathtaking daytrip destinations. With its gentle mountain ranges, lavender lawns, and fields upon fields of flowers—some in hues you never knew existed—the town could make even a colorblind, cranky curmudgeon see rainbows for a day. In addition to its landscape, Furano is famous for its fine grape juice, cheese, and wine.

▐ ▐ TRANSPORTATION AND PRACTICAL INFORMATION. The easiest way to get to Furano from Asahikawa is by **JR train** (80min., 1 per hr., ¥1040; last train back 8:45pm). If you want to save a bit of money, **buses** go to: **Asahikawa Airport** (旭 川空港 ; 1hr., 8 per day, ¥750); **Asahikawa Station** (1½hr., 8 per day, ¥860); **Sapporo** (2½hr.; 1 per hr.; ¥2100, round-trip ¥3950). The two buses from Asahikawa stop at Furano Station, the one from Sapporo stops at Furano's **central bus terminal** (☎23-6001; open 6:30am-6pm), just 5min. on foot from the train station—turn left out of the bus station and follow the main road. In summer (July-Sept.), the **Asaden Bus Company** (あさでん) has comprehensive tours of Furano and the rolling agricultural fields of **Biei** (美瑛). The all-inclusive deal runs daily and is worth the price as it covers most sights listed above plus Biei. The bus departs from the **Asaden Central Bus Terminal**, Asahi Bldg., 8, Miyashita, and returns at 5:30pm. (Departs 9am, returns 5:30pm. ¥3600.) The easiest way to get around is your own car (an absolute must in winter). **Toyota Rent-a-car** (トヨタレンタカー) is across the street and right from the station's exit. (☎23-2100. Open 8am-8pm. ¥5500 for 6hr. MC/V.) Otherwise, the best option is the **summer sight-seeing bus** (☎22-1911; www.cbnet.co.jp/furanobus), which starts at the station and stops at all of the sights above, except the Cheese Factory. (25min. from the station to Tomita Farm and all other stops are along the way; 5 per day 10:10am-4:55pm. ¥150-300 per trip. Departs from platform #4, across the street from the station.) While **bike rental** is available at **Nishi-ni Renta-cycle**, 128, Hinode-chō, be forewarned that giant hills lie ahead. (☎22-2258. ¥500 per 3hr. Open 8am-9pm.) Call **Chūō Hire** (中央ハイヤ ; ☎22-2800) when you're stranded and need a car to pick you up.

    The main **tourist office** (富良野観光案内所), to the right of the station's exit, offers maps, delicious grape juice (¥220), and English pamphlets. (☎23-3388; www.furano.ne.jp. English-speaking staff on occasion. Open daily 9am-6pm.) In an emergency, call ☎110 for **police**, ☎119 for **fire** or **ambulance**.

▐ ▐ ACCOMMODATIONS AND FOOD. The cheapest place to sleep is **Kanari Backpacker's Inn ❶** (Hoshi ni Negai wo Pension; 星に願いをペンション), a 5min. walk from the winery near the lavender fields. From the station, take the local bus or drive up past the winery and it'll be on the left. The rooms here are cozy and the friendly staff will pick you up from the station if you call a day in advance. When making reservations, make it clear that you want to stay at the hostel and *not* the country-house—the price difference is a good ¥5000. (☎23-1275; www2.ocn.ne.jp/ ~fdas/. Dorms ¥3000. Kitchen available. Countryhouse ¥8500, including breakfast and dinner. Check-in 4pm. Check-out 10am. Reservations recommended.) The owner can set you up with outdoor activities (rafting ¥6000). For last-minute, affordable accommodation, **Akiba Minshuku ❷** (あきば民宿), 4-1, Sagae-chō, is close to the station (5min. on foot). Head left out of the station and take the road parallel to the train tracks about 3½ blocks. (☎22-3205. *Tatami*-style rooms only. Breakfast and dinner included. Free parking. Check-in 3pm. Check-out 9:30am.)

For meals, you can't beat **Country Kitchen Kamushara ❶** (カントリーキチン我夢舎楽), a local hole-in-the-wall that serves cheap, homestyle sandwiches (¥600) and curry (¥800) for half the price they're worth. Exit the station and you'll see it right in front to the left, on the 2nd floor. (☎23-1495. Open daily 9am-10pm.) If you're already among the sights come lunchtime, hold your hunger until you get to Tomita Farm, where the **Melon Cafe ❶** serves decent sandwiches from ¥350, and stands sell fabulous melon and smooth lavender ice cream (¥250).

◙ SIGHTS. To experience the fruits of the town yourself, head first to the town's **winery** (Furano Wine Kōjō; 富良野ワイン工場), Shimizu-yama, where you can observe the wine-making process and stroll the beautiful lavender fields in its backyard. Though there's virtually nothing in the way of an English explanation, the unlimited free samples on the 3rd floor need no translation. (Take the sight-seeing bus to the first stop. ☎22-3242. Open May-Nov. daily 9am-4:30pm; Dec.-Apr. M-F 9am-4:30pm. Free.) From there, go right at the road's fork and follow its curve for about 25min. to the **Furano Grape Juice Factory** (ぶどう果汁工場), Nishigaku Niku, the town's main juice production center where you can see how the unfermented stuff is made and sample the flavors. (Take the sight-seeing bus to the 2nd stop. ☎23-3033. Open May-Sept. daily 9am-5pm. Free.) You'll need your own transport or the sight-seeing bus to get to **Tomita Farm** (ファーム富田)—a flower and lavender wonderland and unquestionably the one sight you *must* get to while in Furano. Though it's often crowded with Japanese tour groups, you can skip the gift shops and sneak out to the less-populated parts of the fields. As you stroll, keep your eyes peeled for the Tomita Lavender Museum, the Lavender Distillation House, and the Perfume House—a series of three museums that focuses on the history of lavender in Furano and its role in the production of commercial products. (Take the sight-seeing bus to the 3rd stop. ☎39-3939. Open daily. Free.)

If you have time, the **Furano Cheese Factory** (ふらのチーズ工場), the region's main milk and cheese producer, is in the opposite direction. Learn about dairy production by watching locals at work or even get your own hands-on butter and ice milk-making session. Free samples once again make up for the lack of English explanation. Take a local bus to the Cheese Factory (10min., 5 per day, last return at 4:10pm) from the station. (☎ 23-1156. Open daily May-Oct. 9am-5pm; Nov.-Apr. 9am-4pm. Closed 1st and 3rd Sa of the month. Free.)

DAISETSU-ZAN NATIONAL PARK
(大雪山国立公園)

What the Japanese named "big (大), snowy (雪), mountains (山)" and the Ainu considered "the garden where the gods play," you will experience as **Daisetsu-zan National Park,** Japan's largest and most rugged specimen of unadulterated, raw nature. In the heart of Hokkaidō, the park is a mountainous expanse of snow-glazed purple peaks, seas of hunter green trees, and the breeding house for almost every animal on the food chain. The region is so massive that one gets the feeling that man does not belong in this realm. Unlike Hokkaidō's other national parks, Daisetsu-zan is not streaked with roads—it's a largely untouched region that pro-

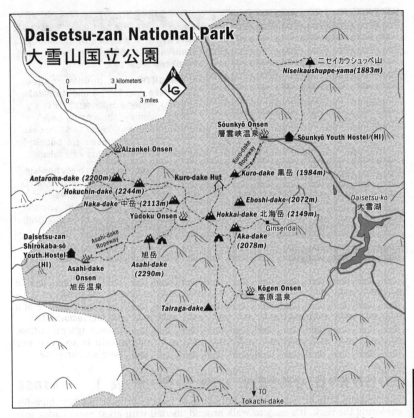

vides the hiker with limitless opportunities to climb for the sky, squat with brown bear families, and imagine the world as it was 1000 years ago. While most visitors come for a few days during the summer, some stay for weeks or months at a time. There's plenty of space, and even in the summer, when hordes of fanny pack-wearing, camera-fumbling tour groups make their way out here, the park appears uncrowded. Make reservations early, gather food and money before leaving the city, and bring your stamina. This is the gods' playground—you'll need the feet of a giant to hold your ground as you climb the jungle gym.

✈ ORIENTATION

Expansive as it is, Daisetsu-zan is easy to navigate once you've got the free maps, the English brochures, and your own A-378 helicopter. If you forgot your aviator license, refer to the **Getting Your Own Helicopter** section (pg. 769), or do like the rest of us and plan your daily hikes and trips from the the park's two main bases— **Sōunkyō Onsen** (層雲峡温泉) and **Asahi-dake Onsen** (旭岳温泉). The former is the larger, situated in the northern part of the park, and the latter is the less-touristed, in the western part. Both are accessible by public transportation, but to get between them, you'll have to go through Asahikawa since mountains prevent any direct route other than hiking. Said hike takes 2-4 days and a whole lotta spirit.

HOKKAIDŌ

AT A GLANCE

AREA: Mountains, mountains, and more mountains. Daisetsu-zan's terrain consists of soaring peaks, deep gorges, sparkling waterfalls, and endless forests. It covers 2300 sq. km (888 sq. mi.).

CLIMATE: Weather changes quickly in the mountains and seasonal temperature shifts can be severe. Winters bottom out at -30°C (-22°F) with lots of snow, and 28°C (82°F) summer heat will sweat your socks off. For forecasts, check the lists at visitor centers and hostels.

CAMPING: Pitching a tent is a great way to get into the wild, but it's by no means necessary, since there are affordable hostels and minshuku in the main areas.

GATEWAYS: It's easiest to go through **Asahikawa** (p. 698) from the west or **Kamikawa** in the east.

HIGHLIGHTS: Most people conquer **Asahi-dake** (旭日岳) and **Kuro-dake** (黒岳), either independently or in a 2- to 4-day journey that crosses both and connects Sōunkyō Onsen to Asahi-dake Onsen. Other must-sees are **Sōunkyō Gorge** (層雲峡) and the waterfalls.

WHEN TO GO: Unless you enjoy frostbite, come between June 20 and September 20 when the hiking and camping weather is ideal. The flowers are nicest in June and July, and fabulous **kōyō** (leaf-changing) season starts early in September.

ON THE WEB   Daisetsu-zan National Park: www.daisetsuzan.or.jp

In the less-traveled south of the park, **Kōgen Onsen** (高原温泉) offers lakeside seats when the leaves start changing in mid-September, and, if you're lonely, it's a good place to befriend a bear. For more info on how to get to Kōgen, inquire at a visitors center. Perhaps the wildest part of the park is around **Mt. Tomuraushi** (トムラウシ山), perfect for those who are seeking beauty and sheer, utter isolation. In the center of Daisetsu-zan National Park, the mountain is so pure and untouched that we had nothing to write about it. Oh yeah, there's a campsite.

SŌUNKYŌ ONSEN (層雲峡温泉)   ☎01658

The pleasant little hot springs town of Sōunkyō Onsen serves as the best base for exploring the park. It's easy to walk around, loaded with great hotel baths, and tame enough not to drive you nuts with its heavy tourism. Best of all, the town is perfectly located for hiking the mountains and walking to the waterfalls.

⌨ TRANSPORTATION AND PRACTICAL INFORMATION. The wheels on the **buses** go round and round, round and round, and round to Sōunkyō Onsen from both eastern and western Hokkaido. From the west, you'll have to go through **Asahikawa,** where national buses chug to the park via **Kamikawa,** some 25km to the northwest (1¾hr., 7 per day, ¥1900; bus boards in front of Asahikawa Station). If you're a JR pass-holder, you might take a train from Asahikawa to Kamikawa (40min.; about 1 per day; express ¥2150, local ¥1040) and then jump the same bus in front of JR Kamikawa Station (30min., 11 per day, ¥770). From the east and south, **Dōhoku Buses** (道北バス ; ☎0166-23-4161) connect Sōunkyō—also via Kamikawa—to: **Kitami** (2hr., 4 per day, ¥2500); **Kushiro** (about 4hr., 2 per day, ¥4790) via **Akan-ko Onsen** (3½hr., 2 per day, ¥3260); **Obihiro** (about 2hr., 2 per day, ¥2200). Reservations are necessary, so call ahead. From **Abashiri,** take a JR train along the Sekihoku Line to **Kitami** (60-70min.; 15 express and local per day; express ¥2650, local ¥1040) and take the bus from there. All buses end up at the **Sōunkyō Bus Station,** 5min. from the center of town. (☎5-3321. Small lockers ¥200. Open 8:30am-5:30pm.) Getting around locally is easy since accommodations and shops cluster in the town's tiny center. You may want to rent a bike for sightseeing—there's a **Rent-a-Cycle** (レンタサイクル) around the corner from the bus station (¥1500 per day). For a taxi, call **Sōunkyō Hire** (層雲峡ハイヤー ; ☎5-3221).

Just inside the main bus stop is the **Sōunkyō Tourist Booth** (層雲峡観光案内 所), Aza Sōunkyō, Kamikawa-chō, where you can get the low-down on the hoe-down. There are some English brochures, and the staff is helpful with booking beds (no charge) and organizing transport, but don't bother stopping if it's hiking info you're after. (☎5-3350. Very little English spoken. Open daily 10:20am-5:30pm.) Instead, head to the nearby **visitors center** (see **Sights**) for all outdoorsy matters, including hikes in other areas of the park. In an emergency, call ☎110 for **police**, ☎119 for **fire** or **ambulance**. Although you won't need much money out here, the **post office**, Sōunkyō, Kamikawa-chō, next to the tourist booth, has an **international ATM**. (☎5-3318. ATM available M-F 9am-5:30pm, Sa 9am-12:30pm.) **Postal code:** 078.

█▐ ACCOMMODATIONS AND FOOD. The only cheap beds in town are at **Sōunkyō Youth Hostel (HI) ❶** (層雲峡ユースホステル), a 10min. walk up the winding path to the left of the ropeway (as you face it). Clean and bustling with an international crowd, the lodge cooks great meals, houses big, comfy beds, and is an invaluable resource for learning about the area. It also has coupons for nearby *onsen* (¥500 per dip). Make reservations in advance, as the only other options nearby are fancy hotels. (☎5-3418; www.youthhostel.or.jp/sounkyo. Laundry ¥200. Breakfast ¥630. Dinner ¥1050. Internet ¥100 per 30min. Dorms ¥2940.) Among the pensions in town, **Minshuku Midori ❷** (民宿みどり) is the cheapest and has simple *tatami* rooms. Shoot straight out of the visitors center, cross the street, and turn left down the main pedestrian street. There's no English sign but you'll see the name of the minshuku in green. (☎5-3315. Check-in 3pm. Check-out 9am. Reservations recommended. ¥3500 per person, with 2 meals ¥6500.) Though there are a few drab *rāmen* joints in town, you're best off eating dinner at your hostel or hotel (from ¥1000) and relying on store-bought goods for lunch. To get to the only supermarket, steer toward town; across the brook from the bus station is **Umetsu Store** (梅津商店). The small selection of noodles will make you wish you'd stocked up on the good stuff before coming to Sōunkyō.

◪ SIGHTS. Start your day at the modern and appealing **Sōunkyō Visitors Center** (層雲峡ビジターセンター), where there's hiking information, videos on the park's natural phenomena (Japanese only), and fabulous photos of scenery and wildlife. The English hiking pamphlets are invaluable; if you don't see them on the rack, ask. You can also buy detailed maps. Follow the main stream toward the ropeway and the center is on the right just before the ropeway parking lot. (☎9-4400. Open June-Oct. daily 8am-6pm; Nov.-May Tu-Su 9am-5pm.) From the center, try exploring **Sōunkyō Gorge** (層雲峡). For a couple hours of amusement, find **Kobako** (小函), an 8km waterway of splashing falls and rigid rock cliffs. The entrance to the falls is about 3km from town, and though you can get there by foot (40min.) or car (5min.), it's best to go by bike so you can take advantage of the gorge's cycling path. Either rent a bike in town (see **Transportation and Practical Information**) or at the parking lot at the gorge entrance (¥1000 per day; ¥1200 per day with rent-and-return privileges). At the time of writing, the part of the cycling path with the best cliff views (the center) was closed. If this situation persists, you can get to the first set of waterfalls from town by biking to the main street, turning right onto the highway, and continuing straight to the first tunnel entrance. Turn right before entering the tunnel and you'll see the parking lot and the falls in front of you. From there, ride down the first part of the path to see the highlights: **Ryu-sei Falls** (流星の滝) and **Ginga Falls** (銀河の 滝). Return to the first tunnel and go through it. On the other side, turn right, and you will now be able to access the tail end of the path to see **Raiman Falls** and **Kinsi Falls**. For more views of the chiseled cliffs, enter the second tunnel in front of you and turn left on the way out—you'll see signs for **Ōbako** (大函), and the parking lot and brook landing are just ahead.

Though few travelers dare to come out during the blistering winter, those who do will find some pretty good and pretty disorganized skiing going on. There are no set trails or ski sessions, but it's common to get an unlimited ropeway/lift-pass (¥3600 per day), bring your own skis, and have your own way like in the good ol' days (from November). For more detailed info, try the visitors center.

■ **HIKING.** Almost everyone who comes to Sōunkyō Onsen makes a point of climbing **Kuro-dake** (黒岳 ; 1984m), a nearby mountain beauty with celestial views. The hike is fairly painless and it only takes a few hours if you use the ropeway. Start at the white and brown **ropeway station,** where you can load up on water and supplies. The route to the peak has three main parts—from the base to the fifth station (1½-2hr.), from the fifth station to the seventh station (30min.), and from there on up (1-1½hr.). The difficulty and duration of the hike will depend on how far you have the ropeway carry you. The toughest should start up the trail to the right of the ropeway station and never look back—it takes about 4hr. up and 2½hr. down without any assistance. Those with an easier route in mind should hop the state-of-the-art **ropeway,** which rockets you up to the fifth station (20min.; every 20min; ¥900, round-trip ¥1650; operates daily June 25 6am-7pm; Aug. 26-Sept. 30 6am-6pm; Oct. 1-15 6am-5pm; Oct. 16-31 7am-4:30pm; Nov. 8am-4:30pm; Dec.-Jan. 9am-4pm; Feb.-Mar. 8am-4pm; Apr.-May 7am-5pm), and then walk 200m to the old-school chairlift nearby. With the **chairlift** (30min.; runs continuously; ¥400, round-trip ¥600) you can reach the seventh station without breaking a sweat and continue from there. The hiking trail is especially rocky from the seventh station to the top. Be careful, especially when descending. Close to the top, the stone steps converge for the first time, and, seconds later, a stunning panorama exposes the surrounding mountaintops.

Some people are so amazed by the views that they can't help but extend their one-day hike into a journey through the mountains. If you're so moved, there are a couple options. The first is **Aka-dake** (赤だけ ; 2078m), a nearby mountain whose views are especially fabulous when the leaves change color. From Kuro-dake's peak it takes about 3hr. to summit Aka-dake, and from there it's another 2½ hr. to descend to its base at **Ginsendai** (銀泉台 ; 1490m). If you want to crash along the way, **Kuro-dake Hut ❶** is some 20min. past Kuro-dake's peak. (Sleeping bag rental ¥1000 per night. Snacks and water ¥300. Blankets ¥300. Open 8am-9pm. ¥1500.) **Hakūn Hut ❶** is another option, about an hour away after you pass Aka-dake's peak (No rentals. ¥1000.) Confirm with an updated schedule, but there should be buses from **Ginsendai** back to **Sōunkyō Onsen** during summer (about 1hr., July-Sept. 2 per day, ¥800). The second option is a 3- or 4-day journey that leads from Kuro-dake to Asahi-dake peak and Asahi-dake Onsen. For more details, inquire at a visitor center and see the **Hiking** section in Asahi-dake (p. 707).

As for hiking practicalities, keep in mind that it's extremely unpleasant climbing in cold rain, especially when clouds block all the beautiful views—check conditions at tourist offices or hostels. If you don't want to take your luggage along for the ride, consider sending it by *takkyūbin* (delivery service) to where you're headed. Those with bee allergies should take precautions, as there are swarms of them toward the tops of the mountains.

ASAHI-DAKE ONSEN (旭日岳温泉) ☎ 0166

Across the mountains from Sōunkyō and about 60km east of Asahikawa sits **Asahi-dake Onsen,** the more subdued hiking base for Daisetsu-zan. The town consists of a single long and winding road, and aside from hotels and the ropeway, there's nothing here but hiking and the great outdoors. Take care of all practical matters before coming, as there are no stores or shops to satisfy your material cravings.

⚡🚌 TRANSPORTATION AND PRACTICAL INFORMATION. When it comes to reaching this remote *onsen* town, there's good news and bad news. The bad news is that it's only accessible by **bus** from Asahikawa; the good news is that it's free in the winter and surprisingly cheap otherwise. **Denki Kidō** (電気起動) runs the buses from Asahikawa's JR station via **Tenjin-kyō, Higashikawa**, and various other local stops (1¾hr.; June 15-Oct. 15 3-4 per day, otherwise 2 per day). Between June 15 and October 15, it costs ¥1000 from Asahikawa, in the off-season absolutely nothing. On the return it's always free, provided you spend at least ¥2000 at one of the town's accommodations (including the youth hostel) or at the ropeway and get a coupon (otherwise it's ¥2000). Since there's no bus station in town, the buses stop along the main road—in front of the ropeway, across the street from the youth hostel, and across the street from the Grand Hotel Taisetsu (グランドホテル大雪). If you're driving, get a good map and plot your route before departing—the roads are tricky and it's not difficult to take a wrong turn. For further information, head to the **visitors center**, 5min. down from the ropeway station. In an emergency, call ☎ 110 for **police**, ☎ 119 for **fire** or **ambulance**. For **currency exchange, postal services, gas**, and the like, your only options are 30km away in the town of Higashikawa. To get there, take the same bus as above.

🏠🍴 ACCOMMODATIONS AND FOOD. Though there's no other budget choice to compare it with, the ◼**Daisetsu-zan Shirokaba-sō Youth Hostel (HI) ❶** (大雪山白樺荘ユースホステル), Asahi-dake Onsen, Higashikawa-chō, is a sublime and spacious inn that redefines "youth hostel." An all-ages international crowd enjoys spotless facilities, luxury dinners, and a soothing outdoor *onsen*. Family-run and staffed with English speakers, the hostel fills up in summer, so make reservations early. (☎ 97-2246; www.ai.wakwak.com/~shirakaba. Check-in 3pm. Check-out 10am. Breakfast ¥600. Dinner ¥1000. Laundry ¥200. Cross-country ski rental ¥300 per day; largest size 28cm—about US men's 10. Members ¥3200, nonmembers ¥4100. Private room ¥4900 per person.) Next door is the **Nutapukaushipe Lodge ❷** (ロッジヌタプカウシペ), which is a bit smaller and cozier. All rooms are *tatami*-style and the log-cabin feel complements the considerate staff. Get decent *rāmen* (¥600) at the in-house restaurant. (☎ 97-2150. Restaurant open noon-5pm. Check-in 3pm. Check-out 10am. No smoking. Reservations recommended. ¥4500 per person.) For camping, head across the street and bear right down the path. The **campsite ❸** offers no elysian views, but it's got a social atmosphere and the management rents cheap equipment. (☎ 97-2544. Open Jan. 20-Sept. 20. 10-person tents ¥520. Air mattresses ¥100. Sleeping bags ¥210. ¥210 per person.)

Most travelers here settle for breakfast and dinner at their lodge and take lunch out to the trails. Hotels and the hostel sell **obentō** lunch sets, which are usually *onigiri* (rice wrapped in seaweed) based, but come with some veggies also. If rice and seaweed three times a day is not your jam, head to the ropeway station where a second-floor restaurant serves mediocre curry rice (¥600), *rāmen* (¥700-750), and *donburi* (¥750). For snacks and drinks to take on your hikes, rely on the ropeway gift store (first floor) and the youth hostel.

🥾 HIKING. Orient yourself at the **visitors center**, Asahi-dake Onsen, Higashikawa-chō, 10min. up the street from the youth hostel. There's an old exhibit on the park's animals and nature, and the English-speaking (or at least understanding) staff is armed with hiking contour maps of the mountains (¥200), portable toilets (free), and three amusing Japanese videos on the surrounding nature (1hr.), flowers (30min.), and animals (10min.). Before hitting the trails, check the weather board (one-week predictions) and ask about local hikes. (☎ 97-2153. Open June-Oct. daily 9am-5pm; Nov.-May Tu-Su 10am-4pm.)

HOKKAIDŌ

One popular trail begins just left of the visitors center and winds through a sea of trees. As you start down the path, you'll cross a little bridge where there's a map of the trails. Continuing left at the fork for 15-20min. leads you to a four-way intersection. Going straight and over the bridge leads you to the rest of the 1hr. course, and going (far) left leads you to the rest of the 30min. course. Both end on the town's main road, and if you turn left and walk straight (15min. for shorter course; 1hr. for longer course), you'll find yourself back at the visitors center.

When it comes to serious hiking, let there be no doubt about it—most people come to conquer Hokkaidō's tallest peak, **Asahi-dake** (旭日岳 ; 2290m). Gleaming gold in the summer and salty-white in the winter, the volcanic wonder is perfect for a dayhike and blessed with some of the most paradisiacal views in the park. On the way up you can either take the **ropeway** (☎97-2234) at the very end of the town's road to the fifth station (10min.; every 15min.; July 1-Oct. 10 ¥1500, round-trip ¥2800; Oct. 11-June 30 ¥1000/¥1800) and then hike to the peak (about 2½hr.), or you can hike the whole way up (4-5hr.) and save a night's worth of accommodation. Whatever you do, climbing down will take you about 1½hr. from the peak to the fifth station, and another 1½hr. to the base on foot. The hike is not particularly dangerous, but there are some steep sections to watch out for, especially since the trail is mostly made up of unstable rocks.

Once at Asahi-dake's summit, if you choose to extend your hike, there several options. One of the shorter routes traces a counter-clockwise loop through the peaks and valleys of **Mamiya-dake** (間宮岳 ; 2185m), **Nakadake-bunki** (中岳分岐), and **Susoaidaira** (裾合平 ; 1690m), eventually ending at Asahi-dake's 5th station, where you can continue down by ropeway or on foot. The hike has flowers along the way, but its main highlight is undoubtedly **Nakadake Rotemburo** (中岳温泉), a free outdoor *onsen* that re-energizes tired hikers' souls and soles at the halfway point between Nakadake-bunki and Susoaidaira. Plan about 6hr. for the hike from base camp, more if you plan on bathing for hours.

A longer route from the peak of Asahi-dake journeys through the mountains, past **Ohachidaira** (御鉢平) and to Sōunkyō Onsen in the park's east. The pilgrimage takes 2-4 days—depending on the weather and your physical condition. Nothing short of amazing, the hike brings you face-to-face with the mountains of the gods. Once you reach **Mamiya-dake** (間宮岳 ; 2185m), an hour from Asahi-dake, you'll have to choose between two routes. To the right is the southern route, which leads to **Arrai-dake** (荒井岳), **Matsuda-dake** (松田岳), and **Hokkai-dake** (北海岳), good for flower-watching, but harder because of a river crossing in the latter half of the hike. To the left is the northern route, which leads to **Nakadake-bunki** (中岳分岐), **Naka-dake** (中岳 ; 2113m), and **Kumono-daira** (雲の平) and makes for an easier, equally scenic hike. The routes converge at a hut 20min. from the peak of **Kuro-dake** (黒岳), where food and water are available (¥300). If you're traveling to Sōunkyō Onsen first, it is possible to do this hike in reverse. For specifics on each leg and safety precautions, check with the visitors center. Take water, food, raingear, and warm clothing—it gets cold at the top. Whatever you do, **stay away from Yūdoku Onsen** (有毒温泉), in the mountains between the northern and southern trails—the hot springs are poisonous and will kill you.

In the winter, cross-country and alpine skiing take over as the main sport, but it's not worth making a special trip out for it. Trails are limited (only 4 alpine) and relatively narrow; trees pose obstacles. Ropeway lift tickets (4-hr. ¥2800, day-pass ¥3800) will get you up the hill, and for good trail information, stop by the visitors center. While they rent equipment there—alpine skis, boots, and poles (¥800 per day; largest-sized boots 28.5cm—US men's 10½), cross-country skis (¥800 per day), and snowshoes (¥800 per day; largest size 27.5cm—US men's 9½)—you're better off getting the cheap stuff at the youth hostel if you're staying there.

ABASHIRI (網走) ☎ 0152

In Abashiri—the gateway to eastern Hokkaidō—two attractions are meant to send shivers down your spine. The first is a sea of snow-topped icebergs that appears in January or February, and the second is a world-*infamous* prison that has housed some of Japan's most dangerous criminals. Abashiri is a nice stop-over in winter, when cross-country skiing and ice fishing take center stage. Summer visitors should spend a day here before heading to Shiretoko National Park.

⌷ TRANSPORTATION. The closest airport is **Memanbetsu Airport** (女満別空港 ; ☎ 74-4182), some 21km out of town and reachable by airport shuttle from the **Abashiri Bus Terminal** (30min., roughly 70min. before flights, ¥750). Flight times and prices for less common destinations change frequently, but you can count on routes to: **Nagoya** (2hr., 2 per day, ¥37,500); **Sapporo** (45min., 6 per day, ¥18,000); **Tōkyō** (1¾hr., 4 per day, ¥35,000). The easiest way to get to Abashiri is by Ohotsuku express JR **train** from Sapporo (5¼hr., 5 per day, ¥9130) or Asahikawa (3½hr., 5 per day, ¥7240). **Local trains** run on the Senmō Line, connecting to Shiretoko-Shari (45min., 9 per day, ¥810), near the national park, and Kushiro (3½hr., 4 per day, ¥3570), farther south. Trains stop at **Abashiri Station**, 2-2, Shinmachi (☎ 43-6197), on the west side of town, just below the Abashiri River. Inside are storage lockers (¥300-500) and a travel agency. Alternatively, cheaper **central buses** run daily from Sapporo Station. (6hr.; every 2hr.; ¥6210, students ¥5600. Reservations required; call ☎ 011-231-0600.) **Local buses** run from the station to the ferry port in **Utoro** (2hr., June 1-Oct. 15 3 per day, ¥2150). All buses stop at **Abashiri Bus Terminal**, South 2, West 1 (☎ 23-2185), just north of the town center beside the Asahikawa River. From the train station, turn right out the exit and take the main road east for about six blocks; it's on the left. (Open daily 6:40am-6pm.) If you're coming from Wakkanai, you'll have to swing through Asahikawa, since no trains travel Hokkaidō's east coast. It's annoying and costly, but not as much as taking the bus and transfering at Nakayubetsu, Monbetsu, Osumu, Esashi, and Hamatonbetsu—if you're out of your mind enough to do it, the total price is ¥9170.

Though Abashiri itself isn't very big, having your own transport makes getting around easier—especially if you're heading to Shiretoko next. **Toyota Rent-a-Lease** (トヨタレンタリース), 2-22-4, Shinmachi, is down the main road as you exit left from the station. (☎ 43-0100. Open daily 8am-8pm.) **Eki Rent-a-Car** (駅レンタカー) is in front of the station. (☎ 43-6197. Open daily 8am-8pm.) Both have similar rates (low-season from ¥6500 per day; high-season ¥8500). All agencies get super busy in July and August, so reserve a car well ahead of time if you're traveling then.

⌷ PRACTICAL INFORMATION. There's a **tourist office** on the right as you exit the station. The staff doesn't speak much English, but they have an English brochure, maps, and pamphlets. (☎ 43-4261; www2s.biglobe.ne.jp/~abashiri. Open daily 9am-5pm. Closed Su Nov.-Dec.). There are a couple **coin laundries** (¥300 per load) by the station, one across the street and left of the station exit, the other left of the exit on the station side of the street. In an emergency, call ☎ 110 for **police**, ☎ 119 for **fire** or **ambulance**. If you're just after the **international ATM**, exit the train station to the left and you'll find a small post office branch on the first block. To **exchange money**, hit up the main **post office**, South 4, East 3-8, which also has an international ATM (available M-F 8:45am-7pm, Sa-Su 9am-5pm). It's east of the town center, 20min. by foot. From the main road in front of the JR station, head east, turn right onto Rte. 39 a block after the bus terminal, and turn left on the main shopping street two blocks up; the post office is five blocks down on the right. (☎ 43-337. Open M-F 9am-4pm; Sa-Su 9am-7pm.) **Postal code:** 093.

⟨⟩ ACCOMMODATIONS AND FOOD. The best kept accommodation secret in town is **Ranpu Minshuku ❶** (民宿ランプ), 3-3-9, Shinmachi, which has free Internet, proximity to the station, and an affable owner. Head to the back of the station and cross the tracks. At the end of the wooden house on the left, go toward the main road and continue straight. It's a 15min. walk. (☎43-3928; www2.ocn.ne.jp/~lamp-in. Check-in noon-midnight. Check-out 10am. Breakfast ¥250. Bike rental ¥300 per hr., ¥1000 per day. Laundry ¥300. ¥2800 per person.) The closest youth hostel is **Abashiri Ryūhyō-no-Oka (HI) ❸** (網走流氷の丘ユース ホステル), 22-6, Aza Meiji, which has very clean rooms and a hilltop view of the Sea of Okhotsk. Take a bus headed for Futatsu-iwa to Meiji-iriguchi (12min., 4 per day noon-5pm, ¥270). From there, follow the signs uphill (10min.). If you take the 5pm bus and call ahead, they'll pick you up at the stop. (☎43-8558; www2.ocn.ne.jpwebsite. Breakfast ¥600. Dinner ¥1000. Laundry ¥200. Check-in 4pm. Check-out 10am. Dorms ¥3250 for members; doubles ¥8500.) A bit out of town, **Abashiri Gensei-kaen Youth Hostel (HI) ❶** (網走原生花園ユースホステル), 208-2, Kitahama, beside Lake Tōfutsu, has exceptionally nice staff who give tips on the area. Hop a JR train to Kitahama (15min., 9 per day, ¥260) and exit the station left. You'll pass a **Seico Mart;** after the second light, bear right after the Lake Tōfutsu sign (とうふつ湖). At the end of the road you'll see the sign; turn right and head all the way down. It's about 20min. by foot. (☎46-2630; www.sapporo.cool.ne.jp/genseikaen. Washer ¥100; dryer ¥100 for 1hr. Cross-country ski rental ¥800 per day. Bike rental ¥200 per hr. Check-in 3:30pm. Check-out 10am. Curfew 10pm. Dorms ¥2900.) Other options crowd the station area; the homely **Abashiri Green Hotel ❸** (網走グリーンホテル), 1-2-9, Shinmachi-chō, is your best bet. (☎43-8080; fax 43-5651. Breakfast ¥1000. Dinner ¥1500. Check-in 3pm. Check-out 10am. No curfew. Singles ¥5500.)

While it's a given that Abashiri has fabulous fish, many rave especially about the juicy crabs. You'll need a car to get to one of the cheaper options, **Irimaru Suisan ❹** (入り丸水産), 39-3, Masu-ura, about 15min. away on the east coast of town. The *kani-don* and *ikura-don* (crab or salmon roe over rice; ¥800) are both great, as are the whole crab plates, which start from ¥4000. (☎43-8890. Open Su-M and W-Sa 11am-5pm.) Right of the station exit is **Cafe Brasserie Anjiro ❷** (あんじろ), 2-2-6, Shinmachi, where the special omelette rice set (without seafood, ¥900) and big salads (¥500) are the way to go. (Open daily 10am-10pm.) If you're hitting the road, the 24hr. **Lawson** next to the station has supplies and phone cards.

◙ SIGHTS. Though Abashiri often gets reduced to Shiretoko's travel hub, it has three museums in its south, reachable by bus. Since they're relatively close, all can be visited in a few hours. The **⊠Hokkaidō Museum of Northern Peoples** (北海道立北方民族博物館), Aza Shiomi, is the best of them, paying deserved tribute to the world's northern indigenous tribes—from the Ainu to the Inuit. Inside are brilliant artifacts, life-sized totem poles, documentaries, and even English translations. (☎45-3888; www.ohotoku26.or.jp/hpohm. Open Tu-Su 9:30am-4:30pm. ¥300, college students ¥100.) To get to the museum, hop a bus from the JR station; it'll drop you off at the door (20min., 1 per hr., ¥330). Taxis cost ¥1200-1300 and take about 10min. From here, exit left onto the main road and continue straight until you see signs for the **Okhotsk Ryū-hyō Museum** (オホーツク流氷館), 245-1, Aza Tentozan. At the signs, turn left and head uphill to the compound of buildings on your right. Not as cool as it sounds, the Ryū-hyō is an unfortunate summer substitute for the city's famous winter glaciers. (☎43-5951; www.ryuhyokan.com. Open daily Apr.-Oct 8am-6pm; Nov.-Mar. 9am-4:30pm. ¥520.) Turn right out of the museum and right on the main road, and follow the signs 1.5km to the chilling **Abashiri Prison Museum** (網走監獄博物館), 1-1, Yobito. The grounds are fairly large and though the prison is neither in its original location nor consists completely of its original buildings, it reveals Japanese life behind bars. Amusing wax figures lighten the experience. To avoid walking, hop the bus from one of the other museums. (☎45-2411. Open daily Apr.-Oct. 8am-6pm; Nov.-Mar. 9am-5pm. ¥1050, students ¥730.)

In the winter, there are two ways to experience Abashiri's sea-splitting glaciers—the free way, looking out from the shoreline, or the paid way, on a heavy-duty tour ship. For the former, consider heading to **Ten-tōzan** peak, just behind the train station, where the views are clear, stunning, and endless, or just keep your eyes peeled out by Kitahama Station. For the more thrilling experience, board one of the **Aurora ice-breaking ships** (おーろら). Buy tickets at the Aurora terminal, at the east of town on the Sea of Okhotsk. To get there, catch a bus or taxi (10min., about ¥1100) from the JR station. (☎43-6000. Tours daily Jan. every 2hr. 9am-3pm; Feb.-Mar. every 1½hr. 9:30am-3:30pm; Apr. every 2hr. 9:30am-3:30pm. ¥3000.) In celebration of the glaciers, the city hosts the **Abashiri Okhotsk Drift Ice Festival** mid-February. The spectacle showcases illuminated snow and ice sculptures and is held in Abashiri Pier Square, on the east side of town (info ☎44-6111).

AKAN NATIONAL PARK (阿寒国立公園) ☎0154

Blessed with a series of navy lakes and massive volcanoes, Akan National Park is known for its beloved green algae, *marimo*, and its Ainu village, **Ainu Kotan** (アイヌコタン). Sweeping into the park, you'll feel like you're getting a firsthand look at the big and busy household of Mother Nature. First are the beautiful children, the caldera lakes—**Akan** (阿寒), **Penketō** (ペンケトー), **Panketō** (パンケトー), **Tarō** (太郎), and **Jirō** (次郎). Then there are the parents—**Mt. O-Akan** and **Mt. Me-Akan**—a highly unpredictable volcanic couple, who've attracted the neighbors' attention since the Missus erupted with steam in the late '50s. The moody group of lakes and mountains cause the climate to swing from -4°F in the winter to 95°C in the summer, allowing visitors to hike when it's warm and ski when the snow's right. It's nice to spend a couple days here while between Daisetsu-zan and Shiretoko, but it's not a priority if you've already seen more impressive Lake Tōya.

▮ TRANSPORTATION.
The only sure way to get to Akan National Park without your own transport is by **bus**, and you'll likely have to transfer. From Asahikawa (4¾hr., 2 per day, ¥4580) and Kushiro (2hr., 5 per day, ¥2650) take an **Akan Bus** to **Akan Kohan**. (☎67-2205; www.akanbus.co.jp. Reservations required.) If you're coming from Shiretoko, take a bus from the **Utoro Terminal** to **Memanbetsu Airport** (1¾hr., 1 per day, ¥2700) and another bus from there to Akan Kohan (4½hr., 1 per day, ¥5890), or, alternatively, take a bus from **Utoro Terminal** to the **Shari JR Station** (50min., 8 per day, ¥1490) and take another bus from there to the station in **Mashū** (1hr., 2 per day, ¥1230) or **Kawayu Onsen** (50min., 2 per day, ¥900). Within the park, infrequent (and very expensive) buses connect Akan Kohan to **Kawayu Onsen** (2¾hr., 3 per day, ¥3250) and **Mashū** (1hr., 3 per day, ¥2030). All arrive and depart from the local bus station in Akan Kohan, on the main road in the north of town.

▮▮ ORIENTATION AND PRACTICAL INFORMATION.
Resting in the heart of eastern Hokkaidō, Akan National Park consists of three main areas—**Akan Kohan Onsen** (阿寒湖畔温泉), **Kawayu Onsen** (川湯温泉), and **Mashū Onsen** (摩周温泉). Each spa town sits by a scenic lake, and while the latter two pair off together northeast, the former hangs by itself in the southeast. Akan Kohan has the most to see and the cheapest accommodations, making it the best choice as a base. As for getting around, you'll need your own wheels unless you have the patience to wait for local buses or the time to hitchhike. (*Let's Go* never recommends hitchhiking.) Consider attacking the park by spending a day in Kohan, and then moving to the surrounding lakes and mountains for a hike or two.

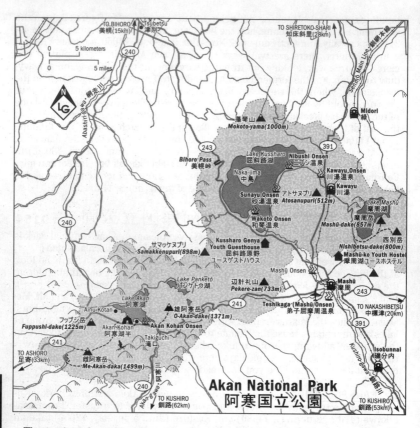

The **tourist information office**, Akan-ko, Akan-chō, is down the street from the local bus station and carries brochures on the town, hiking, and surrounding towns. The one-woman staff makes hotel reservations (for a 10% charge). (☎67-3200. Open daily 9am-6pm.) In an emergency, call ☎110 for **police**, ☎119 for **fire** or **ambulance**. For **money exchange** and an **international ATM**, count on the **Central Post Office**, 2-6-13, Akan-ko Onsen. (☎ 67-2158, exchange available M-F 9am-4pm; ATM available M-F 8:45am-6pm, Sa 9am-5pm, Su 9am-2pm). **Postal code:** 085.

⌂ ⌂ ACCOMMODATIONS AND FOOD. Though there's no youth hostel in Akan Kohan, there are a bunch of cheap minshuku hidden among the flashy hotels. **Kiri Minshuku ❷** (桐民宿), 4-3-26, Akan-ko, Akan-chō, is the best of the bunch, with spotless *tatami* rooms, flavorful meals, and a scorching-hot *onsen*. The laid-back owner speaks some English. From the bus station, cross the street and go down the first street to your right. Make the first left onto the main road and follow it to the tourist shops. The minshuku is on the second floor of the woodworking shop a few doors from the food store. (☎67-2755. Breakfast ¥500. Dinner ¥1500. ¥3500.) If Kiri is full, head a bit farther down the road to **Minshuku Yamaguchi ❷** (民宿山口), 5-3-2, Akan-ko Onsen, Akan-chō, on the right. Though it's a bit more expensive, the owner is great and her bilingual parrot can teach you Japanese. (☎67-2555; www.tabi-hokkaido.co.jp/~yamaguchi. Laundry ¥200. Check-in 2pm. Check-out 10am. ¥4000, with 2 meals ¥5500.) While **Akan-ko Camp-**

site ❶ (阿寒湖畔場) is nothing exciting, it has clean facilities and a friendly crowd lights up the barbecue in summer. The grounds are past the Ainu village—walk up the line of stores, past the Ainu performance center, and bear left across the street. (☎67-3263. Showers ¥100 per 6min. Parking ¥410. Laundry ¥200. 5-person tents ¥2000. Sites ¥400.) If you're stuck in one of the other parts of the park for the night, call upon **Mashū-ko Youth Hostel (HI) ❶** (摩周湖ユースホ ステル ; ☎82-3098; breakfast ¥630; dinner ¥1050; members ¥3360, nonmembers ¥4410) or the **Kussharo Genya Youth Guesthouse (HI) ❶** (屈斜路原野ユース ゲストハウス ; ☎84-2609; members ¥3500, nonmembers ¥4500). Call for directions.

For cheap food, skip the overpriced restaurants by Ainu Kotan and head straight to the local market, **Kanayama Shiten** (カナヤマ支店), 4-3-29, Akan-ko Onsen, Akan-chō. You'll find nice box lunches as well as fruit, veggies, and the works. It's across from Hotel Emerald on the main shopping street. (☎67-2411. Open daily 9am-10pm.) For dinner, head toward the tourist center to **Nabekyū ❸** (奈辺久), a great *tempura* shop. The best deal is the *ten-don* (tempura shrimp over rice; ¥800); other options range ¥1000-2000. (Open daily 11am-3pm and 6-9pm.) At odd hours, count on the 24hr. **Lawson** convenience store, 2-2-36, Akan-ko Onsen, Akan-chō (☎607-4163), at the end of the shopping street toward the tourist center.

◪ **SIGHTS.** The park's sites are concentrated around touristy Akan Kohan. You'll want to check out the *marimo* phenomenon, so for the biggest display of the little green monsters, head to the **Marimo Exhibition Center** (マリモ展示観察セン ター), some 6km away on the little island of Chu-rui (チュルイ島). Inside, you'll find centuries-old *marimo* the size of basketballs and an exhibit describing how the algae form and multiply. Although everything is in Japanese, all you really need is your eyes. To get to the island, take the **sightseeing cruise ship** that departs down the street from the main shopping area, around the corner from Hotel Emerald. The steep price includes a worthwhile 40min. tour of the lake's more remote areas. (Boats every 30-60min. until 5pm. ¥1220. Buy tickets at the dock.) For a look at *marimo*, head to **The Akan Kohan Eco Museum Center** (阿寒 湖畔エコミュージアムセンター), 1-1-1, Akan-ko Onsen, Akan-chō, on the far western end of town. Take the main shopping street toward the tourist office and it's at the end of the road, a 15min. walk. This small display covers the algae's existence throughout the world. Grab an English brochure and check out the forestry and animal exhibits also. (☎67-4100. Open Su-M and W-Sa 9am-7pm.

THE LOCAL LEGEND

TICKLE ME MARIMO

They're big, they're green, and they're multiplying fast enough to take over the entire tourist town of Akan Kohan. What are they? *Marimo!* The spherical little algae that inhabit the bottom of Lake Akan and are so fuzzy and adorable that you'll want to kidnap one to take home and cuddle with.

But keep your scuba gear in the closet, my friend. As rare and desirable as spherical *marimo* might be, they're also an endangered species which can only be found in a few spots in the world—Lake Akan being one of them. Ironically, the species didn't depopulate until the government declared them a national treasure in 1921. This provoked merchants and travelers to take as many *marimo* out of the lake as possible in order to get their hands on an official national treasure.

Today, the species (which can reach a size of 30cm in diameter) has a more optimistic future due to an increase in the Akan community's awareness. Since 1950, the Ainu have honored the algae by holding an annual Marimo Festival, and throughout the town, various museums have worked hard to showcase and explain the green algae to its curious visitors. You, too, can get a feel for the creature by visiting the local sights and buying your own baby *marimo* from one of the town's gift shops. Just remember one thing...keep the tickling to a minimum because your *marimo* will die out of water!

Free.) If you exit the museum to the right and hook around the corner, you'll find yourself along **Yūhodō** (遊歩道), a narrow forest walking path. A pleasant stroll leads you to a quiet part of Akan Lake, home to what the Ainu call **Bokke** (ボッケ), and English speakers would call a mud volcano. Listen for the hisses of bubbling mud on your way down the path, and you can't miss the incessantly erupting brown pool. Just a bit farther along the path is an Ainu **Memorial to Marimo.** If you continue as the path curves around the lake, you'll end up just downhill from where you started. Back on the other end of town is Akan Kohan's very own Ainu village—**Ainu Kotan** (アイヌコタン)—which might as well be Disneyland. Only about 200 Ainu live in Akan Kohan, and, as the line of gift shops indicate, they seem to be too busy selling their culture to actually be living it. The best way to extract a drop of authenticity is to strike up a conversation with one of the Ainu or head up to the Ainu Theater, where excellent free English packets describe the history, culture, and contemporary politics surrounding the indigenous peoples. There are daily song and dance performances (30min., 6 per day, ¥1200).

When the snow buries the pretty lakes and mountains in the winter, don't fret; there's good skiing in the back of town off Rte. 241. To get the slopes, head left from the bus stop on the main road, make your first left, and hike up the hill; it's a 15min. walk. Daily lift tickets run about ¥3000, with lessons and equipment rentals available. Ice skating is also popular, and, a few years back, Asia's first international skating marathon was held on Lake Akan. For skate rentals and skating information, inquire at the the tourist information center.

■ **FESTIVALS.** The **Ainu Marimo Festival** is held every October to pay tribute to the endangered algae, *marimo*. Three days of joyous fireworks and games culminate with a somber climax during which the eldest member of the Ainu community returns a *marimo* back to the lake. If you miss it, consider holding your own *marimo* ceremony by taking a fuzz ball to the bath with you. Beneath Ainu Kohan's plastic-coated shell lies a fabulous *onsen* retreat with over thirty hotels and ryokan. Though you're likely to have a bath wherever you stay, something spacious and tempting waits at **Hotel Emerald** (ホテルエメラルド), right on the town's main shopping street.

■ **HIKING.** The most satisfying way to see the park's lakes and forests is to hike its two highest peaks—**Mt. Me-Akan** (1499m) and **Mt. O-Akan** (1371m). Mt. Me-Akan is higher and easier to climb, and its crater is so large that the gods could use it for putting practice. The main peak of the volcano dates back 15,000 years and numerous eruptions since have given it its unusual, appealing shape. Although there are various routes up the mountain, most opt for the convenient **Nonaka Onsen Course** (野中温泉 コース) since it requires little time (ascent 2hr.; descent 1¼hr.) and offers a stunning view of the range's steamy gray mountains and emerald Lake Onetto. In summer, reach the beginning of the hike by bus (20min., 3 per day July 1-Oct. 20, ¥840) from the Akan Kohan Bus Station, then following signs through a zig-zag path of spruce trees. Be cautious along the steep portions of the hike, especially as you head to the summit after resting at the mountain's ninth station.

Unlike his wife, **Mt. O-Akan** is a dormant volcano that gets much less action when the summer heat kicks in. Perhaps they're divorced. The mountain is about 10,000 years old and attracts serious hikers who want lake views. From Akan Kohan, hop a bus for Kushiro and get off at the trail entrance stop, **Takiguchi** (滝口 ; 5-7min., 5 per day, ¥280). Trudging up the trail, you'll encounter former Siamese lakes Jirō and Tarō, separated soon after birth when Mt. O-Akan erupted on top of them. Continue up the steep part of the trail for a couple hours and by the 5th station, the surroundings start to thin. At the peak, the view of Lake Akan is fabulous.

Whichever peak you climb, be sure to take rain gear as the weather can change suddenly. Locals advise you to make noise and run away if you see bears. For info on other mountain trails—each of which have their own appeal, time requirement, and difficulty—snag the two brochures from the Akan Kohan tourist office.

SHIRETOKO NATIONAL PARK
(知床国立公園)

☎ 01522

Only a couple hours from forgettable Abashiri is the unbelievably wild frontier you've always dreamed of—Shiretoko National Park, a largely undiscovered region on Hokkaidō's remote eastern peninsula. To the Ainu, it was "the end of the world," where land met ocean for one final time in an epic showdown. When you see the steaming hot waterfalls, bundles of misty volcanoes and valleys, and piercing blue sunsets, you may begin to believe it. For the best exploration, you'll need your own car, which you can rent in Abashiri.

⬛ TRANSPORTATION

Getting to Shiretoko is relatively easy, but that's only because there are few options. By **car**, take Rte. 334 from Abashiri or somewhere else north of the peninsula; 2hr. later, you arrive in Utoro—still on Rte. 334. The second option is a **train-bus** combo: take a local JR train from Abashiri to **Shari** (40min., 9 per day, ¥810), then grab a park-bound bus from Shari's JR Station to **Utoro** (50min., 8 per day, ¥1490). Alternatively, take a bus from **Memanbetsu Airport** (女満別空港 ; about 2hr., 1 per day, ¥2700). From Sapporo or Asahikawa, you'll have to go to via Shari or

Abashiri. All buses to the park arrive at **Utoro Bus Terminal** (ウト ロバスターミナル), 170, Utoro-Nishi, Shari-machi, in the center of Utoro town and 10min. from the park entrance. (☎ 4-2054. Open daily 7:45am-4:20pm.) From there you can catch a park shuttle bus (see below) or one of the buses that connect Utoro and Rausu (50min., 2 per day, ¥1310).

🔲 🔃 PRACTICAL INFORMATION AND ORIENTATION

The park's **tourist information center**, 190, Utoro-Nishi, is in the bus terminal building. Although nothing's in English and the staff only speaks Japanese, they're helpful with transportation and general information. (☎ 4-2639. Open daily July-Sept. 8am-7:30pm; Oct.-Nov. 8:30am-6pm; Dec. 9am-5pm; Jan.-Feb. 6 9am-5pm; Feb. 7-Mar. 13 9am-7:30pm; Mar. 14-Apr. 9am-5:30; May-June 8:30am-6pm.) In an emergency, call ☎ 110

HOKKAIDŌ

THE BIG SPLURGE

WATCH OUT FOR THAT TREE!

You've seen the video in the Nature Center, you've peered out from the mountain tops, and you've watched as winged wildlife have flown up to the clouds for a better view—surely you're jealous and in need of a little in-air action yourself. Here in Shiretoko National Park, where the remedy is experience, you can take an overdose of thrills by spending a day paragliding (ハラグライ ダー). The sport is like sky-diving, minus the whole free-falling at terminal velocity bit. A crash course in the sport—first hike or drive up to an elevated peak, then buckle your "chute" on tight, and finally, when the wind's blowing with just the right force, lift off into the great wide open.

As for paragliding in Shiretoko, the best place for an adrenaline rush is through the **Iwaobetsu Youth Hostel**, which has an experienced staff and charges well below the standard prices. If you book a couple days in advance, you'll get door-to-door service (if you're on the Utoro side of the park) and great instruction (Japanese only, but you'll get by) for whatever skill level you're at—virgin or pro. They also provide all of the equipment and take you to a getaway with a fantastic view. So, what are you waiting for? Get signed up to get strapped up, and give your aching feet a rest. *(Available 9am-2:30pm. ¥6000.)*

for **police**, ☎ 119 for **fire** or **ambulance**. There's an **international ATM** at Utoro's **post office**. From the bus terminal exit, head right on the main street, follow it as it bends left, and turn right at the light. (☎ 4-2300; ATM available M-F 8:45am-6pm, Sa-Su 9am-5pm.) **Postal code:** 099.

Encompassing about half of Hokkaidō's eastern peninsula, Shiretoko National Park is a series of mountain ranges and valleys accessed by two gateway towns— **Utoro** in the west and **Rausu** in the east. Utoro is the better base for the park's sights and hikes, as well as for transport and cheap stays. To navigate the park, pick up a bus schedule and a Japanese map from the Utoro tourist office.

▪ ACCOMMODATIONS

Places to stay crowd Utoro and Rausu like fleas on a Japanese poodle. For easiest access to park attractions, stay at the **Shiretoko Iwaobetsu Youth Hostel (HI) ❶** (知床 岩尾別ユースホステル), Aza Iwaobetsu, Shari-chō, Shari-gun, inside the park and about 20min. by car or bus from the Utoro Bus Terminal. Large and homey, the hostel holds nightly info sessions (8:30pm) on the park's sights and activities. Make reservations in summer, when the place fills to the lid with Japanese backpackers. Hop a park-bound bus from Utoro's bus terminal. (15min.; 4 per day Apr. 28-Oct. 31 except July 29-Aug. 20 when they run every 20min; fewer in off-season. ¥490.) It'll take you straight to the hostel. If the buses are only running as far as the Nature Center (late in the day and in off-season), call the hostel and they'll pick you up at the bus terminal. (☎ 4-2311; www.noah.ne.jp/shiretoko-ax. Breakfast ¥500. Dinner ¥1000. Check-in by 8pm. Laundry ¥200; dryer ¥100 per 30min. Sea-kayaking ¥8000 per 3hr., paragliding ¥6000 per 6hr. Members ¥2900; nonmembers ¥3500. Add ¥2000 for private room if available. Reservations recommended.) Just outside the park, across from the Utoro Bus Terminal, is the **Taiyō Minshuku ❷** (太陽民宿), 150, Utoro-Nishi, Shari-chō, Shari-gun. Though a bit disheveled, the friendly inn includes two meals in the price and is an unbeatable deal. (☎ 4-2939. Flexible check-in. ¥4000 per person.) If you'd rather camp, head to the **Onsen Kokusetsu Campsite ❶** (温泉国設キャンプ場), Rausu-chō yu-no-sawa, in Rausu. Free and just across from an irresistible *rotemburo* (outdoor *onsen*), the grounds are undoubtedly the best pitch in the park. Getting here is difficult without your own transport—take a bus from the Utoro Bus Terminal to Rausu (see above for info) and ask the bus driver to let you off at the site. Some report success hitching rides to the campground, though *Let's Go* never recommends hitchhiking. If you're driving, take Rte. 344 from the bus terminal (about 1hr.) and look for the site on the left, 6-7min. after you cross a big, orange bridge.

◘ FOOD

More often than not, the growling sounds you hear in the park will be your own stomach telling you that it's time for lunch; take a box meal and snacks out to the trails with you. Both **Seico Mart** (セイコーマート) 156, Utoro-Higashi, Shari-chō, Shari-gun, in Utoro town next to the post office (☎2-5012; open 24hr.) and Shiretoko Iwaobetsu Youth Hostel offer good options. For a wider selection of fresh veggies, fruit, and cup-o-noodles, cross the street from the Utoro Tourist Office to **Mitai** (みたい), 213, Utoro-Higashi. (☎4-2425. Open June-Sept. daily 9:30am-6:30pm; Oct.-May M-Sa 9:30am-6:30pm.) Otherwise, most people eat at their lodgings—if you stay at the youth hostel, you'll see why: the help-yourself-style meals are something to look forward to. While there aren't restaurants in Utoro to get excited about, Rausu is a different story. If you're there for a meal, consider splurging at the *sashimi* specialist, **Hirose ❸** (ひろ瀬) 57, Fujimi-chō, Rausu-chō. The joint is so undercover that even most locals don't know about it, and if you have to wait, it's only because the chef is still down by the sea reeling in your order. The *uni-don* (sea urchin roe; ¥2500) is fabulous, but for a cheap sampling of the freshest crab, shellfish, salmon, and snail you'll ever taste, go with the ¥1700 *sashimi* lunch set. From the campsite, head down Rte. 344 for about 10min. and go left at the fork. Make the second left and the first right and you'll see the sign mid-way down the block. (☎01538-7-3388. Open daily 10am-10pm.)

◉ SIGHTS

An easy way to approach the park is to divide it into two regions. Start in the park's west (near Utoro), which houses most of the highlights, and only head east to Rausu if you have extra time and your own transport.

> **❗ ANIMALS GONE WILD** Thousands of bears, foxes, deer, and other wild-life live in the park. To preserve your well-being, as well as theirs, keep driving speeds under control—animals often jump into the road. Avoid hiking alone, especially in the fall at dawn and dusk. Many Japanese carry bear-scaring bells (¥800 at the Nature Center), but noisemakers are probably only necessary if you're doing really off-the-beaten-path hiking.

UTORO AND THE PARK'S WEST

Let the natural wonders begin. On your way into the park, stop at **Oshin Koshin Waterfalls** (オシンコシン滝), some 7km before Utoro on Rte. 334. The clean-cut falls, which freeze solid in winter, are up the stairs on the left of the building. (Parking usually available. Not accessible by public transportation. Free.) From there, it's about 30min. through Utoro and the park entrance to the **Shiretoko Nature Center** (知床自然センター), 531, Aza Iwaobetsu, Shari-chō, a transport hub for the sights below and for some of the park's best hikes. At the center, catch an entertaining film that describes the park's seasons (20min., 1 per hr., ¥500), pick up a detailed semi-English map (¥200), and grab a bite to eat. (☎4-2114. Open daily Apr. 20-Oct. 20 8am-5:40pm; Oct. 21-Apr. 19 9am-4pm.) The first attraction, the **Shiretoko Goko Lakes** (知床五湖), are about 9km north. Watch out for bears—they're known to show up here. Backtrack to the fork to the falls and go right this time; a 20min. drive leads you uphill to **▨Kamuiwakka-no-Yu Falls** (カムイワッカの湯), a bathing experience too incredible to believe. Soothingly hot and straight from the mountains, the geo-thermal river and waterfalls here create *rotemburo* (outdoor open baths) well

HOKKAIDŌ

worth the 30min. hike upstream. For comfort, take a pair of flip-flops or go ancient Japanese style by renting a pair of *waraji* (straw slippers), available at the start of the climb or back at the youth hostel.

You can rely on the park's **shuttle bus** to get to most of the sights above. It runs from the Utoro Bus Terminal to the Nature Center, Iwaobetsu Youth Hostel, Shiretoko Goko Lakes, and Kamuiwakka-no-yu Falls. Tickets are sold at the bus terminal, the Nature Center, and the youth hostel. (Operates Apr. 28-Oct. 31, 4 per day, round-trip from Utoro Bus Terminal to Kamuiwakka ¥1800.) From July 29 to August 20, cars are prohibited from driving to Kamuiwakka-no-yu. As compensation, the park increases its park-bound bus (every 20min. 6:50am-7:20pm daily).

RAUSU AND THE PARK'S EAST

About 40min. from the youth hostel is the fishing village of **Rausu**, where fabulous fish and views of Russia are the main highlights. The area has a few eclectic attractions that make a nice half-day trip, but not much else. You'll need your own car, so don't come if you have to bank on buses or the weather's not good.

Once there, skip the town and head straight for the peninsula's eastern coast, where you can check out the fisherman culture and **Hikari-goke** (ひかり苔), a small cluster of caves with rare glowing moss beneath the rocks. Though you may not be overly impressed, it's worth stopping as the moss grows nowhere else in Japan. To get there, head into Rausu on Rte. 334, bear left at the fork after passing the campsite and *rotemburo* and turn left on the main road in town. There's only one coast road and you can't miss it. (Viewable June-Oct. Free.) Another 20min. down the coast by car leads you to stupefying **Seseki Onsen** (セセキ温泉), a *rotemburo* literally on the beach, where cold crashing waves make the water seem that much hotter. As fun as it is, neat-freaks should know that it's a bit dirty and rocky. The *onsen* is not easy to spot—keep your eyes peeled for the sign that says "Seseki 100m." The parking lot is beyond it to the right. (Bring your own towel. Free.) Back in town is **Kunashiri Tenbōtō** (国後展望塔), a popular observatory that provides the best views of Russia and winter drift-ice. Take Rte. 334 into Rausu and turn right just before the school. Make the first right, which hooks back toward you, then follow the loop uphill. (☎01538-7-4560. Open Tu-Su 9am-5pm.) For more on what to do in Rausu and this side of the park, there's a **Visitors Center** (羅臼ビジターセンター), 388, Yunosawa, Rausu-chō, on the left side of Rte. 334 as you head into town. (☎01538-7-2828. Open May-Oct. Tu-Su 9am-5pm; Nov.-Apr. Tu-Su 10am-4pm. Closed Dec. 28-Jan. 10.)

🎿 HIKING

For serious hiking between July and September, consider climbing Shiretoko's highest peak, **Rausu-dake** (羅臼岳 ; 1661m). Taking about 4hr. to climb, the mountain provides a magnificent panorama of the park and Russia in the distance. Though you can climb from either the Utoro or Rausu side of the park, the former is more popular, beginning at **Iwaobetsu Onsen** (岩尾別温泉), reachable by bus from the Nature Center (15min., 2 per day, ¥400). The round-tripround-trip hike can be done in a day (8-9hr.); if you start around 6:45am you'll have ample time to return by nightfall. Overnight climbs are also possible, as there's a free campsite 30min. downhill from Rausu-dake at **Rausu-daira** (羅臼平). For a longer hike, proceed from there across the range's remaining peaks—**Mitsumine-dake** (三ッ峰 ; 1509m), **Sashirui-dake** (サシルイ岳 ; 1564m), **Okkabeke-dake** (オッカバケ岳 ; 1450m), **Minami-dake** (南岳 ; 1459m), **Chienbetsu-dake** (知円別岳 ; 1544m), and **Iou-dake** (硫黄山 ; 1563m), finishing up hedonistically at **Kamuiwakka Yu Falls** (カムイワッカ湯の滝 ; see **Sights**). The roughly 10km shebang takes 2-3 days, and while the hike is mostly of an intermediate level, some difficult and dangerous portions follow Chienbetsu-dake. Before heading out, consult the Nature Center, which also has detailed info on trails, campsites, and weather conditions.

WAKKANAI (稚内) ☎0167

Wakkanai sounds like the Japanese slang for "I don't know" (*wakannai*), which is the response that you will likely get when you ask what there is to do here. The small port town of Wakkanai can only go so far to mask that there's little of interest in Wakkanai. This trading center and fishing port is attention-worthy for its delicious fish and its interesting twin neighbors, **Rishiri-Rebun-Sarobetsu National Park.** Try to use the town as a departure point for these islands.

◰ TRANSPORTATION. Wakkanai Airport (稚内空港) is east of the main town; shuttle buses to the airport leave from Sōya Bus Terminal. (30min., usually 1hr. before flights, ¥590.) Flights to: **Ōsaka Kansai** (about 2½hr., June-Sept. 1 per day); **Sapporo** (50min., 1-2 per day); **Tōkyō Haneda** (about 2hr., 1-2 per day). Call the airport info line for an up-to-date schedule (☎27-2121). **Wakkanai Station** (稚内駅), the transport hub for the city, is 10min. from the harbor and at the southern end of town. (☎23-2583. Open 6am-10pm.) **JR express trains** run to **Asahikawa** (3½hr., 4 per day, ¥7560) and **Sapporo** (5hr., 4 per day, ¥9660); other final destinations require a change in Asahikawa or Sapporo. Long distance buses stop at **Sōya Bus Station** (宗谷バスターミナル), 2-11-29, Chūō, a 3min. walk from the train station—turn right out of the station onto the side street, and the bus station shows up on the left. (☎23-5510; www.soyabus.co.jp. Open 5am-6pm.) Buses operate to **Asahikawa** (4¾hr.; 1 per day, 6am from Wakkanai, 5:10pm from Asahikawa; ¥4350) and **Sapporo** (6hr.; 5 per day; ¥5500, round-trip ¥10,000; June-Oct. 11pm overnight option). At certain times of the day buses depart from the **ferry terminal** or **Hokutō Kankō** (北東観光), but they always stop at the the Sōya Bus Station, so it is more reliable to board there. The ferry terminal, 1-4-1, Kaiun, is a 10min. walk behind the train station to the north. Catch ferries to **Rishiri Island** (1¾hr.; May-Sept. 5 per day, Oct.-Apr. 2-3 per day; from ¥1880, from ¥9790 with vehicle) and **Rebun Island** (1½-2hr.; May-Sept. 5 per day, Oct.-Apr. 2-3 per day; from ¥2100/¥11,120.) Wakkanai also has an **International Ferry Port** (国際旅客ターミナル), which has boats to **Korsakov** (コルサコフ) in **Sakhalin, Russia** (5½hr.; 1 per day at 10am; one-way from ¥20,000, round-trip from ¥30,000).

Wakkanai town is traversable by foot, but call **Wakkanai Taxi** (稚内タクシー) if you need a ride (☎22-5151. Open 24hr.) If you're more comfortable in your own set of wheels, **Nippon Rent-a-car** (日本レンタカー), in Sōya Bus Station, will rent you a car. (¥6000 for 9hr., July-Aug. ¥9000. Open 8am-5pm.)

◱ PRACTICAL INFORMATION. Inside Wakkanai Station is a small **tourist booth** (稚内市観光案内所) with English brochures and maps. The staff is helpful but does not speak English. (☎22-2384. Open June-Sept. daily 10am-6pm; Oct.-May M-Sa 10am-6pm.) Outside the station's exit are **lockers** (¥300-500). There are smaller lockers in the Sōya Bus Station (¥200). In an emergency, call ☎110 for **police,** ☎119 for **fire** or ambulance. For **money exchange** and an **international ATM** (ATM open M-F 8:40pm-7pm, Sa-Su 9am-5pm), head to the **Central Post Office** (中央郵便局), 2-15, Chūō, a 7min. walk away, a few blocks from the station's exit on the main road. (☎23-4271. Open M-F 9am-7pm, money exchange open until 4pm.) **Postal code:** 097.

⌂⌂ ACCOMMODATIONS AND FOOD. While accommodation in Wakkanai is cheap enough to keep you happy for a night, it doesn't compare with the hostels on the islands. Nevertheless, if you have no other option, the cheapest of the bunch is the **Moshiripa Youth Hostel (HI) ❶** (モシリパユースホステル), 2-9-5, Chūō, a 7min. walk from the station. Although the staff here is not exuberant in their welcoming and very strict when it comes to booking, the hostel has clean dorms and nice facilities, and it's popular among Japanese bikers. Reservations and hostel membership are musts. (☎24-0180. Breakfast ¥600. Dinner ¥1000. Check-in 3-8pm. Check-out 10am. Dorms ¥3360.) A more hospitable option is the **Wakkanai Youth Hostel (HI) ❶** (稚内ユースホステル), 3-10-1, Komadōri, which lures travelers with a social atmosphere and younger crowd. Although the hostel is farther from the ferry port, frequent trains run back to Wakkanai Station. Take bus #31 (15min., 1 per hr., ¥210) from Sōya Bus Station to Minami Shōgakkō (Minami Elementary School; 南小学校), continue in the direction of the bus, and follow the youth hostel's signs, or take a JR train to Minami-Wakkanai Station, turn right out of the exit, and follow the road to Otsubo Restaurant. From there, turn right again, go under the tracks, and the hostel signs are on the left. (☎ 23-7162. Check-in 3-8pm. Curfew 9:30pm. Breakfast ¥600. Members ¥2900, nonmembers ¥3900; singles ¥5000.) Also consider **Tenboku Ryokan ❷** (天北旅館), 2nd fl., 2-11-10, Chūō, right near the station and full of tiny, old-fashioned singles. Although there's more flexibility, the clientele tends to be older and they hit the sack early. Head right out of the station and onto the little side street—it's 3 min. down on the right, close to Sōya Bus Station. (☎23-3501. No English spoken. Car rental ¥2900 for 3hr., ¥3500 for 6hr. Check-in 2pm. Check-out 9am. Western-style singles ¥3500, *tatami*-style ¥4200. With breakfast ¥5260.) Even closer to the station, **Saihate Ryokan ❷** (さいはて旅館), 2-11-16, is a slightly better-looking choice with few foreign guests. (☎23-3556. Reservations required. Singles ¥4500, doubles ¥9000.)

The highlight of Wakkanai is its fresh fish. For lunch, stroll through the **Kita Fish Market** (北市場) where you can entice your appetite with samples from the various vendors. (Open daily 8am-6pm.) To seal the deal, go upstairs to **Yume Hiroba ❷** (夢広場), 2-1-5, Kaiun-chō, a pseudo-fish warehouse and the restaurant version of the marketplace. The "dream market" serves everything from delicious sushi and fried fish to crab salads (¥600) and seafood *rāmen* (¥1500). Exit the station and hook around the right until you get to the path that leads back there. The building is bright green. (☎24-5366. Open 11am-3pm and 5-10pm.) In the evening, try **Take-chan ❷** (竹ちゃん), 2-8-7, Chūō, a good dinner option that serves tasty fish dishes. Though everything's in Japanese, the colorful menus have pictures. Try the *tendon* (*tempura* veggies and fish over rice; ¥900) if you're hungry, and the out-of-this world sushi if you've got the budget. (☎22-7130. Open daily 10am-2pm and 5-11pm.)

◨❒ SIGHTS AND ENTERTAINMENT. Any free time you have in Japan's northernmost city is best spent in **Wakkanai Park** (稚内公園), a sprawling hill-top expanse glowing with green grass and small waterways. Inside are monuments including the **Gate to Ice and Snow,** which pays tribute to old Japanese settlements on Russia's Sakhalin, and the **Monument to the Nine Ladies,** which honors postal workers who committed suicide after Japan's defeat in WWII. To get to the monuments, follow the signs at the park's entrance in front of the ropeway exit. The park also has a towering observatory with a tiny museum on Wakkanai history and a panoramic viewing point of the port's surroundings. When the weather's good, you can see both Rishiri-tō and Rebun-tō in the west, and from late August to October you can even see Sakhalin, 43km to the north. (Open May-Oct. Tu-Su 9am-5pm. ¥400.)To get to the park, head south from the station and either take the mini-style ropeway (¥210) or walk up the trail beside it. While you're waiting for the ferry, you might want to check out the **North Breakwater Dome** (427m long), just east of the ferry port. Resembling a concrete wave suspended by numerous pillars, Wakkanai's city symbol has become a festive hangout for motorcyclists, budget travelers, and other loiterers. It's especially fun in the summer when the scene has people grilling fresh fish and throwing back beers to acoustic jamming.

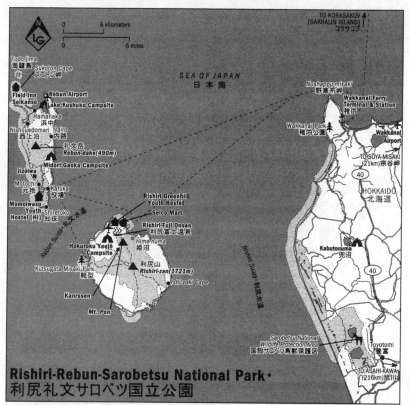

Rishiri-Rebun-Sarobetsu National Park •
利尻礼文サロベツ国立公園

RISHIRI-REBUN-SAROBETSU NATIONAL PARK
(利尻礼文サロベツ国立公園)

A devilish duo of superb hiking, expansive ocean views, and sporty weather, Rishiri-tō and Rebun-tō might be described as the Hokkaidō of Hokkaidō—a remote nature get away that offers a few days on the mountains and near the sea. Each island has its own charismatic flare—**Rishiri Island** is round and sky-reaching, with rugged mountain peaks and rigorous hiking trails, and **Rebun Island** is windy and flatland, covered with grassy slopes and gorgeous summer flowers. The islands deserve at least a couple days each and should be visited in the early summer, when the tour guide companies are still waiting for their prime stock—camera toters of the 40-70 year-old bracket—to go on holiday. Pseudo-hikers will have been weeded out and left back in the Daisetsu-zan gift stores. From galaxy-gazing to mountain climbing, Rebun-tō and Rishiri-tō have what it takes to become the star performers of your itinerary. Make reservations early and load up with cash ahead, because as dazzling as these starlets are, you don't want to be stranded.

RISHIRI-TŌ (利尻島)　　　　☎ 01638

Though snow-covered and too cold to hike in the winter, Rishiri's sparkling showcase volcano **Rishiri-zan** (利尻山 ; 1721m) is the main reason people come to the island. The picturesque peak is often compared to Mt. Fuji, though it doesn't take a volcano expert to notice that Rishiri-zan is far more peak-filled than Fuji, making it harder to climb.

▣▣ TRANSPORTATION AND PRACTICAL INFORMATION. Rishiri is connected to the outside world via **Rishiri Airport** (利尻空港), 5km northwest of town. Catch a local bus from Oshidomari Port (20min., 2 per day at 11:40am and 2:10pm, ¥3100) or a taxi (about ¥1400) to reach the airport. Flights are available to **Sapporo** (50min., 1 per day, ¥20,000). Rishiri can be reached by **ferry** from either **Wakkanai** or **Rebun-tō**. For information on ticket prices and departure times, see **Transportation** under Wakkanai (p. 719). Ferries connect Rebun's **Kafuka Port** and Rishiri's **Oshidomari Port** (鴛泊港 ; 40min.; 2 per day, Jan.-Feb. 1 per day; ¥730), and Kafuka Port and **Kutsugata Port** (沓形港 ; on the western side of Rishiri; 40min.; May-Sept. only, 2 per day, both in the afternoon; ¥730). It's easier to land in Oshidomari Port, where you'll be closer to the youth hostel and other essential services.

To navigate the island, you'll want your own form of transportation. In theory, buses exist, but they're infrequent and indirect, and bound to mess up your hiking schedule. **Car rental** is expensive (around ¥7000 for 3hr., ¥10,000 for 6hr.), but available at **Toyota Rent-a-lease** (トヨタレンターリース ; ☎9-2300; open daily 8am-6pm) and its competitors, most of wihch are lined up in front of the ferry port's exit. To the right is a little shack that has **bike** and **motor-scooter rentals.** (☎2-1046. Open daily 8am-5pm. Bikes ¥400 per hr., ¥2000 per day. Motor-scooters ¥1000 per hr., ¥4000 per day.) **Fuji Hire** (富士ハイヤー ; ☎2-1181) provides taxis.

Inside Oshidomari Port, a **tourist booth** has some information in English. The friendly staff will book accommodations and provide you with you a portable potty if you're in need. (☎2-2201; www.town.rishirifuji.hokkaido.jp. Open Apr 15.-Oct. 15 daily 8am-6pm.) **Luggage storage** is available in the ferry station (¥300-500). While there's nowhere you can change money on the island and traveler's checks will rarely be accepted, there is an **international ATM** in the **post office,** Oshidomari Aza-honchō, Rishiri-fuji-chō. (☎2-1009. Open M-F 8am-6pm. ATM open M-F 8:45am-6pm, Sa 9am-5pm, Su 9am-2pm.) To get there from the station, head out and turn right onto the main road. Turn left just as you ascend the slope.

▣▣ ACCOMMODATIONS AND FOOD. Sleep for cheap by camping or staying at the **Rishiri Green Hill Youth Hostel (HI)** ❶ (利尻グリーンヒルユースホステル), 35-5, Oshidomari Aza Fujino, Rishiri Fuji-chō, about 25min. from the terminal on foot, and 15min. by bus. The hostel is spacious and lively with sing-alongs and late-night chats. Exit right from the station, curve around the slope onto the main road, and continue straight for another 20min.—the hostel will be on your right past the large look-out rock. Buses from the station stop at the hostel (15min.; depart 9:57, 11:54am, 2:24, 5:34pm; ¥150). Unfortunately, these departure times don't coincide with ferry arrivals. (☎2-2507. Washer ¥200; dryer ¥100 per 30min. Breakfast ¥500. Bike rental ¥1500 per day. Guitars for use. ¥2900, nonmembers ¥3900.)

Of the island's many free campsites, the best is on the west side of the island inside **Kutsugata Misaki Park** ❶ (沓形岬公園キャンプ場). The site is about 13km west of Oshidomari Port; a bus departs from the port to the campsite. (40min., 5 per day, ¥730). If your main mission is hiking, try **Hokuroku Yaejō** ❶ (北麓キャンプ場), 4km south of the port. Though the camp is buried in the trees and can get busy, it's tough to complain about the location at the foot of the ascent to Rishiri-zan. Groups take advantage of the cheap bungalows. Take a bus (10min., 3 per day, ¥150) from the port to Rishiri Fuji Onsen, and then continue on up the road for about 20min. (☎2-2394. Check-in 9am. Check-out 10:30am. Free to pitch tents. Bungalow up to 4 people ¥2000.) For upscale accommodation, **Misaki Pension** ❹ (みさきペンション) is fairly priced given the meals, *sentō* (bath), and port-side location. Exit right out of the port, sidle around the dock of boats, and you'll see it. (☎2-2176. Check-in 2pm. Check-out 10am. ¥8500 per person.)

For groceries, snacks, and supplies, **Seico Mart,** about 10min. from the youth hostel (on foot) in the direction of town, is your only option. It's on the main road through town, about a 20min. walk from the port. (☎2-1962. Open daily 6am-11pm.)

⑤ HIKING. Hiking Rishiri-zan is not to be taken lightly. The most convenient starting point is a few kilometers west of Oshidomari Port at the Hokuroku Camping Ground (see below for directions). From there on up, about nine bases dot the path before the final ascent to the mountain's northern peak (the southern peak is higher, but unsafe to climb). Standing beside the shrine at the peak, you should see Russia, Rebun, and Wakkanai. Take enough water with you since there isn't any past base 3. If you feel nauseous or too tired to continue at any point, don't hesitate to retire. Take emergency numbers (police ☎4-2110; hospital ☎4-2626) and climb with others. Groups usually head out from the Green Hill Youth Hostel around 3am, so you might stay there the night before hiking.

If the intensity of Rishiri-zan sounds unappealing, there are plenty of less strenuous hikes. A good 3-4hr. hike begins at the same Hokuroku campsite and heads to **Kanrosen** (観路線), a forest brook said to have the purest water in all of Japan. Fill up a jug before continuing left toward **Mt. Pon** (ポン山) and **Mt. Kopon** (コポン山), where the views aren't as brilliant as those on top of Rishiri-zan, though the hike is challenging and makes for a good workout. Alternatively, circle the island (56km) at your own pace. In order to do this, you'll want to pick up the brochure and packet at the tourist office and get an early start so you can complete the circle. While the fastest means of transportation is by car (2hr.) or motor-scooter (3hr.), even a bike (7-8hr.) or your own two feet (12-14hr.) can do the job. Heading east from Oshidomari Port, find the sights by following the clear and well-placed road signs. The highlights of the island are: **Hime-numa** (姫沼 ; 5km from the port), a man-made pond named after the type of salmon (*himemasu*) released in the water upon its inception; **Ishi-zaki Cape** (石崎), a fabulous look out point off the highway with a view of Rishiri-zan; and **Otatomari-numa** (オタトマリ沼), a lake in the south that's worth at least 30min. of traipsing around. Bikers have the option of taking the special **cycling route** (24.9km; about 2½hr.), which begins southeast of Oshidomari at Cape Nozuka and reaches the Rishiri Sports Park in the west. The route is not too difficult and many travelers have found it easier and just as scenic as circling the island. When you finish your journey, indulge with a hot bath in town at **Rishiri Fuji Onsen** (利尻富士温泉), 40min. by foot from the Hokuroku Campsite. From the port, hop the bus to Rishiri Fuji Onsen. (¥400 for bath. Open daily 11am-9pm. Closed 1st and 3rd Su of the month from Nov.-Apr.)

REBUN-TŌ (礼文島)   ☎01638

As different as Rebun-tō is from Rishiri-tō in topography and shape, the island's hiking is just as prodigious and its ocean views are just as mesmeric. The island has a natural charm that's evident in its rather undeveloped coastlines and barren center, and when the weather's good, the views of Rishiri-zan are almost better than they are on Rishiri itself. To make the most of your time, inquire about hikes at your hostel, and pick up maps and brochures from the tourist office (see below). If you don't have your own transport, it's worth staying at one of the hostels because they will arrange drop-offs and pick-ups for your daily plans.

◪⑰ TRANSPORTATION AND PRACTICAL INFORMATION. On the northern coast, **Rebun-tō Airport** (礼文空港) is temporarily out of service. Call for the current status (☎7-2175). There are **ferries** to Rebun-tō from Rishiri's northern and western ports—**Oshidomari** and **Katsugata**—as well as from **Wakkanai Port.** (For info on prices and departures, see **Transportation** in Wakkanai p. 719.) Boats arrive on the southern end of the island at **Kafuka Port.** While there are **car rental** agencies at the port's exit, they charge the same prices—¥7000 for 3hr. and ¥14,000 per day— try **Toyota Rent-a-car.** (☎6-1117. Open 7am-6:30pm.) To the left side of the stores as you exit the station is **Rent-a-bike Cycle** where you can rent **bikes** or **motor-scooters** for daily excursions. (Bikes ¥500 per hr., ¥2000 per day; scooters ¥1000/¥5000.)

For **tourist information**, look left as you enter the station from the boat landing—the staff at the counter books accommodations and provides English pamphlets. (☎ 6-2655. Open daily Apr. 16-Oct. 15 8am-5pm.) Rebun-tō is hard to traverse without your own transportation. Six local bus routes cover the island, but they are slow, infrequent, and expensive. In an emergency, call ☎ 110 for **police**, ☎ 119 for **fire** or **ambulance.** The island has nowhere to exchange money, though your ATM card might work at the **Central Post Office** (中央郵便局), Kafuka-mura Aza Tonnai, Rebun-chō, on the main road in town. Exit right from the station, make your second left, then a quick right onto the main road. It's a couple places up on the left. (☎ 6-1760. Open M-Sa 9am-6pm, Su 9am-12:30pm. ATM open M-F 8:45am-6pm, Sa 9am-5pm, Su 9a-2pm). **Postal code:** 097.

⚏ ACCOMMODATION AND FOOD. Accommodation in Rebun is scattered, with the upscale places centering around Kafuka Port, and the cheaper stuff gravitating towards the northern and western coasts. Though it's an hour's drive away on the north side of Rebun, **⚏Field Inn Seikansō ❸** (Field Inn 星観荘), Sukoton Hoshi Daira, Funadomari-mura, Rebun-chō, is a dream hostel, sitting like a lone duck on the magnificent Japan Sea coast. If you're coming on your own, take a bus headed to Sukoton (スコトン) from the ferry port and get off at Seikansō (星観荘 ; 1¼hr., 4 per day, ¥1180). The hostel is a bit more expensive than average, but the meals, sing-alongs, and views make it worth every yen. At night meeting, the owner explains (in Japanese) the various hikes and sights in the area. (☎ 7-2818. Guitar for use. Free *shōchū*—Japanese vodka. Washer ¥200; dryer ¥100 per 30min. Dorms ¥5500.) The other loved option, closed at the time of writing, is the **Momoiwasō Youth Hostel (HI) ❶** (ももいわそうユースホステル), on Rebun's southwest coast. The hostel is a party of young and rowdy packers who trek by day and dance like rockstars by night. The tentative plan is to re-open in June 2004, but call ahead to confirm. It's a 15-20min. drive from Kafuka. (☎ 6-1421.)

As for camping, the best place to pitch a tent is on **Lake Kushuko ❶** (久種湖), where the waterside views are fantastic and the facilities are convenient. From the port, hop a Sōya Bus (宗谷バス) headed toward Funadomari (船泊), get off at Byōin-mae (病院前), and head toward the lake. The place is on the northern side of the island and has bungalows also. (☎ 7-3110. Open May-Aug. Check-in 1-7pm. Check-out 11am. ¥500; bungalow ¥2000, fits up to 4 people.) For nearby camping, pitch a tent at the **Midori Gaoka Site ❶** (緑ヶ丘公園), 6km up the eastern coast from the ferry port. To get there, take the same bus as above but get off at Kafugai (香深井 ; 10-15min., 6 per day, ¥280.) While the views don't compare to Lake Kushuko, the area lives up to its name of "green hill park" with an abundance of trees and pleasant walking trails. (☎ 6-1797. Open May-Oct. ¥500.)

Although you will likely eat most meals at your hostel or hotel, if you find yourself craving a sit-down meal, then **Isoroku ❹** (いそろく), might appeal to you with its local specialty, *chan-chan teishoku* (¥800). The dish consists of fried fish *(hokke)*, *miso* soup, and a few side dishes. There's a breakfast special for early birds (¥500). *Onigiri* (rice wrapped in seaweed; ¥200) and *rāmen* (¥600) are the menu's features. (☎ 6-2724. Open daily 7am-8pm.) The biggest supermarket in town is the **Kumiai Store,** which has canned foods and snacks for the camping crowd. Exit right out of the station, make your second left, and it's on the right around the end of the block. (☎ 6-1547. Open M-F 9am-4:30pm, Sa 9am-3pm.)

⚏ HIKING. While Rebun-tō's **Hachi-jikan course** is certainly the most dramatic of its hikes, it's by no means the only way to experience the island's offerings. One of the less intense, yet just as fulfilling courses is **Yo-jikan course,** which traces the island's northwestern peninsula, **Sukoton.** Running 12km, the course begins at **Hamanaka** (浜中), on the northern coast, sticking to the shoreline and allowing for great angles of Misaki Cape and the Japan Sea. If it's raining, stick to one of the more inland routes where the winds aren't as severe.

Come summer (June especially), you belong among the wildflowers of Rebun-tō, and for the best immersion, you'll want to take the **Momojiri Course** (桃知), some 6km long and requiring about 2-3hr. of moderate hiking. The trail begins at **Shiretoko** (知床)—a point on the southern end that's reachable by bus (15min., 3 per day, ¥300)—and works its way up and down the island slopes to a gigantic magma rock at **Momoiwa Observatory** (桃岩 ; 249.5km). If you continue, you'll find yourself on the **Momoiwa Course** (about 1½hr.), which runs through the hilly slopes to Kafuka Port. From the Momoiwa Observatory, it is possible to walk down to the main highway, turn left into the tunnel, and follow the road to the west coast of the southern peninsula. The hiking course you have entered is called **Jizōiwa** (地蔵 岩), and it will lead you to the fishing village of **Motochi** (元地), where fresh scallop and shellfish skewers (¥300) and *uni-don* (¥1200-2600) are sold in the village.

Those looking for some time to themselves might skip the usual hikes for a trip to the haunting **Todo-jima** (トド島), an uninhabited island just off the northern coast of **Sukoton.** The lonely island has nothing on it—but then again, that's why it's so appealing. You can stroll around like Robinson Crusoe and get some entirely new views of Rebun and Rishiri. Getting here requires negotiating with one of the local fishermen. If you're serious about experiencing Rousseau's natural state of man, at least for a couple of hours, your best bet is to stay at the Field Inn (see below) where the owner can arrange the trip for you. (About 3hr. round-trip, including time on the island. Trips subject to weather.)

HOKKAIDŌ

APPENDIX

GLOSSARY

Ainu: indigenous people of Hokkaidō
anime: Japanese animation
bakufu: shōgunate
basho: *sumō* tournament
bentō: Japanese lunch box
bijutsukan: art museum
biwa: Japanese lute
bokujō: pasture; ranch
bonsai: dwarfed tree
buyō: dance
bushidō: the Way of the Warrior; the *samurai* ethos
-chan: suffix used for the name of close friends or young children
-chō: suffix meaning district or neighborhood
-chōme: modern suffix for a municipal sub-district
konbini: convenience store
daimyō: Japanese feudal lord
daruma: round doll with no legs, red body, white face, and no pupils; make a wish when you fill in one pupil and if it comes true, fill in the other; prevalent around New Year's; named after Bodhidharma, a Zen monk who meditated for so long his legs became useless
depāto: department store
Diet: Japanese National Assembly
donburi: rice with toppings in a bowl
eki: station
fugu: blowfish
furigana: *kana* written above or to the right of *kanji* to indicate pronunciation
futsū: regular train
gagaku: music played in the Imperial Court
gaijin: foreigner
gaikokujin: a more formal and politically correct word for foreigner
geisha: a professional Japanese woman trained in the arts of conversation, dancing, and singing to entertain men
go: a strategy game played with black and white stones, typically played by old Japanese men
Golden Week: four national holidays within seven days create a weeklong vacation, one of Japan's three biggest holiday seasons, the end of April through the beginning of May
habu: a poisonous snake in Okinawa
haiku: form of Japanese poem with three lines of five, seven, and five syllables, often depicting on the seasons or nature

hakubutsukan: museum
hanabi taikai: fireworks festival
hashi: 1. Japanese eating utensils; two slender sticks; chopsticks 2. bridge
hiragana: the Japanese cursive syllabary
Hokkaidō: one of Japan's four major islands
Honshū: one of Japan's four major islands
ikebana: flower arranging
iki: bound
irrashaimase: welcome
-ji: suffix for a Buddhist temple
jinja (jingū/gū): term for Shintō shrine
kabuki: a modernized form of Japanese *nō* theater, featuring male performers and stylized movements, dances, and songs to produce comedies and tragedies
kaisoku: rapid train
kaiten-zushi: conveyor belt sushi
kami: god
kamikaze: a Japanese pilot of WWII, trained to make a suicidal crash attack
kankō annaijo: tourist information center
kanpai: cheers!; "dry glass"
kanji: Chinese ideograms
katakana: Japanese syllabary used to write foreign words
kawa (gawa): river or canal
keigo: honorific Japanese
keitai: cell phone; appendage to the body
kimchi: Korean pickled cabbage
kimono: traditional Japanese robe, wide sleeves and tied at the waist with an *obi* belt, made of colorful fabric
kōban: police station
kōen: park
kofun: ancient tomb
konbu: kelp (rhymes with "help")
-ku: suffix for a major municipal subdivision of the city
kyūkō: express train
Kyūshū: one of Japan's four major islands
-machi: a synonym for *-chō*, a suffix for district or neighborhood
-mae: a suffix for in front of
maiko: *geisha*-in-training; a fantabulous researcher for Central Honshū
manga: comic strip
manga kissa: an establishment equipped with *manga* and other amenities
matsuri: festival
meishi: business card
minshuku: bed and breakfast
miso: soybean paste

mochi: pounded sticky rice; a traditional New Year's food; the cause of a handful of elderly deaths every New Year's

mon: gate

nō: classical Japanese theater, incorporating stylized music, dance, and dress

nori: dried seaweed

Obon: Buddhist festival and national holiday in August (or July depending on the lunar calendar), which celebrates the return of ancestors' spirits

okonomiyaki: Japanese pancake

omiyage: gift

onsen: hot spring

origami: Japanese art of paper folding

oshibori: wash cloth

otaku: "house-broken no-life geek"

pachinko: a mindless, pointless, money-sucking slot-machine-like game found on every block of Tōkyō and around every train station in Japan; bends rules of legality to exist

rakugo: comic storytelling

rōmaji: Roman alphabet used for Japanese transliteration

rotenburo: outdoor bath

ryokan: inn

Ryūkyū: traditional name for the islands of Okinawa

sadō: tea ceremony

sake: rice wine

sakura: cherry blossom

salaryman: Japanese business men

-san: suffix meaning Mr. or Mrs.

samurai: Japanese warrior

seppuku: suicide by disembowelment; practiced by Japanese *samurai*

Shikoku: one of Japan's four major islands

shima (jima): island

shinkansen: bullet train

shōchū: Japanese vodka

shodō: calligraphy

shōen: manor

shōgun: a military ruler of pre-modern Japan

shugo: a military governor of medieval provinces

shukubō: lodging in a shrine or temple

sumi-e: monochrome (black ink) drawing

sumō: Japanese pastime; large men wrestle in a rink while wearing little clothing

tanuki: raccoon dog; symbol of mischief

tani (dani): valley

takoyaki: battered and fried octopus balls

tanka: Japanese verse of five lines, the first and third having five syllables and the rest having seven

tatami: woven rice-straw mat

teishoku: set meal

tempura: deep-fried seafood or vegetables

-tera (dera): suffix for Buddhist temples

tokkyū: limited express train

tonkatsu: breaded and fried pork

torii: gate to a shrine

tsunami: a monstrous ocean wave created by an underwater disturbance (i.e. earthquake, volcanic eruption)

typhoon: hurricane

ukai: cormorant fishing

ukiyo-e: Japanese prints

washi: traditional Japanese paper

yamabushi: "those who sleep in the mountains;" followers of the ancient Japanese religion of mountain asceticism

yukata: lighter, summer version of kimono

Zen: a branch of Buddhism that uses meditation, self-contemplation, and intuition to attain enlightenment

NATIONAL HOLIDAYS

DATE	HOLIDAY
January 1	New Year's Day
Second Monday of January	Coming-of-Age Day
February 11	National Founding Day
March 20 or 21	Vernal Equinox Day
April 29	Greenery Day
May 3	Constitution Memorial Day
May 5	Children's Day
Third Monday of July	Maritime Day
Third Monday of September	Respect-for-the-Aged Day
September 23 or 24	Autumnal Equinox Day
Second Monday of October	Health-Sports Day
November 3	Culture Day
November 23	Labor Thanksgiving Day
December 23	Emperor's Birthday

JAPANESE PRONUNCIATION GUIDE

a	as in father	ae	two separate sounds: **ah-eh**
i	as in Giovanni	ai	as in chai tea
u	as in super	ei	as in eight
e	as in penalty	ie	two separate sounds: **ee-eh**
o	as in no	ue	two separate sounds: **oo-eh**
g	always hard g, as in goofy	s	never z, always soft s, as in soap

HIRAGANA

a	あ	i	い	u	う	e	え	o	お
ka	か	ki	き	ku	く	ke	け	ko	こ
sa	さ	shi	し	su	す	se	せ	so	そ
ta	た	chi	ち	tsu	つ	te	て	to	と
na	な	ni	に	nu	ぬ	ne	ね	no	の
ha	は	hi	ひ	hu	ふ	he	へ	ho	ほ
ma	ま	mi	み	mu	む	me	め	mo	も
ya	や	–	–	yu	ゆ	–	–	yo	よ
ra	ら	ri	り	ru	る	re	れ	ro	ろ
wa	わ	–	–	–	–	–	–	–	–
nn	ん	–	–	–	–	–	–	–	–
ga	が	gi	ぎ	gu	ぐ	ge	げ	go	ご
za	ざ	ji	じ	zu	ず	ze	ぜ	zo	ぞ
da	だ	ji	ぢ	zu	づ	de	で	do	ど
ba	ば	bi	び	bu	ぶ	be	べ	bo	ぼ
pa	ぱ	pi	ぴ	pu	ぷ	pe	ぺ	po	ぽ

KATAKANA

a	ア	i	イ	u	ウ	e	エ	o	オ
ka	カ	ki	キ	ku	ク	ke	ケ	ko	コ
sa	サ	shi	シ	su	ス	se	セ	so	ソ
ta	タ	chi	チ	tsu	ツ	te	テ	to	ト
na	ナ	ni	ニ	nu	ヌ	ne	ネ	no	ノ
ha	ハ	hi	ヒ	hu	フ	he	へ	ho	ホ
ma	マ	mi	ミ	mu	ム	me	メ	mo	モ
ya	ヤ	–	–	yu	ユ	–	–	yo	ヨ
ra	ラ	ri	リ	ru	ル	re	レ	ro	ロ
wa	ワ	–	–	–	–	–	–	–	–
nn	ン	–	–	–	–	–	–	–	–
ga	ガ	gi	ギ	gu	グ	ge	ゲ	go	ゴ
za	ザ	ji	ジ	zu	ズ	ze	ゼ	zo	ゾ
da	ダ	ji	ヂ	zu	ヅ	de	デ	do	ド
ba	バ	bi	ビ	bu	ブ	be	べ	bo	ボ
pa	パ	pi	ピ	pu	プ	pe	ぺ	po	ポ

JAPANESE PHRASEBOOK

NUMBERS	ROMAJI	JAPANESE	NUMBERS	ROMAJI	JAPANESE
0	rei	れい	9	ku/kyū	九
½	nibun no ichi	二分の一	10	jū	十
1	ichi	一	11	jū-ichi	十一

NUMBERS	RŌMAJI	JAPANESE	NUMBERS	RŌMAJI	JAPANESE
2	ni	二	12	jūni	十二
3	san	三	20	nijū	二十
4	shi/yon	四	21	nijū-ichi	二十一
5	go	五	100	hyaku	百
6	roku	六	200	nihyaku	二百
7	nana/shichi	七	1000	sen	千
8	hachi	八	10,000	man	万

THE BASICS	RŌMAJI	JAPANESE
Hello	konnichiwa	こんにちは
Goodbye	sayonara	さよなら
How are you?	ogenki desuka?	お元気ですか？
Please	onegaishimasu	お願いします
Thank you	arigatō (gozaimasu)	ありがとう（ございます）
You're welcome	dōitashimashite	どういたしまして
Yes	hai	はい
No	iie	いいえ
Help!	tasukete!	助けて！
I'm sorry	gomennasai	ごめんなさい
Either is fine	docchi de mo ii	どっちでもいい
It doesn't matter (don't worry about it)	daijōbu desu	大丈夫です
What's your name?	onamae wa nan desuka?	お名前は何ですか？
My name is...	watashi no namae wa ...	私の名前は ...
I	watashi	私
you	anata/kimi	あなた・君
he/she	kare/kanojo	彼・彼女
plural: we, you, they	usually use the singular, but for emphasis, add -tachi to singular: *watashi-tachi, anata-tachi*	私たち・あなたたち
to have	arimasu	あります
to not have	arimasen	ありません
okay	daijōbu/okke	大丈夫・オッケー
not okay	yokunai	良くない
to want, would like	hoshii	欲しい
to not want	hoshikunai	欲しくない
Do you have...?	...arimasuka?	... ありますか？
I want ...	...ga hoshii	... が欲しい
I don't speak Japanese	watashi wa nihongo ga hanasemasen	私は日本語が話せません
Do you speak English?	eigo ga hanase masuka?	英語が話せますか？
I can't hear you	kikoemasen	聞こえません
Speak more slowly	motto yukkuri hanashite kudasai	もっとゆっくり話してください
Repeat that	mōichido onegaishimasu	もう一度お願いします
I don't understand	wakarimasen	わかりません
I need help	tetsu datte kudasai	手伝ってください
What time do you open?	nanji ni hiraki masuka?	何時に開きますか？

THE BASICS	RŌMAJI	JAPANESE
What time do you close?	nanji ni shimari masuka?	何時に閉まりますか？
restroom	otearai	お手洗い
man	dansei	男性
woman	josei	女性
toilet paper	toiretto pēpā	トイレットペーパー
Western toilet	seiyō toiretto	西洋トイレット
Japanese toilet	wafū toiretto	和風トイレット
big	ōkii	大きい
small	chiisai	小さい

DIRECTIONS	RŌMAJI	JAPANESE
Where is...?	...wa doko ni arimasuka?	...はどこにありますか？
How do I get to ...?	dō yatte...ni iki masuka?	どうやって ... に行きますか？
I want to go to...	...ni ikitai desu	... に行きたいです
How far is...from here?	...wa koko kara dono kurai tōii desuka?	...はここからどのくらい遠いですか？
How long does it take to get to...?	...made dono kurai kakari masuka	...までどのくらいかかります
north	kita	北
south	minami	南
east	higashi	東
west	nishi	西
left	hidari	左
right	migi	右
front, forward	mae	前
back, rear	ushiro	後
center, middle	mannaka, chūshin	真中、中心
upper, above, ascend	ue	上
lower, below, descend	shita	下
to enter/entrance	hairu/iriguchi	入る・入口
to exit/exit	deru/deguchi	出る・出口
far, distant	tōii	遠い
close, near/nearby	chikai	近い

TRANSPORTATION	RŌMAJI	JAPANESE
I would like to go to...	...ni ikitai desu	... に行きたいです
ticket office	mado guchi	窓口
ticket	kippu	切符
I want to make a reservation	yōyaku o tsukuri tai desu	予約をつくりたいです
I want to buy a ticket to...	...e no kippu o kaitai desu	...への切符を買いたいです
one-way ticket	katamichi kippu	片道切符
round-trip ticket	ōfuku kippu	往復切符
schedule	jikokuhyō	時刻表
What time does it leave?	shuppatsu wa nanji desuka?	出発は何時ですか？
What time does it arrive?	tōchyaku wa nanji desuka?	到着は何ですか？
How long does it take?	nanji kan/nan pun kakari masuka?	何時間・何分かかりますか？

TRANSPORTATION	RŌMAJI	JAPANESE
locker	rokkā	ロッカー
airplane	hikōki	飛行機
airport	hikōjō	飛行場
train	densha	電車
bullet train	shinkansen	新幹線
train station	eki	駅
platform	hōmu	ホーム
bus station	basu tāminaru	バスターミナル
sleeper train	shin dai sha	寝台車
boat	fune	船
docks	hatoba	波止場
I want to get off	koko de oritai desu	ここで降りたいです
subway	chikatetsu	地下鉄
taxi	takushi	タクシー
bicycle	jitensha	自転車
I want to rent a bicycle	jitensha o karitai desu	自転車を借りたいです
insurance	hoken	保険

MONEY	RŌMAJI	JAPANESE
money	okane	お金
yen	en	円
one yen	ichi en	一円
ten yen	jū en	十円
one hundred yen	hyaku en	百円
cash	genkin	現金
US dollars	doru	ドル
credit card	kurejitto kādo	クレジットカード
Can I use a foreign credit card?	gaikoku no kurejitto kādo o tsukae masuka?	外国のクレジットカードを使えますか？
bank	ginkō	銀行
change money	ryōgae	両替
Can I exchange money here?	koko de ryōgae dekimasuka?	ここで両替できますか？
price	nedan	値段
pay/pay for	harau	払う
How much does it cost?	ikura desuka?	いくらですか？
inexpensive	yasui	安い
expensive	takai	高い
I want a receipt	ryōshūsho o morae masuka	領収書をもらえますか

HEALTH & EMERGENCY	RŌMAJI	JAPANESE
I am sick	watashi wa byōki desu	私は病気です
I don't feel well	kibun ga warui desu	気分が悪いです
hurt/pain	itami	痛み
My head hurts	atama ga itai desu	頭が痛いです
My stomach hurts	onaka ga itai desu	おなかが痛いです
I'm allergic to...	...no arerugii ga arimasu	...のアレルギーがあります
I feel nauseous	kimochi ga warui desu	気持ちが悪いです

HEALTH & EMERGENCY	RŌMAJI	JAPANESE
I've caught a cold	kaze o hiki mashita	かぜを引きました
AIDS	eizu	エイズ
diarrhea	geri	下痢
hepatitis	kanen	肝炎
hospital	byōin	病院
Where is the hospital?	byōin wa doko ni arimasuka	病院はどこにありますか
doctor	isha	医者
shot/injection	chūsha	注射
pharmacy	yakkyoku	薬局
medicine	kusuri	薬
antibiotic	kōseibusshitsu	抗生物質
aspirin/painkiller	asupirin/itamidome	アスピリン・痛み止め
condom	condōmu	コンドーム
contraceptive	hinin	避妊
Fire!	kaji!	火事！
police	keisatsu	警察
Thief (pickpocket)!	dorobō!	泥棒！
My money/passport has been stolen.	watashi no okane/pasupōto ga nusumarete shimaimashita	私のお金・パスポートが盗まれてしまいました
I've lost my money/passport.	okane/pasupōto o nakushi mashita	お金・パスポートを無くしました
danger/dangerous	kiken	危険
Leave me alone!	yamete!	やめて！
Harasser!	chikan!	痴漢！

ACCOMMODATIONS & FOOD	RŌMAJI	JAPANESE
hotel	hoteru	ホテル
hostel	hosuteru	ホステル
inn	ryokan	旅館
tourist home	minshuku	民宿
room	heya	部屋
dormitory	ryō	寮
single room	hitori beya	一人部屋
double room	futari beya	二人部屋
triple room	sannin beya	三人部屋
bed	beddo	ベッド
check-in/-out	chekku in/auto	チェックイン・アウト
key	kagi	かぎ
deposit	hoshōkin	保証金
air-conditioning	reibō	冷房
free breakfast	asagohan tsuki	朝ご飯付
I am vegetarian	watashi wa bejetarian desu	私はベジタリアンです
I don't eat meat	oniku ga taberaremasen	お肉が食べられません
I am on a diet	daietto shite imasu	ダイエットしています
How many people are in your party?	nanmei sama desuka?	何名様ですか？

COMMUNICATIONS	RŌMAJI	JAPANESE
post office	yūbinkyoku	郵便局
letter	tegami	手紙
envelope	fūtō	封筒
postcard	hagaki	はがき
stamp	kitte	切手
air mail	eameru	エアメール
surface mail	funabin	船便
registered mail	kakitome yūbin	書留郵便
Poste Restante	kyokudome yūbin	局留め郵便
telephone	denwa	電話
pay phone	kōshū denwa	公衆電話
phone card	terefon cādo	テレフォンカード
long-distance call	chōkyori denwa	長距離電話
international call	kokusai denwa	国際電話
I want to make a long-distance phone call	chokyori denwa o shitai desu	長距離電話をしたいです
What is the number for...?	...no denwa bango wa nandes-uka?	...の電話番号は何ですか？
Internet cafe	intānetto cafe	インターネットカフェ
computer	konpūtā	コンピューター
I want to get on the Internet	intānetto o tsukaitai desu	インターネットを使いたいです
I want to send an email	iimeru o okuritai desu	イーメールを送りたいです
How much is it per hour?	ichijikan wa ikura desuka?	一時間はいくらですか？

PASSPORT & VISA	RŌMAJI	JAPANESE
passport	pasupōto	パスポート
visa	biza	ビザ
embassy	taishikan	大使館
consulate	ryōjikan	領事館

LEISURE	RŌMAJI	JAPANESE
film	eiga	映画
I want to watch a film	eiga o mitai desu	映画を見たいです
movie theater	eigakan	映画館
music	ongaku	音楽
music concert	consāto	コンサート
opera	opera	オペラ
sports	supōtsu	スポーツ
stadium	sutajiamu	スタジアム
to play (a sport)	(supōtsu) o asobu	スポーツを遊ぶ
soccer	sakkā	サッカー
table tennis	pinpon	ピンポン
basketball	basuketto bōru	バスケットボール
swimming (pool)	pūru	プール
martial arts	kakutogi	格闘技
How old are you?	nansai desuka?	何歳ですか？

LEISURE	RŌMAJI	JAPANESE
I am...years old	watashi wa...desu	私は ... です
What do you do (what is your occupation)?	oshigoto wa nandesuka?	お仕事は何ですか？
I am a student/I go to school	gakusei desu	学生です
I am a teacher/I teach school	sensei desu	先生です
I work	shakaijin desu	社会人です
I am retired	intai shimashita	引退しています
bar	izakaya	居酒屋
nightclub	kurabu	クラブ
cover	kabā chāji	カバーチャージ
massage	massāji	マッサージ
sauna	sauna	サウナ
karaoke	karaoke	カラオケ

TIME	RŌMAJI	JAPANESE	TIME	RŌMAJI	JAPANESE
minutes	fun/pun	分	week	shū	週
hour	ichijikan	一時間	Monday	getsuyōbi	月曜日
...o'clock	...jikan	... 時間	Tuesday	kayōbi	火曜日
What time is now?	nanjidesuka?	何時ですか？	Wednesday	suiyōbi	水曜日
morning	asa	朝	Thursday	mokuyōbi	木曜日
noon	ohiru	お昼	Friday	kinyōbi	金曜日
afternoon	gogo	午後	Saturday	doyōbi	土曜日
evening	yūgata	夕方	Sunday	nichiyōbi	日曜日
night	yoru	夜	month (moon)	tsuki	月
midnight	mayonaka	真夜中	Months are referred to numerically starting with Jan.; suffix *gatsu* means "month":		
daytime	hiruma	昼間	January	ichigatsu	一月
nighttime	yoru	夜	February	nigatsu	二月
now	ima	今	year	nen	年
day	nichi	日	last year	kyonen	去年
today	kyō	今日	2004	nisen yo nen	二千四年
yesterday	kinō	昨日	past	kako	過去
tomorrow	ashita	明日	future	mirai	未来

FOOD	RŌMAJI	JAPANESE	FOOD	RŌMAJI	JAPANESE
to eat	taberu	食べる	chopsticks	hashi	箸
supermarket	sūpā	スーパー	buffet	baikingu	バイキング
restaurant	resutoran	レストラン	snacks	oyatsu	おやつ
to go	mochikaeri	持ち帰り	kosher	tekihoshokuhin	適法食品
delivery	haitatsu	配達	fast food	fasuto fūdo	ファストフード
waitstaff/ waitress	ueitoresu	ウエイトレス	McDonald's	makudonarudo	マクドナルド
menu	mennū	メニュー	hamburger	hanbāgu	ハンバーグ
check/bill	okanjō	お勘定	fried rice	chāhan	チャーハン
napkin	napukin	ナプキン	noodles	menrui	めん類
fork	fōku	フォーク	spaghetti	supagetti	スパゲッティ

FOOD	RŌMAJI	JAPANESE	FOOD	RŌMAJI	JAPANESE
knife	naifu	ナイフ	udon noodles	udon	うどん
spoon	supūn	スプーン	ramen noodles	rāmen	ラーメン
bowl	wan	お椀	bean curd/tofu	tōfu	豆腐
plate	osara	お皿	curry	karē	カレー
delicious	oishii	おいしい	dumplings	gyōza	ギョーザ
hot (temp.)	atsui	熱い	egg	tamago	卵
cold	tsumetai	冷たい	bread	pan	パン
Not too much...	sukuname	少なめ	beef	gyūniku	牛肉
wasabi	wasabi	わさび	chicken	toriniku	とり肉
pepper	koshō	コショウ	fish	sakana	魚
salt	shio	塩	lamb	kohitsuji no niku	子羊の肉
soy sauce	shōyu	醤油	pork	butaniku	豚肉
vegetables	yasai	野菜	seafood	kaisanshokuhin	海産食品
corn	tōmorokoshi	とうもろこし	shrimp	ebi	海老
cucumber	kyūri	キュウリ	to drink	nomu	飲む
mushrooms	kinoko	きのこ	beverage	nomimono	飲み物
peas	endō	エンドウ	water	omizu	お水
fruit	kudamono	果物	bottle	botoru	ボトル
apple	ringo	りんご	cup	koppu	コップ
banana	banana	バナナ	hot water	oyu	お湯
grape	budō	ぶどう	tea house	ochashitsu	お茶室
peach	momo	もも	cafe	kafe	カフェ
pineapple	painappuru	パイナップル	tea	ocha	お茶
watermelon	suika	水果	coffee	kōhii	コーヒー
yogurt	yōguruto	ヨーグルト	beer	biiru	ビール
milk shake	miruku shēki	ミルクシェーキ	soft drinks	sofuto dorinku	ソフトドリンク
white rice	shiroigohan	白いご飯	Coke	kokakōra	コカコーラ

PLACES	RŌMAJI	JAPANESE	PLACES	RŌMAJI	JAPANESE
sea	umi	海	What country are you from?	kokuseki wa nan desuka?	国籍は何ですか？
river	kawa	川	Japanese	nihonjin	日本人
lake	mizu-umi	湖	foreigner	gaijin	外人
pond	ike	池	Are you going out?	odekake desuka?	お出かけですか？
waterfall	taki	滝	glacier	hyōga	氷河
island	shima	島	cave	dōkutsu	洞窟
peninsula	hanto	半島	hot springs	onsen	温泉
beach	umi	海	countryside	inaka	田舎
forest	mori	森	downtown	toshin	都心
grasslands	sōgen	草原	city	toshi	都市
desert	sabaku	砂漠	country	kuni	国
plateau	kōgen	高原	road	michi	道

PLACES	ROMAJI	JAPANESE
mountain	yama	山
park	kōen	公園

WEATHER	ROMAJI	JAPANESE
weather	otenki	お天気
How's the weather?	otenki wa dōdesuka?	お天気はどうですか？
weather forecast	tenki yohō	天気予報
clear	hare	晴れ
sun	taiyō	太陽
cloudy	kumori	曇り
humid	shitsu ga takai	質が高い

PLACES	ROMAJI	JAPANESE
street	dōri	通り
boulevard or avenue	ōdōri	大通り

WEATHER	ROMAJI	JAPANESE
Is it going to rain?	ame ga furu yotei desuka?	雨が降る予定ですか？
rain	ame	雨
thunderstorms	raiu	雷雨
typhoon	taifū	台風
flood	kōzui	洪水
umbrella	kasa	かさ
snow	yuki	雪

CLIMATE

Avg. Temperature, Precipitation	January			April			July			October		
	°C	°F	mm	°C	°F	mm	°C	°F	mm	°C	°F	mm
Tōkyō	8	46	67	15	58	152	28	82	374	19	66	143
Ōsaka	7	45	52	15	58	78	29	84	43	20	68	127
Sapporo	-3	26	132	6	43	124	22	72	194	12	53	25
Fukuoka	8	46	71	15	58	83	28	82	150	20	68	87
Naha	18	64	87	21	69	394	28	82	368	26	79	95

MEASUREMENT

Japan uses the metric system of measurement. One unconventional measurement used in Japan is the "tatami mat" or *jō*, used to measure rooms of a house or apartment. The size of a tatami mat varies by region, but hovers around 1.6 sq. m.

MEASUREMENT CONVERSIONS

1 inch (in.) = 25.4mm	1 millimeter (mm) = 0.039 in.
1 foot (ft.) = 0.30m	1 meter (m) = 3.28 ft. = 1.09 yd.
1 yard (yd.) = 0.914m	1 kilometer (km) = 0.62 mi.
1 mile (mi.) = 1.61km	1 gram (g) = 0.035 oz.
1 ounce (oz.) = 28.35g	1 kilogram (kg) = 2.202 lb.
1 pound (lb.) = 0.454kg	1 milliliter (ml) = 0.034 fl. oz.
1 fluid ounce (fl. oz.) = 29.57ml	1 liter (L) = 0.264 gal.
1 square mile (sq. mi.) = 2.59 sq. km	1 square kilometer (sq. km) = 0.386 sq. mi.

DATES

The Japanese system for indicating **years** combines the era (named for the reigning emperor) with a number indicating the year of the era. The Heisei era began with the accession of Akihito in 1989, and, thus, 2004 is Heisei 16.

The eras of the modern period have been the **Meiji** (1868-1912), the **Taishō** (1912-1926), the **Shōwa** (1926-1989), and the **Heisei** (1989 to present). To convert Meiji dates to standard Western format, add 1867 to the reign year (Meiji 33 = 33+1867 = 1900). For Taishō dates, add 1911; Shōwa dates, 1925; and Heisei dates, 1988.

LET'S GO'S *ESSENTIAL JAPANGLISH*

Japanese is hard. I know this, you know this. Still, putting together a modest collection of phrases will make a big difference. Combine the Japanese word lists in the appendix (p. 726) with the information here, and you're good to go.

THE BAD NEWS. Japanese has four different writing systems. The most difficult are the Chinese characters called **kanji.** *Kanji* can have as many as 30 strokes; adding or forgetting a line changes the meaning from "big" (大), to "fat" (太), to "dog" (犬), with potentially disastrous results. Since *kanji* also have multiple pronunciations, literacy is quite a feat. The less ambitious could spend a week or two learning to read **hiragana** and **katakana** instead. Each has 46 phonetic characters—with fewer than 3 strokes each, they're fairly simple. Often station names are written in *hiragana* so children can read them. More useful to the traveler is *katakana*, used to spell foreign words like *bīru* (beer) and *kōhī* (coffee). And you already know the ever-popular **rōmaji,** the standard Roman alphabet.

THE GOOD NEWS. You know more Japanese then you think. Anyone who's seen a samurai film can muster a *sayōnara* or *konnichiwa*, and the band Styx has installed the (highly useful) phrase "Domo Arigatō Mr. Roboto" into the popular lexicon. You'll also be happy to learn that modern Japanese has been infused with many English loanwords, which quickly bulks up your vocabulary. Every Japanese high school graduate has sat through years of English class, so in desperate straits, try carefully pronounced English and see if your buddy understands. Pocket dictionaries facilitate chit-chat, and it's pretty easy to learn the basics, so here are some tried-and-true tips for learning Japanese on the go.

PURONUNSHIĒSHON-DŌ (THE WAY OF PRONUNCIA-TION). If you were to step into a cab in Japan and ask for the "Malibu Beach Hotel," you would likely be met with a stare of profound confusion. First off, all Japanese syllables, except "n," end in vowels. The English pronunciation of the words "beach" or "hotel" sounds like gibberish to a Japanese cab driver, so try pronouncing each syllable as if it ended with a vowel. There is no "l"-sound in Japanese, which means that most imported words that contain an "l" are transliterated with an "r"-sound. Heading back to our example, you can see that the best way to tell the cab driver where to go would be to say "*Maribu Beachi Hoteru.*"

"I SUSHI LIKE" (OR: SUBJECT-OBJECT-VERB ORDER). If you've been thinking to yourself thus far that Japanese is one backwards language, you're absolutely correct. Perhaps the most difficult part of learning Japanese is that sentences have a totally different order from European languages. This means that all sentences follow Subject-Object-Verb order; often the last word of a sentence is the most important one.

YOUR NEW BEST FRIENDS. If there is one verb that you should you learn during your entire trip to Japan, let it be *desu* (the final u is not pronounced), which is equivalent in many ways to the English verb "to be." If you add **ka** to the end of a sentence, it turns your statement into a question. Now all you need to do is add **nan** (what), **doko** (where) or **ikura** (how much) in front of *desu*, and you're on the way to communicating in Japanese. *Nan desu ka? Doko desu ka? Itsu desu ka?* (What??? Where??? When???)

JUST SAY "NO." Japanese uses a number of particles to separate the parts of a sentence, but they're hard to learn without formal instruction. Particles act almost like prepositions, but they always come *after* the word they modify. The particle "*no*", written " の " denotes possession. It's helpful for specifying what you're after. If you want "the bus to Ishikawa", try "*Ishikawa no basu.*" Other particles of note: "*ni*" (に), which often means "at," "*e*" (へ) which means "to," and "*wa*" (は), which marks the main topic. "*To*" (pronounced "toe," written " と ") joins nouns, as in "*sushi to sashimi.*" Bringing us to...

PULLING IT ALL TOGETHER. Now that you're warmed up, here are a few of phrases to try out:

Kore wa ikura desu ka.
- How much does this cost?
O-namae wa nan desu ka.
- What is your name?
...wa doko desu ka.
- Where is [the]...
... no basu wa doko desu ka.
- Where is the bus to…?
And finally...

ON GETTING WHAT YOU WANT. Politeness wins friends. Period. In a restaurant, or sitting next to the Kirin tap, catch your host's attention with a quick *sumimasen* ("excuse me"), then simply say what you want followed by "... *o onegai shimasu*" ("... please"). On your way out, thank your host with "*gochisōsama deshita*" ("it was a feast"). Walk out confidently, remembering that with practice, even you can speak Japanese.

-Matthew D. Firestone

INDEX

A

Abashiri 709–711
accommodations 25–28
 booking 27
 long-term 28
adapters 24
adventure tours 33
Ago-wan 472
AIDS 21
Aikawa 280
Ainu 85, 682, 694, 695, 714
airfares 37
airmail 33
airports
 Akita Airport 311
 Aomori Airport 317
 Asahikawa Airport 698
 Fukuoka Airport 584
 Hakodate Airport 670
 Haneda Airport 111
 Hiroshima Airport 479
 Ishigaki Airport 658
 Itami Airport 396
 Izumo Airport 512
 Kagoshima Airport 619
 Kansai International Airport 396, 432
 Kerama Airport 654
 Kōchi Airport 553
 Komatsu Airport 359
 Kumamoto Airport 614
 Matsumoto Airport 334
 Matsuyama Airport 566
 Memanbetsu Airport 709
 Miyako Airport 654
 Miyazaki Airport 628
 Nagasaki Airport 596
 Nagoya Airport 378
 Naha International Airport 640
 Narita Airport 110
 New Chitose Airport 684
 Niigata Airport 274
 Noto Airport 369
 Ōita Airport 606
 Okadama Airport 685
 Ōsaka International Airport 432
 Rebun-tō Airport 723
 Rishiri Airport 722
 Sado Airport 274
 Sendai Airport 286
 Takamatsu Airport 538
 Tokushima Airport 529
 Wakkanai Airport 719

Yaku-shima Airport 633
Yonago Airport 512
Aizu-Wakamatsu 267–271
Akan National Park 711–715
Akasaka 116
Akihabara 119
Akihito 84
Akita 311–314
alcohol 18
Alternatives to Tourism 57–74
 studying abroad 63
 volunteering 59
 working 69
Anbō 633
animals 76
anime 104
Aomori 317–321
Aoshima 632
Aoyama 117
Arashiyama 428
architecture
 modern 104
 traditional 98
Arita 593
art history 97
arts 97
 aesthetics 102
Asahi-dake Onsen 706–708
Asahikawa 698–701
Asakusa 117
Ashikaga Takauji 79
Ashikaga Yoshinori 79
Ashizuri Misaki 563
Aso-San 605
Asuka 458
Asukadera 78
Atami 234
ATM cards 13
atomic bomb 83, 479, 482, 486, 596, 597
Awaji-shima 525–528

B

bakufu 79
Bandai-Asahi National Park 272
bargaining 16
baseball 106
Bashō Matsuo 285
bathing 95
Battle of Midway 82
bears 30, 31, 77
Beppu 605–614
bicycling 48

Bijodaira 358
bonsai 101
books, recommended 107
bubble economy 83
Buddhism 78, 89
budgeting 15
bunraku 100
buses 45
bushidō 80
business hotels 26

C

calling cards 35
cameras and film 24
campers 33
camping 28–33
 equipment 31
capsule hotels 27
cars. See driving
castles 98
 Bichū-Matsuyama-jō 517
 Fukue-jō 595
 Fukuoka 590
 Gifu 386
 Gujo Hachiman 387
 Hagi 508
 Hikone-jō 474
 Himeji-jō 477
 Hirosaki-jō 316
 Hiroshima-jō 489
 Hiwasa 536
 Imperial Palace, Kyōto 413
 Imperial Palace, Tōkyō 161
 Inuyama 389
 Iwakuni-jō 499
 Kanazawa 366
 Kōchi 559
 Kokura-jō 583
 Kumamoto-jō 618
 Matsue-jō 515
 Matsumoto 337
 Matsuyama 570
 Morioka 308
 Nagahama 475
 Nago Castle Hill 652
 Nagoya 383
 Nakagusuku 646
 Nijō-jō 413
 Okayama-jō 523
 Ōsaka-jō 436
 Sendai 292
 Shimabara-jō 604
 Shuri-jō 645
 Takamatsu 543
 Tokushima 533

MAP INDEX

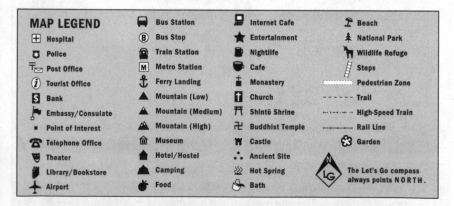

MAP LEGEND

Symbol		Symbol		Symbol	
⊞	Hospital	🚌	Bus Station	🖥	Internet Cafe	⚓	Beach
✪	Police	Ⓑ	Bus Stop	★	Entertainment	🌲	National Park
⊤☑	Post Office	🚂	Train Station	🍸	Nightlife	🦌	Wildlife Refuge
ⓘ	Tourist Office	Ⓜ	Metro Station	☕	Cafe	/	Steps
$	Bank	⚓	Ferry Landing	✝	Monastery	Pedestrian Zone
🏴	Embassy/Consulate	▲	Mountain (Low)	⊞	Church	-----	Trail
▪	Point of Interest	▲	Mountain (Medium)	丌	Shintō Shrine	—·—·—·→	High-Speed Train
☎	Telephone Office	▲	Mountain (High)	卍	Buddhist Temple	——→	Rail Line
♨	Theater	🏛	Museum	🏰	Castle	✿	Garden
📕	Library/Bookstore	🏨	Hotel/Hostel	∴	Ancient Site	
✈	Airport	▲	Camping	♨	Hot Spring	The Let's Go compass always points NORTH.
		🍎	Food	🛁	Bath	